HISTORY AND BIBLIOGRAPHY OF AMERICAN NEWSPAPERS 1690-1820

CLARENCE S. BRIGHAM

Reprinted from the 1947 edition,
with the 1961 additions and corrections,
with the permission of
the American Antiquarian Society.

VOLUME ONE

GREENWOOD PRESS, Publishers
Westport, Connecticut

Poynter Institute for Media Studies
Library

DEC 1 9 '86

Library of Congress Cataloging in Publication Data

Brigham, Clarence Saunders, 1877-1963.
History and bibliography of American newspapers, 1690-1820.

Reprint of the 1947 ed. published by the American Antiquarian Society, Worcester, Mass., which was a revision of a work first issued in the Proceedings of the American Antiquarian Society, 1913 to 1927, under title: Bibliography of American newspapers, 1690-1820; and of the 1961 ed. of additions and corrections, which was reprinted from the Society's Proceedings for April 1961.
Includes indexes.
1. American newspapers—Bibliography. 2. American newspapers—History. I. Title.
Z6951.B86 1976 [PN4861] 016.071'3 75-40215
ISBN 0-8371-8677-3

Trim Size

Original edition 7¾ x 10¾
Reprint edition 6 × 9

Copyright 1947 by the American Antiquarian Society
Copyright © 1975 by the American Antiquarian Society

All rights reserved

Originally published in 1947 by American Antiquarian Society, Worcester, Massachusetts

Reprinted with the permission of American Antiquarian Society

Reprinted in 1976 by Greenwood Press
A division of Congressional Information Service, Inc.
88 Post Road West, Westport, Connecticut 06881

Library of Congress catalog card number 75-40215

ISBN 0-8371-8677-3 SET
    0-8371-8681-1 Vol. 1
    0-8371-8682-X Vol. 2

Printed in the United States of America

10 9 8 7 6 5 4 3 2

CONTENTS

VOLUME I

INTRODUCTION	ix–xvii
BIBLIOGRAPHY OF NEWSPAPERS	1–1175
ALABAMA	3
ARKANSAS	10
CONNECTICUT	11
DELAWARE	77
DISTRICT OF COLUMBIA	87
FLORIDA	109
GEORGIA	111
ILLINOIS	135
INDIANA	138
KENTUCKY	146
LOUISIANA	182
MAINE	195
MARYLAND	218
MASSACHUSETTS	271
MICHIGAN	422
MISSISSIPPI	423
MISSOURI	431
NEW HAMPSHIRE	435
NEW JERSEY	492
NEW YORK	527

VOLUME II

NORTH CAROLINA	758
OHIO	783
PENNSYLVANIA	824
RHODE ISLAND	994
SOUTH CAROLINA	1023
TENNESSEE	1054
TEXAS	1069
VERMONT	1071
VIRGINIA	1103
WEST VIRGINIA	1169
ERRATA	1176
LIST OF LIBRARIES	1177
LIST OF PRIVATE OWNERS	1189
INDEX OF TITLES	1193
INDEX OF PRINTERS	1367
ADDITIONS AND CORRECTIONS	1511

AMERICAN
NEWSPAPERS
1690–1820

History and Bibliography of American Newspapers

1690–1820

BY

CLARENCE S. BRIGHAM

VOLUME ONE

AMERICAN ANTIQUARIAN SOCIETY
WORCESTER, MASSACHUSETTS
1947

COPYRIGHT 1947
BY THE AMERICAN ANTIQUARIAN SOCIETY

PRINTED AT THE HARVARD UNIVERSITY PRINTING OFFICE
CAMBRIDGE, MASS., U.S.A.

DEDICATED TO

GEORGE FRANCIS BOOTH
AND
HARRY GALPIN STODDARD

WHOSE FRIENDLY INTEREST
HAS MADE POSSIBLE
THE PUBLICATION OF THIS WORK

CONTENTS

VOLUME I

INTRODUCTION	ix–xvii
BIBLIOGRAPHY OF NEWSPAPERS	1–1175
ALABAMA	3
ARKANSAS	10
CONNECTICUT	11
DELAWARE	77
DISTRICT OF COLUMBIA	87
FLORIDA	109
GEORGIA	111
ILLINOIS	135
INDIANA	138
KENTUCKY	146
LOUISIANA	182
MAINE	195
MARYLAND	218
MASSACHUSETTS	271
MICHIGAN	422
MISSISSIPPI	423
MISSOURI	431
NEW HAMPSHIRE	435
NEW JERSEY	492
NEW YORK	527

VOLUME II

NORTH CAROLINA	758
OHIO	783
PENNSYLVANIA	824
RHODE ISLAND	994
SOUTH CAROLINA	1023
TENNESSEE	1054
TEXAS	1069
VERMONT	1071
VIRGINIA	1103
WEST VIRGINIA	1169
ERRATA	1176
LIST OF LIBRARIES	1177
LIST OF PRIVATE OWNERS	1189
INDEX OF TITLES	1193
INDEX OF PRINTERS	1367

INTRODUCTION

This Bibliography is really the outgrowth of a suggestion made by the late William MacDonald, at one time professor of history at Brown University and later editorial writer in New York. In a paper on "Some Bibliographical Desiderata in American History," read before the American Antiquarian Society in October, 1911, Professor MacDonald called attention to the urgent need of a bibliography of American newspapers. He said: "The importance of newspapers as historical sources has been, if not underestimated, at least scantily recognized, by historians; and with the exception of our associate, Professor McMaster, few writers of comprehensive histories have made either extended or systematic use of them. Yet I have come to believe that neither our political nor our social development can be truly set forth until the wealth of data hidden in newspapers and magazines has been opened up and made available. It is to the newspapers that we must go, for example, to complete our information about the growth of colonial commerce, manufactures, and agriculture; the influence of English politics on the political activities and public opinion of the colonies; the progress and character of the Revolutionary agitation of the eighteenth century; the reasons for the success of the Federal Constitution, one of the most interesting topics awaiting its finished treatment; and about the nature and growth of slavery. . . . A newspaper bibliography is pre-eminently our own task; since nowhere else is there a collection of such material comparable to our own. I do not underrate the magnitude of the work; it is, perhaps, the most considerable undertaking of a bibliographical sort that now needs to be done, although a well-organized co-operative plan would lighten the labor. Once definitely accomplished, however, and with the partial or complete files now extant located and listed, the historian would be in a position to begin the work, which we all realize has got to be done, of writing large sections of American history over again, as well as of taking up numerous important topics which as yet, for lack of such assistance, lie neglected."

It was early in 1913 that I began upon this monumental task, blithely believing that five years would finish it. But the work had to be done only on evenings and Sundays, and the amount of travel necessary was far underestimated. I spent part of the summer in 1913 journeying to New York, Philadelphia, and Washington, having already covered the larger New England libraries in order to examine their newspaper files. The first installment appeared in the *Proceedings* in October, 1913, covering the States from Alabama to Indiana.

The plan of publication was to write a brief historical account of each newspaper, with exact dates of changes of titles and names of publishers, followed by a checklist of all files located. The decision was made to limit the final date to the year 1820, partly because this was the date chosen by Evans for the final year of his great American Bibliography, also because it covered the beginnings of printing in the middle west, but chiefly because the bibliography had to stop somewhere and to extend it into later decades might cause the entire undertaking to fall under its own weight. Incidentally, it was the choosing of this final date which caused the editors of the Union List of Newspapers, published in 1937, to begin their massive checklist with the year 1821.

In the summer of 1914 my vacation period was spent in a long journey through the Southern States and back through Kentucky, Tennessee, Missouri, Indiana, and Illinois. Subsequent trips to Maryland, New Jersey, New York, and Pennsylvania were made in following summers. New England was near at hand and its libraries were frequently visited. In the far-away States my usual process was to cover the large libraries in the leading city or State capitol and then to hire an automobile to visit the smaller towns. In this way in the course of the entire undertaking I explored about four hundred cities and towns this side of the Mississippi River and travelled about ten thousand miles. At least four different trips were made to the South and West to reexamine files or to visit towns previously omitted. As material was gathered, gradually the installments were printed in the *Proceedings* of this Society, the last being installment No. XVIII in the *Proceedings* of April, 1927.

Since the final installment was printed in the *Proceedings* for 1927, revision has been constantly in progress. The reexamination of known files, the discovery of new files, and especially extended research into the history of the newspapers have combined to make the earlier portions of the Bibliography almost unrecognizable. Furthermore, the decision has been made to list all files more in detail. Where previously it was deemed sufficient to describe a file as scattering or incomplete, in the revision the files are listed in detail, recording all dates and all omissions. Although this procedure rendered the list of far more value, it resulted in a great amount of time and labor, requiring in many cases revisiting such libraries as possessed the files.

A study of the Bibliography shows interesting statistical results. In the period from 1690 to 1820, there were 2120 different newspapers published. Of this total the six New England States had 447 papers, the six Middle Atlantic States from New York to Maryland had 1023 papers, the ten Southern States from Virginia to Louisiana had 425 papers, and the seven Western States had 225 papers. The city which from the beginning to 1820 had the

INTRODUCTION

most newspapers was New York with 138, followed by Philadelphia with 107, and Boston with 73.

The six largest collections of newspapers before 1820 are in the American Antiquarian Society which has 1496 titles, the Library of Congress with 936 titles, Harvard with 732 titles, the New York Historical Society with 634 titles, the New York Public Library with 480 titles, and the Wisconsin Historical Society with 415 titles. Since the exact record is of some interest and shows where the largest number of newspapers of each State can be found, it is here appended in tabular form.

	AAS	LC	HARV	NYHS	NYPL	WHS	TOTAL TITLES	NONE FOUND
Alabama	7	6	. .	. .	. .	3	15	5
Arkansas	1	1	. .	. .	. .	. .	1	. .
Connecticut	73	47	39	33	29	21	78	. .
Delaware	17	9	7	5	2	1	20	2
District of Columbia	32	28	17	10	8	12	37	3
Florida	. .	. .	. .	. .	. .	. .	2	1
Georgia	33	16	14	7	5	5	50	7
Illinois	3	4	. .	. .	. .	. .	5	. .
Indiana	10	5	1	. .	. .	1	20	2
Kentucky	39	29	20	4	3	14	88	25
Louisiana	12	5	7	2	. .	10	25	1
Maine	37	20	25	15	7	8	40	. .
Maryland	59	43	36	25	19	24	93	9
Massachusetts	170	125	110	101	80	78	175	1
Michigan	2	1	. .	1	1	1	2	. .
Mississippi	10	10	5	3	3	. .	19	2
Missouri	2	5	. .	. .	1	2	8	1
New Hampshire	63	50	38	41	27	16	68	1
New Jersey	39	23	24	18	21	9	71	2
New York	332	164	136	192	151	75	434	28
North Carolina	41	19	18	6	1	5	62	6
Ohio	63	23	17	10	4	16	99	13
Pennsylvania	227	128	89	91	55	45	368	57
Rhode Island	26	20	15	20	13	9	32	1
South Carolina	36	25	17	12	9	17	59	8
Tennessee	16	19	5	1	. .	3	42	7
Texas	. .	. .	. .	. .	. .	. .	2	1
Vermont	50	28	34	13	9	10	54	1
Virginia	89	75	54	23	34	27	127	7
West Virginia	7	8	4	1	1	3	24	3
	1496	936	732	634	480	268	2120	194

As is shown in the above list, there are 194 newspapers, out of the total of 2120, of which not a single copy can be located, although they are known to have existed. Furthermore, 196 newspapers are represented in the six libraries by unique issues, found in no other library in the country. In this category the American Antiquarian Society has 118, the Library of Congress has 34, Harvard has 26, the New York Historical Society has 9, the Wisconsin Historical Society has 6, and the New York Public Library has 3.

The mortality in newspapers before 1821 was notable. Over half of the total of 2120 papers in this period, to be exact, 1118 papers, expired before they had reached two years of existence, 1002 papers lived from two to four years, 541 from five to nine years, 302 from ten to nineteen years, 106 from twenty to twenty-nine years, 34 from thirty to thirty-nine years, 15 from forty to forty-nine years, and 10 continued from fifty to eighty-seven years. Of course this takes into account only the history of the papers before 1821, as many continued on for a long period after that year.

The newspaper which sustained the longest continuous publication during the period to 1820 was the *Pennsylvania Gazette*, which was published from 1728 to 1815, a total of 87 years. It is true that for several weeks during the Revolution, when the British troops occupied Philadelphia, the paper was forced temporarily to suspend, but it soon resumed publication, and with continuous volume numbering. The next paper in the line of succession was the *Maryland Gazette*, published for 75 years from 1745 to 1820. The practically complete file of this paper in the Maryland State Library is one of the outstanding files owned by any American library. Then follows the *Boston News-Letter*, published for 72 years from 1704 to 1776, the *New Hampshire Gazette* published for 64 years from 1756 to 1820, the *Newport Mercury* published for 62 years from 1758 to 1820, the *Providence Gazette* published for 58 years from 1762 to 1820, the *Connecticut Gazette* published at New London for 57 years from 1763 to 1820, the *Connecticut Courant* published at Hartford for 56 years from 1764 to 1820, the *Connecticut Journal* published at New Haven for 53 years from 1767 to 1820, and the *Pennsylvania Journal* published for 51 years from 1742 to 1793. This honor list comprises all the papers published continuously for over fifty years. It should be considered that so far as this schedule is concerned, the final date is 1820. Many of the papers continued long after that year and some even are published today, with a record of nearly two hundred years of continuous publication.

To the bibliographer unique titles, single years and short files are interesting, but to the researcher it is the long files which have historical value. The following statistical record shows the comparative size of the collections in the six largest libraries, so far as long files are concerned. In this record a library is credited with a file if it is continuous and at least 90% complete. Most of the files recorded are virtually complete, but the omission of a few issues in a year does not cause the exclusion of the file.

INTRODUCTION

	TOTAL	AAS	LC	NYHS	NYPL	HARV	WHS
2 to 4 years	1002	323	236	146	90	104	85
5 to 9 years	541	112	69	50	37	26	23
10 to 19 years	302	61	34	21	12	7	10
20 to 29 years	106	25	14	8	5	2	3
30 to 39 years	34	14	8	3	1	1	1
40 to 49 years	15	6	2	0	1	0	0
50 years and over	10	1	0	0	1	0	0
		542	363	228	147	140	122

The above record of long continuous files concerns the holdings of only the six largest newspaper libraries. In many cases the longest and best file of a paper is to be found in a State or local historical society which possesses only the papers of its own locality. Yet it is also true that a great many papers are to be located in the best, and often the only, files in one of the large national collections. This is certainly true of the Antiquarian Society collection which has more titles and more long files for at least a dozen States than are to be found in any one library in those States.

There are many and varying reasons for the size of the six national collections. The State Historical Society of Wisconsin, under the active guidance of Lyman C. Draper and Reuben G. Thwaites, built up a large collection during the last half of the nineteenth century, and its *Catalogue of Newspapers* published in 1911 is still one of the standard reference books on the subject. The Harvard University collection is chiefly strong for the years 1795 to 1808 when Christoph D. Ebeling was acquiring newspapers for his history of America. The purchase of the Ebeling collection in 1818 gave Harvard the largest known representation of papers for those thirteen years gathered by anyone. Ebeling obtained them from the Reverend William Bentley of Salem, and I often contrast them with the value of the files of German periodicals which Bentley received in return and which upon his death he left to the American Antiquarian Society. The New York Public Library and the New York Historical Society have always collected early newspapers and even in recent years have added constantly to their holdings. The Library of Congress, with unquestionably the largest existing collection of American newspapers, if one takes into account the papers of the last seventy-five years, has been actively acquiring newspapers for half a century past, and next to the Antiquarian Society, is stronger than any other library even in the early period.

The American Antiquarian Society collection was established, as everyone who is interested knows, by Isaiah Thomas, patriot printer of the Revolution and founder of this Society. He retained most of the newspapers which came to him through exchange for a long period, certainly until 1801, when he turned the printing business over to his son. Then again, when he was preparing his History of Printing in America, he caused to be inserted in newspapers generally throughout the country a notice of his forthcoming work, in which he asked all printers to send him copies of their newspapers. He bought long important files when they came to his notice. Most of them were purchased in 1810, before any historical societies, with one exception, had been established. Some of the files were the *Boston Evening Post*, 1735–1775, which cost Mr. Thomas $60; the *American Weekly Mercury*, 1719–1746, which cost $70; the *New York Weekly Journal*, 1733–1751, which cost $30; and the *Pennsylvania Gazette*, 1735–1775, which cost $180. The prices are startling compared with present-day values.

After Isaiah Thomas' death, the Antiquarian Society continued to acquire newspaper files, although only casually. During the last thirty-seven years, since the present director has been in office, the purchase and exchange of newspapers has been one of our most important activities. In 1880, according to the list in the United States 1880 Census, the Society's collection of pre-1820 newspapers numbered 911 volumes. Today it numbers nearly 3000 volumes and portfolios. The collection certainly has been trebled for the period previous to 1820, and increased fourfold from 1821 to 1865. Also, until recently, about thirty currently issued files have been received and bound, these covering the entire country. For the period previous to 1821, a conservative estimate would be that the Society owns nearly half a million issues of newspapers, available for the use of the investigator.

This is a bibliography of newspapers, and magazines have been excluded, left for some later writer who might compile a checklist of such periodical publications. The distinction between newspapers and magazines is sometimes difficult to draw. The test of a newspaper is generally the inclusion of current news, but the printing of advertisements, marriage and death records, and the fact that the publication calls itself a newspaper even if it has the appearance of a magazine, have all been taken into consideration.

Papers are invariably entered under their exact title. If titles changed, even though volume numbering was continuous, the correct title is the place of entry. But if a paper changed its title for only a brief time, and then resumed its former title, the entire file is entered under the earlier title. In the Index of Titles at the end of the work of course all titles are alphabetically entered, with reference to the proper entry.

In the locating of files, these are listed in order of importance, and generally speaking, the earlier files are listed first. Files listed with inclusive dates are presumed to be complete, or practically complete. In a long file, covering several years, no attempt has been made to list a few missing issues, as this would extend the checklist beyond reasonable proportions. Nor have mutilated copies been so noted. If issues are missing or mutilated in long files, they may well be found in the scattering files of other libraries, which are exactly listed. The word "scattering" has been sparingly used, and then only when several complete files are somewhere consultable. "Scattering issues" means only a few issues in a year, generally not worth exact listing in view of the existence of complete files. "Scattering file" means that the library has from one third to one half of the issues in a given year. "Fair," also sparingly used, and then when complete files exist elsewhere, means that a library has eighty to ninety percent of the issues in a given year. The above types of phraseology are used only in the case of common newspapers where many good files are to be located. In the case of rare newspapers, all issues, wherever located, are exactly entered.

Supplements are not entered except in the case of rare newspapers, where even supplements may be the only issues existing. Some newspapers issued each year as many as fifty supplements and postscripts, and it is to be presumed that if a library has a complete file for a given year, such a file would include the supplements. Meticulous listing of supplements, mutilations, and occasional missing copies must be left to future detailed checklists for local areas. Photostats are not listed except in the case of rare newspapers, although all of the larger photostat undertakings are recorded, with lists of the libraries owning such files. Facsimiles are generally not listed except that reference is frequently made to such a facsimile issue where it might deceive a collector or a library.

In the period before the adoption of the new calendar in 1752, double dating was frequently used on newspapers between January 1 and March 25 of each year. A paper issued on January 17, 1736, might be dated in the head-line as January 17, 1735, or sometimes January 17, 1735–1736. It is entered in the Bibliography under its proper date of 1736. Also in the early eighteenth century issues, a paper issued on April 24, 1704, might be dated April 17 to April 24, 1704. Of course the correct date of publication was April 24.

There are no symbols used in listing the files, thus obviating the constant turning to a key list of libraries to find where a file is to be found. An index, with details of addresses, is provided both for libraries and private owners.

No statement in any previous bibliography or in any local history has been accepted unless specifically quoted. Local histories, however useful they have been to this compiler, are often inaccurate, due to the inability to locate files and to the frequent dependence upon tradition. The many newspapers advertised "to be published" and for which subscriptions were often taken, are not included unless there is proof that they were established. Fully half of the newspapers so advertised never reached the fact of publication. Yet such advertisements are mentioned if the announcement helps bibliographically.

Much research has been put into the effort to identify the first names of printers. Death and marriage notices, local manuscript records, and contemporary references in newspapers have all helped to reveal the Christian names of many otherwise unidentified printers. Early town directories, of which the American Antiquarian Society has a nearly complete collection, have provided many solutions. Although hundreds of names have been found, many remain still unidentified, perhaps later to be found in census reports and town tax lists or by the research of local historians. In the Antiquarian Society is being developed a card catalogue of printers and publishers before 1821, which in time will give the desired biographical information, as part of its catalogue of American imprints, arranged chronologically, geographically, and by printers.

As I look back upon the preparation of this Bibliography, I realize the immense amount of aid that I have received from numerous scholars interested in its publication. The late Professor Charles H. Hull, of Cornell, spent the winters of 1914 and 1915 in the South making a study of printed and manuscript resources of the States from Virginia to Louisiana. Entirely without solicitation he examined hundreds of Southern newspaper files to find material which might assist me in the work of compilation. The actual physical work must have taken him hundreds of hours and aided me in an immeasurable degree. For thirty years Joseph Gavit, of Albany, Acting Librarian of the New York State Library, has written me hundreds of letters listing newspapers and recording information regarding printers. Another constant source of help was the late Douglas C. McMurtrie, whose work in early American printing made him a leading authority in that field, and who is today succeeded by his capable assistant, Albert H. Allen. There are others who have aided me far beyond the answering of queries pertaining to their own files — Henry S. Parsons of the Library of Congress and Virginia S. Burnett of the Rutgers University Library, James O. Knauss and Alfred L. Shoemaker who have solved many of my problems regarding German newspapers, Elmer T. Hutchinson with his knowledge of early printers, Gaylord P. Albaugh who is covering so thoroughly the field of early religious newspapers, and Robert W. G. Vail who during and since his stay in Worcester has always shown the deepest interest in my undertaking. But if I made acknowledgement to all of those who have assisted me, the list would constitute practically a complete roster of the 510 libraries and the 125 private owners listed in the Indexes at the end of this Bibliography.

I realize that my greatest debt in the publication of this Bibliography is to my secretary, Mrs. Dorothea E. Spear. She has prepared the elaborate indexes of titles and publishers, which are not routine tasks but call for the widest knowledge of historical and biographical source material. Also she has read with me all of the proof, which means concentrated accuracy, not to mention the repeating of well over a million words and figures.

The correspondence which has been gathered during over thirty years of compilation constitutes about 15,000 letters and is filed in an arrangement by State and town. Since these letters contain many facts not included in the Bibliography, and much additional material on newspapers published after 1820, they will be carefully preserved for future reference.

When Professor MacDonald told me thirty-five years ago that such a Bibliography was urgently needed by the historian, I believed him. I have never lost my faith in the value of newspapers as tools of research, and the constant use made of our files for thirty years has proved the thesis. The usefulness of newspapers as sources of historical study is often overlooked by libraries. Since they are difficult to acquire and since they take up considerable shelf room, they are frequently rejected in favor of source material not nearly so useful in research. I doubt whether any contemporary expression of printed opinion and fact, both for national and local history, measures up to the newspaper. No history of a town or city can be written without recourse to its newspapers. In the eighteenth and early nineteenth centuries even the advertisements have unique value in social and economic study. In the wider fields of history, whether state or national, the whole trend of events is reported at regular intervals, in the printing of documents and letters, in the arguments of partisan communications, and in editorial opinion. The newspaper is omnivorous. Not only political history, but religious, educational and social history, find place in its pages. Literature, especially essays and poetry, was constantly supplied to its readers. If all the printed sources of history for a certain century or decade had to be destroyed save one, that which could be chosen with the greatest value to posterity would be a file of an important newspaper.

CLARENCE S. BRIGHAM

AMERICAN
NEWSPAPERS
1690–1820

ALABAMA

Blakeley Sun, 1818–1819.

Semi-weekly and weekly. Established December 12, 1818, by Gabriel F. Mott, under the title of "The Blakeley Sun, and Alabama Advertiser." Proposals for the establishment of the paper were published in the St. Stephens "Halcyon," dated October 15, 1818. Although a semi-weekly publication, it was changed to a weekly during the summer months, the change occurring on May 18, 1819. The "Mobile Gazette" of Aug. 25, 1819, stated that the Blakeley Sun "has been discontinued for several weeks past." Yet it must have been later reestablished, as the "Mobile Commercial Register" of Dec. 27, 1821, refers to the "Blakeley Sun."

Am. Antiq. Soc. has Dec. 12, 1818–June 2, 1819.
Ala. Dept. of Archives has Mar. 23, 30, 1819.
Wis. Hist. Soc. has May 7, 1819.

[Cahawba] Alabama Watchman, 1820+.

Weekly. Established Aug. 8, 1820, by A[ugustina] Parsons, with the title of "Alabama Watchman." The last issue located is that of Dec. 15, 1820, vol. 1, no. 19, but the paper was undoubtedly continued until after 1820. In the Savannah "Georgian" of May 3, 1820, is an advertisement by Augustina Parsons proposing to publish at Cahawba the "Alabama Watchman."

Lib. Cong. has Aug. 8–25, Sept. 15–Oct. 20, Nov. 3, 17, 24, Dec. 8, 15, 1820.
Wis. Hist. Soc. has Aug. 8, 1820.

Cahawba Press and Alabama Intelligencer, 1819–1820+.

Weekly. Established June 12, 1819, judging from the date of the first issue located, that of July 10, 1819, vol. 1, no. 5, published by William B. Allen, with the title of "Cahawba Press and Alabama Intelligencer." Proposals for the paper, dated June 1, 1819, were printed in the "Mobile Gazette" of June 30, 1819. The issue for July 15, 1820, was published by Allen & Lamar [William B. Allen and ―― Lamar]. The issue for Dec. 30, 1820, was published by Allen & Brickell [William B. Allen and Richard B. Brickell]. Continued after 1820.

Am. Antiq. Soc. has July 10, 17, 1819; July 15, 1820.
Lib. Cong. has Dec. 30, 1820.

[Claiborne] Alabama Courier, 1819–1820+.

Weekly. Established Mar. 19, 1819, by Tucker & Turner [———— Tucker and ———— Turner], with the title of "Alabama Courier." Continued after 1820. "Turner & Tucker" had previously attempted to start a newspaper at Pensacola, to be called the "Pensacola Gazette" (see Natchez "Mississippi State Gazette" of Sept. 23, 1818), but it presumably never was established.

Am. Antiq. Soc. has Mar. 19, Apr. 9, July 9, Aug. 20, 1819.

Florence Gazette, 1820+.

Weekly. In the Library of Congress is a copy of the "Florence Gazette" of Aug. 19, 1824, vol. 5, no. 27, published by P. Bertrand, showing that this paper must have been established early in the year 1820. In the Clarksville, Tenn., "Town Gazette" of Aug. 9, 1819 is printed an advertisement of proposals for the "Florence Gazette," to be published by P[eter] Bertrand. The paper is quoted in the "Louisville Public Advertiser" of Mar. 18, 1820, and in the Lexington "Western Monitor" of Aug. 29, 1820. The "National Intelligencer" of Oct. 28, 1820, states that the paper was established by P. Bertrand in January 1820.

[Fort Stoddert] Mobile Centinel, 1811–1812.

Weekly. Established May 23, 1811, by Miller and Hood [Samuel Miller and John B. Hood], with the title of "The Mobile Centinel." The place of publication was Fort Stoddert, where the printers located before they were able to enter Mobile. Fort Stoddert was then in Mississippi Territory, but later in Alabama. The only two issues located are those of May 30, 1811, vol. 1, no. 2, published at Fort Stoddart and Jan. 29, 1812, vol. 1, no. 16, published at Fort Stoddert. The numbering would show intermittent publication. The "Natchez Gazette" of June 27, 1811 records the receipt of a file of the "Mobile Centinel" up to June 6, lately established at "Fort Stoddart" by Miller and Hood, and prints long quotations from these issues. There is also a lengthy quotation from the issue of June 6 in the Augusta, Ga., "Columbian Centinel" of July 22, 1811.

According to an advertisement in the Knoxville "Western Centinel" of June 30, 1810, Harry Toulmin proposed to publish "The Mobile Mercury, or Tombigbe & Alabama Advertiser," the advertisement being dated at Fort Stoddert, Mar. 10, 1810, but there is nothing to show that the paper was ever established.

Ala. Dept. of Archives has May 30, 1811; Jan. 29, 1812.

[Huntsville] Alabama Republican, 1816–1820+.

Weekly. Established in August 1816, judging from the date of the first issue located, that of July 15, 1817, vol. 1, no. 46, published by Thos. B. Grantland. The "Huntsville Republican" is quoted in the Chillicothe "Weekly Recorder" of Aug. 28 and Sept. 4, 1816. Its title was first the "Huntsville Republican," which was changed to the "Alabama Republican," with the issue of Feb. 10, 1818. Beginning with Apr. 11, 1818, the paper was edited by J[ohn] Boardman, and published by Thos. B. Grantland. This firm was dissolved Oct. 20, 1818, and beginning with the issue of Oct. 31, the paper was published by J. Boardman. Continued after 1820.

> Ala. Dept. of Archives has Aug. 5, 1817; Sept. 2, 1817–Aug. 5, 1819; Sept. 15–Dec. 29, 1820.
> Lib. Cong. has Jan. 9, 16, Feb. 6–Mar. 8, 20–Apr. 3, 17–May 15, 29–July 3, 15, 22, Aug. 5–Dec. 4, 18, 25, 1819; Jan. 22–Feb. 26, Mar. 11–25, Apr. 8, 22–Sept. 1, 15–Nov. 10, 24–Dec. 29, 1820.
> Howard-Tilton Lib., New Orleans, has July 15, 29, 1817.
> Am. Antiq. Soc. has Apr. 18, 1818; Apr. 3, Aug. 5, 1819.
> N. Y. State Lib. has Aug. 5, 1819.

Huntsville Gazette, 1816.

Weekly. The only issue located is that of Dec. 21, 1816, vol. 1, no. 25, published by John B. Hood, with the title of "Huntsville Gazette." It was published in what was then termed Mississippi Territory, but in that portion which became Alabama Territory in 1817. The Columbia, S. C., "Telescope" of Sept. 17, 1816 mentions the "Huntsville Gazette."

> Lib. Cong. has Dec. 21, 1816.

[Huntsville] Madison Gazette, 1812–1816.

Weekly. The earliest copy located is that of Oct. 19, 1813, vol. 2, no. 73, published by T[homas] G. Bradford & Co., with the title of "Madison Gazette," showing that the paper must have been established in May or June, 1812. It was published in what was then termed Mississippi Territory, but in that portion which was organized into Alabama Territory in March, 1817. The only other copies located are those of May 10, 1814, vol. 2, no. 102 and Feb. 27, 1816, no. 196, both published by Wm. W. Parham. An Act of the Mississippi General Assembly, Nov. 25, 1812, ordered that a certain advertisement should be printed in the "Madison Gazette" ("Statutes of Mississippi Territory," 1816, p. 56). There is a reference to the "Madison Gazette" in the New Orleans "Louisiana Gazette" of May 22, 1813; also a reference to William W. Parham, editor of the Madison Gazette, in the Harrodsburg, Ky., "Lighthouse" of May 27, 1815.

> Am. Antiq. Soc. has Oct. 19, 1813.
> Howard-Tilton Lib., New Orleans, has May 10, 1814.
> Miss. Dept. of Archives has Feb. 27, 1816.

Huntsville Republican, see **[Huntsville] Alabama Republican.**

Mobile Centinel, see [**Fort Stoddert**] **Mobile Centinel.**

[Mobile] Commercial Advertiser, 1819.

In the "Blakeley Sun" of Mar. 12, 1819 is the statement: "We have received the first number of the Commercial Advertiser, printed at Mobile by Messrs. Miller & Fitzgerald" [presumably Isaac Miller and John Fitzgerald]. The "National Intelligencer" of Apr. 17, 1819, records the fact of its establishment and says that the first issue was published on Mar. 9. Miller & Dade had previously advertised in the "Blakeley Sun" of Dec. 22, 1818, that they planned a paper at Mobile with the title of "The Florida Star," but Miller must have taken on a new partner to publish the "Commercial Advertiser." Judging from the title and volume numbering of the "Mobile Gazette & Commercial Advertiser" of Apr. 6, 1819, vol. 3, no. 3, published by Cotten & Miller, the two papers consolidated in March 1819, indicating that the "Commercial Advertiser" lasted for only a few issues. No copies located.

Mobile Gazette, 1813–1820+.

Weekly and semi-weekly. The earliest known issues are entitled "Mobile Gazette Extra," dated July 23 and Aug. 4, 1813, and published by J[ames] Lyon. But since there is no volume numbering, there is no clue to the time of establishment. A letter from Gov. David Holmes to J. Lyon, dated at Mobile, May 2, 1813 (in Journal of Exec. Proceedings in Mississippi Dept. of Archives and History) refers to the publication of U. S. laws in "the Mobile Gazette." J. Lyon, in a letter to the Secretary of the Treasury, May 17, 1813, transmits a copy of his newspaper, the Mobile Gazette (C. E. Carter, "Territorial Papers," vol. 6, p. 367). There is a tradition in Mobile that the first Mobile paper was published by George Childs in 1814 ("Memorial Record of Alabama," 1893, vol. 2, p. 165), but there seems to be no reference to him in the early records and nothing to prove the assumption. Godwin B. Cotten in the "Mobile Gazette" of June 23, 1819 stated that the paper was first established under his management in the infancy of the town, which would mean 1813. There was surely a paper with this title in 1814, as the town records in April 1814 ordered that certain advertisements should be published in the "Mobile Gazette" (Hamilton's "Colonial Mobile," p. 442). Erwin Craighead, writing a history of the Mobile Register in that paper for Sept. 2, 1907, quotes early Mobile town records to show that in 1815 and 1816 votes were ordered printed in the "Mobile Gazette."

The paper must have been reestablished or a new volume numbering adopted in 1817. There are located issues of the "Mobile Gazette," for July 14 and Nov. 3, 1818, published semi-weekly by G[odwin] B. Cotten, but without any volume numbering. The next issue located is that of Apr. 6, 1819, vol. 3, no. 3, published by Cotten & Miller, with the title of "Mobile Gazette & Commercial Advertiser." Isaac Miller disposed of his interest to Daniel B. Sanderson on

May 18, 1819 and the paper was then published by Cotten & Sanderson. Sanderson had joined with Thomas Eastin in advertising proposals (see "Blakeley Sun, and Alabama Advertiser" of Dec. 15, 1818) for publishing the "Republican Constellation" at Cahawba, Ala., but since he so soon took on the "Mobile Gazette," the Cahawba paper presumably was never begun. In the Mobile Gazette of May 4, 1819, it was announced that during the summer months the paper would be published weekly. In the issue of June 23, 1819 Cotten announced that he had sold out to Sanderson and this issue was published by Daniel B. Sanderson. With the issue of June 30, 1819, Robert R. Dade was taken into partnership and the firm name became Sanderson & Dade. The paper was suspended with the issue of Sept. 22, until Oct. 27, 1819, on account of the fever. Sanderson died Sept. 29, 1819, and from Oct. 27, 1819 to January 1820, Dade published the paper alone. In the "Mobile Gazette" of Jan. 5, 1820, Christopher Dameron advertised proposals for a new semi-weekly at Mobile, to be called the "Alabama Gazette," to be published as soon as printing materials arrived from Philadelphia, and to be sent to those who had previously subscribed for the Pensacola Commercial Advertiser. Evidently Dade induced Dameron to abandon his scheme, for the Feb. 2, 1820 issue of the "Mobile Gazette" bore the imprint of Dade & Dameron, and from that time to after 1820 it was published by this firm. The title was changed to "Mobile Gazette & Com'al Advertiser" with the issue of May 3, 1820 and to "Mobile Gazette & General Advertiser" with the issue of July 27, 1820. With the issue of Oct. 3, 1820, it reverted to a semi-weekly, although a country paper, without heading, was also published weekly. Continued after 1820.

Cotten, on Aug. 7, 1819, advertised proposals for a new paper at Mobile to be called "The Alabamian" (see "New Orleans Daily Chronicle" of Sept. 13, 1819), but there is nothing to show that it was established.

Justus Wyman, in his "Geographical Sketch of Alabama Territory" (ms. printed in Ala. Hist. Soc. Trans., vol. 3, pp. 107–127), says that there were two newspapers at Mobile in 1819, but only the "Mobile Gazette" is now known, unless one includes the "Commercial Advertiser" previously noted. The Huntsville "Alabama Republican" of Jan. 8, 1819 states that there were then four papers in Alabama, which might mean those at Blakeley, Huntsville, Mobile and St. Stephens. The "Mobile Gazette" of Aug. 25, 1819 states: "There are no less than six newspapers published in the state, exclusive of our own. They are published at Huntsville, St. Stephens, Claiborne, Cahawba, Tuscaloosa and Mooresvill. Each of them is a weekly paper and of a small size."

Thomas W. Streeter, Morristown, N. J., has July 23, 1813, Extra.
Am. Antiq. Soc. has Aug. 4, 1813, Extra.
Univ. of Chicago has July 14, 1818.
Wis. Hist. Soc. has Nov. 3, 1818.
Lib. Cong. has Apr. 6, May 25–June 9, 23–July 21, Aug. 25–Sept. 8, 22, Oct. 27, Nov. 10, 17, Dec. 15, 1819; Jan. 5, Feb. 2, 23, Mar. 1, 15, 22, Apr. 4–June 15,

29–July 20, Aug. 3, 10, 24, 31, Sept. 14–28, Oct. 10, 20, 27, Nov. 10, Dec. 1, 8, 15, 22, 29, 1820. Also Apr. 27, May 4, 1819; Oct. 6, 1820 of country edition.

[Mooresville].

The "Mobile Gazette" of Aug. 25, 1819, states that there was a weekly newspaper published at "Mooresvill," Ala., in August 1819. No copy, however, has been located.

St. Stephens Gazette, 1816.

There is a reference to the St. Stephens, M. T., Gazette in the New Brunswick "Fredonian" of May 16, 1816. St. Stephens was then in Mississippi Territory in that part which became part of Alabama Territory in 1817. Possibly "Gazette" may have been used as a synonym for newspaper, meaning the "Halcyon."

[St. Stephens] Halcyon, 1815–1820+.

Weekly. Established in 1815, judging from the date of the first regular issue located, that of Jan. 9, 1819, vol. 4, no. 34, although in the issue of May 1, 1820, Thomas Eastin, the editor, refers to his six years' conduct of the paper since its commencement. Its full title was "The Halcyon, and Tombeckbe Public Advertiser." With the issue of Oct. 16, 1820, Joseph DeJeane became the publisher. An Extra of June 2, 1818 has no imprint or volume numbering. Continued after 1820.

> Lib. Cong. has Jan. 9, 18, Feb. 8–Mar. 1, 15, 22, Apr. 5, May 3–July 12, Aug. 9, Oct. 11, 18, Nov. 29–Dec. 20, 1819; Jan. 10–Mar. 7, 20–Apr. 10, May 1–15, 29–June 19, July 3, Aug. 14–28, Sept. 11, Oct. 2, 16–30, Nov. 20, 27, 1820.
> Am. Antiq. Soc. has June 28, Dec. 18, 1819.
> T. W. Streeter, Morristown, N. J., has June 2, 1815, Extra.

Tuscaloosa Republican, 1819–1820+.

Weekly. Thomas B. Grantland advertised in the "Mississippi State Gazette" of Dec. 12, 1818, proposals for the "Alabama Observer" to be published at the Falls of the Black Warrior, Alabama Territory. Presumably this paper never was established, as the "Mobile Gazette" of Apr. 23, 1819 advertised proposals for publishing "a weekly newspaper at Tuscaloosa (falls Black Warrior) to be entitled the Tuscaloosa Republican." In the Huntsville "Alabama Republican" of May 15, 1819, the editor states: "We have received one number of the Tuscaloosa Republican, printed at the falls of the Black Warrior." The "Mobile Gazette" of July 21, 1819, quotes from "The Tuscaloosa Republican" of July 1. In the "Nashville Gazette" of July 28, 1819, there is a reference to the "newspaper recently commenced at the falls of the Black Warrior." In the Charleston "City Gazette" of July 29, 1819, and the St. Stephens "Halcyon" of Oct. 16, 1820, there are references to the Tuscaloosa Republican. No copies have been located. That it was published by Thomas M. Davenport is shown by a reference in the Huntsville "Alabama Republican" of Sept. 18, 1819, which speaks of "Mr. Davenport" as the publisher. In the Library of Congress is an issue of the Tuscaloosa "American Mirror" of Jan. 3, 1824, vol. 5, no. 28, published by Thomas M. Davenport, which would show that the paper was established early in 1819, but had undergone a change of title.

ARKANSAS

[Arkansas Post] Arkansas Gazette, 1819–1820+.

Weekly. Established Nov. 20, 1819, by William E. Woodruff, at the Post, or village, of Arkansas in Arkansas Territory, with the title of "Arkansas Gazette." Robert Briggs was admitted to partnership, and beginning with the issue of March 4, 1820, the paper was published by Woodruff & Briggs. Continued after 1820.

Lib. Congress has Nov. 20, 1819–Dec. 30, 1820.

Ark. Hist. Commission has Nov. 20, 25, 1819; Jan. 8–Feb. 19, Mar. 11–May 6, 20–June 3, 17, 24, July 8–Aug. 26, Sept. 9–Dec. 30, 1820.

Am. Antiq. Soc. has Nov. 20, 1819; Apr. 8–29, May 13–July 1, 29–Aug. 26, Sept. 9–Oct. 7, Nov. 13 suppl., Dec. 2, 1820.

CONNECTICUT

Bridgeport Advertiser, 1806–1810.

Weekly. Established Apr. 10, 1806, judging from the date of the first issue located, that of June 5, 1806, vol. 1, no. 9, published by Hezekiah Ripley, with the title of "Bridgeport Advertiser." The last issue located is that of Jan. 5, 1809, vol. 3, no. 143. It was discontinued probably in the spring of 1810.

Bridgeport Pub. Lib. has June 5, 1806; Jan. 5, 1809.
Yale has Nov. 13, 1806.
Conn. State Lib. has June 11, 1807.
Am. Antiq. Soc. has Sept. 1, 1808.

[Bridgeport] American Telegraphe, 1800–1804.

Weekly. A continuation of the "American Telegraphe" of Newfield, the name of which village was changed to Bridgeport in October, 1800. The first issue with the Bridgeport imprint is that of Nov. 5, 1800, vol. 6, no. 44, printed by Lazarus Beach, with the title of "American Telegraphe." In the "Farmer's Journal" of Danbury of Sept. 29, 1801, Beach announces, under the date of Sept. 23, 1801, that he has sold his paper at Bridgeport, of which he had served as editor for seven years. "The business now passes into other hands," he states. An editorial in the "Farmer's Journal" of Jan. 26, 1802, indicates that Beach had "retaken the establishment of the 'Telegraphe.'" The issues from Sept. 29 to Dec. 15, 1802 were printed by Samuel Mallory for Beach and Mallory. The issues from July 20, 1803 to June 6, 1804 were published by Samuel Mallory. The "Republican Farmer" of Danbury, in the issue of Feb. 29, 1804, states, "Died, at Bridgeport, a few days ago, after a lingering illness, the 'American Telegraphe,' in the tenth year of its age." But this assertion must have been premature, as the paper was continued certainly until June 6, 1804, vol. 10, no. 23.

Conn. State Lib. has Nov. 5, 12, 1800; May 2, 1804.
Bridgeport Pub. Lib. has Mar. 7, 14, Apr. 25, June 6, 1804.
Lib. Congress has Jan. 14, 1801.
Am. Antiq. Soc. has July 22, Sept. 16, 1801; Dec. 15, 1802; July 20, 1803.
Martin Welles, Hartford, has Sept. 29, Oct. 6, 1802.

[Bridgeport] Connecticut Courier, 1814–1820+.

Weekly. Established June 1, 1814, judging from the date of the earliest issue located, that of Aug. 3, 1814, vol. 1, no. 10, published by N[athaniel] L. Skinner, with the title of "Connecticut Courier." It was continued by Skinner until after 1820.

Yale has Aug. 3, Nov. 2, Dec. 21, 1814; Feb. 22, Mar. 22, 29, Apr. 12, 1815; Aug. 28, 1816.
Bridgeport Pub. Lib. has Sept. 6, Dec. 27, 1815; Jan. 10, 24, Feb. 14, 1816; Oct. 29, Nov. 26, Dec. 31, 1817; Jan. 7, July 15, 1818.
N. Y. Pub. Lib. has Feb. 7, 1816; Mar. 19, 1817; Apr. 27, Sept. 26, 1819.
New Haven Col. Hist. Soc. has Feb. 21, 1816.
Shelton, Conn., Lib. has Nov. 27, 1816.
Conn. State Lib. has Jan. 10, 1820.
Am. Antiq. Soc. has June 21, Oct. 4, 1820.

Bridgeport Gazette, 1810–1811.

Weekly. Established May 16, 1810, judging from the date of the first issue located, that of June 27, 1810, vol. 1, no. 7, published by J[ ] Bulkley, with title of "Bridgeport Gazette." Before Aug. 15, 1810, the paper was disposed of to Byrne and Webb [Samuel H. Byrne and Samuel Webb], and was published by them as far as the last issue located, that of Jan. 9, 1811, vol. 1, no. 35.

Am. Antiq. Soc. has June 27, Aug. 15, Oct. 24, 31, 1810; Jan. 9, 1811.
Lib. Congress has Oct. 24, 1810.

Bridgeport Herald, 1805–1806.

Weekly. Established Feb. 28, 1805, by Samuel Mallory, with the title of "Bridgeport Herald." References to its establishment and editorial policy may be found in the Litchfield "Witness" of Oct. 30, 1805, and Mar. 26, 1806. The last issue located is that of Jan. 9, 1806, vol. 1, no. 43, and the paper was probably discontinued in the spring of 1806.

Am. Antiq. Soc. has Mar. 7, Oct. 25, 1805.
Yale has June 13, 1805.
Harvard has July 4, Aug. 1, 1805.
N. Y. Hist. Soc. has Jan. 9, 1806.

[Bridgeport] Patriot of Seventy-Six, 1804.

Weekly. Established July 11, 1804, judging from the first and only issue located, that of Aug. 1, 1804, vol. 1, no. 4, published by Samuel Mallory, with the title of "Patriot of Seventy-Six."

Bridgeport Pub. Lib. has Aug. 1, 1804.

[Bridgeport] Republican Farmer, 1810–1820+.

Weekly. Established Apr. 25, 1810, by Stiles Nichols & Co., with the title of "Republican Farmer." On Jan. 1, 1812, Stiles Nichols and Ephraim F. Nichols announced a dissolution of partnership, and the paper was thenceforth continued by Stiles Nichols until Oct. 21, 1812, when it was conducted by Nichols & Barnum [Stiles Nichols and Charles P. Barnum]. With the issue of Apr. 28, 1813, the firm name again became Stiles Nichols & Co., which, on Dec. 1, 1814 was changed to Stiles Nichols & Son [Roswell S. Nichols]. In the spring of 1818, the paper reverted to the proprietorship of Stiles Nichols, and so remained until after 1820.

> Am. Antiq. Soc. has Apr. 25, May 9, June 20, July 4, Aug. 1, 15, 22, Sept. 12–26, Nov. 21, 1810; Jan. 9, 23, Feb. 6, 20, 27, Mar. 20, Apr. 3, May 15, July 3, 31, Aug. 7, Oct. 16, 23, Nov. 6, Dec. 4, 1811; Jan. 15, June 24, July 22, Sept. 16, 1812; Jan. 6, Nov. 3, Dec. 22, 1813; Jan. 12, Feb. 9, Apr. 20, July 20, 27, Aug. 31, Sept. 21, 28, Oct. 12, Dec. 14, 1814; Mar. 8, 1815; Feb. 12, July 2, 9, 1817; Mar. 4, June 10, Sept. 9, 1818; May 26, 1819; Sept. 27, Oct. 4, 18, 1820.
> Bridgeport Pub. Lib. has May 23, Oct. 17, 31, Dec. 5–19, 1810; Feb. 6, Apr. 17, May 15, Aug. 7–21, Sept. 4–Oct. 16, 30, 1811; Oct. 7, 14, Nov. 4, Dec. 9, 1812; Jan. 2, 6, June 2, 9, Sept. 8, Dec. 22, 29, 1813; Jan. 26–Feb. 23, Mar. 23, 30, Apr. 13–27, May 18, 25, 1814; Mar. 1, 15, Oct. 11–Nov. 1, 22, Dec. 6, 13, 1815; Jan. 31, Feb. 14–28, 1816; Jan. 6, Mar. 5, 1817; Aug. 26, Sept. 23, Oct. 7, 1818; Apr. 7, June 23, July 14, 21, Aug. 11, 1819.
> Yale has May 23, July 4, 1810.
> Shelton, Conn., Lib. has Oct. 24, 1810; May 22, June 12, 1811.
> N. Y. Hist. Soc. has Aug. 26, 1812.
> Martin Welles, Hartford, has Nov. 14, 1810; Feb. 24, 1813–July 10, 1816, fair.
> Wesleyan Univ. has June 29, 1814.
> Lib. Congress has Dec. 16, 1818; Dec. 1, 1819.
> Wis. Hist. Soc. has Apr. 14, 1819.

[Brooklyn] Independent Observer, 1820+.

Weekly. Established in July 1820, judging from the earliest issue located, that of Dec. 18, 1820, vol. 1, no. 25, published by Henry Webb, 2nd, with the title of "Independent Observer, and County Advertiser." The "National Intelligencer" of Oct. 28, 1820, records the receipt of the initial issue of July 10, 1820, published by Henry Webb, 2nd.

> Am. Antiq. Soc. has Dec. 18, 1820.

[Danbury] Connecticut Intelligencer, 1809–1810.

Weekly. Established Dec. 6, 1809, by John C. Gray, with the title of "The Connecticut Intelligencer." The name was changed to "The Connecticut Intelligencer and Farmer's Aid" between Apr. 4 and June 6, 1810. The last issue located is that of Nov. 7, 1810, vol. 1, no. 41.

> Am. Antiq. Soc. has Dec. 6, 1809; Jan. 31, Mar. 14, Apr. 4, June 6, Nov. 7, 1810.

[Danbury] Day, 1812.

Weekly. Established May 12, 1812, by John C. Gray, with the title of "The Day." The last issue located, that of Dec. 15, 1812, vol. 1, no. 30, did not appear until Dec. 22, because of the death of the proprietor's wife, Esther Gray, on Dec. 13.

Am. Antiq. Soc. has May 19, June 9, Dec. 15, 1812.

[Danbury] Farmers Chronicle, 1793–1796.

Weekly. Established on June 17, 1793, judging from the date of the first known issue, Aug. 5, 1793, vol. 1, no. 8, published by Edwards Ely with the title of "Farmers Chronicle." On Apr. 20, 1795, Ely took Stiles Nichols into partnership and the paper was thenceforth published by Ely & Nichols. In the issue of Sept. 19, 1796, vol. 4, no. 38, the last located, it was announced that the firm of Ely & Nichols would be dissolved on Sept. 27, and that the business would be conducted by Nathan Douglas and Stiles Nichols. This firm started a paper on Oct. 3, 1796, with a new title, "Republican Journal," which see.

> Am. Antiq. Soc. has Aug. 5, Sept. 2, 23, Nov. 4, Dec. 16, 1793; Jan. 6, Apr. 28, May 19, June 30, Sept. 22, Dec. 15, 1794; Apr. 20, July 6, Aug. 3, 10, 24, Nov. 2, 16, Dec. 28, 1795; May 23–June 20, July 11, Aug. 1, Sept. 5, 1796.
> Boston Athenæum has Sept. 23, Nov. 25, 1793; Feb. 8, 1796.
> Phil. Lib. Co. has Sept. 30, Oct. 14, 21, 1793; Nov. 9, 1795; June 13, 20, 1796.
> Pequot Lib., Southport, has Nov. 4, Dec. 23, 30, 1793.
> Danbury Lib. has May 12, 1794.
> Harvard has Dec. 8, 1794; Jan. 5, Feb. 23, Mar. 9, 23, 30, May 25, June 22, July 6–20, Nov. 9, Dec. 28, 1795; Jan. 4, Aug. 8, 29, Sept. 5, 19, 1796.
> Lib. Congress has Mar. 16, 1795.
> Conn. Hist. Soc. has July 11, 1796.
> Bridgeport Pub. Lib. has July 18, 25, 1796.

[Danbury] Farmer's Journal, 1790–1793.

Weekly. Established Mar. 18, 1790, by Nathan Douglas and Edwards Ely, with the title of "The Farmer's Journal." It was discontinued presumably with the issue of June 3, 1793, vol. 4, no. 13, and the partners established two rival newspapers, the "Republican Journal," and the "Farmers Chronicle," which see.

> Am. Antiq. Soc. has Mar. 18, 1790–Dec. 26, 1791; Jan. 2–Mar. 19, Apr. 2–June 18, July 2–Aug. 18, Sept. 8–Oct. 13, 27–Dec. 29, 1792; Jan. 5, 12, 28–Feb. 11, Mar. 25–Apr. 8, 22, May 6, 27, 1793.
> Danbury Lib. has Apr. 7, 1790–Feb. 25, Mar. 11, 1793.
> N. Y. Hist. Soc. has Mar. 18, 1790–Mar. 8, 1791.

Yale has Apr. 1, 1790–Dec. 26, 1791, fair; Jan. 9, 30, Mar. 5, Sept. 29, 1792.
Lib. Congress has Mar. 25, Apr. 7, 15, May 6, June 3, 1790; Apr. 26, June 27, 1791; Aug. 18, 1792.
Bridgeport Pub. Lib. has Sept. 16–30, 1790; Jan. 4, Mar. 15, Apr. 19, June 13, 1791; Apr. 9, 16, 1792.
N. Y. Pub. Lib. has June 3, 1790.

[Danbury] Farmers Journal, 1800–1803.

Weekly. Established Apr. 7, 1800, judging from the date of the earliest issue located, that of Apr. 14, 1800, vol. 1, no. 2, published by Nichols & Morse [Stiles Nichols and Samuel Morse], with the title of "Farmers Journal." In June 1800 Morse retired from the firm to publish "The Sun of Liberty," and Stiles Nichols became sole publisher. By April, 1801, Nichols had taken Thomas Rowe into partnership and the paper was published by Nichols & Rowe. Between May 18 and Sept. 7, 1802, it reverted to Stiles Nichols, and he was the publisher as far as the issue of Feb. 1, 1803, vol. 3, no. 147. With the issue of Feb. 8, 1803, the title was altered to "Farmers Journal and Columbian Ark," a new numbering was started, the size was changed from folio to a quarto of eight numbered pages, and the publishers became Stiles Nichols & Co. In May or June, 1803, the title was shortened again to "Farmers Journal," and the size reverted to folio. The last issue located is that of Sept. 6, 1803, vol. 1, no. 31. The "Republican Farmer" was established Nov. 16, 1803.

Fairfield Hist. Soc. has Apr. 14, 1800.
Conn. Hist. Soc. has July 2, 1800.
Harvard has Apr. 14, June 16, 30, July 21, 28, Sept. 29, Oct. 27, Nov. 10–24, Dec. 8, 22, 29, 1801; Jan. 12, 26, Feb. 9, Apr. 20, May 18, 1802; Jan. 1, Mar. 1, July 26, 1803.
Danbury Lib. has May 5, 1801.
Am. Antiq. Soc. has Oct. 1, 1800; July 14, 1801; Apr. 6, 13, 1802; Feb. 1, Apr. 26, July 5, Aug. 16–Sept. 6, 1803.
Troy Pub. Lib. has Sept. 22, 1801.
N. Y. Hist. Soc. has Sept. 7, 1802; Feb. 15–May 3, 1803.
Lib. Congress has Feb. 1, Sept. 6, 1803.

Danbury Gazette, 1813–1814.

Weekly. Established on June 22, 1813, judging from the date of the first known issue, that of Aug. 3, 1813, vol. 1, no. 7, published by Nathaniel L. Skinner, with the title of "Danbury Gazette." The last issue located is that of Mar. 29, 1814, vol. 1, no. 41. Skinner removed to Bridgeport soon afterwards.
Lib. Congress has Aug. 3, 24–Sept. 28, Oct. 12, 26, Nov. 16–Dec. 14, 28, 1813; Jan. 4, 11, 25, 1814.

Am. Antiq. Soc. has Sept. 14, Nov. 23, Dec. 14, 1813; Jan. 11, 25, 1814.
Conn. Hist. Soc. has Oct. 5, Dec. 21, 1813; Feb. 22, Mar. 1–29, 1814.

[Danbury] New-England Republican, 1804–1809.

Weekly. Established July 18, 1804, by Gray & Steele [John C. Gray and Oliver Steele], with the title of "New-England Republican." John C. Gray became sole proprietor with the issue of January 23, 1805, and continued the paper until late in the year 1809. The last issue located is that of Nov. 16, 1808, vol. 5, no. 218. In the first issue of the Danbury "Connecticut Intelligencer," Dec. 6, 1809, Gray stated that "some weeks since" he had announced his intention of discontinuing the "New England Republican."

Wis. Hist. Soc. has July 18, Aug. 15, 29–Sept. 19, Oct. 14, 21, Nov. 14, 28–Dec. 26, 1804; Jan. 9, 23, 30, Feb. 13–Apr. 10, 24, May 1, 22, 29, 1805; Nov. 16, 1808.
Am. Antiq. Soc. has July 18, Oct. 31, 1804; Mar. 27, Apr. 17, May 29, Aug. 21, Dec. 11, 1805; Feb. 26, Mar. 5, Oct. 7, Nov. 12, Dec. 17, 1806; Jan. 6, Oct. 19, Nov. 16, 1808.
Yale has Aug. 29, Sept. 19, Oct. 17, Nov. 7, 1804; Jan. 23, 30, Mar. 13–27, Apr. 10–May 15, June 5, July 3–31, 1805.
Harvard has Sept. 12, 19, 1804; Jan. 2, 1805; Jan. 22, Feb. 12, 26–June 3, July 1, 29, Sept. 30, 1806.
N. Y. Pub. Lib. has July 25, 1804.
Conn. State Lib. has July 25, 1804.
N. Y. Hist. Soc. has Sept. 19, 1804; July 13, Oct. 12, 1808.
Pequot Lib., Southport, has Sept. 26, 1804.
Palmer Lib., Conn. Coll., New London, has Mar. 6, 1805; May 25, June 1, July 13–27, 1808.
Boston Athenæum has Dec. 26, 1804; Jan. 30, 1805.
Bridgeport Pub. Lib. has Aug. 14, 1805.
Univ. of Pittsburgh has May 8, 1805.
Lib. Congress has June 12, 1805.
Martin Welles, Hartford, has Aug. 7, 1805.
N. Y. State Lib. has Nov. 20, 1805.
Trinity Coll., Hartford, has Jan. 13, 1808.
Danbury Lib. has Apr. 6, 1808.
James H. Miller, Stamford, has Aug. 10, 1808.

[Danbury] Republican Farmer, 1803–1809.

Weekly. Established Nov. 16, 1803, by Thomas Rowe & Company, with the title of "Republican Farmer." In June, 1804, Joseph Hutchinson became the proprietor, and was succeeded by Hutchinson & Nichols [Joseph Hutchinson and Stiles Nichols] on Nov. 28, 1804, and this firm by Nichols & Rowe [Stiles

Nichols and Thomas Rowe] on Dec. 12, 1804. With the issue of Dec. 4, 1805, Stiles Nichols became sole proprietor. At some time between Feb. 24 and Apr. 6, 1808, Stiles Nichols & Son became proprietors, being followed on Oct. 19, 1808, by Stiles Nichols & Milton F. Cushing. Stiles Nichols again assumed sole proprietorship in June, 1809. The paper was discontinued soon after, but revived again with new numbering, vol. 1, no. 1, Aug. 16, 1809, by Ephraim F. Nichols, & Co. The last issue located is that of Sept. 6, 1809, vol. 1, no. 4. The paper was removed to Bridgeport, where on Apr. 25, 1810, it was reestablished by Stiles Nichols & Co.

> Am. Antiq. Soc. has Nov. 16–30, 1803; Jan. 18, July 11, Aug. 29, 1804; Jan. 2, Oct. 2, 1805; Feb. 19, May 14, June 18, July 9, Aug. 6, 1806; Dec. 16, 30, 1807; Oct. 12, 19, Dec. 7, 1808; Feb. 22, Mar. 8–29, June 28, July 5, Aug. 23–Sept. 6, 1809.
> Harvard has Dec. 21, 1803; Feb. 29, Mar. 7, 14, Apr. 4, 11, May 16, 23, July 18, Aug. 1, Sept. 12, Oct. 3, 1804; Jan. 2, 9, Mar. 13, 20, Apr. 3, 10, 24, May 1, 22, June 12, July 24, Aug. 7–21, Sept. 18, Oct. 2–16, Nov. 27, Dec. 11, 1805; Jan. 1–15, 29, Feb. 5, Mar. 5, 19–Apr. 9, 23, May 7–21, June 4, 11, 30, July 2, 23, Aug. 6, 20, Oct. 8, Nov. 19, 1806; Sept. 16, Oct. 7, 1807; June 22, Aug. 3, 17, 24, Sept. 7, 21–Oct. 19, Nov. 9, 30, Dec. 7, 1808.
> Wis. Hist. Soc. has July 18–Aug. 8, 22, 29, Sept. 12–Oct. 17, Nov. 14, 28–Dec. 26, 1804; Jan. 16, Feb. 6, 13, 27–Mar. 13, Apr. 3, 10, May 8, 22, 29, 1805; Jan. 29, 1806.
> Bridgeport Pub. Lib. has Dec. 12, 1804; Apr. 3, 1805; Jan. 8, Feb. 5, 1806; June 8, Nov. 9, 1808.
> Troy Pub. Lib. has Feb. 22, 29, July 4, 1804.
> New Haven Col. Hist. Soc. has Nov. 11, 1807.
> N. Y. Pub. Lib. has Nov. 23, Dec. 30, 1807; Jan. 20, Feb. 17, May 11, July 13, 1808.
> Ridgefield, Conn., Lib. has Jan. 6, 1808.
> Danbury Lib. has Apr. 6, 1808.
> Boston Athenæum has May 3, 17, 24, 1809.
> Lib. Congress has Aug. 23, 1809.

[Danbury] **Republican Journal**, 1793.

Weekly. Established June 17, 1793, judging from the date of the earliest issue located, that of July 1, 1793, vol. 1, no. 3, published by Nathan Douglas, with the title of "Republican Journal." Discontinued with the issue of Dec. 9, 1793, according to Douglas' advertisement in the "Farmers Chronicle" of Dec. 16, 1793.

> Boston Athenæum has July 1, Sept. 2, 9, Oct. 14, Nov. 4, 18, 1793.
> Am. Antiq. Soc. has July 15, Aug. 5, Sept. 23, Nov. 4, 1793.

[Danbury] Republican Journal, 1796–1800.

Weekly. Established Oct. 3, 1796, by Douglas & Nichols [Nathan Douglas and Stiles Nichols], with the title of "Republican Journal." The last issue located is that of Feb. 10, 1800, vol. 4, no. 173. The partnership was dissolved on Mar. 31, 1800, and Nichols became one of the editors of the "Farmers Journal" of Danbury in April, 1800.

> Harvard has Oct. 3, 31, Dec. 19, 1796; Jan. 16, Feb. 6–20, Mar. 27–Apr. 10, May 22, 29, July 3, 10, Sept. 18, Oct. 23, 1797; Jan. 5, Mar. 26, Apr. 2, 30, May 14, Sept. 10, 17, Nov. 5, 1798; Apr. 1, May 27, June 3, 1799.
> Am. Antiq. Soc. has Oct. 10, 17, 31, Nov. 21, 28, 1796; Jan. 9, 16, Feb. 6–Mar. 6, Apr. 3–17, May 15, 29–June 12, 26–July 24, Aug. 14, 28–Oct. 2, 30, Nov. 6, 27, Dec. 11–25, 1797; Jan. 1–15, Feb. 5–26, Mar. 26, Apr. 2, 16–May 21, June 4–18, Oct. 1, 29, 1798; Feb. 11, Mar. 18, July 15, 1799; Jan. 6, 1800.
> Yale has Oct. 31, 1796.
> Martin Welles, Hartford, has June 12, 1797.
> Rutgers Univ. has Oct. 2, 1797.
> Conn. Hist. Soc. has Dec. 30, 1799; Jan. 6, 1800.
> Univ. of Notre Dame Lib. has Oct. 16, 1797.
> Bridgeport Pub. Lib. has Mar. 6, 1797; Feb. 10, 1800.

[Danbury] Sun of Liberty, 1800.

Weekly. Established June 24, 1800, judging from the earliest issue located, that of July 1, 1800, vol. 1, no. 2, published by Samuel Morse, with the title of "The Sun of Liberty." The third issue was not published until July 30. In this issue of Oct. 8, 1800, vol. 1, no. 13, it was announced that the paper would be removed to Norwalk after that issue, which would cause a suspension of one week. See under Norwalk "Sun of Liberty."

> Minn. Hist. Soc. has July 1, 30–Sept. 10, 24, Oct. 1, 1800.
> Am. Antiq. Soc. has Aug. 13, Oct. 8, 1800.
> N. Y. State Lib. has Sept. 3–24, 1800.
> Conn. State Lib. has July 30, 1800.
> Yale has Sept. 24, 1800.

Fairfield Gazette, 1786–1789.

Weekly. Established July 13, 1786, judging from the earliest issue located, that of Oct. 26, 1786, vol. 1, no. 16, published by Miller & Forgue [Stephen(?) Miller and Francis Forgue], with the title of "The Fairfield Gazette." Before Feb. 15, 1787, this firm took Peter Bulkeley into partnership under the firm name of Miller, Forgue and Bulkeley, and lengthened the name of the paper to "The Fairfield Gazette; or, the Independent Intelligencer." This firm was dissolved

CONNECTICUT 19

early in August, 1787, Forgue & Bulkeley thenceforth being the firm name. The last issue located is that of Sept. 23, 1789, vol. 3, no. 49.

    Am. Antiq. Soc. has Oct. 26, 1786; Feb. 15, 22, Mar. 1, 8, May 10, June 7, July 25, Aug. 15, 29–Sept. 12, Nov. 15, 1787; Jan. 30, Mar. 12, Apr. 9–30, July 16, 23, Oct. 1, 1788; Feb. 25, June 17, Sept. 23, 1789.

    Fairfield Hist. Soc. has Feb. 22, Dec. 19, 1787.

    Bridgeport Pub. Lib. has May 28, 1788.

[Hartford] American Mercury, 1784–1820+.

Weekly. Established July 12, 1784, by Barlow and Babcock [Joel Barlow and Elisha Babcock], with the title of "The American Mercury." Barlow retired, and beginning with the issue of Nov. 14, 1785, the paper was published by Elisha Babcock. The title was altered to "American Mercury" with the issue of June 30, 1794. With the issue of Jan. 6, 1813, Elisha Babcock took his son Charles into partnership under the firm name of Elisha Babcock & Son, who continued the paper until after 1820.

    Yale has July 12, 1784–Dec. 26, 1820.

    Conn. Hist. Soc. has July 26, 1784–Dec. 26, 1820.

    Am. Antiq. Soc. has July 19–Dec. 27, 1784; Jan. 3, 1785–Dec. 21, 1789, fair; Jan. 4, 1790–Dec. 25, 1797; Jan. 1–Feb. 22, Mar. 8–22, Apr. 5–26, May 10–31, June 14, 21, July 5, Sept. 13, Oct. 4, 18–Nov. 1, 15–29, 1798; Jan. 17–Feb. 7, Mar. 7, 21, Apr. 4, 18–May 2, 23, 30, June 27, July 11, 25, Aug. 8, 15, 29–Nov. 14, Dec. 5, 19, 1799; Jan. 2, 1800–Dec. 25, 1806; Jan. 8, June 4, Oct. 15, 1807; Jan. 7, 1808–Dec. 28, 1809; Jan. 4, Feb. 1–22, Mar. 22, Apr. 5, 19, May 24, 31, June 28, July 19–Aug. 2, 16, Sept. 27, Dec. 6–27, 1810; Jan. 3–May 2, 16, June 6, 20–July 11, Aug. 1, 15, Sept. 19, Oct. 24–Nov. 7, 28–Dec. 12, 1811; Jan. 1, 8, Feb. 5, 26–Mar. 18, May 6–Dec. 30, 1812; Jan. 6, 1813–Dec. 31, 1816; Jan. 7, 1817–Dec. 29, 1818, fair; Jan. 5, 1819–Dec. 26, 1820.

    Conn. State Lib. has Sept. 6, 20, Dec. 27, 1784; Jan. 3, Feb. 28, Mar. 28, Apr. 11, 18, May 2, 16, 23, June 6, 13, July 25–Aug. 15, Sept. 12, Oct. 10–31, Dec. 12, 1785; Jan. 30, Feb. 6, 27, Mar. 13, Apr. 24–May 29, June 12, 26–July 10, Aug. 7, Sept. 11–25, Oct. 30, Nov. 6, 1786; Jan. 29, Feb. 5, 26, Mar. 5, 26, Apr. 16, June 25, July 16, 23, Aug. 20–Sept. 10, Oct. 1, 8, 22, Nov. 12, 19, 1787; Jan. 21–Feb. 11, Mar. 10–24, Apr. 21, May 5, Aug. 11, 25, Sept. 1, 15, Oct. 27, Nov. 10–24, 1788; Mar. 2–Apr. 13, June 1, July 27–Aug. 24, Sept. 21, Nov. 2, 9, Dec. 14, 28, 1789; Feb. 22, Mar. 15, Apr. 5, 12, July 19, Nov. 1–Dec. 27, 1790; Jan. 2, 23–Mar. 5, 19, Apr. 16, 30, May 7, 21, 28, June 11, 18, Sept. 10, 17, Oct. 1, 22, Dec. 24, 1792; Jan. 7, 1793–May 29, 1797, fair; June 19, 26, July 17–Aug. 7, Sept. 4, 25–Oct. 9, 1797; Jan. 1, 1798–Dec. 26, 1799; Jan. 9, 16, 30, Apr. 3, 17–May 1, June 5, July 3–17, Aug. 21, Oct. 2, 30–Dec. 11, 1800; Jan. 15, 29, Feb. 12, 26, Mar. 12, July 9, Aug. 6, Sept. 10, 17,

Oct. 1, 1801; Jan. 7, 1802–Dec. 21, 1809; Feb. 8, 22, 1810–Dec. 21, 1813; Jan. 4–18, Feb. 1, 8, Apr. 5, May 3, 10, 24, 31, July 12, 26, Aug. 9–23, Oct. 4, 11, 25, Nov. 1, Dec. 27, 1814; Jan. 31, Mar. 14, 29, Apr. 12, 19, June 7, Aug. 30, Sept. 6, 20–Oct. 11, 25, Nov. 15–Dec. 5, 1815; Jan. 2, 23, 30, Mar. 26, Sept. 17, 24, Oct. 29, Nov. 12–26, Dec. 10–31, 1816; Jan. 14, 1817–Dec. 28, 1819; Jan. 4, 11, 25–Feb. 8, 22–Mar. 7, 21–Apr. 11, May 2, 9, June 20–July 4, 25, Aug. 22, Sept. 26–Oct. 17, Nov. 7, 14, Dec. 26, 1820.

Lib. Congress has Oct. 18, 25, Nov. 22, 29, Dec. 13, 1784; Jan. 10–24, Feb. 14, Mar. 7, 21, 28, Apr. 11–25, May 30, June 6, 20–July 11, 25, Aug. 15–29, Sept. 12–26, Oct. 24, 31, 1785; Mar. 13, Sept. 4, 1786; Apr. 27, 1789; Jan. 11, 1790; Mar. 28, 1791; Jan. 2, Feb. 27, 1792–Dec. 25, 1797, fair; Jan. 1, Feb. 22, Apr. 26, May 17, 31, 1798; Jan. 3, 1799–Dec. 25, 1800; Jan. 8, 1801–Dec. 31, 1804, fair; Apr. 25, Sept. 12, Nov. 21, Dec. 19, 26, 1805; Mar. 27, Apr. 17, July 17, 31, Aug. 7, 21, Oct. 2, 9, 23, Nov. 6, 13, 1806; Nov. 26, 1807; Apr. 28, 1808–Dec. 29, 1809, fair; Feb. 1, Mar. 22, Sept. 27, Dec. 6, 1810; Jan. 3, Feb. 21–Mar. 7, 21, May 16, June 20, July 11, Dec. 5, 1811; May 13, 20, June 24, July 1, Aug. 5–Dec. 30, 1812; Jan. 20, 1813–Dec. 31, 1816, fair; Jan. 7, 21, Feb. 4, Apr. 15, May 27, June 10, 17, July 8–22, Aug. 5, 12, Sept. 30, Oct. 21, Nov. 4, Dec. 9, 1817; Feb. 10, 17, Mar. 10, 17, Apr. 7–21, May 26, June 23, Sept. 8, 22, Oct. 20, 27, Nov. 10, 17, Dec. 1, 22, 29, 1818; Jan. 5, 1819–Dec. 26, 1820.

N. Y. Pub. Lib. has Mar. 21, 28, Apr. 18, May 2, 1785; Feb. 27, 1786; Jan. 15, July 9, 1787; Mar. 3, June 23–July 7, Aug. 18, Sept. 29, Oct. 6, 1788; Jan. 11–25, Feb. 8, 22–Mar. 22, May 24, June 21, 1790; Feb. 7–Dec. 19, 1791, fair; Jan. 2, 16, Feb. 6, 20, Mar. 12, 26, Apr. 9, 23–May 7, 21, Sept. 3, Oct. 22, 1792; Jan. 7, 1793–Sept. 12, 1796, fair; Jan. 16, 1797; Jan. 25, Mar. 15–Dec. 20, 1798, fair; Jan. 10, Apr. 25, Dec. 12–26, 1799; Jan. 2, 1800–Sept. 17, 1801; Jan. 14, 1802–Dec. 29, 1803; Jan. 5, 1804–Mar. 20, 1806, fair; Oct. 25, 1810; Feb. 7, 1811; Jan. 1, Apr. 29, Sept. 9, 1812; May 5, 12, June 29, Aug. 10, Oct. 5–26, 1813; Sept. 20, 27, Oct. 15, 1814; Feb. 11–Apr. 15, May 20, 27, June 10, 1817; June 20–July 4, 1820.

Va. State Lib. has Mar. 3, 1788–Sept. 7, 1795.

Kent Lib., Suffield, has Jan. 4, 1798–Sept. 24, 1807.

Minn. Hist. Soc. has Apr. 15, 1793; July 29, 1802–Aug. 15, 1805; Mar. 1–15, July 3–24, Aug. 7–21, Sept. 18, Oct. 2, 9, 1806; Apr. 28, 1808–Oct. 11, 1810, fair; Jan. 25, 1814–May 3, 1815, fair.

Boston Pub. Lib. has July 26, Aug. 2, 30–Oct. 11, 25–Nov. 8, 22–Dec. 13, 27, 1784; Jan. 10–Feb. 4, 21, Mar. 21–Apr. 11, 25, May 9, 23, June 6, 20, July 4, 25, 1785; Oct. 20, 1788; Dec. 14, 1789; Apr. 4–May 16, 30, June 6, 27, July 4, 18–Sept. 26, Oct. 17–Nov. 7, 28–Dec. 26, 1791; Jan. 2, 30, Feb. 13–27, Mar. 12–Apr. 16, May 7, 21, June 4–18, July 2–Sept. 24, Oct. 22, Nov. 5, 12, 26, Dec. 10–31, 1792; Jan. 7, 21, 28, Feb. 11–Mar. 4, 25, Apr. 18, 29, May 20, June 10, Oct. 21, Nov. 18, Dec. 16, 30, 1793; Apr. 7, May 26, Aug. 4, 1794; Mar. 2, 23, 30, 1795; Aug. 24, 1813.

CONNECTICUT

Martin Welles, Hartford, has Aug. 30, 1784–June 20, 1785; July 11–25, Aug. 15–Sept. 12, Oct. 31, Nov. 14–Dec. 12, 1785; Jan. 2–16, 30, Feb. 6, 27, Mar. 27, Apr. 10, July 10, 17, 1786; Oct. 25, Dec. 20, 1790; Apr. 20, 1795; Jan. 11, Mar. 28, Apr. 25, May 16, 30, June 13, July 18, Aug. 15, 29–Sept. 19, Oct. 3–17, Nov. 14–28, Dec. 12–26, 1796; Jan. 16, Feb. 27–Mar. 13, Apr. 3, 24, June 5–19, July 31, Sept. 4, 1797; Mar. 4, 8, Apr. 19, 26, Oct. 18, 1798; Apr. 10, 1800; Jan. 1, 1801–Feb. 3, 1803, fair; Mar. 15, July 7, Sept. 8, 1803; Mar. 15, July 26, Aug. 16, 1804; Jan. 2, 1806–Dec. 27, 1810, fair; July 18, Aug. 29, Oct. 10, 24, Nov. 7, 14, 28–Dec. 12, 1811; Jan. 22, Feb. 5, 19, Mar. 25, Apr. 1, May 27, June 17, 24, Aug. 12, 19, Sept. 2, 9, 23–Oct. 14, 28, Nov. 18, Dec. 16, 23, 1812; Jan. 6, 27–Feb. 10, Mar. 3, Apr. 7–21, May 5–19, June 8, 15, July 6, Aug. 10, Sept. 28, Oct. 9–23, Nov. 9, 16, 30, Dec. 7, 21, 1813; Jan. 11, 18, Feb. 8, 15, June 14, July 12, Aug. 9, Sept. 6, 20, Oct. 4–Nov. 8, 29, Dec. 27, 1814; Jan. 10, 21, 31, Feb. 28, Mar. 7, 22, Apr. 5–19, 1815; Jan. 30, Feb. 13, 20, Mar. 12, Apr. 9, 23, 30, May 28, June 18, July 16, 23, Aug. 6, 27, Sept. 3, 10, Oct. 8, 13, Dec. 24, 31, 1816; Jan. 7, 1817–Dec. 26, 1820.

Mass. Hist. Soc. has Aug. 16, Nov. 15–29, Dec. 27, 1784; Jan. 10, Mar. 21, Apr. 11, 1785; Jan. 22, 1787; Jan. 23, Feb. 6–27, Mar. 12–26, 1792; Mar. 8, 1798.

N. Y. Hist. Soc. has Sept. 27, Oct. 25, 1784; Jan. 24–Dec. 19, 1785, fair; Jan. 9, 23, Feb. 20, Apr. 10, July 31, 1786; Mar. 17, 1788; Jan. 26, Apr. 20, June 8, Sept. 28, 1789; Mar. 8, 1790; Feb. 7, 1791; May 14, Oct. 8, 1792; Apr. 29, 1793; Feb. 5, May 21, Nov. 12, 1801; July 22, 1802–Dec. 26, 1805; Jan. 2, 16, 30, Feb. 6, Mar. 6, 13, Apr. 10–May 22, June 12, 19, July 3–17, 31, Aug. 14, 21, Sept. 4–18, Oct. 2, 16, 23, Nov. 6, 27, Dec. 4, 25, 1806; Jan. 15–29, Feb. 12, 26, Mar. 12, 19, May 7, Oct. 1, 1807; Oct. 6, 13, Nov. 3, 10, 1808; Mar. 21, Aug. 8, 1811; Feb. 22, 1812; Jan. 18, 1814; Mar. 13, 1817; Sept. 28, 1819.

Long Id. Hist. Soc. has Apr. 5, 1790–Mar. 21, 1791; Dec. 21, 1795–Dec. 12, 1796; July 3, 1800–Dec. 31, 1807; Jan. 12, 1809–Dec. 30, 1817.

Harvard has June 20, Sept. 26, Nov. 14, 1791; July 16, 1792; Dec. 15, 29, 1794; Jan. 26, Feb. 23–Mar. 30, Apr. 1, June 1, 22, July 6, 20, Aug. 3, Oct. 19–Nov. 16, 1795; Jan. 4, 1796–Nov. 3, 1803, fair; Apr. 12, 1804–Nov. 26, 1807, fair; Aug. 11, Sept. 29, Oct. 6, Nov. 3, 10, Dec. 8, 22, 1808.

Wis. Hist. Soc. has July 8, 1791; Oct. 6, 1794–Aug. 31, Nov. 23–Dec. 21, 1795; Jan. 4–Feb. 8, 1796; July 25, 1799; Sept. 24, 1801–Dec. 1, 1803; Jan. 5, Apr. 5, 19, June 7, July 5, Aug. 23, 30, Nov. 15–Dec. 6, 20, 1804; Jan. 3, Feb. 7–Mar. 7, Apr. 11–May 16, 30–June 13, 27–July 11, Aug. 15, 29, Sept. 5, 19, Oct. 3–17, Nov. 28, 1805; Feb. 13, May 15, Sept. 11, 1806; July 23, 30, Aug. 13, Sept. 3, 10, Oct. 1, 15, 22, Dec. 24, 1807; Jan. 28, Mar. 10, 17, June 2, Sept. 8, Dec. 22, 1808; Jan. 26, Apr. 27, July 6, 27, Aug. 3, 24, Sept. 14, 28, Nov. 2, Dec. 28, 1809; Jan. 25, Mar. 29, May 17, June 28, Sept. 13–27, 1810; Feb. 14,

Mar. 7, Apr. 11, May 16, June 6, 27, July 4, Aug. 22, Sept. 12, Oct. 10, 31–Nov. 21, 1811; Sept. 15, Nov. 10, 1818.

Dartmouth has July 12–Aug. 16, 30–Nov. 22, Dec. 6–27, 1784; Jan. 3–Feb. 7, Mar. 14, Apr. 11, May 2–16, 30, 1785.

Boston Athenæum has Aug. 13, 1787; Oct. 12, 1795–Oct. 2, 1797; Mar. 4, 1802–Mar. 1, 1804; Nov. 20, 1806; July 28–Nov. 10, 1808; Apr. 20, 27, 1809.

New Haven Colony Hist. Soc. has May 28, 1792; Feb. 10–Mar. 31, June 2, 1794; June 7, 1798; Mar. 10, 1803; Feb. 20, 1806; Jan. 1, 1812–Feb. 21, 1815; Dec. 15, 1818.

Otis Library, Norwich, has Jan. 7, Apr. 22, 29, May 13, 27, 1802–Dec. 29, 1803.

Trinity has Jan. 7, 1808–June 6, 1820, fair.

Cornell has Apr. 6, 1809; Sept. 7, 1809–Dec. 27, 1810.

Rutgers Univ. has July 22, 1802–Dec. 29, 1803; Jan. 3–Dec. 5, 1805; Mar. 6–Aug. 21, 1806; Oct. 6, 13, 1808.

Several libraries have single or a few scattering issues.

[Hartford] Connecticut Courant, 1764–1820+.

Weekly. Established Oct. 29, 1764, although this issue was a specimen or prospectus, numbered 00. This prospectus stated that the first issue would appear on Nov. 19, 1764, but since the first known issue, that of Dec. 3, 1764 (no. 2) makes no mention of being delayed in any way, it is probable that the first issue appeared on Nov. 26. The changes in the title were as follows: "The Connecticut Courant," Oct. 29, 1764–Nov. 3, 1766; "The Connecticut Courant; and the Weekly Advertiser," Nov. 10, 1766–Apr. 4, 1767; "The Connecticut Courant," Apr. 11, 1767–May 31, 1774; "The Connecticut Courant, and Hartford Weekly Intelligencer," June 7, 1774–Feb. 10, 1778; "The Connecticut Courant," Feb. 17, 1778; "The Connecticut Courant, and the Weekly Intelligencer," Feb. 24–Apr. 28, 1778; "The Connecticut Courant," May 5, 12, 1778; "The Connecticut Courant, and the Weekly Intelligencer," May 19, 1778–Jan. 2, 1781; "The Connecticut Courant and Weekly Intelligencer," Jan. 9, 1781–Sept. 2, 1783; "The Connecticut Courant, and Weekly Intelligencer," Sept. 9, 1783–Mar. 14, 1791; "The Connecticut Courant," Mar. 21, 1791–Oct. 4, 1809; "Connecticut Courant," Oct. 11, 1809–1820+.

The changes in the names of the publishers were as follows: Thomas Green, Oct. 29, 1764–Apr. 19, 1768; Green and Watson [Thomas Green and Ebenezer Watson], Apr. 25, 1768–Mar. 19, 1771; Ebenezer Watson (Watson died Sept. 16, 1777), Mar. 26, 1771–Sept. 15, 1777; no name of publisher given, Sept. 22, 1777–Dec. 30, 1777; Watson and Goodwin [Hannah Watson and George Goodwin], Jan. 6, 1778–Feb. 23, 1779; Hudson & Goodwin [Barzillai Hudson and George Goodwin], Mar. 2, 1779–Nov. 14, 1815; George Goodwin & Sons, Nov. 21, 1815–Dec. 26, 1820+.

Conn. Hist. Soc. has Oct. 29, Dec. 3–31, 1764; Jan. 7–21, Mar. 4, 11, 25, Apr. 1, 29–Oct. 14, Dec. 30, 1765; Jan. 6, 1766–Dec. 26, 1820.

Connecticut

Yale has May 6, 13, Aug. 26, Sept. 16, 30, Oct. 7, 28, 1865; Jan. 6–Feb. 3, Mar. 31, May 12, Sept. 22, Oct. 20, 1766; Sept. 14, 28, 1767; Jan. 2, 30, Feb. 13, Mar. 27, Apr. 3, 17, 24, May 22, June 5, 12, 26, July 10, 31, Aug. 28–Sept. 18, Oct. 9–Dec. 4, 1769; Dec. 17, 1771; Feb. 9, May 11, 1773; Apr. 12–26, May 24, Sept. 19, 26, Oct. 17, Dec. 12, 1774; Jan. 2–16, 30, Apr. 10, 17, May 8–June 19, July 3, 24–Sept. 4, 25, Oct. 16, 23, Nov. 6, 13, Dec. 4, 11, 1775; Jan. 22–Dec. 30, 1776; Jan. 6, Feb. 10, 17, Mar. 17–Apr. 28, May 12, 19, July 28, Aug. 11, Sept. 8, 22, Oct. 28, Nov. 4, 18, 25, Dec. 16, 23, 1777; Jan. 13, 1778–Dec. 28, 1784, fair; Jan. 4, 1785–Dec. 26, 1820.

Lib. Congress has Aug. 11, 25, Sept. 8, 22, 29, Oct. 20–Nov. 10, 24–Dec. 22, 1766; Jan. 5, 1767–Dec. 28, 1773, fair; Jan. 4, 1774–Dec. 31, 1782; Jan. 7–Sept. 2, 23, Oct. 14, Nov. 4, 18, Dec. 2–16, 1783; Mar. 16, Apr. 6, 20, 27, June 1, 15, 29, Aug. 31, Sept. 7, 21–Oct. 5, Nov. 9, 30, Dec. 21, 1784; Jan. 4, 1785–Nov. 26, 1798; Jan. 7, 1799–Dec. 26, 1820.

Am. Antiq. Soc. has May 12, Dec. 1, 1766; Apr. 27, Oct. 19, Nov. 30, 1767; Jan. 23, 1769; July 16, 1770; Sept. 21, 1773; Aug. 16, 1774; May 1, 22, July 24, Nov. 13, 27, Dec. 11, 1775; Jan. 1, 1776–Dec. 30, 1783, fair; Jan. 6, 13, Feb. 3, 10, 24–Mar. 23, Apr. 6, 13, 27, May 18–June 15, 29, July 13–Aug. 3, Sept. 14, 21, Oct. 12–26, Nov. 9–30, Dec. 21, 1784; Jan. 4–Dec. 26, 1785; Jan. 2, 1786–Dec. 29, 1788, fair; Jan. 5, 1789–Dec. 30, 1793; Jan. 6–Dec. 29, 1794, fair; Jan. 12–May 18, June 1, 29, July 13–27, Aug. 10–24, Sept. 7, 21, Oct. 19, Nov. 9, 23, Dec. 28, 1795; Jan. 11–25, Mar. 21, May 23–Dec. 26, 1796; Jan. 2, 9, 23–Mar. 27, Apr. 10–May 1, 22, June 26–Aug. 21, Sept. 11–Oct. 2, 16–Dec. 25, 1797; Jan. 1, 29, 1798–Dec. 26, 1820.

Conn. State Lib. has July 21, 1766; Apr. 20, July 13–27, Sept. 7, 1767; July 28, 1772; Jan. 26, 1773; May 24, July 19–Dec. 26, 1774; Jan. 2–May 22, Sept. 11, Oct. 2, 1775; Jan. 29, Feb. 5, Mar. 18, Apr. 1, 22, Aug. 12, Sept. 16, Oct. 7, Nov. 18, Dec. 2–16, 30, 1776; Jan. 20, Mar. 31, June 16, Nov. 25, 1777; Nov. 24, 1778; Jan. 5, May 4, June 15, 29, July 20–Aug. 3, Sept. 14–28, Oct. 12, Nov. 16, 1779; Feb. 15, 22, May 9–June 6, 27–Aug. 22, Sept. 12, Nov. 7–28, 1780; Jan. 23, Mar. 6, June 12, Aug. 28, Nov. 13, 1781–Nov. 25, 1783, fair; Feb. 24–Mar. 9, Apr. 6, May 4, 25, June 1, Oct. 12, 1784; Jan. 18, 1785–Dec. 31, 1789, fair; May 17, 1790; Aug. 29, 1791; Feb. 20, Mar. 19, Dec. 31, 1792; Jan. 7, 1793–Dec. 26, 1820.

N. Y. Pub. Lib. has Aug. 10, 1767; Mar. 27, 1769; Dec. 18, 1770; Mar. 12, 1771; Dec. 5, 1774; Apr. 29–May 13, June 3–Oct. 21, Nov. 4–Dec. 9, 1776; Apr. 7, May 5, 1777; Apr. 21, May 26–Aug. 25, Sept. 8–29, 1778; Feb. 23–Mar. 9, Apr. 20, Aug. 3, Sept. 7, 28, Nov. 23, Dec. 14, 1779; Jan. 4, 1780–Apr. 26, 1785; July 17, Aug. 14, 1786; Apr. 9, 1787–Feb. 16, 1789; June 21, Aug. 2, 1790; Sept. 17, 1792; Nov. 11, 1793; Aug. 4, 1794; Jan. 12, Feb. 23, Mar. 16, May 4, 11, July 27, Aug. 17, Sept. 14, 21, Oct. 5, Dec. 14, 21, 1795; Jan. 4, 1796–Dec. 26, 1820.

Wis. Hist. Soc. has Sept. 6, 1774; May 2, Oct. 3, 1780; Dec. 4, 1786–May 31,

1790; Jan. 31, 1791–Dec. 30, 1793; Feb. 24–Oct. 20, 1794; Nov. 2, 9, 16, 1795; May 6, 1799–Dec. 26, 1820.

N. Y. State Lib. has Apr. 19, June 28, Sept. 12, Oct. 10, 17, 1774; Apr. 28, Dec. 2, 1777; Jan. 6, 20, Feb. 10–24, Mar. 17, 31–Apr. 14, May 5, 12, 26–June 30, July 21, 28, Aug. 11–Sept. 1, 15, 22, Oct. 13–27, 1778; Oct. 29, 1787; Apr. 10, 1794; July 10, 1797–Dec. 22, 1800, fair; Aug. 30, 1802–Dec. 12, 1804, fair; Jan. 7, 1807–Dec. 28, 1808; Jan. 25–Sept. 20, 1809, fair; Jan. 9, 1811–Dec. 28, 1813.

N. Y. Hist. Soc. has Jan. 14, Mar. 11, June 24, Sept. 16, 1765; Mar. 3, Sept. 29–Oct. 13, 1766; Apr. 27, Oct. 19, 1767; Feb. 8, May 2, 9, Oct. 3, 1768; Jan. 2–Nov. 13, 1769, fair; Apr. 16, July 2, 16, 1770; Mar. 5, May 14, 1771; Apr. 7, 1772; Dec. 19, 1774; Apr. 3, 10, May 1–15, June 12, July 10, 17, 31, Nov. 27, 1775; Jan. 29, Feb. 5, 19–Mar. 11, 25, Apr. 8, May 13–Sept. 2, 30, Oct. 14, 28, Nov. 11, 18, Dec. 9, 23, 1776; Jan. 13, Mar. 17, Apr. 7, 28, May 5, 1777; May 5, June 9, 16, 30, Sept. 15, Oct. 20, 1778; Jan. 5, 1779–Dec. 26, 1780; Jan. 9, Feb. 20, Apr. 3, Nov. 27, Dec. 4, 11, 1781; Mar. 12, 19, Apr. 2, June 25, July 30, Sept. 3, 10, Oct. 8, Dec. 10, 1782; Jan. 14, 28, Feb. 11, July 1, 29–Aug. 12, 26, 1783; Apr. 20, May 18, Nov. 28, 1784; Jan. 25, Mar. 15, 22, Apr. 5, 12, 26, 1785; Feb. 20, 1786; Feb. 26, May 21, July 2, 16, 23, Aug. 6, Sept. 17, Oct. 8, Dec. 17, 1787; Aug. 18, 25, Sept. 29, 1788; Feb. 9, Aug. 31, 1789; Jan. 28, Feb. 4, 25, Mar. 4, 22–Apr. 5, 26–May 10, June 14, 28, Sept. 6, 1790; May 23, 30, Sept. 26, 1791; Apr. 9, Aug. 20, Dec. 17, 1792; Jan. 7, 21–Feb. 4, 18, Mar. 4, May 6, 1793; Jan. 5–Dec. 28, 1795; Dec. 18, 25, 1797; Jan. 1, 22, Mar. 12, 19, Apr. 2–Dec. 31, 1798; Jan. 21, 28, Feb. 18, Mar. 4–Apr. 1, 15–May 6, June 3, 17–Aug. 26, Sept. 16–Dec. 23, 1799; Jan. 6, 1800–Dec. 26, 1820, fair.

Mass. Hist. Soc. has June 17, 24, 1765; Sept. 1, 29, Oct. 6, 1766; Apr. 10, May 1, 15, 29, June 19, 1769; Mar. 26, June 9, Sept. 17, 1770; Jan. 29, Apr. 7, May 7, 14, July 16, 30, Sept. 3, 24, Dec. 17, 31, 1771; Feb. 4, Apr. 21, May 5, 12, July 21, 28, 1772; Apr. 27, Dec. 7, 1773; May 24, June 21, Aug. 9, Dec. 12, 1774; Apr. 17, 24, Sept. 11, Dec. 11, 1775; Feb. 12, Apr. 22, June 17, July 8, 29, Oct. 14, 28, Nov. 25, Dec. 2, 1776; June 2, 16, Sept. 29, Oct. 14, 1777; May 5, July 7, Sept. 1, Nov. 10, Dec. 15, 22, 1778; Jan. 19, May 11, Oct. 26, Nov. 2, 16, Dec. 21, 1779; Jan. 18, Feb. 15, Mar. 21, Aug. 22, Sept. 19, Dec. 19, 26, 1780; Jan. 9, Feb. 13, Oct. 2, Nov. 6, 20, Dec. 18, 25, 1781; Mar. 26, Apr. 2, 30, May 7, 14, 28, June 25, July 16, Sept. 10, Nov. 19, 1782; Feb. 18, May 13, 1783; Feb. 3, Mar. 2, 16, July 27, Sept. 14, 1784; Jan. 4, 18, Apr. 12, 19, Dec. 19, 1785; Mar. 13, 1786; Feb. 5, 1787; Jan. 2–Nov. 13, Dec. 4, 25, 1797; Feb. 12, 19, Mar. 5, 19, May 28, July 23, 1798; Jan. 7, 1799–Dec. 28, 1801; Apr. 20, Nov. 23, 1803; Jan. 4, 1804–Dec. 31, 1806; Jan. 21–Apr. 1, 22–May 13, June 10–July 8, Oct. 28, Nov. 4–18, Dec. 16, 1807; Jan. 6, 1808–Dec. 30, 1817; June 23, 1818; July 11, 18, 1820.

Martin Welles, Hartford, has Dec. 28, 1767; Feb. 6, 1769; Sept. 10, 1770; Dec. 12, 19, 1774; Aug. 14, Oct. 30, Nov. 20–Dec. 4, 1775; Feb. 19–Mar. 11,

CONNECTICUT 25

Apr. 1, 15, May 13, 27, June 3, July 22, Sept. 23, Nov. 11, 1776; Jan. 6, Feb. 3–17, Mar. 3, 17, 24, Apr. 21, 28, June 16–30, July 7, Aug. 18, 25, Sept. 29, Oct. 21, Nov. 4, 11, 1777; Jan. 6–27, Feb. 10, 17, Mar. 24, Apr. 7, 14, 28–June 30, July 14, 21, Aug. 18, 25, Sept. 8, 22, 29, Nov. 10–Dec. 22, 1778; Jan. 12, May 4, 25, Aug. 17, 24, 1779; Oct. 17, 1780; June 26, 1781; Sept. 10, 1782; Jan. 28, Apr. 1, May 13–June 10, 24, July 8, 22, Sept. 2, 16–30, Nov. 4, Dec. 23, 1783; Jan. 6, Mar. 12, 23, June 22, 29, Aug. 31, Oct. 26, 1784; Jan. 4, 18–Feb. 22, Mar. 15–Apr. 5, 19, May 23–June 27, July 11–Aug. 29, Sept. 19–Oct. 3, 24–Nov. 14, 28, Dec. 5, 19, 1785; Feb. 9, May 4–July 2, 16–Aug. 20, Sept. 3, 24, Oct. 1, 20, Nov. 5–19, Dec. 3–31, 1787; Jan. 14–Apr. 14, May 5–26, 1788; Aug. 3, Nov. 30, 1789; Sept. 20, 27, Oct. 18, 1790; Jan. 3, Mar. 7, 14, Apr. 4, 25, May 2, 16–30, June 20, July 11, Aug. 1, 15–Sept. 5, 19, Oct. 10, 17, Nov. 7, 21, 28, 1791; Feb. 20, Mar. 19, May 7, 28, June 18, Oct. 8, Dec. 17–31, 1792; Jan. 7, 1793–Dec. 31, 1806, fair; Jan. 14–28, Feb. 18–Mar. 4, 25, Apr. 8, 15, May 6–27, June 17, July 1, Aug. 5, 19–Dec. 30, 1807; Jan. 6, 1808–Dec. 26, 1820, good.

Boston Pub. Lib. has May 13, 27, June 24, July 1–22, Aug. 12, 19, Sept. 30, Oct. 14, Nov. 4, 25, 1776; Mar. 24, July 21, 28, Aug. 18, 25, Sept. 8, 22, 29, Nov. 15, 1777; Apr. 28, May 26, June 16, 30–July 14, 28–Sept. 8, Oct. 27, Nov. 3, 17, Dec. 15, 1778; Feb. 9, 16, Mar. 16, Apr. 26, May 11, June 29, July 6, 1779; Mar. 21, Apr. 25, 1780; Apr. 17, Aug. 7, 14, Oct. 9, Nov. 20, Dec. 4–18, 1781; Feb. 5, 1782; July 13, 1784; Feb. 1, 1785; Jan. 28, June 2, July 7–Dec. 29, 1788; Jan. 5, 1789–July 4, 1790, fair; Feb. 7, 1791–July 18, 1792, fair; Sept. 17, 24, 1792; Dec. 9, 1793; Mar. 17, Apr. 17, June 2–July 28, Aug. 18–Sept. 29, 1794; Aug. 24, 1795; Mar. 28–Dec. 26, 1796, fair; Jan. 2–Dec. 25, 1797; Jan. 1–Dec. 31, 1798, fair; Jan. 7, 1799–Dec. 27, 1809; Nov. 3, 1812; Jan. 7–Dec. 30, 1817.

Bronson Lib., Waterbury, has Aug. 17, 1779; Jan. 20, Apr. 20, May 4, 18, June 8–22, July 27, Aug. 3, Sept. 7, Oct. 5, Nov. 9, Dec. 14, 1784; Jan. 11–25, Mar. 3, Apr. 5, 1785; Mar. 10, 1788; Mar. 23, 1789; July 12, 1790; Apr. 12, 1802; July 27, 1803; Aug. 1, 8, 1804; Jan. 9–Feb. 13, Mar. 27, Apr. 17–June 5, July 24, 1805; Oct. 22, 1806; May 12, June 9, 16, July 14, 1812; Feb. 2, 1813; Mar. 7, 14, May 31, 1815; June 11, 18, 1816.

Dartmouth Coll. Lib. has Nov. 20, Dec. 11, 1781; Jan. 1–Dec. 31, 1782, fair; Jan. 7, 1783–Dec. 28, 1784; Feb. 15–Mar. 8, 29, Apr. 5, 19, 26, 1785; Jan. 2, 1786–Dec. 29, 1794; Jan. 7, 1799–Dec. 27, 1809; Jan. 3–Dec. 26, 1810, fair; Jan. 9, Feb. 20, Mar. 13–Apr. 3, 17, May 1, 15–29, July 24, Dec. 31, 1816; June 17, 1817–Dec. 26, 1820, fair.

Boston Athenæum has Mar. 19, 1782–Aug. 19, 1783, fair; Feb. 11, 18, Mar. 8, 15, Apr. 12, 19, May 24, June 21, 1790; June 17, 24, July 29, Oct. 7, 14, 1793; Nov. 3, 1794–Dec. 30, 1796; Jan. 19, July 1, 29–Aug. 19, Sept. 2, Nov. 4, Dec. 30, 1799.

New Haven Colony Hist. Soc. has Sept. 1, 1778; Sept. 26, 1780; Sept. 9, 1783–May 18, 1784; July 18, 1785–Dec. 31, 1787; Jan. 19–Nov. 23, 1795, fair;

Apr. 3, 1797–Nov. 25, 1799; June 8–Dec. 28, 1801; Feb. 1–Aug. 30, 1802, scattering; Jan. 5–Dec. 28, 1803, fair; Jan. 4, 1804–Dec. 27, 1809; Jan. 5, 1819–Dec. 26, 1820.

Hartford Courant Office has Jan. 6, 1784–Dec. 26, 1820.

Case Mem. Lib., Hartford Seminary, has Jan. 4, 1804–Dec. 26, 1820.

Univ. of Mich. (Clements) has Jan. 19, 1767; July 8, 1776; Sept. 29, 1777; June 23, 1778; Aug. 24, Oct. 26, 1779; Jan. 16, 1781; Sept. 10, 1782; Mar. 18, 1783; Jan. 21, 1788; July 20, 1789; Apr. 26, 1790; May 9, Oct. 31, 1791; Dec. 2, 9, 1793; Jan. 13–Aug. 25, 1794, fair; Oct. 12–Dec. 28, 1795; Jan. 4, 1796–Nov. 6, 1797; Feb. 12–Dec. 31, 1798, fair; Jan. 7, 1799–Dec. 25, 1811; Jan. 1, Sept. 29, Oct. 6, 1812; June 8, 1813; Jan. 10–Dec. 26, 1815; Sept. 10, 1816; Mar. 17, Aug. 25, Dec. 22, 1818; Oct. 3, Nov. 7, 1820.

Univ. of Chicago has Jan. 6, 1784–Dec. 18, 1786, fair; Jan. 7–Oct. 11, 1790; Jan. 3, 1791–Nov. 24, 1812, fair; May 4, 18, June 1, July 20, Aug. 3–17, Sept. 7, 14, 22, Oct. 12–26, Nov. 16, 1813; Apr. 5, May 24–Dec. 25, 1814, fair; Jan. 3–Nov. 7, 1815, fair; Mar. 26, June 25, July 30, Aug. 6, Dec. 10, 1816; Jan. 14, Feb. 11, 25, Mar. 4, 18, Apr. 15, June 10, July 7, 22, Aug. 19, Sept. 9, 30, Oct. 14, 28, Nov. 11, 1817.

Va. State Lib. has June 3, 1793–Mar. 7, 1796.

Harvard has May 7, 14, 28, June 4, 18, July 2, 16, 1792; Jan. 5, 19, 26, Feb. 23, Mar. 2, 16, June 15, 22, July 6, 20, Aug. 3, Sept. 14, Oct. 12, 1795; Jan. 11, May 9, 16, June 20, July 11, Aug. 1–Sept. 19, Oct. 3–31, Nov. 14, Dec. 5, 19, 26, 1796; Jan. 2, 16–Feb. 20, Mar. 20, 27, Apr. 17, May 1, 29–June 26, July 10, 17, Sept. 18, Oct. 2–16, Nov. 20, Dec. 18, 1797; Jan. 8, 22, 29, Feb. 19, Mar. 19, 26, Apr. 9, May 14, June 11, July 9, Sept. 3, 17, 24, Oct. 8, 22, 29, 1798; Sept. 2, 16, 23, Nov. 11, Dec. 2, 16–30, 1799; Jan. 20, 1800–Dec. 30, 1807, fair; May 18, Aug. 10–24, Sept. 21, Oct. 5, 26, Nov. 9–23, Dec. 14–28, 1808.

Long Id. Hist. Soc. has Oct. 27, 1794–Dec. 14, 1795; Dec. 19, 1796–Feb. 27, 1797; Jan. 14, 1799–Dec. 21, 1819.

Hist. Soc. Penn. has Mar. 27, July 17, Sept. 11, 18, Oct. 23–Nov. 6, 1769; Nov. 2, 1779; Nov. 11, 1783; Jan. 5–Dec. 28, 1795; Jan. 2, 1797–Dec. 31, 1798.

Trinity Coll. has Jan. 19, 1795–Dec. 30, 1799, fair.

York Inst., Saco, has Jan. 3, 1798–Apr. 10, 1805.

Western Reserve Hist. Soc. has Jan. 28–Dec. 23, 1799; Jan. 5, Feb. 16, 23, Aug. 10–Dec. 28, 1801; Jan. 4, 1802–Dec. 27, 1814; Apr. 1, 1817–Dec. 26, 1820.

Univ. of Ill. has May 8, July 10, Oct. 2–23, 1797; Jan. 1, Feb. 19, July 16, Sept. 3, Oct. 1, Nov. 26, 1798; Feb. 11, 1798–Dec. 26, 1815, fair.

Duke Univ. has Jan. 18, Mar. 21, Aug. 22, 1780; Mar. 20, Nov. 27, 1781; Mar. 19, Apr. 23, July 9, Sept. 10, 24, Dec. 10, 17, 31, 1782; Feb. 25, Mar. 4–May 6, 20, June 10–July 15, 29, Aug. 12–Sept. 2, 1783; Sept. 17, 1787; Mar. 15, 1790–Dec. 31, 1792, fair; Jan. 8, 1798–Dec. 29, 1802, fair; Jan. 4, 1814–Dec. 26, 1815, and other scattering issues.

Hartford Times has Jan. 7, 1807–Dec. 26, 1820.
Phil. Lib. Co. has Dec. 30, 1799–Dec. 28, 1801; Jan. 5, 1803–Dec. 23, 1807, fair.
Detroit Pub. Lib. has Jan. 4, 1802–Dec. 28, 1803.
Penn. State Lib. has June 1805–Jan. 1806.
Cornell Univ. has Sept. 6, 1809–Dec. 29, 1810, fair.
Rutgers Univ. has Apr. 22–Dec. 23, 1776; Dec. 22, 1800–July 16, 1806, scattering issues; Mar. 7, 1810–Mar. 13, 1811, fair; Jan. 5, 1813–Dec. 5, 1820, scattering issues.
Middlesex Co. Hist. Soc., Middletown, has Jan. 2, 1816–Dec. 28, 1819.

[Hartford] Connecticut Intelligencer, 1804.

Weekly. Established Mar. 17, 1804, by Oliver Steele, with the title of "The Connecticut Intelligencer." The last issue located is that of May 8, 1804, vol. 1, no. 8. Discontinued during the year. Steele became one of the editors of the "New England Republican" at Danbury in July, 1804.

Long Id. Hist. Soc. has Mar. 24–May 8, 1804.
Harvard has Apr. 14, 24, May 8, 1804.
Am. Antiq. Soc. has Mar. 17, Apr. 24, 1804.
Duke Univ. has Apr. 14, 1804.

[Hartford] Connecticut Mirror, 1809–1820+.

Weekly. Established July 10, 1809, by Charles Hosmer, with the title of "Connecticut Mirror." The following were the changes in proprietorship: Charles Hosmer, July 10, 1809–Dec. 2, 1811; Hale and Hosmer [Horatio G. Hale & Charles Hosmer], Dec. 9, 1811–Nov. 21, 1814; Charles Hosmer, Nov. 28 (printed 21), 1814–May 13 (printed 18), 1816; Benjamin L. Hamlen, May 20, 1816–May 12, 1817; Hamlen & Newton [B. L. Hamlen and Abner Newton, Jr.], May 19, 1817–Aug. 24, 1818; for the Proprietors, Aug. 31, 1818–Oct. 12, 1818; Stone & Lincoln [William L. Stone and Simeon Lincoln], Oct. 19, 1818–May 29, 1820; S[imeon] Lincoln, June 5, 1820–1820+.

Am. Antiq. Soc. has July 10, 1809–Dec. 25, 1820.
Yale has July 10, 1809–Dec. 25, 1820.
Conn. Hist. Soc. has July 10, 1809–Dec. 25, 1820.
Conn. State Lib. has July 10, 1809–Dec. 25, 1820, good.
Ohio Arch. & Hist. Soc. has July 10, 1809–Dec. 25, 1820, fair.
Hist. Soc. Penn. has July 10, 1809–June 22, 1818; June 28, 1819–Dec. 25, 1820.
Wis. Hist. Soc. has July 17, 1809–Dec. 28, 1818.
Pequot Lib., Southport, has July 10, 1809–June 22, 1818.
Lib. Congress has July 10, 1809–Nov. 17, 1817, fair; Sept. 14, Dec. 28, 1818; Apr. 5, May 3, Aug. 2, 9, 1819; July 10, Sept. 11, 1820.

N. Y. Hist. Soc. has July 10, 1809–June 28, 1813; July 19, 26, Aug. 9–Sept. 13, 27, Nov. 8, 15, 29–Dec. 20, 1813; Apr. 11, May 9, Oct. 10, 1814; July 10, 1815; June 24, July 1, 1816; Nov. 16, Dec. 7, 1818; Jan. 11, Feb. 1, 8, Mar. 29, May 10, June 7, 14, 28, Aug. 16, 1819; Apr. 24, May 29–June 12, Oct. 2, 1820.
Cornell Univ. has July 10, 1809–Aug. 7, 1815.
Dartmouth has Jan. 1, 1810–Dec. 25, 1815.
Western Reserve Hist. Soc. has July 10, 1809–July 17, 1815.
N. Y. Pub. Lib. has July 10, 1809–Dec. 27, 1813; Jan. 3, 1814–Dec. 4, 1815, fair.
Trinity Coll. has July 10, 1809–June 26, 1815.
Martin Welles, Hartford, has July 10, 1809–Dec. 19, 1814, fair; Jan. 2, 1815–June 23, 1817; Jan. 5, Feb. 9, July 20, 1818; Feb. 22, Mar. 29, May 10, 17, 31, June 7, July 12–Sept. 20, Oct. 4, 18–Nov. 1, 29, Dec. 13, 27, 1819; Jan. 3–Apr. 17, May 1–June 5, July 10, 17, 31, Oct. 23, 1820.
Case Mem. Lib., Hartford Seminary, has July 10, 1809–Dec. 28, 1812.
Boston Athenæum has July 10, 1809–July 1, 1811.
Keokuk Pub. Lib. has Dec. 17, 1810–June 5, 1814.
N. Y. State Lib. has Jan. 14–June 17, Oct. 7–28, Dec. 2, 1811; Jan. 13–Dec. 21, 1812; Feb. 1–Dec. 20, 1813.
Univ. of Ill. has July 8, 1811–June 28, 1813.
Univ. of Mich. (Clements) has Apr. 9, May 7, 14, June 18, 25, July 9, 23, 30, Nov. 5–Dec. 31, 1810; Mar. 4, 11, 25, May 27–June 10, July 24, Aug. 5, 1811; July 13, Sept. 21, Nov. 2, 1812; July 28, Aug. 11, 25, 1817.
Mass. Hist. Soc. has Sept. 20, 27, 1813; Jan. 2–Aug. 7, 1815; June 22, July 27, Aug. 10, Sept. 7, 1818; July 10, 17, Aug. 14–28, 1820.
Rutgers Univ. has June 10, July 1–15, 29, Aug. 12–Sept. 30, Nov. 4, Dec. 23, 1811.
Univ. of Texas has June 25–Sept. 10, 1810; Mar. 11, 25–Apr. 8, May 20, 27, 1811.
Univ. of Chicago has Apr. 2, June 25, July 16, Nov. 19, 1810; May 12, July 14, 21, Aug. 4, Nov. 17, Dec. 8, 1817; Jan. 5, Mar. 2, 16, 1818.

[Hartford] Freeman's Chronicle, 1783–1784.

Weekly. Established Sept. 1, 1783, by Bavil Webster, with the title of "The Freeman's Chronicle: or, the American Advertiser." Beginning with the issue of June 3, 1784, the paper was published by Z[ephaniah] Webster. The last issue located is that of July 8, 1784, vol. 1, no. 45.

Lib. Congress has Sept. 1–Oct. 20, 1783.
Am. Antiq. Soc. has Sept. 8–29, Oct. 13–27, Nov. 10, 1783; Jan. 5, 19, 26, Feb. 9, Mar. 1, 15, Apr. 12, May 10–24, June 3–24, July 8, 1784.
Yale has Sept. 29–Nov. 10, 1783.
Mass. Hist. Soc. has Mar. 1, 15, 1784.

Hartford Gazette, 1794–1795.

Semi-weekly and weekly. Established as a semi-weekly Jan. 13, 1794, by Beach & Storrs [Lazarus Beach and Roger Storrs], with the title of "The Hartford Gazette." The title was changed to "Hartford Gazette" with the issue of Feb. 10, 1794, to "The Hartford Gazette: and Universal Advertiser" early in July 1794, to "Hartford Gazette: and the Universal Advertiser" on July 21, 1794, and to "Hartford Gazette" on Oct. 13, 1794. The original publishers were changed to L. Beach & Co., Apr. 21, 1794, and to Beach and Jones [Lazarus Beach and Ira Jones], Oct. 13, 1794. The paper was at first a small quarto, but was enlarged to folio size in July, 1794. It was changed from a semi-weekly to a weekly with the issue of Feb. 19, 1795. The last issue was that of Mar. 19, 1795, vol. 2, no. 118. Beach and Jones removed to Newfield, where they established the "American Telegraphe," Apr. 8, 1795.

Watkinson Lib., Hartford, has Jan. 13–June 26, 1794.
Am. Antiq. Soc. has Jan. 27, Feb. 6, 17, Apr. 28, May 12, 29, Sept. 22, Oct. 2, 6, Nov. 24, Dec. 11, 15, 22, 25, 1794; Jan. 4–12, 26, 1795.
Conn. Hist. Soc. has July 14, 1794–Mar. 5, 1795.
Lib. Congress has July 17–Aug. 14, 21–Sept. 29, Oct. 16, 1794–Mar. 19, 1795.
Boston Pub. Lib. has May 29, Dec. 11, 1794.
Harvard has Dec. 25, 1794; Jan. 15, 19, 26, Feb. 19, Mar. 19, 1795.
N. Y. Hist. Soc. has Oct. 27, 1794.

[Hartford] New Star, 1796.

Published by Apollos Kinsley. This curious little paper, entitled "The New Star," was 16mo in size, 5¾ by 4¼ inches, and had no numbering. Apparently but one issue was printed, that of Feb. 2, 1796. It contained the following announcement: "This small paper is printed for the purpose of making experiments with a model of a Printing Press, on a new plan, lately invented by the Printer hereof. Though the press is by no means complicated, it puts the ink on the types, carries in the papers and prints two sheets at a time, and will deliver them well printed at the rate of more than two thousand sheets in an hour, by the labor of one person only." For an account of Apollos Kinsley as an inventor, see "Memorial History of Hartford County," vol. 1, pp. 469, 563.

Am. Antiq. Soc. has Feb. 2, 1796.

[Hartford] Times, 1817–1820+.

Weekly. Established Jan. 1, 1817, by F. D. Bolles & Co. [Frederick D. Bolles and John M. Niles]. The title was changed with the issue of Nov. 16, 1819, from "The Times" to "The Times, and Weekly Advertiser." Further changes in the names of publishers were as follows: F. D. Bolles for John M. Niles, Mar. 2,

1819–June 15, 1819; for John M. Niles, June 22, 1819–Sept. 21, 1819; Bowles & Francis [Samuel Bowles and John Francis], Sept. 28, 1819–1820+.

    Hartford Times Office has Jan. 1, 1817–Dec. 26, 1820.
    Conn. Hist. Soc. has Jan. 14, 1817–Dec. 26, 1820, fair.
    Conn. State Lib. has Jan. 1, 1817–Dec. 28, 1819.
    Martin Welles, Hartford, has Jan. 7, 1817–Jan. 20, 1818.
    Long Id. Hist. Soc. has Jan. 14, 28, Feb. 4, Aug. 19, 1817; Jan. 6, 1818–Dec. 26, 1820.
    Am. Antiq. Soc. has Jan. 1, 21, Feb. 18, May 13, Dec. 30, 1817; Aug. 25, 1818; Feb. 8, Apr. 11, Nov. 7, 1820.
    Lib. Congress has Apr. 1, May 13, Sept. 9, Dec. 16, 1817; Apr. 13, 1819; Apr. 4–Nov. 7, 1820.

[Litchfield] Collier's Litchfield Weekly Monitor, see Litchfield Monitor.

Litchfield County Monitor, see Litchfield Monitor.

[Litchfield] Farmer's Monitor, see Litchfield Monitor.

Litchfield Gazette, 1808–1809.

    Weekly. Established Mar. 16, 1808, by Hosmer & Goodwin [Charles Hosmer and Oliver Goodwin], with the title of "Litchfield Gazette." Discontinued with the issue of May 17, 1809, vol. 2, no. 10.

    Conn. State Lib. has Mar. 16, 1808–May 17, 1809.
    Conn. Hist. Soc. has Mar. 16, 1808–Mar. 8, 1809.
    N. Y. Hist. Soc. has Mar. 16, 1808–Mar. 1, 1809.
    Am. Antiq. Soc. has Mar. 30, June 8, 1808–May 17, 1809.
    Case Mem. Lib., Hartford Seminary, has June 8, 1808–May 17, 1809, fair.
    Litchfield Hist. Soc. has Apr. 27, Sept. 28, Oct. 5, 26, Dec. 7, 28, 1808; Jan. 4, 25, Mar. 15, Apr. 5, May 10, 17, 1809.
    Lib. Congress has May 11, 1808.
    Wis. Hist. Soc. has June 1, 1808.

Litchfield Journal, 1818.

    Weekly. Established Mar. 11, 1818, judging from the date of the first known issue, that of Apr. 8, 1818, vol. 1, no. 5, published by I[saiah] Bunce, with the title of "Litchfield Journal." In the issue of Oct. 20, 1818, vol. 1, no. 33, it was announced that the paper would be published but a short time longer.

    Litchfield Hist. Soc. has Apr. 8–Oct. 20, 1818.
    Am. Antiq. Soc. has Aug. 4, 1818.
    Duke Univ. has Aug. 4, 1818.

Litchfield Monitor, 1784–1807.

Weekly. Established Dec. 21, 1784, by Collier and Copp [Thomas Collier and William Copp]. It experienced the following changes of name: "The Weekly Monitor, and American Advertiser," Dec. 21, 1784–Mar. 1785; "The Weekly Monitor," Mar. or Apr. 1785–Nov. 28, 1786; "The Weekly Monitor. And Litchfield Town and County Recorder," Dec. 5, 1786–June 4, 1787; "The Weekly Monitor," June 11, 1787–Dec. 31, 1787; "Collier's (Litchfield) Weekly Monitor," Jan. 7, 1788–June 16, 1788; "The Weekly Monitor," June 23, 1788–Apr. 20, 1789; "Weekly Monitor. And the Litchfield Advertiser," Apr. 27, 1789–June 8, 1789, and suspended with the latter issue; revived Nov. 17, 1789, carrying the name of "Weekly Monitor" to the issue of Dec. 4, 1790; "Litchfield-County Monitor," Dec. 11, 1790–Jan. 3, 1791; "Litchfield Monitor," Jan. 10, 1791–Jan. 4, 1792; "The Monitor," Jan. 11, 1792–Aug. 20, 1794; "Litchfield Monitor," Aug. 27, 1794–June 3, 1795; "Litchfield Monitor, and Agricultural Register," June 10, 1795–May 11, 1796; "Weekly Monitor," May 18, 1796–Feb. 21, 1798; "The Monitor," Feb. 28, 1798–Feb. 26, 1800; "The Farmer's Monitor," Mar. 5, 1800–Dec. 10, 1800; "The Monitor," Jan. 21, 1801–June 8, 1803; "Litchfield Monitor," June 15, 1803–July 1, 1807.

The succession of editors was as follows: Collier and Copp [Thomas Collier and William Copp], Dec. 21, 1784–Dec. 12, 1785; Thomas Collier, Dec. 19, 1785–Sept. 8, 1788; Collier and Adam [Thomas Collier and Robert Adam], Sept. 15, 1788–June 8, 1789; Thomas Collier, Nov. 17, 1789–Jan. 4, 1792; Collier and Buel [Thomas Collier and David Buel], Jan. 11, 1792–Feb. 24, 1796; Thomas Collier, Mar. 2, 1796–Feb. 27, 1805; Thomas Collier & Son [Thomas & Thomas G. Collier], Mar. 6, 1805–Sept. 3, 1806; Thomas Collier, Sept. 10, 1806–July 1, 1807. The last issue located is that of July 1, 1807, vol. 21, no. 1137, although there is an issue lacking first page for July 29, 1807.

> Litchfield Hist. Soc. has Nov. 14, 1786–Dec. 31, 1787; Jan. 7–Apr. 28, May 12–Dec. 29, 1788; Jan. 5, 12, Feb. 2, Mar. 16, 1789–Dec. 26, 1792; Jan. 2, 23, 30, Feb. 13, 20, Mar. 13, 27–Apr. 10, 24–May 15, 29–June 26, July 10–Dec. 25, 1793; Jan. 1, 1794–Dec. 25, 1799; Jan. 1–Feb. 26, Sept. 3, Oct. 15, 1800; Jan. 14, 28, Feb. 11, Mar. 4, 25, Apr. 15, 22, May 20, July 1, Aug. 5, 19, Sept. 16–Dec. 30, 1801; Jan. 6–Dec. 29, 1802; Jan. 5–July 13, 1803; Aug. 15, Sept. 19, Nov. 28, 1804; Sept. 11, 25, 1805; Mar. 12–26, Apr. 9, 23, 30, May 14–June 4, 25–July 16, Aug. 6, 13, 27–Sept. 10, 24–Oct. 15, 29–Nov. 19, Dec. 10–31, 1806; Jan. 7–Feb. 4, 18–Mar. 18, Apr. 1, 15, 22, May 6–June 17, July 1, 29, 1807.
>
> Am. Antiq. Soc. has Feb. 1, Mar. 1–15, Apr. 26, June 28, July 5, 19, Aug. 9, 23, Nov. 1, 15–29, 1785; Jan. 3, 17, 24, Feb. 7–Apr. 11, 25, May 23–June 20, Oct. 3, 10, Dec. 12, 26, 1786; Jan. 9–30, Feb. 20, Mar. 5, 19, May 7, 21–June 4, July 2, 16, 30–Aug. 13, Sept. 3–17, Nov. 12, Dec. 3, 17, 24, 1787; Jan. 21–Feb. 4, Apr. 7–21, July 14, 28, Aug. 11, 18, Sept. 1, 15–29, Oct. 13, 20, Nov. 10, 24, Dec. 22, 1788; Apr. 13, 20, May 4, 11, Dec. 8, 22, 1789;

Jan. 19–Apr. 24, May 8–Sept. 20, Oct. 4, 25, Nov. 22, 29, 1790; Jan. 3, 17, 24, Feb. 9, 23, Mar. 2–16, 30–Apr. 27, May 25, June 8–July 13, 27, Aug. 10, 24–Oct. 5, 19, Nov. 2–Dec. 14, 1791; Jan. 11–Feb. 8, 22, 29, Mar. 21–Apr. 11, 26, May 9–23, June 6, 27, July 11, Aug. 1, 8, Sept. 19–Oct. 10, Nov. 28, Dec. 5, 1792; Mar. 13, 27, Apr. 3, June 12, July 10, 24, 31, Sept. 4, Nov. 6, 13, 1793; Jan. 1, 15, 29, Feb. 5, 19–Dec. 31, 1794; Jan. 7, Mar. 4, Apr. 29–May 13, June 24, July 8–22, Aug. 12, 26, Nov. 18, Dec. 30, 1795; Jan. 13, 1796– Dec. 31, 1800, fair; Nov. 25, 1801; Apr. 21, June 16, 1802; May 18, 1803; Apr. 23, 1805; July 30, Aug. 6, 1806.

Yale has Feb. 21, 1785; Feb. 13, 1787–Dec. 29, 1788, fair; Jan. 5–Feb. 16, Mar. 2–30, Apr. 20, 27, May 25–Nov. 17, Dec. 1, 15–29, 1789; Jan. 12–Feb. 23, Mar. 9–May 22, June 7, 14, July 5, 26, Aug. 2, 16–30, Sept. 20, 27, 1790; Jan. 10, Feb. 9, 23, Mar. 9, 23, Apr. 13–27, May 11, 25, June 27, Aug. 3, 10, 31–Sept. 14, Oct. 5–19, 1791; Mar. 14, 28, Apr. 11, May 2, 16, 30, Aug. 1, Oct. 24–Nov. 14, 28, Dec. 12–26, 1792; Jan. 2, 16, Feb. 20–Mar. 27, Apr. 10, 1793; July 31, Aug. 28, Sept. 11, 1799.

Harvard has Feb. 11, 25–Mar. 11, 25, Apr. 8, 22, May 6, 13, 27, June 17, July 15, 29, Nov. 3, Dec. 30, 1795; Mar. 30, Apr. 6, 1796; Mar. 8, May 31, June 14, Aug. 10, Sept. 6, 13, Oct. 8, 25, Nov. 15–29, Dec. 20, 27, 1797; Jan. 3, Feb. 14–28, Mar. 14, Apr. 18, May 16–June 6, 27, July 11, Aug. 22, Oct. 31–Nov. 21, Dec. 12, 26, 1798; Jan. 2, 16, Feb. 13–27, Mar. 27, Apr. 10– May 1, June 19, Sept. 4–18, Oct. 30, Nov. 20, 1799; Jan. 22, Feb. 12, 19, Mar. 5, 12, Apr. 2–30, May 14, 21, June 11–25, July 30–Sept. 17, Oct. 1, 15, 22, Nov. 12, 19, Dec. 3, 10, 1800; Jan. 21, Feb. 4–Mar. 18, Apr. 8–22, May 6– June 3, 24, July 8–Oct. 28, Nov. 18, Dec. 2, 30, 1801; Jan. 13, 27–Feb. 17, Apr. 14, 28, May 12–26, June 9, July 14, Aug. 18, Sept. 1–22, Oct. 6, 27, Nov. 10–24, Dec. 29, 1802; Jan. 5, 19, 26, Feb. 9, 23–May 18, June 1–15, 29–July 27, Aug. 10, 17, 31, Sept. 14, 28, Oct. 5, Nov. 2–30, Dec. 14, 1803; Jan. 18–Feb. 8, 22–Apr. 11, 25–May 30, June 20–July 4, Aug. 15–Sept. 19, Nov. 21–Dec. 26, 1804; Jan. 2–Apr. 3, May 15–29, Sept. 25, Oct. 16, Nov. 6, 1805; Jan. 22, Apr. 30, May 14–28, 1806; Apr. 15, 1807.

Conn. Hist. Soc. has Dec. 22, 1789; Feb. 2, 23–Mar. 9, 23–Apr. 20, May 8, 15, 29–July 12, Aug. 16, 30–Sept. 20, 1790; Jan. 17, Feb. 9, May 25, July 27, Nov. 2, 1791; Jan. 11–Mar. 14, 28–Apr. 18, May 2, 30–June 21, July 4– Aug. 29, Sept. 12–Dec. 26, 1792; Feb. 26–Mar. 12, 26–Apr. 30, May 14– June 11, 25, July 2, 16–Nov. 26, Dec. 17, 24, 1794; Mar. 23, July 20, Aug. 17, Sept. 7, Oct. 5, 19, 26, Dec. 7, 14, 28, 1796; Feb. 8, Mar. 22, 29, Apr. 19, May 3, 31–July 22, Aug. 9–23, Sept. 13, Oct. 18, Nov. 8, 1797; Jan. 31, Feb. 7, Mar. 28, Apr. 18, May 30, Nov. 14, 1798; Feb. 6, 20–Mar. 6, 20, Apr. 3, 10, 24–May 8, 29, June 5, 19–July 10, 24–Sept. 18, Oct. 2–Dec. 18, 1799; Jan. 1, 22, 29, 1800.

N. Y. Pub. Lib. has Dec. 21, 1784; Jan. 4–Feb. 15, Mar. 1, 8, Apr. 12, 1785; Oct. 20, 1788; Jan. 12, Feb. 9, Mar. 16, Apr. 27, 1789; June 14, 1790; Aug. 24,

Oct. 5–Nov. 9, 23, 1791; Mar. 26, 1800; Jan. 15, 29, Mar. 12, 26–Apr. 9, 23, May 7, 14, June 4, 11, July 9, 23, Aug. 13, 27, 1806.

N. J. Hist. Soc. has Feb. 20, Apr. 17, Sept. 18, Oct. 16, 1793; Feb. 6, June 11, July 2, 23, Nov. 26, 1794; Feb. 11, 18, Mar. 4, Apr. 1, May 13, July 15, 1795; May 18, June 9, 15, July 6, 20, Aug. 3, 10, Sept. 28–Oct. 12, Nov. 30, Dec. 21, 1796; Jan. 4, 25, Feb. 15, Mar. 22, 29, Apr. 12, 19, May 17, 24, Aug. 23, 1797.

Gunn Lib., Washington, Conn., has July 25, Sept. 26, Oct. 3, Nov. 7, Dec. 12–26, 1792; Aug. 7, 1793–Dec. 28, 1796, fair.

Lib. Congress has Apr. 3, May 29, 1793; Oct. 5, 1796; July 18, 1798–Feb. 12, 1800, fair; Dec. 3, 1800; Apr. 14, 1802.

Mass. Hist. Soc. has Mar. 15, 1785.

Wis. Hist. Soc. has June 27, 1792; Aug. 13, 1794; Mar. 4, Oct. 21, 28, 1795.

N. Y. Hist. Soc. has Jan. 7, 1795; Jan. 6, 1796; July 31, 1799; July 25, 1804; Dec. 25, 1805; Dec. 24, 1806.

Conn. State Lib. has Aug. 31, 1791; Feb. 6, 1794; Jan. 25, Apr. 5, Sept. 20, 1797; July 17, 1799; June 1, 1803.

New Haven Col. Hist. Soc. has June 27, 1792; Oct. 14, 1795.

Martin Welles, Hartford, has May 16, June 20–July 11, Dec. 5, 1798; Jan. 2, Apr. 17, July 10, 31, Sept. 25, Oct. 2, 1799; Jan. 8, Feb. 19, 26, 1800.

Univ. of Ill. has Aug. 15, Oct. 17, Nov. 7, 14, 1804; Jan. 9, 23, June 26, July 10, Sept. 4, 1805.

Minn. Hist. Soc. has July 30, 1787.

Western Reserve Hist. Soc. has Jan. 1, Nov. 12, 1800.

Derby, Conn. Pub. Lib. has July 11, 1804.

Colgate Univ. Lib., Hamilton, has Oct. 31, 1804.

Litchfield Republican, 1819–1820+.

Weekly. Established May 12, 1819, by I. Bunce [Isaiah Bunce]. Continued after 1820.

Litchfield Hist. Soc. has May 19–Sept. 20, Oct. 4–Nov. 22, Dec. 6–20, 1819; Jan. 17–Apr. 3, 17–May 15, 29, June 12–Dec. 18, 1820.

Am. Antiq. Soc. has July 1, Dec. 20, 1819; Apr. 10–May 1, 22, 1820.

[Litchfield] Weekly Monitor, see **Litchfield Monitor.**

[Litchfield] Witness, 1805–1807.

Weekly. Established Aug. 14, 1805, by Timothy Ashley with the title of "The Witness." In April, 1806, Ashley was convicted of libel and imprisoned. With the issue of April 16, 1806, Selleck Osborn announced that he had purchased Mr. Ashley's interest, and henceforth published the paper. In the issue of May 27, 1807, he stated that the paper had not been issued for two weeks previous. The numbering shows no issue for June 10, 1807. The paper suspended with the issue of June 24, 1807, vol. 2, no. 93.

Am. Antiq. Soc. has Aug. 14, 1805–June 24, 1807.
Litchfield Hist. Soc. has Aug. 21, 1805–June 24, 1807.
Conn. Hist. Soc. has Aug. 21, 1805–June 24, 1807.
Yale has Aug. 21, 1805–June 24, 1807.
N. Y. State Lib. has Sept. 18, 1805–June 3, 1807, fair.
Martin Welles, Hartford, has Sept. 25, 1805–May 27, 1807, fair.
Duke Univ. has Sept. 25–Oct. 9, 23–Nov. 20, Dec. 4, 25, 1805; Jan. 8, 15, 29, Feb. 5, 19–July 2, 16, 23, Sept. 10, 24, Dec. 3, 24, 31, 1806; Feb. 18–25, Mar. 11, 18, Apr. 8, 15, May 4, 1807.
Lib. Congress has Oct. 9–30, Dec. 4, 1805; Jan. 15, 1806–June 24, 1807.
Boston Athenæum has Nov. 13, 1805; Dec. 10, 1806–Feb. 18, 1807.
Wis. Hist. Soc. has Dec. 18, 1805–June 24, 1807.
New Haven Col. Hist. Soc. has Nov. 6, 1805.
Arkansas Hist. Comm. has Oct. 30–Nov. 13, 1805.
Harvard has Apr. 2, 23, 30, May 14–June 18, July 2, 9, 23, Aug. 13, 20, Sept. 17, 24, Oct. 8, 15, Nov. 12, 19, Dec. 10, 24, 31, 1806; Feb. 4, June 24, 1807.
Univ. of Mich. (Clements) has Jan. 22, Feb. 5, 26, May 7, 21–June 4, Sept. 24, Nov. 12, Dec. 10, 1806; Feb. 11, June 3, 1807.
Long Id. Hist. Soc. has Apr. 2, 1806; Mar. 18, 1807.
N. Y. Pub. Lib. has Mar. 4, 1807.
Western Reserve Hist. Soc. has Mar. 18, 1807.

[Middletown] **Connecticut Spectator**, 1814–1815.

Weekly. Established Apr. 20, 1814, by Loomis & Richards [Simeon L. Loomis and Seth Richards], with the title of "Connecticut Spectator." This partnership was dissolved, and with the issue of Mar. 29, 1815, Seth Richards became the publisher. The last issue located is that of Apr. 10, 1816, vol. 2, no. 104.

Conn. Hist. Soc. has Apr. 27, 1814–Apr. 10, 1816.
Middlesex Co. Hist. Soc. has Apr. 20, 1814–Apr. 12, 1815.
N. Y. Hist. Soc. has Apr. 20, May 4, 11, 25–July 20, Aug. 10–Sept. 21, Oct. 5–Dec. 14, 1814; Jan. 4, 11, 25–Mar. 29, Apr. 12–26, May 10–31, June 28–July 26, Aug. 16, Sept. 6, 20, Nov. 15, 22, 1815.
Martin Welles, Hartford, has May 17–June 1, 15, 29–July 13, 27, Aug. 10, Oct. 12–Dec. 28, 1814; Jan. 4–18, Feb. 8–Mar. 8, 29, Apr. 5, 26–May 10, Oct. 25, Nov. 22, 1815.
Conn. State Lib. has July 13, 27, Aug. 10, 1814; Mar. 15–Oct. 25, 1815.
New London Co. Hist. Soc. has Apr. 20, July 20, Sept. 7, 1814.
Ohio Arch. & Hist. Soc. has June 29, July 6, 20, 27, Aug. 10, 17, 31, Sept. 7, Oct. 5, 1814.

Am. Antiq. Soc. has Aug. 17, Oct. 26, Nov. 23, 1814; Jan. 4, 18, Feb. 1, 8, May 10, 24, July 12, 19, Aug. 30, Oct. 18, Nov. 1, 1815.
Lib. Congress has Oct. 5, Dec. 28, 1814; Jan. 4–Apr. 5, 1815.
Wesleyan Univ. has Apr. 27, 1814.
Wis. Hist. Soc. has Sept. 21, 1814.

[Middletown] **Middlesex Gazette**, 1785–1820+.

Weekly. Established Nov. 8, 1785, by Woodward and Green [Moses H. Woodward & Thomas Green], with the title of "The Middlesex Gazette." With the issue of Nov. 5, 1787, it was called "The Middlesex Gazette, or, Fœderal Adviser." The office was destroyed by fire on Jan. 28, 1792, and there were no issues from Jan. 28 to Feb. 25, 1792, with which issue the title became "The Middlesex Gazette, or, Federal Adviser," immediately changed to "The Middlesex Gazette" on Mar. 3, 1792. With the issue of Aug. 19, 1793, the title became "Middlesex Gazette'" which was retained until after 1820. Moses H. Woodward published the paper from June 20, 1789 to Oct. 6, 1797, when he resigned the business to T[ertius] Dunning, who began publication with the issue of Oct. 13, 1797. With the issue of Oct. 3, 1800, Tertius Dunning took his brother John into partnership under the firm name of T. and J. B. Dunning. With the issue of June 7, 1810, T. Dunning became sole proprietor and continued the paper until after 1820.

Conn. Hist. Soc. has Nov. 8, 1785–Dec. 28, 1820.
Am. Antiq. Soc. has Nov. 22–Dec. 27, 1785; Jan. 24–Feb. 13, 27, Mar. 27, May 8, 22, 1786–Dec. 29, 1792, fair; Jan. 12–Feb. 23, Mar. 9, 23–Apr. 20, May 4, 25–June 15, Oct. 12, 26, Nov. 16, 23, Dec. 7–28, 1793; Jan. 4, 1794–Dec. 22, 1797; Jan. 5, Mar. 2, 16, Apr. 20, 27, Oct. 19, 1798; Jan. 3–Dec. 19, 1800, fair; Nov. 2, 1801; Feb. 28–Mar. 14, 28, Apr. 11–Sept. 5, 26, Oct. 7, 1803; Mar. 9, 1804; Apr. 5, 12, 1805; Jan. 10, 1806–Dec. 28, 1809, fair; Jan. 25, Oct. 4, 1810; Apr. 11–July 11, 25, Aug. 8–22, Sept. 12, 26–Oct. 31, Nov. 14, 1811; Apr. 2, May 21, 28, July 23, Aug. 6, 27, Sept. 10, 24, Oct. 8–22, 1812; Jan. 14–28, Apr. 29, June 10, July 22, Aug. 5–26, Dec. 9, 1813; Feb. 24–Nov. 24, Dec. 8, 29, 1814; Jan. 5–Feb. 2, July 13, 20, 1815; Feb. 29–Oct. 31, Nov. 14, 28, 1816; Jan. 9, 1817; Jan. 1, 22–Dec. 10, 1818, fair; Mar. 25, Apr. 29, Aug. 12, 1819; Mar. 16, Apr. 6–June 15, 29–July 13, Aug. 24–Nov. 2, 23–Dec. 7, 28, 1820.
Wesleyan Univ. has Jan. 3, 1786–Jan. 1, Aug. 20, 1787; Sept. 26, 1789; Jan. 9, 1790–Dec. 29, 1797, fair; Oct. 4, 1799–Dec. 2, 1803; Oct. 26, 1804; Jan. 17–Oct. 24, Dec. 5, 1806; Jan. 9, 30, 1807–Dec. 28, 1809, fair; Dec. 30, 1813; Nov. 20, 1817; Sept. 10, 1818.
Conn. State Lib. has Dec. 6, 1785–Dec. 11, 1786; July 2, 1791; Mar. 14, 1795; July 31, 1796; Oct. 6, 1797–May 24, 1799; Sept. 5, 1803–Dec. 21, 1804; Sept. 20–Oct. 25, Nov. 15, Dec. 20, 27, 1805; Jan. 17, 31, Feb. 7, 28, 1806;

Jan. 7, 1808–Dec. 27, 1810; June 24–Dec. 9, 1813, fair; Feb. 9, Apr. 20, 27, May 25–June 29, July 13–27, Aug. 10, 31, Nov. 9–Dec. 7, 21, 28, 1815; Jan. 4, 1816–Dec. 17, 1818; Jan. 21–Dec. 28, 1820, fair.

Middlesex Co. Hist. Soc. has Jan. 22–Mar. 26, May 14, Nov. 5, 1787–Oct. 24, 1789; May 1, July 24, Nov. 6, 13, Dec. 4–18, 1790; Feb. 12, Mar. 5, Apr. 2, 23, June 11, 18, July 2, Sept. 17, Oct. 1–Dec. 31, 1791; Jan. 7, 1792–July 21, 1797, fair; June 26, 1801; Oct. 12, 1809; June 2–16, 30–Sept. 15, 29, Oct. 20, Nov. 3–17, Dec. 8–29, 1814; Jan. 5–Nov. 23, 1815, fair; June 13, Nov. 28, 1816; June 19, Oct. 23, Nov. 6, 1817; Mar. 12, 1818; Feb. 18–Oct. 24, 1819, fair; Nov. 2, 1820.

Russell Lib., Middletown, has June 18, Sept. 17, Oct. 15–Nov. 5, 26, Dec. 31, 1791; Aug. 10, 1793; Aug. 23–Sept. 13, Oct. 11, 25–Nov. 15, 29–Dec. 6, 1794; Aug. 5, 12, Oct. 21, 28, Nov. 11, 18, Dec. 2, 23, 30, 1796; Jan. 20, Feb. 3, 10, 1797; Jan. 5, 12, Nov. 17, 24, 1798; Jan. 23–Nov. 23, 1801; May 16–Dec. 9, 1803, fair; Feb. 10–Dec. 14, 1804, fair; Feb. 8, 15, Mar. 1, Oct. 25, Nov. 1, 15, 29, Dec. 6, 13, 1805; Mar. 7–Oct. 17, 1806; May 5, 1808–Dec. 26, 1811, fair; June 8, 1815; Mar. 27, May 15, July 24, Aug. 28, Sept. 25, 1817; Feb. 5–Dec. 2, 1818, fair.

Yale has Nov. 8, Dec. 27, 1785; Jan. 3–May 1, Aug. 21–Dec. 25, 1786; Jan. 1–Oct. 8, 1787; Oct. 13, 1792; Feb. 22, 1802–Dec. 23, 1803; Sept. 5, 1816; June 29, 1820.

Mass. Hist. Soc. has Jan. 22, 29, Feb. 12, Dec. 31, 1787; Sept. 5, Oct. 3, 1789; Mar. 5, 1791; Mar. 16, 1798; May 17, 1799; Mar. 28, 1800; Mar. 13–27, Apr. 17, May 8, 1801; Mar. 1, 1802; Apr. 18, 1803; Apr. 27, 1809.

Library of Congress has May 22, June 12, July 17, 24, Aug. 7, Sept. 4–18, Oct. 30–Dec. 25, 1786; Jan. 1, 15–Feb. 5, 19–Mar. 26, Apr. 9–23, May 28–July 9, 23, Aug. 6, 13, 1787; Sept. 8–Oct. 6, 1788; Sept. 26, Dec. 12, 1789; Jan. 2, 9, 23, 30, Feb. 13, 27, Mar. 20, Apr. 10, 24–May 8, June 5–19, July 17–Aug. 14, 28–Sept. 18, Oct. 2, Nov. 6, 27, Dec. 4, 18, 25, 1790; Jan. 1, 15, 29–Mar. 5, Apr. 9, June 4–18, July 2, 9, 23–Sept. 3, Nov. 12, Dec. 3–17, 1791; Mar. 17, May 19, 1792; Mar. 23, Dec. 28, 1793; Feb. 8, Apr. 19, May 24, June 14, July 5, 26, Sept. 27, Oct. 11, Nov. 1, Dec. 27, 1794; Jan. 3, Feb. 14, 28–Mar. 14, May 9, 16, June 20–Sept. 18, Nov. 6, 27, Dec. 18, 25, 1795; Feb. 5–19, May 6–27, July 8, 15, 29, Sept. 23, Oct. 14–Dec. 30, 1796; Jan. 20–Sept. 22, 1797; June 8, Sept. 14, 21, Oct. 5, 1798; Jan. 11, May 17, July 5, Aug. 9, Nov. 1, 1799; July 18, 1800; Feb. 1, Mar. 8, Oct. 25, Nov. 8, Dec. 20, 1802; Jan. 3, Feb. 21, Apr. 11, Oct. 7, 1803; Apr. 6, Dec. 7, 1804; Apr. 5, 1805; Jan. 31, Feb. 21, 28, May 17, June 13, 27, July 18, 25, Aug. 22, Oct. 3, Nov. 7, 1806; Mar. 27, Apr. 24, June 19, July 10, 17, 31, Aug. 28, Oct. 16–Nov. 13, 1807; Jan. 21, Apr. 7, May 26, 1808; Jan. 5–19, Feb. 2–May 25, June 8, 22, 29, July 13–27, Aug. 17, 31, 1809; June 14, Aug. 2, 30, Oct. 4, Nov. 22, 1810; Aug. 6, 1812; Apr. 1, Sept. 30, 1813; Feb. 24, Mar. 24, 31, May 19, June 2–16, 30, July 7, Sept. 22, Oct. 6, 27, 1814;

Jan. 19, Mar. 9, May 25, 1815; June 20, 1816; Jan. 30, 1817; June 4, July 9, Oct. 15, Dec. 3, 10, 24, 1818; Mar. 25, 1819.
N. Y. Hist. Soc. has Sept. 3, 1787–Dec. 26, 1789; Feb. 27, 1790; Sept. 15, 1797; Sept. 26, Nov. 7, 1816.
Martin Welles, Hartford, has Oct. 1, 1787; Aug. 18, 1788; Dec. 4, 11, 1790; Feb. 19, Dec. 10, 1791; Nov. 13, 1795; Oct. 11, 1796; Feb. 24, 1797; Dec. 14, 1798; Jan. 11, 1802–Mar. 28, 1803; Dec. 21, 1804; Mar. 22, Apr. 12, 26, 1810; Oct. 31, Dec. 12, 1811; Oct. 23, 1817.
New Haven Col. Hist. Soc. has Oct. 8, Nov. 19, 1787–July 28, 1788; Aug. 11, 18, 1788; Oct. 3, 1789; Oct. 20, 1792; Oct. 27, 1797.
Harvard has May 5, 12, June 2, 16, 1792; Dec. 27, 1794; Jan. 3, Feb. 7–Mar. 7, 21, May 23, 30, June 13–27, July 31, Aug. 21, Oct. 9, 1795; Feb. 19, 1796–Dec. 14, 1798, fair; Jan. 18, Mar. 1, Apr. 19, 26, May 31–June 14, July 12, Aug. 16, 23, Sept. 13, Oct. 25, Nov. 8, 22, 1799; Feb. 14, 1800–Dec. 28, 1801, fair; Jan. 18, Sept. 6, 1802; Jan. 17, 24, Apr. 4, June 20, Oct. 21, 28, Dec. 2, 9, 23, 30, 1803; Jan. 20–Dec. 28, 1804, fair; Jan. 11, Feb. 1, 15, Mar. 8–Apr. 26, July 12, 1805.
Minn. Hist. Soc. has Oct. 6, 1797–Aug. 24, 1798; Dec. 16, 1816.
Boston Athenæum has June 1, 15, July 27, Aug. 17, 24, Sept. 7, Nov. 2, 1793.
Phil. Lib. Co. has Oct. 12, 1793; Nov. 6, 27, Dec. 4, 1795; Mar. 18–Apr. 1, 15, 22, May 13, 20, 1796; Apr. 20, 1798.
N. Y. Pub. Lib. has Aug. 18, 1788; June 26, 1790; Oct. 13, 1792; Aug. 2, 1794; June 29, 1798.
Boston Pub. Lib. has Apr. 10, 1790; Nov. 17, 1792; Aug. 31, 1798.
Univ. of Mich. has Mar. 20, 1790.
Los Angeles Museum Lib. has Dec. 8, 1792.
Wis. Hist. Soc. has June 23, 1792; Apr. 12, 1794; Sept. 25, 1795; July 14–Dec. 29, 1808; Dec. 10, 1818.
Univ. of Ill. has Feb. 14, 1800; Jan. 2, Aug. 14, 1801; July 5, Dec. 13, 1805; Jan. 24, Feb. 28, Apr. 4, 1806.

[**New Haven**] **Belles-Lettres Repository,** 1808.

Weekly. Established Mar. 5, 1808, by Samuel Woodworth, with the title of "The Belles-Lettres Repository." It was of quarto size, eight pages to the issue, and had the appearance of a magazine, but since it contained current news, it might be listed as a newspaper. The last issue located is that of Apr. 16, 1808, vol. 1, no. 7.

New Haven Colony Hist. Soc. has Mar. 5–Apr. 16, 1808, lacking only the first and last leaves of the file.
Stratford Lib. has Mar. 12–Apr. 16, 1808.
Yale has Apr. 16, 1808.

New-Haven Chronicle, 1786–1787.

Weekly. Established Apr. 18, 1786, by Daniel Bowen, with the title of "The New-Haven Chronicle." The heading of the paper contained a large cut of a View of the City of New Haven, which, however was omitted with the issue of Apr. 17, 1787. The last issue located is that of Sept. 11, 1787, vol. 2, no. 73.

> Am. Antiq. Soc. has Apr. 25, May 9, 23, 30, June 13, 20, July 4, 25–Sept. 26, Oct. 10–Dec. 5, 26, 1786; Jan. 2, 9, 23–Feb. 6, 20, Mar. 6–Apr. 3, May 1, 8, 22, June 5, 26, July 10, 31, Aug. 14, 28, Sept. 11, 1787.
>
> New Haven Colony Hist. Soc. has Apr. 25, May 30–July 4, 18–Aug. 8, 22–Nov. 21, Dec. 26, 1786; Jan. 2–30, Feb. 13, 20, Mar. 6–July 24, Aug. 7–29, Sept. 11, 1787.
>
> Mass. Hist. Soc. has Oct. 3, 1786; Jan. 30, Apr. 10, 1787.
>
> Lib. Congress has Dec. 12, 1786.

[New Haven] Columbian Register, 1812–1820+.

Weekly. Established Dec. 1, 1812, by Joseph Barber, with the title of "Columbian Register." The title was changed to "Columbian Register, and True Republican" with the issue of Mar. 21, 1818, but reverted to "Columbian Register" with the issue of Oct. 17, 1818. It was continued by Barber until after 1820.

> Yale has Dec. 1, 1812–Dec. 30, 1820.
>
> New Haven Pub. Lib. has Dec. 1, 1812–Dec. 27, 1817; Oct. 17, 1818–Dec. 30, 1820.
>
> New Haven Colony Hist. Soc. has Jan. 4, 1814–Dec. 21, 1816, fair; Jan. 3, 1818–Dec. 30, 1820.
>
> Am. Antiq. Soc. has Dec. 1, 15, 1812; Jan. 5, Feb. 9, June 1, July 6, 20, 27, Aug. 17, Nov. 9, 1813; Jan. 25–Feb. 22, Mar. 8, 29, Apr. 12, May 17, 31, June 21, Aug. 2, 16, 30–Oct. 4, 18, 25, Nov. 8, 22–Dec. 6, 1814; Jan. 17, 24, Mar. 14, 28, Apr. 8, May 20, 27, June 17, Aug. 19, Oct. 2, 28, Nov. 11, 18, 1815; Jan. 27, Feb. 3, 17, Mar. 30, Apr. 20, May 11, 25, June 8, 22, Aug. 10–Dec. 28, 1816; Jan. 4, 1817–Aug. 22, 1818; Sept. 26–Oct. 10, 1818; Mar. 23, Aug. 7, 1819; Mar. 28, Apr. 22, Dec. 30, 1820.
>
> Martin Welles, Hartford, has Feb. 2, Mar. 2, 23, 1813–Sept. 20, 1814; Oct. 13, 1814–Sept. 23, 1815; Jan. 4, Sept. 14, 21, Oct. 5, 19–Nov. 9, 30–Dec. 21, 1816; Jan. 18–Feb. 15, Mar. 1, 8, Apr. 1, 19–Aug. 9, 30–Sept. 27, Oct. 11, 25–Nov. 29, Dec. 20, 27, 1817; Jan. 3–17, Oct. 17–Dec. 29, 1818; Mar. 2–16, Apr. 6, 13, May 18–31, June 12, 22–July 6, 20, Aug. 3–Dec. 7, 21, 28, 1819; Jan. 25, Feb. 1–19, Mar. 11, 21–Apr. 4, 18–June 13, 27–Nov. 14, 28–Dec. 26, 1820.
>
> Minn. Hist. Soc. has May 11, 1813–Apr. 26, 1814, fair; Jan. 10, 1815–Dec. 28, 1816.
>
> Trinity Coll. has Aug. 12, 1815–Dec. 30, 1820, fair.

N. Y. Pub. Lib. has Aug. 10, 24, 31, Dec. 7, 1813; Dec. 27, 1814; Mar. 19, Apr. 16, June 11, 29, July 9, 16, Aug. 15–29, Sept. 10–Nov. 5, Dec. 24, 1816; Jan. 4, 11, 25–Mar. 15, Apr. 12, May 17, 24, June 7, 14, 28, July 5–Sept. 5, Oct. 11, Nov. 15, 1817; Feb. 22–Mar. 7, 28, Apr. 4, 25, May 16, June 13, Oct. 24, 31, 1818.

Bronson Lib., Waterbury, has Aug. 16–Dec. 27, 1814; Jan. 10, 17, May 22, June 26–July 10, 24, Aug. 7, 26, Sept. 4, 1815.

Lib. Congress has Nov. 29, 1814; Aug. 3, 1816; Jan. 11, Feb. 22, Mar. 15, May 3, 1817; Jan. 2, 1819–Dec. 30, 1820.

Conn. Hist. Soc. has Oct. 4, 1814; Mar. 30, May 25, Dec. 28, 1816; Jan. 4–21, Feb. 1, Mar. 22, Apr. 19–May 3, 24, 31, June 14–28, July 26, Aug. 2, 16, Sept. 13–Oct. 4, Nov. 29, 1817; Mar. 21, Apr. 11, May 16, 30, June 6, 1818.

New London Co. Hist. Soc. has Jan. 4, Sept. 7–21, Oct. 5–Nov. 9, 23–Dec. 21, 1816; Jan. 11–Sept. 6, 1817.

Rutgers Univ. has May 10, 1817–May 2, 1818.

Conn. State Lib. has Feb. 2, May 18; June 15, 29, July 6, Oct. 12, 19, 1813; Feb. 1, Apr. 5, 19, Aug. 30, Sept. 13, Nov. 1, Dec. 6, 13, 1814; Jan. 10, 1815; Apr. 26, May 10, 1817.

Long Id. Hist. Soc. has May 25, 1813.

Wesleyan Univ. has June 28, 1814.

N. J. Hist. Soc. has Oct. 4, 1814.

Wis. Hist. Soc. has Dec. 12, 1818.

Boston Athenæum has June 18, 1820.

[New Haven] **Connecticut Gazette**, 1755–1768.

Weekly. Established Apr. 12, 1755, by James Parker, with the title of "The Connecticut Gazette." Beginning with the issue of Dec. 13, 1755, it was published by James Parker and Co. Thomas, in his "History of Printing," records that John Holt was the editor and the junior partner of the firm, getting out the paper, while Parker was concerned in printing enterprises in New York and New Jersey. (For Holt's connection with Parker, see Beverly McAnear's "James Parker versus John Holt" in N. J. Hist. Soc. Proc., 1941, vol. 59, p. 77.) Holt removed to New York in the summer of 1760, announcing that the business of the "Connecticut Gazette" would be carried on "as usual" by Thomas Green. Green remained with the paper until its suspension with the issue of Apr. 14, 1764, no. 471. The imprint was J. (or James) Parker & Co. from 1755 to 1764.

There was an attempt to revive the paper in July 1764, according to an unique prospectus in the New Haven Colony Historical Society. This broadside headed "To the Publick" and signed by Benjamin Mecom at New Haven on June 18, 1764, stated that "the Company connected with James Parker, Esq; so far as related to the Printing Business in this Place, is, in a Manner, totally dissolved. As Mr. Parker's Attorney, I have lately taken Possession of the Press and Types, and began to work, on my own Account, at the same House. On Friday the

Sixth Day of July next, I shall revive and publish The Connecticut Gazette, if I am sufficiently encouraged to begin it so soon." Presumably Mecom did not receive sufficient encouragement. "The Connecticut Gazette" was revived by Benjamin Mecom on July 5, 1765, although the issue for this date was a "sample" issue numbered 0. The issue for July 12, 1765, no. 472, continued the former numbering. At this time a broadside was issued, entitled "To the Publick of Connecticut," and signed at the end, "Printed by B. Mecom." It begins, "Perhaps there never was a more unpromising Time for the Encouragement of another News-paper." Copies of this broadside are in the A. A. S. and Yale, being placed in the Yale file of the "Connecticut Gazette" after the issue of July 12, 1765. The paper was published by Mecom until it was finally discontinued with the issue of Feb. 19, 1768, no. 596. It was enlarged from small to large folio with the issue of Aug. 2, 1765.

Yale has Apr. 12–July 5, Aug. 16, 30–Sept. 20, Oct. 4–Nov. 8, 22–Dec. 27, 1755; Jan. 3–Dec. 25, 1756; Jan. 8–Mar. 5, July 2, Aug. 13, Oct. 1, 8, 1757; June 10, July 8, 15, 29, Aug. 5, Sept. 9, 30, Oct. 7, 21, Nov. 4–Dec. 30, 1758; Jan. 13, 27, Feb. 3, Mar. 3, Apr. 14, 21, May 5, 19, June 9, Nov. 10, Dec. 1, 15, 1759; Mar. 8, Apr. 5, May 31, June 14–July 12, 26, Oct. 4, Nov. 1, Dec. 6–27, 1760; Jan. 3–May 23, June 5–27, Aug. 1–22, Sept. 12–26, Oct. 10–Nov. 7, 28–Dec. 12, 1761; Jan. 2, 16–Mar. 6, 27–Apr. 17, May 1–June 5, 19–Sept. 18, Oct. 9–Nov. 27, Dec. 11–25, 1762; Jan. 1, 8, 22, Feb. 26, Mar. 5, 19, Apr. 2, May 7, 14, June 18–July 9, Aug. 6, 13, 27, Nov. 3, 19–Dec. 10, 1763; Jan. 7, Feb. 4, 18, 25, Mar. 17–Apr. 14, 1764; July 5–Oct. 11, 25–Dec. 27, 1765; Jan. 3–Sept. 6, 20–Nov. 15, 29–Dec. 13, 1766; Jan. 12–24, Feb. 7–Mar. 14, 28–Apr. 18, May 2–16, 30, June 13–Aug. 1, 15–Oct. 10, 31, Nov. 21–Dec. 25, 1767; Jan. 1, 23, Feb. 19, 1768.

Lib. Congress has May 29–June 26, July 31, Sept. 11, 1756; Jan. 22, Feb. 19, June 4, July 30, Aug. 6, 20, 27, Sept. 24, Oct. 1, 15–29, 1757; May 13, July 8, Aug. 5, Nov. 4, Dec. 16, 1758; Feb. 3, 10, Mar. 3, 17, 31, Apr. 7, May 12–June 2, 16, 23, July 7, 14, Aug. 11–Sept. 1, 1759; Nov. 15, 1760; Jan. 10–31, July 17, Aug. 8, Oct. 17, Dec. 5, 1761; Apr. 3–Dec. 25, 1762; July 5, 12, Aug. 2–30, Sept. 13–Oct. 4, Nov. 1, 15, 29, Dec. 13–27, 1765; Jan. 3–24, Feb. 14–28, Mar. 15–Apr. 26, May 10–Oct. 25, 1766; Feb. 7, Apr. 11, Oct. 17, Nov. 7, 1767; Feb. 19, 1768.

Conn. Hist. Soc. has Sept. 13, 1755; Dec. 4, 1756; July 2, 1757; Mar. 29, May 17, 1760; Aug. 15, 1761–June 5, 1762; Jan. 10, 1766.

Mass. Hist. Soc. has Dec. 20, 1755; Jan. 15, Oct. 22, 1757; May 5, Oct. 27, 1759; July 24, 1762; July 23, Aug. 27, Dec. 31, 1763; Feb. 11, 1764; Aug. 2, 1765; July 12, 26, Sept. 6, 27, Nov. 1, 1766.

Am. Antiq. Soc. has May 3, 1755; Sept. 18, 1756; Mar. 12, July 16, Aug. 6–20, Sept. 17, Oct. 8, 1757; July 12, 1765; Jan. 12, 1767.

Martin Welles, Hartford, has Mar. 6, 13, May 15, 1756; June 2, Dec. 22, 1759; June 12, 1762.

N. Y. Pub. Lib. has Aug. 9, Sept. 20, 1755; Jan. 3, Oct. 23, 1756; Jan. 30, Mar. 27–Apr. 17, May 29, June 26, July 3, 17–Aug. 7, 21, Nov. 13–27, Dec. 18, 1762; Jan. 24, 1766.

N. Y. Hist. Soc. has Jan. 8, 1756; July 9, 1757; July 22, Aug. 19, 1758; Nov. 5, 1763.

Bridgeport Pub. Lib. has Aug. 21, 1756; Apr. 29, June 24, 1758; Jan. 7, 1766.

Litchfield Hist. Soc. has Apr. 3, 10, 1756.

Peck Lib., Norwich, has Apr. 17, 24, July 3, 1756.

N. Y. State Lib. has Oct. 8, 1757; Mar. 28, 1761.

New Haven Col. Hist. Soc. has June 18, 1764 (Prospectus); Oct. 18, 1765.

Phil. Lib. Co. has Sept. 20, Oct. 4, 1765.

[New Haven] Connecticut Herald, 1803–1820+.

Weekly. Established Nov. 1, 1803, with the title of "Connecticut Herald." In the initial issue the prospectus is signed by J[acob] Griswold and the imprint states that the paper is printed "for the Proprietor," changed in the issue of Nov. 8, 1803 to "Proprietors." In the issue of Nov. 15, 1803, the imprint became Comstock, Griswold & Co. [Seth Comstock and Zechariah Griswold]. This firm dissolved, and beginning with the issue of Dec. 18, 1804, the paper was published by Comstock, Steele, & Co., Oliver Steele having been taken into partnership. This issue stated that Jacob Griswold, who was leaving the paper, had been only employed as editor, although his brother Zechariah was a proprietor. The issue of Dec. 11, 1804, announced that the "Herald" had absorbed the "Connecticut Post and New Haven Visitor" under date of Nov. 20, 1804. Subsequent publishers of the "Herald" were as follows: Comstock, Steele, & Co., Dec. 18, 1804–July 23, 1805; Oliver Steele & Co., July 30, 1805–July 23, 1811; Walter & Steele [Joel Walter and Oliver Steele], July 30, 1811–Mar. 9, 1813; Oliver Steele, Mar. 16, 1813–Oct. 1816; Henry C. Flagg, proprietor, and Steele & Gray, printers, Oct. 15, 1816–Oct. 7, 1817; H. C. Flagg and J. C. Gray, Oct. 14, 1817–Oct. 5, 1819; John C. Gray, Oct. 12, 1819–1820+. Beginning with the issue of Mar. 17, 1818, the title was changed to the "Connecticut Herald, and General Advertiser."

New Haven Colony Hist. Soc. has Nov. 1, 1803–Dec. 26, 1820.

Am. Antiq. Soc. has Nov. 1, 1803; Jan. 31, Feb. 21–Mar. 27, Apr. 10–June 26, July 10–Aug. 14, Sept. 4, 18–Dec. 24, 1804; Jan. 1, 1805–Dec. 31, 1811; Mar. 24, 1812–Feb. 22, 1814; June 7, 1814–Dec. 26, 1815; Nov. 5, 12, 26, Dec. 17, 1816; Jan. 7, 28, Feb. 18, 25, Mar. 11–Apr. 15, 29, May 6, 27–June 11, 29, July 15, Aug. 5, 19, Sept. 2–Dec. 23, 1817; Jan. 13, Feb. 3–May 5, 19–June 9, 30–Oct. 20, Nov. 3–24, Dec. 8–29, 1818; Jan. 5–19, Feb. 2, 16, Mar. 2–23, Apr. 13, 27–May 11, 25–June 22, July 6–20, Aug. 10, 17, 31–Sept. 14, Oct. 5, 26, Nov. 2, 16–Dec. 14, 28, 1819; Jan. 18–Mar. 14, May 2–July 4, 18–Aug. 15, 29–Sept. 18, Oct. 3–17, Nov. 7–Dec. 26, 1820.

Yale has Jan. 1, 1805–Dec. 28, 1813; Aug. 9, 1814; Jan. 3–Dec. 26, 1815;

Jan. 2–Mar. 26, Aug. 13, Sept. 24, 1816; Feb. 25, Mar. 11, Apr. 8, 1817–Dec. 26, 1820. They had Dec. 13, 1803; Jan. 3, 17, Feb. 14, 28, Mar. 13, Apr. 3, June 12, July 3, 17, Aug. 7, 21, Sept. 4, Oct. 9, 16, 30, Dec. 4–24, 1804, but this file not found since 1920.

Conn. State Lib. has Nov. 20, 1804–Jan. 5, 1808; Mar. 8, 1808–Apr. 11, June 20–Aug. 29, 1809; Aug. 21, 1810; June 28, Aug. 23, 1814; Jan. 24, 1815; June 25, 1816; Sept. 9, 1817.

Western Reserve Hist. Soc. has Dec. 4, 1804–Oct. 21, 1806.

Martin Welles, Hartford, has May 22, 1804; Mar. 12, Aug. 6, Oct. 15, Nov. 5, 1805; Jan. 21, Apr. 1, 15, May 20, June 10, Aug. 12, 19, Oct. 14, 1806; Sept. 8, Nov. 17, 1807; Apr. 5, 12, June 14, 28, Dec. 13, 1808; Jan. 3, 1809–Mar. 10, 1812, fair; May 5, June 7, Sept. 1, Nov. 3, 1812; June 7, 1814.

Lib. Congress has June 25, July 9, 23, 30, Aug. 20, Oct. 15–27, Nov. 26, Dec. 17, 1805; Sept. 15, Dec. 29, 1807; Jan. 17–31, Mar. 7, 14, Oct. 25, 1809–Dec. 25, 1810; Jan. 22, Feb. 12, Mar. 5, Dec. 17, 1811; Jan. 7–Dec. 29, 1812; Jan. 5–June 8, 22, 29, Aug. 3, 17, Sept. 14, Nov. 30–Dec. 28, 1813; May 16, Dec. 19, 1815; Feb. 6–Mar. 26, Oct. 29, Dec. 3, 1816; Sept. 9, Oct. 21, Nov. 4, 18, Dec. 9, 16, 1817; Feb. 17, Mar. 10, 17, Aug. 4, 1818; Mar. 9, June 8, 15, Aug. 17, 1819; July 25–Aug. 8, Sept. 18, Oct. 24, Nov. 7, 1820.

Conn. Hist. Soc. has Nov. 20, 1804; Apr. 16, Dec. 3, 10, 24, 1805; Feb. 25, Mar. 11, 25, May 6, June 3, Dec. 2, 16, 1806; Jan. 6, Feb. 24, May 26, July 7, Nov. 24–Dec. 8, 1807; Apr. 26, May 24, Nov. 29, 1808; Apr. 28, Sept. 22, Nov. 10, 1812; Jan. 5–Feb. 9, 23–May 11, 25, June 8–July 20, Aug. 10, 31, Sept. 14, Oct. 5–Nov. 16, 30, Dec. 7, 21, 28, 1813; Feb. 22, 1814; Mar. 14, Sept. 19, 1815; Aug. 5, Oct. 7, Dec. 9, 1817; Mar. 3, July 7, Sept. 29, Nov. 10, 1818; Aug. 31, 1819; July 25, Oct. 17, 1820.

Harvard has Nov. 15, 1803; Nov. 20, 1804; Jan. 1, 15, 22, 1805; Feb. 4, 18, Apr. 1, 8, May 27, 1806; July 28, Aug. 18, 1807; Dec. 13, 20, 1808.

N. Y. Hist. Soc. has June 25, Sept. 3, Nov. 26, 1805; Feb. 24, Mar. 24, July 28, Oct. 27, Nov. 17, 1807; Jan. 12, Apr. 19, 26, 1808; Dec. 12, 1809; Aug. 21, 1810; Jan. 1, 1811–Dec. 29, 1812, fair.

Bronson Lib., Waterbury, has Apr. 5, 1808; Nov. 26, Dec. 10, 17, 1811; Dec. 8, 29, 1812; Jan. 5, 12, Feb. 23–Mar. 9, Apr. 13, 20, May 11, June 1, 15, 22, July 4, Oct. 17, 1815; Oct. 13, 1818.

Duke Univ. has July 31–Sept. 4, 18, Oct. 16, 23, 1810; Mar. 5, 19, Apr. 9, May 21, 28, 1811; Aug. 11, 1812; Feb. 9, 23, Mar. 16, 30, May 18, June 1, 1813; Nov. 18, 1817; Feb. 2, 1819.

N. Y. State Lib. has Jan. 7–Dec. 29, 1812.

[New Haven] Connecticut Journal, 1767–1820+.

Weekly. Established Oct. 23, 1767. It experienced the following changes of title: "The Connecticut Journal; and New-Haven Post-Boy," Oct. 23–Dec. 25,

CONNECTICUT

1767; "The Connecticut Journal, and New-Haven Post-Boy," Jan. 1, 1768–Apr. 10, 1772; "The Connecticut Journal, and the New-Haven Post-Boy," Apr. 17, 1772–Aug. 23, 1775; "The Connecticut Journal, & New-Haven Post-Boy," Aug. 30–Sept. 6, 1775; "The Connecticut Journal," Sept. 13, 1775–Dec. 26, 1792; "Connecticut Journal," Jan. 2, 1793–Jan. 3, 1799; "Connecticut Journal & Weekly Advertiser," Jan. 10–Mar. 28, 1799; "Connecticut Journal," Apr. 4, 1799–Dec. 29, 1808; "Connecticut Journal and Advertiser," Jan. 5–June 29, 1809; "Connecticut Journal," July 6, 1809–Jan. 20, 1818; "The Connecticut Journal," Jan. 27, 1818–1820+.

The changes in the names of the publishers were as follows: Thomas and Samuel Green, Oct. 23, 1767–Dec. 27, 1798; Thomas Green, Jan. 3, 1799; Thomas Green and Son, Jan. 10, 1799–Dec. 29, 1808; Thomas Green and Company, [Thomas Green, Thomas Green, Jr., and Thomas Collier], Jan. 5, 1809–June 29, 1809; Eli Hudson, July 6, 1809–June 27, 1814; Hudson & Woodward [Eli Hudson and Thomas Green Woodward], July 4, 1814–Jan. 30, 1816; Eli Hudson, Feb. 6, 1816–Oct. 8, 1816; for the Proprietor, Oct. 15, 1816–Feb. 25, 1817; S. Converse [Sherman Converse], Mar. 4, 1817–1820+.

Yale has Oct. 23, 1767–Dec. 26, 1820.

Lib. Congress has Oct. 30–Nov. 20, Dec. 4–25, 1767; Jan. 1, 15–Feb. 5, 19, 26, Mar. 11, 18, Apr. 1, 8, 22–May 13, June 3, 24, July 29, Aug. 5, 1768; Dec. 15–29, 1769; Jan. 5–19, Feb. 2, 9, 23, Mar. 9, 16, 30, Apr. 6, 20, May 4–June 22, July 6–Aug. 3, 17, 31–Sept. 21, 1770; July 19, Oct. 11, Nov. 8, 22, Dec. 27, 1771; May 15, 22, June 19, July 3, 24, Oct. 9, Dec. 11, 18, 1772; Mar. 5, Apr. 9, 16, July 16, 30, Sept. 3, Oct. 8, 15, 29–Nov. 12, 26, Dec. 10, 17, 31, 1773; Jan. 14, 1774–Dec. 6, 1775, good; Apr. 10, 24, May 29–June 12, July 3–24, Aug. 7–21, Sept. 11–25, Dec. 4, 18, 25, 1776; Jan. 8, 1777–Dec. 29, 1778, good; Jan. 13, 27, Feb. 3, 17–Mar. 31, Apr. 14–June 23, July 7–28, Aug. 11, 25–Oct. 6, Nov. 3, 17, Dec. 29, 1779; Jan. 19, 26, Feb. 9, Mar. 1–15, 29–June 15, 29–Dec. 28, 1780; Jan. 4, 1781–Dec. 29, 1784, good; Jan. 5–June 1, 15, Nov. 9, 23, Dec. 21, 28, 1785; Feb. 1, Mar. 22, Aug. 30, Dec. 13, 27, 1786; Jan. 10, Feb. 14, 28, Mar. 7–21, May 16, 23, July 18, Aug. 8, 15, Sept. 5, 19, 26–Oct. 31, Nov. 14–Dec. 12, 1787; Jan. 2–June 11, 25–Nov. 5, 19–Dec. 31, 1788; Feb. 4, 18–Dec. 30, 1789; Jan. 6, 1790–Sept. 5, 1820.

Am. Antiq. Soc. has Feb. 26, 1768; July 20, Sept. 7–Nov. 2, 16, 1770; Dec. 14, 1774; Jan. 25–Feb. 8, 22, Mar. 1, 15–29, Apr. 12–26, May 10–June 7, Sept. 13, Oct. 11, 1775; Mar. 27–Apr. 17, 1776; Jan. 15, 1777–Dec. 29, 1778, fair; Jan. 20, Feb. 10–Mar. 10, 24, 31, Apr. 14–28, May 12–June 2, 16–July 7, Aug. 11, 25, Sept. 8, 22–Oct. 20, Nov. 3, 17, Dec. 8, 15, 29, 1779; Jan. 5–Feb. 2, Mar. 29–May 4, 18–June 15, 29–Aug. 24, Sept. 7–Oct. 5, 26–Nov. 30, Dec. 21, 28, 1780; Jan. 4, 1781–Dec. 31, 1783, fair; Feb. 18, 25–Mar. 10, 24, 31, May 26–Oct. 13, 27–Dec. 29, 1784; Jan. 12–Mar. 30, Apr. 21–May 11, June 8–July 6, 27, Aug. 10, 17, Sept. 21, 28, Dec. 7, 14, 1785; Jan. 11–Feb. 22, Mar. 8, 22–Apr. 20, May 3, Oct. 4, Nov. 22, Dec. 6, 20, 27, 1786; Jan. 3, 1787–Dec. 30, 1789, fair; Jan. 6, 1790–Dec. 29, 1803; Jan. 5–19,

Feb. 2–23, Mar. 8–Nov. 8, 22, Dec. 6–27, 1804; Jan. 3, 24, 31, Feb. 14, 28–Mar. 14, 28, Apr. 4, 18, May 9, 30, June 13, July 4–18, Aug. 1, 29, Sept. 12, 26, Nov. 7, 21, 27, 1805; Jan. 2, 1806–Dec. 29, 1808; Jan. 5–July 6, 20–Oct. 5, 19, Nov. 16–30, 1809; Jan. 11, Mar. 22, May 3–17, June 7, 14, Oct. 18, Nov. 1, 15, Dec. 13, 27, 1810; Jan. 3–Dec. 26, 1811, fair; Jan. 30, Feb. 13, Mar. 12, 26, Apr. 2, May 28, June 4, July 2, 16, 23, Aug. 6, 20–Sept. 10, 24, Oct. 1, 15, 29, Nov. 19, 23, Dec. 6, 14, 1812; Jan. 18–Dec. 13, 1813; Jan. 3, 1814–Dec. 30, 1817, fair; Jan. 27–Feb. 10, Mar. 3, 17, Apr. 7, 14, 28–May 26, June 23–July 7, 28, Aug. 11–Sept. 15, Nov. 24, Dec. 15, 1818; Mar. 2, 16, Apr. 20, May 18, July 6, Aug. 31, Sept. 7, 28, Oct. 5, 19, Nov. 23, 30, Dec. 14, 1819; Jan. 4, 25, Feb. 1, 15, May 30, June 27, July 18, Aug. 1, Sept. 19, 1820.

Mass. Hist. Soc. has Feb. 12, Mar. 25, July 1, Sept. 23–Oct. 7, 1768; Apr. 7, June 23, 1769; May 18, June 15, July 6, 20, 1770; Feb. 1, 15, Apr. 12, 19, May 17, 31, June 7, July 5, 19, Sept. 6, 27, Oct. 11, 1771; May 15, June 19, 1772; Mar. 19, Apr. 2, Oct. 15, 1773; Mar. 25, Apr. 1, 8, May 13, 20, June 24, July 1, 8, 22–Aug. 25, Sept. 9–Oct. 21, Nov. 25, Dec. 2, 14, 1774; Dec. 6, 1775; Apr. 24, May 22, June 26, July 31, 1776; Mar. 26, May 28, 1777; Sept. 30, 1778; Jan. 13, 27, Sept. 15–29, Nov. 3–17, 1779; Feb. 9, Dec. 28, 1780; Mar. 8–22, Aug. 16, Sept. 27, Oct. 18, 25, Nov. 29, Dec. 6, 1781; Jan. 31, Feb. 21, Mar. 14, May 2, June 20, July 11, Aug. 29, 1782; Apr. 10, 1783; Feb. 25, Sept. 27, 1784; Jan. 19, Feb. 16, 1785; Mar. 8, Apr. 5, 20, 1786; Feb. 21, Mar. 21, 1787; Feb. 2, 1792; Jan. 2, 1793–Dec. 25, 1794; Feb. 18–Mar. 17, 31–Apr. 13, 27–July 20, Aug. 3–Sept. 14, 28–Oct. 12, 26–Nov. 23, 1796; Aug. 24, 1809; Nov. 23, 1819.

Martin Welles, Hartford, has June 16, July 6, Aug. 4, 11, 1769; Apr. 8, 1774; June 21, 1775; May 14, 21, July 23, Sept. 24, Nov. 12, Dec. 3, 1777; Mar. 11, 25, May 6, Oct. 7, Dec. 29, 1778; Sept. 29, 1779; May 25, July 13, 1780; May 17, 31, June 21, Aug. 2, Sept. 20, Oct. 25, Dec. 12, 20, 1781; Jan. 17, 1782; Mar. 13, Sept. 10, 24, Nov. 5–26, Dec. 10, 1783; Jan. 21, June 23, 1784; Feb. 21, 1787; June 25, Sept. 24, 1788; Mar. 18, July 8, 22, 1789; June 30, Nov. 24, 1790; Feb. 23, Mar. 2, May 25, June 1–15, July 13, Sept. 7, 1791; Jan. 11, Sept. 26, Oct. 31–Dec. 26, 1792; Jan. 2, 1793–Dec. 25, 1794; Jan. 1–Feb. 5, Mar. 5, Apr. 29, June 10, Aug. 5, Nov. 5, 1795; Mar. 3, July 13–27, Oct. 19, Dec. 14, 1796; Jan. 4–Dec. 28, 1797; Jan. 11, Feb. 1, Sept. 19, Oct. 17, Nov. 15, Dec. 27, 1798; Sept. 4, 18, Oct. 2, 16, 31, Dec. 12, 26, 1799; Jan. 2, Mar. 6, 27, Apr. 10, May 28, June 11, July 9, 16, 30, Aug. 27, Sept. 10–24, Nov. 20, Dec. 4, 18, 1800; Jan. 1, 1801–Dec. 23, 1802, fair; Jan. 6, 13, 27, Feb. 10, 24, Mar. 3, 17–31, Apr. 17–Aug. 25, Sept. 15–Nov. 17, Dec. 1–15, 29, 1803; Jan. 5, 12, Feb. 23, 1804; Jan. 23, Feb. 13, July 10, 1806; Jan. 1–Dec. 31, 1807, fair; Jan. 28, Feb. 11, 18, Mar. 3, 17, 24, Apr. 7–21, May 4, 19, June 2, 9, 23–July 7, Aug. 11, 18, Sept. 1, 22–Oct. 6, Nov. 10, 17, 1808; Jan. 5–June 29, Aug. 24, Sept. 14, 21, Oct. 5, 26, 1809; Sept. 13, 1811; Feb. 22, Mar. 1, 22, 29, Apr. 12, May 10, 1813; Jan. 3–Feb. 14, 28–

CONNECTICUT 45

Mar. 21, Apr. 11, 18, May 2, 23, 30, June 27, July 4, 18–Aug. 1, 15–Sept. 5, 19–Dec. 26, 1814; Dec. 17, 1816; Jan. 7, 14, Feb. 25, Mar. 4, 11, Apr. 8, 29, May 6, 27, June 3, Sept. 2, Dec. 9, 16, 30, 1817; Apr. 14, May 5, June 30, Nov. 7, Dec. 19, 26, 1818; Apr. 27, May 4, 11, 25, June 1, 15–29, July 13, 27, Aug. 3, 17–31, Nov. 16, 30, Dec. 14, 21, 1819; Jan. 4–Mar. 14, 28–Apr. 11, May 23–June 6, Oct. 3, 17, 31–Nov. 14, 1820.

Conn. Hist. Soc. has Jan. 17, 1772; Feb. 22, May 31–July 26, 1775; Feb. 26, Apr. 30, May 21, Nov. 12–26, Dec. 17, 31, 1777; Jan. 21–Mar. 11, 25–May 13, 27, June 3, 24, July 1, 15–29, Aug. 12, Sept. 2, 16–30, Oct. 14, Nov. 11, 18, Dec. 2, 1778; Feb. 24, Mar. 3, 31, Apr. 14, 21, May 5, 19, 26–June 9, Sept. 1, 1779; Feb. 9, Apr. 20, May 25, June 1, 15, July 6–27, Aug. 17, 24, Sept. 21, Oct. 26, Nov. 2, 16, 23, 1780; Jan. 4, 11, 25, Feb. 8, Mar. 1, 29, Apr. 12–May 2, 24, June 7, 21–July 26, Aug. 23, Sept. 13, 20, Oct. 18, Nov. 1, 22, Dec. 6–27, 1781; Feb. 7, 21, Mar. 14–28, Apr. 24, May 9, 20, July 4, Aug. 15, 29, Nov. 14, 21, Dec. 19, 1782; Jan. 16, 30, Feb. 13–Mar. 6, Apr. 17, May 22–June 5, July 16–Sept. 10, 24–Oct. 8, 22, Nov. 5–26, Dec. 10, 24, 1783; June 9–Dec. 29, 1784; Jan. 26, Feb. 2, 23, 1785; Jan. 2–Feb. 27, May 28, June 2, Sept. 17, Oct. 8–Nov. 5, 26, 1788; Feb. 18, Mar. 11, 18, Apr. 15, 29, June 10, July 8, 29–Sept. 2, 23, Oct. 21, 28–Nov. 18, Dec. 2, 9, 16, 30, 1789; Jan. 6, 1790–Dec. 25, 1800, fair; Jan. 1, Feb. 12, Mar. 19, May 27–June 10, Dec. 17, 1801; Mar. 17, June 9, Aug. 11–25, Sept. 15, 1803; Jan. 29, Aug. 27, Sept. 24, Oct. 1, 22, Nov. 12–Dec. 10, 24, 31, 1807; Sept. 22, 29, 1808; June 29, 1809; Feb. 21, Mar. 28, Aug. 15, Dec. 5, 1814; Nov. 10, 1818–Dec. 26, 1820.

New Haven Col. Hist. Soc. has Feb. 17, 1769; Nov. 13, 1776; July 1, 1778; June 7, 1786–Dec. 21, 1809.

N. Y. Pub. Lib. has July 22, 1768; Jan. 27, 1769; Jan. 5, 1770, Mar. 13, 1772; Jan. 1, Apr. 9, Oct. 8, 15, Nov. 12, Dec. 31, 1773; Jan. 28, Feb. 11, Mar. 18, Apr. 22, May 13, July 15, Oct. 21, Dec. 14, 28, 1774; Jan. 4, Mar. 8, 15, Apr. 12, June 14, July 12, Oct. 18, 25, Nov. 1, 1775; Aug. 5, 1778; Jan. 6, 1779; June 28, 1781; Mar. 14, 1782; May 26, 1784–May 25, 1785; Apr. 18, 1787; Mar. 19, Aug. 20, 1788; May 26, 1790; Oct. 31, 1792; Apr. 23, 1794; Jan. 1, Mar. 5, Apr. 29, June 3, July 8, 15, Aug. 19, Sept. 23, Nov. 19, 1795; June 1, 15, 22, Oct. 19–Nov. 2, Dec. 7, 1796; Apr. 5, 1797; July 4, 1798; Oct. 31, 1799; Mar. 6, July 16, 1800; Sept. 2, Nov. 5, 1801, May 9, 23–Oct. 3, 24–Nov. 21, 1820.

N. Y. Hist. Soc. has Aug. 25, Oct. 27, 1769; Feb. 23, Mar. 9, 1770; July 22, Oct. 21, 28, Dec. 9, 1774; Apr. 5, Aug. 9, Nov. 22, 29, Dec. 13, 1775; Sept. 4, 1776; Jan. 30, July 2, 30, Sept. 2, Dec. 10, 1777; Mar. 25, Apr. 21, May 6, June 17, Nov. 11, 1778; Jan. 6, Mar. 17, Apr. 7, Aug. 18, 1779; July 13, 1780; June 21, 28, 1781; Oct. 18, 1786; Nov. 3, 1790; Nov. 16, 1791; Jan. 15–Dec. 10, 1795; May 4, 1796; Mar. 24, 1803; May 12, Sept. 22, Oct. 6, Nov. 3, 10, 1808; May 21, 1812.

Bronson Lib., Waterbury, has Feb. 26, Dec. 29, 1773; Oct. 7, 1774; Aug. 28, Sept. 11, 18, Oct. 2–16, 30–Nov. 20, Dec. 11, 1776; Mar. 18, July 29, 1778; Jan. 20, Apr. 23, July 23, Aug. 11, 18, Oct. 20, 1779; Jan. 5, 12, Feb. 16, Apr. 12, 20, Sept. 7, 1780; Oct. 11, Dec. 20, 1781; Dec. 5, 1782; Jan. 9, 16, Mar. 27, Apr. 10, Aug. 20, 1783; Nov. 28, 1787; Mar. 19, Apr. 9, May 14, 28, Sept. 10, Oct. 8, 15, Nov. 12–Dec. 10, 31, 1788; Jan. 7, 21, Apr. 29, May 6, June 17, July 15, 29–Aug. 12, Sept. 30, Oct. 14, 28, Nov. 4, Dec. 23, 1789; Jan. 27, Feb. 17, Apr. 28, May 5, 19–June 9, 23–July 21, Aug. 4, Sept. 8, Oct. 6, 1790; May 14, 1794; July 15, 1795; Sept. 28, 1796; Dec. 26, 1799; Jan. 9–23, Feb. 20, 27, Dec. 4, 1800; Mar. 28, 1805; Oct. 15, 1807; Aug. 8, 1811; Sept. 6, 1813; Feb. 20, 1815; Oct. 14, 1817; Oct. 6, 27, Nov. 11, Dec. 15, 22, 1818; May 11, 1819; Apr. 4, 1820.

Shelton, Conn., Lib. has July 19, 1775–Oct. 29, 1783, fair; Sept. 24, 1794; Sept. 30, 1795–Nov. 6, 1806, fair; July 16, Aug. 13–Sept. 17, 1807; July 7, Aug. 24, 1808; Jan. 12, 1809.

N. Y. State Lib. has Jan. 21, Feb. 25, Apr. 8, 29, May 27, June 3, July 15, Sept. 16, 1778; July 20, Aug. 24, Nov. 16, 1780; July 19, Aug. 23, Nov. 1, 1781; May 30, 1782; Apr. 17, Oct. 22, Dec. 24, 1783; June 30–July 21, Aug. 11, 1784; May 23, 1787; Jan. 2, 16–30, Feb. 20, Apr. 16, July 9, 23, Aug. 20, 1788; Mar. 4, July 1, 29, Aug. 19, 26, Nov. 11, 1789; Jan. 6, Feb. 24, Apr. 7, July 7, Sept. 29, 1790; Jan. 5, Feb. 2, Mar. 9, 30, Apr. 6, 13, 27–May 11, June 8, 22, 29, July 20, Aug. 3, 10, Sept. 7, 14, 28–Oct. 12, Nov. 23, 1791; Jan. 11, Feb. 1, 15, June 6, Aug. 1–Sept. 19, Oct. 10–31, Nov. 14–28, Dec. 26, 1792; Jan. 31, June 19, July 3, Nov. 6, 1793; Jan. 23, Feb. 13, Mar. 27, Apr. 23, May 21, June 18, July 9, Oct. 29, Nov. 6, 20, Dec. 11, 1794; Jan. 1, 1795–Dec. 13, 1798, fair; Jan. 24, Mar. 14, July 10, Oct. 9, Nov. 14, Dec. 12, 1799; Jan. 30, Feb. 13, Mar. 6, 13, Apr. 3–17, 30, May 7, 21, 28, June 4, 25, July 16, 23, Dec. 4, 1800; Jan. 8, Feb. 5, Mar. 12, 26, Apr. 23, May 13, June 3, July 22, Aug. 26, Sept. 16, Dec. 10–24, 1801; Feb. 18, Mar. 4, 11, June 10, July 8, Aug. 26, Sept. 9, 23, Oct. 7, 14, Nov. 11, 18, Dec. 9, 16, 1802; Jan. 13, 20, Feb. 10, Mar. 3, 17–31, Sept. 1, 8, Oct. 27, Nov. 10, 17, 1803; Feb. 2, 16, May 17, Aug. 9, Sept. 20, 1804; Jan. 24, 1805; Feb. 6, 13, Mar. 6, 20, July 31, Aug. 14, Oct. 2, 9, 30, Nov. 13, 27, Dec. 11, 18, 1806; Jan. 15, 29, Feb. 5, Mar. 26, May 28, June 25, July 2, 23, Dec. 3, 10, 1807; Mar. 28, Apr. 4, 11, May 17, June 6, Aug. 22, Nov. 28, Dec. 5, 26, 1811; Feb. 22, Mar. 22, 29, Apr. 26, May 3–17, June 7, July 26, Aug. 30, Sept. 13, Nov. 8, Dec. 6, 1813; Jan. 3–Dec. 26, 1814, fair; Apr. 2, July 9, 16, Aug. 20, 27, Sept. 10, 17, 1816.

Western Reserve Hist. Soc. has Dec. 10, 1783; Nov. 28, 1792–Dec. 31, 1795, fair; Jan. 7, 14, 1796; Dec. 14, 1797; Sept. 19, 1798; Feb. 20, Oct. 23–Nov. 6, Dec. 12, 26, 1815; Jan. 16, 1816–Dec. 28, 1819, fair.

Conn. State Lib. has June 22, Oct. 5, 1791; Jan. 17, 1793; Mar. 10, 1796; May 16, July 25, Dec. 6, 1798; Aug. 20, 27, Sept. 24–Oct. 15, 30, Nov. 26, Dec. 11–25, 1800; Feb. 19, Apr. 2–23, May 13, June 3–17, July 22, 29, Sept. 23–

CONNECTICUT 47

Oct. 7, 21, Nov. 5, 12, Dec. 10, 17, 1801; Jan. 21, June 24, July 8, 15, 29, Aug. 12, Sept. 16, 30, Oct. 14–Nov. 4, 24, 1802; Jan. 13, 27–Feb. 24, Mar. 10, 24–Apr. 7, 28–June 2, July 14, 21, Nov. 3–Dec. 29, 1803; Jan. 5–Mar. 29, 1804; Nov. 6, Dec. 4, 18, 25, 1806; Jan. 15, 29, Feb. 5, 26, Apr. 2, 9, 23, May 7, July 9, Aug. 20, Dec. 3, 31, 1807; Jan. 7, 21–Mar. 3, 17–31, June 9, Aug. 4, 11, 25, Sept. 1, 22, 1808; Feb. 28, 1811; Feb. 22, Mar. 1, 22, 29, Apr. 12, May 10, Sept. 13, 1813; Mar. 4, 11, 1817.
Boston Pub. Lib. has Feb. 11–June 3, July 1–29, 1789; Apr. 21, 1790–July 14, 1803, fair.
Wis. Hist. Soc. has Jan. 4, Dec. 26, 1792; Sept. 9, 16, Oct. 29, 1795; Jan. 7, 1796–Dec. 26, 1799; Jan. 1–Dec. 31, 1801; July 18, 1814; Dec. 8, 1818.
Harvard has Feb. 26, Mar. 12, 1795; Mar. 22, June 14, 21, July 5, Sept. 13, 27, Oct. 4–26, Nov. 9–Dec. 28, 1797; Jan. 4, 1798–Aug. 2, 1804, fair; Feb. 13, Mar. 13–Apr. 3, 24, Aug. 14, 1806.
Princeton has Jan. 13, 1790–Aug. 10, 1791.
Phil. Lib. Co. has Oct. 29–Dec. 10, 1795; Jan. 21, Mar. 24–Apr. 27, May 18, 25, June 8–22, July 13, 20, Aug. 10, 17, 1796.
Derby, Conn., Pub. Lib. has Feb. 25, 1796–Dec. 28, 1797, fair.
Duke Univ. has June 24, 1801; Dec. 1, 1803; Oct. 31, 1814; Jan. 2, 1815–July 16, 1816, fair.
Middlesex Co. Hist. Soc., Middletown, has July 11, 1814–May 1, 1815, fair.
Univ. of Mich. (Clements) has Dec. 14, 1774; June 26, 1776; Jan. 11, 1781; Apr. 28, 1790; Sept. 5, Dec. 26, 1792; Jan. 1, 1795; Apr. 24, 1806; July 4, 1811.

[New Haven] Connecticut Post, and New Haven Visitor, 1803–1804.

Weekly. A continuation in numbering, but change of title, of the "Visitor." The initial number, with the title of "Connecticut Post, and New Haven Visitor," was published on Nov. 3, 1803, vol. 2, no. 1, printed for J. Walter [Joel Walter]. The last issue was published on Nov. 14, 1804, vol. 3, no. 3, and on Nov. 20 the paper was bought out by the "Connecticut Herald."

Yale has Nov. 3, 1803–Nov. 8, 1804.
Harvard has Nov. 3–Dec. 15, 29, 1803; Jan. 5–Feb. 16, Mar. 1–15, 29, Apr. 5–May 31, June 28–Aug. 2, 16, Sept. 6–27, Oct. 11–25, Nov. 8, 14, 1804.
Lib. Congress has Nov. 10, 17, Dec. 15, 1803; Jan. 26–Feb. 9, 1804.
New Haven Col. Hist. Soc. has Nov. 17, 1803; July 26, 1804.
Am. Antiq. Soc. has Jan. 19, Mar. 8, 15, Sept. 13, 1804.
N. Y. Pub. Lib. has Feb. 23, 1804.
Long Id. Hist. Soc. has Apr. 12, 1804.
Colgate Univ., Hamilton, has Apr. 26, 1804.

[New Haven] Federal Gazetteer, 1796–1797.

Weekly. Established Apr. 2, 1796, by Tiebout & O'Brien [John Tiebout and Edward O'Brien], with the title of "Federal Gazetteer." Between Aug. 23 and Oct. 4, 1796, Tiebout retired and the paper was published thenceforth by Edward O'Brien & Co. The last issue located is for Apr. 5, 1797, vol. 2, no. 53. Tiebout & O'Brien in 1795 were printers in New York, to which city the former returned after his New Haven experience.

Harvard has Apr. 9, 16, 30, 1796; Feb. 22, 1797.
Phil. Lib. Co. has Apr. 9–23, 1796.
Yale has May 17, 31–June 14, July 26–Aug. 9, 23, Oct. 4, Dec. 14, 21, 1796; Feb. 1, 1797.
Am. Antiq. Soc. has Aug. 9, Dec. 21, 1796; Apr. 5, 1797.

New-Haven Gazette, 1784–1786.

Weekly. Established May 13, 1784, by Meigs, Bowen and Dana [Josiah Meigs, Daniel Bowen and Eleutheros Dana], with the title of "The New-Haven Gazette." This firm was dissolved, and with the issue of Feb. 9, 1786, vol. 2, no. 92, the paper was published by Meigs and Dana. This issue, moreover, was its last under the name of "The New-Haven Gazette." Bowen began the publication of the "New-Haven Chronicle," Apr. 18, 1786, and Meigs & Dana established the "New Haven Gazette and Connecticut Magazine," Feb. 16, 1786, which see.

Yale has May 13, 1784–Feb. 9, 1786.
Conn. Hist. Soc. has May 13, 1784–Sept. 22, Dec. 29, 1785; Jan. 19, Feb. 9, 1786.
Lib. Congress has May 13–Dec. 30, 1784; Jan. 27, Feb. 10, 24, Mar. 10, 17, Apr. 14, May 26–June 9, 30–July 14, Sept. 1, Oct. 20, 1785; Jan. 5–Feb. 2, 1786.
Am. Antiq. Soc. has June 17, July 1, 15–29, Oct. 7, Nov. 11–25, Dec. 23, 30, 1784; Jan. 6–Dec. 29, 1785; Jan. 5, 26, Feb. 9, 1786.
Hist. Soc. Penn. has July 1, 1784–Feb. 2, 1786, badly mutilated.
New Haven Col. Hist. Soc. has Aug. 26, 1784; Jan. 27, Feb. 10, 24, Mar. 10, 17, Apr. 14, 1785–Feb. 9, 1786.
N. Y. Pub. Lib. has Jan. 20, Feb. 17–Apr. 7, May 26–June 16, 30, July 7, 28, Aug. 18–Sept. 15, 29, Oct. 6, 20–Nov. 17, Dec. 1–15, 1785; Jan. 5, 1786.
Shelton, Conn., Lib. has Sept. 2, 9, Oct. 14, 28, Nov. 4, 18, Dec. 2, 1784.
N. Y. Hist. Soc. has Apr. 14, 1785–Jan. 26, 1786.
Trinity Coll. has Oct. 14, 1784–Feb. 3, Apr. 21, 28, Nov. 23, Dec. 1, 1785.
Mass. Hist. Soc. has Nov. 11, 18, 1784; Jan. 27, Feb. 17, 24, Mar. 17, Apr. 7, 14, 1785.
Western Reserve Hist. Soc. has Feb. 24, 1785.

CONNECTICUT

New-Haven Gazette, 1791.

Weekly. Established Jan. 5, 1791, by Abel Morse, with the title of "The New-Haven Gazette." It was of quarto size, eight pages to the issue and paged continuously. It was discontinued with the issue of June 29, 1791, vol. 1, no. 26.

Am. Antiq. Soc. has Jan. 5–19, Feb. 9, 16, Mar. 2–16, Apr. 6, 20, May 4–June 29, 1791.
New Haven Col. Hist. Soc. has Jan. 12–Apr. 20, May 4–18, June 1–29, 1791.
Yale has Mar. 9–June 15, 1791.
N. Y. Pub. Lib. has Jan. 19, 1791.
Lib. Congress has May 4, 1791.

New-Haven Gazette, and Connecticut Magazine, 1786–1789.

Weekly. Established Feb. 16, 1786, by Meigs & Dana [Josiah Meigs and Eleutheros Dana], with the title of "The New-Haven Gazette, and the Connecticut Magazine." The partnership was dissolved and with the issue of Aug. 2, 1787, the paper was published by Josiah Meigs. It was a quarto of eight pages and title pages and indexes were provided for vols. 1 to 3. With the issue of Jan. 15, 1789, vol. 4, no. 1, it was enlarged to small folio, with the title of "The New-Haven Gazette, and Connecticut Magazine." The last issue located is that of June 18, 1789, vol. 4, no. 23.

Conn. Hist. Soc. has Feb. 16, 1786–June 18, 1789.
Yale has Feb. 16, 1786–Jan. 1, 1789.
Am. Antiq. Soc. has Feb. 16, 1786–Dec. 25, 1788; Jan. 1, 15, Feb. 12, 26, 1789.
N. Y. Hist. Soc. has Feb. 16, 1786–Dec. 25, 1788.
New Haven Colony Hist. Soc. has Feb. 16, 1786–Dec. 11, 1788.
Wis. Hist. Soc. has Feb. 16, 1786–Dec. 4, 1788.
Pequot Lib., Southport, has Feb. 16, 1786–Nov. 27, 1788.
N. Y. Pub. Lib. has Feb. 16–Dec. 28, 1786; Jan. 11–Dec. 27, 1787, fair; Jan. 31–Mar. 6, Apr. 10, July 3, Sept. 25, Oct. 9–30, 1788.
Lib. Congress has Feb. 16, 1786–Dec. 27, 1787; Jan. 10–Dec. 11, 1788, fair; Feb. 26, 1789.
Boston Pub. Lib. has Feb. 16, 1786–Dec. 27, 1787; May 8, 22, 29, June 12, 19, July 31, Aug. 21, Sept. 4, 18, 25, Dec. 6, 1788.
Mass. Hist. Soc. has Feb. 16, 1786–Feb. 15, 1787; Mar. 22, 1787; Jan. 10–Dec. 18, 1788.
Newberry Lib. has Feb. 16, 1786–Dec. 27, 1787.
N. Y. State Lib. has Feb. 16, 1786–Dec. 27, 1787.
Boston Athenæum has Feb. 16, 1786–Dec. 27, 1787.
Bridgeport Pub. Lib. has Feb. 16, 1786–Feb. 15, 1787.
Martin Welles, Hartford, has Feb. 16, 1786–Jan. 31, 1788, fair; June 18, 1789.
Univ. of Mich. (Clements) has Feb. 16, 1786–Dec. 13, 1787, fair.
Univ. of Minn. has Feb. 16, 1786–Feb. 15, 1787.

N. Y. Soc. Lib. has Oct. 5, 1786–Dec. 27, 1787.
New Haven Pub. Lib. has Feb. 23–Dec. 28, 1786; Mar. 29–Nov. 1, 15–Dec. 13, 1787.
Conn. State Lib. has Mar. 9–Dec. 21, 1786, fair; Jan. 18, Feb. 1, 8, May 10, 1787; Jan. 17, Feb. 21, Mar. 20, Apr. 3, May 15, 22, Aug. 28, Oct. 23, 1788.
Troy Pub. Lib. has Nov. 9, 1786–Dec. 20, 1787.
Western Reserve Hist. Soc. has Feb. 22–Dec. 27, 1787.
Dartmouth has May 17, July 19, Aug. 2–30, Sept. 20–Oct. 4, 18–Nov. 8, 29, Dec. 20, 27, 1787; Mar. 20, Apr. 17, May 1, 29, July 24, Oct. 2, 9, 1788.
Cornell Univ. has May 31–Nov. 29, 1787.

[New Haven] Herald of Minerva, 1802.

Weekly. Established Oct. 19, 1802, with the title of "The Herald of Minerva; or, Columbian Ark, and Washington Fortress," printed by W[illiam] W. Morse, for Jacob Griswold, Jun. It was of quarto size, with eight numbered pages to the issue. The last issue located is that of Nov. 16, 1802, no. 5.

Am. Antiq. Soc. has Oct. 26, Nov. 2, 16, 1802.
Conn. State Lib. has Nov. 9, 1802.

[New Haven] Messenger, 1800–1802.

Weekly. Established Jan. 2, 1800, by Read & Morse [Ezra Read and William W. Morse], with the title of "The Messenger." The partnership was dissolved, and with the issue of Feb. 12, 1801, the paper was published by William Walker Morse. It was temporarily discontinued with the issue of Apr. 2, 1801, but renewed with the issue of Sept. 29, 1801. The paper was discontinued with the issue of Aug. 9, 1802, vol. 3, no. 112. Morse began printing the "Visitor" at New Haven, Oct. 30, 1802.

Yale has Jan. 2, 9, 30–Feb. 13, 27–May 6, 20–June 17, July 9, 16, 30–Aug. 20, Sept. 3, 24–Oct. 8, Nov. 13, 27–Dec. 11, 25, 1800; Jan. 1, 8, 29, Sept. 29, 1801; Jan. 5–Aug. 9, 1802.
New Haven Col. Hist. Soc. has Jan. 2, Feb. 6–May 6, 20, June 3–Dec. 25, 1800; Jan. 8–Feb. 26, Mar. 5, 26, 1801; Jan. 19, May 31, June 7, 1802.
Harvard has Jan. 16, Apr. 15–June 24, July 9–30, Aug. 20, Sept. 3, 10, 24, Oct. 1, 15–Dec. 25, 1800; Jan. 1–Feb. 26, Mar. 19–Apr. 2, Sept. 29, Oct. 13, Nov. 17, Dec. 1, 29, 1801; Jan. 12, 19, 1802.
Am. Antiq. Soc. has Mar. 13, 27, Apr. 1, 15, 22, May 27, July 30, 1800; Sept. 29–Oct. 27, 1801; Feb. 2, Mar. 16, 23, Apr. 26, May 3, 24–June 7, 21, 28, July 12, 19, Aug. 2, 9, 1802.
Duke Univ. has Mar. 27, Apr. 1, 1800.
N. Y. Hist. Soc. has July 2, 1800.
Long Id. Hist. Soc. has Jan. 1, 1801.
Martin Welles, Hartford, has Jan. 22, 1801.

[New Haven] Sun of Liberty, 1801.

Weekly. A continuation, without change of numbering, of "The Sun of Liberty" of Norwalk. The last number printed at Norwalk was for July 15, 1801, vol. 1, no. 52. The first at New Haven was for Aug. 26, 1801, vol. 2, no. 1, whole no. 53, published by Samuel Morse, with the title of "The Sun of Liberty." Discontinued after a few numbers. The last issue located is that of Nov. 4, 1801, vol. 2, no. 11. Morse went to Savannah, where he began publishing the "Georgia Republican" in August, 1802.

Minn. Hist. Soc. has Aug. 26, Sept. 2, 1801.
Lib. Congress has Aug. 26, 1801.
Am. Antiq. Soc. has Aug. 26, Sept. 9, 30, 1801.
Yale has Sept. 9, 1801.
Martin Welles, Hartford, has Sept. 9, 1801.
Harvard has Sept. 30, 1801.
Rutgers Univ. has Nov. 4, 1801.

[New Haven] Visitor, 1802–1803.

Weekly. Established Oct. 30, 1802, printed by William W. Morse, for the editor [Joel Walter], with the title of "The Visitor." It was of quarto size, eight pages to the issue, and paged continuously. Beginning with the issue of Dec. 11, 1802, the paper was printed for J. Walter [Joel Walter]. The last issue was that for Oct. 25, 1803, vol. 1, no. 52, after which it was enlarged to folio size and title changed to the "Connecticut Post, and New Haven Visitor," which see.

Am. Antiq. Soc. has Oct. 30, 1802–Oct. 25, 1803.
Yale has Oct. 30, 1802–Oct. 25, 1803.
Martin Welles, Hartford, has Oct. 30, 1802–Oct. 25, 1803.
Lib. Congress has Oct. 30, 1802–Oct. 25, 1803, fair.
Conn. Hist. Soc. has Oct. 30, 1802–Jan. 25, 1803.
Conn. State Lib. has Nov. 20–Dec. 25, 1802; Jan. 11–Feb. 8, Mar. 8, 15, Apr. 19, May 10–31, 1803.
N. Y. Hist. Soc. has Dec. 11, 25, 1802; Feb. 22, Apr. 19, 26, July 26, Aug. 16, Sept. 13, 1803.
Univ. of Mich. (Clements) has Jan. 1, 1803.
Duke Univ. has Aug. 9, 1803.

New-London Advertiser, 1795.

Weekly. Established Mar. 2, 1795, judging from the date of the first known number, that of Mar. 16, 1795, vol. 1, no. 3, published by Thomas C. Green,

with the title of "The New-London Advertiser." Apparently continued for only a few issues. The last issue located is that of Apr. 13, 1795, vol. 1, no. 7.
Harvard has Mar. 16, Apr. 13, 1795.
Lib. Congress has Mar. 23, 1795.

[New London] Bee, 1797–1802.

Weekly. Established June 14, 1797, by Charles Holt, with the title of "The Bee." The paper was suspended from Sept. 5 to Nov. 14, 1798, on account of a "malignant disorder" in the city. Holt was tried for libel in 1800 and suspended his paper with the issue of Apr. 2, 1800. He brought out a "Supplement" on May 21, 1800, in which he stated that it was uncertain when the next paper would appear. After having received a fine and a sentence in prison, he revived the paper with the issue of Aug. 27, 1800. He finally discontinued the paper at New London with the issue of June 23, 1802, vol. 5, no. 228, and removed to Hudson, N. Y., where he began publishing a paper with the same title on Aug. 17, 1802.

- N. Y. Hist. Soc. has June 14, 1797–Dec. 25, 1799, good; Jan. 1, 1800–Mar. 17, 1802, fair.
- Yale has Sept. 13, Nov. 15–Dec. 27, 1797; Jan. 3–July 25, Aug. 8–29, Nov. 14–Dec. 26, 1798; Jan. 2–Dec. 25, 1799, fair; Jan. 1, 1800–June 23, 1802.
- Am. Antiq. Soc. has June 21, Aug. 16–Sept. 20, Oct. 4, 11, Nov. 1, 15, 29, Dec. 6, 13, 1797; Jan. 3–17, 31, Feb. 14, 28, Mar. 21, Apr. 25–May 16, June 6, July 4–Dec. 26, 1798; Jan. 2, 1799–Dec. 30, 1801; Jan. 6–Apr. 21, May 19, 26, June 23, 1802.
- Lib. Congress has June 21–July 13, 26–Aug. 16, Sept. 20, Oct. 18–Dec. 27, 1797; Jan. 3, 10, 24–June 27, July 11–Aug. 8, Nov. 28, Dec. 5, 1798; Jan. 2, 16–Feb. 6, Mar. 6, 13, Apr. 3, 24, May 8, 15, 29, June 12, July 3, 24, Aug. 21, Sept. 4, 18, Oct. 9, 16, 30–Nov. 27, Dec. 11–25, 1799; Jan. 1, 8, Feb. 12–Apr. 2, May 21, 1800; Apr. 15, May 6, 1801.
- Minn. Hist. Soc. has July 29–Sept. 30, Nov. 18, 1801–June 23, 1802.
- Harvard has July 6–19, Nov. 15, 22, 1797; Nov. 14, 1798; May 1, July 3, 1799; Sept. 3, Oct. 1, Nov. 5, 1800; Jan. 7, 14, Feb. 4–25, Mar. 18, 25, Apr. 15, 22, May 6, 20–June 17, July 1–Aug. 12, 26, Sept. 23–Oct. 21, Nov. 4–Dec. 2, 16–30, 1801; Jan. 13, 27–Mar. 3, 17–Apr. 7, 21–May 5, 19, June 2, 9, 23, 1802.
- Conn. Hist. Soc. has Sept. 5, Dec. 12, 1798; Jan. 2, 23, Feb. 6, Mar. 4, Oct. 9, 1799; Feb. 12, 26, Mar. 5, Oct. 8, Nov. 12, Dec. 10, 1800; May 6, 13, July 15, Sept. 2, 9, 23–Dec. 2, 16–30, 1801; Jan. 6–27, Feb. 10–24, Mar. 17–31, Apr. 14, 21, May 26, 1802.
- Mass. Hist. Soc. has Oct. 9, 1799; Dec. 10, 1800; July 22, 1801.
- Martin Welles, Hartford, has June 21, Sept. 6, 1797; May 2, 1798; Apr. 2, 1800; Nov. 11, 18, Dec. 9–30, 1801; Jan. 6–Apr. 28, June 2, 9, 1802.
- Essex Inst. has May 15–June 26, July 17, 31, Aug. 12, Oct. 16, Nov. 27, 1799.
- Long Id. Hist. Soc. has June 6, Aug. 29, Sept. 5, 1798.

CONNECTICUT 53

N. Y. Pub. Lib. has Sept. 20, Dec. 13, 1797; Mar. 28, June 6, 1798.
Phil. Lib. Co. has Jan. 24, Mar. 7–28, Apr. 11–25, May 16–July 11, 25, Aug. 8–Sept. 5, Nov. 14–Dec. 26, 1798.
Troy Pub. Lib. has Apr. 4, June 6–20, July 11, Aug. 1, 22, 1798.
Arkansas Hist. Comm. has July 4, Nov. 21, Dec. 26, 1798.
Conn. State Lib. has Apr. 10, 1799; Dec. 24, 1800; Jan. 14, Mar. 25, May 20, June 24, July 15, 22, Aug. 12, 1801.
N. Y. State Lib. has Aug. 27–Oct. 15, Dec. 17, 24, 1800; Jan. 7, 14, Mar. 4–25, Apr. 8, 22, May 6–Sept. 23, Oct. 28, 1801.
Wis. Hist. Soc. has Aug. 9, 1797.
Boston Athenæum has Jan. 28, Mar. 4, 1801.
New London Co. Hist. Soc. has Nov. 18, 1801.

[New London] Connecticut Gazette, 1763–1820+.

Weekly. Established Nov. 18, 1763, by Timothy Green under the title of "The New-London Gazette." In the Conn. Historical Society is a copy of a prospectus dated Oct. 12, 1763. On Dec. 17, 1773, the title was changed to "The Connecticut Gazette and the Universal Intelligencer." On May 11, 1787, the title was shortened to "The Connecticut Gazette." Timothy Green took his son Samuel into partnership and on Mar. 13, 1789, the firm name was changed to Timothy Green and Son, and on May 9, 1793, to Samuel Green. On July 3, 1794, the title was altered to "Connecticut Gazette," and on Jan. 1, 1800, to "Connecticut Gazette, and the Commercial Intelligencer," which was retained until Mar. 6, 1805, upon which date it was again called "Connecticut Gazette," and published by Cady & Eells [Ebenezer P. Cady and Nathaniel Eells]. This co-partnership was dissolved and beginning with the issue of June 3, 1807, Ebenezer P. Cady published the paper. From May 18, 1808, until after 1820, Samuel Green was the publisher.

Conn. Hist. Soc. has Nov. 18, 1763–Nov. 9, 1764; Aug. 22, 1766; Nov. 14, 1766–Dec. 27, 1820.
Yale has Aug. 2, 23–Sept. 13, 27–Oct. 11, 25–Nov. 15, Dec. 20, 27, 1765; Jan. 17–Feb. 14, May 23–Dec. 26, 1766; Jan. 16, 1767–Dec. 30, 1774; May 12, 1775; Jan. 12, 1776–Oct. 17, 1780; May 18–June 8, Nov. 30, 1781; Jan. 7, 1785–Dec. 31, 1795; Jan. 7–Aug. 11, Sept. 22, Dec. 29, 1796; Jan. 19, Feb. 2–Mar. 2, 30, Apr. 13–May 11, June 28, July 12–26, Aug. 16–Sept. 13, Oct. 4, Nov. 23, 1797; Jan. 3, 1798–Oct. 30, 1799, fair; July 29, Aug. 12, 26, Sept. 2, Oct. 28, Nov. 4, Dec. 2, 30, 1801; Jan. 20, Feb. 3, 17, July 2–16, Aug. 18, Sept. 1–Oct. 20, Nov. 3–Dec. 29, 1802; Jan. 5, 1803–Dec. 19, 1804, fair; Jan. 2, 1805–Dec. 27, 1820.
Am. Antiq. Soc. has Nov. 18, 1763; Aug. 29, 1766; Jan. 23, Apr. 10, June 6, Aug. 7, 1767; Apr. 7, June 16, Oct. 20, Nov. 10, Dec. 1–22, 1769; Jan. 26, Feb. 2, 16–Apr. 6, 20, 27, May 4, 18, June 15, 29, July 13, 20, Aug. 3, 10,

24, 31, Sept. 21, 28, Oct. 19, Nov. 2–Dec. 21, 1770; Jan. 4–Feb. 22, **Mar. 8,** 15, 29–Apr. 26, June 7, 14, 28–July 12, 26, Aug. 9, 23, Nov. 8, 1771; June 12, Oct. 30, Dec. 11, 1772; Jan. 8, June 4, 1773; July 1, Aug. 5–Dec. 30, 1774; Jan. 6–Feb. 3, 17, Mar. 3, 17, 31, Apr. 14, 21, May 5–26, June 9–Aug. **18,** Sept. 1, 15, 29–Oct. 13, 27, Nov. 10–24, Dec. 8, 22, 29, 1775; Jan. 5, 19–**Feb.** 16, Mar. 1–15, 29, Apr. 12, 26, May 3, 16–June 7, 21, 28, July 12–Dec. 27, 1776; Jan. 3–Oct. 10, 1777; Mar. 13, Apr. 17–Dec. 25, 1778; Jan. 1, 1779–Dec. 26, 1780, fair; Jan. 2, 1781–Dec. 25, 1789; Jan. 8, 1790–Dec. 22, 1792, **fair;** Feb. 7–June 13, Aug. 1, Sept. 19, Oct. 3, 10, 31, Nov. 13–Dec. 5, 19, 26, 1793; Jan. 2, 1794–Dec. 31, 1800; Jan. 7–Mar. 25, May 13, July 1–Dec. 30, 1801, fair; Jan. 6–Dec. 29, 1802; Jan. 5–Feb. 16, Mar. 16, July 20, Aug. 17–Sept. 7, 28–Oct. 12, 1803; Jan. 25, Feb. 22–Mar. 28, Apr. 11–May 2, 16, June 6, Sept. 12–Oct. 3, 1804; Jan. 2, 1805–Dec. 27, 1809; Jan. 17, Feb. 7, Apr. 25, May 30, June 13, July 4–25, Aug. 29, Sept. 19, 26, Dec. 5, 19, 1810; Jan. 2, 1811–Dec. 29, 1813; Jan. 5–Feb. 2, Apr. 6, 1814–Dec. 27, 1815; Jan. 24–Feb. 28, Mar. 13–Apr. 17, May 1–15, 29–June 12, July 10, 24, Sept. 11–Nov. 13, Dec. 25, 1816; Jan. 15, 22, May 7, July 9, 23, Aug. 13, Oct. 8, 22, 1817; June 10, July 1, 8, 22, Aug. 5, 19, 26, Sept. 9–23, Oct. 21, Nov. 4, Dec. 2–23, 1818; Jan. 20–May 19, June 2–16, 30–Oct. 27, 1819; Jan. 5, Mar. 22–Dec. 27, 1820.

N. Y. Hist. Soc. has Nov. 25, 1763; Mar. 21, May 16, Oct. 17–Nov. 21, Dec. 26, 1766; Feb. 20, June 19, Dec. 4, 1767; Mar. 4, Aug. 19, Sept. 23, Nov. 11, 18, 1768; Feb. 24, Mar. 10, Aug. 18, Sept. 8, 22, 30, Nov. 17, 24, 1769; Jan. 24, 31, Feb. 21, Mar. 6–Apr. 3, 17–May 1, 29, June 5, 19–July 17, Aug. 7–Oct. 16, 30, Dec. 18, 25, 1772; May 14, Sept. 17, Nov. 5, Dec. 17, 1773; Apr. 1, 22, July 8, 22, Sept. 16, 1774–Dec. 28, 1781; Feb. 1–Dec. 6, 1782; Jan. 3–17, Feb. 7–21, Mar. 7, Apr. 18, 25, May 23, June 13, July 11, 18, Aug. 1, 29, Nov. 28, Dec. 19, 26, 1783; Jan. 16, Feb. 27, Apr. 30, 1784; Aug. 12, Sept. 9, Oct. 21, Nov. 4, 1785; Jan. 5, Feb. 17, Mar. 3, Apr. 14, June 30, Oct. 27, Nov. 10, 24, 1786; Apr. 20, May 4, Aug. 24, 31, 1787; Feb. 1, July 4, 11, 1788; Jan. 23–Dec. 18, 1789; Mar. 17, Apr. 28, May 26, June 23, July 7, 21, Aug. 4, 18, Sept. 1, 15, Oct. 13, Nov. 10, 23, Dec. 8, 1791; Jan. 19–Dec. 6, 1792, fair; Oct. 31, Nov. 7, 1793; June 26–Dec. 25, 1794; Jan. 1–15, Feb. 12–Apr. 9, 23, May 7, 21, June 4–18, July 9–30, Aug. 27, Sept. 3, 17, Oct. 22–Dec. 31, 1795; Jan. 7–21, Feb. 4, 25, Mar. 3, 17–Dec. 29, 1796; Jan. 12, 26–June 21, July 26, Aug. 16–30, Sept. 20, 27, Nov. 1, 8, Dec. 20, 27, 1797; Jan. 10, 1798–Dec. 25, 1799; Jan. 15, 29–Feb. 26, Mar. 12–Nov. 19, Dec. 3, 1800–Sept. 22, 1802; Sept. 3, 10, 1806; Jan. 4–Dec. 30, 1807; Oct. 19–Nov. 9, 1808; Jan. 4, 18–Mar. 22, Apr. 12, May 10, July 12, 26–Aug. 9, Sept. 20, Oct. 18, Nov. 8, 1809; Jan. 2–Dec. 25, 1811; May 6, 20–June 3, 24, July 8, 15, 29, Aug. 26, Sept. 2, 16, Oct. 14, Nov. 18, Dec. 23, 1812; Jan. 5, 12, Mar. 2, 9, June 29, 1814; Jan. 4, Mar. 8, 1815; Nov. 20, Dec. 3, 1816; July 16, 1817; Mar. 11, 1818; Apr. 14, Oct. 6, 1819.

CONNECTICUT 55

Lib. Congress has Apr. 20, Sept. 14, 1764; July 15, Aug. 5, 1768; Sept. 16, Dec. 23, 1774; Mar. 3, June 3, 16, Oct. 27, 1775; Mar. 29, Nov. 15, Dec. 20, 1776; Feb. 14, June 6, 1777; July 3–17, Aug. 7, 21, Sept. 18, Oct. 2, 9, 30, Nov. 13, Dec. 4, 11, 1778; Jan. 1, 15, 29–Mar. 5, Apr. 8–June 3, Sept. 15, 1779; Jan. 5–26, Feb. 16, May 26, Aug. 18, Sept. 8, Oct. 10, 1780; Jan. 9– Dec. 7, 1781; May 10, Aug. 9, Oct. 11, 25, Nov. 1, 1782; May 2, 16, 1783; Jan. 30, Feb. 13–Mar. 26, Apr. 9–June 18, July 2–30, Aug. 20, Sept. 3, 17– Dec. 17, 1784; Aug. 12, 1785; Mar. 31, Apr. 21, 1786; July 27, Oct. 19, Dec. 14, 21, 1787; Jan. 4, 11; Feb. 1, 29–Mar. 28, Apr. 11–May 9, June 20– July 25, Sept. 5–19, Oct. 3, 10, 24, Nov. 7, Dec. 5–26, 1788; Jan. 2–Dec. 25, 1789, fair; Jan. 1, 8, Aug. 13, Oct. 22, Nov. 12, Dec. 24, 1790; May 12, June 9, July 7, Aug. 18, Sept. 15, Dec. 29, 1791; Jan. 12, 19, Feb. 16, Mar. 2–Apr. 5, 19, 26, May 10, 17, June 14, 28, July 5, 19, 26, Aug. 23– Nov. 15, Dec. 6, 1792; Mar. 14–Apr. 4, 18, May 2–23, June 6, Sept. 19, Dec. 5, 1793; Jan. 9, Mar. 27, Apr. 3, June, 19, 26, July 24–Oct. 9, 23, Nov. 13, 26, 1794; Apr. 16, 23, Mar. 12, May 7, June 11, 25, July 16, 23, Aug. 6, 13, 27, Sept. 3, 17, Oct. 15–29, Nov. 12–Dec. 31, 1795; Jan. 7– July 28, Aug. 11–Dec. 29, 1796; Feb. 2–June 28, July 12, 19, Aug. 9, 16, 30–Dec. 6, 1797; Jan. 3, 10, Mar. 7–28, Apr. 11, June 6, 27, Aug. 29, Sept. 5, 19, Oct. 24–Nov. 14, 1798; Feb. 13, Apr. 3–24, May 8, 29–Aug. 28, 1799; Jan. 8, Feb. 12–Mar. 26, Apr. 9–July 16, 30, Aug. 6, 20–Dec. 17, 1800; Feb. 4, 11, 1801; Jan. 12, Feb. 2, 16, Mar. 2, July 20, Aug. 24, 1803; Feb. 1, 29, July 18, Sept. 5, 12, 1804; Jan. 16, Feb. 13–27, Mar. 20, 27, Sept. 10, 1805; Oct. 29, Nov. 19, 26, Dec. 17, 1806; Jan. 21, Feb. 18, Mar. 11– Dec. 23, 1807, fair; Jan. 27–Dec. 7, 1808, fair; Aug. 9, 1809; Jan. 2, 1811– Dec. 29, 1813, fair; May 4, 25, June 1, Aug. 3–Dec. 7, 1814; Jan. 4–Feb. 8, 22–Mar. 15, 29–Apr. 26, June 7–21, Aug. 23, Sept. 13, 1815; Jan. 6, 1819– Dec. 27, 1820, fair.

Mass. Hist. Soc. has Apr. 6, 1764; Feb. 22, June 7, Aug. 2, Sept. 20, 27, 1765; Apr. 25, 1766; Aug. 14, 21, Sept. 11, 18, Dec. 18, 1767; July 24, Dec. 2, 1768; Jan. 6, 27, Feb. 3, Mar. 17, 24, Apr. 7–28, May 12, 19, June 2, 16, July 21, 28, Sept. 29, Dec. 15, 1769; Apr. 13, May 18, June 1–15, Aug. 17, Sept. 14, Nov. 23, 1770; Feb. 22, Mar. 1, Aug. 9, 1771; May 15, Aug. 21, 1772; Jan. 29, Apr. 2, 1773; Aug. 5, Dec. 30, 1774; Apr. 7, May 12, Sept. 15, Oct. 27, Nov. 24, Dec. 8, 1775; Jan. 5–Nov. 8, 1776, fair; Feb. 14, Mar. 21, Apr. 18, May 2, 30, June 6, 13, 1777; Nov. 27, 1778; May 20, 1779; Jan. 19, Mar. 22, Apr. 5, May 5, June 30, July 28, Aug. 25, 1780; Jan. 2, 23, Feb. 16, Apr. 27, July 6, Sept. 21, 28, Nov. 2, 16, 1781; Jan. 18–Feb. 1, Mar. 1, 15, Apr. 5, 12, May 3, 24, 31, June 14, July 12–26, Aug. 9, 16, 30–Sept. 27, 1782; June 27, 1783; July 30, 1784; Jan. 28–Feb. 11, Mar. 25, Apr. 8, 1785; Sept. 15, Dec. 22, 1786; Dec. 24, 1790; Jan. 7, 1791; Mar. 29, 1792; Dec. 26, 1793; Jan. 2, 16–Feb. 6, Mar. 13, 20, Apr. 3, 10, 24, June 5, 1794; Sept. 18, Oct. 30, Nov. 13, 26, Dec. 18, 1794; Jan. 8, Feb. 19, 26, Mar. 19, 26, Apr. 16–May 7, July 9–23, Aug. 6, 20, Sept. 10, Dec. 17, 24, 1795; Feb. 11–25,

Apr. 7, June 30, Aug. 4, 25, Sept. 15–29, Oct. 20, Nov. 10, Dec. 1, 15, 29, 1796; Jan. 5, Feb. 2–23, Mar. 2, 9, May 11, 25, June 10, 15, Nov. 22–Dec. 6, 1797; Mar. 7, 28, Apr. 18, 25, May 23, June 27, July 4, Aug. 29, Sept. 5–Nov. 7, Dec. 19, 1798; Jan. 9, 30, Apr. 24, May 1, 8, 29, 1799; Mar. 26–Apr. 9, Aug. 13, Oct. 8, Nov. 10–24, 1800; Apr. 7, May 20, 1801; Dec. 21, 1803; June 7, 1820.

N. Y. Pub. Lib. has July 10, 1767; Dec. 2, 1768; June 22, 1770; Oct. 23, 1772; July 22, 1774; Apr. 21, May 2, Aug. 8, Sept. 29, Oct. 20, Nov. 10–Dec. 1, 15, 29, 1775; Jan. 5, 1776–Dec. 26, 1777, fair; Jan. 2–30, May 22–Dec. 25, 1778, fair; Jan. 1–Dec. 29, 1779; Jan. 5, 1780–Dec. 28, 1781, fair; Jan. 11, 25, Feb. 8, Apr. 5, Sept. 13–Oct. 18, Nov. 8–Dec. 27, 1782; Jan. 3–Dec. 26, 1783, fair; Jan. 16, 23, 1784; June 22, July 20, Aug. 3, Sept. 14, Oct. 5–19, Nov. 2–Dec. 7, 21, 28, 1787; Jan. 11, Feb. 1–Mar. 7, 21–Apr. 25, May 9–June 6, 20–July 11, Dec. 26, 1788; Jan. 2, 9, Mar. 6, June 5, Aug. 7, 14, 1789; Jan. 8–Mar. 19, May 14–June 4, 18, 25, Aug. 6, 27, 1790; Jan. 14–Apr. 1, 14, 21, Sept. 29–Dec. 29, 1791; Jan. 5–19, June 14–28, July 12–Dec. 27, 1792; Jan. 3–Dec. 26, 1793, fair; Jan. 2–16, 29, Mar. 20, Apr. 3, Sept. 11, 1794; Jan. 29–Feb. 26, Mar. 12–26, Apr. 9–23, Nov. 5–Dec. 31, 1795; Jan. 7, 1796–Dec. 27, 1797, fair; Jan. 10–24, Feb. 7–Mar. 7, 21, 28, Sept. 19, 1798; Feb. 6, 13, 27–Mar. 20, Apr. 3, 10, 1799; Mar. 12, May 28, 1800; Apr. 15, July 22, 29, 1801; June 9–Dec. 29, 1802, fair; Mar. 21, 30, June 6, July 18, 25, Aug. 15, 29, Sept. 19–Oct. 3, 31, 1804; Jan. 2–Aug. 28, Dec. 18, 1805; Jan. 1, Feb. 19, 26, Apr. 23, Aug. 27–Sept. 10, Oct. 1, 15, 1806; Jan. 21, July 1, 15, Sept. 16, Nov. 4, 1807; Jan. 6, Mar. 23–June 1, 1808; May 31, July 26, Dec. 20, 1809; Nov. 7, 1810; Jan. 1–Dec. 25, 1811; Feb. 19, 26, July 29, Aug. 5, 26–Oct. 7, 21, Nov. 4–18, Dec. 2, 9, 23, 30, 1812; Jan. 27, Feb. 3, Mar. 3, 10, Apr. 7–May 12, June 2, July 14, Sept. 7–Oct. 13, Nov. 17–Dec. 1, 1813; Jan. 12, May 11, Dec. 14, 1814; Feb. 22, May 31, Aug. 30, Nov. 1, 1815; Apr. 23, June 18, 25, July 30, Oct. 22, Dec. 24, 1817; Jan. 7–Dec. 9, 1818, fair; Apr. 28, July 7, Oct. 27, Nov. 17, 1819; Apr. 26, May 3, June 14–28, July 19–Aug. 2, 30–Sept. 20, Oct. 4, 1820.

New London Co. Hist. Soc. has Mar. 17, 1769; June 3, 1774; Sept. 14, Oct. 22, 1787; Mar. 28–Dec. 19, 1788; Mar. 27, May 1, July 3, Sept. 25, Oct. 23, Nov. 13, 20, Dec. 4, 11, 1789; Jan. 15, Feb. 19, Mar. 19, 1790; May 10, 24, Aug. 30, Sept. 13, Oct. 4–25, Nov. 8, 28, Dec. 6, 20, 1892; Jan. 3, 31, Feb. 28, Mar. 14, 28, Apr. 11, May 2, 23, June 6, July 4, Aug. 1, Sept. 26, Oct. 10, Nov. 7, 21, 1793; Jan. 9–Feb. 27, Mar. 13, 27–Apr. 17, May 8–July 31, Aug. 14, 28, Sept. 5, 25, Oct. 2, 16, 30, Nov. 6, 20, Dec. 18, 1794; Jan. 15, 29–Feb. 12, 26, Mar. 12, 26, Apr. 9, 23, May 7, 21, June 4, 18, July 2, 16, 23, Aug. 6, 13, 27–Dec. 31, 1795; Jan. 7–Dec. 29, 1796; Jan. 5, 19–Mar. 2, Apr. 6, 13, 27–Dec. 27, 1797; May 16, June 27, July 18, Aug. 8, Sept. 12–Oct. 3, 17, 24, 1798; Jan. 9, 30, Feb. 6, Mar. 6–20, Apr. 3–Nov. 13, Dec. 25, 1799; Jan. 22, 1800–Dec. 23, 1801, fair; Jan. 13–27, Feb. 3–17, Apr. 21, 28, July 28, Sept. 8, 15, Oct. 6, Nov. 3, 24, Dec. 1, 22, 1802; Jan. 5–Feb. 9,

CONNECTICUT 57

Mar. 2, 23–May 4, June 22, July 13, 27, Aug. 17–Sept. 14, 1803; Jan. 4–Dec. 26, 1804; Jan. 9–Mar. 6, 20–Apr. 3, 17–May 15, 29, Sept. 11, Oct. 16, 23–Dec. 18, 1805; Jan. 1, 1806–Mar. 5, 1817; Mar. 26, Apr. 2, 9, June 18–Dec. 10, 24, 1817; Jan. 21, 1818–Dec. 27, 1820.

Conn. State Lib. has Aug. 25, 1769; Jan. 24, 1772; June 24, 1774–Aug. 29, 1777, fair; Sept. 18, Oct. 30, 1778–Oct. 31, 1780, fair; May 16, June 6, Nov. 21, 1783; Mar. 26, May 14, 21, June 25, July 23, Aug. 6, Oct. 1, 15, Nov. 26, 1784; Feb. 4, Mar. 25, Apr. 8, 1785–Dec. 15, 1786; Mar. 30, July 6, Aug. 17, Sept. 21, Dec. 7, 1787; Jan. 4, Feb. 1, 15, 22, Mar. 7, Apr. 18–May 2, Oct. 3, 1788; Jan. 9, 16, Feb. 27, Mar. 6, July 24, Aug. 21, Sept. 18, Oct. 30, Nov. 13, 1789; Nov. 19, 1790; Mar. 8, Apr. 5, 19, May 17, Oct. 4, 1792; Aug. 1, 1793–Dec. 26, 1798; Jan. 2–Sept. 18, Nov. 27, Dec. 25, 1799; Jan. 1, 1800–Dec. 30, 1801, fair; Jan. 6, 1802–Dec. 26, 1804; Jan. 2–30, May 15, July 10, 1805; Feb. 12, May 21, Dec. 3, 1806; Oct. 14, 28, Nov. 4, 1807; June 15–29, July 13, Nov. 30, 1808; Feb. 22, May 17, Oct. 18, 25, Nov. 29, Dec. 20, 1809; Jan. 3, 31, Mar. 14, May 2, 9, June 6, 13, July 4, Dec. 12, 1810; Feb. 27, May 1, 1811; Jan. 1, Apr. 29, Dec. 9, 23, 1812; Feb. 10, May 12, Sept. 8, 29, Oct. 20, 1813; July 14, 1819; Jan. 19, 1820.

Martin Welles, Hartford, has Feb. 3, Nov. 3, Dec. 1, 8, 1769; Nov. 2, 1770; Jan. 19, Feb. 16, 1776; Aug. 1, 1777; Nov. 14, 1780–May 25, 1781, fair; July 6, 13, Aug. 31, Sept. 28, Oct. 5, Dec. 14, 28, 1781; Jan. 4, Feb. 22, Mar. 22, Apr. 12, 19, May 10–31, June 21, July 26–Aug. 9, Sept. 6, 27, Oct. 11, 25, Nov. 1, 8, 29–Dec. 13, 1782; Jan. 3, 1783; Oct. 22, 29, Nov. 12, 26–Dec. 31, 1784; Jan. 7, 1785–Nov. 17, 1786, fair; Nov. 21, 1788; Feb. 6, Aug. 7, Nov. 6, Dec. 4, 18, 1789; Aug. 27, Sept. 24, 1790; June 30, Aug. 18, Oct. 6, 1791; Feb. 16, 1792; Feb. 21, Apr. 18, 1793; Apr. 24, 1794; Feb. 12, 1795; Dec. 6, 1797; Jan. 16, May 22, Nov. 20, 1799; June 11, 1800; Mar. 4, 1801; Feb. 29, 1804–Nov. 4, 1806, fair; Oct. 3, Nov. 14, 1808; Feb. 15, July 19, Sept. 13, 1809; Mar. 7, Aug. 15, Nov. 14, 1810; Jan. 9, Feb. 13, Apr. 10–May 15, June 12–July 11, 31–Sept. 11, 25–Oct. 23, Nov. 13, Dec. 4, 1811; Oct. 28, Dec. 23, 1812; May 14, 1817; Dec. 23, 1818.

Buffalo Hist. Soc. has Dec. 29, 1779–Sept. 15, 1780; Dec. 7, 1787–Oct. 10, 1788; Jan. 7–Dec. 30, 1801.

Case Mem. Lib., Hartford Seminary, has Aug. 13, 1795–Sept. 18, 1799; Jan. 1, 1800–Dec. 26, 1804.

Minn. Hist. Soc. has June 9–July 14, Sept. 1–Dec. 26, 1780; Jan. 2, 9, Feb. 9, 16, Mar. 2–Apr. 6, 20–June 29, 1781; Mar. 22, 1782; Aug. 22–Dec. 26, 1783; Jan. 9–23, Mar. 5–Apr. 9, June 25, 1784–Feb. 14, 1793; Mar. 6, 1794–Aug. 6, 1795; Aug. 11, 1796–Aug. 14, 1800; Jan. 7, 1801–Aug. 10, 1803.

Hist. Soc. Penn. has Mar. 1–15, Apr. 5–June 14, Nov. 15, 1776–Dec. 26, 1777; Aug. 28, Dec. 11, 1778; Jan. 15, Mar. 5, Apr. 22, May 20, July 8, Sept. 8, 29, Oct. 13, Dec. 15, 1779; June 23, Aug. 4, Oct. 6, 1780.

Duke Univ. has May 5, 27–June 10, July 8, 14, Aug. 18, Sept. 8, Oct. 6–27, Dec. 29, 1779; Mar. 29, Apr. 21, May 5–June 9, 30, July 7, 21, Oct. 24,

Nov. 28, Dec. 26, 1780; Feb. 23, Mar. 2, 16, May 4, 25, 1781; Mar. 5, Apr. 2, 9, 23, June 4, July 23, Aug. 6, 13, Sept. 10, 24, Oct. 29, Nov. 12, 26, Dec. 3, 31, 1784; Jan. 7, 14, Feb. 18, Mar. 4, Apr. 29, May 13, 27, June 3, July 1, 15–Sept. 16, 30, Oct. 7, Nov. 11, 25, Dec. 16, 1785; Jan. 5, 1786–Dec. 28, 1787, fair; July 3, Aug. 14, 1789; Dec. 25, 1799; May 19, 1802; Aug. 3, 10, 24, 1803; Jan. 2, 1805.

British Museum has Dec. 24, 1784–Dec. 29, 1786.

Bridgeport Pub. Lib. has Jan. 5–Nov. 28, 1780; Oct. 3, 1783–Oct. 8, 1784, fair.

Stonington Hist. Soc. has Mar. 23, 1770; Mar. 7, Sept. 17, 1788; Jan. 1, 1806–Dec. 27, 1809; Mar. 6–Dec. 25, 1811; Jan. 13, 1813–Dec. 28, 1814; Jan. 15–June 25, 1817; Jan. 7, 1818–Dec. 28, 1819.

Wis. Hist. Soc. has Mar. 14, 1766; Apr. 6, 1787–Sept. 29, 1791; May 23, 1793; July 17–Oct. 2, 1794; May 11, Dec. 20, 1797; July 25, 1798; Feb. 27, 1799–July 1, 1801; Dec. 8, 1813; Dec. 16, 1818.

East Hampton Free Lib. has July 15, 1785–Dec. 29, 1786, fair.

Rutgers Univ. has Mar. 16, 1770; June 9–23, Oct. 13, 27, 1775; Nov. 29, 1776; May 30, 1777; June 5, 1778; May 28, 1780; June 6–Oct. 17, 1798, fair; Jan. 6, 13, 27, Feb. 3, 17, Mar. 3, June 2, Oct. 20, Dec. 1, 1802; Jan. 16–Feb. 6, Mar. 13, 27–Apr. 17, May 29, Oct. 23, 1805.

Peck Lib., Norwich, has June 28, July 5, Aug. 23, Oct. 11, 18, Nov. 1–22, 1776; Nov. 18, 1785; Oct. 2, 1789.

Harvard has Jan. 8, 1795–Dec. 9, 1807, fair.

Arkansas Hist. Comm. has Feb. 19, 1795–Mar. 3, 1797; July 5, 1797–Jan. 3, 1798, fair.

N. J. Hist. Soc. has Apr. 18, 1798–Apr. 9, 1800; Mar. 27, 1805.

Phil. Lib. Co. has Oct. 11, 1765; Nov. 5, 19–Dec. 3, 1795; Jan. 7, 28, Mar. 17, 31–Apr. 14, 28, May 12–June 2, 16, July 14, 28–Aug. 11, 1796.

Univ. of Mich. (Clements) has Sept. 7, 1764; Jan. 4, Mar. 15, Apr. 5, June 7, 21, Sept. 20, Oct. 4, Nov. 8, 1765; July 11, Aug. 22, Nov. 28, Dec. 19, 1766; Mar. 27, July 24, Aug. 7, 14, Dec. 11, 1767; Jan. 15, 1768; June 23, 1775; Sept. 6, 1776; June 22, July 6, Sept. 21, 1781; Sept. 27, 1782; Mar. 21, 1788; Oct. 4, 1792; Feb. 9, 16, 1803; Dec. 2, 1812.

Western Reserve Hist. Soc. has July 3, 1767; June 29–Sept. 7, 1788; Nov. 21, 28, Dec. 12, 1788; Jan. 23, May 1, Nov. 27, 1789; Mar. 8, 22, Apr. 26, May 3, 24, 31, Aug. 30, Oct. 4, Dec. 13, 1792; Feb. 7, 14, Apr. 11, 1793; Mar. 13, 1794; Mar. 12, Aug. 27, 1795; Apr. 14, 1796; Sept. 29, Oct. 20, 1802; Nov. 23, 1803; Apr. 4, 1804; Jan. 9, 1805; Feb. 19, 1806; Aug. 9, 1815.

Several libraries have a few scattering later issues found in other files.

New-London Gazette, see [New London] Connecticut Gazette.

[New London] Republican Advocate, 1818–1820+.

Weekly. Established Feb. 18, 1818, judging from the date of the earliest issue located, that of Apr. 15, 1818, vol. 1, no. 9, published by Clapp & Francis

[Joshua B. Clapp and Simeon Francis], with the title of "The Republican Advocate." It was so continued until after 1820.

> Lib. Congress has Apr. 15, 29, Sept. 2, Oct. 14, 28, Dec. 16, 30, 1818; Jan. 13, 27, Feb. 10, 1819; Jan. 5–Dec. 27, 1820.
> Am. Antiq. Soc. has May 13, June 3, July 8, 15, Aug. 5, Sept. 9–23, Oct. 7, Dec. 2, 23, 30, 1818; Jan. 20, Feb. 3, Mar. 10, 17, 31, June 16, 23, July 14, Aug. 4, 25, Sept. 15, Oct. 20–Dec. 8, 1819; June 14, 1820.
> New London Co. Hist. Soc. has Jan. 6, 1819–Dec. 27, 1820.
> Stonington Hist. Soc. has Aug. 19–Sept. 2, 1818; Feb. 17, Mar. 24, May 19, 1819.
> Long Id. Hist. Soc. has Nov. 18, 1818.
> Wis. Hist. Soc. has Dec. 9, 1818.
> Western Reserve Hist. Soc. has Sept. 22, 1819.
> Martin Welles, Hartford, has Dec. 15, 1819.
> Univ. of Mich. (Clements) has June 14, 1820.

[New London] Springer's Weekly Oracle, see **[New London] Weekly Oracle.**

New-London Summary, 1758–1763.

Weekly. Established Aug. 8, 1758 (Thomas, Hist. of Printing, ed. 2, vol. 2, p. 87, is authority for this date, as I have not located the first number). The earliest issue located is that of Sept. 29, 1758, no. 8, published by Timothy Green, with the title of "The New-London Summary, or, the Weekly Advertiser." In May or June, 1763, the title was shortened to "The New-London Summary." The last issue located is that of Sept. 23, 1763, no. 268. Green died Oct. 3, 1763 ("Boston Post," Oct. 10, 1763), and the paper was discontinued soon after. It was immediately succeeded by the "New London Gazette," established Nov. 18, 1763, by Timothy Green, nephew of Timothy.

> Conn. Hist. Soc. has Sept. 29, Oct. 27, Dec. 8, 29, 1758; Jan. 5, Feb. 2–23, Aug. 3–Sept. 28, 1759; Mar. 7, May 9, June 6, 13, Aug. 15–Dec. 26, 1760; Jan. 2–July 17, 1761; Feb. 26, May 14, June 18, Dec. 31, 1762; Jan. 21, Feb. 18, June 24, 1763.
> Am. Antiq. Soc. has Mar. 21, Aug. 22, 1760; Mar. 27, Apr. 10–May 8, June 19, July 24, Aug. 14, Oct. 23, 30, Nov. 20, 27, Dec. 25, 1761; Mar. 19, Apr. 9, June 11, 18, July 2, 23, Aug. 13, Oct. 8, 22–Nov. 5, 19, 26, Dec. 10, 24, 1762; Jan. 7, 14, 28, Feb. 11, Mar. 4, Apr. 8, June 17–July 22, Aug. 5–Sept. 23, 1763.
> New London Co. Hist. Soc. has Jan. 26, 1759; May 30, 1760; Aug. 14, Dec. 18, 1761; Feb. 4, 1763.
> Mass. Hist. Soc. has Oct. 15, 1759, extra; Apr. 29, June 24, 1763.
> Lib. Congress has May 22, 1761.
> N. Y. Pub. Lib. has June 4, 1762.
> Martin Welles, Hartford, has Dec. 24, 1762.

A photostat set, containing all known issues, was reproduced by the Conn. Hist. Soc. in 1930, and is to be found in the following libraries: — Conn. Hist. Soc., Conn. State Lib., Yale, New London Co. Hist. Soc., Am. Antiq. Soc., N. Y. Pub. Lib., N. Y. Hist. Soc., Columbia Univ., N. Y. State Lib., Grosvenor Lib., Univ. of Chicago, Newberry Lib., Univ. of Illinois, Western Reserve Hist. Soc., Univ. of Michigan, Duke Univ., and Huntington Lib.

[New London] **True Republican,** 1807.

Weekly. Established July 1, 1807, by Avery & Spooner [——— Avery and Alden Spooner], with the title of "True Republican." This paper was really a successor of the Norwich paper of the same name. The editors, in their prospectus, announced that it would be called the "Republican Day," but finally decided to continue the old name. The last issue located is that of Nov. 25, 1807, vol. 1, no. 22.

Am. Antiq. Soc. has July 1, 8, Aug. 5, Sept. 16, 30, Oct. 14, 1807.
Harvard has July 8, Aug. 5, 1807.
Western Reserve Hist. Soc. has July 29, Aug. 19, Nov. 25, 1807.
Lib. Congress has Aug. 5, Sept. 23, 1807.
Pequot Lib., Southport, has Nov. 4, 1807.

[New London] **Weekly Oracle,** 1796–1801.

Weekly. Established Oct. 22, 1796, by James Springer, with the title of "Weekly Oracle." It was at first a small folio but with the issue of Oct. 21, 1797, it was enlarged in size and the title changed to "Springer's Weekly Oracle." The last issue located is that of Oct. 27, 1801, vol. 5, no. 258.

Watkinson Lib., Hartford, has Oct. 22, 1796–Oct. 7, 1797.
Harvard has Jan. 21, Mar. 18, 25, June 3, 10, July 8, 15, Nov. 11, 18, 1797; Jan. 6, 1798; Mar. 18, 25, Apr. 29, May 13–27, June 10–24, July 22–Aug. 5, 19, 26, Sept. 9, 16, 30–Oct. 21, Nov. 11, 25, Dec. 23, 1799; Jan. 13–Apr. 21, May 5–19, June 2–23, July 14–Aug. 11, 26, Sept. 2, 16–30, Oct. 14, 21, Nov. 4–25, Dec. 9–30, 1800; Jan. 6, 27, Feb. 10, Apr. 7, 21–May 5, 19–Aug. 4, 18–Sept. 8, 29–Oct. 13, 27, 1801.
Am. Antiq. Soc. has Nov. 26, 1796; Aug. 12, Nov. 11, 1797; Jan. 13, Sept. 3 Nov. 19, 1798; Jan. 28, Nov. 4, 11, 1799; Jan. 27, Mar. 17, 1800; Feb. 17, Apr. 14, 1801.
New London Co. Hist. Soc. has Oct. 28, Nov. 4, 18–Dec. 16, 30, 1797; Jan. 6, Mar. 24, May 12, July 14, 28, Nov. 26, Dec. 10, 1798; Feb. 4, Mar. 4, Apr. 1, June 10, Aug. 12, Sept. 23, Nov. 18, 1799; Feb. 10, 24, Mar. 24, June 16, 23, July 7, Dec. 1, 1800; Jan. 6, Apr. 1, June 23, Sept. 29, 1801.
Mass. Hist. Soc. has Nov. 4, 1797; Jan. 6, June 30, 1798; May 6, June 17, Sept. 23, Dec. 9, extra, 1799; Dec. 16, 1800; Mar. 17, May 19, 1801.

Troy Pub. Lib. has June 23, July 21, Aug. 6–27, Nov. 12, 26, Dec. 17, 1798; Jan. 13, 1800; Sept. 22, 1801.
N. Y. Hist. Soc. has Nov. 19, 1796; Sept. 16, 1797.
N. Y. Pub. Lib. has Mar. 4, 1797; Jan. 13, 1798; Jan. 14, Apr. 8, Sept. 2, 1799; May 26, 1800; Jan. 27, May 5, 12, Aug. 11, 1801.
Western Reserve Hist. Soc. has Apr. 6, May 19, Dec. 24, 1798.
Yale has Apr. 7, 28 extra, 1798.
Lib. Congress has Apr. 28, 1798; Dec. 1, 1800.
Phil. Lib. Co. has June 16, 1798.
Conn. Hist. Soc. has Dec. 30, 1799; Jan. 6, 1800.
Williams Coll. has Dec. 30, 1799.
Wis. Hist. Soc. has May 19, 1800.
Boston Athenæum has Nov. 25, 1800.
Long Id. Hist. Soc. has Mar. 10, 1801.

[Newfield] **American Telegraphe**, 1795–1800.

Weekly. Established, Apr. 8, 1795, by Beach and Jones [Lazarus Beach and Ira Jones], with the title of "American Telegraphe." This firm dissolved partnership with the issue of July 6, 1796, and henceforth Lazarus Beach was sole proprietor. The name of the paper was enlarged, July 13, 1796, to the "American Telegraphe, & Fairfield County Gazette," but was shortened again, Apr. 5, 1797, to the "American Telegraphe." In October, 1800, the village of Newfield was incorporated under the name of Bridgeport. The last issue with the Newfield imprint is that of Oct. 29, 1800, vol. 6, no. 43, and beginning with the issue of Nov. 5, 1800, the name of Bridgeport appears in the imprint. For subsequent issues, see under Bridgeport.

Lib. Congress has Apr. 8, 1795–Mar. 29, 1797.
Harvard has Apr. 15, June 24, July 22, Aug. 5, 12, Sept. 9, 1795; Mar. 16–30, June 26, Dec. 23, 1796; Mar. 22, July 5, Nov. 15, 1797; Jan. 3, 1798.
N. Y. Hist. Soc. has Apr. 22, 1795–June 29, 1796; Sept. 16, 1797.
Am. Antiq. Soc. has May 6, July 15, Aug. 26, Oct. 14, Nov. 11, 18, 1795; May 25, June 8–29, July 13, Oct. 19, Nov. 2–16, 1796; Jan. 11, Feb. 15, 22, Apr. 19, Aug. 30, Oct. 18, Nov. 29, 1797; Jan. 10, May 23, 1798, May 15, 1799.
Yale has June 10, 1795; Aug. 8, 15, 1798; Mar. 7, 13, Apr. 3–24, May 14, 21, June 4, 11, 1800.
Wis. Hist. Soc. has Sept. 9–Oct. 14, 28, 1795.
Conn. State Lib. has May 18–Oct. 12, 26–Dec. 20, 1796; Jan. 4–Mar. 22, 1797; Jan. 16–Oct. 29, 1800.
Bridgeport Pub. Lib. has June 10, 1795; July 13, Oct. 5, 1796; Feb. 20, Mar. 10, Apr. 17, July 2, 1800.
New Haven Col. Hist. Soc. has Aug. 9, 1797; Oct. 29, 1800.
Boston Pub. Lib. has July 25, 1798.

Martin Welles, Hartford, has Oct. 31, 1798.
Conn. Hist. Soc. has Dec. 26, 1799.
N. Y. Pub. Lib. has Aug. 13, 1800.
Western Reserve Hist. Soc. has Oct. 22, 1800.

[Newfield] Humming Bird, 1798.

Established Apr. 14, 1798, by L[azarus] Beach, with the title of "The Humming Bird, Or Herald of Taste." It was a magazine in appearance, of quarto size, but included current news and the record of marriages and deaths, and in its initial issue referred to itself as "a paper." The last issue located is that of June 9, 1798, vol. 1, no. 5. Although announced as a weekly, the volume numbering would show that it was published bi-weekly.

Am. Antiq. Soc. has Apr. 14, June 9, 1798.

[Norwalk] American Apollo, 1801–1802.

Weekly. Established Aug. 12, 1801, by Joseph Dennis, with the title of "The American Apollo." The last issue located is that of Mar. 10, 1802, vol. 1, no. 30. Discontinued in May, 1802, according to a notice of the fact in the New London "Bee" of May 19, 1802.

Am. Antiq. Soc. has Aug. 12, 1801; Mar. 10, 1802.
Fairfield Hist. Soc. has Nov. 25, 1801.
Wis. Hist. Soc. has Dec. 2, 1801.

Norwalk Gazette, 1818–1820+.

Weekly. Established May 6, 1818, by Nichols & Price [Roswell S. Nichols and Philo Price], with the title of "Norwalk Gazette." Continued after 1820.

Norwalk Pub. Lib. has May 6, June 3–Dec. 30, 1818; Jan. 6–Apr. 7, May 26–Aug. 18, Sept. 1–Dec. 29, 1819; Jan. 5–Apr. 19, May 3–Dec. 27, 1820.
Am. Antiq. Soc. has May 6, 20, 1818, Nov. 15, 1820.
Martin Welles, Hartford, has Jan. 27, 1819.
Long Id. Hist. Soc. has Mar. 1–15, 29–Apr. 12, 26–May 17, 31–June 21, Aug. 2, 1820.

[Norwalk] Independent Republican, 1802–1803.

Weekly. Established June 17, 1802, by Joseph Dennis, with the title of "The Independent Republican," continuing the advertisements of "The American Apollo." Dennis had issued proposals for a paper to be called the "Independent Whig," but changed his title when he found that there was already a Philadelphia paper of that name (New London "Bee," May 12, 1802). The last issue located is that of Apr. 6, 1803, vol. 1, no. 41.

Am. Antiq. Soc. has June 17, 1802.
Harvard has Sept. 29–Oct. 13, 27–Nov. 9, Dec. 7, 29, 1802; Jan. 5, 19–Feb. 9, 23–Mar. 16, 30, Apr. 6, 1803.
Boston Pub. Lib. has Feb. 23, 1803.

[Norwalk] **Sun of Liberty,** 1800–1801.

Weekly. A continuation, without change of numbering, of the "Sun of Liberty" of Danbury. The last number printed at Danbury was for Oct. 8, 1800, vol. 1, no. 13, and the first issue at Norwalk was that of Oct. 21, 1800, vol. 1, no. 14, published by Samuel Morse, with the title of "The Sun of Liberty." The last number printed at Norwalk was for July 15, 1801, vol. 1, no. 52, after which the paper was removed to New Haven. See under New Haven.

Minn. Hist. Soc. has Oct. 21, 28, Nov. 18–Dec. 30, 1800; Jan. 6–Mar. 17, Apr. 7, 21–June 24, July 8, 15, 1801.
Long Id. Hist. Soc. has Nov. 18, 25, 1800; May 27, 1801.
N. Y. Hist. Soc. has Mar. 10, 1801.
Am. Antiq. Soc. has Mar. 17, 1801.
Harvard has July 15, 1801.

[Norwich] **Chelsea Courier,** see [Norwich] **Courier.**

[Norwich] **Connecticut Centinel,** 1802–1807.

Weekly. A continuation of the "Norwich Packet," the first issue with the new name of "The Connecticut Centinel" being that of Feb. 16, 1802, vol. 29, no. 1457, the numbering continuing that of the "Packet." Published by John Trumbull until his death Aug. 14, 1802. Beginning with Aug. 17, 1802, the paper was published for Lucy Trumbull, his widow. With the issue of Aug. 23, 1803, it was published by Charles E. Trumbull, who shortened the title on Sept. 22, 1803, to "Connecticut Centinel," and with the issue of July 17, 1804, by his brother, Henry Trumbull, whose name thus appears in the imprint until Nov. 19, 1805. The issues thenceforth to Oct. 27, 1807, vol. 34, no. 1753, which is the last located, were published by S. Webb [Samuel Webb] for Henry Trumbull.

Harvard has Feb. 16–Mar. 16, Apr. 13–27, May 11, 25–June 22, July 6, Aug. 17, 31, Sept. 14, 28–Nov. 9, 23–Dec. 14, 28, 1802; Jan. 11–Mar. 22, Apr. 19, May 3–17, 31–June 14, July 5, 19, Sept. 6–Oct. 4, 18, Nov. 8, Dec. 6–27, 1803; Jan. 17–31, Feb. 14–Mar. 6, 20–Apr. 10, 24, May 1, June 14, 26–July 17, 1804; July 21, Aug. 4, 18, 1807.
Conn. State Lib. has Feb. 16–Dec. 28, 1802; Jan. 4, 25, Feb. 8–July 12, Aug. 2, Sept. 6, 1803; June 12, Aug. 14, Sept. 11, 1804; Apr. 9, July 2, Oct. 29, 1805; June 24, 1806; Apr. 21, June 16, Aug. 11, Oct. 13, 1807.
Am. Antiq. Soc. has May 11, Oct. 19, Dec. 14, 1802; Feb. 1, July 19, Aug. 16–

30, Nov. 29, Dec. 27, 1803; Mar. 13–27, May 22, 1804; Jan. 29, June 11, 18, July 2, 30, Aug. 13, 20, Sept. 3, 24, Oct. 1, 1805; Jan. 7, Feb. 4, 11, Mar. 4, 18, Apr. 1, 8, 22, May 6, June 17, Oct. 7, 28–Nov. 11, Dec. 9, 16, 1806; July 7, Sept. 29, 1807.
Lib. Congress has Apr. 13–27, July 13, Aug. 3, 10, 1802; Feb. 10–May 12, 26–July 14, 1807.
Conn. Hist. Soc. has Mar. 23, May 11, July 6, 13, Sept. 21, 28, Oct. 19–Nov. 30, Dec. 14, 1802; Apr. 10, 1804; Jan. 1, 1805–Mar. 11, 1806, fair; Jan. 6–27, July 28–Oct. 27, 1807.
N. Y. Hist. Soc. has July 20, Dec. 14, 1802.
Martin Welles, Hartford, has Nov. 15, Dec. 20, 1803.
Westerly, R. I., Pub. Lib. has Apr. 5, 1803.
Grinnell Coll. Lib. has Jan. 24, 1804.
New London Co. Hist. Soc. has Apr. 3, 1804.
New Haven Col. Hist. Soc. has May 12, 1807.

[Norwich] **Courier**, 1796–1820+.

Weekly. Established Nov. 30, 1796, by Thomas Hubbard under the name of "The Chelsea Courier." With the issue of May 31, 1798, the title was changed to "The Courier." The paper was published by Russell Hubbard beginning with the issue of Nov. 20, 1805; by Thomas Hubbard & Son with the issue of Nov. 19, 1806; and by Russell Hubbard with the issue of Jan. 20, 1808. The title was changed to "Norwich Courier" with the issue of Mar. 22, 1809. Beginning with the issue of Feb. 12, 1817, the paper was published by Hubbard & Marvin [Russell Hubbard and Theophilus R. Marvin], and with Feb. 17, 1819, by Russell Hubbard, who continued it until after 1820.

Norwich Bulletin Office has Nov. 30, 1796–Oct. 15, 1800; Jan. 14, Feb. 18, 1801–Dec. 15, 1802; Mar. 20, 1805; Mar. 16, 1808; June 5, July 3, 10, 24, Aug. 21, Oct. 30, Nov. 6, 1811; Jan. 8, Mar. 11, Apr. 1, 1812; Aug. 4–18, Sept. 8–Oct. 6, 20–Dec. 29, 1813; Jan. 5, 12, Feb. 9–Mar. 30, Apr. 13, May 4, 11, 25–June 8, 29, July 13, Sept. 7, 14, 28, Nov. 9, Dec. 7, 28, 1814; Jan. 11, 25, Feb. 8, June 21, Sept. 27, 1815; June 12, Aug. 14–Dec. 25, 1816; Apr. 21–Dec. 27, 1820.
Otis Lib., Norwich, has Nov. 30, 1797–Dec. 25, 1811; Nov. 17, 1813–Dec. 27, 1820.
Conn. State Lib. has Jan. 1, 1800–Nov. 17, 1802; Jan. 19, Feb. 16, Mar. 9, 30, Apr. 13, May 25, June 8–22, Nov. 16, Dec. 14, 1803; Apr. 22, 1807; Oct. 23, 1811–May 26, 1813; Aug. 25, 1813–Nov. 5, 1817; July 15, 29, 1818.
Am. Antiq. Soc. has Nov. 30, 1796–Nov. 23, 1797; Jan. 8, Feb. 26, Nov. 5, Dec. 10, 1800; Sept. 30, 1801; Aug. 4, 1802; Oct. 26, 1803; Mar. 21, 1804; June 18–July 23, Aug. 13–Oct. 15, 1806; Apr. 22, 1807; Aug. 16, 1809; Feb. 14, June 6, 13, July 18–Aug. 1, Sept. 26, Oct. 17, 24, 1810; Apr. 10, Nov. 13–

Dec. 25, 1811; Jan. 1, 1812–Nov. 10, 1813; Jan. 5, Aug. 17, 1814; July 26, Aug. 9, 16, 1815; Aug. 4, Sept. 29, 1819.

Conn. Hist. Soc. has Nov. 30, 1796; Jan. 25, 1797–May 31, 1798; Jan. 1, 1800; May 27, 1801–Nov. 11, 1807; Oct. 14, 1812.

Harvard has Nov. 30, Dec. 21, 28, 1796; Jan. 4–Feb. 1, 15–Apr. 12, 26, July 12, Nov. 22, Dec. 28, 1797; Jan. 4, 11, Feb. 1, 8, Mar. 1–22, Apr. 12–26, May 24–June 14, July 5, 12, 26, Aug. 16–Sept. 13, Oct. 25–Nov. 8, 22–Dec. 5, 20, 1798; Jan. 23, Feb. 13, Mar. 27–Apr. 10, May 1, 8, 22–June 5, 19, July 3, 10, 24–Sept. 18, Oct. 2, 9, 30–Nov. 13, 27, Dec. 4, 25, 1799; Sept. 24, Oct. 22, 29, Nov. 26, Dec. 3, 17, 24, 1800; Jan. 7, 28, Feb. 18, 25, Mar. 11, 25, Apr. 1, 15, 29–May 20, June 3–July 1, 15, 29, Aug. 12, 26, Sept. 16–Oct. 7, 21, Nov. 4, 18–Dec. 2, 16–30, 1801; Jan. 6–Mar. 3, 24, 31, Apr. 14–May 5, 19–June 30, July 14–28, Aug. 18, Sept. 1–Dec. 29, 1802; Jan. 5–Mar. 9, 30, Apr. 13, 20, May 4–June 22, July 6, 20, Aug. 3–24, Sept. 7–Nov. 16, Dec. 7, 21, 28, 1803; Jan. 4, 25–Feb. 15, 29, Apr. 11, 25–May 9, 23–June 6, 27–Aug. 15, 29–Nov. 14, 28–Dec. 26, 1804; Jan. 2–Feb. 6, 20–Mar. 27, Apr. 10–May 15, 29–Aug. 7, Sept. 4, 18, Oct. 2, 1805.

New London Co. Hist. Soc. has Feb. 15, Mar. 8, 29, 1798; Jan. 8, Mar. 26, Apr. 9, 1800; June 15, 1803–May 9, 1804; Jan. 2, 23–Feb. 6, Apr. 17, May 15, Oct. 9, 1805; Jan. 1, Mar. 5–26, Apr. 16–30, May 14, June 4, 18, 25, July 9, 16, 30, Aug. 6, 20, 27, Sept. 17, 24, 1806; Dec. 28, 1808; Jan. 18, 1809; Feb. 7–Mar. 28, May 9, June 13, 27–July 18, Aug. 1, 15, 22, Sept. 12–26, 1810; Jan. 30, Feb. 6, Apr. 3, May 8, 22–June 12, July 3, 17, Aug. 28, Oct. 2, 9, Dec. 4, 1811; Jan. 8, Feb. 5, 26, Mar. 25, Apr. 1, 22, June 10–24, Aug. 26, Nov. 11, Dec. 16, 1812; Jan. 27, Feb. 24, Mar. 3, Apr. 14–28, Sept. 22, 29, Oct. 13, 20, Nov. 24, 1813; Feb. 16, Apr. 20, May 11–25, June 8, July 13, 27–Aug. 10, 31, Oct. 19–Nov. 2, 23, Dec. 7, 21, 28, 1814; Apr. 5–Oct. 25, Dec. 13, 1815; Apr. 2, 1817–Dec. 25, 1820.

Martin Welles, Hartford, has Feb. 22, July 5, Aug. 16, Nov. 1, 1797; Feb. 8–Apr. 5, 1798; June 16, 1802; Nov. 7, 1804; Apr. 8, 22, Sept. 30, 1807; Sept. 20, Oct. 4, 1809; Mar. 6, Apr. 30, May 22–June 5, 16, 19, Aug. 7, Sept. 4, 25, Oct. 2, 16, Nov. 13, 20, Dec. 4, 18, 25, 1811; Aug. 11, 1813; Nov. 2, 1814; Apr. 12, 26, July 10, 17, Dec. 6–20, 1815; Apr. 3, May 8–22, 1816; Oct. 8, 1817; Jan. 28, Mar. 18, June 10, Sept. 23, 1818; Jan. 18, June 23, 1819; Oct. 11, 1820.

Yale has Nov. 13, 1799; Jan. 8, 15, 29, June 25, July 16–Oct. 15, 29–Dec. 31, 1800; Jan. 7–Mar. 4, 18–Apr. 1, 15–July 1, 15, 22, Aug. 5–Oct. 7, 21–Nov. 11, 25–Dec. 23, 1801; Apr. 22, 1807; Feb. 1, Aug. 2, 9, Sept. 6, 1809; Jan. 3, Feb. 7, 1810; May 6, 1812; Apr. 28, 1819.

N. Y. Hist. Soc. has Jan. 4–Nov. 22, 1797; May 17, 24, June 7, 28, 1798; Jan. 4, 1815–Dec. 17, 1817.

N. Y. Pub. Lib. has Sept. 2, 1812; Dec. 7, 28, 1814; Jan. 4–Mar. 1, 15–Apr. 26, May 17, 24, Oct. 4, 11, Nov. 22, 29, Dec. 13, 20, 1815; Jan. 3, 10, 24, Mar. 27, Apr. 10, 1816; Mar. 25, Apr. 15–May 13, June 17, July 8, 22–Aug. 5,

Sept. 9, Oct. 7–21, Nov. 4–25, Dec. 9–30, 1818; Jan. 6–27, Feb. 17, Mar. 3, 10, Apr. 28, May 12, 19, June 9–July 7, Sept. 15, 22, Nov. 17, Dec. 1, 22, 29, 1819; Jan. 26, Feb. 2, 16–Apr. 5, 21, May 3–17, 31, Aug. 2, 16, Sept. 13, Oct. 18, Nov. 1, 15, 1820.

Lib. Congress has Nov. 15, 22, 1797; Sept. 13, 1798; Mar. 21, 1804; Apr. 22, May 27, 1807; May 25, 1808–May 31, 1809; Dec. 7, 1814; Apr. 19, 1815.

Western Reserve Hist. Soc. has June 28, 1798; July 30, Aug. 6, 1806; July 13, 1814; Feb. 17, Mar. 10, 1819.

Buffalo Hist. Soc. has Nov. 13, 20, Dec. 4, 1799–Jan. 8, 1800.

N. Y. State Lib. has Jan. 1, 1800.

Williams Coll. has Jan. 1, 1800.

New Haven Col. Hist. Soc. has Feb. 26, 1800; July 29, 1801.

Duke Univ. has May 27, June 24, Sept. 2, 9, 23, Oct. 6, Dec. 2, 1812; Jan. 6, 20, Feb. 3, Aug. 18, Oct. 6, 1813.

Wis. Hist. Soc. has June 1, 1808; Dec. 2, 1818.

Grinnell Coll. Lib. has Jan. 29, 1812.

Rutgers Univ. has Oct. 28, 1812.

Wesleyan Univ. has June 29, 1814.

Thompson, Ct., Lib. has June 28, 1815.

Univ. of Mich. (Clements) has May 13, 1818.

[Norwich] Native American, 1812–1813.

Weekly. Established Mar. 4, 1812, by S[amuel] Webb, with the title of "The Native American." The last issue located is that of June 16, 1813, no. 67. In this issue Webb announces that he has been called into service in the war.

Am. Antiq. Soc. has Mar. 4–May 6, June 24, July 1, 22, Aug. 19, Oct. 14, Dec. 23, 1812; May 12, June 16, 1813.

Lib. Congress has June 3–17, Sept. 2, 23, Oct. 14, 28, Nov. 4, Dec. 9–23, 1812; Jan. 6, 13, 27–Mar. 24, Apr. 14–28, 1813.

Conn. State Lib. has Sept. 30, Oct. 7–21, 1812; Jan. 20, 1813.

Martin Welles, Hartford, has Apr. 14, 21, May 12, 26, 1813.

Yale has June 3, 1812.

Norwich Packet, 1773–1802.

Weekly. Established Oct. 7, 1773, judging from the date of the earliest issue located, that of Nov. 4, 1773, vol. 1, no. 5, published by Alexander Robertson, James Robertson, and John Trumbull. From Nov. 20, 1775 to May 13, 1776, the imprint was given as Robertsons and Trumbull. The Robertsons, who were Loyalists, went to New York in 1776, and beginning with the issue of May 20, 1776, the paper was published by John Trumbull, who continued it until Feb. 9, 1802, vol. 29, no. 1456, after which the title was changed to "The Connecticut Centinel," which see.

The changes in the title of the paper were as follows: — "The Norwich Packet. And the Connecticut, Massachusetts, New-Hampshire, and Rhode-Island Weekly Advertiser," Oct. 7, 1773–Dec. 22, 1777 (frequent change of period to semicolon and the word "and" to "&"); "The Norwich Packet," Dec. 29, 1777–June 1, 1779; "The Norwich Packet; and the Weekly Advertiser," June 8, 1779–Oct. 18, 1781; "The Norwich Packet, and the Weekly Advertiser," Oct. 25, 1781–Sept. 26, 1782 (suspended and resumed Oct. 30, 1783); "The Norwich Packet; or, the Chronicle of Freedom," Oct. 30, 1783–Apr. 7, 1785; "The Norwich-Packet, or, the Country Journal," Apr. 14, 1785–Feb. 1, 1787; "The Norwich Packet. And the Country Journal," Feb. 8, 1787–Jan. 22, 1790; "The Norwich-Packet & Country Journal," Jan. 29, 1790–Sept. 24, 1790; "Vox Populi Norwich Packet," Oct. 1, 1790–June 2, 1791; "Norwich Packet," June 9, 1791–May 17, 1792; "The Norwich Packet," May 24, 1792–Nov. 20, 1794; "Norwich Packet," Nov. 27, 1794–Aug. 21, 1795; "The Norwich Packet," Aug. 26, 1795–June 23, 1796; "Norwich Packet," June 30, 1796–Feb. 9, 1802.

Am. Antiq. Soc. has Nov. 25–Dec. 16, 1773; Aug. 25, Sept. 15, 1774; Feb. 16, Aug. 7, Sept. 4, Oct. 2, 16–Dec. 25, 1775; Jan. 1, 1776–Dec. 26, 1780; Jan. 2–July 26, Sept. 13, 20, Oct. 4–Dec. 27, 1781; Jan. 3–Sept. 26, 1782; Oct. 30–Dec. 25, 1783; Jan. 1–July 29, Aug. 12–Sept. 23, Oct. 14–Nov. 4, Dec. 30, 1784; Jan. 6, 13, 27, Feb. 10–Mar. 10, 31–Apr. 21, May 5, June 9–23, July 7–Sept. 8, 29, Oct. 6, 20–Nov. 10, 23, Dec. 15, 1785; Jan. 5, 19–Mar. 2, 16–30, Apr. 13, 20, May 11, 18, June 1, 8, 22, July 6–27, Aug. 17, 24, Sept. 14–Dec. 28, 1786; Jan. 4–Feb. 8, 22–Mar. 22, Apr. 5–Sept. 27, Oct. 18–Nov. 8, 22, Dec. 6–27, 1787; Jan. 3–31, Feb. 14, 28–Mar. 13, 27, Apr. 24, May 1–Aug. 14, 28–Oct. 31, Nov. 7, 21, Dec. 12, 19, 26, 1788; Jan. 2–23, Feb. 6–20, Mar. 6, 13, Apr. 3, May 29, June 12, 26, July 10–Sept. 25, Oct. 8, 23–Nov. 13, 27, Dec. 4, 18, 25, 1789; Jan. 8–22, Feb. 5–June 4, 18–Aug. 13, Sept. 3–Nov. 19, Dec. 3–31, 1790; Jan. 7, 14, 28–Mar. 4, 18–Apr. 8, 22–May 19, June 9, 23–Aug. 11, 25, Sept. 1, 15–Nov. 23, Dec. 1–15, 1791; Jan. 5–Feb. 23, Mar. 1, 8, 22, 29, Apr. 4–19, May 3–17, 31, June 14–Aug. 2, 16–Dec. 13, 29, 1792; Jan. 17–31, Feb. 14, 21, Mar. 21, Apr. 4–18, May 2, 16, 23, June 6, 20, Aug. 1, 8, Sept. 5–26, Oct. 10, 17, Nov. 21, 28, Dec. 19, 1793; Feb. 20, 1794–Dec. 31, 1795; Jan. 7–June 23, July 7–Aug. 4, Sept. 1, 15, 29, Oct. 6, 20, Nov. 17–Dec. 1, 15, 29, 1796; Jan. 19–Feb. 16, Mar. 2, 16–30, Apr. 13–May 11, June 1, 22, 29, July 11–25, Aug. 8, 15, 29–Oct. 17, 31–Nov. 21, Dec. 12, 19, 1797; Jan. 2, 17–30, Feb. 13, 27–Mar. 20, Apr. 3, 17, 24, May 8–June 19, July 3, Sept. 4, Oct. 2, 9, Nov. 28, Dec. 5, 19, 26, 1798; Jan. 23, 30, Mar. 6, June 27, Aug. 15, 1799; Jan. 23, Feb. 20, Mar. 6, Apr. 3, 24, Sept. 9, 1800; Mar. 31, Apr. 21, Nov. 24, 1801; Jan. 26, Feb. 2, 1802.

Conn. State Lib. has Oct. 28, 1773–Dec. 29, 1774; Jan. 5–July 24, Oct. 2, 1775; Nov. 20, 1783–Oct. 19, Nov. 22, 1786; Oct. 5, 1787; Nov. 14, 1788–Dec. 25, 1789; Dec. 12, 1793; June 12, Oct. 23, 1794; Mar. 2, 1797–Feb. 13, 1798; Aug. 21, Dec. 12, 19, 1798; Aug. 22, Dec. 12, 1799; May 6, July 1, Aug. 5, Sept. 30, Oct. 14, Nov. 4, 18, Dec. 2, 16, 1800; Jan. 6, 1801–Feb. 9, 1802.

Otis Lib., Norwich, has Nov. 16, Dec. 14–28, 1778; Jan. 4–Feb. 22, Mar. 8, Apr. 13–27, May 11, 25, June 8, 15, 29, July 27, Aug. 10–24, Sept. 22, Oct. 5, Nov. 16–30, Dec. 14–28, 1779; Jan. 4, 25, Feb. 1, 15, 29, Mar. 14–28, May 11, 18, June 1, 15, July 20, Aug. 10–31, Oct. 31, 1780; Oct. 7, 1784; May 12, 26, 1785; Sept. 7, 1786–Jan. 23, 1789; Oct. 8, 1790–Dec. 31, 1795, fair; Feb. 23, 1797–Feb. 13, 1798.

N. Y. Hist. Soc. has Jan. 29, 1776–Oct. 20, 1777, fair; Nov. 14, 1780; Feb. 22, 1787; Feb. 20–Mar. 13, 27, Oct. 8, 1789; Nov. 23, 1791; Feb. 6, 1794–Feb. 4, 1796; Apr. 21, 1796–Jan. 5, 1797.

Lib. Congress has July 14–Aug. 4, 18, 1774; Mar. 16, Oct. 2, 23, Nov. 6, Dec. 25, 1775; Jan. 8, Feb. 26, Apr. 1, 8, 29, July 29, 1776; Jan. 5, Apr. 14, 1777; Mar. 16, May 11, June 1, Aug. 31, Sept. 14, 1778; Apr. 20, Aug. 17, Sept. 14, Nov. 16, 1779; May 4, 1780; June 21, Dec. 20, 27, 1781; Jan. 3–31, Feb. 14, 21, June 20, July 11–25, Aug. 8, Sept. 19, 1782; Apr. 1, Aug. 19, Oct. 21, 1784; July 21, Nov. 23, 1785; Jan. 4, Apr. 5, June 7, 1787; Mar. 6, Apr. 24, Nov. 14–Dec. 26, 1788; Jan. 2–Dec. 25, 1789; Jan. 1–Apr. 16, 30–Aug. 6, Sept. 10, Dec. 10, 1790; Feb. 25, May 12, June 2, 9, July 6–Dec. 29, 1791; Jan. 5, 1792–Dec. 25, 1794, good; Feb. 5, 18, 26, Apr. 9, May 8, July 10, 17, 31, Aug. 14, 21, Sept. 16, Nov. 12, Dec. 23, 1795; Mar. 31, May 19–June 2, 23, July 7, 14, 1796; Aug. 29, 1799; Jan. 12, 19, 1802.

Mass. Hist. Soc. has Nov. 4, 1773; Jan. 27, Nov. 17, 1774; Jan. 19, Feb. 2, Apr. 13, 1775; Feb. 12, 19, May 13, July 22–Aug. 5, Nov. 11, 1776; Mar. 8, Dec. 28, 1779; Mar. 21, Dec. 19, 1780; Jan. 16, 30, Mar. 8, 1781; Jan. 10, Mar. 14, 21, Apr. 18, May 2, 30, 1782; Nov. 27, 1783; Mar. 11, 18, Apr. 29, 1784; June 30, 1791; Feb. 9, 16, Mar. 8, 29, 1792.

Peck Lib., Norwich, has Dec. 16, 23, 1773; Nov. 15, 1781; Jan. 11–Dec. 13, 1787; Jan. 19, 1792–Dec. 19, 1793; Jan. 5, 1797–Dec. 26, 1798; Jan. 23–Dec. 30, 1800.

N. Y. Pub. Lib. has May 19–Aug. 18, Sept. 15, 22, Oct. 6, 20–Nov. 3, 24, Dec. 8, 15, 1774; Jan. 19, Feb. 23, Mar. 16, 23, Apr. 20, May 18, June 8, 15, Aug. 28, 1775; Oct. 20, 1777; Feb. 27, Apr. 17, 1794; May 29, 1775; June 2, 1796; Jan. 9, 1799.

New London Co. Hist. Soc. has Mar. 10, 1774; Sept. 30, Dec. 1, 9, 23, 30, 1784; Jan. 27–Feb. 10, Mar. 10, 24, Apr. 28, June 2, 23, 30, July 14, 28, Sept. 29, 1785; May 11, 1786; Apr. 5, 1787; Apr. 24–May 29, June 12–Oct. 16, 1794; Oct. 14, 1795; Jan. 7, 1796.

Norwich Bulletin Office has Mar. 8, June 28, July 19, Aug. 23, Oct. 25–Dec. 29, 1792; Jan. 3, 1793–Oct. 9, 1794.

Conn. Hist. Soc. has Oct. 2, 1775; Mar. 4, Dec. 9, 1776; Dec. 14, 1778; Mar. 21, July 27, Oct. 10, 31, 1780; Jan. 30, Apr. 12–May 4, Nov. 15, 1781; Feb. 7–28, May 30, June 13–July 11, 25, Aug. 1, 15, 26, 1782; Nov. 6, Dec. 10, 18, 1783; Jan. 22, Feb. 19, 26, Mar. 11, May 6, 13, June 24, July 1, 22, 29, Aug. 12, Nov. 18, 1784; Sept. 29, Oct. 6, Nov. 23, 1785; Jan. 19, May 18, Aug. 24, Nov. 9–22, Dec. 7, 1786; Jan. 4, 25, Feb. 1, Mar. 15, 22, Apr. 26,

Connecticut

May 3, July 26, Sept. 6, Nov. 8, 15, Dec. 13, 20, 1787; Mar. 13, 27, May 1, 22, 29, June 12–July 3, Aug. 14, Sept. 18, 25, Oct. 2–16, 31, Nov. 14, Dec. 19, 1788; Jan. 30, Feb. 6–27, Mar. 13–27, May 1–15, 29, July 10, 31–Aug. 14, 28, Sept. 4, 11, Nov. 6, Dec. 18, 25, 1789; Jan. 5, 1792; Jan. 3, 1793–Feb. 13, 1794; Jan. 8, Feb. 26, Mar. 5, 26, Apr. 16, June 5–19, July 3, 17, 31, Aug. 4, Sept. 9, 16, 30, Oct. 14, 28, Nov. 12, 26, 1795; Jan. 19, Feb. 2, 9, July 11, Sept. 26, Oct. 31, 1797; Dec. 26, 1799–Dec. 30, 1800; Jan. 6, Feb. 10, 17, Apr. 7, 14, May 5, 12, June 2, 9, Sept. 8, Oct. 13, Nov. 24, Dec. 1, 1801; Jan. 5, 1802.

Martin Welles, Hartford, has Apr. 15, May 13, 1776; Nov. 6–Dec. 18, 1783; Jan. 3, Feb. 5–Mar. 11, Apr. 1, 8, 22, 29, May 13, June 10, 24, July 8, 22, 29, 1784; May 19, Sept. 1, 1785; Oct. 19, 26, Nov. 16–Dec. 21, 1786; Jan. 25, Feb. 22, Mar. 15, 22, Apr. 5, 19, May 10–31, June 14, 21, July 5, 12, 26–Aug. 9, 23, Sept. 13, 27, 1787; Oct. 29, 1790; Mar. 11, June 16, 1791; Jan. 2, 1800.

New Haven Col. Hist. Soc. has Nov. 22, Dec. 7–28, 1786; Jan. 11, 25, Mar. 8, 15, 29, Apr. 12–May 3, 17, June 7, 21, July 12–Sept. 6, 20, Oct. 5, Nov. 1, 8, 22, 29, Dec. 27, 1787; Jan. 3, 10, 31, Feb. 14, 21, Apr. 10–24, May 8–July 3, 24, 1788.

Harvard has Feb. 5–Mar. 5, 26, May 15, 22, June 12, 19, July 17–31, Aug. 14, 21, Sept, 9, Nov. 19, Dec. 31, 1795; Feb. 18, Apr. 21, June 30, July 28, Aug. 11–25, Sept. 8–22, Oct. 6, 20–Nov. 3, Dec. 22, 29, 1796; Jan. 5, 12, 26, Feb. 2, 16–Mar. 30, Apr. 13, 20, May 25, June 22, July 11, 18, Oct. 10, 17, Nov. 14–Dec. 19, 1797; Jan. 9, 23–Feb. 6, Mar. 6, May 15, 29, July 3, 31, Aug. 14, 28–Sept. 18, Nov. 7, 21, Dec. 19, 1798; Jan. 9–30, Feb. 20, 27, Mar. 20–Apr. 17, May 2–16, 30–June 20, July 4, 25–Oct. 24, Nov. 7, 21, 28, Dec. 26, 1799; Jan. 2, 16–Feb. 20, Mar. 13, 27, Apr. 10–May 6, 20, June 3, 17–July 29, Sept. 2–Dec. 30, 1800; Jan. 6–27, Feb. 10, 24–June 30, July 14–28, Aug. 11, 25, Sept. 1, Oct. 6–Nov. 3, 17, Dec. 1, 8, 22, 29, 1801; Jan. 5, 12, 26–Feb. 9, 1802.

Bridgeport Pub. Lib. has June 21, 28, July 12, 26–Aug. 16, Sept. 13, 20, Oct. 4–18, Nov. 8–22, Dec. 20, 27, 1781; Jan. 10–24, Feb. 7–21, Mar. 21–Apr. 4, 18–May 9, 23, June 6–July 4, 18–Aug. 8, 1782; Oct. 30, Nov. 13–27, Dec. 18, 25, 1783.

Westerly, R. I., Pub. Lib. has Dec. 9, 16, 1773.

Western Reserve Hist. Soc. has Dec. 16, 1773; Nov. 17, 1774; June 3, 1776; Jan. 16, 1781; Apr. 12, 1787; Sept. 8, 1791; Oct. 7, 1795.

Pocumtuck Valley Mem. Lib., Deerfield, Mass., has Aug. 29, 1782; Nov. 18, 1784; June 16, Aug. 11, 1785; Feb. 5, 1795.

Yale has Feb. 12, 1776; Oct. 2, 1788.

Boston Pub. Lib. has July 29, 1776; Feb. 19, 1784; Apr. 14, July 14, 1785; May 22, 1788.

Thompson, Conn., Lib. has Nov. 11–Dec. 30, 1784.

Buffalo Hist. Soc. has Nov. 10, 1785.

New London Co. Hist. Soc. has May 11, 1786.

Duke Univ. has Apr. 16, 1787; May 19, 1791.
Hist. Soc. Penn. has Mar. 13, 1789.
Long Id. Hist. Soc. has Dec. 16, 1800; Feb. 17, 1801.

[Norwich] **True Republican,** 1804–1806.

Weekly. Established June 20, 1804, by Sterry & Porter [John Sterry and Epaphras Porter], with the title of "True Republican." Proposals for publishing this paper were printed in the "Connecticut Centinel" of Mar. 27, 1804, signed by John Sterry and Epaphras Porter. John Sterry left the firm in June, 1806, apparently on June 11, and henceforth the paper was published by C. Sterry & E. Porter [Consider Sterry and Epaphras Porter]. The last issue located is that of Nov. 5, 1806, vol. 3, no. 17. In the Norwich "Connecticut Centinel" of Nov. 4, 1806, is a reference to the recent discontinuance of the "True Republican."

> Am. Antiq. Soc. has June 20, July 11, Aug. 8, 29, Oct. 1, Nov. 7, 1804; Mar. 27, Apr. 3, June 26, 1805; May 14, July 23, 1806.
> Harvard has July 4–Aug. 8, 22–Sept. 19, Oct. 3–17, 31–Nov. 14, 1804; Jan. 9–Feb. 13, 27–Apr. 10, May 22, June 5–19, July 3–24, Aug. 7–21, Sept. 4, 18–Nov. 6, 20–Dec. 4, 18, 25, 1805; Jan. 8, 15, 29–Feb. 12, 26, Mar. 12, 19, Apr. 9, May 14, 21, June 4, Aug. 6, 20, 27, Sept. 10, 17, Oct. 8–22, Nov. 5, 1806.
> Rutgers Univ. has June 26–Aug. 28, Sept. 11–Nov. 6, 27–Dec. 25, 1805; Jan. 1–May 14, 28, 1806.
> Conn. Hist. Soc. has July 11, 1804.
> Univ. of Chicago has Aug. 8, 1804.
> New London Co. Hist. Soc. has Aug. 15, 1804.
> Westerly, R. I., Pub. Lib. has Oct. 24, 1804.
> New Haven Col. Hist. Soc. has Mar. 20, 1805.
> Martin Welles, Hartford, has Apr. 10, 1805.
> N. Y. Pub. Lib. has May 8, Aug. 7, 1805; July 30, Aug. 6, 1806.
> Boston Athenæum has Mar. 26, Oct. 1, 1806.
> Lib. Congress has July 30, Aug. 6, 1806.
> Stonington Hist. Soc. has July 30, Aug. 6, 1806.

[Norwich] **Vox Populi Norwich Packet,** see **Norwich Packet.**

[Norwich] **Weekly Register,** 1791–1795.

Weekly. Established Nov. 29, 1791, by Ebenezer Bushnell, with the title of "The Weekly Register." Bushnell took in Thomas Hubbard as partner, and beginning with the issue of June 12, 1792, the paper was published by Bushnell & Hubbard. Bushnell retired and beginning with the issue of Oct. 1, 1793, Thomas Hubbard was sole publisher. The paper was discontinued with the issue of Aug. 19, 1795, vol. 4, no. 39.

Otis Lib., Norwich, has Nov. 29, 1791–Nov. 19, 1793.
Yale has Nov. 29, 1791–Nov. 20, 1792.
Am. Antiq. Soc. has Dec. 6, 1791–Dec. 25, 1792; Jan. 1–Feb. 12, 26, Mar. 12– May 14, June 11–Sept. 24, Oct. 8–Nov. 5, 19–Dec. 31, 1793; Jan. 7–Mar. 11, 25, Apr. 15–Oct. 7, 21–Nov. 18, 1794; Jan. 6–Feb. 17, Mar. 3–24, Apr. 21, 28, May 13, June 10–24, July 29–Aug. 12, 1795.
Duke Univ. has Dec. 13–27, 1791; Jan. 10, 24, Sept. 25, Oct. 16, Dec. 25, 1792; Apr. 9, 1793.
Lib. Congress has Jan. 10, 1792–May 20, 1794; Mar. 24, 1795.
Conn. Hist. Soc. has May 3, Sept. 11–Nov. 20, 1792; Sept. 10, 17, 1793; May 27, June 10, 24–Sept. 16, 1794.
N. Y. Hist. Soc. has Oct. 29, Nov. 19, 26, Dec. 10–24, 1793; Jan. 14–Apr. 8, 22, May 6, June 24, July 1, 15–Aug. 5, 19, Sept. 16, Oct. 7–21, Dec. 2, 1794; Jan. 13, 27, 1795.
New London Co. Hist. Soc. has Dec. 3, 1793–Dec. 16, 1794.
N. Y. Pub. Lib. has June 12, 1792; Jan. 15, May 14, 1793; Oct. 7, Nov. 4, 25, 1794; Feb. 24, 1795.
Harvard has Dec. 9, 16, 1794; Jan. 27, Feb. 3, 17, 24, Mar. 31, May 27, June 17, July 8–22, Aug. 12, 19, 1795.
Mass. Hist. Soc. has Jan. 10, Feb. 7, Mar. 13, Apr. 10, 1792.
Univ. of Mich. (Clements) has Dec. 4, 11, 25, 1792.
Phil. Lib. Co. has Oct. 1, 1793.
Long Id. Hist. Soc. has Apr. 28, June 10, 1795.

[Sharon] Rural Gazette, 1800–1801.

Weekly. Established Mar. 31, 1800, judging from the date of the first issue located, that of June 9, 1800, vol. 1, no. 11, published by E[liott] Hopkins, with the title of "Rural Gazette." The name of Eliott Hopkins appears in the 1800 Census under Sharon. Trumbull, in his "List of Books printed in Conn.," p. 146, notes a copy of the initial issue of Mar. 31, 1800, seen by him, but not now located. The last issue located is that of July 13, 1801, vol. 2, no. 16.

Am. Antiq. Soc. has June 9, 1800.
Harvard has Nov. 24, Dec. 15, 1800; Jan. 12, 19, Mar. 23, June 29, 1801.
Conn. Hist. Soc. has Dec. 22, 1800; Jan. 26–Feb. 16, Mar. 2, 23, May 11– June 8, July 13, 1801.
Long Id. Hist. Soc. has Jan. 19, 1801.
N. Y. Hist. Soc. has July 13, 1801.

[Stonington] America's Friend, 1807–1808.

Weekly. Established July 15, 1807, by John Munson, with the title of "America's Friend." The last issue located is that of Sept. 28, 1808, vol. 2, no. 12.

Yale has July 22–Aug. 12, Sept. 2, 16, Oct. 21, Nov. 11, 25, Dec. 9, 16, 24, 1807; Jan. 20, 27, Feb. 3–Apr. 6, 27, May 18, 25, June 8, 15, 29, 1808.
Am. Antiq. Soc. has July 29, Sept. 2, 9, Nov. 4, 25, 1807.
Harvard has July 27, Aug. 24, Sept. 7, 28, 1808.
N. Y. Pub. Lib. has Sept. 2, 1807.
New London Co. Hist. Soc. has Sept. 9, Nov. 25, 1807.

[Stonington] **Impartial Journal**, 1799–1804.

Weekly. A continuation, except for name, of the "Journal of the Times," the first number with the new title of "Impartial Journal" being that of Oct. 8, 1799, vol. 2, no. 1, published by Samuel Trumbull. Discontinued with the issue of May 1, 1804, vol. 6, no. 31.

Harvard has Oct. 8–Nov. 26, 1799; Mar. 4–18, Nov. 18, 25, 1800; Jan. 6, Mar. 19, Apr. 28, June 16–July 7, 21–Aug. 11, 25, Sept. 1, 1801; Aug. 17–31, Sept. 14–Nov. 2, 16, 30–Dec. 28, 1802; Jan. 4–18, Mar. 8, 29, Apr. 19, May 3–31, June 21, July 5, Aug. 9, Oct. 4, Nov. 1, 1803; Mar. 6, 1804.
N. Y. Hist. Soc. has Nov. 12, Dec. 3–24, 1799; Jan. 28, Feb. 11–25, Mar. 18, Apr. 15–May 27, 1800; Feb. 24–May 12, 26, June 2, Aug. 25–Sept. 22, Oct. 27, 1801.
Conn. Hist. Soc. has Mar. 4–Sept. 30, 1800.
Am. Antiq. Soc. has Sept. 16, Dec. 2, 1800; Aug. 4, 11, Sept. 29, Oct. 6, 1801; Feb. 8, 22, 1803.
Westerly, R. I., Pub. Lib. has Dec. 23, 1800; Apr. 28, 1801; Sept. 7, 1802; Aug. 30, 1803.
Stonington Hist. Soc. has Jan. 3–May 1, 1804.
Williams Coll. has Dec. 31, 1799.
Brown Univ. (Rider) has Nov. 11, 1800.
Conn. State Lib. has Nov. 4, 1800.
Lib. Congress has Dec. 2, 1800.
Long Id. Hist. Soc. has Mar. 10, 1801.
N. Y. Pub. Lib. has Aug. 30, 1803; Jan. 24, 1804.

[Stonington] **Journal of the Times**, 1798–1799.

Weekly. Established Oct. 10, 1798, by Samuel Trumbull, with the title of "Journal of the Times." Enlarged from small to large folio Jan. 2, 1799. The last issue located with this title is that of Sept. 17, 1799, vol. 1, no. 50. The title was changed Oct. 8, 1799, to "Impartial Journal," which see.

Conn. Hist. Soc. has Oct. 10, 1798–Sept. 17, 1799.
Am. Antiq. Soc. has Nov. 14, 1798; Apr. 23, 1799.
Harvard has Jan. 9, 16, Feb. 13, Mar. 19, Apr. 2, May 21, June 4, 18, July 16, Aug. 6–20, Sept. 3, 17, 1799.

[Stonington-port] **Patriot,** 1801–1802.

Weekly. Established July 24, 1801, by S. Trumbull [Samuel Trumbull], under the title of "The Patriot, or, Scourge of Aristocracy." It was of octavo size, paged, and with signature marks. Although apparently a magazine, it referred to itself as a newspaper and included current news. It was discontinued with the issue of July 30, 1802, vol. 1, no. 52, which issue stated that the paper would be suspended, but later would be brought out in folio form. The volume had a title page followed by a prospectus to subscribers. In the Stonington "Impartial Journal" of Feb. 22, 1803, is an advertisement asking prospective subscribers of "The Patriot, &c" to send in their names to Samuel Trumbull, editor of the "Impartial Herald." There is nothing to show that it was reestablished.

Am. Antiq. Soc. has July 24, 1801–July 30, 1802.
N. Y. Hist. Soc. has July 24, 1801–July 30, 1802.
Yale has July 24, 1801–June 18, July 2–30, 1802.
Brown Univ. has July 24–Nov. 27, Dec. 25, 1801; Jan. 1–July 9, 23, 1802.
Univ. of Mich. (Clements) has Aug. 28, 1801–July 23, 1802, fair.
Conn. State Lib. has July 24–Aug. 14, Sept. 11, 1801; May 21, June 11, 1802.
Conn. Hist. Soc. has Aug. 28–Dec. 25, 1801; Jan. 1–29, Feb. 12, May 21–June 18, July 2–30, 1802.
Lib. Congress has Oct. 23, 30, Nov. 13–Dec. 25, 1801; Jan. 1–Apr. 30, May 14–July 30, 1802.
Harvard has Sept. 11, 18, Oct. 2, 9, 23–Dec. 4, 18, 25, 1801; Jan. 1–Mar. 19, Apr. 2, 9, 30–May 21, June 18–July 30, 1802.

[Suffield] **Impartial Herald,** 1797–1799.

Weekly. Established June 14, 1797, by H. & O. Farnsworth [Havila and Oliver Farnsworth], with the title of "Impartial Herald; A Periodical Register of the Times." Beginning with the issue of July 17, 1798, the paper was published by Gray & Albro [Edward Gray and Rescome D. Albro], who adopted with that date a new series of numbering, and shortened the title to "Impartial Herald." Beginning with Dec. 25, 1798, the paper was published by Edward Gray alone. The last issue located is that of June 11, 1799, vol. 1, no. 48.

Kent Memorial Lib., Suffield, has June 14–Dec. 27, 1797; Jan. 3–May 2, 16, June 6, July 17, 1798–June 11, 1799.
Am. Antiq. Soc. has June 14, 28–Dec. 27, 1797; Jan. 3–June 6, 18–July 9, Nov. 13, 20, 1798; Mar. 5, 1799.
Wesleyan Univ. has June 14, 28–Dec. 27, 1797; Jan. 3–24, Feb. 7–Apr. 25, May 16–June 11, Aug. 21–Dec. 25, 1798; Jan. 2–Apr. 2, 16–June 11, 1799.
Harvard has June 14–28, Aug. 31–Sept. 20, Oct. 11, 25, Nov. 8–22, Dec. 13, 1797; July 17, 31–Aug. 14, Sept. 11, 18, Oct. 9, Nov. 6, 20, 27, Dec. 18, 1798; Jan. 1, 8, Feb. 12, Apr. 23–May 7, 21, June 4, 1799.

Wis. Hist. Soc. has Apr. 18–May 9, 1798.
Conn. Valley Hist. Soc., Springfield, has May 2–July 2, 1798.

[Windham] Advertiser, 1818–1819.

Weekly. A continuation, without change of volume numbering, of the Windham "Register, and, Country Advertiser." The earliest issue located of "The Advertiser" is that of May 7, 1818, no. 62, published by S[amuel] Webb. An advertisement, dated Apr. 14, 1818, in this issue, requesting payments due the previous publishers, Henry Webb 2d & Co., would seem to show that the title was changed on Apr. 9, 1818. "The Advertiser" was of quarto size, was printed on a single leaf, bore no imprint and contained only advertisements without any reading matter. The only exceptions to this were that occasional issues contained marriage and death notices, and that the issue of July 2, 1818 comprised four pages of Public Acts. The issue of June 11, 1818 stated "The Advertiser is circulated gratis through the county of Windham." The last issue located is that of Mar. 4, 1819, no. 105, although there is a fragment of Mar 11, 1819.

Yale has May 7–21, June 11, 18, July 2–23, Aug. 13–Sept. 3, 24, Oct. 15–Nov. 5, 19, Dec. 3, 1818; Jan. 7, 28–Mar. 11, 1819.

Windham Herald, 1791–1816.

Weekly. Established Mar. 12, 1791, by John Byrne, under the title of "The Phenix; Or, Windham Herald." The title was shortened to "Windham Herald" with the issue of Apr. 19, 1798. Beginning with Mar. 29, 1811, John Byrne took his son, Samuel H. Byrne, into partnership and the paper was published by J. Byrne and Son. It was discontinued by them with the issue of Mar. 30, 1815, but revived, with a continuation of the numbering, by Samuel Green on July 27, 1815. Beginning with the issue of Oct. 19, 1815, the imprint is "Printed and published by Benjamin G. Willett for Samuel Green." The issues for June 6 and 13, 1816, were "Printed and published by Benjamin G. Willett," and from June 20, 1816, to Sept. 19, 1816, vol. 26, no. 1316, "Printed and published for Samuel Green," upon which latter date the paper was discontinued.

Am. Antiq. Soc. has Mar. 12, 1791–Dec. 27, 1804; Jan. 3–Feb. 28, July 4, Oct. 17, 1805; Nov. 6, Dec. 4, 1806; May 18, Aug. 3, 1809; June 22, Nov. 23, Dec. 7, 14, 1810; Nov. 1, 22, 1811; Jan. 28, Feb. 4, Apr. 1, 29, Sept. 10, Nov. 18, 1813; Mar. 3, June 16, Oct. 13, 1814; Feb. 2, 1815; Mar. 7, June 20, July 4, 1816.

Conn. Hist. Soc. has Apr. 23, 1791–Dec. 27, 1804; May 5–June 2, 23–July 14, Aug. 11–25, Sept. 8–Oct. 20, 1808.

Yale has Dec. 10, 1791; Aug. 25, Nov. 19, 1792; Sept. 18, Oct. 1, 1796; Aug. 5, Sept. 23, 1797; Mar. 13, July 10, 1800; Jan. 2, 1801; Nov. 25, Dec. 2, 1802; Jan. 2–Dec. 25, 1806; Jan. 7–Dec. 29, 1808; Jan. 12, Feb. 16, Mar. 9, 1809; Jan. 4–Dec. 27, 1811; Jan. 7, 1813–Sept. 19, 1816.

CONNECTICUT 75

Lib. Congress has Apr. 23, June 11, 18, Oct. 29, Nov. 19, Dec. 3–31, 1791; Jan. 14–28, Feb. 18, 25, Mar. 10, 17, Apr. 7, 21, May 5–19, June 9–July 28, Aug. 25–Sept. 15, Oct. 6–20, Nov. 3–17, Dec. 1–15, 29, 1792; Jan. 5–19, Feb. 9, 16, Mar. 9–June 15, 29–Aug. 10, 24–Sept. 21, Oct. 5–Nov. 2, 16–Dec. 14, 28, 1793; Jan. 4, 18–Mar. 15, 29–June 14, 1794; Feb. 7, 14, 28, Mar. 14, Nov. 14, 1795; Apr. 19, May 17, 31, July 19, Oct. 4–18, Nov. 15, 22, Dec. 6, 20, 27, 1798; Jan. 10–31, Feb. 28, Mar. 21, May 30, Aug. 29, Sept. 12, 26, Oct. 3, 10, Nov. 29–Dec. 26, 1799; Jan. 2–Feb. 20, Mar. 13, Apr. 17, 24, Aug. 7, Oct. 2, Nov. 6, 1800; Feb. 10, Aug. 11–25, Sept. 1, Oct. 6, 1803; Mar. 15, 22, 1804; Dec. 31, 1807; Feb. 16, 1810–Feb. 7, 1812.

N. Y. Hist. Soc. has Jan. 5, 1793; Mar. 28, Apr. 18–May 23, June 6–Dec. 12, 26, 1795; Jan. 16, 30, Feb. 13–27, Mar. 26–May 14, 28–Nov. 19, Dec. 3–31, 1796; Jan. 7–Mar. 24, Apr. 15, 21, May 19, June 9, 16, 30, July 14–Aug. 5, Sept. 1, 22, Oct. 13, Nov. 9, Dec. 14, 1797; Feb. 8–22, Mar. 22, Apr. 12–May 3, 17–31, June 14, 21, July 19, Oct. 18, Nov. 15–29, Dec. 20, 27, 1798; May 9, 1799–Dec. 19, 1800; Oct. 29, 1801; May 6, Sept. 9, 1802; June 30, 1803; May 24, Aug. 9, 1804; May 21, 1807; Nov. 16, 1809; June 8, 1810.

Harvard has Feb. 22, Oct. 25, Dec. 20, 1794; Feb. 21, 28, 1795; June 9, 16, 30, July 14, Aug. 11, Sept. 8, 15, 29, Nov. 2, 16–Dec. 7, 21, 1797; Jan. 4–Feb. 1, 15, 22, Mar. 15, 22, Apr. 5, 12, 26, May 10–31, June 21, 28, July 12–Aug. 30, Sept. 13, Nov. 8–22, Dec. 6, 13, 1798; Feb. 7, 21–Mar. 21, Apr. 4–June 13, 27, July 25, Aug. 8–29, Sept. 12–Oct. 24, Nov. 7, 21, 1799; Jan. 9–Feb. 13, Mar. 6–Apr. 17, May 1, 22–June 12, 26–July 24, Sept. 11, 25, Oct. 9, 23, Nov. 20, 1800; Jan. 2, 23–Feb. 13, 27, Mar. 6, 20–Apr. 2, Oct. 1, 29, 1801.

Martin Welles, Hartford, has Sept. 8, 1792; May 21, 1796; Apr. 19, 1798–Nov. 20, 1800, fair; Dec. 16, 1802; Sept. 10, 1812; Apr. 15, 1813.

Thompson, Conn., Lib. has Nov. 7, 21, 1795; Mar. 18, 1797; Aug. 1, 15, 1799; Jan. 2–Mar. 29, June 12, July 17, Oct. 30, Nov. 28, 1800; Mar. 13, Apr. 19, July 2, Dec. 24, 1801; Apr. 8, 1802; Jan. 6, 13, Feb. 17, Apr. 14, 21, May 5–19, June 9–23, July 7, Aug. 4, 18–Sept. 1, 15, 22, Oct. 6, 13, 27–Dec. 29, 1803; June 7, July 19, Aug. 16, Sept. 20, Nov. 16, Dec. 13, 20, 1804; Jan. 3, 10, Feb. 18, 1805; May 22, June 5, Aug. 14, 1806; Jan. 29, 1807; June 16, Sept. 15, 22, 1808; Jan. 12, Aug. 10, 1809; Dec. 21, 1810; Mar. 8, Apr. 5–19, May 3, 24, June 7, 28–July 19, Aug. 16–Sept. 13, 27, Oct. 18, 25, Nov. 8–22, Dec. 6, 1811; Jan. 10, 17, 31–Feb. 14, Mar. 6, 13, Apr. 2, Sept. 24, Nov. 27, Dec. 3, 1812; Mar. 18, 1813; Nov. 17, 1814; Feb. 16, Mar. 16, 1815.

Windham Lib. has Mar. 8, 1798–Feb. 20, 1800.

Conn. State Lib. has Aug. 25, 1792; Apr. 4, Aug. 29, 1795; Oct. 13, 1797; Apr. 26, July 19, 1798; Mar. 21, 1799; Jan. 2, Mar. 6, 1800; Aug. 27, 1801; Feb. 25, 1802; Mar. 31, 1803; Oct. 29, 1807; June 9, July 28, Aug. 4, 1808.

Univ. of Mich. (Clements) has Apr. 4, May 9, 16, June 27, July 11, 18, Aug. 8, 22, 29, Nov. 14, 21, 1795; May 14, 28–June 11, July 16, Sept. 24, Oct. 1,

15–Nov. 5, 19, Dec. 3, 17, 24, 1796; Dec. 27, 1798; Jan. 24, Aug. 29, Dec. 5, 1799.

N. Y. Pub. Lib. has May 21, Nov. 19, 1796; Jan. 14, 1802; Nov. 7, 1805.

Robert C. Byrne, Hatfield, Mass., has Mar. 12, 1791.

Western Reserve Hist. Soc. has Nov. 19, 1801.

Univ. of Ill. has Oct. 21, 1802.

Hist. Soc. Penn. has May 3, 1804.

New Haven Col. Hist. Soc. has July 16, 1807.

Middlesex Co. Hist. Soc. has Dec. 15, 1814.

[Windham] Phenix, see **Windham Herald.**

[Windham] **Political Visitant,** 1819–1820.

Weekly. Established early in November, 1819, judging from the first and only issue located, that of May 15, 1820, vol. 1, no. 29, published by Henry Webb, 2d, with the title of "The Political Visitant."

Boston Athenæum has May 15, 1820.

[Windham] **Register,** 1817–1818.

Weekly. Established Mar. 6, 1817, by Samuel Webb, with the title of "The Register." The size of the paper was quarto. At some time before the close of the year 1817, Henry Webb, 2d & Co. became the publishers, the size was enlarged to folio, and the title was changed to "The Register, and, Country Advertiser." The last issue located is that of Dec. 11, 1817, vol. 1, no. 41, but the title is included in a list of Connecticut newspapers of January 1818, printed in the Hartford "Times" of Feb. 2, 1818. The paper was continued by Samuel Webb as "The Advertiser" (which see), without change of volume numbering, apparently in April 1818. An advertisement in "The Advertiser" of May 7, 1818, dated Apr. 14, 1818, requests that debts due to Henry Webb, 2d & Co. should be paid. This would seem to show that the change of title and publisher took place with the issue of Apr. 9, 1818.

Am. Antiq. Soc. has Mar. 13, Apr. 10, Dec. 11, 1817.

DELAWARE

Dover Argus, 1804.

In the Portland "Eastern Argus" of May 31, 1804, is the following: "Messrs. Aitken & Freeman have established a Republican Paper at Dover, (Delaware) entitled, 'The Dover Argus, or Delaware Spy.'" No copy located, although the issue of June 13 is quoted in the "Eastern Argus" of July 5, 1804. The Wilmington "Mirror of the Times" of May 23, 1804, says, "A new Republican paper has lately been set up at Dover, in this State, entitled if we recollect, (for the editors have not sent us their paper) The Dover Argus, or Delaware Advertiser." The Hudson, N. Y., "Bee" of July 24, 1804, refers to the recent establishment of "The Dover Argus, and Delaware Advertiser," published semi-weekly by Aitken & Freeman. Aitken & Freeman were probably Robert S. Aitken and John Freeman. Since a paper with the title of "The Argus and Delaware Advertiser" appears at Newcastle in 1805, with the volume numbering carrying its establishment back to July 1804, it seems probable that the "Argus" was discontinued at Dover at this time and was removed to Newcastle, especially as the "Constitutionalist" was established at Dover in August 1804.

[Dover] Constitutionalist, 1804–1805.

Weekly. Established Aug. 9, 1804, judging from the date of the earliest issue located, that of Sept. 6, 1804, vol. 1, no. 5, published by J[ohn] B. Wootten & P[resley] Allee, with the title of "The Constitutionalist; or The Defender of the People's Rights." The last issue located is that of July 11, 1805, vol. 1, no. 36. The paper is referred to in the Wilmington "Mirror of the Times" of Oct. 23, 1805.

Am. Antiq. Soc. has Sept. 6, 27, 1804; Jan. 17, 24, Feb. 7, Apr. 15, July 11, 1805.
Del. Hist. Soc. has Sept. 19, 1804.

[Dover] Federal Ark, 1802–1803.

Semi-weekly. Established Sept. 14, 1802, by William Black, with the title of "The Federal Ark." The publisher intended to remove to Wilmington in October, but was prevented by the presence of a fever epidemic at the latter town. In October and November he could issue his paper only weekly. His last issue at Dover was that of Feb. 21, 1803, vol. 1, No. 40, and the following issue was published at Wilmington.

Del. Hist. Soc. has Sept. 14, 1802–Feb. 21, 1803.
Am. Antiq. Soc. has Sept. 17, Nov. 23, 1802.
Hist. Soc. Penn. has Oct. 8, 1802.

[Dover] Friend of the People, 1799.

Semi-weekly. Established Sept. 14, 1799, judging from the first and only issue located, "The Friend of the People," vol. 1, no. 5, for Sept. 28, 1799, published by William Black.

Harvard has Sept. 28, 1799.

[Dover] National Recorder, 1820+.

Weekly. Established in July 1820, judging from the date of the earliest issue located, that of Oct. 19, 1820, vol. 1, no. 15, published by Samuel F. Shinn, with the title of "National Recorder." Continued after 1820.

Del. Hist. Soc. has Oct. 19, 1820.
Am. Antiq. Soc. has Nov. 23, Dec. 7, 21, 1820.

Newcastle Argus, 1804–1805.

Semi-weekly. Established in July 1804, judging from the date of the earliest issue located, that of May 8, 1805, vol. 1, no. 84, published by John Barber, under the title of "The Argus and Delaware Advertiser." With the issue of May 21, 1805, the title was changed to the "Newcastle Argus." The last issue located is that of Aug. 9, 1805, vol. 2, no. 24. John Freeman was probably the printer in 1804, having removed from Dover. John Freeman, called "printer of New Castle, Del.," was married at Philadelphia, Nov. 22, 1804 (Philadelphia "Aurora," Nov. 27).

Harvard has May 8, 11, 15, 21, 24, 28, 31, June 4, 1805.
Am. Antiq. Soc. has Aug. 9, 1805.

[Wilmington] American Watchman, 1809–1820+.

Semi-weekly. Established Aug. 2, 1809, by James Wilson, under the title of the "American Watchman; and Delaware Republican." The title was shortened to the "American Watchman" with the issue of Jan. 1, 1814. Wilson sold out the establishment, and beginning with the issue of July 19, 1817, the paper was published by Selleck Osborn, with a new series of numbering. Continued after 1820.

Del. Hist. Soc. has Aug. 2, 1809–Dec. 31, 1814; May 4, 8, 29, June 1, Aug. 24, Sept. 7–14, 25, Oct. 2–12, 19, 23, Nov. 2, 20, Dec. 11, 21, 28, 1816; Jan. 4, 1817–Dec. 29, 1819; Jan. 1–July 12, 21, 1820.

Am. Antiq. Soc. has Aug. 2–Dec. 30, 1809, fair; Jan. 3, 1810–June 29, 1811; July 6, 1811–Nov. 19, 1814, fair; Jan. 7, 18, Feb. 22, Mar. 1, Apr. 19, 26, May 6, 17, June 24, July 5, Aug. 2, 5, 12, 23–30, Sept. 9, 23, Oct. 25, Nov. 8, Dec. 6, 1815; Jan. 6–13, 27, Apr. 24, May 15, June 26, July 6, 13, 27, Oct. 2,

1816; Jan. 4, Feb. 18, Mar. 29, Apr. 26, May 7, June 4, July 16, 23, Aug. 9, Sept. 13, 1817; Sept. 26, Oct. 17, 28, Nov. 4, 1818; Feb. 3, June 26, Oct. 4, Dec. 29, 1819; Jan. 8, 22, Feb. 16, 23, Mar. 1–8, 22, 29, May 17, 1820.
Phil. Lib. Co. has Jan. 1, 1812–Dec. 28, 1816.
Lib. Congress has Sept. 30, 1809; July 25, 1810; Mar. 7, Dec. 2, 1812; July 1, 1815; Aug. 21, 1816; Apr. 23, June 2, 1817; Jan. 2, 1819–Dec. 29, 1820.
Mrs. Henry S. Young, Elkton, Md., has Jan. 3–Dec. 28, 1816.
Hist. Soc. Penn. has July 18–Dec. 29, 1820.
Univ. of Del. has Aug. 28, 1813.
Ohio Hist. & Phil. Soc. has Sept. 11, 1813.
N. Y. Hist. Soc. has Dec. 24, 1814; Dec. 9, 1815.
Richard S. Rodney, Wilmington, has Jan. 6, 16, 1819.

Wilmington Courant, 1762.

The chief authority for the publication of this paper is Isaiah Thomas, who in his "History of Printing in America," ed. 2, vol. 2, p. 154, says: "The first and only newspaper published before 1775, in what is now the state of Delaware, made its appearance in Wilmington about the year 1762, entitled, if my information is correct, the 'Wilmington Courant,' printed and published by James Adams, for the short period of six months; when, for want of encouragement, it was discontinued." William McCulloch, writing in 1814, referred to Thomas's statement and said "My information does not embrace the title of the paper he attempted, but it was different from this" (Am. Antiq. Soc. Proc. Apr. 1921, p. 132). William Nelson, in his "Notes toward a History of the American Newspaper" 1918, p. lxviii, says "Thomas gives the name of this paper as the *Courant*, but I am informed that *Chronicle* is correct."

The paper was surely published at Wilmington in 1762, even if there is no contemporary reference to the title. James Adams advertised in "The Pennsylvania Gazette" of June 10, 1762, that he would publish a weekly paper at Wilmington, to begin July 9. Wilmington news of July 30 was printed in "The Pennsylvania Gazette" of Aug. 5; news of Sept. 10 in the issue of Sept. 16; news of Dec. 17 in the issue of Dec. 23. In the Gazette of Apr. 21, 1763, James Adams advertised books for sale at his printing-office in Wilmington. Wilmington news of July 30, 1762 was printed in "The New York Mercury" of Aug. 9, and news of Sept. 10 in the issue of Sept. 20. Wilmington news of Dec. 17, 1762 was printed in "The New York Gazette; or, the Weekly Post-Boy" of Dec. 30.

[Wilmington] Delaware and Eastern-Shore Advertiser, 1794–1799.

Semi-weekly. Established May 14, 1794, by S. & J. Adams, & W. C. Smyth, with the title of "The Delaware and Eastern-Shore Advertiser." Beginning with May 28, 1794, the imprint was Sam. & John Adams and W. C. Smyth. William C. Smyth removed, and beginning with the issue of Mar. 18, 1795, the paper was published by Samuel & John Adams. The last issue located is that of Dec. 26, 1799, no. 578.

    Hist. Soc. Penn. has May 14, 1794–May 13, 1795; Dec. 13, 17, 24, 1798; June 20, 1799.

    Am. Antiq. Soc. has May 31, June 7, July 5, Aug. 23, Sept. 3, 6, Oct. 11, Nov. 15, Dec. 7, 10, 20–27, 1794; Jan. 14, Feb. 4, 7, 18, Apr. 8, 25, 1795; Jan. 2, Feb. 22, July 11, Oct. 20, 1796; Apr. 2, May 3, 1798; Mar. 4, 14, 1799.

    Harvard has Mar. 4, 11, 14, 21, 25, Apr. 1, 25, June 17–24, July 1, 4, Aug. 1, 5, 1795; Jan. 9, Mar. 24, Apr. 14–21, 28, May 12, 16, 30, June 2, 13, 20, 27, 30, July 7, 14, 18, 25–Aug. 4, 15, 22–29, Sept. 5, 12–19, Oct. 3, 6, 24, 31–Nov. 7, 14–24, Dec. 8–29, 1796; Jan. 19, 26, Feb. 2–27, Mar. 6, 16–23, Apr. 6–May 1, Nov. 2, 13, 1797; Aug. 1, 1799.

    Del. Hist. Soc. has June 28, 1794–Feb. 25, 1795; July 15, Aug. 12, 1795; May 19, 1796; Sept. 7, 1797; Feb. 26, 1798; Aug. 22, 29, Sept. 5, 12, 19, 26, 1799.

    Wilm. Inst. Lib. has June 13, 1796; May 4, 1797–Dec. 26, 1799, fair.

    Lib. Congress has Jan. 31, Mar. 21, June 13, Oct. 10, 1795.

    Phil. Lib. Co. has Oct. 17, 24, 31, Nov. 7, 11, 18, 1795; Jan. 20, 1796.

    Richard S. Rodney, Wilmington, has June 13, 1796.

[Wilmington] **Delaware Courant,** 1786–1787.

    Weekly. Established in September, 1786, judging from the date of the earliest issue located, that of May 5, 1787, vol. 1, no. 35, published by Samuel and John Adams, with the title of "The Delaware Courant, and Wilmington Advertiser." The Hist. Soc. Penn. has a prospectus for this paper, headed "To the Public" and signed by James Adams, Junior, and Samuel Adams, May 17, 1786, yet all the known issues were published by James' two brothers, Samuel and John. The last issue located is that of Sept. 8, 1787, vol. 2, no. 53.

    Am. Antiq. Soc. has May 5, 12, 26, June 2, July 7, 14, 21, Aug. 4, 11, 18, Sept. 1, 8, 1787.

[Wilmington] **Delaware Freeman,** 1810.

    Weekly. Established Sept. 21, 1810, by Risley and Skinner [Jeremiah B. Risley and Robert Skinner], with the title of "The Delaware Freeman." The last issue located is that of Oct. 27, 1810, vol. 1, no. 6.

    Am. Antiq. Soc. has Sept. 21, 29, Oct. 27, 1810.

[Wilmington] **Delaware Gazette,** 1785–1799.

    Weekly, semi-weekly and tri-weekly. Established June 14, 1785, judging from the date of the earliest issue located, that of June 28, 1785, vol. 1, no. 3, published weekly by Jacob A. Killen, with the title of "The Delaware Gazette." At some time between this date and Jan. 18, 1786, the title was changed to "The

Delaware Gazette; or, the Faithful Centinel." In July or Aug. 1786, the title was altered to the "The State Gazette; or, the Faithful Centinel," but between November 1786, and March 1787, it was changed back to its former title. With the issue of Apr. 11, 1787, the paper was transferred to Frederick Craig and Company [F. Craig, Peter Brynberg and Samuel Andrews]. Soon after Nov. 22, 1788, the title was shortened to "The Delaware Gazette," and between May and Sept. 1789, lengthened to "The Delaware Gazette, and General Advertiser." Early in Sept. 1789, probably on Sept. 2, publication was changed from weekly to semi-weekly, but weekly publication was resumed on Nov. 21, 1789. On Mar. 5, 1791, the firm was dissolved, the paper was transferred to Peter Brynberg and Samuel Andrews, and the title shortened to "The Delaware Gazette." Beginning with Sept. 8, 1795, the paper was changed to a semi-weekly, and was published for Robert Coram, by Bonsal & Starr [Vincent Bonsal and Caleb Starr]. Coram died Mar. 9, 1796, and with the issue of Mar. 15, the paper was printed by Bonsal & Starr. Beginning with the issue of Sept. 6, 1796, it became a tri-weekly and was reduced in size to small 4to. Beginning with the issue of Oct. 29, 1796, the paper was published by W[illiam] C. Smyth, although it was stated that Smyth had owned the paper since Sept. 7, 1796. With the issue of Nov. 5, 1796, it was again made a semi-weekly and enlarged to folio size.

In September and October 1798, the paper was suspended because of the yellow fever epidemic, and a small quarto single sheet entitled "The Wilmington Mercury" was published by Smyth under the authority of the Health office, "printed occasionally and delivered gratis to the patrons of the Delaware Gazette." The issues located date from Sept. 16 to Oct. 25, 1798, all without volume numbering. The first issue with the resumed title was that of Oct. 27, 1798, no. 870, entitled "The Delaware Gazette," published weekly by W. C. Smyth. With the issue of Mar. 14, 1799, it was published semi-weekly by Bonsal & Niles [Vincent Bonsal and Hezekiah Niles] for Vaughan & Coleman [John Vaughan and Daniel Coleman]. It was discontinued with the issue of Sept. 7, 1799, no. 946, when it was stated that after a short suspension its successor would be the "Delaware Gazette and Mirror of the Times," to be published by James Wilson. Wilson established on Nov. 20, 1799, the "Mirror of the Times," which see.

Am. Antiq. Soc. has July 5, Aug. 16, Nov. 22, 1786; Apr. 11, May 23, July 4, Aug. 8, Oct. 10, 17, 31, Dec. 19, 1787; Nov. 22, 1788; Apr. 25, Sept. 9, 19, 23, Oct. 10, Nov. 14, 21, 28, Dec. 19, 1789; Jan. 16, 30, Feb. 20, Mar. 27, Apr. 3, May 1, 8, June 19, 1790; June 16–July 28, Aug. 11–25, Sept. 15, 22, Oct. 6–Dec. 8, 22, 29, 1792; Jan. 5–Dec. 21, 1793; Jan. 18–Mar. 15, 29–May 17, June 28, July 12, 19, Aug. 9, 23, 30, Sept. 13, 27–Oct. 11, 25, 1794; Aug. 15, Sept. 15–22, Oct. 9, 1795.

Del. Hist. Soc. has Jan. 18, Apr. 12, 1786; Jan. 10, 1789–Dec. 25, 1790; Apr. 2, Sept. 17, 1791; Oct. 13, 1792; Jan. 5, 12, 26, Feb. 9, 16, Aug. 31, Dec. 21, 1793; Feb. 1, Oct. 4, 1794; Mar. 14, Aug. 15, Sept. 8–Dec. 2, 8–29, 1795; Jan. 1–Aug. 30, Dec. 3, 1796; Feb. 25–Mar. 4, 11, 18–Apr. 1, 19, May 3, 10–July 5, 12–22,

29, Aug. 2, 5, 1797; Mar. 24, Oct. 27, 1798; Mar. 14–Sept. 7, 1799; and Wilmington Mercury, Sept. 22, 23, 24, 25, Oct. 8, 9, 15, 16, 17, 21, 22, 25, 1798.

Harvard has July 2–16, Sept. 17, Nov. 12–26, 1791; Mar. 7, Apr. 18 extra, May 30, June 13, Aug. 15, 1795; Mar. 8, 22, Apr. 1, 8, 22, 29, May 3, 13, 17, June 28, July 12–18, 29, Aug. 2, 12, 19–Sept. 2, 10, 13, Oct. 1, 6–22, Nov. 1–16, 23, Dec. 3–17, 24, 31, 1796; Jan. 7, 14, 28–Feb. 22, Mar. 1–18, 25–Apr. 5, 12–19, 26, 1797.

Lib. Congress has Mar. 28, 1787; Apr. 2, July 16, Aug. 27, 1791; May 5, Dec. 1, 1792; June 15, Oct. 19, 26, 1793; Feb. 21, Aug. 22, 1795; June 7, 1796; Feb. 4, 8, May 27, 1797; Feb. 20, 1799.

Hist. Soc. Penn. has July 30, 1791–Jan. 21, 1792; Sept. 22, 1792; May 4, 1793.

N. Y. Hist. Soc. has June 28, 1785; Mar. 23–July 27, 1799.

Richard S. Rodney, Wilmington, has Nov. 22, 1788; Sept. 3, 1791.

N. Y. Pub. Lib. has Apr. 2–23, 1791; May 24, 1794.

Buffalo Hist. Soc. has Oct. 11, 1794.

Phil. Lib. Co. has Oct. 30, 1795; July 5, 1796; June 23, 1798.

Univ. of Del. has Jan. 5, 1793.

[Wilmington] **Delaware Gazette,** 1809–1810.

Semi-weekly. Established July 8, 1809, by Joseph Jones, with the title of "The Delaware Gazette." The last issue located is that of June 30, 1810, vol. 1, no. 101.

Del. Hist. Soc. has July 8–Aug. 2, Sept. 23–Oct. 21, Dec. 6–16, 23, 27, 1809; Jan. 6, 13–31, Feb. 14, Mar. 14, 24–Apr. 18, May 12–30, June 6, 1810.

Am. Antiq. Soc. has Aug. 2, 5, 26, Nov. 25, 29, Dec. 1, 9, 23, 30, 1809; Jan. 13, 17, 31, Feb. 7–14, Mar. 17–24, Apr. 4, 7, 14, 21, 25, May 2–16, June 6, 30, 1810.

Lib. Congress has July 12, 15, 22, 1809.

Hist. Soc. Penn. has Aug. 16, 1809.

[Wilmington] **Delaware Gazette,** 1814–1820+.

Semi-weekly. Established Apr. 19, 1814, by M[oses] Bradford, with the title of "The Delaware Gazette." Beginning with the issue of Nov. 10, 1814, the title was lengthened to "Delaware Gazette and Peninsula Advertiser." With the issue of Jan. 1, 1817, Bradford disposed of the paper to William A. Miller, who published it until 1820. Samuel Harker then purchased the paper, and beginning with the issue of Feb. 23, 1820, published it under the shortened title of "Delaware Gazette," and with a new series of numbering. It was continued after 1820.

Del. Hist. Soc. has Apr. 19, 1814–June 7, 1817; Aug. 6, 13, 20, Sept. 6, Oct. 25, Nov. 22, Dec. 10, 13, 31, 1817; Aug. 5, Sept. 12–Oct. 31, Nov. 7, 11, 18–Dec. 30, 1818; Mar. 27, Sept. 4, Nov. 6, 20, Dec. 15, 1819; Feb. 23–Dec. 29, 1820.

Wilm. Inst. Lib. has Apr. 18, 1815–Dec. 29, 1820.

Am. Antiq. Soc. has Apr. 19, 1814–Apr. 13, 1815; June 13, Aug. 22, 29, Sept. 5, Oct. 5, 1815; Apr. 4–Dec. 26, 1816; Jan. 1–15, Feb. 5, 12, 15, 26, Mar. 1–12, 19–29, Apr. 2, 5, 12–19, May 3–14, 21, 1817; May 13, 20, 1818; Nov. 17, 1819; Mar. 4, Apr. 1, Aug. 18, Sept. 22, 29, Oct. 17, Nov. 24, Dec. 15, 1820.

Hist. Soc. Penn. has Apr. 11, 13, May 2, 1815; Apr. 18, 1816; Dec. 29, 1819.

Lib. Congress has June 13, 1815; Apr. 2, 9, June 4, 1817; Jan. 6–Dec. 29, 1819; Feb. 26–Dec. 29, 1820.

Wis. Hist. Soc. has Nov. 25, 1818.

Mass. Hist. Soc. has Aug. 18, 1820.

[Wilmington] **Delaware Patriot,** 1816.

Semi-weekly. Established July 9, 1816, by William S. Buell, under the title of "Delaware Patriot, and Eastern Shore Advertiser." The last issue located is that of Oct. 4, 1816, vol. 1, no. 25.

Am. Antiq. Soc. has July 9, 16, 23, Aug. 2, 9, 13, 27, Sept. 13, 17, 24, 28, Oct. 4, 1816.

H. Armour Smith, Yonkers, N. Y., has July 30, 1816.

[Wilmington] **Delaware Statesman,** 1811–1813.

Semi-weekly. Established July 10, 1811, by William Riley, with the title of "The Delaware Statesman." The last issue located is that of July 24, 1813, vol. 2, no. 104.

Del. Hist. Soc. has July 10, 13, 24, Aug. 14, Sept. 7, 18–Oct. 5, 12, Nov. 13, Dec. 4, 18, 1811; Jan. 8, 11, 25, Feb. 5, 12, Mar. 7, May 9, 13–30, July 11, Aug. 5, 8, 15, Sept. 2, 5, 16, Oct. 24, Nov. 18, 25, Dec. 30, 1812; Mar. 17, Apr. 7, May 1, 15, 19, July 17, 24, 1813.

Am. Antiq. Soc. has July 10, 24, 27, Aug. 3, Nov. 6, 1811; Feb. 5, Mar. 7, Aug. 26–Sept. 5, 12, 19, 26, 30, Oct. 3, 28, Nov. 7, 11, 21, Dec. 9, 1812; Jan. 16, 20, Feb. 10, 13, July 3, 1813.

N. Y. Hist. Soc. has Oct. 16, 1811; June 24, 1812.

Lib. Congress has Nov. 20, 1811.

[Wilmington] **Federal Ark,** 1803–1804.

Semi-weekly. A continuation, without change of volume numbering, of "The Federal Ark" published at Dover by William Black in 1802–1803. It was removed to Wilmington, where the first issue was that of Feb. 28, 1803, vol. 1, no. 41, published by Black & Smyth [William Black and William C. Smyth] with the title of "The Federal Ark." At some time between Apr. 13 and July 27, 1803, William Black became sole publisher. The last issue located is that of June 13, 1804, vol. 2, no. 172. In July 1804 Black left on a voyage to Charleston, S. C., and on the return trip in September was lost at sea (see "Raleigh Register," Nov. 26, 1804).

> Del. Hist. Soc. has Feb. 28–Mar. 5, 12, 16, 23, 30, Apr. 2, 13, July 27–Oct. 19, 26–Nov. 2, 1803; Jan. 4–June 13, 1804.
> Am. Antiq. Soc. has June 22, July 23–Aug. 3, 17, 24, 1803; Jan. 18, Feb. 8, Mar. 3–17, 31, Apr. 4, 1804.
> Harvard has July 9, Nov. 12, Dec. 31, 1803; May 30, 1804.

Wilmington Mercury, 1798, see **[Wilmington] Delaware Gazette,** 1785–1799.

[Wilmington] Mirror of the Times, 1799–1806.

Semi-weekly. Established Nov. 20, 1799, by James Wilson, under the title of the "Mirror of the Times, & General Advertiser." With the issue of Jan. 2, 1805, the size of the paper was reduced to quarto, and an index and title-page at the end of the year were promised. No issues were published from Apr. 2 to May 14, or from June 21 to July 23, 1806, and publication throughout 1806 was irregular. The paper was discontinued with the issue of Aug. 22, 1806, vol. 7, no. 680.

> Del. Hist. Soc. has Nov. 20, 1799–Aug. 22, 1806.
> Am. Antiq. Soc. has Jan. 18, 22, Feb. 19, 26, Mar. 5, 12, Apr. 5, May 17, July 23, Sept. 17, Oct. 18, Nov. 19, 26, 29, Dec. 3, 17, 1800; Jan. 14, Feb. 14, 21, 28, Mar. 21, Apr. 25, May 16, 23, June 6, 20, July 15, 25, Sept. 23, Nov. 14, 1801; Jan. 20, Mar. 31, June 19, 23, Dec. 18, 1802; Jan. 1, 8, 22, Feb. 2, 16, 19, Mar. 12, 19, 30, Apr. 6, 20, 27, May 4, 7, 25, June 4, 18, 22, July 13, 16, 27, 30, Aug. 3, 13–Sept. 7, 14, 21, 28, Oct. 1, 8, 29, Nov. 2, 16, 19, 26, Dec. 14, 24, 28, 1803; Jan. 4–June 27, Aug. 1, 4, 11, 18–Sept. 1, 8, 15–29, Oct. 10, 13, 20–Nov. 21, 28, Dec. 1, 12, 15, 22, 25, 1804; Jan. 2–Feb. 2, 9, 13, 20–Mar. 30, Apr. 6–24, May 8, 11, 18–25, June 1–8, 15, 19, 29, July 3, 10–20, 27–Sept. 14, 21–Oct. 26, Nov. 2, 9, 13, 20, 27, Dec. 18, 1805; Jan. 1–July 31, Aug. 7, 19, 22, 1806.
> Harvard has Jan. 29, Feb. 5, 8, 19, 26, Mar. 8, 15, 29, Apr. 2, 9, 16, 19, May 10, June 7–14, 21, 28–July 4, 12, 19, 25, Aug. 6, 9, 20, 23, 30, Sept. 13, Oct. 18, 25, Nov. 8, 19–Dec. 24, 31, 1800; Jan. 3–21, 28–Feb. 25, Mar. 4, 7, 14–25, Apr. 8–25, May 2, 6, 16, 20, 27, 30, June 10, 17, 24–July 8, 15, 22–Sept. 26, Oct. 3, 10, 17–24, 31–Nov. 7, 14, 21–28, Dec. 5–30, 1801; Jan. 6–Mar. 13, 20–Apr. 17, 24–May 5, 12–29, June 5–12, 19–July 7, 12–Aug. 14, 21, Sept. 4, 18–25, Oct. 1, 13, Nov. 10–Dec. 18, 25, 29, 1802; Jan. 1–22, 29–Feb. 23, Mar. 2, 5, 12–23, 30–Apr. 6, 13, 20–May 28, June 4, 11, 18, 22, 29–July 30,

Aug. 6, 13, 20–31, Sept. 7–21, Oct. 1–15, 22–Nov. 5, Dec. 10, 24, 1803; Jan. 4, 14, 18, 23, Feb. 1–11, 18, Mar. 17–24, Apr. 18, 21, 28, May 5, 9, 16, 19, 26, June 2, 23–July 11, 18–28, Aug. 8, 15, 18, 25–Sept. 5, 12–Oct. 10, Nov. 7–Dec. 5, 12, 19, 22, 1804; Jan. 2–30, Feb. 6, 9, 20, 27, Mar. 6, 9, 16, 20, 27–Apr. 13, 20, 24, May 4, 11, 18, 25, June 5–19, 26–July 13, 20–Aug. 28, Sept. 7–21, 28, Oct. 1, 12, 16, 26–Nov. 9, 23, 27, Dec. 18, 21, 28, 1805; Jan. 1, 4, 11, 22, 29, Mar. 1, 15, 22, 29, May 16, June 5–14, 21, July 29, Aug. 2, 5, 1806.

N. Y. Hist. Soc. has June 28, 1800–Dec. 30, 1801; June 25, 29, July 9, 1803.

Wilm. Inst. Lib. has Aug. 3, 1805; Jan. 11, 15, Feb. 1–12, 19, 22, Mar. 1–8, 19, 26, Apr. 2, May 16, 23–30, June 11–21, July 23, 26, 1806.

Duke Univ. has Jan. 30, Feb. 2, 20, Mar. 9, 30–May 1, 25, June 1, 8, 12, July 13, 31–Sept. 4, 11, 18, 28, Oct. 1, 1805.

Lib. Congress has Jan. 14, Feb. 14, Mar. 14, 1801; May 23, Oct. 13, 1804; Sept. 28, Oct. 16, Nov. 13, 1805.

N. Y. Pub. Lib. has Dec. 7, 1799; May 14, 1800.

Yale has Jan. 2–Dec. 28, 1805.

Mrs. Henry S. Young, Elkton, Md., has Jan. 1–Aug. 22, 1806.

Mass. Hist. Soc. has Mar. 7, 1804.

Mrs. H. C. Evans, Wilmington, has Nov. 19, 1800–Dec. 30, 1801.

[Wilmington] Monitor, 1800–1802.

Weekly and semi-weekly. Established Feb. 1, 1800, by W. C. Smyth [William C. Smyth] under the title of "The Monitor; or, Wilmington Weekly Repository." It was published as a weekly until June, 1800, when it was changed to a semi-weekly and the title altered to "The Monitor, & Wilmington Repository." Between May and August 1801 the title was again changed to "The Monitor; or, Delaware Federalist." The paper was suspended for a while in 1802. The last issue located is that of Sept. 1, 1802, vol. 3, no. 168.

Harvard has Feb. 8, Sept. 20, Oct. 1, 29, Nov. 5, 8, 15, 22, 26, Dec. 3, 10–17, 1800; Jan. 21, Oct. 21–Nov. 4, 5, Dec. 5, 9, 24, 1801; Sept. 1, 1802.

Del. Hist. Soc. has June 11, Sept. 20, 1800; May 23, Aug. 8, Oct. 24, Nov. 16, 1801.

N. Y. Hist. Soc. has Oct. 7, 1800.

Lib. Congress has Feb. 7, Oct. 14, Nov. 7, 1801.

Am. Antiq. Soc. has Oct. 21, 1801.

Richard S. Rodney, Wilmington, has Nov. 4, 1801.

[Wilmington] Museum of Delaware, 1804–1809.

Weekly. Established June 23, 1804, judging from the date of the earliest issue located, that of Sept. 8, 1804, vol. 1, no. 12, published by Joseph Jones, with the title of "The Museum of Delaware." Yet the Wilmington "Mirror of the Times" of June 6, 1804, states that the first issue of the "Museum of Delaware" will appear on June 30. In 1806, the title was changed to "The Museum of Delaware, & General Advertiser." The issue of June 17, 1809, vol. 4, no. 258, announced that the paper would be discontinued upon July 1, 1809, in favor of the "Delaware Gazette," to be established by Joseph Jones.

>Del. Hist. Soc. has Nov. 10, 1804; Jan. 3, 17–Apr. 18, May 2–June 20, July 4, 18, Aug. 1, 8, Sept. 5, 26, Oct. 10, 31–Dec. 12, 1807; Jan. 9–23, Feb. 20–Mar. 5, July 23–Aug. 20, Sept. 3, 10, 24–Oct. 22, 1808; Jan. 14–Feb. 4, 18–Mar. 13, 1809.
>Am. Antiq. Soc. has Sept. 8, 1804; Sept. 14, 1805; Feb. 14, Apr. 18, Dec. 12, 1807; Dec. 17, 31, 1808; Jan. 14, Feb. 4, 11, 25–Mar. 25, Apr. 24, May 8, June 17, 1809.
>Lib. Congress has May 20, June 3–17, 1809.

[Wilmington] State Gazette, see **[Wilmington] Delaware Gazette,** 1785–1799.

DISTRICT OF COLUMBIA

Alexandria, see under **Virginia.**

[Georgetown] Cabinet, 1800–1801.

Tri-weekly and daily. Established Aug. 26, 1800, by J[ames] Lyon, with the title of "The Cabinet." The paper, of folio size, was issued tri-weekly, with the titles and imprints of two successive numbers printed as a two column heading on the second and fourth pages. The place of printing is given only as "District of Columbia," but the advertisements and reading notices show that it was printed at Georgetown. On Sept. 3, 1800, the editor stated that on that day he began daily publication, and on Sept. 8 referred to the paper as a "Daily" in the imprint, but distribution was still undoubtedly tri-weekly. In November 1800 there was a four weeks' suspension and the paper then appeared as a daily, of quarto size, with a front page title "The Cabinet." A country paper was also issued weekly. The last issue located is that of Mar. 6, 1801, vol. 1, no. 113. In the first number of his "National Magazine," under date of Oct. 21, 1801, Lyon expressed his regrets at having been compelled to discontinue "The Cabinet." There is a contemporary reference to this paper printed in the "Penn. Mag. of Hist. and Biog.," vol. 13, p. 126.

> N. Y. State Lib. has Aug. 26–Oct. 14, Nov. 20, Dec. 4, 6–12, 15–17, 19–24, 27–31, 1800; Jan. 2–9, 27, 30, 1801.
> Long Id. Hist. Soc. has Dec. 12, 13, 1800.
> Am. Antiq. Soc. has Dec. 30, 1800; Feb. 4, Mar. 4, 1801.
> Lib. Congress has Jan. 5, Mar. 4, 1801.
> Hist. Soc. Penn. has Mar. 6, 1801.

[Georgetown] Centinel, & Country Gazette, 1796–1800.

Weekly. Established in May, 1796, by Green, English, & Co. [Charles D. Green, David English and Samuel Hanson], as a country edition of their semi-weekly "Centinel of Liberty." The earliest issue located is that of June 30, 1797, vol. 2, no. 6, entitled "The Centinel, & Country Gazette." Hanson, who was editor, retired on July 23, 1799, and the firm name became Green & English. The last issue located is that of Mar. 21, 1800, vol. 5, no. 12, but the paper undoubtedly was continued as long as the semi-weekly issue, until November 1800.

> Harvard has June 30, July 7, Aug. 11, Sept. 1, 8, 29, 1797; Mar. 2, 1798.
> Pratt Free Lib., Baltimore, has Oct. 6, 1797.
> Am. Antiq. Soc. has Jan. 5, 1798.
> Schenectady Co. Hist. Soc. has Jan. 10–Mar. 21, 1800.

[Georgetown] Centinel of Liberty, 1796–1800.

Semi-weekly. Established May 24, 1796, by Green, English & Co., [Charles D. Green, David English and Samuel Hanson], under the name of "The Centinel of Liberty, and George-town Advertiser." With the issue of Jan. 4, 1799, the title was changed to "The Centinel of Liberty, and George-town and Washington Advertiser," and with Sept. 17, 1799, to "The Centinel of Liberty, or George-town and Washington Advertiser." With the issue of July 23, 1799, Samuel Hanson, who was editor, retired and the firm name became Green & English. The paper was discontinued under this title on Nov. 14, 1800, vol. 5, no. 89, when Green & English established in its stead a daily paper, "The Museum and Washington and George-town Daily Advertiser."

> Harvard has May 27, June 7, 17, 28, July 1, 8–15, 22, 29–Aug. 12, 19, 26, 30, Sept. 6, 23, 30, Oct. 7, 14, 21, Nov. 11, 18, 22, 29, Dec. 2, 9, 16, 23, 1796; Jan. 6, 13, 17, 24, 27, June 2, Aug. 22, Sept. 15, Oct. 10, 13, Nov. 17, 21, 1797; Feb. 20, Mar. 2, 1798.
> Lib. Congress has June 24, 1796; Dec. 25, 1798; Jan. 4, 1799–Nov. 14, 1800.
> Phil. Lib. Co. has May 31, June 7, 10, 14, 17, 1796.
> Am. Antiq. Soc. has Dec. 29, 1796; Apr. 15, 25, May 2, 16, July 11, Aug. 18, Sept. 1, 12, 19, 1797; Jan. 2, 5, 16, 23, Feb. 2, 6, Mar. 12, June 15, 1798; Jan. 8, Dec. 24, 1799.
> Georgetown Univ. has May 31, 1796.
> Pratt Free Lib., Baltimore, has Apr. 25, 1797.
> N. Y. Pub. Lib. has Jan. 25, Mar. 1, 1799.

[Georgetown] Columbian Chronicle, 1793–1796.

Semi-weekly. Established Dec. 3, 1793, by S. Hanson [Samuel Hanson], with the title of "The Columbian Chronicle." In April or May 1794, Isaac Briggs was admitted to partnership and the paper was thenceforth published by Hanson & Briggs. Between October and December 1794, James Priestley was made a partner in place of Briggs, and the paper was thenceforth published by Hanson & Priestley. This firm was dissolved and with the issue of Apr. 24, 1795, the paper was published by Samuel Hanson. James Priestley became a bookseller in Georgetown and later removed to Baltimore to become principal of Baltimore Academy. The last issue of the paper located is that of May 10, 1796, no. 251, and the paper is referred to as "the late Columbian Chronicle" in the prospectus of "The Centinel of Liberty" of May 24, 1796.

> Am. Antiq. Soc. has Dec. 3, 1793; May 20, July 15, Aug. 22, 1794; Jan. 20, 23, June 23, 1795.
> Lib. Congress has Feb. 25, Mar. 25, 1794.
> Buffalo Hist. Soc. has Sept. 30, Oct. 10, 1794.
> Harvard has Feb. 3, Mar. 3, 6, May 12, 22, June 2, 12, 19–July 7, 17, 21, 28,

Aug. 4, 11, 14, 21, 25, Sept. 8, Oct. 6, 1795; Jan. 8, 19, Feb. 24, Mar. 4, Apr. 1, 8, 12, 26, May 3, 10, 1796.
Wis. Hist. Soc. has Mar. 13, 1795.
Univ. of Ga. has June 26, 1795.

[Georgetown] Columbian Repository, 1803–1804.

Weekly. Established Sept. 30, 1803, by Bradford & Burgess [Thomas G. Bradford and B——— Burgess], with the title of "Columbian Repository." These publishers had intended to publish a newspaper at Alexandria to be called "The Mercury" (see advertisement in Georgetown "Olio" of June 30, 1803), but in the initial issue of the "Columbian Repository" stated that patrons of the Mercury would be served with the Repository. The paper was of quarto size, with eight numbered pages, although occasionally reduced to four pages. With the issue of Oct. 28, 1803, the name of the printing firm disappeared from the imprint, and although there was nothing henceforth to show the name of the printer, there was nothing to show that it was not printed by Bradford & Burgess. The last issue located is that of Feb. 3, 1804, vol. 1, no. 19.

Harvard has Sept. 30–Nov. 5, 10, 25–Dec. 23, 1803; Jan. 13, 20, Feb. 3, 1804.

[Georgetown] Daily Federal Republican, 1814–1816.

Daily. Established Jan. 4, 1814, as a daily issue of the "Federal Republican," which see. The numbering was continuous with the previous tri-weekly issue. The title was "Federal Republican," Jan. 4–Jan. 17, 1814; "Daily Federal Republican," Jan. 18–Nov. 26, 1814; "Federal Republican," Nov. 28, 1814–Feb. 21, 1815; and "Daily Federal Republican," Feb. 22, 1815–Apr. 3, 1816. Although there was no imprint, the publishers were Alexander C. Hanson and Jacob Wagner. For other information regarding the printers, see under "Federal Republican." The last issue of the daily was that of Apr. 3, 1816, vol. 12, no. 1756. The paper was then removed to Baltimore and united with the "Baltimore Telegraph" under the title of "Federal Republican and Baltimore Telegraph," Apr. 4, 1816, vol. 1, no. 1.

Md. Hist. Soc. has Jan. 4, 1814–Apr. 3, 1816.
Am. Antiq. Soc. has Jan. 4–Apr. 4, May 31, July 13, Oct. 5, 1814; Apr. 9, 1815–Apr. 3, 1816.
Lib. Congress has Mar. 26, Apr. 6, 30–Dec. 29, 1814, fair; Apr. 10–July 16, Nov. 6–Dec. 30, 1815; Jan. 1–13, 16–23, 25–30, Feb. 1, 2, 9, 12, 17–20, 22–26, Mar. 2, 5, 12–16, 20, 21, 23, 26, 27, 29, 30, Apr. 1, 1816.
Univ. of Texas has Jan. 4–Apr. 13, 1814, fair.

[Georgetown] Federal Republican, 1812–1816.

Tri-weekly and semi-weekly. Removed from Baltimore because of the demolition of its office, June 22, 1812, by a mob. The paper was printed at Georgetown, as a tri-weekly, after five weeks' interval, on July 27, 1812, vol. 6, no. 845. This issue was distributed at Baltimore the same day, but a personal attack on one of the editors closed that city henceforth to the paper. The editors at Baltimore were Alexander C. Hanson and Jacob Wagner, and they continued in that capacity at Georgetown, although in no case does either of their names appear in the imprint. Jacob Wagner signs an editorial in the issue of Sept. 6, 1813. Robert Read advertises as acting "for the Proprietors" in the issues of July 12, 1813, and Jan. 13, 1815. In April 1815, James B. Carter advertises as doing all kinds of printing at the office of the Federal Republican. Hanson was elected a member of Congress in March 1813. The title of the paper at first was "Federal Republican, and Commercial Gazette," but with the issue of Dec. 27, 1813, it was shortened to "Federal Republican." On Jan. 4, 1814, the paper appeared as a daily (see under "Daily Federal Republican"). The tri-weekly edition was continued as a paper "for the Country," but with the issue of Apr. 26, 1814, it was changed to a semi-weekly. From Jan. 5 to Apr. 22, 1814, the paper was without heading or title. The last issue of the semi-weekly was on Apr. 2, 1816, vol. 10, no. 1313, after which the paper was removed to Baltimore and united with the "Baltimore Telegraph."

Am. Antiq. Soc. has Aug. 3, 1812–Apr. 2, 1816.
Md. Hist. Soc. has Aug. 3, 1812–Apr. 2, 1816.
N. Y. Hist. Soc. has Aug. 3, 1812–Apr. 2, 1816, fair.
Boston Pub. Lib. has Aug. 19, 1812–Mar. 29, 1816, fair.
Univ. of Mich. (Clements) has Aug. 3, 1812–Dec. 31, 1813; Jan. 3, 1814–Sept. 8, 1815, fair; Feb. 2, 14, 16, 18, Mar. 14, 1816.
Cincinnati, Young Men's Mercantile Lib., had July 27, 1812–May 1814, examined by me in 1918, but they disposed of their newspaper collection in 1927, and this file cannot now be traced.
Lib. Congress has Aug. 7, 1812–Dec. 29, 1813; Jan. 2–Mar. 30, Apr. 29, May 31, June 7, 14, July 12, Aug. 5, 19, Oct. 7–Dec. 30, 1814; Jan. 3, 1815–Mar. 29, 1816, fair.
N. Y. Pub. Lib. has Aug. 3, 1812–Feb. 7, 1815.
Brown Univ. has Aug. 24, 1812–Dec. 29, 1815.
N. Y. State Lib. has Aug. 12, 1812–Apr. 22, 1814; May 27–Oct. 21, Dec. 13, 1814; Feb. 21, July 4, Sept. 26, Oct. 3, 1815; Mar. 15, 1816.
Wis. Hist. Soc. has Aug. 3, 1812–Dec. 22, 1813, fair; Apr. 4, May 12, 1815.
Duke Univ. has Aug. 17, 1812–Dec. 31, 1813, fair; Apr. 26, May 10, 20, June 7, 10, 28, July 8, Aug. 19, 26, Sept. 16, 30, Oct. 28, 1814; May 26, Sept. 22, 1815; Jan. 19, 1816.
Yale has Aug. 5, 1812–Dec. 31, 1813; Apr. 26–Dec. 23, 1814, fair; June 13, 1815.
Harvard has Aug. 13, 1812–Aug. 25, 1813.
Essex Inst. has Aug. 19, 1812–Aug. 23, 1813.
Conn. Hist. Soc. has Aug. 19, 1812–Aug. 16, 1813.

Univ. of Texas has Oct. 4, 1812–May 26, July 23–Dec. 31, 1813; June 24–Sept. 27, 1814.
N. Y. Soc. Lib. has Jan. 22, 1813–Feb. 16, 1814.
Ohio Arch. & Hist. Soc. has Feb. 28, 1815–Apr. 2, 1816.
Mass. Hist. Soc. has Aug. 14, 1812; Apr. 19, Dec. 20, 1813; Jan. 3, June 28, July 22, 29, Nov. 15, Dec. 13, 1814; Jan. 13, Feb. 10, 24–Mar. 17, 24–Apr. 4, 11–25, May 5, 30, June 2, 9, 13, 30–July 18, 25, Sept. 15, 22, Oct. 6, 10, Nov. 14, 1815.
Chicago Hist. Soc. has Aug. 24, Sept. 7, 9, Oct. 14–21, 1812; Feb. 22, 1813.

[Georgetown] **Friend of the People**, 1800.

Fortnightly. Established by James Lyon in the District of Columbia, presumably in August 1800. It was evidently printed at Georgetown since it was published in conjunction with Lyon's other paper, "The Cabinet," which was printed at Georgetown. The title is known from an advertisement in "The Cabinet," from Aug. 26 to Sept. 23, 1800, where it is stated "The Friend of the People, a political paper, by the Editor of the Cabinet, is published in the District of Columbia every two weeks, at one dollar a year." The advertisement also states that the paper was formerly published at Richmond, Va. The New London "Bee" of Oct. 15, 1800, states that "The Friend of the People" had been unavoidably suspended for some time, but was now resumed. The title is mentioned in "The Cabinet," in November 1800, in advertisements of the "National Magazine," but was omitted from this advertisement after Nov. 20, 1800. No copies located.

[Georgetown] **Independent American**, 1809–1811.

Tri-weekly and semi-weekly. Established in July, 1809, by Edgar Patterson, with the title of "Independent American." Beginning with the issue of Oct. 6, 1810, it was published by Thomas & Leakin [John Thomas and Thomas Leakin]. The last issue located is that of Dec. 29, 1810, vol. 2, no. 21. Issues to July 3, 1810, were tri-weekly; from July 7, 1810, to Dec. 11, 1810, were semi-weekly; from Dec. 13, 1810, were tri-weekly. In the "National Intelligencer" of Mar. 23, 1811, Thomas advertised that the "Independent American" would be sold at public auction on that day.

N. Y. Hist. Soc. has Oct. 28, 1809–Dec. 29, 1810.
Lib. Congress has Aug. 26, Oct. 7, 24, Nov. 23, 1809; Apr. 14, 21, May 10, July 11, 21, Oct. 3, 1810.
Am. Antiq. Soc. has Jan. 16, 18, Feb. 3, 20, Mar. 6, 13, 20, 29, 31, Apr. 3, 7, 10, 14, 19, 21, May 8, 10, 15, 19–24, 31, June 2, 7, 9, 21, 26–30, July 11, 18, 21, 28, Aug. 4, 8, 18–Sept. 1, Oct. 17, 1810.

[Georgetown] **Messenger,** 1816–1817.

Semi-weekly and tri-weekly. Established as a semi-weekly, Apr. 17, 1816, by James C. Dunn & Co., with the title of "The Messenger." Beginning with Dec. 10, 1816, it was issued tri-weekly. The last issue was for Oct. 24, 1817, vol. 1, no. 203, after which the paper was continued under the new title of the "National Messenger," which see.

Lib. Congress has Apr. 17, 27, May 1, 8–18, 25–July 24, 31–Aug. 24, 31–Sept. 7, 14, 21, 28, Oct. 9, 12, 19–Dec. 31, 1816; Jan. 2–Feb. 24, Mar. 3–12, 24, 26, Apr. 4–14, 18–30, May 5–June 25, 30, July 2, 9, 14–18, 28–Aug. 4, 8, 13, 15, 20–29, Sept. 8, 12, 19, 29–Oct. 3, 8, 13–24, 1817.

Am. Antiq. Soc. has May 1, 15, June 15, 19, 22, July 6, 27, Aug. 7, 10, 24, 28, 31, Sept. 4, 11–25, Oct. 2–Nov. 2, 9–Dec. 19, 24, 28, 31, 1816; Jan. 2–Feb. 14, 19–24, Mar. 10, 14, 19–Apr. 2, 7, 14–18, 23–May 23, 28, June 2, 4, 9, 16, 20, 30–July 4, 18, 1817.

Duke Univ. has Sept. 21, Oct. 10, 23–30, Nov. 20–27, Dec. 7–17, 24, 28, 1816; Jan. 9, 11, 16, 18, 21, 25–30, Feb. 1, 7, 10, 14, 21, 24, Apr. 23, 28, 30, May 2, 7, 12, 21, 23, June 16, 1817.

[Georgetown] **Metropolitan,** 1820+.

Tri-weekly. Established Jan. 26, 1820, by William Alexander Rind, Jun., with the title of "The Metropolitan." The first number was a specimen issue and the second number did not appear until Feb. 5. Continued after 1820.

Lib. Congress has Jan. 26–Dec. 30, 1820.
Am. Antiq. Soc. has Jan. 26–Dec. 30, 1820, fair.
Filson Club, Louisville, has May 30, June 13, Aug. 12, 15, 29, 1820.
Duke Univ. has May 9, 1820.

[Georgetown] **Museum,** 1800–1802.

Daily and tri-weekly. Established Nov. 18, 1800, by Green & English [Charles D. Green and David English], under the name of "The Museum and Washington and George-town Daily Advertiser." It was really a continuation of the "Centinel of Liberty," since the advertisements were continued from that paper. Although started as a daily, only the first two numbers were so issued, and on Nov. 27, 1800, the title was changed to "The Museum and Washington and George-town Advertiser," with the intention of publishing a tri-weekly. The first eight issues were published on Nov. 18, 19, 24, 27, Dec. 2, 4, 9, 10 and from then on publication was tri-weekly. It was discontinued with the issue of Jan. 22, 1802, vol. 2, no. 10, after which the paper was sold to Rind and Prentiss, who merged it into the "Washington Federalist" of Georgetown.

A weekly issue for the country was also published, apparently beginning on Nov. 21, 1800. The earliest issue located is that of Jan. 16, 1801, vol. 1, no. 9, entitled "The Washington Museum." This consisted of the news pages of the issues of Jan. 14 and 16 printed on a double leaf, with a single leaf of the issue of Jan. 12 laid in. The numbering was continued independently of the regular tri-weekly issue, and the last number located is that of Jan. 11, 1802, vol. 1, no. 46 (error for 56).

Lib. Congress has Nov. 18, 1800–Jan. 22, 1802.
Am. Antiq. Soc. has Nov. 18, 1800; Jan. 7, 1801.
Md. Hist. Soc. has Dec. 9, 29, 1800; Jan. 16–Sept. 4, 21, Oct. 16–30, Nov. 9, 27–Dec. 11, 1801; Jan. 4, 1802, mostly weekly issues.
Annapolis, Md., Land Office, Chancery Papers, has Dec. 31, 1800.

[Georgetown] Museum; Georgetown Advertiser, 1809.

Weekly and semi-weekly. Established Jan. 21, 1809, with the title of "Museum; Georgetown Advertiser," by William Rind, Junior, "under the sanction of his father, late proprietor of the Washington Federalist." It was of small quarto size and was at first issued as a weekly, but was changed to a semi-weekly with the issue of Aug. 19, 1809. The issue for Oct. 10, 1809, vol. 1, no. 41, is the last located and was probably the last published. On the editorial page at the top of the first column the title is "Museum, and Georgetown Advertiser."

Lib. Congress has Jan. 21–July 11, Aug. 15–22, 29–Oct. 10, 1809.

[Georgetown] National Messenger, 1817–1820+.

Tri-weekly. A continuation of the "Messenger," but with the new name of "National Messenger" and a new series of numbering. The first issue is for Oct. 27, 1817, new series, vol. 1, no. 1, published by James C. Dunn & Co. [James C. Dunn and William A. Rind, Jr.], which firm name after four numbers was changed to Dunn & Rind, Jr. Rind withdrew from the firm, and beginning with the issue of Dec. 14, 1818, the paper was published by Dunn & Co. There is no publisher's name given from Aug. 21 to Dec. 4, 1820, after which the paper was published by James C. Dunn for the Proprietors. Continued after 1820.

Lib. Congress has Oct. 27, 1817–Dec. 31, 1818; Jan. 2, 1819–Dec. 29, 1820, fair.
Am. Antiq. Soc. has Mar. 9, May 29, July 15, Dec. 31, 1818; July 21, 1819; July 17, 1820.
Wis. Hist. Soc. has Dec. 4, 1818.

[Georgetown] Olio, 1802–1803.

Weekly. Established July 1, 1802, by Benjamin Parks & Co., with the title of "The Olio." It was of quarto size, each issue containing eight numbered pages. With the issue of Dec. 23, 1802, Parks became sole publisher. The last issue located is that of Aug. 4, 1803, vol. 2, no. 6. It was discontinued in September

1803, according to an advertisement signed by B. Parks in the first issue of the Georgetown "Columbian Repository" of Sept. 30, 1803.

Am. Antiq. Soc. has July 1, 1802–June 23, 1803.
N. Y. Pub. Lib. has Sept. 2, Nov. 4–25, Dec. 9–30, 1802; Jan. 6–Feb. 3, 17, 1803.
Conn. Hist. Soc. has Feb. 3–July 28, 1803.
Harvard has May 13–Aug. 4, 1803.
Lib. Congress has Oct. 21, 1802; Apr. 8, 15, 1803.

[Georgetown] Senator, 1813–1814.

In the "National Intelligencer" of Nov. 25, 1813, and in the "Federal Republican" of Nov. 26, 1813, Ebenezer H. Cummins announced that he would establish early in December 1813 a tri-weekly newspaper, of folio size, to be called "The Senator," and although containing intelligence and essays, to be devoted primarily to reporting the proceedings of the senate. Judging from advertisements in the "Federal Republican" of Jan. 6, 1814, and in the "National Intelligencer" of Mar. 1, 1814, publication was commenced as scheduled, although the editor refused to exchange newspapers and admitted that he had been able "only to exhibit a miniature specimen of the design as originally contemplated." The paper was referred to in the "Federal Republican" of Mar. 11, 1814, and apparently continued at least to April, 1814. No copies have been located.

[Georgetown] Spirit of 'Seventy-Six, 1811–1814.

Semi-weekly. A continuation, without change of numbering, of "The Spirit of 'Seventy-Six" published at Washington. Apparently the first Georgetown issue was that of Feb. 22, 1811, vol. 3, no. 47. This issue was without name of printer, but the issue of Mar. 1, 1811 was published by J. M. & J. B. Carter [John M. and James B. Carter] for the benefit of the widow and orphan children of Edward C. Stanard. Beginning with the issue of May 21, 1813, the imprint became Ebenezer H. Cummins, & John M. Carter. Cummins was ousted from the firm (see "Federal Republican," Nov. 17, 1813), and with the issue of Nov. 16, 1813, the paper was published by John M. & J[ames] B. Carter. It was suspended soon afterwards, but was revived in February 1814, by James B. Carter, who adopted the same title, but a new numbering. The issue of Mar. 4, 1814, vol. 1, no. 4, is the last located.

Boston Athenæum has Feb. 22, Mar. 1, 5, 12, 1811.
Am. Antiq. Soc. has Feb. 26, Apr. 16, May 3, 21, Aug. 2, Nov. 5, 29, 1811; Dec. 4, 18, 22, 1812; Jan. 1, 12, July 20, Oct. 1, 1813.
Lib. Congress has May 10, 1811; Aug. 11, 25, Sept. 8, Dec. 22, 1812; Apr. 30, May 18, 1813; Mar. 4, 1814.
Hist. Soc. Penn. has May 15, 19, 29, June 9–23, July 10–21, Aug. 21, Sept. 15–22, Oct. 2, Nov. 10, 13, 20–Dec. 11, 18–29, 1812; Jan. 1, 15–22, 29–Feb. 16,

Mar. 2–23, 30–Apr. 9, 16, May 11, 18, 25, June 1–8, 15, July 13, 16, 23, 27, Aug. 3, 10, 24, Sept. 7, Oct. 1, 5, Nov. 16, 1813.

N. Y. State Lib. has Sept. 8–15, 29–Oct. 9, 16, 23, 27, Nov. 24, 1812; Jan. 19, Apr. 23, 30, 1813.

Georgetown Univ. has Sept. 14, 28, Oct. 1, 1813.

[Georgetown] **Times, and Patowmack Packet,** 1789–1791.

Weekly. Established Feb. 12, 1789, judging from the date of the first issue located, that of Apr. 23, 1789, vol. 1, no. 11, published by Charles Fierer, with the title of "The Times, and Patowmack Packet." Evidently Fierer established the paper with Christian Kramer, since Kramer in the "Maryland Journal" of Apr. 14, 1789, dating his communication at George Town on April 12, advertised that he had "commenced Partnership with a certain Charles Fierer, in a Printing-Office in George-Town, Patowmack River" and that since Fierer had violated the articles of their agreement, no one should pay any money to said Fierer without a written order from Kramer. The advertisement at first spelled the name Frierer, which was corrected to Fierer with the issue of Apr. 24. Georgetown at this time was in Maryland, not having been transferred to the District of Columbia until January 1791. Between December 1789 and April 1790, the name of the publishers had changed to Charles Fierer and Thomas U. Fosdick. They continued as publishers as far as the last issue traced, that of July 6, 1791, no. 124.

Am. Antiq. Soc. has Oct. 14, Nov. 25, 1789; Apr. 21, May 12–26, June 23, 30, July 21–Aug. 18, Sept. 8–29, Oct. 13–27, Nov. 17, Dec. 22, 1790; Feb. 2, 16, Apr. 6, 1791.

Lib. Congress has Apr. 23, 1789.

Harvard has July 6, 1791.

[Georgetown] **Washington Federalist,** 1800–1809.

Tri-weekly, daily and semi-weekly. Established Sept. 25, 1800, as the "Washington Federalist," with the imprint "Printed by William Alexander Rind, for himself and John Stewart." Although the name of Washington was in the title, the office was located at Georgetown. At first a tri-weekly, the paper became a daily with the issue of Nov. 24, 1800, but omitting the Saturday issue. It so continued during the session of Congress until Feb. 24, 1801, then was published as a tri-weekly from Feb. 26 to Dec. 4, 1801, then as a daily during the session of Congress from Dec. 7, 1801 to May 5, 1802, then as a tri-weekly from May 7, 1802 to July 11, 1804, then as a semi-weekly from July 16, 1804 to Aug. 3, 1808, then as a tri-weekly from Aug. 9, 1808 to June 20, 1809. During most of this period, "Country papers" were also issued without the title heading.

Beginning with the issue of May 12, 1801 (no issues were printed from May 2 to May 12) the paper was published by William Alexander Rind; with the issue of Sept. 9, 1801, by Rind and Prentiss [W. A. Rind and Charles Prentiss]; with the issue of Mar. 23, 1802, by William A. Rind & Co.; and with the issue of June 1, 1803, by William A. Rind. The Wilmington, Del., "Mirror of the Times" of Jan. 14, 1804, referred to the "Washington Federalist" as "edited by Elias B. Caldwell, clerk of the supreme court of the United States." With the issue of Oct. 28, 1807, Jonathan S. Findlay assumed charge of the paper as editor, although Rind's name appeared as printer, and Georgetown appeared in the imprint. On Aug. 9, 1808, Jonathan S. Findlay's name appeared as sole publisher and a new series of numbering was adopted accompanying the whole numbering. The last issue was that of June 20, 1809, no. 2090, in which it was announced that the paper had been sold to Edgar Patterson, who proposed publishing "The American Federalist" on July 1. In its stead he published "The Independent American," which see.

 Am. Antiq. Soc. has Sept. 25, 30, Oct. 7–Dec. 31, 1800; Jan. 1–Mar. 3, Apr. 18, May 12, 16–Dec. 31, 1801; Jan. 1–May 7, Sept. 13, Nov. 12, Dec. 10–31, 1802; Jan. 3–10, 14, 17, Feb. 2, 4, 11, 16, 23, Mar. 14, 16, Oct. 19–Nov. 25, 30–Dec. 5, 9, 12, 14, 19–23, 28, 30, 1803; Jan. 2–Mar. 26, Apr. 9, 16, 18, 23, May 7, 9, June 11, 13, Aug. 4, 15, 18, 29–Sept. 8, 15–22, 29, Oct. 13, 27, Nov. 14–24, Dec. 8, 29, 1804; Feb. 13, Mar. 16, May 18, June 12, 19, 26, 29, July 6, Nov. 6, Dec. 4, 7, 14–28, 1805; Jan. 1–Apr. 19, 1806; Oct. 28, 1807–June 20, 1809, of the regular issue. Also May 12–Oct. 1, Dec. 17, 22, 1802; Jan. 3–Mar. 2, 9, 16, 23, Apr. 4, 8, 13, 18, Aug. 10, 31, Sept. 7, 14, 19, 1803; Jan. 20, 23, Feb. 3, 22–Apr. 30, May 14–July 9, Aug. 11, Oct. 3, 10, 24, Nov. 3, 10, Dec. 8, 15, 24, 1804; Jan. 5–June 22, 1805, fair, of country issues.

 Lib. Congress has Oct. 30, 1800–Sept. 8, 1804, fair; Sept. 12, 15, 26, Oct. 13–20, Nov. 7, 17, 28, 1804; Jan. 12, 30, Feb. 20–27, Mar. 2, 13, Apr. 10, May 15, 22–29, June 5, 12, Sept. 3, 11, 14, Nov. 21, 23, Dec. 18, 28, 1805; Mar. 5, 1806; Apr. 8, 22, July 18, 29, Oct. 31, Dec. 2–31, 1807; Jan. 2, 1808–Mar. 2, 1809, fair; Mar. 21, 1809, of regular issues. Also Dec. 31, 1800; Jan. 2–12, 22, 26, Feb. 6, 16–Mar. 3, 1801; Mar. 10, May 21, 28, June 16, July 21, Aug. 4, 11, 18, 25, Sept. 1, 15, Oct. 6, 20, Nov. 26, Dec. 15, 1802; Jan. 3, 21, 26, 28, Feb. 4, 9, 22, 1803; Feb. 24, 29, 1804; Apr. 9, June 11, July 9, 1808, of country issues.

 N. Y. Hist. Soc. has Oct. 23, Nov. 28, Dec. 10, 17, 19, 22, 23, 31, 1800; Jan. 1–June 28, Sept. 3–Dec. 31, 1801, fair; Jan. 1, 1802–Oct. 20, 1804, fair; Jan. 5–Mar. 30, Apr. 20, 24, Nov. 6, 23, 30, Dec. 18–28, 1805; Jan. 1, 4, 11–18, 25–Feb. 19, 1806; Apr. 2, 21, 1808; mostly regular issues.

 Wis. Hist. Soc. has Oct. 30, 1800–Oct. 13, 1802, fair; Dec. 13–24, 29, 31, 1808.

 Harvard has Oct. 7, 21, Nov. 28, Dec. 24, 31, 1800; Jan. 2, 6, 9, 13, 16, 21, 22, Feb. 3–9, 12, 17–28, Mar. 10, 26, Apr. 1, 7, 18, 29, May 14, 16, 21, June 1, 5–10, 17–July 10, 15–Aug. 3, 10, 17, 19, 24–28, Sept. 2, 9–Oct. 7, 12–16, 21–Nov. 9, 13–23, Dec. 7, 12–15, 1801; Mar. 2, 9, May 10, June 18, Oct. 20, 29, 1802; Mar. 14, 1803; Oct. 13, 1804; regular issues. Also Mar. 1, Apr. 16,

May 31, June 4, July 9, Oct. 27, Nov. 3, 5, Dec. 3, 13, 29, 1802; Mar. 18, June 8, 15, 17, July 8, Oct. 28, Nov. 7, 16, 30, Dec. 2, 1803; Jan. 13, 1804; July 16, Sept. 24, 1806; country issues.

Yale has Sept. 28, 1801–Sept. 24, 1802; Mar. 7, 1808; Jan. 31, Feb. 16, 1809; regular issues.

Univ. of Mich. (Clements) has Nov. 28, 1800; Jan. 8–Mar. 31, fair, May 1–5, 7, 10, July 14, Sept. 8, 1802; Oct. 31, Dec. 5–31, 1807; Jan. 3–Mar. 2, 1809.

Boston Athenæum has Jan. 3–June 20, 1809.

Duke Univ. has Sept. 23, Nov. 16, Dec. 2, 1801–Apr. 2, 1802, fair; Dec. 23, 1807; Jan. 6, Mar. 16, 1808.

Univ. of Chicago has July 19, 1802; Mar. 7–Nov. 28, 1803, fair; Jan. 9–Dec. 1, 1804, scattering, regular issues; Dec. 13, 1802–Dec. 15, 1804, scattering, country issues.

Mass. Hist. Soc. has Dec. 7–19, 1801; Feb. 2, 1803; Feb. 19, 1806; Apr. 14, 1808; Mar. 18, 1809.

Boston Pub. Lib. has May 13, 1803; Nov. 10–29, 1808; Feb. 18, 1809.

Md. Hist. Soc. has July 22, 24, Aug. 12, 1801.

Hist. Soc. Penn. has Mar. 5, 1801.

Univ. of Rochester has Nov. 8, 1808.

[Georgetown] **Washington Museum,** see **Museum,** 1800–1802.

Georgetown Weekly Ledger, 1790–1793.

Weekly. Established Apr. 17, 1790, by M. Day and W. Hancock [probably Matthias Day and William Hancock], for the Proprietor, with the title of "The George-Town Weekly Ledger." In August or September 1791, Alexander Doyle became the publisher and continued in that capacity until the spring of 1792, when he was succeeded by James Doyle. The last issue located is that of Oct. 5, 1793, vol. 4, no. 26.

Am. Antiq. Soc. has May 1, 15, June 5, 26, July 10, Aug. 14, Sept. 4, 11, Dec. 11, 1790; Mar. 19, Apr. 9, May 14, June 18, 25, with supplements, Aug. 6, 1791; Jan. 28, Feb. 4, Mar. 31, Dec. 15, 1792; Aug. 24, 1793.

Harvard has June 18–July 2, 23, Sept. 17, Oct. 1, Nov. 26, 1791.

Lib. Congress has Feb. 18, Mar. 31, Sept. 22, 1792; Feb. 16, Oct. 5, 1793.

Newton B. Collinson, Edgewater, Md., has Sept. 10, 1791.

Wis. Hist. Soc. has July 28, 1792.

Washington Advertiser, 1796.

Semi-weekly. Established with the title of "The Washington Advertiser," Mar. 9, 1796, by John Crocker & Co., who took over the establishment of the "Impartial Observer," continuing its advertisements. In May, 1796, John Crocker assumed the sole proprietorship. The last issue located is that of May 11, 1796.

vol. 1, no. 19. The paper was of quarto size, paged, and eight pages to the issue.

Harvard has Mar. 12, 16, 23, 26, Apr. 9–20, 27, May 7, 11, 1796.
Am. Antiq. Soc. has Mar. 9, 23, 1796.

Washington Advertiser, 1800.

Daily and tri-weekly. Established Nov. 20, 1800, by Brown & Snowden [Matthew Brown and Samuel Snowden], with the title of "Washington Advertiser." The paper was announced in the Georgetown "Centinel of Liberty" of July 22, 1800, and published its prospectus on Aug. 12, 1800. The first issue, of quarto size, is the only one located and probably the only one published. It announced that it would be published daily during the sessions of Congress, and tri-weekly during the recess. Lack of encouragement forced the editors to discontinue publication in Washington and on Nov. 24, 1800, the office was removed to Alexandria (see "Washington Federalist" for Nov. 25, 1800) where, on Dec. 8, 1800, S. Snowden & Co. established the "Alexandria Advertiser," using the type and style of set-up that had been intended for the "Washington Advertiser."

Am. Antiq. Soc. has Nov. 20, 1800.
Boston Pub. Lib. has Nov. 20, 1800.

[Washington] American Literary Advertiser, 1802–1804.

Weekly. Established Mar. 27, 1802, by the Franklin Press, with the title of "American Literary Advertiser." Within a few weeks the names of the publishers were given as James Lyon and Richard Dinmore. About the first of December 1802, the paper was removed from Washington to Alexandria, where the imprint was given merely "District of Columbia." The last issue located is that of Mar. 20, 1804, vol. 3, no. 104. The Am. Antiq. Soc. has a "Prospectus" dated May 7, 1802.

Am. Antiq. Soc. has Mar. 27, June 18, Oct. 1, 1802; Feb. 18, June 25, July 29–Aug. 19, Sept. 2, 9, 1803; Prospectus May 7, 1802.
Harvard has Sept. 24–Oct. 8, Nov. 11, 18, Dec. 16, 24, 1802; Jan. 7–28, Feb. 11, Mar. 23–Apr. 8, 29, May 6, 27, June 10, 25, July 1, 29, Sept. 2, 16, 23, 1803.
Lib. Congress has June 10, 1803; Mar. 20, 1804.

[Washington] Apollo, 1802.

Established May 1, 1802, by W. Duane & Son [William and William J. Duane], with the title of "The Apollo." It was announced that the paper would be published daily or tri-weekly as occasion might require, and that the second number would appear as soon as 500 subscribers were found. The first number is the only one that has been traced, and was undoubtedly the only one issued.

Am. Antiq. Soc. has May 1, 1802.

[Washington] **Atlantic World,** 1807.

Weekly. Established Jan. 19, 1807, by John Wood, with the title of "Atlantic World." The prospectus announced that the paper would be published by John Wood, late editor of the "Western World of Kentucky." The second issue did not appear until Feb. 3 and was published by John Wood and Thomas W. White, as was also the issue of Feb. 10. The issues of Mar. 24 and 31, vol. 1, no. 10, were published by John Wood & Jehiel Crossfield, and are the last located. The Newark "Centinel of Freedom" of June 9, 1807, stated that John Wood, editor of the Atlantic World, had absconded, leaving his partner in the lurch, and that the paper had been discontinued.

Lib. Congress has Jan. 19, Mar. 24, 1807.
Am. Antiq. Soc. has Feb. 3, 10, Mar. 24, 31, 1807.

Washington City Gazette, 1800.

Charles Cist, under date of July 21, 1800, sent out a printed circular to Postmasters throughout the country, beginning: "Herewith you will receive a specimen of the Washington City Gazette, which I propose to publish after the 1st of October next." He requested the Postmasters to obtain subscribers and to send the lists soon, "that their papers may be duly forwarded." No copies of this paper have been located. The American Antiquarian Society has a copy of the printed circular.

Washington City Gazette, 1814.

Tri-weekly and weekly. Established Jan. 5, 1814, by William Elliot as a tri-weekly, judging from an advertisement in the "National Intelligencer" of Jan. 4, 1814, although the earliest issue located is that of Jan. 17, 1814, vol. 1, no. 5, entitled "Washington City Gazette." George Watterston was editor of the paper, according to an account which he wrote in later years (see his "Picture of Washington," 1840, p. 77). Elliot took Daniel Rapine into partnership and beginning with the issue of either Feb. 25 or Feb. 28, 1814, the paper was published by William Elliot & Co. With the issue of Nov. 5, 1814, Elliot again became sole proprietor, changing the paper to a weekly and reducing it in size to a quarto of eight pages, with pagination. In the issue of Dec. 17, 1814, vol. 1, no. 138, the last located, the publisher announced that he intended to engage in another line of business and that the paper was for sale.

Am. Antiq. Soc. has Jan. 17–28, Feb. 2, 9, 18–23, 28, Mar. 4, 11–16, 28, 30, Apr. 6–11, 15, 18, 25, 29–May 4, 13, 16, 23, 29, June 6, 13, 15, 20–24, 29,

July 1, 6–11, 15–22, 27, Aug. 3, 8, 12, 17, Sept. 2, Nov. 5, 12, Dec. 10, 17, 1814.

Cincinnati Pub. Lib. has Mar. 7, May 2, 16, 18, 1814.

[Washington] City of Washington Gazette, 1817–1820+.

Daily and tri-weekly. Established Oct. 27, 1817, according to an announcement in the "Washington City Weekly Gazette" of Oct. 18, 1817. Entitled "City of Washington Gazette," it was published by Jonathan Elliot as a continuation of his "Washington City Weekly Gazette," without change of numbering, although a "new series" was commenced. Published as a daily and also a tri-weekly "for the country," and continued until after 1820.

Lib. Congress has Dec. 4, 1817–Dec. 30, 1820, of daily, with only a few issues missing. Also Nov. 24, Dec. 3, 1817; Jan. 16, June 22, July 29, Aug. 31, 1818; Sept. 2, 1818–Dec. 4, 1820, fair, of country issues.

N. Y. Hist. Soc. has Nov. 12, 20, 21, Dec. 4–10, 16, 1817; Jan. 3, 1818–Dec. 29, 1819; May 8, Dec. 1, 1820, of daily.

Am. Antiq. Soc. has Jan. 31, Feb. 19, 20, Mar. 28, 30, Apr. 2, July 6, 16, 27, 31, Aug. 26, 29, Sept. 26, Oct. 12, 14, 31, 1818; Feb. 2, 20, May 6, 25, June 1, 8, Aug. 14, 21, 28, Sept. 21, 1819; Jan. 1–Dec. 30, 1820, fair, of daily. Also Nov. 19, 26, 1817; Nov. 6, Dec. 19, 1818; May 17, 26, 31, June 4, 7, Aug. 4, 26, Oct. 8, 1819; Jan. 5, 10, 12, Feb. 9, 16, 18, Mar. 6, 22, 27, Apr. 14–21, 28, May 1–26, June 5, 26, July 24–Aug. 9, 16, 23, 25, Sept. 6, 13–27, Oct. 2, 9, 13, 16, Nov. 15, 17, 22, 27, Dec. 6, 8, 15–22, 29, 1820, of country issues.

N. Y. Pub. Lib. has Apr. 7, Dec. 8, 17, 22, 31, 1819; Jan. 10–14, 19, 21, 26, Feb. 7–11, 21, July 12, Dec. 27, 1820, of country issues.

Princeton has Feb. 4, 10, 1819; Mar. 23, 28, 29, Apr. 19, 27, May 6, 8, 23, 24, June 1–3, 1820.

Univ. of Mich. (Clements) has May 26, June 7, 1819; Jan. 10, 17, 20, Apr. 28, June 2, 24, July 28, Aug. 8, Sept. 11, 1820, of daily.

Wis. Hist. Soc. has Dec. 3, 1818.

Detroit Pub. Lib. has Feb. 18, 1820.

Duke Univ. has June 30, 1820.

N. Y. State Lib. has Nov. 13, 1820.

Washington City Weekly Gazette, 1815–1817.

Weekly. Established Nov. 25, 1815, by Jonathan Elliot, with the title of "Washington City Weekly Gazette." It was of quarto size and paged. Discontinued with the issue of Oct. 18, 1817, no. 100, when it was stated that on Oct. 27, it would be published in folio size as a tri-weekly under the name of the "City of Washington Gazette," which see.

Lib. Congress has Nov. 25, 1815–Oct. 18, 1817.
N. Y. Pub. Lib. has Nov. 25–Dec. 30, 1815; Jan. 6–20, Feb. 3–Apr. 20, May 4–Aug. 31, Oct. 19–Nov. 9, Dec. 14–28, 1816; Jan. 4–25, Mar. 1, 8, Apr. 5–June 28, July 19–Aug. 16, 30–Sept. 20, Oct. 18, 1817.
Am. Antiq. Soc. has Feb. 10, Mar. 2, 16, Apr. 20, May 11, 18, 1816; Jan. 4, Mar. 1, Apr. 5, 19, 26–May 10, 24–June 14, July 26, Aug. 9, 1817.
Duke Univ. has June 15, 1816.

[Washington] **Daily National Intelligencer,** 1813–1820+.

Daily. Established Jan. 1, 1813, as a daily, by Gales & Seaton [Joseph Gales, Jr., and William W. Seaton], with the title of "Daily National Intelligencer." Continued by this firm, together with their tri-weekly edition, until after 1820. For the earlier tri-weekly paper, see "National Intelligencer."

There are many scattering files and issues in various libraries, but only the longer files are here listed. Most libraries have the tri-weekly issue, which was mailed generally throughout the country.

Amer. Antiq. Soc., Lib. Congress, Hist. Soc. Penn., Cornell Univ., and Washington, D. C., Pub. Lib. have Jan. 1, 1813–Dec. 30, 1820.
Western Reserve Hist. Soc. has May 11–Dec. 31, 1813; July 2–Dec. 31, 1814, fair; Jan. 2, 1815–Dec. 30, 1820.
Johns Hopkins Univ. has Jan. 5, 1814–Dec. 30, 1815; Jan. 1, 1817–Dec. 31, 1819.
N. Y. Pub. Lib. has Mar. 5–Apr. 8, 11–16, July 2, 1814; Jan. 4, 1815–Dec. 28, 1820, fair.
Mass. Hist. Soc. has Dec. 4, 1813; Jan. 2, 1815–Dec. 30, 1820.
Univ. of Texas has Jan. 3, 1815–Dec. 27, 1816, fair; Jan. 7–Nov. 13, 1818; Jan. 2, 1819–Oct. 21, 1820.
Duke Univ. has Jan. 3–Dec. 29, 1815; Jan. 1–31, Mar. 1–31, May 1–June 30, Nov. 21–Dec. 31, 1818; Jan. 1–Dec. 31, 1819; Feb. 24–Dec. 31, 1820.
Wis. Hist. Soc. has July 1–Dec. 31, 1814; Jan. 25–Dec. 30, 1815; Jan. 1–Dec. 31, 1817; Jan. 1, 1819–Dec. 30, 1820.
N. Y. Hist. Soc. has Feb. 2–Oct. 27, 1813; Jan. 15, 1818–Mar. 19, 1819, fair.
Univ. of Chicago has Dec. 1, 1817–Nov. 20, 1818, fair; July 1–Dec. 29, 1819, fair.
Filson Club, Louisville, has Nov. 26, 1818–Sept. 19, 1820, fair.
Many libraries have scattering issues.

Washington Expositor, 1807–1809.

Weekly. Established by Richard Dinmore on Nov. 14, 1807, judging from the date of the first issue located, that of Nov. 21, 1807, vol. 1, no. 2. It was of folio size, and its full title was the "Washington Expositor, and Weekly Register." This form of publication was soon discontinued, and on Jan. 2, 1808, a new paper was published by Dinmore & Cooper [Richard Dinmore and William Cooper], with new numbering and with the shortened title of "Washington Expositor." It was of quarto size, paged and provided with an index. The last issue located is that of Jan. 6, 1809, vol. 1, no. 54, evidently the last published.

N. Y. State Lib. has Nov. 21, 28, Dec. 4, 1807; Jan. 2, 16, Mar. 26, Apr. 2, 1808.
Am. Antiq. Soc., Lib. Congress and Wis. Hist. Soc. have Jan. 2, 1808–Jan. 6, 1809.
N. Y. Hist. Soc. has Dec. 4, 1807.

Washington Federalist, see [Georgetown] **Washington Federalist.**

Washington Gazette, 1796–1798.

Semi-weekly and weekly. Established June 15, 1796, by Benjamin More, with the title of "The Washington Gazette." It was first published as a semi-weekly, but beginning with the issue of Sept. 16, 1797, it became a weekly. The issue of July 26, 1797, announced that publication would not proceed until it was attended by some profit to the publisher, and the next number appeared on Sept. 16, 1797. The last issue located is that of Mar. 24, 1798, vol. 2, no. 35, upon which date the editor announced, "I shall not be able to continue the publication of the Washington Gazette except some friend should lend a helping hand." This was undoubtedly the last issue.

Lib. Congress has June 15, 1796–Dec. 23, 1797; Jan. 13–27, Feb. 10, 17, Mar. 3–24, 1798.
Am. Antiq. Soc. has June 18, 1796–Mar. 24, 1798.
Harvard has July 6, 9, 16, 20, 27–Sept. 3, 10, 17, 21, Oct. 1–29, Nov. 9, 16, Dec. 3–14, 21, 24, 31, 1796; Jan. 4, 11, 14, 21–Feb. 25, Mar. 4–11, 18–Apr. 22, 29, June 24, July 1–12, Sept. 16, 30–Oct. 14, Nov. 11, 18, Dec. 2, 1797; Jan. 13, Mar. 3, 10, 1798.
Phil. Lib. Co. has June 11, 22, 25, July 6, 9, Aug. 3, 13, 1796.
N. Y. Pub. Lib. has June 22, 25, July 6, 13, 16, Oct. 26, 1796; Feb. 27, 1797.
Univ. of Mich. (Clements) has Mar. 24, 1798.

[Washington] Impartial Observer, 1795–1796.

Weekly and semi-weekly. Established May 22, 1795, by T[homas] Wilson under the name of the "Impartial Observer, and Washington Advertiser," judging from the date of the earliest issue located, that of June 12, 1795, vol. 1, no. 4. The paper was of quarto size, paged and with eight pages to an issue. On September 14, 1795, publication became semi-weekly. The last issue located is that of Oct. 1, 1795, vol. 1, no. 23. ·Thomas Wilson died Feb. 22, 1796, after which John Crocker & Co. took over the paper, continued the advertisements and changed the title to "The Washington Advertiser," which see.

Harvard has June 19, July 17, 31, Aug. 7, 14, Sept. 5, Oct. 1, 1795.

Wis. Hist. Soc. has June 12, Aug. 21, Sept. 14, 1795.
Am. Antiq. Soc. has June 26, July 17, Aug. 14, 1795.
Lib. Congress has July 3, 1795.

[Washington] Monitor, 1808–1809.

Tri-weekly. This succeeded "Colvin's Weekly Register," a sixteen page octavo magazine, which was published from Jan. 16 to Apr. 30, 1808. In the issue of Apr. 30, J. B. Colvin announced that this was his last issue as a magazine and that thenceforth a tri-weekly publication would appear, "in the shape of a newspaper." On May 12, 1808, J[ohn] B. Colvin established a tri-weekly paper, entitled "The Monitor." It was at first a small folio, but with the issue of Nov. 5, 1808, was enlarged to large folio. Beginning with the issue of Mar. 4, 1809, the plan of the paper was changed, the size was reduced to small folio, and a new numbering was adopted with pagination. The tri-weekly publication was not always adhered to. The last issue located is that of June 20, 1809, vol. 1, page 167. Colvin, in an advertisement dated Aug. 3, 1809, in the "National Intelligencer" of Aug. 4, stated that he had been compelled to relinquish his establishment through lack of subscriptions and that he would dispose of his press and types.

Am. Antiq. Soc. has May 12, 1808–June 20, 1809, nearly complete.
Harvard has May 14, 24–28, June 4, 7, 11–16, 21, July 9, 12, 26–Aug. 16, 23–Sept. 1, 6, 17–29, Oct. 4, 8, 11, 20, 22, 27–Nov. 1, 15–24, Dec. 3–8, 13, 15, 24, 1808; Apr. 22, 1809.
Lib. Congress has May 19, 31, June 16, July 2, 9, 14, 19, 21, 28, Aug. 2, 4, 16, 23, 26, Sept. 1, 6, 17–27, Oct. 1–6, 11, 15, 20, 22, 29, Nov. 1, 10, Dec. 3, 8, 13–31, 1808; Jan. 3–14, 19, 24, Feb. 9, 23, 25, Mar. 11, 14, 23, Apr. 22, May 11, 16, 18, 23–27, June 10, 1809.
N. Y. State Lib. has June 4, 11, 16, July 2, Sept. 17, 27, Oct. 1, 13, 15, 20, 22, Nov. 12, 19, Dec. 13, 1808; Jan. 10, 12, 1809.
Wis. Hist. Soc. has May 31, 1808; Apr. 25, May 30, June 8, 1809.
N. Y. Hist. Soc. has Nov. 24, 29–Dec. 20, 27, 31, 1809.
Duke Univ. has June 28, 1808.
Univ. of Mich. (Clements) has Oct. 11, 1808.
Del. Hist. Soc. has Feb. 4–May 6, 1809.
Conn. Hist. Soc. has Mar. 16–June 15, 1809.

Washington Museum, see [Georgetown] Museum.

[Washington] National Intelligencer, 1800–1820+.

Tri-weekly and semi-weekly. Established Oct. 31, 1800, by Samuel Harrison Smith, under the title of the "National Intelligencer and Washington Advertiser." In the issue of May 21, 1810, it was stated that the paper was conducted by Samuel H. Smith and Joseph Gales, Jun., and printed by Smith. Smith soon retired, and beginning with the issue of Sept. 3, 1810, the paper was published by Joseph Gales, Jun. Beginning with the issue of Nov. 27, 1810, the title was shortened to the "National Intelligencer." On Oct. 31, 1812, it was announced that the editor had taken into partnership Mr. William W. Seaton, "late joint conductor, with Mr. Joseph Gales, Sen'r, of the Raleigh Register," and with the issue of Nov. 3, 1812, the firm name became Gales & Seaton. When the "Daily National Intelligencer" (q. v.) was started on Jan. 1, 1813, the tri-weekly was continued without change of numbering, as a paper "for the country." On Mar. 17, 1819, it was announced that the paper would be published three times a week during sessions of Congress and twice a week in recess. It was therefore a semi-weekly from Mar. 17 to Mar. 20, 1819; a semi-weekly from Mar. 23 to May 8, 1819; a semi-weekly from May 12 to Nov. 13, 1819; a tri-weekly from Nov. 16, 1819, to Aug. 12, 1820; a semi-weekly from Aug. 16, 1820, to Nov. 11, 1820; and a tri-weekly from Nov. 14, 1820, to after the close of the year. Gales & Seaton continued the paper until after 1820.

There are many scattering sets of the tri-weekly "National Intelligencer," but only the longer files are here listed. Almost every large library in the country has scattering issues, and a complete check-list would require a volume in itself. For the daily publication see under "Daily National Intelligencer."

Am. Antiq. Soc. and Lib. Congress have Oct. 31, 1800–Dec. 30, 1820.
Va. State Lib. has Oct. 31, 1800–Aug. 20, 1802; Dec. 3, 1802–Dec. 30, 1820.
Western Reserve Hist. Soc. has Oct. 31, 1800–Oct. 31, 1804; Jan. 2, 1805–Dec. 30, 1806, fair; Jan. 2, 1807–Dec. 31, 1814; Jan. 3–Dec. 30, 1815, fair; Jan. 2, 1816–Dec. 30, 1820.
Hist. Soc. Penn. has Oct. 31, 1800–Nov. 11, 1801; Apr. 7, 1802–Dec. 30, 1820.
Univ. of Mich. (Clements) has Oct. 31, Nov. 21–26, Dec. 3–10, 17, 22, 26–31, 1800; Jan. 5, 1801–Dec. 31, 1802, fair; Jan. 5, 1803–Dec. 30, 1805; Jan. 3, 1806–Dec. 29, 1809, fair; Jan. 1, 1810–Dec. 30, 1820.
Boston Athenæum has Nov. 28, 1800–Dec. 31, 1804; Jan. 2, 1807–Dec. 30, 1820.
Boston Pub. Lib. has Nov. 24, 1800–Dec. 30, 1801, scattering file; Jan. 6, 1802–Nov. 23, 1808, fair; Jan. 2, 1809–Dec. 30, 1820.
Essex Inst. has Oct. 1803–Dec. 30, 1820.
Harvard has Jan. 4, 1802–Dec. 28, 1808; Jan. 29, 1811–Dec. 20, 1820.
N. Y. Hist. Soc. has Mar. 1, 1802–Dec. 28, 1820, fair, with 1812, 1815, and 1817 somewhat incomplete.
Washington, D. C. Pub. Lib. has Nov. 5, 1800–Oct. 30, 1813.
Wis. Hist. Soc. has Jan. 2, 1804–Oct. 29, 1806; Jan. 2, 1807–Nov. 4, 1808; Nov. 1, 1809–Dec. 30, 1813; Sept. 6, 1814–Dec. 30, 1820.
Mass. Hist. Soc. has Jan. 1, 1806–Dec. 31, 1816; Jan. 25, 1817–Dec. 30, 1820, fair.
Md. State Lib. has Dec. 8, 1806–Nov. 29, 1817; Jan. 2, 1819–Dec. 30, 1820.
Tenn. Hist. Soc. has Oct. 31, 1800–July 29, 1805, fair; Apr. 23–May 14, 1806;

DISTRICT OF COLUMBIA 105

Oct. 15, 1806–Apr. 18, 1808, fair; July 20, 1811; Nov. 21, 1812–June 1, 1814; Nov. 1, 1814–Mar. 29, 1817, fair; Dec. 4, 1817–Dec. 30, 1820, fair.
Duke Univ. has Jan. 9–Oct. 30, 1801; Nov. 2, 1807–Dec. 30, 1808; Dec. 1, 1809–July 2, 1810; Mar. 5, 1811–Nov. 4, 1813, fair; Jan. 1, 1814–Dec. 30, 1820, fair.
Conn. Hist. Soc. has Dec. 9, 1801–June 30, 1803; Mar. 14–July 29, 1808; Dec. 26, 1808–Dec. 30, 1820.
Yale has Nov. 5, 1802–Oct. 31, 1803; Jan. 5–Nov. 30, 1807; Nov. 6, 1811–Oct. 31, 1812; Jan. 1, 1814–Dec. 30, 1820.
N. Y. Pub. Lib. has Nov. 9, 1804–Nov. 8, 1809; Jan. 1, 1810–Dec. 30, 1815; Dec. 4, 1817–Dec. 30, 1819, scattering file; Jan. 1–Dec. 30, 1820, fair.
Dartmouth has Nov. 23, 1804–Dec. 5, 1805; Jan. 12–June 5, Oct. 27–Dec. 30, 1807; Jan. 20–Dec. 16, 1808, scattering; Jan. 6, 9, 11, June 28, Nov. 29, Dec. 30, 1809; Jan. 1, 1810–Dec. 31, 1811, fair; Jan. 2–Dec. 29, 1812; Mar. 11, 1813–Dec. 30, 1820.
Chicago Hist. Soc. has Nov. 1, 1805–Jan. 30, 1807; Nov. 23, 1808–Nov. 21, 1812; Feb. 29, 1816–Dec. 30, 1820.
Univ. of Kansas has Nov. 14, 1808–Oct. 30, 1809; Nov. 2, 1810–Dec. 30, 1820.
Phil. Lib. Co. has Nov. 22, 1809–Dec. 30, 1820.
N. J. State Lib. has Nov. 25, 1801–Dec. 29, 1810.
Univ. of Va. has Sept. 5–Dec. 30, 1803, fair; Jan. 2, 1804–Dec. 30, 1805; Jan. 1–Oct. 31, 1806, fair; Nov. 6, 1807–Apr. 15, 1808, fair; Apr. 25, 1808–Oct. 31, 1810; Nov. 2, 1811–Nov. 4, 1813, fair; Dec. 25, 1819–Dec. 30, 1820, fair.
Univ. of Chicago has Oct. 31, 1800–Nov. 11, 1801, fair; Jan. 4, 1802–Jan. 6, 1806, scattering file; Dec. 19, 1808–Dec. 29, 1809, scattering file; Jan. 1, 1810–Dec. 31, 1817, fair; Jan. 2, 1819–Dec. 30, 1820.
Md. Hist. Soc. has Jan. 2, 1809–Oct. 31, 1811; July 2, 1812–Dec. 30, 1813; Jan. 1–Dec. 30, 1820.
Howard-Tilton Lib., New Orleans, has Jan. 2, 1812–Dec. 28, 1820.
Univ. of Texas has Jan. 2, 1812–Dec. 21, 1820.
Kenyon Coll. Lib., Gambier, Ohio, has Mar. 22, 1814–July 18, 1820.
Johns Hopkins Univ. has Oct. 23, 1807–June 30, 1812.
N. J. Hist. Soc. has Jan. 4, 1808–Nov. 4, 1813.
N. Y. State Lib. has Oct. 1, 1804–Dec. 30, 1805; Nov. 13, 1807–Oct. 31, 1810; Sept. 3, 1811–Dec. 31, 1812, fair; Nov. 2, 1813–Oct. 25, 1814; June 3–Oct. 30, 1817, fair; Jan. 1–Dec. 30, 1820, fair.
Brown Univ. has Dec. 1, 1810–Dec. 31, 1814, fair; Jan. 2, 1817–Dec. 30, 1820.
Mo. Hist. Soc., St. Louis, has Nov. 28, 1811–Nov. 14, 1812; Feb. 28, 1815–Dec. 30, 1819.
Bath, Me., Patten Lib., has May 27, 1813–Nov. 17, 1818; Jan. 1, 1819–Dec. 30, 1820.
Ohio Hist. & Phil. Soc. has Apr. 10–Nov. 6, 1813, fair; Jan. 1, 1814–May 2, 1815, fair; Oct. 24, 1815–Sept. 3, 1816, fair; Jan. 1–Dec. 30, 1820.

St. Louis Univ. has Aug. 12–Nov. 11, 1801; Jan. 4–Dec. 28, 1802.
La. State Univ. has July 28, 1802–Dec. 11, 1805; Jan. 1–Dec. 27, 1810.
Peabody Coll., Nashville, Tenn., has Oct. 21, 1803–Nov. 19, 1806; Feb. 3, 1807–Sept. 26, 1808, fair.
Univ. of Ga. has Jan. 6–June 3, Aug. 4–Dec. 29, 1805, fair; Jan. 2–Sept. 4, 1807, scattering file; Feb. 12, 1810–Dec. 28, 1815, fair; Jan. 7–Dec. 25, 1817, fair.
Iowa State Dep't of History has Dec. 2, 1808–Jan. 8, 1810.
Cincinnati Pub. Lib. has July 31, 1813–July 27, 1815; Jan. 1–Dec. 31, 1818.
Alexandria, Va., Lib. has Jan. 3–Dec. 30, 1815; Jan. 1, 1818–Sept. 8, 1819.
Many libraries have scattering issues, found in other files.

[Washington] National Intelligencer, daily, see [Washington] Daily National Intelligencer.

[Washington] Spirit of 'Seventy-Six, 1809–1811.

Semi-weekly. A continuation, without change of numbering, of the paper of this name which had been established at Richmond, Sept. 13, 1808. It was removed to Washington toward the end of 1809, as the last located Richmond issue is Nov. 4, 1809, vol. 2, no. 16, and the first located Washington issue is Dec. 29, 1809, vol. 2, no. 24, published by Edward C. Stanard, with the title of "The Spirit of 'Seventy-Six." The publisher advertised in the "National Intelligencer" of Nov. 29, 1809, that the printing apparatus had at length arrived from Richmond, and that publication would begin at Washington within four days. It probably did begin on December 5. Stanard died Dec. 8, 1810, but the issues of Dec. 11–25 continue his name in the imprint. That of Dec. 28 omits it and states that communications should be sent to John M. Carter at his office in Georgetown. The issue of Feb. 15, 1811, vol. 3, no. 45, is the last located issue published at Washington, and the paper was discontinued there with either this or the succeeding issue. For further issues, see under Georgetown.

N. Y. Hist. Soc. has Jan. 26–Dec. 28, 1810.
Boston Athenæum has Dec. 29, 1809; Jan. 2, 26, June 12, 15, July 17–Aug. 7, 14–Sept. 14, 21, 25, Oct. 2, 5, 12–23, 30, Nov. 2, 9–Dec. 18, 25, 28, 1810; Jan. 1, 4, 15, 18, 25–Feb. 5, 12, 15, 1811.
Am. Antiq. Soc. has Jan. 12, 16, 26, Mar. 2, May 29, Aug. 14, 17, 28, Oct. 23, 1810.
Lib. Congress has Apr. 6, June 12, 19, 29, July 13, Sept. 28, 1810.

[Washington] Universal Gazette, 1800–1814.

Weekly. A continuation, without change of numbering, of "The Universal Gazette" of Philadelphia. The last issue published at Philadelphia was for

DISTRICT OF COLUMBIA 107

Sept. 11, 1800, vol. 2, no. 148, and the first at Washington was for Nov. 6, 1800, vol. 2, no. 149, entitled "The Universal Gazette." This paper, published by Samuel Harrison Smith, was virtually a weekly edition of the "National Intelligencer," and was subject to the same editorial changes. With the issue of Sept. 6, 1810, the name of Joseph Gales, Jun., replaced that of Smith in the imprint, and the title was shortened to "Universal Gazette"; and with the issue of Nov. 6, 1812, the firm name became Gales & Seaton. The paper was discontinued with the issue of May 13, 1814, vol. 11, no. 848.

Am. Antiq. Soc. has Nov. 6–Dec. 24, 1800; Feb. 12, 19, Mar. 4, Apr. 2, May 14, June 11, 25, July 20, Dec. 17, 24, 1801; Jan. 21, Feb. 4, 18–Apr. 29, Aug. 12, Sept. 16, Oct. 14–28, Dec. 9–30, 1802; Jan. 6, 1803–Dec. 26, 1805; Jan. 16, Feb. 27, Mar. 13, Apr. 3–June 19, July 3, 17–Sept. 4, 25–Oct. 30, Dec. 11–25, 1806; Jan. 1–Sept. 3, 17–Dec. 31, 1807; Jan. 7–Mar. 24, Apr. 14, 21, May 5–June 16, July 7, 21, 28, Aug. 11, 18, Sept. 1–29, Oct. 13–Dec. 29, 1808; Jan. 5, 1809–Dec. 28, 1810; Jan. 4–Feb. 22, Mar. 22, 29, Apr. 10, May 3, 10, 24–July 12, 26, Aug. 9–Sept. 20, Oct. 11–Dec. 27, 1811; Jan. 3–July 31, Aug. 14–Sept. 11, Oct. 2, 16–Dec. 25, 1812; Jan. 1–Mar. 19, Apr. 2–May 14, 28–Oct. 15, 29, Nov. 12–Dec. 10, 24, 31, 1813; Jan. 7–May 13, 1814.

Lib. Congress has Nov. 6–Dec. 24, 1800; Jan. 10, 22–Mar. 19, Apr. 2–May 28, June 11–25, July 9–Sept. 10, 24–Oct. 15, 29, Nov. 12–Dec. 17, 1801; Jan. 7–21, Feb. 18, Mar. 11, 18, Apr. 22, May 13–27, June 10, 24, July 8–29, Aug. 12, 19, Sept. 23, Oct. 28, Nov. 11, Dec. 16, 1802; Jan. 20, Feb. 3, 17, Mar. 3, 10, 24–Apr. 14, 28, May 12, 26, June 23, 30, July 21, 28, Aug. 11, 18, Sept. 8–29, Nov. 17–Dec. 1, 15–29, 1803; Jan. 5, 1804–Dec. 26, 1805; Jan. 16–Dec. 25, 1806; Jan. 8–22, Feb. 5–May 14, 28–July 16, 30–Sept. 3, 17–Oct. 15, 29–Dec. 31, 1807; Jan. 7–Feb. 25, Mar. 10, 17, 31, May 12, 26–Dec. 29, 1808; Jan. 5, 1809–Apr. 19, May 10, 1810; Jan. 4–Feb. 15, June 14, July 26, Aug. 23, Sept. 20, Nov. 1, 15, 1811; Jan. 17, 24, Feb. 21, 28, Mar. 6, 13, Apr. 3, 10, May 15, June 19, Nov. 20–Dec. 25, 1812; Jan. 1–Feb. 26, Apr. 30, May 28, July 2, 30, 1813; Apr. 22–May 6, 1814.

Hist. Soc. Penn. has Nov. 6, 1800–Dec. 30, 1802; Jan. 6, Nov. 24, Dec. 29, 1803; Mar. 19, Dec. 6–20, 1804; Jan. 3–Feb. 28, 1805; Feb. 4, 1808; Apr. 19, May 24, 1810; Nov. 6, Dec. 11, 1812.

York Inst., Saco, Me., has Nov. 6, 1800–Dec. 30, 1802.

Univ. of Mich. (Clements) has Nov. 6, 27, Dec. 11, 18, 1800; Feb. 19, 1801; Jan. 21–Apr. 30, May 27–June 17, Aug. 5, 12, Dec. 16, 30, 1802; Jan. 6–Feb. 24, June 16, 23, Oct. 20, Nov. 3–Dec. 29, 1803; Jan. 5, 26, Feb. 9, Mar. 1–22, Apr. 5–June 14, July 5, 19, Aug. 2, 23, Sept. 6, 20–Oct. 11, Nov. 1–Dec. 27, 1804; Jan. 3–Mar. 7, Apr. 25, July 4, Aug. 22, Sept. 12, Dec. 5, 26, 1805; Jan. 2, 30, Feb. 20–Apr. 17, May 1–29, June 12–July 3, 17–Aug. 21, Sept. 4, 18, Oct. 23–Nov. 6, 27–Dec. 4, 1806; Jan. 1, 8, Feb. 5–Mar. 5, 26–Apr. 23, May 7, 28–June 18, July 9, 30, Aug. 6, Sept. 17, Oct. 15, 29,

Nov. 5, 19, Dec. 3, 1807; Apr. 8, Sept. 15, 1808; Mar. 30, Aug. 10, 1809; May 10, June 7, July 19, Aug. 2, 9, Sept. 13, 20, 1810; Nov. 15, 1811.

Phil. Free Lib. has Nov. 6, 1800–Mar. 11, 1802.

Peabody Inst., Baltimore, has Nov. 6, 1800–Dec. 24, 1801.

Va. Hist. Soc. has Nov. 6, 1800–Dec. 24, 1801, fair.

Harvard has Dec. 4, 18, 1800; Jan. 8, 15, 29, Feb. 4, Mar. 4, 19, 26, Apr. 16, 30, May 7, 21–June 4, 25–July 9, 30, Aug. 13, 20, Sept. 3, 10, 24–Oct. 8, 22, 29, Nov. 19, Dec. 3–17, 31, 1801; Apr. 1, May 27, June 3, 17, Sept. 11, Oct. 21, 1802; Apr. 19, 1804.

Dartmouth has Dec. 12, 1805–Jan. 22, 1807; Nov. 15, 1811–Nov. 6, Dec. 4, 1812; Jan. 1, 1813–May 13, 1814.

N. Y. Hist. Soc. has Nov. 6–27, Dec. 11–24, 1800; Nov. 10, 1803; Dec. 19, 1805; Mar. 20, 1806; Jan. 15, 29, 1807; Nov. 17, Dec. 1–22, 1808; Jan. 12, 26, Feb. 23, Mar. 9, Apr. 6, 1809.

Wis. Hist. Soc. has Dec. 12, 1805–Mar. 27, Dec. 4, 1806; Nov. 10–Dec. 29, 1808.

Long Id. Hist. Soc. has Dec. 28, 1810–May 15, 1811.

Mass. Hist. Soc. has Nov. 15, 1804; Jan. 24, Feb. 28, 1805; Nov. 5, 1807; Jan. 18, Feb. 1, 8, Dec. 14, 1810; Nov. 15, 22, 1811; Feb. 14, 28, Mar. 6, 27, 1812; Jan. 8, 1813.

N. Y. State Lib. has Dec. 25, 1806; Aug. 25, 1808; Mar. 23, Dec. 14–28, 1810; Jan. 11–Feb. 22, Nov. 8–Dec. 27, 1811; Jan. 3–Apr. 10, June 5, 19, Nov. 6, 1812.

Rutgers Univ. has Feb. 21, Dec. 25, 1812; June 18, July 16, 1813; Jan. 7, 1814.

Duke Univ. has Nov. 20, 27, 1800; Dec. 18, 26, 1806; Jan. 22, July 9, Nov. 12, 26, Dec. 3, 17, 24, 1807; Jan. 7, 14, Feb. 11–25, 1808; Jan. 11, 1811.

Md. Hist. Soc. has May 22–July 3, 17–31, Aug. 14–Sept. 10, 25–Oct. 2, 23, Nov. 13, Dec. 4, 1806; Sept. 3, 17–Oct. 29, Dec. 17, 1807; Feb. 11–Mar. 10, Oct. 17, 1808.

Boston Athenæum has Nov. 13–27, 1800.

Yale has Feb. 19, 1801; Jan. 27–Feb. 17, Dec. 1, 1803; Dec. 27, 1804; Jan. 10, Mar. 27, 1806.

Boston Pub. Lib. has Feb. 22, Mar. 1, 1811.

FLORIDA

[Fernandina] El Telegrafo de las Floridas, 1817.

Weekly. Established early in December 1817, but no copy located. The "Charleston Courier" of Dec. 19, 1817 has the following announcement:

"El Telegrafo de las Floridas. An attentive correspondent at St. Marys, forwarded to us by the last mail, the first number of a weekly newspaper under the above title, printed in Spanish at Amelia Island. It announces a meeting of the Representatives of the Floridas, under a discharge of artillery, on the 1st inst. when Col. Irwin was elected President of that body, and steps were taken for the complete organization of the new republican government. The paper abounds in editorial remarks upon the future destinies of the Republic of Florida, and with sentiments of contempt and detestation for the government of Spain. Its object is to furnish a record of passing events in that island, with interesting extracts from American and other foreign papers."

For a discussion of Aury's piratical government at Fernandina, on Amelia Island, see "Florida Historical Society Quarterly," July 1928, vol. 7, pp. 31–56. The newspaper established by his government must have expired almost immediately, as his forces were subjugated by the American war vessels on Dec. 23, 1817.

[Pensacola] see under Alabama, [Claiborne] Alabama Courier.

[St. Augustine] East-Florida Gazette, 1783–1784.

Weekly. Established Feb. 1, 1783, judging from the date of the earliest issue located, that of Mar. 1, 1783, vol. 1, no. 5, printed by Charles Wright for John Wells, Jr., with the title of "The East-Florida Gazette." There are quotations from the "East-Florida Gazette" of Feb. 22 and Mar. 8, 1783, in the Philadelphia "Independent Gazetteer" of Apr. 5, 1783. In the "Gazette of the State of Georgia," of May 8, 1783, there is a reference to the St. Augustine paper of Apr. 19, also to the "East Florida Gazette Extraordinary" of Apr. 21. William Charles Wells was really the publisher of the paper. In his "Two Essays," London, 1818, he prints a memoir of himself, in which he describes his career at St. Augustine, where he arrived at the first of the year in 1783. He states: — "Immediately afterwards, I began to publish a weekly newspaper in my brother's name; the first thing of the kind ever attempted in that country." He says that he went to Charleston in the summer of 1783, soon returned to St. Augustine, and embarked for England in May 1784.

A communication to Miller's "South Carolina Gazette" of Aug. 13, 1783, denounces Dr. William Charles Wells for returning to Charleston "bringing in the vessel with him a gazette printed at Augustine under his auspices wherein the good people of these States are insulted." The same paper of Oct. 4, 1783, mentions that a sloop had lately left Charleston for Augustine carrying Dr. Wells as a passenger. The same paper of Apr. 1, 1784, says "the printer has received the East-Florida Gazette of the 22d March." John Wells is known to have published at least two books at St. Augustine in 1784, the titles of which may be found in the Brinley Catalogue, no. 4346, and in Evans' "American Bibliography," no. 18490. The last issue located of the "East-Florida Gazette" is that of May 17, 1783, vol. 1, no. 16.

> British Public Record Office, London, has Mar. 1, May 3, 17, 1783. Reproduced in facsimile by D. C. McMurtrie, with an introduction, Evanston, 1942. Copies in most of the larger libraries.

St. Francisville, see under **Louisiana.**

GEORGIA

[Athens] Foreign Correspondent, see [Athens] Georgia Express.

Athens Gazette, 1814–1820.

Weekly. Established Feb. 17, 1814, by Hodge & M'Donnell [John Hodge and Alexander M'Donnell], with the title of "Athens Gazette." With the issue of Nov. 9, 1815, the partnership was dissolved and the paper was published by John Hodge; with the issue of Nov. 16, 1815, by Hodge & Co.; and with the issue of Apr. 25, 1816, by John Hodge. The issue of May 8, 1817, is numbered vol. 4, no. 9, The next issue located, that of Mar. 28, 1818, vol. 4, no. 49, was published by Samuel W. Minor. The last issue located is that of Oct. 20, 1820, vol. 8, no. 21.

> Univ. of Ga., Athens, has Feb. 17, 1814–Feb. 6, 1817, fair; Apr. 3, 10, May 8, 1817.
> Ga. State Lib. has Dec. 9, 1819; Oct. 20, 1820.
> Washington Mem. Lib., Macon, has Oct. 27, 1814.
> Duke Univ. has Mar. 25, 1818.

[Athens] Georgia Express, 1808–1813.

Weekly. Established May 14, 1808, judging from the date of the first issue located, that of July 23, 1808, vol. 1, no. 11, published by M'Donnell & Harris [Alexander M'Donnell and Eli Harris], with the title of "Georgia Express." With the issue of Mar. 25, 1809, the partnership was dissolved and Alexander M'Donnell became sole publisher. With the issue of July 22, 1809, the title was changed to "Foreign Correspondent & Georgia Express." Sometime in 1811, the title reverted to "Georgia Express," and the firm of publishers became M'Donnell & Gaines [Alexander M'Donnell and Xenophon J. Gaines]. With the issue of Oct. 9, 1812, Alexander M'Donnell again assumed the proprietorship. The last issue was that of Aug. 13, 1813, vol. 5, no. 262. M'Donnell joined in establishing the "Athens Gazette," Feb. 17, 1814.

> Univ. of Ga., Athens, has Aug. 6, 1808–Dec. 22, 1810, fair; Jan. 3, 1812–Aug. 13, 1813, fair.
> Washington Mem. Lib., Macon, has July 23, 1808; Jan. 7, 1809.
> Am. Antiq. Soc. has Oct. 6, 1810.

Augusta Chronicle, 1789–1820+.

Weekly, semi-weekly and tri-weekly. A continuation, under the name of "Georgia. The Augusta Chronicle and Gazette of the State," of "The Georgia

State Gazette or Independent Register." The first issue with the new title was that of Apr. 11, 1789, vol. 3, no. 132, published by John E. Smith. Smith died Feb. 1, 1803, but his name remained in the imprint for the remainder of the year. In January 1804 the paper was taken over by Dennis Driscol and the title shortened to "Augusta Chronicle." Driscol died Mar. 10, 1811, and the paper was thenceforth published by Adams & Duyckinck [George Adams and Benjamin T. Duyckinck]. With the issue of Dec. 24, 1813, George Adams assumed the sole proprietorship. With the issue of Dec. 20, 1816, the paper was published by Kean & Duyckinck [John E. Kean and Benjamin T. Duyckinck] and was changed to a semi-weekly. With the issue of Aug. 20, 1817, the paper was published by Kean, Duyckinck & Pearre [George W. S. Pearre] and the title was lengthened to "Augusta Chronicle, and Georgia Gazette," and again altered to "Augusta Chronicle & Georgia Gazette" with the issue of June 17, 1818. Beginning with the issue of Mar. 29, 1819, the paper became a tri-weekly. Pearre sold out his interests to John K. M. Charlton, and beginning with the issue of Aug. 23, 1819, the paper was published by Kean, Duyckinck & Charlton. With the issue of Nov. 13, 1820, the title was again shortened to "Augusta Chronicle," and the semi-weekly issue was renewed. Duyckinck retired, and beginning with the issue of Nov. 17, 1820, the paper was published by Kean & Charlton. Continued after 1820.

Univ. of Ga. has Apr. 11, 1789–Nov. 23, 1799; June 21, 1800–Oct. 8, 1803; Dec. 31, 1803; Jan. 28, 1804–Dec. 30, 1809; Mar. 31, 1810–Nov. 15, 1811, fair; Jan. 3, 1812–Dec. 31, 1819.

Lib. Congress has Apr. 11, 1789–July 14, 1792; Mar. 21–May 23, June 6–Aug. 8, 22–Sept. 12, 26–Oct. 10, 24, 31, Nov. 14–Dec. 5, 19, 1795; May 9, 1801; Dec. 2, 1809; Nov. 15, 22, 1816; Jan. 2, 1819–Dec. 29, 1820.

Ga. Hist. Soc. has June 5, 1790–Jan. 3, 1801; Aug. 30, 1801.

Am. Antiq. Soc. has Aug. 4, Nov. 17, 1792; Aug. 3, 31, Dec. 28, 1793; May 24, June 14, 21, 1794; Jan. 10, 17, Mar. 7, 1795; Jan. 9–Feb. 20, Mar. 19–June 11, Aug. 27–Oct. 1, 15–Nov. 12, 26–Dec. 31, 1796; Oct. 11, Dec. 27, 1800; Jan. 3, 1801–Dec. 18, 1802, fair; Feb. 7–Dec. 26, 1807; Jan. 2, 23, Feb. 20, Mar. 5, 19, Apr. 2–23, May 7, 28–Aug. 27, Sept. 10, 17, Oct. 1–Dec. 3, 17, 1808; Jan. 7–Dec. 23, 1809; Dec. 1, 1810; Apr. 5, 1817; May 6, 1818; June 9, 1819.

Harvard has Jan. 31, Feb. 7, May 30, June 27–July 25, Aug. 8, Sept. 19, Nov. 7, Dec. 26, 1795; Jan. 16–30, Feb. 13, Mar. 12–26, July 2, 16, 30, Aug. 6, 20, 27, Sept. 17–Oct. 1, 15–29, Nov. 19–Dec. 31, 1796; Jan. 14–Feb. 11, 25, Mar. 4, Apr. 15, 1797.

Ga. State Lib. has May 31–June 28, July 12, 19, Aug. 16–Dec. 27, 1811; Jan. 3–May 29, June 12–Oct. 23, Nov. 6–Dec. 25, 1812; Jan. 1–Oct. 22, Nov. 26–Dec. 31, 1813; Jan. 7–Oct. 28, Dec. 9, 1814; Feb. 3, 17–Oct. 27, Nov. 10–Dec. 29, 1815; Jan. 5–July 26, 1816.

Hist. Soc. Penn. has Feb. 2, 1793; Jan. 18, 1794; June 20, 1795.

Conn. State Lib. has Nov. 19, 1796; Apr. 26, May 3, 1800.

Boston Pub. Lib. has June 14, 1794.
N. Y. Hist. Soc. has June 13, 1801.
Duke Univ. has Feb. 27, 1802.
N. Y. Pub. Lib. has Nov. 13, 1802.
Boston Athenæum has Mar. 8, 1806.
Univ. of Chicago has Oct. 4, Nov. 1, 1817; May 30, July 11, 25, Aug. 1, 1818.
Ga. Dept. af Archives, Atlanta, has June 23, 1804; Apr. 12, 1806; July 18, 1820.
Washington Mem. Lib., Macon, has Dec. 27, 1811.

[Augusta] Columbian Centinel, 1803–1811.

Weekly. Established in July, 1803, judging from the date of the first issue located, that of July 3, 1804, vol. 1, no. 49, published by George F. Randolph, with the title of "Columbian Centinel." With the issue of Jan. 24, 1807, the publishers became George F. Randolph & Co.; and with the issue of June 3, 1809, Samuel Hammond, who continued certainly as far as Aug. 10, 1810. Subsequent publishers are indicated only by scattering issues: Samuel Hammond & John H. Pike on Dec. 7, 1810; Wm. Sims, Jun., for the Proprietors, from June 18 to Aug. 19, 1811; and William Sims, Jun., for the Proprietor, Oct. 14, 1811. Samuel Hammond, Jr., advertises, over the date of June 3, 1811, that he was sole proprietor from May 27, 1809 to Feb. 2, 1811. John H. Pike, over the same date of June 3, 1811, cautions against payment to Samuel Hammond, Jr., as he himself was joint editor, joint proprietor and sole printer of the newspaper from Sept. 1, 1810 to Feb. 2, 1811. William Sims, Jr., began a new and additional numbering from June 11, 1811. There was a lapse of four numbers previous to the issue of Oct. 14, 1811, which William Sims, Jr., published "pro tempore" for the proprietor, with the statement that he had "a prospect" of being able to issue future numbers regularly. An advertisement, dated April, 1814, in the "Monitor" of Washington, Ga., of May 21, 1814, requests persons indebted "to any of the Proprietors of the Augusta Columbian Centinel Printing Office, prior to 2d February, 1811" to call at the office of the "Mirror of the Times" to settle their respective accounts. The issue of Oct. 14, 1811, vol. 9, no. 425, however, is the last located. The "Augusta Herald" of Jan. 19, 1815, records the death, on Jan. 14, of Samuel Hammond, Jr., "formerly Proprietor and Editor of the Columbian Centinel."

Univ. of Ga., Athens, has Aug. 2, 1806–Sept. 12, 1807, fair; Jan. 7–Dec. 23, 1809, fair.
Am. Antiq. Soc. has July 3, 1804; Nov. 1, 1806; Aug. 1, 1807; June 25, Nov. 12, 1808; June 10, 1809; Feb. 10, Aug. 10, Dec. 7, 1810; June 18, July 2, 22–Aug. 19, Oct. 14, 1811.

Augusta Gazette, 1785–1786.

No issues of this paper have been located, but it is mentioned in contemporaneous newspapers. The "South Carolina Gazette and Public Advertiser" of

Aug. 30, 1785, says, "A printing office has lately been established in the town of Augusta, by Mr. G. Hughes, who publishes a weekly paper there, and we are told, meets with very liberal encouragement." The same journal, of Sept. 29, 1785, quotes from "The Augusta Gazette of September 24th." There are other contemporaneous references to the paper, the last found being in the "Columbian Herald" of Charleston of Sept. 30, 1786, which quotes from the "Augusta Gazette" of Sept. 24, 1786. John E. Smith established the "Georgia State Gazette" at Augusta on Sept. 30, 1786. Greenberry Hughes, the publisher referred to, became one of the publishers of "The Charleston Evening Gazette," Aug. 7, 1786.

An article in the Augusta "Daily Constitutionalist" of Oct. 21, 1858, refers to a paper published in Savannah in 1774 and says that "some years later a paper was edited in Augusta by Augustus C. Geo. Elholm. He was a chivalrous Dane, for a long time the Adjutant General of the State." But no proof of his editorship has been found, or whether he was connected with the "Augusta Gazette."

[Augusta] Georgia Advertiser, 1819–1820+.

Tri-weekly and semi-weekly. Established March, 1819, judging from the date of the earliest issue located, that of May 12, 1819, vol. 1, no. 16, published by T[ippo] S. Hannon, with the title of "Georgia Advertiser." It was issued at first three times a week (see proposals in "Georgian" of March 12, 1819, also notice of first issue in Savannah "Columbian Museum" of Apr. 6, 1819), but after a few issues, it became a semi-weekly. The last issue located is that of Aug. 14, 1819, vol. 1, no. 43, although it is quoted in the "Columbian Museum" of Nov. 19, 1819. The marriage of Tippo S. Hannon, "editor of the Georgia Advertiser," to Eliza Hammond, at Augusta, on Apr. 23, 1820, is recorded in the "Raleigh Register," May 5, 1820. The paper was combined with the "Augusta Chronicle" in 1822.

Lib. Congress has May 12, Aug. 14, 1819.

[Augusta] Georgia Gazette, 1816.

Weekly. The only issues located are from Feb. 5 to Mar. 11, 1816, vol. 7, nos. 381–386. The full title was "The Georgia Gazette and General Advertiser" and the publishers were Pearre & Groves [George W. S. Pearre and ——— Groves]. Judging from the volume numbering, the paper was apparently a continuation of the "Mirror of the Times," which see. Under date of Nov. 4, 1816, Pearre advertised for sale the plant of the "Georgia Gazette," stating that he had to leave the State soon ("American Advocate" of Louisville, Ga.).

Am. Antiq. Soc. has Feb. 5–19, Mar. 11, 1816.

GEORGIA 115

[Augusta] Georgia State Gazette, 1786-1789.

Weekly. Established Sept. 30, 1786, by John E. Smith, under the name of "The Georgia State Gazette or Independent Register." It was so called to the issue of Apr. 4, 1789, vol. 3, no. 131, after which it was called "Georgia. The Augusta Chronicle and Gazette of the State." See under "Augusta Chronicle."

Lib. Congress has Oct. 21, 1786–Sept. 15, Oct. 13–Dec. 1, 22, 29, 1787; Jan. 5, 1788–Apr. 4, 1789.
Univ. of Ga. has Oct. 14, 1786–Apr. 4, 1789.
Am. Antiq. Soc. has Nov. 4, 1786.
Univ. of Mich. (Clements) has Jan. 26, 1788.

Augusta Herald, 1799-1820+.

Weekly and semi-weekly. Established as a weekly July 17, 1799, by Randolph & Bunce [George F. Randolph and William J. Bunce], with the title of "Augusta Herald." With the issue of Aug. 20, 1800, Randolph retired from the firm and the paper was conducted by William J. Bunce. On July 11, 1804 (see article on early Georgia newspapers in Augusta "Daily Constitutionalist" of Oct. 21, 1858), the paper began to be published by Hobby & Bunce [William J. Hobby and William J. Bunce]. On Dec. 31, 1816, publication was changed to semi-weekly. Beginning with the issue of July 29, 1817, the firm was dissolved and the paper was conducted by William J. Bunce. It was continued after 1820.

Randolph & Bunce also issued a "Monthly Herald," a quarto sheet of four pages, of which Univ. of Ga., Athens, has Apr. 5, May 10, 1800, vol. 1, nos. 1 and 2, and the Univ. of Ga. (DeRenne Lib.) has May 10, 1800.

Augusta Chronicle office once had a file of the Herald, which included July 15, 1801–June 29, 1803, July 11, 1816–June 30, 1818, and Oct. 1, 1819–June 27, 1820, but these were destroyed by fire in November 1921, shortly before the remainder of their file was sold to the University of Texas.
Univ. of Ga., Athens, has July 17, 1799–June 17, 1801, fair; Oct. 7, 1801–July 7, 1802, fair; Oct. 6, 1802–Apr. 25, 1804, fair; Oct. 6, Dec. 6, 1804–Aug. 14, 1806, fair; Nov. 24–Dec. 29, 1808; Jan. 5–26, Feb. 9, Apr. 6, 13, May 4–June 8, 1809; Feb. 8, 15, Mar. 29, Nov. 8, Dec. 6, 1810; Jan. 2–Dec. 31, 1812; Sept. 1, 1814–June 27, 1816; Jan. 7, 1817–Dec. 29, 1818; Feb. 1, 1820.
Am. Antiq. Soc. has July 24–Aug. 7, 21–Oct. 30, Nov. 13, Dec. 4–25, 1799; Jan. 7–July 9, 1800; May 13, 20, 1801; Apr. 3, 1806; Apr. 25, 1811; Jan. 19–Dec. 28, 1815.
Univ. of Texas has July 10, 1806–June 28, 1810; Apr. 13, 1819; June 30–Dec. 29, 1820.
Duke Univ. has May 12, 1802; July 1, 1813–June 22, 1815; May 5, 1820.
Ga. State Lib. has Jan. 21, Feb. 4–July 8, 1801.
Lib. Congress has Jan. 15, 1800; May 6, 1801; Nov. 20, 1818; Nov. 23, Dec. 9, 1819.

Conn. Hist. Soc. has Jan. 15, 1800.
N. Y. Pub. Lib. has Nov. 10, 1802.
Washington Mem. Lib., Macon, has June 13, 1804.
Ga. Dept. of Archives, Atlanta, has Dec. 4, 11, 1806.
Univ. of N. C. has Nov. 28, 1811.
N. Y. Hist. Soc. has July 6, 1815.
Univ. of Chicago has July 17, 1818.

[Augusta] **Mirror of the Times,** 1808–1814.

Weekly. Established Oct. 17, 1808, judging from the date of the first issue located, that of Oct. 31, 1808, vol. 1, no. 3, published by Daniel Starnes & Co., with the title of "Mirror of the Times." The last issue known is that of Sept. 2, 1813, vol. 5, no. 259, but there is a reference to the paper in the "Monitor" of Washington, Ga., of May 21, 1814.

Am. Antiq. Soc. has Oct. 31, Nov. 28, 1808; May 22, 29, June 19, July 3, 1809; Dec. 3, 1810; Oct. 28, 1811.
Prof. Charles H. Hull, Ithaca, N. Y., owned Sept. 2, 1813, but now not located.

[Augusta] **Monthly Herald,** see **Augusta Herald.**

[Augusta] **Southern Centinel,** 1793–1799.

Weekly. Established June 6, 1793, by A[lexander] M'Millan, with the title of the "Southern Centinel, and Universal Gazette." Beginning with the issue of Dec. 5, 1793, the title was changed to the "Southern Centinel, and Gazette of the State" and the imprint to "Printed by Alexander M'Millan." The last number located is that of Nov. 7, 1799, vol. 6, no. 338.

Ga. Hist. Soc. has June 6, July 4, 1793–Nov. 7, 1799.
Am. Antiq. Soc. has Nov. 28, 1793–May 31, 1798, fair.
Harvard has Feb. 5, 12, Mar. 5, June 4, 1795; Jan. 21, Mar. 16, 29, Apr. 21–May 5, 19, June 23, July 7–21, Aug. 4, Sept. 1, 8, 22, 29, Oct. 20, Nov. 3, 24, Dec. 8, 29, 1796; Jan. 19–Feb. 9, 23, Mar. 2, 16, 23, Apr. 13, 1797.
Ga. Dept. of Archives, Atlanta, has Apr. 23, 1795.
Conn. State Lib. has July 30, 1795.

Darien Gazette, 1818–1820+.

Weekly. Established Oct. 26, 1818, judging from the date of the first issue located, that of Jan. 4, 1819, vol. 1, no. 11, published by M'Intyre & Millen [Archibald C. M'Intyre and John Millen], with the title of "Darien Gazette." The issue of Jan. 24, 1820, was published by John Millen & Co., and those in November–December 1820 by Millen & Maxwell [John Millen and ——— Maxwell]. Continued until after 1820.

GEORGIA 117

Am. Antiq. Soc. has Jan. 4, 1819; Jan. 24, 1820.
Ga. State Lib. has Nov. 4–Dec. 30, 1820.

[Greensborough] **Georgia Observer,** 1806.

The Sparta "Farmer's Gazette" of Sept. 20, 1806, mentions "The Georgia Observer, a paper published in Greensborough." No copy located.

[Greensborough] **Selector,** 1820.

The "National Intelligencer" of Oct. 28, 1820, notes the establishment of a new newspaper at Greensborough, Ga., entitled "The Selector" and published weekly by Pierce & Robinson [———— Pierce and ———— Robinson] and says that it commenced Aug. 5, 1820. No copy located.

[Louisville] **American Advocate,** 1816.

Weekly. Established Feb. 15, 1816, by Wheeler & Clarke [no. 3 reads George W. Wheeler & James Clarke], with the title of "American Advocate." The last issue located is that of Nov. 28, 1816, vol. 1, no. 41.

Ga. Hist. Soc. has Feb. 22–Nov. 28, 1816.

[Louisville] **American Standard,** 1812.

Weekly. Established Jan. 16, 1812, judging from the first and only issue located, that of May 14, 1812, vol. 1, no. 18, published by A. Wright and D. Clarke with the title of "American Standard." In the Athens "Georgia Express" of Feb. 7, 1812, are proposals, over date of Dec. 26, 1811, signed by Ambrose Wright and David Clarke, to print at Louisville a weekly newspaper to be entitled the "American Standard." The paper is referred to as the "Louisville Standard" in the Milledgeville "Georgia Journal" of Sept. 2, 1812.

Am. Antiq. Soc. has May 14, 1812.

Louisville Courier, 1811–1812.

Weekly. Established Aug. 21, 1811, with the title of "The Louisville Courier," published by George W. Wheeler, for Harvey & Dowsing [———— Harvey and ———— Dowsing]. The last issue located is that of Oct. 30, 1811, vol. 1, no. 11, but the paper is referred to in the Milledgeville "Georgia Journal" of Jan. 15, 1812.

Harvard has Aug. 21, Sept. 25, Oct. 9, 23, 30, 1811.

Louisville Gazette, 1798–1811.

Weekly. Established in November, 1798, judging from the date of the earliest issue located, that of Aug. 20, 1799, vol. 1, no. 39, published by Elisha H. Waldo, with the title of "The State Gazette, and Louisville Journal." Waldo continued to publish the paper certainly through Dec. 24, 1799, vol. 2, no. 57. When on a visit to Charleston, he died July 25, 1801, according to a notice in the Charleston "Times" of July 27. The "Waldo Genealogy," 1883, p. 119, in recording the date of his death, refers to him as "being at the time State Printer of Georgia." Judging by the volume numbering of the paper, his death must have been followed by a short suspension of publication, as the next issue located is that of May 12, 1802, vol. 4, no. 162, published by Ambrose Day & James Hely, with the title of "The Louisville Gazette; and Republican Trumpet." They must have assumed charge in 1800, as the editor of the "Augusta Herald," in the issue of June 25, 1800, refers to the editors as Ambrose Day and James Hely; and in the issues of Sept. 9 and 30, 1801, refers to the "Republican Trumpet" and "Trumpeter Hely." After an apparent suspension of six months, judging from the volume numbering, the paper was reestablished on Nov. 19, 1803, published by Day & Hely for Abner Hammond, with the title of "Louisville Gazette. And Republican Trumpet." This partnership was dissolved, and with the issue of Jan. 23, 1805, the paper was published by Ambrose Day for Abner Hammond. Issues for Oct. 24, 1806, and May 22, 1807, were published by Ambrose Day. In August, 1809, George W. Wheeler is mentioned as "co-editor of the Louisville Gazette." The Thomas list of papers issued in the first part of the year 1810 (Thomas, "History of Printing," ed. 2, vol. 2, p. 303) mentions the "Louisville Gazette" as published by Day & Wheeler. The title was shortened before 1810 to "Louisville Gazette." An issue for May 4, 1810, was published by Ambrose Day & Co. On Aug. 14, 1810, this partnership was dissolved and Ambrose Day became sole publisher and so continued to the date of the last issue located, that of Mar. 2, 1811, no. 557. The paper was discontinued in 1811. Ambrose Day advertises in "The Louisville Courier" of Oct. 9, 1811, that he, as "late editor of the Louisville Gazette," proposes to publish a paper at Eatonton, Ga., to be called the "Georgia Press."

Univ. of Ga., Athens, has Aug. 20–Sept. 10, Dec. 10–24, 1799.
Am. Antiq. Soc. has May 12, 1802; Dec. 21, 28, 1803; May 15, 22, 1807; May 4, Sept. 11, Nov. 20, Dec. 1, 11, 1810; Jan. 26, Feb. 2, 19, Mar. 2, 1811.
Harvard has Nov. 26, Dec. 14–28, 1803; Jan. 4, Feb. 15, Mar. 21, 28, Apr. 25, May 2, 23, 30, June 20, 27, July 11, 25–Aug. 29, Oct. 10, 17, 1804; Jan. 16, 23, 1805; Oct. 24, 1806; Mar. 20, 1807.

[Louisville] Independent Register, 1801.

Weekly. Established July 2, 1801, judging from the first and only issue located, that of Aug. 13, 1801, vol. 1, no. 7, published by James Smylie, with the title of "The Independent Register."

Lib. Congress has Aug. 13, 1801.
Univ. of Ga., Athens, has Aug. 13, 1801.

GEORGIA   119

[Louisville] State Gazette, 1799, see **Louisville Gazette**.

[Milledgeville] **Georgia Argus**, 1808–1816.

Weekly. Established in March, 1808, judging from the date of the first issue located, that of July 5, 1808, vol. 1, no. 16, published by Dennis L. Ryan, with the title of "Georgia Argus." In the latter part of 1811, Nicholas Childers became the publisher and so continued until January or February 1814, when John E. Kean took over the paper. With the issue of May 11, 1814, Kean took Walter Jones into partnership and the paper was published by Kean & Jones. Between Nov. 8, 1814, and Jan. 3, 1816, the paper was taken over by Jones & Hightower [Walter Jones and Pleasant R. Hightower], who discontinued it with the issue of Feb. 14, 1816, vol. 8, no. 47, and then started the "Milledgeville Republican."

Am. Antiq. Soc. has July 5, 1808; Apr. 25, Dec. 19, 1809; Apr. 10, Aug. 1, 8, 1810; June 12, 1811; June 24, July 29, Oct. 7, 1812; Sept. 15, 1813; May 18, June 1, 8, Aug. 10, 1814; Jan. 3, 10, 17, 31, Feb. 7, 14, 1816.

Harvard has Jan. 16, 23, Feb. 6, 13, May 22, July 10, 17, Aug. 7, Sept. 11, Oct. 2, 23, 1811; Feb. 5, 26, Mar. 25, Apr. 1, 15, June 3, July 8–22, Aug. 12, 26, Dec. 9, 16, 1812; Feb. 10, 17, Mar. 3, 17–31, Apr. 14, June 2–23, July 7, 21, Aug. 4–18, Sept. 1, Oct. 6, 20, Dec. 1, 1813; Jan. 12, Mar. 9, 30, May 4, Sept. 21, Nov. 8, 1814.

Ga. State Coll. for Women, Milledgeville, has Jan. 9–Dec. 26, 1810, fair.

Univ. of Ga., Athens, has Sept. 1, 1813.

[Milledgeville] **Georgia Journal**, 1809–1820+.

Weekly. Established Nov. 3, 1809, by Seaton Grantland, with the title of "The Georgia Journal," changed to "Georgia Journal" with the issue of July 10, 1811. Published by Grantland until Oct. 30, 1811, beginning with which issue he admitted his brother into partnership, under the firm name of Seaton & Fleming Grantland. Fleming Grantland died Jan. 28, 1819, and S. Grantland sold out to John B. Hines, editor of the "Reflector," and beginning with the issue of Feb. 23, 1819, the paper was published by John B. Hines. Beginning with the issue of June 29, 1819, the paper was published by Camak & Hines [James Camak and John B. Hines]. Continued after 1820.

Univ. of Ga., Athens, has Nov. 3, 1809–Dec. 5, 1810, fair; Jan. 30, Feb. 6, 27, Mar. 6, 20, Apr. 3, 17–May 15, July 17, Aug. 7, Sept. 11, 18, Nov. 6, Dec. 25, 1811; Jan. 1–Dec. 30, 1812, good; Jan. 6, Mar. 10, 31, Apr. 14, June 9–23, Aug. 4, Sept. 22–Oct. 20, Dec. 15, 1813; Jan. 5, 1814–Dec. 26, 1820.

Am. Antiq. Soc. has Dec. 12, 1809; Jan. 9, Mar. 27–Apr. 10, 24, May 1, 15, 22, June 5–July 18, Aug. 1–29, Sept. 12, 19, Nov. 14, 1810; Jan. 15, 29, Feb. 12, 26, Mar. 11, 25, Apr. 8, 22–May 20, June 3–July 1, 15, 29, Aug. 12,

19, Sept. 2, Oct. 14, Nov. 4, 1812; Jan. 19, 26, Mar. 16–30, Apr. 13–27, June 1, 15, Sept. 28, Oct. 5, Nov. 9, 1814; Jan. 3, May 10, June 7, Aug. 9, 16, Sept. 27, Oct. 18, Nov. 8–29, Dec. 13, 1815; Jan. 10–Mar. 6, 20–Apr. 3, 24–June 5, 19–July 31, Aug. 14–Nov. 6, 27, Dec. 11, 25, 1816; Jan. 1, 14, 28, Mar. 18, Apr. 8, 29, May 6, June 17–July 1, 22, Aug. 26, Sept. 2, 23, Mar. 10–Apr. 7, 21, May 5, June 9, 16, 30–July 14, 28, Aug. 11, 18, Sept. 1, 22, Oct. 6, 20, Nov. 10–Dec. 29, 1818; Jan. 5, 12, 26–Mar. 30, May 4, 11, 25, June 1, 15–Aug. 24, 1819; Feb. 1–Mar. 14, Apr. 11–May 2, 16, June 13, 20, July 4–18, Aug. 15–29, Dec. 26, 1820.

Mrs. David Ferguson, Milledgeville, has Oct. 27, 1813–Oct. 16, 1816.

Harvard has May 29, June 19, 26, July 10, 17, 31–Sept. 11, Oct. 9, 16, Nov. 20, Dec. 11, 1811; Jan. 7, 15, Feb. 26, Mar. 11, Apr. 8, June 3, 17, July 29, 1812; Mar. 10, June 9, July 21, Aug. 4, Sept. 29, Oct. 20, 1813.

Lib. Congress has Jan. 12, 1819–Dec. 26, 1820.

Emory Univ., Atlanta, has Oct. 24–Dec. 26, 1820.

Ga. State Coll. for Women, Milledgeville, has Jan. 6, 1817; Jan. 27–Feb. 24, 1818; Dec. 21, 28, 1819; Jan. 11–25, Sept. 12, 19, Nov. 14, 1820.

Univ. of Chicago has Oct. 27, 1818.

Duke Univ. has June 6, 1820.

[Milledgeville] Georgia Republican, 1819.

Weekly. Established by Jones & Denison [Walter Jones and Henry Denison] in September 1819, according to a reference to the initial number in the "Georgian" of Savannah of Sept. 21, 1819; also to the Proposals which promised the paper on Sept. 14, as published in the "Georgian" from May to Sept. 1819. The "National Intelligencer" of Nov. 16, 1819, records the receipt of the first number, dated Sept. 14, 1819. Henry Denison died Oct. 30, 1819 (Milledgeville, "Georgia Journal"). The "Georgian" of Jan. 17, 1820, states, under date of Jan. 6, 1820, that the printing office of the "Georgia Republican" had been bought by S. Grantland and R. M. Orme, who found that the subscriptions to the "Republican" were insufficient to support it, and proposed to publish another paper to be called the "Southern Recorder," at Milledgeville, to appear in February, 1820. No issues of "Georgia Republican" located.

Milledgeville Intelligencer, 1806–1816.

Weekly. Established in June or July 1806. In the "Augusta Chronicle" of July 26, 1806, there is an announcement that those who subscribed to the "Milledgeville Intelligencer" are informed that the first three numbers are published and may be had by applying at the post-office. The only issue located, that of Nov. 22, 1808, vol. 3, no. 124, published by A[lexander] McMillan, with the title of "Milledgeville Intelligencer," would date the establishment back to June 1806. An issue of June 9, 1808, is referred to in the "Georgia Argus" of July 5, 1808. The paper is mentioned in Isaiah Thomas' list of 1810 ("Hist. of Printing," ed. 2, vol. 2, p. 303), as published by A. McMillan. The "Augusta Chronicle" of Oct. 11, 1816 quotes the "Milledgeville Intelligencer."

Wis. Hist. Soc. has Nov. 22, 1808.

[Milledgeville] **Reflector,** 1817–1819.

Weekly. Established Nov. 12, 1817, by J[ohn] B. Hines, with the title of "The Reflector." The last issue located is that of Feb. 2, 1819, vol. 2, no. 5. The paper was united with the "Georgia Journal" by John B. Hines, according to his statement in the "Georgia Journal" of Feb. 23, 1819.

Lib. Congress has Nov. 12, 1817–Feb. 2, 1819.
Am. Antiq. Soc. has Apr. 21, 1818.
Univ. of Ga. has June 9, 1818.
Univ. of Chicago has July 28, 1818.

Milledgeville Republican, 1816.

Weekly. Established Feb. 21, 1816, by Jones & Hightower [Walter Jones and Pleasant R. Hightower], judging from the date of the first issue located, that of Mar. 20, 1816, vol. 1, no. 5, entitled "Milledgeville Republican." Jones advertised in the Milledgeville "Georgia Journal" of May 8, 1816, that he was authorized to receive debts due the late firm of Jones & Hightower.

Am. Antiq. Soc. has Mar. 20, 27, 1816.

[Milledgeville] **Southern Recorder,** 1820+.

Weekly. Established Feb. 15, 1820 by Grantland and Orme [Seaton Grantland and Richard M. Orme], with the title of "Southern Recorder." Continued after 1820.

Emory Univ., Atlanta, has Feb. 15–Dec. 26, 1820.

[Mount Zion] **Missionary,** 1819–1820+.

Weekly. Established in May 1819, judging from the date of the earliest issue located, that of Jan. 28, 1820, vol. 1, no. 36, published by Jacob P. Norton, with the title of "The Missionary." Continued after 1820.

Am. Antiq. Soc. has Jan. 28, Mar. 3, 1820.
Ga. Dept. of Archives, Atlanta, has Apr. 7, 1820.

[Petersburg] **Georgia and South Carolina Gazette,** 1806.

The "Augusta Herald" of Oct. 23, 1806 mentions "The Georgia and South Carolina Gazette" printed at Petersburg on the 2nd instant, and on Nov. 27,

1806, mentions "the Petersburg paper of the 13th instant." No copy located. Petersburg was in Elbert County, Georgia, about 53 miles north of Augusta, near the South Carolina line (see C. C. Jones, "Dead Towns of Georgia," p. 237).

[Savannah] American Patriot, 1812.

Semi-Weekly. Established Apr. 14, 1812, by Mitchell and Pratt [John S. Mitchell and Charles M. Pratt], with the title of "The American Patriot." Discontinued with the issue of June 5, 1812, vol. 1, no. 16, upon which day Mr. Mitchell was attacked by a mob and severely maltreated. He issued several broadsides concerning the occurrence, the last one, on June 8, 1812, stating that the "American Patriot" had been discontinued.

Ga. Hist. Soc. has Apr. 14–June 8, 1812.

N. Y. Hist. Soc. has Apr. 14, 17, 24, 28, May 5, 12, 15, 26, 29, June 5, 1812.

[Savannah] Columbian Museum, 1796–1820+.

Semi-weekly, tri-weekly and daily. Established as a semi-weekly Mar. 4, 1796, by Powers & Seymour [Titus Powers and Gurdon I. Seymour], under the name of the "Columbian Museum & Savannah Advertiser." Powers died July 26, 1797, and beginning with the issue of July 28, 1797, Gurdon I. Seymour became sole publisher. Beginning with the issue of Dec. 12, 1797, the paper was published by Gurdon I. Seymour and Philip D. Woolhopter. They admitted Francis Stebbins to the firm with the issue of Mar. 12, 1802, under the firm name of Seymour, Woolhopter & Stebbins. Stebbins retired and beginning with the issue of June 16, 1804, the publishers were again Seymour & Woolhopter. Seymour retired and Philip D. Woolhopter became sole proprietor beginning with the issue of July 17, 1809. Francis Stebbins purchased half of the Museum early in 1815 and is "now editor" (Hudson, N. Y. "Northern Whig," May 30, 1815), but since no files of the paper are available for 1815–1816, it is not known how long he remained. Beginning with the issue of Feb. 3, 1817, the paper was united with the "Savannah Gazette," under the title of the "Columbian Museum and Savannah Daily Gazette," published by Kappel, Crow & Co., and numbered vol. 1, no. 1. Woolhopter retired, later dying Feb. 11, 1818.

At first a daily and a tri-weekly paper for the country were published, but beginning with the issue of May 10, 1817, only a tri-weekly edition was issued, the numbering being continuous with that of the daily issue and the word "Daily" being omitted from the title. Edward Crow withdrew from the firm and beginning with the issue of May 31, 1817, the paper was conducted by Michael J. Kappel & Co. Beginning with the issue of Nov. 10, 1817, the daily issue was resumed, and the word "Daily" restored to the title. At the same time the earlier numbering of the "Columbian Museum" was resumed, the issue for Nov. 10 being numbered vol. 22, no. 3420; new series, vol. 1, no. 162. The tri-weekly country issue was continued. From June 16 to Oct. 17, 1818, the paper was issued as a tri-weekly and the word "Daily" omitted from the title. Upon

GEORGIA 123

Oct. 19, 1818, the daily was resumed. With this issue, it was announced that the copartnership between Michael J. Kappel, Cosam E. Bartlet and James Mork had been dissolved by the death of Mork on Oct. 12, and that the paper would, beginning with Oct. 19, be published by Kappel & Bartlet. As in 1818, tri-weekly issues only were issued from June 1 to Oct. 23 in 1819, and from June 3 to Nov. 4 in 1820, and the word "Daily" omitted from the title. A fire in the Museum office on Jan. 11, 1820, caused a suspension of issues on Jan. 12 and 14. Continued after 1820.

Ga. Hist. Soc. has Mar. 4, 1796–Dec. 31, 1799; Jan. 3, 1800–Dec. 29, 1801, good; Jan. 1–Dec. 29, 1802; Jan. 4–Dec. 31, 1803, fair; Jan. 4–Dec. 29, 1804; Jan. 18, 1806–June 4, 1812; Aug. 10, Sept. 14, 1812; Feb. 3, 1817–Dec. 30, 1820.

Am. Antiq. Soc. has Mar. 22, 1796–Dec. 31, 1799, good; Jan. 3–Sept. 26, Oct. 10, 1800; Aug. 4–Dec. 29, 1800, good; Sept. 17, Oct. 15–Dec. 31, 1802; Jan. 4, 1803–Dec. 26, 1804, fair; Feb. 22, 1806; Oct. 9, 13, 23, 30, Nov. 3, 10, 13, 20, Dec. 18, 1807; Jan. 29, Feb. 12, Mar. 11, 25, Apr. 8, 19, 22, May 3, 6, June 3, 17–28, July 1–Dec. 30, 1808, fair; Jan. 7, Mar. 28, 1811; Jan. 16, Feb. 20, 1812; Nov. 25, 1813; May 8, 1815; Feb. 3, 1817–Dec. 31, 1819, good; Jan. 1–Dec. 28, 1820, fair.

Emory Univ., Atlanta, has Mar. 2, 1798–Mar. 3, 1804; Mar. 5, 1806–Mar. 1, 1810.

Lib. Congress has Mar. 4–May 6, 31–Dec. 30, 1796; Jan. 3–Mar. 7, 14, 17, Apr. 4, 7, 21, 28–May 9, 16–23, 30, June 6–16, 30, July 4, 11, 14, 21, 28–Aug. 8, 19–Sept. 1, 8, 12, 19, 26, 29, Oct. 24, 27, Dec. 1, 5, 15–29, 1797; Jan. 5–12, 19–26, Feb. 2, 16–23, Mar. 9–May 1, 8–18, June 1, 8, 12, 22–July 6, 13, Aug. 14, Sept. 14, 18, 25–Oct. 2, 12, 23, Nov. 13, 20, Dec. 18, 1798; Jan. 8–Dec. 31, 1799; June 13, July 4, 18–29, Aug. 5–15, 29, 1800; May 8, 1801; Mar. 11, 18, Apr. 1, May 6, June 11, 25, July 2, 13, 16, Aug. 17, 20, Oct. 5, Nov. 2, 5, Dec. 17, 1803; Feb. 25, May 5, July 28, Oct. 17, Nov. 24, 1804; Nov. 10, 13, Dec. 18, 1807; June 17, July 12, 1808; July 12, Nov. 26–Dec. 12, 20–31, 1817; Apr. 10, July 25, 1818; Mar. 4, 11, June 15, Aug. 21, 1819.

Harvard has Mar. 15, 25, Apr. 1, 15, 29, May 27, June 3, 7, 14–28, July 5, 8, 15–26, Aug. 2, 9–Sept. 2, 9–Nov. 15, 22–29, Dec. 6–30, 1796; Jan. 3–24, 31–Mar. 3, 17–Apr. 4, 11, 14, 26, May 5–16, 23, 30–June 9, 16–27, Oct. 27, Dec. 15, 22, 1797; June 28, July 2, 16, Aug. 9, 1799; Feb. 18, Mar. 21, May 27, July 11, Nov. 21, 28, Dec. 16, 23, 1800; Jan. 2, 9, Feb. 10, 17, Mar. 6, 10, Apr. 7, 24, May 8, 15, June 26, July 7–17, 24–31, Aug. 7, 11, 21, 28, Sept. 22–Oct. 2, 1801; Apr. 13, 16, Oct. 1, Nov. 2, 1802; Sept. 21, 1803; Oct. 17, 1804; Oct. 20, 1807.

Univ. of Ga. has Apr. 15, 1796–Feb. 27, 1798; Aug. 13, 1802–May 16, 1804, fair; Jan. 6–Dec. 22, 1814, good; Jan. 26, 1815; Dec. 11, 1818; Nov. 15, 16, 1820.

Phil. Lib. Co. has Apr. 29–May 10, 20, June 7, 10, 17, 28, July 1, 15–26, Aug. 2, 1796.
Boston Pub. Lib. has Aug. 12, Sept. 2, 16, 23, 27, Oct. 4–11, Nov. 4, 22, Dec. 6, 9, 1796; Apr. 28, June 6, 1797.
Samuel B. Adams, Savannah, has Mar. 3, 1797–Feb. 7, 1798.
N. Y. Hist. Soc. has Mar. 2, 1798–Mar. 1, 1799.
N. Y. Pub. Lib. has June 8, 15, 19, 29, Aug. 2, 1796.
Mass. Hist. Soc. has Oct. 4, 11, 1796.
Duke Univ. has Sept. 5–23, 1800; Apr. 12, July 13, 23, Aug. 3, 13, 24, 27, Sept. 17, 1803.
Hist. Soc. Penn. has Jan. 16, 1815.
Wis. Hist. Soc. has Jan. 24, 1817; Dec. 10, 1818.

[Savannah] **Daily Georgian**, see [Savannah] Georgian.

Savannah Daily Republican, see [Savannah] Republican.

[Savannah] **Daily Savannah Republican**, see [Savannah] Republican.

[Savannah] **Federal Republican Advocate**, 1807.

Semi-weekly. Established July 27, 1807, by John Carmont & Co. [John Carmont and John Dougherty], according to proposals in the Savannah "Patriot and Commercial Advertiser" of July 20, 1807, which paper it succeeded. John Dougherty, one of the proprietors of the Federal Republican Advocate, died at Savannah Sept. 10, 1807 (Savannah "Republican" Sept. 12, 1807). The earliest issue located is that of Sept. 21, 1807, vol. 1, no. 17, published by John Carmont & Co., with the title of "Federal Republican Advocate, and Commercial Advertiser." With the issue of Dec. 31, 1807, the name of John Carmont appeared alone in the imprint. The last issue located is that of Feb. 1, 1808, vol. 1, no. 55.

Am. Antiq. Soc. has Sept. 21, 1807.
Ga. Hist. Soc. has Oct. 5, 22, 1807.
Univ. of Ga., Athens, has Oct. 8, 15–29, Nov. 9, 16, Dec. 3, 7, 14–21, 31, 1807; Jan. 4, 28, Feb. 1, 1808.

Savannah Gazette, 1817.

Tri-weekly. Established Jan. 14, 1817, by Michael J. Kappel, with the title of "Savannah Gazette." Only eight numbers were issued, the last being that of Jan. 30, 1817, vol. 1, no. 8, after which the paper was united with the "Columbian Museum" and published under the name of the "Columbian Museum and Savannah Gazette," which see.

Ga. Hist. Soc. has Jan. 14–30, 1817.
Am. Antiq. Soc. has Jan. 14, 18, 21, 25, 30, 1817.
Lib. Congress has Jan. 18, 1817.

[Savannah] **Gazette of the State of Georgia**, 1783–1788.

Weekly. Established Jan. 30, 1783, by James Johnston, with the title of "The Gazette of the State of Georgia." The last issue with this title was that of Oct. 16, 1788, no. 299, after which it was changed to "The Georgia Gazette," which see.

Ga. Hist. Soc. has Jan. 30, 1783–Oct. 26, 1786; Jan. 4, 1787–Oct. 16, 1788.
Am. Antiq. Soc. has Mar. 13, 20, Apr. 24–July 3, 17–Aug. 14, 28–Oct. 16, 30–Dec. 25, 1783; Jan. 1, 1784–Dec. 22, 1785; Aug. 31, 1786; Feb. 15–June 14, 28–Dec. 27, 1787; Jan. 3–Mar. 27, Apr. 10–Sept. 4, 18, 25, Oct. 9, 16, 1788.
Lib. Congress has Feb. 27–Mar. 20, Apr. 3–May 8, 22, 29, June 12–July 3, 17–31, Aug. 14, Sept. 4–18, Oct. 2–Nov. 27, Dec. 25, 1783; Jan. 1–June 10, 24–Sept. 23, Oct. 14–Dec. 30, 1784; Jan. 6–Sept. 15, 29–Dec. 22, 1785; Jan. 19, Oct. 19, Dec. 14, 1786; Mar. 15, May 24, 31, July 26, Sept. 13, 20, Oct. 25, Nov. 1, 1787; Feb. 7, Sept. 18, 1788.
Tenn. State Lib. has Apr. 5, 1787–Oct. 16, 1788.
Telfair Academy, Savannah, has Mar. 20, Apr. 24, May 1, 22–July 3, 17–Aug. 14, 1783; Jan. 29, Feb. 19–Mar. 11, Apr. 15, June 10, 24–July 22, Aug. 5, Sept. 2, 23, 1784.
N. Y. Pub. Lib. has Mar. 3, 1785.
Univ. of Ga. has Apr. 28, 1785.
Amer. Philos. Soc. has Oct. 19, 1786.

[Savannah] **Georgia Gazette**, 1763–1776.

Weekly. Established Apr. 7, 1763, by James Johnston, with the title of "The Georgia Gazette." Suspended with the issue of Nov. 21, 1765, on account of the stamp-act, and not revived until May 21, 1766. It was then published continuously by Johnston until 1776, when it was discontinued because of the war. The last number located is that of Feb. 7, 1776, no. 644. For Johnston's career during 1776–1783, see D. C. McMurtrie's "Pioneer Printing in Georgia" in the Georgia Historical Quarterly for June 1932, vol. 16, pp. 77–113, also reprinted in pamphlet form.

Mass. Hist. Soc. has Apr. 7, 1763–May 23, 1770.
Ga. Hist. Soc. has Jan. 5–Dec. 28, 1774; Jan. 11, 25, Feb. 1, Mar. 22, 29, Apr. 19, 26, May 17–July 19, Aug. 2–Dec. 27, 1775; Jan. 3–Feb. 7, 1776.
Yale has May 28, June 4, July 2, 9, Sept. 3, 1766.
British Pub. Rec. Office has June 27–July 11, 1770; Dec. 16, 1772; June 16,

1773; Aug. 24–Sept. 28, Oct. 12, Nov. 2, Dec. 14, 1774; Jan. 18, 25, June 14, July 12, 26, Sept. 27, Dec. 6, 27, 1775.

Lib. Congress has July 27, Aug. 10, 31–Sept. 28, Oct. 12, 1774; June 21, Aug. 23–Sept. 6, 20, 1775.

Univ. of Mich. has Mar. 8, Apr. 5, 1764.

Am. Antiq. Soc. has Feb. 7, 1765; July 16, 23, 1766; Nov. 23, 1774.

Mo. Hist. Soc., St. Louis, has Aug. 30, 1775.

A photostat reproduction of the file from Apr. 7, 1763 to May 23, 1770 was made by the Mass. Hist. Soc., which is in the following libraries: Am. Antiq. Soc., J. Carter Brown Lib., Mass. Hist. Soc., N. Y. Pub. Lib., N. Y. State Lib., Grosvenor Lib., Lib. Congress, Univ. of Ga., Newberry Lib., Univ. of Ill., Wis. Hist. Soc.

[Savannah] Georgia Gazette, 1777–1778.

No copies of this paper have been located, but that it was published in 1777–1778 is shown by several contemporaneous references in Charleston newspapers. "The South-Carolina and American General Gazette" of Aug. 28, 1777 quotes from the "Georgia Gazette." The same journal, for Sept. 25, 1777, quotes from the "Georgia Gazette" of Sept. 15, 1777. In the same journal for Oct. 16, 1777, there is a letter to the editor written from Savannah on Sept. 22, 1777, referring to "a Piece in the last Georgia Gazette," which the editors of the Charleston paper remarked "were intended to have been published in the Georgia Gazette but the printers have discontinued the publication of their paper for some time." That it was soon reestablished is shown by an article in the "South-Carolina and American General Gazette" of Mar. 12, 1778, quoting from the "Georgia Gazette" of Mar. 5, 1778.

That this Savannah paper was published is also evidenced by the records of the Executive Council of Georgia, requiring that certain resolves should be printed in "the Gazette," or "the Gazette of this State" (see votes of Jan. 29, Feb. 9, Mar. 9 and Mar. 10, 1778, in "Revolutionary Records of Georgia," vol. 2, pp. 18, 29, 48 and 52). William Lancaster, who printed several pamphlets at Savannah in 1777 and 1778, was undoubtedly the printer of the newspaper. The disturbed conditions in Georgia in the spring of 1778 evidently caused the temporary suspension of the paper. On Aug. 25, 1778 the Executive Council acted upon a petition for establishing Edward Welch in the printing business in Savannah. On Aug. 31 it was ordered that William Lancaster should appear before the council "to shew cause why the Types and other printing utensils purchased by the public and intended for him, should not be again returned to the public at what they cost, the said William Lancaster not have complied with his engagements respecting the said Types and utensils" (*Idem*, vol. 2, p. 98). Lancaster refused to give up the press and on Sept. 11, 1778 the Council resolved that the press and types should be impressed for public use and be placed in the hands of Edward Welch. This apparently was done and Welch reestab-

GEORGIA   127

lished the newspaper, as on Nov. 25, 1778 the Council voted that a certain resolve should be published in "the next Gazette" (*Idem*, vol. 2, p. 121). In December 1778 Savannah was captured by the British and all public business came to an end.

[Savannah] Georgia Gazette, 1788–1802.

Weekly. A continuation of "The Gazette of the State of Georgia," but without change of numbering, the first issue with the new name of "The Georgia Gazette" being that of Oct. 23, 1788 (no. 300), published by James Johnston. Beginning with the issue of Jan. 7, 1790, the paper was published by James and Nicholas Johnston. The title became "Georgia Gazette" with the issue of Jan. 2, 1794. It was suspended with the issue of Nov. 24, 1796 (no. 722), because of the great Savannah fire, but was revived on Sept. 2, 1797 (no. 723), by Nicholas Johnston under the firm name of N. Johnston & Co. Nicholas Johnston died on Oct. 20, 1802, and the issue of Oct. 21, 1802 has no publishers' imprint given. Beginning with the issue of Oct. 28, 1802, James Johnston is given as printer. The last issue was that of Nov. 25, 1802, no. 996, upon which date James Johnston announced that the firm of N. Johnston and Co. was dissolved by the death of Nicholas Johnston and the poor health and advanced age of James Johnston.

Ga. Hist. Soc. has Oct. 23, 1788–Nov. 25, 1802.
Am. Antiq. Soc. has Oct. 23, 1788–Dec. 30, 1790; Mar. 1–29, Nov. 22, Dec. 20, 1792; Jan. 17, 24, Feb. 28, May 16, July 11, 18, Aug. 8, 29, Sept. 12, 19, Oct. 10–24, Nov. 14, 28, Dec. 26, 1793; Jan. 9–June 5, July 3–17, 31–Dec. 25, 1794; Jan. 1–Mar. 5, 19, Apr. 2–30, May 14–Aug. 27, Sept. 10–Dec. 31, 1795; Jan. 7, 14, Feb. 11–Mar. 3, 17–May 12, 26–June 16, July 7–Nov. 3, 1796; Sept. 2, 1797–Nov. 25, 1802.
Tenn. State Lib. has Oct. 23, 1788–Dec. 24, 1789.
Lib. Congress has June 4, 1789; Jan. 7, 1790–Dec. 29, 1791; Dec. 26, 1793; Mar. 6, 20, May 22, 29, Sept. 25, Oct. 30, Nov. 27, 1794; Apr. 16, Nov. 19–Dec. 10, 24, 1795; Oct. 13, 1796; Feb. 23, Aug. 9, Dec. 20, 1798; Feb. 14, 21, May 9–June 18, Aug. 1–22, Oct. 17, Nov. 7, 21, 1799; Jan. 9, 16, Feb. 6, 20, Mar. 13–Apr. 17, May 1–July 17, 31–Aug. 14, 28–Oct. 2, 16–Nov. 20, Dec. 4–25, 1800; Jan. 1–22, Feb. 12, 19, Mar. 5, 12, 26–Apr. 30, May 14–Dec. 17, 31, 1801; Jan. 7–Oct. 28, 1802.
Univ. of Ga., Athens, has Nov. 6, 1788; Jan. 19, 1798–Jan. 21, 1802.
Harvard has May 26, June 2, 16, 23, 1791; Aug. 1, 1793; Jan. 29, Feb. 5, 19, Apr. 9, 16, May 28–June 11, 25, July 9, 23, Aug. 6, 20, Dec. 17, 1795; Mar. 24, Apr. 28, May 5, June 2, 23, July 7–Oct. 20, Nov. 24, 1796; Mar. 28, Apr. 18, May 2–30, June 27, July 18, Sept. 5, 26, 1799; July 31, Oct. 23, Nov. 20, 27, Dec. 25, 1800; Feb. 12–Mar. 26, Apr. 9–May 21, June 4, 18–July 9, 23, Aug. 6, Sept. 24, Oct. 8, 22–Dec. 31, 1801; Jan. 7, 14, Feb. 18, Mar. 4, 11, Apr. 1, 22, 29, May 13–27, June 17, 24, July 8–22, Aug. 5, 26, Sept. 23, Oct. 21–Nov. 25, 1802.

Duke Univ. has Jan. 2, 1794–Sept. 22, 1796; Sept. 2, 1797; Aug. 9, Dec. 20, 1798; Feb. 14, 21, May 9, 23–July 18, Aug. 8, 15, 1799; Jan. 2–Dec. 18, 1800.
N. Y. Hist. Soc. has Aug. 29, 1789.
N. Y. Pub. Lib. has Apr. 14, May 5–26, 1791.
Univ. of Texas has Oct. 31, 1793.

[Savannah] Georgia Journal, 1793–1794.

Semi-weekly. Established Dec. 4, 1793, by James Carey, under the title of "The Georgia Journal: and Independent Federal Register." The last issue located is that of Feb. 19, 1794, vol. 1, no. 23.

Ga. Hist. Soc. has Dec. 4, 1793–Feb. 19, 1794.
Hist. Soc. Penn. has Dec. 4, 1793.
Am. Antiq. Soc. has Dec. 25, 28, 1793; Jan. 1, 1794.

[Savannah] Georgia Republican, 1802–1807.

Weekly and semi-weekly. Established Aug. 21, 1802, by Lyon and Morse [James Lyon and Samuel Morse], under the name of the "Georgia Republican & State Intelligencer," changed from a weekly to a semi-weekly with the issue of Oct. 23, 1802. Morse died July 26, 1805, and beginning with the issue of Aug. 2, 1805, the paper was published for James Lyon and the widow of Samuel Morse. John F. Everitt signed the announcement regarding the continuation of the paper, stating that Lyon was in Kentucky. Beginning with the issue of Jan. 3, 1806, it was published by Everitt and McLean [John F. Everitt and Norman McLean] and the title shortened to the "Georgia Republican." This partnership was dissolved and beginning with the issue of Jan. 2, 1807, the paper was published by John F. Everitt. The last issue with this title was that of Mar. 6, 1807, vol. 5, no. 19. On Mar. 10, 1807, the title was changed to "The Republican; and Savannah Evening Ledger," which see.

Univ. of Ga., Athens, has Aug. 21, 1802–Dec. 2, 1803; Jan. 3, 1804–Dec. 3, 1805; Jan. 3, 1806–Feb. 20, 1807.
Ga. Hist. Soc. has Dec. 15, 1802; Jan. 1, 5, 12, 29, Mar. 3, 7, 31, Apr. 28, May 19, 30, June 23, Oct. 18, Dec. 15, 1803; Jan. 3, 13, 24, Apr. 24, May 4, 8, 29, June 19, 26, 29, July 13, 24, 31, Aug. 14, Sept. 11, 25, Oct. 5–Dec. 24, 1804; Jan. 10, 14, 21, Feb. 7, Mar. 11, 21, Apr. 11, May 2–13, Oct. 25, Dec. 17, 1805; Jan. 3, 1806–Mar. 6, 1807.
Lib. Congress has Jan. 12–Mar. 7, 17–28, Apr. 7–May 12, 19–June 13, July 22–Aug. 8, 15, 19, Oct. 11–Nov. 29, Dec. 9, 16, 1803; Mar. 23–June 22, 29–Sept. 28, Oct. 12–Dec. 24, 1804; Jan. 7–28, Feb. 4–25, Mar. 4–28, 1805; Jan. 2–Mar. 6, 1807.
Am. Antiq. Soc. has Sept. 4, 1802; Apr. 18, May 23, 30, June 2, Sept. 27, 30, Oct. 18, 1803; Feb. 24, 28, Mar. 6, Apr. 3, Oct. 5, Nov. 26, 1804; Feb. 14, Aug. 2, 16, Oct. 15, 22, 1805.

Harvard has Oct. 16, 27, Nov. 3, 10, 17, 20, 27, Dec. 1, 18, 22, 1802; Jan. 5, 12, 19, 22, Feb. 10, 17, 24, Mar. 7, 17–31, Apr. 18–June 2, 9, 13, 1803.

[Savannah] **Georgian,** 1818–1820+.

Daily and tri-weekly. Established Nov. 25, 1818, by J[ohn] M. Harney with the title of "The Georgian." The first number states that there is to be a daily paper and also a country paper. The second number states that the paper will be published daily during the winter and spring, and tri-weekly during the summer. From Dec. 24, 1818, to Feb. 15, 1819, J. M. Harney's name is not in the imprint, and there is no clue to the publisher, but the name appears in later issues. Title changed to "The Daily Georgian" with the issue of Jan. 1, 1819. Issued as a tri-weekly from June 1, 1819, to Oct. 19, 1819, and as a daily thereafter. In the issue of Mar. 3, 1820, the imprint is changed from "Published by John M. Harney" to "Edited by John M. Harney," and the announcement is made that the paper had been transferred on Feb. 19, and that N[athaniel] H. Olmstead would attend to the management, while Harney would be the editor. Continued after 1820.

Ga. Hist. Soc. has Nov. 25, 1818–Dec. 30, 1820.
Univ. of Ga., Athens, has Dec. 31, 1819; Jan. 4–June 29, fair, Aug. 1, 1820.
Am. Antiq. Soc. has Jan. 4, 6, 1819; Apr. 5, 1820.
Wis. Hist. Soc. has Nov. 28, 1818.
Lib. Congress has June 8, 1819.

[Savannah] **Morning Chronicle,** 1817–1819.

Daily and tri-weekly. Established late in the year 1817. An advertisement in the "Columbian Museum" of July 12, 1817, states that the "Morning Chronicle" will be published daily from Nov. 1 to June 1, and tri-weekly from June 1 to Oct. 31, also that publication will start as soon as printing materials arrive. The issues of May 8 and 20, 1818, nos. 156 and 166, were published by Samuel Ker, and state that the paper is published daily during the winter and spring months, and tri-weekly during the summer months. The issue of Dec. 7, 1818, no. 237, was published tri-weekly. The issue of June 28, 1819, no. 344, was published tri-weekly by Samuel Ker.

Am. Antiq. Soc. has May 8, 20, 1818; June 28, 1819.
Wis. Hist. Soc. has Dec. 7, 1818.

[Savannah] **Patriot,** see [Savannah] **Southern Patriot.**

Savannah Price Current, 1818–1820.

Weekly. Established Nov. 14, 1818, by Oliver Steele, with the title of "Savannah Price Current and Public Sale Report." It was of quarto size, with financial and marine news on the first two pages, with second leaf blank. In December 1818 the title was changed to "Savannah Wholesale Prices Current," and William C. Barton joined Steele as publisher under the firm name of Barton & Steele. Early in 1819 Steele retired in favor of Richard W. Edes, the firm becoming Barton & Edes; and R[obert] Raiford, by whom the paper was "Corrected every Thursday," was evidently editor. On May 8, 1819, Henry P. Russell displaced Barton in the firm, which became Russell & Edes. The last issue located is that of May 18, 1820, vol. 2, no. 28.

Am. Antiq. Soc. has Nov. 21, 1818; Mar. 18, May 20, 1819; May 18, 1820.
Harvard Business Lib. has Dec. 31, 1818.

[Savannah] **Public Intelligencer**, 1807–1809.

Tri-weekly and semi-weekly. Established Apr. 7, 1807, by Norman M'Lean and William E. Barnes, as a tri-weekly, with the title of "Public Intelligencer." It was changed to a semi-weekly with the issue of June 23, 1807. Barnes retired from the firm, and beginning with the issue of Oct. 20, 1807, the paper was conducted by Norman M'Lean. It was discontinued with the issue of Feb. 3, 1809, vol. 2, no. 88.

Ga. Hist. Soc. has Aug. 14, 1807–Feb. 3, 1809.
Am. Antiq. Soc. has Apr. 18–25, May 7–12, 21, 30–June 6, 16, 20, 30, July 7, 14, 24, 28, Aug. 7, 11, 21, Sept. 8, Nov. 27, 1807; May 15, 22, 26, July 12, 22, 29, Aug. 23, Sept. 2, 9, 27, Oct. 7, 18, 1808.
Harvard has Apr. 9–16, 23–28, May 7, June 16, 18, 30, July 7, 21–28, Sept. 11, 15, 25, Oct. 20, Nov. 10, 1807.

[Savannah] **Republican**, 1807–1820+.

Tri-weekly and daily. A continuation, but without change of numbering, of the "Georgia Republican." The first issue with the new name of "The Republican and Savannah Evening Ledger" was that of Mar. 10, 1807 (vol. 5, no. 20). Published tri-weekly by John F. Everitt, but beginning with the issue of May 28, 1807, by Everitt & Evans [John F. Everitt and John J. Evans]; and beginning with the issue of June 28, 1810, by John J. Evans. Evans died on Jan. 15, 1813, and beginning with the issue of Jan. 23, 1813, the imprint read "Published for John J. Evans." On Mar. 4, 1813, Allen M'Lean and Mary Evans advertise to have his accounts settled, and with the issue of Mar. 9, 1813, the paper was purchased and published by Frederick S. Fell. With the issue of June 18, 1816, the name was shortened to "Savannah Republican." Beginning with the issue of Mar. 11, 1817, Fell took Archibald C. M'Intyre into partnership, publishing under the name of Frederick S. Fell & Co. Beginning with the issue of Oct. 13, 1817, the paper was issued as a daily and the name changed to "Daily Savannah Republican," the numbering being continuous. A tri-weekly edition for the country was also issued. From June 24 to Oct. 15, 1818, the regular tri-weekly replaced the daily, the title reverting with the issue of June 24 to "Savannah Republican." Beginning with the issue of June 24, 1818, the partnership between Fell and M'Intyre was dissolved, and the paper published by Frederick S. Fell. With the issue of Oct. 16, 1818, the daily issue was resumed, the title changing to "Savannah Daily Republican." From July 8 to Oct. 16, 1819, and from June 13 to Nov. 4, 1820, the regular tri-weekly replaced the daily, the title changing to "Savannah Republican." Upon Oct. 19, 1819, and Nov. 6, 1820, the daily issues were resumed, the title changing to "Savannah Daily Republican." Continued after 1820.

- Univ. of Ga., Athens, has Mar. 10, 1807–Dec. 30, 1815; Jan. 7, 1817–Dec. 29, 1820.
- Lib. Congress has Mar. 10, 1807–Dec. 30, 1812; Jan. 4, 1814–Dec. 28, 1815; June 18, 1816–Dec. 30, 1820.
- Ga. Hist. Soc. has Mar. 12, 1807–Mar. 4, 1813.
- Am. Antiq. Soc. has Mar. 21, 1807–Dec. 30, 1812, good; Oct. 9, 16, 1813; Jan. 22, 1814; Jan. 17, Apr. 4, June 22, 29, Aug. 29, 1815; Aug. 3, 8, 31, Sept. 3, 19, 28, 1816; Apr. 15, Sept. 4, Oct. 4, Nov. 7, 13, 1817; Jan. 3, 10, 17, 20, 24, Feb. 14, 17, Mar. 19, 24, Apr. 2, 4, 9, 23, May 7, 28, 30, June 4, 9, 20, Sept. 1, 5, 8, 29, Oct. 13, 17, 1818; May 27, July 6, 27, 1819.
- Harvard has Mar. 19–31, Apr. 7–11, 16, 21, 23, 30–May 16, 21–30, June 4, 9, 13–25, July 2, 4, 9–13, 21–30, Aug. 6–20, 27–Sept. 8, 12, 17–29, Oct. 13–31, Nov. 3, 17, 19, Dec. 3, 15, 1807.
- Duke Univ. has Mar. 10, 15, 17, 22–29, Apr. 2, 5, June 7, July 5, 19, 28, Aug. 11, 20, Sept. 1, 22, 24, 29, Oct. 8, 13, 18–27, Nov. 5–19, 26, Dec. 1, 8, 1808; Apr. 28, May 29, Dec. 4, 1810.
- N. Y. Hist. Soc. has May 31, 1817.
- Wis. Hist. Soc. has Dec. 2, 1818.
- Univ. of Rochester has Apr. 20, 1819.
- Boston Athenæum has Mar. 11, 24, 1820.

[Savannah] **Royal Georgia Gazette,** 1779–1782.

Weekly. Established Jan. 21, 1779, by John Daniel Hammerer, judging from the date of the first issue located, that of Feb. 11, 1779, no. 4, entitled "The Royal Georgia Gazette." Between Mar. 11 and Aug. 12, 1779, the paper was taken over by James Johnston. The last issue located is that of June 6, 1782, no. 171. The British had evacuated Savannah in May 1782. On July 15, 1782, Johnston, banished from the State as a Royalist, informed the House of Assembly that he "had left the Printing Materials belonging to this State in the hand of Mrs. Johnston his wife." In August 1782 the Assembly passed an Act including Johnston's name among those who could return to the State upon payment of a fine, and in October he was back in Savannah, under the protection of the State, in order to "print for the public, and his press already prepared for that purpose" ("Revolutionary Records of Georgia," vol. 3, p. 125 and "Georgia Historical Quarterly" 1917, vol. 1, p. 332. For Johnston's career, see D. C. McMurtrie's "Pioneer Printing in Georgia," 1932, pp. 25-32). In January 1783 Johnston established "The Gazette of the State of Georgia," which see.

> Lib. Congress has Feb. 11, Mar. 11, 1779; Jan. 3, 24, Mar. 14, 21, Apr. 25, May 23, 30, June 6, 1782.
> British Museum has Aug. 12, 19, 1779; July 27, Aug. 3, 31, Sept. 7, 28, Oct. 12, 1780; Dec. 7, 1780–Mar. 22, 1781. The issues in the British Museum from Aug. 12, 1779 to Oct. 12, 1780 were reproduced in facsimile in 1942 by D. C. McMurtrie, Evanston, Ill., copies of which are to be found in most of the larger libraries.
> Univ. of Ga., Athens, has Nov. 25–Dec. 23, 1779; Jan. 6–27, 1780.
> British Pub. Rec. Office has Mar. 23, June 8, 1780.
> N. Y. Hist. Soc. has Jan. 4–Dec. 27, 1781.
> Hist. Soc. Penn. has Jan. 24–Feb. 14, Mar. 7, 1782.

[Savannah] Southern Patriot, 1804–1807.

Semi-weekly. Established Nov. 10, 1804, by James Hely, with the title of "The Southern Patriot." Hely sold the paper to John Dougherty, who began publishing it with the issue of Oct. 2, 1806. Title changed to "The Patriot and Commercial Advertiser" with the issue of Oct. 27, 1806. Dougherty admitted John Carmont to partnership and beginning with the issue of Jan. 15, 1807, the paper was published by Dougherty and Carmont. Discontinued with the issue of July 20, 1807, vol. 3, no. 171, to be succeeded by the "Federal Republican Advocate."

> Harvard has Nov. 14–21, Dec. 5, 8, 22, 28, 1804; Jan. 4–11, 18–29, Feb. 1, 19, Mar. 1–8, 15, 22, Apr. 2–23, May 3, 10–28, June 4, 7, 21, 29–July 12, 30, Aug. 2, 30–Sept. 6, 17–27, Oct. 4–11, 22, 25, Nov. 12–22, Dec. 17, 24, 27, 1805; Jan. 10, Feb. 6, 13, 20, Mar. 13, 24, 27, Apr. 17, 24, May 1, 12–22, June 16, 23, July 14, 1806.
> Ga. Hist. Soc. has Jan. 28, Feb. 27, July 21, Aug. 4–Oct. 27, Dec. 1–29, 1806; Jan. 1–12, 19, Feb. 9–Mar. 26, Apr. 2–9, 16, 23–June 18, 25–July 20, 1807.
> Am. Antiq. Soc. has July 26, 1805; Jan. 31, Feb. 6, Mar. 10, 24, 1806.

[Savannah] Wholesale Prices Current, see Savannah Price Current.

[Sparta] Farmer's Gazette, 1803–1807.

Weekly. Established June 3, 1803, by Day & Ryan [Ambrose Day and Dennis L. Ryan], with the title of "Farmer's Gazette." The partnership was dissolved and Dennis L. Ryan succeeded to the sole ownership on Sept. 16, 1803. The last issue located is that of Aug. 29, 1807, vol. 4, no. 198. Probably discontinued soon afterward, as Ryan commenced publishing the "Georgia Argus" at Milledgeville in March, 1808.

Harvard has June 3, 17, July 15, 29, Sept. 2, 16, 23, Oct. 14–Dec. 1, 23, 1803; Jan. 6, 20–Feb. 18, Mar. 3, 31, Apr. 7, 21, 28, May 26–June 9, 23–July 7, Sept. 22, Oct. 13, 27, Dec. 15, 22, 1804; Jan. 5, 12, Feb. 2, 16, 23, Mar. 16–Apr. 6, 20–May 4, 18–June 22, July 6, 20–Aug. 3, 17, Sept. 21, 28, Oct. 19, Nov. 16, 23, Dec. 7, 14, 28, 1805; Jan. 25, Mar. 15–29, Apr. 26, May 17, 31, June 21, July 5, 12, Aug. 9–Sept. 13, Nov. 2, 1806; May 2, 1807.

Univ. of Ga., Athens, has Aug. 16–Sept. 6, 20, Oct. 10–25, Nov. 8, Dec. 6, 13, 1806; Jan. 17–Feb. 14, Mar. 7, 14, 28, Apr. 4, 25–June 6, July 11, Aug. 29, 1807.

Am. Antiq. Soc. has June 17, Sept. 16, Oct. 28, 1803; Aug. 16, 1806; Mar. 7, 14, May 23, 1807.

Yale has Jan. 6, 1804; Aug. 8, 1807.

[Washington] **Friend and Monitor,** 1815.

Weekly. Established Jan. 13, 1815, by John K. M. Charlton, who had bought the "Monitor" from David P. Hillhouse and consolidated it with the "Friend" (presumably a paper which he had proposed issuing). The issue for Jan. 13, vol. 1, no. 1, entitled "The Friend and Monitor," is dated 1814 instead of 1815, but the error was corrected in the next issue. The last issue located is that of Dec. 22, 1815, vol. 1, no. 50. Charlton established "The News" at Washington on Jan. 19, 1816.

Ga. Hist. Soc. has Jan. 13–Feb. 10, 24–Apr. 7, 21, 28, May 12–June 30, July 21, Aug. 4, 18–Sept. 15, 29, Oct. 6, 20, Nov. 3, 17, Dec. 1–22, 1815.

Duke Univ. has June 23, 1815.

Washington Gazette, 1800–1801.

A letter from David P. Hillhouse to George R. Gilmer, Feb. 4, 1851 (printed in "Washington [Ga.] Chronicle," May 15, 1899) states that the "Monitor" was established in 1800 as the "Washington Gazette" by Alexander M'Millan, who sold it in 1801 to David Hillhouse, who changed the title to the "Monitor." No copies located.

[Washington] **Monitor,** 1801–1815.

Weekly. Established in February 1801, judging from the date of the first issue located, that of Feb. 23, 1805, vol. 5, no. 209, published for S[arah] Hillhouse, with the title of "Monitor." The "Monitor" was at first published by David Hillhouse. He died Mar. 24, 1803 ("Hillhouse Historical and Genealogical Collections," 1924, p. 142), and the paper was henceforth published for his widow Sarah Hillhouse. In 1811 or early in 1812, her son, David P. Hillhouse, assumed proprietorship of the paper and published it until the issue of Jan. 6, 1815, vol. 14, no. 724, when he sold out to John K. M. Charlton. See under "Friend and Monitor."

Univ. of N. C. has Nov. 2, 1805–July 19, 1806; Aug. 2, 1806–Feb. 6, 1808; Mar. 11, 1809–Dec. 29, 1810.
Duke Univ. has Feb. 23–Oct. 26, 1805, although not found since 1930.
Ga. State Lib. has June 15, 29, Aug. 17–Sept. 14, Oct. 12, Dec. 21, 28, 1805; Jan. 5–Mar. 22, 1806.
Ga. Hist. Soc. has Dec. 30, 1809; Jan. 6, Feb. 3–Apr. 7, May 5–June 2, 23–Aug. 11, 25–Dec. 8, 1810; Jan. 9–Mar. 27, Apr. 17, 24, May 8, 15, 29–Dec. 25, 1813; Jan. 6, 1815, extra.
Am. Antiq. Soc. has June 30, Aug. 4, Dec. 8, 15, 1810; Jan. 26, Feb. 23, Mar. 2, Apr. 13, 20, 1811; Mar. 7, 1812; Apr. 3, Oct. 9, 1813; Mar. 5, May 21, July 2, Aug. 6, 1814.
Harvard has Sept. 28, 1805.
Mrs. Ida A. Wright, Washington, Ga., has Jan. 7, Feb. 25, 1809.
Univ. of Ga., Athens, has Feb. 4, 1809.
Mrs. Gari Melchers, Falmouth, Va., has Jan. 21, 1809.
Ga. Dept. of Archives has Aug. 30, 1806.
Yale has July 29, 1809.

[Washington] News, 1816–1820+.

Weekly. Established Jan. 19, 1816, by John K. M. Charlton, judging from the date of the first issue located, that of Feb. 23, 1816, vol. 1, no. 6, entitled "The News." Charlton became the publisher of the "Augusta Chronicle" in August, 1819, and presumably was succeeded by Philip C. Guien, who was the publisher of the paper in June 1821.

Am. Antiq. Soc. has Feb. 23, 1816; Apr. 4, 1817; Apr. 9, 1819.
Duke Univ. has Apr. 1, 1816; Aug. 22, Sept. 5, 1817.
N. Y. Hist. Soc. has June 15, 1821.

ILLINOIS

Edwardsville Spectator, 1819–1820+.

Weekly. Established May 29, 1819 by Hooper Warren, with the title of "Edwardsville Spectator." Continued after 1820.

St. Louis Merc. Lib. has May 29, 1819–Dec. 26, 1820.
Lib. Congress has May 29–July 10, 24–Oct. 16, 30, Nov. 27–Dec. 25, 1819; Jan. 1–May 29, June 13–Nov. 7, 21–Dec. 26, 1820.
Chicago Hist. Soc. has Apr. 18–June 27, July 11–Aug. 22, Sept. 5, 19–Dec. 26, 1820.
Am. Antiq. Soc. has June 5, Sept. 25, 1819; Aug. 22, 1820.
Alonzo P. Walton, Schenectady, N. Y., has July 31, 1819.
Ohio Hist. & Phil. Soc. has Sept. 11, 1820.

[Kaskaskia] Illinois Herald, 1814–1816.

Weekly. Established in May 1814, judging from the date of the earliest and only issue located, that of Dec. 13, 1814, vol. 1, no. 30, published by Mathew Duncan, with the title of "The Illinois Herald." Duncan in the imprint spelled his first name "Mathew," although in a paper previously published by him at Russellville, Ky., "The Farmer's Friend," and later in Pope's "Laws of Illinois" printed in June 1815, he spelled it "Matthew." The "Illinois Herald" is referred to in several issues of the Paris, Ky., "Western Citizen" from May 28 to Oct. 8, 1814; in the Chillicothe "Weekly Recorder" of May 17, 1815; and in the Cincinnati "Liberty Hall" of Oct. 16 and 30, 1815. Samuel R. Brown, in his "Western Gazetteer" 1817, p. 27, in describing Kaskaskia in 1816, says there is a "printing office, from which is issued a weekly newspaper entitled the 'Illinois Herald.'" In 1816 Duncan sold his paper to Daniel P. Cook, who established in its stead "The Western Intelligencer."

Ill. State Hist. Lib. has Dec. 13, 1814.

[Kaskaskia] Illinois Intelligencer, 1818–1820.

Weekly. A continuation of the "Western Intelligencer," without change of numbering, the first issue with the new name of "The Illinois Intelligencer" being that of May 27, 1818, new series, vol. 1, no. 39, old series, vol. 2. Published by Blackwell & Berry [Robert Blackwell and Elijah C. Berry]. Beginning with the third volume, Sept. 1818, the new series of numbering was dropped. The issue for Oct. 14, 1820, vol. 5, no. 6, announced that this was the last number published at Kaskaskia, and that the next number would be published at Vandalia. See under Vandalia.

St. Louis Merc. Lib. has May 27, 1818–May 12, 1819.
Lib. Congress has Jan. 13–27, Feb. 10–Mar. 3, 17–May 26, June 9–Oct. 6, 27–Dec. 1, 15–29, 1819; Jan. 5–17, 31–Mar. 4, 25, Apr. 8, 22–May 13, 27–June 10, July 22, Aug. 7–Sept. 23, Oct. 7, 14, 1820.
Chicago Hist. Soc. has Sept. 16, 1818; Mar. 10, June 16, July 21, 28, 1819.
Am. Antiq. Soc. has July 1, 1818.

[Kaskaskia] Western Intelligencer, 1816–1818.

Weekly. Established Apr. 24, 1816, judging from the date of the first known issue, that of May 15, 1816, vol. 1, no. 4, published by Dan'l P. Cook & Co., [Robert Blackwell], with the title of "The Western Intelligencer." With the issue of May 29, 1816, Robert Blackwell was admitted to partnership, and the paper was published by Cook & Blackwell. The issue for Sept. 10, 1817, is numbered "new series, no. 2, vol. 1," and is published by Berry & Cook [Elijah C. Berry and Daniel P. Cook] showing that on Sept. 3, 1817, the new firm had signalized their partnership with a new numbering. With the issue of Oct. 23, 1817, the publishers again changed, this time to Berry and Blackwell, which with the issue of Feb. 4, 1818, was transposed to Blackwell and Berry. The last issue with the name of "Western Intelligencer" was on May 20, 1818, new series, vol. 1, no. 38, old series, vol. 2, after which the name was changed to "The Illinois Intelligencer," which see.

St. Louis Merc. Lib. has May 15–June 25, July 9, 24–Sept. 5, Oct. 2, 23–Dec. 25, 1816; Jan. 1–Feb. 19, Mar. 5, 12, May 7–21, July 2, Sept. 10–Dec. 25, 1817; Jan. 1–Feb. 11, 25–May 20, 1818.
Am. Antiq. Soc. has Apr. 29, 1818.

[Shawneetown] Illinois Emigrant, 1818–1819.

Weekly. Established late in May 1818, judging from the following statement in the Kaskaskia "Illinois Intelligencer" of June 3, 1818: "We have received the first number of a newspaper printed at Shawnoe-town, in this territory, entitled, 'The Illinois Emigrant,' and edited by Mess. Eddy and Kimmel." The earliest issue located is that of June 17, 1818, vol. 1, no. 3, published by Eddy & Kimmel [Henry Eddy and Allen W. Kimmel], with the title of "The Illinois Emigrant." Allen Kimmel's father, Peter Kimmel, actually projected the paper, according to a letter written by him to Nathaniel Pope, Dec. 22, 1817 (in U. S. Dept. of State Archives), but presumably he put his son in charge, as a notice of the dissolution of the firm, May 27, 1820, referring to their previous conduct of the Illinois Emigrant, was signed by Henry Eddy and A. W. Kimmel.

No issues were published between June 5 and June 23, and between June 23 and Aug. 21, 1819, because of lack of paper. The last issue with this title was that of Sept. 18, 1819, vol. 1, no. 54, after which it was changed to "The Illinois Gazette," which see.

It has been frequently stated in Illinois histories that this paper was at first called the "Shawnee Chief," but no paper of this name is known, nor is there any evidence that such a paper existed. Mr. Frank W. Scott writes me under date of Jan. 10, 1914: "My search has convinced me that there never was a 'Shawnee Chief,' because as early as June 8, 1818, an agent wrote a letter to the editor of the 'Emigrant,' saying: 'I received your first number and the terms of subscription.' A similar letter from another correspondent is dated July 17, 1818. These letters clearly refer to a preliminary number of the paper used as a prospectus to be placed in the hands of agents who were to solicit subscriptions. This also shows that the 'Illinois Emigrant' was not merely a new title for an old paper, but a new title for a new paper. It was projected as early as May, 1818, because the letter of June 8 includes a long list of subscribers secured at various towns." The fact that the first issue was specifically referred to in a contemporaneous newspaper as the "Illinois Emigrant," as noted above, is sufficient proof to discard the theory that it was at first called the "Shawnee Chief." Possibly this latter title was confused with the "Shawnee Chief" published at Shawneetown in 1844 (issue of Aug. 3, 1844 in Am. Antiq. Soc.).

Am. Antiq. Soc. has Oct. 17, Dec. 26, 1818; Mar. 6, 1819.
Lib. Congress has Jan. 9, 23–Mar. 27, Apr. 10–May 22, June 5, 23, Aug. 21– Sept. 18, 1819.
Ohio Hist. & Phil. Soc. has June 17, 1818.
Univ. of Ill. has June 24, 1818, although not located in 1944.

[Shawneetown] **Illinois Gazette,** 1819–1820+.

Weekly. A continuation of the "Illinois Emigrant," without change of numbering, the first issue with the new title of "The Illinois Gazette" being that of Sept. 25, 1819, vol. 2, no. 1. The paper was published by Eddy & Kimmel [Henry Eddy and Allen W. Kimmel], until Kimmel sold his interests to James Hall, and beginning with the issue of May 27, 1820, it was published by Hall & Eddy. Continued after 1820.

Lib. Congress has Sept. 25, 1819–Mar. 9, 30, Apr. 6, 20–June 10, July 1–Sept. 9, 30, Oct. 14, Nov. 11, Dec. 2, 1820.
Chicago Hist. Soc. has Mar. 16, July 29, Aug. 5, 1820.

[Vandalia] **Illinois Intelligencer,** 1820+.

Weekly. A continuation, without change of numbering, of "The Illinois Intelligencer" published at Kaskaskia. The first number of "The Illinois Intelligencer" published at Vandalia was that of Dec. 14, 1820, vol. 5, no. 7, published by Blackwell & Berry [Robert Blackwell and William Berry, who had displaced his brother Elijah C. Berry upon removal of the paper to Vandalia]. With the issue of Dec. 23, 1820, the paper was published by Brown & Berry, Robert Blackwell having sold his interests to William H. Brown. Continued after 1820.

Lib. Congress has Dec. 14, 23, 1820.

INDIANA

Brookville Enquirer, 1819-1820+.

Weekly. Established Feb. 5, 1819, by John Scott, and Co., under the title of "The Brookville Enquirer, and Indiana Telegraph." The prospectus in the first issue stated that since the publication of the "Plain Dealer" had ceased by the dissolution of the copartnership of its late proprietors, the subscribers proposed publishing a new paper; signed by M[iles] C. Eggleston, D[aniel] J. Caswell, William C. Drew and John Scott. This firm was dissolved, and beginning with the issue of Oct. 1, 1819, the paper was published by B. F. Morris & Co. [Bethuel F. Morris, Daniel J. Caswell and William C. Drew]. With the issue of Mar. 2, 1820, the title was shortened to "Brookville Enquirer." The paper was continued after 1820.

Lib. Congress has Feb. 5, 19–Mar. 5, 19–Apr. 9, 23–May 28, June 18, July 2–23, Aug. 6–20, Sept. 10–Nov. 26, Dec. 24, 31, 1819; Jan. 7–Feb. 18, Mar. 2, 16–June 20, July 4–18, Aug. 1–15, 29–Dec. 26, 1820.

Ind. State Lib. has Mar. 5, 1819; Mar. 9, Apr. 13, 1820.

[Brookville] Plain Dealer, 1816-1819.

Weekly. Established Oct. 22, 1816, judging from the date of the first issue located, that of Nov. 5, 1816, vol. 1, no. 3, printed by Benjamin Ogle, Jr., for B[ethuel] F. Morris, with the title of "The Plain Dealer." The earliest advertisements, however, are all dated Oct. 16, 1816. David Thomas, in his "Travels through the Western Country," 1819, p. 194, refers to the paper as being published by B. F. Morris in February 1818, and it is quoted in the Cincinnati "Western Spy" of June 6, 1818. It was discontinued in January 1819, to be succeeded by "The Brookville Enquirer." The first issue of the Enquirer on Feb. 5, 1819 continued advertisements from the Plain Dealer carrying the earlier volume numbers, the latest being no. 103, Dec. 1, 1818. There was also an advertisement in the Enquirer, dated Jan. 5, 1819, referring to its being published in the "Plain Dealer and White Water Gazette," of Brookville, Ind. In the National Archives, State Dep't. Papers, is a letter from Guernsey G. Brown, Feb. 5, 1819, saying that he has sold his share in the "Plain Dealer and White Water Gazette" to John Scott & Co., who were to change the name to the "Brookville Enquirer."

Am. Antiq. Soc. has Nov. 5, 12, 1816.

[Charlestown] Indiana Intelligencer, 1818-1820+.

Weekly. Established in June 1818, judging from the first and only issue located, that of July 27, 1820, vol. 3, no. 110, published by Lingan & Dunkin [Joseph A. Lingan and L―――― L. Dunkin], with the title of "The Indiana

Intelligencer." The Vincennes "Indiana Centinel" of June 19, 1819 refers to this paper as having been edited about two months previously by Dr. [Elias] McNamee. It also is quoted in the Corydon "Indiana Gazette" of June 19, 1819, and the Madison "Indiana Republican" of June 19, 1819, and is mentioned in the Vincennes "Indiana Centinel" of Sept. 11, 1819. Continued after 1820.

Am. Antiq. Soc. has July 27, 1820.

[Corydon] **Indiana Gazette,** 1816–1820+.

Weekly. Established in November 1816, judging from the date of the first issue located, that of Feb. 15, 1817, vol. 1, no. 12, published by Brandon & Lodge [Armstrong Brandon and John Lodge], with the title of "The Indiana Gazette." Lodge removed to Madison in December 1817. In February 1818 according to David Thomas "Travels through the Western Country," p. 194, the publisher was A. Brandon. By Jan. 9, 1819, the firm name had become A. & J. Brandon [Armstrong and Jesse Brandon]. With the issue of July 3, 1819, this firm became Brandon & M'Cullough, Randall M'Cullough having purchased an interest. M'Cullough retired from the firm, and beginning with July 6, 1820, the paper was published by Brandon & Co. [Armstrong Brandon & Co.]. Continued after 1820.

Lib. Congress has Aug. 9, 1817; Jan. 9–Nov. 27, Dec. 11–25, 1819; Jan. 1–Mar. 30, Apr. 13, 20, May 4–June 1, 15, 22, July 6, 13, 27–Dec. 28, 1820.
Henry Co. Hist. Society, New Castle, Ind., has Feb. 15, 1817 (photostat in Ind. State Lib.).
Am. Antiq. Soc. has June 21, 1817.

[Corydon] **Indiana Herald,** 1816–1818.

Weekly. Established in 1816, by Cox & Nelson [Isaac Cox and Reuben W. Nelson]. The Cincinnati "Liberty Hall" of Sept. 25, 1816 mentions the "Indiana Herald," a new paper published at Corydon. The paper is quoted in the Ind. House Journal of Dec. 6, 1816, p. 56; the Vincennes "Indiana Centinel" of Mar. 28, 1817; the Madison "Indiana Republican" of Sept. 16, 1817; the Savannah "Republican" of May 7, 1818; the Vincennes "Western Sun" of May 30, 1818; and the Lawrenceburg "Dearborn Gazette" of Aug. 17, 1818. David Thomas, in his "Travels through the Western Country," 1819, p. 194, lists the paper as in existence in February 1818, edited by R. W. Nelson, but in a note says: "We learn that the Herald is discontinued at Corydon, and the Indianian, by the same Editor, is now published at Jeffersonville." No copy located.

[Jeffersonville] **Indianian,** 1818–1820+.

Weekly. Established Sept. 20, 1818, according to a record of the receipt of the first issue in the "National Intelligencer" of Nov. 7, 1818, which stated that the paper was edited by R. W. Nelson and printed by Isaac Cox. The first issue located is that of Nov. 13, 1819, vol. 2, no. 3, edited by R[euben] W. Nelson and printed by Isaac Cox, with the title of "The Indianian." David Thomas in his "Travels" states that Nelson removed from Corydon to publish his new newspaper at Jeffersonville. The Corydon "Indiana Gazette" of Aug. 10, 1820, quotes a letter to "The Indianian" addressed to Messrs. Nelson & Cox and dated Aug. 2, 1820. The Edwardsville, Ill., "Spectator" of Aug. 29, 1820, quotes from "The Indianian," published by Messrs. Nelson and Cox. The last issue located is that of June 8, 1820, vol. 2, no. 33. The paper was presumably continued after 1820, and subsequent publishers moved the press to Indianapolis in 1822.

Ohio Arch. & Hist. Soc. has Nov. 13, Dec. 4–18, 1819; Jan. 1, 23, Mar. 10, 24–Apr. 7, 20, 27, May 18, June 8, 1820.

[Lawrenceburg] Dearborn Gazette, 1817–1819.

Weekly. Established in December 1817, judging from the date of the first and only issue located, that of Aug. 17, 1818, vol. 1, no. 35, published by B[———] Brown & Co., with the title of "Dearborn Gazette." David Thomas, in his "Travels," 1819, p. 194, states that it was published by B. Brown in February 1818. The "History of Dearborn, Ohio and Switzerland Counties," 1885, p. 176, states "The printer of the establishment is remembered to have been Steele Sampson," although I find no further proof of this statement. The paper must have suspended about a year after its establishment, as the Corydon "Indiana Gazette" of May 22, 1819, states that "The Dearborn Gazette is at length resuscitated." The Vincennes "Indiana Centinel" of Sept. 11, 1819 says: "The Dearborn Gazette . . . has again given up the ghost. . . . It is thought that this exit is final and conclusive. . . . A stranger, calling itself The Indiana Oracle, has arisen upon its remains." Yet the Dearborn Gazette must have been revived, for in July 1823, "The Indiana Oracle" was united with it, under the title of "The Indiana Oracle and Dearborn Gazette."

H. L. Hodell, Cincinnati, has Aug. 17, 1818 (photostat in Am. Antiq. Soc.).

[Lawrenceburg] Indiana Oracle, 1819–1820+.

Weekly. Established Sept. 1, 1819, judging from the date of the earliest issue located, that of Sept. 29, 1819, vol. 1, no. 5, published by Dunn & Russell [Isaac Dunn and ——— Russell], with the title of "The Indiana Oracle." The paper was so continued until after 1820.

Ind. State Lib. has Sept. 29–Nov. 17, Dec. 8–29, 1819; Jan. 5–Apr. 8, 22, May 13–June 12, 26–Oct. 3, 1820.

Duke Univ. has Apr. 15, 1820.

[Lexington] **Cornucopia of the West,** 1816.

Weekly. The only issue located is that of June 8, 1816, vol. 1, no. [torn], published by Madox and Brandeberry [D———— T. Madox and ———— Brandeberry], with the title of "The Cornucopia of the West." This issue contains the notice "To the Public. The Cornucopia of the West, originally designed for the publication of Geographical, Statistical, Agricultural, Commercial & Historical investigations of the western territories, has dwindled down into a weekly newspaper." There is a reference to the paper in the Vincennes "Western Sun" of July 20, 1816. The "Indiana Register," of Vevay, of Sept. 30, 1816 says: "D. T. Madox, editor of the late Cornucopiæ of the West, is a candidate for the senatorial clerkship."

Ind. State Lib. has June 8, 1816.

[Lexington] **Western Eagle,** 1815–1816.

Weekly. Removed in 1815 from Madison to Lexington and there continued without change of volume numbering. The first issue at Lexington was that of July 8, 1815, vol. 3, no. 1, published by Jacob Rhoads, with the title of "The Western Eagle." The last regular issue published was that of Jan. 6, 1816, vol. 3, no. 26.

Ind. State Lib. has July 8–22, Aug. 5–19, Sept. 24–Oct. 21, Nov. 4–Dec. 9, 1815.
Ind. Hist. Soc. has Sept. 9, 16, Oct. 28, Dec. 16, 23, 1815; Jan. 6, 1816.

[Madison] **Indiana Republican,** 1817–1820+.

Weekly. Established Jan. 2, 1817 by Samuel Pelham, with the title of "Indiana Republican." With the issue of Dec. 13, 1817, Pelham retired, and John Lodge became the publisher. In January 1819 Copeland P. L. Arion, Lodge's brother-in-law, became a partner, under the firm name of Lodge and Arion, who continued the paper until after 1820.

Ind. State Lib. has Jan. 16, 1817–Dec. 5, 1818.
S. Arion Lewis, Los Angeles, has Jan. 23, 1819–Oct. 5, 1820 (film reproduction in Ind. State Lib.).

[Madison] **Western Eagle,** 1813–1815.

Weekly. Established May 26, 1813 by S. M. Levenworth and W. Hendricks [Seth M. Levenworth and William Hendricks], with the title of "The Western Eagle." This partnership was dissolved and beginning with the issue of Sept. 10, 1813, the paper was published by Hendricks & Camron [William Hendricks and William Camron]. Hendricks resigned as editor in favor of Jacob Rhoads, and the paper was published by Rhoads & Camron beginning with the issue of Apr. 8, 1814, vol. 1, no. 43. This is the last Madison issue located. The paper was removed to Lexington in July 1815, and there continued by Rhoads without change of volume numbering.

Jefferson Co. Hist. Soc., Madison, has May 26, 1813.
Am. Antiq. Soc. has Aug. 6, Sept. 10, 24–Nov. 5, Dec. 3, 17–31, 1813; Jan. 14, Feb. 4–25, Mar. 18, Apr. 1, 8, 1814.

New-Albany Chonicle, 1820+.

Weekly. Established Sept. 30, 1820, judging from the date of the earliest issue located, that of Nov. 11, 1820, vol. 1, no. 7, published by E[benezer] Patrick, with the title of "New-Albany Chronicle." The issue of Jan. 13, 1821 (file for 1821 in Am. Antiq. Soc.), was published by M[ason] C. Fitch & M[atthew] Patrick.

Am. Antiq. Soc. has Nov. 11, 18, 1820.

[Salem] Tocsin, 1818–1820+.

Weekly. Established by Patrick and Booth [Ebenezer Patrick and Beebe Booth], on Mar. 17, 1818, judging from the date of the first issue located, that of Mar. 31, 1818, vol. 1, no. 3, entitled "The Tocsin." According to Stevens, "History of Washington County, Indiana," p. 383, Booth retired in March 1819, to be succeeded by E. Patrick. The issue of July 5, 1819 was published by Ebenezer Patrick; those of Jan. 8 and Apr. 8, 1820 by E. & M. Patrick [Ebenezer and Matthew Patrick]; and that of June 10, 1820 by Ebenezer Patrick. The paper was continued until after 1820, although Ebenezer Patrick removed to New Albany in the fall of 1820.

Am. Antiq. Soc. has Mar. 31, May 5, 1818; July 5, 1819.
Washington Co. Hist. Soc., Salem, Ind., has Jan. 8, June 10, 1820.
Salem Pub. Lib. has Apr. 8, 1820.

[Vevay] Independent Examiner, 1819–1820+.

In the Corydon "Indiana Gazette" of June 5, 1819 is the statement: "We have received the first number of a paper printed at Vevay, denominated the 'Independent Examiner,' which is edited by Stephen C. Stevens. We hope it will be more permanent in its existence than the papers formerly printed in that Town." The "National Intelligencer" of July 28, 1819, records the establishment of the paper, which it says was begun the last week in May. There are references to the Vevay Examiner in the Madison "Indiana Republican" of July 10, 1819; in the Vincennes "Western Sun" of September and October 1819; and in the Corydon "Indiana Gazette" of Nov. 13, 1819, which prints a letter addressed to the "Independent Examiner." No copies in 1819–1820 located. The Indiana

State Library has the issues of Feb. 15 and Mar. 22, 1821, vol. 2, nos. 62 and 66, published by John Douglass.

[Vevay] Indiana Register, 1816–1819.

Weekly. Established June 17, 1816, judging from the date of the first issue located, that of July 8, 1816, vol. 1, no. 4, printed and published by William C. Keen, with the title of "The Indiana Register." The printed "Proposals" were dated April 1816, and signed by William C. Keen (see C. E. Carter, "Territorial Papers of U. S.," vol. 8, p. 432). In 1817 a new partnership was formed and the paper was published by John F. Dufour, William C. Keen and Robert Burchfield, under the firm name of Dufour, Keen, & Co. According to David Thomas, "Travels," 1819, p. 194, the paper was published by J. F. Dufour in February 1818. It was quoted in the Cynthiana, Ky., "Guardian of Liberty" of July 25, 1818. It was discontinued before June 1819, according to the Corydon "Indiana Gazette" of June 5, 1819. P. Dufour, in "The Swiss Settlement of Switzerland County, Indiana," 1925, p. 110, says that in about 1819 the title was "Indiana Register and Vevay and Ghent Advertiser." The paper was revived by Keen in 1824, judging from an issue of Jan. 30, 1824, vol. 1, no. 3.

National Archives, State Dep't. Papers, has "Proposals," April 1816 (photostat in Lib. Congress and Am. Antiq. Soc.).
Lib. Congress has July 8, 1816.
Am. Antiq. Soc. has Sept. 16, 30, 1816; Nov. 25, 1817.

[Vincennes] Indiana Centinel, 1817–1820+.

Weekly. Established Mar. 14, 1817, by Samuel Dillworth and Charles Keemle, with the title of "Indiana Centinel." In 1818, according to a reference in the "Western Sun" of Nov. 28, 1818, it was published by Elias McNamee. Early in 1819 it was published by N. Blackman for Willis Fellows. The issue of May 29, 1819, states that "this paper, previous to its late transfer, was the exclusive property of Doctor McNamee and B. J. Ball." With the issue of Oct. 23, 1819, Fellows retired and the paper was published by N[athan] Blackman. Beginning with the issue of Apr. 15, 1820, the title was changed to "Indiana Centinel & Public Advertiser," although the issues of Aug. 19 and Sept. 2, 1820, were much reduced in size because of scarcity of paper and were titled "Indiana Centinel." With the issue of Dec. 2, 1820, the paper was published by N. Blackman, but also had the imprint "W[———] H. Johnston, Printer." Continued after 1820. W. H. Johnston had previously published in the Vincennes "Western Sun" of Oct. 9, 1819 proposals for "The Western Patriot," to be printed in Evansville, Ind., but probably never established.

Am. Antiq. Soc. has Mar. 14–Apr. 4, 18, 25, 1817; June 19, July 3, Aug. 21, 1819; Jan. 1, 15–Feb. 12, 26, Mar. 4, Apr. 8, June 24, Dec. 30, 1820.

Ind. State Lib. has May 22–July 3, 17, 24, Aug. 14–Dec. 25, 1819; Jan. 1–Aug. 12, Sept. 2, Oct. 28–Dec. 30, 1820.
Lib. Congress has Dec. 11–25, 1819; Jan. 1–Sept. 2, Oct. 28–Dec. 2, 30, 1820.

[Vincennes] **Indiana Gazette**, 1804–1806.

Weekly. Established July 31, 1804, by E[lihu] Stout, with the title of "Indiana Gazette." The date of the first issue of this paper has generally been conjectured as July 4, 1804, but the issue of Aug. 7, 1804, vol. 1, no. 2, gives every indication that the first issue was on July 31, 1804. The printing office was burned out in April 1806 ("Ind. Mag. of History," vol. 31, p. 127), and the paper was succeeded by the "Western Sun." The last issue located is that of Apr. 12, 1806, vol. 2, no. 20, owned by H. S. Cauthorn, Jr., and reproduced in the Centennial Edition of the "Western Sun," July 4, 1904. Joseph Charless advertised in the Bardstown, Ky., "Candid Review" of Sept. 1, 1807, that he would establish the "Indiana Gazette" at Vincennes to begin about Oct. 1, 1807, but he could not carry out his intentions and went to St. Louis, where he started the "Missouri Gazette," July 12, 1808.

Harvard has Aug. 7–21, Sept. 11–Oct. 2, 16, 23, 1804.
Am. Antiq. Soc. has Aug. 7–28, Oct. 23, 1804; Aug. 7, 14, 1805.
Univ. of Texas has Apr. 10, 1805.
Ind. State Lib. has Feb. 15, 1806.
Mrs. H. S. Cauthorn, Jr., Portland, Ore., has Apr. 12, 1806.

[Vincennes] **Western Sun**, 1807–1820+.

Weekly. Established July 4, 1807, by E[lihu] Stout, with the title of "The Western Sun." With the issue of Aug. 1, 1807, the publishers became Elihu Stout and George C. Smoot. There were no issues published from Oct. 3 to Nov. 17, 1807, due to the absence of Mr. Stout in Kentucky and to the illness of Mr. Smoot. With the issue of Nov. 17, 1807, Jonathan Jennings took Mr. Smoot's place in the firm, which became Stout & Jennings. Stout resumed sole proprietorship with the issue of Dec. 23, 1807. The paper was suspended from Oct. 27 to Dec. 8, 1810, from Jan. 5 to June 15, 1811, from Aug. 3 to Nov. 9, 1811, from Feb. 22 to Mar. 7, 1812, from Mar. 20 to July 10, 1813, from Oct. 30 to Dec. 11, 1813, and from Sept. 16 to Dec. 16, 1815, as well as omitting occasional issues. The title was changed to "The Western Sun & General Advertiser" with the issue of Dec. 6, 1817. The printing office was destroyed by fire Feb. 28, 1819, but most of the material was saved, except a large quantity of paper (Kaskaskia "Illinois Intelligencer" of Mar. 31, 1819). No issues therefore were published between Feb. 20 and Mar. 20, 1819. With the issue of June 26, 1819, the title was altered to "Western Sun & General Advertiser." Beginning with the issue of Oct. 2, 1819, the paper was published by Stout & Osborn [Elihu

Indiana

Stout and John W. Osborn], but with the issue of Oct. 7, 1820, Osborn retired and it was henceforth published by Elihu Stout. Continued after 1820.

Ind. State Lib. has July 11, 1807–Dec. 30, 1820, with but few issues missing.
Lib. Congress has Jan. 28, May 6, 13, 27–June 10, July 1–15, Aug. 5–19, Sept. 2, Dec. 16, 30, 1809; Dec. 9, 1812; Jan. 2, 16, 23, Feb. 6–20, Mar. 20, Apr. 3–May 29, June 12–Aug. 21, Sept. 11–Oct. 30, Nov. 13, 27–Dec. 11, 1819; Jan. 1–22, Feb. 12–Apr. 22, May 6, 20, July 1, 8, 22–Aug. 19, Oct. 7, 14, 28–Dec. 23, 1820.
Am. Antiq. Soc. has May 13, 1809; July 21, Aug. 4, 1810; Sept. 20, 1817; Aug. 5, Oct. 7, 1820.
Chicago Hist. Soc. has Sept. 5, 1807; May 24, 1817.
Wis. Hist. Soc. has Oct. 17, 1818.

KENTUCKY

[Augusta] **Bracken Sentinel,** 1820.

Weekly. Established Jan. 29, 1820, judging from the date of the earliest issue located, that of Apr. 22, 1820, vol. 1, no. 13, published by C[harles] D. M'Manaman, with the title of "Bracken Sentinel."
Ohio Hist. & Phil. Soc. has Apr. 22, May 13, Aug. 19, Sept. 2, 9, 1820.

Augusta Whig, 1818.

No copy located. Established presumably in 1818, since it was first authorized to print State advertisements, Dec. 11, 1818 (Ky. Acts, 27th Ass'y, p. 597).

[Bairdstown] **Candid Review,** 1807–1811.

Weekly. Established early in 1807 by P[eter] Isler & Co. Judging from the date of the first issue located, that of July 14, 1807, vol. 1, no. 23, entitled "Candid Review," it would have been established on Feb. 11, but Morse's "American Gazetteer," 3rd edition, 1810, says: "The 1st No. of the 'Candid Review,' a newspaper, was printed in this town, Jan. 1807, by P. Isler." The last issue located is that of Aug. 27, 1810, vol. 4, no. 178. The issues from Sept. 1, 1807, to Aug. 27, 1810, were published by P. Isler. There is a reference to the "Candid Review" and P. Isler in the Lexington "Reporter" of Aug. 3, 1811. The name of the town was spelled "Bairdstown" throughout.

Harvard has July 14, 1807.
Am. Antiq. Soc. has Sept. 1, 8, Oct. 7, 1807; June 20, Dec. 12, 1809; July 9, Aug. 27, 1810.
Univ. of Chicago has Dec. 9, 1807; Mar. 29, 1808.
Filson Club, Louisville, has Mar. 22, 1808.

[Bardstown] **Impartial Review,** 1806.

Proposals for this paper, signed by Peter Isler & Co., and dated October 1806, were printed in the Danville "Informant" of Dec. 2, 1806. It was established presumably in 1806, since it was first authorized to print State advertisements, Dec. 9, 1806 (Littell's Laws, vol. 3, p. 343). It is possible that this was the title at first selected for the "Candid Review," which was established by Peter Isler & Co. early in 1807.

Bardstown Repository, 1812–1820+.

Weekly. There is an advertisement of the prospective publication of this paper, which is signed by James McAllister, in the Lexington "Kentucky Gazette" of Jan. 21, 1812. That it was established in February, 1812, would be assumed from the volume numbering of the earliest issue located, that of June 29, 1814, vol. 3, no. 19, published by William Bard with the title of "Bardstown Repository." William Bard printed pamphlets at the Bardstown Repository Office in 1812. Bard continued the paper until March, 1815, when he formed a partnership with George C. Smoot under the firm name of Bard and Smoot, with a new series volume numbering. With the issue of May 4, 1815, the partnership was dissolved and William Bard published the paper alone, restoring the old volume numbering. With the issue of May 23, 1815, a partnership was formed with John P. Edrington under the firm name of Bard & Edrington, with a new series volume numbering. In 1816, apparently in February, John P. Edrington began publishing the paper alone, again with a new series volume numbering, and so continued it to the last issue located, that of June 23, 1819, vol. 4, no. 17, whole no. 381. The Danville "Olive Branch" of June 2, 1820, records the marriage, on May 18, of Marquis Barnett, editor of the Bardstown Repository, to Matilda G. Thomas. Barnett printed at Bardstown from 1819 to after 1820, and pamphlets late in 1820 bore the imprint of the Repository Office.

Am. Antiq. Soc. has June 29, July 6, Aug. 3, 17, Nov. 16, Dec. 7, 1814; Feb. 9, Mar. 16, 23, Apr. 13–May 30, 1815; Sept. 4–25, Oct. 16, 30, 1816.
Western Ky. State Teachers Coll., Bowling Green, has June 23, 1819.

[Bardstown] **Telescope**, 1815.

No copy located. Established presumably in 1815, as it was first authorized to print State advertisements, Feb. 8, 1815 (Ky. Acts, 23rd Ass'y, p. 434).

[Bardstown] **Western American**, 1803–1805.

Weekly. Established by F[rancis] Peniston, Sept. 6, 1803, with the title of "The Western American." In the issues of September 1803, the place of imprint was spelled Bairdstown, but thereafter Bardstown. The last Bardstown issue located is that of May 17, 1805, vol. 2, no. 89. Judging by the numbering of Louisville issues the paper was suspended in the fall of 1805, or earlier. Peniston advertised in the "Kentucky Gazette" of Lexington, Oct. 31, 1805, proposals for the "Louisiana Herald" to be published at St. Louis, but there is no evidence to show that it was ever established. In 1806, Peniston removed "The Western American" to Louisville, where on Jan. 30, 1806, he brought out the paper with the same title, and without change of numbering. See under Louisville.

Am. Antiq. Soc. has Sept. 6, 13, Oct. 13, Nov. 3, 10, 18, Dec. 16–30, 1803; Feb. 17, Mar. 2, June 1, 22, 29, Oct. 19–Nov. 2, 16, Dec. 7, 28, 1804.
Wis. Hist. Soc. has Nov. 23, 30, 1804; Mar. 8, 22, May 3–17, 1805.
Univ. of Chicago has Jan. 11, Mar. 15, 29, Apr. 5, 20, 1805.

[Bowling Green] Backwoodsman, 1820+.

No copy for 1820 located. First authorized to print State advertisements, Feb. 14, 1820 (Ky. Acts, 28th Ass'y, p. 970). Manuscript Court records of Warren County show that the editor in May, 1821 was Lewis Dillard. In the National Archives, State Dept. Papers, accompanying a letter of Nov. 3, 1822, from Lewis Dillard, is a copy of "The Backwoodsman" for Nov. 2, 1822, vol. 2, no. 36, indicating that the paper was established in February 1820.

[Bowling Green] Christian Advocate, 1820+.

No copy located. Established presumably in 1820, since it was first authorized to print State advertisements, Dec. 21, 1820 (Ky. Acts, 29th Ass'y, p. 162). Manuscript Court records of Warren County show that the editor in February 1821 was Lewis Dillard.

[Bowling Green] Southern Gazette, 1819.

No issue of this paper has been located, but the "National Intelligencer" of Apr. 24, 1819, lists the initial issue of the "Southern Gazette" of Bowling Green, published weekly by Thomas Green on Mar. 20, 1819. It is also referred to in the Frankfort "Argus" of Apr. 30, 1819.

[Bowling Green] Southern Patriot, 1819.

The Lexington "Kentucky Gazette" of May 14, 1819, states: "The Southern Patriot, of Bowling Green, Ky., is a paper of recent date, and highly respectable pretensions."

[Cynthiana] Guardian of Liberty, 1817–1820.

Weekly. Established Jan. 4, 1817, by John G. Keenon & Co., with the title of "Guardian of Liberty." It was suspended, for lack of support, with the issue of Dec. 27, 1817, but was revived by John G. Keenon with the issue of Mar. 7, 1818. Beginning with the issue of Jan. 26, 1819, it was published by J. G. & Adam C. Keenon. The last issue located is that of Mar. 13, 1819, vol. 2, no. 52. The "Guardian of Liberty" is quoted in the "Louisville Public Advertiser" of Jan. 12, 1820.

Univ. of Chicago has Jan. 18–Oct. 4, 18–Dec. 6, 27, 1817; Mar. 14–Apr. 18, May 11–Aug. 8, 22–Sept. 19, Oct. 3, 1818–Mar. 13, 1819.
Am. Antiq. Soc. has Jan. 11, 1817.

[Danville] Globe, 1812.

No copy located, but an issue of "The Globe" of May 26, 1812, "printed at Danville, Kentucky," is referred to in the "American Watchman" of Wilmington, Del., of June 17, 1812.

KENTUCKY 149

[Danville] **Impartial Observer**, 1810–1811.

Weekly. A continuation, without change of title or numbering, of "The Impartial Observer" of Lexington. The last issue at Lexington was that of Nov. 17, 1810, vol. 1, no. 13, and the first at Danville, Dec. 3, 1810, vol. 1, no. 14. The Danville issues were published by Edward Prentiss & Co., with the title of "The Impartial Observer." The last issue located is that of Jan. 22, 1811, vol. 1, no. 21.

Harvard has Dec. 10, 1810; Jan. 1, 8, 22, 1811.

[Danville] **Informant**, 1805–1810.

Weekly. Established Sept. 3, 1805, by Ogilsby & Demaree [Samuel Ogilsby and Samuel R. Demaree], with the title of "The Informant." In June or July, 1806, Samuel R. Demaree assumed the sole proprietorship. The last issue located is that of Mar. 3, 1807, vol. 2, no. 25, although the paper is listed in Thomas's list of 1810 (Amer. Antiq. Soc. Trans. vol. 6, p. 303), without name of publisher.

Chicago Hist. Soc. has Sept. 3–17, Nov. 5–19, 1805; May 13, July 29, Aug. 5, Sept. 9, Nov. 25, Dec. 2, 1806.
Harvard has Dec. 10, 1805; Jan. 21, Sept. 16–30, Oct. 14, 21, 1806.
Filson Club, Louisville, has Apr. 3, 1806.
Circuit Clerk's Office, Harrodsburg, Ky., has May 5, 1806.
Lib. Congress has Mar. 3, 1807.

[Danville] **Lighthouse**, 1813–1816.

Evidently established in 1813, since it was first authorized to print State advertisements, Dec. 24, 1813 (Ky. Acts, 22nd Ass'y, p. 125). J[oseph] A. Woodson was printing at Danville in 1813. A poetical editorial in the Winchester "Kentucky Advertiser" of Feb. 22, 1817, refers to Dr. Anthony Hunn's various newspaper ventures and includes a paper conducted by him called the "Light-house." Since there was a paper by the same name published a Harrodsburg, in the same county, in 1814, it is presumable that the place of publication was changed. See under Harrodsburg. Yet Samuel R. Brown, in his "Western Gazetteer," 1817, p. 95, referring to Danville in 1816, says there is "a printing office, in which is published a newspaper called the 'Light House.'"

[Danville] **Mirror**, 1804.

Weekly. Established Sept. 3, 1804, by J[ohn] Adams, with the title of "The Mirror," printed "at the house belonging to Mr. William Owens." The last issue located is that of Oct. 24, 1804, vol. 1, no. 7.

Harvard has Sept. 3, 1804.
Chicago Hist. Soc. has Oct. 24, 1804.

[Danville] Olive Branch, 1820+.

Weekly. Established in March 1820, judging from the date of the first issue located, that of Apr. 7, 1820, vol. 1, no. 2, published by James Armstrong, with the title of "Olive Branch." In this issue the publisher referred to a lapse of two weeks since the previous issue. The "National Intelligencer" of May 30, 1820, records the receipt of the first number issued on Mar. 24, 1820. With the issue of Apr. 14, 1820 the title was changed to "Olive Branch, and Union of the West," with Apr. 21, 1820, to "Olive Branch, and Western Union," and with May 12, 1820, to "The Olive Branch and Western Union." Continued after 1820.

Centre College, Danville, has Apr. 7–June 30, July 14, 21, Aug. 11–Oct. 13, Nov. 4–18, Dec. 2, 16, 1820.

[Danville] People's Friend, 1818.

No copy located. Established presumably in 1818, since it was first authorized to print State advertisements, Dec. 11, 1818 (Ky. Acts, 27th Ass'y, p. 597).

[Flemingsburg] Star, 1819–1820.

The "National Intelligencer" of Nov. 16, 1819, states that "The Star" was established as a weekly paper the last Saturday in September 1819, but without mention of name of publisher. It was first authorized to print State advertisements, Dec. 15, 1819 (Ky. Acts, 28th Ass'y, p. 809). The only copy located is that of July 29, 1820, vol. 1, no. 45, published by Peter Akers, with the title of "The Star."

Ohio Hist. & Phil. Soc. has July 29, 1820.

[Frankfort] American Republic, 1810–1812.

Weekly. Established June 26, 1810, by H[umphrey] Marshall, with the title of "The American Republic." The last issue located is that of Apr. 17, 1812, vol. 2, no. 95. The "Argus" of Frankfort of June 24, 1812, refers to the recent discontinuance of the "American Republic" and the withdrawal of Mr. Marshall from political life.

Lexington Pub. Lib. has June 26, 1810–Apr. 3, 1812.
Univ. of Chicago has Aug. 17, Oct. 12–Nov. 9, 23–Dec. 28, 1810; Jan. 4, 17–Mar. 22, Apr. 5–Aug. 2, Sept. 20–Oct. 11, Nov. 18, 1811; Apr. 10, 1812.
Am. Antiq. Soc. has July 3, Oct. 5, 19, 1810; Mar. 1, 8, 29, 1811.
Chicago Hist. Soc. has Oct. 19, 1810.
Filson Club, Louisville, has Nov. 2, 1810; Nov. 8, 15, 1811; Feb. 7, 28, Mar. 13, Apr. 3, 10, 1812.
Wis. Hist. Soc. has Nov. 2, 9, 30, Dec. 21, 28, 1810.

Lib. Congress has Dec. 28, 1810.
Ky. State Hist. Soc. has Feb. 22, 1811; Apr. 10, 17, 1812.
Ohio Hist. & Phil. Soc. has Jan. 10, 17, 1812.

[Frankfort] **Argus of Western America**, 1808–1820+.

Weekly. Established Jan. 27, 1808, by William Gerard, with the title of "The Argus of Western America." It was first issued in octavo size, each issue of 16 pages; but although having the appearance of a magazine, it published current news and was in reality a newspaper. On Aug. 27, 1808, the size of the paper was changed to a quarto of eight pages, and on Nov. 16, 1808 the firm name of the publishers became Wm. Gerard & Moses O. Bledsoe. With the issue of Feb. 6, 1809, the paper became a folio of four pages. With the issue of Apr. 15, 1809, this firm dissolved and the paper was published by Wm. Gerard alone. Between Nov. 7, 1812, and Feb. 24, 1813 (probably in January, 1813), Gerard admitted Elijah C. Berry to partnership under the firm name of Gerard & Berry, and changed the title to "Argus of Western America." With the issue of Nov. 1, 1816, the firm became Gerard & Kendall [William Gerard and Amos Kendall]. In May, 1817, the firm became Kendall & Russells [Amos Kendall, Gervas E. and John B. Russell] who continued the paper until after 1820.

Am. Antiq. Soc. has Feb. 3–17, Mar. 3, 17–July 28, Aug. 11, Nov. 16, 1808; Feb. 6, 18, 25, Mar. 11, 18, Apr. 8–22, May 16, 30, June 7, July 19, Aug. 2 extra, Sept. 6, 1809; Jan. 13, 27, Mar. 10, July 7, Sept. 29, Oct. 20, 1810; Sept. 19, 1812; July 23, Aug. 13, 1814; Apr. 24, 1818; Apr. 30, June 4, July 23, 1819.

Lib. Congress has Apr. 21, 28, May 12, 19, June 2, 9, July 21, 1808; Jan. 27, 1810; Oct. 31, 1812; Sept. 4, 1818; Jan. 1–Apr. 30, May 14–Sept. 17, Oct. 1–Nov. 19, Dec. 3–31, 1819; Jan. 7, 21–Feb. 17, Mar. 2–16, 30–May 11, 25–Dec. 28, 1820.

N. Y. Hist. Soc. has Jan. 27–Mar. 17, 31, Apr. 7, 21–June 9, 23, July 7–Aug. 11, Sept. 17–Oct. 19, Nov. 2–23, 1808.

Filson Club, Louisville, has Aug. 27, 1808–Jan. 28, 1809; Mar. 4, 1812; Jan. 19, 26, Feb. 9, 16, Mar. 1–22, May 5, June 28, Aug. 2, 9, 1816; Feb. 14, May 2, 1817; Sept. 25, Oct. 2, 1818; Nov. 19, 26, Dec. 17–31, 1819; Jan. 14, 21, Feb. 2, 17, Mar. 2–May 11, 25, June 1, 15, 29–Oct. 5, 1820.

Harvard has Sept. 1–29, Oct. 20–Nov. 3, 17, Dec. 14, 1810; Jan. 21, Feb. 13–27, Mar. 13, 20, Apr. 3–24, May 15, 29–June 12, July 3–17, 1811; Apr. 1–15, May 20, June 24, July 1, Aug. 5, 19, Sept. 26, 1812; Feb. 17, 24, Mar. 29, Apr. 3, 17, June 5, 19, 26, July 17, Aug. 14, Sept. 11, Oct. 9, 23, Nov. 20, 27, Dec. 8, 1813; Jan. 1, 8, Feb. 12, Mar. 5, 12, Apr. 2, 23–May 7, 21–June 11, Sept. 3, 10, 24, Oct. 8, 22, Nov. 10, 13, 19, Dec. 10, 1814.

Calvin M. Fackler, Danville, Ky., has Feb. 3–June 23, 1808.

Univ. of Chicago has Jan. 11, July 19, Aug. 2, 23, Oct. 4–Nov. 1, 29–Dec. 6, 1816; Jan. 17, Feb. 7, 21, Apr. 18, 25, May 30, Oct. 17, Nov. 7, Dec. 5–19,

1817; Jan. 2, Feb. 13, May 1, 22, July 24, Aug. 21, Sept. 18, Dec. 11, 18, 1818; Jan. 15–Feb. 5, 16, Mar. 19, Apr. 2, July 2, Aug. 13, Oct. 29, Dec. 17, 31, 1819; Apr. 20, Dec. 28, 1820.

Ky. State Hist. Soc. has Dec. 6, 14, 1810; Sept. 25, 1818; Dec. 17, 1819.

Ohio Hist. & Phil. Soc. has Dec. 23, 30, 1812; Nov. 13, 1813; June 9, 1815.

Univ. of Pittsburgh has Nov. 27, 1811.

Mass. Hist. Soc. has Aug. 19, 1812.

Western Ky. State Teachers Coll., Bowling Green, has May 8, July 3, Aug. 7, Sept. 4–18, 1813.

Lexington Pub. Lib. has Sept. 22, 1815; Jan. 26, 1816.

Centre Coll., Danville, has May 10, 1816.

Univ. of Ill. has July 23, 1819, extra.

[Frankfort] **Commentator**, 1817–1820+.

Weekly. Established by Moses O. Bledsoe on Jan. 3, 1817, judging from the date of the earliest issue located, that of Jan. 17, 1817, vol. 1, no. 3, entitled "The Commentator." The next issue located is that of July 4, 1817, published by Bledsoe & Farnham [Moses O. Bledsoe and John H. Farnham]. Farnham, between July and October 1818 (see "Autobiography of Amos Kendall," 1872, pp. 191–194), retired from the firm, and Moses Owsley Bledsoe became sole proprietor. With the issue of May 7, 1819, Bledsoe sold out and the paper was published by J. H. & W. B. Holeman [Jacob H. and William B. Holeman]. With the issue of June 1, 1820, J[acob] H. Holeman became sole publisher and so continued until after 1820.

Wis. Hist. Soc. has Jan. 17, 1817.

Filson Club, Louisville, has Feb. 24, Mar. 16, Apr. 27, June 8, 29, July 6, Aug. 3–Oct. 5, 1820.

Howard-Tilton Lib., New Orleans, has July 4–18, Aug. 8–29, Nov. 14, 1817.

Am. Antiq. Soc. has July 10, 1818; June 25, 1819.

Ohio Hist. & Phil. Soc. has Oct. 16, 1818; Dec. 14, 1820.

Chicago Hist. Soc. has Jan. 1, 1819–Dec. 20, 1820.

Lib. Congress has Jan. 1–Feb. 5, 19–Mar. 19, Apr. 2–June 11, 25–July 2, 16–Dec. 30, 1819; Jan. 6, 20–Feb. 10, 24–Sept. 21, Oct. 19–Nov. 16, Dec. 7–28, 1820.

Western Ky. State Teachers Coll., Bowling Green, has May 21, 1819.

Ky. State Hist. Soc. has Dec. 8, 1819.

[Frankfort] **Guardian of Freedom**, 1798–1805.

Weekly. Established May 8, 1798, by John Bradford & Son [James M. Bradford], under the title of "The Guardian of Freedom." Apparently the paper was suspended in May 1800, presumably with the issue numbered vol. 2, no. 52. The issue of Oct. 2, 1801, vol. 3, no. 1, whole no. 105, stated that the paper was

KENTUCKY 153

resumed after having been suspended for some time. The original partnership was dissolved and the paper published by James M. Bradford beginning with the issue of Dec. 11, 1801. With the issue of Feb. 8, 1804, it was transferred to E. C. Berry (Elijah Conway Berry, beginning with the issue of Feb. 4, 1805). The last issue located is that of Mar. 25, 1805, vol. 5, no. 284.

Lib. Congress has May 8, 1798–Feb. 28, 1799; Oct. 2, 1801–Dec. 28, 1803.

Am. Antiq. Soc. has June 19, Oct. 30, 1798; July 7, 1802, June 15, Aug. 3, 17, 24, Dec. 28, 1803; May 26, 1804.

Univ. of Chicago has May 30, 1799; June 30, July 7, Nov. 24, 1802; July 20, 1803; Jan. 18, Feb. 1, 15–May 12, 26–June 2, 16–30, July 14–28, Aug. 11, 27–Oct. 1, Nov. 14, 28, 1804; Jan. 10, Feb. 11, Mar. 25, 1805.

Harvard has Aug. 22, 1799; Oct. 2, 9, Nov. 6, 13, 27–Dec. 11, 25, 1801; Jan. 1, 15–Feb. 12, 26, Mar. 12–Apr. 9, May 13–26, June 9–Aug. 4, 18, 25, Sept. 8–Nov. 10, Dec. 22, 1802; Jan. 5, 19, Feb. 9, Mar. 2, 16, 30, May 11, June 8, 22, July 13, 27, Aug. 17–Sept. 7, 28, Oct. 12, Nov. 2, 23, 30, Dec. 14, 21, 1803; Jan. 18, Feb. 15, 29, Mar. 17, 24, Apr. 14–May 12, June 9–30, July 21, Aug. 4, Sept. 3, Nov. 28, Dec. 13–27, 1804; Jan. 21, Feb. 4, 11, 25–Mar. 11, 1805.

Filson Club, Louisville, has Oct. 10, 1799; Aug. 17, 1803.

Mrs. Frank G. Nifong, Columbia, Mo., has Dec. 23, 1799.

N. Y. Hist. Soc. has July 14, 1802.

Long Id. Hist. Soc. has Sept. 29, Oct. 6, 27, 1802.

Chicago Hist. Soc. has June 15, Aug. 31, Sept. 7, 1803.

Western Ky. State Teachers Coll., Bowling Green, has Apr. 21, 28, May 12, 26, June 2, 30–July 28, Sept. 24, Oct. 1, 22, 29, Dec. 5, 1804.

[Frankfort] **Kentucky Journal,** 1795.

Weekly. Established Nov. 7, 1795, judging from the first and only issue located, that of Dec. 5, 1795, vol. 1, no. 5, printed by Benjamin J. Bradford, with the title of "The Kentucky Journal."

Am. Antiq. Soc. has Dec. 5, 1795.
Phil. Lib. Co. has Dec. 5, 1795.

[Frankfort] **Kentucky Palladium,** see **Palladium.**

[Frankfort] **Palladium,** 1798–1816.

Weekly. Established Aug. 9, 1798, by Hunter & Beaumont [William Hunter and William H. Beaumont], with the title of "The Palladium: A Literary and Political Weekly Repository." With the issue of Dec. 19, 1799, Wm. Hunter became sole publisher. With the issue of Oct. 22, 1803, the title was shortened to "The Palladium." At some time between May and October 1809 Hunter took George W. Pleasants into partnership, under the firm name of W. Hunter &

G. W. Pleasants. In the issue of Nov. 25, 1809, Hunter announced that he had sold out his interest in favor of Robert Johnston, and with the issue of Dec. 2, 1809, the firm name became Johnston and Pleasants. On Apr. 8, 1812, George Washington Pleasants, one of the editors of the paper, died, aged 23, and the issues from Apr. 15, through May 6, 1812, bore the name of Robert Johnston as publisher. With the issue of May 13, 1812, the paper was published by Johnston and Pleasants, but whether it was published in behalf of the deceased editor or by one of his relatives is not stated. In September 1814, the paper was published by Robert Johnston, and late in the same year, probably in November, by Johnston and Buchanan [Robert Johnston and Joseph Buchanan], who altered the title to "Kentucky Palladium" and started a new series of numbering in addition to the old series. In 1815 or 1816 Robert Johnston became sole publisher. In March 1816 the paper was purchased and published by G[ervas] E. and J[ohn] B. Russell. In the "Argus of Western America" of Mar. 22, 1816, is recorded the marriage of Gervas E. Russell, "one of the editors of the Kentucky Palladium," to Miss Harriet Branham, on Mar. 17. The last issue located is that of Sept. 6, 1816, vol. 19, no. 8, new series, vol. 2, no. 42. The Cincinnati "Liberty Hall" of May 12, 1817 records the discontinuance of the "Kentucky Palladium" with the issue numbered vol. 19, no. 42 and states that it was taken over by the "Argus of Western America."

Univ. of Chicago has Aug. 9, 1798–Apr. 20, 1809.
Wis. Hist. Soc. has Aug. 9, 1798–Oct. 13, 1803.
Ky. State Lib. has Oct. 23, Nov. 6–27, Dec. 25, 1798; Jan. 22, 29, Feb. 12, 28, Mar. 21–Apr. 4, 18, 25, May 9–July 25, Aug. 8–29, Sept. 26–Nov. 7, 21, 28, Dec. 12, 19, 1799; Jan. 16, Feb. 6, 27–May 29, June 12, 26, July 3, 17, 31–Aug. 21, Sept. 4–Oct. 2, 30–Dec. 9, 23, 30, 1800; Jan. 6–Feb. 24, Mar. 10–24, Apr. 7–May 12, 26–July 7, 28–Aug. 25, Sept. 8, 15, 29, Oct. 16–30, Nov. 13–Dec. 18, 1801; Jan. 8, Feb. 5, Mar. 18, Apr. 15–May 6, 27, June 3, 17–July 1, 15–Sept. 23, Oct. 7–Nov. 4, 18–Dec. 2, 16–30, 1802; Jan. 6–20, Feb. 3–Mar. 17, Apr. 7, 1803.
Harvard has Dec. 4–25, 1801; Jan. 1, 22–Feb. 5, 25–Aug. 26, Sept. 9–Oct. 7, 21–Dec. 30, 1802; Jan. 13–Mar. 17, 31–Apr. 14, May 5, 12, 26–June 9, 23, 30, July 14, 28–Aug. 11, Sept. 8–Oct. 15, 29–Nov. 12, 26, Dec. 3, 17–31, 1803; Jan. 7–Mar. 3, 17, 31, Apr. 14, 21, May 5–19, June 9, 23–July 21, Sept. 1, 22–Oct. 13, Nov. 3–Dec. 15, 1804; Jan. 5, 12, Feb. 2, 23, Mar. 9, Apr. 6–May 4, 18, 25, June 8, 22–July 6, 20, 27, Aug. 10–Sept. 14, 28, Oct. 12, 26, Nov. 11–Dec. 1, 16, 23, 1805; Jan. 2, 9, 23, 30, Feb. 20–Mar. 13, 27–Apr. 24, May 22, 29, Aug. 7–28, Sept. 18, Oct. 2, Nov. 6, 13, 27–Dec. 25, 1806; Jan. 1, 15, Feb. 5, 1807; Jan. 19, Feb. 9, Mar. 2, 16, 30–Apr. 20, May 4, 18–June 1, 15, 29, July 6, 20–Aug. 17, 31, Sept. 21–Nov. 8, 27, Dec. 11, 1811; Jan. 1, 8, 22, 29, Feb. 19, Mar. 11, Apr. 1–22, May 20, 27, June 24–July 15, Aug. 5, 19, 26, Sept. 16, 30, Nov. 4–Dec. 16, 1812; Jan. 20, 27, Feb. 10, 24, Mar. 17–Apr. 28, May 26, June 2, 19, July 3, 10, 1813.

Filson Club, Louisville, has Jan. 6, Nov. 20, 1801; July 15, 1803; Nov. 10, 24, 1804; Dec. 16, 1805; May 22, June 19–July 24, Aug. 7–Dec. 25, 1806; Jan. 15–May 14, 28–July 23, Aug. 6–27, Sept. 10–Oct. 8, 22–Nov. 19, Dec. 3–24, 1807; Mar. 24, 1808; Nov. 4, 25, 1809–July 15, 1812; Nov. 14, 1812; Sept. 18, 1813.

Am. Antiq. Soc. has Dec. 25, 1798; Nov. 29, 1802; Feb. 24, July 21, 28, 1803; May 26, June 30, 1804; Feb. 9, 16, Mar. 2, 9, Apr. 20, May 11, 18, June 1, 1805; Nov. 5, 1807; Apr. 21, 29, 1808; July 14, Sept. 29, Oct. 20, 1810; Mar. 2, May 4, Aug. 17, 24, Sept. 21–Oct. 5, 18–Nov. 22, Dec. 18, 1811; Jan. 15, July 29, 1812; Nov. 20, 1813; Sept. 6, 1816.

Lib. Congress has Apr. 21, 1801; Nov. 18–Dec. 1, 1805; Oct. 9–23, 1806; Feb. 19, Mar. 5, Apr. 16, June 4, Aug. 13, 27, Sept. 6, Dec. 3, 10, 1807; Nov. 13, 1815; July 19, 1816.

Hist. Soc. Penn. has Nov. 13, 1798.

Ohio Hist. & Phil. Soc. has Mar. 7, 1799.

N. Y. Pub. Lib. has June 29, 1805.

Univ. of Pittsburgh has Oct. 30, 1806; Nov. 27, 1811.

Boston Athenæum has Mar. 27, Nov. 27, 1806; Feb. 5, 1807.

Western Ky. State Teachers Coll., Bowling Green, has Dec. 25, 1813; Sept. 24, 1814.

Lexington Pub. Lib. has Oct. 30, Dec. 4, 18, 25, 1815; Feb. 26, Mar. 18, 1816.

Ky. State Hist. Soc. has Apr. 30, 1814.

[Frankfort] **Pulse,** 1816.

Samuel R. Brown, in his "Western Gazetteer," 1817, p. 98, describing Frankfort in 1816, states that there is a paper published there called the "Pulse." No copy located.

[Frankfort] **Western World,** 1806–1810.

Weekly. Established July 7, 1806, with the title of "The Western World," published for Joseph M. Street & Co. John Wood was co-editor (see issue of Nov. 1, 1806; also account of establishment of paper in Humphrey Marshall's "History of Kentucky," 1824, v. 2, p. 377). William Hunter, who printed "The Palladium," in his issue of July 10, 1806, referred to the establishment of "The Western World" by Joseph M. Street and John Wood, and stated that he had been engaged to print the paper for them, without assuming any financial or editorial responsibility. With the issue of Nov. 22, 1806, the editors obtained a press of their own and issued the paper from the press of Joseph M. Street & Co. With the issue of Dec. 18, 1806, John Wood removed to publish the "Atlantic World" at Washington, and the paper was issued "from the press of Joseph M. Street." Street became involved in a libel suit, and with the issue of June 29, 1809, sold the paper to Gore & Barnes [Henry Gore and Troilus

Barnes]. The Frankfort "Argus of Western America" of Sept. 6, 1809, accuses Humphrey Marshall of being editor, with Gore and Barnes as his printers. With the issue of Nov. 2, 1809, the partnership was dissolved, and the printer became Henry Gore, who announced in the issue of June 8, 1810, vol. 4, no. 206, the last located, that he would discontinue the paper with the issue of June 22, 1810. In this issue was the announcement, signed by Humphrey Marshall, that the paper would be succeeded by the "American Republic."

 Am. Antiq. Soc. has July 12–Aug. 16, 30–Dec. 25, 1806; Jan. 8–Feb. 12, 26, Mar. 5, 19, 26, Apr. 9–30, May 14–June 18, July 2–Aug. 13, 27–Oct. 1, 22–Nov. 5, 1807; Apr. 27, June 8, 1810.
 Filson Club, Louisville, has July 26–Nov. 15, 27–Dec. 18, 1806; Jan. 29, Feb. 12–July 30, Aug. 13–Dec. 31, 1807; Feb. 11, 1808–June 8, 1810.
 Wis. Hist. Soc. has Oct. 25, 1806–Apr. 2, 1807; Dec. 17, 31, 1807; Jan. 7, 14, Oct. 6–Nov. 10, 1808.
 Ky. State Hist. Soc. has Aug. 9, 1806–Aug. 4, 1808.
 Harvard has Sept. 13, Oct. 18, Nov. 2, 15, 27, Dec. 11–25, 1806; Jan. 8, 22, Feb. 12, 1807.
 Univ. of Pittsburgh has July 7, 26, Aug. 2, 23, Oct. 4, 11, Nov. 1, 1806.
 Lib. Congress has Sept. 13, 20, Oct. 4–Nov. 27, Dec. 18, 1806; Feb. 19–Mar. 5, May 14, Sept. 17, 1807; Jan. 26, 1810.
 N. Y. State Lib. has Sept. 20–Oct. 4, Nov. 27, 1806.
 N. Y. Hist. Soc. has Dec. 18, 1806; Jan. 7, 22, Feb. 5, May 14, 28, June 18, July 2, 9, Aug. 27, Sept. 24, 1807.
 Univ. of Chicago has July 7, 1806.
 Boston Athenæum has Jan. 22, 29, 1807.
 Chicago Hist. Soc. has Jan. 7, 1808.

[Georgetown] **Minerva,** 1814–1816.

 Weekly. Apparently this paper was a continuation of "The Telegraph." Benjamin S. Chambers acquired "The Telegraph" in October, 1812, and adopted a new volume numbering; the issue of Dec. 22, 1813, the last known with this title, was vol. 2, no. 13. The earliest issue located of "The Minerva" is that of May 14, 1814, vol. 2, no. 32, which would carry the date of establishment back to October 1812, with the probable change of title early in 1814. This issue of "The Minerva" was published by Henderson & Chambers [Thomas Henderson and Benjamin S. Chambers]. The issue of Feb. 18, 1815, the next located, was published by Thomas Henderson, but an advertisement therein, dated Nov. 5, 1814, implies that it was previously published by B. S. Chambers. There is a reference to "The Minerva," edited by Thomas Henderson, in the Lexington "Western Monitor" of June 16, 1815. An "Almanac for 1816," published toward the end of 1815, was printed by Henderson and Reed [Thomas Henderson and ―――― Reed] at Georgetown. Perrin, "Pioneer Press of Kentucky," p. 60, notes an issue of Oct. 12, 1815, vol. 4, no. 4, edited by Amos Kendall, but entitled the "Minerva Press." The last issue was that of Jan. 16, 1816 (see "Autobiography of Amos Kendall," 1872, p. 164).

Cincinnati Pub. Lib. has May 14, 1814.
Am. Antiq. Soc. has Feb. 18, 1815.

[Georgetown] Minerva Press, 1815–1816, see Minerva.

Georgetown Patriot, 1816–1820.

Weekly. Established Apr. 20, 1816, with the title of "Georgetown Patriot," edited by Amos Kendall, and printed and published by Shellers and Lyle [——— Shellers and John N. Lyle]. The same imprint occurs in December, 1816. In November, 1816, Kendall left Georgetown to become an editor of the "Argus" at Frankfort. The last issue located of the "Georgetown Patriot" is that of May 10, 1817, vol. 2, no. 56, edited by William Sebree and printed by John N. Lyle. The paper is quoted in the Cynthiana "Guardian of Liberty" of Apr. 4, 1818; the "Louisville Public Advertiser" of June 24, 1820; and the Lexington "Western Monitor" of Oct. 17, 1820. In the Frankfort "Argus of Western America" of June 1, 1820 is a record of the marriage of W[illiam] B. Holeman, "Editor of the Georgetown Patriot," to Sarah A. Stewart of Frankfort, on May 28, 1820.

Filson Club, Louisville, has Apr. 20–Dec. 14, 1816.
Wis. Hist. Soc. has Apr. 20, 1816.
Am. Antiq. Soc. has Sept. 14, 21, 1816; May 10, 1817.

[Georgetown] Telegraph, 1811–1813.

Weekly. Established in June 1811, judging from an editorial mention in the Lexington "Kentucky Gazette" of July 3, 1811, noting the "appearance of the second issue of the Georgetown Telegraph edited by Shadrach Penn." The earliest issue located, that of Sept. 25, 1811, vol. 1, no. 10, entitled "The Telegraph," was published by Shadrach Penn. In this issue the editor states that "two months have now elapsed since the publication of the first number." Perrin, in his "Pioneer Press of Kentucky," p. 59, mentions an issue of Apr. 9, 1812, published by Penn. For Penn's later career, see under "American Statesman," of Lexington. The paper was evidently transferred in October, 1812, to Benjamin S. Chambers, who began a new volume numbering, for the next issue located is that of Apr. 22, 1813, vol. 1, no. 29, published by Benjamin S. Chambers. The last issue located is that of Dec. 22, 1813, vol. 2, no. 13. Chambers seems to have later changed the title to "The Minerva," which see.

Am. Antiq. Soc. has Sept. 25, 1811; July 22, Sept. 29, Dec. 22, 1813.
Lib. Congress has Apr. 22, 1813.

[Georgetown] **Wasp and Independent Gazette, 1820.**

No copy located. Established presumably in 1820, since it was first authorized to print State advertisements, Nov. 16, 1820 (Ky. Acts, 29th Ass'y, p. 31).

[Glasgow] **Green River Telegraph, 1818–1819.**

No copy located. Established presumably in 1818, since it was first authorized to print State advertisements, Dec. 11, 1818 (Ky. Acts, 27th Ass'y, p. 597). The "National Intelligencer" of Jan. 16, 1819, under the heading of newspapers recently established, records the "Green River Telegraph" published at Glasgow, Ky., by Gaines and Williams [Herbert P. Gaines and ––––– Williams]. There are references to this paper in the Lexington "Western Monitor" of June 15, 1819, and in the "Nashville Gazette" of Aug. 7, 1819. Manuscript Court records of Warren County show that the editor was Herbert P. Gaines in February to May 1819. Gaines wrote to Worsley at Lexington, Oct. 19, 1819, asking for a journeyman printer (Draper MSS. in Wis. Hist. Soc., 6 CC 94).

[Glasgow] **Kentucky Patriot, 1818.**

Weekly. Established Aug. 19, 1818, judging from the first and only copy located, that of Sept. 30, 1818, vol. 1, no. 7, published by A[lbert] A. James, with the title of "The Kentucky Patriot and Glasgow Gazette." That it succeeded Iredale's paper is shown in the Barren County Deed and Will Book G, 155, where William H. Iredale records on Aug. 10, 1818, that he has sold to Albert A. James all his interest in the "Kentucky Patriot and Glasgow Gazette," together with all the apparatus and material (Eva Mae Barton's thesis on "History of Journalism in Glasgow").

William H. Jones, Jr., Glasgow, has Sept. 30, 1818.

[Glasgow] **Patriot, 1814–1818.**

The first and only issue of which there is knowledge is that of July 18, 1814, vol. 1, no. 8, published by Iredale and Taylor [William H. Iredale and ––––– Taylor], with the title of "The Patriot," which issue was reproduced in the Louisville "Courier Journal" of Feb. 5, 1928. The original was at that time owned by Mr. Charles W. Hesson of Louisville. Clippings of five chancery advertisements attached to affidavits from the editors of the Patriot, dating from 1815 to 1818, have been located — three, of Mar. 9, 1815, Aug. 23, 1817, and Mar. 9, 1818, in the Western Kentucky State Teachers College Library at Bowling Green; and two, of June, 1815, and Apr. 27, 1816, in the Barren County Circuit Court files at Glasgow. (The information regarding the chancery advertisements is from a thesis on "A History of Journalism in Glasgow," written by Eva Mae Barton for a master's degree at the George Peabody College for Teachers in 1934.)

This paper was first authorized to print State advertisements, Jan. 19, 1814 (Ky. Acts, 22nd Ass'y, p. 155). Manuscript Court records of Warren County show that the editor was William H. Iredale in August, 1814. In the Lexington "Reporter" of Sept. 11, 1816, is recorded the marriage, on Sept. 4, of William H. Iredale, of Glasgow, Ky., editor of the "Patriot and Political Advertiser," to Mary Spotswood.

[Glasgow] **People's Friend**, 1820.

The "National Intelligencer" of May 30, 1820, records the receipt of the first issue, Apr. 1, 1820, of "The People's Friend," published at Glasgow, Ky., by Woodson and Gill [Joseph A. Woodson and ——— Gill]. No copy located.

[Harrodsburg] **Impartial Observer**, 1815.

No copy located. Established presumably early in 1815, as it was first authorized to print State advertisements, Feb. 6, 1815 (Ky. Acts, 23rd Ass'y, p. 397).

[Harrodsburg] **Light House**, 1814–1815.

Weekly. The only issue located is that of May 27, 1815, vol. 2, no. 97, published by Gordon and M'Murtry [——— Gordon and ——— M'Murtry], with the title of "Light House." This numbering would show that it was established in July, 1813, and since there was a paper of this name published at Danville, in the same county, in 1813, it is probable that the paper was established at Danville and removed to Harrodsburg. An imperfect copy of July 1814 contains a notice requesting other printers to send their papers to Harrodsburg, instead of Danville. Joseph Buchanan, in an advertisement in the Lexington "Reporter" of Sept. 17, 1814, refers to his recent purchase of the "Light House" at Harrodsburg, and states that it will take the place of his proposed "Sensorium of Literature and Politics" which was to have been published at Lexington. The Lexington "Kentucky Gazette" of Sept. 26, 1814, says: "We received today a number of the Light House, a paper published at Harrodsburg, the first which has appeared under the direction of its new editor, Dr. Buchanan." This was Dr. Joseph Buchanan, who two months later was one of the editors of the "Kentucky Palladium" of Frankfort. Moore & Gordon [——— Moore and ——— Gordon] were printing at Harrodsburg in September 1814, and may have been the printers of Buchanan's paper.

Ohio Hist. & Phil. Soc. has July 1814.
Univ. of Chicago has May 27, 1815.

[Harrodsburg] **National Pulse**, 1816–1817.

Weekly. Established Nov. 16, 1816, judging from the date of the earliest issue located, that of Dec. 7, 1816, vol. 1, no. 4, published by Anthony Hunn, with the title of "The National Pulse." The issue for Nov. 8, 1817, vol. 1, no. 52, states that it was the final number, since the publisher was compelled to give his time to the increased "duties of the medical profession." An editorial in the Winchester "Kentucky Advertiser" of Feb. 22, 1817 is addressed "To Doct. Anthony Hunn, Editor of the National Pulse."

Filson Club, Louisville, has Dec. 7, 1816.
Ohio Hist. & Phil. Soc. has Aug. 23, Sept. 6, 13, Nov. 8, 1817.

[Henderson] **Columbian,** 1820.

No copy located. Established presumably in 1820, since it was first authorized to print State advertisements, Dec. 27, 1820 (Ky. Acts, 29th Ass'y, p. 210). A partial file for 1824 is in the Lib. Congress, beginning with Sept. 11, 1824, vol. 3, no. 28, which would indicate the date of establishment in March, 1822. If there was a paper of this name at Henderson in 1820, its publication was suspended for quite a time, or another paper of the same name was begun in 1822.

[Hopkinsville] **Kentucky Republican,** 1819–1820.

Weekly. The Lexington "Kentucky Gazette" of Jan. 7, 1820 says, "We have received the first two numbers of the 'Kentucky Republican,' published at Hopkinsville, Ky., by Putnam Ewing." The only issue located is that of July 29, 1820, vol. 1, no. 26, published by Putnam Ewing with the title of "Kentucky Republican."

Ohio Hist. & Phil. Soc. has July 29, 1820.

[Hopkinsville] **Western Eagle,** 1813.

Weekly. Established Jan. 1, 1813, judging from the date of the first and only issue located, that of Feb. 12, 1813, vol. 1, no. 7, published by Henry L. Cartwright & Co., with the title of "Western Eagle."

Western Ky. State Teachers Coll., Bowling Green, has Feb. 12, 1813.

[Hopkinsville] **Western Hemisphere,** 1818–1819.

There is a quotation from this paper in the Winchester "Kentucky Advertiser" of Aug. 1, 1818. It is also referred to in the "Nashville Gazette" of Aug. 7, 1819, and in the Lexington "Kentucky Reporter" of Aug. 25, 1819.

[Lancaster] **Examiner,** 1810.

No copy located. Established presumably early in 1810, as it was first authorized to print State advertisements, Jan. 23, 1810 (Littell's Laws, vol. 4, p. 126).

[Lancaster] **Kentuckian,** 1819–1820.

No copy located. Established late in 1819 or possibly early in 1820, as it was first authorized to print State advertisements, Jan. 7, 1820 (Ky. Acts, 28th Ass'y, p. 822).

[Lancaster] **Political Theatre,** 1808–1810.

Weekly. Established Nov. 11, 1808, by M. & J. Norvell [Moses and Joshua Norvell], with the title of "Political Theatre." The last issue located is that of July 26, 1809, vol. 1, no. 35. The paper appears in Thomas's 1810 list as published by Moses Norvell.

Am. Antiq. Soc. has Nov. 18–Dec. 10, 1808; Jan. 17, Feb. 7, 1809.
Lib. Congress has July 26, 1809.

Lexington Advertiser, see [Lexington] **Western Monitor.**

[Lexington] **American Statesman,** 1811–1813.

Weekly. Established July 20, 1811, printed by Thomas T. Skillman for Watson & Overton [Samuel E. Watson and Samuel R. Overton] with the title of "American Statesman." The issue of Nov. 9, 1811, is as above; that of Nov. 23 has no name of publisher; and that of Dec. 17 is printed by Thomas T. Skillman for Watson and Co., intervening issues not being located. The early issues of 1812 bear the last imprint up to the issue of Apr. 18, 1812. This is printed and published by Thomas T. Skillman, and has a valedictory statement signed by Samuel E. Watson announcing his own retirement and stating that the editorial department would thereafter be conducted by S. R. Overton. The paper was purchased and published in August, 1812, by Shadrach Penn, Jun. In July 1813, the title was changed to "American Statesman, and Columbian Register." The issue of Oct. 30, 1813, vol. 3, no. 121, is the last located. In the O'Reilly MSS., no. 631, in the Rochester Hist. Soc. is a letter written by Henry C. Sleight, in which he states that he purchased (apparently in 1813) the newspaper published by Shadrach Penn, but that the enterprise was not successful, so that he began the "Western Monitor" in August 1814. Sleight, however, calls Penn's paper the "Lexington Advertiser," which would mean that his memory erred or that Penn had altered his title. H. C. Sleight advertised in the Lexington "Reporter" of Dec. 4, 1813 that he wished to sell a complete printing outfit suitable for a country newspaper. In the "Kentucky Gazette" of Dec. 6, 1813, he advertises that he has commenced the business of book and job printing, and refers to the recent last number of his newspaper.

Am. Antiq. Soc. has July 20, Aug. 31, Sept. 7, 21, 28, Nov. 2, 9, 1811; Mar. 10, Apr. 18, 1812; Aug. 14, 1813.
Harvard has July 20, Aug. 31, Oct. 26, Nov. 23, Dec. 17, 1811; Apr. 18, 1812.

N. Y. State Lib. has Oct. 2, 9, 23–Nov. 21, Dec. 19, 1812; Apr. 10, May 1, June 19, Oct. 30, 1813.
Lib. Congress has Oct. 12, 26, 1811.
Ohio Hist. & Phil. Soc. has Dec. 31, 1811.

[Lexington] Castigator, 1818–1820.

Weekly. Established in November, 1818, judging from the date of the first issue located, that of Apr. 14, 1819, vol. 1, no. 22, published by X[enophon] J. Gaines, with the title of "The Castigator." The last issue located is that of Jan. 22, 1820, vol. 2, no. 7. Gaines died Aug. 23, 1820. It is of quarto size and should be considered a magazine rather than a newspaper. It does contain, however, news of current interest.

Lexington Pub. Lib. has Apr. 14, July 24, 1819; Jan. 22, 1820.

[Lexington] Impartial Observer, 1810.

Weekly. Established Aug. 25, 1810, judging from the date of the earliest issue located, that of Sept. 15, 1810, vol. 1, no. 4, entitled "The Impartial Observer." The first publishers were B[ertrand] Guerin & J[———] Wooldridge (see their advertisement in the Frankfort "Palladium" of July 14, 1810), but this firm was dissolved on Sept. 7, 1810. The issue of Sept. 15, 1810, was published by B. Guerin & E. Prentiss [Bertrand Guerin and Edward Prentiss]. The last issue printed at Lexington was on Nov. 17, 1810, vol. 1, no. 13, after which the paper was removed to Danville. See under Danville.

Harvard has Sept. 15, 22, Nov. 3, 10, 17, 1810.

[Lexington] Independent Gazetteer, 1803–1806.

Weekly. Established Mar. 29, 1803, by Charless & Peniston [Joseph Charless and Francis Peniston], with the title of "Independent Gazetteer." This partnership was dissolved May 10, 1803, and the paper published by J. Charless. On August 16, 1803, Charless took Robert Kay into partnership and the paper was published by Charless & Kay. With the issue of Sept. 27, 1803, Charless relinquished his interests and Robert Kay became sole publisher. With the issue of Mar. 16, 1804, the paper was purchased and published by T[homas] Anderson, who continued to publish it up to the last issue located, that of Nov. 16, 1805, vol. 3, no. 33. The "Kentucky Gazette" of Lexington, Feb. 6, 1806, states, "The publication of the Independent Gazetteer, having been suspended, the editor of the Kentucky Gazette proposes issuing his paper twice a week."

Univ. of Chicago has Mar. 29, Apr. 19, May 3, 17, 24, June 7–28, July 12–26, Aug. 9, 16, Sept. 6–Nov. 15, Dec. 13, 1803; Mar. 6, 1804.
Am. Antiq. Soc. has Apr. 19, 26, May 31, July 26, Sept. 6, 27, Dec. 20, 1803; Jan. 9, 17, 24, Feb. 21, Mar. 16, Apr. 6, 13, Oct. 26, 1804.

Harvard has Oct. 19, Nov. 2–23, Dec. 7–21, 1804; Jan. 11, 18, Feb. 1–15, Mar. 8, 15, 29, Apr. 12, May 10, 17, June 14, 21, July 12, Nov. 16, 1805.
Chicago Hist. Soc. has July 26, 1803.
N. Y. Pub. Lib. has Sept. 28, 1804.
Boston Athenæum has Dec. 7, 1804.
Lib. Congress has June 14, 1805.

[Lexington] **Kentucky Gazette,** 1787–1820+.

Weekly and semi-weekly. Established Aug. 11, 1787, by John and Fielding Bradford, under the title of "The Kentucke Gazette." With the issue of June 7, 1788, Fielding Bradford retired and the paper was published by John Bradford (called J. Bradford from Sept. 17, 1796 to Dec. 30, 1797). With the issue of Mar. 14, 1789, the title was slightly altered to "The Kentucky Gazette"; on May 5, 1792 to "Kentucky Gazette"; and on Jan. 4, 1797, to "The Kentucky Gazette," and the issue changed to semi-weekly. With the issue of Jan. 3, 1798, it reverted to the weekly issue, and on Jan. 31, 1798, changed its title to "Kentucky Gazette." On Jan. 2, 1799, the title again reverted to "The Kentucky Gazette." With the issue of Apr. 2, 1802, John Bradford transferred the paper to his son Daniel Bradford, who with the issue of Jan. 18, 1803, changed the title to "Kentucky Gazette and General Advertiser." With the issue of Feb. 19, 1806, the paper became a semi-weekly, but reverted to a weekly on Jan. 3, 1807. With the issue of Apr. 11, 1809, the title was shortened to "Kentucky Gazette," which was retained until after 1820. With the issue of Oct. 3, 1809, Bradford transferred the paper to Thomas Smith. In the issue of Aug. 18, 1812, Smith stated that he was enlisting for service in Canada, and that the editorship would devolve upon his brother-in-law, William W. Worsley. The imprint, however, did not change. With the issue of Sept. 21, 1813, Smith admitted John Bickley to partnership under the firm name of Smith & Bickley. With the issue of Oct. 3, 1814, this firm sold out to F[ielding] Bradford, Jr., who, with the issue of June 2, 1817, sold to Jno. Norvell & Co. On Jan. 2, 1815, a new series volume numbering was begun. With the issue of Feb. 27, 1818, John Norvell became sole publisher. With the issue of Mar. 5, 1819, the paper was transferred to Joshua Norvell & Co. [Joshua Norvell, Ignatius T. Cavins, and James Armstrong]. With the issue of Aug. 6, 1819, the paper was published by Norvell & Cavins, and with that of July 27, 1820, by I. T. Cavins, who continued it until after 1820.

Lexington Pub. Lib. has Aug. 18–Dec. 22, 1787; Jan. 5–Mar. 29, Apr. 12–May 24, June 7–Sept. 13, 27–Dec. 27, 1788; Jan. 3–Apr. 25, June 6–Dec. 26, 1789; Jan. 2–Aug. 2, Dec. 4–18, 1790; Jan. 1–Mar. 26, Apr. 9–June 4, 18–July 23, Oct. 8–Dec. 31, 1791; Jan. 7–Sept. 8, Nov. 24–Dec. 29, 1792; Jan. 5–Mar. 2, 16–Apr. 27, May 11–July 13, 27–Dec. 28, 1793; Jan. 4–May 17, 31–June 14, 28–Aug. 2, Sept. 20–Dec. 27, 1794; Jan. 3–Aug. 22, Sept. 19–Dec. 26, 1795; Jan. 2–Mar. 26, Apr. 9–Dec. 31, 1796; Jan. 4, 1797–Dec. 28, 1802; Jan. 4–

June 26, Aug. 2–Dec. 27, 1803; Jan. 3, 1804–Dec. 29, 1806; Jan. 3, 1809–Dec. 30, 1816; Jan. 6–Sept. 20, Oct. 4–Nov. 29, Dec. 13–27, 1817; Jan. 10, 17, Feb. 7–Aug. 7, 21–Sept. 11, 25–Dec. 25, 1818; Jan. 1–Dec. 17, 31, 1819; Jan. 7–June 22, July 6, 20–Sept. 14, Oct. 12, 19, Nov. 16, Dec. 14, 1820.
Univ. of Chicago has Mar. 8, Sept. 6, 20, 1788; Feb. 8, 1794; Oct. 10, 1795; Jan. 16, 1796; Sept. 9–23, 1797; July 11–Aug. 1, 15–Sept. 12, Oct. 3, 10, Nov. 21, 1798; Mar. 14, May 16–June 27, Aug. 15–Sept. 26, Oct. 10–Nov. 28, Dec. 19, 26, 1799; Jan. 2, 9, 23–Feb. 27, Mar. 20–Apr. 3, 17, May 8, 22–June 26, July 10–24, Aug. 7–21, 1800; Feb. 14, Apr. 26, May 3, June 21–July 12, Aug. 2, 16, 30, Sept. 13, 27, Oct. 4, 25, Nov. 1, 15, 22, Dec. 27, 1803; Jan. 3, Mar. 27, Apr. 3, 17–May 1, 15, 29–June 19, 25, July 24, Oct. 2, Nov. 20, 1804; Mar. 5, Apr. 9–May 21, 28, Nov. 14, 1805; Aug. 14, Sept. 4, 18, 22, Oct. 27, Nov. 3, 6, 17, 1806; Sept. 22, Oct. 20, 1807; Jan. 12, Mar. 8, 15, Apr. 19–May 31, June 14–28, July 12–Aug. 16, Oct. 25, Nov. 8–22, Dec. 5, 13, 1808; Apr. 18, July 25, Sept. 19, Oct. 24, 1809; Jan. 2, May 29, July 17, 24, Aug. 21, Sept. 11, 25, 1810; Jan. 8, 15, 29, Feb. 26, Mar. 5, 19–Apr. 2, 23, May 21, June 4, 18–July 16, 30, Aug. 6, 27, Sept. 3, Oct. 1, 15, Nov. 5, Dec. 3, 10, 31, 1811; Jan. 14–28, Feb. 25, Mar. 3, 31, Apr. 14–28, May 26–June 30, July 14, Aug. 4, 18–Sept. 1, Oct. 20, 27, Nov. 24–Dec. 22, 1812; Jan. 26, Mar. 2, 16, Apr. 20, May 25, July 13, 27, Sept. 14, Oct. 19, Nov. 1, Dec. 6, 20, 1813; Jan. 10, 17, 31, Feb. 14, June 13, 27, Aug. 15, 22, Sept. 5, 26, Oct. 31–Nov. 14, 1814; Jan. 2–23, Feb. 6, 27, Mar. 20, 27, Apr. 17, May 8, 29, June 5, 19, July 10, 17, Aug. 7, Sept. 18, Oct. 2, Nov. 6, Dec. 19, 1815; Jan. 15, Feb. 5, 19, Mar. 25, Apr. 8, 29, May 6, 20, 27, June 10, 24, July 22, Aug. 12, 26, Sept. 2, 30–Oct. 14, 28, Nov. 11, Dec. 9, 16, 1816; Jan. 27, Feb. 3, Mar. 3, 17–31, Apr. 14, May 5, 12, June 9, 28, July 12–Aug. 16, 30, Oct. 18, 25, Nov. 22, Dec. 6, 13, 27, 1817; Jan. 24, 31, Apr. 3, 24, May 8, June 12, July 3, 31, Sept. 25, Nov. 6, Dec. 4, 11, 1818; Jan. 8, 22–Feb. 12, 26, Mar. 5, 26, Apr. 2, 30, June 4, 11, July 2, 16, 23, Aug. 6, 20, Sept. 10, 17, Nov. 26, Dec. 10, 17, 1819.
Lib. Congress has Mar. 1, Nov. 8–Dec. 27, 1788; Jan. 3–June 6, July 11–25, 1789; Sept. 24–Dec. 17, 31, 1791; Jan. 21–Apr. 28, May 12, 19, June 9, 16, Nov. 17–Dec. 29, 1792; Jan. 5–Mar. 2, 30–Apr. 20, May 4–July 27, Aug. 10, 1793; Apr. 18–June 20, July 4–Dec. 26, 1798; Jan. 2–Apr. 11, 25–May 9, 1799; May 22, 1800; Feb. 16, 1801; Apr. 11, 1807; June 20, 1809; Jan. 30, 1810, Mar. 17, 1812; July 29, Aug. 5, 26, Sept. 2, Oct. 14, 1816; Mar. 10–24, Nov. 15, 1817; Jan. 1–June 11, 25–Dec. 31, 1819; Jan. 7–May 5, 19–Aug. 10, 24–Oct. 12, 26–Dec. 21, 1820.
Am. Antiq. Soc. has Mar. 15, July 12, 1794; May 9, 1798; Nov. 7, 14, 1799; Jan. 23, 30, Oct. 27, Nov. 10, Dec. 22, 1800; Dec. 5, 25, 1801; July 23, Sept. 10–24, 1802; June 21, Aug. 9, 16, Sept. 20, 27, Oct. 11, Dec. 27, 1803; Jan. 3, 10, Feb. 21, Mar. 6, Apr. 3, 10, June 19, July 10, Aug. 7, 14, Oct. 16, Nov. 13, 27, Dec. 25, 1804; Feb. 12, May 7, June 25, Aug. 27, Sept. 17, Oct. 31–Nov. 14, 1805; Jan. 2–Feb. 26, Mar. 1–12, 26, Apr. 2–9, 16, 19, 30–May 6, 13–20, 31–June 14, 21, 28, July 5, 26–Aug. 25, Sept. 25, 29, Oct. 6–13, 27,

KENTUCKY 165

Nov. 3, 10–Dec. 1, 15–25, 1806; Feb. 14, 28, Apr. 4, 28, May 5, 19, 26, July 21, Aug. 18, 25, Dec. 29, 1807; Jan. 26, Feb. 16–Mar. 1, 15, Apr. 5–May 10, 24–June 14, 28–July 26, Aug. 23, 30, Sept. 13, Oct. 4–18, Nov. 1–15, Dec. 5, 20, 1808; Jan. 10, Feb. 7, 20, 27, Mar. 13–Apr. 11, 25, May 9–30, June 13, 20, July 11, 25, Aug. 1, 15, Sept. 12, 19, Oct. 17, Nov. 21, 28, Dec. 19, 26, 1809; Jan. 16–Feb. 13, 27–Mar. 20, Apr. 24, May 8, June 5, Sept. 18, 1810; Jan. 9, Feb. 27, Mar. 27–Apr. 10, May 1, Oct. 9, 1815; Sept. 9, Nov. 4, 1816; July 26, 1817; Jan. 8, Mar. 26, 1819; Jan. 21, 1820.

Harvard has May 28, June 4, 18–July 16, 30, Aug. 13–27, Sept. 10–24, Oct. 22–Dec. 31, 1796; Jan. 4–11, 28–Feb. 25, Mar. 4–29, June 3, 7, 14, July 8, 12, 29, Aug. 2, Sept. 2, 6, 16, 27–Oct. 4, 18, 21, 28–Nov. 4–18, Dec. 2, 6, 1797; Jan. 10, 24, Feb. 7, 14, Apr. 11, 25, June 20–July 4, 18, Aug. 1, 1798; May 23, June 20–July 4, 18–Aug. 8, 22–Oct. 24, Nov. 7, 1799; Dec. 5–25, 1801; Jan. 1–Mar. 5, 19, 26, Apr. 9, 16, May 7, 14, 28–June 4, 18–Sept. 24, Oct. 5–Dec. 7, 21, 28, 1802; Jan. 4–Mar. 8, 22–Apr. 19, May 10–July 19, Aug. 2, 9, 23, 30, Sept. 20–Oct. 4, 18–Nov. 15, 29–Dec. 27, 1803; Jan. 10, 17, Feb. 7–28, Mar. 13, 27, Apr. 10–24, May 8, 15, June 25, July 3–31, Aug. 28–Oct. 9, 23–Nov. 20, Dec. 25, 1804; Jan. 7, 22, Feb. 12, 26, Mar. 12, 19, Apr. 2, 16, 30, May 7, 28, June 4, 25–July 23, Aug. 13–Sept. 17, Oct. 31–Nov. 14, 28, 1805; Jan. 2–23, Feb. 22–Mar. 5, Apr. 2, 5, 12–19, May 6, 13, 27, Aug. 2, 7–14, Sept. 22, Oct. 6, 9, Nov. 3, 10–Dec. 1, 8, 15, 18, 1806; Feb. 28, Apr. 5, 12, May 2–16, June 9, 16, July 21, Aug. 18, 25, Oct. 13, Dec. 8, 29, 1807; Jan. 5, Feb. 16, 23, Mar. 15, Apr. 12, 19, May 10, 24–June 28, July 12–Aug. 9, 23–Sept. 13, Oct. 4, 18, 25, Nov. 8, 15, 29, Dec. 5, 1808; Sept. 4, Oct. 23, Nov. 13, Dec. 3, 18, 1810; Apr. 30, May 14, 21, Sept. 10, Oct. 1–15, Nov. 5, 12, Dec. 3–31, 1811; Jan. 14, Feb. 18, Mar. 24–Apr. 21, June 23, Aug. 18, 25, Sept. 15–29, Oct. 27, Nov. 17–Dec. 8, 1812; Jan. 5, 26, Feb. 23, Mar. 2, 23, 30, Apr. 20, June 1, 8, July 6–Aug. 24, Sept. 7, Oct. 12, 19, Dec. 13–27, 1813; Jan. 10, 24, Feb. 21, Mar. 7, 21, Apr. 4–18, May 2, 30, June 6, Sept. 5, 19, 26, Oct. 10, 24, Nov. 7, 21–Dec. 12, 1814.

Wis. Hist. Soc. has Nov. 24, 1787; Feb. 23, Mar. 1, 15–Apr. 5, 26, May 31–Sept. 13, Oct. 4–Nov. 29, 1788; Feb. 26, 1791; Apr. 14, 28, June 9, Sept. 1, 22, Oct. 13, Nov. 17, 1812; July 13, Aug. 3, 1813; Feb. 28, Mar. 21, 1814.

Filson Club, Louisville, has Mar. 1, 15–Apr. 5, May 3, Sept. 13, 27, Dec. 20, 1788; Aug. 8, 1789; Sept. 22, Dec. 8, 1792; Oct. 12, Nov. 16, 1793; May 17–31, July 12–26, Aug. 9, 23, 1794; Jan. 9, 1800; Jan. 29, 1802; Sept. 27, 1803; Oct. 23, 1804; May 14, Nov. 21, 1805; Nov. 17, 1806; Jan. 30, 1815; Apr. 22, June 10, 1816; May 29, Oct. 16, 1818; Jan. 29, Mar. 19–Apr. 23, May 15–June 11, 25, July 2, 16–Aug. 13, Sept. 3, 17, 24, Oct. 8–Nov. 5, 1819.

Ky. State Hist. Soc. has July 11, 1795; Aug. 13, 1796; Apr. 11, Nov. 28, 1799; Aug. 23, 1803; Oct. 24, 1805; Apr. 9, 16, Sept. 22, Dec. 1, 1806; Oct. 6–20, Nov. 10, 24, Dec. 1, 15–29, 1807; Feb. 23–Apr. 26, 1808; Aug. 28, 1818 extra.

Cincinnati Pub. Lib. has Feb. 28, 1814–Dec. 25, 1815; Jan. 15–Dec. 23, 1816.

Ind. State Lib. has Jan. 2, 1815–July 15, 1816.

Univ. of Ky., Lexington, has Jan. 8–Feb. 5, Mar. 4–May 27, June 10–July 8,

22–Aug. 26, Sept. 9–23, Oct. 7, 21–Dec. 30, 1816; Jan. 6–June 21, July 5, 1817.

Va. State Lib. has July 11, 1798, extra; July 25, 28, Dec. 1, 1807; Apr. 10, 1810; Apr. 25, 1814.

Boston Athenæum has Dec. 19, 1805; Dec. 11, 25, 1806; Jan. 3, 17, 25, Feb. 7, 1807; June 10, 1816.

Duke Univ. has Jan. 24, 1795.

Univ. of Texas has Nov. 23, 1802.

Chicago Hist. Soc. has May 8, 1810.

N. Y. Pub. Lib. has June 5, 1800; May 29, 1815.

Ohio Hist. & Phil. Soc. has Aug. 3, 31, 1820.

All the known issues from 1787 to 1800 inclusive were reproduced by the Univ. of Michigan Library in photostat, of which there are sets in the following libraries: — Amer. Antiq. Soc.; John Carter Brown Lib.; N. Y. Hist. Soc.; Lib. Congress; Duke Univ.; Lexington Pub. Lib.; Filson Club, Lexington; West Ky. Teachers Coll., Bowling Green; Univ. of Chicago; Newberry Lib.; Univ. of Illinois; Western Reserve Hist. Soc.; Ind. State Lib.; Mo. Hist. Soc.; Mercantile Lib., St. Louis; Clements Lib., Univ. of Mich.; Wis. Hist. Soc.; Minn. Hist. Soc.; Univ. of Texas; Huntington Lib.

[Lexington] **Kentucky Reporter**, see [Lexington] **Reporter**.

Lexington Public Advertiser, 1820+.

Semi-weekly. Established Jan. 5, 1820, by Daniel Bradford, with the title of "The Lexington Public Advertiser." Continued after 1820.

Lexington Pub. Lib. has Jan. 5–Dec. 30, 1820.

[Lexington] **Reporter**, 1808–1820+.

Weekly and semi-weekly. Established Mar. 12, 1808, by Worsley and Overton [William W. Worsley and Samuel R. Overton], with the title of "The Reporter." It was published weekly, but from 1808 to 1813 it was published semi-weekly during the sessions of the legislature. With the issue of July 8, 1809, Overton retired and the paper was published by William W. Worsley. With the issue of Feb. 14, 1816, it was published by Worsley & Smith [William W. Worsley and Thomas Smith]. With the issue of Oct. 3, 1817, the title was changed to "Kentucky Reporter." Worsley retired and with the issue of Mar. 10, 1819, the paper was published by Thomas Smith, who continued it until after 1820.

Lexington Pub. Lib. has Mar. 12, 1808–Dec. 25, 1813; Jan. 1–July 23, Aug. 12, 20, Sept. 10, 1814; Feb. 1, Apr. 7, May 3, 24, 31, June 14, Aug. 9, 23, Sept. 6, 13, 27, Oct. 11–Nov. 1, Dec. 6, 20, 1815; Jan. 3, 1816–Dec. 29, 1819; Apr. 4–May 9, 23, 30, July 4–Oct. 10, 1820.

KENTUCKY 167

Am. Antiq. Soc. has Mar. 12, 1808–Mar. 25, 1809; Apr. 1, 15, 29, May 13, June 3, 20, July 1, 8, 18, 22, Aug. 19–26, Sept. 9, 16, Oct. 21, 24, 31, Nov. 7, 11, Dec. 2–30, 1809; Jan. 6, 1810–Dec. 25, 1813; Jan. 1–Aug. 12, 1814; Feb. 1, May 3, Aug. 23, Sept. 6, 13, 27, Oct. 11, 25, Nov. 1, Dec. 6, 1815; Jan. 3, 1816–Dec. 27, 1820.
Cincinnati Pub. Lib. has Mar. 12, 1808–Dec. 30, 1810; Jan. 6, 1815–Dec. 24, 1817.
Univ. of Chicago has Dec. 8, 1810; Jan. 11–Dec. 26, 1812; Jan. 23–Dec. 25, 1813; Jan. 1–July 9, 25–Aug. 20, Sept. 3, 1814; Jan. 13, Feb. 8–13, Mar. 6, 17, 31, Apr. 12, 26, May 19–Aug. 4, 18–25, Sept. 8–Dec. 22, 1815; Jan. 5, 19–Apr. 12, May 3–July 12, 24–Dec. 27, 1816; Jan. 1–15, 29, Feb. 21–June 11, July 2–Sept. 3, Oct. 8–Dec. 31, 1817; Jan. 7, 21–Feb. 11, 25–Apr. 1, 15–Dec. 30, 1818; Jan. 6, Feb. 17–Mar. 31, Apr. 14–May 19, June 16, 23, July 7–21, Aug. 11–Sept. 8, 22, 29, Nov. 10–Dec. 1, 29, 1819; Feb. 16, Mar. 29, Apr. 26, May 3, 24, June 7, 14, July 19, Aug. 16, 23, Sept. 13–Oct. 4, 25, Nov. 27, Dec. 11, 1820.
Hist. Soc. Penn. has Mar. 12, 1814–Aug. 20, 1817.
Filson Club, Louisville, has July 2, 1814–June 14, 1815; May 6, 1818–Nov. 10, 1819.
Lib. Congress has May 14, 1808; Mar. 30, Dec. 10, 1811; Jan. 18–Dec. 26, 1812; Apr. 13, Sept. 18–Dec. 25, 1813; Jan. 15–July 9, 1814; Mar. 29, June 21, July 12, Aug. 23, Nov. 1, 22, Dec. 20, 1815; Jan. 3, Mar. 6–20, May 1, 29, June 12, 19, Aug. 7–21, Sept. 4, 18, Oct. 2–16, Nov. 6–Dec. 25, 1816; Feb. 28, Apr. 16, July 30, Aug. 6, 1817; Jan. 28, Feb. 25–Mar. 11, May 20–June 3, July 1, 8, Sept. 23, Oct. 28, Nov. 4, 25, 1818; Jan. 13–Oct. 20, 1819; June 14, Aug. 16, 1820.
Harvard has May 14, 21, June 4, July 9, Aug. 13, Sept. 1, 8, 26, Oct. 3, 17, Nov. 7, 1808; Jan. 26, Apr. 1, 1809; Sept. 15, Oct. 6, 20, 27, Nov. 5, 17, 24, Dec. 15, 1810; Jan. 12, June 8, 15, July 20, Aug. 3–17, 31, Sept. 14–Oct. 12, 26, Dec. 14–21, 1811; Jan. 21, 28, Feb. 4, Mar. 21, 24, 31, Apr. 4, 11, 25, June 13, 1812.
Chicago Hist. Soc. has Jan. 23, 1809; Sept. 1, 1810; May 4, 1811, Apr. 7, 1812; Nov. 6, 1813.
Ohio Hist. & Phil. Soc. has Oct. 31–Nov. 14, Dec. 26, 1812; Jan. 2, 9, 1813; May 2, 9, June 27, July 4, 18, Sept. 10, 19, 26, Oct. 10–24, Nov. 7, 21, 28, Dec. 5, 31, 1817; Jan. 14, Mar. 11, 18, Apr. 8, 15, July 22–Aug. 12, 1818; Feb. 3, 17, 1819; Feb. 16, July 26, 1820.
Wis. Hist. Soc. has June 9, 26, July 31, Aug. 2, Sept. 4–18, Oct. 2, 9, Nov. 20, 1813; Jan. 29, Mar. 12, Apr. 16, July 30–Aug. 20, Sept. 3, 10, Dec. 31, 1814; Nov. 4, 1818.
Howard-Tilton Lib., New Orleans, has Jan. 3–Mar. 21, Apr. 11–June 6, 20–Nov. 1, 28–Dec. 31, 1817.
Univ. of Pittsburgh has Nov. 9, 26, 1811.
N. J. Hist. Soc. has Sept. 4, 1816.

Univ. of Ill. has Mar. 28, 1817.
Ky. State Hist. Soc. has Apr. 23, 1817.

[Lexington] **Stewart's Kentucky Herald,** 1795–1803.

Weekly. Established in February, 1795, judging from the date of the first issue located, that of June 30, 1795, vol. 1, no. 20, published by James H. Stewart, with the title of "Stewart's Kentucky Herald." The last of the Lexington issues located is that of Aug. 2, 1803, vol. 9, no. 444. After an interruption of a year or more, the paper was removed to Paris in 1805, where it was continued by James H. Stewart under the same name. The first Paris issue located is that of Nov. 25, 1805, vol. 9, no. 489. See under Paris.

Lexington Pub. Lib. has June 30, Aug. 18, 1795.
Univ. of Chicago has Nov. 17–Dec. 1, 29, 1795; Jan. 26, Feb. 2, Oct. 18 extra, 25, 1796; Jan. 30, Feb. 5, 19, 26, Mar. 12, July 23, 1799; Feb. 10, May 19, 1801; Mar. 30, May 25, 1802.
Ohio Hist. & Phil. Soc. has Oct. 6, 1795.
Harvard has Feb. 14, 1797; Apr. 26, May 17, Aug. 2, 1803.
Bancroft Lib., Berkeley, Cal., has June 6, 1797.
Ky. State Hist. Soc. has Oct. 24, 1797.
Filson Club, Louisville, has Feb. 13, 1798; Feb. 5, Apr. 23, Dec. 3, 1799; Dec. 15, 1801; Feb. 9, 1802.
Am. Antiq. Soc. has Mar. 25, 1800; Aug. 18, Sept. 15, Oct. 27, Nov. 3, 1801.
Lib. Congress has Apr. 17, Sept. 25, 1798; Mar. 12, 1799; Apr. 21, 1801.
N. Y. Hist. Soc. has Aug. 20, 1799.
B. H. Trees, Lexington, has July 8, 1800 (A.A.S. has photostat).
Ky. State Teachers Coll., Bowling Green, has Oct. 14, 1800.

[Lexington] **Western Monitor,** 1814–1820+.

Weekly. Established Aug. 3, 1814, by Fishback & Sleight [James Fishback and Henry C. Sleight], with the title of "The Western Monitor." With the issue of May 5, 1815, Sleight retired and Fishback took Thomas T. Skillman into partnership under the firm name of Fishback & Skillman. With the issue of Aug. 11, 1815, the paper was published by Thomas T. Skillman, with William G. Hunt as editor. In the issue of Oct. 17, 1818, William Gibbes Hunt announced that he had become sole proprietor and publisher as well as editor, and he so continued until after 1820. With the issue of Oct. 24, 1818, the title became "Western Monitor," and with May 25, 1819, the words "Lexington Advertiser" were added above the title as part of the device.

Am. Antiq. Soc. has Aug. 3, 1814–Dec. 20, 1817; May 2, Nov. 28, 1818; Mar. 6, 20, Apr. 3–24, May 8, 25, June 1, 22–Sept. 7, 28–Nov. 2, 23, Dec. 14–28, 1819; Jan. 4, 18–Feb. 1, 22–Mar. 7, 21, 28, May 2, 23, 30, June 13, July 11, Aug. 1, 15–Sept. 19, Oct. 3–31, 1820.

Wis. Hist. Soc. has Oct. 21, Dec. 16, 1814; Jan. 6, 13, 27–Feb. 24, Mar. 10–June 2, 16, July 14–Sept. 8, 22, Oct. 13, 27–Nov. 10, 24, Dec. 1, 22, 29, 1815; Jan. 5, 19–Feb. 16, Mar. 1–22, Apr. 5, 12, 26–Sept. 20, Nov. 8–29, 1816; Nov. 21, 1818.
Ind. State Lib. has Nov. 18, 1814; Jan. 6, Feb. 17, 24, Mar. 17, 24, Apr. 28, May 26, Oct. 20, Nov. 3, 24–Dec. 22, 1815; Feb. 16, Mar. 1, 8, 29, Apr. 5, 26–May 10, 24–July 19, 1816.
Univ. of Chicago has Dec. 23, 1814; Jan. 20, June 23, 30, Oct. 6, Dec. 15, 1815; Dec. 6, 13, 1816; Jan. 24, 1818; Feb. 27–Apr. 24, May 8–June 1, 22, 29, July 13, 27–Nov. 2, 16–30, Dec. 14–28, 1819; Jan. 4–Feb. 1, 15–Mar. 28, May 2, 23, 30, June 12, July 4–18, Aug. 1, 15–Oct. 31, 1820.
Lib. Congress has June 21, July 5, Nov. 22, 1816; Jan. 9, 1819–Dec. 19, 1820.
Lexington Pub. Lib. has Jan. 3–24, Feb. 7, 21–Mar. 14, Apr. 18–June 6, 27, July 25–Aug. 15, 29, Sept. 5, Oct. 3, 24–Dec. 26, 1818; Jan. 2–Dec. 28, 1819; Jan. 11–Feb. 22, Mar. 7–May 9, 23–June 13, 27–Oct. 17, Nov. 14, 1820.
Filson Club, Louisville, has June 13, Aug. 8–22, Sept. 5–Dec. 26, 1818; Jan. 16–Feb. 20, Mar. 6, 13, 27–Apr. 17, May 18, June 1–Sept. 21, Oct. 5–Nov. 9, 1819.
Howard-Tilton Lib., New Orleans, has July 12, Sept. 13, Oct. 25, Nov. 8, 15, 1817.
Ohio Hist. & Phil. Soc. has Apr. 25, May 2, 1818; Feb. 26, Mar. 6, May 25, 1819; Oct. 3, 1820.
Ohio Arch. & Hist. Soc. has Sept. 9, 1814.
N. Y. State Lib. has Oct. 7, 1814.
Duke Univ. has June 30, 1815; May 9, 1817.
Univ. of Ill. has Jan. 2, 1819.

[Lincoln County] **Lamp,** 1807–1808.

Weekly. Established in August 1807, judging from the only issue located, that of Jan. 12, 1808, vol. 1, no. 24, "Published in Lincoln County, at Dr. Anthony Hunn's, near Capt. James Hickman's plantation, by S. Ogilsby and Co," with the title of "The Lamp." An editorial in the Winchester "Kentucky Advertiser" of Feb. 22, 1817, in referring to Dr. Anthony Hunn's newspaper ventures, mentions his establishing the "Lamp." In the Lancaster "Political Theatre" of Dec. 10, 1808, is an advertisement referring to "The Lamp" of May 2, 1808. The county seat of Lincoln County was Stanford. The "Farmer's Almanac" for 1809 was printed at "Lincoln County" by Samuel Ogilsby & Co.

Univ. of Chicago has Jan. 12, 1808.

Louisville Correspondent, 1812–1817.

Weekly. Established in September, 1812, judging from the date of the first issue located, that of Jan. 13, 1813, vol. 1, no. 19, published by Farquar & Smoot

[William Farquar and George C. Smoot], with the title of "Louisville Correspondent." Smoot retired early in 1814 (certainly before May 11) and the paper was printed by J[oshua] Gore for William Farquar. Farquar sold the paper to William Tompkins, who began publishing it with the issue of Sept. 7, 1814. With the issue of Oct. 5, 1814, the imprint was changed to William Tompkins & Co. With the issue of Apr. 10, 1815, Tompkins admitted Robert Miller to partnership under the firm name of Tompkins & Miller. With the issue of Sept. 11, 1815, the paper was sold to Mann Butler, who in October, 1815, added to the imprint the name of James Hughes as printer. With the issue of Nov. 27, 1815, Butler admitted William Wood to partnership under the firm name of Butler & Wood. Wood died May 29, 1816, but the imprint was continued until the issue of Sept. 9, 1816, when the paper was published by Butler & Hughes (James Hughes having purchased Wood's interest). With the issue of Feb. 17, 1817, the paper was purchased by E[lijah] C. Berry, who continued publishing it as far as the last issue located, that of June 28, 1817, vol. 5, no. 43. Berry went to Kaskaskia, Ill., where he became an editor of "The Western Intelligencer" in September, 1817. The Chillicothe "Supporter" of Nov. 4, 1817 notes the discontinuance of the "Louisville Correspondent." The Lexington "Western Monitor" of Nov. 22, 1817, states that the "Correspondent" at Louisville has been succeeded by the "Kentucky Herald."

 Am. Antiq. Soc. has May 11, July 6, 20, 27, Aug. 17–Sept. 7, 21–Nov. 23, Dec. 21, 1814; Jan. 4, 11, 27–Feb. 13, 27–Mar. 20, Apr. 3, 10, May 8, 15, June 26, July 10–24, Aug. 14–28, Sept. 11, 25, Nov. 6, Dec. 11–25, 1815; Jan. 1–22, Feb. 5, 19, Mar. 11, June 3, 10, 24–July 8, Aug. 5, 19, 26, Sept. 9–Oct. 7, 21–Nov. 4, 25, Dec. 2, 1816; Jan. 6, 13, 27–Mar. 29, Apr. 12, 26, May 3, June 28, 1817.

 Lib. Congress has Jan. 13, 1813; Aug. 5, 1816; Apr. 12, 1817.
 Filson Club, Louisville, has July 28, 1813; Jan. 15, 1816.
 Univ. of Chicago has Oct. 26, 1814; Apr. 24, 1815.
 Chicago Hist. Soc. has Feb. 13, 1815.

[Louisville] **Farmer's Library**, 1801–1810.

 Weekly. Established in January, 1801, judging from the date of the earliest issue located, that of Dec. 7, 1801, vol. 1, no. 47, entitled "The Farmer's Library; or, Ohio Intelligencer," and published by Samuel Vail. At some time between May 19, 1803, and Feb. 15, 1804, the title was shortened to "The Farmers' Library" and was published by Samuel Vail and E[lijah] C. Berry. Vail & Berry had formed their partnership certainly by September 1803. This partnership was dissolved and with the issue of Feb. 25, 1804, the paper was published by Samuel Vail, as was also the issue of Mar. 3, 1804. The only later issues located are those of Oct. 26, Nov. 2, 1805, published by Joshua Vail; and Apr. 16, 1806 to July 23, 1807, printed for the proprietors by S. Vail. The title of the paper appears in Thomas's 1810 list (Amer. Antiq. Soc. Trans. vol. 6, p. 303), but no name of publisher is given. Samuel Vail & Co. advertised proposals for the "Missouri Correspondent, and Illinois Gazette" at St. Louis in the Louisville "Western American" of July 23, 1806, but the paper never materialized. Vail entered the army as an ensign in May 1808.

Univ. of Chicago has Feb. 18, 25, Mar. 11, Apr. 1, 8, Aug. 26–Sept. 9, Oct. 14, Nov. 4–18, 1802; Feb. 15, 25, Mar. 3, 1804; Oct. 26, Nov. 2, 1805; Apr. 16, 23, 1806; July 23, 1807.

Harvard has Dec. 7, 1801.

Filson Club, Louisville, has May 6, 1802; Feb. 3, May 19, 1803; Apr. 2, 1807.

Louisville Gazette, 1807–1812.

Weekly. Established Nov. 24, 1807, by Joseph Charless, under the title of "Louisville Gazette, and Western Advertiser." The last issue located bearing his name as printer is that of Apr. 5, 1809, v. 2, no. 72. Charless had established the "Missouri Gazette" at St. Louis, July 12, 1808, but retained his name in the imprint of the Louisville paper. In the "Louisville Gazette" of Apr. 5, 1809, was an advertisement for subscription to the "Missouri Gazette," where "a capable editor is employed." In the "Missouri Gazette" of July 26, 1809, Charless mentions that he had disposed of his printing-office in Kentucky. The "Louisville Gazette" appears in Thomas's 1810 list, with the name of Gerard Brooks as publisher. There is an issue of the "Louisville Gazette" for Mar. 15, 1811, published by Rannells & Smoot [probably David V. Rannells and George C. Smoot], but no volume number is given since this issue was not of regular size, owing to lack of paper. The "Louisville Gazette" is referred to in the Lexington "Kentucky Gazette" of Apr. 14, 1812.

Amer. Antiq. Soc. has Dec. 1–15, 1807; Jan. 12–Feb. 2, Mar. 1, 1808; Apr. 5, 1809.

Lib. Congress has Jan. 4, 1809.

Wis. Hist. Soc. has Mar. 15, 1811.

[Louisville] Kentucky Herald, 1817–1820+.

Weekly. Established in November, 1817, judging from the date of the earliest issue located, that of July 22, 1818, vol. 1, no. 37, published by H[alsey] Deming, with the title of "Kentucky Herald & Mercantile Advertiser." It was first authorized to print State advertisements, Jan. 2, 1818 (Ky. Acts, 26th Ass'y, p. 322). The "Kentucky Herald" is quoted in the "Louisville Public Advertiser" of Sept. 2, 1820; and the Louisville "Herald" in the "Edwardsville [Ill.] Spectator" of Dec. 19, 1820. The issue of Nov. 8, 1820, was published by Deming, who probably continued the paper after 1820.

Ohio Hist. & Phil. Soc. has Oct. 28, Nov. 18, 1818.

Am. Antiq. Soc. has June 9, 1819.

Univ. of Chicago has June 30, 1819.
Filson Club, Louisville, has July 22, 1818; Nov. 1, 8, 1820.

[Louisville] **Public Advertiser,** 1818–1820+.

Weekly and semi-weekly. Established June 30, 1818, by S[hadrach] Penn, Jun. It was a weekly and its title was "Public Advertiser" up to Jan. 23, 1819. With the issue of Jan. 27, 1819, the title was changed to "The Louisville Public Advertiser," and the issue to a semi-weekly. There was also a weekly edition, without front page title or volume numbering. Continued by Penn until after 1820.

Lexington Pub. Lib. has June 30, 1818–Dec. 18, 1819; Jan. 1–8, 1820.
Univ. of Chicago has July 21–Aug. 25, Sept. 8–Dec. 8, 22–29, 1818; Jan. 5–May 1, 12–Sept. 1, 8, 1819–Dec. 30, 1820.
Lib. Congress has Apr. 28, Aug. 28, Oct. 9–Dec. 29, 1819; Jan. 19–Dec. 30, 1820.
Am. Antiq. Soc. has May 5, 1819; Jan. 19, 26, Feb. 19, Mar. 1–Apr. 5, 15–26, May 6, 13–20, 27, June 3, 7, 21–July 8, 15–26, Aug. 2–12, 19–30, Sept. 6–13, 20–Oct. 7, 14–21, 28–Nov. 22, 29–Dec. 20, 27, 30, 1820.
Duke Univ. has Apr. 22, May 6, 1820.

[Louisville] **Western American,** 1806.

Weekly. A continuation of the "Western American" of Bairdstown, without change of numbering. The first Louisville issue was on Jan. 30, 1806, vol. 3, no. 1, published by F[rancis] Peniston, with the title of "The Western American." The last Louisville issue located is that of Sept. 11, 1806, vol. 3, no. 32.

Am. Antiq. Soc. has Feb. 6, 13, 27, Apr. 9, 16, May 7–21, June 4, 25, July 16, 23, Sept. 11, 1806.
Univ. of Chicago has Mar. 6–20, 1806.
Lib. Congress has Apr. 23, 1806.

[Louisville] **Western Courier,** 1811–1820+.

Weekly. Established in November, 1811, judging from the date of the earliest issue located, that of Aug. 28, 1812, vol. 1, no. 42, published by Thomas Crawford, Jun., with the title of "The Western Courier." The paper was taken over by Nicholas Clarke at some time between Nov. 5 and Dec. 22, 1812. Clarke published it up to the last issue located that of Dec. 2, 1820, vol. 10, no. 9. The paper is quoted at length in the "Louisville Public Advertiser" of Aug. 5 and Aug. 30, 1820. It was continued after 1820.

Chicago Hist. Soc. has Aug. 28, Oct. 15, Nov. 5, 1812.
Harvard has Oct. 1, 15–29, Dec. 22, 1812; Feb. 9, 16, Mar. 23, July 6–20, Aug. 17, 1813.

Wis. Hist. Soc. has Nov. 16, 30, 1813–Sept. 26, 1816.
Am. Antiq. Soc. has June 13, 1814; June 1, Oct. 5, 1815.
Univ. of Chicago has Apr. 20, 1815; Apr. 10, 17, 1817.
Filson Club, Louisville, has Apr. 1, Dec. 2, 1820.
Princeton Univ. has Apr. 1, 1820.

[Maysville] Eagle, 1814–1820+.

Weekly. Established in June, 1814, under the title of "The Eagle," judging from the date of the earliest issue located, that of Mar. 3, 1815, vol. 1, no. 40, published by J. H. & R. Corwine [Joab H. and Richard Corwine]. The paper is referred to as published by the Corwines in the "Kentucky Almanac" for 1815, printed in the latter part of 1814. Richard Corwine died Dec. 19, 1815, and the paper was published by Joab H. Corwine. With the issue of May 3, 1816, it was published by James C. Pickett, who continued it (according to an advertisement in the issue of Aug. 30, 1816) through the issue of Aug. 9, 1816. With the issue of Aug. 30, 1816, it was published by Chalfant & Berry [Thomas? Chalfant and William C. Berry]. With the issue of Jan. 10, 1817, the paper was transferred to Grinstead & Co., which firm name was later called William Grinstead & Co., and W. Grinstead & Co. With the issue of Nov. 14, 1817 the paper was transferred to A[aron] Crookshanks, who published it to the last issue located, that of Mar. 27, 1818, vol. 4, no. 42. According to Collins, "History of Kentucky," 1874, vol. 2, p. 560, the paper was sold by Crookshanks on Nov. 1, 1820, to Lewis Collins, who published it for many years afterwards.

Am. Antiq. Soc. has Mar. 3, 1815; Jan. 26, Aug. 30, Sept. 13–Oct. 4, Nov. 8, 22, 29, Dec. 13, 1816; Jan. 10–Mar. 7, 21–Apr. 4, 25–May 23, June 6, 13, 27–July 25, Aug. 22–Sept. 5, 26, Oct. 3, Nov. 7–21, Dec. 5, 1817; Jan. 2, 9, Feb. 6, 27, Mar. 20, 27, 1818.
Lib. Congress has July 19, 1816.
Filson Club, Louisville, has Jan. 24, 31, Feb. 28, Mar. 21, 28, July 4, 25, 1817.

[Mount Sterling] Laurel, 1818–1819.

Weekly. No copy located. Established evidently in 1818, since it was first authorized to print State advertisements, Dec. 11, 1818 (Ky. Acts, 27th Ass'y, p. 597). In the Winchester, Va. "Republican Constellation" of Sept. 19, 1818, is a quotation from the "Laurel" of Aug. 15. In the "Mobile Gazette" of July 20, 1820, there is a quotation from the "Kentucky Laurel" referring to a declaration filed in the "Laurel" office, Apr. 19, 1819.

[Paris] Instructer, 1818.

Weekly. Established May 2, 1818, by James M. Lilly. This is the only issue located, and bears the title of "Instructer" printed merely as a column heading in the first page. W. H. Perrin, in his "Pioneer Press of Kentucky," p. 66, says that this paper "was afterward removed to Millersburg, in the same county, where it shortly after died a natural death, and where the editor also died of consumption." The Chillicothe, Ohio, "Weekly Recorder" of July 27, 1820, records the recent death of James M. Lilly, "editor of the Instructor, lately printed in Paris."

Am. Antiq. Soc. has May 2, 1818.

[Paris] Kentucky Herald, 1806.

Weekly. Established Apr. 17, 1806, vol. 1, no. 1, with the title of "The Kentucky Herald," but with no printer's name or indication of who published it. The advertisements were in continuation of those in "Stewart's Kentucky Herald" of Mar. 27, 1806, and the type and format were the same as of that paper. On May 8, 1806, appeared another issue of the "Kentucky Herald," also vol. 1, no. 1, published by Robert K. M'Laughlin, & Co., continuing the advertisements of the two previous papers. No further issues can be located.

Harvard has Apr. 17, May 8, 1806.

[Paris] Rights of Man, 1797–1798.

Weekly. Established in May, 1797, judging from the date of the earliest issue located, that of Aug. 30, 1797, vol. 1, no. 14, published by Darius Moffett, with the title of "Rights of Man, or the Kentucky Mercury." The last issue located is that of Jan. 10, 1798, vol. 1, no. 33.

Harvard has Aug. 30, Sept. 6, 27, Oct. 11, 25, Nov. 8, 15, 1797; Jan. 10, 1798.

[Paris] Stewart's Kentucky Herald, 1805–1806.

Weekly. A continuation of the paper of the same title published at Lexington, without change of numbering. The last Lexington issue located is that of Aug. 2, 1803, vol. 9, no. 444, and the first Paris issue located is that of Nov. 25, 1805, vol. 9, no. 489, entitled "Stewart's Kentucky Herald." All of the known Paris issues are published by James H. Stewart, except the last located, that of Mar. 27, 1806, vol. 9, no. 503, which has no printer's name. This paper was apparently succeeded by the "Kentucky Herald," which see.

Harvard has Nov. 25, Dec. 2, 16, 30, 1805; Jan. 13, 20, Mar. 6, 27, 1806.

[Paris] Western Citizen, 1808–1820+.

Weekly. Established in February, 1808, under the title of "The Western Citizen," judging from the date of the first issue located, that of Nov. 17, 1808, vol. 1, no. 42, printed by J[ohn] A. Grimes. Perrin, in his "Pioneer Press of Kentucky," p. 56, prints a letter which notes an issue of Nov. 3, 1808, vol. 1, no. 30 (this numbering does not harmonize with the located copy of Nov. 17,

1808), and which states that the early files of the paper were destroyed by fire. In 1809, the paper was purchased by Joel R. Lyle, who published it until after 1820.

Am. Antiq. Soc. has Dec. 24, 1808; Feb. 26–Aug. 20, Sept. 3–Dec. 31, 1814; Jan. 7–June 10, 24–Dec. 27, 1815; Jan. 3, 10, 1816.
Transylvania Coll., Lexington, has Sept. 5, 1812; Feb. 27, Apr. 10, May 1, 22, June 5, 19, Aug. 14, Sept. 11, Oct. 2, 9, 23, Nov. 6, 20, 1813; Oct. 23, Nov. 19, 26, Dec. 10, 17, 31, 1814; Jan. 21, Mar. 18, 25, May 6, July 19, 26, Aug. 9, 16, Sept. 6, Nov. 15, 22, Dec. 13, 20, 1815; Jan. 10, Feb. 28, Mar. 20–Apr. 3, 24, May 8, June 5, 19, July 24, Aug. 7, 14, Sept. 4, 25–Nov. 6, 20, Dec. 11, 25, 1816; Jan. 8, 15, 29, Feb. 19, Mar. 5, 19, 26, Apr. 9, 23, May 7, 14, 28, July 23, 30, Aug. 13–26, Sept. 9–30, Oct. 14, 28, Dec. 16–30, 1817; Jan. 13, Feb. 3, 24, Mar. 31, Apr. 14, 28–May 12, 26, June 2, 23, 30, Sept. 15–29, Oct. 20, Dec. 1, 1818; Mar. 9, Nov. 16, Dec. 7, 28, 1819; Jan. 4, Apr. 4, May 9, June 13, 27, Aug. 8, 15, Sept. 5, Oct. 3, 24, 31, Nov. 14, 21, Dec. 26, 1820.
Ky. State Hist. Soc. has Jan. 4–Feb. 1, 15–Mar. 14, Apr. 4, 18, May 2, 16–June 6, 20–July 4, 18–Oct. 10, 1812; Jan. 26, 1813; Feb. 13, 1815; Mar. 23, 1819.
Kentuckian-Citizen office, Paris, has Nov. 17, 1808.
Lib. Congress has Dec. 31, 1808.
Univ. of Chicago has Nov. 24, 1810; June 15, 1811.
Louisville Pub. Lib. has Feb. 8, 1812.

[Richmond] **Globe,** 1809–1810.

Weekly. Established, under the title of "The Globe" in November, 1809, judging from the date of the first issue located, that of Jan. 24, 1810, vol. 1, no. 12, printed by Ruble, Harris & Co. [Thomas W. Ruble and E. Harris]. The junior editor was probably Eli Harris, who had resigned from the "Georgia Express" at Athens in March 1809. The issues from July 12, 1810, to Oct. 17, 1810, vol. 1, no. 50, the last located, were printed by Ruble & Harris.

Am. Antiq. Soc. has Jan. 24, July 12, Aug. 1, Oct. 17, 1810.
Chicago Hist. Soc. has Jan. 24, 1810.

[Richmond] **Luminary,** 1811–1820+.

Weekly. Established under the title of "The Luminary," in July, 1811, judging from the date of the first issue located, that of Aug. 14, 1811, vol. 1, no. 5, published by John A. Grimes. The last issue located published by Grimes is that of Feb. 12, 1814. The next issue found is that of Mar. 8, 1816, published by Peter Bertrand, who printed at Richmond in the latter part of 1815. In this issue is an advertisement, dated Feb. 2, 1816, requesting settlement of all debts due John A. Grimes, also the firm of Grimes & Brooking. Joseph Turner printed at Richmond from 1816 to after 1820, issuing his imprints from "the office of the Luminary." The issue of July 14, 1820, vol. 9, no. 52, was published by Joseph Turner, who states editorially that this issue "completes the fourth volume of the Luminary, since under the management of the present proprietor."

Am. Antiq. Soc. has Jan. 18, Feb. 8, 22, 1812; Feb. 12, 1814; Mar. 8, 1816.
Harvard has Aug. 14, 1811.
Ohio Hist. & Phil. Soc. has July 14, 1820.

[Russellville] **Farmer's Friend**, 1808–1813.

Weekly. Established in December, 1808, judging from the date of the first issue located, that of Oct. 2, 1809, vol. 1, no. 44, published by Matthew Duncan, with the title of "The Farmer's Friend." Before May 25, 1810, the title was altered to "Farmer's Friend." The last issue located is that of Dec. 14, 1810, vol. 3, no. 2. Manuscript Court records of Warren County show that the editor was James M. Duncan in June 1811 to August 1812. Yet Matthew Duncan printed at Russellville in 1813; and a document in the National Archives, Dep't of State Papers, undated, but of 1813, urges that the printing of federal laws be given to J. Gwin of the "Sovereign People" in place of M. Duncan, editor of the "Farmer's Friend," who "has declined printing his paper."

Lib. Congress has Oct. 2, 1809; May 25, Oct. 26, Dec. 14, 1810.
Filson Club, Louisville, has Oct. 27–Dec. 22, 1809.
Am. Antiq. Soc. has Sept. 14, 1810.

[Russellville] **Mirror**, 1806–1812.

Weekly. Established Nov. 1, 1806, by Adams and Mitchell [John Adams and William Mitchell], with the title of "The Mirror." With the issue of Mar. 20, 1807, the paper was published solely by John Adams. The Russellville "Farmer's Friend" of Nov. 3, 1809, prints an amusing and poetic account of the recent "death" of the Mirror, but if this account was true, the paper was evidently revived. In 1810 it was sold to Ira Woodruff & Co., which is the publishers' name appearing in Thomas's 1810 list. It was so published up to the last issue located, that of Jan. 29, 1812, vol. 5, no. 4.

Harvard has Nov. 1, 7, 21, Dec. 12, 19, 1806; Jan. 9, 30, Mar. 13, Apr. 3, June 27, July 4, 18, 25, Aug. 8–22, Sept. 5, 26, Oct. 20, 1807; Mar. 24, June 2, 16, 23, July 14, 21, Oct. 10, 27, Nov. 10, Dec. 8, 15, 1808.
Am. Antiq. Soc. has Nov. 7, 14, 1806; Feb. 27, Mar. 13, 27, Apr. 3–17, May 1, 8, July 4, 18, Aug. 8, 22–Sept. 12, Oct. 20, Dec. 1, 1807; Mar. 24, 1808; Jan. 5, 1809.
Va. State Lib. has Nov. 14, 1806.
Chicago Hist. Soc. has May 8, 1807; June 30, July 7, 1808.
Univ. of Chicago has Jan. 29, 1812.

KENTUCKY

[Russellville] **Sovereign People**, 1813–1814.

Weekly. Established in June, 1813, judging from the date of the first and only issue located, that of Nov. 24, 1813, vol. 1, no. 22, published by John Gwin & Co., with the title of "The Sovereign People." Gwin & Co. "declined" their paper shortly before October 1814 (letter of Oct. 17, 1814 in National Archives, State Dep't Papers).

Wis. Hist. Soc. has Nov. 24, 1813.

[Russellville] **Weekly Messenger**, 1814–1820+.

Weekly. Established in January, 1814, judging from the date of the earliest issue located, that of Jan. 26, 1819, new series, vol. 6, no. 4, published by Putnam Ewing, Jr., with the title of "The Weekly Messenger." Some broadsides of 1815 were "printed at the office of the Weekly Messenger, Russellville," and there are Russellville 1816 pamphlets with the imprint of Henry C. Sleight. Sleight, in a biographical letter (O'Reilly MSS., no. 631, in Rochester Hist. Soc.), states that he went to Russellville soon after May 5, 1815 and "started" a weekly paper there entitled "The Messenger," which he sold out in 1817. In September, 1819, the paper was purchased by Charles Rhea. With the issue of Sept. 2, 1820 Rhea took George B. Crutcher into partnership under the firm name of Rhea & Crutcher. With the issue of Oct. 14, 1820, the imprint became C. Rhea, & Co. Between Nov. 18 and Dec. 5, 1820, Charles Rhea again became sole proprietor and continued the paper after 1820.

Manuscript Court records of Warren County show the record of payments for Chancery advertisements to Crumbaugh & Sleight [——— Crumbaugh and Henry C. Sleight] as editors in May 1815; to H. C. Sleight in August 1816; to George B. Crutcher in August 1817; to Putnam Ewing, Jr., in February–May 1819; and to Charles Rhea in May 1820. Putnam Ewing, Jr., was printing at Russellville in the latter part of 1818.

Documents in the National Archives, State Dep't Papers, have the following references to this paper: — letter of Oct. 17, 1814, requesting appointment of Crombaugh & Rea [Crumbaugh & Rhea], editors of the "Weekly Register" [error for "Weekly Messenger"?], as printers of U. S. Laws; record of payment, July 18, 1815, to Crumbaugh & Rhea for printing U. S. Laws (this appears in printed "Accounts of Receipts and Expenditures" for 1815); letter, Oct. 12, 1820, from Charles Rhea, stating that he had purchased the Weekly Messenger from Putnam Ewing on Sept. 4, 1819; letter, Apr. 8, 1820, from George B. Crutcher, "late editor of the Weekly Messenger," having succeeded Henry C. Sleight.

Lib. Congress has Jan. 26–May 29, 1819; Jan. 11–Feb. 1, 15–Mar. 28, Apr. 8– Aug. 19, Sept. 2–Nov. 11, Dec. 5, 19, 1820.

[Shelbyville] **Impartial Compiler,** 1818–1820.

Weekly. Established in May, 1818, judging from the earliest issue located, that of Apr. 30, 1819, vol. 1, no. 49, no name of publisher given, entitled "Impartial Compiler." Joshua D. Grant was printing at Shelbyville in 1818–1820, and presumably was the printer of this paper. The "Shelbyville Compiler" is quoted in the "Louisville Public Advertiser" of Mar. 11, 1820. The issue of May 27, 1820, vol. 3, no. 1, entitled "Impartial Compiler," was published by Joshua D. Grant.

Lib. Congress has Apr. 30, 1819.
Ohio Hist. & Phil. Soc. has May 27, 1820.

[Shelbyville] **Kentuckian,** 1814–1816.

Weekly. Established evidently in 1814, since it was first authorized to print State advertisements Dec. 19, 1814 (Ky. Acts, 23rd Ass'y, p. 237). In the "Louisville Correspondent" of May 11, 1814, George C. Smoot issued a prospectus to publish at Shelbyville a weekly paper to be called "The Kentuckian," which he hopes will appear about the first of July. The Shelbyville "Kentuckian" of July 2 is quoted in the Washington, Ky., "Union" of July 23, 1814; and the paper is also quoted in the Lexington "Reporter" of July 19, 1815, and in the Hamilton, Ohio, "Miami Intelligencer," of Oct. 12, 1815. It may have been continued to 1816, as Cox & Ballard [——— Cox and ——— Ballard] were printing at Shelbyville in that year. No copy located.

[Shelbyville] **Republican Register,** 1804.

No copy located. Established presumably in 1804, since it was first authorized to print State advertisements Dec. 15, 1804 (Littell's Laws, vol. 3, p. 192).

[Springfield] **Western American,** 1818.

No copy located. Established presumably in 1818, since it was first authorized to print State advertisements, Dec. 11, 1818 (Ky. Acts, 27th Ass'y, p. 597).

[Washington] **Dove,** 1808–1814.

Weekly. Established late in August, 1808, judging from the earliest issue located, that of Feb. 17, 1810, vol. 2, no. 26, published by Corwine & Co., with the title of "The Dove." The issue of Mar. 21, 1812, vol. 4, no. 23, whole no. 179, was printed by J. H. & R. Corwine [Joab H. and Richard Corwine]. Berry & Denny advertise in the Chillicothe, Ohio, "Fredonian" of July 22, 1808, that they soon intend to establish "The Dove" at Washington. Berry was undoubtedly William C. Berry, who is known to have been a printer at Washington early in 1808 (see his marriage notice in the Chillicothe "Scioto Gazette" of

May 30, 1808). The paper was first authorized to print State advertisements, Feb. 9, 1809 (Littell's Laws, vol. 4, p. 53). It appears in Thomas's 1810 list, as published by Berry & Corwine. It was probably published until 1814, as J. H. and R. Corwine removed to Maysville in that year to publish "The Eagle." J. H. and R. Corwine and J. C. Picket issued proposals in the Georgetown "Telegraph" of Sept. 25, 1811, for a new paper to be called the "Kentucky Enquirer," to be published about November at Washington. "The publication of the Dove will be entirely suspended if the present contemplated establishment succeeds; if not, it will appear as usual." Since the "Dove" was not suspended for at least several months afterwards, it is probable that the new paper was never published.

Ky. State Hist. Soc. has Feb. 17, 1810.
Harvard has Mar. 21, 1812.

[Washington] **Mirror,** 1797–1799.

Weekly. Established, under the title of "The Mirror," on Sept. 16, 1797, by Hunter & Beaumont [William Hunter and William H. Beaumont], judging from the earliest issue located, that of Sept. 30, 1797, vol. 1, no. 3. This firm also established "The Palladium" at Frankfort on Aug. 9, 1798, and published the two papers simultaneously until Dec. 19, 1799, when "The Mirror" was discontinued.

Univ. of Chicago has Sept. 30, Oct. 7, 21, 1797–June 16, 1798.
Lib. Congress has Oct. 21, 1797–Sept. 4, 18, 1799.
Am. Antiq. Soc. has Nov. 30, 1798.

[Washington] **Republican Auxiliary,** 1806–1810.

Weekly. Established in August, 1806, judging from the date of the first and only issue located, that of Aug. 15, 1807, vol. 1, no. 52, published by Robert Richardson, with the title of "Republican Auxiliary." The Frankfort "Western World" of Sept. 27, 1806, refers to the "Republican Auxiliary." A paper called the "Auxiliary" appears as published at Washington, with no editor given, in Thomas's 1810 list.

Lib. Cong. has Aug. 15, 1807.

[Washington] **Union,** 1814–1820+.

Weekly. Established on Jan. 4, 1814, judging from the date of the earliest issue located, that of Mar. 8, 1814, published by David V. Rannells, with the title of "The Union." Rannells continued to publish it until 1817 or later. In fact he was printing at Washington with Lewis Collins in 1819–1820, and by himself in 1821. The paper was continued until after 1820.

Am. Antiq. Soc. has Mar. 8, 29, Apr. 19, May 3, 10, 24, June 11–July 2, 16, 23, Aug. 6, 13, 27, Sept. 10, Oct. 22, Nov. 5, 12, Dec. 3, 17, 24, 1814; Jan. 7– Mar. 17, 31, Apr. 7, 21–May 12, 26, June 9, 16, 30, July 14, 21, Aug. 11– Sept. 1, 15–29, Oct. 20, Nov. 3, 17, Dec. 1–29, 1815; Jan. 5–Feb. 9, Mar. 15, 29–Apr. 19, May 3, 10, 31–July 12, 26–Aug. 9, 23, Sept. 6–Oct. 11, Dec. 6– 27, 1816; Jan. 3–Feb. 14, 28–May 9, 1817.
Mass. Hist. Soc. has Mar. 15, 1816.

[Washington] Weekly Messenger, 1803.

Weekly. Established on June 2, 1803, judging from the date of the earliest issue located, that of June 16, 1803, vol. 1, no. 3, published by Jonathan Smith Findlay & Company, with the title of "The Weekly Messenger." The last issue located is that of Oct. 6, 1803, vol. 4, no. 175.

Am. Antiq. Soc. has June 16, 23, Sept. 15, Oct. 6, 1803.
Univ. of Texas has July 21, 1803.

Winchester Advertiser, 1814–1815.

Weekly. Established Aug. 5, 1814, by Martin & Patten [William W. Martin and Nathaniel Patten, Jr.], with the title of "Winchester Advertiser." With the issue of Oct. 29, 1814, the title was shortened to "The Advertiser." The last issue located is that of June 14, 1815, vol. 1, no. 46. In July, 1815 this firm was succeeded by Patten & Finnell, who changed the title to "Kentucky Advertiser," which see.

Am. Antiq. Soc. has Aug. 5, Sept. 2, 23, Oct. 15, Nov. 19, Dec. 10, 24, 31, 1814; Jan. 21, Feb. 4, 11, Mar. 4, 11, 25, Apr. 29, May 6, 24, 31, June 14, 1815.
Wis. Hist. Soc. has Aug. 12–Dec. 10, 1814; Nov. 9, 1816.
Univ. of Chicago has Jan. 14, 21, Feb. 4, 1815.

[Winchester] Kentucky Advertiser, 1815–1819.

Weekly. A continuation, without change of numbering, of "The Advertiser" of Winchester. The first issue with the new title of "Kentucky Advertiser" was published in July, 1815, by Patten & Finnell [Nathaniel Patten, Jr., and Nimrod L. Finnell]. The title was changed to "The Kentucky Advertiser" in November or December, 1815. With the issue of Aug. 3, 1816, Finnell retired, and the paper was published by Nathaniel Patten, Jr. With the issue of July 26, 1817, vol. 3, no. 156, Patten apparently suspended the paper on account of arrears in subscription. It was revived in September, 1817, judging from the date of the issue of June 13, 1818, vol. 4, no. 194, published by N. L. Finnell. The firm of Dillard & Hukill was printing at Winchester in the summer of 1819, at the Office of the "Kentucky Advertiser" although there is nothing to show that they were associated with the newspaper. In July, 1819 (according to a statement in the

"Kentucky Gazette," of Lexington, of July 30, 1819), James Armstrong purchased the paper. The next issue located, that of Oct. 30, 1819, vol. 6, no. 5, whole no. 265, is published by J. Armstrong, and has the title changed to "Kentucky Advertiser Farmer's Magazine." This is the last issue located. Armstrong removed to Danville, where he began publishing the "Olive Branch," in March 1820.

Am. Antiq. Soc. has Aug. 2, 9, Sept. 13, 20, Oct. 21, 28, Nov. 11, Dec. 9-30, 1815; Jan. 6, 27-Mar. 30, Apr. 13-May 25, June 15, 29, July 6, 20, 27, Aug. 10-Sept. 14, 28, Oct. 5, Nov. 9, 23, Dec. 7, 21, 28, 1816; Jan. 11-Feb. 1, 15-Apr. 5, 26, June 28, 1817.

Univ. of Chicago has Aug. 10, 31, Sept. 14-Oct. 12, 26, Nov. 2, 23, Dec. 7, 21, 28, 1816; Jan. 4, July 19, 1817; June 13, Aug. 1, 1818.

Wis. Hist. Soc. has Nov. 9, 1816.

Lib. Congress has Oct. 30, 1819.

[   ] **Kentucky Telegraphe,** 1798.

No copy located. Established evidently in 1798, since it was first authorized to print State advertisements, Dec. 22, 1798 (Littell's Laws, vol. 2, p. 228). Unfortunately the name of the town where it was printed is not mentioned in the Act.

LOUISIANA

[Alexandria] **Louisiana Herald,** 1818–1820+.

Weekly. The earliest issue located is that of Mar. 20, 1819, vol. 1, no. 25, entitled "Louisiana Herald," published by George F. Tennery, implying that the paper was established in October, 1818. In January, 1820, Tennery was succeeded as publisher by Benjamin M. Stokes. In the National Archives, State Dep't Papers, is a letter from Stokes, Jan. 21, 1820, stating that he had purchased the paper from Tennery. He sold the paper back to Tennery, who resumed the proprietorship with the issue of Apr. 22, 1820 and so continued until after 1820.

Am. Antiq. Soc. has Mar. 20, 27, 1819.
Lib. Congress has Jan. 21, 28, Feb. 11, 18, Mar. 17–31, Apr. 22, May 6–June 10, 24–July 15, 29–Sept. 9, 30–Nov. 4, 25, Dec. 2, 1820.

[Alexandria] **Louisiana Planter,** 1810.

Weekly. Established Apr. 17, 1810, judging from the date of the first and only issue located, that of May 15, 1810, vol. 1, no. 5, published by Benj. M. Stokes, with the title of "The Louisiana Planter."

N. Y. Hist. Soc. has May 15, 1810.

[Alexandria] **Louisiana Rambler,** 1817–1818.

Weekly. The only issues located are those of Mar. 28, and Apr. 11, 1818, new series, vol. 2, nos. 5 and 7, published by Hugh Chain, with the title of "Louisiana Rambler." This would imply that the paper was established, or reestablished, early in 1817. In the "Washington Republican" of Natchez, Miss., of Apr. 9, 1817, is the following notice: "Married at Alexandria, on Thursday evening last, Mr. Hugh Chain, one of the editors of the 'Louisiana Rambler,' to Miss Matilda Anderson, both of that place." The "National Intelligencer" of Sept. 8, 1818, records the death, in a quarrel, of Hugh Chain, editor of the Louisiana Rambler, on July 19. The paper was evidently then discontinued, as the "Louisiana Herald" was established as its successor late in 1818.

Am. Antiq. Soc. has Mar. 28, Apr. 11, 1818.

[Alexandria] **Red-River Herald,** 1813.

Weekly. The only issue located is for Sept. 10, 1813, vol. 1, new series, no. 4, size large quarto, published by Thomas Eastin, with the title of "Red-River Herald."

Harvard has Sept. 10, 1813.

LOUISIANA

Baton-Rouge Gazette, 1819–1820+.

Weekly. Established Feb. 6, 1819, judging from the earliest issue located, that of June 5, 1819, vol. 1, no. 18, published by Morison & Devalcourt [―――― Morison and T―――― Devalcourt], with the title of "Baton-Rouge Gazette." It was printed half in English and half in French, with the French title of "Gazette de Baton-Rouge" on the third page. It was continued after 1820.

Am. Antiq. Soc. has June 5, 1819; July 8, 1820.
H. Louis Cohn, Baton Rouge, has Dec. 11, 25, 1819.
C. P. Manship, Baton Rouge, has Jan. 1, 1820.
Univ. of Pittsburgh has Nov. 29, 1820.

[Jackson] Feliciana Gazette, 1820+.

Weekly. Established Dec. 23, 1820, judging from the earliest issue located, that of Dec. 30, 1820, vol. 1, no. 2, published by Blackburn & Fishburn [―――― Blackburn and Philip Fishburn], with the title of "Feliciana Gazette." The paper was continued after 1820.

Univ. of Texas has Dec. 30, 1820.

[Natchitoches] El Mexicano, 1813.

The only known issue is that of June 19, 1813, vol. 1, no. 2, entitled "El Mexicano." It bore no imprint, but like its immediate predecessor, the "Gaceta de Texas," the volume numbering of which it continued (see under Nacogdoches, Texas), was undoubtedly printed by Aaron Mower, and edited by José Alvarez de Toledo and William Shaler. It was a folio single sheet and was printed in Spanish and English. The editors state "Great will undoubtedly be the surprise of those who after having seen the first number of the 'Gaceta de Texas,' are informed that it saw the light only to die and resuscitate again, on the banks of the Red river, under the title of 'The Mexican.'"

A full discussion of this paper and the reasons for its establishment is contributed by Ike H. Moore to the "Southwestern Historical Quarterly" of October 1935, vol. 39, pp. 83–99, but this article was written before the discovery of the original issue. Further light on the subject is in Kathryn Garrett's article in the "Southwestern Historical Quarterly" of January 1937, pp. 200–215.

State Dep't Archives, Special Agents MSS, William Shaler, 1810, II, contains the original issue of June 19, 1813. Photostats are in the Lib. Congress, Am. Antiq. Soc., Univ. of Texas, and San Jacinto Museum at Houston.

[Natchitoches] Gaceta de Texas, see under Nacogdoches, Texas.

[New Orleans] Ami des Lois, 1809–1820+.

Tri-weekly and daily. Established in November, 1809, judging from the date of the first issue located, that of Jan. 2, 1810, vol. 1, no. 20, entitled "L'Ami des Lois." It was published as a tri-weekly by Leclerc & Co., although Thomas in his 1810 list states that it was published by Hilaire Leclerc. The first two pages were in French and the last two in English, with a column heading on third page, "Friend of the Laws." A broadside prospectus in the State Department at Washington (Bureau of Rolls and Library, Claiborne Correspondence) states that the paper will appear on Nov. 16, 1809 and will be "edited and published by Hilaire Leclerc, the elder." With the issue of May 11, 1810, the imprint was changed from Leclerc & Co. to J[ohn] Leclerc & A[ugust] Provosty. At some time in 1810 or 1811 J. Leclerc became sole publisher. The "Natchez Gazette" of Aug. 15, 1811, records under date of Aug. 3, that "Yesterday was committed to prison, Mr. John LeClerc, Editor of the Friend of the Laws . . . ten days imprisonment." With the issue of May 22, 1815, publication was changed from tri-weekly to daily and the title changed to "L'Ami des Lois et Journal du Soir." With the issue of Feb. 22, 1819, the paper was sold to James M'Karaher and the title changed to "L'Ami des Lois et Journal du Commerce," with the column heading on the last page, "Friend of the Laws and Commercial Journal." A tri-weekly issue for the country, without title, was also published. In the first week in April, 1820, the paper was transferred to A[rnould] DuBourg and P[――――] Cherbonnier, who changed it to a tri-weekly on August 3, 1820. On Nov. 25, 1820, this firm of publishers announced that they had sold the paper and that beginning with the issue of Nov. 30 it would be published daily instead of tri-weekly. It was presumably sold to Michel de Armas and Jn. Bte. Maureau, since their names appear as publishers in the early issues of 1821.

> Charles Titcomb, New Orleans and New York, has Jan. 2, 1810–Feb. 20, 1819. This file has been in storage for many years and in 1944 Mr. Titcomb writes me that it is not accessible.
> New Orleans City Archives has June 1–Nov. 4, 1813; Jan. 4–Nov. 29, 1814; Jan. 2, 1816–Dec. 31, 1818; July 1–Sept. 29, 1819; Jan. 2–Mar. 30, Aug. 12, 1820.
> Wis. Hist. Soc. has Jan. 18, 1810.
> La. State Museum has June 18, 1812, Jan. 6–Sept. 20, 1814; May 4–Aug. 31, 1818, fair; Jan. 2–Mar. 29, Apr. 6–Nov. 25, 1820.
> Am. Antiq. Soc. has Mar. 17, 18, 1818; Mar. 20, 1819.
> Yale has Jan. 24, 1815.
> Duke Univ. has Dec. 31, 1817.

New-Orleans Chronicle, 1818–1819.

Daily. Established July 13, 1818 by Thomas W. Lorrain, with the title of "The New-Orleans Chronicle." The title within three months was changed to

"New-Orleans Daily Chronicle." The last issue located is that of Sept. 14, 1819, vol. 3, no. 327. A tri-weekly issue for the country was also issued, with the column heading of "New-Orleans Chronicle," but without volume numbering. The "Port-Gibson (Miss.) Correspondent" of Dec. 25, 1819, records the marriage of Thomas W. Lorrain, editor of the "New Orleans Chronicle."

> Am. Antiq. Soc. has July 14, 1818; Mar. 4, Sept. 13, 14, 1819.
> Wis. Hist. Soc. has Oct. 21, 1818.

[New Orleans] Courrier de la Louisiane, 1807–1820+.

Tri-weekly. Established Oct. 14, 1807. The paper was printed in both French and English, the first two pages in French, with the title "Courrier de la Louisiane," and the last two pages in English, with a column heading "Louisiana Courier." The first few issues had no publisher's imprint, but the prospectus, undated, is signed by J. B. Thierry & Co. Jean Baptiste Simon Thierry had come to America from Paris about 1805. With the issue of Nov. 23, 1807, the name of the publisher was given as Thierry & Co. [Thierry and Jean Dacqueny]. With the issue of Apr. 21, 1809, James W. Smith was added to the firm, which became Thierry, Dacqueny & Smith, but with the issue of Aug. 23, 1809, Smith retired and it became Thierry & Dacqueny. Between June 11 and July 4, 1810, J. B. Thierry assumed sole proprietorship. Thierry died Mar. 6, 1815, and the paper was transferred to J[oseph] C[harles] de St. Romes, who continued it until after 1820.

Throughout most of this period, a weekly issue "for the country" was also published. Issues from Aug. 25, 1809 to Feb. 20, 1811 were entitled "Courrier de la Louisiane pour la Campagne," and issues from Nov. 27, 1811 to after 1820 were without title except column headings.

> La. State Museum has Oct. 14, 1807–Oct. 16, 1809; Oct. 17, 1810–Oct. 12, 1814; Oct. 16, 1815–Dec. 29, 1820.
> New Orleans City Archives has July 4–Dec. 5, 1810; July 29–Nov. 29, 1811; Jan. 6–Dec. 31, 1813; Nov. 18, 21, 25, 1814; Jan. 3, 1816–Dec. 27, 1820.
> Harvard has Oct. 23–30, 1807; May 9, 11, 20, June 1, 8, 10, July 18–22, Aug. 3, 5, 29–Sept. 2, Dec. 12–23, 1808; Sept. 21, Oct. 15, 23, 1810; Nov. 27–Dec. 18, 1811; Feb. 19, Apr. 29, July 8, 29, Sept. 16, 30, Oct. 7, 1812, country issues.
> Am. Antiq. Soc. has Mar. 9, 14, Apr. 6, 18–22, May 9, 13, June 3, July 13, 15, Aug. 3, 8, 12, 1808; and June 11, 1810, tri-weekly; Nov. 14, 1810; Aug. 9, 1816; Apr. 6–20, 1818; Apr. 19, 1819; and Apr. 3, Nov. 13, 1820, country issues.
> Lib. Congress has Sept. 19, 1814, tri-weekly; and Feb. 20, 1811; Feb. 1, 1819–Dec. 11, 1820, fair, country issues.
> Duke Univ. has Apr. 20, 1808.
> Wis. Hist. Soc. has Apr. 29, 1808; Nov. 11, 16, 1818.
> U. S. Dept. of State Archives has Sept. 30, 1808; Jan. 18, 1809.

Univ. of Pittsburgh has Oct. 7, Nov. 6, 8, 1811.
Tulane Univ. has Jan. 25, 1815.
Elrie Robinson, St. Francisville, La., has Apr. 19, 1815.

New-Orleans Daily Chronicle, see New-Orleans Chronicle.

[New Orleans] Echo du Commerce, 1808–1809.

Daily. Established Sept. 23, 1808, judging from the first and only issue located, that of Sept. 28, 1808, vol. 1, no. 5, published by Theodore Lamberté, with the title of "L'Echo du Commerce." It was a small folio, was published every day but Sunday, included news and advertisements, and was printed in French and English. The English title, carried as a column heading, was "The Commercial Echo." Gov. Claiborne, in a letter of Nov. 18, 1809 ("Claiborné Official Letter Books," vol. 5, p. 16), said: "There was lately a daily paper called the *Echo* printed in French and English, but has been discontinued."

Wis. Hist. Soc. has Sept. 28, 1808.

[New Orleans] Friend of the Laws, see Ami des Lois.

[New Orleans] Gazette de la Louisiane, see Louisiana Gazette.

[New Orleans] L'Ami des Lois, see Ami des Lois.

[New Oleans] Lanterne Magique, 1808–1809.

Weekly. The "New York Herald" of July 9, 1808, records the receipt of the first four numbers of "La Lanterne Magique, lately set on foot at New Orleans." The only copy located is that of Nov. 20, 1808, vol. 1, no. 5, published by Johnson & Ravenscraft [——— Johnson and ——— Ravenscraft], with the title of "La Lanterne Magique." It was published every Sunday and printed in both French and English. It was of folio size and declared that its policy was political and literary. This issue of Nov. 20, 1808, appeared after a suspension of apparently five months. An editorial says that the paper "went asleep, principally in consequence of a dearth of amusing matter. . . . Scarcely had three of our numbers made their appearance, when the legislature, as if to spite us, adjourned *sine die*." The receipt of several numbers of "La Lanterne Magique" is noted in the Natchez "Mississippian" of Jan. 19, 1809. Gov. Claiborne, in referring to it in a letter of Mar. 17, 1808, states that proposals had been issued for "The Majic Lantern;" and in a letter of Nov. 18, 1809, says that it was nominally edited by a Frenchman named Daudet ("Official Letter Books of W. C. C. Claiborne" vol. 4, p. 167 and vol. 5, p. 16). This was undoubtedly Alexis Daudet, who edited a pamphlet of French songs entitled "Le Chansonnier des Graces," New Orleans, printed by Th. Lamberté, 1809 (Copy in Am. Antiq. Soc.).

Wis. Hist. Soc. has Nov. 20, 1808.

[New Orleans] **Louisiana Advertiser**, 1820+.

Semi-weekly, tri-weekly and daily. Established Apr. 19, 1820, by Sampson & Lorrain [John P. C. Sampson and Thomas W. Lorrain], as a semi-weekly. It was made a tri-weekly with the issue of Apr. 25, 1820, and a daily on June 19, 1820. The partnership was dissolved Aug. 19, 1820, and the paper published by J. P. C. Sampson. Sampson died Aug. 25, 1820 (see long obituary in "L'Ami des Lois" of Sept. 9, 1820), and was succeeded as publisher by P[———] Wood. At some time between Nov. 18 and Dec. 8, 1820, James Beardslee became the publisher and continued the paper until after 1820.

Wis. Hist. Soc. has Apr. 19–May 20, 25–June 24, 28–Aug. 4, 15, 16, 19, 21, Nov. 8, 18, Dec. 8–15, 18–20, 25, 1820.

[New Orleans] **Louisiana Courier**, see Courrier de la Louisiane.

[New Orleans] **Louisiana Gazette**, 1804–1820+.

Weekly, semi-weekly, tri-weekly and daily. Established July 24, 1804, by John Mowry, under the title of "The Louisiana Gazette." Although announced as a semi-weekly, lack of support compelled weekly publication until, with the issue of Jan. 15, 1805, it became a semi-weekly. It so continued until Apr. 3, 1810, with which issue it became a daily and was published by John Mowry & Co., under the title of "The Louisiana Gazette and New-Orleans Daily Advertiser." A semi-weekly issue was also published, with the title of "The Louisiana Gazette for the Country," and the scheme of volume numbering differing from that of the daily issue. Beginning with the issue of Sept. 6, 1811, the paper was published as a tri-weekly, the title changing to "The Louisiana Gazette and New-Orleans Advertiser," but with the issue of Nov. 4, 1811, it resumed daily publication and its former title. Again, with the issue of Aug. 11, 1812, the paper was changed to a tri-weekly and the title to "The Louisiana Gazette and New-Orleans Advertiser." John Mowry died, as the result of a duel, on Nov. 21, 1813, and the paper was transferred to David M'Keehan. When the paper changed from a daily to a tri-weekly, the country issue changed from a semi-weekly to a weekly. Between Oct. 27, 1814, and Mar. 7, 1815, the paper was transferred to Godwin B. Cotten, and between Mar. 30 and Apr. 4, 1815, the title was changed to "The Louisiana Gazette and New-Orleans' Mercantile Advertiser." With the issue of Jan. 18, 1816, the paper was sold to William Bruner, who apparently gave up the country issue. With the issue of Jan. 13, 1817, the paper became a daily, but this lasted only until Feb. 18, 1817, when it resumed tri-weekly publication. Bruner admitted Charles W. Duhy to partnership, and with the issue of Apr. 12, 1817, the paper was published by Bruner & Duhy. In May (certainly by May 31), 1817, the paper was brought out with the first two pages in French and the last two pages in English, with the two titles, "Louisiana Gazette" and "Gazette de la Louisiane." Beginning with the issue of Jan. 31, 1818, it was published daily. Bruner died Mar. 8, 1820, and beginning with the issue of Mar. 13, 1820, the paper was conducted by C. W. Duhy, who continued it until after 1820.

New Orleans City Archives has July 31, 1804–Mar. 31, 1812; June 9–Oct. 27, 1814; Mar. 28–Dec. 5, 19, 1815; Jan. 2, 1816–May 24, 1817; June 26, 1817–Dec. 2, 1819; Jan. 10–Dec. 26, 1820.

U. S. Dep't of State Archives has July 24, 1804.

Am. Antiq. Soc. has May 28, Oct. 8, Dec. 3, 1805; Jan. 24, 28, Feb. 25, 1806; June 6, 1810, daily; May 29, June 1, 26, 29, Dec. 24, 27, 1810, semi-weekly; Feb. 11, Mar. 25, 28, Apr. 1, 4, 1811, semi-weekly; May 22, Oct. 23, 1813, weekly; Feb. 24, Sept. 20, 1814, weekly; May 4, 1815, weekly; Feb. 19, July 11, 1818, daily.

La. State Museum has Apr. 4, 1812–Apr. 3, 1813; May 27–June 28, Oct. 2–Dec. 20, 1817; Jan. 5–Dec. 30, 1819.

Wis. Hist. Soc. has Mar. 17, 20, 24, 1807; Nov. 19–21, 1818.

N. Y. Hist. Soc. has Mar. 3, 1807; Oct. 4, 1816; Apr. 3, 5, 8, 10, 24, May 1, 3, 17, 20, 24, 1817.

Edward A. Parsons, New Orleans, has Mar. 7, Apr. 15, 1815.

Yale has Mar. 19, 1818.

[New Orleans] Mensagero Luisianes, 1809–1811.

Semi-weekly. Established in September 1809, judging from the earliest issue located, that of Oct. 13, 1810, vol. 2, no. 110, published in Spanish and English by Don Joaquin de Lisa, with the title of "El Mensagero Luisianes." The paper is entered in Thomas's 1810 list of newspapers ("History of Printing in America," ed. 2, vol. 2, p. 305), as "The Messenger (El Mensagero)," with Boniquet given as the publisher. A postscript, or "Postillon," of Dec. 11, 1810, has no imprint. Issues of Mar. 15 and 23, 1811, vol. 2, nos. 152 and 155, carry the names of Don Joaquin de Lisa and Don Joseph Antonio Boniquet as publishers.

U. S. State Dept. (Archives) has Oct. 13, 1810.

Seville, Spain, Archivo General de Indias, has Dec. 11, 1810 (photostat, Am. Antiq. Soc.).

Havana Archives has Mar. 15, 23, 1811 (see Perez, "Guide to Cuban Archives," p. 105).

[New Orleans] Misisipi, 1808–1810.

Semi-weekly. Established Sept. 10, 1808, judging from the earliest issue located, that of Oct. 12, 1808, vol. 1, no. 10, published in Spanish and English, with the title of "El Misisipi," by William H. Johnson & Co., "at the office of the Louisiana Gazette." It was of quarto size. The issue of Dec. 10, 1808, vol. 1, no. 27, was published "en la imprenta de la Luisiana Gaceta, por J. R." This

LOUISIANA 189

may have been Jean Renard, who was an active printer at New Orleans at the period. The paper is quoted in the Natchez "Mississippian" of Jan. 19, 1809, and in the New York "American Citizen" of Feb. 11, 1809. Thomas, in his record of newspapers published in the first part of 1810 ("History of Printing," ed. 2, vol. 2, p. 305), lists this paper as a semi-weekly published by Wm. H. Johnson & Co.

Wis. Hist. Soc. has Oct. 12, 1808.

Seville, Spain, Archivo General de Indias, Papeles de Cuba, Legajo 185, has Dec. 10, 1808 (photostat Am. Antiq. Soc.).

[New Orleans] Moniteur de la Louisiane, 1794-1814.

Weekly, semi-weekly and tri-weekly. The earliest issue recorded is that of Aug. 25, 1794, no. 26, published by L[ouis] Duclot, with the title of "Moniteur de la Louisiane," a small octavo newspaper of four pages (reproduced in La. Hist. Soc. Publications, vol. 1, no. 4). The next issue located is that of Sept. 4, 1800, no. 187, an octavo newspaper without any indication of the publisher's name. It was then a weekly and since if it had been published regularly it would have been established in February, 1797, the conclusion would be either that there had been a lapse in publication or that the editor succeeding Duclot had begun a new volume numbering. There are occasional references to the early paper. The issue of Jan. 1, 1811, states that the "Moniteur," since Nov. 13, 1797, has been the "depot" of Government Acts; Winthrop Sargent in a letter of Apr. 20, 1799, to Timothy Pickering, refers to enclosing a copy of the "Louisiana Moniteur" ("Miss. Territorial Archives," vol. 1, p. 142); and the paper is quoted in the Philadelphia "Courrier Français" of Feb. 19, 1798. Issues from Aug. 14, 1802 (no. 304) to Nov. 26, 1803 (no. 371), were of quarto size and without publisher's imprint. With the issue of Dec. 3, 1803 (no. 372) as dated, but not issued until Dec. 12, the paper was published by J.B.L.S. Fontaine [Jean Baptiste Leseur Fontaine]. In March 1804, judging by subsequent volume numbering, publication was changed to semi-weekly. In 1806 the size was changed from quarto to folio. The paper became a tri-weekly with the issue of Dec. 18, 1810. With the issue of Jan. 3, 1811, Fontaine sold out the paper to Toulouse & LeFaux [C. Morane Toulouse and Louis F. M. LeFaux]. With the issue of May 24, 1812, the partnership was dissolved and LeFaux became sole proprietor. The paper reverted to a semi-weekly with the issue of June 8, 1814. The last issue located is that of July 2, 1814, no. 1641.

The "Moniteur" was undoubtedly the first Louisiana newspaper. "Le Courrier du Vendredi" of 1786, mentioned by William Nelson in his Bibliography ("N. J. Archives," ser. 1, vol. 11, p. lxxxvi), was not a Louisiana newspaper, so Mr. Nelson informed me in response to my query regarding it. Jean Baptiste Leseur Fontaine, who died July 4, 1814, in his will left to the city of New Orleans his file of the "Moniteur."

W. H. Wilson, of New Orleans, once owned the issue of Aug. 25, 1794, but this was since destroyed by fire (see "Papers of Bibliog. Soc.," v. 14, p. 128). Fortunately, however, it was reproduced in facsimile, as noted above.

La. State Museum has Aug. 14, 1802–Nov. 26, 1803; Feb. 28, 1807; Aug. 9, 1809; Jan. 3, 1811–Dec. 31, 1812; July 3, 1813; Apr. 21, 1814.

New Orleans City Archives has Oct. 22, 1806–Jan. 1, 1811; Jan. 6, 1813–July 2, 1814.

Duke Univ. has Jan. 2–Dec. 30, 1813.

Mrs. T. P. Thompson, New Orleans, has Sept. 4, 1800; May 10, 1806.

Bibliothèque Nationale, Paris, has May 28–June 18, Dec. 3, 19, 1803; Jan. 7, Feb. 11, 18, 1804 (photostats in Lib. Congress).

Chicago Hist. Soc. has May 28, Dec. 3, 1803.

Edward A. Parsons, New Orleans, has Dec. 24, 1803.

U. S. Dep't. of State Archives has July 26, 1804.

Howard-Tilton Lib., New Orleans, has Aug. 16, 1804; Aug. 24, 1811.

Donaldsonville, La., Clerk of Courts Office, has Jan. 3, 1805.

Seville, Spain, Archivo General de Indias, Papeles de Cuba, Legajo 142, has July 6, 1805 (photostat in Lib. Congress).

Wis. Hist. Soc. has May 7, 1808.

Edward Eberstadt, New York City, has Jan. 2, July 19, 1804.

Edward L. Tinker, New York City, has Feb. 21, 1810; Sept. 22, 1812.

[New Orleans] **Orleans Gazette**, 1804–1820+.

Tri-weekly, semi-weekly, daily and weekly. Established Dec. 20, 1804, by James M. Bradford, with the title of "The Orleans Gazette; and Commercial Advertiser." It was at first a tri-weekly, but was changed to a semi-weekly in June, 1805. Bradford admitted Thomas Anderson into partnership in December, 1805, or January, 1806, and the firm name became Bradford & Anderson. In 1807, apparently in December, it became a daily, with the title of "The Orleans Gazette; and Commercial Daily Advertiser." It remained a daily until 1810 or 1811, when it became a semi-weekly. In 1810 and after, the title was "Orleans Gazette & Commercial Advertiser." In 1809, apparently on Aug. 4, John Hill replaced Bradford and firm became J. Hill & T. Anderson. Hill died Oct. 28, 1810, and Thomas Anderson became sole publisher. Anderson died Aug. 18, 1811, and was succeeded by Jo. Bar. Baird, according to an issue of May 25, 1812 (Joseph B. Baird had issued proposals for the "Florida Herald" in December, 1810, to be issued at Baton Rouge, but there is no evidence to show that it was published). Baird was succeeded by the firm of Baird & Wagner, according to an advertisement under their name in the "Louisiana Gazette" of Aug. 8, 1812; and this firm, by Peter K. Wagner in 1813 or 1814, but since there are only occasional issues for this period, the exact dates of change of firm name cannot be given. The regular issue was changed from a semi-weekly to a tri-weekly on Aug. 10, 1812. Peter K. Wagner continued as publisher until after 1820.

Beginning with December 20, 1804, a country paper was issued weekly, with a volume numbering of its own, at first under the title of "The Orleans Gazette, For the Country," which title was a two column heading on the fourth page. There were several slight changes in this heading; in 1808 and 1812 the title of "Orleans Gazette for the Country" occupied the front page, and in 1818–1820, there was no title except column heading.

Am. Antiq. Soc. has Dec. 22, 29, 1804; Jan. 5, 12, 26–Feb. 16, Mar. 9, 23–Apr. 20, May 11, 25, June 1, 1805; Aug. 20, 1808; Nov. 8, 1810; June 6, 1811; May 25, 1812; Mar. 21, Apr. 28, 1818; Mar. 22, 1819, of country issues; June 28, July 24–Aug. 10, Sept. 18, 1805; Mar. 12, 19, 26, Apr. 26–May 3, June 28, July 5, 19–30, Aug. 13, Oct. 9, 16, 20, 1806; Feb. 5, Nov. 16, 1807; June 5, 1810; Apr. 22, 1814; Mar. 23, 1818, of regular issues.

Harvard has Dec. 29, 1804; Jan. 12–Mar. 16, Apr. 6, 20, 27, May 11, 18–June 1, 1805, of country issues; June 28, July 17, 20, Aug. 7, 10, Sept. 4–21, Nov. 16–21, 1805; Feb. 1, Mar. 22–29, Apr. 19, 26, May 10, 14, June 11, 14, 25–July 12, 23, 26, Aug. 9, 13, 28–Sept. 4, 22–Oct. 16, 30, 1806; Feb. 2, 5, Mar. 9, July 13, 20–30, Aug. 13, 24, 31, Sept. 21, 24, Oct. 1–8, 15, Nov. 16–23, 1807, of regular issues.

Lib. Congress has Apr. 20, 23, June 18, July 13, Aug. 17, Oct. 19, 26, 29, 1807; Jan. 5, 1816, of regular issues; Apr. 16, Sept. 3, 1808; Sept. 8, 15, 1809; Feb. 23, 1819–June 15, 1820, fair, of country issues.

La. State Univ. has May 29, June 4, Oct. 16, 17, 1816; Jan. 4, 8, 13, 15, 20–24, Feb. 7, 17, 26, Apr. 17, May 13–July 26, fair; Sept. 13, Dec. 9, 13, 18, 24, 1817; Apr. 9, 1818; Jan. 6–Dec. 30, 1819, fair, country issues.

La. State Museum has Apr. 13, 1805; Mar. 5, 1807; Sept. 18, 1812, regular issues.

U. S. Dep't of State Archives has Dec. 31, 1804, extra; Apr. 13, 1805, extra; Apr. 2, 1808.

Yale has Mar. 9, 1805.

Wis. Hist. Soc. has Oct. 23, 1818.

[New Orleans] Telegraphe, 1803–1812.

Semi-weekly and tri-weekly. Established Dec. 14, 1803, by Beleurgey et Renard [Claudius Beleurgey and Jean Renard], with the title of "Le Telegraphe, et le Commercial Advertiser." It was printed in both French and English. In 1804 Renard withdrew and C. Beleurgey became sole proprietor. In 1805 or 1806 (apparently in January, 1806) the paper was changed from a semi-weekly to a tri-weekly, and the title became "Telegraphe, et le Commercial Advertiser & New-Orleans Price Current." In 1807, the title was changed to "The Telegraphe et le General Advertiser." In 1810, and perhaps before, a weekly edition for the country was issued, entitled "Telegraphe de la Campagne." Between Nov. 8, 1810, and Feb. 9, 1811, the paper was obtained and published by Jean Dacqueny, and the title changed to "Telegraphe Louisianais and Mercantile Advertiser." The last issue located of this series and with this publisher is that of Oct. 10, 1811. On Apr. 2, 1812, a new series was established with the same title, but new volume numbering, published by Kohlheim & Mitchell [——— Kohlheim and ——— Mitchell], who announced that they had purchased the paper from Dacqueny. It was still a tri-weekly in French and English. The last issue located is that of Apr. 18, 1812, vol. 1, no. 8.

Am. Antiq. Soc. has Dec. 17, 1803; Jan. 25–Feb. 8, 1804; Aug. 23, 30, Sept. 4, 1806; Oct. 13, 1807; Feb. 25, 1808; Apr. 15, 1809; Nov. 1, 8, 1810; Apr. 7–11, 1812.
Lib. Congress has Oct. 17, 22, Dec. 12, 1807; Apr. 5, 1808.
Harvard has Feb. 9–14, Mar. 30, Apr. 20–25, May 2, July 20, Aug. 29, 31, Sept. 12, Oct. 5, 10, Nov. 5, 1811; Apr. 2–18, 1812.
La. State Museum has July 21, 1804; Mar. 11, Apr. 8, 1809.
U. S. Dept. of State Archives, has June 3, 1806.
Wis. Hist. Soc. has May 7, 1808.

[New Orleans] **Trumpeter**, 1811–1812.

Weekly. Established in October 1811, judging from the date of the only issue located, that of Oct. 10, 1812, vol. 1, no. 53, published in French and English by Toulouse & Mitchell [C. Morane Toulouse and ——— Mitchell].

Harvard has Oct. 10, 1812.

[New Orleans] **Union**, 1803–1804.

Weekly and semi-weekly. Established Dec. 13, 1803, by J[ames] Lyon & Co., under the title of "The Union; or, New-Orleans Advertiser and Price Current." With the issue of Jan. 9, 1804, the word "or" was omitted from the title. Although announced as a semi-weekly, the paper was published weekly until February, 1804, when the semi-weekly issue was established and also a weekly issue "for the country." By Mar. 16, 1804, J. Lyon had become sole proprietor, but the paper was "Edited by J[ohn] Kidder in the absence of J. Lyon." By September, Kidder's name was omitted from the imprint, and the paper was published by J. Lyon. In December, 1804, the establishment was bought by James M. Bradford, who on Dec. 20, 1804, brought out a new paper entitled "The Orleans Gazette."

Harvard has Dec. 20, 27, 1803; Jan. 9, 17, Sept. 4, 1804, of regular issue; May 29, Aug. 15, Sept. 19, 27–Oct. 11, 20, Nov. 14–28, 1804, of country issue.
Am. Antiq. Soc. has Jan. 9, 23, July 11, Oct. 11, 1804, of regular issue; Feb. 23, Mar. 1, 15, May 25, 29, Sept. 27, Nov. 14, 21, 1804, of country issue.
U. S. Dept. of State Archives has Mar. 16, 1804 suppl.

[St. Francisville] **Asylum,** 1820+.

Weekly. Established in January 1820, judging from the earliest copy located, that of July 20, 1820, vol. 1, no. 27, published for the Editors by F[ielding] Bradford, with the title of "The Asylum, and Feliciana Advertiser." It was continued by Bradford after 1820, as there is a file for 1821-22 in the Library of Congress. The "National Intelligencer" of Mar. 2, 1820, records the fact of its establishment by F. Bradford and states that the first number was issued Jan. 18, 1820.

Ohio Hist. and Phil. Soc. has July 20, 1820.

[St. Francisville] **Florida Sentinel,** 1816-1818.

This paper is known only through references to it in contemporaneous newspapers. In the "Louisiana Gazette" of Oct. 21, 1816, is a description of a ball at St. Francisville, taken from the "Florida Sentinel" and dated Sept. 21, 1816. In the "Potsdam [N. Y.] Gazette" of Aug. 8, 1817, there is an article quoted from the "St. Francisville (West-Florida) Centinel" of June 17, 1817. It is referred to as the "Florida Centinel" in the Lexington "Kentucky Gazette." of Oct. 25, 1817, and in the Cynthiana, Ky., "Guardian of Liberty" of Nov. 29, 1817. There is another reference to the "Florida Sentinel" in "L'Ami des Lois" of Apr. 28, 1818. The name is accounted for by the fact that that section of Louisiana between the Mississippi and Pearl Rivers was called West Florida, and had been annexed to Louisiana by Act of Congress approved Apr. 14, 1812.

[St. Francisville] **Louisianian,** 1819-1820.

Weekly. Established May 8, 1819, by William M'Laran, with the title of "The Louisianian." It was suspended from July 17 to Sept. 11, 1819, because of the illness of the editor. The last issue located is that of May 27, 1820, vol. 1, no. 44.

Lib. Congress has May 8-Dec. 11, 1819; Jan. 8, Feb. 12, Mar. 11-May 27, 1820.

[St. Francisville] **Time Piece,** 1811-1816.

Weekly. Established by James M. Bradford, Apr. 4, 1811, judging from the date of the first issue located, that of Apr. 25, 1811, vol. 1, no. 4. The place of publication is given as St. Francisville, West Florida, which name is accounted for by the fact that the section between the Mississippi and Pearl Rivers was called West Florida and was annexed to Louisiana by Act of Congress approved Apr. 14, 1812. The last issue located is an extra of Jan. 17, 1815, but without volume numbering. The paper is quoted in the Zanesville "Muskingum Messenger" of Jan. 24, 1816.

Am. Antiq. Soc. has Apr. 25, May 30, June 6, July 4, 11, 25, Aug. 1, 15, 22, Sept. 12, 19, 1811; June 10, Sept. 16, 1813; June 16, 1814; Jan. 17, 1815, extra.
Harvard has May 2–23, June 20, Aug. 8, 22, Sept. 12, Oct. 10, 24, 1811; May 7, June 25, Oct. 3, 8, 1812.
Yale has Aug. 22, 1811.
La. State Museum has Aug. 20, 1812.
Miss Louise Butler, Bains, La., has Aug. 26, 1813.
Elrie Robinson, St. Francisville, has Sept. 30, 1813.

[**St. Louis**], see under **Missouri**.

MAINE

[Augusta] **Edes' Kennebec Gazette**, see **Kennebec Gazette**.

[Augusta] **Herald of Liberty**, 1810–1815.

Weekly. Established by Peter Edes on Feb. 13, 1810, with the title of "Herald of Liberty," as a continuation of the "Kennebec Gazette," although with a change of title and a new volume numbering. Late in 1811, apparently in December, he placed the name of his son, Peter Edes, Jun., in the imprint and started a new volume numbering. But in 1813, at some time between Jan. 16 and Oct. 9, he placed his own name again at the masthead. The last issue located is that of Sept. 2, 1815, vol. 4, no. 186, and the paper was discontinued very soon afterwards, as Edes established the "Bangor Weekly Register" on Nov. 25, 1815.

Me. Hist. Soc. has Feb. 13–Dec. 25, 1810; Apr. 23, May 14–July 16, Aug. 6, 13, 27–Oct. 15, 29, 1811; Sept. 5, 1812; Jan. 1, 8, 1814.
Am. Antiq. Soc. has Feb. 20, Mar. 20–Apr. 17, May 15, Oct. 2, 16, 23, Nov. 6, 1810; Apr. 16, 30, May 21, July 16, Aug. 13, 1811; Dec. 19, 1812; Jan. 16, Oct. 9, 23, 1813; Jan. 7, 28, Aug. 19–Sept. 2, 1815.
Me. State Lib. has Mar. 20, Apr. 10, 24, 1810; Feb. 12, 1812.
Yale has Apr. 30, July 16, 1811.
York Inst., Saco, has June 25, 1814.

[Augusta] **Kennebec Gazette**, 1800–1810.

Weekly. Established by Peter Edes, Nov. 14, 1800, with the title of "The Kennebec Gazette," as a continuation of the "Kennebec Intelligencer," although with a change of title and a new volume numbering. The place of publication was at first at Hallowell, but the office was removed to Augusta with the issue of Sept. 11, 1801, vol. 1, no. 43, upon which date the name was changed to "Edes' Kennebec Gazette." This heading was used until Apr. 21, 1803, when the name of "The Kennebec Gazette" was resumed. The paper was suspended from Feb. 11 to Mar. 28, 1804, because of a fire which destroyed Edes' printing office, and again from Nov. 21, 1804, to Jan. 16, 1805, because of lack of support. With the issue of May 23, 1804, the title was altered to "Kennebec Gazette." Beginning with the issue of Aug. 8, 1805, Peter Edes took his son Benjamin into partnership under the firm name of Peter Edes & Son, but this was changed back to Peter Edes as sole publisher with the issue of Apr. 18, 1806. The last issue was that of Feb. 6, 1810, vol. 10, no. 263. On Feb. 13, 1810, the name of the paper was changed to "Herald of Liberty," which see.

Me. Hist. Soc. has Nov. 14, 1800–Aug. 20, 1802; Oct. 21, 1802–Dec. 15, 1803; Apr. 4–Sept. 20, Oct. 4–Nov. 21, 1804; Jan. 16–May 29, June 13–27, July 11,

18, Aug. 8, 1805; Apr. 17–Aug. 7, 21, Sept. 11, 25–Oct. 23, Nov. 6–Dec. 25, 1807; Feb. 19, 1808.
Harvard has Nov. 14–Dec. 26, 1800; Jan. 2–July 31, Aug. 14–28, Sept. 11–Nov. 6, 27, Dec. 11–25, 1801; Jan. 8–Feb. 12, 26, Mar. 5, 19–Apr. 23, May 7, 14, June 4–July 23, Aug. 6, 20–Sept. 3, 24, Oct. 1, 14, 21, Nov. 4–Dec. 23, 1802; Jan. 6–Mar. 24, Apr. 7, 21, 28, May 19, 26, June 9–Dec. 22, 1803; Mar. 28, Apr. 18, 25, May 9, 16, 30, June 21–Aug. 16, Sept. 13, 20, Oct. 11–Nov. 1, 14, 21, 1804; Jan. 16, 30, Feb. 13–Mar. 27, Apr. 10, 24, May 8, 22–June 13, 27, July 4, 18–Aug. 15, Sept. 5–19, Oct. 24–Nov. 21, Dec. 6–27, 1805; Jan. 3, 10, Feb. 14, 21, Mar. 7–21, Apr. 11, 25, May 16–June 20, July 4, 18–Aug. 8, 22, 29, Sept. 12, Oct. 3–17, 31–Nov. 14, 1806; Feb. 27, 1807.
Am. Antiq. Soc. has Mar. 27–Apr. 10, 1801; Oct. 21, Nov. 25, 1802; Jan. 20, Aug. 18, Nov. 24, Dec. 1, 1803; Apr. 3, 1805; Mar. 7, May 30–June 27, July 18–Aug. 1, Sept. 19, Oct. 10, Nov. 28, Dec. 12, 1806; Jan. 16, Feb. 27, Mar. 27, 1807; Mar. 18, Apr. 29, 1808; Nov. 25–Dec. 9, 1809; Feb. 6, 1810.
Kennebec Hist. Soc. has Aug. 2, 7, 21, Sept. 11, Oct. 2–16, Nov. 13–Dec. 4, 18, 1801; Jan. 15, Mar. 19–Apr. 2, May 7, 28, July 2, 16, Aug. 13–Sept. 3, Dec. 16, 1802; Jan. 6, 20, Feb. 10, 1803.
Me. State Lib. has Dec. 30, 1802; Nov. 27, 1807; Nov. 25, 1808; Nov. 25, Dec. 2, 9, 1809; Feb. 6, 1810.
Boston Pub. Lib. has Dec. 11, 1801.
Yale has June 18, 1802.
Lib. Congress has Dec. 12, 1806.

[**Augusta**] **Kennebeck Intelligencer,** 1795–1800.

Weekly. Established by Peter Edes, Nov. 21, 1795, with the title of "Kennebeck Intelligencer," in the northern part of the town of Hallowell, in that part now called Augusta. Hallowell was divided Feb. 20, 1797, and the northern part was called Harrington; beginning therefore, with the issue of Mar. 18, 1797, Harrington appears in the imprint as the place of publication. On June 9, 1797, the name of Harrington was changed to Augusta, and beginning with the issue of June 30, 1797, Augusta appears as the place of publication. With the issue of July 26, 1799, the place of publication is again called Hallowell. On Aug. 30, 1799, the word "Kennebeck" in the title was changed to "Kennebec." With the issue of June 6, 1800, vol. 5, no. 218, the paper was discontinued. It was revived, however, on Nov. 14, 1800, under the name of the "Kennebec Gazette," which see.

Harvard has Nov. 21, Dec. 26, 1795; Feb. 13, Mar. 12, May 3, 20, June 3, 17–Aug. 26, Sept. 9–Oct. 7, 21–Dec. 17, 31, 1796; Jan. 7–Apr. 8, 21, June 9, 16, 30, Sept. 29, Oct. 17–31, Dec. 19, 26, 1797; Jan. 9, 30–Mar. 6, 20, Apr. 10, May 1, 8, July 6, Aug. 10, 24–Nov. 10, 24, Dec. 8, 29, 1798; Feb. 2, 9, 23, Mar. 2, May 10–24, June 7, 14, July 26–Aug. 16, 30–Oct. 11, 1799; Jan. 18, Feb. 1–15, Mar. 1–15, 29–May 16, June 6, 1800.

Am. Antiq. Soc. has Nov. 28, 1795; Jan. 2, 9, Feb. 27, May 10, 20, June 17, July 8, 22, Aug. 26, Oct. 7, 21, 29, Dec. 3, 24, 31, 1796; Jan. 28–Mar. 11, 25, Apr. 1, 15, 21, May 5–26, June 9, July 28–Aug. 25, Sept. 15, 22, Oct. 10–31, Nov. 14, 28, Dec. 12, 19, 1797; Jan. 2–Mar. 27, Apr. 24, May 8, June 12, 18, July 13, 20, Sept. 7, 14, Oct. 12, Nov. 3, 17–Dec. 15, 29, 1798; Jan. 5, 12, Feb. 9, Mar. 2, Dec. 7, 1799; Mar. 29–Apr. 12, 1800.
Me. Hist. Soc. has Feb. 6–27, Oct. 7–Nov. 12, 1796; Feb. 4, May 19, 26, 1797; Feb. 20–Mar. 13, 1798; Jan. 12, May 10–31, 1799; Apr. 5, 1800.
Phil. Lib. Co. has Nov. 21, 28, 1795; Jan. 9, 16, 1796.
Mass. Hist. Soc. has May 12, 1797.
Me. State Lib. has June 9, 1797.
Essex Inst. has June 23, Aug. 25, Sept. 1, 15, 29, 1797.
Lib. Congress has July 7, Aug. 11, 18, Oct. 24, 1797.
N. Y. Hist. Soc. has Nov. 10, 1798.
Kennebec Hist. Soc. has June 21, 28, July 12, Aug. 2, 9, Sept. 6, 20, 1799.
Hallowell Lib. has Jan. 4, 1800.

Augusta Patriot, 1817.

Weekly. Established Mar. 7, 1817, by James Burton, Jun., with the title of "Augusta Patriot." The last issue located is that of Aug. 15, 1817, vol. 1, no. 24, and the paper was probably discontinued before the close of the year, since Burton took charge of the "Bangor Register" in December, 1817.

Am. Antiq. Soc. has Mar. 7, June 13, July 11–25, 1817.
N. Y. Hist. Soc. has June 13, Aug. 15, 1817.
Bangor Pub. Lib. has Aug. 8, 1817.

Bangor Register, see Bangor Weekly Register.

Bangor Weekly Register, 1815–1820+.

Weekly. Established Nov. 25, 1815, by Peter Edes, with the title of "Bangor Weekly Register." Suspended with the issue of Aug. 23, 1817, when Edes sold out to James Burton, Jr. Burton resumed publication of the paper on Dec. 25, 1817, continuing the volume numbering. At some time between Dec. 10, 1818, and Mar. 4, 1819, the title was changed to "Bangor Register." The paper was continued after 1820. A reprinted issue, dated Nov. 16, 1816, was made up of items taken from issues of 1815 and 1816.

Am. Antiq. Soc. has Nov. 25, 1815–Dec. 28, 1816; Jan. 11–25, Mar. 8, 15, May 17, 1817; Feb. 5, 1818; Mar. 4, Aug. 5, Nov. 18, 1819.
Bangor Pub. Lib. has Nov. 25, Dec. 30, 1815; Jan. 13–Feb. 17, May 4, 18, June 8, July 13–Aug. 10, 25–Sept. 14, Oct. 26, Nov. 16, 23, Dec. 14–28, 1816; Mar. 4, 25, Apr. 8, Sept. 2, 9, 30, 1819. It once had a complete file, which was destroyed in the fire of Apr. 30, 1911.

Me. Hist. Soc. has Aug. 31, Nov. 16, 1816; Nov. 23, 1820.
Mass. Hist. Soc. has Nov. 16, 1816.
Wis. Hist. Soc. has Dec. 10, 1818.
Miss Amy C. Witherle, Castine, has May 20, July 22, Dec. 23, 1819.

[Bath] **Maine Gazette,** 1820+.

Weekly. Established Dec. 8, 1820, by Torrey and Simpson [Joseph G. Torrey and John S. Simpson], with the title of "Maine Gazette." Continued after 1820.

Am. Antiq. Soc. has Dec. 8–29, 1820.
Harvard has Dec. 8–29, 1820.
Wis. Hist. Soc. has Dec. 8, 1820.
Lib. Congress has Dec. 15, 22, 1820.

[Belfast] **Hancock Gazette,** 1820+.

Weekly. Established July 6, 1820, by Fellowes & Simpson [Ephraim Fellowes and William R. Simpson], with the title of "Hancock Gazette." Beginning with the issue of Dec. 14, 1820, the title was changed to the "Hancock Gazette and Penobscot Patriot." Continued after 1820. Griffin, in his "History of the Press of Maine," p. 158, says that William Biglow was "its first editor."

Am. Antiq. Soc. has July 6–Dec. 28, 1820.
Belfast, Republican Journal office has July 6–Dec. 28, 1820.
Belfast Free Lib. has Oct. 5, 19, 26, Nov. 9–Dec. 28, 1820.
Univ. of Mich. (Clements) has Aug. 10, 1820.

[Brunswick] **Maine Intelligencer,** 1820+.

Weekly. Established Sept. 23, 1820, by Joseph Griffin, with the title of "Maine Intelligencer." It was printed by Griffin, and according to Griffin's "Press of Maine," p. 73, was edited by John M. O'Brien. It was of quarto size, eight pages to an issue, and although in appearance a magazine, was really a newspaper. Continued after 1820.

Am. Antiq. Soc. has Sept. 23–Dec. 29, 1820.

[Buckstown] **Gazette of Maine,** 1805–1812.

Weekly. Established July 25, 1805, by William W. Clapp, under the name of the "Gazette of Maine. Hancock Advertiser," which with the issue of July 2, 1807, was changed to "Gazette of Maine. Hancock and Washington Advertiser." With the issue of Apr. 20, 1811, Clapp sold out to Anthony H. Holland. It was announced, in the issue of Apr. 17, 1812, vol. 7, no. 39, that the paper would be suspended for a month because of the editor's intended absence, and it probably was not again established. The name of Buckstown was changed to Bucksport in 1817.

Bowdoin has July 25, 1805–June 26, 1806.
Harvard has Aug. 1, 8, 22–Sept. 26, Oct. 17, 31–Nov. 14, 28, Dec. 12, 1805; Jan. 2, 9, 23, Feb. 13, Mar. 13, 20, Apr. 3–17, May 1, 15, June 5, July 17–Aug. 7, 28, Sept. 25, Oct. 2, 1806; Dec. 24, 1808; July 20–Dec. 27, 1811; Jan. 3–Feb. 7, 21–Mar. 27, Apr. 10, 17, 1812.
Am. Antiq. Soc. has July 25, Oct. 17, 1805; July 2, 1807; Feb. 10, Mar. 3, 17, May 5, 19, July 21, 28, Aug. 11, 18, Sept. 1, Oct. 13, 27, Dec. 8, 1810; Mar. 23, Apr. 6, 20, May 4, Dec. 13, 1811; Jan. 10, 31, Mar. 20, Apr. 10, 1812.
E. L. Beazley, Bucksport, has Oct. 10–31, Nov. 21, 28, 1805; Jan. 2, 9, 23, 30, Feb. 13–Apr. 24, May 8–June 5, 26–July 10, 24, 1806.
Me. Hist. Soc. has July 3–Oct. 9, 23–Dec. 25, 1806; Jan. 1, 8, 22, Feb. 12, 26, Mar. 12–Apr. 23, May 7, 21, June 18–July 30, Aug. 20–Sept. 3, 17, Oct. 1–15, 29–Nov. 12, 26–Dec. 31, 1807; Jan. 7–June 30, 1808; July 21, Oct. 27, 1810; Apr. 6, 1811.
Dartmouth has Apr. 3, 1806.
Belfast Free Lib. has May 5, 1808.
Bangor Pub. Lib. has Sept. 9, 1809.
Yale has May 4, 1811.
N. Y. Pub. Lib. has Feb. 7, 1812.

[**Castine**] **Columbian Informer**, 1802.

Weekly. Established Apr. 22, 1802, by David J. Waters & Co. [David J. Waters and Enoch H. Rust], under the name of the "Columbian Informer; and the Eastern Advertiser." The first issue was numbered vol. 4, no. 1, in continuation of Waters' previous paper, the "Castine Journal." With the issue of May 13, 1802, David J. Waters became sole publisher. The last issue located is that of July 1, 1802, vol. 4, no. 9. Waters established the "Penobscot Patriot" at Hampden in January 1803.

Harvard has Apr. 29–May 13, June 10–July 1, 1802.

[**Castine**] **Eagle**, 1809–1812.

Weekly. Established Nov. 14, 1809, by Samuel Hall, with the title of "The Eagle." The paper was discontinued with the issue of Dec. 14, 1811, vol. 2, no. 50. The editor, however, issued two or three sheets during the "Electioneering Campaign," according to an extra of Mar. 19, 1812.

Am. Antiq. Soc. has Nov. 28, 1809–Dec. 14, 1811.
Miss Amy C. Witherle, Castine, has Nov. 14–28, Dec. 19, 26, 1809; Jan. 9–July 3, 24, Aug. 7, 14, 28–Oct. 30, 1810.

Miss Anna C. Witherle, Castine, has Nov. 14–Dec. 26, 1809; Jan. 2–June 5, 19–Aug. 21, Sept. 4–Nov. 20, Dec. 4–25, 1810; Jan. 1–May 7, 21–Dec. 14, 1811, also Nov. 21–Dec. 26, 1809; Jan. 2–Apr. 24, May 8–June 5, 19, July 3–Oct. 23, 1810.
Me. Hist. Soc. has Jan. 9, 1810–Dec. 14, 1811, fair.
Lib. Congress has Feb. 6, Apr. 24, June 5, July 10–24, Aug. 7, 14, Sept. 18, Oct. 16, 23, 1810; Feb. 19, Mar. 5, June 4, 1811.
Me. State Lib. has Apr. 10, 1810.
Mass. Hist. Soc. has Mar. 5, 1811.
Essex Inst. has Apr. 16, 1811.
N. Y. Pub. Lib. has June 4, 1811.
Hist. Soc. Penn. has Mar. 19, 1812.

Castine Journal, 1799–1801.

Weekly. Established Jan. 2, 1799, by David J. Waters, under the title of "The Castine Journal, and Universal Advertiser." The title was changed to the "Castine Journal, and the Eastern Advertiser" with the issue of May 1, 1799. Discontinued with the issue of Oct. 30, 1801, vol. 3, no. 49.

Harvard has Jan. 2, 9, Feb. 13, 27, Mar. 20, Apr. 24, May 1, 15–June 19, July 31, Oct. 11, Nov. 8, 15, 26, Dec. 10, 24, 1799; Jan. 14, Feb. 4, Apr. 3, Aug. 8, Sept. 19, Nov. 7, 28, 1800; Jan. 30, Apr. 3, May 7, 22–July 17, Aug. 21, 28, Sept. 18, Oct. 9–23, 1801.
Am. Antiq. Soc. has Feb. 6–20, Mar. 13, 20, May 8, Sept. 25, Oct. 18, 1799; Jan. 21, June 6, Dec. 26, 1800; Jan. 2, 30, Feb. 13, Apr. 10, Oct. 30, 1801.
N. Y. Hist. Soc. has Jan. 2, 16–Feb. 13, 27, Mar. 13–Apr. 10, 24, 1799.
Miss Anna C. Witherle, Castine, has Jan. 16–Nov. 8, 29–Dec. 31, 1799.
Miss Amy C. Witherle, Castine, has Dec. 31, 1799; Jan. 14, 28–Mar. 4, 18–Apr. 25, May 9–July 25, Aug. 8–Dec. 26, 1800.
N. Y. Pub. Lib. has Jan. 9, 1799.
Me. Hist. Soc. has Mar. 13, 1799.
Me. State Lib. has May 8, 1799.
Essex Inst. has July 17, 1799.
Lib. Congress has Aug. 29, 1800.

Eastport Sentinel, 1818–1820+.

Weekly. Established Aug. 31, 1818, by Benjamin Folsom, under the title of the "Eastport Sentinel and Passamaquody Advertiser," which spelling was corrected in 1819 to Passamaquoddy. Continued after 1820.

Machias County Court House has Mar. 20, 1819–Dec. 30, 1820.
Eastport Pub. Lib. has Aug. 28, 1819–Dec. 30, 1820.

Am. Antiq. Soc. has Aug. 31, Sept. 7, 28, 1818; Mar. 27–Apr. 17, July 31, 1819; Feb. 26, Oct. 21, 1820.
Wis. Hist. Soc. has Dec. 7, 1818.
Me. Hist. Soc. has Apr. 17, 1819.

[Falmouth] **Cumberland Gazette,** 1786.

Weekly. A continuation, but with volume numbering omitted, of "The Falmouth Gazette," the first issue with the new name of "The Cumberland Gazette" being that of Apr. 7, 1786. Published by Thomas B. Wait. Part of Falmouth was incorporated as Portland on July 4, 1786, and the name of the latter town appeared in the imprint with the issue of July 20, 1786. See under Portland. The last Falmouth issue was that of July 13, 1786.

Me. Hist. Soc. has Apr. 7–July 13, 1786.
Am. Antiq. Soc. has Apr. 7–June 29, July 13, 1786.
Portland Pub. Lib. has Apr. 7–May 25, June 8–22, 1786.
Mass. Hist. Soc. has Apr. 13, 1786.

Falmouth Gazette, 1785–1786.

Weekly. Established Jan. 1, 1785, by Titcomb and Wait [Benjamin Titcomb, Jr., and Thomas B. Wait], under the name of "The Falmouth Gazette and Weekly Advertiser." Titcomb retired from the firm and beginning with the issue of Feb. 16, 1786, Thomas B. Wait was sole proprietor. The last issue with this title was that of Mar. 30, 1786, vol. 2, no. 65. With the issue of Apr. 7, 1786, the title was changed to "The Cumberland Gazette," which see.

Me. Hist. Soc. has Jan. 1–22, Feb. 5–Apr. 23, May 7–Dec. 31, 1785; Jan. 7–Mar. 30, 1786.
Am. Antiq. Soc. has Jan. 1–Apr. 2, 16, 23, May 7–June 25, July 9–Sept. 17, Oct. 15–Nov. 12, Dec. 3–31, 1785; Jan. 7, 14, Feb. 2, 16–Mar. 9, 23, 30, 1786.
Mass. Hist. Soc. has Jan. 1–Nov. 19, Dec. 3–17, 1785.
Lib. Congress has Jan. 8, Feb. 19–Mar. 12, 26, 1785.
Portland Pub. Lib. has Jan. 1, 8, 22, Feb. 5–Mar. 12, 26, Apr. 2, 16, 23, May 7–21, June 4, 11, July 9–23, Aug. 13, 27–Sept. 17, Oct. 15, 22, Nov. 12, 26, Dec. 24, 31, 1785; Feb. 2, 23–Mar. 9, 23, 1786.
Yale has Feb. 19, 26, Mar. 26, 1785.
Boston Pub. Lib. has Feb. 2, 1786.
Many libraries have the facsimile issue of Jan. 1, 1785, printed in 1885.

[Fryeburg] **Russel's Echo,** 1798–1799.

Weekly. Established Feb. 22, 1798, by Elijah Russel, under the title of "Russel's Echo: or, the North Star." Although the issue of Feb. 22, is vol. 1, no. 1, yet there is an implication that there was a previous issue, and Feb. 29, (which should be Mar. 1) is vol. 1, no. 3. The paper was published quite irregularly. With the issue of Nov. 28, 1798, after a lapse of two months, the title was shortened to "Russell's Echo," the printer changing the spelling of his name from Russel to Russell. It was suspended, for want of paper, with the issue of Jan. 11, 1799, vol. 1, no. 27, and was probably not revived.

Samuel Souther, in his "Centennial Celebration of Fryeburg," 1864, p. 37, says that there was once a complete file of "Russel's Echo" in the library of Fryeburg Academy. It has long since disappeared, and was probably burned when the Academy building was destroyed by fire in May 1850.

Harvard has Feb. 22, 29, Apr. 5, May 17, 31, July 11, Aug. 14, 28, Nov. 28, Dec. 31, 1798; Jan. 11, 1799.
Am. Antiq. Soc. has Apr. 19, May 3, 17, June 7, 1798.
Miss Anna Barrows, Fryeburg, has Mar. 22, 1798.

[Hallowell] **American Advocate**, 1810–1820+.

Weekly. Established Jan. 23, 1810, by Nathaniel Cheever, with the title of "American Advocate." The American Antiquarian Society has the "Proposals" dated Aug. 23, 1809 and signed in autograph by 121 subscribers. The title was changed to the "American Advocate and Kennebec Advertiser" with the issue of July 23, 1814. Cheever sold out to Samuel K. Gilman, who began publishing it, under the name of S. K. Gilman, with the issue of July 25, 1818. Continued after 1820.

Hallowell Lib. has Jan. 23, 1810–Dec. 30, 1820.
Am. Antiq. Soc. has Jan. 23, 1810–Dec. 28, 1816; Jan. 4–Feb. 15, Mar. 8–Apr. 12, May 24–Nov. 29, Dec. 13–27, 1817; Jan. 3–Dec. 26, 1818; Jan. 2, 9, 30–Dec. 25, 1819; Jan. 1–Apr. 15, 29, May 6, July 22–Sept. 16, 30–Dec. 30, 1820.
N. Y. Hist. Soc. has Jan. 23, 1810–Jan. 14, 1813; Jan. 21, 1815–Jan. 13, 1816.
Me. Hist. Soc. has Jan. 23, Feb. 6, 13, 27, Mar. 13, 20, Apr. 3–May 8, 22, June 7, July 12, Aug. 9, Sept. 6, Oct. 11–25, 1810; Feb. 6, Mar. 20–Apr. 3, 17, May 15–June 5, 19, Aug. 28, Sept. 25, Oct. 22, Dec. 17, 1811; Mar. 31, Apr. 7, May 5, 19, Oct. 8, 1812; Jan. 7, 28, Mar. 11, 1813; Jan. 22–Dec. 31, 1814; Jan. 7, 1815–Dec. 30, 1820.
Duke Univ. has Jan. 23–June 28, July 12, Aug. 9–23, Sept. 6, 27–Nov. 1, 15–Dec. 6, 19, 26, 1810; Jan. 2, 16–30, Feb. 20, 27, Mar. 13–Apr. 3, May 1, 8, 22, June 19, July 24, Aug. 7, 28, Sept. 4, 25, Oct. 2, 15, 29–Dec. 17, 1811; Jan. 7–28, Feb. 11–June 9, July 9–23, Aug. 6, 27, Sept. 3, 17–Oct. 1, 15, Nov. 5–Dec. 3, 24, 31, 1812; Jan. 14–28, Mar. 4, 11, 25–Apr. 22, May 15, June 19, July 3, 31, Aug. 14, 21, Sept. 4–18, Oct. 2, 16, Nov. 13, Dec. 11, 18, 1813; Jan. 1, 22, Feb. 5, 26–Mar. 26, Apr. 9–23, May 7, 14, 28, June 11–July 30, Aug. 20–Sept. 3, 17, 24, Oct. 8, 22–Nov. 19, Dec. 3, 1814; Jan. 14–May 6, June 10–Sept. 16, 30, Oct. 14–28, Nov. 11–Dec. 16, 30, 1815; Jan. 20–May 4,

18–June 29, July 13–Aug. 31, Sept. 14, 28, Oct. 5, 26–Dec. 28, 1816; Jan. 4–Feb. 1, 15, Mar. 15–Apr. 12, May 24–Nov. 29, Dec. 13, 20, 1817.

Boston Pub. Lib. has Aug. 14, Sept. 4, 18, Oct. 2–Nov. 26, Dec. 24, 1811; Jan. 14–28, Feb. 25, Mar. 3, 31, Apr. 7, 21, May 5, June 9, Aug. 6, 13, 27, Sept. 10, Oct. 1, 15–Nov. 19, Dec. 31, 1812; Jan. 7–Feb. 25, Mar. 11–Dec. 11, 1813; Jan. 1, 8, 1814; Jan. 21–Feb. 18, Mar. 4, 18, Apr. 8–May 13, June 3, 17–29, Aug. 5, 12, 26–Sept. 16, Oct. 7, 28–Nov. 25, Dec. 9, 16, 30, 1815.

Bowdoin has Jan. 21, 28, Mar. 31, June 16, July 16, Aug. 13, Nov. 12, 1812; July 3, 1813; Feb. 5, 26, Apr. 23–May 7, 28, June 4, 25, July 16, 1814; Jan. 21, Apr. 8, 22, May 13–June 10, July 22, Aug. 5, 12, 26, Sept. 16–30, Nov. 4, Dec. 23, 1815; Apr. 27, July 20, Aug. 3, 24, Sept. 7, Oct. 5, 12, 26, Nov. 2, 23–Dec. 7, 21, 28, 1816; Jan. 4–18, Feb. 1, 22–Mar. 8, Apr. 5, 19–May 17, 31–June 21, Aug. 2, 16–30, Sept. 20, Nov. 22–Dec. 6, 20, 27, 1817; Jan. 10, Feb. 21, Apr. 18, May 16, 23, July 25, 1818–Dec. 30, 1820.

Lib. Congress has Sept. 20, Oct. 11, 1810; Oct. 2, 1811; Jan. 21, 1813–Jan. 14, 1815; Apr. 25, 1818; Oct. 16, Nov. 20, 1819.

Mass. Hist. Soc. has Jan. 7–June 25, July 30–Dec. 31, 1812.

Portland Pub. Lib. has Apr. 4, 25, May 9, June 20, Nov. 7, 21, Dec. 19, 1818; Jan. 9, Feb. 6, Mar. 6–20, Apr. 10, May 8, June 19, July 10, 17, Aug. 14, Sept. 4, Oct. 16–30, Nov. 20, Dec. 4, 25, 1819; Jan. 29, Apr. 29, 1820.

York Inst., Saco, has Jan. 16, 1819; Jan. 8–Dec. 30, 1820.

Univ. of Mich. has July 16, 1812.

Me. State Lib. has May 8, Sept. 25, 1819.

[Hallowell] **Eastern Star,** 1794–1795.

Weekly. Established in August, 1794, judging from the date of the first issue located, that of Jan. 20, 1795, vol. 1, no. 25, published by Howard S. Robinson, with the title of "The Eastern Star." The paper was discontinued with the issue of July 28, 1795, vol. 1, no. 52, and Robinson joined T. B. Wait and J. K. Baker in establishing "The Tocsin" at Hallowell, Aug. 4, 1795.

Am. Antiq. Soc. has Feb. 17–Mar. 10, 24, Apr. 7, 21, June 30, July 14, 1795.
Harvard has Feb. 17, Mar. 17, May 19–June 2, 16, 30, July 21, 1795.
Wis. Hist. Soc. has Jan. 20, Mar. 17, July 6, 1795.
Me. Hist. Soc. has Feb. 17, 1795.

Hallowell Gazette, 1814–1820+.

Weekly. Established Feb. 23, 1814, by Goodale & Burton [Ezekiel Goodale and James Burton, Jr.], with the title of "Hallowell Gazette." Burton withdrew from the firm, and Ezekiel Goodale became sole publisher beginning with the issue of Apr. 5, 1815. With the issue of Sept. 13, 1820, the publishers became Goodale, Glazier & Co. [Ezekiel Goodale, Andrew Master and Franklin Glazier]. The paper was so continued until after 1820.

Hallowell Lib. has Feb. 23, 1814–June 21, 1820.
Am. Antiq. Soc. has Feb. 23, Mar. 9, 23, 30, Apr. 27, May 11, June 15, Dec. 7–21, 1814; Jan. 17–Dec. 18, 1816; Jan. 1–Dec. 31, 1817; June 10–Aug. 12, Sept. 2–23, Nov. 18–Dec. 2, 1818; Jan. 27–May 12, June 10, Aug. 11, Oct. 13, 1819; Jan. 26–Nov. 29, 1820.
York Inst., Saco, has Jan. 7–Dec. 30, 1818; Jan. 5–Dec. 27, 1820.
Me. State Lib. has Jan. 10–Dec. 25, 1816.
N. Y. Hist. Soc. has Jan. 1–Dec. 31, 1817.
Me. Hist. Soc. has Feb. 8, Aug. 2, 1815; Sept. 18, 1816; July 9, 30, Aug. 13–27, 1817; Nov. 24, 1819.
Mass. Hist. Soc. has Sept. 16, 1818; Mar. 29, 1820.
Wis. Hist. Soc. has Dec. 16, 1818.

[Hallowell] Kennebec Gazette, see [Augusta] Kennebec Gazette.

[Hallowell] Kennebeck Intelligencer, see [Augusta] Kennebeck Intelligencer.

[Hallowell] Tocsin, 1795–1797.

Weekly. Established Aug. 4, 1795, by Wait, Robinson & Baker [Thomas B. Wait, Howard S. Robinson and John K. Baker], with the title of "The Tocsin." Robinson retired on Jan. 15, 1796, and the paper was published by Wait & Baker. They sold out to Benjamin Poor, whose imprint first appears with the issue of Sept. 30, 1796. The last issue located is that of Aug. 25, 1797, and the paper was discontinued soon afterwards, since an advertisement dated Jan. 1, 1798, in the "Wiscasset Telegraph" of Jan. 23, 1798, referring to the town of Hallowell, says "Not long since, a Paper was published in this place, but it is now no more." "The Tocsin" was peculiar in that it had no volume numbering.

Harvard has Aug. 4, 28, 1795; Mar. 12, 19, May 20, July 29, 1796; Apr. 1, June 16, 30, 1797.
Am. Antiq. Soc. has Feb. 27, May 10, June 3, July 15, Aug. 26, Dec. 31, 1796; Mar. 4, 18, Apr. 1–15, May 5, Aug. 4, 18, 25, 1797.
Hallowell Lib. has Apr. 16–June 17, July 1, 22, Aug. 5, 26, Sept. 9, 16, 30–Nov. 5, Dec. 3, 10, 24, 1796; Jan. 14, Feb. 4–Mar. 18, Apr. 15–28, June 9, 1797.
Me. Hist. Soc. has Apr. 28, May 5, July 7, 1797.
Lib. Congress has Oct. 2, 1795.

[Hampden] Penobscot Patriot, 1803.

Weekly. Established in January, 1803, by David J. Waters, with the title of the "Penobscot Patriot, and the Hancock & Washington Advertiser." The first issue located is that of Feb. 26, 1803, vol. 1, no. 6, and the last, that of Mar. 26, 1803, vol. 1, no. 10. Several of the advertisements in these issues are dated late in 1802, showing that the paper was probably a continuation of Waters' "Columbian Informer" of Castine. Griffin, in his "Press of Maine," p. 112, states that Waters went to Richmond, Va., about 1804, where he died within a few months.

Harvard has Feb. 26, Mar. 19, 26, 1803.

[Harrington] Kennebeck Intelligencer, see [Augusta] Kennebeck Intelligencer.

[Kennebunk] **Annals of the Times**, 1803–1805.

Weekly. Established Jan. 13, 1803, by S[tephen] Sewall, with the title of "The Annals of the Times." It was discontinued with the issue of Jan. 3, 1805, vol. 2, no. 52.

Harvard has Jan. 13–Feb. 3, 17, 24, Mar. 17–31, May 5, 19–June 2, 16, 30, July 7, 21, 28, Aug. 11, 25, Sept. 1, 15–Dec. 8, 22, 1803; Jan. 12, Feb. 9, Mar. 8, 15, Apr. 26–May 17, 31, June 7, 28–July 19, Aug. 2–Sept. 13, Oct. 11–25, Nov. 8, 22–Dec. 20, 1804; Jan. 3, 1805.
Am. Antiq. Soc. has Apr. 7, July 14, Sept. 7–29, 1803; Feb. 2, Mar. 1, 15, 22, 1804.
Dartmouth has May 12, 1803.
York Inst., Saco, has Sept. 15, 1803.
Essex Inst. has Oct. 11, 1804.

[Kennebunk] **Eagle of Maine**, 1802.

Weekly. Established July 1, 1802, by J[ohn] Whitelock. The last issue located is that of Sept. 30, 1802, vol. 1, no. 14.

Harvard has July 1, 22, 29, Sept. 9, 23, 30, 1802.

Kennebunk Gazette, 1805.

Weekly. Established Mar. 20, 1805, by William Weeks, with the title of "Kennebunk Gazette." Discontinued with the issue of July 31, 1805, vol. 1, no. 20. The publisher removed to Saco, where he established the "Freeman's Friend" on Aug. 21, 1805.

Harvard has Mar. 20–Apr. 3, 17–May 8, 29–June 26, July 10–24, 1805.
N. Y. Hist. Soc. has Mar. 27–July 31, 1805.
Am. Antiq. Soc. has Mar. 20, 27, Apr. 10, 24, June 5, July 24, 1805.

[Kennebunk] **Weekly Visiter**, 1809–1820+.

Weekly. Established June 24, 1809, by James K. Remich, with the title of "Weekly Visiter." So continued until after 1820, although in 1821 the title was changed to "Kennebunk Gazette."

York Inst., Saco, has June 24, 1809–Dec. 30, 1820.
Am. Antiq. Soc. has July 24, 1809–June 8, 1811; Aug. 17, 1811–June 12, 1813; June 18, 1814; Jan. 27, Feb. 3, June 15, 1816–May 23, 1818; July 31, 1819; June 10–Dec. 30, 1820.
Kennebunk Free Lib. has May 15, June 19, 1813–June 11, 1814; June 8, 1816; June 7, July 5, Oct. 11, 1817; Mar. 14, Apr. 4, 25–Dec. 26, 1818; Jan. 2, 1819–June 3, 1820.
Lib. Congress has Oct. 28, 1809; Apr. 4, 1812; June 17, 1815–June 1, 1816; May 3, 1817.
Me. State Lib. has Oct. 3, 1818; Feb. 6, Apr. 10, 24–May 8, 29, 1819.
Me. Hist. Soc. has Jan. 14, 28, 1815.
N. Y. Pub. Lib. has Apr. 4, 1818.
Wis. Hist. Soc. has Dec. 19, 1818.
Essex Inst. has July 10, 1819.

Portland Commercial Gazette, 1803–1804.

Weekly. Established Nov. 16, 1803, by E[lezer] A. Jenks, with the title of "Portland Commercial Gazette," to feature commercial news hitherto contained in "Jenks' Portland Gazette." The paper was at first a folio, but in April 1804 was reduced to quarto. It carried no volume numbering. The last issue located is that of Aug. 30, 1804, although it was evidently discontinued with the issue of Nov. 8, 1804, as appears from an editorial in "Jenks' Portland Gazette" of Nov. 12, 1804.

Am. Antiq. Soc. has Nov. 16, 1803–Mar. 28, 1804; June 21, 1804.
Lib. Congress has Nov. 23–Dec. 28, 1803; Jan. 4, 18, Feb. 1, 8, 29–Mar. 21, 1804.
Harvard has Nov. 23–Dec. 14, 1803; Jan. 11, Feb. 1, 22, Apr. 11, May 2, 9, 24, 31, June 21–July 12, 26, Aug. 16, 23, 1804.
Dartmouth has Nov. 16, 30, 1803.
Mass. Hist. Soc. has Nov. 30, 1803; Jan. 4, Feb. 15, 1804.
Me. Hist. Soc. has Feb. 15, Aug. 2, 30, 1804.

[Portland] Cumberland Gazette, 1786–1791.

Weekly. A continuation of "The Cumberland Gazette" of Falmouth, which town was incorporated as Portland in 1786. The first issue with the Portland imprint was that of July 20, 1786, and with the same title. The paper was published by Thomas B. Wait and carried no volume numbering. With the issue of Sept. 25, 1789, the title was shortened to "Cumberland Gazette." The last issue with this title was that of Dec. 26, 1791, when to avoid confusion with another Portland paper of a similar name, the title was changed to the "Eastern Herald," which see.

MAINE 207

Me. Hist. Soc. has July 20–Sept. 28, Nov. 9–Dec. 29, 1786; Jan. 5, Feb. 9–Dec. 27, 1787; Jan. 3–Feb. 14, 28–Dec. 25, 1788; Jan. 1, 15–June 26, July 10, 17, Aug. 28, Oct. 2, 9, 1789; Feb. 1, 8, Mar. 1–Apr. 5, 26, May 10, 24–June 21, July 5, 26, Aug. 2, 16, 30, Sept. 6, Oct. 11, 25, Nov. 8–Dec. 6, 20, 27, 1790; Jan. 10, 24–Feb. 7, Apr. 18, May 2, 16–June 13, July 4, 25, Aug. 1, 15, 22, Sept. 5, 19, Oct. 3, 10, Nov. 7–28, Dec. 26, 1791.

Portland Pub. Lib. has Aug. 10–Oct. 26, Nov. 9–Dec. 1, 15–29, 1786; Jan. 5–Nov. 22, Dec. 6–27, 1787; Jan. 3–Feb. 14, 28–Dec. 25, 1788; Jan. 8–22, Feb. 5–Mar. 5, 19–June 26, July 10–Sept. 11, 25–Oct. 9, Nov. 30–Dec. 14, 1789; Jan. 11, Feb. 1–Apr. 5, 19–May 10, 24–Dec. 27, 1790; Jan. 10–Dec. 26, 1791.

Am. Antiq. Soc. has July 20–Sept. 28, Oct. 19, Nov. 2, 17–Dec. 29, 1786; Jan. 5–Nov. 9, 22–Dec. 27, 1787; Jan. 3–Feb. 14, 28–Apr. 10, 24–June 26, July 10–Dec. 25, 1788; Jan. 1, 8, 22, 29, Feb. 12–Mar. 5, Apr. 2–30, May 14, 29, June 12, July 10, Aug. 14, 28–Sept. 18, Oct. 9, Nov. 9–23, Dec. 7, 14, 28, 1789; Feb. 1–15, Mar. 1–May 10, 24–Sept. 27, Oct. 11–Dec. 27, 1790; Jan. 3–Feb. 7, Mar. 7–Sept. 5, 19–Oct. 10, 24–Dec. 26, 1791.

N. Y. Hist. Soc. has Jan. 18, 1790–Dec. 26, 1791.

Mass. Hist. Soc. has Nov. 24, 1786; Jan. 5, 12, Feb. 9, 1787.

Lib. Congress has Jan. 5, Sept. 27, 1787.

[Portland] **Eastern Argus**, 1803–1820+.

Weekly. Established Sept. 8, 1803, by Day & Willis [Calvin Day and Nathaniel Willis, Jr.], with the title of "Eastern Argus." Day retired from the firm, and beginning with the issue of Nov. 8, 1804, Nathaniel Willis, Jr., became sole publisher. With the issue of Oct. 18, 1805, Willis omitted the "Junior" after his name. He admitted Francis Douglas to partnership and beginning with the issue of Jan. 7, 1808, the firm name became Willis and Douglas. Willis retired and beginning with the issue of Oct. 6, 1808, Francis Douglas became sole proprietor and so remained up to the time of his death, Sept. 3, 1820. The next few issues after this date have no publisher's name given, but beginning with the issue of Nov. 7, 1820, Thomas Todd and Susan Douglas, widow of the late proprietor, became the publishers under the firm name of Thomas Todd & Co. With the issue of Nov. 8, 1815, the title was altered to "The Eastern Argus." Although regularly a weekly, the paper was published semi-weekly during the meetings of the Maine Constitutional Convention, Oct. 12–Nov. 2, 1819, and also during the session of the legislature, June 9–July 4, 1820. Continued after 1820.

Portland Pub. Lib. has Sept. 8, 1803–Dec. 26, 1820.

Bowdoin has Sept. 8, 1803–Dec. 29, 1808; Aug. 31, 1809–Sept. 6, 1815; Nov. 8, 1815–Dec. 26, 1820.

Patten Lib., Bath, Me., has Mar. 22, 1805–Dec. 26, 1820.

Am. Antiq. Soc. has Sept. 8, 1803–June 7, 1805; Sept. 13, 27, Oct. 18, Nov. 8–22, 1805; Jan. 17, 1806–Dec. 28, 1809; Jan. 1, 18–Feb. 15, Mar. 1, 15, 22,

June 28, July 5, Aug. 30, Oct. 18–Nov. 1, Dec. 13, 1810; Jan. 3, 1811–Dec. 30, 1813; Jan. 13, Feb. 10, Mar. 31, Apr. 28, May 26, June 23–July 7, Aug. 11, Oct. 13, 27–Nov. 24, 1814; Jan. 5–19, Feb. 2, 23, Mar. 9, 30, July 12, 26, Aug. 23, Sept. 6, 20–Oct. 4, 18, Nov. 1–29, Dec. 20, 27, 1815; Jan. 17–Feb. 13, 27, Mar. 19, 26, Apr. 30, May 7, 15, 29–June 12, 26, July 10–Nov. 6, 20, 25, Dec. 17, 1816; Jan. 21, 28, Feb. 11, 18, Mar. 4–18, Apr. 8, 22, May 13, 20, Sept. 30–Oct. 14, Nov. 11, 18, Dec. 9, 1817; Jan. 20, 27, Mar. 3, Apr. 7–21, June 2, July 21, Aug. 25, Sept. 8, Oct. 6, 20, 27, Dec. 29, 1818; Jan. 26, Feb. 2, 23–Mar. 30, Apr. 13–27, May 11, June 1, 15, July 3, 20–Aug. 3, 17, 31, Oct. 5–Nov. 2, 16, 30–Dec. 21, 1819; Jan. 4–Dec. 26, 1820.

Me. Hist. Soc. has Dec. 30, 1803; Apr. 20, July 19, Sept. 6, 13, Oct. 4, 11, Nov. 1, 8, 23, Dec. 7, 14, 1804; Jan. 11, 1805–Sept. 11, 1806, fair; Jan. 1, 1807–Dec. 29, 1808; Mar. 30, July 6–Dec. 28, 1809; Jan. 4–Mar. 8, 1810; Apr. 4, June 6, 1811; Jan. 2, 1812–Nov. 4, 25, Dec. 30, 1813; Jan. 6, 13, Mar. 3, 31, 1814; Jan. 12, Mar. 2, Sept. 20, 27, Dec. 20, 1815; Apr. 2, July 17, 24, Aug. 7–Sept. 4, 1816; Feb. 11, 1817; Nov. 10, 1818; Jan. 5–Dec. 28, 1819, fair; Mar. 14, Apr. 25, May 16, June 27–Dec. 26, 1820.

Boston Athenæum has Sept. 8, 1803–Sept. 5, 1811; Nov. 25, 1816.

Mass. Hist. Soc. has Sept. 8, 1803–Aug. 27, 1807; Feb. 14, 1815; Jan. 16, July 17, 31–Oct. 9, 23, 30, 1816.

Harvard has Sept. 15, 1803–Dec. 8, 1808, fair.

N. Y. Hist. Soc. has Sept. 6, 1805–Aug. 27, 1807; Jan. 7–Feb. 25, 1808; Jan. 24–May 30, Aug. 29, Nov. 20, 1811; Jan. 9–Dec. 31, 1812.

N. Y. State Lib. has Sept. 8, 1803–Aug. 30, 1805.

Lib. Congress has Nov. 25, 1803–Aug. 30, 1805; Jan. 15, Feb. 12, Mar. 12, 26, Apr. 23, Dec. 17, 1807; May 19, June 2, 9, July 7–21, Aug. 4, Sept. 1, 8, Oct. 20, Nov. 3, 1808; Feb. 1, 1810; Apr. 4, May 9, 16, June 6, 20, 27, Aug. 22, 1811; Jan. 16–Dec. 31, 1812; May 20, Nov. 4, 1813; Nov. 3, 1814; Jan. 12, 1815; June 26, Nov. 20, 1816; Sept. 30, 1817; Dec. 22, 1818; Jan. 5, 1819–Dec. 26, 1820.

Duke Univ. has Mar. 14, Apr. 11, May 29, Aug. 21, Sept. 4–Nov. 27, Dec. 11–25, 1806; Jan. 1, 1807–Dec. 29, 1808; Jan. 5–Mar. 9, 23–Apr. 13, 27, Aug. 10, 24, Dec. 21, 28, 1809; July 16, 1812.

York Inst., Saco, has Dec. 28, 1804; Jan. 3, 1806–Dec. 31, 1807.

Boston Pub. Lib. has June 30, 1808; Sept. 14, 1809; Jan. 2, 1812–Dec. 29, 1814; Feb. 16, Aug. 28, 1816; June 30, 1818–Dec. 28, 1819; Mar. 14, Nov. 7, 1820.

Wis. Hist. Soc. has Jan. 1–Dec. 27, 1810; Jan. 2–Dec. 31, 1812, fair; Sept. 25, 1816; Dec. 15, 1818.

Me. State Lib. has Mar. 16, 1809; Jan. 9, 1812–Dec. 29, 1814; Apr. 13, July 20, 1819; Aug. 7, 1820.

Chicago Pub. Lib. has Jan. 5, 1815–Dec. 31, 1816.

N. Y. Pub. Lib. has Aug. 6, 1812; Jan. 5, 1819–Dec. 26, 1820.

Univ. of Mich. (Clements) has July 12, 1804; Mar. 22, 1805; July 23, 1807; Jan. 14–Dec. 29, 1808; Feb. 16, 23, Aug. 24, 1809; Jan. 25, Feb. 15, Mar. 28,

MAINE 209

May 2, 9, 23, 30, June 16–July 11, 25–Aug. 15, Sept. 19, 26, Oct. 12, Dec. 26, 1820.

Essex Inst. has July 14, Sept. 22, Nov. 3, 1814; Jan. 5–Mar. 9, 1815; June 12, 1816; Apr. 29, May 6, 20, 1817, Sept. 19, 1820.

[Portland] **Eastern Herald**, 1792–1804.

Weekly and semi-weekly. A continuation of the "Cumberland Gazette," the first issue with the new name of "The Eastern Herald" being Jan. 2, 1792, published by Thomas Baker Wait. Like its predecessor, the paper bore no volume numbering. In 1796, John K. Baker bought out and consolidated this paper and the "Gazette of Maine," the first issue with the new title, "The Eastern Herald and Gazette of Maine," being Sept. 3, 1796, published by John Kelse Baker. At the same time, the paper was made a semi-weekly, but resumed the weekly issue upon Sept. 9, 1797. With the issue of Mar. 5, 1798, Baker admitted Daniel George to partnership, and the paper was published by Baker and George. With this issue, moreover, the paper was headed "vol. XIV," it having previously possessed no volume number whatever. The partnership was dissolved and with the issue of Nov. 3, 1800, vol. 17, no. 1, the new firm of Russell and George [Elijah Russell and Daniel George] was established. With the issue of Dec. 29, 1800, the title was changed to "Russell & George's Eastern Herald & Maine Gazette." Russell retired and with the issue of Feb. 2, 1801, the paper was published by Daniel George and the title changed to "The Eastern Herald & Maine Gazette," the title again slightly changing, Feb. 15, 1802, to "The Eastern Herald and Maine Gazette." George died Feb. 4, 1804. No publisher's name was henceforth given and the paper was discontinued with the issue of Dec. 31, 1804, vol. 21, no. 5.

York Inst., Saco, has Jan. 2, 1792–Nov. 26, 1804.

Portland Pub. Lib. has Jan. 2, 1792–Dec. 24, 1795; Jan. 6, 1796–Dec. 25, 1797, fair; Jan. 15–29, Feb. 12–Mar. 19, Apr. 2, 9, 23–May 7, 21, June 4–18, July 9–23, Aug. 13, 27, Sept. 3, 24, Oct. 15, 22, Nov. 12–26, Dec. 10–31, 1798; Jan. 7–Feb. 4, 18, 25, Mar. 11, 18, Apr. 15, May 13, 27–July 8, 20, Aug. 12, 19, Sept. 2, 9, 23, Oct. 14, 28, Nov. 4, Dec. 2, 16–30, 1799; Jan. 20–Feb. 3, 24, May 5, June 2, 16, Aug. 4, Sept. 8, 1800; Jan. 19–Feb. 2, Mar. 30–Apr. 13, 27, May 4, 25, June 8, 22, 29, July 13–Aug. 24, Sept. 7, 14, 28, Oct. 12, 26, Nov. 9–Dec. 21, 1801; Jan. 11, 1802–Dec. 31, 1804, fair.

Am. Antiq. Soc. has Jan. 2, 30–Mar. 5, 19, 26, Apr. 16–May 14, 28, June 11–25, July 9, 23–Sept. 10, 24, Oct. 22, Nov. 12–26, Dec. 17, 1792; Jan. 10–24, Feb. 14, Mar. 21, Apr. 4–18, May 3, 11, 25, Aug. 10, Sept. 21, 1793; Jan. 6, May 10–July 5, 19–Dec. 29, 1794; Jan. 26, Feb. 9, 16, Mar. 2, Apr. 13–27, July 20, Aug. 17, 24, 1795; Mar. 3, 10, Apr. 27, May 30, June 6, 20, July 4, 25, Sept. 14, 24, Oct. 15, 24, Nov. 10–17, Dec. 12, 16, 1796; Jan. 12, 26, 30, Feb. 9, 13, 20, 23, Mar. 6–16, 23, 30, Apr. 10, 19–29, May 6, 13, 20, 24, June 24, July 1, 22, 29, Aug. 5, 19, Sept. 30, Oct. 14, 30, Dec. 4, 18, 25, 1797; Jan. 15–Mar. 19,

Apr. 9, 30, May 28, June 18, 25, July 9, Sept. 10, Oct. 29–Nov. 12, 26–Dec. 17, 1798; Jan. 7, 14, Feb. 25, Mar. 11, 18, Dec. 2, 1799; Mar. 24, June 9, Oct. 6, 20–Nov. 3, 1800; Apr. 11, July 18, Aug. 22, Sept. 5, 19–Oct. 3, 1803.

Harvard has May 14, 21, June 11, July 2, 1792; Feb. 16, 1795–Dec. 31, 1804, fair.

Me. Hist. Soc. has Jan. 16, 30, Feb. 27, Mar. 19, Apr. 2, 23–May 7, June 4, 11, 25–July 16, 30, Aug. 6, 20, 27, Sept. 17, 24, Oct. 8–22, Nov. 12–Dec. 24, 1792; Jan. 17, Feb. 7, 21–Mar. 21, Apr. 4, 18, June 1–15, July 13, Aug. 24, Sept. 14, Oct. 5–Nov. 2, 25, Dec. 30, 1793; July 26, Dec. 15–29, 1794; Jan. 5, 1795–Aug. 29, 1796; Oct. 24, 1796; Jan. 12, Feb. 20, 23, 1797; Dec. 16, 1799; Nov. 10, 1800; Jan. 5, Mar. 30, Dec. 28, 1801; July 30, Sept. 17, 1804.

N. Y. Hist. Soc. has Jan. 16, 1792–Dec. 16, 1793; fair, Nov. 17, 1794–Nov. 20, 1795, fair; Feb. 15, 1796; Jan. 26–Feb. 6, 20, 23, Mar. 13, 1797.

Mass. Hist. Soc. has Jan. 30–Feb. 13, Mar. 5–26, 1792.

Lib. Congress has Feb. 27, 1792; Mar. 23, Apr. 6, Sept. 21, 1795; Feb. 13, Mar. 13, 30, 1797; July 8, Oct. 14, 1799.

Phil. Lib. Co. has Oct. 22, 29, Nov. 12–Dec. 3, 1795; Jan. 6, Mar. 3–17, 31, Apr. 7, 21, May 2, 23–June 6, 20, July 4–25, Aug. 8, 1796.

Me. State Lib. has June 7, 1794.

Univ. of Chicago has Oct. 13, 1794.

N. Y. Pub. Lib. has Oct. 20, 1794.

Essex Inst. has Jan. 12, 1797; Sept. 23, Oct. 21, 1799.

[Portland] Freeman's Friend, 1807–1810.

Weekly. A continuation, in name and volume numbering, of the "Freeman's Friend" of Saco, published by William Weeks. The first issue at Portland was that of Sept. 19, 1807, vol. 3, no. 1, published by William Weeks, with the title of "Freeman's Friend." Weeks' office was destroyed by fire on Jan. 17, 1808, and beginning with the issue of Jan. 23, 1808, he published his paper at the office of J. M'Kown. The paper was suspended with the issue of Feb. 13, 1808, and resumed with the issue of May 21, 1808. Weeks admitted John M'Kown to partnership and beginning with the issue of June 18, 1808, the firm name was Weeks & M'Kown. Weeks retired to take charge of the "New Hampshire Gazette" at Portsmouth and beginning with the issue of June 17, 1809, the paper was published by J. M'Kown. It was discontinued with the issue of June 9, 1810, vol. 5, no. 26.

Am. Antiq. Soc. has Sept. 19, 1807–June 10, 1809; Aug. 12–26, Nov. 4, 25, 1809; May 12, 1810.

Me. Hist. Soc. has Sept. 26, 1807–Feb. 13, 1808; May 21, 1808–Dec. 30, 1809; June 2, 9, 1810.

Portland Pub. Lib. has Sept. 16–Oct. 14, 28–Dec. 9, 1809; Jan. 7–Feb. 17, Mar. 3, 17–Apr. 21, May 5–June 9, 1810.

MAINE 211

N. Y. State Lib. has May 21, 1808–June 10, 1809.
Wis. Hist. Soc. has Jan. 6–June 9, 1810.
Univ. of Mich. (Clements) has Sept. 19, Nov. 14, 28, Dec. 26, 1807; July 23, 30, 1808.
N. Y. Hist. Soc. has Oct. 17, Nov. 14–Dec. 26, 1807; Jan. 2–30, Feb. 13, 1808.
Harvard has Oct. 17, Dec. 5, 1807; Aug. 6, 20, Sept. 3–Oct. 15, Nov. 5, 12, 26–Dec. 10, 24, 1808.
Boston Pub. Lib. has Oct. 22, 1808; Feb. 18, Mar. 4, June 10, Aug. 5, 12, 1809; Jan. 13, Mar. 3, 10, 1810.
Lib. Congress has June 18, 1808.
Mass. Hist. Soc. has Sept. 10, 1808.

[Portland] Gazette, 1798–1820+.

Weekly. Established as "The Gazette" Apr. 16, 1798, by Elezer Alley Jenks. The title was changed to "Jenks' Portland Gazette" with the issue of Apr. 29, 1799, and to "Jenks' Portland Gazette. Maine Advertiser," with the issue of Sept. 27, 1802; but the title was again shortened to "Jenks' Portland Gazette" with the issue of Oct. 31, 1803, and further shortened to "Portland Gazette" with the issue of Mar. 18, 1805. Jenks disposed of the paper to Isaac Adams and William Jenks, Jun., with the issue of July 16, 1805, and the title was changed to "Portland Gazette, and Maine Advertizer" with the issue of July 23. Jenks retired and Isaac Adams became sole publisher beginning with the issue of July 21, 1806. Beginning with the issue of Sept. 19, 1808, the paper was published by Arthur Shirley. With the issue of Dec. 26, 1808, the title became "Portland Gazette, & Maine Advertiser"; with Jan. 30, 1809, "Portland Gazette, and Maine Advertiser"; and with Oct. 26, 1812, "Portland Gazette, and Maine Advertiser." With the issue of Sept. 19, 1814, Joshua Shirley was admitted to partnership [A. & J. Shirley] and remained until 1819, when Arthur Shirley again assumed the proprietorship. The title was shortened to "The Portland Gazette" with the issue of Apr. 7, 1818. In many of the issues from 1815 to 1818, the names of the publishers were not given. In Oct. 1819 and June 1820, the paper was published semi-weekly during the session of the legislature. The paper was continued after 1820.

Me. Hist. Soc. has Apr. 16, 23, May 14, 1798–Apr. 22, 1799; July 15–29, Aug. 12, Dec. 30, 1799; Feb. 3, 24, Mar. 3, Apr. 28, 1800–July 25, 1803; Sept. 19, 1803; Mar. 10, Apr. 7, 28, 1804–Apr. 15, 1805; Apr. 29, July 16, 1805–July 14, 1806; Jan. 12–26, Feb. 9–23, Mar. 23–May 11, 25–July 27, Aug. 10–Sept. 14, 28–Oct. 12, Nov. 2–Dec. 21, 1807; Jan. 4, 1808–July 3, 1809; Aug. 7–21, Nov. 20, 27, Dec. 25, 1809; Jan. 1, 1810; Jan. 28, Mar. 18, Sept. 30, 1811; Apr. 27, June 1, Aug. 31, 1812; Mar. 15, Apr. 12, Aug. 2, Nov. 8, 29, 1813; Mar. 21, Apr. 2, June 27, July 2, 11, 25, Oct. 3, 31–Nov. 14, 1814; Jan. 30, Feb. 6, 27, Sept. 20, Dec. 19, 1815; Feb. 6, 13, 27, Mar. 12, Apr. 2, May 7–

June 11, July 16–Sept. 3, 17–Oct. 8, 29–Nov. 19, Dec. 28, 1816; Sept. 30, Nov. 4, 1817; Jan. 6, Feb. 10, Apr. 21, Dec. 15, 1818; Feb. 16, 1819; Feb. 22, 29, Oct. 10, 1820.

Portland Pub. Lib. has May 21, June 11, 18, July 9, 16, 1798; Feb. 25, Apr. 29– June 3, 17, Aug. 26, Sept. 23–Nov. 18, Dec. 2–16, 1799; Jan. 6–Feb. 25, Apr. 6, 27–Dec. 29, 1800; Jan. 5–Mar. 9, Apr. 7, 1801–Dec. 17, 1802; Jan. 3–17, 31–Feb. 14, 28–Apr. 25, May 9–Dec. 31, 1803; Jan. 7–Apr. 21, May 5–July 9, 30–Nov. 26, Dec. 17–31, 1804; Apr. 22, 1805–Apr. 11, 1808; Mar. 20, Apr. 10, Sept. 4, 1809–Sept. 3, 1810; Apr. 15–Oct. 21, Nov. 4, 11, 25–Dec. 30, 1811; Jan. 6–Feb. 17, Mar. 2–30, Oct. 19–Nov. 2, 1812; Sept. 6, 1813–Aug. 29, 1814; Jan. 22, July 29, Dec. 23, 1817; Apr. 14, June 23, Aug. 18, Sept. 22, 1818; Nov. 9, 1819; Jan. 4, June 19, Dec. 12, 1820.

Am. Antiq. Soc. has Apr. 23, May 14–28, June 11–Sept. 17, Oct. 8–Nov. 12, 26– Dec. 31, 1798; Jan. 7–Apr. 15, 29–Dec. 30, 1799; Jan. 6–Apr. 21, May 5– June 24, July 14–Aug. 11, Sept. 1–Oct. 13, Nov. 10–Dec. 1, 15, 22, 1800; Jan. 5–26, Feb. 23, Mar. 30, Apr. 6, 20–May 4, 18, June 1, 15–July 13, Aug. 3, 10, Sept. 14, 28, Dec. 28, 1801; Jan. 4, 18–Feb. 1, 15, 22, Mar. 15, 29– Apr. 26, May 10, 31–Aug. 30, Sept. 13, 27–Oct. 11, 25–Dec. 6, 20, 1802; Jan. 10, 17, 31–Feb. 14, Mar. 21–Apr. 4, 18, 25, May 9, 30, June 20, July 4, Aug. 8–Sept. 26, Oct. 10, 31–Nov. 26, Dec. 31, 1803; Jan. 7–Dec. 17, 31, 1804; Apr. 15, June 3, July 9, Sept. 16, 23, Oct. 7, 14, Dec. 2, 1805; Feb. 17, Apr. 7, June 2, 16–Dec. 29, 1806; Jan. 5, 1807–Dec. 25, 1809; Feb. 5, 12, Mar. 12, 19, Apr. 16, June 18, 25, Aug. 6, 13, Sept. 10, 24, Oct. 22, 1810; Jan. 7, 14, 28, Feb. 11–Mar. 4, 18–Apr. 1, May 27, June 3, July 15, Aug. 26, Sept. 9, 30, Oct. 14, 21, Nov. 18–Dec. 16, 1811; Jan. 13, Feb. 3, Mar. 2, 23, Apr. 20, May 18–June 1, 22, Aug. 10, 31, Nov. 23, 30, 1812; Jan. 4–Apr. 12, May 10– Dec. 27, 1813; Jan. 10, 24–Dec. 26, 1814; Jan. 2, 16–Feb. 6, Apr. 10, 17, May 8, 15, July 24, 31, Sept. 4, 1815–Dec. 28, 1816; Jan. 4, May 13, Nov. 23, 1817; Apr. 21–May 5, July 21, 28, Oct. 13, 27, 1818; Aug. 10, 17, Sept. 7– Nov. 23, Dec. 7–28, 1819; Jan. 4–Dec. 26, 1820.

N. Y. Pub. Lib. has May 6, 1799–Apr. 19, 1802; Aug. 1, 1803–Dec. 24, 1804; July 16, 1805–Aug. 28, 1809; July 8, 1811; Mar. 20–Dec. 26, 1815; Sept. 2, 1817–Oct. 27, 1818; Jan. 4–Dec. 26, 1820.

Essex Inst. has Dec. 2, 16, 1799; Jan. 13, 1806–Dec. 28, 1807; Jan. 15, 1810– Dec. 28, 1812; Jan. 2–Dec. 21, 1816; Sept. 2, 9, 1817; Jan. 4–Dec. 26, 1820.

Boston Pub. Lib. has Mar. 31, 1806; Sept. 4, 1809; Mar. 12, Apr. 16, 1810; Jan. 7, 1811–Sept. 30, 1817; Jan. 13, 1818–Dec. 28, 1819; Mar. 14, 1820.

Mass. Hist. Soc. has May 28, 1798–Apr. 21, 1800; Apr. 27, 1801–Apr. 15, 1805; Oct. 17, 1808; Sept. 27, Dec. 26, 1815; Jan. 2–Apr. 30, July 9–Nov. 5, 1816; June 22, July 6–Aug. 10, 31, Sept. 7, 21–Nov. 16, 1819.

Boston Athenæum has Apr. 29, 1799–Jan. 19, 1807; Jan. 18, 1808; May 22, July 24, 1809; May 27, 1811; Sept. 20, 1815; Sept. 3, 24, Oct. 8, 22–Nov. 5, 1816; Apr. 8, 15, May 13, 20, July 1, 1817; Jan. 26, 1819; Jan. 4, 18, Mar. 7, 28, 1820.

MAINE 213

York Inst., Saco, has Apr. 23, July 9, 1798–June 30, 1800; Jan. 5, 1801–Nov. 26, 1804; Dec. 30, 1817; Mar. 7, May 23–Dec. 26, 1820.
Harvard has Aug. 13, 1798; Jan. 7, Mar. 4, 11, 1799; Sept. 23, 1799–Dec. 26, 1808, fair.
Lib. Congress has Apr. 23, May 14–28, June 18, 25, July 16, Aug. 6, 13, Oct. 15, 22, Nov. 12, 19, 1798; Feb. 11, 25, May 20, 1799–Mar. 10, 1800; Feb. 9, 1801; May 31, June 14, July 5, 19–Aug. 2, 16, Oct. 25, Nov. 8–29, 1802; Mar. 21, Apr. 4, 25, July 4, Aug. 22, 29, Nov. 7, 1803; Feb. 4, 11, 25, Mar. 3, 31–Apr. 21, May 5, 12, June 4, 25, Sept. 17, Oct. 1–15, 29, Nov. 5, Dec. 17, 1804; Jan. 27, Sept. 29, 1806; Jan. 5, 19–Feb. 16, 30, Mar. 16, May 25, Aug. 10, 24, 31, Sept. 14–28, Oct. 12, 19, Nov. 2, 16, 30, 1807; Jan. 4, 1808–Dec. 25, 1809; Sept. 30, 1811; Jan. 24, Feb. 22, 1814; Jan. 30, May 8, 1815; Jan. 2–Dec. 28, 1816; Apr. 11, 25, May 16, 1820.
Yale has Nov. 12, 1798–Mar. 4, 1799; Jan. 2–Dec. 25, 1809; Aug. 27, 1816.
Wis. Hist. Soc. has Jan. 1–Dec. 31, 1810; Jan. 5, 19–May 25, June 8–July 6, 20–Aug. 3, 17, 24, Sept. 7–21, Oct. 12–Dec. 14, 28, 1812; Dec. 15, 1818.
Bowdoin has Apr. 15, 1817–Apr. 7, 1818; Apr. 20–Oct. 28, Nov. 30, 1819; Feb. 8–Mar. 7, 21–May 9, 23–July 25, Aug. 8–Sept. 26, Oct. 10–Dec. 26, 1820.
Duke Univ. has Aug. 6, 1804; Sept. 20, Oct. 4–Nov. 8, 1815; Jan. 9–Aug. 27, 1816.
Dartmouth has Nov. 19, 1803; Apr. 8, Oct. 14, 1805; Nov. 9, 1819; July 11–Aug. 1, 15–Oct. 31, Nov. 28–Dec. 12, 26, 1820.
Bangor Pub. Lib. has June 24–July 8, 1799.
N. Y. Hist. Soc. has Dec. 25, 1799; Aug. 19, Dec. 16, 1811; May 25, June 1, July 13, Aug. 10, 31, Sept. 21, Oct. 12, Nov. 9–23, 1812.
Me. State Lib. has Dec. 3, 1803; Aug. 27, Oct. 15, Dec. 3, 1804; July 29, Oct. 28, 1805; Apr. 7, 1806; Feb. 2, Mar. 23, 1807; Jan. 4, Aug. 22, Sept. 12, 19, 1808; Jan. 8, Apr. 23, 30, Sept. 3, 1810; Mar. 25, Sept. 9, 1811; May 11, 1812; Feb. 1, 15, May 24, July 19, Aug. 16, Dec. 20, 1813; Mar. 7, July 25, 1814; Jan. 9, 23, Feb. 20, Mar. 19, Oct. 8, 1816; June 3, 1817; Feb. 10, June 23, Sept. 1, Oct. 27, 1818; Apr. 13, July 20, Aug. 24, 1819; May 2, 23, June 22, Aug. 15, Sept. 5, Nov. 7, Dec. 5, 19, 26, 1820.

[Portland] Gazette of Maine, 1790–1796.

Weekly. Established Oct. 8, 1790, by Benjamin Titcomb, Jun., with the title of "Gazette of Maine." Its last issue was that of Aug. 29, 1796, vol. 6, no. 308, and on Sept. 3, 1796, it was consolidated by John K. Baker with "The Eastern Herald."

York Inst., Saco, has Jan. 12, 1792–Aug. 29, 1796.
Am. Antiq. Soc. has Oct. 15–28, Nov. 11–26, Dec. 9–30, 1790; Jan. 6–27, Feb. 10, 17, Mar. 3–17, Apr. 1–June 3, 17, July 1–Sept. 9, 23–Nov. 18, Dec. 1, 8, 29, 1791; Jan. 19, Feb. 2–June 1, 15–29, July 13–Aug. 10, 24–Oct. 18, Nov. 1–

Dec. 20, 1792; Jan. 3–17, 31, Feb. 14, 21, Mar. 7–Apr. 4, 18–May 4, 25, Aug. 3, 31, Sept. 9, Nov. 4, 1793; Jan. 13, Mar. 3, Apr. 21, May 17, Aug. 23, 1794; Jan. 26, Feb. 9, 23, Apr. 6, 20, June 22, July 6, 13, Aug. 3, 10, 24, Sept. 7, Nov. 5, 12, Dec. 24, 1795; Mar. 10, May 30, 1796.
N. Y. Hist. Soc. has Oct. 8–Dec. 16, 30, 1790; Jan. 20–Feb. 10, Mar. 17–May 27, June 10, 17, July 8–Sept. 2, 16, 30–Oct. 14, 28, Nov. 25, Dec. 8, 1791.
Me. Hist. Soc. has Oct. 22, Nov. 4–Dec. 30, 1790; Jan. 6, Mar. 10, Apr. 7–May 27, 1791; July 13, 1792; Apr. 25, Nov. 11, 1793; Jan. 27, Oct. 13, 1794; Jan. 26, 1795.
Lib. Congress has Dec. 9, 23, 30, 1790; Feb. 3, 17–Mar. 3, 17–Apr. 1, 14–28, May 12, July 8–29, 1791; Aug. 3, 1792; June 8, 15, 1793; Jan. 19, 26, Apr. 6, Sept. 21, Nov. 26, 1795; May 16, 1796.
Harvard has Feb. 16, Mar. 2, 9, May 25, June 15, 29, July 13, Nov. 12, Dec. 31, 1795; Feb. 11, 18, Mar. 10, 24, 31, Apr. 14, May 9, 23, July 4–Aug. 1, 15, 22, 1796.
Mass. Hist. Soc. has Feb. 16–Mar. 22, Apr. 5, 1792.
Phil. Lib. Co. has Oct. 14, 1793; Jan. 7, 1796.

[Portland] Herald of Gospel Liberty, 1810–1811.

Bi-weekly. Established at Portsmouth, N. H., Sept. 1, 1808, by Elias Smith, with the title of "Herald of Gospel Liberty." The opening Address says: "A religious Newspaper, is almost a new thing under the sun; I know not but this is the first ever published to the world." The paper was removed to Portland with the issue of Apr. 27, 1810, vol. 1, no. 44. Elias Smith was the publisher, but the issues from Nov. 23, 1810, to Mar. 1, 1811, bore also the name of John P. Colcord as printer. The paper was removed to Philadelphia with the issue of July 5, 1811. The last Portland issue, therefore, was on June 21, 1811, vol. 3, no. 74. The paper was of quarto size and had continuous pagination.

Am. Antiq. Soc., Lib. Congress, Congregational Lib. of Boston, N. H. Hist. Soc., N. H. State Lib., Wesleyan Univ., N. Y. Hist. Soc., Antioch College, Penn. State Lib., Presbyterian Theol. Sem. of Chicago, and Chicago Theol. Sem. have Apr. 27, 1810–June 21, 1811.
Hist. Soc. Penn. has Apr. 27, 1810–June 21, 1811, fair.
Mass. Hist. Soc. has Apr. 27–Aug. 17, 1810.
Univ. of Mich. (Clements) has Apr. 27–Aug. 17, 1810.
Defiance Coll., Defiance, Ohio, has July 6, 1810–June 21, 1811.

[Portland] Jenks' Portland Gazette, see [Portland] Gazette.

Portland Magazine, 1805.

Weekly. Established May 11, 1805, by William Jenks, Jun., with the title of "Portland Magazine." It contained current news, both national and local, as well as marriage and obituary notices, and except for its title could well be classed as a newspaper. It was of quarto size and paged continuously. The last issue located is that of June 8, 1805, vol. 1, no. 5. Jenks became joint proprietor of the "Portland Gazette" in July, 1805.

Am. Antiq. Soc. has May 11–June 8, 1805.
Harvard has May 11, June 1, 1805.
Lib. Congress has May 11, 1805.

[Portland] Oriental Trumpet, 1796–1800.

Weekly. Established Dec. 15, 1796, by John Rand, with the title of "Oriental Trumpet." Rand admitted William Burdick to partnership, and beginning with the issue of Apr. 25, 1798, the title was changed to the "Oriental Trumpet. Or, The Town and Country Gazette" and was published by Rand and Burdick. With the issue of Nov. 14, 1799, the title was slightly altered to "Oriental Trumpet: Or, Town and Country Gazette." Burdick withdrew from the firm with the issue of Nov. 5, 1800, vol. 4, no. 202, which is the last located.

Harvard has Dec. 15–29, 1796; Jan. 5, 12, Feb. 9, Mar. 9–Apr. 6, 26, June 21, July 5, 12, Oct. 3, Nov. 16, 30, Dec. 14, 28, 1797; Jan. 4–25, Feb. 8, 22–Mar. 8, Apr. 12, 19, Sept. 12, 19, 1798; Feb. 28, Mar. 24, Apr. 11, 24, May 15, July 17–Aug. 7, 21, Sept. 4–25, Oct. 9–Dec. 4, 19, 1799; Jan. 9–Feb. 13, Mar. 6, 13, 27–Apr. 24, May 7–July 30, Aug. 13–Sept. 24, Oct. 8, 15, 29, Nov. 5, 1800.
Am. Antiq. Soc. has Dec. 29, 1796; Jan. 5, 19, Feb. 9, 16, Mar. 2–30, Apr. 13, 26, May 3, 17, 31, June 14, 21, July 12, Aug. 16, 23, Oct. 3, 11, Nov. 2, 9, Dec. 7–28, 1797; Jan. 4, 18–Feb. 8, 22–Mar. 22, Apr. 5, 19–May 30, June 13, 27, July 11, 18, Oct. 3, 18, Nov. 15–Dec. 13, 27, 1798; Jan. 10, 17, Feb. 14, 28, Mar. 24, May 29, 1799; Apr. 24, 1800.
Me. Hist. Soc. has Jan. 19, May 3, June 28–July 12, Dec. 28, 1797; June 6, Aug. 15, 29, 1798; Jan. 9, 16, 1800.
Lib. Congress has Dec. 13, 1798.
N. Y. Hist. Soc. has Nov. 14, 1799.

[Portland] Russell & George's Eastern Herald, see Eastern Herald.

[Saco] Freeman's Friend, 1805–1807.

Weekly. Established Aug. 21, 1805, by William Weeks, with the title of "Freeman's Friend." He published it until Aug. 15, 1807, vol. 2, no. 52, when he removed to Portland, and there continued its publication. See under Portland.

Lib. Congress has Aug. 21, 1805–Aug. 15, 1807.
Harvard has Aug. 21, 28, Sept. 11–Oct. 2, 16–Nov. 6, 27, Dec. 11–25, 1805; Jan. 1–15, 29, Feb. 12, 26–Mar. 19, Apr. 2, 9, 30, May 14–June 11, 25–July 16,

30, Aug. 20, 27, Sept. 20–Nov. 1, 29, Dec. 13, 20, 1806; Jan. 3, 10, 31, Feb. 7, Mar. 7, Apr. 4, 11, May 2, 9, 23, 30, June 13, 20, July 11, Aug. 1, 8, 1807.
Am. Antiq. Soc. has Aug. 21, Sept. 25, Oct. 2, Nov. 6, Dec. 25, 1805; Mar. 12, 19, May 21, July 23, 30, Aug. 20–Sept. 10, Oct. 4, Nov. 1, 8, 1806; Jan. 3, 31, Feb. 7, 21, Mar. 14, May 9–30, June 20–July 11, Aug. 1, 15, 1807.
York Inst., Saco, has Aug. 21, 1805–Feb. 26, Mar. 12, 1806.
Me. Hist. Soc. has Sept. 10, 1806; Mar. 28–May 9, 30–June 13, July 4–Aug. 15, 1807.
N. Y. Hist. Soc. has July 2, Nov. 15, Dec. 6, 13, 1806; Jan. 17, 31, Mar. 7–21, Apr. 4, May 2, Aug. 15, 1807.
Dartmouth has Aug. 1, 1807.

Wiscasset Argus, 1797–1798.

Weekly. Established Dec. 23, 1797, by Laughton & Rhoades [Daniel Laughton and Ebenezer Rhoades], with the title of "Wiscasset Argus." The last issue located is that of Jan. 13, 1798, vol. 1, no. 4, and the paper was soon afterwards discontinued.

Am. Antiq. Soc. has Dec. 30, 1797; Jan. 6, 1798.
Harvard has Jan. 6, 13, 1798.

[Wiscasset] Eastern Repository, 1803–1807.

Weekly. Established June 16, 1803, by Babson and Rust [John Babson and Enoch H. Rust], with the title of "Eastern Repository." The paper was discontinued and the partnership dissolved Sept. 7, 1807, according to an advertisement in the Wiscasset "Republican" of Oct. 7, 1807. The last issue located is that of June 23, 1807, vol. 5, no. 1.

Am. Antiq. Soc. has June 16, 30, Aug. 18, Sept. 15, 1803, Mar. 6, 13, 1804; Aug. 6, 1805; Apr. 22, 29, Aug. 12, Oct. 28, Nov. 18, 25, 1806; Feb. 17, Mar. 17, Apr. 7, June 23, 1807.
Harvard has June 30–Aug. 25, Sept. 8–Oct. 13, 27, Nov. 3, 22–Dec. 20, 1803; Jan. 3, 10, 24, Feb. 14, 21, Mar. 13–27, Apr. 10, 24, May 1, June 5, 26, July 10–Aug. 14, Sept. 4, 11, 25–Oct. 9, 23, Nov. 13–Dec. 25, 1804; Jan. 15, 1805.
Univ. of Ill. has Oct. 30, Dec. 11, 1804; Jan. 1, 29, 1805.
Me. Hist. Soc. has Mar. 6, 1804.
Dartmouth has July 23, 1806.

[Wiscasset] Lincoln Telegraph, 1820+.

Weekly. Established Apr. 27, 1820, by Samuel B. Dana, with the title of "Lincoln Telegraph." Continued after 1820.

Am. Antiq. Soc. has Prospectus of Feb. 15, 1820; May 11, 1820.

Me. Hist. Soc. has Apr. 27, 1820.
York Inst., Saco, has Dec. 14, 1820.

[Wiscasset] **Republican,** 1807–1808.

Weekly. Established by Thomas Loring, Sept. 23, 1807, with the title of "The Republican," judging by the date of the first issue located, that of Oct. 7, 1807, vol. 1, no. 3. The last issue located is that of Jan. 27, 1808, vol. 1, no. 18.

Am. Antiq. Soc. has Oct. 21, 28, Nov. 11, 18, 1807; Jan. 27, 1808.
Harvard has Oct. 7, 1807.

Wiscasset Telegraph, 1796–1799.

Weekly. Established Dec. 3, 1796, by J. N. Russell and H. Hoskins [Joseph N. Russell and Henry Hoskins], with the title of "The Wiscasset Telegraph." The partnership was dissolved under date of Apr. 1, 1797, when Henry Hoskins became sole publisher. With the issue of Mar. 18 or 25, 1797, the title became "Wiscasset Telegraph," but in the summer of 1797 reverted to "The Wiscasset Telegraph." In October or November, probably with the issue of Nov. 17, 1797, Hoskins admitted John W. Scott into partnership, under the firm name of Henry Hoskins and John W. Scott, who continued certainly until the issue of Oct. 23, 1798. The last issue located, that of Mar. 9, 1799, vol. 3, no. 5, was published by Henry Hoskins.

Harvard has Dec. 10–24, 1796; Jan. 7, Apr. 1, June 20, Dec. 1, 8, 22, 1797; Jan. 23, June 1, 15, July 6, 20, Sept. 7, 14, Oct. 23, 1798.
Am. Antiq. Soc. has Jan. 7, Feb. 11, Mar. 4, 11, 25, Apr. 1, 25, May 9, 30, June 13, Sept. 19, Nov. 24, Dec. 1, 1797; Jan. 12, Feb. 13, Mar. 17, May 25, 1798.
Me. Hist. Soc. has May 23–June 20, Dec. 1, 1797; Mar. 9, 1799.

MARYLAND

Abingdon Patriot, 1805–1807.

Weekly. Established by Daniel P. Ruff on Sept. 17, 1805, judging from the date of the first and only issue located, that of Oct. 1, 1805, vol. 1, no. 3. The full title was "The Abingdon Patriot, and Harford County Gazette." It was discontinued with the issue of Apr. 21, 1807, according to an article in the Baltimore "Federal Gazette" of Apr. 25, 1807.

Lib. Congress has Oct. 1, 1805.

[Annapolis] Maryland Gazette, 1727–1734.

Weekly. Established in September, 1727, judging from the date of the first issue located, that of Dec. 10, 1728, no. 65. In the "American Weekly Mercury," Philadelphia, of Sept. 28, 1727, is a news item dated Annapolis, Sept. 16, 1727, and it is possible that this was the date of the first issue of "The Maryland Gazette." There are occasional quotations from the Annapolis paper in the "Mercury" in 1727 and 1728; and in the issue of June 13, 1728, is an advertisement for the apprehending of Nicholas Classon, a printer by trade, 21 years of age, who "formerly lived with William Parks Printer in Annapolis." This first located issue of Dec. 10, 1728, was published by William Parks, with the title of "The Maryland Gazette," as are all subsequent issues to Dec. 22, 1730, no. 171, the last issue located of the early series. It was continued longer, certainly to March, 1731, as is shown by a bill from William Parks, March 1, 1730/31, for printing in the Gazette advertisements of St. Ann's Parish (Md. Hist. Mag., v. 8, pp. 158, 163). During this period, Parks had been in England (see issue of June 9, 1730) and had also set up a press at Williamsburg, Va., where, according to the "American Weekly Mercury" of July 15, 1731, he advertises that he is residing. In December, 1732, the Annapolis paper was revived by W. Parks, and E. Hall [William Parks and Edmund Hall], under the title of "The Maryland Gazette Reviv'd," as is shown by the issue of Feb. 2, 1733, no. 9. The issues from Feb. 2 to Mar. 16, 1733, bore this title, but from Apr. 13, 1733, to Nov. 29, 1734, were entitled "The Maryland Gazette." Between Apr. 20 and Dec. 28, 1733, William Parks had become sole publisher. The last issue located of this new series is that of Nov. 29, 1734, no. 90, and the paper was discontinued either with this issue or soon afterwards. Samuel Ogle, Governor of Maryland, under date of Nov. 22, 1737, wrote "As we have not a Press here at present, I have given Directions to the Bearer of this to get a good Number of Proclamations printed in Philadelphia" (Penn. Col. Records, v. 4, p. 253).

The John Carter Brown Library in 1925 reproduced in photostat all the known issues, which set is to be found in the following libraries: Amer. Antiq. Soc.,

Conn. State Lib., Duke Univ., Grosvenor Lib., John Carter Brown Lib., Lib. Congress, Md. Hist. Soc., Md. State Lib., Mass. Hist. Soc., Newberry Lib., N. Y. Hist. Soc., N. Y. Pub. Lib., N. Y. State Lib., Pratt Lib. of Baltimore, Univ. of Chicago, Univ. of Ill., Univ. of Mich., Va. Hist. Soc., Va. State Lib., Western Reserve Hist. Soc., Wis. Hist. Soc., and Yale.

Md. Hist. Soc. has Dec. 10, 1728–Feb. 11, 25–May 6, 20, 27, June 10–July 22, 1729.

N. Y. Pub. Lib. has June 3, Oct. 28, 1729; Mar. 3, 17, 31, May 26, June 9, 16, Oct. 20, Dec. 1, 15, 22, 1730; Feb. 2, 9, Mar. 16, Apr. 13, Dec. 28, 1733; Jan. 18, May 24, July 19, Aug. 2, 9, Sept. 27, Nov. 1, 22, 29, 1734.

British Museum (Burney Coll.) has Apr. 29, May 20, June 3–17, July 15, 22, 1729.

U. S. Naval Academy, Annapolis, has Mar. 15, 1734.

[Annapolis] **Maryland Gazette,** 1745–1820+.

Weekly. Established Jan. 17, 1745, by Jonas Green, under the title of "The Maryland Gazette." With the issue of Oct. 26, 1758, William Rind was admitted to partnership and the paper was published by Jonas Green, and William Rind. In consequence of the Stamp Act, the paper was suspended for a time in 1765. The issue of Oct. 10, 1765, no. 1066, was headed "The Maryland Gazette, Expiring: In uncertain Hopes of a Resurrection to Life again." On Oct. 17, an unnumbered issue was published, entitled "A Supplement to the Maryland Gazette, of last Week"; on Oct. 24, there appeared another issue entitled "Second Supplement to the Maryland Gazette, of the Week before last"; and on Oct. 31, another issue, entitled "Third and Last Supplement to the Maryland Gazette, of the Tenth Instant." These three issues were published by Jonas Green. On Dec. 10, 1765, was published an issue entitled "An Apparition of the late Maryland Gazette," which announced its revival within a few weeks. On Jan. 30, 1766, there appeared "The Maryland Gazette, Reviving," no. 1067, resuming the former numbering and published by Jonas Green. This was followed by "The Maryland Gazette, Revived," no. 1068, on Feb. 20, 1766; and "The Maryland Gazette," no. 1069, on Mar. 6, 1766, after which publication proceeded regularly. Jonas Green died on Apr. 11, 1767, and beginning with the issue of Apr. 16, 1767, the paper was published by his widow, Anne Catherine Green. With the issue of Jan. 7, 1768, she admitted her son into partnership, under the firm name of Anne Catherine and William Green (spelled Catharine Jan. 28, 1768, and after). William Green died in August, 1770, and with the issue of Aug. 23, 1770, the paper was published by Anne Catharine Green. With the issue of Jan. 2, 1772, it was published by Anne Catharine Green and Son [Frederick Green]. Mrs. Green died Mar. 23, 1775, and beginning with the issue of Mar. 30, 1775, the paper was published by Frederick Green. It was temporarily suspended with the issue of Dec. 25, 1777, but was revived by Frederick and Samuel Green with the issue of Apr. 30, 1779. This firm name was changed to F. and S. Green with the issue of Mar. 14, 1782, and to Frederick and Samuel Green with the issue of Oct. 2, 1788. In January, 1811, both these editors died within a week of each other, Samuel on Jan. 6, and Frederick on Jan. 12, and beginning with the issue of Jan. 16, 1811, the paper was published by Jonas Green, son of Frederick and grandson of the founder (see "Md. Republican," Sept. 20, 1813). The title was changed to "Maryland Gazette, and Political Intelligencer" with the issue of Jan. 28, 1813, although shortage of paper caused a reversion to the earlier title and a reduction in size, from Sept. 8 to Oct. 6, 1814. The paper was continued by Jonas Green until after 1820.

A microfilm reproduction of the Maryland Gazette, 1745–1820, was issued by the Yale University Library in 1938, which was acquired by the following libraries: — Am. Antiq. Soc., Boston Pub. Lib., Yale, Dartmouth, N. Y. Pub. Lib., N. Y. Hist. Soc., Columbia, Coll. of City of N. Y., Grosvenor Lib. of Buffalo, Princeton, Hist. Soc. Penn., Temple Univ., Lib. Congress, Md. State Lib., Peabody Inst. Baltimore, Pratt Lib. Baltimore, Univ. of Virginia, Duke Univ., Ohio State Univ., Newberry Lib., Univ. of Chicago, Univ. of Illinois, Univ. of Missouri, Clements Lib. Univ. of Mich., Wis. Hist. Soc., Univ. of Texas, Huntington Lib., Univ. of Calif. Berkeley.

 Md. State Lib., Annapolis, has Apr. 26, 1745–Dec. 28, 1820, one of the most complete newspaper files existing.

 Md. Hist. Soc. has Apr. 26, 1745–Dec. 30, 1746; Feb. 3–June 30, July 14, 28–Sept. 1, 22–Oct. 14, Nov. 18, Dec. 9–23, 1747; Jan. 6–Feb. 24, Mar. 30, Apr. 13, May 18, 25, June 15–July 27, Aug. 10, 31, Sept. 7, Oct. 19, Nov. 23, 30, 1748; Jan. 4, 1749; Mar. 12, 1752–Dec. 27, 1764; Aug. 1, 22, 1765; Feb. 20, Aug. 7, 1766; Jan. 22, Feb. 19, Mar. 12, 26, Apr. 9, 1767–Dec. 1, 1768; Mar. 23, Apr. 13, 27, June 8, 22, July 6, 13, 27–Aug. 24, Sept. 28, Oct. 5, Dec. 28, 1769; Jan. 25, 1770; Nov. 28, 1771; Jan. 2, 1772; Jan. 14, 1773–Dec. 18, 1777, fair; Jan. 6–June 30, July 28–Nov. 17, Dec. 22, 1785; Apr. 6, May 4, 11, 25–Aug. 3, 17–Sept. 7, 21–Nov. 23, 1786; Jan. 4, 1787–Dec. 25, 1788; Jan. 1, May 21, June 4, 18, July 2, 16, 23, Aug. 6–27, Sept. 10, 17, Oct. 1, 15, 1789–Dec. 30, 1790; Jan. 13, 1791–Dec. 21, 1797, fair; May 16, 1799; Sept. 4, Dec. 4, 1800; Apr. 19, 1809–June 12, 1811; July 9, Aug. 20, 1812; Feb. 18–Sept. 30, fair, Dec. 29, 1813; Jan. 5, 19–29, May 26, June 9, July 7, Sept. 22–Oct. 6, 1814; Jan. 19, Feb. 2, Mar. 2, 30, Apr. 13–May 4, 18, June 1, 15, 22, July 6–20, Aug. 3–17, 31, Sept. 21, 28, 1815; June 6, Aug. 15, Sept. 26, Oct. 24, 1816; Aug. 7, 28, Dec. 4, 1817; Jan. 15, Sept. 3, Oct. 22, Dec. 24, 1818; Jan. 14, Mar. 11, Apr. 29, May 20, 27, June 10, Aug. 19, Sept. 9, 30, Dec. 9, 1819; Feb. 3, 10, Mar. 2, Nov. 9, 1820.

 Lib. Congress has Apr. 22, Dec. 30, 1746; Oct. 26, 1748; Apr. 16, 1752–Oct. 30, 1755, fair; July 9–Oct. 1, 1761; Oct. 6, 1763; Jan. 26–Dec. 20, 1764; Jan. 3, Feb. 21, Mar. 14, May 9, 30–July 11, 25, 1765–Sept. 25, Oct. 16–30, Nov. 13–Dec. 26, 1766; Jan. 1, 15–Feb. 12, Mar. 26–Apr. 9, May 14–28, June 11–25, Oct. 8, 1767; May 19, June 2, 16, July 21, Aug. 4, 18–Sept. 8, 29, Oct.

MARYLAND

6, 20, 27, Nov. 10–Dec. 1, 1768; May 11, 1769; Mar. 7, June 27, July 4, Oct. 17, 1771; Apr. 22–Dec. 23, 1773; May 26, 1774; Mar. 28, May 23, June 27, 1776; Apr. 10, 1777; Aug. 5, 19, 26, 1784; May 25, July 27, Aug. 3, 17, Sept. 28, Oct. 5, 19–Nov. 2, 30, 1786; Jan. 4, 18, Feb. 15, 22, June 21, 28, Aug. 2, 9, Sept. 27, Oct. 4, 25–Dec. 6, 1787; May 1, 1788; Jan. 14–Feb. 11, 25, Mar. 4, 18–May 13, 27–July 1, 15–Aug. 5, 19, Sept. 2–Oct. 14, 28– Dec. 30, 1790; Jan. 20, 27, 1791; May 17, 24, Sept. 20, 1792; Apr. 18, 1793; May 14, 1795–May 10, 1798; Sept. 4, Nov. 20, 1800; May 14, 1801; Jan. 26, Nov. 22, 1804; Jan. 24, Mar. 21, 1805; July 31, 1806; May 26, 1808; Nov. 1, 1809; May 23, June 6, 13, July 11, 18, 1810; June 5, 1817.

Am. Antiq. Soc. has Dec. 12, 1754; Mar. 15, May 24, June 14, 21, Aug. 16, 23, Nov. 8, 1764; Aug. 28, 1766; Apr. 9, 1767; Jan. 6, 1774–Dec. 21, 1775; Feb. 29, Mar. 21, Apr. 11, May 2–16, July 4, 1776; Mar. 29, 1781; May 16, 1782; Jan. 23, Mar. 27, Apr. 17, June 12, 26, July 17, Aug. 14, Sept. 4, 18, Oct. 16, 30, 1783; May 19, 26, Dec. 22, 1785; Jan. 5, 12, Feb. 9, 16, Mar. 2, 9, 30, Apr. 20–May 11, 25–June 15, July 6, 20, 27, Aug. 10, 24, 31, Sept. 14–28, Oct. 19–Nov. 9, 30, Dec. 14, 28, 1786; Jan. 4–Feb. 8, Mar. 8, 22–May 10, 24–July 12, 26, Aug. 9–Sept. 6, 20–Nov. 15, 29–Dec. 20, 1787; Mar. 20, Dec. 18, 25, 1788; Jan. 22–Feb. 26, Mar. 12–26, Apr. 9–23, May 7, July 23, Aug. 13–Sept. 10, Oct. 1, Nov. 5, 19–Dec. 31, 1789; Jan. 14, 28, Feb. 25, Mar. 25, Apr. 8, 22, May 6–20, June 3–Aug. 19, Sept. 2–Oct. 14, 28, Nov. 4, 18–Dec. 30, 1790; Jan. 13, 27–Mar. 3, 31, Apr. 14, 28, May 12, June 2, 30, July 7, 28–Aug. 11, 25, Sept. 15, Oct. 13, 20, Nov. 3, Dec. 1, 1791; Jan. 12– Feb. 23, Mar. 8–22, Apr. 12–26, May 10, 17, 31–Sept. 28, Oct. 11, 18, Nov. 1, 15–29, Dec. 13–27, 1792; Jan. 3, 10, 24–Feb. 21, Mar. 7–Apr. 11, 25–May 9, 23–June 13, July 18, Dec. 12, 26, 1793; Apr. 17, Aug. 21, Sept. 18, 1794; July 9, 1795; Oct. 25, 1798; Feb. 27, 1812; Apr. 25, Aug. 29, 1816; Jan. 30, Dec. 4, 1817; July 13, 1820.

Wis. Hist. Soc. has Apr. 10–Dec. 24, 1760; Jan. 7, 1762–Sept. 1, 1763; Jan. 15– Dec. 10, 1767; Aug. 2, Oct. 18, 1781–July 31, 1783; Jan. 1–Dec. 2, 1784; Mar. 10, 17, Apr. 7, 14, July 14, Aug. 18–Sept. 8, 29–Nov. 10, Dec. 1, 8, 1791; Jan. 5, June 21, 28, 1792; Aug. 27, 1795.

Comdr. J. T. Bowers, Annapolis, has Mar. 28, 1750–Dec. 11, 1751.

Va. State Lib. has Jan. 24, 1750; Jan. 2–Aug. 27, 1752; Sept. 14, 1752–Dec. 27, 1753; Jan. 10–May 16, 1754.

Peabody Lib., Baltimore, has Mar. 7–Apr. 4, 25–Nov. 28, Dec. 19, 1754.

N. Y. Hist. Soc. has July 24, 31, Aug. 14, 1755; Sept. 2, 1756; Jan. 13, 1763; Sept. 17, 1779; Mar. 17, 1785; Feb. 14, Aug. 8, 1793; May 17, 31, June 7, July 12, Nov. 29–Dec. 13, 1809; Jan. 3, 10, 24, 31, Feb. 21–Mar. 7, May 2, 30, June 20, 27, July 25–Aug. 8, 22, Sept. 5, 12, 26, Oct. 10, 17, Nov. 7, 14, 28, Dec. 12–26, 1810; Jan. 16–30, Feb. 20, Mar. 6–20, Apr. 10, 1811.

Dist. of Col. Pub. Lib., Georgetown Branch, has Jan. 4, 1776–Dec. 18, 1777.

Mass. Hist. Soc. has Oct. 19–Nov. 9, 1748; July 10, 17, 1755; July 7, Sept. 8, 15, 1757; May 25, 1769; Apr. 19, July 12, Sept. 6, 1770; May 30, June 6, 27,

Sept. 19, 1771; Apr. 23, May 7, 1772; Mar. 25, 1773; Jan. 12, Dec. 21, 1775; May 9, July 11, Sept. 12, Oct. 3, 10, 31, 1776; Feb. 6, 1777.
Yale has May 15, 22, 1760; Mar. 14, Aug. 1, 8, 22–Oct. 10, 31, 1765; Jan. 30, Mar. 6, 13, Apr. 10, May 15, Sept. 4, 1766; Jan. 26, Mar. 9, 1775.
Harvard has July 25, 1765; July 17, 1777; June 23–Sept. 29, Nov. 17, 24, 1791; Mar. 5, 12, May 28, June 11–July 2, 16, 30, Aug. 13, 27, 1795; Feb. 11, Mar. 3, 17–Apr. 14, June 30, July 7, 21–Aug. 11, 25, Sept. 1–15, Oct. 6–20, Nov. 10–Dec. 1, 22, 1796; Jan. 5, 12, 26–Mar. 16, 30–Apr. 27, Aug. 17, Sept. 7, 21–Oct. 5, 19, Nov. 2, 9, 30, Dec. 28, 1797; Jan. 18, Feb. 1, 8, 22, Mar. 8, 22, 29, Apr. 12, May 10–24, June 7–21, Aug. 16–30, Oct. 18–Nov. 1, 15, 22, 1798; Jan. 3–17, Feb. 14, 28, Mar. 14, Apr. 4–May 16, 30, June 13, July 25, Aug. 1, 15, Sept. 19, Oct. 10, 31, Nov. 21, Dec. 26, 1799; Jan. 9–30, Mar. 6, 20, Apr. 3, 10, 24, May 1–June 19, July 3, 10, 24, Aug. 21, Sept. 18, Oct. 2, 16, 23, Nov. 6–20, Dec. 4–18, 1800; Jan. 1–Feb. 5, 19–Mar. 12, 26, Apr. 9–June 4, 18, 25, July 9, Aug. 13, 20, Sept. 3, 10, Oct. 1, 15–29, Nov. 12, 26–Dec. 31, 1801; June 16, Aug. 25, 1803.
British Museum has May 10, 1749; Feb. 15, 1770; June 20, 1771; Mar. 4, 25, Sept. 9, 1773; July 6, Aug. 17, 1775; June 13–Oct. 3, 1776; Mar. 6–Aug. 7, 1777; May 14, June 11, 25, July 16, Sept. 17, Oct. 29, Nov. 12, 1779; Jan. 16–Nov. 6, 1783; Dec. 2, 1784; Jan. 6, 1785–Aug. 10, 1786; Sept. 27, 1787–July 29, 1790; Jan. 7, 1819–Dec. 28, 1820.
Phil. Lib. Co. has Oct. 10, 24, 31, 1765; Apr. 14, 1768; Sept. 19, 26, 1793; Oct. 22–Nov. 26, 1795; Jan. 7–21, Feb. 25, Mar. 3, 17, 24, Apr. 7–21, May 26–June 16, 30–July 14, 28, 1796.
Georgetown Univ. has July 18, 1754.
Johns Hopkins Univ. has Aug. 7, 1755; Oct. 30, 1777.
Del. Hist. Soc. has Oct. 5, 1758.
Pratt Lib., Baltimore, has July 18, 1765; Nov. 28, 1793; Dec. 25, 1817; Jan. 1–Feb. 5, 1818.
N. Y. Pub. Lib. has Feb. 6, 1772, Oct. 27, 1780; July 31, 1794.
Rutgers Univ. has June 24, 1773.
Univ. of Mich. (Clements) has Jan. 12, 1775.
N. Y. State Lib. has May 11, 1775.
Duke Univ. has Apr. 21, Nov. 10, 1784.
Univ. of Ga. has June 30, 1785.

[Annapolis] **Maryland Gazette, and Annapolis Advertiser,** 1779.

Weekly. Established in April, 1779, judging from the date of the earliest issue located, that of July 9, 1779, vol. 1, no. 15, published by James Hayes, Jun., and entitled "The Maryland Gazette, and Annapolis Advertiser," a single sheet only. The only other known issue is an "Extraordinary," no. 17, presumably published July 23, 1779. Hayes had been publishing "The Maryland Gazette, and Baltimore General Advertiser" (see under Baltimore), and upon the suspension of that paper early in 1779, went to Annapolis, where his activity apparently caused the revival of the "Maryland Gazette," by Frederick and Samuel Green, on Apr. 30, 1779.

Lib. Congress has July 9, 1779.
Md. Hist. Soc. has [July 23], Extraordinary.

[Annapolis] Maryland Republican, 1809–1820+.

Weekly and semi-weekly. Established June 17, 1809, by John W. Butler, with the title of "The Maryland Republican." It was published weekly, except during the sessions of the assembly, when it was published semi-weekly. With the issue of July 1, 1811, Butler disposed of the paper to Jehu Chandler. The last regular issue was that of June 21, 1817, upon which date Chandler announced a new semi-weekly paper, and thereafter issued weekly extras of a single page only to bridge the interval before the commencement of the new series. Extras were issued on June 28, July 5, 12, 19, 26. The first issue of the new series appeared on July 17, 1817, with the title of "The Maryland Republican and Political and Agricultural Museum." It was a semi-weekly, although the second issue did not appear until Aug. 7, 1817. Continued after 1820.

Md. Hist. Soc. has June 17, 1809–Sept. 30, 1812; July 3, 1813–Dec. 30, 1820.
Md. Hall of Records, Annapolis, has July 22, 1809–Dec. 22, 1810.
Am. Antiq. Soc. has Sept. 2, Nov. 11, 1809; Jan. 20, Mar. 17, Apr. 21–June 2, 23–July 14, 28–Sept. 1, 15, 29, Nov. 13–Dec. 15, 1810; Feb. 23, Mar. 2, 23, Apr. 6–May 11, June 1–22, July 1, 8, 29, Aug. 15, 22, Sept. 11, 18, Oct. 2, 9, 30, Nov. 11–29, Dec. 20–30, 1811; Jan. 15, Feb. 12–26, Mar. 25–Apr. 15, 29, May 6, 27, June 24–Aug. 12, 26, Sept. 9, Oct. 7–Nov. 4, 23–Dec. 4, 14, 18, 25, 1812; Jan. 1, 6, 13, Mar. 10, 24, Apr. 3, June 5, Sept. 25, Nov. 6, Dec. 11, 14, 21, 25, 1813; Jan. 1, Feb. 19, 23, Mar. 19, Apr. 30, May 7, 1814; Dec. 23, 1817; Mar. 6, 1820.
Lib. Congress has July 1, 1811–June 20, 1812; Dec. 21, 1816; Jan. 2, 1819–Nov. 27, Dec. 9, 1820, fair.
Wis. Hist. Soc. has July 22, Sept. 9–23, Oct. 7, 1809.
Pratt Lib., Baltimore, has July 29, 1809; May 26, 1810; Dec. 8, 1818–Feb. 13, 1819, fair.
Howard-Tilton Lib., New Orleans, has Dec. 16, 1809; Dec. 13, 1811.
Univ. of Pittsburgh has Dec. 2, 13, 1811.

[Baltimore] American, 1799–1820+.

Daily. Established May 14, 1799, by Alex. Martin, under the title of "American. And Daily Advertiser." With the issue of Nov. 30, 1801, the title was altered to "American. And Baltimore Daily Advertiser." With the issue of May 17, 1802, Martin transferred the paper to Thomas Burling, who on Aug. 17, 1802, transferred it to W. Pechin, although there was an announcement that John B.

Colvin would assist for a while in the editorial department. In July, 1802, the title was "American and Mercantile Daily Advertiser," and in September, 1802, "American, and Commercial Daily Advertiser," although no file exists to give exact dates of change. Beginning with Jan. 1, 1803, the paper was published by Pechin & Frailey [William Pechin and Leonard Frailey]. This firm was dissolved and the paper conducted by William Pechin, beginning with the issue of Aug. 12, 1805. With the issue of July 2, 1810, the firm was enlarged to W. Pechin & G. Dobbin & Murphy. [William Pechin, George Dobbin and Thomas Murphy] and the title changed to "American & Commercial Daily Advertiser." On Dec. 3, 1811, George Dobbin died, but the name of the firm remained unchanged, his share in the business being retained for the benefit of his widow. In September 1814, when the British attacked Baltimore, the paper was published intermittently. The issue of Sept. 10 was followed by unnumbered single page issues on Sept. 12, 15 and 16, but the regular issue was resumed on Sept. 20, 1814. With the issue of July 4, 1815, the firm added William Bose under the firm name of Pechin, Dobbin, Murphy & Bose. With the issue of July 1, 1817, this was changed to Dobbin, Murphy & Bose, who continued the paper until after 1820. The name of Dobbin in the firm only represented the family interest, or perhaps Catharine Bose Dobbin, George Dobbin's widow. His oldest son did not enter the firm until after 1820. A tri-weekly country paper was also issued from 1800 to 1820, with column headings and with various minor changes of title.

Md. Hist. Soc. has May 14–June 29, July 2, 4–Nov. 16, 25, Dec. 6–12, 1799; June 6–Dec. 31, 1800, fair; Jan. 1–7, 30–May 2, fair, Aug. 5, Sept. 4, 1801; July 7, 1804–Dec. 30, 1820.

Am. Antiq. Soc. has May 18, Nov. 20, 1799; Oct. 20, 1800; Jan. 17, 19, 26, Feb. 6, July 6–Dec. 15, 1801; Aug. 23, Sept. 4, 1802; Feb. 25, Dec. 7, 1804; Jan. 1–Dec. 31, 1805, fair; Jan. 3, 8, 11, 20, 23, 24, 29, Feb. 4, 5, Mar. 29, July 1, 1806–Feb. 15, 1808; Jan. 3–June 30, Sept. 19, Oct. 4, 5, 30, Dec. 28, 1809; July 3, 1810–Dec. 30, 1820, of the daily. Also Feb. 2, Apr. 13, 27, June 24, July 16, Aug. 14, Sept. 23, Nov. 23, 1801; July 12, Aug. 23, Sept. 3, Nov. 10, 22, 29, Dec. 3, 6, 17, 1802; Jan. 21, Aug. 1, 26, Sept. 30, Oct. 14, 19, Nov. 18, 21, Dec. 2, 23, 1803; Jan. 11, 23, Feb. 17, 29, Apr. 18, May 16, 21, Aug. 3, 24, 1804; Jan. 14, 28, Mar. 1, 1805; Jan. 19, Apr. 28, June 18, Aug. 25, 1806; Nov. 25, Dec. 21, 1807; June 9, 18, Oct. 19, 1808; July 10, Aug. 16, Oct. 18, 25, Nov. 17, Dec. 1, 29, 1810; Jan. 3, 5, 24, Feb. 12, 23, Mar. 5, June 22, July 16, 18, Aug. 13, 17, Sept. 3, 21, 24, Nov. 28, Dec. 10, 31, 1811; Jan. 30, July 24, Sept. 22, 1812; May 13, Oct. 26, Nov. 2, 30, Dec. 21, 1813; Jan. 6, 8, 22, Feb. 1, Mar. 1, Apr. 2, Aug. 20, Sept. 8, 10, 24, Oct. 8, Dec. 15, 1814; July 11, 1815, of the tri-weekly.

Peabody Inst., Baltimore, has Jan. 1, 1808–Dec. 30, 1820.

Harvard has of the daily, Dec. 28, 1799; Jan. 24, Apr. 22, 1800; Mar. 3, 23, Apr. 28–30, 1802; Jan. 10, 1803; Aug. 7–Nov. 13, 1804, fair; and of the tri-weekly, July 30, Nov. 14, Dec. 5, 1800; Jan. 19, 23, Feb. 23, June 26, 28, 1801; July 7, 1801–Jan. 23, 1809, fair.

Pratt Lib., Baltimore, has July 16, 1802; July 2–Dec. 31, 1805, fair; Jan. 1, 1807–Dec. 31, 1808; Apr. 8, 11–13, July 12–Oct. 3, 1809, fair; July 31, Aug. 21, 23, 27, 1810; Jan. 1–Dec. 31, 1811, fair; Jan. 1, 1812–Dec. 31, 1813; Jan. 1–June 30, July 14, Sept. 7, Dec. 10, 1814; July 15, 1815; Jan. 2, 1818–Dec. 30, 1820.

Wis. Hist. Soc. has Nov. 23, 1799–May 13, 1800; Jan. 1–June 30, 1806; June 13–Oct. 5, fair, Oct. 20, Nov. 8, 16, 22, 27, Dec. 1, 3, 8, 10, 22, 1810; Jan. 1–Feb. 18, 1811; Jan. 17, July 8, 1812; June 4, 9, 15, July 13, 1813; Jan. 1–June 30, 1814; Aug. 12, Dec. 16, 1815.

Lib. Congress has July 23, Dec. 24, 1807; Jan. 16, 18, Mar. 14, Apr. 4, 5, 18, Dec. 24, 1808; Apr. 1, June 6, July 4, 6, 7, 10, 11, Sept. 9–13, Oct. 2, 31, 1809; Feb. 10, Mar. 24, Apr. 6, 23, July 7–Dec. 31, 1810, fair; Jan. 2–Sept. 21, 1811, fair; Jan. 1–June 30, 1812; May 10, 28, 31, Aug. 11, Sept. 21, Oct. 13, 25, 26, 29, 1814; Aug. 10, 22, 23, 28, Sept. 4, Oct. 2, 5, 6, 28, 31, Nov. 4, Dec. 2, 6, 7, 11–16, 18–22, 1815; Jan. 11–Feb. 17, Mar. 16, June 8, July 29, Sept. 17, 19, 30, Oct. 2, 5, 7, Dec. 21, 28, 1816; Jan. 14, 21, 22, Mar. 4–8, 11, 21, 24, May 26, July 3, 4, 14, 29, 30, Aug. 8, 30, Sept. 10, 11, 15, 17–20, 29, Oct. 4, 7, 9, 31, Nov. 15, 18, Dec. 27, 31, 1817; Jan. 1, 1818–Dec. 29, 1820, fair.

N. Y. Pub. Lib. has Feb. 11, 1803; Feb. 20–June 19, 1805; Feb. 6–28, May 27–Sept. 12, 1806, fair; Jan. 29–Feb. 16, Nov. 3, Dec. 7–31, 1807, fair; Jan. 1–July 31, fair, Sept. 26, 1808; Jan. 9–28, Apr. 4, June 2–Dec. 29, 1809, fair; May 4, June 6, 16–18, July 7, 19, Sept. 4, 14, 26, 27, 1810; Jan. 26, Feb. 1, 2, 22, 25–Mar. 1, 5, 22, 23, 1811; Aug. 4, 5, 8, Sept. 21, 1812; also Nov. 14, 1800 of the tri-weekly.

N. Y. Hist. Soc. has Feb. 9, 18–Apr. 25, May 11, 12, 18–July 2, 21, Aug. 1, 2, 1803; July 6, 1810; Jan. 1–June 30, 1812; Feb. 25, 1813–June 30, 1814.

Mrs. Nelson Gutman, Baltimore, Md., has July 2, 1810–Dec. 31, 1811.

Mass. Hist. Soc. has Dec. 4, 1805; July 7, 9, 10, 17, 1807; May 14, 1811; Dec. 31, 1817; Oct. 22, 1818; Jan. 29, July 10, 1820.

Duke Univ. has Feb. 9–May 24, 1811, fair.

Many libraries have a few scattering or single issues.

[Baltimore] **American Farmer**, 1819–1820+.

Weekly. Established Apr. 2, 1819, by John S. Skinner. The paper was in a way a continuation of the "Maryland Censor," whose subscribers received the "American Farmer" until the termination of their subscriptions in August, 1819. No name of printer is given from Apr. 2 to Apr. 23, 1819; it was printed by Ebenezer French from Apr. 30 to June 18; no name from June 25 to July 26; by Ebenezer French from July 23 to Sept. 10; and by Joseph Robinson from Sept. 17, 1819, to Mar. 10, 1820. It was published throughout by John S. Skinner until after 1820, and was of quarto size, with pagination, title-page and index. Although more properly a magazine, it is included in this list, since the early issues, at least, contain current Baltimore news and death notices.

Files are to be found in nearly all of the larger historical libraries of the country.

[Baltimore] American Patriot, 1802–1803.

Weekly and tri-weekly. Established Sept. 18, 1802, printed and published by S. M'Crea [Samuel M'Crea] for the editor [Dennis Driscol], with the title of "American Patriot." A specimen number had been issued on Sept. 4, 1802, also with the numbering vol. 1, no. 1. No paper was issued from Dec. 18, 1802, to Jan. 11, 1803, upon which latter date it was brought out as a tri-weekly. Driscol sold out his interest and beginning with the issue of Apr. 16, 1803, the paper was published by M'Crea & Kennedy [Samuel M'Crea and Samuel Kennedy]. It was suspended for a short while after the issue of July 19, 1803, but was revived with the issue of Aug. 6, 1803, upon which latter date it was published by S. Kennedy. With the issue of Aug. 16, 1803, the title was changed to "American Patriot and Fell's Point Advertiser." The last issue located is that of Oct. 15, 1803, vol. 1, no. 125, in which it was announced that the paper would be issued as a daily during the ensuing week. There is no evidence to show that it was so issued.

Md. Hist. Soc. has Sept. 4, 25, 1802–Oct. 15, 1803.
Harvard has Sept. 4, Oct. 16–Nov. 6, 20, Dec. 4–18, 1802; Jan. 11–15, 20–25, 29, Feb. 8, 17–24, Mar. 3–8, 15–19, 26–31, Apr. 5–19, 23–26, 30–May 5, 10, 14–28, June 2–11, 16–21, 25, 30, July 2, 7–14, 19, Aug. 9, 27, Sept. 1–6, 15, 24, Oct. 4, 6, 1803.
Am. Antiq. Soc. has Nov. 20, 27, 1802; Mar. 8, 19, Apr. 5, 30, May 26, July 2, 14, 1803.
N. Y. State Lib. has Apr. 30, 1803.
Lib. Congress has June 7, 1803.
N. Y. Hist. Soc. has Aug. 20, 1803.

[Baltimore] City Gazette, 1797.

Daily. A continuation, but without change of numbering, of the "Baltimore Telegraphe." The change of title was made about Jan. 1, 1797 (see under the "Baltimore Telegraphe"), the full title being "City Gazette, and Daily Telegraphe," published by Clayland, Dobbin & Co. [Thomas E. Clayland and Thomas Dobbin]. Between Apr. 12 and June 22, 1797, the title was again changed to "The Telegraphe and Daily Advertiser," which see.

Am. Antiq. Soc. has Feb. 11, 18, 1797.
Harvard has Mar. 16–Apr. 12, 1797.

MARYLAND

Baltimore Correspondent, 1809.

No copy of this paper has been located and it is known only through the reprint of a poem "Aus dem Baltimore Correspondent" in the "Readinger Adler" of Feb. 21, 1809. Christian Cleim was the German printer in Baltimore in this year and may have printed the paper.

Baltimore Daily Intelligencer, 1793–1794.

Daily. Established Oct. 28, 1793, upon the foundation of the "Baltimore Daily Repository," continuing the advertisements and using the same type, but adopting the new title of "Baltimore Daily Intelligencer" and a new volume numbering. It was published by Yundt and Patton [Leonard Yundt and William Patton]. The last issue with this title was that of Oct. 29, 1794, vol. 1, no. 311, after which it was continued by the new firm of Yundt and Brown, as the "Federal Intelligencer," which see.

Md. Hist. Soc. has Oct. 28, 1793–Oct. 29, 1794.
Lib. Congress has Oct. 29, 1793–Oct. 29, 1794.
St. Louis Univ. has Oct. 29, 1793–June 23, 1794.
N. Y. Hist. Soc. has Oct. 28, 1793–Feb. 28, 1794.
Pratt Lib., Baltimore, has Dec. 19, 1793; Jan. 11, 24–Oct. 29, 1794, fair.
Univ. of Pittsburgh has Jan. 2–Oct. 29, 1794.
Am. Antiq. Soc. has Jan. 15–18, 22, 23, Apr. 12, 19, 30, May 1, 12–15, June 13, 25, July 30, 31, Aug. 25, 26, Sept. 4, 9, 17, Oct. 4, 25, 1794.
Peabody Inst., Baltimore, has Mar. 1–Oct. 29, 1794, fair.
Univ. of Chicago has Mar. 3–Oct. 26, 1794, fair.
Johns Hopkins Univ. has Jan. 2–Apr. 28, 1794.
Georgetown Univ. has June 2–30, 1794.
Univ. of Mich. (Clements) has July 25–Aug. 1, 1794.
N. Y. Pub. Lib. has Aug. 1, 2, 27, Sept. 16, 1794.
Hist. Soc. Penn. has Feb. 12, 1794.
N. Y. State Lib. has Sept. 29, 1794.
Buffalo Hist. Soc. has Oct. 18, 1794.

Baltimore Daily Repository, 1791–1793.

Daily. Established Oct. 24, 1791, by David Graham, with the title of "Baltimore Daily Repository." It was of quarto size. With the issue of Apr. 29, 1793, it was enlarged to folio size and published by D. Graham, L. Yundt and W. Patton [David Graham, Leonard Yundt and William Patton]. The last issue located is that of Oct. 19, 1793, vol. 2, no. 621, and it was probably discontinued with this issue, to be succeeded by the "Baltimore Daily Intelligencer," which see.

Md. Hist. Soc. has Oct. 26, 1791–Apr. 23, 29–Oct. 19, 1793.
Peabody Inst., Baltimore, has Oct. 24, 1791–Apr. 16, 1792.

Lib. Congress has Oct. 25, 1791–Aug. 30, 1792; Apr. 29–Oct. 19, 1793.
Am. Antiq. Soc. has Nov. 15, 16, Dec. 5, 6, 19, 20, 26, 27, 1791; Jan. 7, 19, 23, 27, Feb. 2, 20–22, 27, 28, Mar. 13, 15, 23, 24, Apr. 18, 19, May 7–10, 16, 17, 26–June 5, 8–23, 27, 28, 30–Dec. 31, 1792; Jan. 1–12, 15–Feb. 4, 6–22, 26, 28–Mar. 2, 5–9, 13–27, 29–Apr. 4, 8–19, 22–24, 26, 27, 30, May 2, 11, 16, 20, 23, 25, 30, June 4, 6, 8, 26, Aug. 24, 27, 29, Oct. 9, 10, 1793.
N. Y. Hist. Soc. has Feb. 2–Oct. 3, 1792.
Hist. Soc. Penn. has Feb. 17–Dec. 19, 1792; Sept. 18, Oct. 1, 1793.
Univ. of Mich. (Clements) has Dec. 31, 1791; Jan. 2–June 29, July 25, Aug. 17, 18, Oct. 19, 20, Dec. 22, 1792; Feb. 6, 7, Mar. 16, Apr. 1, 22, 23, June 22, Sept. 5, 1793.
Pratt Lib., Baltimore, has Jan. 7, 19; Feb. 2, Mar. 24, 27–28; Apr. 9, 14, 19–21, May 15; July 3–5, 11–17, 19, 23–25, 27–28; Aug. 1–3, 6–7, 13, 15–18, 27–30; Sept. 3–4, 6–7, 10–11, 13–15, 18–20, 26–29; Oct. 5–9, 12–18, 22–31; Nov. 2–Dec. 31, 1792; Jan. 1–Apr. 27, 1793.
Yale has Oct. 22, 1792–Apr. 22, 1793, fair.
Phil. Lib. Co. has Sept. 16–Oct. 1, 1793.
N. Y. State Lib. has May 10, 1793.

[Baltimore] **Democratic Republican, 1802.**

Weekly, semi-weekly and daily. Established Feb. 10, 1802, judging from the date of the first issue located, that of Mar. 17, 1802, vol. 1, no. 6. The full title was "The Democratic Republican; or, Anti-aristocrat," published weekly by Cornelius Firebrand, junior [John B. Colvin]. The paper was of quarto size and each issue was of 8 pages, with pagination. The imprint reads "Printed by Samuel Sower, for the Editor." With the issue of Apr. 7, 1802, the paper was issued semi-weekly, the size was enlarged to folio, and the number of pages reduced to four, the editor's address being signed by John B. Colvin. The issue of Apr. 10 bears the imprint "Printed by S. Sower for J. B. Colvin." With the issue of May 6, 1802, the paper was issued tri-weekly, and the issue of May 8 announced that Colvin would have the paper printed at his own house. The imprint then becomes "Printed & published by John B. Colvin." The last issue in this form was that of May 21, 1802, vol. 1, no. 23. After an interval of ten days, the paper was brought out in new form, the issue of May 31, 1802, being numbered vol. 1, no. 24. It bore the new title of "Democratic Republican; and Commercial Daily Advertiser," and was published by W. Pechin, "assisted in the editorial labors by J. B. Colvin." Although entitled a daily, it was June 15, 1802, before the paper was really issued daily. The last issue located is that of Aug. 13, 1802, vol. 1, no. 76. On Aug. 17, 1802, William Pechin and John B. Colvin took control of the "American."

Harvard has Mar. 17, 24, Apr. 7, 10, 21, May 6, 8, 15–21, 31, June 15–18, 21–30, July 2, 6, 8–12, 14, 17, 21–23, 26, 28–30, Aug. 2, 4, 5, 9–11, 13, 1802.

MARYLAND

[Baltimore] Dunlap's Maryland Gazette, 1775–1778.

Weekly. Established May 2, 1775, by John Dunlap under the title of "Dunlap's Maryland Gazette; or the Baltimore General Advertiser." The issue of July 11, 1775, was entitled "Dunlap's Maryland Gazette; Baltimore General Advertiser," but on July 18 it reverted to "Dunlap's Maryland Gazette; or, the Baltimore General Advertiser." In May and June, 1778, several issues were printed in reduced size because of scarcity of paper, and the title shortened to "Dunlap's Maryland Gazette." The last issue with the title of "Dunlap's Maryland Gazette; or, Baltimore General Advertiser" was on Sept. 8, 1778, vol. 4, no. 176. With the issue of Sept. 15, 1778, the paper was published by James Hayes, Junior, and the title changed to "The Maryland Gazette, and Baltimore General Advertiser," which see. Hayes then stated that he had carried on the business for Mr. Dunlap for "upwards of three years past."

Md. Hist. Soc. has May 2–Dec. 26, 1775; Jan. 2–May 28, June 19–Dec. 24, 1776; Feb. 11–July 29, Aug. 12–Sept. 23, Oct. 28, Nov. 4, 18–Dec. 23, 1777; Jan. 6–June 23, July 21–Aug. 18, Sept. 1, 8, 1778.
Pratt Lib., Baltimore, has July 11, 25, Aug. 8, 22–Nov. 14, 28–Dec. 12, 26, 1775; Jan. 2–Oct. 22, Nov. 5, 19, 26, Dec. 10–31, 1776; Jan. 7–21, Feb. 4–Sept. 30, Oct. 14–28, Nov. 11–Dec. 2, 16–30, 1777; Jan. 6–Sept. 8, 1778.
Wis. Hist. Soc. has Feb. 20, 1776.
Lib. Congress has July 23, Aug. 6, 1776.
British Museum has Apr. 21, May 5, 19, 26, Aug. 25–Sept. 8, 1778.
N. Y. Pub. Lib. has Sept. 8, 1778.

[Baltimore] Eagle of Freedom, 1796.

Tri-weekly. Established July 4, 1796, judging from the date of the first issue located, that of July 15, 1796, vol. 1, no. 6, published by Pechin & Wilmer [William Pechin and James J. Wilmer], under the title of "The Eagle of Freedom; or, the Baltimore Town & Fell's Point Gazette." The last issue located is that of July 27, 1796, vol. 1, no. 11.

Harvard has July 15, 20, 22, 27, 1796.
Phil. Lib. Co. has July 15, 20, 22, 25, 1796.

[Baltimore] Edwards's Baltimore Daily Advertiser, 1793–1794.

Daily. A continuation of "The Baltimore Evening Post," the change of title occurring in October, 1793. The numbering, however, was continuous. The earliest issue located of "Edwards's Baltimore Daily Advertiser" is that of Oct. 21, 1793, vol. 2, no. 394, published by Philip Edwards. This was the title through Oct. 4, 1794. The issue of Nov. 1, 1794, is entitled "Edwards's Balt. Daily Advertiser," the issues from Nov. 15 to 20, 1794 are entitled "Edwards's Balt Daily Advertiser," and that of Dec. 18, 1794, "Edwards's Daily Advertiser."

The last issue located is that of Dec. 18, 1794, vol. 3, no. 753, but on Jan. 1, 1795, Edwards bought an interest in the "Maryland Journal" and consolidated his paper with it.

> Am. Antiq. Soc. has Oct. 29, 31, Nov. 14, Dec. 24, 30, 31, 1793; Jan. 8, 9, 29, 30, Feb. 25, Apr. 21, 22, 30, May 1, 10, July 16, 18, Aug. 1, 18, 19, Oct. 3, 4, Nov. 1, 15, 1794.
> Md. Hist. Soc. has Nov. 8–18, 20, 21, 23–26, Dec. 4, 5, 9, 10, 12, 17–21, 24, 1793; Jan. 1–4, Feb. 8, 11, 12, Mar. 31, Apr. 2, May 20, July 25, Aug. 30, 1794.
> Pratt Lib., Baltimore, has July 2, 3, 9, Aug. 13, 16, Sept. 5–8, 10, 12, 29, 1794.
> Phil. Lib. Co. has Oct. 21, 1793.
> Lib. Congress has July 25, Nov. 19, 20, 1794.
> Buffalo Hist. Soc. has Oct. 1, 1794.
> N. Y. Pub. Lib. has Dec. 18, 1794.

[Baltimore] Edwards's Daily Advertiser, see Edwards's Baltimore Daily Advertiser.

Baltimore Evening Post, 1792–1793.

Daily. Established July 13, 1792, by Philip Edwards, with the title of "The Baltimore Evening Post." With the issue of July 31, 1792, the title was changed to "The Baltimore Evening Post and Daily Advertiser." With the issue of Oct. 24, 1792, Edwards changed the title to "The Baltimore Morning Post and Daily Advertiser," which title he kept for only two days, publishing a morning issue on Oct. 25, and then in the evening of Oct. 25 returning to his former title. With the issue of Oct. 30, 1792, the title was shortened to "The Baltimore Evening Post." In October, 1793, the title was changed to "Edwards's Baltimore Daily Advertiser," which see. There was no change in the numbering, the issue of "The Baltimore Evening Post" of Sept. 30, 1793, being vol. 2, no. 378, and that of "Edwards's Baltimore Daily Advertiser" of Oct. 21, 1793, being vol. 2, no. 394.

> Am. Antiq. Soc. has July 13–Dec. 31, 1792; Jan. 11, 12, 14, Mar. 2, Apr. 25, 27, July 18–20, 1793.
> Lib. Congress has July 28, 1792.
> Pratt Lib., Baltimore, has Sept. 27, Oct. 3, Nov. 30, 1792.
> Phil. Lib. Co. has Sept. 17–19, 21, 24, 27–30, 1793.

Baltimore Evening Post, 1805–1811.

Daily. Established Mar. 25, 1805, by J. Cook & Co. [John Cook and George Bourne], under the title of "Baltimore Evening Post: Mercantile Daily Advertiser." With the issue of June 10, 1805, the title was shortened to "Baltimore

MARYLAND 231

Evening Post." Cook sold out his interest to George Bourne, who began publishing the paper with the issue of Aug. 31, 1805. With the issue of Nov. 27, 1805, the paper was published by Hezekiah Niles. Leonard Frailey was admitted to partnership and with the issue of Sept. 8, 1806, the paper was published by Niles & Frailey. With the issue of July 11, 1809, Frailey withdrew from the firm, and the paper was again published by Hezekiah Niles. The paper was transferred to Thomas Wilson, who began publishing it with the issue of June 11, 1811. The last issue was that of June 22, 1811, vol. 13, no. 78, after which it was changed to a morning paper and the title altered to "The Sun," which see. A country paper was also issued tri-weekly, with the column heading of "Baltimore Evening Post."

Md. Hist. Soc. has Mar. 25, 1805–June 22, 1811.
N. Y. Hist. Soc. has Mar. 25–Dec. 17, 1805; Sept. 25, 1806–Mar. 21, 1807; July 2–Dec. 31, 1810.
Lib. Congress has Mar. 25–May 29, 1806; Mar. 21–Sept. 14, 1808; Aug. 1, 1809–Jan. 31, 1810; Sept. 26, 1810–June 10, 1811 of the daily; May 26, June 2, Nov. 25, Dec. 11, 1807; Apr. 9, May 14, 17, 21, 1808; Aug. 19, Nov. 9, Dec. 9, 23, 1809; Feb. 3, 6, Mar. 10, May 31, July 5, 12, Aug. 28, 1810, of the tri-weekly.
British Museum has Mar. 25, 1805–Mar. 17, 1808; Sept. 27, 1809–Dec. 31, 1810.
Pratt Lib., Baltimore, has Jan. 1–June 30, 1806, fair; Jan. 14, July 9, 30, Sept. 18, Oct. 2, 1807; Aug. 18, 24, 25, 31–Sept. 29, 1808, fair; Jan. 2–Dec. 31, 1809, fair; Feb. 23–Apr. 19, 1811, fair.
Harvard has Mar. 25, 1805–Dec. 31, 1808, tri-weekly, fair.
Peabody Lib., Baltimore, has Mar. 25, 1805–Mar. 31, 1806, fair; Sept. 29–Dec. 29, 1808.
Loyola Coll., Baltimore, has Mar. 25–Dec. 31, 1805.
Phil. Lib. Co. has Aug. 29, 1807–Sept. 1, 1810, of the tri-weekly; and Jan. 1–June 30, 1810, of the daily.
N. Y. Pub. Lib. has Mar. 25–June 24, 1805; June 2, Sept. 5, 1806; Mar. 22, 23, 28, Apr. 14, May 4, 26, June 6, 9, 27, July 16, 30, Aug. 4, 24, 30, Sept. 6, 30, Dec. 16, 1808; Jan. 4, Feb. 15, 20, Mar. 23, Apr. 8, 11, 19, 20, May 1, 4, 26, June 6, 9, 27, July 16–31, 1809.
Wis. Hist. Soc. has Sept. 27, 1808–Mar. 24, 1809; Mar. 25–Nov. 30, 1810; May 4, 1811.
Hist. Soc. Penn. has Aug. 1, 1809–Mar. 13, 1810; Mar. 5–May 31, 1811.
Am. Antiq. Soc. has Mar. 25, 28, Aug. 19, 26, 28, 29, 1805; Mar. 28–Dec. 30, 1809; Aug. 22, 1810, of the daily; and Feb. 22, Aug. 12, 21, Sept. 2, 11, 27, Oct. 4, 28, Nov. 1, 20, 1806; Jan. 3, 13, 24, 27, Feb. 10, 17, Mar. 17, 21, 26, 28, Apr. 11, 14, May 19, June 6, 9, July 28, Oct. 6, 1807; Mar. 12, Apr. 19, June 28, Nov. 8, Dec. 15, 17, 31, 1808; Feb. 16, 25, Mar. 28, June 15, 22–27, July 1, 13, 15, 22, Aug. 10, 24, 29, Sept. 23, 26, Dec. 5, 28, 1809; Jan. 4, 11, 18, 23, 25, Feb. 15, Mar. 27, May 5, 9, 15, 19, June 2, 7, 30, July 14, 31,

Sept. 1, Oct. 18, Nov. 3, 8, Dec. 22, 1810; Jan. 3, Apr. 16, 18, May 11, 1811, of the tri-weekly.

Boston Pub. Lib. has Jan. 1–June 30, 1810.

Univ. of Chicago has July 8, 1806; Mar. 23, July 8, Sept. 23, 29, 1807.

N. Y. State Lib. has Dec. 6, 29, 31, 1807; Sept. 30, Dec. 24, 1808; Jan. 5, Feb. 14, 1809; May 17, 1810; Apr. 13, 1811 of the tri-weekly.

Howard-Tilton Lib., New Orleans, has June 27, 28, Dec. 30, 31, 1808; Apr. 27, 1811.

Joseph Katz, Baltimore, has June 2–Sept. 24, 1806; June 2–Sept. 24, 1810.

Mrs. Nelson Gutman, Baltimore, Md., has Jan. 2–June 22, 1811.

[Baltimore] **Federal Gazette,** 1796–1820+.

Daily. A continuation, but without change of numbering, of the "Federal Intelligencer," the change of title occurring with the issue of Jan. 1, 1796, vol. 4, no. 673, published by Yundt & Brown [Leonard Yundt and Matthew Brown], with the title of "Federal Gazette & Baltimore Daily Advertiser." This firm dissolved and with the issue of Jan. 1, 1807, the paper was published by John Hewes. It was then transferred to William Gwynn, who began publishing it with the issue of Jan. 1, 1813, and continued it until after 1820. A country paper, tri-weekly, was also issued, certainly from 1807 to after 1820.

Md. Hist. Soc. has Jan. 1, 1796–Dec. 30, 1820.

Peabody Lib., Baltimore, has Jan. 1, 1796–Dec. 31, 1813; July 1, 1814–Dec. 30, 1815; July 1, 1816–Dec. 31, 1818; July 1, 1819–Dec. 30, 1820.

Lib. Congress has Jan. 2, 1796–Dec. 31, 1799; Jan. 2–Feb. 17, July 1–Dec. 31, 1800; Feb. 9, Mar. 9–June 30, Aug. 4–Dec. 29, 1801; Jan. 1, 1803–Dec. 31, 1813; Apr. 23, 25, May 18, 21, 23, June 1, Aug. 24, 1814; Aug. 16, 17, 23, 30, Sept. 6, Oct. 4, 5, 1816; Apr. 27, 1818; Jan. 25, Feb. 6, 1819; Jan. 22, 26, Oct. 6, Nov. 8, 1820. Also June 12, 29, Aug. 24, Nov. 24, 25, 30, Dec. 3, 1807; Apr. 12, 1811; July 7, 1812; and Oct. 28, 1814 of the tri-weekly.

Pratt Lib., Baltimore, has Jan. 1, 1796–Dec. 27, 1799; Feb. 18, July 1–Dec. 31, 1800, fair; July 1–Dec. 31, 1802; July 26, 1803; Jan. 3–Mar. 31, 1804, July 1–Dec. 31, 1805, fair; Jan. 24, Mar. 17, July 23, 1807; Nov. 7, 1808–Dec. 30, 1809; Feb. 22, Mar. 17, 30, 31, Oct. 6, 11, Dec. 4, 21, 1810; Jan. 1–May 27, June 14, 1811; Mar. 4, June 20, 1812; Oct. 29, 1814; Aug. 2, 1815; Jan. 1, 1816–Dec. 31, 1817; Nov. 9, 15, 1808; Jan. 24, Nov. 23, 1809; Mar. 25, Aug. 9, 1817; Nov. 19–Dec. 31, 1818; Jan. 2–Feb. 23, May 4, 13, 1819; Feb. 8, 1820, of the tri-weekly.

Univ. of Pittsburgh has Jan. 2–Dec. 31, 1796; July 5, 1797–June 26, 1799; July 1, 1801–June 30, 1802; Jan. 1, 1803–June 30, 1804; Jan. 1–June 30, 1806; Jan. 1–Dec. 31, 1807; Sept. 1, 1809–Feb. 26, 1810.

Wis. Hist. Soc. has Jan. 1–Dec. 31, 1796; Jan. 7–Dec. 30, 1797; July 1–31, Aug. 12–Dec. 31, 1799; Jan. 1–Dec. 31, 1801; Jan. 19–Mar. 31, fair; Apr. 13, 16, 23, May 26, 27, Dec. 8–30, 1802; Jan. 1–June 30, 1803; Jan. 2–June 30,

MARYLAND

1804; Nov. 10–Dec. 31, 1808; July 2, 1810–June 29, 1811; Feb. 3, Mar. 6, May 1, 1816; Apr. 13–May 31, July 1–Oct. 31, 1820.
British Museum has Jan. 1–Dec. 31, 1796; Jan. 1–July 1, 1805; Jan. 1–Dec. 31, 1806; July 1, 1807–June 30, 1808; Jan. 2, 1809–Dec. 31, 1810; July 1, 1811–June 30, 1812; Jan. 1–June 30, 1813; Jan. 1, 1814–June 30, 1815; July 1, 1816–June 30, 1817; Jan. 1–June 30, 1818; Jan. 1, 1819–Dec. 30, 1820.
Hist. Soc. Penn. has July 1, 1796–Dec. 30, 1804.
N. Y. Hist. Soc. has Jan. 1–June 30, 1796; Sept. 25, 1797–Nov. 23, 1798, fair; July 21–Dec. 31, 1807; May 8, 1809–Feb. 24, 1813.
Yale has Jan. 1–June 30, Nov. 7, 1796; Dec. 13, 1798–Apr. 24, 1799; July 1–Dec. 30, 1803; Jan. 1, 1806–Dec. 31, 1807; Dec. 12, 1815.
Univ. of Chicago has Mar. 29, 1796–Dec. 29, 1797, fair; Jan. 3–June 29, 1799, fair; Mar. 27, 29, Apr. 11, 12, 1806; July 3, 25, 28, Nov. 2, 4, 9, Dec. 3, 1807; Nov. 24, 25, 1818.
N. Y. Pub. Lib. has Jan. 1, 1796–Mar. 10, 1797; Jan. 1, 18, Mar. 2, Apr. 24, 1799; Dec. 15, 16, 1803; Dec. 24, 1804; July 29, 1808.
Boston Pub. Lib. has July 18–Dec. 31, 1800; Jan. 2, 1804–June 30, 1805; Jan. 1, 1806–Dec. 30, 1807; Jan. 2, 1809–Dec. 31, 1812; Jan. 1–June 30, 1819.
Am. Antiq. Soc. has Jan. 1–June 30, Oct. 8, Nov. 11, 1796; Feb. 10, 11, 23, Mar. 14–Dec. 30, 1797, fair; Jan. 3, 6–Mar. 7, 16, 29, Apr. 24, 26, 27, May 5, June 21, Aug. 30, Sept. 1, 3, 18, Oct. 2, 9, 25, Nov. 6, 1798; Jan. 1–Dec. 31, 1799; Mar. 26, Apr. 25–Dec. 13, 30, 31, 1800; Jan. 1, 2, 5, 10, 17, 20, Feb. 3, 5, 7–28, Apr. 27, May 16, 1801; Mar. 6, 1804; Feb. 28, 1805; Feb. 8, Aug. 21, Nov. 11, Dec. 4–31, 1806; Jan. 4–May 28, June 13–17, 21, 1808; Apr. 13, Dec. 6, 1809; Feb. 8, 9, Mar. 8, May 18, Aug. 24, 25, Sept. 1, 22, 1810; Jan. 8, Feb. 2, 4, Mar. 16, Sept. 27, 1811; Mar. 6, Apr. 8, 20, July 3, 9, 1812; Mar. 19, 1813; Dec. 26, 1814; Jan. 25, July 18, Oct. 27, 1815; Aug. 6, 1819. Also Apr. 7, 12, 1808; Jan. 21, July 7, 1812; Feb. 16, Nov. 19, 1816; Jan. 15, 1817; May 28, Aug. 28, 1818; Jan. 28, June 29, July 1, 3, 1819 of tri-weekly.
Univ. of Mich. (Clements) has Feb. 19, Apr. 6, 8, 11, 12, 16, May 2–5, 9–11, 18, July 15, 28, Nov. 4, 8, 10–Dec. 30, 1796, fair; Jan. 3–June 30, fair, Sept. 30, Oct. 3, Nov. 16, Dec. 2, 30, 1797, fair; Jan. 3–Dec. 31, 1798, fair; July 1–Dec. 31, 1799, fair; July 7, 1812.
N. Y. State Lib. has Jan. 1–May 9, June 24, July 13, 14, Sept. 21, 1796; July 3–Dec. 30, 1797; Jan. 1–June 28, 1799; Apr. 2–June 30, 1804; Jan. 1–Mar. 2, 1807; Feb. 6, 10, Aug. 11, 15, 19, 1809; July 27, Aug. 1, 6, Sept. 12, 29, 1810; July 21, 1812.
Boston Athenæum has Jan. 3, 1806–Dec. 31, 1808.
Loyola Coll., Baltimore, has Jan. 2–June 27, 1800; Feb. 1–June 9, 1804.
Harvard has Jan. 4–Mar. 31, 1796; Feb. 16, Mar. 18, Apr. 3, 4, 10, Aug. 15, 18, 26, Oct. 6, 7, 17, 1797; Jan. 20, 28, Sept. 1, 17, 18, 1798; July 24, 1799; Nov. 6, 29, 1800; Apr. 6–Dec. 31, 1801, fair; Jan. 2–15, Feb. 13, Mar. 23, Sept. 11, Oct. 11, 12, 15, Dec. 23, 1802; Jan. 7, May 14, 17, 25, June 3, 10, 14, 27, July 16, 27, 29, Sept. 4, Nov. 1, 5, 7, 10, 1803; Jan. 26, 27, June 16, 29, Sept. 4,

Nov. 1, 1804; Jan. 3, June 28, 1805; Aug. 20, Sept. 1, 6, 11, 12, 17, 30, Oct. 7, 15, 23, 27, 29, Nov. 4, 7, 10, 11, 26, 28, Dec. 1, 4, 10, 15, 1806; Jan. 9, 13, 19, Feb. 5, 9, 20, 28, Mar. 10, 16, 30, Apr. 21, 1807.

Chicago Hist. Soc. has Jan. 1–30, 1799; Jan. 8, 1811–Nov. 28, 1812, fair.

Charleston Lib. Soc. has Jan. 2–Dec. 30, 1797.

Duke Univ. has Jan. 1, 1796–Dec. 30, 1797, fair; Mar. 29, Aug. 26, Dec. 3, 4, 1799; Dec. 10, 26, 1804; Jan. 1–June 29, 1805; Aug. 30–Nov. 5, 1808; July 11, 15–18, 22–26, 29, Aug. 9, 10, 1814; Aug. 1–6, Sept. 22, 1818.

Phil. Lib. Co. has Jan. 18, 25–Feb. 2, Mar. 4, 16–Apr. 30, May 18, June 2–Aug. 11, 1796; Dec. 12, 1811–Mar. 6, 1812, fair.

Johns Hopkins Univ. has Jan. 11–Dec. 31, 1799; Apr. 2, 15, 18, 20–30, 1803; July 5–Dec. 27, 1815.

Goucher College, Baltimore has May 20, 1807; May 25, June 15, 1810; Sept. 9, 23, Nov. 5, 1811; Apr. 18, May 6, 9, 19, June 8, 10, 17, 18, 20, 26, Sept. 29, Nov. 21, 1812; Apr. 1–Dec. 30, 1815, fair; Feb. 1, 3, 5, Mar. 15–May 31, 1816, fair; Feb. 5, 7, 8, Mar. 4, 5, May 5, 8, 9, 21–31, June 24, July 12, 22, 1817; May 9, July 22, Sept. 30, 1818; Feb. 5, Apr. 16, 1819.

Martin Memorial Lib., York, Pa., has Jan. 2–June 30, 1800.

Univ. of Va. has Jan. 1–Feb. 26, 1803; Dec. 14, 1804.

Several libraries have single or scattering issues.

[Baltimore] **Federal Intelligencer,** 1794–1795.

Daily. A continuation, but without change of numbering, of the "Baltimore Daily Intelligencer," the change of title occurring with the issue of Oct. 30, 1794, vol. 2, no. 312. The full title was "Federal Intelligencer, and Baltimore Daily Gazette." Published by Yundt and Brown [Leonard Yundt and Matthew Brown]. The last issue with this title was that of Dec. 30, 1795, vol. 3, no. 672, the paper being continued as the "Federal Gazette," which see.

Md. Hist. Soc. has Oct. 30, 1794–Dec. 30, 1795.

Pratt Lib., Baltimore, has Oct. 30, 1794–Dec. 30, 1795.

Am. Antiq. Soc. has Nov. 13, 20, Dec. 22, 30, 1794; Jan. 1–Dec. 30, 1795.

Lib. Congress has Oct. 30–Dec. 30, 1794; Jan. 1–Mar. 18, 20–Sept. 1, 3, 7, 9–15, 19–Oct. 1, 3–8, 10–15, 17–29, 31–Nov. 9, Dec. 9, 21, 1795.

Univ. of Chicago has Oct. 30–Dec. 30, 1794.

Peabody Lib., Baltimore, has Oct. 30–Nov. 17, 19–25, 27–Dec. 1, 3–14, 16–30, 1794; Jan. 1–Dec. 30, 1795.

Univ. of Pittsburgh has Oct. 30–Dec. 10, 1794.

N. Y. Hist. Soc. has Dec. 27, 1794; Jan. 2–June 29, 1795.

Boston Athenæum has July 2–Dec. 30, 1795.

Hist. Soc. Penn. has July 2–Dec. 30, 1795.

Univ. of Mich. (Clements) has Jan. 1–Feb. 21, 24–Mar. 17, 23–26, 28–Apr. 11, 14–May 5, June 18–22, July 29, 30, Aug. 5, 26, Sept. 15, Nov. 6, Dec. 28, 1795.

Wis. Hist. Soc. has Nov. 1–Dec. 31, 1794; July 14, 22, 29, 31, Aug. 1, Sept. 2, Oct. 6, 14, 19, 27, 30, 31, Nov. 11, Dec. 3, 15, 24, 1795.
N. Y. Pub. Lib. has Dec. 19, 22, 1794; Jan. 23, 26, 30, Feb. 18, 24, Mar. 3, 5, 9, 11, 17, 24, 26, 27, 30, Apr. 8, 10, 13, 18, 20, 23, 24, May 7, 16, 20, June 6, 15, 1795.
Joseph Katz, Baltimore, has Mar. 9, 10, Apr. 25, June 25–30, July 3, 7, 9, 10, 21, Aug. 25, 27–29, Nov. 4, 5, 13–21, Dec. 25, 26, 30, 1795.
N. Y. State Lib. has Nov. 7–Dec. 30, 1795.
Harvard has Apr. 9, June 11–25, 1795.
Phil. Lib. Co. has Aug. 24, Oct. 15, 26, 27, 30, Nov. 3, 13, 14, 19–Dec. 1, 8–10, 1795.
Va. Hist. Soc. has Jan. 13, Oct. 27, 30, 31, 1795.
Duke Univ. has June 24, Nov. 2, 3, 7, 10, Dec. 18, 23, 1795.
Univ. of Va. has Mar. 12, 1795.
Huntington Lib. has Dec. 26, 1795.

[Baltimore] **Federal Republican,** 1808–1812, 1816–1820+.

Tri-weekly and daily. Established July 4, 1808, under the title of "Federal Republican & Commercial Gazette," printed and published for the Proprietors [Alexander C. Hanson and Jacob Wagner] by Joseph Robinson. From Apr. 5 to Apr. 21, 1809, no printer's name was given. Although announced as a daily, it was published as a tri-weekly until Apr. 24, 1809, when a daily and tri-weekly country paper were issued. With this issue, moreover, it was printed and published for the Proprietors by John L. Cook. With the issue of Oct. 5, 1809, it was united with the "North American." The name of "Federal Republican & Commercial Gazette" was retained, but a new volume numbering was adopted and the name of printer was omitted. Thomas states in his 1810 list that the paper was published for the proprietors by Wagner & Hanson [Jacob Wagner and Alexander C. Hanson], and the Baltimore Directories of 1810 and 1812 give Jacob Wagner as editor of the Federal Republican. Hanson was a proprietor from 1808 to 1819. Because of the demolition of its office by a mob on June 22, 1812, the paper was removed to Georgetown, D. C., where it was published for nearly four years (see under District of Columbia — Georgetown). The last issue published at Baltimore was that of June 22, 1812, vol. 6, no. 844, and the first at Georgetown, June 27, vol. 6, no. 845. The last issue published at Georgetown was that of Apr. 3, 1816, vol. 12, no. 1756. With the issue of Apr. 4, 1816, the paper was united with the "Baltimore Telegraph" under the new title of "Federal Republican and Baltimore Telegraph" published in Baltimore by Paul Allen & Co. It adopted a new volume numbering and issued a daily, also a semi-weekly country paper, the latter with the regular title and a numbering of its own. With the issue of Dec. 2, 1816, the paper was published by Allen, Edes, & Co., it being announced that Messrs. Allen & Hanson [Paul Allen and Alexander C. Hanson] had purchased of Thomas H. Hill his share in the paper, and had taken in Benjamin Edes as partner. With the issue of Aug. 14, 1818, the paper was published by Benjamin Edes & Co. With the issue of Jan. 4, 1819, the paper was published by Benj. Edes & Jas. P. Heath, it being announced that Heath had purchased from A. C. Hanson his one-third interest in the paper. With the issue of Feb. 22, 1820, Heath retired and the paper was published by Benjamin Edes. Continued after 1820.

 Am. Antiq. Soc. has of the regular issue July 4, 1808–Dec. 31, 1810; Jan. 1–Apr. 4, Oct. 5–Dec. 31, 1811; Jan. 1–Mar. 11, Apr. 3, 4, 7, 17, June 18, 1812; Apr. 27, Oct. 5–Dec. 28, 1816; Jan. 1–June 30, Nov. 7, 1817; July 15, Aug. 14, 1818; Jan. 1–Nov. 24, 1819. Also of the country issue Apr. 25, 1809–Dec. 29, 1810; Jan. 1, Mar. 28, Sept. 26, 1811; Jan. 2–June 20, 1812; Apr. 13, 17, 24, 27–May 22, June 5, 12, 15, 26, 29, July 13, 17, 31, Aug. 10–21, Sept. 14, 25, Oct. 2, 8, 18, 29, Nov. 1, 15–22, Dec. 3, 10, 20, 24, 1816; Jan. 2, 28, Feb. 11, June 3, Nov. 4, 1817; Mar. 3, July 31, Aug. 14, Sept. 4, 11, 22, 25, Oct. 9, 13, Nov. 10, 17, 20, 1818; Jan. 7, Feb. 18–25, May 5, 26, Oct. 3, 1820.

 Md. Hist. Soc. has July 6, 27, Aug. 8–15, 19, 22, 26, Sept. 2, 9–14, 21, Oct. 10, 19, 21, 28, 31, Nov. 11, Dec. 5, 1808; Jan. 23, June 5, 19–Dec. 29, 1809, fair; Jan. 1, 1810–June 22, 1812; Apr. 4, 1816–Dec. 31, 1817; Jan. 4, 25, 27, Feb. 11, 1819; Nov. 3, 1820.

 N. Y. Pub. Lib. has July 29, Aug. 26, Sept. 14, Oct. 3–7, Nov. 14–Dec. 30, 1808; Jan. 2, 1809–June 20, 1812.

 Pratt Lib., Baltimore, has Nov. 28, 1808–July 25, 1809; Sept. 23, Oct. 19, 21, 1809; Jan. 1–Dec. 31, 1810; Jan. 1–Dec. 31, 1811, fair; Jan. 1–Apr. 30, May 25–30, June 17–22, Aug. 3–12, 1812; Sept. 28, 1816; May 12, 1818; Jan. 4, 25, 27, Feb. 11, Mar. 18, 20, Apr. 3, 9, 17, 1819; July 25, Oct. 13, 17, 1820. Also of the country issue July 1, Sept. 12–Dec. 30, 1810, fair; Jan. 2–9, 25, 27, Feb. 1, 6–15, 27, Mar. 1, Oct. 4, Dec. 8, 1810; May 26, 1812.

 Wis. Hist. Soc. has July 20, Aug. 19, 22, Dec. 12, 16, 23, 26, 1808; Jan. 1–Dec. 31, 1810; Dec. 4, 5, 20, 21, 27, 28, 1811; Jan. 1–June 20, 1812, fair; Jan. 3, 1817–Dec. 30, 1820, fair.

 N. Y. Hist. Soc. has Oct. 5, 1809–Dec. 31, 1810; Apr. 6, 1816–Apr. 4, 1820, fair.

 Lib. Congress has of the regular issue Jan. 16–Dec. 28, 1809; Jan. 2–4, 8, 20, Feb. 2, 8, Mar. 17, 20, 22, June 29, July 30, Aug. 1, Sept. 17, 1810; Jan. 14, 1811; Feb. 4, 1812; Dec. 31, 1816–Aug. 20, 1817; Apr. 17, 21, 24, May 1, June 19, 30, July 17, 21, 31, Aug. 4, 18, 25, Sept. 1, Dec. 8, 1818; Jan. 11, May 18, June 2, Aug. 5, 1819; Nov. 28, 1820. Also of the country issue June 23, July 1, Oct. 2, 1809; Oct. 20, 1809–Jan. 31, 1812; Feb. 8, 15, Mar. 31, 1812; Apr. 6–Nov. 29, 1816; Jan. 10, 1817–Mar. 31, 1818.

 Dartmouth has July 6, 15–25, Aug. 5–10, Sept. 21, 1808; May 29, 1810–June 20, 1812; Oct. 13, 27, 29, Nov. 8–Dec. 15, 1813, all tri-weekly.

 Peabody Lib., Baltimore, has Oct. 5, 1809–Dec. 31, 1811.

 Boston Athenæum has Jan. 2, 1809–Dec. 31, 1810, partly daily and partly tri-weekly; Feb. 4, 7, 1811; also Jan. 3, 1817–Dec. 11, 1818 of the country paper.

MARYLAND 237

N. Y. Soc. Lib. has Dec. 15, 1809–Jan. 9, 1810.
Boston Pub. Lib. has Dec. 18, 1810–Feb. 9, 1811, fair; Feb. 19, Nov. 19, Dec. 12, 1811; Jan. 29, 31, Mar. 2, 3, 24, 29, 30, 1812.
Univ. of Chicago has Oct. 5, 1811–Apr. 6, 1812; Feb. 10, June 2, 1818.
Univ. of Mich. (Clements) has Apr. 20, Nov. 1, Dec. 6–10, 1816; Jan. 24–31, May 6, Aug. 1, Sept. 30, Nov. 7–11, 18–25, Dec. 9, 1817; Jan. 2–6, Feb. 3, May 5, June 2, 12, July 28, Aug. 4–7, Sept. 11, 25–29, Oct. 6, 16–20, Nov. 3, 1818; Jan. 19, Feb. 9, Mar. 30, July 6–9, Nov. 23, 30, 1819; Feb. 18, 1820, all semi-weekly; Feb. 27, 1809; Apr. 4–Sept. 30, 1817, daily.
Harvard has July 20–25, Aug. 8, 24, Oct. 10, 12, Dec. 14, 1808.
Ohio Arch. & Hist. Soc. has Apr. 6–Dec. 31, 1816, fair, country edition.
Lehigh Univ. has May 9–Nov. 28, 1820, country edition.
Mass. Hist. Soc. has May 4, 1816; Dec. 7, 1818; Dec. 11, 1819; May 6, 1820.
Yale has Jan. 18, 30, 1809.
Goucher College, Baltimore, has June 8, 1810; May 13, 1812.
N. Y. State Lib. has Aug. 26, 1817.
Filson Club, Louisville, has July 20, Oct. 1, 1819.

[Baltimore] Fell's-Point Telegraphe, 1795.

Tri-weekly. Established Mar. 4, 1795, according to the first issue located, that of Mar. 6, 1795, vol. 1, no. 2, published by John W. Allen, with the title of "Fell's-Point Telegraphe." It was of quarto size. The last issue located is that of June 1, 1795, vol. 1, no. 39, with which issue the title was altered to "Fells-Point Telegraph." The paper was undoubtedly soon thereafter discontinued, as Allen became a joint editor of the "Maryland Journal," June 18, 1795.

Harvard has Mar. 6, 9, May 13, 1795.
Am. Antiq. Soc. has Mar. 13, Apr. 17, 20, May 20, 29, June 1, 1795.

[Baltimore, German Newspaper] 1786.

No copy of this paper has been located, nor is its name known, but its existence is authenticated by the following advertisement in the "Maryland Journal" of June 16, 1786. "The subscriber respectfully informs his Friends in particular, and the Public in general, that he commenced the Publication of his German Newspaper Yesterday, and intends to continue it Weekly. Subscriptions for the same, are taken in by him, at his Printing-Office in Market-Street, nearly opposite the Green-Tree, at the small Price of Ten Shillings per Annum; Five Shillings of which is paid at the time of Subscribing, the better to enable him to prosecute his Undertaking. All Kinds of Printing, in the German, performed, by Henry Dulheuer. Baltimore, June 15, 1786."

Baltimore Intelligencer, 1798–1799.

Tri-weekly. Established by William Pechin, Mar. 7, 1798. The paper was of quarto size and the full title was "The Baltimore Intelligencer." The issue of

Mar. 7, 1798, is vol. 1, no. 1, and that of June 4, 1798, is vol. 1, no. 39, but that of Oct. 31, 1798, is vol. 3, no. 103. Possibly Pechin made his volume numbering refer to the establishment of his "Eagle of Freedom," begun in 1796. The last issue located is that of Jan. 26, 1799, vol. 3, no. 140, although the paper was undoubtedly continued to May, 1799, when it was transferred to Alexander Martin, who began publishing the "American," May 14, 1799. Martin states in his initial issue that he is distributing his paper to the former subscribers of the "Intelligencer," lately conducted by Mr. Pechin.

Md. Hist. Soc. has Mar. 7–Apr. 11, 16–June 4, 1798.
Am. Antiq. Soc. has Mar. 30, Dec. 12, 1798; Jan. 12, 1799.
Harvard has Oct. 31, Nov. 12, Dec. 3, 10, 27, 1798; Jan. 15, 26, 1799.

[Baltimore] **Journal of the Times**, 1818–1819.

Weekly. Established Sept. 12, 1818, with the title of "Journal of the Times," published by Schaeffer & Maund [Frederick G. Schaeffer and Thomas Maund], and edited by Paul Allen. It was an octavo, each issue containing sixteen numbered pages. It was strictly a magazine without advertisements or local news, and the only reason for including it here was because of its journalistic title and the fact that it featured a weekly summary of national news. It was discontinued with the issue of Mar. 6, 1819, vol. 1, no. 26, and was superseded on Apr. 8, 1819, by a daily paper entitled the "Morning Chronicle," with the same printers and editor.

Am. Antiq. Soc., Lib. Congress, Md. Hist. Soc., Peabody Lib., Johns Hopkins, N. Y. State Lib., N. Y. Pub. Lib., Boston Pub. Lib., Boston Athenæum, Mass. Hist. Soc., Harvard, Univ. of Mich., and other libraries have files of this publication.

[Baltimore] **Maryland Censor**, 1818–1819.

Weekly. Established Aug. 19, 1818, by William F. Redding. The "Frederick-Town Herald" of Sept. 19, 1818, reprinting from the "Easton Gazette" and referring to the establishment of the "Maryland Censor," said "there is little doubt but that the Maryland Censor is nothing more or less than the famous and infamous People's Advocate, published in that city during the warmly contested election of 1816, resuscitated and furnished with a new name and appendage." The last issue located is that of Feb. 3, 1819, vol. 1, no. 25, and the paper was discontinued soon afterwards, as its office was bought out by the "American Farmer," the first number of which was published Apr. 2, 1819.

Am. Antiq. Soc. has Aug. 19, 26, Sept. 2, 16, 30, Oct. 21, 28, Nov. 11–25, 1818; Jan. 20, 1819.
Md. Hist. Soc. has Sept. 9, 16, 30–Dec. 30, 1818; Jan. 27, Feb. 3, 1819.
Lib. Congress has Aug. 19, 1818.

Wis. Hist. Soc. has Dec. 16, 1818.
Univ. of Chicago has Jan. 5, 1819.

[Baltimore] **Maryland Gazette,** 1778–1779, 1783–1792.

Weekly and semi-weekly. A continuation of "Dunlap's Maryland Gazette." The first issue with the new title of "The Maryland Gazette, and Baltimore General Advertiser" appeared on Sept. 15, 1778, vol. 4, no. 177, published by James Hayes, Junior. The last Baltimore issue located is that of Jan. 5, 1779, vol. 4, no. 163 (should be 193). Hayes went to Annapolis, where in April, 1779, he established "The Maryland Gazette, and Annapolis Advertiser" (see under Annapolis). The Baltimore paper was revived by John Hayes, May 16, 1783, with a new volume numbering, and with practically the same title, the "Maryland Gazette: or, the Baltimore General Advertiser." With the issue of Oct. 31, 1783, Jacob A. Killen was admitted to partnership under the firm name of J. Hayes and J. A. Killen, later changed to Hayes and Killen. With the issue of Apr. 9, 1784, the partnership was dissolved, and the paper published by John Hayes. With the issue of May 24, 1785, the paper became a semi-weekly. With the issue of Jan. 10, 1786, the title was altered to the "Maryland Gazette; or, the Baltimore Advertiser." It reverted to its weekly issue on May 23, 1786, but again became a semi-weekly on Feb. 27, 1787. Hayes discontinued the paper with the issue of Jan. 6, 1792, vol. 9, no. 757.

Pratt Lib., Baltimore, has Sept. 15, 1778–Jan. 5, 1779; May 16, 1783–Jan. 6, 1792.
Md. Hist. Soc. has Sept. 15, 1778–Jan. 5, 1779; May 16, 1783–Dec. 30, 1791.
Lib. Congress has Jan. 5, 1779; June 27, 1783–May 13, 1785; Jan. 27, 31, Mar. 14, 24, 31, Apr. 25, May 23, 1786–Dec. 28, 1787; June 24, Dec. 2, 16, 19, 26, 1788; Jan. 2–Apr. 14, May 5–Nov. 13, 24–Dec. 18, 1789; Aug. 13, Oct. 8, Dec. 28, 1790.
Peabody Lib., Baltimore, has May 16, 1783–May 7, 1784; Jan. 4–Dec. 30, 1788; Jan. 5–Oct. 26, 1790.
N. Y. Pub. Lib. has Oct. 24, Nov. 14, 1783; May 24, 1785–May 16, 1788; Jan. 22, 1790–Nov. 18, 1791, fair.
Am. Antiq. Soc. has Nov. 7, Dec. 5, 1783; Apr. 8, 29, 1785; Jan. 3–May 19, June 13, 27, Aug. 1, Oct. 24, Nov. 28, Dec. 26, 1786; Jan. 2, 9, 23, Feb. 27, Mar. 6–20, 27–Apr. 10, 17–24, May 4–11, 18, June 1, July 6, 13, 27, Aug. 17, 24, 1787; May 20, 1788–Jan. 6, 1792.
Harvard has June 20–Sept. 10, 1784; Feb. 11–Dec. 23, 1785; Dec. 16, 1788; June 21–July 29, 1791.
N. Y. Hist. Soc. has Jan. 20–Nov. 24, 1789; Jan. 7, 1791.
Loyola Coll., Baltimore, has May 19, 1789–May 18, 1790.
British Museum has Sept. 15–Oct. 27, 1778; June 28, July 29, 1785; Mar. 17, 1786; Nov. 16, Dec. 18, 1787; Sept. 8, 18–Oct. 20, 30–Nov. 6, 1789.

Univ. of Mich. (Clements) has July 9–16, 1784; June 22, July 6, 27, Oct. 12, 1787.
Thomas G. Strohm, Baltimore, has Jan. 7–Dec. 30, 1785.
Yale has Dec. 27, 1785–Jan. 17, 1786.
Hist. Soc. Penn. has Jan. 4, Oct. 25, 1787.
Dickinson Coll., Carlisle, Penn., has Aug. 5, 1785.
Ohio Arch. & Hist. Soc. has Nov. 28, 1788.
Filson Club, Louisville, has Dec. 23, 1788.
Western Reserve Hist. Soc. has June 14, 1791.

[Baltimore] Maryland Journal, 1773–1797.

Weekly, semi-weekly, tri-weekly and daily. Established as a weekly Aug. 20, 1773, by William Goddard, under the title of "The Maryland Journal, and the Baltimore Advertiser." Goddard's name was omitted from the imprint from Feb. 13 to May 3, 1775, and beginning with the issue of May 10, 1775, the paper bore the imprint of his sister, M. K. Goddard [Mary K. Goddard]. In January 1777 the experiment was tried of issuing the paper semi-weekly, but was then abandoned. On June 15, 1779, Goddard announced that Eleazer Oswald was admitted to partnership, but there was no change in the imprint, and the partnership kept up for only about two years. Goddard and Oswald advertised in the Maryland Journal of Apr. 10, 1781, that they had formed a design of printing European classics, that they renounced all share in the newspaper, and that they wished success for "the Printress of the Maryland Journal." The name of M. K. Goddard throughout this period was the only one in the imprint. The paper was changed to a semi-weekly with the issue of Mar. 14, 1783. With the issue of Jan. 2, 1784, William Goddard resumed the editorship and the paper was published by William and Mary Katherine Goddard, although this was the only issue published by them as a firm, the issue for Jan. 6 and thenceforth being published by William Goddard alone. With the issue of Jan. 25, 1785, Goddard admitted Edward Langworthy to partnership and the paper was published by Goddard and Langworthy. This firm was dissolved, and with the issue of Jan. 31, 1786, the paper was published by William Goddard. With the issue of Aug. 7, 1789, he took James Angell into partnership and the paper was published by W. Goddard and James Angell. With the issue of Feb. 22, 1793, James Angell became sole publisher. With the issue of Nov. 1, 1793, the paper was published by James Angell & Paul J. Sullivan, and was issued tri-weekly. With the issue of June 11, 1794, James Angell again became sole publisher, and with the issue of Oct. 17, 1794, the paper reverted to a semi-weekly. With the issue of Oct. 31, 1794, Angell disposed of his interest to Francis Brumfield & Co. With the issue of Jan. 1, 1795, the paper was united with "Edwards's Baltimore Daily Advertiser," under the name of the "Maryland Journal, and Baltimore Universal Daily Advertiser," and was published as a daily by Philip Edwards & Co. With the issue of June 18, 1795, the firm name was changed to P. Edwards & J. W. Allen [Philip Edwards and John W. Allen]. The title was changed to "Maryland Journal & Baltimore Advertiser," with the issue of Oct. 26, 1795. The partnership was dissolved and the paper published by Philip Edwards with the issue of June 20, 1796. With the issue of Aug. 2, 1796, Edwards took William C. Smyth into partnership under the firm name of Edwards & Smyth, and changed the title to "Maryland Journal & Baltimore Daily Advertiser." This partnership terminated on Sept. 8, 1796, and the paper was continued by Philip Edwards. Because of a fire on Dec. 4, 1796, the paper was suspended with the issue of Dec. 3, but resumed publication upon Dec. 27, 1796. With the issue of Jan. 2, 1797, Edwards retired and the paper was published by D. Finchete Freebairn. The paper was suspended with the issue of Feb. 28, 1797, but resumed publication under the proprietorship of Philip Edwards, with the issue of Mar. 21, 1797, the title being shortened to "Maryland Journal." It was discontinued with the issue of July 1, 1797, no. 3429.

Md. Hist. Soc. has Aug. 20–Sept. 25, Oct. 16–Dec. 30, 1773; Jan. 8–Mar. 3, 31, May 28–July 16, Aug. 24, Sept. 7, 21, Oct. 26–Nov. 30, Dec. 19, 26, 1774; Jan. 2, 9, 23, 30, Feb. 13–27, Mar. 13, 29–June 21, July 5–Nov. 8, 22–Dec. 27, 1775; Jan. 3–Feb. 28, Mar. 13–27, Apr. 10–May 1, 15, 22, June 12–July 17, 31–Sept. 25, Oct. 2, 16, 30, Dec. 11, 18, 30, 1776; Jan. 1, 8, 16, 22–Dec. 30, 1777; Jan. 6, 1778–July 1, 1797.

Pratt Lib., Baltimore, has Nov. 25–Dec. 16, 1777; Jan. 13, 1778–Dec. 28, 1787; Mar. 28, Sept. 16, 26, Oct. 7, 1788; Dec. 8, 1789; Jan. 1, 1790–Dec. 30, 1794.

Am. Antiq. Soc. has Aug. 20, Sept. 4, 9, 1773; May 22, 1775; Mar. 20, May 1, July 17, Oct. 9, Nov. 27, 1776; Jan. 28, Feb. 11–Mar. 18, Apr. 1–July 1, 15–29, Aug. 12, 19, Sept. 16, 1777–Dec. 26, 1780; Jan. 2, 9, Mar. 27–Apr. 10, May 8, June 26, Aug. 28, Sept. 11, 25–Oct. 16, Nov. 20, 27, Dec. 25, 1781; Jan. 1–Dec. 24, 1782; Jan. 7, 14, 28, Mar. 25–Apr. 4, June 10, 24, 27, July 29, Aug. 1, 15–22, 29–Sept. 19, 30, Oct. 3, 10–17, 28, 31, Nov. 11–18, Dec. 12, 1783; Jan. 2–Dec. 31, 1784, fair; Jan. 4, 7, Feb. 22–Dec. 30, 1785; Jan. 3, Feb. 14–Aug. 8, fair, Sept. 12, 15, Oct. 3, 31, Nov. 7, 28, Dec. 1, 19, 1786; Jan. 2, 16, Feb. 2, 20, Mar. 20–27, Apr. 6–Dec. 28, 1787, fair; Jan. 1, 1788–Dec. 30, 1794; Jan. 6, 8, 12, 14, Feb. 6, 7, June 19, 30, July 7, 31–Aug. 28, Sept. 9, 19, Oct. 28, 30, Nov. 3, 6, 13, 17, 1795; Jan. 16, 23, Apr. 6–15, May 10, 14, 23, 24, June 3, 7, 14, 24, 28, July 6, 8, 16, Aug. 10, Sept. 17, Oct. 11, 15, 22, Nov. 1–18, 1796; Jan. 10, 1797.

Lib. Congress has Nov. 7, 1774; July 19, Aug. 9, Nov. 1, 1775; Apr. 24, July 10, Aug. 28, Dec. 11, 1776; Feb. 4, Oct. 14, Nov. 11, 25–Dec. 16, 1777; June 16, Dec. 15, 1778; July 6, 20–Aug. 24, Sept. 7–Nov. 2, 16, 23, 1779; Feb. 1, 8, Mar. 14, June 13, 20, July 4–18, Aug. 1, Oct. 17, 24, 1780, Feb. 6, 27, Apr. 24, May 8, June 19, Oct. 2, 23, 1781; Apr. 30, May 7, July 9, Sept. 10, 17, Oct. 1, 29–Nov. 12, 26–Dec. 10, 31, 1782; Jan. 14–Dec. 30, 1783, fair; Apr. 27, July 23, Dec. 28, 1784; Apr. 8, Sept. 20, Oct. 4, 28, Nov. 4, 18, 25, Dec. 6, 23, 1785; Jan. 24, 1786–Dec. 30, 1788, fair; Jan. 2, 1789–Dec. 30, 1791; Jan. 3,

1792–Dec. 23, 1793, fair; Jan. 29–Nov. 25, 1794, fair; Jan. 15, Oct. 13, 1795; Sept. 23, 1796.

British Museum has Aug. 21, 1776; Jan. 22, 1777–Feb. 2, 1779; Mar. 23, June 22, 29, 1779; June 25, 1782–Oct. 31, 1783; Jan. 2–Dec. 31, 1784; Feb. 8, Mar. 29, Apr. 12, May 3–July 1, 1785; Jan. 3–Aug. 8, 1786; Sept. 21, 1787–July 27, 1790.

N. Y. Hist. Soc. has Aug. 31, Dec. 19, 1774; Mar. 13, 29, June 7, Aug. 2, Sept. 6, 20, Oct. 4, 11, 1775; Mar. 20, June 12, 1776; Jan. 8, Mar. 18, June 17, 24, July 22, 29, Sept. 2–16, Oct. 7, 28, Nov. 4, Dec. 23, 30, 1777; Jan. 6, 1778–Jan. 26, 1779, fair; July 23–Oct. 29, 1782; Apr. 15, Oct. 24–Nov. 11, 21, 25, Dec. 2–9, 1783; Jan. 4, 1785–Dec. 31, 1790; Feb. 14, 1792.

Hist. Soc. Penn. has Mar. 18–May 10, May 27, June 10, 1777; Jan. 2, 1784–July 18, Oct. 24, 1788; Jan. 2, 1789–Oct. 28, 1791; Dec. 23, 1792.

N. Y. Pub. Lib. has Sept. 4, 1776; Mar. 18, Apr. 1, May 6, June 17, July 22, 1777–Dec. 29, 1778, fair; July 27, 1779; Oct. 24, 1780; Jan. 2, May 7, June 8, Aug. 20, Oct. 8, 12, 1784; Jan. 7–Dec. 30, 1785, fair; Jan. 24, May 23, Aug. 22, Dec. 19, 1786; June 1–Aug. 31, 1787; Jan. 1, 1788–Dec. 30, 1793.

Harvard has Jan. 14, 1783–Sept. 17, 1793, fair; Jan. 1, 25, Sept. 19, 1796; Apr. 10, 17, 1797.

Duke Univ. has Apr. 28–Sept. 22, 1778; Jan. 22, 29, Apr. 30, May 21, 28, June 25, July 30, Sept. 10, 17, 22, Nov. 19, 1782; Jan. 27, 1784; July 18, Oct. 3, 1788; Jan. 2, 1789–Dec. 27, 1793, fair.

Wis. Hist. Soc. has Mar. 31, Sept. 14, 1774; Apr. 5, 1775; Apr. 10, June 5, 1776; Sept. 29, 1778; Oct. 2, 1781–July 8, 1783; May 28, Oct. 5, Nov. 9, 1784; Sept. 27, 1785; Jan. 2–Dec. 25, 1787; Feb. 9, 12, 1790; July 27, 1792, Oct. 1, 1793; July 25, Aug. 30, Oct. 10, 1795.

Boston Pub. Lib. has Jan. 12–Dec. 14, 1779, fair; May 1, 1787; Dec. 18, 1789; Aug. 13, 1790; July 19, 1791; Apr. 3, Aug. 1, Oct. 23, Nov. 6, 1792.

Univ. of Mich. (Clements) has July 6, 20, Nov. 16, 1779; Oct. 2, 1781; July 23, 1784; May 23–Dec. 22, 1786, fair; Feb. 16–Dec. 21, 1787, fair; Jan. 18, 1788–Dec. 30, 1791, fair; Jan. 17–20, 27, 31, Mar. 6, Apr. 17, 20, May 18, Aug. 21, 1792; Feb. 8, July 30, Dec. 4, 11, 1793; July 25, 30, Aug. 1, 1794.

Peabody Lib., Baltimore, has Nov. 5, 1782–Oct. 10, 1783, fair; Feb. 17–Apr. 18, 1786; Jan. 1–Dec. 30, 1788; June 23, 1789; June 14, 24, July 1, 5, 22, Aug. 26, Sept. 30, Nov. 11, 1791.

Yale has Jan. 4–Dec. 30, 1785; Mar. 4, 1788; Apr. 8, May 6, July 26, 1791; Mar. 20, 1792–Jan. 1, 1793, fair.

Loyola Coll., Baltimore, has Aug. 18, Sept. 12, Oct. 13, Nov. 28, Dec. 26, 1786; Aug. 15, Sept. 23, 1788; Jan. 1–Dec. 28, 1790.

Univ. of Pittsburgh has Jan. 6–Dec. 25, 1789.

Mass. Hist. Soc. has Oct. 20, 1778; Jan. 5, Apr. 6, 1779; Oct. 2, 1781, Jan. 15, 29, Apr. 2–16, 30, May 14, June 25, July 23, Sept. 10, 24, Oct. 22, Dec. 17, 1782; Mar. 25, 28, 1783; Mar. 25, 1785; Mar. 23, 1790; July 13, 1792.

Newberry Lib., Chicago, has Aug. 1–Sept. 29, 1786.

Phil. Lib. Co. has Sept. 20, 24, 27, 1793; Mar. 31, July 20, Aug. 24, 1795.
Rutgers Univ. has July 1, 1777; Apr. 18, 22, 29, 1778; Jan. 24, Oct. 27, 1786; Apr. 3, 10, Sept. 4, Nov. 16, 1787; Apr. 18, 22, 29, 1788; Sept. 29, 1789; Mar. 12, 1790.
Johns Hopkins Univ. has Dec. 18, 1773; Apr. 19, May 10, 1775.
Western Reserve Hist. Soc. has Sept. 10, 1784; July 31, Sept. 25, Dec. 14, 1787; Feb. 10, 1789; Dec. 24, 1790; Aug. 3, Dec. 9, 1791; Aug. 14, 1792.
Several libraries have single, or a few scattering, issues.

[Baltimore] **Mechanics' Gazette,** 1815.

Daily. Established Mar. 14, 1815, by Thomas Wilson & Co., under the title of the "Mechanics' Gazette; and Merchants' Daily Advertiser." With the issue of July 7, 1815, James [?] M'Evoy was admitted to the firm under the name of Wilson & M'Evoy, and the size of the paper enlarged from quarto to folio. A tri-weekly country paper was also established. With the issue of Aug. 26, 1815, this firm was dissolved and the paper edited by Thomas Wilson for John Robb. The last issue located is that of Sept. 13, 1815, vol. 1, no. 90–53.

Md. Hist. Soc. has May 4–June 19, 21–July 1, 3, 7–Aug. 16, 18–23, 26–Sept. 9, 13, 1815.
Am. Antiq. Soc. has Mar. 14, 29, Apr. 27, May 17, 18, July 12, 1815.

[Baltimore] **Morning Chronicle,** 1819–1820+.

Daily. Established Apr. 8, 1819, with the title of "Morning Chronicle & Baltimore Advertiser," edited by Paul Allen, and printed and published by Schaeffer & Maund [Frederick G. Schaeffer and Thomas Maund]. It succeeded the "Journal of the Times," an octavo magazine edited by Paul Allen and published by Schaeffer & Maund. A tri-weekly country paper was also published. With the issue of Sept. 30, 1820, the paper was printed by Thomas Maund, Allen continuing as editor. Continued after 1820.

Md. Hist. Soc. has Apr. 8, 1819–Dec. 30, 1820.
Wis. Hist. Soc. has Apr. 8, 1819–Apr. 7, Oct. 9–Dec. 30, 1820.
Lib. Congress has Apr. 8–Oct. 7, 1819 of the daily; and Sept. 2, Dec. 4, 1819 of the tri-weekly.
Lehigh Univ. has Sept. 1–27, 1820.
Am. Antiq. Soc. has Apr. 8, June 18, 1819; May 5, 1820, of the daily; and May 20, 1819; Mar. 4, Nov. 16, 1820 of the tri-weekly.
Goucher College, Baltimore, has Oct. 7, 1819.
Univ. of Ga. has Jan. 17–Feb. 19, 1820, fair.
Pratt Lib., Baltimore, has Jan. 26, 1820.

Baltimore Morning Post, see **Baltimore Evening Post,** 1792–1793.

[Baltimore] Museum, see National Museum.

[Baltimore] National Museum, 1813–1814.

Weekly. The prospectus issue, one of the most pretentious announcements ever put forth by an American editor, was entitled "The Museum and Weekly Gazette," dated Aug. 27, 1813, and signed by Camill. M. Mann, M.D. The initial issue entitled "National Museum, and Weekly Gazette," appeared Nov. 13, 1813, published by Camill. M. Mann, and printed by G[eorge] Dobbin and [Thomas] Murphy. George Dobbin had died in 1811, and his name represented the family interest. It was of quarto size, eight numbered pages to the issue, and included domestic news, essays, and marriage and death notices. With the issue of Dec. 11, 1813, it was printed by J[oseph] Robinson for Camill. M. Mann, and with Jan. 8, 1814, printed for Camill. M. Mann. With the issue of Jan. 29, 1814, the title was changed to "National Museum, and Weekly Gazette of Discoveries, Natural Sciences, and the Arts." The last issue located is that of Mar. 12, 1814, vol. 1, no. 16.

Am. Antiq. Soc. and N. Y. State Lib. have Prospectus of Aug. 27, 1813.
N. Y. Hist. Soc. has Nov. 13, 27–Dec. 18, 1813; Jan. 15–Mar. 12, 1814.
Univ. of Penn. has Nov. 13, 27, Dec. 4, 1813; Jan. 8–Mar. 12, 1814.

[Baltimore] Neue Unpartheyische Baltimore Bote, 1795–1798.

Weekly and tri-weekly. Established in March 1795, judging from the first and only copy located, that of May 4, 1796, no. 59, published by Samuel Saur, with the title of "Der Neue Unpartheyische Baltimore Bote und Marylander Staats-Register" (see also G. C. Keidel, "Earliest German Newspapers of Baltimore," 1927, p. 8). It was presumably discontinued in 1797 or 1798. Saur, in his prospectus of Jan. 4, 1799 for the "Baltimore Postbote," refers to his previous German newspaper.

Baltimore Municipal Museum has May 4, 1796 (photostat in Md. Hist. Soc.).

[Baltimore] North American, 1808–1809.

Daily. Established Jan. 11, 1808, by Jacob Wagner, with the title of "The North American and Mercantile Daily Advertiser." The colophon on last page stated that it was "Printed for the Editor by Peter K. Wagner." A tri-weekly country paper was also published. The last issue was that of Oct. 3, 1809, vol. 4, no. 521, after which it was merged with the "Federal Republican," which see.

Md. Hist. Soc. has Jan. 11, 1808–July 8, 1809; Aug. 5–Oct. 3, 1809.
Boston Athenæum has Jan. 11–Dec. 31, 1808 of the daily; and Jan. 11–Oct. 3, 1809 of the tri-weekly.

Lib. Congress has Jan. 11–Dec. 15, 1808; Mar. 4, 7, 14, Apr. 14, July 13, 18, 21, 27, 1809 of the daily; and Jan. 26, 1808–Sept. 21, 1809 of the tri-weekly.
Am. Antiq. Soc. has Jan. 15–Dec. 8, 1808, fair; Mar. 17, 21, 1809 of the daily; and Nov. 17, 1808 of the tri-weekly.
Pratt Lib., Baltimore, has Feb. 5, 1808–Jan. 12, 1809, fair.
Peabody Lib., Baltimore, has July 1–Oct. 3, 1809.
Wis. Hist. Soc. has July 28, Sept. 22, 1808.
Howard-Tilton Lib., New Orleans, has July 29, 31, 1809.
Georgetown Univ. has Sept. 20, 1809.
British Museum has Sept. 29, 1809.

[Baltimore] **Palladium of Freedom,** 1787.

Daily. Established Aug. 2, 1787, judging from the first and only issue located, that of Aug. 8, 1787, vol. 1, no. 6, published by Maurice Murphy and Richard Bowen, with the full title of "The Palladium of Freedom; or, the Baltimore Daily Advertiser." A contemporaneous inscription on this copy, apparently in the hand of William Goddard, says, "First Daily Paper at Balt., continued a few weeks. The Publishers abdicated under Cover of the Night."

Am. Antiq. Soc. has Aug. 8, 1787.

Baltimore Patriot, 1812–1820+.

Daily. Established Dec. 28, 1812, by Ebenezer French & Co., with the title of "Baltimore Patriot." The second issue did not appear until Jan. 4, 1813, but thereafter the paper was published daily. With the issue of Aug. 18, 1813, the size of the paper was enlarged and the title changed to "Baltimore Patriot & Evening Advertiser." With the issue of Mar. 31, 1814, the paper was published by Munroe & French [Isaac Munroe and Ebenezer French]. French disposed of his interest to John Norvell, and with the issue of May 22, 1815, the publishing firm became Munroe & Norvell. Norvell removed from Baltimore and with the issue of Feb. 12, 1817, the paper was published by Isaac Munroe. With the issue of May 1, 1817, the title was changed to "Baltimore Patriot & Mercantile Advertiser." Continued by Munroe after 1820. A tri-weekly country paper, without heading, was also published from 1812 to after 1820.

Md. Hist. Soc. has Dec. 28, 1812–Dec. 30, 1815; Jan. 2, 1817–Dec. 30, 1820 of the daily; and July 8, 1816; Jan. 2–Dec. 30, 1819, fair; Jan. 6, Feb. 4, Apr. 27, July 10, Sept. 20–25, Oct. 13, 24, 30, Nov. 13, 27, Dec. 4, 1820 of the tri-weekly.
Lib. Congress has Mar. 13–Aug. 17, 1813; Jan. 3, 1814–Aug. 31, 1815; Jan. 29, Mar. 15, Apr. 11, May 4, June 9, July 13, Aug. 12, 15, 16, 20, 1816; Apr. 30, Aug. 19, Sept. 9, 1817; Jan. 1, 1818–Dec. 30, 1820 of the daily; and Sept. 10, 1813–Aug. 18, 1814; May 27–Dec. 28, 1815; Feb. 15, Mar. 1, 1817; May 19, 1819, of the tri-weekly.

Peabody Inst., Baltimore, has Dec. 28, 1812–Dec. 29, 1815; Jan. 1–Dec. 31, 1818.
Boston Athenæum has Jan. 1, 1814–June 30, 1817; Jan. 1, 1818–Dec. 30, 1820 of the daily.
N. Y. Hist. Soc. has Dec. 28, 1812–Aug. 17, Dec. 24, 1813.
Wis. Hist. Soc. has Jan. 1, 1813–Dec. 31, 1815; Dec. 15, 1818.
Pratt Lib., Baltimore, has Jan. 7–Dec. 30, 1813; Jan. 14–July 13, Oct. 1, 26, 1814; Jan. 28, Feb. 18, Aug. 3, 1815; Mar. 21, 1818.
Am. Antiq. Soc. has Feb. 9, Apr. 21, 30, May 13, 1813; July 1–Sept. 9, 20–Dec. 31, 1814; June 29, July 13, 1815; Apr. 8, May 11, 17, Aug. 9, Dec. 30, 1819; May 18, 1820 of the daily; and Jan. 14, May 18, Aug. 2, 17, 24, 28, 1813; Feb. 3, 10, Mar. 8, Apr. 16, 19, Aug. 11, Dec. 31, 1814; Feb. 14, Mar. 11, 21, Aug. 3, Sept. 7, 1815; Jan. 30, Mar. 30, Apr. 2, 1816; Mar. 26, Oct. 31, Dec. 8, 1818; Feb. 9, 1819; Oct. 12, 1820 of the tri-weekly.
Mass. Hist. Soc. has Feb. 14, 1818; Dec. 10, 1819; Jan. 7, June 13, 1820.
Johns Hopkins Univ. has Sept. 1, 1815.

[Baltimore] **People's Advocate,** 1816.

A democratic paper repeatedly referred to in the file of "The People's Friend" from May to September, 1816. The only issue located is the first leaf of Apr. 24, 1816, vol. 1, no. 19, entitled "The People's Advocate," but with the leaf missing containing the imprint. "The People's Friend" of Sept. 13, 1816, mentions the paper as having "ceased to exist."

Md. Hist. Soc. has Apr. 24, 1816.

[Baltimore] **People's Friend,** 1816.

Weekly. Established May 25, 1816, with the title of "The People's Friend," printed for the proprietors at 39 Water Street, the office of the "Federal Republican." A federalist paper issued to combat the democratic party during the election of 1816. No issues were published from Aug. 29 to Sept. 13. The last issue located is that of Sept. 27, 1816, vol. 1, no. 18.

Md. Hist. Soc. has May 25–Sept. 27, 1816.

[Baltimore] **Porcupine,** 1804.

In the "Federal Gazette" of Aug. 18, 1804, it is stated that a new paper of quarto size, entitled the "Porcupine," by Archy Touchstone, made its appearance on Aug. 16, from the office of Messrs. Wane and Murphy [John Wane and Thomas Murphy]. No copy located.

Baltimore Postbote, 1799–1800.

In the "Baltimore Intelligencer" of Jan. 12, 1799, Samuel Saur has an advertisement dated Jan. 5, announcing the publication of a tri-weekly newspaper, the "Baltimore. Postbote," to begin by the middle of January. He states that friends were dissatisfied that he had not continued his previous German paper, and requested that he publish another. E. F. Leyh, in a volume on the German press of Baltimore (quoted by G. C. Keidel, "Earliest German Newspapers of Baltimore," 1927, p. 4) states that he knew of an issue of the "Baltimore Post" in 1799, published by Samuel Saur, but presumably he meant "Post" as synonymous with "Bote." Saur in his "Neue Hoch-Deutsche Americanische Calender" for 1800 states that he has been publishing a tri-weekly newspaper for a considerable time (quoted in full in J. O. Knauss, "Social Conditions among the Pennsylvania Germans," 1922, p. 193). No copy of the "Baltimore Postbote" has been located.

Baltimore Price-Current, 1803–1820+.

Weekly. Established Feb. 14, 1803, by Joseph Escavaille with the title of "Baltimore Price-Current," and printed at the Anti-Democrat office. With the issue of Aug. 13, 1803, it was printed at no. 14 So. Charles Street; with the issue of Feb. 4, 1804, by Wane and Murphy [John Wane and Thomas Murphy]; with the issue of Aug. 29, 1805, by G. Dobbin & Murphy '[George Dobbin and Thomas Murphy]; with the issue of Feb. 26, 1810, by Hunter & Robinson [James A. Hunter and Joseph Robinson]; and with the issue of Apr. 21, 1810, by Joseph Robinson. Escavaille published it throughout this period and until after 1820. The title was changed to "Baltimore Weekly Price Current" with the issue of Jan. 3, 1805, and to "Baltimore Price Current" with the issue of June 26, 1813. It was a paper of quarto size.

Md. Hist. Soc. has Feb. 14, 1803–Dec. 30, 1820.
Phil. Lib. Co. has Jan. 1, 1807–Dec. 26, 1812.
Pratt Lib., Baltimore, has Jan. 3, 1805–Dec. 25, 1806.
Lib. Congress has Sept. 20, 27, Oct. 18, 25, 1804; Feb. 21, Mar. 7–28, May 2, 23, 1805; May 24, 31, 1817.
Goucher Coll. Lib., Baltimore, has July 15, 1809; Sept. 5, 1818; May 29, 1819.
Univ. of Mich. (Clements) has May 14, 1808.

Baltimore Recorder, 1810.

Weekly. Established June 9, 1810, judging from the first and only issue located, that of June 16, 1810, vol. 1, no. 2. The full title was "The Recorder; or, Summary of Foreign, Domestic, and Literary Intelligence," and the paper was printed by John Westcott, Jun.

Am. Antiq. Soc. has June 16, 1810.

[Baltimore] Republican, 1802–1804.

Daily and tri-weekly. Established as a daily Jan. 1, 1802, under the title of "The Republican; or, Anti-Democrat," by Prentiss and Cole [Charles Prentiss and John Cole]. With the issue of May 14, 1802, it was changed to a tri-weekly. A weekly country paper was also established. With the issue of Aug. 4, 1802, the firm was dissolved and the paper published by Charles Prentiss. Prentiss sold out to George L. Gray, who began publishing the paper with the issue of June 1, 1803. It was discontinued with the issue of Dec. 30, 1803, vol. 2, no. 233. It was Gray's intention to start a daily, but lack of support made him give up the project, and on Jan. 14, 1804, he issued a "Valedictory Appendix" of four pages.

Md. Hist. Soc. has Jan. 1, 1802–Dec. 30, 1803; Jan. 14, 1804.
Pratt Lib., Baltimore, has Jan. 1–Dec. 31, 1802; July 1, Oct. 31, Nov. 2, 1803.
Peabody Lib., Baltimore, has Jan. 1–Dec. 30, 1802.
N. Y. Hist. Soc. has Jan. 1–Dec. 30, 1802; Aug. 17, 1803.
Harvard has Jan. 9, 1802–Jan. 14, 1804, fair; also June 29, July 7, Sept. 15, 1802; Feb. 17, 23, Apr. 20, 1803 of the weekly paper.
N. Y. Pub. Lib. has Jan. 29–Dec. 29, 1802; Mar. 16–23, Apr. 6–13, June 8–July 6, 1803.
Wis. Hist. Soc. has Jan. 1–Mar. 31, May 12, July 2–Dec. 31, 1802.
Am. Antiq. Soc. has Jan. 1–July 21, 26–Aug. 6, 11, 16, 18, 30–Sept. 10, 15, 17, 22–Oct. 20, Nov. 26, Dec. 20, 1802; Feb. 14, 21, Apr. 10, Oct. 19, Nov. 2, 1803; also Aug. 10, Sept. 7, 21, 28, Nov. 9, 1803 of the weekly paper.
Lib. Congress has Jan. 23–Oct. 22, 1802.
Duke Univ. has Feb. 1–Nov. 29, 1802.
Ohio Arch. & Hist. Soc. has Mar. 11–Dec. 24, 1802, fair.
Yale has Oct. 19–Nov. 21, 1803.
Boston Pub. Lib. has June 27, Sept. 4, Nov. 16, 1803.

[Baltimore] Scourge, 1810.

Weekly. Established May 26, 1810, judging from the date of the first issue located, that of June 2, 1810, vol. 1, no. 2, entitled "The Scourge." The heading reads "By Titus Tickler, Esq. & Co.," and the imprint "Printed and Published by Samuel Magill, agent for the Proprietors." The last issue located is that of Nov. 24, 1810, vol. 1, no. 26.

Md. Hist. Soc. has June 2–Oct. 13, 1810.
Am. Antiq. Soc. has Aug. 18, Nov. 24, 1810.
N. Y. Hist. Soc. has Nov. 3, 1810.

[Baltimore] Sun, 1811–1813.

Daily. Established by Thomas Wilson on June 24, 1811, entitled "The Sun." It was the immediate successor of the "Baltimore Evening Post," the last issue of which was on June 22, 1811, and bore the inscription "Late Baltimore Evening Post" in the heading. The last issue located of "The Sun" is that of Jan. 29, 1813, vol. 4, no. 480. A tri-weekly country paper was also issued.

Baltimore City Lib. had June 24–Dec. 31, 1811; July 2, 1812–Jan. 29, 1813, but since the library was abolished in 1934, this file has not been located. It was listed for me in 1917 by Dr. George C. Keidel.

Pratt Lib., Baltimore, has July 1, 1811–Dec. 31, 1812.

Mrs. Nelson Gutman, Baltimore, Md., has June 24–Dec. 31, 1811.

Am. Antiq. Soc. has July 11, 1811; Apr. 2, 8, 1812; also Aug. 24, Sept. 17–26, Oct. 15, 26, Dec. 5, 14, 1811; Jan. 11, 16, 30, Feb. 15, 25, Mar. 17, 21, 28, Apr. 2, 1812 of the tri-weekly edition.

N. Y. State Lib. has Apr. 28, May 2, June 16–20, Aug. 8, 15, Oct. 15–22, 27, Nov. 14, Dec. 15, 1812 of the tri-weekly edition.

Md. Hist. Soc. has Aug. 7, Sept. 18, Dec. 23, 1812; Jan. 7, 1813.

Lib. Congress has Sept. 26, Nov. 2, 1811 of the tri-weekly.

Howard-Tilton Lib., New Orleans, has Oct. 27, Dec. 7, 1811.

N. Y. Hist. Soc. has Dec. 6, 1811.

N. Y. Pub. Lib. has Nov. 18, 1812.

[Baltimore] Sunday Monitor, 1796.

Weekly. Established with the title of "Sunday Monitor," Dec. 18, 1796, by Philip Edwards, who refers to this issue as "a specimen of what he humbly hopes will entitle him to future favour." Perhaps the only number issued. Edwards advertised in the "Maryland Journal" of Dec. 27, 1796, that he was resigning the printing business and that D. Finchete Freebairn would continue the Monitor if sufficient subscribers were speedily obtained.

Md. Hist. Soc. has Dec. 18, 1796.

[Baltimore] Sunday Morning's Messenger, 1819.

The "National Intelligencer" of July 28, 1819, records the receipt of the first issue, July 18, 1819, of "Sunday Morning's Messenger," established at Baltimore by Ebenezer French. No copy located.

Baltimore Telegraphe, 1795–1807.

Daily. Established Mar. 23, 1795, published by Clayland, Dobbin & Co. [Thomas E. Clayland and Thomas Dobbin], with the title of "The Baltimore Telegraphe." About Jan. 1, 1797 (surely between Dec. 19, 1796, and Feb. 11, 1797), the title was changed to "City Gazette and Daily Telegraphe," but without any change in the volume numbering. Between Apr. 12 and June 22, 1797, the title was changed to "The Telegraphe and Daily Advertiser" and the firm name to T. E. Clayland & T. Dobbin, the volume numbering still being continuous. Clayland died Dec. 4, 1797, but there was no immediate change in the imprint. Beginning with the issue of Jan. 1, 1799, the paper was published by Thomas Dobbin, who continued it as far as the last issue located, that of Feb. 6, 1807, no. 3733. Dobbin died Feb. 10, 1808.

Peabody Lib., Baltimore, has Mar. 23, 1795–Sept. 23, 1796; July 1, 1797–June 30, 1798; Jan. 1, 1799–June 30, 1801; Jan. 2, 1804–June 29, 1805.
Md. Hist. Soc. has Oct. 2, 1797–Dec. 31, 1806.
Harvard has Apr. 11, June 18, 26, 1795; Jan. 7–Mar. 31, Apr. 21, May 27, 28, June 17, 18, Oct. 7, Dec. 19, 1796; Mar. 16–Apr. 12, June 14, 16, 22, 27–30, July 1, 7, Aug. 9, 18, 24, Oct. 10, Nov. 9, Dec. 19, 29, 30, 1797; Jan. 1, 3–5, 8, 11, May 17, Aug. 31, Sept. 17, 18, 1798; Feb. 26, Mar. 4, 7, Apr. 5, June 28, July 9, Nov. 13, 1799; Jan. 22, Apr. 14, 15, 17, 18, 21–25, 28, 30, May 7, 26, 31, June 2, 9, 16, 25, July 26, 30, Aug. 7, 8, 14, 21, 22, 27, 30, Sept. 1, 11, 15, 24, 1800–Feb. 6, 1807, fair.
Am. Antiq. Soc. has May 14, June 22, 23, 30, July 6, 7, 13–16, Aug. 4, 11, 14, 15, 26, 27, Sept. 9, 10, 23–Dec. 31, 1795; Jan. 1–Mar. 28, July 8, Aug. 10, 1796; Oct. 13, 27, Nov. 15, 18, 1797; Jan. 17, 25, Feb. 16, 21, Mar. 8, 15, 21, 23, Apr. 12, 16, 18, 30, May 26, July 12, Sept. 13, 20, Nov. 28, 1798; Feb. 2, 1799; Jan. 3, Mar. 26, Apr. 16, May 10, Sept. 5, 10, 20, Oct. 22, 31, Nov. 6, 8, Dec. 3, 23, 1800; Feb. 2, May 4, Aug. 15, 21, 26, Sept. 15, 29, Oct. 7, Nov. 10, 11, Dec. 21, 1801; Apr. 3, June 2, 7, July 16, Oct. 6, 13, Nov. 30, Dec. 1, 3, 7–9, 29, 1802; Jan. 24, Feb. 4, 14, 23, 26, Mar. 2, 16, Apr. 2, 13, 18, 26, May 13, June 4, 16, 25, July 15, 21, Aug. 2, 11–Sept. 29, fair, Oct. 14, Nov. 5, 17, Dec. 5, 1803; Jan. 28, Feb. 28, Mar. 2, 13, June 4, 6, 12, 14, 28, Aug. 10, 22, Sept. 6, 8, Oct. 5, Dec. 1, 25, 1804; Feb. 21, Apr. 23, 1805; Feb. 18, May 9, July 15, Sept. 7, Nov. 20, Dec. 5, 9, 1806; Jan. 11, 1807.
Lib. Congress has May 11–16, Aug. 26, Nov. 9, Dec. 7–10, 1795; Mar. 1, 7, Sept. 22, Oct. 18, 1796; June 28, 1797; July 4, 6, Aug. 1, 7, 1798; Mar. 12, Dec. 17, 1799; Feb. 18, 20, 1801; Jan. 1–Dec. 31, 1805.
Phil. Lib. Co. has Mar. 15–Aug. 20, 1796; Jan. 15–Dec. 18, 1806.
N. Y. Hist. Soc. has July 1–Dec. 31, 1800, fair; Sept. 10, 1806.
Wis. Hist. Soc. has Nov. 10, 1798; July 1–Dec. 31, 1805.
Pratt Lib., Baltimore, has Dec. 21, 1799; Sept. 5, 1800; Jan. 29, 1802.
Howard-Tilton Lib., New Orleans, has July 4, 1801; Jan. 23, Mar. 17, Apr. 15, Nov. 18, Dec. 1, 1802.
N. Y. State Lib. has June 4, 10, 1800.

Baltimore Telegraph, 1814–1816.

Daily. Established by Allen & Hill [Paul Allen and Thomas H. Hill] on May 17, 1814, judging from the volume numbering and advertisements of the first issue located, that of June 9, 1814, vol. 1, no. 21. The full title was "Baltimore Telegraph and Mercantile Advertiser." Thomas Howard Hill had advertised in the Baltimore "American" of Dec. 28, 1813, proposals for publishing

"The Baltimore Correspon͡ ͡ ɪt and Merchant's, Manufacturer's and Mechanic's Daily Advertiser." The last issue located is that of Feb. 9, 1816, vol. 4, no. 472. A paper "for the country" was also issued. On Apr. 4, 1816, it was united with the "Federal Republican" under the title of "Federal Republican and Baltimore Telegraph."

N. Y. Hist. Soc. has June 23, 30, Oct. 20, 22, 26, 31, Nov. 3, 7, 8, 11, 12, 15, 17, 19, 22, 24, 28, 30, Dec. 1, 10, 15, 17, 21, 23, 27–29, 31, 1814; Apr. 18, 1815.
Pratt Lib., Baltimore, has Nov. 30, 1814–May 15, 1815; Feb. 9, 1816.
Hist. Soc. Penn. has Jan. 2–Dec. 30, 1815.
Lib. Congress has June 9, July 4, Aug. 24, 1814.
Md. Hist. Soc. has Nov. 1, 1814; Dec. 9, 13, 1815.
Howard-Tilton Lib., New Orleans, has Sept. 18, 21, 1815.

[Baltimore] **Weekly Museum,** 1797.

Weekly. Established Jan. 8, 1797, by John Smith and Christopher Jackson, with the title of "The Weekly Museum." It was issued on Sunday. Each issue contained eight pages numbered, and the size was octavo. Although published in magazine form, it contained current news and advertisements, and could be considered a newspaper. With the issue of Apr. 16, 1797, Christopher Jackson became sole publisher. The last issue located is that of May 28, 1797, vol. 1, no. 21.

Md. Hist. Soc. has Jan. 8–Feb. 12, 26–May 28, 1797.
Harvard has Feb. 5, 12, 1797.

Baltimore Weekly Price Current, see **Baltimore Price-Current.**

[Baltimore] **Whig,** 1807–1814.

Weekly and daily. Established, under the title of "Whig, or Political Telescope," on Sept. 24, 1807, judging from the date of the first issue located, that of Oct. 15, 1807, vol. 1, no. 4. The earliest advertisements, however, are dated Sept. 28, 1807, and this was possibly the date of the first issue. The paper was at first issued as a weekly, but beginning with the issue of Oct. 22, 1807, it was published daily. It was ostensibly published by the "Democratic Republican Association, or, Whig Club," but the editor, as is shown by the issues of Nov. 9 and 16, 1807, was Baptis Irvine. In "The Case of Baptis Irvine, in a Matter of Contempt of Court," published at Baltimore, 1808 (copy in Amer. Antiq. Soc.), it is stated, p. 5, "The Whig was established by a company of persons during the last summer, and Mr. Irvine was engaged as the Editor." With the issue of Dec. 7, 1807, the title was changed to "The Whig," although the heading of the editorial column continued under the old title until Feb. 6, 1808. The issue of Oct. 15, 1807, was printed by John W. Butler. Beginning with the issue of

Oct. 22, 1807, the paper was "Printed at No. 3, N. Gay-Street"; with the issue of Feb. 6, 1808, it was "Printed & Published (for the Proprietors,) by Joseph Robinson"; and with the issue of May 23, 1808, after a suspension of three weeks, it was "Printed & Published by B. Irvine." With the issue of July 2, 1810, the title was changed to the "Baltimore Whig." With the issue of Oct. 22, 1810, Samuel Barnes was admitted to partnership and the paper published by Irvine & Barnes. With the issue of Aug. 2, 1813, Barnes removed to Fredericktown, and the paper was transferred to Cone and Norvell [Spencer H. Cone and John Norvell]. The last issue located is that of May 6, 1814, at which time the "Whig" was absorbed by the "American." A country paper was issued tri-weekly throughout most of this period.

N. Y. Pub. Lib. has Oct. 15, 1807–Dec. 31, 1810, fair.
Md. Hist. Soc. has June 1, 1808–June 30, 1812; also July 4, 7, 1810; Jan. 5–Dec. 27, 1811; Jan. 2–Dec. 30, 1813 of the tri-weekly.
Pratt Lib., Baltimore, has July 1–Dec. 31, 1808, fair; Jan. 3–June 28, 1811, fair; Sept. 2, 1811.
Wis. Hist. Soc. has Apr. 28, 1809–Apr. 30, 1810.
Marietta Coll. has Sept. 29, 1809–Dec. 12, 1810, tri-weekly.
Lib. Congress has Nov. 16, 26, 27, Dec. 11, 1807; Nov. 25, 28, Dec. 22, 27, 1809; Jan. 15, July 2–Dec. 30, 1811, fair; Nov. 23, 1812–July 14, 1813; Sept. 6–Nov. 30, 1813; May 3–6, 1814; also Nov. 25, 28, Dec. 22, 27, 1809; Feb. 5, 17, June 9, Aug. 7, 23, 1810; Mar. 9, 21, 23, Apr. 4, Sept. 26, Oct. 1, 1811 of the tri-weekly.
Am. Antiq. Soc. has Oct. 22, Nov. 5, 6, 9, 12, 16, 20, 27–30, Dec. 2, 1807; Apr. 26, May 27, July 29–Dec. 31, 1808; Jan. 2–Mar. 27, July 6, 1809; Mar. 30, June 9, July 4, Dec. 1, 8, 1810; Jan. 2, 11, Feb. 11, 20, Mar. 13, Dec. 2, 1811; Apr. 3, 20, 1812; July 24, Oct. 28, Nov. 16, 18, Dec. 8, 1813; Mar. 22, 23, 1814; also Dec. 5, 8, 29, 31, 1807; Jan. 7, 14, 16, Feb. 25, 27, Mar. 12, 17, 19, 29, 31, Apr. 7, June 14, 18, 23, July 2, 12, 26, 28, Aug. 16, 23, 30–Sept. 22, Oct. 13, 20, 25, 27, Dec. 3, 1808; Feb. 21, 25, Mar. 4, May 20, June 29, Nov. 18, 1809; Mar. 10, June 7, Aug. 2, 9, 21, Oct. 4, Nov. 13, 1810; Jan. 1, 15, 31, Apr. 25, June 18, July 18, Aug. 17, 22, 29, Sept. 7, 17, 21, Oct. 1, Nov. 7, 16, 29, Dec. 20, 1811; Jan. 31, Mar. 4, Apr. 20, Aug. 14, Sept. 3, Oct. 13, 1812; Feb. 16, July 24, Nov. 20, Dec. 30, 1813; Jan. 29, Feb. 1, Mar. 26, Apr. 7, 12, 16, 28, 1814 of the tri-weekly.
N. Y. State Lib. has Dec. 31, 1807; May 25, 1808; May 1, Dec. 1, 1809; Jan. 9, Feb. 9, Mar. 17, Apr. 21, May 2, 1810; Apr. 12–16, 1811; Apr. 27, June 16, July 15, 28, 31, Aug. 8, 21, Sept. 8–Nov. 20, 1812, fair; May 21, July 9, Sept. 11, Nov. 20, 25, 27, 29, 1813; Jan. 7–10, 13, 15, Feb. 24, Apr. 2, 1814.
Petersburg, Va., Pub. Lib. has Jan. 21–Dec. 30, 1809, country edition.
Hist. Soc. Penn. has Jan. 1–Aug. 10, 1811.
Johns Hopkins Univ. has Apr. 1–May 20, 1811.
Yale has July 9–Dec. 27, 1811.

MARYLAND 253

Harvard has Nov. 3, 1807; Sept. 19–Dec. 27, 1808, mostly tri-weekly.
Univ. of Mich. (Clements) has Sept. 12–15, 1808.
Univ. of Pittsburgh has Nov. 4, Dec. 10, 14, 16, 1811; Jan. 15, 22, 1812.
Howard-Tilton Lib., New Orleans, has Feb. 3, 1808; Apr. 25, 1814.
Univ. of Texas has Sept. 26, 1812.

[Bel Air] **Bond of Union,** 1820+.

Weekly. Established in February 1820, judging from the first and only issue located, that of Oct. 4, 1821, vol. 2, no. 32, published by William Coale, Jr., with the title of "Bond of Union and Harford County Weekly Advertiser." It was probably a successor to the "Bond of Union" established by William Coale at Havre-de-Grace in 1818. The "National Intelligencer" of May 30, 1820, records the receipt of the initial issue, Feb. 29, 1820, of "The Bond of Union" published at Bel-Air, Md., by William Coale, Jr.

Pratt Lib., Baltimore, has Oct. 4, 1821.

[Chestertown] **Apollo,** 1793.

Semi-weekly. Established Mar. 19, 1793, judging from the date of the first issue located, that of Mar. 26, 1793, vol. 1, no. 3. It was published by G[eorge] Gerrish and R[obert] Saunders, Jr., with the full title of "The Apollo; or, Chestertown Spy." With the issue of Apr. 19, 1793, it was published by Robert Saunders, Jr., who changed the title to "Chestertown Gazette" with the issue of July 26, 1793. The last issue located is that of Dec. 31, 1793, vol. 1, no. 85.

Md. Hist. Soc. has Mar. 26–June 14, 21–July 9, 16, 19, 26, 30, Aug. 9, 13, 30–Sept. 6, 13–Oct. 18, Nov. 1–15, 22–29, Dec. 13, 17, 31, 1793.
N. Y. Hist. Soc. has Apr. 12, 1793.
Am. Antiq. Soc. has May 10, 1793.
Harvard has July 23, 1793.

Chestertown Gazette, see [Chestertown] **Apollo.**

[Cumberland] **Allegany Freeman,** 1813–1818.

Weekly. Established by S[amuel] Magill on Nov. 20, 1813, judging from the date of the first issue located, that of Dec. 11, 1813, vol. 1, no. 4, entitled "Allegany Freeman." The last issue located is that of July 27, 1816, vol. 3, no. 37. The editor is given as F[rederick] A. Wise in a list of Maryland newspapers in "Niles' Weekly Register" of Dec. 27, 1817. It is stated in the "Maryland Republican" of Mar. 7, 1818, that this paper was to be "relinquished" with the issue of Feb. 28, 1818, and there is a reference to its recent discontinuance in the

Fredericktown "Political Examiner" of Apr. 1, 1818. Wise established "The Westmoreland Republican" at Greensburg, Penn., on Apr. 25, 1818.

Am. Antiq. Soc. has Dec. 11, 1813; Jan. 8, 15, 1814.
Md. Hist. Soc. has June 29, July 27, 1816.

[Cumberland] **Alleghany Federalist, 1815–1817.**

Weekly. Established in March 1815, judging from the first and only issue located, that of July 6, 1816, vol. 2, no. 70, published by Wm. Magruder, with the title of "The Alleghany Federalist." It is noted as "recently discontinued" in a list of Maryland newspapers in "Niles' Weekly Register" of Dec. 27, 1817.

Md. Hist. Soc. has July 6, 1816.

[Cumberland] **American Eagle, 1809.**

Weekly. Established Feb. 8, 1809, by G[———] P. W. Butler & Co., to succeed Butler's other paper, "Cumberland Impartialist." The only known issue of "The American Eagle" is that of Feb. 15, 1809, vol. 1, no. 2. Butler removed to Huntingdon, Penn., in July 1809.

Am. Antiq. Soc. has Feb. 15, 1809.

Cumberland Gazette, 1814.

Weekly. It is stated in W. H. Lowdermilk's "History of Cumberland," 1878, p. 301, that the "Cumberland Gazette" was established by William Brown Jan. 13, 1814. The only copy located is that of July 21, 1814, vol. 1, no. 28, published by William Brown, with the title of "Cumberland Gazette." This evidently is the William Brown who published the "Hagers-Town Gazette" from 1809–1813.

Am. Antiq. Soc. has July 21, 1814.

Cumberland Impartialist, 1808–1809.

Weekly. Established in January, 1808, judging from the date of the only issue located, that of Jan. 24, 1809, vol. 1, no. 52, published by G[———] P. W. Butler, with the title of "The Cumberland Impartialist." Discontinued with this issue and succeeded by "The American Eagle."

Am. Antiq. Soc. has Jan. 24, 1809.

[Cumberland] **Western Herald, 1818–1819.**

Weekly. Established in March, 1818, judging from the date of the first issue located, that of Apr. 5, 1819, vol. 2, no. 4, published by Joseph Smith, with the title of "Western Herald & Cumberland Weekly Advertiser." The only other issue located is that of Apr. 12, 1819.

Univ. of Chicago has Apr. 5, 12, 1819.
Am. Antiq. Soc. has Apr. 12, 1819.

[Easton] **Eastern Shore General Advertiser,** see [Easton] **Republican Star.**

Easton Gazette, 1817–1820+.

Weekly. Established in December, 1817, judging from the date of the first issue located, that of July 6, 1818, vol. 1, no. 30, published by Alexander Graham under the title of "Easton Gazette, and Eastern Shore Intelligencer." Continued after 1820.

Md. Hist. Soc. has Dec. 14, 1818–Dec. 23, 1820.
Am. Antiq. Soc. has July 6, 1818.
Pratt Lib., Baltimore, has Mar. 11, 1820.

[Easton] **Herald,** see [Easton] **Maryland Herald.**

[Easton] **Maryland Herald, 1790–1804.**

Weekly. Established May 11, 1790, by James Cowan, the full title being "The Maryland Herald, and Eastern Shore Intelligencer." Cowan issued a prospectus "To the Public" dated June 3, 1789. The title was changed to "Herald and Eastern Shore Intelligencer" on Oct. 29 or Nov. 5, 1799. Cowan discontinued the paper with the issue of Nov. 13, 1804, vol. 15, no. 748.

Md. Hist. Soc. has prospectus of June 3, 1789; May 11–June 1, Aug. 3–31, Sept. 14–Oct. 26, Nov. 16–Dec. 28, 1790; Jan. 4–Feb. 8, 22–June 14, 28–Sept. 6, Oct. 11, Nov. 15, 1791; May 1, 1792–Dec. 27, 1796, fair; Apr. 11, 1797–Nov. 13, 1804, fair.
Am. Antiq. Soc. has May 18–Aug. 17, 31, Sept. 7, 21–Oct. 5, 19, Nov. 16, Dec. 14, 21, 1790; Mar. 8, Apr. 12, 26, June 28, Aug. 16, 30, Sept. 6, 13, Oct. 4, 1791; Jan. 24–Feb. 7, May 8, June 19, 26, July 3, 17, 31, Sept. 18, 1792; Feb. 12, Mar. 12, July 16, 1793; Aug. 28, 1798; Jan. 17, Mar. 13, June 26, 1804.
Harvard has June 7, 28, July 5, 19, Nov. 15, 1791; Feb. 24, Mar. 24, May 19, June 9, 16, Nov. 10, 1795; May 17, 24, June 7, 21, July 5–19, Aug. 2–23, Sept. 6–27, Oct. 11–25, Nov. 15, 22, Dec. 6–27, 1796; Jan. 10–24, Feb. 14, 28, Apr. 18, 1797.
Lib. Congress has July 24, 1792; Aug. 26, 1794; Aug. 7, 21–Sept. 4, 25, Oct. 2, Nov. 20, 27, Dec. 11, 1798; July 30, Nov. 19, 1799; Dec. 16, 1800.
Phil. Lib. Co. has Oct. 27–Nov. 10, Dec. 1, 1795.

Wis. Hist. Soc. has Mar. 10, 1795, Feb. 19, 26, May 7, July 30–Aug. 20, Sept. 24–Oct. 22, 1799.

Pratt Lib., Baltimore, has Oct. 12, 1790; photostat of prospectus, June 3, 1789.

[Easton] **People's Monitor**, 1809–1815.

Weekly. Established by Samuel B. Beach Mar. 4, 1809, with the title of "The People's Monitor." Beach continued the paper certainly as far as Feb. 24, 1810. The issues from July 7, 1810, to Apr. 13, 1811, were published by Henry W. Gibbs; and those from June 6, 1812, to Dec. 23, 1815, by Nicholas S. Rowlenson. Owing to the absence of papers for the intervals between these periods the exact dates of change of proprietorship cannot be determined. The last issue located is that of Dec. 23, 1815, vol. 7, no. 363.

Am. Antiq. Soc. has Mar. 4–Nov. 4, 18, Dec. 2–30, 1809; Jan. 6–Feb. 24, July 7, 14, 1810; Feb. 2, 23, Apr. 13, 1811; June 6, 20, Aug. 8, 15, Sept. 12, 19, Oct. 3, 10, Dec. 26, 1812; Jan. 2, 9, Feb. 27, Mar. 6, Nov. 27, Dec. 4, 1813.

Wis. Hist. Soc. has Jan. 9–Dec. 25, 1813.

Md. Hist. Soc. has Apr. 29, June 3, 17, Nov. 4, 1809; Dec. 8, 1810; June 11, 1814; Jan. 7–Nov. 25, Dec. 9, 23, 1815.

Harvard has Mar. 25, Apr. 1, 1809.

Yale has Sept. 2, 16, Oct. 7, 1809.

Dartmouth has Apr. 1, 1809.

N. Y. State Lib. has Apr. 29, 1809.

[Easton] **Republican Star**, 1799–1820+.

Weekly. Established late in August 1799, judging from the date of the first issue located, that of Feb. 11, 1800, vol. 1, no. 25, published by Thomas Perrin Smith. The full title was "Republican Star, or, Eastern Shore Political Luminary." With the issue of Sept. 7, 1802, the paper was brought out in new form and with the title "Republican Star or Eastern Shore General Advertiser." An alternate system of numbering was begun, vol. 1, no. 1, and vol. 4, no. 157. With the issue of Sept. 20, 1814, the title was changed to the "Republican Star"; with that of Sept. 27, 1814, to "Republican Star or General Advertiser"; and with that of Jan. 7, 1817, to "Republican Star and General Advertiser." Smith continued the paper until after 1820.

Md. Hist. Soc. has Sept. 7, 1802–Dec. 26, 1820.

Wis. Hist. Soc. has Sept. 7, 1802–Dec. 26, 1820.

Am. Antiq. Soc. has Feb. 11, 1800; Mar. 13, June 26, 1804; Jan. 15, 1805; June 17, Sept. 2, Oct. 14, 1806; July 10, Oct. 2, 1810; Feb. 26, Mar. 12, Aug. 6, 1811; Feb. 11, 1812; May 31, June 21, 28, July 26, Aug. 2, 16, 23, Sept. 13, 1814; June 13, 1815.

Harvard has Oct. 16, Nov. 13–Dec. 25, 1804; Jan. 1–22, Feb. 5–Apr. 9, 30,

May 7, June 4–25, July 9–Nov. 19, Dec. 3, 10, 24, 31, 1805; Jan. 28, Apr. 1, June 24, 1806.
N. Y. Hist. Soc. has Dec. 8, 15, 1807; Jan. 26, Feb. 2, Mar. 15, Apr. 5, 12, 26, May 10, 24, June 14–Dec. 27, 1808; Jan. 3–Dec. 26, 1809; Jan. 9, 23, Feb. 6–Mar. 6, 27–May 29, June 12, 19, July 3, 10, 24–Dec. 25, 1810; Jan. 1–Apr. 16, May 7–June 15, July 9–Sept. 3, 17, Oct. 1, 8, 1811.
Lib. Congress has Dec. 23, 1800; Aug. 30, 1808; Feb. 9, Apr. 6, Sept. 14, Oct. 12–Nov. 2, 30, 1813; Oct. 10, 1815; Mar. 17, 1818; Jan. 5, 1819–Dec. 26, 1820.
Pratt Lib., Baltimore, has Oct. 11, 1803; Oct. 11, 1808.
Easton Star-Democrat office has Dec. 27, 1803; May 3, 1808.

[Elizabethtown] **Maryland Herald,** 1797–1820+.

Weekly. Established Mar. 2, 1797, by Thomas Grieves, under the title of "The Maryland Herald, and Elizabeth-Town Advertiser." Beginning with the issue of June 8, 1797, the imprint reads "Elizabeth (Hager's) Town." Elizabethtown was the original name of Hagerstown, but gradually was displaced by the later and permanent name. With the issue of Feb. 26, 1801, the title was changed to "The Maryland Herald, and Elizabeth-town Weekly Advertiser," and with the issue of Feb. 22, 1804, to "The Maryland Herald, and Hager's-Town Weekly Advertiser," Hagerstown replacing Elizabethtown in the imprint. With the issue of Mar. 10, 1813, Stewart Herbert, son of the founder of "The Washington Spy," was taken into partnership and the paper published by Thomas Grieves & Stewart Herbert. They continued the paper until after 1820.

Md. Hist. Soc. has Mar. 2, 1797–Feb. 15, 1805; Oct. 2, 1816; Sept. 17, 1817; Apr. 27, May 4, 1819; Dec. 12, 1820.
Hagerstown Herald-Mail office has Mar. 3, 1802–Feb. 8, 1804; Mar. 7, 1804–Dec. 26, 1820.
Washington Co. Lib., Hagerstown, has Mar. 3, 1802–Oct. 14, 1812, fair; Mar. 10, 1813–Dec. 26, 1820, fair.
Pratt Lib., Baltimore, has Dec. 8, 1802; Oct. 5, 12, Dec. 14, 21, 1803; Dec. 14, 1804; Feb. 8, Mar. 1, 1805–Feb. 10, 1809; Dec. 16, 30, 1812; Feb. 10, 1813–Dec. 26, 1820.
Harvard has Mar. 2, 9, 16, 30, Apr. 13, 20, 1797.
Lib. Congress has Apr. 23, 1801.
Rutgers Univ. has Sept. 7, 1803.
Univ. of Texas has July 12, 1805.
Am. Antiq. Soc. has Aug. 15, 1810.

[Elizabethtown] **Washington Spy,** 1790–1797.

Weekly. Established in June, 1790, judging from the date of the first issue located, that of Aug. 26, 1790, no. 9, published by Stewart Herbert under the title of "The Washington Spy," and with the imprint of "Elizabeth-(Hager's)

Town." Elizabethtown was the early name of Hagerstown. Herbert died on Mar. 3, 1795, and the issue of that day was published by Phebe Herbert. Beginning with the issue of Mar. 10, 1795, the paper was published by Phebe Herbert and John D. Cary. This partnership was dissolved with the issue of Apr. 21, 1796, and the paper printed by Phebe Herbert as sole publisher. With the issue of July 27, 1796, the name of the publisher was omitted from the imprint, which referred only to the "Office of the Washington Spy." The last issue located is that of Feb. 1, 1797, no. 339. The paper was succeeded, Mar. 2, 1797, by the "Maryland Herald," published by Thomas Grieves, who married Phebe Herbert.

Md. Hist. Soc. has Aug. 26, Sept. 2, 16, Oct. 14–28, Nov. 18, Dec. 2, 16–30, 1790; Jan. 6–27, Feb. 10–Mar. 30, Apr. 13–Sept. 12, Oct. 12–Dec. 28, 1791; Jan. 4, 11, 25, Feb. 8–22, Mar. 7–July 25, Aug. 8, 15, 29, Sept. 19–Dec. 28, 1792; Jan. 11–Mar. 29, Apr. 19–May 3, 31–June 21, July 5–26, Aug. 9–Oct. 18, Nov. 1, 15–Dec. 20, 1793; Jan. 3–Apr. 23, May 3–Aug. 13, 27–Oct. 14, 28–Dec. 30, 1794; Jan. 6–20, Feb. 10, Apr. 21, 28, May 12–July 28, Aug. 11–Dec. 3, 17–31, 1795; Jan. 6, 21–Feb. 25, Mar. 10, 17, Apr. 7–27, May 11, 25–Aug. 3, 17–Sept. 14, 28–Oct. 12, 26, Nov. 16–Dec. 21, 1796; Jan. 18, 1797.

Harvard has June 15–July 6, Sept. 21, 28, Nov. 23, 1791; Mar. 10, June 16, 1795; May 25–June 29, 1796; Feb. 1, 1797.

Am. Antiq. Soc. has Oct. 28, Nov. 25–Dec. 9, 1790; June 2, 1795.

Phil. Lib. Co. has June 15–29, 1796.

[Fredericktown] **Bartgis's Federal Gazette,** 1794–1800.

Weekly. A continuation of "Bartgis's Maryland Gazette," with same numbering, but new title of "Bartgis's Federal Gazette, or the Frederick-Town and County, Weekly Advertiser." The new title was undoubtedly assumed in 1794, although the first issue located is that of Feb. 26, 1795, vol. 3, no. 145, published by Matthias Bartgis. With the issue of Aug. 30, 1797, the title was changed to "Bartgis's Federal Gazette, or the Frederick County Weekly Advertiser." The last issue of this title located is that of Apr. 23, 1800, vol. 7, whole no. 415, and before the end of the year the title was changed to "Bartgis's Republican Gazette," which see.

Md. Hist. Soc. has July 21–Aug. 11, Sept. 8–29, Oct. 27, Nov. 3, Dec. 1–29, 1796; Jan. 5, 12, Feb. 9–Mar. 9, 23, 30, Apr. 20–Oct. 25, Nov. 8–Dec. 27, 1797; Jan. 3–Mar. 14, 28–Apr. 11, 1798; Sept. 11–25, 1799.

Mrs. Anna L. Morgan, Washington, D. C., has Sept. 5, 1798–Apr. 12, 1800. Am. Antiq. Soc. and Lib. Congress have photostats of Sept. 5, 1798 and Dec. 25, 1799, from this file.

Harvard has Feb. 26, Mar. 12, June 11, 1795; Jan. 7, Mar. 17, Apr. 14, May 26, June 2, 30, Aug. 4, 1796; Aug. 28, 1799; Feb. 12, Apr. 23, 1800.

Phil. Lib. Co. has Apr. 21, 28, June 9, 1796.
Am. Antiq. Soc. has Jan. 23, 1799.

[Fredericktown] Bartgis's Maryland Gazette, 1792–1794.

Weekly. Established by Matthias Bartgis, May 22, 1792, under the title of "Bartgis's Maryland Gazette, and Frederick-Town Weekly Advertiser." It was of small quarto size, but was enlarged to folio with the issue of Apr. 4, 1793, and reduced again to quarto with the issue of May 23, 1793. The last issue located is that of Jan. 23, 1794, no. 88, soon after which the title was changed to "Bartgis's Federal Gazette," which see.

Md. Hist. Soc. has May 22–June 12, 26, July 3, 17, 31–Aug. 28, Sept. 11, 25, Oct. 2, 16, 30–Dec. 25, 1792; Jan. 1–Mar. 12, 28, Apr. 11, 25, May 2, 16, 30–Dec. 19, 1793; Jan. 2–23, 1794.

[Fredericktown] Bartgis's Marylandische Zeitung, 1785–1789.

Bi-weekly. The only copy located is that of Feb. 18, 1789, no. 89, published by Matthias Bartgis, with the title of "Bartgis's Marylandische Zeitung." If issued bi-weekly, this would carry the date of establishment back to October 1785. In the "Maryland Chronicle" of Jan. 18, 1786, Bartgis announced his intention of establishing a post to carry "my English and German News-papers" to nearby towns. Another advertisement in the same paper, dated June 4, 1787, advertises for a partner to take the management of the "Printing-Office in the English and German language, and two public papers in this town." Bartgis was already then preparing to establish printing offices at Winchester, Va., and York, Penn.

Am. Antiq. Soc. has Feb. 18, 1789.

[Fredericktown] Bartgis's Republican Gazette, 1800–1820+.

Weekly. A continuation of "Bartgis's Federal Gazette," the volume numbering being the same, but the title changing to "Bartgis's Republican Gazette." The new title was undoubtedly assumed in 1800, although the first issue located is that of Feb. 11, 1801, vol. 8, no. 30, whole no. 457, published by Matthias Bartgis. The title changed to "Bartgis's Republican Gazette, and General Advertiser" between Jan. 22 and Mar. 12, 1814; to "The Republican Gazette and General Advertiser" between Jan. 7, 1815, and Mar. 23, 1816; and back to "Bartgis's Republican Gazette, and General Advertiser" between Mar. 30, 1816, and Feb. 1, 1817. The name of the publisher, at first Matthias Bartgis, was changed to M. Bartgis & Son [Matthias E. Bartgis] between Sept. 23, 1815, and Mar. 16, 1816; to M. Bartgis & Company between Dec. 21, 1816, and Jan. 25, 1817; to M. Bartgis by Feb. 1, 1817; to M. Bartgis & Burke [William B. Burke] between July 12 and Aug. 23, 1817; and to Matthias Bartgis between Sept. 5 and Nov. 21, 1818. Published by Bartgis until after 1820.

Md. Hist. Soc. has Feb. 11, 18, Apr. 8, May 20, Aug. 5, Dec. 9–30, 1801; Jan. 6, 13, 27–Mar. 17, 31–Apr. 28, Aug. 6–Dec. 31, 1802; Jan. 7–Sept. 9, 23–Dec. 30, 1803; Jan. 6–June 29, July 13, Sept. 21, Oct. 12, 19, Nov. 2, 1804; Jan. 4, 18, Feb. 1–Mar. 15, Apr. 12, May 3, June 14, 21, July 5, 1805; Feb. 7, Mar. 7, 14, Apr. 18, May 2, 9, 23, Oct. 17–31, Nov. 14, 21, 1806; Jan. 23–May 15, June 12–26, 1807; Nov. 26–Dec. 31, 1808; Jan. 7–Feb. 25, Mar. 25–Apr. 8, May 20–July 1, 15–Aug. 19, Sept. 9–Oct. 7, 28, 1809; Jan. 20–Feb. 17, Mar. 3–24, Apr. 7–May 5, 19, June 23, July 14–Aug. 4, 18–Sept. 1, 15–Dec. 29, 1810; Jan. 5–Dec. 28, 1811; Jan. 11, Feb. 1–Mar. 21, Apr. 4, 18–May 30, June 13, July 4, 25, Aug. 8–29, Sept. 12, Oct. 3, 24–Nov. 14, Dec. 26, 1812; Jan. 2, 23, Feb. 13–27, Mar. 20, Apr. 3–17, May 8–June 5, July 10, 24, Aug. 7, 28, Sept. 4, 18, Oct. 2–23, Nov. 13, Dec. 4–25, 1813; Jan. 1–15, Mar. 12, 19, Apr. 2, 16, May 28, June 11–25, July 9–23, Nov. 19, 1814; Mar. 25, Sept. 10, 1815; Oct. 26, Dec. 14, 1816; Mar. 8, Apr. 12, May 31–July 5, Aug. 23–Oct. 4, Nov. 1, 15–Dec. 27, 1817; Jan. 3–Feb. 7, 28–Mar. 14, 28, Apr. 4, 25–May 16, 30–Aug. 29, Nov. 21, Dec. 5, 19, 26, 1818; Jan. 2–16, 30–Mar. 6, 20–Dec. 18, 1819; Jan. 8–22, Mar. 18, 25, July 29, Sept. 30, Oct. 7, Nov. 11, 1820.

Lib. Congress has Feb. 18, 1801; July 22, 1809; Feb. 17, Nov. 24, Dec. 8, 15, 1810; Feb. 9–23, Mar. 16–May 18, June 29, July 20, 27, Aug. 10, 24–Sept. 7, 21, Oct. 5, 19, Nov. 16, Dec. 28, 1811; Apr. 18, May 2, Oct. 10, 1812; Apr. 17, July 10, 1813; Mar. 23, 1816; Apr. 6, Aug. 30, 1817; Dec. 19, 1818; Jan. 9, 16, 30, Feb. 13–27, Mar. 20–May 8, 22, Sept. 23, 1819.

Am. Antiq. Soc. has June 17, 1801; Jan. 21, Feb. 18, 25, Mar. 18, Oct. 28, Nov. 18, Dec. 9, 1803; Mar. 2, Aug. 10, 1804; Jan. 18, Feb. 1, 1805; Mar. 7, July 1, 1806; Mar. 4, 1809; May 26, 1810; Apr. 10, 1813; Sept. 3, Dec. 31, 1814; Feb. 1, 1817; Feb. 13, May 22, 1819.

Harvard has Nov. 25, 1801; Oct. 29–Nov. 19, Dec. 3, 17–31, 1802; Jan. 7–Feb. 25, Mar. 11, 25, Apr. 1, 15, 29–June 3, 24–July 29, Aug. 19–Oct. 14, 28, 1803; July 13–27, Aug. 10, Sept. 7, 28–Nov. 2, 16, 30, Dec. 7, 21, 28, 1804; Jan. 4–Feb. 15, Mar. 1–July 12, 26, Aug. 23–Sept. 6, 27, Oct. 4, 25, Nov. 1, 15–Dec. 27, 1805; Jan. 31, Feb. 7, Apr. 4, 11, 25, May 2, 16–June 27, Oct. 3, 24, Nov. 28, Dec. 19, 1806; Jan. 30, Feb. 6, Apr. 3, 17, 24, 1807.

N. Y. Hist. Soc. has Apr. 10–June 5, 19, July 3, 18, Aug. 8, 29, Sept. 5, 26, Oct. 10, 24–Nov. 28, 1807.

Univ. of Texas has June 24, 1803.

Univ. of Ill. has June 28, 1805.

[**Fredericktown**] **Freiheitsbothe**, 1810.

Weekly. Established Apr. 7, 1810. The only copy located is entitled "Der Freiheitsbothe," Apr. 14, 1810, vol. 1, no. 2, published by C[harles] T. Melsheimer. Melsheimer was publishing the "Plain Dealer" in 1813.

MARYLAND 261

Am. Antiq. Soc. has Apr. 14, 1810.

[Fredericktown] General Staats-Bothe, 1793.

Bi-weekly. In the Philadelphia "Neue Philadelphische Correspondenz" of Mar. 19, 1793, is an advertisement stating that at Fredericktown, Md., Matthias Bartgis, printer, had since the beginning of the year issued bi-weekly a folio newspaper with the title of "General Staats-Bothe." In the "Chesnuthiller Wochenschrift" of June 18, 1793, is a quotation from the "General Staats-Bothe" of Fredericktown, Md. No copy located.

[Fredericktown] General Staatsbothe, 1810–1813.

Weekly. Established in March 1810, judging from the date of the only issue located, that of Dec. 27, 1811, vol. 2, no. 91, published by M[atthias] E. Bartgis and Co., with the title of "Der General Staatsbothe, und Wahre Republicaner." In 1812 Matthias E. Bartgis of Fredericktown offered for sale a German establishment "The General Staatsbothe," with all its printing apparatus, and stating that it had a respectable subscription of about 500 subscribers (see advertisement in "Susquehanna Waterman" of Columbia, Penn., Mar. 12, 1812). In "Bartgis's Republican Gazette" for Feb. 13, 1819, is an advertisement dated Nov. 28, 1818, which evidently refers to this paper. It is signed by M. Bartgis and reads: "All those that are indebted to the subscriber, for the German Newspaper, that was printed from the year 1810 to 1813, which was three years," etc.

Am. Antiq. Soc. has Dec. 27, 1811.

Frederick-Town Herald, 1802–1820+.

Weekly. Established by John P. Thompson, June 19, 1802, with the title of "Frederick-Town Herald," and continued by him until after 1820.

Peabody Lib., Baltimore, has June 19, 1802–Dec. 30, 1820.
Am. Antiq. Soc. has June 19, 1802–June 2, 1804; Jan. 26, Feb. 2, 23, 30, Apr. 13, June 15–Nov. 16, 30–Dec. 28, 1805; Jan. 4, 18, Feb. 1–15, Mar. 15–May 17, 31–June 21, July 5–Dec. 27, 1806; Jan. 3, 1807–June 4, 1808; June 10–Nov. 25, Dec. 16, 30, 1809; Jan. 6–Feb. 24, Mar. 10–Apr. 21, May 5, 19–June 2, 23, Aug. 11, 1810; Feb. 2, Dec. 7, 1811.
Wis. Hist. Soc. has June 19, 1802–June 9, 1804, June 18, 1807–June 4, 1808.
Md. Hist. Soc. has June 19, 1802–June 11, July 9, 1803; Feb. 25, 1804; Nov. 25, 1809; Mar. 30, 1811; Sept. 12, Oct. 3, 24, Nov. 21, 1812; Mar. 27, Oct. 23, 1813; May 7, Aug. 6, 1814; Jan. 28, Oct. 14, 1815; Apr. 19, 1817; Jan. 30, Oct. 2, 1819; Feb. 5, Apr. 8, 1820.
Pratt Lib., Baltimore, has Aug. 27–Dec. 31, 1803, Jan. 7–Aug. 11, Sept. 15, Oct. 6–27, 1804; Jan. 12, 19, Feb. 9–Mar. 16, 30–Apr. 20, May 4–June 1, Oct. 12, 1805; Nov. 1, 1817.
Md. State Lib. has June 19, 1802–June 11, 1803.

Univ. of Chicago has Apr. 30, May 28, 1803; Feb. 4–Mar. 17, 31–May 26, June 16–Aug. 25, Sept. 8–29, Oct. 27–Nov. 10, Dec. 15, 1804.
Lib. Congress has July 6, 1805; Aug. 4, Nov. 3, 1810; Sept. 26, Oct. 10, 24, 1812; Mar. 20, Aug. 21, Oct. 23, 30, 1813.
Duke Univ. has Aug. 20, 1803; Mar. 10, 17, 1804.
Georgetown Univ. has June 16, 23, July 21, Sept. 8, 15, 1804.
N. Y. Hist. Soc. has Dec. 4, 1805; Jan. 11, 18, Feb. 1, Apr. 5, 1806.
Harvard has Apr. 7, Nov. 10, 1804.
Yale has Mar. 24, 1804.
Univ. of Texas has May 4, 1805.
Artz Lib., Frederick, has Nov. 12, 1808.

[Fredericktown] **Hornet**, 1802–1814.

Weekly. Established June 22, 1802, under the title of "The Hornet," published by M[atthias] Bartgis in a small quarto, with four pages to each issue. The issue of Nov. 9, 1802, announced that in future the paper would be edited by Bartgis and Underwood [Matthias Bartgis and William B. Underwood]. But there was no imprint until the issue of Dec. 28, 1802, when the paper was "Printed by Matthias Bartgis." Underwood resigned to go to Pennsylvania to establish the "Gettysburg Gazette" on Jan. 21, 1803. With the issue of June 21, 1803, the title was changed to "Hornet" and the size to folio, and the whole of the last page was printed in German. Upon Dec. 23, 1806, the paper was sold to "one of its original editors," William B. Underwood, and the German page was given up. Either then or by Jan. 13, 1807, a new volume numbering was adopted, since the issue of Mar. 17, 1807, published by William B. Underwood, is vol. 1, no. 10. The last issue of this series located is that of June 23, 1807, and the paper was suspended immediately afterwards, to be succeeded by "The Independent American Volunteer" established by Underwood on July 8, 1807.

On Feb. 1, 1809, "The Hornet" was revived, published by M. Bartgis and with a new volume numbering. The size was small quarto. With the issue of Aug. 9, 1809, the size was enlarged to folio and the title changed to "The Hornet; or, Republican Advocate." With the issue of Aug. 22, 1810, the paper was published by M[atthias] E. Bartgis. The last issue located of this series is that of Oct. 9, 1811, vol. 3, no. 35. It was again revived July 21, 1813, with new volume numbering and under the title of "The Hornet," printed by M. Bartgis & Co., and of small quarto size. It was discontinued with the issue of July 6, 1814, vol. 1, no. 52.

Am. Antiq. Soc. has June 22, 1802–June 21, July 5, Sept. 13, Oct. 4, 22, 1803; Mar. 6, 1804; Apr. 9, Dec. 3, 1805; Feb. 1, July 12, 1809; Jan. 17, July 4, Nov. 14, 1810; Dec. 22, 1813; Mar. 23, Apr. 6, 27, June 29, 1814.
Northumberland Co. Hist. Soc., Sunbury, Pa., has June 22, 1802–June 14, 1803; Feb. 1, 8, 1809.
Md. Hist. Soc. has June 29, Nov. 9, Dec. 21, 1802; Mar. 15, July 12, 1803–

Dec. 31, 1805; Jan. 7–Mar. 11, 25, Aug. 5, 1806; Aug. 9, 1809–Oct. 9, 1811.
Lib. Congress has Aug. 2–Dec. 27, 1803; Jan. 3–Mar. 20, Apr. 3–Oct. 23, Dec. 25, 1804; Jan. 1, 20, Mar. 12–26, Apr. 16–30, May 14, June 4, Sept. 17, 24, Oct. 15, 22, Nov. 19, 26, Dec. 10, 17, 1805; Jan. 7–Feb. 11, 25, Mar. 18–Apr. 1, 15–May 6, June 17–Nov. 18, 1806; Nov. 28, Dec. 12, 1810; Jan. 9, 23, Apr. 24, June 12, 19, July 3, Aug. 7, 1811; July 21–Oct. 6, 20–Dec. 29, 1813; Jan. 12–26, Feb. 9–Mar. 9, 23–May 18, June 15–July 6, 1814.
Harvard has Oct. 12, 1802; Jan. 11, 25, Apr. 12, May 24, June 14, 21, Aug. 9–30, Sept. 20, Oct. 25, Dec. 13, 1803; Jan. 17, Feb. 7, Apr. 24, May 1, 15, 29, June 19–Aug. 7, 21–Sept. 4, 25, Nov. 6–20, Dec. 11, 18, 1804; Jan. 1, June 11, 1805; Dec. 2, 1806; Jan. 6, Mar. 17, 24, Apr. 7, 14, 28, May 12, 26, June 2, 16, 23, 1807.
Univ. of Ill. has May 14, Dec. 10, 31, 1805; Feb. 11, 25, Mar. 11, 1806.
Univ. of Texas has June 25, 1805; Mar. 13, 1811.
Ohio Hist. & Phil. Soc. has June 22, 1814.

[Fredericktown] **Independent American Volunteer,** 1807–1808.

Weekly. Established by William B. Underwood, July 8, 1807, with the title of "The Independent American Volunteer." Underwood resigned his proprietorship and beginning with the issue of Jan. 6, 1808, the paper was published "at the office of the Republican Gazette." The Gettysburg, Pa., "Adams Centinel" of Jan. 13, 1808, states that Mr. Underwood withdrew from the editorship on Dec. 30, 1807, and then quotes the Fredericktown "Republican Advocate" to the effect that the "Volunteer" had expired. But evidently it was continued under the proprietorship of M. Bartgis. The last page began to be printed entirely in German, having at the heading "Gedruckt: bey M[atthias] Bartgis." With the issue of June 15, 1808, the paper was published at M. Bartgis' Printing-Office. The last issue located is that of Dec. 28, 1808, vol. 2, no. 78. On Feb. 1, 1809 Bartgis revived "The Hornet."

Md. Hist. Soc. has July 22–Dec. 16, 30, 1807; Jan. 6–June 29, July 13–27, Aug. 10–Sept. 28, Oct. 12, Nov. 2–23, Dec. 7, 28, 1808.
Harvard has Sept. 9, Oct. 28, Nov. 11, 18, 1807; Jan. 20–Feb. 10, Mar. 2–16, 30, Apr. 13–27, May 18, 25, June 8, 15, 29–July 13, 27–Aug. 24, 1808.
Am. Antiq. Soc. has July 8, 15, Aug. 19, 26, 1807.

[Fredericktown] **Maryland Chronicle,** 1786–1788.

Weekly. Established Jan. 4, 1786, by Matthias Bartgis, under the title of "The Maryland Chronicle, or the Universal Advertiser." The last issue located is that of May 28, 1788, vol. 3, no. 126. In 1788 or 1789 the title was changed to "The Maryland Gazette; or, the Frederick Advertiser," which see.

Md. Hist. Soc. has Jan. 18–Dec. 6, 20, 27, 1786; Jan. 3–July 18, Aug. 1–29, Sept. 12–Dec. 12, 1787.

Am. Antiq. Soc. has June 27, July 4, Aug. 8–29, Sept. 19, 26, Oct. 10–31, Nov. 14, 21, Dec. 5, 1787; May 28, 1788.
N. Y. Pub. Lib. has May 21, 1788.
Western Reserve Hist. Soc. had June 25, 1788, according to C. B. Galbreath's "Newspapers and Periodicals in Ohio," but cannot locate this issue.

[Fredericktown] **Maryland Gazette**, 1788–1789.

Weekly. Evidently, judging from the volume numbering, a continuation of "The Maryland Chronicle, or the Universal Advertiser." The only issue located, that of Dec. 2, 1789, no. 202, was published by Matthias Bartgis, with the title of "The Maryland Gazette; or, the Frederick Advertiser." The change of title must have been made in 1788 or 1789.

N. Y. State Lib. has Dec. 2, 1789 (Am. Antiq. Soc. has photostat).

[Fredericktown] **Maryland Gazette**, 1790–1792.

Weekly. Established in February, 1790, judging from the date of the first issue located, that of Dec. 11, 1790, vol. 1, no. 43. This issue was entitled "The Maryland Gazette, and Frederick Weekly Advertiser," and was published by John Winter. Sometime in the first half of the year 1791, the name "Frederick" in the title was changed to "Frederick-Town." The last issue located is that of Oct. 4, 1791, vol. 2, no. 33. Bartgis evidently obtained the paper in May, 1792, changing the title to "Bartgis's Maryland Gazette."

Harvard has July 5–Aug. 2, Sept. 20, Oct. 4, 1791.
Am. Antiq. Soc. has Dec. 11–25, 1790.

[Fredericktown] **Plain Dealer**, 1813–1814.

Weekly. Established in June, 1813, judging from the date of the earliest issue located, that of July 29, 1813, vol. 1, no. 7, published by C[harles] T. Melsheimer & Co., with the title of "Plain Dealer." Between May 25, and Oct. 19, 1814, the title was changed to "Plain Dealer & Political Intelligencer," published by C. T. Melsheimer. The last issue located is that of Oct. 26, 1814, vol. 2, no. 20.

Md. Hist. Soc. has July 29, Aug. 19, 26, Sept. 16, 1813; Oct. 19, 26, 1814.
Am. Antiq. Soc. has July 29, Aug. 19, Sept. 30, 1813.
Lib. Congress has July 29, 1813.
Harvard has May 25, 1814.

[Fredericktown] **Political Examiner**, 1813–1820+.

Weekly and semi-weekly. Established Aug. 9, 1813, by Samuel Barnes, with the title of "Political Examiner." The second number was on Aug. 18, and from then to Sept. 29, publication was semi-weekly. With the following number the weekly issue was resumed and continued. With the issue of Feb. 16, 1814, the title was changed to "Political Examiner & Public Advertiser." Continued by Samuel Barnes until after 1820.

Am. Antiq. Soc. has Aug. 9, 18, 21, 28, Sept. 8, Oct. 15, 29, Nov. 12, 26–Dec. 24, 1813; Jan. 26–Feb. 16, Mar. 16, 23, Apr. 6–27, June 15, 29, July 27, Aug. 10, 31–Sept. 28, Oct. 12, Nov. 23, Dec. 7, 1814; Mar. 22, May 3, Nov. 22, 29, Dec. 27, 1815; Feb. 28, Apr. 10, 17, May 15, June 12, July 24, Dec. 18, 1816; Aug. 6, 1817–July 28, 1819.
Lib. Congress has Mar. 22, 1815; Jan. 6, 13, 27–Nov. 24, Dec. 8–29, 1819; Jan. 12–Apr. 26, May 10–31, June 21–July 5, 19, 26, Aug. 23–Nov. 15, 29–Dec. 20, 1820.
Harvard has Aug. 9, 18, Oct. 15, 1813.
Md. Hist. Soc. has July 13, Oct. 5, 1814; Sept. 27, Nov. 1, 1815; Nov. 4, 1818; Feb. 10, 1819; Aug. 9, 1820.
Duke Univ. has Sept. 1, 1813.

[Fredericktown] **Republican Advocate**, 1802–1808.

Weekly. Established Dec. 6, 1802, by John B. Colvin, with the title of "Republican Advocate." In the issue of Dec. 12, 1806, Colvin announced his retirement as editor, and this was the last issue to bear his name in the imprint. The four subsequent issues bore no publisher's name, but in the issue of Jan. 16, 1807, the paper was bought and published by Silas Engles. The last issue located is that of Dec. 15, 1808, vol. 6, no. 311.

Am. Antiq. Soc. has Dec. 6, 1802–Dec. 12, 1806; Jan. 16, Feb. 6, 27, Mar. 6, 27, Apr. 3, 17, Nov. 5, 1807.
Harvard has Dec. 6, 17–31, 1802; Jan. 21–Feb. 11, 25, Mar. 11, May 6–20, June 3, 17, July 1, 15, 22, Aug. 5, 19, 26, 1803; Jan. 6, 27, Feb. 3, Mar. 2, 9, Apr. 27, May 4, June 15, July 13–Aug. 10, Sept. 7, Oct. 5, 12, Nov. 16, 30–Dec. 28, 1804; Jan. 4, 18, Feb. 22, Mar. 1, Apr. 5, 19, 26, May 10, 17, June 14, July 26–Aug. 23, Sept. 13–Oct. 18, Nov. 8, 15, 29–Dec. 13, 27, 1805; Jan. 3–17, Feb. 21–May 2, 16–June 13, 27, July 11, Aug. 1–Sept. 5, Oct. 3–24, Nov. 21, 28, Dec. 12, 19, 1806; Jan. 23–Feb. 6, Mar. 13, Apr. 3, 10, 24, May 1, 15–29, June 11, July 2, 16–30, Aug. 13–Oct. 8, 29, Nov. 5, 26, 1807; Aug. 4, 11, 25, Sept. 8–22, Oct. 6, 27, Nov. 10, 17, Dec. 8, 15, 1808.
Lib. Congress has Dec. 6, 1802–Nov. 15, 1805.
Md. Hist. Soc. has Jan. 28, Oct. 14, Nov. 11, 18, 1803; Feb. 17, Mar. 3, 23, July 27, Aug. 10, Oct. 5, 1804; June 14, Nov. 15, 1805.
Univ. of Ill. has Mar. 7, 1806.
Wis. Hist. Soc. has June 2, 1808.

[Fredericktown] **Republican Gazette**, see **Bartgis's Republican Gazette**.

[Fredericktown] **Rights of Man, 1794–1800.**

Weekly. Established by John Winter on Jan. 22, 1794, judging from the first issue located, that of Feb. 5, 1794, vol. 1, no. 3, entitled "Rights of Man." The next issue found is that of Mar. 26, 1794, published by John Winter and John D. Cary. Between Mar. 4 and May 13, 1795, the paper was again acquired by John Winter. The last issue located is that of Nov. 5, 1800, published by Winter. Many of the issues had no volume numbering.

> Harvard has Mar. 4, May 13, 27–June 17, July 1, 29–Aug. 19, Sept. 2, Nov. 25, Dec. 30, 1795; Jan. 27, Mar. 23–Apr. 6, May 4–18, June 8, 15, 29–Aug. 10, 24, Sept. 7–21, Oct. 5–28, Nov. 16, Dec. 7–28, 1796; Jan. 4–Mar. 15, 29, Apr. 12, 1797.
> Md. Hist. Soc. has Feb. 5, Nov. 26, 1794; Aug. 1, Sept. 5, 12, 1798; June 18, Nov. 5, 1800.
> N. Y. Hist. Soc. has Mar. 26, 1794.

[Fredericktown] **Star of Federalism, 1816–1820.**

Weekly. The earliest issue located of the "Star of Federalism" is that of Apr. 5, 1817, which has on one margin "no. 19," and on the other "Uniontown, vol. 1, no. 50." The paper was established at Uniontown, Md., in March, 1816, and removed to Fredericktown in November, 1816. The Fredericktown issues were published by Charles Sower. The issue of Nov. 20, 1818, says "This day's paper completes the second year since its commencement in Frederick." The last issue located is that of Mar. 24, 1820, no. 174, also "Uniontown, vol. 4, no. 49, total 198." Sower died Oct. 18, 1820, and his plant was purchased by the "Frederick-Town Herald."

> Md. Hist. Soc. has Apr. 5, 19, 26, Aug. 29, Dec. 5, 1817; June 26–Dec. 25, 1818; Jan. 1–Mar. 19, Apr. 2, 9, 23, May 21, June 11–Aug. 6, 27, Nov. 19, 1819; Mar. 24, 1820.
> Artz Lib., Frederick, has Mar. 19, 1819.
> Pratt Lib., Baltimore, has Oct. 1, 1819.

Georgetown, see under **District of Columbia.**

Hagers-Town Gazette, 1809–1814.

Weekly. Established May 16, 1809, judging from the date of the earliest issue located, that of May 23, 1809, vol. 1, no. 2, published by William Brown, with the title of "Hagers-Town Gazette." The last issue located is that of June 15, 1813, vol. 5, no. 214, published by William Brown. Brown established the "Cumberland Gazette" at Cumberland, Md., in January 1814. In the Hagerstown "Maryland Herald" of Dec. 21, 1814, is an advertisement, dated Dec. 17, 1814, and signed by Henry Sweitzer as Trustee, advising that "the Printing establishment of the late Hagerstown Gazette" would be sold for the benefit of the creditors of William McPherrin. Scharf's "Western Maryland" states that William McPherrin owned the Hagerstown Gazette in June 1813, and made an assignment to Henry Sweitzer in December 1814.

Lib. Congress has May 23, 1809–June 15, 1813.
Am. Antiq. Soc. has Dec. 19, 1809; June 12, Aug. 28, 1810.
N. Y. Pub. Lib. has Jan. 26, 1813.

[Hagerstown] **Maryland Herald**, see under **Elizabethtown**.

[Hagerstown] **Torch Light**, 1814–1820+.

Weekly. Established in November, 1814, according to a reference to it in the Fredericktown "Political Examiner" of Nov. 23, 1814. It is quoted in the Chambersburg, Pa., "Democratic Republican" of Nov. 21, 1815, and Jan. 23, 1816, as published by William D. Bell. J. T. Scharf, in his "History of Western Maryland," vol. 2, p. 1143, states that the paper was established by O[tho] H. W. Stull and a few other Hagerstown men, with William D. Bell as editor. This agrees with a list of Maryland newspapers, printed in "Niles' Weekly Register" of Dec. 27, 1817, which includes the Hagerstown "Torch Light" as published by Mr. Stull. The "York (Penn.) Recorder" of Dec. 15, 1818, records the marriage of William D. Bell, editor of the "Torch Light" to Miss Susanna Harry, both of Hagerstown, on Nov. 24, 1818. The only issue located is that of June 15, 1819, vol. 5, no. 32, published by William D. Bell, with the title of "The Torch Light & Public Advertiser." The paper was continued by Bell until after 1820.

Lib. Congress has June 15, 1819.

[Hagerstown] **Wacht-Thurm**, 1815.

Weekly. Established Mar. 24, 1815, judging from the date of the only issue located, that of Apr. 21, 1815, vol. 1, no. 5, published by Johann F. Koch, with the title of "Der Wacht-Thurm und Oeffentlicher Anzeiger."

Moravian Archives, Bethlehem, Penn., has Apr. 21, 1815.

[Hagerstown] **Washington Spy**, see under **Elizabethtown**.

[Hagerstown] **Westliche Correspondenz**, 1795–1820+.

Weekly. Established in June, 1795, judging from the date of the earliest issue located, that of Sept. 28, 1796, no. 68, published by Johann Gruber and entitled "Die Westliche Correspondenz und Hägerstauner Wochenschrift." A new series, however, must have been started in June, 1799, since the volume numbering of the next issue located, that of Mar. 12, 1801, is no. 90. This issue is entitled "Die Westliche Correspondenz" and is also published by Johann Gruber. The paper is mentioned frequently in contemporaneous newspapers previous to 1811, and is listed by Thomas in his 1810 list (Amer. Antiq. Soc. Trans., vol. 6, p. 301) as published by John Gruber. The issue of Feb. 27, 1813, no. 714, is entitled "Die Westliche Correspondenz, und Hägerstauner Wochenschrift," and published by Johann Gruber. Later in 1813 Gruber took Daniel May as a partner, under the firm name of Gruber & May. In October 1813 Daniel May married Gruber's daughter (Sunbury "Northumberl. Republicaner," Oct. 23, 1813). An issue of "Die Westliche Correspondenz" of Dec. 30, 1825, published by J. Gruber & D. May, was numbered "31st year, no. 27," which would carry the date of establishment back to June, 1795.

Berks Co. Hist. Soc., Reading, has Sept. 28, 1796.
Hist. Soc. Penn. has May 17, 1798.
Lib. Congress has Mar. 12, 1801.
Penn. State Lib. has Feb. 27, 1813.

[Havre-de-Grace] Bond of Union, 1818–1819.

Weekly. Established in January, 1818, judging from the date of the first issue located, that of Apr. 23, 1818, vol. 1, no. 16, published by William Coale, with the title of "The Bond of Union." The paper was apparently suspended from Sept. 1818 to Jan. 1819, since the issue of Jan. 21, 1819, vol. 1, no. 37, which was entitled "Bond of Union," states "It is now four months since the appearance of this paper." In 1820 Coale, or perhaps his son, established a paper with this same title at Bel Air, Md.

Am. Antiq. Soc. has Apr. 23, 30, 1818.
Pratt Lib., Baltimore, has Jan. 21, 1819.

[Rockville] Centinel of Freedom, 1820.

Weekly. Established Jan. 7, 1820, judging from the only issue located, that of Jan. 14, 1820, vol. 1, no. 2, published by John Webber, with the title of "Centinel of Freedom." This paper had previously been advertised in the Georgetown "National Messenger" of Apr. 26, 1819, as the "Centinel of Freedom" to be published at Rockville by John S. Gallaher and Cyrus R. Saunders, to begin in June 1819. Evidently this earlier publication was premature.

Am. Antiq. Soc. has Jan. 14, 1820.

Rockville Courier, 1819.

Weekly. Established Sept. 6, 1819, judging from the first and only issue located, that of Sept. 27, 1819, vol. 1, no. 4, published by Andrew Kennedy, for the Proprietor, with the title of "The Rockville Courier." Yet the "National Intelligencer" of Nov. 16, 1819, records the receipt of the first number of the

MARYLAND 269

Rockville Courier, published by Andrew Kennedy, and says that it was issued on Sept. 8, 1819.

Lib. Congress has Sept. 27, 1819.

Rockville Journal, 1818.

No copy located. There is a quotation from a paper with this title in the Fredericktown "Political Examiner" of Mar. 11, 1818.

[Rockville] Maryland Register, 1807–1808.

Weekly. Established by Matthias E. Bartgis on Mar. 20, 1807, judging from the date of the earliest issue located, that of Apr. 3, 1807, vol. 1, no. 3. The size of the paper was quarto, and the full title "The Maryland Register & Montgomery Advertiser." The only other issue located is that of June 2, 1808, vol. 1, no. 45, also published by Bartgis.

Am. Antiq. Soc. has Apr. 3, 1807.
Wis. Hist. Soc. has June 2, 1808.

[Rockville] True American, 1820+.

An issue of the "True American & Farmer's Register" of Mar. 10, 1824, vol. 5, no. 6, published by J[ulius] A. Bingham, would seem to show that this paper was established in January 1820. In 1828 a paper was published at Rockville called the "Maryland Journal & True American."

Lib. Congress has Mar. 10, 1824.

[Uniontown] Engine of Liberty, 1813–1816.

Weekly. Established Sept. 9, 1813, judging from the issue of Oct. 14, 1813, vol. 1, no. 6, published by Charles Sower, with the title of "Engine of Liberty, and Uniontown Advertiser." William McCulloch, in his Additions to Thomas' History of Printing (Am. Antiq. Soc. Proceedings, April 1921, p. 161), says that Charles Sower removed from Norristown, Penn., to Uniontown, Md., soon after 1812, and established a newspaper there. The last issue located is that of June 15, 1815, vol. 2, no. 39, in which Sower announces the sale of the publication to John Harris, who was to continue the paper. The paper presumably existed until the establishment of the "Star of Federalism" in 1816. In the Fredericktown "Star of Federalism" of Aug. 29, 1817, William Hodgkiss of New Market, Md., advertises to collect all debts due John Harris or himself for the "Engine of Liberty."

Prof. William R. Taylor, Ann Arbor, Mich., has Oct. 14–Dec. 30, 1813; Jan. 6–Feb. 17, Mar. 3–Aug. 11, Sept. 22, 29, Oct. 13, 1814–Apr. 20, June 1, 15, 1815.
Md. Hist. Soc. has Feb. 23, Mar. 23, Apr. 20, 1815.

[Uniontown] Star of Federalism, 1816.

Established by Charles Sower in March 1816, and later, probably in November 1816, removed to Fredericktown (Scharf's "History of Western Maryland," vol. 2, p. 857). There is a reference to the "Star of Federalism" in a letter dated at Uniontown, June 6, 1816, in the Baltimore "Federal Republican." In the Fredericktown "Star of Federalism" of Oct. 16, 1818, there is a reference to its founding at Uniontown. No copy located. See also under Fredericktown.

Westminster Chronicle, 1818.

The "National Intelligencer" of Dec. 17, 1818, records the establishment of the "Westminster Chronicle," at Westminster, Md., printed by William B. Burke, and states that the first issue appeared in November. No copy located.

[Westminster] Observer, 1817–1818.

No copy located. In a list of Maryland newspapers in "Niles' Weekly Register" of Dec. 27, 1817, the name of the editor is given as George Keatinge. The "Baltimore American" of Feb. 5, 1818, prints the action of the Maryland legislature authorizing the arrest of George Keatinge for an article in "The Observer" of Jan. 23, 1818. There is a reference to this paper and its editor, "Mr. Keating," in the Fredericktown "Political Examiner" of Apr. 1, 1818; also another reference in the Annapolis "Maryland Republican" of Mar. 7, 1818.

MASSACHUSETTS

[Boston] Agricultural Intelligencer, 1820.

Weekly. Established Jan. 7, 1820, by William S. Spear, under the title of "Agricultural Intelligencer, and Mechanic Register." It was of quarto size, with eight numbered pages to each issue. Though primarily agricultural, the paper included current news, both local and national, marriage and death notices, and advertisements. It was suspended with the issue of July 7, 1820, vol. 1, no. 26.

Am. Antiq Soc. has Jan. 14–July 7, 1820.

[Boston] American Apollo, 1792–1794.

Weekly. Established Jan. 6, 1792, by Belknap & Young [Joseph Belknap and Alexander Young], with the title of "The American Apollo." It was of octavo size, each number containing eight or twelve pages consecutively numbered, and including also a separately paged issue of the publications of the Massachusetts Historical Society. The partnership was dissolved, and with the issue of May 18, 1792, the paper was published by Joseph Belknap, and with that of May 25, 1792, by Belknap & Hall [Joseph Belknap and Thomas Hall]. The issue of Sept. 28, 1792, vol. 1, no. 39, was the last published in magazine size and the last to contain the extra pages of Historical Society publications (see Mass. Hist. Soc. Proc., vol. 1, p. xxv). The first issue to be published in folio newspaper form was that of Oct. 5, 1792, vol. 2, no. 1, published by Belknap and Hall, with the title of "American Apollo." With the issue of July 10, 1794, this partnership was dissolved and the paper was published by Joseph Belknap. The issue of Dec. 25, 1794, vol. 3, no. 69, was unquestionably the last published.

Am. Antiq. Soc. and Boston Athenæum have Jan. 6, 1792–Dec. 25, 1794.
Boston Pub. Lib. has Jan. 6, 1792–Dec. 25, 1794, fair.
Mass. Hist. Soc. has Jan. 6, 1792–Dec. 27, 1793; Jan. 2, 30–Feb. 13, 27–May 1, 15–June 19, July 3, 10, 24–Aug. 28, Sept. 11, 25–Oct. 9, 23–Nov. 6, Dec. 18, 25, 1794.
Lib. Congress has Jan. 6–Dec. 28, 1792; Jan. 25, 1793–Dec. 25, 1794, fair.
N. Y. State Lib. has Jan. 6–Dec. 31, 1792; Jan. 11, 25, Feb. 8, 15, Mar. 1–15, 29–Apr. 19, May 10, 17, 31, June 7, 21–Aug. 16, Sept. 6, 13, 27–Dec. 27, 1793; Jan. 30, Feb. 6, Mar. 6–27, Apr. 17, 24, May 23, June 5, July 3, 10, 31, Aug. 7, 28, Sept. 11, Oct. 23, 1794.
Univ. of Mich. (Clements) has Jan. 6–Oct. 23, Dec. 7, 14, 28, 1792; Jan. 18, Feb. 1–Mar. 15, Apr. 5, 12, 26, May 10, 17, 31–June 14, 1793; Jan. 2, 9, Mar. 6, Sept. 25–Oct. 9, 23–Nov. 6, 1794.
Portland Pub. Lib. has Oct. 1, 1792–Feb. 27, 1794.

Harvard has Jan. 6–Sept. 28, 1792; July 12, 1793–Dec. 25, 1794.
Wis. Hist. Soc. has Jan. 6–Dec. 31, 1792; Mar. 22, Oct. 18, Nov. 15, 22, 1793; Mar. 6, Apr. 17, May 15–Aug. 20, Sept. 11–Nov. 27, Dec. 11, 25, 1794.
Dartmouth has Oct. 5, 1792–Sept. 27, 1793.
Chicago Hist. Soc. has Oct. 26, 1792–July 5, 1793; Nov. 13, 1794.
N. Y. Pub. Lib. has Nov. 2, 1792; Jan. 18, June 28, Aug. 16, 30, Oct. 25, Dec. 27, 1793; Mar. 27, Apr. 17, June 12, 19, July 17, Sept. 11, 25, Oct. 2, Nov. 6, 13, 27, Dec. 4, 25, 1794.
Mass. State Lib., Congregational Lib. Boston, Western Reserve Hist. Soc., and Detroit Pub. Lib. have Jan. 6–Sept. 28, 1792.
Yale has Jan. 6–Sept. 28, 1792, fair.
Univ. of Chicago has Jan. 6–Sept. 14, 1792.
Grosvenor Lib., Buffalo, has Jan. 6–Sept. 14, 1792, fair.
Newberry Lib. has Feb. 24, Mar. 9–May 11, June 1, July 6–27, Aug. 17, 1792.
Essex Inst. has Oct. 5, Nov. 2–16, 1792; Feb. 22, Apr. 6, Nov. 22, 1793; Jan. 2, Feb. 13, Mar. 6, Sept. 25, Dec. 18, 1794.
Bowdoin Coll. has Jan. 27–Apr. 13, 1792, fair.
N. Y. Hist. Soc. has Jan. 13–Sept. 28, 1792; Oct. 4, 1793; Jan. 2, 30–Mar. 6, 20, 27, Apr. 17, May 15, July 17, Sept. 18, Oct. 30, 1794.
Rutgers Univ. has Jan. 6, 20, 27, Feb. 10, 17, Mar. 2–Apr. 13, 27, Mav 4, July 6, 1792.
Univ. of Me. has Oct. 12, Dec. 31, 1792; Jan. 4, Oct. 18, 1793.
Huntington Lib. has June 15, 22, 1792.
Phil. Lib. Co. has Apr. 11, 18, 1793.
Cincinnati Pub. Lib. has Dec. 21, 1792.
Duke Univ. has July 19, 1793; Sept. 25, 1794.

[Boston] **American Herald,** 1784–1788.

Weekly and semi-weekly. A continuation, without change of numbering, of the "Boston Evening Post." The full title was "The American Herald: and the General Advertiser," published by Edward E. Powars, and the first issue was on Jan. 19, 1784, vol. 3, no. 117, published weekly. Beginning with the issue of Apr. 5, 1784, the title was shortened to "The American Herald," and with the issue of Apr. 26, 1784, it was published by Powars and Willis [Edward E. Powars and Nathaniel Willis]. With the issue of Sept. 20, 1784, the title was shortened to "American Herald." With the issue of July 17, 1786, the paper was published by Edward Eveleth Powars, changed in the imprint to Edward E. Powars with the issue of Aug. 14, 1786, and reverting to Edward Eveleth Powars on Nov. 20, 1786. With the issue of Jan. 14, 1788, the title was changed to "The American Herald: and Federal Recorder," but with the succeeding issue of Jan. 21, reverted to "American Herald," and thenceforth throughout 1788, the word "The" was alternately omitted from and included in the title. With the issue of Feb. 28, 1788, the paper became a semi-weekly. The paper was discontinued at Boston with the issue of June 30, 1788, vol. 7, no. 367, and removed to Worcester, where it was re-established with the issue of Aug. 21, 1788, vol. 8, no. 368. See under Worcester-American Herald.

Mass. Hist. Soc. has Jan. 19, 1784–June 30, 1788.
Am. Antiq. Soc. has Feb. 2, 1784–June 19, 1788, fair.
Boston Pub. Lib. has Jan. 19–Dec. 27, 1784; Jan. 3–17, 31–Feb. 28, Mar. 28, May 16, June 27, Sept. 5, Oct. 3, 10, 24, Nov. 14, 28, Dec. 19, 26, 1785; Jan. 9–Dec. 18, 1786, fair; Apr. 2, 23, May 14, 21, July 30, Sept. 17, Oct. 8, 22, Nov. 26, Dec. 10, 31, 1787; Jan. 7–Mar. 6, 17–31, Apr. 7, 10, 18, 28, May 5, 1788.
Boston Athenæum has Jan. 19, 1784–Dec. 26, 1785; Jan. 2–30, Feb. 13, 20, Mar. 6, 20, Apr. 3, 10, 24, June 19, 26, July 24, Sept. 4, 25, Oct. 30, Nov. 6, Dec. 11, 25, 1786.
Lib. Congress has Feb. 16, 1784–Dec. 26, 1785, fair; Jan. 2, 9, 30, Feb. 6, 20–Mar. 6, 20–May 1, 15, 29, June 5, 19, Aug. 21, Sept. 4, 11, 25–Oct. 9, 23–Nov. 6, Dec. 11, 25, 1786; Jan. 15, 29, 1787; Jan. 14, 21, Feb. 11–25, May 5, 12, 1788.
Harvard has Jan. 19–Dec. 27, 1784.
Wis. Hist. Soc. has Jan. 24, 1785–Dec. 31, 1787.
N. Y. Hist. Soc. has Mar. 8, Apr. 5, 19, June 14–July 5, Aug. 2, 23, Sept. 6, 27–Oct. 11, Nov. 15, Dec. 6–27, 1784; June 6, 27, Aug. 8, Oct. 3, Nov. 14–28, Dec. 12, 1785; Jan. 16, 30, Feb. 13, 27–Mar. 13, 27, Apr. 3, June 26, Oct. 16, 30, Nov. 20–Dec. 4, 18, 25, 1786; May 28–June 18, July 2, 16, 30–Sept. 3, 30, Oct. 8–Dec. 31, 1787; Jan. 7–21, Feb. 25–Mar. 6, 20, 24, May 29, 1788.
N. Y. State Lib. has June 28, July 12, 19, Aug. 2, 16–30, Sept. 27, Oct. 4, 25–Nov. 8, 22–Dec. 6, 20, 27, 1784; Jan. 3, 17–Feb. 14, Mar. 14, 28, Apr. 4, Aug. 8, 29, Oct. 10, 24–Nov. 14, 28, 1785; Feb. 20, Apr. 17, 24, Dec. 4, 1786; Jan. 22, Feb. 26, Oct. 29, 1787; Feb. 18–Mar. 16, 1788.
N. Y. Pub. Lib. has Sept. 20, Nov. 15, Dec. 6, 1784; May 9, 16, 1785; Jan. 2, 9, Feb. 27, Mar. 13, 27–Apr. 10, 24, May 1, 15, July 24, 31, Sept. 18, 25, Oct. 9, 1786; June 11, Dec. 24, 31, 1787; Jan. 21, Feb. 4, 28, Mar. 3, 20, 31, Apr. 10, 1788.
Univ. of Mich. (Clements) has May 17, 1784; June 27, Nov. 28, Dec. 5, 19, 1785; Feb. 6, Mar. 13, Sept. 4, Oct. 16, Nov. 27, 1786; Feb. 26–Mar. 12, Sept. 10, Dec. 3, 17, 1787.
Duke Univ. has Mar. 15, Apr. 12, Aug. 16–30, Nov. 1, 8, 22, Dec. 6, 1784.
Chicago Hist. Soc. has Nov. 29, 1784; May 1, 1786.
Hist. Soc. Penn. has Mar. 13, 1786.
Me. Hist. Soc. has Apr. 17, 1786.

[Boston] **American Herald,** 1790, see **Saturday Evening Herald.**

[Boston] American Journal, 1785.

Weekly. Established Feb. 22, 1785, judging from the date of the first issue located, that of Mar. 15, 1785, vol. 1, no. 4, published by William Barrett, with the full title of "The American Journal and Suffolk Intelligencer." The last issue located is that of July 12, 1785, vol. 1, no. 21.

Am. Antiq. Soc. has Mar. 15, 22, June 7, 21, July 12, 1785.
Mass. Hist. Soc. has Mar. 15, Apr. 19, July 5, 1785.
Lib. Congress has Mar. 29, 1785.
Essex Inst. has June 21, 1785.
Harvard has July 5, 12, 1785.

[Boston] American Republican, 1809.

Weekly. Established Mar. 13, 1809, by Everett & Munroe [David Everett and Isaac Munroe], entitled "American Republican," as a weekly edition of their "Boston Patriot." Meeting with little support, it was discontinued with the issue of Apr. 3, 1809, vol. 1, no. 5.

Patten Lib., Bath, Me., has Mar. 13–Apr. 3, 1809.
Lib. Congress has Mar. 13, 27, 1809.
Am. Antiq. Soc. has Mar. 20, Apr. 3, 1809.
N. Y. Hist. Soc. has Mar. 27, Apr. 3, 1809.
Boston Pub. Lib. has Apr. 3, 1809.

[Boston] Argus, 1791–1793.

Semi-weekly and weekly. A continuation, without change of numbering, of the "Herald of Freedom," the first issue with the new name of "The Argus" being published semi-weekly by John Howel on July 22, 1791, vol. 6, no. 36. With the issue of Sept. 2, 1791, all volume numbering was omitted. With the issue of Oct. 25, 1791, the paper was published by Edward Eveleth Powars. The paper was changed from a semi-weekly to a weekly with the issue of July 3, 1792, but reverted to a semi-weekly with the issue of Apr. 12, 1793. The last issue located is that of June 28, 1793.

Am. Antiq. Soc. and Mass. Hist. Soc. have July 22, 1791–June 28, 1793.
Boston Athenæum has July 26–Nov. 18, 25–Dec. 30, 1791; Jan. 3–31, Feb. 14, 28, Mar. 16, 23–Apr. 6, 13, 17, May 1–25, June 15, 26, Sept. 25–Oct. 16, Nov. 13–27, Dec. 25, 1792; Feb. 5, 26–Apr. 12, 23–May 14, 21–June 4, 11, 14, 1793.
Lib. Congress has July 29, Aug. 2, 16–26, Sept. 2, 13, 30–Nov. 4, 11, 15, 25, Dec. 9, 23, 1791; Jan. 10–Dec. 25, 1792, fair; Jan. 1–June 28, 1793.
Boston Pub. Lib. has July 26–Aug. 9, 16–Sept. 16, 27–Nov. 18, 25, Dec. 9–23, 30, 1791; Jan. 6, 13, 17, 31, Mar. 13–23, 30, May 18, 25, 29, June 1, 5, 19, July 10, Aug. 21, Sept. 11, Oct. 16, 1792; Jan. 8, 15, May 14, 17, 28, 1793.

Harvard has July 22–Aug. 23, 30–Sept. 6, 13–20, 27–Oct. 7, 28, Dec. 16–23, 1791; June 19, 26, July 3, 17, 31, Aug. 14, Sept. 11, 25, Oct. 2–16, Nov. 13, Dec. 4, 1792; Mar. 12, 1793.

Trinity Coll., Hartford, has Sept. 23–Oct. 4, 1791; Jan. 3, 1792–June 28, 1793, fair.

N. Y. Pub. Lib. has Sept. 2, Oct. 18, 28–Nov. 11, 1791; Mar. 13, Oct. 16, 1792; Feb. 19, Mar. 19, June 25, 1793.

Univ. of Mich. (Clements) has July 29, Aug. 2, Sept. 13, Nov. 4, 1791; June 26, 1792; June 25, 1793.

Essex Inst. has Sept. 20, 1791; Jan. 6, Dec. 4, 1792.

[Boston] **Auction Advertiser,** 1816.

Daily. Established Oct. 10, 1816, judging from the only copy located, that of October 11, 1816, vol. 1, no. 2, published by Tileston & Parmenter [Ezra B. Tileston and James Parmenter], with the title of "Auction Advertiser." It contained only advertisements and was issued free of charge. It was of small quarto size.

Boston Pub. Lib. has Oct. 11, 1816.

[Boston] **Censor,** 1771–1772.

Weekly. Established Nov. 23, 1771, with the title of "The Censor," published by E[zekiel] Russell. It was a political magazine rather than a newspaper, somewhat in the style of the "Tatler" or "Spectator," but its occasional "Postscripts" bore every appearance of being newspapers and contained certain local news and a large number of advertisements. It was of folio size and paged. The last issue located is that of May 2, 1772, vol. 2, no. 7.

Mass. Hist. Soc. and Boston Pub. Lib. have Nov. 23, 1771–May 2, 1772.
Boston Athenæum has Nov. 23, 1771–Apr. 11, 1772.
Am. Antiq. Soc. has Nov. 23, 1771–Mar. 21, Apr. 4, 1772.
Lib. Congress has Nov. 23, 1771–Feb. 22, 1772.
N. Y. State Lib. has Dec. 14, 28, 1771; Jan. 25, Feb. 1, 1772.
N. Y. Pub. Lib. has Jan. 18, 25, Feb. 8, 15, 1772.

[Boston] **Christian Watchman,** 1819–1820+.

Weekly. Established May 29, 1819, by True & Weston [Benjamin True and Equality Weston], with the title of "Christian Watchman." It was of quarto size and paged. With the issue of Nov. 20, 1819, vol. 1, no. 26, this size was discontinued, and upon Dec. 4, 1819, the paper was enlarged to folio size and the title changed to "Christian Watchman & Baptist Register." On Jan. 27, 1820, the printing office was destroyed by fire, and there were no issues on Jan. 29 and Feb. 5, the paper being resumed on Feb. 12, 1820. It was thus continued until after 1820.

Am. Antiq. Soc., Brown Univ., Andover Newton Theol. Sem., Colgate Univ., Pratt Inst. of Brooklyn, and Ohio State Lib. have May 29, 1819–Dec. 30, 1820.
Yale has May 29–Nov. 20, Dec. 4, 1819–Dec. 30, 1820.
Boston Athenæum has May 20–Nov. 20, 1819; July 8, Dec. 16–30, 1820.
Boston Pub. Lib. has Dec. 4, 1819–Dec. 30, 1820.
Harvard has Dec. 4, 1819–Dec. 30, 1820.
N. Y. Hist. Soc. has Dec. 4, 1819–Dec. 30, 1820.
Western Reserve Hist. Soc. has May 29–Nov. 20, 1819.
Congregational Lib., Boston, has May 29, June 12, 1819; Jan. 8, Apr. 8–Oct. 28, 1820, fair.
N. Y. Pub. Lib. has May 29, 1819.
Lib. Congress has Feb. 12, 1820.
Univ. of Chicago has Dec. 16–30, 1820.

Boston Chronicle, 1767–1770.

Weekly and semi-weekly. Established Dec. 21, 1767, by Mein and Fleeming [John Mein and John Fleeming], with the title of "The Boston Chronicle." A broadside "Proposals" was issued Oct. 22, 1767. It was a weekly, of quarto size, paged and each issue containing eight pages. The first two numbers were reprinted in varying form at the close of 1768. With the issue of Jan. 2, 1769, it was enlarged to folio size and issued semi-weekly. It was discontinued with the issue of June 25, 1770, vol. 3, no. 26. Of the three volumes published, each had a title-page and the first had an Index of six pages.

Am. Antiq. Soc. has Oct. 22, Dec. 21, 1767–June 25, 1770; also reprints of Dec. 21, 28, 1767.
Boston Athenæum, Cornell, Mass. Hist. Soc., Mass. State Lib., N. Y. Hist. Soc., and Wis. Hist. Soc. have Dec. 21, 1767–June 25, 1770.
Boston Pub. Lib. has Dec. 21, 1767–June 17, 1770.
British Museum has Dec. 21, 1767–June 7, 1770.
Univ. of Mich. (Clements) has Dec. 21, 1767–Dec. 28, 1769; Jan. 1–June 11, 1770, fair.
Lib. Congress has Dec. 21, 1767–Dec. 28, 1769; Jan. 4–11, 22, Feb. 22, 26, Mar. 19, May 14, 17, June 4, 14, 18, 1770.
N. Y. State Lib. has Dec. 21, 1767–Dec. 28, 1769; Jan. 11, 30, Feb. 22, Mar. 5, Apr. 30, May 10, 17, 1770.
N. Y. Pub. Lib. has Dec. 21, 1767–Dec. 28, 1769; Feb. 15, 19, Apr. 19, 1770.
Harvard, Yale, and Univ. of Chicago have Dec. 21, 1767–Dec. 28, 1769.
Essex Inst. has Dec. 21, 1767–Dec. 18, 1769.
Bowdoin, Conn. Hist. Soc., Detroit Pub. Lib., Long Id. Hist. Soc., N. J. Hist. Soc., Hist. Soc. Penn., Univ. of Texas, and Univ. of Ill. have Dec. 21, 1767–Dec. 26, 1768.
Chicago Hist. Soc. has Dec. 21, 1767–Dec. 12, 1768.

Dartmouth has Dec. 21, 1767–Dec. 5, 1768.
Iowa State Dep't of History has Jan. 4–Dec. 26, 1768.
York Inst., Saco, has Feb. 15–Dec. 12, 1768.
Ohio Arch. & Hist. Soc. has Jan. 2–Dec. 18, 1769.

[Boston] Columbian Centinel, 1790–1820+.

Semi-weekly. A continuation, without change of numbering, of the "Massachusetts Centinel," the first issue with the new name being on June 16, 1790, vol. 13, no. 27, published by Benjamin Russell. With the issue of Oct. 5, 1799, the title was altered to "Columbian Centinel. & Massachusetts Federalist." The character "&" in the title was changed to "and" with the issue of Nov. 13, 1799, and was altogether omitted with the issue of July 5, 1800. With the issue of May 4, 1803 the title was changed to "Columbian Centinel; and Massachusetts Federalist"; and with June 8, 1803, to "Columbian Centinel & Massachusetts Federalist." With the issue of Sept. 5, 1804, the title became "Columbian Centinel. Massachusetts Federalist," the last two words being in a wreath in a center ornament. With the issue of Sept. 6, 1809, the imprint read "Printed by William Burdick for the Proprietor," changed on Oct. 25, 1809, to "Printed by William Burdick for B. Russell." With the issue of May 18, 1814, it was merely "Printed for Benjamin Russell," and on Jan. 17, 1816, it was "Printed for Benjamin Russell by E. G. House" [Eleazer G. House.] With the issue of Jan. 3, 1818, the title was shortened to "The Columbian Centinel," changed again on Jan. 21, 1818, to "Columbian Centinel. American Federalist." With the issue of Mar. 4, 1818, the paper was "Printed for Benjamin Russell," changed on Jan. 2, 1819, to "Printed by Thomas Hudson for Benjamin Russell." Continued after 1820.

Am. Antiq. Soc., Boston Athenæum, Boston Pub. Lib., Lancaster Pub. Lib., Mass. Hist. Soc., Mass. State Lib., N. E. Hist. Gen. Soc., Harvard, Essex Inst., Dartmouth, N. Y. Hist. Soc., N. Y. State Lib., Long Id. Hist. Soc., Lib. Congress, Univ. of Mich. (Clements), Univ. of Ill., Wis. Hist. Soc., and British Museum have practically complete files, June 16, 1790–Dec. 30, 1820.

Yale has Jan. 1, 1791–Dec. 30, 1820.
Bowdoin has June 19, 1790–Mar. 24, 1819.
Cornell has Jan. 1, 1791–Dec. 30, 1797; Jan. 2, 1799–Dec. 30, 1820.
N. Y. Pub. Lib. has June 16, 1790–Dec. 31, 1817; Jan. 7, 24, May 6, 1818–Dec. 15, 1819, fair; Jan. 1–Dec. 30, 1820.
Minn. Hist. Soc. has June 16, 1790–Oct. 5, 1791, fair; Jan. 4, 1792–Dec. 28, 1793, fair; Jan. 1, 1794–Dec. 30, 1820.
Hist. Soc. Penn. has Feb. 16, 1791–Dec. 31, 1794; Jan. 2, 1796–Dec. 31, 1803; Jan. 2, 1805–Dec. 30, 1820.
Detroit Pub. Lib. has June 16, 1790–Mar. 8, 1794; Nov. 26, 1794–Dec. 30, 1797, scattering file; Jan. 3, 1798–Dec. 31, 1800; May 23–Dec. 26, 1801; Jan. 1–Dec. 31, 1803, fair; Jan. 5, 1805–Dec. 30, 1818, fair.

Univ. of Chicago has June 16–Dec. 29, 1790; Jan. 4–Dec. 26, 1792, fair; Jan. 4–Dec. 24, 1794, fair; Mar. 8, 1797–Dec. 15, 1802, fair; Sept. 3, 1803–Dec. 30, 1818, fair; Jan. 1–Dec. 2, 1820; and a few other scattering issues.

Conn. Hist. Soc. has July 3–Dec. 29, 1790; Mar. 13–Dec. 28, 1793; Mar. 12, 1794–Sept. 5, 1795; Jan. 6, 1796–June 24, 1797; Jan. 31–June 27, 1798; Jan. 2, 1799–Mar. 1, 1806; Aug. 2–Dec. 31, 1806; Aug. 1, 1807–Dec. 31, 1817; Jan. 2, 1819–Dec. 30, 1820.

Old Colony Hist. Soc., Taunton, has Jan. 15, 1796–Dec. 29, 1798; Jan. 12, 1799–Dec. 30, 1820.

Duke Univ. has Aug. 7, Nov. 17, Dec. 22, 1790; Apr. 20, 1791–Apr. 21, 1792, fair; Jan. 2, 1793–Aug. 30, 1794, fair; May 2, Oct. 21, 31, Dec. 9, 1795; Jan. 2, 1796–Dec. 30, 1820, fair.

Williams Coll. has Sept. 14, 1791–Dec. 30, 1797, fair; Jan. 3, 1798–Dec. 29, 1813.

Phil. Lib. Co. has June 23, Oct. 10, 1793; Jan. 8–Nov. 16, 1794, fair; June 17–July 11, 1795; Oct. 3, 1795–Sept. 29, 1798, scattering issues; Jan. 1, 1800–Dec. 29, 1819, fair.

Univ. of Minn. has Jan. 2–Nov. 20, 1793; Jan. 11–Dec. 31, 1794; Jan. 2, 1796–Apr. 29, 1797; Jan. 10–Dec. 23, 1801, fair; Jan. 4, 1804–Dec. 31, 1806; Jan. 4, 1809–Dec. 30, 1820.

Trinity Coll., Hartford, has Apr. 1, 1801–Dec. 29, 1802; Jan. 4–Dec. 29, 1804; Jan. 1, 1806–Dec. 28, 1816.

Washington Univ., St. Louis, has Jan. 3, 1801–Dec. 30, 1809; Jan. 1, 1812–Dec. 29, 1813; Jan. 21, 1815–Dec. 30, 1820.

Western Reserve Hist. Soc. has June 16, 1790–Dec. 30, 1795; Jan. 2, 1802–Dec. 29, 1804, fair; Jan. 2, 1805–Dec. 27, 1817; Jan. 2, 1819–Apr. 8, 1820, fair.

Chicago Hist. Soc. has Mar. 16, 1791–Mar. 9, 1793; Feb. 22–Dec. 31, 1794, fair; Jan. 1–Dec. 31, 1806; Jan. 3–July 29, 1807; Jan. 2, 1808–Dec. 30, 1815; and a few other scattering issues.

Cincinnati Pub. Lib. has June 16, 1790–Dec. 28, 1793; May 28, 1794–Dec. 31, 1800; Nov. 24, 1804–Dec. 28, 1805; July 16, 1806–July 23, 1808; July 29, 1809–Dec. 30, 1812; Jan. 1, 1814–Dec. 30, 1815.

Brown Univ. has Dec. 4, 1799–Dec. 31, 1800; Aug. 12, 1801–June 11, 1814.

Me. Hist. Soc. has Jan. 14–Dec. 26, 1792; Jan. 1, 1794–Dec. 23, 1795; Jan. 4–Dec. 30, 1797; Sept. 5, 1798–Mar. 2, 1799; June 10, 1807–Dec. 31, 1808.

Bangor Hist. Soc. has Jan. 3–Dec. 30, 1795; Jan. 1–Dec. 31, 1800; Jan. 1, 1803–Dec. 29, 1804; Jan. 3–Dec. 26, 1810.

Portland Pub. Lib. has Mar. 4, 1797–Mar. 3, 1798; Mar. 10–Dec. 25, 1802, scattering file; Dec. 7, 1814–Aug. 16, 1817, fair.

Newberry Lib. has Jan. 4, 1792–Dec. 21, 1793, fair; Jan. 17–Aug. 1, 1795, fair; Mar. 16, 1796–Nov. 15, 1798, scattering file; Apr. 17–Dec. 14, 1799, fair; Jan. 29, 1800–Jan. 3, 1801; Jan. 2–Dec. 31, 1808, fair; Jan. 2–Dec. 29, 1813.

Taunton Pub. Lib. has Jan. 4, 1804–Dec. 30, 1812.

Univ. of Texas has Jan. 4–Aug. 22, 1804; Jan. 1–Aug. 27, 1806; Oct. 24, 1807–Dec. 28, 1816.
Lowell Pub. Lib. has June 16, 1790–Sept. 7, 1793; Jan. 30, 1802–Sept. 1, 1804.
Cambridge Pub. Lib. has Jan. 4–Dec. 29, 1804; July 18, 1807–Dec. 29, 1810; Jan. 2–Dec. 29, 1813.
Va. State Lib. has Jan. 4, 1797–Jan. 1799.
Hamilton Coll., Clinton, N. Y., has Oct. 24, 1798–Aug. 24, 1799; Nov. 8, 1800–Sept. 5, 1801, fair.
Univ. of Me. has May 18–Dec. 15, 1793; Jan. 10–June 24, 1795; Jan. 4–June 28, 1797; July 14–Dec. 29, 1798; Jan. 7–Aug. 19, 1801, fair; Oct. 23, 1819–Nov. 18, 1820, fair.
Buffalo Hist. Soc. has Apr. 30, 1791–Feb. 22, 1820, scattering file.
Univ. of Pittsburgh has Jan. 1–Dec. 31, 1814; Jan. 3–Dec. 28, 1816.
Smith College has Jan. 1–Dec. 31, 1791.
Rutgers Univ. has Feb. 25–Dec. 1, 1792; and a few other scattering issues.
Many libraries have scattering issues.

[Boston] Columbian Detector, 1808–1809.

Weekly and semi-weekly. Established as a weekly Nov. 18, 1808, which is the date of the first regular issue, vol. 1, no. 1. There was also a prospectus issue numbered vol. 1, no. 1, one copy dated Nov. 7, and another Nov. 9. The title was "The Columbian Detector," printed for the editors by Snelling & Simons [Samuel G. Snelling and William Simons]. With the issue of Nov. 25, 1808, the paper was "Printed for the Editors" by unnamed printers "at No. 5 Devonshire Street"; and with the issue of Jan. 27, 1809, it was printed by Eben[ezer] French for the Editors. With the issue of Feb. 14, 1809, the title was changed to "Columbian Detector," and the publication was changed to semi-weekly. The paper was discontinued with the issue of May 19, 1809, vol. 1, no. 41, when it was sold out to the "Boston Patriot."

Am. Antiq. Soc., Boston Athenæum, Mass. Hist. Soc., and Lib. Congress have Nov. 7, 18, 1808–May 19, 1809.
Ohio Arch. & Hist. Soc. has Nov. 9, 18, 1808–May 19, 1809.
Boston Pub. Lib. has Nov. 9, 18, Dec. 9, 23, 1808; Jan. 6–May 19, 1809.
Univ. of Mich. (Clements) has Nov. 18, Dec. 2, 16, 1808; Feb. 14, Mar. 7, 14, Apr. 11, May 9, 12, 1808.
Duke Univ. has Nov. 7, 18, Dec. 16, 1808; Feb. 10, 1809.
Mass. State Lib. has Mar. 3, 7, 21–28, Apr. 18, May 5, 9, 19, 1809.
Wis. Hist. Soc. has Jan. 20, 27, Mar. 3, 10, Apr. 25–May 19, 1809.
Harvard has Nov. 18, 1808.
N. Y. Hist. Soc. has Nov. 18, 1808.
Portland Pub. Lib. has Dec. 16, 1808.
N. Y. Pub. Lib. has Dec. 30, 1808.

Western Reserve Hist. Soc. has Dec. 30, 1808.
Essex Inst. has Jan. 6, 1809.
Me. Hist. Soc. has Feb. 14, 1809.

[Boston] Commercial Gazette, 1796–1797, see Boston Price-Current.

Boston Commercial Gazette, 1816–1820, see Boston Gazette, 1800–1820.

[Boston] Compass, 1818–1819.

First issued on June 6, 1818, with the title of "The Compass," published by "Paul and Others." It was of quarto size, paged, and without advertisements. The "New England Galaxy" of June 12, 1818, in referring to this issue of the paper, said that its "professed object is to advocate the claims of Mr. Clay to the presidency." The issue of Aug. 1, 1818, vol. 1, no. 2, has in the imprint "published weekly," but states "We shall not yet commence the regular publication of this paper, but as soon as a sufficient number of subscribers are obtained to warrant its regular publication, we shall go on with it. Until then it will be issued occasionally, and notice will be given in the papers of the time it will appear." But no further issues were published until July 3, 1819, vol. 1, no. 1, when a new series was started, published at the office of Thomas Badger, Jun., by "Paul and Others." The next issue was on Aug. 7, 1819, published every Saturday by Joseph Dixon, Jun., and edited by "Paul and Others." The issue of Aug. 21, 1819, vol. 1, no. 4, is the last located.

Boston Athenæum has June 6, Aug. 1, 1818; July 3, Aug. 7, 21, 1819.
Am. Antiq. Soc. has Aug. 1, 1818.
N. Y. Hist. Soc. has Aug. 1, 1818.

[Boston] Constitutional Telegraph, 1799–1802.

Semi-weekly. Established Oct. 2, 1799, with the title of "The Constitutional Telegraph," published at Parker's Printing Office [Samuel S. Parker]. With the issue of Jan. 1, 1800, the title was changed to "The Constitutional Telegraphe." With the issue of July 19, 1800, the paper was published by Jonathan S. Copp for the proprietor. With the issue of Oct. 1, 1800, the paper was published by John S. Lillie. In March, 1802, Lillie was sentenced to three months imprisonment for libel, and with the issue of Apr. 10, 1802, the paper was published by J[ohn] M. Dunham. It was discontinued with the issue of May 22, 1802, vol. 4, no. 276, and the "Republican Gazetteer" published in its stead. (See Buckingham's "Specimens of Newspaper Literature," vol. 2, p. 308; and "Diary of William Bentley," vol. 2, p. 319, and vol. 3, p. 254).

Boston Athenæum has Oct. 2, 1799–Dec. 31, 1800; Jan. 14, 21, Apr. 11, 1801; Jan. 7–May 19, 1802.
Lib. Congress has Oct. 2–30, Nov. 9–20, 27–Dec. 28, 1799; Jan. 1, 4, 8, Feb. 22,

26, Mar. 19, 22, 29–Apr. 16, May 17, Oct. 11, 22, 25, Nov. 15–22, 29–Dec. 13, 1800; Jan. 7–June 6, 13–July 11, 18–Sept. 30, Nov. 7, 21–28, Dec. 5, 9, 1801; Jan. 2–May 22, 1802.

Am. Antiq. Soc. has Nov. 6, 23, Dec. 7, 14–28, 1799; Jan. 1–June 18, 25–Dec. 31, 1800; Jan. 3–Dec. 30, 1801; Jan. 16, Feb. 10, Mar. 17, 1802.

Mass. Hist. Soc. has Oct. 5, 16, 19, 30–Nov. 6, 23, Dec. 11–21, 1799; Jan. 1–May 7, 14, 18, 25–June 11, 28–Aug. 30, Sept. 6, 13, 20–Dec. 31, 1800; Jan. 3–June 17, 24–Aug. 22, 29–Oct. 28, Nov. 4, 7, 14–Dec. 9, 23, 26, 1801; Jan. 16, 23, Feb. 6, 20, 27, Mar. 10–24, Apr. 7, 14, May 19, 22, 1802.

Boston Pub. Lib. has Jan. 1–Dec. 31, 1800; Jan. 3–Mar. 28, Apr. 4–15, 22, 29, May 9–23, June 3, 10, 13, 24–July 1, 11–Aug. 12, 22–Sept. 30, Oct. 10–Dec. 30, 1801; Jan. 2–May 22, 1802.

Dartmouth has Nov. 23, 1799; Jan. 1–Feb. 15, 22–May 14, 21–Aug. 6, 13–30, Sept. 27–Oct. 29, Nov. 5–22, 29–Dec. 27, 1800; Jan. 7–Feb. 7, 18, 25–July 22, 29, Aug. 1, 8, 12, 19–Nov. 7, 14–Dec. 30, 1801; Jan. 2–May 22, 1802.

Yale has Oct. 5–20, 29–Dec. 21, 1799; Jan. 1–Dec. 24, 1800.

Portland Pub. Lib. has Nov. 29, 1800–Feb. 27, 1802.

N. Y. State Lib. has Dec. 14, 1799; Mar. 29, Apr. 2, Aug. 13, 1800; Nov. 7, 1801; Jan. 16–May 12, 1802, fair.

Harvard has Oct. 2–9, 1799; Sept. 27, Oct. 1, 1800; Sept. 26, 30, Nov. 25, Dec. 2–30, 1801; Jan. 2–Mar. 31, Apr. 7–May 22, 1802.

Me. Hist. Soc. has Oct. 15, 1800; Feb. 11–Dec. 30, 1801.

Essex Inst. has Jan. 4–Aug. 23, 1800, fair; July 4, 1801; Apr. 7–May 22, 1802.

Univ. of Mich. (Clements) has Mar. 26, Sept. 13, 1800; Jan. 14, Apr. 8, June 13, 17, Sept. 9, 16, 23–Oct. 14, 1801.

Long Id. Hist. Soc. has July 26, Aug. 9, 16, Oct. 25, Dec. 27, 1800; Jan. 3, Mar. 18, 1801.

Wis. Hist. Soc. has Sept. 19, 1801; May 1–22, 1802.

N. J. Hist. Soc. has Nov. 19, Dec. 17, 1800; Feb. 28, Mar. 11, 1801.

Univ. of Ill. has Dec. 2, 5, 26, 1801; Jan. 23, 1802.

Conn. Hist. Soc. has Dec. 28, 1799; Jan. 1, 1800.

N. Y. Pub. Lib. has May 23, 1801.

Rutgers Univ. has May 27, 1801.

[Boston] Continental Journal, 1776–1787.

Weekly. Established May 30, 1776, by John Gill under the title of "The Continental Journal, and Weekly Advertiser." Gill disposed of the paper to James D. Griffith, who began publishing it with the issue of Apr. 28, 1785, slightly changing the title to "The Continental Journal, and the Weekly Advertiser." Because of the State tax on advertisements, he discontinued the paper with the issue of June 21, 1787, vol. 10, no. 591.

Boston Athenæum has May 30, 1776–Dec. 30, 1784; Jan. 6–Sept. 15, Oct. 6–Nov. 3, 24, 1785.

Am. Antiq. Soc. has June 20, 1776–Dec. 31, 1778; Jan. 7–May 13, 27, June 3, 17–July 8, 22, Aug. 12–Sept. 2, 16–Nov. 18, Dec. 2, 10, 23, 1779; Jan. 6, 13, Feb. 10–June 8, 22–July 27, Aug. 10, 17, 31–Nov. 9, 23–Dec. 28, 1780; Jan. 4–Feb. 15, Mar. 1–22, Apr. 5, 19–June 7, 21–July 26, Aug. 23–Dec. 27, 1781; Jan. 3–17, Feb. 7–28, Mar. 14–Apr. 11, 25–June 27, Aug. 1–Oct. 3, 17, 31, Nov. 14, Dec. 5, 19, 26, 1782; Jan. 2, 1783–Dec. 30, 1784; Jan. 6–Aug. 18, Sept. 1–15, Oct. 6–27, Nov. 10–Dec. 1, 16, 29, 1785; Jan. 19, Feb. 16–Mar. 2, 16–June 22, July 6–Aug. 3, 31, Sept. 14, 28–Nov. 9, 23, 30, Dec. 28, 1786; Mar. 8–May 17, 31–June 21, 1787.

Lib. Congress has June 27–July 11, Aug. 8, 15, 29, Sept. 12–Dec. 26, 1776; Jan. 9–Dec. 25, 1777; Jan. 8, 15, 29, Feb. 5, 19, Mar. 5–Apr. 9, 30–June 4, 18–Dec. 31, 1778; Jan. 14, 28–July 8, Aug. 5–Oct. 7, 21–Dec. 30, 1779; Jan. 6, 13, Feb. 10–Mar. 2, 23, Apr. 6, 13, 27, May 11, 25–Sept. 2, 28–Oct. 5, 19, 26, Nov. 9–30, Dec. 14, 21, 1780; Jan. 4–Aug. 30, Sept. 13–27, Oct. 11–Dec. 27, 1781; Jan. 3–Mar. 14, Apr. 11–25, May 9–23, June 6, 20, July 4, 25, Aug. 15–Sept. 26, Oct. 10, 24–Dec. 26, 1782; Jan. 2–July 17, 31, Aug. 7, 21–Sept. 11, 25–Dec. 25, 1783; Jan. 1, 1784–Dec. 29, 1785; Jan. 5–Aug. 17, 31–Sept. 21, Oct. 12–26, Nov. 9–Dec. 15, 1786.

Mass. Hist. Soc. has May 30, 1776–Dec. 31, 1778; Jan. 7–Apr. 22, May 7–June 3, 17–July 22, Aug. 5–Dec. 2, 16–30, 1779; Jan. 6–Mar. 2, 23–Oct. 5, 19–Dec. 28, 1780; Jan. 4, 1781–Dec. 30, 1784; Jan. 6, 13, 27, Feb. 17, Mar. 10, 24, 31, Apr. 14, May 5, 26–July 28, Sept. 1, Nov. 17, 1785; Jan. 12, 19, Feb. 2, 9, Mar. 16, 30–Apr. 20, June 1, 22, Aug. 10, 17, Sept. 14, Nov. 16, 30, Dec. 20, 1786; Jan. 4, 18, Feb. 15, 22, Mar. 8, 29, Apr. 5, 1787.

Boston Pub. Lib. has June 20, Aug. 2, 15, Sept. 5–Dec. 26, 1776; Jan. 2, 1777–Dec. 27, 1781; Jan. 3–Feb. 28, Mar. 14, Apr. 26, May 2, 16, Oct. 3, Dec. 19, 1782; Jan. 16, 30–Feb. 27, Mar. 13–Apr. 10, May 8–July 3, 17, Aug. 7, 14, 28–Nov. 27, Dec. 12, 18, 1783; Jan. 15–Feb. 19, Mar. 4–18, Apr. 8–29, May 27–June 17, July 1–15, 29–Sept. 23, Oct. 7–Nov. 4, 26, Dec. 2, 16, 23, 1784; Jan. 6–Mar. 31, Apr. 28–May 19, June 9–30, July 14–28, Oct. 6, 27, Nov. 24, 1785; Mar. 2, 23–Apr. 13, 27–May 18, June 8, July 6–20, Sept. 14, Oct. 12, 1786; Mar. 29, May 17, 1787.

York Inst., Saco, has Jan. 4, 1781–Feb. 8, 1787, fair.

N. Y. State Lib. has May 30, June 20, July 4–Dec. 26, 1776; Jan. 2–Sept. 4, Nov. 6, Dec. 11, 18, 1777; Jan. 1–Dec. 17, 1778, fair; Mar. 18–Dec. 30, 1779, fair; Jan. 6, Feb. 24, Mar. 2, 23, Apr. 20–May 4, 18, June 1, 29, July 21–Aug. 3, Sept. 14, Oct. 5, Nov. 2, 16, 30, Dec. 8, 1780; Jan. 18, 1781–Dec. 26, 1782, fair; Jan. 9, 16, 30, Feb. 13, May 16, June 12, July 3, 1783; Jan. 1–Dec. 30, 1784, fair; Apr. 13, 1786.

N. Y. Pub. Lib. has June 6, 13, July 25–Dec. 26, 1776; Jan. 2–Dec. 25, 1777; Jan. 1–15, 29, Feb. 5, 19–Mar. 19, Apr. 2–July 23, Aug. 6, 13, 27, Sept. 3, 17–Dec. 10, 24, 31, 1778; Jan. 21, Feb. 4, 18–Mar. 18, Apr. 1, 8, May 7, 13, 27, June 3, July 1, 22, Aug. 5–Dec. 30, 1779; Jan. 6–July 27, Aug. 24, 31, Oct. 5, 19–Nov. 2, 23–Dec. 8, 1780; Jan. 11, Feb. 1–Mar. 8, Apr. 26, May 10, 17, 31, July 19, Nov. 15, 1781; Nov. 29, Dec. 5, 19, 26, 1782; May

MASSACHUSETTS 283

1–16, 29, Aug. 14, Dec. 25, 1783; Jan. 1, July 1, 1784; Apr. 21, 1785; Jan. 5, Aug. 3, 1786.
Dartmouth has May 30–Dec. 26, 1776; Jan. 23, Feb. 6, 20, Mar. 6, 20, Apr. 10, 24, May 8–July 24, Aug. 7–Sept. 18, Oct. 9–Nov. 27, 1777; Jan. 1–Dec. 31, 1778; Jan. 7–21, Feb. 11, 18, Mar. 4–June 3, 17–July 1, 15, 22, Aug. 5–26, Sept. 9–Oct. 14, 28–Nov. 25, Dec. 10, 23, 30, 1779; Jan. 6, 13, Feb. 24, Mar. 2, 16–May 18, June 1, 8, 22–July 13, 27-Aug. 31, Sept. 14–Dec. 28, 1780.
Hist. Soc. Penn. has Mar. 13, Apr. 3, 24, July 17, 31–Aug. 14, 28–Sept. 18, Oct. 2–16, Nov. 6–27, 1777; Jan. 8–Apr. 2, 16–Oct. 15, 29–Dec. 31, 1778; Jan. 7, 1779–Apr. 21, 1785.
Wis. Hist. Soc. has Aug. 15, Oct. 10, 1776; July 17–Aug. 7, 21, Sept. 4, 18–Oct. 2, 30, Nov. 13, 21, Dec. 4, 19, 1777; Jan. 1, 22, Feb. 26, Apr. 2, May 7–Dec. 31, 1778; Jan. 7–Mar. 11, 25, Apr. 8, May 13–July 29, Aug. 12–Dec. 30, 1779; Jan. 6, 13, Feb. 10–May 4, 1780; Jan. 23, Mar. 8, 15, Apr. 12–June 7, Aug. 16–30, Sept. 20, Oct. 18, 25, Nov. 8, 22–Dec. 6, 1781; May 12–Aug. 4, 25–Sept. 15, 29, Oct. 13–Dec. 22, 1785; Jan. 12, 26–Feb. 23, Mar. 9, 23, Apr. 7–27, May 18, 25, 1786.
N. Y. Hist. Soc. has Aug. 29–Oct. 3, 24–Dec. 26, 1776; Jan. 2–16, 30–May 9, 23–Aug. 14, 28–Nov. 27, Dec. 11–25, 1777; Jan. 8, 15, 29, Feb. 12–Mar. 12, Apr. 30, May 5, 28, June 4, 18–July 16, 30–Dec. 31, 1778; July 22, Aug. 5–26, Oct. 7, 21, Nov. 11–24, 1779; Jan. 6, Feb. 3, 10, 24–Mar. 9, 23–Apr. 13, 27–June 8, July 6–Aug. 10, 24–Dec. 14, 28, 1780; Feb. 15, Apr. 19, May 17, 24, June 7–July 26, Aug. 16–Sept. 13, 27–Oct. 11, 25–Dec. 27, 1781; Jan. 3–Mar. 28, July 18, Aug. 22, Sept. 5, 12, 26, Nov. 21, 29, 1782; Nov. 6, 1783; Jan. 29, Feb. 5, Mar. 18, May 13, June 24, Sept. 16, 23, 1784.
Univ. of Mich. (Clements) has July 4, Aug. 2–Dec. 26, 1776; Jan. 2, 16–May 15, 29–June 26, July 10–Aug. 7, 21–Dec. 25, 1777; Jan. 1–June 11, 25–Sept. 3, 17, Oct. 1–29, Nov. 12, 19, Dec. 3–31, 1778; Jan. 7–21, Feb. 18, Mar. 4, 11, Apr. 8, May 27, June 3, July 15, Aug. 12–26, Sept. 9, Dec. 2, 10, 1779; Jan. 6, Mar. 2, June 15, 29, July 13, 27, Aug. 3, Oct. 19, 1780; Jan. 25, Feb. 1, 22, Mar. 8, Apr. 12, 19, May 4, June 7, 21, July 12, Aug. 9–23, Sept. 13, 20, Oct. 11, 18, Nov. 1–29, Dec. 14–20, 1781; Jan. 3, 17, Feb. 21, Mar. 7, May 9, June 6, 20, July 25, Aug. 15, 29–Sept. 26, Nov. 7, 21–Dec. 12, 1782; Jan. 16, Feb. 27–Mar. 13, 27, Apr. 10, 17, May 22–June 12, July 3, 17, 24, Sept. 11, 25, Oct. 2, 1783; Jan. 1, Feb. 12, Apr. 16, June 17, 1784; June 30, 1785; Apr. 20, 1786.
Duke Univ. has Nov. 7–Dec. 26, 1776; Jan. 23, Feb. 6, 13, 27, May 6, 20–Apr. 10, May 29, June 5, 26, July 3, Aug. 14, 1777; Jan. 8, Mar. 26, Apr. 30, May 7, July 9, 16, 30–Aug. 20, Sept. 3, 17, 24, Oct. 8, 22, Nov. 12, Dec. 17, 1778; Sept. 2, Oct. 21, 1779; July 13, Aug. 10, Oct. 26, 1780; Apr. 19, May 4, Aug. 9, Sept. 20, Oct. 11, 18, Nov. 15–29, Dec. 14, 20, 1781; Feb. 21, Mar. 7, June 6, 20, Sept. 5, Nov. 7, Dec. 5, 1782; Jan. 16, 1783.
Harvard has May 30, June 6, 20–July 4, 25–Aug. 15, 29–Dec. 26, 1776; Jan. 2, 1777–Dec. 3, 1778; Jan. 20, 27, 1780; Jan. 3, 24–Nov. 7, 1782.
Essex Inst. has Dec. 13, 1776; Feb. 13, Mar. 20, 27, May 2, 15, June 12, 26,

Aug. 21, 28, Nov. 27, 1777; May 7, 28, July 9, Oct. 29, 1778; Jan. 7, Mar. 4, May 7–Aug. 5, 19–Sept. 23, Oct. 14–Nov. 18, Dec. 23, 1779; Mar. 9, Oct. 12, Dec. 8, 1780; Sept. 27, 1781; Jan. 31, Feb. 14, May 16, 1782; July 17, 1783. Yale has Aug. 6, 13, 1778; Sept. 14, 1780; Dec. 6, 14, 1781.

[Boston] Courier, 1795–1796.

Semi-weekly. Established July 1, 1795, by Sweetser & Burdick [Benjamin Sweetser and William Burdick], with the title of "The Courier." With the issue of Oct. 21, 1795, the title was changed to "The Courier. Boston Evening Gazette and Universal Advertiser." With the issue of Dec. 9, 1795, the partnership was dissolved and the paper published by Benjamin Sweetser alone. With the issue of Dec. 19, 1795, the title was altered to "The Courier. Boston Evening Gazette, and General Advertiser." The last issue published was that of Mar. 5, 1796, vol. 2, no. 20, since the printing office was burned out on Mar. 9. Sweetser purchased the "Federal Orrery" about a month later, and on Nov. 3, 1796, changed its name to "The Courier and General Advertiser." For an account of this latter paper, see under "Federal Orrery."

Mass. Hist. Soc. has July 1–Dec. 30, 1795.
Am. Antiq. Soc. has July 4, 11, 29, Aug. 5, 12, Sept. 9, 23, Oct. 17, 24, 31, Nov. 4–21, Dec. 5, 19, 30, 1795; Jan. 2–Mar. 5, 1796.
Lib. Congress has July 1, 4, 18–Aug. 1, 26–Sept. 12, Oct. 3, 21, 24, 31, Nov. 4, 11, Dec. 2, 5, 1795; Jan. 6, Feb. 20, 24, 1796.
Phil. Lib. Co. has Oct. 21, 28, Nov. 4, 14, 21–28, Dec. 5, 1795; Jan. 6, 16, 23, 27, 1796.
Essex Inst. has Aug. 11, Nov. 18, 25, 1795; Jan. 23, Feb. 10, 13, 1796.
Harvard has Aug. 19, 1795; Feb. 13, 20, 1796.
Boston Pub. Lib. has Nov. 4, 1795; Feb. 20, 27, 1796.
N. Y. Pub. Lib. has Oct. 24, 1795.
Duke Univ. has Nov. 7, 1795.

Boston Courier, 1805–1809.

Weekly. Established June 13, 1805, by B[enjamin] Parks & Co., with the title of "Boston Courier," as a country edition of the semi-weekly "Democrat." With the issue of Jan. 2, 1806, this firm was dissolved, the announcement being signed by Benjamin Parks and Benjamin True, and the paper was conducted by Benj. Parks. With the issue of Aug. 6, 1807, Parks engaged Selleck Osborn to take editorial charge of the paper, but Osborn's illness apparently did not allow him to serve in this capacity for more than a few weeks. At no time did his name appear in the imprint. The last issue located is that of May 4, 1809, vol. 6, no. 47, and the paper was undoubtedly discontinued soon after, as Parks established the "Daily Advertiser" on June 5, 1809.

Am. Antiq. Soc. has June 13–Dec. 26, 1805; Jan. 2–16, 30–Feb. 20, July 31–

MASSACHUSETTS 285

Dec. 25, 1806; Jan. 1, 1807–Dec. 29, 1808; Jan. 5, 12, Feb. 2, 16–Mar. 2, 16–30, Apr. 13–May 4, 1809.
Boston Athenæum has June 13–Aug. 15, Oct. 3, 1805; Jan. 2, 9, Feb. 6, 13, 27, Mar. 6, Oct. 30, 1806; Feb. 19, Mar. 5–19, Apr. 8, 16, May 7–July 30, Oct. 29, Nov. 12, 25, Dec. 2, 24, 1807; Jan. 14–Feb. 11, Mar. 17, 24, Apr. 14, Aug. 11–Sept. 22, Oct. 13, 27–Dec. 29, 1808; Jan. 5–Feb. 30, Mar. 13, Apr. 13, 27, May 4, 1809.
Boston Pub. Lib. has June 13, 1805–June 11, 1807.
Lib. Congress has July 11, 31, Aug. 15–Oct. 24, Nov. 7–Dec. 12, 26, 1805; Jan. 2–July 31, 1806; May 28, June 4, July 30, Aug. 13, Sept. 3–Dec. 31, 1807; Jan. 7–Feb. 11, 25, Mar. 3, 31, Apr. 14, May 19, 1808.
Dartmouth has July 31, Aug. 22, 1805; Nov. 20, 1806; Jan. 8–Feb. 12, 26–Apr. 23, May 7–21, June 25, July 2, 16, 23, Aug. 6, Sept. 17, 1807.
N. Y. Hist. Soc. has Apr. 28–July 21, Aug. 4–Dec. 1, 1808.
Mass. Hist. Soc. has June 27, Aug. 22, 29, 1805; Sept. 3–17, Nov. 19–Dec. 17, 1807; Jan. 7–28, Feb. 11, Oct. 27, 1808; Apr. 27, 1809.
N. J. Hist. Soc. has June 27, Aug. 22, 29, 1805.
Univ. of Mich (Clements) has Oct. 10, 1805; Jan. 7, 1808.
Harvard has June 13, 1805.

[Boston] **Courier and General Advertiser,** 1796, see **Federal Orrery.**

[Boston] **Courier de Boston,** 1789.

Weekly. Established Apr. 23, 1789, printed by Samuel Hall. An undated Prospectus was issued in an octavo pamphlet of eight pages. The paper was of quarto size, paged and eight pages to the issue. The name of the editor is not given in the imprint, but Isaiah Thomas, in his "History of Printing," 1874, vol. 1, p. 178, states that the paper was printed for Joseph Nancrede, who taught French at Harvard College. The address to the public was printed in the "Massachusetts Centinel" of Jan. 3, 1789, signed by P. J. G. de Nancrede, who generally called himself Joseph de Nancrede. It was discontinued with the issue of Oct. 15, 1789, no. 26.

Am. Antiq. Soc. has Apr. 23–Oct. 15, 1789, and Prospectus.
Boston Athenæum, Boston Pub. Lib., Mass. Hist. Soc., Mass. State Lib., Harvard, Essex Inst., N. Y. Hist. Soc., and Lib. Congress have Apr. 23–Oct. 15, 1789.
Forbes Lib., Northampton, has Apr. 23–Oct. 8, 1789.
Wis. Hist. Soc. has Apr. 23–July 16, 30–Oct. 1, 15, 1789.
Univ. of Mich. (Clements) has Apr. 23–Sept. 3, 17–Oct. 1, 15, 1789.
N. Y. Pub. Lib. has Apr. 23, 1789.

[Boston] **Courier Politique,** 1792–1793.

Weekly. Established Dec. 10, 1792, with the title of "Le Courier Politique de l'Univers." No copy of this paper has been located, but the prospectus is published in the "Columbian Centinel" of Nov. 21, 1792, in which it is stated "The paper will be published on the Monday of every week, and consist of four pages quarto. The first number will be delivered at Boston, the 10th of December next. . . . Subscriptions will be received at Boston by J. Bumstead, Printer, Union Street, near the Market, by the Editor of the Centinel, and by the different Printers, in the United States and in the West Indies." In the "Columbian Centinel" of Dec. 12, 1792 is the statement "A new paper commenced publishing in this town, on Monday last [Dec. 10], called the 'Political Courier of the World,' in French and English, in columns corresponding with each other. . . . The Editor is a man of talents." There is a reference to the issue of Dec. 24, 1792, in the "Centinel" of Dec. 26, 1792. There are also references to the paper in the "Writings of J. Q. Adams," vol. 1, p. 125, and in the "Diary of William Bentley," vol. 1, p. 415. In the Library of the American Antiquarian Society is a letter from Louis de Rousselet to Isaiah Thomas, dated Nov. 18, 1792, soliciting his support of the paper and stating that he could be addressed at Joseph Bumstead's printing-office. Apparently the last issue of the paper was on Jan. 14, 1793. In the "Columbian Centinel" of Jan. 19, 1793, is an advertisement of M. Rousselet, "Editor of the Courier Politique de l'Univers," stating that he had been suddenly called to the Island of Guadaloupe, that he was "unable to complete the task he had undertaken" and that subscribers could have their money returned at Joseph Bumstead's printing-office. In the "Independent Chronicle" of Jan. 24, 1793, is the following notice: "Sudden Death. Died (at Olympia) after a few weeks of existence, the offspring of an aristocratical Genius *Le Courier de l'Univers.* . . . The remains are to be entombed with its ancestors, at Guadaloupe." An account of this paper by Percival Merritt is printed in the "Publications of the Colonial Society of Massachusetts" vol. 24, pp. 296–299.

A few years later another attempt was made to establish a French newspaper in Boston. There exists an undated "Prospectus du Courier des Deux Mondes," presumably printed in 1794, whereby Joseph Nancrede asked for subscriptions to a paper with this title. The Prospectus is in the Essex Institute, with photostat copy in American Antiquarian Society; the paper was to be a weekly of four pages. No copy of the paper has been found and it probably was never published. The "Salem Gazette" of Feb. 25, 1794, under the heading of "Proposals for Printing," states that subscriptions will be taken at Carlton's Bookstore in Salem for "A Weekly Paper, in the French language, to be published in Boston."

Boston Daily Advertiser, 1796–1797, see **Polar Star.**

[Boston] Daily Advertiser, 1809.

Daily. Established June 5, 1809, with the title of "The Daily Advertiser," B. Parks, printer. This initial issue, which is of quarto size, is the only one located. Benjamin Parks may have published this one issue in the form of a prospectus.

Am. Antiq. Soc. has June 5, 1809.

Boston Daily Advertiser, 1813–1820+.

Daily. Established Mar. 3, 1813, under the name of "Boston Daily Advertiser," published by Wm. W. Clapp and edited by Horatio Biglow. It was issued in connection with the "Repertory," the latter paper being really a tri-weekly issue of the "Daily Advertiser," and carrying a heading at the top of the first column on the second and fourth pages of "Daily Advertiser, and Repertory." The tri-weekly issues with this heading ran only from Mar. 4 to May 29, 1813, and are listed under "The Repertory." With the issue of Apr. 30, 1813, the "Boston Daily Advertiser" was "published by Clapp & Biglow," changed on May 1, 1813, to "W. W. Clapp & H. Biglow." With the issue of Apr. 7, 1814, the paper was sold to Nathan Hale, who became the publisher, W. W. Clapp continuing as printer. With the issue of Mar. 17, 1815, Clapp's name disappeared from the imprint, and with the issue of Sept. 16, 1817, S[olomon] G. Low became the printer. Low continued as printer and Nathan Hale as publisher until after 1820.

Boston Athenæum has Mar. 3, 1813–Dec. 30, 1820.

Am. Antiq. Soc. has Mar. 3, 1813–Dec. 30, 1820, except for a few issues in 1818–1820.

Mass. Hist. Soc. has Mar. 3–Dec. 31, 1813; Jan. 1–Dec. 31, 1814, fair; Jan. 2, 1815–Dec. 30, 1820.

Boston Pub. Lib. has Mar. 3, 1813–May 31, 1814; Sept. 1, 1814–Dec. 30, 1820.

Chicago Hist. Soc. has June 12, 1813–Oct. 21, 1819.

Lib. Congress has Mar. 3–Dec. 31, 1813; Jan. 13, 1814–Dec. 22, 1815, scattering file; Jan. 22–Dec. 31, 1816, fair; Jan. 3–Nov. 28, 1817, scattering file; Jan. 1, 1818–Sept. 26, 1820.

Wis. Hist. Soc. has Mar. 3–May 29, Oct. 28, 1813–Nov. 5, 1814, fair; May 18–Nov. 3, 1815, fair; Jan. 31, June 5–8, 12, 13, July 29, Aug. 17, 1816; Jan. 3–Dec. 30, 1818; Sept. 3, 1819–Dec. 30, 1820, fair.

N. Y. Hist. Soc. has Mar. 3–Dec. 31, 1813; Apr. 9, July 1, 1814–Apr. 4, 1816, fair; June 24, 25, Nov. 18, 19, 1816; Dec. 27, 1817; Nov. 5, 1818; Feb. 19, 20, July 5, 1819.

Essex Inst. has Mar. 3, 1813–June 30, 1814; Dec. 8, 1814–Aug. 5, 1820, scattering issues; Nov. 16–Dec. 30, 1820.

N. Y. State Lib. has Mar. 3–May 28, Aug. 7, Dec. 10, 1813; Jan. 7, 18, Feb. 10–June 30, fair, July 6, 29, Aug. 10, 30, Sept. 12, 1814; May 28, July 8–11, 19–31, Aug. 2, 3, 5–9, 12–15, 25, Sept. 30, Oct. 6, 11, 14, 25, Nov. 4, 6, 1815; Dec. 27, 1816.

Mass. State Lib. has Dec. 1, 1813–Feb. 26, 1814, fair; Oct. 9, 20, 1815; Aug. 7, Sept. 3, 1816; Apr. 14, May 28, 31, June 2, 6, 9–12, 1817; Jan. 30, Feb. 12, Aug. 28, Oct. 8, 9, 13, 1818.

Harvard has Mar. 27, July 2–Dec. 31, 1813, fair; Jan. 2–Mar. 31, 1815; May 19, 1819–Mar. 2, Nov. 20–Dec. 30, 1820.
Univ. of Mich. (Clements) has Mar. 3–12, Apr. 15, May 3, 15, June 17, Oct. 15, 19, Nov. 2, 4, Dec. 31, 1813; Feb. 18, Mar. 2, 14, Apr. 22, 1814; Jan. 10, Aug. 24, 1815; Aug. 6, Dec. 25, 1816; Jan. 4–Sept. 18, 1817, scattering issues; July 3, 1818–Sept. 21, 1820, scattering issues.
Duke Univ. has Dec. 10, 1814–May 17, 1815; Mar. 4–June 29, 1818, scattering issues.

[Boston] Degrand's Boston Weekly Report, see Boston Weekly Report.

[Boston] Democrat, 1804–1809.

Semi-weekly and tri-weekly. Established as a semi-weekly Jan. 4, 1804, by True & Parks [Benjamin True and Benjamin Parks], who bought the "Gazetteer" and established "The Democrat" in its place. Associated with them as editor was John M. Williams, who wrote under the pseudonym of "Anthony Pasquin." Williams soon had a disagreement with the proprietors and published an unfriendly advertisement in the "Columbian Centinel" of June 27, 1804, which advertisement was repudiated by True & Parks in the "Democrat" of June 30, 1804. Williams's connection with the paper evidently ceased at this time. With the issue of Jan. 1, 1806, the firm was dissolved and the paper published by Benjamin Parks alone. With the issue of Aug. 1, 1807, Parks engaged Selleck Osborn to take editorial charge of the paper, but Osborn's illness apparently did not allow him to serve in this capacity for more than a few months. At no time did his name appear in the imprint. He was commissioned 1st lieutenant in the Mass. light dragoons, July 8, 1808 (Heitman, "Historical Register," 1903). Beginning with the issue of May 9, 1809, the paper was issued tri-weekly and on a single sheet. The last issue located is that of May 25, 1809, vol. 6, no. 43, and the paper was undoubtedly discontinued soon after. Beginning with June 13, 1805, a weekly country edition of the "Democrat" was published under the name of the "Boston Courier."

Boston Athenæum has Jan. 4, 1804–May 25, 1809.
Am. Antiq. Soc. has Jan. 4, 1804–Dec. 31, 1808, fair; Jan. 4–14, 25–Feb. 11, 18, 25, May 18, 23, 1809.
Harvard has Jan. 4, 1804–Dec. 31, 1808.
Lib. Congress has Jan. 4, 1804–Mar. 22, 1809, fair.
Mass. Hist. Soc. has Jan. 7, Feb. 22–Mar. 7, June 16, July 14, Aug. 29–Sept. 12, 19, 29, Oct. 13, 24, 27, Nov. 3, 10, 28, Dec. 1, 8, 29, 1804; Jan. 15, 19, 26, Feb. 2–20, 27–Mar. 27, Apr. 13, 20, 24, May 4, 8, 25–June 8, 22, July 3, 17, 27, Aug. 7, 17, Sept. 7, 18, Oct. 23, Nov. 20, 27–Dec. 14, 21–28, 1805; Jan. 4, 11, Feb. 8, 19, Apr. 9, 30, May 31, June 28, July 30, Aug. 2, 23, Nov. 19, 27, Dec. 20, 1806; Apr. 1, 4, 18, Aug. 19, 29–Sept. 23, Oct. 3–10, 31, Nov. 8, 14,

25, 28, Dec. 2, 9, 19, 1807; Jan. 6–Dec. 28, 1808, fair; Jan. 4, 21–28, Feb. 4, 11–18, 25, Mar. 4, May 3, 16, 1809.
Essex Inst. has Jan. 11, 1804; Mar. 16, July 3, Aug. 28, Sept. 4, 14, Oct. 19, 1805; Jan. 1, 22, Mar. 1, 5, 15, Aug. 27, 1806–Feb. 1, 1809.
N. Y. State Lib. has Apr. 6, May 1–June 8, fair, Aug. 17, Oct. 9, 12, 30, Nov. 2–Dec. 25, 1805, fair; Jan. 1–May 21, fair, July 16–Aug. 30, fair, Oct. 29–Nov. 5, 29, 1806; Jan. 17, 21, 28, Feb. 11, 14, Mar. 9, 21, Apr. 11–May 6, July 22, 29, Aug. 22–Dec. 30, 1807, fair; Jan. 13, 1808–May 16, 1809, fair.
Boston Pub. Lib. has Jan. 7–Feb. 11, 22, 25, July 4, Sept. 1, 1804; Mar. 16, 1805; Jan. 22, Mar. 12, Aug. 23, 1806; Jan. 17, June 13, Aug. 1, 1807–Dec. 31, 1808; Jan. 4–May 25, 1809.
Bangor Pub. Lib. has Jan. 4, 1804–Feb. 15, 1806, fair.
N. J. Hist. Soc. has June 2, 1804–Oct. 23, 1805, fair.
Univ. of Mich. (Clements) has Jan. 4–Dec. 26, 1804, fair; Jan. 23, Feb. 20, Mar. 2, 6, 16, May 4, 8, 18, June 5, 8, 15, Oct. 5, 1805; Jan. 4–Feb. 16, 1806; Mar. 26, Apr. 30, June 4, 1808.
N. Y. Hist. Soc. has Oct. 24, 1807–Apr. 27, 1808.
Bath, Patten Free Lib. has Jan. 30, 1808–May 25, 1809.
Yale has Jan. 7–Aug. 18, 1804, scattering file; Jan. 4–Mar. 4, 1809.
Wis. Hist. Soc. has Feb. 22, 1804; May 15, July 27, Nov. 23, 1805; Apr. 12, June 14, 28, July 12, 23, Sept. 6, 17, 24, 1806; Sept. 5, 1807; June 25, July 16, 20, Sept. 14, 1808; Feb. 1, 1809.
Dartmouth has May 2, Oct. 20, 1804; Feb. 9, Mar. 2, 16, Apr. 17, 20, 1805.
Duke Univ. has Jan. 2, 9, 16, 19, 1805; June 1, Sept. 10, 1808.

Boston Evening Gazette, 1795–1796, see [Boston] Courier.

[Boston] Evening Gazette, 1814–1816.

Weekly. Established Aug. 20, 1814, by William Burdick, with the title of "Evening Gazette, and General Advertiser." At first there were two editions, one on Saturday afternoon and one on Saturday evening. In the issue of Oct. 15, 1814, vol. 1, no. 9, although the heading title was not changed, the imprint on the last page gave the title as "Evening and Morning Gazette, &c," and stated that the paper was published every Saturday evening and Sunday morning. Therefore on Oct. 16 and Oct. 23, 1814, vol. 1, nos. 9 and 10, there was published a "Morning Gazette, and General Advertiser." In the issue of Oct. 29, 1814, it was stated that the Sunday morning paper was given up and the former scheme of two editions on Saturday would be resumed. With the issue of Sept. 16, 1815, the paper was enlarged from small to large folio. With the issue of Feb. 24, 1816, the paper was printed by E[phraim] C. Beals, for Wm. Burdick, but with the issue of Apr. 27, 1816, it was again printed and published by William Burdick. The last issue with this title was that of Aug. 10, 1816, vol. 2, no. 52, after which it was continued as the "Boston Intelligencer," which see.

Am. Antiq. Soc., Boston Athenæum, Boston Pub. Lib., Essex Inst., and Wis. Hist. Soc. have Aug. 20, 1814–Aug. 10, 1816.

Mass. Hist. Soc. has Aug. 20, 1814–Sept. 9, 1815; Jan. 27, Feb. 3, 10, Mar. 30, June 1, 8, 15, 1816; and the "Morning Gazette" Oct. 16, 23, 1814.

Brown Univ. has Aug. 20, 1814–Aug. 12, 1815; Mar. 30–Aug. 10, 1816.

Stow, Mass., Randall Lib. has Aug. 20, 1814–Sept. 9, 1815.

Williams Coll. has Aug. 20, 1814–Sept. 2, 1815.

Lib. Congress has Aug. 20, Sept. 3–Nov. 26, Dec. 3, 31, 1814; Jan. 7, 1815–Aug. 10, 1816.

Grosvenor Lib., Buffalo, has May 6, 1815–Aug. 3, 1816.

N. Y. Hist. Soc. has July 15, Aug. 5, Sept. 9, 23, 30, Oct. 14, Nov. 4, 1815–Aug. 10, 1816.

Hist. Soc. Penn. has Oct. 21, 1815–Aug. 10, 1816.

N. Y. Pub. Lib. has Sept. 16, 23, Oct. 7–Dec. 30, 1815; Jan. 6–Mar. 2, 16, 23, Apr. 6, 13, May 4, 25–July 13, Aug. 3, 10, 1816.

Univ. of Mich. (Clements) has Sept. 17, Nov. 19–Dec. 31, 1814; Jan. 7–28, Feb. 11–Mar. 11, Apr. 1–May 6, 27–July 22, Aug. 5, 19, 1815.

Duke Univ. has Sept. 24, 1814; June 3–July 8, 22, 1815; Aug. 24, 1816–July 12, 1817.

Boston Evening-Post, 1735–1775.

Weekly. Established Aug. 18, 1735, by T[homas] Fleet under the title of "The Boston Evening-Post." The paper was really a continuation of "The Weekly Rehearsal," since Fleet's last number of "The Weekly Rehearsal" was on Aug. 11, 1735, no. 202, and the first issue of "The Boston Evening-Post" was on Aug. 18, 1735, no. 203. The second issue of the "Post," however, on Aug. 25, 1735, was no. 2, and thereafter the numbering was continuous. Thomas Fleet died July 21, 1758, and the issue of July 24, 1758, was published by his sons Thomas Fleet and John Fleet, although it was not until the issue of July 31, 1758, that the change of names occurred in the imprint. With the issue of Jan. 5, 1761, the firm name was changed in the imprint to T. and J. Fleet. In defiance of certain provisions of the Stamp Act, the issues from Nov. 4, 1765, to May 19, 1766, inclusive, refrained from giving the imprint with the names of the publishers. The paper was discontinued with the issue of Apr. 24, 1775, no. 2065.

Am. Antiq. Soc. has Aug. 18, 1735–Apr. 24, 1775, a remarkable colonial file, lacking only a score out of nearly 2100 issues.

Mass. Hist. Soc. has Jan. 19, 1736–Dec. 26, 1737, fair; Jan. 23, 1738–Dec. 27, 1742, scattering file; Jan. 10–Dec. 19, 1743; Feb. 6–Dec. 31, 1744, scattering; Jan. 7, 1745–Dec. 31, 1750; Jan. 7, 1751–Dec. 29, 1755, fair; Jan. 5, 1756–Dec. 12, 1757, scattering file; Jan. 9, 1758–Dec. 28, 1761, fair; Jan. 4, 1762–Apr. 24, 1775.

MASSACHUSETTS 291

Boston Pub. Lib. has Apr. 5, 19, June 7, 1736; Nov. 14, 1737; May 29, 1738; Dec. 10, 1739; June 1–Dec. 31, 1741, fair; Jan. 4, Nov. 15, 1742; Jan. 10, 1743–Dec. 2, 1751; Jan. 6–Feb. 17, Mar. 2, 16, May 4, July 27, 1752–Dec. 27, 1756; Jan. 3–Dec. 19, 1757, fair; Jan. 9, 1758–Dec. 28, 1761, scattering file; Jan. 4, 1762–Apr. 24, 1775.
N. Y. State Lib. has Nov. 12–26, 1739; June 29, July 27, 1741; Sept. 27–Oct. 11, Nov. 1, 1742; Nov. 21, 1743; Apr. 30, 1744; Jan. 14, 1745–Dec. 5, 1748, fair; Jan. 2–Oct. 16, 1749, scattering file; Jan. 8–Dec. 24, 1750, fair; Feb. 4, 11, Apr. 15, June 3, 24, 1751; Jan. 6, 1752–Dec. 17, 1753, scattering file; Apr. 29, Oct. 7, 1754; Mar. 24, May 19, Sept. 8, 1755; Feb. 27, Aug. 7, Dec. 4, 25, 1758; Feb. 5–Dec. 24, 1759, scattering file; Feb. 4, Mar. 3, May 26, 1760; Feb. 23, Mar. 16, Aug. 31, Nov. 23, 1761; Feb. 1, 1762–Apr. 17, 1775, fair.
Boston Athenæum has Dec. 15, 1740; Jan. 5, Feb. 16, Mar. 23, May 18, Sept. 14–28, Oct. 12, 19, Nov. 9–23, 1741; Jan. 4, 1742–Dec. 1, 1746, fair; Jan. 5, June 29, July 27, Dec. 14, 1747; Mar. 14, July 18, 1748; Jan. 30, 1749; Feb. 12, Sept. 24, Dec. 31, 1750; June 10, Sept. 23, 1751; Jan. 7–Dec. 23, 1754; Jan. 2, 1758–Dec. 29, 1760; Nov. 30, 1761; June 28, 1762; July 25, Aug. 1, Sept. 12, 19, Oct. 3, 1763; Jan. 7, 1765–Apr. 17, 1775.
British Museum has Aug. 22, 1743–Apr. 10, 1775, fair.
Essex Inst. has Oct. 24, 1743–Oct. 29, 1744, scattering file; Feb. 4, 1745; Jan. 5–Mar. 23, June 29, Dec. 14, 1747; Dec. 3, 1750; Jan. 28, 1751; Aug. 17, 1752–Apr. 28, Nov. 24, 1755; Jan. 19, 1756–Nov. 30, 1761, fair; Jan. 4, 1762–Dec. 11, 1769; Jan. 1–Dec. 17, 1770, fair; Feb. 18–Dec. 2, 1771, scattering; Jan. 6–Dec. 21, 1772, fair; Jan. 18–Nov. 15, 1773, scattering; Jan. 3, 1774–Apr. 24, 1775.
Lib. Congress has Sept. 24, 1739; Feb. 11, Oct. 6, 1740; July 13, 20, Oct. 12, 26, Nov. 16, 1741; Jan. 18, 25, Apr. 19, 1742; Jan. 17–Dec. 19, 1743, scattering; Jan. 9–Feb. 26, Apr. 16–Dec. 17, 1744; Feb. 3–Oct. 6, 1746, scattering; Aug. 29, Oct. 3, 1748; July 31, Aug. 14, 21, Sept. 4–18, Oct. 9, 16, 1749; May 28, 1750; Apr. 8, 22, 1751; Mar. 5–Dec. 17, 1753, fair; Jan. 7–Dec. 30, 1754; July 28, Aug. 11, 1755; Jan. 5–Dec. 20, 1756, fair; Apr. 4, 18, Sept. 5, 1757; Jan. 1, 15, July 2–16, Aug. 27, Oct. 8, Nov. 5, 12, 1759; Jan. 14–Feb. 4, 25, Mar. 3, Apr. 28, June 23, 1760; Jan. 5, 1761–Dec. 27, 1762, fair; Jan. 3–July 25, fair, Dec. 12, 26, 1763; Jan. 2, 1764–Dec. 30, 1765, scattering; Jan. 6, 1766–Dec. 26, 1768, fair; Jan. 2, 1769–Dec. 28, 1772; Jan. 4–Dec. 27, 1773, fair; Jan. 3, 1774–Apr. 17, 1775.
Wis. Hist. Soc. has Aug. 8, 1737; Jan. 26–Dec. 14, 1741, fair; July 2–Dec. 31, 1750, fair; Dec. 30, 1751; Feb. 12, 1753; Oct. 14, 1754; Feb. 13, 1758–July 30, 1759, scattering; Jan. 25, 1762; May 30, Aug. 29–Sept. 26, 1763; Jan. 7, 1765–Dec. 22, 1766, fair; Feb. 6, 1769–Dec. 31, 1770, scattering; Jan. 7–Feb. 11, Apr. 22–Nov. 11, 1771; Feb. 3–Dec. 28, 1772, scattering; Jan. 4, Mar. 29, Dec. 13–27, 1773; Jan. 10–Dec. 26, 1774, fair; Jan. 2, Mar. 13, 1775.
N. Y. Hist. Soc. has July 5, 1742; Feb. 3, 24, Mar. 3, 10, 1746; Mar. 23, 1747;

Mar. 21, May 9, June 27, 1748; Feb. 27, Sept. 4, 1749; Jan. 22, Oct. 29, 1750; Apr. 22, 29, May 20, 1751; May 14, Oct. 8, Nov. 26, Dec. 17, 1753; Mar. 1, 15, Oct. 18, 25, Nov. 15, Dec. 13, 1756; Jan. 31–Dec. 26, 1757, fair; Feb. 20, Apr. 17, May 1–29, June 12, Oct. 9, 16, 1758; May 18, 1761; Feb. 15, 1762; Mar. 14, 1763; May 7, June 4, 11, 25, 1764; Feb. 10, 1766; July 20, 1767; Aug. 1, 15, Sept. 26, 1768; Sept. 25–Nov. 20, Dec. 11–25, 1769; Jan. 1–Dec. 31, 1770; Oct. 7, 21, Dec. 2, 30, 1771; Jan. 13, June 1, Nov. 23, 1772; Apr. 12, 26, June 21, July 12, Aug. 23, Sept. 20, Oct. 4, Dec. 13, 1773; Jan. 3, Mar. 21, June 20, July 18, Sept. 12, Oct. 24, Nov. 7, 14, Dec. 19, 1774; Jan. 9–Mar. 27, Apr. 17, 24, 1775.

N. Y. Pub. Lib. has Sept. 5, Oct. 24–Nov. 14, 1743; Sept. 29, 1746; Feb. 1–Nov. 28, 1748, fair; Oct. 22, 1750; Apr. 22, 1751; Sept. 25, Nov. 27, 1752; Apr. 2, July 9, 1753; Jan. 28–Feb. 18, June 10, Aug. 5, 1754; Jan. 20, Sept. 8, 29, Dec. 1, 15, 1755; Feb. 9, Aug. 2, Oct. 11, 1756; May 30, June 27, 1757; Oct. 15, Dec. 24, 1759; Jan. 28, 1760; Jan. 19, 1761; Jan. 4, 1762–June 13, 1763, scattering; May 7, Oct. 29, 1764; Jan. 21, 1765–Oct. 19, 1767, scattering; Jan. 4, 1768–Dec. 24, 1770, fair; Feb. 25, Aug. 12, 26, Oct. 28, 1771; Jan. 20, Feb. 10, 17, Mar. 9, Apr. 6, 20, Aug. 10, 1772; Apr. 12–Dec. 20, 1773, scattering; Jan. 3, 1774–Apr. 24, 1775, fair.

Univ. of Mich. (Clements) has Feb. 16, 1736; Aug. 20, 27, Oct. 22–Nov. 5, 19, 26, 1739; Jan. 21–Feb. 4, 18, Mar. 10, 24, 31, June 16, July 21, 1740; July 5, Sept. 27–Dec. 27, 1742; May 30, Sept. 19, Nov. 28, 1743; Feb. 4, 25, Nov. 11, 1745; Feb. 3, 17, Apr. 28, May 12, June 9, 16, 30, Nov. 10, 1746; Jan. 19, 26, Apr. 27, June 1, 8, July 27, Sept. 21, 28, 1747; Jan. 11, 25, Feb. 1, Mar. 14, Apr. 11, May 9, Oct. 24, 31, 1748; Jan. 8–Dec. 17, 1750, scattering; Nov. 6, 20, Dec. 11, 1752; Aug. 13, Oct. 8, 1753; Jan. 17, 24, 1754; Feb. 10, Mar. 17, 1755; Oct. 10, 1757; Nov. 6, 1758; Feb. 5, 12, Mar. 19, 26, July 16, 30, Sept. 17, Oct. 29, 1759; Apr. 21, 28, May 26, 1760; Feb. 9, Apr. 13, Aug. 31, 1761; July 19–Dec. 20, 1762, scattering; Jan. 31–Dec. 26, 1763; Jan. 9, 1764–Apr. 17, 1775, fair.

Harvard has Jan. 2, 1744–Dec. 30, 1745; Apr. 21–Dec. 29, 1746, fair; Jan. 12, 1747–Oct. 24, 1748, scattering; Apr. 3, 10, 1749; Jan. 28–July 15, 1751; Jan. 20, Nov. 27, 1752; July 29–Dec. 23, 1754, scattering; July 5, 1762; Mar. 10, 24, June 9, 1766; Dec. 26, 1768; Jan. 2–Dec. 25, 1769, fair; Jan. 1–Dec. 31, 1770; Jan. 14, Apr. 8, May 20, Sept. 16, Dec. 16, 1771; Apr. 6, 1772; Aug. 30, 1773–Jan. 23, 1775, scattering.

Portland Pub. Lib. has Jan. 31, 1763–Dec. 28, 1767.

Duke Univ. has Mar. 3, 17, June 9, 1740; June 28, Aug. 23, Oct. 25, 1742; Jan. 17, Feb. 21, June 27, July 11, 18, Nov. 7, 1743; Feb. 4, 1745; Apr. 28, 1746; Sept. 21, 1747; Apr. 2, 30, 1750; Feb. 2, 1756; Oct. 29, 1759; Dec. 21, 1761; Mar. 7, June 6, 1763; Mar. 4, 1765–Dec. 29, 1766, fair; Aug. 24, 1767; June 6, Aug. 8, 15, 1768; Jan. 30–Feb. 13, Mar. 20–Dec. 25, 1769, fair; Jan. 1, Feb. 19, Sept. 10, 1770; Feb. 25, June 3, Sept. 9, Dec. 9, 1771; May 25, Nov. 30, 1772; Jan. 11–Dec. 13, 1773, fair; Sept. 19, 1774; Jan. 9, Feb. 6, 13, 1775.

Yale has May 30, Nov. 28, 1743; Jan. 14, 21, Mar. 18, 1745; May 6, 1751; Jan. 21, Aug. 12–Dec. 30, 1765; Jan. 6–Oct. 20, 1766, scattering; June 12, July 24, Aug. 21, Oct. 9, Nov. 6, 13, 1769; Oct. 22, 1770; Oct. 25, 1773; June 27, Oct. 24, 1774.

Newport Hist. Soc. has Feb. 23–Nov. 23, 1767, fair.

Phil. Lib. Co. has Feb. 16, 23, 1741; July 26, Aug. 16, 23, Sept. 6, Oct. 18, Nov. 1, 1742; Jan. 3, Feb. 14–28, Mar. 21, Apr. 11, May 2–16, June 20–Aug. 1, 15–29, Sept. 12–26, Oct. 10–Nov. 21, Dec. 12–26, 1743; Apr. 15, 1745; Jan. 20–July 21, Aug. 11–Sept. 1, 22–Oct. 13, Nov. 10, 17, Dec. 8, 15, 29, 1746; Jan. 5–Feb. 16, Mar. 9–Apr. 20, May 11–Aug. 3, 17–31, Sept. 21–Oct. 5, 19–Nov. 30, 1747; Jan. 4, 11, 25, Feb. 1, 21, Mar. 21–May 30, June 13–July 4, 25, Aug. 1, 15, 22, 1748; Feb. 6, Mar. 13, Apr. 3, May 1, 8, Aug. 28, Sept. 4, Dec. 18, 1749; Jan. 1, 8, 22, July 30, Aug. 27, Sept. 24, Nov. 5–19, Dec. 10, 24, 1750; Mar. 4–18, Apr. 1, May 6, 13, 27, June 3, 17, July 1, 29, Sept. 30, Oct. 14, 1751; Feb. 10, 17, Mar. 23, 1752; Apr. 22, July 8, 29, Sept. 2, 9, 23, Oct. 7, 28, 1765; Jan. 13, 27, 1766.

Univ. of Minn. has Jan. 30, Mar. 6, Apr. 10, May 22, June 5, July 3, Aug. 7, 14, Nov. 6, 1769; Nov. 19, 1770.

Dartmouth has Jan. 1–15, Feb. 12, Oct. 22, Nov. 12, 1770; Sept. 21, 1772; Apr. 25, June 13, Sept. 26, Oct. 10, Nov. 21, 1774; Apr. 10, 1775.

Hist. Soc. Penn. has Nov. 11, Dec. 2–30, 1765; Mar. 8, Apr. 5, May 24, 1773.

Many libraries have single or a few scattering issues.

[Boston] Evening Post, 1778–1780.

Weekly. Established Oct. 17, 1778, by White and Adams [James White and Thomas Adams], with the title of "The Evening Post; and the General Advertiser." The last issue with this title was that of Feb. 26, 1780, and with the issue of Mar. 9, 1780, the title was changed to "The Morning Chronicle; and the General Advertiser," although the numbering was continuous. The issues of Mar. 23 and Apr. 20, 1780, were of smaller size and have the shortened title of "The Morning Chronicle & General Advertiser." The paper was discontinued with the issue of May 11, 1780, vol. 2, no. 83.

Mass. Hist. Soc. has Oct. 17, 1778–Oct. 30, Nov. 13–Dec. 25, 1779; Jan. 1–15, Feb. 12–May 4, 1780.

Am. Antiq. Soc. has Oct. 17–Nov. 7, 21–Dec. 5, 19, 26, 1778; Jan. 2–Feb. 27, Mar. 13–July 10, 24–Nov. 13, 27–Dec. 25, 1779; Jan. 1–Mar. 23, Apr. 6, 20–May 11, 1780.

Boston Pub. Lib. has Oct. 17–31, Nov. 28, Dec. 5, 26, 1778; Jan. 9–Feb. 6, 20, 27, Mar. 13–Apr. 10, May 1, 8, 22, 29, June 19–July 10, 24–Aug. 7, Sept. 11, Oct. 2, Nov. 13, Dec. 4, 18, 1779; Jan. 1, 15–Feb. 5, 19, Mar. 16, Apr. 20, May 4, 11, 1780.

Lib. Congress has Oct. 17–31, Nov. 14, Dec. 5–26, 1778; Jan. 2–Mar. 6, 27, Apr. 3, 17–May 15, 29–Oct. 16, Nov. 6–Dec. 11, 25, 1779; Jan. 1–22, Mar. 16, 1780.

N. Y. State Lib. has Nov. 7–Dec. 26, 1778; Jan. 9, 16, 30, Feb. 20–Mar. 6, 20–May 1, 15, 22, June 26, July 3, Aug. 21, Oct. 2–16, Nov. 13, 27–Dec. 11, 25, 1779; Jan. 1, Feb. 12–26, 1780.
Univ. of Mich. (Clements) has Nov. 14–28, 1778; Jan. 2–Aug. 21, Sept. 4–Oct. 9, Nov. 13, 27, Dec. 11, 18, 1779.
Dartmouth has Oct. 24–Dec. 26, 1778; Jan. 2–Feb. 27, May 8–29, 1779.
Boston Athenæum has Nov. 28, 1778; Apr. 3, 17, May 8, 22, June 5, July 24, 1779; Mar. 9, 1780.
Duke Univ. has Jan. 9, 16, 30, Feb. 20, Mar. 27, Apr. 17, May 15, Oct. 16, 1779.
N. Y. Hist. Soc. has July 31, 1779; Feb. 5, 1780.
N. Y. Pub. Lib. has Apr. 24, July 31, 1779.
Hist. Soc. Penn. has May 15, 1779.

Boston Evening-Post, 1781–1784.

Weekly. Established Oct. 20, 1781, by Edward E. Powars, under the title of "The Boston Evening-Post: and the General Advertiser." The last issue with this title was that of Jan. 10, 1784, vol. 3, no. 116, after which Powars changed the name of the paper to the "American Herald," which see.

Am. Antiq. Soc. has Oct. 20, 1781–Dec. 28, 1782; Jan. 11, 25–Feb. 8, Mar. 1–May 3, 17, 1783–Jan. 10, 1784.
Lib. Congress has Oct. 20, 1781–Dec. 28, 1782; Jan. 11–Mar. 15, 29–July 5, 19–Nov. 22, Dec. 6, 20, 1783–Jan. 10, 1784.
Boston Athenæum has Oct. 27, 1781–Dec. 27, 1783.
Boston Pub. Lib. has Dec. 8–22, 1781; Jan. 12, Feb. 16, Mar. 2, 16, May 11–25, June 8, 15, 29–July 27, Aug. 10, 31, Sept. 7, 21, Oct. 5, 12, 26–Dec. 28, 1782; Jan. 11, Feb. 8, Mar. 1, 15, 22, Apr. 5, May 10–June 28, July 12, 19, Aug. 2–16, 30–Sept. 27, Oct. 11, Nov. 1, 8, 22, Dec. 6–27, 1783.
N. Y. Pub. Lib. has May 18, 25, June 15, July 6, 20, Aug. 3, 17, Sept. 7–21, Oct. 5, 26, Nov. 9, 23, 30, 1782; Feb. 8, Mar. 15, 22, May 10, 31, June 14, Aug. 2, 9, Sept. 13, Nov. 1, Dec. 20, 1783.
N. Y. State Lib. has Nov. 10, Dec. 29, 1781; Jan. 19, Apr. 5, May 11, 25, June 1, July 13–27, Aug. 24, Sept. 28–Oct. 12, 1782; May 24, 1783.
Hist. Soc. Penn. has Sept. 28–Oct. 26, Nov. 23, Dec. 21, 1782; Jan. 25, Feb. 15, Apr. 19, 26, May 10, 1783.
Univ. of Mich. (Clements) has Oct. 20, Dec. 15, 1781; May 4, 11, 25, June 1, July 20, Aug. 10, Sept. 28, Nov. 9, 1782.
N. Y. Hist. Soc. has June 8, Aug. 10, 1782; Apr. 12, 26, Aug. 23, Nov. 22, 1783; Jan. 3, 1784.
Harvard has Nov. 17, 24, 1781; Jan. 3, 10, 1784.
Essex Inst. has Feb. 1, 1783.
Ohio Arch. & Hist. Soc. has Jan. 3, 1784.

[Boston] **Exchange Advertiser, 1784-1787.**

Weekly. Established Dec. 30, 1784, by Peter Edes, with the title of "The Exchange Advertiser." Because of the advertisement tax it was reduced in size to small folio with the issue of Aug. 3, 1786. It was discontinued with the issue of Jan. 4, 1787, vol. 2, no. 105. There is a humorous account of its "decease" in the "Massachusetts Centinel" of Jan. 6, 1787.

Mass. Hist. Soc. has Dec. 30, 1784; Jan. 6–May 19, June 2–Nov. 17, Dec. 1, 8, 1785; Jan. 5–Aug. 31, Oct. 5, 12, Nov. 9, 16, 30, Dec. 7, 1786; Jan. 4, 1787.
Am. Antiq. Soc. has Dec. 30, 1784; Jan. 13–Apr. 28, May 19, June 16–Sept. 29, Oct. 13, Nov. 17–Dec. 1, 16–29, 1785; Jan. 5–Mar. 2, 30–Apr. 13, 27, May 11, 18, June 1, 22, 29, July 13–27, Aug. 24, 31, Sept. 14, 21, Oct. 5, Nov. 2–23, Dec. 15, 21, 1786.
N. Y. State Lib. has Dec. 30, 1784–May 25, 1786; July 6, 27, 1786.
Lib. Congress has Jan. 27–Apr. 28, May 12, 19, June 16, 23, July 14, Aug. 18, Sept. 1, 8, 22, Oct. 6, 13, 27, Nov. 3, 17, Dec. 1, 29, 1785; Jan. 5–19, Feb. 2–16, Mar. 2–23, Apr. 7–20, May 11–June 15, 29, July 13–27, 1786.
N. Y. Hist. Soc. has Feb. 17, 1785; Jan. 12–26, Feb. 9–Mar. 23, Apr. 13–Sept. 21, Oct. 5, 19–Dec. 21, 1786.
Univ. of Mich. (Clements) has Jan. 13, 27–Mar. 17, 31–Apr. 21, July 7, 21, 28, Aug. 18, Sept. 1–29, Nov. 24, Dec. 1, 1785.
Boston Pub. Lib. has Dec. 30, 1784; May 26, June 16, July 21, 1785; Jan. 5, Feb. 2, 1786.
Yale has Feb. 3, 17, 24, Mar. 17, July 21, 1785.
N. Y. Pub. Lib. has Jan. 5, Feb. 2, Mar. 30, Apr. 7, 1786.
Essex Inst. has Nov. 3, 1785.

[Boston] **Federal Gazette, 1798.**

Daily and semi-weekly. Established Jan. 1, 1798, by Caleb P. Wayne, with the title of "Federal Gazette and Daily Advertiser." With the issue of Mar. 8, 1798, the paper was changed from a daily to a semi-weekly and the title was changed to "Federal Gazette and General Advertiser." It was discontinued with the issue of Mar. 26, 1798, vol. 1, no. 60.

Am. Antiq. Soc., Boston Athenæum and Mass. Hist. Soc. have Jan. 1–Mar. 26, 1798.
Boston Pub. Lib. has Jan. 1, 2, 8–10, 12, 25, 27–Feb. 17, 20, 21, 24–28, Mar. 8, 26, 1798.
Long Id. Hist. Soc. has Jan. 1–Feb. 28, 1798.
Lib. Congress has Jan. 2, 3, 5, 6, 11–16, 18–24, 27–29, 1798.
Phil. Lib. Co. has Feb. 9–Mar. 19, 1798.
Univ. of Ill. has Jan. 1–9, 1798.
Harvard has Jan. 8, 11, 12, 22, 1798.

[Boston] **Federal Orrery,** 1794–1796.

Semi-weekly. Established Oct. 20, 1794, with the title of "Federal Orrery," edited by Thomas Paine, and printed by Weld and Greenough [Ezra W. Weld and William Greenough]. With the issue of Apr. 23, 1795, the paper was printed by Ezra W. Weld, and with the issue of June 1, 1795, by Alexander Martin. With the issue of Apr. 21, 1796, Paine sold the paper to Benjamin Sweetser, who became both editor and publisher. With the issue of Nov. 3, 1796, Sweetser changed the name of the paper to "The Courier and General Advertiser," continuing, however, the volume numbering. The paper was undoubtedly discontinued with the issue of Dec. 8, 1796, vol. 5, no. 15.

Am. Antiq. Soc. and Mass. Hist. Soc. have Oct. 20, 1794–Dec. 8, 1796.

Boston Athenæum has Oct. 20, 1794–Nov. 10, 17–24, Dec. 5, 1796.

Boston Pub. Lib. has Oct. 20, 1794–Sept. 12, Oct. 6, 10, 17–Nov. 3, 14, 28, Dec. 8, 1796.

N. Y. Pub. Lib. has Oct. 20, 1794–Dec. 31, 1795; Jan. 4–Apr. 25, May 2–9, 19–30, June 6–27, July 7, 18–Sept. 15, 22, Oct. 27–Nov. 17, 28, Dec. 1, 8, 1796.

Harvard has Oct. 20, 1794–Dec. 31, 1795; Jan. 4–Apr. 21, May 5, 12, 23, 26, June 9, 13, July 21–Aug. 4, 11–18, 29, Oct. 3, 10, 20, 24, Nov. 14, Dec. 5, 8, 1796.

Wis. Hist. Soc. has Oct. 20–Dec. 29, 1794; Jan. 1, 1795–Apr. 18, 1796, fair; May 2, 5, 12, 23, 26, July 21, Aug. 11, 1796.

Lib. Congress has Oct. 20, 1794–Dec. 28, 1795, fair; Jan. 4–Dec. 5, 1796, scattering file.

N. Y. Hist. Soc. has Oct. 20, 1794–Oct. 19, 1795.

Hist. Soc. Penn. has Oct. 20, 1794–Oct. 15, 1795.

N. Y. State Lib. has Oct. 20, 1794–Sept. 28, 1795, fair; Dec. 28, 1795–Oct. 31, 1796, fair.

Essex Inst. has Nov. 27, 1794–Apr. 18, 1796, scattering file.

Univ. of Chicago has Oct. 20, Nov. 13, 17, Dec. 1, 1794–Dec. 28, 1795, scattering file.

Univ. of Mich. (Clements) has Dec. 1, 1794–Apr. 27, 1795, scattering file; June 4, July 6, Oct. 19, Nov. 23, 1795; Jan. 7, Mar. 21, Oct. 17, 20, 1796.

Phil. Lib. Co. has Feb. 19, 23, Sept. 14, Nov. 2, 20, 23, 30, 1795; Jan. 4, 25, Mar. 14–Aug. 8, 1796, scattering.

Long Id. Hist. Soc. has Jan. 26, 1795; Sept. 8–Oct. 24, 1796.

Western Reserve Hist. Soc. has Nov. 10, 1794.

Univ. of Ill. has Nov. 3, 1796.

Me. Hist. Soc. has Dec. 8, 1796.

[Boston] **Fredonian, 1810.**

Weekly. Established Feb. 20, 1810, published for the editors by E[leazer] G. House with the title of "The Fredonian." The names of the editors are not given. The paper was discontinued with the issue of May 15, 1810, vol. 1, no. 13.

Am. Antiq. Soc. has Feb. 20–May 15, 1810.
Bath, Patten Free Lib. has Feb. 20–Mar. 27, 1810.
Mass. Hist. Soc. has Feb. 20, 27, Mar. 13, 20, Apr. 3, 1810.
Boston Pub. Lib. has Mar. 20, 1810.
Lib. Congress has May 8, 1810.

Boston Gazette, 1719–1798.

Weekly. Established Dec. 21, 1719, printed by J[ames] Franklin and published by William Brooker. Brooker's name does not appear in the imprint but he acknowledges his proprietorship in the issue of Jan. 11, 1720. The title was "The Boston Gazette," although the words "New-England" were printed in smaller type above the title and were so printed through 1752. In August, 1720 (with the issue of either Aug. 8, 15, or 22), the paper was printed by S[amuel] Kneeland. With the issue of Sept. 26, 1720, the paper was printed by S. Kneeland for Philip Musgrave. Musgrave died May 18, 1725, and since the next known issue after this event, that of July 19, 1725, is printed by S. Kneeland for Thomas Lewis, it is probable that Lewis immediately succeeded Musgrave as publisher. With the issue of Apr. 25, 1726, the paper was published by Henry Marshall and Thomas Lewis, no printer's name being given. Lewis died of an apoplectic fit on Jan. 14, 1727 (see the account of his death in the "American Weekly Mercury" of Feb. 7, 1727), and was succeeded by Henry Marshall as sole publisher. No printer's name was given, although it is probable that Bartholomew Green, Jr., was the printer. With the issue of June 19, 1727, the paper was printed by B. Green, Jun., for Henry Marshall. Marshall died Oct. 4, 1732, and with the issue of Oct. 9, 1732, it was printed by B. Green, Jun., for John Boydell. Upon Green's father's death, the "Jun" was omitted with the issue of Jan. 1, 1733. With the issue of Apr. 1, 1734, B. Green was sole publisher. The last known issue printed by B. Green is that of Sept. 13, 1736, and the next issue located, that of Oct. 11, 1736, is published by John Boydell and printed by S. Kneeland and T. Green [Samuel Kneeland and Timothy Green]. Boydell died Dec. 11, 1739, and the issue of Dec. 17, 1739, announced that the paper would be carried on for the benefit of the family of the late publisher. Hannah Boydell, the widow, died Oct. 15, 1741, and with the issue of Oct. 19, 1741, S. Kneeland and T. Green became the proprietors. They incorporated with it the "New-England Weekly Journal," changing the title on Oct. 20, 1741, to "The Boston Gazette, or New England Weekly Journal," altered on Oct. 27, 1741, to "The Boston Gazette, or, Weekly Journal." With the issue of Jan. 3, 1753, S. Kneeland began publishing the paper alone (although his name did not appear in the imprint during 1753) and altered the title to "The Boston Gazette, or, Weekly Advertiser." With this issue, moreover, he commenced a new volume numbering. Kneeland sold out the paper to Benjamin Edes and John Gill, who began publishing it with the issue of Apr. 7, 1755. With this issue they commenced a new volume numbering and changed the title to "The Boston Gazette, or Country Journal," altered with the issue of Apr. 5, 1756, to "The Boston-Gazette, or, Country Journal," and with the issue of Apr. 12, 1756, to "The Boston-Gazette, and Country Journal." Owing to the exigencies of war, Edes & Gill temporarily suspended the paper with the issue of Apr. 17, 1775, and their partnership was dissolved. Benjamin Edes went to Watertown and began printing the paper with the issue of June 5, 1775, the title being the same and the numbering continuous. The last Watertown issue was that of Oct. 28, 1776, after which Edes returned to Boston and continued the paper with the issue of Nov. 4, 1776. With the issue of Apr. 12, 1779, Benjamin Edes took his two sons, Benjamin, Jr., and Peter, into partnership, publishing the paper under the firm name of Benjamin Edes and Sons, and altering the title to "The Boston Gazette, and the Country Journal." Peter Edes withdrew from the partnership with the issue of Nov. 1, 1784, and the paper was published by Benjamin Edes and Son (Benjamin Edes, Jr.). With the issue of Jan. 6, 1794, they changed the title to "The Boston Gazette, and Weekly Republican Journal." The partnership was dissolved and with the issue of June 30, 1794, the paper was published by Benjamin Edes. It was discontinued with the issue of Sept. 17, 1798, no. 2293.

This newspaper has been reproduced in photostat by the Mass. Historical Society for 1719–1742, which set is to be found in the following libraries: — Am. Antiq. Soc., Boston Athenæum, Boston Pub. Lib., John Stewart Bryan, University of Chicago, Columbia Univ., Conn. State Lib., Essex Inst., Grosvenor Lib. Buffalo, Harvard, Univ. of Ill., John Crerar Lib., Lib. Congress, Md. Hist. Soc., Mass. Hist. Soc., Mass. State Lib., Univ. of Mich., Univ. of Minn., N. Y. Hist. Soc., Newberry Lib., Univ. of N. C., Princeton, R. C. B. Thruston, and Yale.

Am. Antiq. Soc. has Jan. 4–25, Feb. 15, Mar. 14, Apr. 11, 25, May 9–30, June 20, 27, July 11, 18, Aug. 1, 22–Oct. 17, 31, Nov. 7–21, Dec. 5, 12, 1720; Jan. 2, 16–Mar. 20, Apr. 3–17, 27–May 8, June 19, 1721; Jan. 1, July 2, 23, 30, Nov. 12–26, 1722; Apr. 15, June 3, 24, 1723; Apr. 13, 1724; Apr. 26, 1725; Apr. 24, Nov. 13, 1727; Jan. 1, 1728; Nov. 15, 1731; Feb. 7, May 8, June 26, Oct. 2, 1732; Jan. 8, Oct. 15, 1733; Oct. 21, Nov. 25, 1734; June 23, 1735; May 31, Sept. 13, 1736; Mar. 7, May 23, Oct. 24, 1737; Feb. 20, June 26, Sept. 4, Nov. 6, 13, 27, Dec. 4, 1738; Jan. 8–Feb. 5, May 7, 28, Aug. 20, 27, Dec. 10, 17, 1739; Feb. 25, Apr. 14–May 5, 26, June 9, 30, Aug. 4–25, Sept. 8, 29, 1740; Jan. 5, 12, Apr. 13–27, Aug. 10, Oct. 5, 19, Nov. 10, 17, Dec. 1–22, 1741; Jan. 19, Feb. 2, Mar. 2, May 18, 25, July 13, Aug. 10, 24, Sept. 7, Nov. 16, 1742; Jan. 4, 1743–Dec. 25, 1744; Jan. 1, 1745–Dec. 23, 1746, fair; Jan. 6, 1747–Dec. 31, 1751; Mar. 17, Sept. 19, Nov. 21, 1752; Jan. 3–Dec. 25, 1753; May 28, July 16, Aug. 6–20, Sept. 3–17, 1754; Jan. 14, 21, Feb. 11,

Massachusetts

Apr. 7–Dec. 29, 1755; Jan. 5–Dec. 27, 1756; Jan. 3–Mar. 28, Apr. 25, June 27, Oct. 3, 1757; Jan. 2, 1758–Dec. 27, 1762; Jan. 10–24, Apr. 25, May 9, June 13–27, July 11, 18, Aug. 22, Oct. 10, Dec. 12, 1763; Feb. 27, 1764–Dec. 30, 1765, fair; Jan. 6, 1766–Dec. 26, 1768; Jan. 16, 1769–Dec. 30, 1782; Jan. 6, 1783–Dec. 30, 1793, fair; Jan. 6, 1794–Sept. 17, 1798.

Mass. Hist. Soc. has Dec. 21, 1719; Jan. 4, 11, Mar. 7, Oct. 3–Dec. 26, 1720; Jan. 16, 1721–July 27, 1724, fair; Jan. 18, 1725; Apr. 18, July 18, Aug. 1, Dec. 26, 1726; May 1, 1727; Sept. 16, 1728–Apr. 21, 1729, fair; Jan. 4, 18, Feb. 8–22, Mar. 15, 22, Apr. 5–26, June 21, July 5–19, Aug. 16, 30–Sept. 27, Oct. 18, Nov. 8, 22, 29, Dec. 13, 27, 1731; Jan. 3, 17, 31–Feb. 14, Mar. 13–27, Apr. 17, May 8, 15, June 5, 19, July 17, Aug. 21, 28, Oct. 16, 1732; Mar. 18, Sept. 16, 1734; Feb. 2, Aug. 9, 1736; Jan. 2–16, 30, Feb. 6, May 8, 15, June 5, Aug. 21, Sept. 4, Dec. 18, 1738; Jan. 15, 22, Feb. 12–Mar. 19, Apr. 9, 30, May 28, June 18, July 2, 9, 30–Aug. 13, 27–Sept. 24, Nov. 5, 26–Dec. 17, 1739; Jan. 28, Mar. 3, June 30, Dec. 8, 1740; Mar. 30, Apr. 13–27, May 25, June 22, 29, Oct. 20–Nov. 17, Dec. 1, 8, 22, 29, 1741; Jan. 26, Mar. 25, Aug. 31, 1742; Jan. 11, Feb. 1, 8, June 21, July 5, Aug. 30, Sept. 20, Oct. 18, Dec. 20, 1743; Feb. 14, Apr. 10, June 24, Aug. 21, Sept. 25, Oct. 2, Nov. 27, Dec. 25, 1744; Jan. 8, Feb. 5, Apr. 2, 16, 23, May 7, 14, 28–July 9, Aug. 6, Nov. 5, 12, 26, 1745; Jan. 7, 21, Feb. 11, 18, Mar. 18, 25, June 3, Sept. 16, Nov. 11, 25, Dec. 9–23, 1746; Jan. 6, 1747–Dec. 11, 1753, fair; Jan. 1, 1754–Dec. 25, 1758; Jan. 1, 1759–Dec. 29, 1760, fair; Jan. 5, 1761–Dec. 30, 1782; Jan. 6, 1783–Dec. 12, 1785, fair; Jan. 2, Apr. 24, May 8, 15, June 5–19, Sept. 11, Oct. 16, Dec. 18, 25, 1786; Jan. 1–Dec. 3, 1787, fair; Feb. 4–18, Mar. 3, Oct. 20, Dec. 8, 1788; Jan. 12, 19, Feb. 9–23, Mar. 30, June 22, 29, Aug. 31, Dec. 7, 28, 1789; Feb. 22, Mar. 29, Nov. 22, 1790; Jan. 3, 1791–Sept. 17, 1798.

Wis. Hist. Soc. has Feb. 17–Nov. 30, 1724, fair; Mar. 1, Apr. 5, 12, May 17, July 19, 1725–Dec. 29, 1729; Jan. 12, 1730–Dec. 31, 1731, fair; Jan. 3, Nov. 20, 27, Dec. 18, 1733; Jan. 1, 22, Feb. 12, Mar. 5, 26, Apr. 23, May 21, 28, 1733; June 17–Aug. 19, 1734; June 23–July 7, Aug. 4–25, 1735; June 21, Oct. 11–Dec. 20, 1736; Jan. 19–Nov. 17, 1741, fair; Feb. 17, May 26–July 21, Sept. 1, 8, Oct. 13, 20, 1747; Jan. 5, Mar. 1–June 14, fair; Oct. 4, Nov. 1, Dec. 6, 1748; Jan. 17, 24, Feb. 14, May 30, June 13–July 11, 1749; Apr. 3, 10, May 1–29, Oct. 9, 1753; May 7–28, 1754; Feb. 18, Mar. 18, June 2–Dec. 15, 1755, fair; Mar. 1–22, July 26, Aug. 2, 23, Oct. 18, Nov. 15, 22, Dec. 6, 27, 1756; Jan. 3–Nov. 7, 1757, fair; Jan. 2, 1758–Dec. 15, 1760; Jan. 12–Feb. 23, June 1–Sept. 7, 1761; Jan. 25–Dec. 13, 1762, fair; Jan. 16–Sept. 24, 1764, fair; Jan. 7–Dec. 30, 1765, fair; Jan. 6–Dec. 22, 1766; Mar. 9, 16, 30, 1767; Mar. 20, May 29–Oct. 23, 1769, fair; Jan. 8–Nov. 5, 1770, scattering; Feb. 25, Mar. 25, Aug. 5, Oct. 14, 28, 1771; Jan. 6, 1772–Dec. 26, 1774; Mar. 6, July 31, 1775; Jan. 29, 1776–Sept. 4, 1780, fair; June 4, July 30, Sept. 10, Nov. 12, Dec. 3, 1781; Jan. 14–Dec. 16, 1782, fair; June 9, 1783–June 11, 1798, scattering issues.

Dartmouth has Oct. 27, Dec. 15, 22, 1729; Jan. 5–12, 27–Feb. 23, Mar. 9, Apr. 27, Sept. 14, Oct. 5, 12, Nov. 2, 16–Dec. 28, 1730; Jan. 4–25, Feb. 15, Mar. 1, 15, 29–Apr. 26, May 10, 31–July 19, Aug. 2–16, 30–Oct. 4, 18–Nov. 8, 22–Dec. 13, 27, 1731; Jan. 3–Feb. 14, 28–Mar. 27, Apr. 10, 24–May 22, June 5, July 3–17, 31–Aug. 14, 28–Oct. 30, 1732; Jan. 1, 15–Mar. 5, Apr. 2–23, May 7–29, June 11–25, July 16, Aug. 6–Oct. 29, 1733; Nov. 4–25, Dec. 9–30, 1734; Jan. 6–May 26, June 16–Aug. 25, Sept. 8–Dec. 29, 1735; Jan. 5, 1736; May 23, 1737; Aug. 3–17, 1767; Jan. 24–June 27, Aug. 1–22, 1774, fair; Jan. 23, 1775–Sept. 22, 1783, fair; Nov. 29, 1785–May 9, 1788; Sept. 30–Oct. 10, 31, 1788; Mar. 18, 1793–Feb. 24, 1794, scattering.

Boston Athenæum has Oct. 21, 1723; Feb. 3–24, 1724; May 3, 1736; Dec. 11, 1738; Mar. 10, 1740; Aug. 10, 1741; Mar. 16, May 11, 1742; Apr. 10, July 24, 1744; May 21, 28, 1745; May 27, Oct. 28, 1746; Jan. 6, 1747; Mar. 20, 1750; Sept. 24, 1751; Jan. 3, 1753–Dec. 24, 1754, fair; Feb. 23, Sept. 20, 1756; Jan. 30, Mar. 6, June 5, Oct. 23, 30, Nov. 20, Dec. 25, 1758; Jan. 7–Dec. 29, 1760; Feb. 16, 1761–Dec. 20, 1762; Feb. 28, Apr. 4, May 2, July 25–Dec. 5, 1763; Feb. 13, 1764–Dec. 31, 1781; Jan. 28–Dec. 30, 1782, fair; Dec. 27, 1784; Feb. 14, Apr. 4, Aug. 8, 29, Nov. 21, 28, 1785; June 12, Sept. 18, Dec. 4, 1786; June 11, Oct. 1, 1787; Jan. 26, 1789; Jan. 18, Feb. 1, 15, Aug. 30, Nov. 15, 1790; May 30, Aug. 8, 1791; June 4, 1792; Aug. 28, 1797; Mar. 12, Aug. 6–27, 1798.

Boston Public Library has Apr. 25, Aug. 22, 1720; Mar. 6, 1721; July 30, 1722; Aug. 5, Sept. 2–Oct. 14, 1723; July 30, 1733; Feb. 25, Mar. 25, Apr. 1, 1734; Oct. 25, 1736; Jan. 17, 24, 1737; Apr. 7, 28, 1740; Apr. 20, Nov. 17, 24, 1741; Mar. 30, 1742; Jan. 11, Mar. 8, 22–Apr. 12, May 17, 24, Aug. 2, Nov. 1, 1743; May 29, June 12, 19, Aug. 7, 14, 28–Sept. 25, Oct. 16, 30–Nov. 27, 1744; July 16, Aug. 20, 1745; Mar. 3, 17–Nov. 10, 24–Dec. 22, 1747; Feb. 9, 23, Mar. 8–29, Apr. 19–June 7, July 5, 12, Aug. 2, 16, 30, Sept. 27, 1748; Jan. 10, 17, Feb. 14–Mar. 7, Apr. 4, 11, May 2, July 4, Aug. 15, 22, Sept. 12–26, Oct. 24, 1749; Apr. 17, May 22, July 10–24, 1750; Mar. 5, Apr. 16, May 28, Sept. 24, 1751; June 16, 1752; Jan. 3–Aug. 28, Nov. 13, 1753; Apr. 14, 1755–Dec. 20, 1756, fair; Jan. 3–Feb. 7, Apr. 4, May 2, 23, June 6, 20, July 4, 11, 25, Aug. 1, 15–29, Sept. 12–Oct. 3, 31, Nov. 28, Dec. 12–26, 1757; Apr. 17, May 1, 8, June 5, 26, July 10, 24, Aug. 21–Sept. 4, Oct. 2, 16, 30, Nov. 6, 1758; Mar. 26, Aug. 6, Oct. 8, 1759; Jan. 14–Dec. 29, 1760; Feb. 9, Mar. 2–16, Apr. 27, July 6, Oct. 5, Nov. 30, 1761; Feb. 15, Mar. 1, July 12, Oct. 4, Dec. 13–27, 1762; Feb. 7, 14, Apr. 18, May 9, 30–July 4, 18, Sept. 26, 1763; Jan. 2–30, Mar. 12, 19, Apr. 2, 9, May 7, 28, July 9, 23–Aug. 13, Oct. 8, Nov. 12, 1764; Jan. 7, 1765–Dec. 29, 1777; Jan. 12, 1778–Dec. 27, 1784, fair; Feb. 7, 14, 28, Mar. 14–May 16, June 20, 27, July 18, Aug. 29, Nov. 28, 1785; Jan. 2–Dec. 25, 1786; Jan. 1, 1787–Dec. 29, 1788, fair; Jan. 5, 1789–Dec. 26, 1791; Jan. 2, 1792–Sept. 17, 1798, fair.

N. Y. Pub. Lib. has Nov. 1, 1736–Aug. 20, 1739; Mar. 15, 22, 1743; Oct. 9, 1744; May 27, 1746; Jan. 13, May 5, June 9, 16, Dec. 16, 1747; Feb. 16,

MASSACHUSETTS 301

1748; Feb. 21, Aug. 1, 1749; Feb. 6–May 1, 1753; Sept. 1, Oct. 20, Nov. 17, 1755; Feb. 23, Aug. 30–Nov. 8, Dec. 13, 20, 1756; Jan. 3, 1757–Nov. 6, 1758; Mar. 19, 1759–Nov. 3, 1760, scattering; July 27, 1761; Aug. 30, Sept. 13, 1762; Jan. 3, 10, 31, Feb. 7, 21, 28, Apr. 4, July 4, 25, Nov. 7, 1763; Apr. 30, Sept. 17, Oct. 29, 1764; Jan. 7, May 13, 1765; Jan. 13–Dec. 22, 1766, fair; Feb. 23–Nov. 16, 1767, fair; Jan. 11–Dec. 26, 1768, fair; Jan. 2, 1769–Dec. 27, 1773; Jan. 3, 1774–Apr. 17, 1775, scattering; Oct. 28, 1776–Dec. 19, 1785, fair; Jan. 9, Nov. 27, 1786; Jan. 1–Nov. 26, 1787; Jan. 21, 1788–Sept. 10, 1798, fair.

Lib. Congress has July 13, 1724; July 4–Sept. 26, 1726; Apr. 1, 1734; Oct. 31, 1737; Feb. 26, Mar. 12, Apr. 9, May 28, Aug. 27, Dec. 10, 1739; Jan. 28, June 30, Sept. 1, 8, Oct. 6–20, 1740; Oct. 27–Nov. 10, 1741; Dec. 21, 1742; Feb. 1, 1743; July 9, 1745; Apr. 22, May 13, Sept. 16–30, 1746; Feb. 10, Mar. 24, 31, Apr. 14, 21, May 12, 26, June 2, July 7–Oct. 13, Nov. 10–24, Dec. 15, 22, 1747; Feb. 9, Apr. 19, May 3, 1748; May 2, Sept. 19, 1749; Jan. 16, Apr. 10, 17, 1750; Jan. 7, June 16, 1752; Jan. 23, Aug. 28, Sept. 4, 1753; Sept. 3, 1754; Mar. 11, Apr. 14, 21, May 5–19, June 9, Sept. 8–Nov. 24, Dec. 8, 15, 1755; Feb. 16, 1756–Dec. 25, 1758, fair; Mar. 26, July 30, Sept. 17, Dec. 31, 1759; Jan. 14, 21, Feb. 4, 18, Apr. 28, May 19, 26, June 23–July 7, Oct. 27, Nov. 24, 1760; Jan. 5, 1761–Dec. 26, 1763, fair; Jan. 2, 1764–Dec. 22, 1777; Jan. 5, 1778–Dec. 29, 1783, fair; Jan. 5, 1784–Dec. 25, 1797; Jan. 1–Sept. 17, 1798, fair.

Essex Inst. has June 8, Nov. 30, 1742; Sept. 17, 1745; Oct. 7, 1746; Apr. 17, 1753; June 18, 1754; Apr. 7, 1755–Dec. 31, 1764; Feb. 24, June 2–Dec. 29, 1766; Feb. 8, Apr. 4, July 4, 25, Aug. 1, 15–29, 1768; Mar. 20, 1769; Oct. 15, 1770; Apr. 1–June 22, 1771, fair; Feb. 24, Mar. 23, Dec. 21, 1772; Mar. 29, Oct. 25, Dec. 27, 1773; June 18, 25, Aug. 22, Oct. 10, 24, Nov. 14, 21, Dec. 5, 1774; July 18, 1774–Dec. 4, 1775, scattering; Jan. 1, 1776–Dec. 30, 1782, fair; Jan. 13, 1783–Nov. 13, 1786, scattering; July 14, 1788; Feb. 9, 16, 1789; Feb. 1–Dec. 6, 1790, scattering; Nov. 14, Dec. 26, 1791; May 21, June 18, 1792.

Harvard has Dec. 11, 1738; Apr. 12, 1743; Nov. 6, 27, Dec. 18, 1744; Jan. 8, Nov. 26, 1745; Apr. 3, Nov. 6, 1750; Dec. 31, 1754; Apr. 7, 1755–Mar. 29, 1756; Sept. 18, Oct. 2, Nov. 20, Dec. 25, 1758; Jan. 22, Aug. 6, Oct. 29, Nov. 5, Dec. 17, 1759; Feb. 4, 1760–Jan. 19, 1767, scattering; Jan. 11, 1768–Dec. 27, 1784; Oct. 9, 1786; June 27, July 18, 1791; Sept. 24, 1792; May 30, 1796–Sept. 10, 1798, fair.

Yale has Jan. 16, Aug. 7, 1758; Mar. 15, 1762–Dec. 31, 1764, fair; Aug. 5, 1765–Jan. 12, 1767, fair; Jan. 4, 1768–Dec. 24, 1770; Jan. 21–Dec. 30, 1771, fair; Oct. 5, 1772; Jan. 25, 1773–Dec. 25, 1775, scattering file; Jan. 13, 1777–Dec. 28, 1778; Oct. 15, 29–Nov. 12, 1781; Feb. 25, Apr. 1, May 20, July 22, 1782; Jan. 10, 1785–July 7, 1788.

N. Y. Hist. Soc. has June 6, 1737; Sept. 14, Oct. 5, 12, 1741; Mar. 8, 1743; Jan. 16, 23, Mar. 13, 1753; Jan. 15–June 25, 1754; Jan. 28, 1755; Jan. 10–Dec. 12, 1757; Mar. 6, 1758–Aug. 27, 1759, fair; Jan. 7–Dec. 22, 1760, fair;

Jan. 26, 1761–Dec. 12, 1768, scattering; Jan. 2, 1769–Dec. 31, 1770; Feb. 25, 1771–Dec. 15, 1777, scattering file; Oct. 19, 1778–Sept. 12, 1796, scattering issues.
British Museum has Dec. 11, 1721; Jan. 15, 29, Mar. 19, May 21, 28, 1722; May 27, 1765–Feb. 20, 1775, fair.
Univ. of Mich. (Clements) has May 28, 1739; Mar. 26, 1748; May 12, Nov. 3, 1755; May 3–Dec. 6, 1756, fair; Feb. 21–Mar. 7, 21, 1757; July 24, 1758; Nov. 5, 26, 1759; June 30, Sept. 1, 22, Oct. 6, 1760; Apr. 6, July 6, 20, Dec. 21, 1761; Jan. 11–Dec. 27, 1762, scattering; Jan. 3, Mar. 7, 14, Aug. 29, Nov. 14, Dec. 26, 1763; Jan. 2, 1764–Dec. 26, 1768, scattering file; Jan. 2, 1769–Dec. 27, 1773; Jan. 10–Oct. 10, 1774, fair; Feb. 13, 1775–Dec. 23, 1782, scattering file; Dec. 29, 1783; Mar. 8, 1784; Apr. 25, 1785; Mar. 5, Apr. 23, 1787; Feb. 16, 1789; Jan. 18, 1790–Nov. 7, 1791, scattering file; Jan. 14, 1793; Mar. 3, 1794–Oct. 9, 1797, scattering; Aug. 20, Sept. 10, 1798.
Bowdoin Coll. has Dec. 20, 1756–Dec. 26, 1757; Oct. 14, 1771–Dec. 20, 1773.
N. Y. State Lib. has Apr. 21, 28, July 28, Dec. 15, 29, 1747; Jan. 26, Feb. 9, 23, May 31, June 7, 1748; Feb. 7, May 2, 9, 1749; Jan. 30, Feb. 13, Mar. 27, Apr. 10, Oct. 30, 1750; Dec. 10, 17, 1751; Mar. 24, 1752; Oct. 25–Nov. 8, Dec. 6, 1756; Feb. 7, June 6, Nov. 28, 1757; Jan. 9, Apr. 17, May 15, 29, June 12, July 24, Aug. 7–28, Sept. 25, Oct. 2, Nov. 6, 20, 1758; Jan. 5, 12, Mar. 2, July 27, Nov. 2, 23, 30, Dec. 21, 28, 1761; Jan. 11, Apr. 19–Dec. 27, 1762; Jan. 17, 24, Mar. 28, Aug. 22, 29, 1763; Jan. 2, 1764–Dec. 29, 1766; May 4, 1767–Aug. 1, 1774; Oct. 31, Dec. 19, 1774; Jan. 2, Feb. 6, Apr. 3, Oct. 9, 23, Nov. 20, 1775; 1776–1785, scattering issues; Jan. 31, 1791–Jan. 21, 1793, scattering issues.
Duke Univ. has June 28, Oct. 11, Nov. 8, 22, 1756; Dec. 12, 1757; June 23, 1760; Aug. 9, Sept. 6, Nov. 8, 22, Dec. 6, 1762; Jan. 3, 1763; Jan. 30, Feb. 6, Nov. 19, 1764; Feb. 4, Apr. 1–Nov. 25, 1765, fair; May 12–26, Sept. 15, Dec. 29, 1766; Feb. 2, 1767–Dec. 26, 1768, scattering file; Jan. 9, 1769–Dec. 19, 1774, fair; Oct. 30, 1775–Oct. 26, 1789, scattering issues.
Hist. Soc. Penn. has Jan. 21, 1760; Jan. 25, 1762; Oct. 10, 1768; Jan. 8, 1770–Dec. 21, 1772; Feb. 1, 15, 1773; June 5–Dec. 25, 1775; Jan. 1–Sept. 16, 1776, fair; Jan. 6–Sept. 29, 1777, fair; Feb. 23, June 15–29, 1778; Feb. 3, Nov. 17, 1783; Apr. 18, 1785.
Amherst Coll. has July 17–Sept. 25, 1727; Dec. 29, 1783–Mar. 15, 1784.
British Pub. Rec. Office has Dec. 1, 1729; Aug. 31, Oct. 12, 1730; July 12, 1731; June 17, Dec. 9, 1734; May 17, 24, 1736; Apr. 21, June 2, 1740; Oct. 31, 1774.
Portland Pub. Lib. has July 25, 1757; Jan. 31, June 6, Nov. 28, 1763; May 13, July 15, Aug. 12, Sept. 16, Nov. 25, 1765; Jan. 13, May 26, Aug. 11, 18, 1766; Feb. 23, 1767; Jan. 19, 1778; Apr. 7, 1788.
Phil. Lib. Co. has Jan. 14, Feb. 4, 25, Apr. 8, July 8, 15, 29, Sept. 2–Nov. 4, Dec. 16, 23, 1765; Mar. 17, 1766; Oct. 14, 1793; Nov. 16–Dec. 7, 1796; Mar. 14–Apr. 4, 18–May 2, 30–July 18, Aug. 1, 15, 1796.
Newberry Lib. has Aug. 18–Sept. 8, Dec. 15, 1794; Jan. 12, 1795.

R. I. Hist. Soc. has Dec. 24, 1733.
Conn. State Lib. has Aug. 30, 1736.
Many libraries have single or a few scattering issues represented in other collections.

Boston Gazette, 1800–1820+.

Semi-weekly. A continuation, without change of volume numbering, of "Russell's Gazette." The first issue, of which the full title was "Boston Gazette, Commercial and Political," was that of Oct. 9, 1800, vol. 9, no. 11. It was published by John Russell & James Cutler, the two having formed a partnership on this date. With the issue of Jan. 3, 1803, the title was shortened to "Boston Gazette," published by Russell and Cutler. With the issue of Sept. 2, 1813, Simon Gardner was taken into partnership and the paper published by Russell, Cutler & Co. With the issue of Jan. 1, 1816, the title was changed to "Boston Commercial Gazette," although the word "Commercial" was in much smaller type than the rest of the title. With the issue of Jan. 2, 1817, it was printed in the same size of type. Cutler died Apr. 29, 1818, but the surviving partners waited until June 25 before they announced the continuation of the partnership, and it was not until the issue of June 29, 1818, that the firm name of Russell & Gardner appeared in the imprint. The "Boston Commercial Gazette" was continued by them until after 1820.

Am. Antiq. Soc., Boston Athenæum, Boston Pub. Lib., Mass. Hist. Soc., Essex Inst., and Lib. Congress have practically complete files, Oct. 9, 1800–Dec. 28, 1820.

N. Y. State Lib. has Oct. 9, 1800–Jan. 14, 1802; May 20, June 24, July 1, Aug. 12, 1802; Jan. 3, 1803–Feb. 17, 1820.

Conn. Hist. Soc. has Oct. 9, 1800–Dec. 30, 1805; May 4, 1809–June 1, 1812, Jan. 4, 1813–Dec. 28, 1820.

Bath, Me., Patten Lib., has Jan. 8, 1801–Dec. 28, 1820, lacking 1809.

N. Y. Hist. Soc. has Oct. 9, 1800–Oct. 28, 1813; Nov. 22, 1813–July 28, 1814, fair; Sept. 29–Dec. 29, 1814, fair; Jan. 9–Dec. 21, 1815, scattering file; Jan. 1, Dec. 9, 23–30, 1816; Jan. 2, 1817–Dec. 30, 1819.

Harvard has Oct. 9, 1800–Dec. 29, 1808, fair; May 15, 1809–Dec. 30, 1811, fair; Jan. 2, 1812–Dec. 28, 1815; Jan. 6–Dec. 18, 1817; Apr. 8, 1819–Dec. 28, 1820.

Univ. of Mich. (Clements) has Oct. 9, 1800–June 25, 1812, fair; July 6, 1812–June 12, 1815, scattering issues; Jan. 2, 1817–Dec. 28, 1820.

Duke Univ. has Oct. 9, 1800–Dec. 30, 1811, fair; 1812–1813, scattering issues; Jan. 2, 1815–Dec. 30, 1816.

Wis. Hist. Soc. has Oct. 9, 1800–Dec. 29, 1806; Feb. 23, 1807–Dec. 26, 1808, fair; Jan. 2, 1809–Dec. 21, 1812; Jan. 11–Dec. 30, 1813, fair; Jan. 2–Dec. 28, 1815.

Chicago Hist. Soc. has Oct. 13–Dec. 8, 1800, fair; Mar. 12–Oct. 8, 1801, scattering; Jan. 3, 1805–Nov. 17, 1817.
Louisville Pub. Lib. has Jan. 3, 1805–Dec. 27, 1810; Jan. 2, 1812–Dec. 30, 1813; Jan. 2, 1815–Dec. 30, 1816.
N. Y. Pub. Lib. has Oct. 9, 1800–Dec. 22, 1806, fair; 1808–1817, a few scattering issues; Jan. 4, 1819–Dec. 28, 1820, fair.
Cambridge Pub. Lib. has Oct. 9, 1800–Dec. 31, 1801; Jan. 21–Sept. 23, 1805; Jan. 4–Dec. 29, 1808.
Washington Univ., St. Louis, has Apr. 13, 1801–Mar. 1, 1802, fair; 1803–1805, scattering; Jan. 2–Dec. 29, 1806; Jan. 4–June 30, 1808; Jan. 2–Dec. 28, 1809.
Dartmouth has May 16–Dec. 14, 1803, fair; Feb. 20, Apr. 26, 1804–Dec. 26, 1805, fair; Feb. 6, 1806–Dec. 21, 1807, fair; Feb. 4–Sept. 29, 1808, scattering issues; July 20, Aug. 3, 19–Dec. 28, 1809; Jan. 1, 1810–Dec. 12, 1816, scattering issues; Jan. 2, 1817–June 14, 1819, fair; Dec. 16–30, 1819; Nov. 6, 1820.
Me. Hist. Soc. has Dec. 7, 1801–Dec. 30, 1802; Jan. 1, 1810–Dec. 21, 1812; Dec. 25, 1815–June 15, 1818.
Taunton Pub. Lib. has Jan. 26, 1804–Dec. 23, 1811.
Yale has Nov. 13, 1800–Dec. 31, 1801; Jan. 6, 1803–Dec. 31, 1804; Jan. 4, 1808–Dec. 28, 1809; and a few other scattering issues.
Western Reserve Hist. Soc. has Mar. 5, 1801–Dec. 29, 1803; Apr. 2–Dec. 31, 1804; Jan. 6–Dec. 18, 1806; Jan. 9–Dec. 28, 1809; Jan. 3, 1811–Dec. 31, 1812; Jan. 3–Dec. 29, 1814; all files lacking a few issues.
Newberry Lib. has June 29, 1812–June 21, 1813; Jan. 3–Dec. 19, 1814.
Rutgers Univ. has Oct. 20, 1800–July 12, 1802.
Brown Univ. has June 25, 1801–Dec. 26, 1803, fair.
Minn. Hist. Soc. has Oct. 14, 1802–Aug. 27, 1804.
Portland Pub. Lib. has Jan. 21, 1805–Dec. 25, 1806, fair.
Univ. of Minn. has Jan. 1–Dec. 31, 1807; Jan. 5–Dec. 28, 1809.
La. State Univ. has Jan. 2–Dec. 31, 1804.
Penn. State Lib. has Oct. 9, 1800–Feb. 2, 1801.
British Museum has Oct. 9, 1800–Apr. 13, 1801.
Ohio Arch. & Hist. Soc. has Jan. 1–Oct. 16, 1801; May 12–Dec. 23, 1802; July 11, 1803–Dec. 31, 1810, scattering issues.
Princeton Univ. has Jan. 4, 1813–Mar. 10, 1814.
Many libraries have scattering issues.

[Boston] Gazetteer, 1803.

Semi-weekly. A continuation, without change of volume numbering, of the "Republican Gazetteer." The first issue of "The Gazetteer" was that of Apr. 2, 1803, vol. 2, no. 1, published by J[ohn] M. Dunham. The word "The" was omitted from the title with the issue of Aug. 20, 1803. With the issue of Oct. 29, 1803, Dunham admitted Benjamin Parks to partnership, under the firm name of

Dunham & Parks. The last issue was that of Dec. 31, 1803, vol. 2, no. 79, as the paper was transferred to True & Parks who established "The Democrat" in its place.

Boston Athenæum, Boston Pub. Lib., Harvard and Wis. Hist. Soc. have Apr. 2–Dec. 31, 1803.
Me. Hist. Soc. has Apr. 2–Sept. 21, 1803, fair.
Mass. Hist. Soc. has Apr. 2–9, 16, 20, July 9, Aug. 10, 24, 27, Sept. 10, Oct. 15–22, Nov. 9, 12, 30, Dec. 10, 1803.
Am. Antiq. Soc. has July 9, 23, 27, Aug. 20–Oct. 8, 15–Dec. 24, 1803.
Lib. Congress has Apr. 9, 30, May 21, June 25, Oct. 5–15, 22, 29, Nov. 5, 23, Dec. 10, 1803.
Univ. of Ill. has May 4, July 2, 1803.

[Boston] Green & Russell's Boston Post-Boy, see Boston Post-Boy.

[Boston] Herald of Freedom, 1788–1791.

Semi-weekly. Established Sept. 15, 1788, by Edmund Freeman and Loring Andrews, under the title of "The Herald of Freedom, and the Federal Advertiser." With the issue of Sept. 15, 1789, the paper was published by Edmund Freeman alone. With the issue of Mar. 16, 1790, the title was shortened to "The Herald of Freedom." With the issue of Apr. 5, 1791, Freeman sold out the paper to John Howel, who shortened the title to "Herald of Freedom." The paper was discontinued with the issue of July 19, 1791, vol. 6, no. 35, being replaced by "The Argus," which continued the old numbering. See under Argus.

Am. Antiq. Soc., Mass. Hist. Soc. and Harvard have Sept. 15, 1788–July 19, 1791.
Boston Pub. Lib. has Sept. 18, Oct. 2–Dec. 4, 15–29, 1788; Jan. 1–Feb. 17, 24, Mar. 3, 6, 17–Apr. 7, 17, 24, May 1, 5, June 9, 12, 23, July 3, 7, 17, Aug. 4, 7, 14–Sept. 1, 8, 15–22, Oct. 2, 13, 23, 27, Nov. 3, 6, 20, 27–Dec. 4. 11–18, 25, 1789; Jan. 1–Dec. 28, 1790, fair; Jan. 7, 18, 21, Feb. 8, 11, 22, Mar. 11, 22, Apr. 1–29, May 13, 20, 24, 31–June 10, 17, 24, 1791.
Essex Inst. has Sept. 18, Nov. 24–Dec. 1, 8–29, 1788; Jan. 1–Dec. 29, 1789, fair; Jan. 1, 5, 12–Feb. 2, 9–16, 23–Mar. 9, 23, Apr. 16, 23, May 11, July 6, Aug. 3, 17, 21, 27, Sept. 7–28, Oct. 5–12, Nov. 2, Dec. 24, 28, 1790; Jan. 4, 11–21, 28, Feb. 11, 22–Mar. 1, Apr. 8, 12, 1791.
Lib. Congress has Sept. 18–Dec. 29, 1788; Jan. 1–Dec. 29, 1789, fair; Jan. 1–Mar. 13, 19–May 28, June 4–11, 25, Aug. 3, 17, 24, 27, Sept. 7, 10, 21, 28, Oct. 5–12, Nov. 2, 1790; Jan. 21, Apr. 5, 8, 15, 19, June 3, 17, July 5, 1791.
N. Y. State Lib. has Sept. 15, 1788–Aug. 21, 1789; Sept. 1, 1789–Mar. 4, 1791, fair; Mar. 18, 22, May 24, June 3, July 19, 1791.
Boston Athenæum has Feb. 10, 20, Mar. 3, 6, Aug. 14, 25, Sept. 22, Oct. 2, 13, 16, 23, Nov. 3–10, 17, 20, Dec. 18, 1789; Jan. 8, 19, Feb. 5, 16, Mar. 9,

Apr. 6, 9, 30, May 2, 7, 11, June 8, 11, July 27, Aug. 27, Nov. 25, 30, Dec. 31, 1790; Mar. 4, May 3, 10, 17, 24, July 19, 1791.

N. Y. Pub. Lib. has Oct. 2, 23, Nov. 6, 17, 20, Dec. 25, 29, 1788; Jan. 1–June 9, fair, Nov. 10, 1789; Feb. 2, June 29, Nov. 16, 19, Dec. 3, 1790; Apr. 8, June 3, 1791.

Mass. State Lib. has Jan. 1–Dec. 29, 1789.

Univ. of Mich. (Clements) has Sept. 25, Nov. 3, 1788; Jan. 6–Dec. 29, 1789, fair; Mar. 12, 1790; Feb. 15, 1791.

Wis. Hist. Soc. has Feb. 13, Mar. 17–May 5, July 28, 1789; Jan. 2–July 13, fair, Aug. 13, 31, Oct. 5, 8, Nov. 12, 16, 1790; May 31, 1791.

Dartmouth has July 14, Aug. 18, 21, Sept. 1, 11, 15, 22, 25, Oct. 6, Nov. 13–27, 1789; Mar. 23, Apr. 13, 1790.

Univ. of Chicago has Jan. 1, 9, Feb. 20, Mar. 3, 17, Apr. 3, May 5, 26, June 3, 1789.

Hist. Soc. Penn. has Jan. 6, 1789; Jan. 12, 22, 29, Feb. 2, Sept. 10, 1790.

Cincinnati Pub. Lib. has Apr. 9, 1790.

[Boston] **Idiot,** 1817–1819.

Weekly. Established Jan. 10, 1818, with the title of "The Idiot, or, Invisible Rambler." There was also a preliminary issue of Dec. 20, 1817. Neither the proprietor's nor printer's name is given, although it is stated to be published by "Samuel Simpleton." The Amer. Antiquarian Soc. has two subscription bills, dated Apr. 5 and July 4, 1818, signed by Henry Trumbull, which would indicate that he was the proprietor. Trumbull published his "Western Emigration, Journal of Doctor Jeremiah Simpleton's Tour to Ohio" in "The Idiot" during 1818, and issued it as a pamphlet the following year. With the issue of Oct. 17, 1818, there is an announcement, "Subscriptions for this paper received by N. Coverly, Milk Street," which would indicate that Nathaniel Coverly was the printer. With the issue of Aug. 29, 1818, the title was slightly altered to "The Idiot, or Invisible Rambler." It was of quarto size, and since it contained marriage and death notices, and current news, both local and domestic, could be considered a newspaper. It was discontinued with the issue of Jan. 2, 1819, vol. 1, no. 52, its establishment having been bought out by the "Kaleidoscope."

Am. Antiq. Soc. has Dec. 20, 1817; Jan. 10, 1818–Jan. 2, 1819.

Mass. Hist. Soc. and Harvard have Jan. 10, 1818–Jan. 2, 1819.

Detroit Pub. Lib. has Jan. 10, 17, Feb. 7–Dec. 24, 1818.

Boston Pub. Lib. has Jan. 10, 1818–Jan. 2, 1819, fair.

Catholic Univ., Washington, D. C., has Jan. 10–Oct. 17, 1818, fair.

Essex Inst. has Feb. 14–Dec. 26, 1818.

N. Y. Hist. Soc. has May 16, July 4, 25, Aug. 1, 29, Sept. 5, Oct. 10, 31, 1818.

Lib. Congress has Aug. 22–Sept. 15, 1818.

[Boston] **Independent Advertiser,** 1748–1749.

Weekly. Established Jan. 4, 1748, by Rogers and Fowle [Gamaliel Rogers and Daniel Fowle], with the title of "The Independent Advertiser." There were evidently no issues published between Oct. 2, 1749, no. 92, and Dec. 5, 1749, no. 93. Discontinued with the issue of Dec. 5, 1749.

Am. Antiq. Soc. has Jan. 4–25, Feo. 8, Mar. 7–Oct. 24, Nov. 7–Dec. 26, 1748; Jan. 2–Sept. 25, 1749.
Boston Pub. Lib. has Jan. 2–Mar. 23, June 6, 1748–Aug. 28, 1749.
Mass. Hist. Soc. has Jan. 4, 11, Feb. 8, 22, Mar. 21, 28, May 9, 30, June 27, July 4, Sept. 5–Oct. 17, Dec. 12, 1748; Jan. 2–Oct. 2, Dec. 5, 1749.
Lib. Congress has Mar. 21, Apr. 11, May 2–16, Aug. 15, 22, Sept. 26, 1748; Jan. 16, 23, Feb. 13–27, Mar. 13–Sept. 4, 18–Oct. 2, 1749.
Wis. Hist. Soc. has Jan. 2–Oct. 2, Dec. 5, 1749.
N. Y. State Lib. has Feb. 6–Sept. 25,.1749.
Harvard has Feb. 6, May 8, July 10, 31, Sept. 25, 1749.
N. Y. Pub. Lib. has June 6, Nov. 7, 1748; Mar. 20, 1749.
N. Y. Hist. Soc. has Apr. 18, May 9, 1748.
Univ. of Mich. (Clements) has Feb. 13, May 1, 8, June 5, 12, 1749.
Hist. Soc. Penn. has Feb. 1, 1748.
Boston Athenæum has June 27, 1748.

[Boston] **Independent Chronicle,** 1776–1820+.

Weekly and semi-weekly. A continuation of "The New-England Chronicle," the first issue with the new title of "The Independent Chronicle" being that of Sept. 19, 1776, no. 422, published weekly by Powars and Willis [Edward E. Powars and Nathaniel Willis]. With the issue of Nov. 7, 1776, the title was changed to "The Independent Chronicle. And the Universal Advertiser." With the issue of Mar. 4, 1779, Powars withdrew from the firm and the paper was published by Nathaniel Willis. With the issue of Jan. 1, 1784, the paper was purchased by Adams and Nourse [Thomas Adams and John Nourse]. There were slight variations in the punctuation in the title on Aug. 16, 1781, Nov. 26, 1784, Mar. 19, 1789, and Oct. 1, 1789, and with the issue of Jan. 29, 1789, the title was shortened to "Independent Chronicle: and the Universal Advertiser." John Nourse died Jan. 2, 1790, and with the issue of Jan. 7, 1790, the paper was published by Thomas Adams. With the issue of Feb. 17, 1791, the title was again "The Independent Chronicle: and the Universal Advertiser." With the issue of July 11, 1793, Isaac Larkin was admitted to partnership under the firm name of Adams and Larkin. With the issue of Aug. 19, 1793, publication was changed from weekly to semi-weekly. Larkin died Dec. 4, 1797, and with the issue of Dec. 7, 1797, the paper was published by Thomas Adams. With the issue of May 13, 1799, Adams transferred the paper and it was printed by Ebenezer Rhoades for the Proprietor (announced as James White). With the issue of May 15, 1800, White gave up his interests and the paper was published by Adams & Rhoades [Abijah Adams and Ebenezer Rhoades]. With the issue of Dec. 21, 1801, the title was shortened to "The Independent Chronicle," shortened again on Jan. 2, 1806, to "Independent Chronicle." With the issue of Oct. 20, 1808, Davis C. Ballard was admitted to the firm, which became known as Adams, Rhoades & Co. With the issue of Jan. 3, 1814, Ballard withdrew and the paper was published by Adams & Rhoades. With the issue of June 4, 1817, Davis C. Ballard and Edmund Wright, Jr., under the firm name of Ballard & Wright, bought the paper and consolidated with it the "Boston Patriot." They published two papers, one the "Independent Chronicle & Boston Patriot (for the country)" which was a continuation, in volume numbering and otherwise, of the semi-weekly "Independent Chronicle"; and the other the "Independent Chronicle & Boston Patriot," which started a new volume numbering with the issue of June 2, 1817, and was a continuation of the daily "Boston Patriot." With the issue of Oct. 1, 1817, the semi-weekly dropped the words "for the country" from the title, and thenceforth for two months, the titles of the semi-weekly and the daily papers were the same. With the issue of Dec. 2, 1817, vol. 2, no. 157, the daily edition changed its name to the "Boston Patriot & Daily Chronicle," for which continuation see under "Boston Patriot." The semi-weekly "Independent Chronicle & Boston Patriot" was continued by Ballard & Wright until after 1820. The "&" in the title was changed to "and" with the issue of Mar. 1, 1820. Ballard died Nov. 29, 1820, but the firm name was continued.

The famous spurious issue of the "Supplement to the Boston Independent Chronicle," no. 705, Mar. 1782, was printed by Benjamin Franklin at Passy, France, containing a fictitious account of a consignment of scalps sent by the Seneca chiefs to Canada, and designed to influence British sentiment. No. 705 of the genuine "Independent Chronicle" was printed Feb. 28, 1782, and the spurious issue, of which there were two editions, was dated Mar. 20, 1782 in a Boston date-line. Both editions are in the Library of Congress, the American Philosophical Society, also in other Franklin collections (see Luther S. Livingston, "Franklin and His Press at Passy," 1914, pp. 58–67).

Am. Antiq. Soc. has complete file, Sept. 19, 1776–Dec. 30, 1820, with supplements, carrier's addresses, etc.

Boston Pub. Lib. has Sept. 19, 1776–Dec. 29, 1791, fair; Jan. 5, 1792–Dec. 30, 1816; Jan. 13–May 1, 1817, scattering; June 4, 1817–Dec. 30, 1820.

Lib. Congress has Sept. 26, 1776–Dec. 25, 1783; Jan. 1, 1784–Dec. 27, 1787, fair; Jan. 3, 1788–Dec. 31, 1798; Jan. 3, 1799–Dec. 29, 1800, fair; Jan. 1, 1801–Dec. 29, 1819; Jan. 1–Dec. 27, 1820, fair.

Boston Athenæum has Sept. 19, 1776–Dec. 23, 1779; Jan. 4, 1781–May 29, 1817; Dec. 3–24, 1817; Jan. 2, 1819–Dec. 30, 1820.

Dartmouth has Feb. 13, 1778–Dec. 30, 1820, fair.

Mass. Hist. Soc. has Sept. 19, 1776–Dec. 28, 1786; Jan. 4–Dec. 20, 1787, fair;

MASSACHUSETTS

Jan. 10–Nov. 13, 1788, scattering; Jan. 29, 1789–Dec. 30, 1790, fair; Jan. 6, 1791–Nov. 5, 1812; Dec. 3, 7, 25, 28, 1812; Jan. 4–Dec. 30, 1813; Jan. 6, 1814–May 9, 1816, fair; Jan. 2–Dec. 31, 1817, scattering; Jan. 3, 1818–Dec. 30, 1820.
Mass. State Lib. has Sept. 19, 1776–Dec. 29, 1794; Jan. 1–Dec. 31, 1795, fair; Jan. 4, 1796–Dec. 31, 1798; Jan. 21–Dec. 30, 1799, fair; Jan. 2, 1800–Dec. 31, 1807; Jan. 21, 1808–Dec. 28, 1809, fair; Jan. 4–Dec. 31, 1810, scattering; Jan. 8–Dec. 30, 1811; Jan. 2–Oct. 5, 1812, scattering; Jan. 4–Dec. 30, 1813.
Essex Inst. has Sept. 19, 1776–Dec. 25, 1777, fair; Jan. 1, 1778–Dec. 27, 1781, scattering file; Feb. 7, 1782–Nov. 28, 1796, scattering issues, Feb. 2, 1797–Nov. 5, 1798, scattering file; Dec. 16, 1799–Dec. 1, 1800, scattering issues; Jan. 12–Dec. 31, 1801, scattering file; Jan. 14–Dec. 2, 1802, scattering issues; Jan. 3, 1803–Dec. 28, 1809; Jan. 3–Dec. 30, 1811; Jan. 4–Dec. 30, 1813; Jan. 10, 1814–Feb. 17, 1817, scattering issues; June 4, 1817–Dec. 30, 1820.
Wis. Hist. Soc. has Oct. 24, 1776; Jan. 23, May 22, Aug. 14, Oct. 9, 16, Nov. 20, Dec. 11, 1777; Jan. 15, 1778–Dec. 30, 1784, fair; Jan. 6, Dec. 8, 1785; Sept. 7, Nov. 30, 1786; Jan. 11, 1787–Nov. 20, 1788, scattering file; Jan. 15–Dec. 31, 1789, fair; Jan. 7, 1790–Dec. 30, 1793, scattering file; Jan. 6, 1794–Dec. 29, 1796, fair; Jan. 2, 1797–Dec. 29, 1800; Jan. 1–Aug. 24, 1801, scattering; Jan. 4, 1802–Nov. 19, 1812, fair; Mar. 22, 1813–Mar. 31, 1814; Jan. 2, 1815–Dec. 30, 1816; June 2, 1817–Dec. 30, 1820.
N. Y. Pub. Lib. has Oct. 3, 1776–Dec. 10, 1778, scattering file; Jan. 7, 1779–Dec. 28, 1780; Jan. 11, 1781–Dec. 26, 1782, fair; Jan. 16, 1783–Dec. 25, 1788, scattering file; Jan. 1, 1789–Dec. 30, 1790; Jan. 6, 1791–Dec. 28, 1795, fair; Jan. 4, 1796–Dec. 30, 1816, Feb. 21, 1818; Oct. 26, Dec. 11, 1819.
N. Y. Hist. Soc. has Sept. 26, 1776–Dec. 14, 1781, scattering file; Jan. 17–Nov. 29, 1782; Jan. 16–Feb. 27, Mar. 20–June 26, Aug. 14, 1783; Jan. 8, 1784; Aug. 25, 1785–Dec. 21, 1786, scattering issues; Sept. 27, 1787; Nov. 20, 1788–Dec. 3, 1789, scattering issues; Jan. 6, 1791–Dec. 27, 1792, fair; May 23, 1793; Jan. 2, 1794–Dec. 27, 1798, fair; Jan. 7–Aug. 22, 1799, scattering; Sept. 2–Dec. 23, 1799; Jan. 9, 16, 23, Mar. 24–Dec. 29, 1800; Jan. 1, 1801–Dec. 30, 1805, fair; July 16, 1807–Dec. 28, 1809; May 7, 1810–Oct. 28, 1813, fair; Jan. 3–Dec. 29, 1814; Mar. 2, 20, Oct. 12, 19, 1815; Jan. 2–May 29, 1817; Dec. 1, 1819–Dec. 30, 1820.
N. Y. State Lib. has Sept. 19, 1776–Dec. 10, 1779, fair; Jan. 6–Nov. 16, 1780, scattering; Jan. 4, 1781–Dec. 26, 1782, fair; Jan. 2, 1783–Dec. 30, 1784; Jan. 6, 1785–Dec. 20, 1787, scattering issues; Jan. 3, 1788–Dec. 31, 1789; 1790–1791, scattering issues; Jan. 5–Dec. 27, 1792, fair; Jan. 3, 1793–Dec. 31, 1795; Jan. 14–Nov. 21, 1796, scattering; Jan. 2, 1797–Dec. 31, 1810; Oct. 7, 1811–Nov. 5, 1812, scattering issues; Jan. 4–Dec. 30, 1813; May 26, 1814–Dec. 28, 1815; June 5, 6, 18, 25, 1817; Jan. 3, 1818–Dec. 30, 1820.
Yale has Apr. 3, 1777–Dec. 28, 1780, fair; Nov. 22, 1781; Aug. 18, 1794; Jan. 12, 1795–Dec. 28, 1809; Jan. 3–Dec. 30, 1811.
Univ. of Mich. (Clements) has Sept. 19, 1776–Dec. 20, 1781, fair; Jan. 3,

1782–Dec. 28, 1786, scattering file; Jan. 4, 1787–Dec. 30, 1790, fair; Jan. 6, 1791–Dec. 31, 1798; Jan. 3, 1799–Dec. 28, 1809, fair; Mar. 7, 1811–Dec. 27, 1817, scattering issues; Jan. 24, 1818–Dec. 30, 1820, fair.

Duke Univ. has Jan. 23, 1777–Dec. 10, 1778, fair; Feb. 18, 1779–June 29, 1780, scattering issues; July 21, 1780–July 18, 1782; May 8, 1783–Jan. 11, 1787, scattering issues; Jan. 3–Dec. 4, 1788, fair; May 31, June 7, Aug. 9, 16, 1792; Dec. 9, 1793; Jan. 2–Dec. 29, 1794; July 9, 1795; Apr. 11, Aug. 1, 1796; Apr. 3, July 20, Dec. 7, 1797; Mar. 7, 18, May 13, 1799; Jan. 2–Sept. 25, 1800, fair; Feb. 12, Apr. 13, Sept. 28, Nov. 16, 1801; Jan. 4–Dec. 13, 1802, scattering file; Jan. 3, 1803–May 29, 1817, fair; Nov. 20, 1817; May 1–Dec. 29, 1819, scattering file.

Univ. of Minn. has June 27, 1799–June 30, 1800; Aug. 4, 1803–Dec. 31, 1804; Jan. 2–June 3, 1806; Jan. 4, 1808–June 29, 1809; Jan. 4–Dec. 30, 1813.

Bath, Me., Patten Lib. has Jan. 14, 1802–May 29, 1817.

Bowdoin has Jan. 2, 1794–Dec. 29, 1797; Dec. 21, 1801–Dec. 29, 1808; Jan. 2, 1812–Dec. 30, 1820.

British Museum has July 14–Dec. 29, 1785; Jan. 5–Feb. 9, Dec. 7, 14, 1786; Feb. 1–Dec. 27, 1787; Jan. 3–Dec. 11, 1788, fair; Mar. 11–Apr. 15, May 13–Oct. 21, 1790; Jan. 13–Nov. 24, 1791; Jan. 1, 1798–Dec. 31, 1807; Mar. 3–May 30, 1808; Jan. 1, 1810–Dec. 31, 1812.

Harvard has Nov. 7–Dec. 26, 1776; Dec. 14, 1780–Dec. 22, 1785; Oct. 19, Nov. 23, 1786–Dec. 27, 1787; June 26, July 3, 1788; Jan. 1, 1789–Dec. 27, 1792; Mar. 14–Dec. 30, 1793, scattering issues; Jan. 9–June 9, Nov. 24–Dec. 8, 1794, fair; Jan. 1–Dec. 31, 1795; Jan. 21–May 30, 1796; Aug. 11, 1796–Dec. 30, 1820.

Hist. Soc. Penn. has Oct. 3, 1776–July 1, 1784; 1784–1786, scattering issues; Mar. 12, 1795–Dec. 28, 1797.

Conn. Hist. Soc. has Jan. 1, 1795–Dec. 29, 1796; Jan. 2–Dec. 28, 1809; Nov. 26, 1812–May 27, 1813.

Union Coll. has Jan. 2–Dec. 28, 1797; Jan. 3, 1805–Dec. 29, 1814.

Western Reserve Hist. Soc. has Jan. 1, 1795–Dec. 28, 1797; Jan. 1, 1801–Dec. 28, 1809; Jan. 3–Dec. 26, 1811; with a few other scattering issues.

York Inst., Saco, has Aug. 31, 1786–Dec. 6, 1804; Feb. 12–Dec. 24, 1810.

Univ. of Chicago has Oct. 24, 1776–July 25, 1793, scattering issues; Jan. 20, 1794–Dec. 29, 1800, fair; Jan. 1, 1810–Dec. 30, 1811.

Chicago Hist. Soc. has Jan. 1, 1784; July 23–Oct. 12, 1795, scattering; Feb. 17, 1806; Dec. 17, 1807; Mar. 21, 24, 1808; Dec. 8, 1808–Feb. 16, 1820, scattering file.

Minn. Hist. Soc. has Sept. 3, 1795–Oct. 16, 1800.

Me. Hist. Soc. has Jan. 29, 1798–Dec. 30, 1802, scattering file; Jan. 3–June 16, 1803; Aug. 1, 1803–Dec. 24, 1807, scattering; Jan. 4, 1808–May 13, 1811, fair.

Portland Pub. Lib. has Jan. 6, 1785–Dec. 28, 1786; Jan. 1–Dec. 28, 1795; Jan. 1–Dec. 31, 1810; Dec. 14, 1812–Jan. 10, 1814.

Amherst Coll. has Nov. 7–21, 1776; June 19, 1783–Apr. 1, 1784.
Bangor Pub. Lib. has Feb. 23, 1792–Mar. 28, 1793.
N. J. Hist. Soc. has Jan. 7, 1804–Dec. 30, 1805.
Los Angeles Pub. Lib. has Jan. 4–Dec. 29, 1796.
Brown Univ. has Jan. 3–Dec. 26, 1805; Jan. 2, 1809–Feb. 26, 1810.
Cincinnati Pub. Lib. has Jan. 3–Dec. 30, 1805.
Univ. of Texas has Jan. 2–Dec. 28, 1815.
Concord, Mass., Pub. Lib. has Aug. 25, 1819–Dec. 30, 1820.
Many libraries have scattering issues.

[Boston] Independent Ledger, 1778–1786.

Weekly. Established June 15, 1778, by Draper & Folsom [Edward Draper and John W. Folsom], with the title of "The Independent Ledger, and American Advertiser." With the issue of July 20, 1778, the title was slightly changed to "The Independent Ledger, and the American Advertiser." The partnership between Draper & Folsom was dissolved on Nov. 3, 1783, although it was not until the issue of Dec. 1, 1783, that the name was changed in the imprint to John W. Folsom. With the issue of Mar. 29, 1784, the size of the paper was slightly increased and the name in the imprint changed to John West Folsom. The paper was discontinued with the issue of Oct. 16, 1786, no. 457.

Mass. Hist. Soc. has June 15, 1778–Oct. 16, 1786.
Boston Athenæum has June 15, 1778–Dec. 26, 1785.
Lib. Congress has June 15, July 13–27, Aug. 10–Nov. 30, Dec. 14–28, 1778; Jan. 4, 18, Feb. 1–May 17, 31, June 14, 28–July 19, Aug. 2, 16, Sept. 13, Oct. 18, Nov. 1, 8, Dec. 6–27, 1779; Jan. 17–Feb. 28, Mar. 13, 20, June 5–26, July 17, 31, Aug. 14, Sept. 4, Oct. 16, 30, Nov. 6, 20, 27, 1780; Jan. 8, 15, Feb. 12, 19, Mar. 19–Apr. 9, 23, May 7, 14, July 16, 30, Sept. 17, 24, Oct. 8, 15, Nov. 12–Dec. 31, 1781; Jan. 28, Feb. 11–Mar. 11, 25, Apr. 1, 22–May 6, 27, June 3, 17, July 22, Aug. 5, 12, 26, Sept. 2, 16–30, Oct. 14, 28–Dec. 2, 16–30, 1782; Jan. 27, Feb. 10, Mar. 17–June 2, 16–Sept. 1, Oct. 6, Nov. 3, Dec. 8, 1783; Jan. 5, 1784–Oct. 16, 1786.
Am. Antiq. Soc. has June 29, July 27–Oct. 12, 26–Dec. 14, 28, 1778; Jan. 18, 25, Feb. 8, 15, Apr. 12–May 10, 24–June 7, July 5, Aug. 2–16, Sept. 13–Oct. 11, Nov. 8, 29, Dec. 20, 1779; Jan. 24, Feb. 7, 28–Mar. 13, Apr. 10–24, May 8–29, June 12, 26, July 24, Aug. 7, 21–Sept. 4, 18, 25, Oct. 16–30, Nov. 27, Dec. 25, 1780; Jan. 1, Feb. 12, Apr. 23, 30, June 4, July 30, Dec. 17, 1781; Mar. 11, Apr. 1, 15, May 13, June 10, 17, Aug. 12, Sept. 16, Oct. 21, 28, Nov. 18–Dec. 30, 1782; Jan. 6, 1783–Dec. 27, 1784; Jan. 3–31, Feb. 14–May 9, 23, June 6–20, July 4, Aug. 22, Sept. 5, 19, Oct. 10–31, Dec. 19, 26, 1785; Jan. 2–16, Feb. 6, 20–Mar. 20, Apr. 3–May 22, June 12, 26, July 3, 17, Aug. 7–21, Sept. 11, 18, Oct. 2–16, 1786.
N. Y. State Lib. has June 15–Aug. 17, Sept. 7, 21–Dec. 28, 1778; Jan. 4, 18–

May 31, June 14–July 12, 26, Aug. 9–23, Sept. 13, Oct. 4, 18, Nov. 1, 8, 29, Dec. 6, 20, 27, 1779; Jan. 3, 17–Feb. 28, Mar. 13–Apr. 3, July 3, 31–Aug. 14, Sept. 4–18, Oct. 16, 23, Dec. 18, 25, 1780; Mar. 26, June 11, 25–July 16, Aug. 27, Sept. 17, 24, Oct. 8–22, Nov. 19–Dec. 3, 17, 24, 1781; Jan. 14, 28–July 1, Aug. 5, 12, Sept. 2–Dec. 30, 1782; Jan. 6–Sept. 8, Oct. 6, 20, 27, Nov. 17, 24, Dec. 8, 1783; Jan. 5–Feb. 9, 23–Dec. 27, 1784; Jan. 3, 17, 31–Feb. 21, Mar. 7, 14, 28, Apr. 11, May 9–Aug. 1, 29, Oct. 31–Nov. 14, Dec. 26, 1785; Jan. 9–Feb. 27, May 22, Aug. 14, 21, Sept. 18, Oct. 9, 1786.

Amherst Coll. has July 13, 20, Aug. 24, Sept. 7–21, Oct. 5, 19–Nov. 2, 30–Dec. 21, 1778; Jan. 4–18, Feb. 22–Mar. 22, Apr. 5, 12, May 3, 17–31, June 21–July 19, Aug. 2–Sept. 6, Nov. 29–Dec. 27, 1779; Feb. 21–Mar. 6, 20, May 22, June 26, July 3, 17, 24, Aug. 14, Sept. 4, 25, Oct. 2, 30, Nov. 6, 20, Dec. 11, 1780; Jan. 8, 29, Mar. 26, Oct. 18–Nov. 12, Dec. 10, 17, 1781; Jan. 7–21, Feb. 4, 25, Mar. 4, Apr. 1–29, May 20, June 3–24, July 8, Aug. 5, 19, Sept. 2, 9, 23, Oct. 7, 21, Nov. 11, 18, Dec. 23, 30, 1782; Jan. 27, Feb. 3, 17, Mar. 10, Apr. 14, 28, May 12, June 30–Sept. 22, Oct. 6–Dec. 22, 1783; Jan. 5–Mar. 8, 22, 29, 1784.

Boston Pub. Lib. has June 22, July 6, Aug. 10–Sept. 21, Oct. 5–26, Nov. 9, 16, Dec. 14, 1778; May 10, Oct. 11, 1779; Feb. 28–Mar. 13, June 26, July 17, Sept. 18, Oct. 30, Dec. 18, 1780; Apr. 9, June 25, Oct. 8, Nov. 26, Dec. 10, 1781; June 10, Sept. 16, Nov. 25, Dec. 16, 1782; Jan. 20, 1783–Dec. 27, 1784, fair; Jan. 3, 24, Feb. 14–Mar. 7, 21, 28, Apr. 11, 18, May 2, June 20, Aug. 1, Oct. 10, 17, 1785; Jan. 2, Feb. 6, 27, Mar. 6, Apr. 3, May 1, 22, Sept. 11, 18, Oct. 2, 9, 1786.

Essex Inst. has Mar. 22, May 17, June 21, Sept. 13–Oct. 11, Nov. 1, Dec. 27, 1779; Feb. 14, July 10, 24–Aug. 14, Sept. 11, 25–Oct. 9, Nov. 6–27, Dec. 18, 25, 1780; Jan. 1, 15–29, Feb. 19, Mar. 5–May 7, 28–June 18, July 2–Oct. 8, Nov. 19–Dec. 24, 1781; Apr. 1, 8, 22, 29, May 20–June 10, July 1–29, 1782; Jan. 27, Apr. 7, Aug. 18, 1783; Jan. 12, Apr. 5, 26, May 17, 31, June 7, 28, July 5, 19, Aug. 2, 16, Oct. 4, 11, 25, Nov. 8, 15, Dec. 20, 1784; Feb. 28, Mar. 21, 1785; Mar. 6, May 1, 1786.

Univ. of Mich. (Clements) has July 20, Aug. 17, Sept. 21, Oct. 5, 12, 26, Nov. 2, 16, 30, 1778; Feb. 8, 15, Mar. 8, 22, Apr. 5, 12, 26–May 17, Sept. 13, Nov. 8, Dec. 13, 1779; Mar. 20, Oct. 30, Nov. 27, 1780; Jan. 15, July 9, Sept. 17, Dec. 10–24, 1781; Jan. 7, 14, Feb. 11, 25–Mar. 11, Apr. 22, May 27, Nov. 4, Dec. 23, 30, 1782; Jan. 13, 27, Feb. 3, 24–Mar. 17, 31–Aug. 4, 18–Dec. 29, 1783; Dec. 12, 1785; Feb. 6, 1786.

N. Y. Pub. Lib. has July 27, Nov. 9, 1778; June 12, Nov. 20, 1780; Apr. 9, 1781; Aug. 12, 1782; Feb. 24, Apr. 14, May 12, June 2–July 14, Aug. 4–18, Sept. 8, 15, Oct. 6, Nov. 10, 17, Dec. 8, 22, 1783; Mar. 29–May 17, 31–July 26, Aug. 9–Dec. 27, 1784; Jan. 3–Mar. 28, 1785; May 22, Sept. 4, Oct. 16, 1786.

Hist. Soc. Penn. has July 6, 1778–June 14, July 5, 12, 26–Aug. 9, 30, Oct. 18, 25, 1779; Nov. 20, 1780; July 22, 1782; Dec. 26, 1785; Jan. 2–Feb. 6, 27, 1786.

MASSACHUSETTS 313

Yale has July 13–Sept. 14, 28–Oct. 12, Nov. 9–Dec. 14, 1778; Jan. 7, 1782; Jan. 13, 1783.
Duke Univ. has July 20, 1778; Feb. 15, Mar. 8, Apr. 5, May 3, 1779; Aug. 21, 1780; Feb. 11, Mar. 11, Apr. 22, 1782; Aug. 11, 1783; Feb. 2, 9, 1784.
N. Y. Hist. Soc. has June 26, July 31, Sept. 18, 1780; June 12, 1786.
Wis. Hist. Soc. has July 20, 1778; May 10, 1779; Oct. 16, 1780.
Dartmouth has Apr. 23, May 7–21, 1781.
Harvard has Apr. 14, Dec. 22, 1783.
Mass. State Lib. has Oct. 10, 1785.

Boston Intelligencer, 1816–1820+.

Weekly. A continuation, without change of numbering, of the "Evening Gazette," the first issue with the new title of "Boston Intelligencer, and Morning & Evening Advertiser," being that of Aug. 17, 1816, vol. 3, no. 1, published by William Burdick & Co. With the issue of Jan. 4, 1817, Burdick relinquished the proprietorship, but no transfer to another proprietor was noted in the paper until the issue of Mar. 8, 1817, when William W. Clapp announced that he had purchased the paper. The name of William W. Clapp & Co. first appeared in the imprint with the issue of Mar. 15, 1817. No publisher's name appeared in the imprint beginning with the issue of May 2, 1818, and it was not until the issue of July 25, 1818, that Clapp's name again appeared, this time without the "Co." With the issue of Oct. 24, 1818, the title was changed to "Boston Intelligencer & Evening Gazette." Clapp continued the paper until after 1820.

Am. Antiq. Soc. and Boston Pub. Lib. have Aug. 17, 1816–Dec. 30, 1820.
Essex Inst. has Aug. 17, 1816–Dec. 30, 1820, fair.
Boston Athenæum has Aug. 17, 1816–Dec. 25, 1819; July 1, 1820.
N. Y. Hist. Soc. has Aug. 17, 1816–Dec. 25, 1819; Jan. 1–Dec. 30, 1820, fair.
Grosvenor Lib., Buffalo, has Aug. 17, 1816–Dec. 25, 1819; Mar. 18, 1820.
Wis. Hist. Soc. has Aug. 17, 1816–Aug. 14, 1819, fair.
Newton Free Lib. has Nov. 9, 1816–Dec. 25, 1819.
Lib. Congress has Aug. 17, 1816–Dec. 27, 1817; Feb. 21, Mar. 21, Apr. 11, 18, May 2, July 25, Sept. 5, Nov. 7, Dec. 19, 1818; Jan. 2–Aug. 21, Sept. 4–18, Oct. 16, Nov. 6, 13, 27–Dec. 25, 1819; Jan. 22–Feb. 12, 26–Mar. 11, 25–Apr. 8, May 6, 20, 27, June 10, 24, July 1, Oct. 7–21, Dec. 16–30, 1820.
Mass. Hist. Soc. has Oct. 19, 1816; Aug. 16, 1817–Oct. 17, 1818; Feb. 20, Mar. 13, May 22, July 3, 1819; Jan. 1–Dec. 30, 1820.
Univ. of Mich. (Clements) has Nov. 9, 1816; Aug. 16, Sept. 6–20, Oct. 11–Nov. 1, 15, 29, Dec. 6, 20, 1817; Jan. 3–17, 31–Feb. 28, Mar. 14, 28–May 23, June 6–July 4, 18–Sept. 12, 26–Oct. 3, 24–Dec. 26, 1818; Jan. 2, 1819–Dec. 23, 1820.
Hist. Soc. Penn. has Aug. 17, 1816–Dec. 27, 1817.
Univ. of Texas has Aug. 16, 1817–Sept. 12, 1818.

Dartmouth has June 13, July 18, Aug. 1–15, Sept. 5, 19, 26, Oct. 17, Nov. 14–Dec. 5, 1818; Jan. 2, 1819–Dec. 30, 1820.
Duke Univ. has Aug. 24–Dec. 28, 1816; Jan. 4, 18–Feb. 1, 15–July 19, 1817.
Yale has Oct. 24, 1818–Nov. 27, 1819.

[Boston] J. Russell's Gazette, 1798–1800, see Russell's Gazette.

[Boston] Kaleidoscope, 1818–1819.

Weekly. Established Nov. 28, 1818, judging from the earliest issue located, that of Dec. 12, 1818, vol. 1, no. 3. "The Kaleidoscope" was published by Hews & Goss [Abraham Hews, Jr., and Sylvester T. Goss] and edited by N[athaniel] H. Wright. With the issue of Jan. 9, 1819, it absorbed a similar paper entitled "The Idiot, or, Invisible Rambler," and changed its title to "Boston Kaleidoscope and Literary Rambler." Wright's last issue as editor was May 8, 1819. With the issue of July 3, 1819, Goss became sole publisher. The last issue located is that of Nov. 6, 1819, vol. 1, no. 49. The paper probably finished with no. 52 on Nov. 27, 1819, as Goss established the "Ladies' Port Folio" on Jan. 1, 1820, and also "The New Hampshire Intelligencer" at Haverhill, N. H., in November 1819. "The Kaleidoscope" was of quarto size, paged, and since it contained marriage and death notices, and a considerable amount of current news, especially local, could be considered a newspaper.

Am. Antiq. Soc. has Dec. 12–26, 1818; Jan. 9–Apr. 24, May 8–June 19, July 3–Aug. 28, Sept. 18, Oct. 23, Nov. 6, 1819.
N. Y. Hist. Soc. has Feb. 6, Apr. 17, May 29, Oct. 23, 1819.

[Boston] Ladies' Port Folio, 1820.

Weekly. Established by Sylvester T. Goss as a magazine, Jan. 1, 1820, with the title of "Ladies' Port Folio." It was of quarto size, and strictly a magazine, without current news or advertisements, although like many magazines it printed marriage and death notices. It ran thus until June 17, 1820, vol. 1, no. 25. On June 24, 1820, Goss changed it to folio newspaper size, with current news and regular newspaper advertisements. The only issue in this form located is that of July 8, 1820, new series vol. 2, no. 3.

Am. Antiq. Soc. has Jan. 1–June 17, July 8, 1820.
Boston Pub. Lib., Lib. Congress, and Harvard have Jan. 1–June 17, 1820.

[Boston] Massachusetts Centinel, 1784–1790.

Semi-weekly. Established Mar. 24, 1784, by Warden & Russell [William Warden and Benjamin Russell] under the title of "The Massachusetts Centinel: and the Republican Journal." With the issue of Oct. 16, 1784, the title was shortened to "The Massachusetts Centinel." The paper was at first of quarto size and title pages were printed for vols. 1 and 2. Warden died Mar. 18, 1786, and with the issue of Mar. 22, the paper was published by Benjamin Russell. With this issue, moreover, the size was enlarged to folio. The last issue with this title was that of June 12, 1790, vol. 13, no. 26, and with the issue of June 16, 1790, the title was changed to "Columbian Centinel," which see.

Am. Antiq. Soc., Boston Athenæum, Lancaster, Mass., Pub. Lib., and Mass. Hist. Soc. have Mar. 24, 1784–June 12, 1790.
British Museum has Mar. 24, 1784–June 12, 1790, nearly complete.
Lib. Congress has Mar. 31–Dec. 29, 1784, fair; Jan. 1, 1785–June 12, 1790.
N. Y. Hist. Soc. has Mar. 24, 1784–June 12, 1790, lacking 16 issues.
Boston Pub. Lib. has Mar. 31–Dec. 22, 1784, fair; Jan. 1, 1785–June 12, 1790.
N. E. Hist. Geneal. Soc. has Mar. 27, 1784–Mar. 19, 1785; Mar. 22, 1786–June 12, 1790.
N. Y. Pub. Lib. has Apr. 7–Dec. 29, 1784, fair; Jan. 1, 1785–June 12, 1790.
Long Id. Hist. Soc. has June 2, 1784–June 12, 1790.
N. Y. State Lib. has Mar. 24–Dec. 4, 1784, fair; Jan. 5, Feb. 19, Mar. 23, 1785–June 12, 1790.
Dartmouth has Mar. 24–Oct. 13, 1784; Mar. 12, 1785–Dec. 31, 1788, fair; Jan. 3, 1789–June 12, 1790.
Mass. State Lib. has Jan. 5, 1785–June 12, 1790, fair.
Univ. of Mich. (Clements) has Apr. 3, Dec. 15, 25, 1784; Jan. 22, 1785–Dec. 30, 1786, fair; Jan. 3, 1787–June 12, 1790.
Wis. Hist. Soc. has Mar. 24, 1784–Dec. 31, 1785, fair; Jan. 7–Mar. 18, Apr. 12, May 24, Apr. 8, 15, 19, July 5, Sept. 27, 1786; Mar. 3–Dec. 29, 1787, fair; Jan. 2, 1788–Dec. 26, 1789; Jan. 2–June 12, 1790, fair.
Detroit Pub. Lib. has Mar. 23, 1785–Sept. 13, 1786; Aug. 25, 1787–June 12, 1790.
Harvard has June 5, 12, July 28, Dec. 25, 1784; Jan. 12, Feb. 5–Dec. 31, 1785, fair; Jan. 4–Mar. 18, 25, Apr. 15, May 13, Sept. 20–Dec. 30, 1786; Jan. 3–Dec. 29, 1787; Jan. 2, 1788–June 12, 1790, fair.
Essex Inst. has Jan. 29–Dec. 31, 1785, scattering file; Feb. 1, 1786–Dec. 26, 1787, a few scattering issues; Jan. 2, 1788–June 12, 1790, fair.
Yale has Jan. 1, 1785–Mar. 18, 1786; Mar. 10, 1787; Sept. 17, 1788–Dec. 30, 1789.
Western Reserve Hist. Soc. has Oct. 30, Nov. 13, 1784; Jan. 1–Mar. 19, 1785; Apr. 8–Sept. 16, 1786, fair; June 13, 1787–May 19, 1790, fair.
Univ. of Chicago has Mar. 24, 1784–Mar. 19, 1785, fair; 1787–1788, scattering issues; Jan. 3, 1789–June 12, 1790, fair.
Univ. of Ill. has Mar. 24, 1787–Mar. 15, 1788; Jan. 3, 1789–June 12, 1790.
Hist. Soc. Penn. has Mar. 24–Sept. 18, 1784; Jan. 23–Sept. 13, 1788.
York Inst., Saco, has Sept. 19, 1787–Sept. 13, 1788.
Williams Coll. has Jan. 2, 1788–Sept. 12, 1789.
Cincinnati Pub. Lib. has Jan. 25, 1788–June 12, 1790, fair.

Duke Univ. has May 5, 15, July 10, 1784; May 25, 1785; Feb. 15, Mar. 15, 29, Nov. 11, 22, 1786; Feb. 14, Mar. 10, July 7, 18, 28, 1787; Feb. 6–Dec. 27, 1788, scattering; Jan. 3, 1789–June 12, 1790, fair.
Conn. Hist. Soc. has Jan. 3, 1789–June 12, 1790.
Keene, N. H., Pub. Lib. has Mar. 25–Sept. 16, 1786.
Smith Coll. has May 12–Dec. 29, 1787.
Cornell has Jan. 10–Dec. 30, 1789.
Me. Hist. Soc. has Jan. 7–Dec. 30, 1789.
Many libraries have a few scattering issues.

[Boston] **Massachusetts Gazette, 1765–1766,** see **Boston News-Letter.**

[Boston] **Massachusetts Gazette, 1768–1769.**

Semi-weekly. Established May 23, 1768, and published semi-weekly, as part of "The Boston Post-Boy & Advertiser" issued by Green & Russell [John Green and Joseph Russell] on Monday, and of "The Boston Weekly News-Letter" issued by R[ichard] Draper on Thursday. The issue of "The Massachusetts Gazette," by the arrangement between the two firms of publishers, appeared therefore on Mondays and Thursdays, as a part of, or accompanying, the "Post-Boy" and the "News-Letter" alternately. The first issue of "The Massachusetts Gazette" was no. 277, which numbering was undoubtedly adopted through reckoning back, although slightly in error, to the first time when the words "Massachusetts Gazette" appeared as part of the title of "Boston News-Letter." The last issue of "The Massachusetts Gazette" in this form was that of Sept. 25, 1769, no. 417. "The Massachusetts Gazette" as part of the "Post-Boy" ran from May 23, 1768, to Sept. 25, 1769, and as part of the "News-Letter" ran from May 26, 1768, to Sept. 21, 1769. This paper is an integral part of the files of the "News-Letter" and the "Post-Boy," with which it is generally bound, but because of its distinctive title, it is here described separately. The issues, however, are listed under the "Boston News-Letter" and the "Boston Post-Boy." For a full discussion of the subject, see the Colonial Society Check-List in "Publications," vol. 9, p. 484.

[Boston] **Massachusetts Gazette, 1785–1788.**

Weekly and semi-weekly. Removed from Salem, where it was entitled "The Salem Gazette," to Boston, where the first issue was published Nov. 28, 1785, vol. 5, no. 216, published by Samuel Hall. Its title was "The Massachusetts Gazette." It was changed from a weekly to a semi-weekly with the issue of Aug. 22, 1786. Beginning with the issue of June 5, 1787, Hall admitted John W. Allen into partnership under the firm name of S. Hall and J. W. Allen. With the issue of Sept. 4, 1787, Hall relinquished his interests and the paper was published by John Wincoll Allen. It was discontinued with the issue of Nov. 11, 1788, vol. 8, no. 486.

MASSACHUSETTS 317

Am. Antiq. Soc., Mass. Hist. Soc., and Lib. Congress have Nov. 28, 1785–Nov. 11, 1788.
Boston Pub. Lib., Essex Inst., N. Y. Pub. Lib., and N. Y. State Lib. have Nov. 28, 1785–Nov. 11, 1788, nearly complete.
Univ. of Mich. (Clements) has Nov. 28, 1785–Nov. 11, 1788, fair.
Dartmouth has Nov. 28, 1785–May 9, 1788; Sept. 30–Oct. 10, 31, 1788.
Yale has Nov. 28, 1785–Dec. 21, 1787, fair.
Wis. Hist. Soc. has Jan. 2, 1786–Dec. 28, 1787; Jan. 1–Nov. 7, 1788, fair.
Univ. of Chicago has Dec. 5, 12, 1785; Jan. 2, 1786–Sept. 26, 1788, fair.
Boston Athenæum has Nov. 28, 1785–Oct. 13, 1786; Oct. 16, 19, 30, 1787–Feb. 29, Mar. 7, 14, Apr. 8, 18, May 2, June 3, July 1, 4, Aug. 5–15, Sept. 16, 19, 1788.
N. Y. Hist. Soc. has Jan. 2–July 31, Aug. 25, Sept. 12, 29, Oct. 3, 6, 13, 24, 27, Nov. 3, 7, 14–Dec. 29, 1786, fair; Jan. 2–July 31, fair, Aug. 7, 14, 21, 31–Sept. 7, 14, 21, 25, Oct. 5, 9, 16, 26, Nov. 6, 30, Dec. 7, 1787; Jan. 1, 4, 11, 14, 25, 29, Feb. 8, 12, 22, 29, Mar. 7–14, 25, Apr. 1, 8–22, 29, May 9, 16, June 3, 27, July 11, 18–29, 1788.
Hist. Soc. Penn. has June 5, 1787–Nov. 11, 1788.
Duke Univ. has Dec. 19, 1785; Jan. 2–Dec. 29, 1786.
Ohio Arch. & Hist. Soc. has Jan. 9–Dec. 19, 1786.
Chicago Hist. Soc. has Jan. 23–July 24, 1786.
Univ. of Minn. has Aug. 7–Dec. 29, 1786.
Amherst Coll. has July 6–Dec. 18, 1787.
Rutgers Univ. has Aug. 29–Sept. 29, Oct. 10, 13, 27, Nov. 10, 24, Dec. 1, 8, 1786; Feb. 16, 1787; Feb. 15, Mar. 4, Apr. 8, 1788.
Harvard has Feb. 16, Mar. 27, 30, May 8, 1787.
Mass. State Lib. has Sept. 4, 14, 18, Oct. 2, 1787.

[Boston] **Massachusetts Gazette and Boston News-Letter,** 1763–1768, 1769–1776, see **Boston News-Letter.**

[Boston] **Massachusetts Gazette and Boston Post-Boy,** 1769–1775, see **Boston Post-Boy.**

[Boston] **Massachusetts Mercury,** 1793–1803.

Tri-weekly and semi-weekly. Established Jan. 1, 1793, with the title of "Massachusetts Mercury," published by Young and Etheridge [Alexander Young and Samuel Etheridge]. It was of quarto size and was issued tri-weekly. With the issue of July 2, 1793, the size of the paper was changed to folio, the issue to semi-weekly and the title to "The Mercury." With the issue of Aug. 9, 1793, the partnership was dissolved and the paper published by Alexander Young alone. With the issue of Apr. 8, 1794, Young admitted Thomas Minns to partnership under the firm name of Young and Minns. With the issue of Dec. 4, 1795, the title reverted to "Massachusetts Mercury," but with the issue of July 8, 1796, was again changed to "The Mercury," and with the issue of Jan. 3, 1797, was changed back again to "Massachusetts Mercury." With the issue of Jan. 2, 1801, the title was changed to "The Mercury and New-England Palladium." The last issue with this title was that of Mar. 8, 1803, vol. 21, no. 19, and with the issue of Mar. 11, 1803, the title was changed to "New-England Palladium," which see.

Mass. Hist. Soc. has Jan. 1, 1793–Mar. 8, 1803.
Am. Antiq. Soc. has Jan. 3, 5, 10, 12, 17–22, 26, 29, Feb. 2, 7, 9, 16, 21, 1793–Mar. 8, 1803.
Boston Athenæum has Feb. 9, 1793–Mar. 8, 1803.
Boston Pub. Lib. has Mar. 23, July 2, 1793–Mar. 8, 1803.
Essex Inst. has Apr. 2–10, 18, May 10, July 2, 1793–Jan. 31, 1794, fair; Apr. 11, 29, July 1, 1794; Feb. 24, 1795; June 3, 1796–Dec. 29, 1797, fair; Jan. 2, 1798–Mar. 8, 1803.
Harvard has May 6, Nov. 8, 22, Dec. 6, 31, 1793; Jan. 14–June 10, 1794, scattering; Feb. 17, 20, Mar. 6, May 26, July 24, Aug. 14, Sept. 4, Dec. 1, 18, 1795; Jan. 1, 1796–Mar. 8, 1803.
N. Y. State Lib. has Jan. 1, 1793–June 27, 1794; Sept. 12, 1794; Apr. 3, 1795–July 5, 1799; Aug. 27, Oct. 8, 15, 18, 25, Nov. 26, 1799; Jan. 3, 1800–Mar. 8, 1803.
Lib. Congress has Jan. 12, Feb. 5–June 28, fair, Aug. 6, Sept. 20, Oct. 1, 1793; Feb. 28, 1794–July 7, 1795, scattering; Aug. 25, 1795–Dec. 29, 1797, fair; Jan. 2, 1798–Mar. 8, 1803.
N. Y. Hist. Soc. has Feb. 14–June 19, 1793; July 2, 1793–July 22, 1794, fair; Jan. 1, 1796–Dec. 29, 1797; Mar. 27, May 25, Aug. 21, 24, Sept. 21, Oct. 26, 30, Nov. 27, Dec. 11, 1798; May 21, 1799–Dec. 26, 1800, fair; Jan. 2, 1801–Mar. 8, 1803.
Wis. Hist. Soc. has Feb. 23, 1793–Dec. 16, 1796, scattering file; Jan. 3, 1797–Dec. 28, 1798; Jan. 1–Sept. 27, 1799, fair; Dec. 31, 1799–Dec. 30, 1800, fair; Jan. 2, 1801–Mar. 8, 1803.
Conn. Hist. Soc. has Jan. 2, 1798–Mar. 8, 1803.
British Museum has July 3, 1798–Mar. 8, 1803.
Univ. of Mich. (Clements) has Apr. 15, Aug. 8, Oct. 28, 31, 1794; July 21, Oct. 30, Nov. 13, 1795; Feb. 19, Apr. 15, 19, July 15, Nov. 18, 1796; Jan. 13, 1797–Dec. 13, 1799, scattering file; Jan. 3, 1800–Mar. 8, 1803.
Me. Hist. Soc. has Sept. 5, 1797–Dec. 2, 1800, fair; Jan. 2–Dec. 29, 1801.
Univ. of Ill. has Jan. 2, 1798–Dec. 31, 1799; July 4, 1800–Dec. 29, 1801.
Yale has Aug. 16, Sept. 27, Nov. 1, 22, 1796; July 14, Sept. 19, 1797; Aug. 10–17, 1798; Jan. 4, 1799–Mar. 4, 1803.
Duke Univ. has July 26–Aug. 6, Sept. 3, 17–24, Oct. 1, 8, 15, 1793; Mar. 7, Apr. 18, 1794; Jan. 1–Dec. 20, 1796, fair; Jan. 10–Feb. 3, 14, 17, Apr. 7, May 2, June 6, July 4–Dec. 29, 1797; Sept. 21–Oct. 2, 9, 16, 19, 26, Dec. 1,

1798; Jan. 25, 1799; Jan. 3, 1800–July 31, 1801; Aug. 4–Dec. 29, 1801, fair; Jan. 7–Mar. 8, 1803.
N. Y. Pub. Lib. has Jan. 3–June 24, July 9, 1793; Feb. 25, Apr. 15, May 9, Oct. 31, 1794; Jan. 2, 13, Oct. 23, Nov. 17, 1795; Jan. 5, May 27, June 21, July 1, 1796–Dec. 29, 1797; Jan. 2–Dec. 28, 1798, fair; Feb. 1, 12, Mar. 22, May 7, 14, 31, June 11, 18, 25, Sept. 24, Dec. 6, 17, 31, 1799; Jan. 3–Dec. 23, 1800, fair; May 22, 1801–Oct. 19, 1802, fair.
Mass. State Lib. has July 2–Dec. 27, 1793; Jan. 2, 1801–Mar. 8, 1803.
Portland Pub. Lib. has July 2, 1793–Feb. 28, 1794.
Congregational Lib., Boston, has Apr. 16, 1799–Apr. 11, 1800.
Phil. Lib. Co. has Oct. 23, 30, Nov. 17, 24, 1795; Jan. 12–26, Mar. 8, 15, Apr. 1, 15, 29, May 27–June 3, 17, 24, July 15–29, Aug. 19, 1796.
Dartmouth has Jan. 2, 1801–Feb. 22, 1803, fair.
Western Reserve Hist. Soc. has Jan. 2, 1801–Dec. 30, 1803.
Trinity Coll., Hartford, has Jan. 2, 1801–Mar. 8, 1803.
Amherst Coll. has Jan. 2, 1801–June 29, 1802.
Bowdoin Coll. has Jan. 2, 1801–Dec. 31, 1802, fair.
Newberry Lib. has July 7, 1795–Dec. 30, 1796, scattering; Jan. 24–Dec. 29, 1797, fair; Jan. 2, 1798–Oct. 8, 1799, scattering; Feb. 23, 1802.
Univ. of Chicago has Nov. 17, 1795; Apr. 6, 13, May 11, 1798; May 21, 31, June 14, 18, July 23, Aug. 20, 1799; Feb. 7–Dec. 23, 1800, fair; Mar. 17–Dec. 29, 1801, fair.
Vassar Coll. has Jan. 2, 1801–Mar. 8, 1803, fair.
Cornell has Jan. 2–Dec. 22, 1801.
Many libraries have single, or a few scattering, issues.

[Boston] **Massachusetts Spy,** 1770–1775.

Tri-weekly, semi-weekly and weekly. Established July 17, 1770, by Z. Fowle and I. Thomas [Zechariah Fowle and Isaiah Thomas], with the title of "The Massachusetts Spy." The size of the paper was small quarto. The first number of July 17, 1770, which had no imprint, was in the nature of a prospectus, the regular publication, which was tri-weekly, beginning with the issue of Aug. 7, 1770, vol. 1, no. 2. The last issue to have the Fowle and Thomas imprint was that of Oct. 11, 1770, and they dissolved partnership soon afterwards, since advertisements printed in the issue of Oct. 18, 1770, show that Fowle had removed from the Spy office, and the original agreement by which Fowle disposed of his printing materials to Thomas, in the possession of the American Antiquarian Society, is dated Oct. 23, 1770. The first issue, however, to have the name of I. Thomas in the imprint is that of Oct. 30, 1770. With the issue of Nov. 5, 1770, the paper was changed to a semi-weekly. The last issue of quarto size was that of Feb. 1, 1771, vol. 1, no. 65. After a short suspension, the paper was resumed with the issue of Mar. 7, 1771, the size being changed to folio, the publication to weekly, and a new volume numbering adopted. With the issue of Oct. 8, 1772, the title was enlarged to "The Massachusetts Spy Or, Thomas's Boston Journal." With the issue of Nov. 3, 1774, the comma after "Or" in the title was omitted. The last issue printed at Boston was that of Apr. 6, 1775, vol. 5, no. 218, after which it was removed to Worcester and re-established on May 3, 1775. See under Worcester.

Am. Antiq. Soc., Boston Athenæum and Mass. Hist. Soc. have July 17, 1770–Apr. 6, 1775.
Lib. Congress has July 17, Aug. 11, Sept. 1, Oct. 27, Nov. 29, Dec. 10, 17–31, 1770; Jan. 7, 14, Apr. 4–Aug. 29, Oct. 3–Dec. 26, 1771; Jan. 2, 16–Feb. 27, Mar. 12–Apr. 23, May 7, June 11, July 2, 9, Sept. 3–17, Oct. 8, 15, 29, Dec. 17, 31, 1772; Jan. 7, 1773–Apr. 6, 1775.
British Museum has Mar. 7, 1771–June 10, 1773; June 2, 1774–Apr. 6, 1775, fair.
John L. Balderston, Beverly Hills, Calif., has 1771–1774.
Boston Pub. Lib. has July 17, Aug. 23, Sept. 1, 13, Oct. 2, 13, 23–Nov. 12, 19, 22, 29, Dec. 7, 17–31, 1770; Jan. 7, 10, Feb. 1, Mar. 9–30, June 27–July 11, Aug. 1, 8, 22, 29, Sept. 12–Oct. 31, Nov. 22, Dec. 19, 26, 1771; Jan. 2, 1772–Apr. 6, 1775, fair.
N. Y. State Lib. has July 17–Dec. 31, 1770; Jan. 3–Feb. 1, July 18, Aug. 22, Oct. 31, Dec. 12, 1771; Feb. 27, Mar. 12, June 18, Aug. 27, Oct. 15, 29, Nov. 12, 1772; Jan. 7, 14, Aug. 12, Oct. 21, Nov. 18, Dec. 2, 16, 23, 1773; Jan. 27, Feb. 10, 17, Mar. 3, 10, 24, Apr. 7, 21–May 19, July 7, 15, Aug. 4, Sept. 1, 8, Oct. 6, Nov. 3–Dec. 8, 29, 1774; Jan. 12, Feb. 2, 16, Mar. 17, 1775.
Worc. Pub. Lib. has July 17, Oct. 30, 1770; Mar. 7, 1771–Feb. 27, 1772.
Taunton Pub. Lib. has May 12, 1774–Apr. 6, 1775.
Univ. of Mich. (Clements) has Apr. 8, Aug. 12, Nov. 11, 18, Dec. 16, 1773; Mar. 3, May 12, June 23, July 7–Aug. 4, Sept. 15, Oct. 6, 13, 27–Dec. 22, 1774; Jan. 5, 12, 26, Feb. 2, 16–Mar. 9, 23–Apr. 6, 1775.
N. Y. Pub. Lib. has Feb. 1, May 2, 16, June 27, Aug. 29, Sept. 4, Oct. 24, Dec. 26, 1771; Mar. 12, 19, Apr. 9, 30–May 28, Sept. 3, 1772; Jan. 7, Feb. 4, Mar. 25, 1773; June 9, Sept. 8, 1774; Jan. 12, Feb. 6, Mar. 17, 23, 1775.
Essex Inst. has July 4, Aug. 22, Sept. 26, Oct. 3, Nov. 7, 14, Dec. 5, 12, 1771; Jan. 2–16, Feb. 27, 1772; Jan. 21, July 29, 1773; Aug. 25, Oct. 13, Nov. 17, Dec. 16, 22, 1774; Feb. 23, Mar. 2, 23, Apr. 6, 1775.
Wis. Hist. Soc. has Sept. 15, 1770; June 25, Nov. 19, 1772; May 27, Sept. 2, 9, 23, 1773; Feb. 17, Mar. 17, Apr. 15, 1774; Mar. 2, 1775.
Harvard has Aug. 15, Nov. 14, 22, 1771; Mar. 12, May 28, 1772; May 12, June 23, July 28, 1774.
Duke Univ. has Dec. 16, 1773; Oct. 6, Dec. 8, 16, 1774; Jan. 26, Mar. 2, 30, 1775.
Western Reserve Hist. Soc. has Feb. 4, 1773; Jan. 5, Feb. 16, Mar. 9, 30, 1775.
N. Y. Hist. Soc. has Jan. 23, Feb. 6, 1772; Mar. 30, 1775.
Hist. Soc. Penn. has Sept. 15, Oct. 20, 1774.

[Boston] **Mercury**, see **Massachusetts Mercury**.

Boston Mirror, 1808–1810.

Weekly. Established Oct. 22, 1808, with the title of "Boston Mirror," vol. 1, no. 1, by Oliver and Munroe [Edward Oliver and Isaac Munroe], as a substitute for a newspaper "The Times" and a magazine "The Emerald." It also absorbed with the issue of Nov. 5, 1808, a magazine, "The Pastime," which had been published at Schenectady, N. Y., by John Howard Payne when a student at Union College. In the "Boston Mirror" of Nov. 5, 1808, the publishers stated that they had "formed a connection" with the Editor of "The Pastime," and Payne wrote a long address regarding his engagement as an editor of the Mirror and his plans for that newspaper. He could not have remained on the paper more than a few weeks, as even then he was preparing for the stage and made his debut in New York on February 24, 1809. With the issue of Apr. 22, 1809, the partnership of Oliver and Munroe was dissolved and the paper published by Edward Oliver. With the issue of Oct. 21, 1809, the size of the paper was reduced to quarto, each issue being paged and containing eight pages. Oliver discontinued the paper with the issue of July 21, 1810, vol. 2, no. 40.

>   Am. Antiq. Soc., Boston Athenæum, and Boston Pub. Lib. have Oct. 22, 1808–July 21, 1810.
>   N. Y. State Lib. has Oct. 22, 1808–July 14, 1810, fair.
>   Mass. Hist. Soc. has Oct. 22, 1808–Dec. 30, 1809.
>   Lib. Congress has Oct. 22, 1808–Oct. 14, 1809.
>   Portland Pub. Lib. has Oct. 22, 1808–Oct. 14, 1809.
>   Harvard has Oct. 22, 1808–Aug. 19, 1809.
>   Conn. Hist. Soc. has Oct. 21, 1809–July 7, 1810.
>   Ill. State Lib. has Oct. 28, 1809–July 7, 1810.
>   N. Y. Hist. Soc. has Oct. 22, 1808–Sept. 23, 1809, fair; Nov. 4, 11, Dec. 16, 23, 1809; Jan. 6–20, Feb. 3–Mar. 3, 10, 24–May 12, 1810.
>   Dartmouth has Nov. 12, 26, 1808; Jan. 21, June 24, 1809.
>   N. Y. Pub. Lib. has Apr. 14, 28, May 5, 1810.
>   Duke Univ. has June 9, 1810.

[Boston] **Morning Chronicle**, see **Evening Post**, 1778–1780.

[Boston] **Morning Gazette**, 1814, see **Evening Gazette**.

[Boston] **New-England Chronicle**, 1776.

Weekly. Removed from Cambridge, Mass., and printed at Boston with the issue of Apr. 25, 1776, no. 401, published by Samuel Hall, with the title of "The New-England Chronicle." For previous issues, see under Cambridge. With the issue of June 13, 1776, Hall sold the paper to Edward E. Powars and

Nathaniel Willis, who began publishing it under the firm name of Powars and Willis. The last issue with the title of "The New-England Chronicle" was that of Sept. 12, 1776, no. 411 (misprint for 421), and with the issue of Sept. 19, 1776, the title was changed to "The Independent Chronicle," which see.

Am. Antiq. Soc., Boston Athenæum and Boston Pub. Lib. have Apr. 25–Sept. 12, 1776.
Essex Inst. has Apr. 25–June 20, July 4–Sept. 12, 1776.
Univ. of Mich. (Clements) has Apr. 25–June 20, July 4–Aug. 22, Sept. 5, 12, 1776.
Mass. Hist. Soc. has Apr. 25–July 11, 25–Aug. 22, Sept. 12, 1776.
Lib. Congress has Apr. 25–July 4, 18, 25, Aug. 8, 15, 29–Sept. 12, 1776.
N. Y. Pub. Lib. has Apr. 25–May 9, 23–July 11, 25, Aug. 2, 15, Sept. 12, 1776.
N. Y. State Lib. has Apr. 25–May 9, 30, June 6, 20, 27, July 11, Aug. 1, 8, Sept. 5, 12, 1776.
Harvard has Apr. 25, May 23–June 6, 20, Aug. 1, 22, 1776.
Wis. Hist. Soc. has Apr. 25–May 16, 30, June 20–July 11, 1776.
Mass. State Lib. has May 2, June 13, 27–Sept. 12, 1776.
Hist. Soc. Penn. has June 6–Sept. 12, 1776.
N. Y. Hist. Soc. has Apr. 25–May 9, 30, Sept. 5, 1776.
Western Reserve Hist. Soc. has Apr. 25, Sept. 12, 1776.
Dartmouth has May 9, July 4, 1776.

[Boston] **New-England Courant**, 1721–1727.

Weekly. Established Aug. 7, 1721, published by J[ames] Franklin with the title of "The New-England Courant." Although the first issue located is that of Nov. 27, 1721, no. 17, the exact date of the establishment of the paper is given in the "Boston News-Letter" of Aug. 14, 1721, which states, "On Monday last the 7th Currant came forth a Third News-Paper in this Town, Entituled, the New-England Courant." James Franklin in his newspaper gave frequent offense to the General Court, which ordered both his imprisonment and the suppression of his paper. At length, with the issue of Feb. 11, 1723, the paper was published under the name of his brother Benjamin Franklin. In his "Autobiography," Benjamin Franklin records that the paper went on under his name for "several months" and it was in October, 1723, that he left Boston. What is supposed to be Benjamin Franklin's own file of the paper, that in the British Museum, ends with Sept. 16, 1723, and on Sept. 30, 1723, James Franklin advertises for a "likely lad for an apprentice." Benjamin Franklin's name was continued in the imprint until the last issue located, that of June 25, 1726, no. 255. Isaiah Thomas, in his "History of Printing," ed. 1874, vol. 2, p. 38, says that "publication ceased in the beginning of the year 1727," and the "Boston News-Letter" of Mar. 9, 1727, speaks of the "Late Courant." There is an account of the paper, with identification of the authors of articles in 1721–1722, in Mass. Hist. Soc. Proceedings, vol. 57, pp. 336–353.

This newspaper, 1721–1726, has been reproduced in photostat by the Mass. Historical Society, which set is to be found in the following libraries: Am. Antiq. Soc., Boston Athenæum, Boston Pub. Lib., British Museum, J. C. Brown Lib., Univ. of Calif., Conn. State Lib., Grosvenor Lib., Huntington Lib., Univ. of Ill., Lib. Congress, Mass. Hist. Soc., Univ. of Mich., Newberry Lib., N. Y. Hist. Soc., N. Y. Pub. Lib., N. Y. State Lib., Hist. Soc. Penn., Western Reserve Hist. Soc., Wis. Hist. Soc., and Yale Univ.

British Museum has Aug. 7–Sept. 11, 25–Dec. 25, 1721; Jan. 1–Oct. 1, 15, 1722–Sept. 16, 1723.

Mass. Hist. Soc. has Nov. 27–Dec. 25, 1721; Jan. 1–Apr. 2, 16–Oct. 15, 29–Dec. 31, 1722; Jan. 7–Oct. 28, Nov. 25, 1723–Dec. 28, 1724; Jan. 4–Mar. 22, Apr. 5, 19–Aug. 21, Sept. 4, 11, 25–Dec. 25, 1725; Jan. 1–Mar. 26, Apr. 9–June 4, 18, 25, 1726.

N. Y. State Lib. has Dec. 4, 1721; Jan. 15, Mar. 12, Apr. 23, May 21, 28, July 30, Sept. 3, 17–Oct. 15, Dec. 10, 1722; Feb. 18, 25, Mar. 18, Apr. 1, 15, May 6, June 17, July 8, Sept. 2–23, Oct. 21, Dec. 2–30, 1723; May 18, June 15, 29–July 27, 1724; May 24, 1725.

Am. Antiq. Soc. has Jan. 8, Feb. 5, July 9, 1722; Feb. 11, Mar. 4, Apr. 1, Aug. 5, Sept. 9, 23, Oct. 14, 21, 1723; June 1, 1724; Jan. 25, Mar. 8, 1725; May 7, 28, 1726.

Wis. Hist. Soc. has June 18–Nov. 5, 1722.

Lib. Congress has June 1, 1724; Dec. 25, 1725; Jan. 8, 29, Feb. 12, 19, Mar. 19, Apr. 30, 1726.

Yale has Mar. 23, Apr. 27, 1724; Apr. 9, 16, 1726.

N. Y. Pub. Lib. has Feb. 4, 1723; Mar. 5, 1726.

Boston Pub. Lib. has Feb. 26, 1722.

Univ. of Mich. (Clements) has Oct. 7, 1723.

Hist. Soc. Penn. has Feb. 4, 1723.

Rutgers Univ. has Feb. 11, 1723; Jan. 15, 1726.

Many libraries have the facsimile of Feb. 11, 1723.

[Boston] **New-England Galaxy**, 1817–1820+.

Weekly. Established Oct. 10, 1817, by Joseph T. Buckingham, under the title of "New-England Galaxy & Masonic Magazine." The masonic department was conducted by Samuel L. Knapp until the summer of 1818 (see J. T. Buckingham, "Personal Memoirs," vol. 1, p. 77). With the issue of June 16, 1820, the name of "Jefferson Clark, printer," was added to the imprint. With the issue of Oct. 13, 1820, the title was shortened to "New-England Galaxy." The paper was continued by Buckingham, with Clark as printer, until after 1820.

Am. Antiq. Soc., Boston Athenæum, Boston Pub. Lib., Mass. Hist. Soc., Essex Inst., N. Y. State Lib., Lib. Congress, York Inst. Saco, and Wis. Hist. Soc. have Oct. 10, 1817–Dec. 29, 1820.

Minn. Hist. Soc. has Oct. 10, 1817–Oct. 8, 1819.
Univ. of Texas has Nov. 14, 1817–Oct. 22, 1819; Aug. 18–Dec. 29, 1820.
Cornell Univ. has Jan. 23, 1818–Nov. 17, 1820, scattering file.
N. Y. Hist. Soc. has Oct. 22, 1819–Dec. 1, 1820.
Dartmouth has Oct. 10–Dec. 26, 1817; Jan. 2–Oct. 9, Nov. 13, 1818.

[Boston] **New-England Palladium,** 1803–1820+.

Semi-weekly. A continuation, without change of volume numbering, of "The Mercury and New-England Palladium," the first issue with the new title of "New-England Palladium" being that of Mar. 11, 1803, vol. 21, no. 20, published by Young and Minns [Alexander Young and Thomas Minns]. With the issue of Jan. 3, 1815, the title was enlarged to "New-England Palladium & Commercial Advertiser." The paper was continued by Young & Minns until after 1820.

Am. Antiq. Soc., Boston Athenæum, Boston Pub. Lib., Mass. Hist. Soc., Harvard, Essex Inst., and Lib. Congress have Mar. 11, 1803–Dec. 29, 1820.
Wis. Hist. Soc. has Mar. 11, 1803–Dec. 30, 1806; Jan. 2, 1807–Dec. 30, 1808, fair; Jan. 3, 1809–Dec. 30, 1817; Sept. 29, 1818–Dec. 31, 1819; Jan. 4–Dec. 29, 1820, fair.
Western Reserve Hist. Soc. has Jan. 3–Dec. 28, 1804, fair; Jan. 1, 1808–Dec. 31, 1816; Jan. 3, 1817–Dec. 29, 1818, fair; Jan. 1–Dec. 28, 1819; Apr. 4–June 16, 1820.
N. Y. State Lib. has Nov. 25, 1803–Dec. 30, 1814, fair; Nov. 14, 1815–Dec. 30, 1817; Feb. 27, Apr. 28, May 29, 1818–Dec. 26, 1820.
N. Y. Hist. Soc. has Mar. 11, 1803–Dec. 31, 1805; Jan. 1, 1808–Nov. 23, 1813; Jan. 27, Mar. 17, 1815; Jan. 2, 1816–Dec. 29, 1820.
Chicago Hist. Soc. has Mar. 11, 1803–Dec. 29, 1818, fair.
Univ. of Ill. has Jan. 3, 1804–Dec. 28, 1810; Jan. 3, 1815–Dec. 29, 1820.
Phil. Lib. Co. has Mar. 11, 1803–Nov. 15, 1811, fair; Jan. 3, 1815–Nov. 28, 1817, fair.
Yale has Mar. 11, 1803–Dec. 31, 1813; Mar. 19–Nov. 10, 1815; Jan. 9–Dec. 31, 1816; Jan. 2–Sept. 26, 1818.
Univ. of Mich. (Clements) has Mar. 11, 1803–Dec. 29, 1807, fair; Jan. 15, 1808–Dec. 21, 1810, scattering file; Jan. 1, 1811–Dec. 31, 1816, fair; Feb. 18, 1817–July 14, 1820, scattering issues.
Rutgers Univ. has Jan. 4, 1803–Dec. 31, 1813; Jan. 2–Dec. 31, 1816; Jan. 2–Dec. 29, 1818.
Washington Univ., St. Louis, has Feb. 17, 1801–Dec. 20, 1803, fair; Mar. 19–Dec. 31, 1805; Jan. 2, 1807–Dec. 29, 1809; Mar. 14, 1815–Dec. 31, 1816; Jan. 2, 1818–Dec. 29, 1820.
Detroit Pub. Lib. has Jan. 1, 1805–Dec. 30, 1806; Jan. 5, 1810–June 11, 1811; Jan. 3, 1812–July 15, 1814, fair; Mar. 11, 1817–Dec. 25, 1818.
Portland Pub. Lib. has Jan. 1, 1813–Dec. 29, 1820.

British Museum has Apr. 5, 1808–Dec. 31, 1811; Oct. 1, 1816–Dec. 30, 1817; Jan. 1–Dec. 31, 1819.
Dartmouth has Mar. 11, 1803–Dec. 18, 1804, fair; June 18, July 26, 1805; Jan. 24–Dec. 19, 1806, fair; Jan. 13–Dec. 22, 1807, scattering; Jan. 19–Dec. 30, 1808, fair; Jan. 6, 1809–Dec. 27, 1814, scattering; Jan. 3–Dec. 29, 1815, fair; Jan. 9, 1816–Sept. 5, 1820, scattering.
Brown Univ. has Jan. 4–Dec. 27, 1803; Jan. 1, 1805–Dec. 30, 1806.
Ct. Hist. Soc. has Mar. 11, 1803–Apr. 25, 1806; Jan. 2–Dec. 29, 1807.
Univ. of Chicago has Jan. 1–Dec. 31, 1805; Jan. 3, 1809–Dec. 29, 1811.
Mass. State Lib. has Jan. 3–Dec. 28, 1804; Jan. 3–Dec. 29, 1809; Jan. 3–Dec. 29, 1812.
Duke Univ. has Mar. 11, 1803–Dec. 28, 1804, fair; Apr. 2, 1805; Feb. 21, 1806; Jan. 23–Dec. 8, 1807, scattering; Mar. 24, Nov. 28, 1809; Mar. 2, July 6, 1810; Mar. 11, 1811; Jan. 1–Dec. 31, 1813; Jan. 3–Dec. 29, 1815, fair; Jan. 12, 1816–Apr. 18, 1817, scattering.
N. Y. Pub. Lib. has June 7, 1803–Nov. 20, 1804, fair; and a few later scattering issues.
Me. Hist. Soc. has Jan. 3, 1809–Dec. 31, 1811, fair.
Univ. of Texas has Jan. 3–Dec. 28, 1804.
Vassar Coll. has Mar. 11–Dec. 30, 1803, fair.

[Boston] New-England Repertory, see Repertory.

[Boston] New-England Weekly Journal, 1727–1741.

Weekly. Established Mar. 20, 1727, by S[amuel] Kneeland, with the title of "The New-England Weekly Journal." With the issue of July 3, 1727, the paper was published by S[amuel] Kneeland & T[imothy] Green. With the issue of Aug. 26, 1735, the hyphen in "New-England" in the title was omitted. The paper was discontinued with the issue of Oct. 13, 1741, no. 981, and incorporated with the "Boston Gazette," also published by S. Kneeland & T. Green.

Mass. Hist. Soc. has Mar. 20–Oct. 30, Nov. 13, Dec. 4–25, 1727; Jan. 1–Feb. 5, 19, Mar. 4–25, Apr. 8–Sept. 9, 23–Dec. 30, 1728; Jan. 6–Mar. 31, Apr. 14–Oct. 20, Nov. 3–17, Dec. 1–29, 1729; Jan. 5–July 27, Aug. 11–Dec. 28, 1730; Jan. 4, 1731–May 1, 15–Dec. 25, 1732; Jan. 1–Feb. 12, 26–Apr. 23, May 7–Nov. 26, Dec. 10–24, 1733; Jan. 14–Sept. 16, 30–Oct. 21, Nov. 4–Dec. 9, 23, 30, 1734; Jan. 6–Sept. 30, Oct. 14–Dec. 16, 30, 1735; Jan. 6–Mar. 2, 16–Dec. 28, 1736; Jan. 4–July 5, 26–Sept. 27, Oct. 11, Nov. 1, 8, 29–Dec. 13, 1737; Jan. 17, Feb. 14, Mar. 7, July 25, Dec. 19, 1738; Jan. 2–Feb. 6, 20–Dec. 25, 1739; Jan. 8–Feb. 12, Mar. 11, 25–June 24, Aug. 19, Sept. 2, 23, 30, Dec. 2, 1740; Jan. 6–Oct. 13, 1741.
Am. Antiq. Soc. has Mar. 20–Dec. 25, 1727; Jan. 1–Apr. 1, 15, 29–June 3, 17–Aug. 5, Nov. 18, 1728; Jan. 13, 20, Feb. 3, 10, Mar. 3, 24, Apr. 21, June 9, Sept. 8–29, 1729; Jan. 12, Apr. 6, May 18, Aug. 17, Dec. 14, 28, 1730; June 7,

July 5, 19, 26, Aug. 16, Sept. 13, 20, Oct. 4, 18–Nov. 1, 1731; Jan. 3, Mar. 13, Apr. 3, 24, July 17, Oct. 2–Dec. 25, 1732; Jan. 8, 22, 29, Feb. 26, Mar. 26–Apr. 9, 23, May 14–July 16, 30, Aug. 6, 27–Oct. 1, 29–Nov. 12, 26–Dec. 24, 1733; Jan. 14–28, Feb. 11, 18, Mar. 11, July 1, 29, Sept. 9, Oct. 28, 1734; July 7, Nov. 4, 25, 1735; Jan. 27, May 18–June 1, 15, 22, July 13–Sept. 28, Oct. 19, Nov. 2–30, Dec. 14–28, 1736; Jan. 4–Dec. 27, 1737; Jan. 3, 31–Feb. 14, Apr. 11, June 6–20, July 11, Aug. 8, Dec. 19, 1738; Feb. 13, Mar. 20, May 15, June 19, July 3–31, Aug. 14, 28, 1739–Dec. 30, 1740; Jan. 6–Mar. 31, Apr. 14–May 26, June 9–July 7, 28, Aug. 4, 18, 25, Sept. 8, 29–Oct. 13, 1741.
Boston Athenæum has Mar. 20, 1727–Dec. 28, 1730; Feb. 1, 15, 1731; Jan. 24, Mar. 6, June 19, July 3, Oct. 2–16, Nov. 13, 1732; Feb. 12, Dec. 3, 1733; Apr. 8, 1734; Jan. 6, 20, 1736.
Harvard has Mar. 20–Apr. 24, May 22, June 26–July 10, Aug. 7, 28–Sept. 11, Oct. 2, 16–Dec. 25, 1727; Jan. 1, 8, Feb. 5, Mar. 4, 18, 25, Apr. 8–22, July 29, Aug. 12–Dec. 30, 1728; Jan. 13, 20, Feb. 3–Apr. 21, May 5–July 14, 28–Sept. 15, 29, Oct. 13–Nov. 3, 24–Dec. 15, 1729; Jan. 12, Feb. 23–Apr. 20, May 4–July 6, Aug. 11, 24–Sept. 14, Oct. 5–26, Nov. 16, 23, 1730; Jan. 4, Mar. 1, Apr. 19, 1731.
Lib. Congress has Apr. 17, 24, May 8–June 26, July 10, 17, Aug. 7, 14, 28, Sept. 11–Dec. 25, 1727; Jan. 1–Dec. 30, 1728; Jan. 6–Apr. 7, 28–June 9, 23–Sept. 15, 1729; Apr. 5, 12, 26–May 31, 1731; Aug. 21, 1732; Nov. 4, 1734; Jan. 6–Dec. 30, 1735; Jan. 6, 13, Feb. 3, 10, 24, Mar. 2, 16–Apr. 13, 27–June 29, July 13, 20, Aug. 3–Dec. 28, 1736; June 14, Dec. 27, 1737; Jan. 8–Feb. 12, Mar. 11, 25–July 1, Aug. 19, Sept. 2, 23, Oct. 14, Nov. 11, Dec. 2, 1740; Oct. 6, 1741.
Boston Pub. Lib. has July 3, 1727; Feb. 12, 26, Apr. 8, 1728; Feb. 24, Mar. 17, Nov. 3, 1729; Oct. 18, 1731; Jan. 1, 1733–Dec. 30, 1734; Feb. 15–May 24, June 7, 14, July 5–Sept. 27, Oct. 11–Nov. 22, Dec. 6, 13, 1737; Feb. 7, 21–Mar. 14, Apr. 4, 18–June 6, 20, July 4–25, Aug. 8–Sept. 12, 26–Nov. 21, 1738; Apr. 24, 1739; Jan. 1–Feb. 26, Mar. 11–May 27, June 10–Sept. 2, 30–Nov. 25, Dec. 9–23, 1740.
N. Y. State Lib. has June 19, July 10, Aug. 14, Sept. 4, 1727; Mar. 3, Apr. 21, Sept. 8, 1729; Dec. 28, 1730; Mar. 8–June 7, 21, July 5–Aug. 9, 23–Sept. 27, 1731; Jan. 10, Feb. 7, Mar. 13, 20, Apr. 3, May 1, 15, 22, June 5–19, July 3, 10, 24–Aug. 14, 28–Sept. 11, Oct. 23, Nov. 13–Dec. 4, 1732; July 2–Aug. 20, Sept. 3–24, 1733; Jan. 14–28, Feb. 11–Mar. 4, 18, Apr. 15, 22, May 6, 28, 1734; Jan. 6, 13, 27, Feb. 10, Mar. 24, Apr. 28, May 5, July 28, Aug. 4, Dec. 16, 1735; Dec. 14, 1736; Mar. 1, Apr. 5, 12, 26–June 28, Sept. 13, 1737; Jan. 29, Apr. 15, 29, May 6, 1740; Mar. 3, Apr. 7, 1741.
N. Y. Hist. Soc. has Apr. 24, 1727, Jan. 4–Feb. 22, Mar. 8, 1731–Dec. 25, 1732; Jan. 17–31, Feb. 14–Mar. 14, Aug. 22–Oct. 24, Nov. 7–Dec. 26, 1738.
Wis. Hist. Soc. has Oct. 2–Dec. 18, 1727; Jan. 1–Mar. 25, Apr. 29, May 20, July 1–Sept. 30, Oct. 28, Dec. 9–23, 1728; Aug. 11, 1729; Jan. 26, Feb. 9–23, Mar. 9–23, Apr. 14, 20, May 11–June 1, 15, July 20, Aug. 3, 24, 31, Sept. 14,

28–Oct. 19, Nov. 2, 16–Dec. 21, 1730; Jan. 10, Mar. 14–May 23, June 6, 13, July 4–18, Aug. 1, 8, 29–Sept. 12, Oct. 3–Dec. 12, 1738; Nov. 6, 1739; Jan. 20, 27, Mar. 3, June 30, July 14, 1741.

Mass. State Lib. has Mar. 26, May 14, 28, June 18–July 9, Aug. 27, Sept. 3, 1733; Jan. 28, 1734; June 22, Aug. 3, Sept. 28, 1736; Jan. 11, Feb. 1, 8, 22, Mar. 29, May 3, 24–June 7, July 26, Aug. 9, 23–Sept. 6, 20, 1737; Oct. 16, 23, Nov. 13, Dec. 4, 18, 1739; Jan. 29, Apr. 29, May 27, 1740; Apr. 14, 1741.

N. J. Hist. Soc. has Apr. 10, July 17, Sept. 4, Oct. 16, 30, Nov. 6, 20, 27, Dec. 18, 1727; Jan. 15, Feb. 5, 26, Mar. 4, Apr. 1, Dec. 30, 1728; Feb. 24, Mar. 3, 31, Apr. 21, 1729; Aug. 11, Oct. 26, 1730.

N. Y. Pub. Lib. has Apr. 21, 1729; Sept. 21, 1730; Apr. 23, June 11, July 9, Oct. 1, 1733; Apr. 29, 1734; Oct. 10, 1738; Mar. 4, 1740.

Univ. of Mich. (Clements) has Mar. 11, Apr. 8, 1728; Mar. 3, 1729; May 31, 1731; May 25, 1736.

British Museum (Burney) has Nov. 30–Dec. 21, 1730.

Western Reserve Hist. Soc. has Dec. 14, 1730.

Many libraries have the facsimile of Apr. 8, 1728.

Boston News-Letter, 1704–1776.

Weekly. Established Apr. 24, 1704, under the title of "The Boston News-Letter," published by John Campbell and printed by B[artholomew] Green. The initial issue has been reproduced in facsimile several times, the best being the photographic reproduction in S. A. Green's "Ten Fac-simile Reproductions relating to Various Subjects," p. 15, where photographs are given of two copies slightly varying in set-up. With the issue of Nov. 10, 1707, the paper was printed by John Allen, with Campbell continuing as publisher. Apparently it was suspended during the last eight months of 1709. In the issue of June 26, 1710, the proprietor states: "This is the last day of the second quarter since the Revival of the News-Letter the first of January last, which had been dropt for eight months after five years experience, for want of any Tollerable encouragement to support it." Yet the volume numbering from Mar. 28, 1709 (no. 258) to Mar. 13, 1710 (no. 308) does not indicate any suspension.

On Oct. 2, 1711, Allen's printing-office was destroyed by fire, and with the issue of Oct. 8, 1711, the paper was again printed by Bartholomew Green, or, as the imprint read "Printed in Newbury Street, for John Campbell Post-Master." The name of B. Green appeared in the imprint as printer with the issue of Oct. 3, 1715. Campbell finally transferred the paper to B. Green who became both publisher and printer with the issue of Jan. 7, 1723. With the issue of Jan. 5, 1727, the title was changed to "The Weekly News-Letter," and a new volume numbering was adopted; but with the issue of Nov. 5, 1730, the title was again changed to "The Boston Weekly News-Letter," and the earlier volume numbering was resumed. Bartholomew Green died Dec. 28, 1732, and beginning with the issue of Jan. 4, 1733, the paper was published by J[ohn] Draper, his son-in-law. With the issue of Sept. 1, 1757, the title was changed to "The Boston News-Letter," and with that of Mar. 25, 1762, to "The Boston News-Letter and New-England Chronicle." John Draper died Nov. 29, 1762, and with the issue of Dec. 2, 1762, the paper was published by his son Richard Draper, although his name did not appear in the imprint. With the issue of Jan. 13, 1763 (dated Jan. 11, by mistake), the paper was printed by Richard and Samuel Draper. With the issue of Jan. 6, 1763, the title was slightly altered to "The Boston News-Letter, and the New-England Chronicle."

With the issue of Apr. 7, 1763, the title was changed to "The Massachusetts Gazette. And Boston News-Letter," which latter change was the result of a vote of the Governor and Council authorizing the publication of all official notices in this paper. With the issue of Apr. 19, 1765, the paper was published and printed by Richard Draper and Samuel Draper. The Stamp Act took effect in November, 1765, and with the issue of Nov. 7, 1765, the Drapers changed the title to "The Massachusetts Gazette"; abandoned the volume numbering, assigning to each issue a zero in place of the usual number; and in defiance of the provisions of the Stamp Act omitted the names of the publishers in the imprint. With the issue of May 22, 1766, upon the receipt of the news of the repeal of the Act, the Drapers reverted to the title "The Massachusetts Gazette. And Boston News-Letter" and resumed the former numbering with no. 3268. Samuel Draper died Mar. 21, 1767, and with the issue of Mar. 26, 1767, the paper was published by Richard Draper.

With the issue of May 26, 1768, the title was changed to "The Boston Weekly News-Letter," and an arrangement was entered into between Draper and Green & Russell, publishers of the "Boston Post-Boy," by which a paper with the title of "The Massachusetts Gazette" was published by the two firms as part of, or accompanying, their respective papers (see under "Massachusetts Gazette," 1768–1769). This arrangement lasted until the issue of Sept. 28, 1769, when the New-Letter changed its title to "The Massachusetts Gazette; and the Boston Weekly News-Letter." With the issue of May 19, 1774, Draper entered into partnership with John Boyle and the paper was published under the firm name of Richard Draper and John Boyle. Draper died June 5, 1774, and with the issue of June 9, 1774, the paper was published by Margaret Draper and John Boyle, changed with the issue of June 30, 1774, to Draper and Boyle. With the issue of Aug. 11, 1774, the firm was dissolved and the paper published by Margaret Draper, although the word "Draper's" was the only form of imprint. The last issue with this imprint which has been located is that of Sept. 7, 1775, and the next issue located, that of Oct. 13, 1775, was printed by J[ohn] Howe. This issue, moreover, was headed "The Massachusetts Gazette: Published Occasionally," although the succeeding issues examined have the regular title. The last issue located is that of Feb. 22, 1776, undoubtedly no. 3769, although the volume numbering is torn from the only located copy. There is a quotation from the issue of Feb. 29, 1776, in the "Boston Gazette" of Mar. 4, 1776.

In a work entitled "An Historical Digest of the Provincial Press," by L. H.

Weeks and E. M. Bacon, all the items relating to American affairs in the News-Letter from Apr. 24, 1704, to June 30, 1707, were reprinted and provided with a good index. Because of the great expense of this work, Volume I only was issued.

This newspaper, 1704-1776, has been reproduced in photostat by the Mass. Historical Society, which set is to be found in the following libraries: — Am. Antiq. Soc., Boston Pub. Lib., J. C. Brown Lib., Univ. of Calif., Univ. of Chicago, Columbia Univ., Essex Inst., Grosvenor Lib., Huntington Lib., Univ. of Ill., Lib. Congress, Mass. Hist. Soc., Univ. of Mich., Newberry Lib., N. Y. Hist. Soc., N. Y. Pub. Lib., N. Y. State Lib., Western Reserve Hist. Soc., Wis. Hist. Soc., and Yale Univ.

The excellence of the Ayer Check-List of Boston Newspapers, 1704-1780, published by the Colonial Society of Massachusetts in 1907 in vol. 9 of its Publications would make it seem unnecessary to repeat much of this information. But during the last thirty years there have been many additions to the holdings of the dozen libraries there listed, and also the holdings of a dozen other libraries could be listed. Therefore the following lists, for those libraries which are included in Ayer, will note only additions and changes, but will give in full the holdings of libraries not included in Ayer.

Mass. Hist. Soc. has Apr. 24, 1704-Feb. 22, 1776, as listed in Ayer, with the following additions: — Feb. 21, 1709; July 24, Nov. 6, 1710; Jan. 22, 1711; May 14, June 4, 1724; Mar. 4-18, Dec. 9, 1725; Apr. 7, 14, June 2-30, 1726; Feb. 16-Dec. 7, 1727; Apr. 24, Mar. 6, June 5, 1729; Apr. 22, June 3, 10. 24, July 1, 1731; Aug. 22, 29, Sept. 12, 1734; Jan. 1-15, Feb. 5-Dec. 30, 1736; Jan. 4-Dec. 27, 1739, complete; Jan. 6-Dec. 29, 1743, complete; Apr. 23, May 7, 1747; Apr. 6, 1749; Aug. 1, 1751; Jan. 23, Sept. 25, 1755; Feb. 14, 1760; Apr. 21, 1763; Jan. 10, 1765-Dec. 28, 1769, complete; July 28, 1774; Jan. 18, 1776.

Am. Antiq. Soc. has Apr. 24, 1704-Jan. 11, 1776, as listed in Ayer, with the following additions: — Aug. 28, 1710; Feb. 27, June 4, 1716; Apr. 21, 1720; Oct. 10, 24, 1723; Mar. 2, 23, 31, Apr. 13-May 25, June 29, July 6, 20-Aug. 10, Sept. 28, 1727; June 21, 1733; Jan. 12-July 5, 19-Nov. 15, 29-Dec. 27, 1744; June 6, 1745; Feb. 12-Mar. 12, 26-Sept. 10, 1747; Mar. 2, 1749; Oct. 31, 1751; July 4, 1755; Mar. 4, Apr. 1, May 27, 1756; Mar. 23, Nov. 9, 1758; Aug. 9, Sept. 20, 27, 1759; Jan. 1-29, Feb. 12-Mar. 19, Apr. 9-May 21, June 4, 11, 25-Dec. 17, 31, 1761; Jan. 7-28, 1762; Jan. 6-Mar. 31, May 26-June 30, July 21-Aug. 12, 25, Sept. 1, 15-29, Dec. 29, 1763; Jan. 26-Feb. 16, Mar. 8, May 10, 24, Oct. 25, 1764; Jan. 3-Oct. 10, 24-Nov. 21, Dec. 6-26, 1765; Jan. 2, 1766-Dec. 31, 1767; Jan. 7, Feb. 4-Mar. 3, 17-Apr. 7, 21-May 12, 1768; May 17, June 28, Aug. 16, 1770; Feb. 14, July 18, Aug. 22, Oct. 10, 1771; July 30, Aug. 6, Dec. 31, 1772; Jan. 7-Nov. 11, 26-Dec. 30, 1773; Feb. 17, 1774; Mar. 17, Dec. 28, 1775.

Boston Pub. Lib. has Nov. 24, 1712-Feb. 1, 1776, as listed in Ayer, with the following additions: — Nov. 24, 1712; Feb. 19, Nov. 13, 1741; Dec. 16, 1742; May 26, 1743; May 30, Oct. 3, 17, 1745; Jan. 16, Feb. 6, 20, Apr. 17, May 29, June 12, July 11, Oct. 30, Dec. 18, 1746; May 7, Aug. 13, Oct. 22, Nov. 12, Dec. 31, 1747; Mar. 30, 1749; Aug. 8, 1751; Jan. 30, Oct. 30, Dec. 25, 1755; May 27, June 10, 17, July 29, Aug. 5, 19–Oct. 7, 21, 28, 1756; Jan. 19, 1758; Feb. 8–June 21, 1759, fair; Oct. 10, 1760; Jan. 22–Oct. 15, 1761, fair; July 1, 1762; Feb. 17, Aug. 18, Sept. 8, 1763; Apr. 19, Sept. 6, Oct. 11, 18, Nov. 8, 30, 1764; Oct. 10, Dec. 19, 1765; Feb. 13, 27, Aug. 28, 1766; Sept. 3, 10, 1767; Jan. 7–28, Feb. 18–Apr. 7, May 12, 19, June 30, Aug. 25, 1768; Jan. 12–Dec. 28, 1769, fair; July 4, Sept. 12, 1771; Jan. 2, 1772–Dec. 30, 1773, fair.

Lib. Congress has June 12, 1710–Jan. 12, 1775, as listed in Ayer, with the following additions: — Sept. 3, 1711; Mar. 21, 1715; Mar. 26, Dec. 10, 1716; June 17, 1717; June 1, 1719–Dec. 24, 1722, almost complete; Jan. 21, 1723–Dec. 22, 1726, fair; May 29, 1729; June 4, 1730; Feb. 27, Mar. 6, July 17, Oct. 2–Dec. 25, 1735; Apr. 2, 8, 22–June 17, Dec. 30, 1736; Jan. 4–Dec. 27, 1739, fair; Jan. 3–Dec. 18, 1740, fair; Sept. 15, 1743; Nov. 28, 1745; Feb. 27, Aug. 7, 1746; Nov. 14, 1751; Jan. 9, 1755; Feb. 26, May 20, June 3, 1756; Oct. 5, 12, 1758; Nov. 6, Dec. 11, 1760; Jan. 1, July 30, Sept. 10, Oct. 1, 15, 1761; Oct. 20, Nov. 3, Dec. 9, 1763; Jan. 7, 1768–Dec. 28, 1769, fair; Jan. 24, Dec. 26, 1771; Jan. 9, Aug. 20, Dec. 10, 17, 1772; Sept. 30, 1773; Jan. 27, Feb. 3, Apr. 7, 1774; Jan. 12, 26–Mar. 2, 23, Apr. 13, 1775.

Harvard has Apr. 24, 1704–Dec. 19, 1771, as listed in Ayer, with the following additions: — Nov. 14, 1740; July 12, 1744; Jan. 3–Dec. 26, 1745; Feb. 6, 27, Mar. 20, 27, Apr. 25, June 26, July 10, 25, 31, 1766; Mar. 5, 12, Apr. 2, 16, 23, 1767; May 13, 1773.

Boston Athenæum has Feb. 19, 1711–June 1, 1775, as listed in Ayer, with the following additions: — Jan. 6, Feb. 10, Mar. 3, 10, July 7, Oct. 14, 20, 1743; Apr. 6, 1749; Oct. 9, 1755; May 27, 1756; June 30, 1774.

N. Y. Hist. Soc. has Apr. 24, 1704–Mar. 30, 1775, as listed in Ayer, with the following additions: — Apr. 1, 1717; Nov. 12, 1724; Oct. 20, Nov. 24, 1726; Nov. 13, 1741; June 2, 1743; May 12, 1757; June 19, 26, 1760; May 31, 1764; May 9, June 27, 1765; Mar. 27, May 22, June 5, July 10, 1766; Feb. 12, 26, Mar. 5, 19, 26, Apr. 23, June 11, July 2, 30, Sept. 24, 1767; Apr. 28, June 9, Aug. 4, 1768; Jan. 26, July 6, 13, Aug. 24, 1769; Jan. 11, 1770–Apr. 13, 1775, fair.

N. Y. Pub. Lib. has Mar. 13, 1710–Apr. 20, 1775, as listed in Ayer, with the following additions: — May 26, 1718; Aug. 21, Nov. 6, 1721; Oct. 15, 1722; July 24, 31, 1760; Feb. 12, Apr. 9, 1761; Feb. 4, 11, Apr. 8, 23, July 29–Oct. 14, 28, 1762; Oct. 3, 1765; June 5–19, July 3, 17–Aug. 14, 28–Sept. 18, Oct. 2, 16–Nov. 6, Dec. 18, 1766; May 28, July 2, 9, Dec. 24, 1767; Jan. 14, 21, Feb. 11–25, July 14, 1768; Mar. 2, 9, Apr. 20–Oct. 5, 19–Dec. 28, 1769; Jan. 18, 1770–Dec. 31, 1772, fair; Jan. 6, 13, Mar. 24, 31, Apr. 28, May 19, 26, Oct. 27, 1774.

N. Y. State Lib. has Aug. 28, 1710; June 27, 1723; May 14, 1741; Jan. 9, Feb.

27, 1746; Feb. 26, May 21, June 4, 11, 25, July 9-23, Aug. 6, 13, 1747; Jan. 7, 14, Mar. 10, 17, June 2, 16, Aug. 25, Oct. 13, Dec. 15, 1748; Mar. 29, July 19, 1750; July 4, 1751; Apr. 25, 1754; Jan. 1, June 25, 1761; Mar. 3, Aug. 4, Sept. 22, 1763; Aug. 2, Sept. 13, Nov. 15, 22, Dec. 27, 1764; Aug. 8, 1765; Mar. 13, Sept. 25, Nov. 28, 1766; Apr. 30, Aug. 6, Oct. 1, Dec. 17-31, 1767; Jan. 14, 1768-Dec. 30, 1773, fair; Jan. 13, Feb. 10, Apr. 15, 28, May 5, 26-June 23, July 7, Sept. 22, Oct. 20, Dec. 1, 22, 1774.

Wis. Hist. Soc. has May 14, 1741-Dec. 26, 1771, as listed in Ayer, with the following additions: — Jan. 18, 1770; Apr. 21, 1774.

Hist. Soc. Penn. has Oct. 11, 1764-Nov. 12, 1767, as listed in Ayer.

Yale has Mar. 24, 1718; Apr. 10, 1760; Jan. 5, 1764; Aug. 8, 15, 29, Sept. 5, Oct. 10-Nov. 14, Dec. 6, 19, 1765; Jan. 2-16, 30-Feb. 27, Mar. 13-Apr. 3, May 1, 15, 22, July 10, Sept. 4, 1766.

Conn. Hist. Soc. has Dec. 5, 19, 1715; Apr. 30, May 7, 21-Aug. 27, Sept. 10-24, Oct. 8-29, Nov. 12-Dec. 31, 1716; Jan. 7-Dec. 30, 1717; Jan. 6-20, Feb. 3-Mar. 10, 24-May 5, 19-Dec. 29, 1718; Jan. 5-May 25, 1719.

Univ. of Mich. (Clements) has Feb. 25, 1725; Oct. 5, 1758; Sept. 20, 1759; Jan. 17, 1760; May 5, Aug. 5, 1762; Feb. 10, 1763; July 12, Oct. 18, 1764; Feb. 7, Apr. 4, May 9, Aug. 15, 22, Sept. 19, Oct. 3, Dec. 19, 1765; Sept. 11, Oct. 2, 23, 1766; Jan. 22, Feb. 26, Mar. 26, May 28, Oct. 15, Nov. 26, 1767; Jan. 7-June 30, fair, July 21, Sept. 1, 1768; Feb. 2-Dec. 21, 1769, fair; Feb. 1, 1770-Dec. 29, 1774, scattering file.

Duke Univ. has Feb. 21, 1765; Mar. 10, 1768-Dec. 21, 1769, fair; Feb. 1, Mar. 1, May 17, June 7, Aug. 16, Sept. 20, Oct. 18, Nov. 1, 1770; Jan. 17, Feb. 21, Mar. 21, Apr. 25, May 9, Oct. 10, 1771; Feb. 20, 1772-Dec. 30, 1773, fair; Feb. 10, 24, Mar. 10, 17, Apr. 15, May 5-19, June 2-16, July 14, 28, Aug. 4, 25, Sept. 15, Dec. 1, 1774.

British Museum has Aug. 29, 1765-Nov. 9, 1775, scattering file.

Mass. State Lib. has Feb. 4, 1717; June 12, 1746; Dec. 4, 11, 1760; Aug. 6, 1761; Sept. 29, 1763; Jan. 17, 1765-Nov. 5, 1767, fair; Nov. 11, 1773.

Newport, R. I., Hist. Soc. has June 6, Sept. 12, Oct. 10-24, Nov. 14, 1751.

Univ. of Minn. has Jan. 7-Dec. 30, 1762.

Essex Inst. has a few scattering issues as recorded in Ayer, but with the following additions: — May 17, June 7, 14, 1770; Feb. 16, June 1, 1775.

Univ. of Va. has Nov. 20, 1721; Jan. 29, 1722.

Dartmouth Coll. has Jan. 11, 1728; May 21, Oct. 8, 1730.

Phil. Lib. Co. has May 16, Aug. 15-29, 1765.

British Pub. Record Office has Oct. 7, 1706; June 29, 1732; May 9, 1734; June 19, 1755.

Williams Coll. has June 11, 1730.

[Boston] **P. P. F. Degrand's Boston Weekly Report**, see **Boston Weekly Report**.

Boston Patriot, 1809–1820+.

Semi-weekly and daily. Established Mar. 3, 1809, by Everett & Munroe [David Everett and Isaac Munroe], as a semi-weekly, with the title of "Boston Patriot." With the issue of Mar. 7, 1810, the partnership was dissolved and Everett transferred his interests to Munroe, serving under him as editor; but it was not until the issue of Mar. 10, 1810, that the imprint read, "Published by Isaac Munroe and edited by David Everett." Munroe formed a partnership with Ebenezer French and with the issue of May 4, 1811, the paper was published by Munroe & French, and edited by David Everett. With the issue of Nov. 9, 1811, Everett's name was omitted from the imprint. With the issue of Jan. 1, 1814, Davis C. Ballard purchased the paper and became the publisher. With the issue of Mar. 9, 1816, the title of the paper was changed to "Boston Patriot and Morning Advertiser." The issue of May 31, 1817, vol. 17, no. 25, was the last semi-weekly issue. Ballard formed a partnership with Edmund Wright, Jr., under the firm name of Ballard & Wright, purchased the "Independent Chronicle," and consolidated it with the "Boston Patriot." They published two papers, one the "Independent Chronicle & Boston Patriot," which was published daily, was assigned a new volume numbering beginning with the issue of June 2, 1817, and was a continuation of the "Boston Patriot"; and the other the "Independent Chronicle & Boston Patriot (for the country)," which was published semi-weekly and was a continuation, in volume numbering and otherwise, of the "Independent Chronicle." With the issue of Oct. 1, 1817, the semi-weekly dropped the words "for the country" from the title, and thenceforth for two months, the titles of the semi-weekly and the daily papers were the same. With the issue of Dec. 2, 1817, vol. 2, no. 157, the daily edition changed its name to the "Boston Patriot & Daily Chronicle." The file of the Patriot, therefore, to be complete should include the daily edition of "Independent Chronicle & Boston Patriot" from June 2 to Dec. 1, 1817. With the issue of Dec. 3, 1817, the "&" in the title was changed to "and." With the issue of July 1, 1819, the title was changed to "Boston Patriot & Daily Mercantile Advertiser." Ballard died Nov. 29, 1820, but the paper was continued under the firm name of Ballard & Wright after 1820.

Boston Pub. Lib. and Essex Inst. have practically complete files Mar. 3, 1809–Dec. 30, 1820.

Mass. Hist. Soc. has Mar. 3, 1809–Mar. 22, 1817; May 17, 1817; Jan. 8–Apr. 17, 1818, scattering; June 2, 1818–Dec. 30, 1820.

Am. Antiq. Soc. has Mar. 3, 1809–Dec. 31, 1817; Jan. 1–Dec. 30, 1818, fair; Jan. 1–July 3, Aug. 7, 1819; Feb. 5, Oct. 19, Nov. 16, 29, Dec. 2, 21, 1820.

Boston Athenæum has Mar. 3, 1809–Dec. 31, 1819.

Bath, Me., Patten Lib. has Mar. 17, 1809–May 31, 1817; Jan. 2, 1818–Feb. 27, 1819; Nov. 1, 1819–June 13, 1820.

Wis. Hist. Soc. has Mar. 3, 1809–May 31, 1817; Jan. 1–June 1, 1818; June 13, 1818–Dec. 31, 1819, scattering file; Jan. 1–Dec. 30, 1820.

MASSACHUSETTS

Mass. State Lib. has Mar. 3, 1809–Feb. 27, 1811; Apr. 15, 1812–July 20, 1814, fair; June 2, 1817–Dec. 30, 1820.
Harvard has Mar. 3, 1809–Dec. 30, 1812; Dec. 2, 1817–June 30, 1819; Jan. 1–Dec. 30, 1820.
Lib. Congress has Mar. 7, 1809–Dec. 30, 1815, fair; Jan. 3–Dec. 21, 1816, scattering file; Jan. 1–Dec. 31, 1817, fair; Jan. 1, 1818–Dec. 30, 1820.
Univ. of Mich. (Clements) has Mar. 3, 1809–Dec. 27, 1815, fair; Feb. 7–Dec. 21, 1816, scattering file; Jan. 8–May 31, 1817, scattering file; Jan. 1, June 17–24, 1818; Jan. 5, June 11, 1819.
N. Y. State Lib. has Mar. 3, 1809–Jan. 15, 1817, fair; Jan. 17–Dec. 31, 1818, fair; Jan. 12–Dec. 30, 1820, scattering.
Me. Hist. Soc. has Mar. 3, 1809–May 3, 1817.
N. Y. Hist. Soc. has Mar. 3, 1809–Dec. 30, 1815; Oct. 28, 1816; June 5, 13, 1818; Dec. 9, 11, 1819; Mar. 9, 1820.
Yale has Mar. 3, 1809–Feb. 1, 1817.
Western Reserve Hist. Soc. has Mar. 3, 1809–Mar. 10, 1813; Oct. 2, 1813–Mar. 11, 1820, scattering issues.
Dartmouth has Mar. 17, Sept. 2, 1809–Dec. 29, 1810; Dec. 12, 16, 1812; Mar. 23, June 8, 1814–Dec. 21, 1816, fair.
Conn. Hist. Soc. has Mar. 3, 1809–Feb. 28, 1810; Apr. 27, 1814–May 17, 1815.
Chicago Hist. Soc. has Mar. 3, 1809–Dec. 31, 1810, fair; Mar. 14–Dec. 30, 1812; Jan. 1–Dec. 31, 1814.
Duke Univ. has Mar. 3, 1810–Aug. 31, 1811; Mar. 14, 1812–Mar. 10, 1813; Jan. 1–Dec. 31, 1814; Jan. 4, 1815–May 28, 1817, fair.
Univ. of Mo. has Mar. 2, 1811–Sept. 4, 1816.
Portland Pub. Lib. has Mar. 3, 1809–Oct. 26, 1811, fair.
Bowdoin Coll. has Mar. 3, 1809–July 21, 1810, fair.
Md. Hist. Soc. has Mar. 3, 1809–Feb. 24, 1810.
La. State Univ. has Mar. 3, 1809–Feb. 28, 1810.
Univ. of Texas has Apr. 1, 1812–May 4, 1814.
Rutgers Univ. has May 20–Sept. 30, 1809, fair; Feb. 3–Dec. 29, 1810, fair; Feb. 13, 1811; Nov. 7, 1812; Jan. 13, 1813–Feb. 11, 1815, fair; Mar. 26–Apr. 30, 1817.
Peabody Lib., Baltimore, has May 20, 1812–Mar. 10, 1813.
Phil. Lib. Co. has Oct. 17, 1812–May 19, 1813, fair.
Hist. Soc. Penn. has Mar. 12, 1814–Dec. 30, 1815.
Ohio Arch. & Hist. Soc. has July 11, Nov. 17, 1810; Mar. 26–Nov. 30, 1814; Jan. 4–Mar. 8, 1815; Apr. 3–May 20, 1816.
N. Y. Pub. Lib. has Mar. 28–Apr. 4, Sept. 1, Oct. 27, 1810; June 8, 1811; Jan. 22, 29, Sept. 19, 1812; May 29, 1813; Mar. 16–Dec. 25, 1816, fair.
British Museum has Oct. 2–Dec. 30, 1820.

[Boston] **Pilot,** 1812–1813.

Semi-Weekly. Established Sept. 25, 1812, under the title of "The Pilot," published by David Everett, and printed by True & Rowe [Benjamin True and Thomas Rowe]. The publisher and printers were also concerned in the publication of the "Yankee," issued weekly, and the matter printed in the two papers was largely the same. The paper received little support, and was discontinued with the issue of Jan. 16, 1813, vol. 1, no. 33. An announcement regarding it was printed in the "Yankee" of Jan. 22, 1813.

Boston Athenæum has Sept. 25, 1812–Jan. 16, 1813.
Essex Inst. has Sept. 25–Dec. 18, 1812; Jan. 1–16, 1813.
Am. Antiq. Soc. has Sept. 25–Dec. 8, 1812; Jan. 1–16, 1813.
N. Y. State Lib. has Sept. 25–Oct. 27, Nov. 6, 10, 17–Dec. 4, 11, 22, 1812; Jan. 1, 1813.
Mass. Hist. Soc. has Sept. 25–Nov. 13, Dec. 4, 29, 1812; Jan. 1, 5, 8, 16, 1813.
N. Y. Hist. Soc. has Oct. 16, 23, 27, Nov. 3–10, 17, 20, Dec. 1, 4, 11–22, 1812.
Bath, Me., Patten Free Lib. has Sept. 25–Oct. 2, 1812.
Boston Pub. Lib. has Oct. 20–Dec. 8, 1812.
Lib. Congress has Oct. 6, 23–30, 1812.

[Boston] **Polar Star,** 1796–1797.

Daily. Established Oct. 6, 1796, printed by Alexander Martin for the Proprietors, with the title of "Polar-Star: Boston Daily Advertiser." Although his name was not mentioned in the imprint, the editor of the paper was John D. Burk (see Buckingham "Specimens of Newspaper Literature," vol. 2, p. 294). With the issue of Oct. 10, 1796, the title was changed in set-up, the words "Polar Star" being placed in the center, dividing the words "Boston Daily" from the word "Advertiser." With the issue of Nov. 14, 1796, the title was changed to "Polar Star and Boston Daily Advertiser." The last issue located is that of Feb. 2, 1797, no. 102, and this was probably the last published.

Boston Athenæum has Oct. 7, 1796–Feb. 2, 1797.
Am. Antiq. Soc. has Oct. 6–Dec. 31, 1796; Jan. 16, 26, 1797.
N. Y. Hist. Soc. has Oct. 7, 8, 12, 14, 16–Nov. 1, 3, 4, 6–11, 14, 16, 17, 19–26, 29–Dec. 9, 13, 14, 19–26, 28, 29, 1796; Jan. 9–11, 28, 1797.
Lib. Congress has Oct. 31–Dec. 9, 19, 22, 1796.
Harvard has Oct. 25, 26, Nov. 29, Dec. 8, 9, 23, 1796; Jan. 4, 30, 31, 1797.
Wis. Hist. Soc. has Nov. 10, 11, 17, 19, 23, 28–Dec. 2, 1796.
Essex Inst. has Dec. 7, 10, 14, 23, 27, 28, 1796; Jan. 13, 14, 18, 25, 26, 1797.
Mass. Hist. Soc. has Oct. 6, 1796.
N. Y. Pub. Lib. has Dec. 7, 1796.

[Boston] **Political Courier,** 1792, see **Courier Politique.**

MASSACHUSETTS 335

[Boston] Post, see Boston Evening Post.

Boston Post-Boy, 1734–1775.

Weekly. Established late in 1734, although the exact date is uncertain. The earliest issue located, that of Apr. 21, 1735, is numbered 23, and reckoning back from this number, the date of the first issue would have been Nov. 18, 1734. But Isaiah Thomas in his "History of Printing" (1874 edition, vol. 2, p. 46) says that the publication was begun in October, 1734. This earliest located issue of Apr. 21, 1735, was entitled "The Boston Weekly Post-Boy," and was "Printed for Ellis Huske." No printer's name is given in the imprint, but Thomas states (*Idem*, vol. 1, p. 127) that John Bushell, "as I have been informed, printed the Boston Weekly Post-Boy, during a short period, for Ellis Huske." With the issue of June 11, 1750, the title was changed to "The Boston Post-Boy." The Post-Boy was suspended for a period between 1754 and 1757. The last issue located of this first series is that of Dec. 23, 1754, no. 1030, and judging from an advertisement in the Boston Evening Post of Dec. 30, 1754, asking subscribers for the Post-Boy to settle their accounts, this may have been the last issue. Thomas, however, says "I believe it was continued until within a few weeks of the time when the provincial stamp act took place, in 1755 (April 30)." Ellis Huske died Apr. 24, 1755. (For a study of the facts regarding the establishment and discontinuation of the Post-Boy, see Mr. Albert Matthews' notes in Colonial Soc. Publications, vol. 9, pp. 465–470.)

The paper was revived on Aug. 22, 1757, by John Green and Joseph Russell, with the title of "The Boston Weekly Advertiser," printed by Green and Russell, and a new volume numbering was begun. With the issue of Jan. 1, 1759, the title was changed to "Green & Russell's Boston Post-Boy & Advertiser," and with the issue of May 30, 1763, changed again to "The Boston Post-Boy & Advertiser." With the issue of May 23, 1768, an arrangement was entered into between Green & Russell and Richard Draper, publisher of the "Boston News-Letter," by which a paper with the title of "The Massachusetts Gazette" was published by the two firms as part of, or accompanying, their respective papers (see also under "Massachusetts Gazette," 1768–1769). The title, however, of "The Boston Post-Boy & Advertiser" was not changed, the most noticeable difference in appearance being the new heading of "The Massachusetts Gazette" at the top of what generally was the third page of the paper. This arrangement lasted until the issue of Oct. 2, 1769, when the Post-Boy changed its title to "The Massachusetts Gazette, and the Boston Post-Boy and Advertiser." With the issue of Apr. 26, 1773, the paper was published by Mills and Hicks [Nathaniel Mills and John Hicks]. With this issue, too, the comma after the word "Gazette" in the title was changed to a semicolon. The last issue located is that of Apr. 17, 1775, no. 921.

The detailed list of holdings given in the Ayer Check-List of Boston Newspapers, 1704–1780, published by the Colonial Society of Massachusetts in 1907 in vol. 9 of its Publications makes it unnecessary to repeat this information. Therefore the following lists, for those libraries which are included in Ayer, will note only the additions of the last thirty-five years. Libraries not included in Ayer have their holdings listed in detail.

Mass. Hist. Soc. has Jan. 1, 1739–Apr. 17, 1775, as listed in Ayer, with the following additions: — Jan. 19, Apr. 5, 19, Aug. 23, 30, Sept. 13, Dec. 27, 1736; Jan. 8, July 23, Oct. 22, Nov. 12, 19, Dec. 3, 10, 1739; Feb. 25, 1740; June 22, 1741; Jan. 17, Feb. 21, Mar. 28, Apr. 18, June 27, 1743; Dec. 17, 1744; Sept. 26, 1748; May 7, 1759; May 5, 1766; May 4, July 6, Aug. 3, 1772; Aug. 8, Sept. 19, 1774.

Boston Pub. Lib. has Jan. 30, 1749–Apr. 10, 1775, as listed in Ayer, with the following additions: — Sept. 28, 1741; Apr. 19, 1742; Jan. 6, 27, Feb. 10, 17, Mar. 3, 10, 31, May 26, June 2, 23, 30, Aug. 4, Sept. 1, Oct. 13–27, Nov. 17, Dec. 29, 1746; Apr. 6, May 4, July 20, Aug. 3, Sept. 7, Nov. 2, 9, 23, 30, Dec. 14, 1747; Mar. 7, May 16, June 20, July 18, Aug. 1, Nov. 13, 1748; Feb. 20–Mar. 6, 27, Apr. 3, 24, May 29, June 19, July 3, 10, Oct. 2, 23, Nov. 20, 1749; June 4, July 23, 30, Sept. 17, Oct. 15, 1750; Jan. 21, May 13, Sept. 9, Oct. 28, Nov. 4, 18, Dec. 9, 1751; Jan. 6, 26–Feb. 10, Mar. 2, 23, 30, Apr. 20, Oct. 2, 1752; Jan. 1, 8, 22, 29, Feb. 12–26, Mar. 5, 19, 26, Aug. 6, Sept. 2, Nov. 26, Dec. 3, 1753; Sept. 2, 1754; Feb. 26, 1759; Oct. 13, 1760; Jan. 4–July 12, Aug. 16–Nov. 22, Dec. 13–27, 1762; Jan. 10, Feb. 7, 28, Mar. 6, 14, May 16, 23, June 6, 20, July 11, 25, Aug. 8, 1763; Sept. 9, 16, Oct. 7, Dec. 9, 16, 1765; Jan. 27, Apr. 28, May 26, June 2, Sept. 15, Nov. 3, 17, Dec. 1, 8, 1766; Jan. 5, 19, Feb. 16, 23, Mar. 2, 23, Apr. 6, May 11, June 8, 15, 29–July 13, Aug. 10, Sept. 14, Dec. 14, 1767; Jan. 11, Feb. 8–Apr. 18, May 2–June 13, July 25–Aug. 8, 22–Sept. 19, Oct. 3–Nov. 7, Dec. 12, 19, 1768; Jan. 9, Feb. 13, Mar. 27, Apr. 10, 24, June 26, July 17, 24, Aug. 28, Oct. 9–Nov. 27, Dec. 11, 25, 1769; Jan. 1, July 30, 1770; Nov. 4, 1771; June 8, 22, July 13, Aug. 10–24, Sept. 21, 28, Nov. 2, 30, Dec. 14, 28, 1772; Jan. 4–Feb. 22, Mar. 8, Apr. 12, 26, May 3, 17–June 21, July 5–19, Aug. 2, 23, Sept. 6–20, Oct. 18, Nov. 1, 22, 29, Dec. 13, 1773; Apr. 4, 11, May 23, Sept. 12, 19, Oct. 17, Nov. 7, 28, 1774; Mar. 13, 1775.

Am. Antiq. Soc. has Apr. 21, 1735–Apr. 17, 1775, as listed in Ayer, with the following additions: — Apr. 26, 1736; Sept. 24, 1739; May 24, 1742; July 29–Nov. 25, Dec. 9–23, 1745; Jan. 6, 13, Feb. 17–Apr. 21, May 5, 12, 26–June 9, 23–July 7, 21–Nov. 17, Dec. 8–29, 1746; Jan. 5–Mar. 2, Dec. 14, 1747; Mar. 6, 1749; Mar. 2, 1752; Sept. 26, 1757; Jan. 1, 1759–Dec. 22, 1760; Jan. 19, Nov. 16, 1761; Feb. 1, 15, May 24, June 14, 21, Aug. 9–Sept. 13, Oct. 18–Nov. 15, 29–Dec. 27, 1762; Jan. 3, 24–Apr. 11, 25–Aug. 8, Nov. 14, 1763; Apr. 16, Dec. 10, 1764; Feb. 4, 1765; Feb. 17, May 26, 1766; Jan. 5, 1767–Dec. 25, 1769; Apr. 15, June 10, Nov. 18, Dec. 16, 1771; Feb. 10, Dec. 7, 1772; Oct. 18, Nov. 8, 1773; June 27, Oct. 31, Dec. 12, 1774; Feb. 27, Mar. 13, 20, Apr. 10, 1775.

MASSACHUSETTS 337

Boston Athenæum has Apr. 12, 1742–Apr. 10, 1775, as listed in Ayer, with the following additions: — June 8, 1767; May 16, June 6–27, July 11–18, Aug. 1–22, Sept. 5, 26–Oct. 10, 24, 31, Nov. 21, Dec. 5, 19, 1774.
Lib. Congress has Jan. 18, 1742–Apr. 17, 1775, as listed in Ayer with the following additions: — Jan. 1, Feb. 5, July 9, Sept. 10, 24, 1739; Jan. 28, Mar. 24–Apr. 7, 21, June 9, 23, July 14, 1740; July 27, Aug. 10, Nov. 9, 1741; Jan. 5–26, Feb. 16, Apr. 13, 27, June 8, Aug. 10, 24, Oct. 12, 26, Dec. 28, 1747; Jan. 25, Feb. 22, May 9, 1748; July 10, Nov. 13, 20, 1749; Sept. 3, 1750; June 3, Sept. 23, Nov. 25, 1751; Mar. 16, 1752; Mar. 12, 1753; May 29, Aug. 7, 1758; Feb. 11, Mar. 17, 31, Apr. 21, Sept. 15, Nov. 24, 1760; Feb. 2, Apr. 27, May 4, Aug. 3, 1761; June 20, 1763; Mar. 5–19, Apr. 9, 16, June 11, July 2, 16, 30, Aug. 6, 20, 27, Sept. 10, 24–Oct. 22, Nov. 19, 26, Dec. 3, 17, 24, 1764; Mar. 25, May 6, 13, July 22, 1765; Jan. 13, Mar. 24, Apr. 7, 21, 28, May 19, June 2, 30, July 21, 28, Aug. 25, Sept. 29, 1766; Jan. 26–Feb. 9, 23–Mar. 16, Apr. 13, 20, May 4, 25, June 1, July 27–Aug. 10, Oct. 26, Nov. 2, 1767; Feb. 22, Mar. 21, Apr. 11, May 9, 23, June 6–July 4, 18, Aug. 1–Sept. 5, 19, 26, Oct. 10–Nov. 7, 21–Dec. 5, 1768; Feb. 6, 20, Mar. 13, May 22, June 5, July 5, 1769; Jan. 1, 1770–Dec. 20, 1773, fair; Feb. 28, Mar. 7, Apr. 11, 1774; Apr. 3, 1775.
N. Y. Pub. Lib. has Mar. 22, 1742–Dec. 5, 1774, as listed in Ayer, with the following additions: — Mar. 11, 1754; Jan. 9–30, Oct. 9, 1758; June 25, Aug. 20–Nov. 5, 19–Dec. 17, 31, 1759; Jan. 7–21, Feb. 11–Mar. 31, Apr. 14–May 5, 19–June 30, Sept. 15–Oct. 13, Nov. 3–Dec. 29, 1760; Jan. 5–19, Feb. 2, 9, 23–Mar. 30, Apr. 13, May 4–Aug. 10, Sept. 28, Nov. 22–Dec. 28, 1761; Feb. 22, Apr. 12, Sept. 27, Dec. 20, 1762; Mar. 7, Sept. 5, Nov. 7, Dec. 19, 1763; May 18, 25, July 20, Oct. 26, Nov. 30, 1767; Jan. 4–Aug. 1, Sept. 12, Oct. 3, 1768; Mar. 7, May 9, 30–June 20, Aug. 8–29, Oct. 17, Nov. 7, 21, Dec. 26, 1774; Jan. 9, 16, 30, Feb. 6, 27, Mar. 6, 20–Apr. 3, 1775.
Wis. Hist. Soc. has Feb. 24, 1766–Apr. 17, 1775, as listed in Ayer, with the following addition: — Nov. 5, 1771.
N. Y. State Lib. has Dec. 7, 1747; Mar. 7, 1748; May 8, June 5, 26, July 17, 31–Aug. 28, Sept. 18, 1749; Aug. 6, 13, Sept. 10, 17, Dec. 31, 1750; Feb. 4, Mar. 11–25, Sept. 9, 1751; Apr. 6, 13, May 4, 11, 1752; Jan. 8, 1753; Jan. 21, Mar. 18, 25, 1754; Sept. 26, Oct. 24, Dec. 5, 12, 1757; Feb. 6, 20, May 29, July 10, Aug. 7–21, Oct. 9, 30, Dec. 4, 1758; Jan. 8, 22, Apr. 2, June 25, July 2, 30, Aug. 27, Sept. 10, Dec. 3, 1759; Feb. 4, Mar. 24, 31, June 30, Nov. 10–Dec. 22, 1760; Jan. 19, 26, Mar. 16–30, Apr. 27, May 4, July 13, 27, Aug. 3, 1761; Feb. 15, Apr. 5, July 5, 12, Aug. 16, Sept. 6, 20, 1762; Mar. 25, Sept. 26, Oct. 24, 1763; Jan. 2–Dec. 31, 1764; Mar. 18, Apr. 1, 15, May 6, 13, June 10, July 22, 1765; Feb. 17, Apr. 7, 21, May 19, 26, Dec. 15, 1766; Jan. 26–Feb. 9, Apr. 27, May 4, June 1, 15, July 13, 20, Dec. 7, 21, 1767; Jan. 4, 18, Feb. 1, 15–Mar. 7, 21, May 2, 9, 23, June 6, 13, 27, July 18, Aug. 1, 15, 22, Oct. 10, Dec. 5, 19, 1768; Jan. 2–Oct. 23, Nov. 6–20, Dec. 4, 18, 25, 1769; July 2, 23, 30, Aug. 13, Oct. 1, 22, Nov. 12, Dec. 17, 24, 1770;

Jan. 7, Mar. 4, Sept. 9, 23, Nov. 11–25, Dec. 9, 30, 1771; Jan. 6–27, Feb. 10, 24, Mar. 23, June 8, Sept. 28, Oct. 5, Nov. 2, 9, 1772; Jan. 4–Feb. 1, 15, 22, Mar. 15–Apr. 19, May 10, June 28, July 5, 19, Aug. 2, Oct. 18–Nov. 8, 29, 1773; Feb. 28, Mar. 7, 28–Apr. 25, May 9, 23, June 20, Sept. 26, Nov. 28, 1774; Mar. 13, Apr. 3, 1775.

British Museum has Mar. 24, Apr. 28, Aug. 11, Oct. 13, Nov. 3, 17, Dec. 1, 1766; Feb. 16, May 4, July 13, Sept. 21, 28, Oct. 12, Nov. 16, Dec. 14, 28, 1767; Feb. 1, 22, 29, Apr. 11, June 20, Sept. 26, Nov. 28, 1768; Jan. 2, 30–Feb. 20, May 22, July 17, Sept. 11, Oct. 9–Dec. 25, 1769; Jan. 1–Feb. 12, May 21–June 18, Sept. 17, Oct. 1, 1770; Apr. 8, Dec. 2, 1771; Jan. 6, Feb. 3, 10, Apr. 20, 27, Aug. 3, Oct. 19, 26, 1772; June 14, Sept. 13, 1773; Jan. 3, 10, 24–Mar. 7, 21, Apr. 4–25, May 9, July 4–Aug. 1, 15–Dec. 26, 1774; Jan. 2–Feb. 13, 27–Mar. 13, 27–Apr. 10, 1775.

Harvard has Jan. 9, 1744–Aug. 23, 1773, as listed in Ayer, with the following additions: — Feb. 25, 1745; Jan. 30, Sept. 24, 1764; Jan. 28, 1765; Feb. 24, Mar. 3, 17–31, May 5, 12, June 16, 30, Aug. 4, 1766; Oct. 1, 1770; Jan. 16, 1775.

Univ. of Mich. (Clements) has June 15, 1747; Jan. 9, Mar. 13, 1758; July 21, 1760; June 8, 1761; Feb. 15, Sept. 20–Oct. 4, 18, Dec. 6, 1762; Feb. 14–Mar. 14, June 6–July 18, Aug. 1, Sept. 12, Oct. 24, Nov. 7, 14, 28, Dec. 5, 1763; July 2, Oct. 15, 1764; Sept. 16, 30, 1765; Nov. 3, 24, 1766; Feb. 2, 9, Mar. 9, 30, Dec. 21, 28, 1767; Feb. 22, June 6, July 11, 18, Aug. 15, Sept. 26, Oct. 10, Dec. 5, 1768; Jan. 29, Apr. 9, 23, May 14, July 30, Oct. 1, 1770; Mar. 11, June 17, Dec. 9, 1771; Feb. 24, Mar. 23, Aug. 17, Nov. 9, Dec. 7, 1772; Mar. 22, 29, Apr. 19, May 10, Aug. 2, Oct. 18, 25, Nov. 8, Dec. 6, 1773; Apr. 11, Sept. 19, 26, Oct. 10, 1774; Feb. 27, Mar. 13, 1775.

N. Y. Hist. Soc. has Sept. 14, 1741; Jan. 7, Feb. 25, Apr. 3–17, June 12–26, July 17–Oct. 16, 1749; Dec. 18, 1758; Dec. 27, 1762; Apr. 10, 1769; June 18, 1770; Jan. 4, 1773; Jan. 9–23, Feb. 6–Mar. 6, 20, 27, Apr. 10, 1775.

Essex Inst. has Mar. 28, 1743; Mar. 5, 1744; Jan. 13, Feb. 10, 1752; Mar. 10, Nov. 17, Dec. 29, 1760; Jan. 5, 1761; Apr. 19, July 19, 1762; Jan. 10, 17, Feb. 7, June 20, Sept. 5, Oct. 31, Dec. 26, 1763; Jan. 9, 1764; Aug. 29, Sept. 5, 1774; Jan. 30, Feb. 13, Apr. 10, 1775.

Yale has Jan. 4, 1762–Dec. 30, 1765, fair; Aug. 5–Sept. 9, Oct. 7–21, Nov. 4–Dec. 30, 1765; Jan. 6–Feb. 24, Mar. 17–Apr. 7, 21, May 5, 26, 1766; Mar. 23, 1767.

Duke Univ. has June 6, Oct. 10, Nov. 14, 1768; Mar. 22, June 7–Aug. 9, 23–Sept. 13, 27–Nov. 8, 29–Dec. 27, 1773; Feb. 7, Nov. 7, 1774; Jan. 9, 1775.

Dartmouth has Sept. 1, 1735; Dec. 19, 1748; Aug. 14, Sept. 11, Oct. 2, 1749; Feb. 19, 1750; Mar. 18, 1751; Dec. 10, 31, 1753; May 27, 1754.

Phil. Lib. Co. has Apr. 1, 22, Sept. 2, 1765; Mar. 10, 1766.

Hist. Soc. Penn. has June 11, 1744.

[Boston] Present State of the New-English Affairs, 1689.

"The Present State of the New-English Affairs" was a broadside issued in 1689 with the imprint at the bottom of the page "Boston, Printed and Sold by Samuel Green, 1689." It carried the heading, or title, at the top of the page, above rules, with a subheading "This is Published to prevent False Reports." Folio in size, it was printed on the recto of a single sheet, with the verso blank. The page is set in two columns, and contains extracts from two letters of Increase Mather, a public news-letter and an order from King William — all concerning New England's attempt to secure new charters from the King. It had no exact date of issue, no volume numbering, and no news other than extracts from the documents which were the cause of its publication. It probably was printed in November 1689 and the last dated document is September 3, 1689.

In the judgment of most bibliographers it has been considered a broadside and not a newspaper. But since some writers believe that it has some of the attributes of a newspaper, and also to complete the record, the title is here included.

The only known copies are in the American Antiquarian Society and in the Massachusetts Archives, vol. 35, p. 83. It has been reproduced in photographic facsimile by William G. Shillaber for the Club of Odd Volumes in 1902, by Samuel A. Green in 1903 in his "Ten Fac-simile Reproductions Relating to Various Subjects," and by T. J. Holmes in his "Increase Mather a Bibliography," 1931, vol. 2, p. 444, with an excellent historical note. Mr. Albert Matthews, who concludes that the publication is a broadside, and not a newspaper, treats of the subject in detail in the "Publications of the Colonial Society of Massachusetts," vol. 10, pp. 310–320.

Boston Price-Current, 1795–1798.

Weekly and semi-weekly. Established as a weekly Sept. 7, 1795, by J. and J. N. Russell [John and Joseph N. Russell], with the title of "The Boston Price-Current; and Marine-Intelligencer." It was at first of quarto size, but with the issue of Mar. 7, 1796, was increased to folio. With the issue of June 27, 1796, the Russell partnership was dissolved, and the paper published by John Russell. With the issue of Sept. 12, 1796, the publication became semi-weekly, and the punctuation of the title was changed so as to read "The Boston Price-Current and Marine Intelligencer." With the issue of Dec. 1, 1796, the heading "A Commercial Gazette" was placed above the title, changed to "Commercial Gazette" with the issue of Dec. 26, 1796, and again to "Russell's Commercial Gazette" with the issue of Sept. 7, 1797, but in neither case was this intended to be part of the title. The last issue with the title of "The Boston Price-Current and Marine Intelligencer" was that of June 4, 1798, vol. 4, no. 26, after which the title was changed to "Russell's Gazette," which see.

Boston Athenæum has Sept. 7, 1795–Sept. 4, 1797.

Mass. Hist. Soc. has Nov. 16, 1795–June 4, 1798, lacking 22 issues.
Am. Antiq. Soc. has Nov. 9, Dec. 14, 1795; Jan. 4–Dec. 26, 1796; Jan. 2–Feb. 27, Mar. 6, 23, Apr. 6, 20, 27, May 27, Aug. 31, Oct. 2–Dec. 28, 1797; Jan. 1–June 4, 1798.
Lib. Congress has Dec. 21, 28, 1795; Jan. 25–Dec. 12, 1796, fair; Jan. 2–Feb. 6, Mar. 6, Apr. 6, May 22, 1797; Jan. 1, 11, 15, Feb. 5, 12, 19–Mar. 5, Apr. 12, May 3–10, 17, 21, 31, June 4, 1798.
N. Y. Hist. Soc. has Oct. 26, 1795; Jan. 18, Feb. 1, Mar. 28, Apr. 18, May 23, June 6, Aug. 1, 29, Sept. 15, 22, Oct. 3, 10, Nov. 24, Dec. 22, 1796; Jan. 26, Apr. 10, June 26, 29, July 31, Aug. 24, 31–Dec. 28, 1797; Jan. 1–11, 18–Mar. 19, 26–Apr. 9, 16–June 4, 1798.
Harvard has Feb. 15, Mar. 21, Apr. 4, 18, May 9, 16, Aug. 8–22, Sept. 8–22, 29, Oct. 6–Nov. 21, Dec. 5–12, 19, 26, 29, 1796; Jan. 2–12, 19, 26–Feb. 16, 27–Mar. 9, 16–23, 30–Apr. 20, 27, May 1, June 26, July 6, 31, Nov. 20, 27, 1797; Jan. 8, 11, Apr. 23, June 4, 1798.
N. Y. State Lib. has Nov. 17, Dec. 16, 19, 26, 1796; Jan. 2–Feb. 27, 1797.
Ct. Hist. Soc. has Jan. 1–June 4, 1798.
Univ. of Mich. (Clements) has Feb. 29–Mar. 28, Apr. 11, 25, May 30, June 20, Sept. 29, Oct. 3, 13, 20, 27–Nov. 10, Dec. 1, 12, 1796; Feb. 26, May 31, June 4, 1798.
Phil. Lib. Co. has Nov. 2, 30, Dec. 7, 1795; Jan. 25, Apr. 11, 25, May 23, June 13, 27, July 11–Aug. 15, 1796.
Wis. Hist. Soc. has Sept. 7, Nov. 16, 1795; Sept. 25–Oct. 9, 1797.
N. Y. Pub. Lib. has Mar. 14, 21, Oct. 20–27, 1796; Feb. 6, 1797; Mar. 29–June 4, 1798.
Boston Pub. Lib. has June 20, Dec. 5, 22, 1796; June 19, July 24, 1797.
Essex Inst. has May 25, 1797; May 28, June 4, 1798.
Duke Univ. has May 17, June 4, 1798.

[Boston] **Publick Occurrences**, 1690.

The first and only issue was that of Sept. 25, 1690, with the title of "Publick Occurrences," and at the bottom of the third page the imprint "Boston, Printed by R[ichard] Pierce for Benjamin Harris, at the London-Coffee-House. 1690." It was headed "Numb. 1," and was announced to be published once a month, or oftener. Since it offended the authorities and was without license, an order was issued by the Governor and Council suppressing it and forbidding its further publication.

This has generally been considered the first genuine newspaper published in America, and is so considered in this work. It had most of the attributes of a newspaper of that day, including a title of the newspaper type, a system of enumeration, a general smattering of current news, and an announcement of continuous publication. None of these attributes are to be found in "The Present State of the New-English Affairs," published in 1689, which should be considered a broadside issued for a specific purpose, rather than a newspaper. (For a full discussion of the subject, see article by Albert Matthews in "Publications of Colonial Society of Mass.," vol. 10, pp. 310–320.)

The only known copy of "Publick Occurrences" is in the Public Record Office of London. It has been reproduced several times, notably in Dr. S. A. Green's "Ten Fac-simile Reproductions relating to Old Boston," 1901, and in Weeks and Bacon's "Historical Digest of the Provincial Press," vol. 1, 1911. The only known copies of the broadside Order of the Governor and Council suppressing the paper are in the American Antiquarian Society and the Massachusetts Historical Society.

Boston Recorder, 1816–1820+.

Weekly. Established Jan. 3, 1816, by Nathaniel Willis, with the title of "The Recorder." With the issue of Jan. 31, 1816, the paper was published by Ezra Lincoln, according to the imprint, although in the text it was stated that Lincoln printed the paper for the editor [Sidney E. Morse]. With the issue of Apr. 10, 1816, it was published by David J. Burr and printed by Ezra Lincoln. With the issue of May 1, 1816, it was published by David J. Burr and printed by Nathaniel Willis. With June 19, 1816, it was printed and published by Nathaniel Willis, who so continued until after 1820. With the issue of Jan. 1, 1817, the title was changed to "Boston Recorder." The editor of the paper from Jan. 3, 1816, to Apr. 1, 1817, was Sidney E. Morse, although his name did not appear at any time in the imprint. In the issue of Apr. 1, 1817, the "Editor" stated that he was giving up his position, and Nathaniel Willis announced himself as sole proprietor. For the controversy as to whether Willis or Morse was the actual founder of the paper, see F. Hudson, "Journalism in the U. S.," 1873, pp. 289–295.

Am. Antiq. Soc., Boston Athenæum, Boston Pub. Lib., Congregational Lib. of Boston, Mass. Hist. Soc., Harvard, Essex Inst., Amherst Coll., Williams Coll., Me. Hist. Soc., Bath Pub. Lib., Dartmouth, Conn. State Lib., Conn. Hist. Soc., Yale, N. Y. Hist. Soc., N. Y. Pub. Lib., N. Y. State Lib., Union Theol. Sem., Lib. Congress, Univ. of Mich. (Clements), Chicago Theol. Sem., Garrett Bibl. Inst., Detroit Pub. Lib., and Wis. Hist. Soc. have Jan. 3, 1816–Dec. 23, 1820.

Univ. of Minn. has Jan. 3, 1816–Dec. 23, 1817; Jan. 30, 1819–Dec. 23, 1820.

York Inst., Saco, has Jan. 3, 1816–Dec. 23, 1817.

Newberry Lib. has Jan. 3–Dec. 24, 1816; Jan. 2–Dec. 18, 1819.

Brown Univ. has Jan. 1–Dec. 16, 1817; Sept. 12–Dec. 26, 1818; Jan. 2–Dec. 18, 1819, fair.

Allegheny Coll. has Jan. 1, 1817–Dec. 26, 1818, fair.

Mass. State Lib. has Jan. 1, 1818–Dec. 23, 1820.

Rutgers Univ. has May 20, 1817–June 23, 1818.

Portland Pub. Lib. has Jan. 2, 1819–Dec. 23, 1820.

Univ. of Texas has July 3, 1819–Dec. 23, 1820.
Princeton Univ. has Feb. 6, 1819–Dec. 23, 1820, fair.
Duke Univ. has Jan. 3–Aug. 30, 1816; Jan. 13, 1818; Jan. 1–Dec. 23, 1820.
Many libraries have single or scattering issues.

[Boston] **Repertory**, 1804–1820+.

Semi-weekly and tri-weekly. Removed from Newburyport where it had been established July 6, 1803, with the name of "New-England Repertory." The last Newburyport issue was on Jan. 21, 1804, vol. 1, no. 57, and the first issue at Boston was on Feb. 3, 1804, vol. 1, no. 58. Upon its removal to Boston, the title was changed to "The Repertory." It was published semi-weekly for John Park. With the issue of Feb. 14, 1809, John Park admitted his brother Andrew W. Park to partnership under the firm name of J. & A. W. Park, but with the issue of July 3, 1810, the paper was again published by John Park. With the issue of July 2, 1811, William W. Clapp took charge of the paper and it was printed and published by William W. Clapp, and edited by John Park. With this issue, moreover, the title was changed to "The Repertory and General Advertiser." The "and" in the title was changed to "&" with the issue of July 23, 1811. With the issue of July 7, 1812, Park withdrew as editor, and the paper was published by William W. Clapp. With the issue of Jan. 1, 1813, a change was made in the set-up of the title, the word "Repertory," in larger type, being placed between the two words "General" and "Advertiser"; but with the issue of Jan. 8, 1813, the title reverted to "The Repertory & General Advertiser."

With the issue of Mar. 4, 1813, the paper was united with the "Boston Daily Advertiser," projected by Horatio Biglow. The "Boston Daily Advertiser" appeared as a daily on Mar. 3, 1813. The Repertory appeared as a tri-weekly issue of the daily on Mar. 4, 1813, published by Wm. W. Clapp and edited by Horatio Biglow, but carried no title except the column heading "Daily Advertiser, and Repertory," at the top of the first column of the second and fourth pages. With the issue of May 1, 1813, the imprint was changed to "Published by W. W. Clapp and H. Biglow." With the issue of June 1, 1813, the paper was issued in new form with a first page title "The Repertory," and resuming the volume numbering of vol. 10, no. 1. With the issue of Apr. 7, 1814, Clapp and Biglow transferred their interest to Nathan Hale, in which issue it was stated at the top of the first column of the second page that the paper was "Edited and Published by Nathan Hale. W. W. Clapp, Printer." During part of 1814, certainly between May 30 and Nov. 18, the tri-weekly issue appeared every week-day, subscribers apparently having their choice of papers issued on Monday, Wednesday and Friday, or Tuesday, Thursday and Saturday. With the issue of Mar. 6, 1815, Clapp's name as printer disappeared from the imprint, which was "Published by Nathan Hale." Although ostensibly published as a tri-weekly, the paper was frequently issued on successive days during 1815 and 1816, and there was much confusion in the volume numbering. Under the title

MASSACHUSETTS 343

of "The Repertory," the paper was continued by Nathan Hale until after 1820. See also under "Boston Daily Advertiser," 1813–1820.

Boston Pub. Lib. has Feb. 3, 1804–Dec. 29, 1812; July 1, 1813–Dec. 30, 1820.

N. Y. Hist. Soc. has Feb. 3, 1804–Feb. 26, 1813; June 1, 1813–Dec. 30, 1820.

Boston Athenæum has Feb. 3, 1804–Feb. 26, 1813; Jan. 3–Dec. 30, 1815; Jan. 2–June 7, 1817; July 2–Dec. 31, 1818; Mar. 7, 14, 23, July 1–Dec. 30, 1820.

Am. Antiq. Soc. has Feb. 3, 1804–Dec. 31, 1814; Jan. 1–Aug. 29, fair, Sept. 8, 12, 17, Oct. 19, 21, Dec. 5, 21, 1815; May 14, June 6, 25, July 4, 15, Sept. 10, 1816; May 20, Oct. 4, 11, Dec. 9, 1817; Jan. 15, Feb. 24, 28, Mar. 5, 7, 17, 21, 31, Apr. 4, 18, 25, 28, Sept. 1, 1818; May 20, 1819–Dec. 30, 1820, fair.

Mass. Hist. Soc. has Feb. 3, 1804–Dec. 29, 1812; Jan. 5, 1813–Dec. 12, 1820, scattering file.

Essex Inst. has Feb. 3, 1804–Feb. 26, 1813; June 1, 1813–Dec. 30, 1816, fair; Jan. 2–Dec. 30, 1817, scattering.

Lib. Congress has Feb. 3, 1804–Dec. 31, 1811, fair; Jan. 3–Dec. 29, 1812; Jan. 22, 1813–July 27, 1815, fair; Jan. 2–June 29, 1816; Apr. 15, 1817; Feb. 25, Mar. 4, Nov. 4, 1819; Jan. 7, 1820.

Dartmouth has Feb. 3, 1804–Dec. 30, 1816, fair; Feb. 1, 1817; Mar. 6, 1819.

N. Y. State Lib. has Feb. 3, 1804–Dec. 29, 1812; Jan. 4–Oct. 27, 1814, fair; May 6, 1816.

N. Y. Pub. Lib. has Nov. 6, 1804–Dec. 29, 1807; Jan. 1, 1808–Dec. 28, 1810; Jan. 1, 4, 1811; July 14, 1812; Nov. 30, 1813; Dec. 28, 1814; Jan. 25–July 14, 1815, fair.

British Museum has Feb. 3, 1804–Dec. 31, 1811.

Harvard has Feb. 3–Dec. 28, 1804, fair; Jan. 1, 1805–Dec. 31, 1811; Jan. 3–Dec. 29, 1812, fair; Feb. 1, 1814.

Chicago Hist. Soc. has Aug. 14, 1804–June 26, 1810.

Wis. Hist. Soc. has Feb. 3–Dec. 21, 1804, fair; Jan. 1–Dec. 31, 1805; Jan. 3, 1806–Dec. 31, 1811, fair; Apr. 17, 1812; Jan. 2–Sept. 28, 1816, fair; July 28, Nov. 5, 1818.

Yale has Jan. 1, 1805–Dec. 28, 1810; Jan. 1–28, July 2–Nov. 1, 1811.

Univ. of Mich. (Clements) has Feb. 17, 1804–Dec. 31, 1805, scattering issues; Jan. 3, 1806–Dec. 29, 1809; Jan. 2–Dec. 28, 1810, fair; Feb. 5, 1811–June 19, 1812, scattering issues; July 3, 1812–Feb. 26, 1813; June 12, 1813–June 15, 1815, scattering issues.

Duke Univ. has Feb. 3, 1804–Dec. 31, 1805; Jan. 14–Dec. 26, 1806, fair; Jan. 6–23, Nov. 6–Dec. 29, 1807; Jan. 6–Sept. 12, 1809; Jan. 24, Mar. 10, 1812; Jan. 1, 1815–June 1, 1816.

Portland Pub. Lib. has Jan. 1–Dec. 29, 1805; Feb. 28–Dec. 30, 1806; June 14, 1808–Dec. 29, 1809.

Conn. Hist. Soc. has May 25, 1809–Dec. 29, 1812; Feb. 16, 1814–Sept. 16, 1815.

New Haven Col. Hist. Soc. has Jan. 3, 1809–Dec. 28, 1810, fair; June 8, 1813–June 8, 1815, fair.

State Teachers Coll., Johnson City, Tenn. has Jan. 3, 1806–Dec. 29, 1807; July 2, 1811–Oct. 6, 1812.
Mass. State Lib. has June 12, 15, Nov. 16, 1804–Dec. 29, 1809; June 1–Dec. 30, 1813.
Brown Univ. has Jan. 4, 1805–Dec. 30, 1806.
Western Reserve Hist. Soc. has Mar. 6–Dec. 28, 1804, fair; Jan. 1–Dec. 31, 1805; Jan. 3, 1806–Dec. 22, 1809, fair; Jan. 2, 1810–July 7, 1812, scattering, and a few other scattering issues.
Rutgers Univ. has Jan. 4–Dec. 27, 1805, fair.
Cornell Univ. has Jan. 8–Dec. 30, 1808.
Wesleyan Univ. has Jan. 1–Nov. 1, 1808.
Cambridge Pub. Lib. has Jan. 1–Dec. 31, 1811.

[Boston] **Republican Gazetteer**, 1802–1803.

Semi-weekly. Established by J[ohn] M. Dunham on May 26, 1802. The "Republican Gazetteer" replaced the "Constitutional Telegraphe," but was given a new volume numbering. The last issue was that of Mar. 30, 1803, vol. 1, no. 89, and on Apr. 2, 1803, the title was changed to "The Gazetteer," which see.

Boston Athenæum and Harvard have May 26, 1802–Mar. 30, 1803.
Lib. Congress has May 26–Dec. 29, 1802; Jan. 1, 5, Feb. 9, 1803.
Boston Pub. Lib. has May 26–June 9, 16–July 31, Aug. 7, 14–Oct. 23, 30–Dec. 29, 1802.
Essex Inst. has June 12–Dec. 4, 1802, fair.
Wis. Hist. Soc. has May 26, 29, 1802; Jan. 1–Mar. 30, 1803.
Am. Antiq. Soc. has June 2, 5, July 3–17, 25, Aug. 4, Sept. 1, 8, 15, 22, 29, Oct. 16, Nov. 10, 17, 24, Dec. 4, 11, 15, 22, 29, 1802; Feb. 16, 23, 1803.
Mass. Hist. Soc. has July 17, Nov. 20, 24, Dec. 22, 1802; Feb. 9, 12, Mar. 12–19, 1803.
Dartmouth has May 26, 29, 1802.
Me. Hist. Soc. has Oct. 30, Dec. 29, 1802; Feb. 23, 1803.
Western Reserve Hist. Soc. has Jan. 29, 1803.

[Boston] **Russell's Commercial Gazette**, 1797–1798, see **Boston Price Current**.

[Boston] **Russell's Gazette**, 1798–1800.

Semi-weekly. A continuation, without change of volume numbering, of the "Boston Price Current." The first issue of "Russell's Gazette. Commercial and Political" was that of June 7, 1798, vol. 4, no. 27, published by John Russell. With the issue of Dec. 17, 1798, the title was changed to "J. Russell's Gazette. Commercial and Political." With the issue of Jan. 9, 1800, Russell transferred the paper to James Cutler. The last issue with the title of "J. Russell's Gazette" was that of Oct. 6, 1800, vol. 9, no. 10, after which the title was changed to "Boston Gazette," which see.

Am. Antiq. Soc., Boston Athenæum, Mass. Hist. Soc., Essex Inst., Conn. Hist. Soc., N. Y. Pub. Lib., and Lib. Congress have June 7, 1798–Oct. 6, 1800.
N. Y. Hist. Soc. and Univ. of Mich. (Clements) have June 7, 1798–Oct. 6, 1800, fair.
Boston Pub. Lib. has July 19, 1798–Apr. 7, 1800.
Wis. Hist. Soc. has Jan. 3, 1799–Oct. 6, 1800.
Penn. State Lib. has Jan. 14, 1799–Oct. 6, 1800.
N. Y. State Lib. has June 11, July 12, Aug. 30, Oct. 15–Dec. 30, 1798; Jan. 7, 28, Feb. 18, Mar. 4–14, 21, 28, Apr. 1, 11–18, July 1–8, 18, Oct. 10, Dec. 5, 1799; Jan. 2–Oct. 6, 1800.
Harvard has July 19, Sept. 17, 20, 1798; Jan. 17, 1799–Oct. 6, 1800, fair.
Duke Univ. has June 14, 18, 25, 28, July 9, 26, Aug. 6, Sept. 20–27, Oct. 11, 1798–Dec. 26, 1799, fair; Jan. 2–Oct. 6, 1800.
Mass. State Lib. has June 13–Nov. 4, 1799, fair; Feb. 24–Oct. 6, 1800.
Chicago Hist. Soc. has May 23, 1799–Oct. 6, 1800, fair.
Trinity Coll., Hartford, has Nov. 4, 1799–Oct. 6, 1800.
Cambridge Pub. Lib. has Jan. 6–Oct. 6, 1800.
British Museum has Apr. 17–Oct. 6, 1800.
Hist. Soc. Penn. has Nov. 19, Dec. 24, 1798; Jan. 7, Feb. 14, 25, July 15, Aug. 15, 22, 29, Sept. 12, Nov. 4, 1799; Apr. 7, May 15, July 3, 1800.

[Boston] **Satirist**, 1812.

Weekly. Established Jan. 16, 1812, with the title of "The Satirist," published by J[ames] L. Edwards, and edited under the pseudonym of "Lodowick Lash'em." The paper was issued irregularly, the thirteen numbers appearing on Jan. 16, Feb. 3, 8, 19, 29, May 14, 21, 28, Apr. 4, 11, 20, May 2, 9. With the issue of Apr. 20, 1812, the title was changed to "The Boston Satirist, or Weekly Museum," and the publisher's name was no longer given in the imprint. It was discontinued with the issue of May 9, 1812, no. 13.

Am. Antiq. Soc., Mass. Hist. Soc. and Lib. Congress have Jan. 16–May 9, 1812.
Boston Pub. Lib. has Jan. 16–May 2, 1812.
Harvard has Mar. 14, 1812.
Univ. of Mich. (Clements) has Apr. 4, 11, 1812.

[Boston] **Saturday Evening Herald**, 1790.

Weekly. Established July 17, 1790, by Edward Eveleth Powars under the title of "The Saturday Evening Herald, and the Washington Gazette." In August, 1790, the title was changed to "The American Herald, and the Washington Gazette." In October, 1790, the title was slightly changed to "American

Herald. And the Washington Gazette." The last issue located is that of Dec. 13, 1790, vol. 1, no. 22.

Am. Antiq. Soc. has July 24, Aug. 30, Sept. 27, Oct. 18–Nov. 22, Dec. 13, 1790.

[Boston] Scourge, 1811.

Established Aug. 10, 1811, with the title of "The Scourge," published by M[errill] Butler and edited under the pseudonym of "Tim Touchstone." It was supposed to be published weekly, but since the issues were frequently several days late in appearance, it may be said to have been published occasionally. Some of the issues went through more than one edition, as is shown by the issues of Aug. 10, Sept. 4, and Sept. 14, in the Antiquarian Society file, which are headed in the first column of the first page "Second Edition." In the issue of Nov. 30, 1811, there is an account of an attack upon the editor, Merrill Butler, "in the office of Mr. James L. Edwards, in which the newspaper called the Scourge is printed." The issue of Dec. 11, 1811, states that on Dec. 3, the editor was sentenced to six months imprisonment for libel, and had begun serving his term. This issue was published "for M. Butler." The record of the case in the Supreme Court referred to Merrill Butler as the printer and to Charles Williams as the publisher (see Providence "Columbian Phenix," Dec. 7, 1811). The issue of Dec. 28, 1811, vol. 1, no. 16, was undoubtedly the last issued. On Jan. 16, 1812, James L. Edwards established "The Satirist."

> Am. Antiq. Soc., Boston Pub. Lib., Mass. Hist. Soc., and Lib. Congress have Aug. 10–Dec. 28, 1811.
> N. Y. Hist. Soc. has Aug. 10–Dec. 11, 1811.
> Cornell Univ. has Aug. 10–Dec. 11, 1811, fair.
> Univ. of Mich. (Clements) has Aug. 21, Sept. 4, Oct. 21, 29, Nov. 20, 27, 1811.
> Harvard has Oct. 19–Nov. 2, 16, 27, 1811.
> Essex Inst. has Oct. 8, Dec. 11, 1811.
> N. Y. Pub. Lib. has Nov. 16, 1811.

Boston Spectator, 1814–1815.

Weekly. Established Jan. 1, 1814, with the title of "The Boston Spectator," printed and published for John Park by Munroe & Francis [Edmund Munroe and David Francis]. With the issue of Nov. 5, 1814, the firm name of the printers became Munroe, Francis & Parker, Samuel H. Parker having entered the firm. John Park continued the paper until the issue of Feb. 25, 1815, vol. 1, no. 61, when it was discontinued. It was of quarto size, paged, and provided with a title page and index.

> Am. Antiq. Soc., Boston Athenæum, Boston Pub. Lib., Mass. Hist. Soc., Harvard, Essex Inst., Brown, Yale, N. Y. Pub. Lib., N. Y. Hist. Soc., N. Y. State Lib., Hist. Soc. Penn., Lib. Congress, Wis. Hist. Soc., Newberry Lib., Univ.

of Chicago, Western Reserve Hist. Soc., Kansas Hist. Soc., Univ. of Minn., Univ. of Calif., and Stanford Univ. have Jan. 1, 1814–Feb. 25, 1815.
Chicago Hist. Soc. has Jan. 1, 1814–Feb. 18, 1815.
Dedham Hist. Soc. has Jan. 1, 1814–Feb. 11, 1815, fair.

[Boston] Times, 1794.

Tri-weekly. Established Oct. 4, 1794, with the title of "The Times: or the Evening Entertainer," published by Hall & Macclintock [Thomas Hall and ——— Macclintock]. In the Antiquarian Society file is a 16mo., 8 page "Proposal" for publishing the paper, dated July 28, 1794. With the issue of Nov. 5, 1794, the paper was published by Thomas Hall. The last issue located is that of Nov. 8, 1794, vol. 1, no. 15.

Am. Antiq. Soc. has July 28 Proposal, Oct. 4, 9, 14, 16, 21, 23, 25, 29, Nov. 3, 5, 8, 1794.
Boston Pub. Lib. has Oct. 4, 9, 14, 16, 29, Nov. 3, 5, 1794.
N. Y. Pub. Lib. has Oct. 18, 21, 23, Nov. 1, 8, 1794.
Wis. Hist. Soc. has Oct. 23, 25, Nov. 5, 8, 1794.
Mass. Hist. Soc. has Oct. 4, 1794.
Lib. Congress has Oct. 4, 1794.
N. Y. Hist. Soc. has Nov. 3, 1794.

[Boston] Times, 1807–1808.

Weekly. Established Dec. 12, 1807, with the title of "The Times," published by Oliver & Munroe [Edward Oliver and Isaac Munroe]. The paper was of quarto size and paged. Although of magazine form, because of its inclusion of death and marriage notices, current news, etc., it should be considered a newspaper, and was so termed by its publishers. The paper was discontinued with the issue of Oct. 15, 1808, vol. 1, no. 45, and in its stead was published the Boston Mirror, which see.

Am. Antiq. Soc., Boston Pub. Lib., Brown Univ., Lib. Congress, La. State Univ., and Wis. Hist. Soc. have Dec. 12, 1807–Oct. 15, 1808.
Harvard has Dec. 12, 1807–Oct. 8, 1808.
Conn. Hist. Soc. has Jan. 23–Oct. 8, 1808.
Mass. Hist. Soc. has Jan. 16, 1808.
N. Y. Hist. Soc. has Mar. 5, Apr. 16, 1808.
Univ. of Mich. (Clements) has Sept. 10, 1808.

Boston Weekly Advertiser, see Boston Post-Boy.

[Boston] Weekly Messenger, 1811–1820+.

Weekly. Established Oct. 25, 1811, by James Cutler, with the title of "The Weekly Messenger." The last issue in folio form was that of Oct. 13, 1815, vol. 4, no. 52. With the issue of Oct. 20, 1815, vol. 5, no. 1, the paper was transferred to Nathan Hale, who changed the title to "Boston Weekly Messenger" and brought it out in magazine size, 16 pages to each weekly number. Although having the appearance of a periodical, it was made up largely of current news taken from Hale's paper, the "Boston Daily Advertiser," and its publisher stated, "It will not be less a news paper than heretofore." Each volume had a title-page and index. The last issue in octavo size is that of June 8, 1820, vol. 9, no. 35. With the issue of June 15, 1820 (vol. 10, or new series, vol. 1, no. 1), the paper was again published in folio size, and was so continued until after 1820.

Am. Antiq. Soc., Boston Athenæum, Boston Pub. Lib., Mass. Hist. Soc., Essex Inst., Yale, and Wis. Hist. Soc. have Oct. 25, 1811–Dec. 29, 1820.
N. Y. Hist. Soc. has Oct. 25, 1811–Oct. 9, 1817; Oct. 22, 1818–Dec. 29, 1820.
Dartmouth has Oct. 25, 1811–Dec. 30, 1814; Jan. 6, 1815–Dec. 29, 1820, fair.
Lib. Congress has Oct. 25, 1811–Oct. 8, 1818; Apr. 22, 1819; Oct. 14, 1819–Dec. 29, 1820.
Mass. State Lib. has Nov. 1, 1811–Oct. 13, 1815; Oct. 17, 1816–Oct. 9, 1817; June 15–Dec. 29, 1820.
Univ. of Chicago has Dec. 11, 1812–Oct. 8, 1818, fair; Oct. 14, 1819–June 1, 1820.
Univ. of Mich. (Clements) has Oct. 25, 1811–Dec. 26, 1816; Jan. 2, 1817–Oct. 8, 1818, fair; June 15–Dec. 29, 1820.
Harvard has Oct. 25, 1811–Oct. 13, 1815; Oct. 17, 1816–Oct. 9, 1817; June 15–Nov. 23, 1820.
British Museum has Oct. 25, 1811–Oct. 13, 1815.
N. Y. State Lib. has Oct. 25, 1811–Oct. 13, 1815.
Marblehead Hist. Soc. has Oct. 25, 1811–Oct. 13, 1815.
Duke Univ. has Oct. 25, 1811–Oct. 13, 1815.
York Inst., Saco, has Oct. 25, 1811–Aug. 11, 1815.
Brown Univ. has Oct. 25, 1811–Oct. 20, 1814; Jan. 1, 1815–May 10, 1818; June 8–Dec. 29, 1820.
Vassar Coll. has Oct. 25, 1811–Oct. 13, 1815; June 15–Dec. 29, 1820.
Chicago Hist. Soc. has Oct. 25, 1811–Oct. 22, 1813; Jan. 14, 1814–Oct. 13, 1815, scattering file.
Rutgers Univ. has Oct. 25, 1811–Oct. 14, 1814.
Univ. of Texas has Oct. 25, 1811–Jan. 18, 1814.
Detroit Pub. Lib. has Oct. 25, 1811–Oct. 15, 1813.
La. State Univ. has Nov. 8, 1811–Oct. 14, 1814.
Rev. Harrison W. Dubbs, Gorham, Me., has May 8, 1812–Sept. 8, 1815.
Providence Pub. Lib. has Apr. 24, 1812–Oct. 14, 1814.
Ohio Arch. & Hist. Soc. has Mar. 6, 1812–Dec. 30, 1814.
Ga. Hist. Soc. has Nov. 6, 1812–Oct. 14, 1814.
Western Reserve Hist. Soc. has Dec. 3, 1813–Oct. 3, 1816, fair.
Hist. Soc. Penn. has Apr. 22, 1814–June 30, 1815.

Bowdoin Coll. has Oct. 20, 1815–Dec. 29, 1820.
Concord, Mass., Pub. Lib. has Oct. 25, 1811–Oct. 15, 1812; June 15–Dec. 29, 1820.
Conn. Hist. Soc. has Oct. 23, 1812–Oct. 8, 1813.
N. Y. Pub. Lib. has Oct. 15, 1818–Sept. 30, 1819, fair.

[Boston] Weekly News-Letter, see Boston News-Letter.

Boston Weekly News-Letter, see Boston News-Letter.

Boston Weekly Post-Boy, see Boston Post-Boy.

[Boston] Weekly Rehearsal, 1731–1735.

Weekly. Established Sept. 27, 1731, with the title of "The Weekly Rehearsal" and "printed by J[ohn] Draper for the Author." Isaiah Thomas states ("History of Printing," 1874 ed., vol. 1, p. 125, and vol. 2, p. 42) that the paper was established by Jeremiah Gridley and that it "was carried on at the expense of some gentlemen who formed themselves into a political or literary club, and wrote for it. At the head of this club was the late celebrated Jeremy [Jeremiah] Gridley, Esq., who was the real editor of the paper." With the issue of Aug. 21, 1732, the paper was printed by Thomas Fleet. This issue, moreover, was the first to have a number, although the number given to it, 47, was an error, as forty-seven issues had already been published, and the issue of Aug. 21, 1732, should have been numbered 48. With the issue of Apr. 2, 1733, Gridley retired and Thomas Fleet became sole proprietor and publisher. The last issue of "The Weekly Rehearsal" was that of Aug. 11, 1735, no. 202, and upon Aug. 18, 1735, it was replaced by "The Boston Evening-Post," which see.

Am. Antiq. Soc. has Oct. 4, 1731–Aug. 11, 1735, lacking Sept. 27, 1731; Apr. 24, 1732; May 7, Nov. 26, 1733; June 3, Sept. 16, 1734.
Mass. Hist. Soc. has Sept. 27–Dec. 27, 1731; Jan. 3–May 8, 22, June 5–Sept. 18, Dec. 11, 1732; Feb. 5, May 28, 1733; Jan. 7, Apr. 8, Aug. 19, Dec. 23, 1734; Mar. 17, 1735.
Boston Pub. Lib. has June 26, 1732; Feb. 5, 1733; Feb. 18, 1734; Aug. 4, 1735.
Lib. Congress has May 1, 8, July 3, Sept. 4, Dec. 25, 1732.
Univ. of Mich. (Clements) has Feb. 5, 1733.
British Public Record Office has May 13, 1734.

Boston Weekly Report, 1819–1820+.

Weekly. Established May 1, 1819, by P[eter] P. F. Degrand, with the title of "Boston Weekly Report of Public Sales and of Arrivals." The first issue was of quarto size, but the second number was enlarged to folio and the title changed to "P. P. F. Degrand's Boston Weekly Report of Public Sales and of Arrivals." With this issue, moreover, it was stated that the paper was printed by E[lisha] Bellamy. It was published by Degrand and printed by Bellamy until after 1820.

Am. Antiq. Soc., Boston Athenæum, Boston Pub. Lib., Portland Pub. Lib., Woburn Pub. Lib., and N. Y. Hist. Soc. have May 1, 1819–Dec. 30, 1820.
Yale has May 8, 1819–Dec. 30, 1820.
N. Y. Pub. Lib. has May 1–Nov. 13, 1819.
Phil. Lib. Co. has May 8–Dec. 25, 1819.
Lib. Congress has May 1, 29, 1819; Jan. 15, 1820.
Essex Inst. has May 8, 1819; Jan. 1–Dec. 30, 1820.

[Boston] Yankee, 1812–1820.

Weekly. Established Jan. 3, 1812, with the title of "The Yankee," published by True & Rowe [Benjamin True and Thomas Rowe] and edited by David Everett. On Sept. 25, 1812, Everett established a semi-weekly newspaper called "The Pilot," printed by True & Rowe, and the matter printed in the two papers was largely the same. In the issue of "The Yankee" for Jan. 22, 1813, True & Rowe announced that "The Pilot" was suspended and that their partnership with Everett was dissolved, and with this issue Everett's name was omitted from the imprint. With the issue of Dec. 31, 1813, the partnership of True & Rowe was dissolved, and Thomas Rowe took Joshua Hooper, Jr., into partnership under the firm name of Rowe & Hooper. This partnership was dissolved and with the issue of Dec. 29, 1815, the paper was published by Thomas Rowe; but with the issue of Feb. 2, 1816, the partnership was resumed, and the paper again published by Rowe & Hooper. The partnership was again dissolved, and with the issue of Jan. 31, 1817, the paper was published by Thomas Rowe. With the issue of May 15, 1818, Rowe disposed of the paper to Benjamin True and Equality Weston, who published it under the firm name of True & Weston. With the issue of Apr. 15, 1819, the title was changed to "Boston Yankee." The last issue published was that of Jan. 20, 1820, vol. 9, no. 5, as a fire destroyed the office on Jan. 27, and the paper evidently was not revived.

Boston Pub. Lib. has Jan. 3, 1812–Jan. 20, 1820.
Am. Antiq. Soc. has Jan. 3, 1812–Dec. 31, 1818; Jan. 7, 1819–Jan. 20, 1820, fair.
Boston Athenæum has Jan. 3, 1812–Dec. 30, 1819.
Lib. Congress has Jan. 3, 1812–Dec. 31, 1813; Jan. 7–Dec. 30, 1814, fair; Jan. 6, 1815–Dec. 20, 1816; Jan. 10, 17, 31, Feb. 21, Mar. 7, Apr. 4, June 6–Dec. 26, 1817; Jan. 2, 1818–Jan. 20, 1820.
Bath, Me., Patten Lib. has Jan. 15, 1813–Dec. 23, 1819.
Mass. Hist. Soc. has Jan. 3–Aug. 21, Sept. 4, 1812–Dec. 31, 1813; Jan. 7–May 20, June 3–Sept. 16, Oct. 14, 28–Nov. 25, Dec. 9, 1814; Jan. 6–June 30, July 14–Dec. 22, 1815; Jan. 19, 26, Feb. 2, 23–Mar. 8, 22, 29, Apr. 19,

May 31, June 21–July 19, Aug. 9–30, Sept. 13–27, Oct. 18, Nov. 1, 15–Dec. 27, 1816; June 6, 13, 27, July 11, Aug. 8, Oct. 31, Nov. 7–28, Dec. 12–26, 1817; Jan. 2–Feb. 20, Mar. 6–Apr. 17, May 29, June 25, July 16, Oct. 8, 1818; Jan. 21, Apr. 1, 1819.

Ohio Arch. & Hist. Soc. has Jan. 3, 1812–Dec. 15, 1815; June 14, 1816; Aug. 26, 1819.

Amesbury, Mass., Pub. Lib. has Feb. 26, 1813; Jan. 13, 1815–Dec. 23, 1819; Jan. 6–20, 1820.

Duke Univ. has Jan. 3, 1812–Dec. 24, 1813.

N. Y. Hist. Soc. has Mar. 27–Dec. 25, 1812; Jan. 1–Mar. 12, Dec. 3, 24, 31, 1813; Jan. 7, 21–Feb. 25, Apr. 15, May 6, 27, Sept. 30–Oct. 21, Nov. 4, 11, Dec. 16, 30, 1814; Jan. 27, Feb. 3, 17–Mar. 10, Apr. 7, 21, Aug. 4, Sept. 22, 1815; Jan. 3, 1817.

Hist. Soc. Penn. has Nov. 4, 1814–Dec. 27, 1816.

Wis. Hist. Soc. has Oct. 9, 1812; Dec. 30, 1814–Dec. 22, 1815; Jan. 6, Dec. 24, 1818.

Detroit Pub. Lib. has June 19, 1812–Dec. 24, 1813, fair.

Essex Inst. has Jan. 3–Nov. 27, 1812; Dec. 17, 1813; Apr. 1, Dec. 2, 1814; June 2, July 21, Aug. 11–Sept. 1, 29, 1815; June 14, Sept. 13, Oct. 4, Dec. 13, 1816; Jan. 31, Feb. 7, May 9, Oct. 3, 1817; Apr. 3, June 4, Dec. 10, 17, 1818; Jan. 7, 14, 1819.

Univ. of Mich. (Clements) has Nov. 20, 1812; June 25, 1813; June 17, Aug. 5, 1814; Jan. 6, 1815–Nov. 15, 1816, fair; Aug. 29, Nov. 14, 1817; Feb. 13, May 9, June 4, July 2, Aug. 27, Nov. 26, 1818; Jan. 14, Feb. 18, Mar. 11, Sept. 9–Dec. 9, 23–30, 1819; Jan. 6–20, 1820.

Yale has Jan. 3–Dec. 18, 1812; Mar. 26, 1813; Dec. 31, 1813–Dec. 23, 1814; Apr. 7, 14, June 30, July 14, Aug. 11–25, Sept. 15, 29, Oct. 6, Nov. 24, 1815; Jan. 5, Apr. 5, May 10, Aug. 23, Oct. 18, 1816.

Springfield City Lib. has Dec. 22, 1815–Nov. 22, 1816, scattering file.

N. Y. State Lib. has Oct. 2, 16, 23, Nov. 13, 1812; Feb. 18, Sept. 23, 1814; Feb. 6, 1818.

Harvard has June 11, 1818.

[Brookfield] **Moral and Political Telegraphe**, 1795–1796.

Weekly. A continuation, without change of numbering, of the "Worcester County Intelligencer." The new title was "The Moral and Political Telegraphe; Or, Brookfield Advertiser" and the first issue was on May 6, 1795, vol. 1, no. 31, published by Elisha H. Waldo. The paper was discontinued with the issue of Aug. 17, 1796, vol. 2, no. 98.

Am. Antiq. Soc. has May 6, 1795–Mar. 30, Apr. 13–Aug. 17, 1796.
Boston Pub. Lib. has May 6–June 3, 17–Sept. 30, Nov. 4, 18, Dec. 30, 1795; Apr. 27–May 11, 25, June 22, 29, July 27, 1796.

Harvard has July 22, Aug. 12, Sept. 9, Dec. 30, 1795.
Essex Inst. has July 29, 1795, Apr. 13, 27, 1796.
Univ. of Mich. (Clements) has Aug. 26, 1795.

[Brookfield] **Political Repository,** 1798–1802.

Weekly. Established Aug. 14, 1798, by Ebenezer Merriam & Co., with the title of "The Political Repository: Or, Farmer's Journal." Discontinued with the issue of May 4, 1802, vol. 4, no. 195.

Am. Antiq. Soc. has Aug. 14, 1798–May 4, 1802.
Boston Athenæum has Feb. 5, 1799; Oct. 21, Nov. 18–Dec. 30, 1800; Jan. 6–Feb. 3, 17, 24, Mar. 10–Apr. 14, 28–May 19, June 2, 16–30, July 21, Aug. 25–Sept. 15, Nov. 3–17, Dec. 7, 22, 1801; Jan. 12, 19, 1802.
N. Y. Pub. Lib. has Oct. 29–Dec. 10, 1799; Feb. 11, Mar. 4–18, Apr. 8–22, May 6, 27, July 8, Sept. 16–Oct. 21, Nov. 4–18, Dec. 9–23, 1800; Jan. 13–27, Feb. 24, Mar. 3, 17–31, Apr. 21–July 28, 1801.
Harvard has Aug. 28, Sept. 6, Oct. 9, Nov. 6, 1798; Jan. 29, Feb. 12, Apr. 16, July 23, 30, 1799; Jan. 21, May 20, 1800; Feb. 3, Mar. 10, Nov. 3–17, Dec. 1–29, 1801; Jan. 5–Feb. 16, Mar. 2–Apr. 27, 1802.
N. Y. State Lib. has Feb. 5, 1799; Oct. 21, Nov. 18–Dec. 30, 1800; Jan. 6–Feb. 3, 17, 24, Mar. 10–Apr. 14, 28–May 19, June 2, 16–30, July 14, 21, Aug. 25–Sept. 15, Nov. 3–17, Dec. 7, 22, 1801; Jan. 5–19, 1802.
Boston Pub. Lib. has Mar. 5–Nov. 19, Dec. 3–24, 1799.
Lib. Congress has Nov. 5, 19, Dec. 3, 31, 1799; Dec. 23, 1800; Mar. 3, May 12, 1801; May 4, 1802.
Troy Pub. Lib. has Apr. 29, May 27, Aug. 5, Sept. 30, 1800; Apr. 14, 28, June 23, July 28, Aug. 18, Sept. 8, 22, Nov. 24, Dec. 29, 1801; Jan. 19, Apr. 6, 1802.
Mass. Hist. Soc. has July 9, 1799.
Conn. Hist. Soc. has Dec. 24, 31, 1799.
Duke Univ. has Mar. 4, Apr. 15, 1800.
Stockbridge Pub. Lib. has Mar. 17, July 21, 1801.
Univ. of Mich. (Clements) has Oct. 13, 27, 1801.
N. Y. Hist. Soc. has Sept. 2, 1800; Feb. 2, 1802.
Long Id. Hist. Soc. has May 19, 1801.

[Brookfield] **Worcester County Intelligencer,** see **Worcester Intelligencer.**

[Brookfield] **Worcester Intelligencer,** 1794–1795.

Weekly. Established Oct. 7, 1794, by Isaiah Thomas and Elisha H. Waldo, with the title of "The Worcester Intelligencer: Or, Brookfield Advertiser." With the issue of Jan. 6, 1795, the title was altered to "The Worcester County Intelligencer: Or, Brookfield Advertiser." The last issue with this title was that of Apr. 28, 1795, vol. 1, no. 30, after which the title was changed to "Moral

MASSACHUSETTS 353

and Political Telegraphe," which see. With this issue of Apr. 28, 1795, Thomas withdrew from the firm.

Am. Antiq. Soc. has Oct. 7, 1794–Apr. 28, 1795.
Boston Pub. Lib. has Oct. 7, 14, 28, 1794–Apr. 28, 1795.
Harvard has Feb. 24–Mar. 17, Apr. 21, 1795.
Univ. of Mich. (Clements) has Apr. 28, 1795.

[Cambridge] New-England Chronicle, 1775–1776.

Weekly. A continuation, without change of volume numbering, of the "Essex Gazette," published at Salem. The last issue of the "Essex Gazette" was that of May 2, 1775, vol. 7, no. 353, and the first issue of "The New-England Chronicle: or, the Essex Gazette" was that of May 12, 1775, vol. 7, no. 354, published by Samuel and Ebenezer Hall. Ebenezer Hall died Feb. 14, 1776, and with the issue of Feb. 22, 1776, the paper was published by Samuel Hall, although his name did not appear in the imprint until the issue of Feb. 29. The last Cambridge issue was that of Apr. 4, 1776, vol. 8, no. 400, after which the paper was removed to Boston.

Am. Antiq. Soc., Boston Athenæum, Mass. Hist. Soc., Harvard, Essex Inst., N. Y. Pub. Lib., Lib. Congress, and Wis. Hist. Soc. have May 12, 1775–Apr. 4, 1776.
Boston Pub. Lib., N. Y. Hist. Soc., N. Y. State Lib., Yale, and Univ. of Mich. (Clements) have May 12, 1775–Apr. 4, 1776, nearly complete.
Mass. State Lib. has June 29, 1775–Apr. 4, 1776, fair.
Portland Pub. Lib. has May 12–Nov. 30, 1775.
Taunton Pub. Lib. has June 15–Dec. 7, 1775.
Duke Univ. has May 25–Dec. 28, 1775, fair.
Dartmouth has May 12, 25, June 15–July 21, Sept. 14, Nov. 30, 1775.
Rutgers Univ. has June 15, 29, Sept. 28, Nov. 30, 1775.
Western Reserve Hist. Soc. has Sept. 7, 21, Oct. 5, Nov. 30, Dec. 14, 21, 1775.

[Charlestown] American Recorder, 1785–1787.

Semi-weekly and weekly. Established Dec. 9, 1785, by Allen and Cushing [John W. Allen and Thomas C. Cushing], with the title of "The American Recorder, and the Charlestown Advertiser." The paper was changed from semi-weekly to weekly with the issue of Aug. 4, 1786. With the issue of Sept. 22, 1786, the publishing firm was dissolved and the paper published by John W. Allen. The paper was discontinued with the issue of May 25, 1787, vol. 2, no. 110.

Mass. Hist. Soc. has Dec. 9, 1785–May 25, 1787.
Univ. of Mich. (Clements), has Dec. 9, 16, 1785–Sept. 15, 29–Dec. 29, 1786; Jan. 5–May 18, 1787.

Am. Antiq. Soc. has Dec. 9–30, 1785; Jan. 3–20, 27–Mar. 10, 17, 24–31, Apr. 7–28, May 5–30, June 13–30, July 7, 11, 18, 25, 29, Aug. 11–Dec. 29, 1786; Jan. 5–May 18, 1787.
Boston Pub. Lib. has Dec. 16–30, 1785; Jan. 3–Sept. 8, 22, Oct. 20, Nov. 3, 10, 24, 31, Dec. 15, 1786; Jan. 5, 19–Feb. 9, Mar. 9–30, 1787.
Boston Athenæum has Dec. 27, 30, 1785; Jan. 3, 6, 13–20, 27–Feb. 14, 21, 24, Mar. 3, 10, 17, 21, 28–Apr. 7, 14–May 12, 19, 26, 30, June 6, 9, 16–July 14, 21–Aug. 11, Sept. 1, 8, Nov. 24, 1786; Feb. 9, 1787.
N. Y. Pub. Lib. has Dec. 9, 1785–Aug. 11, 1786.
N. Y. State Lib. has Dec. 9, 1785–July 4, 29, 1786.
Hist. Soc. Penn. has Aug. 18, 1786–May 25, 1787.
Lib. Congress has Jan. 6, 27, Feb. 10–17, Mar. 10, 21, May 16, 30–June 6, 30, July 25, Sept. 8, 29, Oct. 13, 27, Nov. 3, 17, Dec. 29, 1786; Jan. 19, Feb. 9, 16, 1787.
Me. Hist. Soc. has Jan. 3, 1786.
N. Y. Hist. Soc. has June 23, 1786.
Essex Inst. has Apr. 11, June 20, 1786.
Harvard has May 18, 1787.

[Charlestown] **Bunker-Hill Sentinel**, 1820.

Weekly. A continuation, without change of numbering, of the "Franklin Monitor and Middlesex Republican," the last known issue of which was that of June 3, 1820, vol. 2, no. 18. The earliest issue of the new paper located is that of June 24, 1820, vol. 2, no. 21, the title being Bunker-Hill Sentinel And Middlesex Republican," published by George Clark, & Co., with David Wilson as printer. In the issue of July 29, 1820, vol. 2, no. 24, it is stated that there had been no paper published for the preceding two weeks.

Am. Antiq. Soc. has June 24, 1820.
Boston Pub. Lib. has July 1, 29, 1820.

[Charlestown] **Franklin Monitor**, 1819–1820.

Weekly. Established Jan. 2, 1819, by Bellamy & Green [Elisha Bellamy and Thomas Green], in a paper of quarto size, entitled "Franklin Monitor." With the issue of Feb. 20, 1819, the paper was enlarged to folio and the title was changed to "Franklin Monitor. And Charlestown General Advertiser." With the issue of May 29, 1819, the firm was dissolved and the paper published by Thomas Green. With the issue of Oct. 16, 1819, the title was changed to "Franklin Monitor and Middlesex Republican." On Nov. 27, 1819, Green transferred the paper to David Felt, but the imprint stated merely that it was published "For the Proprietor." With the issue of Jan. 8, 1820, the paper was published by George Clark, & Co., and printed by David Wilson. It was so printed up to the issue of June 3, 1820, vol. 2, no. 18, and within three weeks, it was discontinued under this name and the title changed to "Bunker-Hill Sentinel," which see.

Am. Antiq. Soc. has Jan. 2–Mar. 13, Apr. 10–Dec. 25, 1819; Jan. 1, Apr. 15, 1820.
Boston Pub. Lib. has Apr. 17–May 1, 29, June 5, 19, 26, July 24, 31, Aug. 28, Oct. 23–Nov. 6, Dec. 4, 18, 1819; Feb. 26, Mar. 11–Apr. 8, 22, May 13, 27, June 3, 1820.
Lib. Congress has Feb. 6, July 17, 1819.

[Concord] **Middlesex Gazette,** 1816–1820+.

Weekly. Established Apr. 20, 1816, by Bettis and Peters [William J. Bettis and Joseph T. Peters], with the title of "Middlesex Gazette." During the first year, at some time between November 1816 and March 1817, the firm was dissolved and the paper published by Joseph T. Peters. With the issue of Apr. 18, 1818, the title was changed to "The Middlesex Gazette, & Advertiser." With the issue of Apr. 30, 1819, the title reverted to "Middlesex Gazette," and the paper was transferred to Caleb Cushing. With the issue of Jan. 27, 1820, Joseph T. Peters repurchased the paper and continued it until after 1820.

Essex Inst. has Apr. 5–July 5, 19–Oct. 11, Nov. 15–Dec. 13, 1817; Jan. 3–Mar. 7, 21, 28, 1818; May 7–27, June 10–Sept. 23, Oct. 7, 21, Nov. 4–Dec. 2, 16–30, 1819; Jan. 6, 13, 1820.
Concord Pub. Lib. has Apr. 5, July 19, 26, Sept. 6, 27, Nov. 8, 1817; Mar. 21, Apr. 18–June 6, 20–Sept. 26, Oct. 10–Dec. 26, 1818; Jan. 2–Mar. 13, 27–Apr. 24, Sept. 23, Oct. 7–21, Nov. 4–Dec. 16, 30, 1819; Jan. 13–June 24, July 8–Dec. 30, 1820.
Am. Antiq. Soc. has Apr. 20, June 22, Oct. 5, 1816; July 19, 1817; Apr. 4, 25, May 9, July 18, 25, Nov. 21–Dec. 26, 1818; Jan. 9–23, July 15, Aug. 5, 1819; May 27, Aug. 19, Sept. 23, Oct. 14, 1820.
Rutgers Univ. has Nov. 23, 1816; Aug. 26, Sept. 16, 1819; Mar. 4, Apr. 1, 22, Sept. 30, Oct. 21, 1820.
Me. Hist. Soc. has Sept. 21, 1816.
Mass. Hist. Soc. has Sept. 28, 1816.
Harvard has Oct. 10, 1818.
Wis. Hist. Soc. has Dec. 19, 1818.

[Conway] **Farmer's Register,** 1798.

Weekly. Established Mar. 17, 1798, judging from the date of the earliest issue located, that of Apr. 7, 1798, vol. 1, no. 4, entitled "Farmer's Register," and published by Theodore & A. H[ayden] Leonard. At some time in June or July, 1798, the title was slightly changed to "The Farmers' Register." With the issue of Sept. 8, 1798, the firm was dissolved and the paper was published by Theodore Leonard. The last issue located is that of Oct. 27, 1798, vol. 1, no. 33.

Am. Antiq. Soc. has May 26, June 2, July 28, Sept. 8, 1798.
Pocumtuck Valley Mem. Assoc., Deerfield, has Apr. 7, Oct. 27, 1798.
Phil. Lib. Co. has May 19, Aug. 18, Sept. 1, 1798.
Harvard has Aug. 25, Sept. 1, 8, 1798.
Troy Pub. Lib. has Sept. 8, 1798.

[Dedham] Columbian Minerva, 1799-1804.

Weekly. A continuation, without change of numbering, of "The Minerva," the first issue with the new title of the "Columbian Minerva" being that of Jan. 3, 1799, vol. 3, no. 117, published by Herman Mann. The paper was discontinued by Mann with the issue of Sept. 4, 1804.

Dedham Hist. Soc. has Jan. 3, 1799–Sept. 4, 1804
Harvard has Jan. 10, 1799–Sept. 4, 1804, fair.
Boston Athenæum has Jan. 3, 1799–Dec. 30, 1800, fair; June 23, 1801–Feb. 16, 1802, fair; June 8, 1802–Dec. 27, 1803, fair.
Am. Antiq. Soc. has Jan. 3–Sept. 5, 19, 26, Oct. 17–Nov. 7, 21–Dec. 19, 1799; Jan. 2, 9, 1800; Apr. 21, May 19, 1801; May 25, 1802; Apr. 19, 26, Aug. 16–30, Sept. 20, Oct. 4, 1803–Sept. 4, 1804.
Lib. Congress has Jan. 17–Feb. 21, Mar. 14, Apr. 11, 25, May 2, Aug. 15, Sept. 5, 1799.
Mass. Hist. Soc. has Mar. 7, 1799; Jan. 16, Feb. 27, Mar. 20, 27, Apr. 17, 1800; Apr. 14, 1801; Aug. 24, 1802.
N. Y. State Lib. has Feb. 7, 1804.

Dedham Gazette, 1813-1819.

Weekly. Established Aug. 20, 1813, by Samuel Hall. With the issue of Oct. 29, 1813, the imprint was changed to "Printed by Samuel Hall for the Proprietors"; with that of Nov. 26, 1813, to "Printed for the Proprietors"; and with that of Jan. 6, 1815, to "Printed for the Proprietor." With the issue of May 31, 1816, the paper was published by Abel D. Alleyne, the previous issue having announced that Jabez Chickering, who was a "principal agent in establishing" the paper, had withdrawn as proprietor. With the issue of Jan. 8, 1819, the paper was purchased and published by H. & W. H. Mann [Herman Mann Jr., and William H. Mann]. It was discontinued with the issue of June 25, 1819, vol. 6, no. 46. H. Mann, in his "Annals of Dedham," p. 76, states that before the paper was purchased by the Manns, Jabez Chickering was proprietor, Theron Metcalf was editor and Abel D. Alleyne was printer. The title throughout was "Dedham Gazette."

Dedham Hist. Soc. has Aug. 20, 1813–Aug. 9, 1816; Nov. 22, 1816; Jan. 3, Feb. 14, Mar. 7, 21, Apr. 4, 18, May 2, 16, June 18, Aug. 29, Sept. 5, Oct. 17, Dec. 12, 1817; Jan. 23, Feb. 20, Mar. 13, 20, May 1, June 16, July 10, 24, Oct. 2, 16, Nov. 6, 20, 27, 1818; Jan. 8–June 25, 1819.

MASSACHUSETTS 357

Am. Antiq. Soc. has Aug. 20–Dec. 31, 1813; Jan. 7–Aug. 26, Sept. 9, 23, Nov. 4–Dec. 30, 1814; Jan. 6–27, Feb. 3, 17–Apr. 14, May 5–26, June 9, 16, 30–Aug. 4, 25–Sept. 8, 22, 29, Oct. 20, 27, Nov. 17, 24, 1815; Jan. 19, Feb. 16, Mar. 1, 8, 22–Apr. 5, 19, May 10, June 14, July 26, Aug. 16, 30–Sept. 13, 27–Oct. 18, Nov. 8–Dec. 27, 1816; Jan. 3–Mar. 28, Apr. 11–Aug. 8, Sept. 5, Oct. 10–Dec. 26, 1817; Jan. 2–Apr. 3, 24–May 22, Aug. 14–Dec. 25, 1818; Jan. 1–May 28, June 25, 1819.

James H. Chickering, Dover, Mass., has Aug. 20, 1813–Feb. 24, 1815; Mar. 10, 1815–Aug. 1, 1817, scattering.

Lib. Congress has Jan. 14, Aug. 20, 27, Dec. 31, 1813; Jan. 14, Mar. 25, July 29, Aug. 12, 26, Dec. 2, 1814; Jan. 6, Mar. 10–24, May 19, July 21, 1815; Oct. 9, 1818; Apr. 23, 1819.

Essex Inst. has Aug. 19, 26, Dec. 16, 1814; Feb. 3, 10, Sept. 15, 1815; June 20, 1817.

Wis. Hist. Soc. has Dec. 3, 1813; Apr. 29, 1814; Oct. 27, 1815; Dec. 18, 1818.

Mass. Hist. Soc. has Sept. 17, Oct. 8, 1813.

N. Y. Hist. Soc. has Sept. 24, 1813; Mar. 22, 1816.

N. Y. Pub. Lib. has Nov. 4, 1814.

[Dedham] Minerva, 1796–1798.

Weekly. Established Oct. 11, 1796, by Nathaniel and Benjamin Heaton, with the title of "The Minerva." With the issue of Dec. 7, 1797, the partnership was dissolved, Benjamin Heaton withdrew, and the paper was published by N. Heaton and H. Mann. With the issue probably of Jan. 4, 1798, the paper was published by Herman Mann. With the issue of Mar. 8, 1798, Mann took James H. Adams into partnership under the firm name of H. Mann and J. H. Adams. With the issue of Sept. 20, 1798, the proprietorship reverted to Herman Mann. The last issue with the title of "The Minerva" was that of Dec. 27, 1798, vol. 3, no. 116, after which it was called the "Columbian Minerva" which see.

Harvard has Oct. 11–25, Nov. 29, Dec. 6, 20, 27, 1796; Jan. 3–24, Feb. 14, 28–Apr. 25, Oct. 10, 24–Nov. 29, 1797; Feb. 15, Mar. 1, 8, 22, Apr. 12, 26, May 17, 31–June 14, July 12, Aug. 2–16, Sept. 6–20, Nov. 15, Dec. 13, 27, 1798.

Dedham Hist. Soc. has Nov. 8, 15, Dec. 6, 27, 1796; Apr. 25, Oct. 17–Dec. 7, 1797; Jan. 11–June 28, July 12, Aug. 2–30, Sept. 13–Dec. 6, 20, 27, 1798.

Am. Antiq. Soc. has June 6, Sept. 26, Oct. 31, Nov. 9, 1797; Jan. 25, Apr. 26, June 7, Aug. 30, Oct. 26, Nov. 22, 28, Dec. 30, 1798.

Wis. Hist. Soc. has Mar. 28, May 9, 1797; May 24, 1798.

Mass. Hist. Soc. has Aug. 23, Sept. 20, 1798.

Boston Athenæum has Jan. 18, 1798.

[Dedham] Norfolk Repository, 1805–1809.

Weekly and semi-weekly. Established May 14, 1805, by Herman Mann, with the title of "The Norfolk Repository." It was an eight page quarto, paged, and had a title-page and index at least to vol. 1. It was suspended with the issue of Sept. 17, 1805, vol. 1, no. 19, because of the theft of a portion of its funds, and was resumed with the issue of Mar. 25, 1806, vol. 1, no. 20. With the issue of Sept. 20, 1808, it was reduced from eight to four pages. The weekly issue was discontinued with the issue of Nov. 29, 1808, and on Dec. 6, 1808, a semi-weekly issue was begun, with the title of "Norfolk Repository," which was continued until Dec. 27, 1808. On Jan. 5, 1809, the paper was brought out in folio size, with the title of "Norfolk Repository" and with a new volume numbering, and was "Printed by H. Mann for the Editor" [Titus Strong]. Discontinued with the issue of Dec. 28, 1809, vol. 1, no. 52.

Dedham Hist. Soc. has May 14, 1805–Dec. 28, 1809.
Boston Pub. Lib. has May 14, 1805–Nov. 29, 1808.
Am. Antiq. Soc. has May 14, 1805–Nov. 4, 1806; Sept. 22, Nov. 3–Dec. 29, 1807; Jan. 5–Dec. 20, 1808; Jan. 5, 12, 26, Feb. 2, Mar. 2, 9, 1809.
Harvard has May 14–July 30, Aug. 13–Sept. 17, 1805; Aug. 12, 26, Sept. 30, Oct. 23, 1806; Jan. 20, Feb. 25, Mar. 3, 24, 31, May 12–June 2, 30, Aug. 25–Sept. 15, Oct. 6, 13, Nov. 3, 1807; Aug. 2, 16, 23, Sept. 6, 13, Nov. 1, 1808.
Western Reserve Hist. Soc. has May 14–Sept. 17, 1805; Mar. 25–Nov. 4, 1806.
Lib. Congress has Nov. 11, 1806–Nov. 29, 1808.
Duke Univ. has Nov. 18, 1806–Nov. 3, 1807.
N. Y. Hist. Soc. has Jan. 5–Dec. 28, 1809.
Mass. Hist. Soc. has June 4, 1805; Oct. 27, Nov. 17, 24, Dec. 29, 1807; Jan. 12–Feb. 2, 16, 23, Mar. 8, 15, Apr. 26, May 31–June 21, July 19, 26, Sept. 6, 13, 1808; Oct. 5, 1809.
Wis. Hist. Soc. has Jan. 12, Feb. 9, 16, Mar. 2–16, Sept. 28, 1809.
Long Id. Hist. Soc. has Sept. 9, 1806.
Boston Athenæum has Mar. 8, 1808.

[Dedham] Village Register, 1820+.

Weekly. Established June 9, 1820, with the title of "Village Register, and Norfolk County Advertiser," printed for the Proprietor by H. & W. H. Mann [Herman Mann, Jr., and William H. Mann]. In his "Annals of Dedham," p. 76, H. Mann states that the first proprietor was Asa Gowen. With the issue of Oct. 27, 1820, it was printed by H. & W. H. Mann, for J[onathan] H. Cobb. Continued after 1820.

Am. Antiq. Soc. has June 9–Dec. 29, 1820.
Dedham Hist. Soc. has June 9–30, July 21–Dec. 29, 1820.
Lib. Congress has Sept. 15–Dec. 29, 1820.
Essex Inst. has Dec. 22, 1820.

MASSACHUSETTS 359

[Fairhaven] Bristol Gazette, 1812–1813.

Weekly. A continuation, without change of volume numbering, of the "New-Bedford Gazette," of New Bedford. The last known issue of the "New-Bedford Gazette" is that of July 17, 1812, vol. 1, no. 40, and the earliest known issue of the "Bristol Gazette" is that of July 31, 1812, vol. 1, no. 42, published by Joseph Gleason, Jun. With the issue of Feb. 19, 1813, Gleason disposed of the paper to Paul Taber. It was discontinued with the issue of July 10, 1813, vol. 2, no. 39.

Fairhaven, Millicent Lib. has July 31–Aug. 14, 28–Oct. 2, 16–Nov. 12, 26–Dec. 25, 1812; Jan. 1–15, Feb. 19, Mar. 5–May 21, June 4, 18–July 10, 1813.
New Bedford Pub. Lib. has July 31, Aug. 7, 20–Sept. 25, Oct. 9, 16, 1812; Jan. 8, 29, Feb. 26, Mar. 19, Apr. 2, 16, June 4, 1813.
Am. Antiq. Soc. has Aug. 7, 20, Oct. 23, Nov. 20, Dec. 18, 1812; May 14, 1813.
N. Y. Hist. Soc. has May 28–June 11, 1813.

[Greenfield] Franklin Federalist, 1817.

Weekly. Established May 24, 1817, by Russell Wells, with the title of "Franklin Federalist, and Religious, Scientific, and Literary Repository." The paper was discontinued with the issue of Dec. 29, 1817, vol. 1, no. 32, and was replaced two weeks later by "The Franklin Intelligencer," which see.

Greenfield Gazette Office has May 24–Dec. 29, 1817.
Pocumtuck Valley Mem. Assoc., Deerfield, has May 31–June 21, 1817.
Am. Antiq. Soc. has June 7, July 5, 26, Sept. 20, Dec. 22, 1817.
N. Y. Hist. Soc. has May 24, June 14, Dec. 15, 1817.
Lib. Congress has June 21, 1817.
Dartmouth has Dec. 15, 1817.
N. Y. Pub. Lib. has Dec. 22, 1817.

[Greenfield] Franklin Herald, 1812–1820+.

Weekly. A continuation, without change of volume numbering, of "The Traveller." The first issue with the title of "Franklin Herald" was that of Jan. 7, 1812, vol. 1, no. 48, published by Ansel Phelps. With the issue of May 12, 1812, Phelps took John Denio into partnership with him, under the firm name of Denio & Phelps. With the issue of Nov. 14, 1815, this partnership was dissolved and the paper published by Ansel Phelps. With the issue of June 3, 1817, the partnership of Denio & Phelps was again formed and so continued until after 1820.

Greenfield Pub. Lib. has the S. D. Conant file, Jan. 7, 1812–Dec. 26, 1820.
Harvard has Jan. 7, 1812–Jan. 5, 1813; Dec. 28, 1813–Dec. 26, 1820.
Am. Antiq. Soc. has Jan. 14, May 26, June 2, 23, July 14, 28, Aug. 18, Sept. 8, Oct. 6, Nov. 10, 24, Dec. 1, 22, 29, 1812; Jan. 19, Mar. 23, 30, May 4, July 27,

Oct. 5, 19, Nov. 16, Dec. 14, 21, 1813; Feb. 8, June 7, 14, Aug. 9, 30, 1814; Jan. 31, May 2, June 27, Aug. 1, 15, 29, Oct. 10, 24, Nov. 7, 14, Dec. 12, 1815; Jan. 30, Feb. 20, Mar. 5, 19, Apr. 16, May 21, Sept. 24, Oct. 29, Nov. 12, Dec. 24, 31, 1816; Mar. 18, 25, Apr. 8–29, June 3, 17, Aug. 12, Oct. 7, 21, 28, Dec. 23, 1817; Jan. 13, 20, Apr. 21, May 5, 26, July 28, Sept. 15–29, Nov. 10, 1818; Jan. 26–Feb. 23, Mar. 30, Apr. 20, 27, May 18, June 15, 22, Aug. 10, 24, Sept. 21, Nov. 2, Dec. 28, 1819; Jan. 4, 25, Feb. 8, 15, Mar. 28, Apr. 4, 18, 25, May 9, June 20, July 4, Sept. 5, 1820.

Lib. Congress has Jan. 7, 1812; Jan. 17, May 4, June 8, 15, Aug. 31, 1813; May 3, June 14, Nov. 29, 1814; Jan. 10, Mar. 14, 28, May 16, 30, July 4, 11, Aug. 1, 15–Sept. 19, Oct. 10, 24–Nov. 7, 21, Dec. 12, 1815; Jan. 2, 23, Feb. 13, Apr. 9, 23, May 7, 14, July 2, 9, 23, Oct. 6, 29, Nov. 12, Dec. 24, 1816; Jan. 21, Feb. 4–18, Apr. 3, May 20, 1817; Feb. 10–Mar. 3, 24, May 5–19, June 16, 23, July 14, Aug. 4, 18, Oct. 6, 27–Dec. 15, 1818; Jan. 19, 26, Feb. 16, Mar. 2, 16, 30, Apr. 13, 20, May 11–June 1, 15–July 6, 20–Aug. 17, Sept. 14, 28, Oct. 5, 26, Nov. 2, 23, 30, Dec. 14, 28, 1819; Jan. 4, 11, 25, Feb. 1, 29, Apr. 4–18, May 9–23, July 4, Aug. 15, 22, Sept. 5, 19, Oct. 10, 17, Nov. 7, 28, Dec. 19, 26, 1820.

Pocumtuck Valley Mem. Assoc., Deerfield, Mass. has Jan. 7, 28–Feb. 11, Apr. 4, 28, May 26, June 16–30, Nov. 10, 1812; Sept. 7, Oct. 12, 1813; Jan. 25, Mar. 1, June 7, 28, July 5, Aug. 23, 30, Sept. 20, Oct. 11, 25, Nov. 22, Dec. 13–27, 1814; Jan. 3–Sept. 12, 26, Oct. 10, Nov. 7, 14, 28, Dec. 12, 19, 1815; Jan. 9, 30, Feb. 13, Mar. 5–June 4, Oct. 1, 1816; Apr. 22, July 1, 1817; Jan. 27, Mar. 17, 24, May 26, July 7, 28, Aug. 11, 25, Oct. 6, 13, 1818; May 25, July 6, 13, 27, 1819; Jan. 4, Feb. 8, 1820.

N. Y. Hist. Soc. has Mar. 31, July 28, Oct. 6, Dec. 29, 1812; Jan. 26, Feb. 16, Mar. 23, Apr. 13, July 20, Aug. 24, 1813; Jan. 18, 25, July 5, Oct. 11, Nov. 15, 1814; July 11, Sept. 26, 1815; June 30, July 28, Oct. 27, 1818; Apr. 6, May 4, 18–June 8, July 20, 27, Aug. 17–Sept. 7, 21, Dec. 28, 1819; Sept. 5, 12, 1820.

Duke Univ. has Nov. 24, 1812; June 27, 1815; Apr. 8, Aug. 12, 1817; Sept. 22, 1818; Feb. 16, 1819.

Greenfield Gazette Office has Oct. 5, 1813; Apr. 26, July 5, 1814; Sept. 17, 1816.

Boston Athenæum has Dec. 28, 1813; Jan. 10, 1815.

Essex Inst. has Apr. 14, 1812.

Boston Pub. Lib. has Apr. 13, 1813.

N. Y. Pub. Lib. has Apr. 4, 1820.

[Greenfield] **Franklin Intelligencer,** 1818.

Weekly. Established Jan. 12, 1818, by Russell Wells, with the title of "The Franklin Intelligencer." Although published from the same office as its predecessor, the "Franklin Federalist," it was projected as a different paper with a new volume numbering. The last issue located, and probably the last published, was that of Mar. 23, 1818, vol. 1, no. 11.

MASSACHUSETTS 361

Greenfield Gazette Office has Jan. 12–Mar. 23, 1818.
Lib. Congress has Jan. 19, Mar. 9, 23, 1818.
Am. Antiq. Soc. has Jan. 19, 1818.

Greenfield Gazette, 1792–1811.

Weekly. A continuation, without change of volume numbering, of "The Impartial Intelligencer." The first issue of the "Greenfield Gazette" was that of Aug. 2, 1792, vol. 1, no. 27, published by Thomas Dickman. With the issue of Mar. 5, 1795, the title was changed to "Greenfield Gazette. Or, Massachusetts and Vermont Telegraphe"; and with the issue of Jan. 4, 1798, to "Greenfield Gazette. An Impartial Register of the Times." Dickman sold out to Francis Barker who began publishing the paper with the issue of Aug. 20, 1798, and who changed the title, with the issue of Sept. 1, 1798, to "Greenfield Gazette. A Register of Genuine Federalism." Thomas Dickman bought back the paper and again became publisher with the issue of June 17, 1799. With the issue of June 7, 1802, he sold out the paper to John Denio, who with this issue shortened the title to "Greenfield Gazette." Denio sold out the paper to Ansel Phelps, who changed the title to "The Traveller" with the issue of Feb. 12, 1811. The last issue with the title of "Greenfield Gazette" was that of Feb. 5, 1811, vol. 20, no. 2, whole no. 990.

Greenfield Pub. Lib. has the S. D. Conant file, Aug. 2, 1792–Feb. 5, 1811.
Am. Antiq. Soc. has Aug. 2–Nov. 1, 15–Dec. 6, 20, 27, 1792; Jan. 3–17, 31, Feb. 7–Mar. 28, Apr. 18, May 2–July 25, Aug. 8, Sept. 12, Nov. 28, Dec. 12, 26, 1793; Jan. 2–16, July 17, 31, Aug. 28, Sept. 11, 18, Oct. 9, 30, Nov. 13, 27, Dec. 18, 1794; Jan. 1, 29–Feb. 26, June 25, July 23, 30, Aug. 13, 27, Nov. 5–26, 1795; May 12–June 9, 23, Aug. 25, Sept. 8, 15, Oct. 6–Nov. 17, 1796; Jan. 26–Feb. 23, Mar. 9–30, Apr. 13, 20, May 11, June 15, 22, July 13, 20, Aug. 3–Sept. 28, Oct. 12, 26, Nov. 29, Dec. 21, 1797; Jan. 10–24, Feb. 7–June 25, July 9, 23, Oct. 13–Nov. 12, Dec. 3, 17, 24, 1798; Jan. 21, Feb. 25, Mar. 25, 1799; Jan. 11–Oct. 6, 1800; Jan. 9, Nov. 14, 1801; Apr. 12–Aug. 30, Sept. 13, Oct. 4–Dec. 27, 1802; Jan. 3–31, Feb. 14–Mar. 14, Apr. 18–May 16, June 13–27, July 11–Sept. 26, Oct. 10–Dec. 5, 19, 26, 1803; Jan. 2, 1804–May 15, 1809; Jan. 30, Mar. 13, Apr. 17, June 26, July 24, Sept. 25, 1810.
Pocumtuck Valley Mem. Assoc., Deerfield, Mass., has Sept. 27, Nov. 1, Dec. 6, 27, 1792; Jan. 10, Feb. 7, Apr. 10, Oct. 3, Nov. 28, 1793; Jan. 30–Apr. 24, May 8, July 31–Dec. 25, 1794; Jan. 1–22, Dec. 17, 24, 1795; Jan. 7–Dec. 29, 1796; Jan. 5–19, July 27, Sept. 21–Dec. 28, 1797; Jan. 4, 17, Feb. 28, Aug. 20, Dec. 17, 1798; July 29, 1800; Jan. 16, 1801; Mar. 8, June 28, Dec. 6, 13, 1802; Jan. 10, Feb. 21, 28, Apr. 4, June 20, 1803; Jan. 30, Apr. 9, Oct. 22, 1804; Jan. 28–Dec. 30, 1805; Jan. 6–20, Feb. 3, 24, July 14, 1806; Oct. 5, 12, 26, 1807; Feb. 22, July 25, Nov. 21, 1808; Jan. 23, June 26, Nov. 28, 1809.
Harvard has Feb. 18, 26, May 21, June 18, 25, July 16–30, Oct. 8, Nov. 18,

1795; Mar. 10, 17, Apr. 14, May 12, 26, June 9, 16, July 14, Sept. 1, Oct. 27, Nov. 10, Dec. 22, 29, 1796; Feb. 2, 23, Mar. 16, May 25, June 15, 22, July 13, Aug. 10, 24–Sept. 7, 28, Oct. 5, Nov. 23, 29, Dec. 14, 21, 1797; Jan. 4, 10, 24, Feb. 28, Mar. 14, Apr. 11, 25, June 4, Aug. 20–Sept. 1, Oct. 6, 27, Dec. 10, 1798; Jan. 28, Feb. 25, Mar. 11, Apr. 22, 29, June 3, 10, 24, July 20–Sept. 14, 28, Oct. 5, 19–Nov. 2, Dec. 14, 1799; Jan. 11, 25, Aug. 16, Nov. 14, 21, Dec. 5, 1800; Jan. 4, 1808–Feb. 5, 1811.

Duke Univ. has Aug. 9, 30–Oct. 18, 1792; Feb. 4, 11, Mar. 10, June 2, Sept. 21, 1796; Jan. 5, 12, Mar. 2, 9, June 29, July 13, 20, Nov. 29, 1797; Nov. 3, 1798; Mar. 25, May 6, Aug. 21, Oct. 12, 1799; Mar. 28, Apr. 11, May 2, June 14, Aug. 30, Oct. 6, 31–Dec. 26, 1800; Jan. 2, 9, Feb. 13, 1801; June 14, 21, July 12, 1802; Apr. 4, May 9, Aug. 22, Sept. 12, Dec. 12, 19, 1803; Jan. 2, 9, Mar. 5–19, Apr. 16, 30, June 18, July 9, Sept. 24, Nov. 12, 19, 1804; Jan. 7, Feb. 4, Mar. 18, May 27, June 10, July 8, Nov. 18, Dec. 9, 1805; Mar. 3, Apr. 21, May 5, June 2, 9, 30, Dec. 8, 1806; Apr. 20, June 29, July 13, 27, Aug. 31, Nov. 9, Dec. 7, 1807; Feb. 8, May 2, 23, 30, June 13, July 11, Oct. 3, Nov. 21, 1808; Feb. 6, Mar. 13, 27, June 19, Aug. 28, 1809; Feb. 6, Mar. 27, June 5, July 3, Aug. 7, 21, Sept. 4, Oct. 2, 1810.

Lib. Congress has Apr. 18, 1793; May 12, 1796; Aug. 10, 17, Sept. 7, 1797; Jan. 4, 1800; Jan. 23, 1801; Mar. 7, Dec. 19, 1803; Jan. 2–Dec. 3, 1804, fair; June 29, Aug. 28, Oct. 30, Dec. 21, 1807; Apr. 18, 25, May 30, 1808; Jan. 29, 1811.

N. Y. Hist. Soc. has Sept. 26, Nov. 14, 28, 1803; Mar. 19, Apr. 2, May 7, Oct. 15, Nov. 26, 1804; Jan. 21, Apr. 15, 22, May 13, July 8, Aug. 12, 1805; Jan. 27, 1806; Apr. 27, July 6, 1807; Jan. 18, Mar. 7, 28, Aug. 15, 1808; Apr. 1, Dec. 26, 1809; Jan. 23, Sept. 25, 1810.

Greenfield Gazette Office has Oct. 31, Dec. 12, 26, 1803; Jan. 9, 16, Nov. 19, Dec. 17, 1804; May 9, 1808; Nov. 14, 1809; Apr. 10–24; May 27, 31, July 3, 17, Sept. 11, Nov. 27, Dec. 18, 1810.

Wis. Hist. Soc. has Aug. 14, Sept. 3, 10, 1794; Aug. 15, 1808.

N. Y. Pub. Lib. has July 28, 1796; Aug. 9, 1800; Oct. 25, 1802.

Rutgers Univ. has Jan. 3, 1793.

Conn. Hist. Soc. has Dec. 28, 1799.

Boston Pub. Lib. has Apr. 21, 1806.

Mass. Hist. Soc. has May 5, 1806.

Buffalo Pub. Lib. has Sept. 4, 1809.

[Greenfield] **Impartial Intelligencer,** 1792.

Weekly. Established Feb. 1, 1792, by Thomas Dickman, with the title of "The Impartial Intelligencer." The last issue with this title was that of July 26, 1792, vol. 1, no. 26, and with the issue of Aug. 2, 1792, the title was changed to "Greenfield Gazette," which see.

Greenfield Pub. Lib. has Feb. 8–July 26, 1792.
Am. Antiq. Soc. has Feb. 1, 8, Mar. 7–28, Apr. 12–25, May 9–June 6, 20, 27, July 12–26, 1792.
Pocumtuck Valley Mem. Assoc., Deerfield, has Feb. 29, Apr. 25, May 9, June 13, July 26, 1792.
Mass. Hist. Soc. has Feb. 8, 29, Mar. 21, Apr. 4, 1792.
Wis. Hist. Soc. has June 20, 1792.

[Greenfield] Traveller, 1811.

Weekly. A continuation, but with a new volume numbering, of the "Greenfield Gazette." The first issue of "The Traveller" was that of Feb. 12, 1811, vol. 1, no. 1, published by Ansel Phelps. Phelps retained this title until Dec. 31, 1811, vol. 1, no. 47, and with the issue of Jan. 7, 1812, changed it to "Franklin Herald," which see.

Greenfield Pub. Lib. and Harvard have Feb. 12–Dec. 31, 1811.
Am. Antiq. Soc. has Feb. 19–Mar. 12, Oct. 1, 29, Dec. 17, 1811.
Pocumtuck Valley Mem. Assoc., Deerfield, has June 18–Aug. 13, Dec. 24, 1811.
Los Angeles Museum Lib. has Oct. 15, 1811.

[Haverhill] Essex Patriot, 1817–1820+.

Weekly. Established May 10, 1817, by P[eter] N. Green with the title of "Essex Patriot." With the issue of Dec. 23, 1820, Green disposed of the paper to W[illiam] Hastings, who continued publication until after 1820.

Boston Athenæum has May 10, 1817–Dec. 30, 1820.
Haverhill Pub. Lib. has May 17, 1817–Feb. 21, 1818; Mar. 14–Apr. 4, 18, 25, May 23, 30, June 13, 27, July 4, Aug. 1, Oct. 17, Nov. 14, Dec. 12, 1818; Jan. 30, Feb. 6, 20, 27, Apr. 3, May 1, 1819; Jan. 8, 29, Mar. 18, Apr. 1, 22, Aug. 5, 26, Oct. 7, 1820.
Am. Antiq. Soc. has May 10, 24, June 14, 28–Aug. 2, 30–Oct. 4, 18, Nov. 8–22, Dec. 20, 1817; Jan. 3, 10, 31, Feb. 7, Mar. 14, May 2, June 6, Oct. 31, Nov. 21, 1818; Apr. 3, May 22, June 12, Aug. 7, 14, 28–Nov. 27, Dec. 11–25, 1819; Jan. 1–Feb. 5, Apr. 29, May 6, Dec. 9, 16, 1820.
Essex Inst. has May 17, 31–June 14, July 5, 12, 26, Aug. 9, 23–Dec. 6, 20, 27, 1817; Jan. 3–Feb. 21, Mar. 7, 21, May 9, Dec. 12, 1818; Apr. 3, May 15, Aug. 7, Oct. 23, 1819; Jan. 1, June 24, 1820.
Georgetown, Mass., Peabody Lib. has May 15, 1819–Dec. 30, 1820.
Haverhill Hist. Soc. has May 17, Sept. 13, Oct. 18, Nov. 8, 1817; Jan. 10, May 30, 1818; June 6, 1819; May 27, 1820.
Lib. Congress has July 12, Aug. 30, 1817.

Haverhill Federal Gazette, 1798–1799.

Weekly. Established Oct. 26, 1798, by Seth H. Moore & Chester Stebbins, who announce in the first issue that they have purchased from Angier March the "copyright" of the Impartial Herald, and that the "publication will be continued by them, under the title of the 'Haverhill Federal Gazette.'" In the title, the word "Federal" was placed in an ornament in the center and was in much smaller type. The paper was discontinued with the issue of Nov. 27, 1799, vol. 2, no. 6.

Mass. Hist. Soc. has Oct. 26, 1798–Oct. 25, Nov. 15, 27, 1799.

N. Y. Hist. Soc. has Dec. 28, 1798; Jan. 4–June 21, July 4–25, Aug. 8–Nov. 1, 15–27, 1799.

Am. Antiq. Soc. has Nov. 9–Dec. 14, 28, 1798; Jan. 4, 25, Feb. 15–Mar. 8, Apr. 12, May 24–July 25, Aug. 8, Sept. 5–Oct. 3, 1799.

Harvard has Oct. 26, Nov. 2, 1798; July 4, 18, Aug. 8–29, Sept. 19, 26, Nov. 20, 1799.

Essex Inst. has Nov. 2, 16, Dec. 7, 14, 1798; Jan. 4, 18, Feb. 1, Sept. 26, Nov. 1, 1799.

Haverhill Pub. Lib. has Nov. 23, Dec. 14, 1798; Mar. 1, Oct. 10, 1799.

Lib. Congress has Feb. 8, Sept. 12, 1799.

Duke Univ. has July 11, 1799.

Haverhill Gazette, see **Haverhill Federal Gazette.**

[Haverhill] Guardian of Freedom, 1793–1795.

Weekly. Established Sept. 16, 1793, by E. Ladd and S. Bragg [Eliphalet Ladd and Samuel Bragg], with the title of "Guardian of Freedom." With the issue of Apr. 3, 1794, the paper was published by Eliphalet Ladd. Ladd sold the paper to Samuel Aiken, who began publishing it with the issue of May 29, 1794, but transferred it to Benjamin Edes, jun., with the issue of June 26, 1794. The last issue located is that of Nov. 5, 1795, vol. 3, no. 7.

Am. Antiq. Soc. has Sept. 16, 20, Oct. 11–Nov. 18, Dec. 5–26, 1793; Jan. 9, Feb. 13, Mar. 6–Apr. 17, May 1–22, June 5–19, July 3, 10, Aug. 7, 14, Sept. 18, Oct. 9, Nov. 13, 21, Dec. 25, 1794; Jan. 22, Feb. 19, Apr. 3, 23, May 7, 21, June 11, July 16, Aug. 6–27, 1795.

Haverhill Pub. Lib. has Sept. 16–Oct. 4, 25–Dec. 26, 1793; Jan. 2–Feb. 20, Mar. 13–Sept. 18, Oct. 9, 1794; Aug. 20, 1795.

Mass. Hist. Soc. has Jan. 8, 22–Mar. 12, 26, Apr. 3, 16, 30–May 21, June 11–July 2, 16–Aug. 27, Sept. 10–Oct. 8, 22–Nov. 6, 1795; and "New-Years Verse" of Jan. 1, 1795.

N. Y. Hist. Soc. has June 25–Oct. 1, 22–Nov. 5, 1795.

Lib. Congress has Oct. 11, 1793; Feb. 13, Nov. 6, 1794; Aug. 13, 1795.

MASSACHUSETTS 365

Harvard has Mar. 12, Apr. 16, Aug. 6, 1795.
Essex Inst. has Oct. 25, 1793; July 9, 1795.

[Haverhill] **Impartial Herald,** 1798.

Weekly. Established July 27, 1798, by Angier March, with the title of "Impartial Herald." It was discontinued with the issue of Oct. 19, 1798, vol. 1, no. 13, the establishment being succeeded by the "Haverhill Federal Gazette," which see.

Am. Antiq. Soc. has Aug. 17–Sept. 7, 21–Oct. 19, 1798.
Essex Inst. has July 27, Aug. 31, Sept. 28, 1798.
Harvard has Aug. 3, 31, Sept. 7, 1798.
Haverhill Pub. Lib. has Sept. 28, Oct. 12, 19, 1798.
Lib. Congress has Sept. 14, 21, 1798.

[Haverhill] **Merrimack Intelligencer,** 1808–1817.

Weekly. Established July 2, 1808, by William B. Allen with the title of "Merrimack Intelligencer." With the issue of Feb. 29, 1812, William B. Allen took his brother Horatio into partnership under the firm name of W. B. & H. G. Allen. With the issue of Aug. 28, 1813, the firm was dissolved and the paper published by Horatio G. Allen. With the issue of Jan. 1, 1814, Allen sold out to Greenough and Burrill [William Greenough and Nathan Burrill]. With the issue of Nov. 5, 1814, Greenough retired in favor of Thomas Tileston, who published the paper under the firm name of Burrill and Tileston. With the issue of Jan. 4, 1817, they disposed of the paper to P[eter] N. Green, who discontinued publication with the issue of Feb. 8, 1817, vol. 9, no. 31.

Haverhill Pub. Lib. has July 2, 1808–Dec. 30, 1815; Apr. 27, Sept. 14, 1816.
Boston Athenæum has Sept. 3, 10, 1808; Sept. 23, 1809; June 2, 1810–Feb. 8, 1817.
Essex Inst. has July 2, 1808–Dec. 30, 1809, fair; Jan. 6, 1810–June 25, 1814, good; July 30, Oct. 1, Nov. 26, 1814; Mar. 4, 25, May 13, Sept. 2–Nov. 11, 1815.
Am. Antiq. Soc. has July 23, 30, Sept. 3, Nov. 26, 1808; Jan. 21, 29, May 27, July 15–Sept. 2, Nov. 25, Dec. 9–30, 1809; Jan. 6–27, Feb. 10–Oct. 27, Nov. 10–Dec. 29, 1810; Jan. 5, 12, Mar. 2–June 15, 29–July 13, 27, Aug. 10, 31, Sept. 7, 28, Oct. 12, Nov. 16–Dec. 7, 21, 28, 1811; Feb. 1, Apr. 11, May 2, July 4, Nov. 28, Dec. 19, 1812; Jan. 2–Mar. 6, 20–May 8, 22–Sept. 25, Oct. 9–30, Nov. 13, 20, Dec. 4, 18, 1813; Jan. 1–15, Feb. 12–May 14, 28, June 11, 1814; Sept. 9, Oct. 21, 1815; Jan. 6, Mar. 9, May 4, 25, July 20, Aug. 10, 17, 31, Sept. 7, 21–Dec. 7, 21, 28, 1816; Jan. 4, 1817.
Haverhill Hist. Soc. has July 30, 1808; Apr. 1, May 20, Aug. 5, 12, Dec. 9, 1809; Jan. 20–Oct. 27, 1810, fair; Mar. 2–16, May 18–June 1, 15, 1811; Apr. 11,

May 2, 1812; Jan. 23–Nov. 20, 1813, fair; Jan. 8, Mar. 12, 19, Apr. 2–16, 30, July 16, 23, Aug. 6, 13, Sept. 3–Oct. 15, Nov. 5, 12, 26, Dec. 3, 24, 1814; Jan. 14–Feb. 18, Mar. 25, July 29–Sept. 9, 1815; Feb. 3–Apr. 6, 1816.

Lib. Congress has Dec. 9, 1809; Jan. 20, Apr. 14, May 19, June 30, July 7, Aug. 18, 1810; Sept. 7, 1811; Jan. 4–May 23, June 6–Oct. 17, Nov. 7, 14, 1812; Jan. 23, Feb. 27, Mar. 7, Apr. 17, May 29, June 26, July 24, 31, Aug. 14, 1813; May 4, 1816.

Harvard has Aug. 13, 20, Sept. 3, 24–Oct. 8, 22, Nov. 12, 19, Dec. 10, 24, 1808.

N. Y. Hist. Soc. has Jan. 5, 1811; Aug. 24, 31, 1816.

Haverhill Museum, 1804–1806.

Weekly. Established Dec. 4, 1804, by Francis Gould, with the title of "Haverhill Museum." Gould had bought out the "Haverhill Observer" and continued the advertisements from that paper. Discontinued with the issue of Nov. 22, 1806, vol. 2, no. 52.

Harvard has Dec. 11–25, 1804; Jan. 1–Feb. 5, 19, Mar. 5, 12, 26–Apr. 9, 23, May 7–28, June 11, July 2, 16, 23, Aug. 6–Sept. 17, Oct. 1–Nov. 26, Dec. 10, 17, 31, 1805; Jan. 14, 21, Feb. 4–25, Mar. 11, 25, Apr. 29, May 13, 20, June 17, July 8, 1806.

Haverhill Pub. Lib. has Feb. 5, 12, Mar. 5, 19, 26, Apr. 30, June 11, 18, July 2–Aug. 13, 27, Sept. 10, 17, Oct. 15, Dec. 3–17, 1805; Feb. 4, 11, 25, Mar. 11, 18, Apr. 15–May 13, June 3–July 1, 15–Sept. 16, 30–Oct. 21, Nov. 4, 15, 22, 1806.

Essex Inst. has Dec. 11, 1804; Apr. 2, 16, Oct. 29, 1805; May 20–June 3, July 22, 29, Aug. 12, Nov. 11, 15, 1806.

Am. Antiq. Soc. has Jan. 8, Feb. 19, 26, 1805; Feb. 25, Mar. 18, July 22, Sept. 2, Oct. 21, Nov. 4, 1806.

Haverhill Hist. Soc. has Feb. 19, 1805.

Univ. of Ill. has July 9, 1805.

Boston Athenæum has Oct. 28, 1806.

[Haverhill] Observer, 1800–1804.

Weekly. Established Dec. 5, 1800, by Galen H. Fay, with the title of "The Observer." With the issue of Jan. 7, 1803, the title was changed to "Haverhill Observer." The paper was discontinued Nov. 27, 1804, vol. 4, no. 52, in which issue Fay announced the sale of the paper to Francis Gould. Gould established the "Haverhill Museum" in its place.

Lib. Congress has Dec. 5, 1800–Nov. 27, 1801.

Harvard has Dec. 19, 1800; Jan. 2–16, 30–Feb. 13, Mar. 6, Apr. 17, May 8, 15, 29–June 12, 26, July 10, 24, Sept. 4, 25–Oct. 9, 23, 30, Nov. 13, 20, Dec. 18, 1801; Jan. 1, 8, Feb. 5, Mar. 26, Apr. 2, 16, June 25, July 9, Aug. 20–

MASSACHUSETTS 367

Sept. 3, 24, Oct. 8–22, Nov. 19–Dec. 3, 17–31, 1802; Jan. 7–Feb. 25, Mar. 11, 25–May 13, 27, June 24–July 15, 29, Aug. 5, 19–Sept. 30, Oct. 25–Nov. 22, Dec. 13, 1803; Jan. 10, 24–Feb. 7, 28–Mar. 20, Apr. 3, 17–May 8, 22, July 10–Aug. 14, Sept. 4–25, Nov. 13, 20, 1804.
Haverhill Pub. Lib. has Feb. 13, May 22, 1801; Jan. 1, Mar. 5, May 28, Nov. 19, 1802; Jan. 8–Feb. 11, 25, Mar. 18, 25, Apr. 15, May 27, July 22, Aug. 19, Sept. 23, 30, Nov. 15, 29–Dec. 13, 1803; Jan. 24–Nov. 27, 1804.
Essex Inst. has July 3, Dec. 4, 1801; Mar. 19, Sept. 3, Oct. 1, 1802; May 20, June 3, Sept. 30, Nov. 1, 8, 22, 29, Dec. 13, 20, 1803; Jan. 10, 17, Feb. 7, 28, Mar. 13, 27–Apr. 10, 24, May 1, June 5, 19–July 17, 31, Aug. 21, 28, Sept. 18, 25, Oct. 16–Nov. 20, 1804.
Am. Antiq. Soc. has Dec. 12, 19, 1800; Feb. 27, Sept. 11, 25, Nov. 20, 1801; Jan. 8, 15, Feb. 5–19, Mar. 26, Apr. 9, Sept. 24, Dec. 31, 1802; Feb. 4, Aug. 26–Sept. 9, 1803; Jan. 24, Feb. 28, Mar. 13, 20, June 12, Sept. 18, 1804.
Haverhill Hist. Soc. has Aug. 21, 28, 1801; Apr. 22, May 20, 1803.
N. Y. Pub. Lib. has May 13, 1803.

[Lenox] **Watch Light,** 1808–1809.

Weekly. Established in September, 1808, judging from the earliest issue located, that of Mar. 27, 1809, vol. 1, no. 29, the "Watch Light," published by Eldad Lewis. The last issue noted is that of May 22, 1809, vol. 1, no. 37.

Am. Antiq. Soc. has Mar. 27, May 15, 1809.
Robert C. Rockwell, Pittsfield, who died 1928, had May 22, 1809, now not located.

[Leominster] **Political Focus,** 1798–1799.

Weekly. Established July 5, 1798, by Charles & John Prentiss. With the issue of Mar. 7, 1799, the paper was published by Charles Prentiss alone. The last issue located is that of Dec. 5, 1799, vol. 2, no. 75.

Am. Antiq. Soc. has July 26–Dec. 27, 1798; Jan. 3–Mar. 21, Apr. 4–May 16, 30–June 20, July 4–18, Aug. 1, 15–Nov. 14, 28, Dec. 5, 1799.
Harvard has July 26, Sept. 6, 13, Nov. 15, 29, 1798; Jan. 17, Feb. 14–28, Mar. 14–28, Apr. 11, 18, May 2–23, June 13–July 4, 25–Sept. 26, Oct. 17–Dec. 5, 1799.
Mass. Hist. Soc. has July 12, 26, Aug. 16, Nov. 8, 1798; Apr. 25, May 30–June 13, July 4, 25, Aug. 15–Sept. 5, 19–Oct. 3, 31–Nov. 14, 28, 1799.
Boston Pub. Lib. has Nov. 29–Dec. 20, 1798; Jan. 3–24, Feb. 7, 14, Mar. 14, 21, Apr. 11, May 2, 9, 30, Aug. 29, 1799.
Leominster Pub. Lib. has Sept. 6, 1798; Apr. 18, 1799.
N. Y. State Lib. has Aug. 1, 1799.

[Leominster] **Political Recorder,** 1809–1810.

Weekly. Established in July, 1809, judging from the date of the earliest issue located, that of Mar. 15, 1810, vol. 1, no. 36, with the title of "Political Recorder," published by Salmon Wilder. Discontinued with the issue of July 19, 1810. (See "Leominster Enterprise," June 4, 1873, quoting copy owned by James Bennett.)

Am. Antiq. Soc. has Mar. 22, July 5, 1810.
Leominster Pub. Lib. has Mar. 15, 1810.
Fred E. Bushey, Keene, N. H., has Mar. 29, 1810.

[Leominster] **Rural Repository,** 1795–1797.

Weekly. Established Oct. 22, 1795, by Charles Prentiss with the title of "The Rural Repository." It was discontinued with the issue of Apr. 13, 1797, vol. 2, no. 78.

Am. Antiq. Soc. has Oct. 22–Dec. 31, 1795; Jan. 7–Nov. 17, Dec. 22, 1796; Jan. 19–Mar. 2, 16–Apr. 13, 1797.
Leominster Pub. Lib. has Oct. 22, 1795–Oct. 13, 1796.
Harvard has Dec. 10, 17, 31, 1795; Feb. 11, 18, Mar. 17, 24, Apr. 14–28, May 12, 26, June 9–23, July 7–Sept. 29, Oct. 13–27, Nov. 10–Dec. 8, 22, 29, 1796; Jan. 5–26, Feb. 23–Apr. 6, 1797.
Boston Pub. Lib. has Nov. 19, 1795; Feb. 25, Apr. 14, May 12, 26, June 16, 30, Sept. 15, 22, Oct. 6, 13, 1796.
Lib. Congress has Nov. 12, 19, Dec. 3, 10, 24, 31, 1795; Jan. 14, Mar. 17, 24, 1796.
Phil. Lib. Co. has Nov. 12, Dec. 3, 1796.
Mass. Hist. Soc. has Mar. 31, 1796.
Boston Athenæum has Sept. 8, Oct. 13, 1796.

[Leominster] **Telescope,** 1800–1802.

Weekly. Established Jan. 2, 1800, by Adams & Wilder [Daniel Adams and Salmon Wilder], with the title of "The Telescope: or, American Herald." The paper was discontinued with the issue of Oct. 14, 1802, vol. 3, no. 146.

Am. Antiq. Soc. has Jan. 2–23, Feb. 6–Dec. 25, 1800; Jan. 1–Dec. 24, 1801; Jan. 7–Mar. 11, 25, Apr. 1, 15–May 6, 20–June 10, 24–Sept. 16, Oct. 7, 14, 1802.
Harvard has Jan. 23–Feb. 13, 27, Mar. 6, 20–Apr. 10, 24–May 15, June 5–26, July 10, 24, 31, Aug. 14–Dec. 25, 1800; Jan. 1–Feb. 26, Mar. 12–May 28, June 11–Nov. 26, Dec. 17–31, 1801; Jan. 7–Feb. 4, 18–Mar. 18, Apr. 8–May 27, June 10–Aug. 12, 26–Sept. 30, Oct. 14, 1802.
Leominster Pub. Lib. has Feb. 20–Nov. 27, 1800; Mar. 12, Apr. 9, 23–May 7, Aug. 27, Dec. 10, 1801; Apr. 1, 1802.

Mass. Hist. Soc. has May 15, 29–June 19, July 3–31, Aug. 21–Nov. 6, 1800.
Conn. Hist. Soc. has Jan. 9, 23–Apr. 17, May 15, 22, June 5, 12, July 3, Nov. 6, 1800; July 9, 1801.
Dartmouth has Oct. 1–Dec. 31, 1801.
Essex Inst. has May 7, 1801.

[Leominster] Weekly Messenger, 1806.

Weekly. Established Jan. 23, 1806, judging from the date of the earliest issue located, that of Feb. 6, 1806, vol. 1, no. 3, "The Weekly Messenger, and Farmer's Moral and Political Monitor," published by Salmon & James Wilder. The last issue located is that of Dec. 18, 1806, vol. 1, no. 48.

Dartmouth has Feb. 6, 13, 27–May 15, 1806.
Am. Antiq. Soc. has Feb. 20, Mar. 6, 13, Oct. 23, 30, Dec. 18, 1806.
Leominster Pub. Lib. has Mar. 13, Aug. 28, 1806.
Harvard has Apr. 24, 1806.

Nantucket Gazette, 1816–1817.

Weekly. Established May 6, 1816, by Tannatt & Tupper [Abraham G. Tannatt and Hiram Tupper], with the title of "Nantucket Gazette." With the issue of Oct. 12, 1816, the firm was dissolved and the paper published by A. G. Tannatt. It was discontinued with the issue of Mar. 8, 1817, vol. 1, no. 41. The file in the Boston Public Library was that owned by Lewis G. Pray, a frequent contributor, whose articles are signed in his handwriting.

Boston Pub. Lib. has May 6, 1816–Mar. 8, 1817.
Nantucket Athenæum has May 6, 1816–Feb. 1, 1817.
Am. Antiq. Soc. has May 6–June 3, 24–July 29, Aug. 10, 17, 31–Sept. 21, Oct. 5–Nov. 2, 16–Dec. 14, 28, 1816; Jan. 25–Mar. 1, 1817.
Lib. Congress has Aug. 3, 1816.
Essex Inst. has Sept. 7, 1816.

Nantucket Weekly Magazine, 1817–1818.

Weekly. Established June 28, 1817, by A[braham] G. Tannatt, with the title of "Nantucket Weekly Magazine: Literary and Commercial." It was of quarto size and paged, and although a magazine in name could well be included as a newpaper. It was discontinued with the issue of Jan. 3, 1818, vol. 1, no. 27.

Boston Pub. Lib. has June 28, 1817–Jan. 3, 1818.
Nantucket Athenæum has July 5, 1817–Jan. 3, 1818.
Am. Antiq. Soc. has Sept. 13, 27, Oct. 25, 1817.

[New Bedford] Columbian Courier, 1798–1805.

Weekly. Established Dec. 8, 1798, by Abraham Shearman, Jun., with the title of "Columbian Courier." With the issue of Dec. 3, 1802, the title was changed to "Columbian Courier, and Weekly Miscellany"; and with that of Dec. 2, 1803, to "Columbian Courier, or Weekly Miscellany." Discontinued with the issue of Mar. 1, 1805, vol. 7, no. 13.

> New Bedford Pub. Lib. has Dec. 8, 1798–Dec. 31, 1802; Jan. 7, 1803–Feb. 22, 1805, fair.
> Harvard has July 3, 1799; Jan. 3, 1800–Mar. 1, 1805, fair.
> Am. Antiq. Soc. has Dec. 15–29, 1798; Jan. 26, Feb. 23, Mar. 2, 23–Apr. 6, June 12, Nov. 22, 1799; Mar. 14, June 20, Sept. 26, Dec. 5, 19, 26, 1800; Jan. 2, 23, 30, Feb. 13, Mar. 13, 27, May 8–June 5, July 3–17, 31, Aug. 7, 21, 28, Sept. 18, Oct. 9, 23–Nov. 13, 27, Dec. 18, 1801; Jan. 1–Mar. 5, 19, Apr. 9–30, May 14–June 11, 25–Sept. 3, 17–Oct. 15, Nov. 19, Dec. 3–31, 1802; Jan. 7, 1803–Dec. 28, 1804; Jan. 4–Mar. 1, 1805.
> N. Y. Hist. Soc. has Dec. 15–29, 1798; Jan. 5–Apr. 13, May 4–June 12, 26–July 10, 24–Sept. 18, Oct. 2–Nov. 1, 15, 1799; Mar. 13, May 29, July 3, Dec. 11, 18, 1801; Dec. 17, 1802; Apr. 1, 1803.
> Lib. Congress has Mar. 30, 1799; Jan. 23, 1801; Jan. 8–Feb. 12, 26–Mar. 12, 26–May 21, June 11, 18, July 2, 30, Aug. 27, Sept. 3–17, Oct. 8, 22, Nov. 19, 26, Dec. 10–31, 1802; Jan. 7, 1803.
> N. J. Hist. Soc. has Dec. 6, 1799; May 8, 1801; Aug. 20, Sept. 10, Oct. 8–22, Nov. 5–26, Dec. 10, 17, 1802; Jan. 14, 21, Feb. 11, Mar. 4, 25–Apr. 8, 22, May 6–June 10, July 1–15, 29–Sept. 16, 30, Oct. 7, 21–Dec. 2, 16, 1803; Mar. 30, 1804.
> Duke Univ. has Feb. 25, Mar. 4, Apr. 15, May 27, June 17, 24, July 8, Aug. 5, 19–Sept. 2, Nov. 4, 25, Dec. 2, 1803; Feb. 17, 24, Mar. 9, Apr. 27, July 13, Aug. 10, 31, Oct. 12, Dec. 21, 28, 1804; Jan. 18, Feb. 15–Mar. 1, 1805.
> N. Y. Pub. Lib. has Dec. 2, 1803; Nov. 2, Dec. 14, 1804.
> Old Dartmouth Hist. Soc. has Mar. 7, 1800.
> Long Id. Hist. Soc. has Jan. 23, 1801.

New-Bedford Gazette, 1811–1812.

Weekly. Established Oct. 18, 1811, by Joseph Gleason, jun., with the title of "New-Bedford Gazette." The paper was really a continuation of the "Old Colony Gazette," but with a new volume numbering. The last located issue of the "New-Bedford Gazette" was that of July 17, 1812, vol. 1, no. 40, and within a fortnight the paper was removed to Fairhaven, where it was published as the "Bristol Gazette," which see.

> New Bedford Pub. Lib. has Oct. 18, 1811–July 17, 1812.
> Am. Antiq. Soc. has Oct. 18–Nov. 15, 29, Dec. 13, 1811; Jan. 3. Feb. 21, 28, Mar. 20, May 1, June 12, 26, July 3, 1812.

MASSACHUSETTS 371

N. Y. Hist. Soc. has Nov. 29, 1811; Apr. 24, July 10, 17, 1812.
Lib. Congress has Feb. 24, 1812.
Mass. Hist. Soc. has July 10, 1812.

[New Bedford] Medley, 1792–1799.

Weekly. Established Nov. 27, 1792, by John Spooner, with the title of "The Medley or Newbedford Marine Journal," and so continued until the last issue, that of Oct. 18, 1799, vol. 7, no. 52.

Am. Antiq. Soc. has Dec. 8, 22, 29, 1792; Jan. 5–Mar. 2, 16–Apr. 20, May 3, 24, Nov. 15, 18, 25–Dec. 30, 1793; Jan. 6, 1794–Oct. 18, 1799.
New Bedford Pub. Lib. has Nov. 27, 1792–Nov. 21, 1794; Feb. 13, May 8–Oct. 30, 1795; Nov. 11, 18, Dec. 23, 1796; Jan. 6, Feb. 17, Mar. 31–Oct. 27, 1797; Sept. 14, 1798.
Old Dartmouth Hist. Soc. has Nov. 27, 1792–Oct. 31, 1794.
Duke Univ. has Nov. 18, Dec. 2, 23, 1793; Jan. 13–27, Mar. 10, Apr. 14, May 19, June 2, 9, Sept. 22, 1794; Jan. 2, Feb. 6, 13, 27, Mar. 27–Apr. 10, 24–May 8, June 19, 26, July 31, Aug. 7, 21, Nov. 6, 13, Dec. 18, 1795; Apr. 15, May 20, 27, June 10, July 1–15, 29, Oct. 21, Nov. 4, Dec. 2, 1796; Jan. 13–Feb. 3, 17–Mar. 10, 23–Apr. 28, May 12–26, June 30, July 14, 28, Aug. 11, 18, Sept. 8, 22, Oct. 13–Nov. 3, 17, Dec. 1–15, 29, 1797; Jan. 5–19, Feb. 9–Mar. 2, Apr. 6, 13, 27–June 1, 15, Sept. 7, Nov. 16–Dec. 7, 21, 28, 1798; Jan. 18, 25, Feb. 15, Apr. 5, July 19, Aug. 2, 1799.
Harvard has Feb. 13, 20, Mar. 20, May 22–June 12, 26, July 3, 17–Aug. 7, Sept. 5, Oct. 2, Dec. 18, 1795; Jan. 1, Feb. 6, 26, Aug. 5, 1796; Jan. 5, Feb. 3, Apr. 7, 21, June 2–16, July 14, Sept. 22, Oct. 6, Nov. 3, 17, Dec. 1–22, 1797; Jan. 12, 19, Feb. 2–23, Apr. 6–20, May 18–June 1, 15, 22, July 6, 20, 27, Aug. 17–31, Sept. 14, Oct. 26–Nov. 9, 30, Dec. 14, 1798; Jan. 11, 25, Feb. 15, 22–Mar. 29, Apr. 12, 19, May 3, 10, 24, June 21, July 19, Aug. 9–Sept. 6, 20, 1799.
N. Y. Pub. Lib. has Dec. 29, 1792; Nov. 18, 1793; Mar. 17, Apr. 14, 1794; June 3, 1796.
Lib. Congress has June 2, Oct. 24, 1794; Feb. 23, 1797; Aug. 2, 1799.
Mass. Hist. Soc. has Feb. 26, July 8, 1796.
Wis. Hist. Soc. has Aug. 11, 1794.
Essex Inst. has Feb. 20, 1795.

New-Bedford Mercury, 1807–1820+.

Weekly. Established Aug. 7, 1807, by Benjamin Lindsey with the title of "New-Bedford Mercury." It was so continued until after 1820.

New Bedford Pub. Lib. has Aug. 7, 1807–Dec. 29, 1820.
Am. Antiq. Soc. has Aug. 7, 1807–July 28, 1809; Sept. 8, Oct. 20, Nov. 17,

Dec. 1–15, 1809; Jan. 5, Feb. 9–23, Mar. 9, 30, Apr. 13, 27, May 4, 18–June 1, 29–Aug. 10, Sept. 21–Oct. 26, Nov. 30, Dec. 28, 1810; Jan. 4, 18–Feb. 1, 15–Mar. 1, 15–29, Apr. 12, May 3–17, June 14, 21, July 12–26, Aug. 9, 16, 30, Sept. 27–Oct. 25, Nov. 15, 29–Dec. 13, 1811; Jan. 3, 17, Feb. 21, 28, Mar. 27, 1812–Dec. 30, 1814; Jan. 6–May 5, 19–Oct. 6, 20–Dec. 1, 15–29, 1815; Feb. 16, Mar. 1–15, 31, Apr. 5, Nov. 29, Dec. 27, 1816; Aug. 1, 1817; Apr. 24, Aug. 7, 1818; July 23, Aug. 6, 20, 1819; Jan. 7, Mar. 31, Aug. 11, Sept. 1, 8, 1820.

N. Y. Hist. Soc. has Aug. 14, 1807–Dec. 30, 1808; Jan. 6–27, June 23–Dec. 29, 1809; Jan. 5–July 20, Aug. 3, 10, Sept. 7, 21–Oct. 12, Dec. 28, 1810; Nov. 22, 1811; Oct. 22, 1813; July 1, 1814–Dec. 29, 1820.

Lib. Congress has Mar. 25, Dec. 9, 1808; June 23, 1809; Oct. 12, Dec. 28, 1810; Jan. 18, June 14, 1811; Feb. 25, 1814–Mar. 17, 1815; Nov. 3, 1815; Mar. 28, Aug. 1, 1817.

Old Dartmouth Hist. Soc. has Feb. 15, 1811; July 3, 17, 1812; Jan. 7–Dec. 2, 1814.

Duke Univ. has Apr. 17–May 1, June 26, July 24–Aug. 7, Oct. 16, Dec. 4, 1812; May 14, June 4, 18, Nov. 19, Dec. 3, 1813; May 4, 25, Apr. 1, 15, June 3, July 15, Aug. 5, 19, Sept. 23, 1814.

Miami Co. Hist. Soc., Peru, Ind., has Apr. 15, Oct. 13, Dec. 29, 1815; Jan. 12, 19, Feb. 2, Mar. 1, May 24, 1816; Oct. 5, 19, 26, 1817; July 17, 1818; Apr. 23, Aug. 27, Sept. 10, 17, Oct. 15, 1819; May 19, Dec. 22, 1820.

Harvard has Sept. 11, Oct. 16, Nov. 6, 20, Dec. 11, 1807.

N. Y. Pub. Lib. has Mar. 25, Aug. 5, 1808; Apr. 5, 1816.

Univ. of Mich. (Clements) has May 3, July 19, 1811.

Wis. Hist. Soc. has May 13, 1816; Dec. 18, 1818.

Chicago Hist. Soc. has Oct. 20, 1809.

Mass. Hist. Soc. has June 14, 1816.

Portland Pub. Lib. has Mar. 21, 1817.

[New Bedford] Old Colony Gazette, 1808–1811.

Weekly. Established Oct. 21, 1808, by Billings & Tucker [Elijah Billings and —— Tucker] with the title of "Old Colony Gazette." In June or July, 1809, the firm was dissolved and the paper published by Elijah Billings. In April, 1810, Billings transferred the paper to David Hollis. Discontinued under this title with the issue of Oct. 11, 1811, vol. 3, no. 52, and succeeded by the "New-Bedford Gazette," which see.

Am. Antiq. Soc. has Oct. 21, Dec. 9, 1808; Jan. 6, Feb. 3–17, Mar. 10, 17, 31, May 5, 26, Oct. 6, 20, Nov. 24, 30, Dec. 8, 1809; Jan. 12, 26, Feb. 2, 16, Mar. 9, 30, Apr. 13, May 4, June 8, July 6, 27–Aug. 10, Sept. 28, Oct. 5, 19, 26, Dec. 14, 28, 1810; Jan. 4, 25, Feb. 1, Apr. 5, May 3, Sept. 27–Oct. 11, 1811.

MASSACHUSETTS 373

N. Y. Hist. Soc. has Jan. 20–Feb. 10, May 26, Sept. 8, Nov. 17, 30, Dec. 8, 1809; Mar. 2, 23, 30, Oct. 9, 1810; Jan. 11, Sept. 6, 1811.
New Bedford Pub. Lib. has Feb. 24, Mar. 24, May 12, 26, June 2, Aug. 11, Sept. 8, 1809; Aug. 3, Nov. 23, 1810; Mar. 8, 1811.
Harvard has Nov. 4–Dec. 2, 16–30, 1808; Jan. 20, 1809.
Boston Athenæum has Apr. 28, May 5, 19, 26, 1809.
Old Dartmouth Hist. Soc. has Mar. 29, 1811.
N. Y. Pub. Lib. has Aug. 23, 1811.

[Newburyport] **American Intelligencer**, 1801.

Weekly. Established June 4, 1801, by Ephraim W. Allen, with the title of "American Intelligencer, and General Advertiser." The last issue located is that of July 30, 1801, vol. 1, no. 9.

Conn. Hist. Soc. has June 4–July 30, 1801.
Harvard has June 4–July 2, 23, 30, 1801.

[Newburyport] **Essex Journal**, 1773–1777.

Weekly. Established Dec. 4, 1773, by Isaiah Thomas and Henry-Walter Tinges, with the title of "The Essex Journal and Merrimack Packet: Or, the Massachusetts and New-Hampshire General Advertiser." The first issue, Dec. 4, 1773, was delivered "Gratis," together with a "Supplement" of the same date, and was followed by the second number on Dec. 29, 1773, also with a "Supplement." Thenceforth publication was regular. With the issue of June 22, 1774, there was a slight change in the set-up of the title, with the omission of the comma after the word "Or." With the issue of Aug. 17, 1774, Thomas withdrew from the firm, and a new firm, Ezra Lunt and Henry-Walter Tinges, began publication (changed in the imprint to E. Lunt and H. W. Tinges with the issue of Oct. 12, 1774). With the issue of Dec. 28, 1774, the paper was increased to a larger folio and there was a slight change in the set-up of the title. With the issue of June 30, 1775, the size was decreased to one page because of scarcity of paper, and the title was changed to "The Essex Journal: Or, The Massachusetts and New-Hampshire General Advertiser, &c." The issue of July 14, 1775, was omitted. With the issue of July 22, 1775, Lunt withdrew from the firm and the paper was published by John Mycall and Henry-Walter Tinges. With the issue of Aug. 4, 1775, the paper was reduced to a smaller folio and the title changed to "The Essex Journal, or New-Hampshire Packet." The necessity of publishing reduced issues made slight changes in the title in October and November, 1775, until with the issue of Nov. 17, 1775, the title was changed to its more permanent form, "The Essex Journal and New-Hampshire Packet." With the issue of Jan. 19, 1776, Tinges retired from the firm and the paper was published by John Mycall. With the issue of Nov. 1, 1776, the title was changed to "The Essex Journal: or the New-Hampshire Packet, and the Weekly Advertiser." With the issue of Dec. 12, 1776, the paper was reduced in size and the title shortened to "The Essex Journal." Discontinued with the issue of Feb. 13, 1777, no. 163.

> Boston Athenæum has Dec. 4, 1773–Jan. 26, Feb. 9–Sept. 14, 28–Dec. 28, 1774; Jan. 4–Apr. 19, May 3–Nov. 25, Dec. 8–29, 1775; Apr. 19, May 10–Dec. 26, 1776.
> Mass. Hist. Soc. has Dec. 4, 29, 1773; Jan. 5–19, Feb. 2–June 1, 29, July 13–Sept. 7, 21, Nov. 16, Dec. 21, 28, 1774; Jan. 25, Feb. 1, Mar. 8–Apr. 12, May 13, 26–June 30, July 22–Sept. 8, 22–Oct. 13, Nov. 17, 25, 1775; Jan. 5–19, Feb. 2–Mar. 3, 15, 29, Apr. 26–May 10, 24–June 7, 19–28, July 26–Aug. 30, Sept. 13–27, Oct. 18, Nov. 1, 15–28, Dec. 11–26, 1776.
> Lib. Congress has Feb. 16, Apr. 6, 27–May 11, July 27–Aug. 17, Sept. 7, 14, 28, Oct. 5, Nov. 9, Dec. 14, 1774; Jan. 19–Feb. 15, Mar. 1–Apr. 5, 19, May 3, 13, 26, June 16–July 7, Aug. 4, 25, Sept. 5, 15, Nov. 17, Dec. 8, 1775; Jan. 5, 1776–Feb. 6, 1777.
> Essex Inst. has Jan. 26, Feb. 2, 16, Mar. 2, May 11, June 1–22, Sept. 21, Oct. 26, Dec. 28, 1774; Jan. 4–Feb. 15, Mar. 1–Apr. 19, June 23, July 7, 28, Aug. 25–Sept. 8, 22–Nov. 3, 17–Dec. 29, 1775; Mar. 29, Apr. 12, 19, July 12, Aug. 9–Sept. 13, 27–Oct. 11, Dec. 5, 1776; Feb. 6, 1777.
> Am. Antiq. Soc. has Dec. 4, 1773; Jan. 19, Feb. 2, Apr. 6, 20, May 25, June 8, Aug. 3, 10, Sept. 28, Nov. 2, 1774; Feb. 1, June 3, Sept. 15, Nov. 17, Dec. 15, 1775; Feb. 9, 16, Mar. 1, Apr. 12, 26, May 18–June 1, July 19, Aug. 30, Nov. 28–Dec. 19, 1776; Jan. 9, 23–Feb. 13, 1777.
> N. Y. Hist. Soc. has Jan. 12–Apr. 13, May 4, 11, 25–Nov. 30, 1774; May 3, Nov. 17, 1775; Feb. 2, July 12, 19, 1776.
> Univ. of Mich. (Clements) has Jan. 19, Feb. 23, Mar. 30, Apr. 6, 20–May 11, June 1, July 13, Aug. 3, 10, 24, 1774; Feb. 1, May 13, 1775; Jan. 12, Feb. 9, June 7, Aug. 16, 30, Oct. 18, Dec. 11, 19, 1776; Jan. 2, 16, Feb. 6, 1777.
> N. Y. Pub. Lib. has Jan. 26, Mar. 16, 30, June 15, 1774; Apr. 26, May 3, 13, 1775; Apr. 5, July 26, Sept. 20, Oct. 18–Nov. 1, 1776.
> Wis. Hist. Soc. has June 1, 1774; Jan. 19, Feb. 8, 22–Mar. 15, 29, Apr. 19, 1775.
> N. Y. State Lib. has Mar. 2–Apr. 13, 1774.
> Western Reserve Hist. Soc. has Apr. 26, May 10, 24, June 1, 14, 21, Aug. 16, 1776.
> Harvard has Feb. 2, 1774; Mar. 1, 1775; July 26, 1776.
> Newburyport Pub. Lib. has Jan. 5, Apr. 20, 1774.
> Boston Pub. Lib. has Apr. 27, 1774; Aug. 23, 1776.
> Chicago Hist. Soc. has June 7, Oct. 18, 1776.
> Dartmouth has Apr. 13, 1775.
> Univ. of Minn. has Dec. 1, 1775.
> Hist. Soc. Penn. has Sept. 27, 1776.

[Newburyport] **Essex Journal,** 1784–1794.

Weekly. Established July 9, 1784, by John Mycall, with the title of "The Essex Journal and the Massachusetts and New-Hampshire General Advertiser." With the issue of Dec. 20, 1786, the title was changed to "The Essex Journal & New-Hampshire Packet." With the issue of July 4, 1787, the paper was published by William Hoyt, but with the issue of July 15, 1789, was again published by John Mycall. It was discontinued, under this title, with the issue of Apr. 2, 1794, no. 511, being succeeded by the "Morning Star," which see.

Am. Antiq. Soc. has July 9–Aug. 20, Sept. 10–Oct. 27, Nov. 10–Dec. 1, 15–29, 1784; Jan. 5–Apr. 6, 20–Dec. 28, 1785; Jan. 4–Apr. 19, May 3, 31–July 5, 19–Aug. 9, 23–Oct. 18, Nov. 1–15, Dec. 6–27, 1786; Jan. 3–June 27, July 11–Aug. 15, 29, Sept. 26–Dec. 26, 1787; Jan. 2–Feb. 20, Mar. 5–Apr. 2, 16–Oct. 8, Nov. 5–19, Dec. 3, 10, 24, 31, 1788; Jan. 7–28, Feb. 11, 18, Mar. 25–Apr. 15, May 6–27, June 24, July 8–29, Aug. 12–Sept. 23, Oct. 7–Dec. 30, 1789; Jan. 6–Oct. 27, Nov. 10–Dec. 29, 1790; Jan. 5–19, Feb. 2, 16, Mar. 2–16, Apr. 6–Sept. 7, 21–Oct. 26, Nov. 9–23, Dec. 7, 21, 28, 1791; Jan. 4, 18, Feb. 1–Apr. 25, May 9, 16, June 6–20, July 4, 18–Aug. 8, 22–Oct. 3, 17–Nov. 14, Dec. 5–26, 1792; Jan. 2–Feb. 27, Mar. 13–May 8, 22, June 5, 19, July 17, 31, Aug. 7, 21, Sept. 11, 25–Dec. 25, 1793; Jan. 1–Apr. 2, 1794.

Lib. Congress has July 9–Aug. 27, Sept. 10–Dec. 29, 1784; Jan. 5, 12, 26–Mar. 30, Apr. 13–July 27, Aug. 31, Sept. 21–Dec. 14, 28, 1785; Jan. 4–25, Feb. 8–May 31, June 21–July 12, 26–Aug. 16, Sept. 13–Oct. 25, Nov. 8, 22–Dec. 6, 20, 1786; Jan. 10, Feb. 7, 14, 28, Mar. 7, 21–July 4, 25, Aug. 8, 29, Sept. 19–Oct. 3, 17, Nov. 7, Dec. 5–26, 1787; Jan. 2, 16, 30–Feb. 13, June 25, July 9, Aug. 20, Sept. 24, Oct. 1, 15–Nov. 5, Dec. 10, 31, 1788; Jan. 7–28, Feb. 25–Mar. 18, Apr. 8, 22, May 13, 27, June 3, July 8–Dec. 30, 1789; Jan. 6, 27–Mar. 24, Apr. 7–21, May 5–June 2, 16–July 7, 21–Sept. 1, 15–Oct. 27, Nov. 24–Dec. 15, 29, 1790; Jan. 5–19, Feb. 2–Apr. 6, 20–May 4, 18–June 29, July 13–27, Aug. 17–Sept. 28, Oct. 12–26, Nov. 9, 16, 30–Dec. 28, 1791; Jan. 4, 11, 25–Apr. 18, May 2, 9, June 6–Aug. 29, Sept. 12, 19, Oct. 3–31, Dec. 5–26, 1792; Jan. 2–Mar. 6, 20, Apr. 10, 24–May 8, 22, June 5–Aug. 28, Sept. 11–Oct. 16, 30, Nov. 13–Dec. 25, 1793; Jan. 1–22, Feb. 12–Mar. 5, 19, Apr. 2, 1794.

Essex Inst. has July 9–23, Aug. 6, 13, Sept. 3, Oct. 1, 13, 27, Nov. 17, 24, Dec. 15, 29, 1784; Jan. 5, 19–Mar. 9, 23–Apr. 6, May 18–June 8, 22, July 6, 20–Aug. 17, Sept. 7, 28, Oct. 5, 19–Nov. 2, 16–Dec. 14, 28, 1785; Feb. 1, 15–Apr. 5, June 7, 14, Aug. 30, Oct. 4, 18, Nov. 15–29, 1786; Jan. 3–Dec. 26, 1787; Jan. 2–30, Feb. 13–Mar. 12, 26, Apr. 9, May 14, June 18, July 23, Aug. 13, 20, Sept. 10, Oct. 8–22, Nov. 12–26, Dec. 10, 31, 1788; Jan. 21, 28, Apr. 15, May 6, 13, July 15, 29, Aug. 26–Sept. 16, Oct. 14, 28–Nov. 18, Dec. 9–30, 1789; Jan. 6–Feb. 10, 24–Mar. 17, 31–Apr. 14, 28–May 12, June 9, July 28, Aug. 11–25, Sept. 8–29, Dec. 16, 1790; Jan. 12, Feb. 2–Mar. 23, Apr. 6, 25, May 4, June 22–July 6, 27, Aug. 31, Sept. 7, 21,

Oct. 5, 12, 26, Nov. 2, Dec. 7, 28, 1791; Feb. 8, Mar. 21, Apr. 25, May 16, July 11, 25, Sept. 5, 12, Oct. 31, 1792; Jan. 9, 16, Feb. 13, 20, Apr. 3, 24, May 15, Sept. 11, Oct. 16, Nov. 13, 1793; Jan. 1, Mar. 12, 1794.

N. Y. Pub. Lib. has July 9, 1784–Dec. 28, 1785; Jan. 4–June 28, Sept. 27, Oct. 18, Dec. 6, 20, 1786; Feb. 7, May 2, Nov. 21, 1787; Apr. 21, June 23, Aug. 18, Nov. 24, 1790; Mar. 2, 30, July 20, Nov. 9, 1791; Mar. 7, Oct. 3, 1792; Mar. 6, July 17, Dec. 25, 1793.

N. Y. Hist. Soc. has Nov. 24, 1784; Feb. 2, Nov. 11, 1785; Mar. 22, 1786; May 14, 1788; July 22, 1789; Mar. 10, 24, 31, Apr. 14, Sept. 15–Dec. 8, 22, 1790; Jan. 5–Feb. 2, Apr. 13, 20, 1791; Jan. 4, 11, Feb. 22, 29, Apr. 18, May 2, 30, June 6, 20–July 25, Aug. 8, 15, 29, Sept. 19–Oct. 10, 24, 31, Dec. 5–26, 1792; Jan. 2–May 29, June 12–July 10, 24–Oct. 9, 23–Nov. 13, 27–Dec. 25, 1793; Jan. 1–Feb. 26, 1794.

Newburyport Pub. Lib. has Aug. 27, Sept. 17–Dec. 15, 1784; Feb. 2, Mar. 23, 30, Apr. 13, May 18, July 20, Aug. 31, Sept. 28–Oct. 26, Dec. 28, 1785; Jan. 11, Feb. 15, Mar. 8, 15, 29, May 24, June 7, July 5, 12, 26, Aug. 9–23, Sept. 6, Oct. 11, 18, Nov. 8, Dec. 6, 1786; Sept. 3, Oct. 15, 22, 1788; Feb. 11, 25, Oct. 28, 1789; Mar. 24, Aug. 18, 25, Sept. 29, Oct. 13, Dec. 8, 22, 29, 1790; Jan. 5, 12, Feb. 2–16, Mar. 2–30, Apr. 13, 20, May 4–25, June 15, Sept. 7, 21, Oct. 12, Nov. 2, 1791; Jan. 18, Feb. 1–15, 29, Mar. 14, 28–Apr. 11, 25, May 2, 16, June 13–27, July 25, Aug. 1, 15, Sept. 12, 26–Oct. 24, Nov. 14–Dec. 5, 26, 1792; Jan. 2–Feb. 6, Mar. 6, 20–Apr. 3, 24, May 8, 15, 29, June 5, 26, Aug. 21, Sept. 11, 18, Dec. 4, 18, 1793; Jan. 1, 15, Mar. 19, 1794.

Mass. Hist. Soc. has Aug. 6, Sept. 24, 1784; June 8, Aug. 10, 17, Sept. 21, 1785; May 3, 31, Oct. 18, Nov. 1, 1786; May 2, 1787; Feb. 13, Mar. 12, 1788; Nov. 4, 18, 1789; Jan. 6, 20, June 30, Sept. 22, 1790; Feb. 9, Mar. 9, July 6, Oct. 26, Nov. 2, 1791; Dec. 5, 1792; Jan. 9, Feb. 6, 13, May 1, July 10, 1793.

Wis. Hist. Soc. has July 16, Aug. 6, 27–Sept. 24, Oct. 20, Nov. 10, Dec. 1, 1784; Jan. 5, 26, Mar. 30, June 22, July 20, Aug. 3, Sept. 21, Oct. 19, Nov. 2, Dec. 14, 1785.

Univ. of Mich. (Clements) has July 16, 1784; Jan. 3, 1787; May 21, 1788; Jan. 8, 22, Feb. 19–Mar. 5, 19, 1794.

Boston Athenæum has July 30, Nov. 10, 1784; Feb. 23, Mar. 16, Apr. 6, 1785; Jan. 16, Feb. 6, Oct. 23, 1793.

Duke Univ. has Sept. 5, 1785; June 14, 1786; Mar. 17, 1790; Aug. 8, 1792; Mar. 27, May 22, Oct. 2, 1793.

Harvard has Sept. 6, 1786; May 2, 1787; June 22, July 13, Sept. 7–21, Nov. 2, 1791; May 16, 1792.

Western Reserve Hist. Soc. has July 16, Aug. 27, 1784.
Dartmouth has Apr. 13, 1785; May 24, 1786.
N. Y. State Lib. has May 16, 1787; Mar. 20, 1793.
Phil. Lib. Co. has Oct. 9, 16, 1793.
Boston Pub. Lib. has Mar. 27, 1793.

Newburyport Gazette, 1807.

Semi-weekly. Established Apr. 7, 1807, by Benjamin Edes, with the title of "Newburyport Gazette." The last issue located is that of Sept. 18, 1807, vol. 1, no. 48.

Harvard has Apr. 7, 9, 20, 30, May 4, 18, 28, June 1, 22, July 2–16, 23, Aug. 10, 24–Sept. 3, 10–18, 1807.
Am. Antiq. Soc. has Apr. 7, May 11, July 6, 9, Aug. 10–17, 1807.

Newburyport Herald, 1797–1820+.

Semi-weekly. Established Oct. 31, 1797, with the title of "The Newburyport Herald and Country Gazette," by Barrett & March [William Barrett and Angier March] who consolidated their respective papers, the "Political Gazette" and the "Impartial Herald." With the issue of Dec. 22, 1797, the partnership was dissolved and the paper published by Angier March. With the issue of Apr. 11, 1800, it was published by Chester Stebbins for the Proprietor, but with the issue of Oct. 17, 1800, it was again published by Angier March. Because of ill health March transferred the paper to Allen & Stickney [Ephraim W. Allen and Jeremiah Stickney], who began as publishers with the issue of Aug. 4, 1801. With the issue of June 18, 1802, Stickney disposed of his interests to John Barnard and the paper was published by Allen & Barnard. The title was shortened to "Newburyport Herald" with the issue of Mar. 4, 1803. The partnership was dissolved and the paper published by E. W. Allen with the issue of July 12, 1803. With the issue of Apr. 2, 1805, it was published by Wm. B. Allen for E. W. Allen, and with Dec. 3, 1805, by E. W. Allen. The office was burned out by a fire on May 31, 1811, which caused a reduction to a half-sheet for a fortnight following. The title was changed to "Newburyport Herald. And Country Gazette" with the issue of Dec. 3, 1811. Allen sold the paper to Henry Small, who began publishing it with the issue of Apr. 18, 1815, and changed the title to "Newburyport Herald, and Commercial Gazette"; but with the issue of Oct. 3, 1815, it reverted to E. W. Allen. With the issue of Feb. 16, 1816, it was published for E. W. Allen by B[enjamin] W. Folsom, and with the issue of Mar. 15, 1816, by B. W. Folsom. With the issue of Feb. 4, 1817, it was published by William Hastings for E. W. Allen. With the issue of Apr. 25, 1817, the title was changed to "Newburyport Herald, Commercial and Country Gazette," and it was published by William Hastings for the Proprietors. With the issue of Feb. 4, 1818, E. W. Allen again became publisher, changing the title to "Newburyport Herald." With the issue of June 1, 1819, H[enry] R. Stickney's name appeared as printer, although the name of E. W. Allen remained as publisher. With the issue of Feb. 4, 1820, the name of E. W. Allen as publisher was the only one in the imprint, and so continued until after 1820.

Newburyport Pub. Lib. has Nov. 14, 1797–Aug. 3, 1802; Apr. 12, 1803–Dec. 29, 1820.

Essex Inst. has Oct. 31, 1797–Dec. 31, 1811; Jan. 3–Mar. 30, June 2, Nov. 20, 1812; Jan. 1, 1813–Dec. 30, 1814; May 5, 1815–Sept. 27, 1816; Jan. 3, 1817–Dec. 31, 1819; Apr. 4–Dec. 30, 1820.

Am. Antiq. Soc. has Nov. 3, 1797–Dec. 25, 1798, fair; Jan. 1, 1799–Sept. 30, 1806; Oct. 31, Nov. 4, 11, 1806; Jan. 27, Feb. 6, Mar. 6, 13, 24, May 29–June 5, 12, 16, 26, July 31, 1807; Jan. 1–Dec. 30, 1808, fair; Jan. 3, 1809–Dec. 30, 1814; Feb. 24, 1815–Nov. 5, 1816, fair; Jan. 17, Feb. 14, Mar. 28, July 8, Aug. 8, 29, Sept. 12, 16, Oct. 3, 1817; Apr. 2, 17, 21, May 15, July 17, Aug. 7, 11, Sept. 11, 25, Oct. 13, 20, 27, Dec. 18, 1818; Jan. 19, Apr. 1, May 4, 7, July 6, 9, Aug. 13, Sept. 14, Oct. 1, Nov. 5, Dec. 7, 1819; Jan. 28, Apr. 11, June 2, July 7, Sept. 8, Nov. 7, 10, Dec. 5, 1820.

Harvard has Oct. 31, 1797–Dec. 30, 1808, fair.

Lib. Congress has Oct. 31–Dec. 29, 1797; Jan. 2–Oct. 16, 1798, fair; Jan. 11, Feb. 8, May 7, June 21, Sept. 17, 1799; Jan. 3, Feb. 4, 11, Mar. 7, Oct. 31, Nov. 4, 11, 21, 28, Dec. 16–26, 1800; Jan. 2, 6, 13, 23, 30, Aug. 28, 1801; Dec. 25, 1802; Jan. 21, July 1, 1803; Mar. 16, 1804; Apr. 25–May 2, 16, 30, 1806; Aug. 16–Dec. 30, 1808; May 12, 1809–Dec. 31, 1811, fair; Jan. 7, 17, July 28, Sept. 15, 22, 1812; Mar. 5, 12–23, May 4, 11, 28, June 4, Sept. 17, Nov. 2, 19, 23, Dec. 14, 28, 1813; Jan. 21, Feb. 8, Mar. 1, Apr. 1–12, 1814; Mar. 25, 1817.

N. Y. Hist. Soc. has Nov. 28, 1797–Dec. 11, 1798, fair; Dec. 13, 1799–Aug. 31, 1802, fair; Nov. 5, 16, Dec. 5, 1802; Jan. 21, 1806; Jan. 26, Feb. 26, 1808; July 19, Aug. 6, 16, 1811; Apr. 6, 1812; Mar. 11, Sept. 27, Oct. 4, Dec. 16, 20, 1814; Nov. 14, Dec. 29, 1815; Sept. 6, 13, Oct. 15, Nov. 1, 8, 22, 28–Dec. 6, 31, 1816; Nov. 6, 1819.

Univ. of Mich. (Clements) has Nov. 10, 1797; Oct. 30, 1798; Nov. 12, Dec. 27, 1799; May 30, 1800; May 15, June 23, Aug. 11, 1801; May 24, 1803–Feb. 7, 1804; Mar. 9, 16, 25, Apr. 17, May 4, 1804; Oct. 28, Nov. 22, Dec. 9, 28, 1808; Feb. 14, 1809; Jan. 5–Dec. 25, 1810, fair; Jan. 4, Feb. 1, 15, 26–Apr. 2, 9, 19, May 14, 17, June 28, July 2, Dec. 17, 1811; Apr. 3, Aug. 4, 28, Sept. 8, 1812; Mar. 23, 1813; May 27, July 15, Aug. 9, 1814; Jan. 23, Apr. 16, 23, 30, May 21, July 2, 12, 1816; Jan. 4–Oct. 3, 13–Dec. 29, 1820.

Boston Athenæum has Jan. 3, 7, 17, May 23, Nov. 11, 1800; May 1, 5, 1801; Aug. 23, 1805; July 15, 1806; Jan. 2, Apr. 14, 1807–Mar. 28, 1809; Apr. 25, May 26, 30, Aug. 8, 1809; Jan. 25, Mar. 26, July 9, 1811; May 18, 1813; Feb. 8, 1814; June 6, July 18, Sept. 15, 1815; Jan. 14, May 27, June 20, 1817.

N. Y. State Lib. has Oct. 20, 1801–Apr. 15, 1803; Sept. 8, 1812.

Boston Pub. Lib. has Dec. 8, 1797; Aug. 14, 1798; Feb. 5–Mar. 30, Apr. 6–May 14, 25, July 13, Sept. 10, 21, 24, Oct. 5, 22, 29, Nov. 16, 25, Dec. 3, 7, 1813; Feb. 22, 1814.

Duke Univ. has Jan. 20, July 17–Sept. 29, Nov. 10, 1801; Feb. 22, May 27, Aug. 30, Sept. 28, Nov. 1, 25, 1803; Jan. 6, 13–20, 28, Mar. 9, May 1, June 1, 15, 1804; Mar. 5, 1805; Apr. 19, 1808; Apr. 10, May 15, 22, 25, Aug. 31,

1810; Jan. 4, 11, 22, Mar. 26, Apr. 12, 23–30, May 10, 21, June 2, 25, July 2–12, 1811; Apr. 12, 29, May 10, 20, 27, Oct. 14, Dec. 20, 1814; Apr. 7, 11, 1815; Jan. 2, 16, Feb. 16, 20, 27, Mar. 1, Aug. 27, 1816.

Minn. Hist. Soc. has Dec. 12, 22, 1797; Jan. 5, Feb. 2, 16, May 1, 4, June 16, 22, 29, July 3, 13–30, Aug. 14, 24, Sept. 14, Oct. 30, Nov. 13, 16, 27, 30, Dec. 14, 18, 1798; Jan. 4, 8, 18, Feb. 1, 19, 22, Mar. 5, 12, 19, 26, Apr. 5, May 14–24, 31, June 4, 7, 18, Sept. 3, 6, Oct. 8, 1799; Oct. 28, 1800; June 19, Oct. 2, 9, Nov. 10, 24, Dec. 4, 1801; Jan. 1, 5, 8, 29, 1802.

Univ. of Minn. has June 14, 1799; Apr. 7, June 25, Sept. 24, Oct. 4, 1813; Dec. 1, 1814; Oct. 24, Nov. 21, 1817.

N. Y. Pub. Lib. has Apr. 13, 1798; Aug. 16–23, Sept. 13, 1799; Sept. 25, 1804; Aug. 20, Oct. 11, 1811; Mar. 31, June 26, Aug. 7, 1812; Feb. 9, Mar. 23, July 6, Sept. 10, Oct. 1, 12, 1813; Jan. 25, Feb. 25, Apr. 29, 1814; Mar. 11, 1815.

Long Id. Hist. Soc. has Dec. 26, 30, 1800; Mar. 13, 17, Aug. 7, 1801.

Mass. Hist. Soc. has Mar. 2, 16, 1798; Dec. 3, 1799.

[Newburyport] **Impartial Herald**, 1793–1797.

Weekly and semi-weekly. Established May 18, 1793, by Blunt and Robinson [Edmund M. Blunt and Howard S. Robinson], with the title of "Impartial Herald." With the issue of Feb. 28, 1794, the firm was dissolved and the paper published by Edmund M. Blunt. With the issue of Aug. 23, 1794, Blunt took Angier March into partnership under the firm name of Blunt & March, who with the issue of Dec. 16, 1794, changed the issue to a semi-weekly. With the issue of Sept. 24, 1796, Blunt withdrew and the paper was published by Angier March. The last issue is that of Oct. 27, 1797, vol. 5, no. 380, after which this paper and the "Political Gazette" were consolidated and a new paper published entitled "Newburyport Herald," which see.

Essex Inst. has May 18, 1793–Dec. 29, 1795; Jan. 26, Feb. 2, 5, 12, 23, Mar. 18, June 14, Sept. 3, 27, Nov. 15, Dec. 20, 1796; Jan. 3–Sept. 12, 23–Oct. 21, 27, 1797.

Newburyport Pub. Lib. has Oct. 12, 1793; Nov. 7, 28, 1794; Mar. 3, Apr. 14, May 23–June 6, Oct. 30, 1795–Sept. 20, Oct. 28, 1796.

Am. Antiq. Soc. has Aug. 3, 17, 24, Nov. 2, 9, 15, 29, 1793; Jan. 3–24, Feb. 14, 28, Mar. 28, Apr. 18, 25, May 24, July 19, Aug. 9, Oct. 31, 1794; Jan. 6, 16, 23, Feb. 3, 24, Mar. 3, 6, 13, Apr. 14, 21–May 9, 19, June 23–30, July 7–18, 25, Aug. 1, 11–Sept. 1, 8, Nov. 17–24, Dec. 4, 22, 1795; Mar. 8, May 21, 28, 31, June 7, 11, 18–28, July 9–16, Sept. 17, Oct. 1, 18–Nov. 4, 15–29, Dec. 6, 13, 20, 30, 1796; Jan. 6, 20, 31–Feb. 14, 21–Mar. 21, 28–Apr. 18, 29, June 3, 20–27, July 4, 8, 15, 22, Aug. 5, 8, 15–26, Sept. 12–19, 30–Oct. 7, 14–27, 1797.

Lib. Congress has July 27, Aug. 3, 10, 31, Oct. 26, 1793; Nov. 7, 1794; Feb. 20, May 16, June 27, Aug. 8, 11, Oct. 6, Nov. 24, Dec. 1, 25, 1795; Jan. 5, 19, Mar. 1–8, 29, Apr. 5, 30, June 25, Nov. 1, 1796; Jan. 20–Oct. 24, 1797, fair.

Harvard has Feb. 20, 27, Mar. 6, 13, Apr. 10, 17, June 2, 9, 16, 23, July 4, 14, 18, Aug. 11, 18, Sept. 8, Oct. 10, Dec. 18, 22, 1795; Feb. 12, 16, Mar. 11, 15, 25, Apr. 5, 19, 26–May 3, 10, 21, June 18, 25, 28, July 9, 12, 23–30, Aug. 13, 27–Sept. 3, 13, 24, Oct. 4, 8, 15–25, Nov. 1–18, 25–Dec. 23, 30, 1796; Jan. 6, 10, 17, 20, 27, 31–Feb. 7, 14, 21–Mar. 21, 28–Apr. 7, 15, 18, 29, May 27, 30, Aug. 1, 19, Sept. 2, 16, Oct. 7, 1797.
N. Y. Hist. Soc. has Feb. 16–Dec. 9, 1796; Jan. 27–Sept. 23, 1797.
N. Y. Pub. Lib. has June 22, Nov. 22, 1793; June 7, Dec. 12, 1794; Mar. 3, May 12, July 14–Dec. 25, 1795; Jan. 1–8, 15–26, Feb. 5, 12, 19–Mar. 11, 18–May 21, 28–June 28, July 9, 16–Aug. 13, 20–Sept. 13, 20–Oct. 21, Nov. 1–18, 25, Dec. 6, 9, 1796; Jan. 17, 20, Apr. 1, 1797.
Boston Athenæum has Jan. 10, 1794; Sept. 12, 19, 29, Oct. 17, 27, 30, Dec. 22, 1795; Jan. 1, 5, 19, 26, Feb. 2, 9, 16–23, Mar. 1, 8, 15, 22, 29, Apr. 26, May 17–24, June 21, 28, July 12, 1796.
Phil. Lib. Co. has Apr. 25, Sept. 29, Nov. 3, 17, 24, 1795; Jan. 1, 15, 19, 26, Feb. 23, Apr. 1, 5, 24, Aug. 9, 1796.
Wis. Hist. Soc. has Dec. 26, 1794; Jan. 2, 16, Feb. 6, Mar. 24, 27, Apr. 3, Sept. 1, 22, Nov. 27, 1795.
Newburyport Hist. Soc. has Feb. 3, 1793; July 18, 1796; Sept. 12, 1797.
Mo. Hist. Soc., St. Louis, has Sept. 14, 1793; July 5, 1794.
Rutgers Univ. has Sept. 27, 1796; June 27, 1797.
Amesbury Pub. Lib. has Feb. 10, 1795.
Univ. of Mich. (Clements) has July 8, 1797.
N. Y. State Lib. has Aug. 22, 1797.

[Newburyport] **Independent Whig**, 1810–1811.

Weekly and semi-weekly. Established Mar. 22, 1810, judging from the date of the earliest issue located, that of Apr. 5, 1810, vol. 1, no. 3, published by N[athaniel] H. Wright, with the title of "Independent Whig." With the issue of Oct. 10, 1810, the publication was changed to semi-weekly. On Feb. 5, 1811, his office was destroyed by his political opponents, and it was Mar. 9, 1811, before he was able to bring out another issue of his paper. It was thereafter published weekly. The last issue located is that of May 2, 1811, vol. 2, no. 19. In the "Exeter Constitutionalist" of Exeter, N. H., of May 21, 1811, is an humorous account of the decease of the "Independent Whig" on May 16, 1811. In the "Essex Register" of June 25, 1811, Mr. Wright inserted an article explaining the causes of the discontinuance of his paper.

Am. Antiq. Soc. has Apr. 5, 12, May 3, 17, June 14, 21, July 4, 12, 19, Aug. 2, 16–30, Sept. 13, Oct. 13, 24, 27, Nov. 3–10, Dec. 5, 8, 22, 26, 1810; Jan. 1, 9–19, 30, Mar. 16, 23, 28, May 2, 1811.
Essex Inst. has July 4, Nov. 7, 1810; Jan. 30, 1811.
Univ. of Mich. (Clements) has June 21, Aug. 30, 1810; Jan. 1, 1811.
Boston Athenæum has Nov. 7, 1810; Jan. 26, 1811.

Mass. Hist. Soc. has Mar. 9, 28, 1811.
Amesbury Pub. Lib. has July 4, 1810.
Newburyport Pub. Lib. has Aug. 30, 1810.
Duke Univ. has Nov. 7, 1810.
Newburyport Hist. Soc. has Jan. 1, 1811.

[Newburyport] **Merrimack Gazette,** 1803–1804.

Weekly. Established Mar. 21, 1803, by Caleb Cross, with the title of "Merrimack Gazette." With the issue of Sept. 17, 1803, the title was changed to "Merrimack Gazette, and Essex Advertiser." The last issue located is that of Feb. 11, 1804, vol. 1, no. 48. It was evidently discontinued with the issue of Feb. 18, as the "Newburyport Herald" of Feb. 21, 1804, records: "The 'Merrimack Gazette,' a democratic paper heretofore published in this town, on Saturday last, about meridian, rested from its labors!"

Essex Inst. has Mar. 21–Aug. 20, Sept. 3–Oct. 15, 1803.
Harvard has Apr. 2, 16, 30–May 14, 28, June 11–Aug. 20, Sept. 3, 17–Oct. 15, 29–Dec. 24, 1803; Jan. 7, Feb. 11, 1804.
Amesbury Pub. Lib. has July 1, 9, Aug. 20–Sept. 3, 17, Oct. 1, 8, 1803.
Am. Antiq. Soc. has Apr. 2, Sept. 3, 31, Oct. 8, 1803.
N. Y. Pub. Lib. has May 7, 1803.
Lib. Congress has May 28, 1803.

[Newburyport] **Merrimack Magazine,** 1805–1806.

Weekly. Established Aug. 17, 1805, by Whittingham & John Gilman, with the title of "Merrimack Magazine and Ladies' Literary Cabinet." Although nominally a magazine, it contained vital records and current local and domestic news, and could well be included as a newspaper. It was of quarto size, paged, and provided with a title-page and index. The last issue located, that of Aug. 9, 1806, vol. 1, no. 52, referred to the possible commencement of a second volume.

Newburyport Pub. Lib., Am. Antiq. Soc., Essex Inst., Bowdoin Coll., Univ. of Chicago, and N. Y. State Lib. have Aug. 17, 1805–Aug. 9, 1806.
Boston Pub. Lib. has Aug. 17, 1805–Aug. 9, 1806, fair.
Lib. Congress has Mar. 8, 29–Apr. 12, May 3–July 26, 1806.

[Newburyport] **Morning Star,** 1794.

Weekly. Established Apr. 8, 1794, by Howard S. Robinson, with the title of "The Morning Star." With the issue of May 20, 1794, Robinson admitted Benjamin Tucker to partnership under the firm name of Robinson & Tucker. With the issue of Oct. 14, 1794, the firm was dissolved and the paper published by Benjamin Tucker. It was discontinued with the issue of Dec. 3, 1794, vol. 1, no. 35, Tucker having sold out to Blunt & March, the publishers of the "Impartial Herald."

Newburyport Pub. Lib. has Apr. 8–Dec. 3, 1794.
Essex Inst. has Apr. 8–Nov. 26, 1794.
Am. Antiq. Soc. has Apr. 15–Sept. 30, Oct. 14–Dec. 3, 1794.
Lib. Congress has June 3, July 22, Sept. 16, 1794.
Univ. of Mich. (Clements) has Sept. 2, 23, Nov. 19, 1794.
N. Y. Pub. Lib. has Oct. 21, 1794.

[Newburyport] **New-England Repertory,** 1803–1804.

Semi-weekly. Established July 6, 1803, with the title of "New-England Repertory," published by John Barnard, for John Park. Beginning with the issue of Sept. 3, 1803, the name of John Barnard was omitted from the imprint. The paper was discontinued at Newburyport with the issue of Jan. 21, 1804, vol. 1, no. 57, and was removed to Boston, where it was continued by John Park under the title of "The Repertory."

Am. Antiq. Soc., Boston Athenæum, Boston Pub. Lib., Mass. Hist. Soc., Essex Inst., Newburyport Pub. Lib., Dartmouth, N. Y. Hist. Soc., N. Y. State Lib., and Lib. Congress have July 6, 1803–Jan. 21, 1804.
Harvard has Aug. 27, Sept. 3, 10, 14, Oct. 1, 19, Nov. 30, Dec. 14, 1803.
Univ. of Mich. (Clements) has Aug. 20, Sept. 3, 10, Oct. 1, 5, Nov. 5, 9, 19, Dec. 14, 1803.
Duke Univ. has Dec. 14, 1803.

[Newburyport] **Political Calendar,** 1804–1805.

Weekly and semi-weekly. Established Mar. 26, 1804, with the title of "Political Calendar," published by Caleb Cross and edited by Joshua Lane. It was at first intended to call the paper the "Republican Directory," according to the prospectus. It was also announced as a semi-weekly, but it was not so published until the issue of Apr. 19, 1804. The name of Joshua Lane, as editor, disappeared from the imprint with the issue of May 3, 1804. With the issue of Oct. 1, 1804, the paper became a weekly, and with the issue of Oct. 15, 1804, the title was changed to "Political Calendar And Essex Advertiser." The last issue located is that of June 17, 1805, vol. 2, no. 89.

Harvard has Mar. 26, Apr. 9–May 7, 14, 24–June 7, 25–July 16, 23–Aug. 9, 16, 20, 27–Sept. 6, 13–24, Oct. 1–15, Nov. 5–Dec. 3, 31, 1804; Jan. 7–21, Feb. 4, 11, 25, Mar. 4, 11, 25–May 13, June 10, 17, 1805.
Dartmouth has Mar. 26–Nov. 19, 1804; Apr. 15, 22, May 20, 1805.
Am. Antiq. Soc. has Mar. 26, Apr. 2, 16–23, 30–Aug. 9, 16–Sept. 10, 17–27, Oct. 8–29, Dec. 24, 1804; Jan. 14, 1805.

Essex Inst. has Apr. 16, May 10–17, 28–June 14, Aug. 2, 27, Sept. 3, 17, Oct. 15, 1804; Mar. 11, Apr. 29, 1805.
Me. Hist. Soc. has June 25, 1804.
Wis. Hist. Soc. has Aug. 16, 1804.

[Newburyport] Political Gazette, 1795–1797.

Weekly. Established Apr. 30, 1795, by William Barrett, with the title of "Political Gazette." The last issue was that of Oct. 27, 1797, vol. 3, no. 27, after which this paper and the "Impartial Herald" were consolidated and a new paper published entitled the "Newburyport Herald," which see.

Harvard has Apr. 30–Aug. 20, Sept. 3, 10, 24–Dec. 29, 1795; Jan. 5–Nov. 25, 1796; Jan. 6–Oct. 27, 1797.
Am. Antiq. Soc. has June 11, 25, July 16, Aug. 6–27, Sept. 10, Nov. 17, 24, Dec. 8, 22, 29, 1795; Feb. 2, May 26–June 16, July 7, Aug. 18, Oct. 6–Nov. 4, 18–Dec. 2, 30, 1796; Jan. 6–Apr. 27, May 18, 25, June 15, 29–July 27, Aug. 10–Oct. 27, 1797.
N. Y. Hist. Soc. has Aug. 13–Sept. 3, Oct. 1–27, Nov. 10, 24, Dec. 15–29, 1795; Jan. 5–26, Feb. 16–Mar. 22, Apr. 5, 28–Aug. 18, Sept. 8–Dec. 30, 1796; Jan. 6–Feb. 17, Mar. 3–17, 31–May 11, 1797.
Newburyport Pub. Lib. has Apr. 30, 1795–Jan. 26, 1796; July 21, 1796; Apr. 7, Oct. 12, 1797.
Boston Athenæum has Sept. 10, 1795–Jan. 19, Feb. 2, May 5–June 30, July 14, Aug. 4, 1796.
Lib. Congress has Sept. 10, 17, Oct. 8, 1795; Feb. 16, Sept. 15, 1796; Feb. 17, 24, June 22, Aug. 17, Oct. 27, 1797.
Essex Inst. has Aug. 13, 1795; Dec. 23, 1796; Jan. 6, 27, Feb. 3, May 25, June 15, July 6, Aug. 3, Sept. 7, 1797.
Newburyport Hist. Soc. has Dec. 8, 1795; Aug. 17, 1797.
Rutgers Univ. has Aug. 25, 1796.
Univ. of Mich. (Clements) has Aug. 17, 1797.

[Newburyport] Statesman, 1808–1809.

Semi-weekly. Established Aug. 15, 1808, with the title of "The Statesman," published by W[illiam] Griffin, for the Proprietor. With the issue of Aug. 29, 1808, it was published by Joseph Gleason, Jun'r., the Proprietor. The last issue located is that of Mar. 9, 1809, vol. 2, no. 6.

Am. Antiq. Soc. has Aug. 15–25, Sept. 2–Oct. 27, Nov. 3–Dec. 29, 1808; Jan. 2–Feb. 27, Mar. 9, 1809.
Wis. Hist. Soc. has Aug. 15–Oct. 27, Nov. 3–Dec. 29, 1808; Jan. 2–30, Feb. 6–27, Mar. 9, 1809.

Boston Athenæum has Aug. 15–Oct. 27, Nov. 3–14, 21–Dec. 29, 1808; Jan. 5–30, Feb. 6–27, 1809.
Univ. of Mich. (Clements) has Aug. 15–Oct. 6, 13–27, Nov. 3–10, 21–30, Dec. 8–26, 1808; Jan. 5–Feb. 13, 20–27, 1809.
Harvard has Aug. 29, Sept. 19–29, Oct. 17, 31, Nov. 7, 21, 28, 30, Dec. 8, 22, 29, 1808.
Newburyport Pub. Lib. has Aug. 18, Sept. 29, Nov. 3, 1808; Jan. 5, 30, Feb. 9, 20, 23, Mar. 9, 1809.
Dartmouth has Aug. 18, 29, Sept. 5, 12, 15, 22, 29–Oct. 6, 13–Nov. 3, 10, 21–28, 1808.
Yale has Aug. 29, Sept. 29, Nov. 3, 1808.
Essex Inst. has Sept. 29, Nov. 10, 1808.

[Northampton] **Anti-Monarchist,** 1808–1810.

Weekly. Established Dec. 14, 1808, with the title of "Anti-Monarchist, and Republican Watchman," "Published for the Proprietor. C[————] Sawtell, Printer." In December, 1809, the name of Sawtell, as printer, was omitted and the paper was merely "Published for the Proprietor." There is no clue to the name of the publisher until the issue of Oct. 10, 1810, when Charles Shepherd offers the establishment for sale. The last issue located is that of Dec. 5, 1810, vol. 2, no. 104, and it is probable that the paper finished out the volume to no. 104.

Forbes Lib., Northampton, had Dec. 21, 1808–Dec. 5, 1810 offered in 1926, but did not obtain the file. Present location unknown.
Am. Antiq. Soc. has Dec. 14–28, 1808; Jan. 4, 11, 25–Feb. 15, Mar. 1, 15–Apr. 5, 19, May 3, 10, Sept. 6, 13, Oct. 11–25, Dec. 27, 1809; Jan. 3–31, Feb. 28, Mar. 14–31, Apr. 11, May 9, 16, 30, June 6, July 4–18; Aug. 1, 8, 22, Sept. 5, 19–Oct. 31, Nov. 14, 1810.
Pocumtuck Valley Mem. Assoc., Deerfield, has June 28, July 26, Aug. 16, 30–Sept. 13, Oct. 18, Nov. 22, 1809.
Lib. Congress has Feb. 1, Oct. 18, Nov. 8, 22, 1809; Aug. 29, 1810.
N. Y. Hist. Soc. has Dec. 21, 1808; Jan. 25, Sept. 27, Oct. 4, 1809.
Boston Athenæum has May 3, 10, 24, 1809.
Harvard has Dec. 21, 28, 1808.
Wis. Hist. Soc. has Dec. 21, 1808; Jan. 25, Oct. 11, 1809.
N. Y. State Lib. has Jan. 24, Aug. 8, 1810.
Rutgers Univ. has Aug. 23, 1809.

[Northampton] **Democrat,** 1811–1813.

Weekly. Established Mar. 12, 1811, "printed for the Proprietors," and with the title of "The Democrat." The editor's address refers to "the revival of the republican press in this county," an evident reference to the late "Anti-Monarchist." With the issue of Jan. 7, 1812, the paper was "printed by Galen Ware, for the Proprietors." Beginning with March, 1812, it was printed by Clapp and Ware [Caleb Clapp and Galen Ware]. Charles L. Seeger is referred to in the issue of Apr. 7, 1812, as having been editor for the past twelve months. With the issue of Apr. 7, 1812, the partnership was dissolved and the paper printed by Caleb Clapp. The last issue located is that of Aug. 17, 1813, vol. 3, no. 128.

Am. Antiq. Soc. has Mar. 12–Apr. 2, 23, May 7–21, July 2, 23–Aug. 20, Sept. 17, 24, Oct. 8, 15, 29–Nov. 19, Dec. 3, 10, 24, 1811; Jan. 7, Feb. 11, Mar. 17, Apr. 14–Sept. 8, 22, Oct. 6–Nov. 17, Dec. 2–29, 1812; Jan. 5–Feb. 23, Mar. 9–May 18, June 1–Aug. 17, 1813.

Forbes Lib., Northampton, has Mar. 10, 1812–Mar. 2, 1813.

Univ. of Mich. (Clements) has Aug. 20, Nov. 19, 1811; Apr. 14, May 19, June 9, July 14, Aug. 11, Sept. 1, 22, Oct. 13, Dec. 8, 1812; Feb. 9, June 22, 1813.

Pocumtuck Valley Mem. Assoc., Deerfield, has June 11, 18, 1811; Jan. 14, 1812; Feb. 23, Mar. 2, 1813.

Boston Pub. Lib. has Apr. 14, 1812.

Lib. Congress has May 28, 1811.

Buffalo Hist. Soc. has Nov. 26, 1811.

N. Y. State Lib. has July 21, 1812, extra.

N. Y. Hist. Soc. has Aug. 18, 1812.

[Northampton] **Hampshire Gazette**, 1786–1820+.

Weekly. Established by William Butler, Sept. 6, 1786, with the title of "The Hampshire Gazette," judging from the date of the prospectus and the earliest issue located, that of Sept. 13, 1786, no. 2. The title was changed to "Hampshire Gazette" with the issue of Apr. 18, 1792. With the issue of July 5, 1815, Butler transferred the paper to William W. Clapp, although Clapp allowed Butler's name to stand in the imprint in this issue, and the issue of July 12, 1815, had no name of printer. With the issue of July 19, 1815, Clapp appeared as publisher and the title was changed to "Hampshire Gazette. And Northampton Advertiser." With the issue of Aug. 2, 1815, the title was changed to "Hampshire Gazette. And Publick Advertiser," but with that of Apr. 3, 1816, the "And" was omitted. With the issue of Mar. 5, 1817, Clapp sold out the paper to Bates & Judd [Isaac C. Bates and Hophni Judd], although no publisher's name appeared in the imprint. With the issue of Mar. 12, 1817, the title was changed to "Hampshire Gazette & Public Advertiser." On June 4, 1817, the proprietors announced that they had added Thomas W. Shepard to the firm, and with the issue of June 11, 1817, the imprint was given as "Published by Thomas W. Shepard, & Co." Hophni Judd, one of the proprietors, died Mar. 15, 1818, but Bates apparently continued in the firm. With the issue of Jan. 5, 1819, the "&" in the title was changed to "and," and with the issue of Jan. 4, 1820, the title was shortened to "Hampshire Gazette." So continued until after 1820.

Forbes Lib., Northampton, has Sept. 13, 1786–Oct. 28, 1807; Jan. 6, 1808–Dec. 26, 1820.

Am. Antiq. Soc. has Sept. 27, Nov. 22, 1786; Jan. 31, Feb. 28, Mar. 7, 28, Apr. 4, May 2–23, June 6, 20, July 4, 18, Aug. 1–Sept. 26, Oct. 10–Nov. 7, 21–Dec. 26, 1787; Jan. 2–Aug. 13, 27, Sept. 3, 17, 24, Oct. 15–Nov. 5, 19–Dec. 10, 24, 31, 1788; Jan. 7, 21, Feb. 4, Mar. 4, Apr. 15–Dec. 30, 1789; Jan. 6, 1790–Dec. 11, 1793, fair; Jan. 8, Mar. 5, Apr. 2, 23, May 7, 21, June 4, July 23–Aug. 13, Sept. 3, 17–Dec. 31, 1794; Jan. 7, 1795–Dec. 28, 1796; Jan. 25–Feb. 8, 22–Mar. 15, 29–May 17, 31, June 7, 14, July 19, Aug. 2, 16, 30–Sept. 27, Oct. 11–Nov. 15, 29–Dec. 27, 1797; Jan. 3, 1798–Dec. 24, 1806, fair; Mar. 25, May 20, 27, July 15, 1807; Jan. 13–July 27, Aug. 10, 17, Sept. 7, 21–Oct. 5, 19, Nov. 16, 1808; Jan. 4, 1809–Dec. 26, 1810; Jan. 2, 1811–Dec. 27, 1815, fair; Jan. 3, 1816–Dec. 26, 1820.

Mass. Hist. Soc. has Sept. 20, 1786–Aug. 31, 1796; Aug. 30, 1797–Dec. 26, 1798; Jan. 19, 1803; June 4, 1806; Feb. 10, 1808; Nov. 9, 1819.

N. Y. Hist. Soc. has Feb. 21, Apr. 25, Oct. 3, 1787; Mar. 12–Dec. 10, 1788, fair; July 29, 1789; Mar. 17, May 5, July 21, Aug. 4, Nov. 17, Dec. 1, 1790; Jan. 19–Oct. 12, 1791, fair; Mar. 28, 1792; Feb. 20, 27, Mar. 20, 27, May 29, June 5, July 10, 1793; Feb. 25, Mar. 4, Apr. 8, July 15, Aug. 26, Nov. 18, 1795; Feb. 24–Mar. 23, Apr. 27, May 4, July 6–27, Oct. 5, 26, Nov. 2, Dec. 21, 28, 1796; Feb. 1, 8, 22, Mar. 8, 29, Apr. 12, 19, May 10, 17, June 14, Aug. 30, Sept. 6, Oct. 18, Nov. 8, 1797; Jan. 3, Feb. 14, Nov. 7, 21, 1798; Sept. 18, Nov. 13, 1799; Feb. 5–19, Mar. 12, 26, Apr. 9–30, June 4, July 16, 30, Aug. 6, 20–Sept. 3, 17–Oct. 8, 22, Nov. 5–26, Dec. 10, 24, 1800; Apr. 1, 15, Sept. 2, 9, Dec. 16, 30, 1801; Mar. 30, July 21, Oct. 27, Dec. 23, 1802; Jan. 12–Oct. 5, 1803, fair; Jan. 15, June 7, Oct. 3, 17–Nov. 21, 1804; Mar. 13, May 29, Sept. 4, 1805; Apr. 2, Aug. 6, 1806; Mar. 11, 1807; Nov. 15, 1809; June 4–Dec. 31, 1817.

Lib. Congress has Oct. 29, 1788; Jan. 14, 21, Sept. 23, 1789; Sept. 22, Oct. 20, Nov. 3–17, Dec. 1–15, 29, 1790; Jan. 4, 19–Mar. 16, Apr. 6, 13, May 4, 18, June 22, July 6–27, Aug. 17, Oct. 12–26, Nov. 30, Dec. 21, 1791; Jan. 4, 18, Feb. 15–Apr. 18, July 4–Aug. 29, Sept. 12–Oct. 3, 17, Dec. 5, 1792; Jan. 9, 30, Feb. 20, May 8, Aug. 21, 1793; Jan. 29, Mar. 19, Sept. 17, Nov. 12, Dec. 24, 1794; Sept. 19, 1798; Jan. 1, 8, 1800; Oct. 7, Nov. 4, 1801; Apr. 21–Dec. 22, 1802, fair; Nov. 27, 1805; Feb. 26, May 7, Aug. 20, Sept. 17, Oct. 1, 1806; July 8, 1807; Oct. 31, 1810; Apr. 10, 17, Aug. 21, Sept. 4, 1811; Jan. 29–Feb. 12, Mar. 18, July 8–Dec. 30, 1812; Apr. 14–Aug. 24, Nov. 10, 24, Dec. 1–29, 1813; Jan. 5, 1814–Dec. 27, 1815, fair; Dec. 4, 1816; Mar. 23, 1819; May 23, 1820.

Harvard has May 9, 1792; Jan. 1, 1794–Dec. 30, 1795; Mar. 8–Apr. 26, Oct. 11, Nov. 22, 1797; Jan. 10, May 9, 23, July 11, 1798; Apr. 30, June 4–25, July 16, 30, Aug. 13–27, Sept. 10–Oct. 1, 15–Nov. 5, 19–Dec. 10, 24, 31, 1800; Jan. 7, 1801–Sept. 25, 1805, fair; Nov. 6, 1806; Oct. 7, 1807; Oct. 5, 1808.

Boston Pub. Lib. has Sept. 20, 1786–July 20, 1787; Aug. 22, Sept. 28, Dec. 12,

26, 1787; Jan. 9, 16, 30, Feb. 20, Mar. 5–26, Apr. 9–30, July 16, Aug. 13, Sept. 17, Nov. 5, Dec. 24, 1788; Mar. 4, May 6, 20, July 22–Aug. 26, Sept. 9, 23, 30, 1789; Jan. 20, Mar. 3, Aug. 4, Sept. 22, 1790; Nov. 9, 1791; Apr. 25, May 9, Oct. 17, 1792; Aug. 1–15, 1798; Sept. 14, 1803.
Univ. of Mich. (Clements) has June 13, Dec. 5, 1787; Dec. 31, 1788; Mar. 12, Aug. 11, Nov. 3, Dec. 15, 1790; Jan. 4, Mar. 16, June 1, 8, Aug. 24, Sept. 21, Nov. 9, 23, Dec. 7, 1791; Apr. 25, May 9, June 6, 20, Oct. 24, Nov. 7–28, Dec. 12, 19, 1792; Jan. 2, 16, Mar. 13, July 3, 1793; Oct. 26, 1796; Aug. 27, 1800; Nov. 17, 1802; Apr. 4, 11, June 27, 1804; May 29, June 10, 1805; Oct. 21, 1807; June 22, Aug. 10, 31, 1808; Feb. 22, Sept. 6, 13, 1809; May 29, 1811; Sept. 27, 1815; Oct. 13, 1818.
Springfield City Lib. has Oct. 3, 1787; May 21, Aug. 6, 27–Sept. 10, 1788; May 13, Oct. 14, Dec. 30, 1789; Mar. 24, July 7, 28, 1790; Nov. 3, 17–Dec. 8, 1813; Feb. 16, 1814; Nov. 1, 1815–Nov. 20, 1816.
Easthampton, Mass., Pub. Lib. has Oct. 12, 1796; Aug. 5–Nov. 18, 1801; Feb. 24–May 5, 1802; May 18, 25, June 15, 29, July 6, Sept. 7–28, 1803; Apr. 25, Sept. 5, 1804; Apr. 17, July 3, 10, 1805; Oct. 15, 1806; Apr. 15, July 1, Oct. 7, 1807; June 12, 1811; Apr. 2, 1812; Jan. 6, 1813–Dec. 21, 1814; Jan. 11–Feb. 1, 1820.
N. Y. Pub. Lib. has Feb. 14, 1787; Mar. 2, 1791; Feb. 15, 1792; Nov. 27, 1793; May 15, 1799; July 23, Sept. 3, Oct. 8, 22, Nov. 12, 1800; Mar. 18, 1807; Mar. 24, 1813; Feb. 2, 1814; Nov. 17, 1815; Mar. 9, 1819.
Duke Univ. has Nov. 24, 1790; Feb. 8, 1792; Sept. 12, 1793; Dec. 13, 1797; Dec. 8, 1802; Apr. 20, June 1, 8, Aug. 17, 24, 1803; Apr. 11, May 2, 16, July 25, Sept. 5–19, 1810; Jan. 14, Feb. 18, Nov. 10, 1818; May 16, Aug. 8, Oct. 31, 1820.
Wis. Hist. Soc. has Oct. 2, 1793; Sept. 24, 1794; Apr. 1, Sept. 2, 1795; Aug. 10–31, Sept. 21, Oct. 19, 26, Nov. 9, 16, Dec. 7–28, 1808; Dec. 15, 1818.
Pocumtuck Valley Mem. Assoc., Deerfield, has Jan. 10, 1787; July 30, Nov. 26, 1788; Apr. 8, 1789; Mar. 7, 1792; Apr. 9, 1794; Nov. 4, 1795; May 5, 1799; Jan. 8, 22, July 16, 1800; Oct. 7, 1807; Aug. 22, 1810; Nov. 30, 1811; Dec. 10, 1817.
Western Reserve Hist. Soc. has Sept. 14, 1796.
Essex Inst. has Dec. 11, 1799; Aug. 4, 1818.
Conn. Hist. Soc. has Jan. 8, 15, 1800.
Cornell Univ. has Mar. 13, 1816.
Chicago Hist. Soc. has Apr. 25, May 16, 1820.

[Northampton] Hampshire Register, 1817.

Weekly. Established Jan. 8, 1817, judging from the only issue located, that of Apr. 23, 1817, no. 16, published by Elijah Brooks. This issue, furthermore, was stated to be the last published.

Am. Antiq. Soc. has Apr. 23, 1817.

[Northampton] **Hive**, 1803–1805.

Weekly. Established Aug. 23, 1803, by Thomas M. Pomroy, with the title of "The Hive." It was of quarto size, eight pages to the issue, but manifestly a newspaper. With the issue of Jan. 3, 1804, a new volume numbering was again adopted "in order that each volume may commence and close with the year." A title-page and table of contents were promised at the close of the year. With the issue of Jan. 1, 1805, vol. 2, no. 1, the size was changed to a four-page folio. The paper was discontinued with the issue of Jan. 29, 1805, vol. 2, no. 5, Pomroy having disposed of his establishment to William Butler, publisher of the "Hampshire Gazette."

Am. Antiq. Soc. has Aug. 23, 1803–Dec. 25, 1804; Jan. 8, 1805.
Forbes Lib., Northampton, has Aug. 23, 1803–Dec. 25, 1804.
N. Y. State Lib. has Aug. 30, 1803–Dec. 25, 1804.
Lib. Congress has Aug. 30, 1803–Dec. 25, 1804, fair; Jan. 29, 1805.
Wis. Hist. Soc. has Sept. 20–Oct. 4, 18–Dec. 27, 1803; May 15–Dec. 25, 1804.
Harvard has Sept. 27, Oct. 18, Nov. 1–22, Dec. 6–20, 1803; Jan. 3, 17, 31–Feb. 21, Mar. 13, 20, Apr. 3–24, June 5, July 31, Aug. 14–Sept. 18, Oct. 9–23, Nov. 13, 20, 1804; Jan. 1–22, 1805.
N. Y. Hist. Soc. has Jan. 3–Dec. 25, 1804.
Duke Univ. has Sept. 20–Oct. 18, 1803; Jan. 31, Mar. 13, Apr. 3, 24–May 22, June 5–Aug. 14, 28–Sept. 25, Oct. 9, 16, 1804.
Mt. Holyoke Coll. has Sept. 20–Nov. 29, Dec. 20, 27, 1803.
Univ. of Mich. (Clements) has Apr. 24, May 15, June 5, 1804.
Boston Athenæum has Oct. 16–30, Nov. 13, 20, 1804.
Mass. Hist. Soc. has Mar. 20, 1804.
Yale has Apr. 24, 1804.
Long Id. Hist. Soc. has Sept. 4, 1804.

[Northampton] **Patriotic Gazette**, 1799–1800.

Weekly. Established Apr. 12, 1799, by Andrew Wright with the title of "Patriotic Gazette." Discontinued with the issue of June 23, 1800, vol. 2, no. 63.

N. Y. Pub. Lib. has Apr. 12, 1799–June 23, 1800.
Forbes Lib., Northampton, has Apr. 12, 1799–June 2, 1800.
Am. Antiq. Soc. has Apr. 19, May 3–Aug. 30, 1799; Apr. 14–May 19, June 2, 1800.
Lib. Congress has Apr. 26, May 10, 31, June 14, 21, 1799.
Harvard has June 21, Aug. 23, Oct. 4, 11, 1799; Feb. 6, Mar. 3, May 19, June 2–23, 1800.
Conn. Hist. Soc. has Jan. 2–16, Feb. 6, 13, 24–Apr. 7, 21–June 23, 1800.
Univ. of Mich. (Clements) has Apr. 21, May 5, 1800.

[Northampton] Republican Spy, 1804-1808.

Weekly. Removed from Springfield and established at Northampton with the issue of July 3, 1804, vol. 2, no. 54, published by Timothy Ashley, with the title of "Republican Spy." With the issue of June 4, 1805, the paper was published by Andrew Wright, and with the issue of Aug. 6, 1806, by Andrew Wright "for the Proprietors." With the issue of Jan. 28, 1807, it was taken over and published by Horace Graves. With the issue of July 28, 1807, Graves admitted Ebenezer Clap to partnership, under the firm name of Graves & Clap. The paper was discontinued with the issue of Nov. 16, 1808, vol. 6, no. 281.

Conn. Valley Hist. Soc., Springfield, has July 3, 1804-June 23, 1807.
Harvard has July 3, 17-31, Aug. 28-Oct. 9, 23, Nov. 6, 1804; Jan. 1, 15-29, Feb. 19, 26, Mar. 5, Apr. 2, 9, May 7, 14, June 18, July 23, Aug. 13-Sept. 17, Oct. 1, 8, 22-Nov. 26, Dec. 10-31, 1805; Jan. 14-Feb. 11, 25, Mar. 4, Apr. 8- May 13, 27-June 10, July 15, 30, Aug. 6, 20, Sept. 10, 24, Oct. 8, Nov. 5- 26, Dec. 24, 31, 1806; Feb. 4, 11, Mar. 25-Apr. 15, May 6, 19, June 30, July 7, 21, Aug. 4, 11, Sept. 1, 22, 29, Oct. 13, 27, Nov. 11, 18, 1807.
Am. Antiq. Soc. has July 31, Aug. 21, Nov. 27, Dec. 11, 1804; Feb. 5, Sept. 3- 17, Oct. 8, 22, 29, Nov. 26, Dec. 3, 1805; Feb. 18-Dec. 31, 1806; Jan. 7- Dec. 30, 1807; Jan. 13-Feb. 17, Mar. 2-16, Aug. 3, 10, Sept. 7, 1808.
Lib. Congress has Aug. 28, Sept. 11, 18, Oct. 2, 16-30, Dec. 4, 1804; Feb. 19, June 11, Aug. 6, Oct. 29, Nov. 12, 1805; Jan. 7, 28, Feb. 4, 18, Mar. 25, May 20, July 23, Dec. 24, 1806; Jan. 7-June 23, July 21, Nov. 25, Dec. 16, 1807; Mar. 16, Oct. 26, Nov. 2, 1808.
Wis. Hist. Soc. has Mar. 25, Oct. 22, Nov. 19, Dec. 10, 31, 1806; Jan. 14, Mar. 25, Apr. 8, 1807; Jan. 6-Mar. 23, Apr. 6-20, May 4-June 22, July 6-20, Aug. 3, 31, Sept. 7, 21-Nov. 16, 1808.
Forbes Lib., Northampton, has Apr. 22, May 20, Nov. 12, 1806; Nov. 9, 1808.
Pomona Coll., Claremont, Calif., has Nov. 20, 1804.
N. Y. Pub. Lib. has Feb. 12, 1805; Apr. 29, 1806.
N. Y. Hist. Soc. has Dec. 3, 1806.
Western Reserve Hist. Soc. has Mar. 18, 1807.

[Pittsfield] American Centinel, 1787.

Weekly. Established Sept. 28, 1787, judging from the date of the earliest and only issue located, "The American Centinel," Oct. 19, 1787, vol. 1, no. 4, published by Russell & Storrs [Ezekiel Russell and Roger Storrs]. This statement does not harmonize with that of J. G. Holland, in his "History of Western Massachusetts," vol. 1, p. 465, where it is stated that the paper was established Dec. 1, 1787, judging from the second issue. J. E. A. Smith, in the "Berkshire County Eagle" of Mar. 3, 1887, quotes a copy owned in Pittsfield by Thaddeus Clapp, dated Dec. 18, 1787, vol. 1, no. 9, published by E. Russell. But it was Mr. Clapp who had written the article on newspapers for Holland, and since his paper was in dilapidated condition, he might have read it as Dec. 8, 1787, vol. 1, no. 2. A possible explanation of the volume numbering would be that Russell started a new numbering after the dissolution of the partnership with Storrs.

Robert C. Rockwell, Pittsfield, who died 1928, had Oct. 19, 1787, now not located.

[Pittsfield] Berkshire Chronicle, 1788–1790.

Weekly. Established May 8, 1788, by Roger Storrs, with the title of "The Berkshire Chronicle." With the issue of Dec. 19, 1788, the size of the paper was enlarged and the title changed to "The Berkshire Chronicle, and the Massachusetts Intelligencer." The last issue located is that of Sept. 30, 1790, vol. 3, no. 13.

Berkshire Athenaeum, Pittsfield, has May 15, 1788–June 17, 1790.
Am. Antiq. Soc. has May 8, June 5, 26, July 3, 24, Sept. 4, 25, Oct. 16, 30, Nov. 13, Dec. 19, 1788; Feb. 20, Apr. 24, May 1, 15, Aug. 3, 31, Sept. 21, Oct. 5, Nov. 2, Dec. 7–21, 1789; Jan. 7, 28, Feb. 11, 25, Mar. 11–June 24, July 8, 29–Aug. 12, 26, Sept. 9–30, 1790.
Univ. of Mich. (Clements) has June 19, 1788; Dec. 14, 1789; Aug. 12, 1790.
Lib. Congress has July 17, 1788.
N. Y. Hist. Soc. has Apr. 8, 1790.
R. C. Rockwell, Pittsfield, who died 1928, had June 24, 1790.

[Pittsfield] Berkshire Gazette, 1798–1800.

Weekly. Established Jan. 18, 1798, with the title of "Berkshire Gazette," published by Merrill and Smith [Orsamus C. Merrill and Chester Smith]. In June, 1798, Merrill retired from the firm in favor of Nathaniel Holly, and the paper was published by Holly & Smith. With the issue of Mar. 6, 1799, Holly retired and the paper was published by Chester Smith. The last issue located is that of Feb. 11, 1800, vol. 2, no. 50.

Am. Antiq. Soc. has Jan. 18, 24, Feb. 28, Mar. 28–Apr. 11, 25, July 25, Aug. 1, 22, Sept. 12, Oct. 3, 17, 31, Nov. 7, Dec. 19, 1798; Feb. 13, Mar. 13, July 3, 1799.
Harvard has Jan. 24, Mar. 28, Apr. 4, Aug. 15, 29–Sept. 12, Oct. 17–31, Nov. 14, 1798; Jan. 2, Feb. 27, Apr. 10, 17, May 22, June 5–19, July 31, Aug. 7, 21, Sept. 11, Oct. 16, 23, 1799; Jan. 14, Feb. 4, 11, 1800.
Berkshire Athenaeum, Pittsfield, has Apr. 11, 1798; Feb. 20–Mar. 20, Apr. 3, 10, May 8, 22–June 5, 19, Aug. 28, Sept. 4, 18, 1799.

[Pittsfield] Berkshire Reporter, 1807–1815.

Weekly. Established by H[eman] Willard at Pittsfield, under the name of "The Berkshire Reporter," in January, 1807, the earliest Pittsfield issue located being that of Jan. 17, 1807, vol. 18, no. 889. The paper was a continuation in numbering, although not in title, of the "Western Star," Willard's paper at Stockbridge. With the issue of May 16, 1807, Willard disposed of the paper to Seymour & Smith [Joseph W. Seymour and Milo Smith]. With the issue of Oct. 15, 1808, Seymour retired and the paper was published by Milo Smith & Co. Smith's name disappeared from the imprint late in 1814 or early in 1815 (he was at Stockbridge in 1815 publishing the "Berkshire Herald") and in 1815 the paper was printed by E[———] Cooper, Jun., for the Proprietors. The last issue at Pittsfield was that of Nov. 23, 1815, vol. 26, no. 1351, after which the paper was removed to Stockbridge, consolidated with the "Berkshire Herald" of that town, and continued, without change of numbering, as the "Berkshire Star." See under Stockbridge.

Am. Antiq. Soc. has Jan. 17, 24, Feb. 14, 28, Mar. 14, Apr. 4, 18–June 6, 20, July 25, Aug. 8, 15, 29, Oct. 10–31, Nov. 14, Dec. 5–26, 1807; Jan. 2–16, Feb. 6, 20, Mar. 5–19, Apr. 9, May 14, 28, June 11, 25, Aug. 13–27, 1808; Feb. 4, Mar. 6, Nov. 18, 1809; Jan. 3, 1810–Dec. 28, 1811; Feb. 1, Oct. 22, 1812; Mar. 24, Apr. 21, 28, June 30, Sept. 1, 1814; July 27–Aug. 10, Nov. 2, 16, 1815.

H. Armour Smith, Yonkers, N. Y., has Jan. 31, 1807–Oct. 27, 1809, fair.

Berkshire Athenaeum, Pittsfield, has Oct. 31, 1807; Jan. 3–Mar. 28, Apr. 11–June 13, 27–Dec. 26, 1810; Jan. 5, Mar. 9, May 4, Aug. 17, Sept. 14, Nov. 9, 1811; Feb. 8, Aug. 15, 1812; Jan. 7, 1813–May 19, 1814; July 28, 1814.

N. Y. State Lib. has Feb. 14, 28, Mar. 14, 21, July 14, 1807; Mar. 12–26, July 10, Nov. 26, Dec. 3, 1808; Feb. 4–Apr. 8, 22, 29, May 13–July 8, 22–Sept. 23, Oct. 7, 14, 28–Nov. 18, 29, 1809–Apr. 18, 1810.

Lib. Congress has Aug. 12, 1809; Apr. 25, May 16, June 6, Nov. 7, 1810.

Univ. of Mich. (Clements) has July 11, Oct. 22, 29, 1812; June 1, 1815.

Western Reserve Hist. Soc. has Nov. 2, 1815.

Harvard has Apr. 4, 1807.

Cornell Univ. has Aug. 1, 1807.

Univ. of Ill. has Sept. 24, 1808.

Essex Inst. has June 10, 1809.

Pocumtuck Valley Mem. Assoc., Deerfield, has Nov. 25, 1809.

Wis. Hist. Soc. has Oct. 29, 1812.

Mrs. Raymond L. Buell, Richmond, Mass., has Oct. 27, 1814.

Marblehead Hist. Soc. has Sept. 7, 1815.

[**Pittsfield**] **Sun**, 1800–1820+.

Weekly. Established Sept. 16, 1800, by Phinehas Allen, with the title of "The Sun." With the issue of May 17, 1802, the title appeared only as a column heading on the first page. With the issue of May 23, 1803, the full page heading was resumed and the title changed to "The Pittsfield Sun." The title was changed with the issue of Sept. 15, 1804, to "The Sun"; with July 6, 1805, to

"The Pittsfield Sun"; with Jan. 6, 1806, to "The Pittsfield Sun; or, Republican Monitor"; with Aug. 8, 1807, to "The Pittsfield Sun"; and with Nov. 19, 1817, to "Pittsfield Sun." Continued by Phinehas Allen until after 1820.

Berkshire Athenaeum, Pittsfield, has Sept. 16, 1800–Dec. 27, 1820.
Am. Antiq. Soc. has Oct. 7–Nov. 11, 25–Dec. 9, 24, 1800; Feb. 24, Mar. 17, 23, Apr. 28, May 12, July 14, 28, Sept. 1–15, 29–Oct. 26, Dec. 7, 21, 1801; Jan. 4–Feb. 1, Mar. 8, 29–Apr. 12, 26, May 17, 24, June 21, July 5, 12, 26, Aug. 9–Oct. 4, 25–Nov. 15, Dec. 6, 27, 1802; Jan. 10, 17, 31, Feb. 14–28, Apr. 4, 11, July 4, 11, Aug. 1–Oct. 3, 24–Dec. 26, 1803; Jan. 9, 16, Feb. 13, 20, Mar. 5–26, Apr. 9, 23–May 7, 28, June 4, 9, July 7, 21, 28, Sept. 1, 8, 22–Oct. 6, 27–Nov. 12, Dec. 3, 31, 1804; Jan. 7, 28–Mar. 11, 25–Apr. 15, 29, May 13–27, June 15, 29–July 13, 27–Sept. 14, Oct. 19–Nov. 25, Dec. 9, 23, 1805; Jan. 6, 13, 27, Feb. 3, 17, Mar. 10, 31–Apr. 14, 28, May 17, June 28, July 12–Aug. 9, 23–Nov. 15, Dec. 13, 1806; Feb. 7, 14, 28, Mar. 14, 28, Apr. 4, 18–June 27, July 11, Aug. 8–Sept. 19, Oct. 3–31, Nov. 14–Dec. 12, 26, 1807; Jan. 2–Aug. 27, Sept. 10–24, Oct. 8, 22, Nov. 12, 19, Dec. 3–31, 1808; Jan. 7, 1809–Dec. 27, 1820.

N. Y. Hist. Soc. has Sept. 23, 1800–Sept. 12, 1803, fair; Mar. 25, 1813–July 27, 1815.

Harvard has Jan. 6, Apr. 21–May 5, 19–June 2, 16–July 7, 21, 28, Aug. 11, Sept. 1, 29, Oct. 13–Nov. 9, 23, Dec. 14–28, 1801; Jan. 4–Feb. 15, Mar. 8–Apr. 12, 26, May 3, 24–July 5, 26, Aug. 9, 16, Sept. 6–20, Oct. 4, 11, 25, Nov. 8–22, Dec. 6–27, 1802; Jan. 17–May 2, 23, 30, June 13, 27, July 25, Aug. 22, Sept. 5, 12, Oct. 3, 24, 1803; Mar. 12, 19, Apr. 23, June 23, July 28–Aug. 18, Sept. 1, Oct. 6, 20, Nov. 12–26, 1804; Jan. 21, Feb. 18, Mar. 4, 11, 25–Apr. 8, 29, May 13–June 10, 22, 29, July 20, Aug. 3, Sept. 7, 14, 28–Nov. 25, Dec. 9–30, 1805; Jan. 6–20, Feb. 10–Mar. 3, Apr. 4, 21–May 17, June 7–21, July 12–26, Aug. 9, Sept. 27, Oct. 11, 18, Nov. 22, Dec. 6–27, 1806; Jan. 10–Feb. 14, Mar. 7, 14, 28, Apr. 4, 25, May 2, June 6, 13, July 4, Sept. 5, 26, Oct. 3–17, 1807; Dec. 10–31, 1808.

N. Y. Pub. Lib. has Sept. 15–Oct. 27, Nov. 12–Dec. 17, 31, 1804; Jan. 21–Feb. 18, Mar. 4–Apr. 15, 29, May 13–July 20, Aug. 3–Sept. 7, 21, 28, Oct. 12–Dec. 30, 1805; Jan. 13–Apr. 14, May 10, 17, 31, June 7, 21–July 26, Aug. 9–Oct. 4, 1806; Aug. 19, Sept. 9, 1809; Jan. 17, 31, Feb. 14–Mar. 7, June 20, 27, July 18, Sept. 26–Oct. 10, 24–Dec. 26, 1810; Jan. 5, 19–Mar. 2, 16, 30–July 6, 20–Sept. 7, 1811; Sept. 17–Oct. 1, 15–Dec. 31, 1812; Jan. 7–May 6, 20, June 3–July 22, Aug. 5, 19, 1813; June 16, 30, 1814; June 29, 1815; Sept. 12–Nov. 13, Dec. 4, 11, 25, 1816; Jan. 1–22, Feb. 12–Mar. 5, 19–May 21, June 4, July 2–30, Aug. 13–27, 1817; Sept. 1–Nov. 17, Dec. 1–22, 1819; Jan. 5, 19–Apr. 5, 19–May 17, 31–Aug. 2, 16, 1820.

N. Y. State Lib. has Dec. 16, 1800; June 23, Sept. 15, 1801; July 5–26, Dec. 20, 27, 1802; Jan. 3, Sept. 12, 1803; Mar. 19, 1804; June 10, Sept. 7, 1805; Mar. 17, Apr. 4–21, June 14, 21, 1806; Jan. 10, 1807–Feb. 16, 1811; Mar. 21,

28, Aug. 1, 8, Oct. 1, 1812; Mar. 10, Aug. 25–Sept. 15, Dec. 15–29, 1814; Feb. 2–16, Mar. 29, May 4, 11, June 1, Aug. 3, 17, 31–Sept. 14, Nov. 23, 1815; Sept. 19, Nov. 13, 1816.
Boston Pub. Lib. has Jan..7, 1813–Aug. 29, 1816.
Lib. Congress has Mar. 3, 1801; July 12, 1806; Mar. 7, 1807; Jan. 13–Dec. 29, 1814; Jan. 15, 1817; Jan. 27–Dec. 15, 1819; Jan. 5, 26, Feb. 9–23, Mar. 8, Sept. 7, Nov. 15–Dec. 27, 1820.
Duke Univ. has July 22, 1809; Feb. 28, Apr. 11, 25, May 16, 30, Aug. 29, Nov. 7, 28, Dec. 12, 26, 1810; Mar. 16, Apr. 13, 20, May 4–June 15, Aug. 3, 31, Sept. 14, Oct. 19–Nov. 16, 30, Dec. 7, 1811; Feb. 29, June 27, Aug. 1, 1812; May 6, 1813; Oct. 31, Nov. 20, 1816; Nov. 29–Dec. 13, 1820.
Univ. of Ill. has Dec. 16, 1800; Jan. 6, 20, 27, 1801; Oct. 10, 31–Nov. 14, Dec. 5, 19, 26, 1803; Mar. 19, 26, Apr. 9, 30, May 7, 21, 1804; Jan. 6, Feb. 24, Mar. 10, 1806; Oct. 10, 17, 1807; Nov. 3, 1814.
Stockbridge Pub. Lib. has May 9, 1812; Dec. 2, 16–30, 1813; Jan. 13, 1814; Dec. 4, 11, 1816; May 14, 21, June 4, July 30, 1817; Aug. 5, Sept. 30, Dec. 23, 1818.
Univ. of Mich. (Clements) has May 14, 1808; May 11, 1811; Nov. 5, 1812; Feb. 17, 1814; Nov. 7, 1816; Mar. 18, 25, 1818.
Yale has Aug. 3, Oct. 19, 26, Nov. 16, 30, 1811; June 27, 1812; Dec. 13, 1820.
Long Id. Hist. Soc. has Nov. 11, Dec. 30, 1800; July 28, Aug. 4, 1801.
Essex Inst. has Mar. 1, 1802; Oct. 3, 1807; Sept. 26, 1810; Feb. 4, 1813.
Wis. Hist. Soc. has Dec. 30, 1800; Jan. 10, Aug. 1, 1810; June 23, 1814; July 6, 1815; Nov. 7, 1816; Dec. 16, 1818.
Minn. Hist. Soc. has Jan. 16, 30, Feb. 6, 1808.
Boston Athenæum has Apr. 8, 29, 1809; Mar. 15, 1820.
Buffalo Hist. Soc. has Aug. 26, 1813; Jan. 20, May 26, 1819.

Plymouth Journal, 1785–1786.

Weekly. Established Mar. 19, 1785, by Nathaniel Coverly, with the title of "The Plymouth Journal, and the Massachusetts Advertiser." The last issue located is that of June 13, 1786, vol. 2, no. 65, in which Coverly refers to the possible discontinuance of his paper if subscriptions are not paid.

Am. Antiq. Soc. has Mar. 19, May 17, 31–July 5, 19, 26, Aug. 16, 30–Sept. 20, Oct. 1, Dec. 13–27, 1785; Jan. 3–17, Feb. 14, 28, Mar. 14, 28–June 13, 1786.
Pilgrim Soc. Lib., Plymouth, has Mar. 21, Apr. 18, 1786.
N. Y. Hist. Soc. has Mar. 28, June 6, 1786.

Portland, see under **Maine.**

[Salem] American Eagle, 1790.

This was the title given to the first issue of the "Salem Gazette," Jan. 5, 1790. See under "Salem Gazette," 1790–1820.

[Salem] American Gazette, 1776.

Weekly. Established June 18, 1776, with the title of "The American Gazette: or, the Constitutional Journal." It was "Printed by J. Rogers, at E. Russell's Printing-Office," but Ezekiel Russell was evidently the publisher rather than John Rogers. An unnumbered "Extraordinary" issue was published June 12, 1776; and an "Extraordinary" issue, numbered vol. 1, no. 1, was published June 19. The last issue located is that of July 30, 1776, vol. 1, no. 7, and it is probable that this issue was the last published.

Essex Inst. has June 12, 18–July 30, 1776.
Am. Antiq. Soc. has June 18–July 30, 1776.
Amherst Coll. has June 18–July 9, 23, 30, 1776.
Mass. Hist. Soc. has June 18–July 23, 1776.
Lib. Congress has June 18–July 16, 30, 1776.
Boston Pub. Lib. has June 19, 25, July 9, 16, 1776.
Univ. of Mich. (Clements) has July 16, 23, 1776.

Salem Chronicle, 1786.

Weekly. Established Mar. 30, 1786, by George Roulstone, with the title of "The Salem Chronicle, and Essex Advertiser." The last issue located is that of Aug. 3, 1786, vol. 1, no. 19.

Essex Inst. has Mar. 30–Apr. 20, May 4, 18, 25, June 8–July 6, Aug. 3, 1786.
Am. Antiq. Soc. has Apr. 7, 1786.
N. Y. Hist. Soc. has June 15, 1786.

[Salem] Essex Gazette, 1768–1775.

Weekly. Established Aug. 2, 1768, by Samuel Hall, with the title of "The Essex Gazette." There was also a prospectus signed by Samuel Hall and dated July 5, 1768. With the issue of Jan. 7, 1772, Samuel Hall admitted his brother Ebenezer to partnership and the paper was published by Samuel and Ebenezer Hall. The last issue at Salem was that of May 2, 1775, vol. 7, no. 353, and the next issue was published at Cambridge, May 12, 1775, vol. 7, no. 354, and entitled "The New England Chronicle." See under Cambridge.

Essex Inst. has Aug. 2, 1768–May 2, 1775.
Mass. Hist. Soc. has Aug. 9, 1768–May 2, 1775.
Lib. Congress has Aug. 2, 1768–May 2, 1775, lacking 3 issues.
Am. Antiq. Soc. has Aug. 2, 1768–May 2, 1775, lacking 5 issues.
Yale has Aug. 2, 1768–May 2, 1775, lacking a few issues.
Boston Athenæum has Aug. 16, 1768–June 13, 1769; Aug. 1, 1769–May 2, 1775.
Wis. Hist. Soc. has Aug. 2, 1768–July 28, 1772; Jan. 5, 1773–May 2, 1775.

MASSACHUSETTS 395

N. Y. Hist. Soc. has Sept. 13, 20, 1768; Feb. 21, 28, Apr. 18, May 9, 30–June 13, 27, July 4, 18, 25, Aug. 22–Sept. 12, 26–Oct. 10, 24–Nov. 7, 28, Dec. 5, 26, 1769; Jan. 2, 16, 23, Mar. 27, Apr. 3, May 22–June 5, 19, Sept. 18–Dec. 25, 1770; Jan. 1–Feb. 26, Mar. 12–26, Apr. 9, 16, 30, May 7, 28–June 25, July 9, 30–Dec. 31, 1771; Jan. 7, 1772–Dec. 28, 1773; Jan. 11, 18, Feb. 8, 15, Mar. 15, Apr. 5, 26, June 18, July 5–19, Oct. 4, 1774; Jan. 3–May 2, 1775.
N. Y. Pub. Lib. has Aug. 2–Dec. 27, 1768; Jan. 3–July 25, Aug. 8, 29, 1769; Feb. 6, 20, Apr. 3, 17–May 1, 22, June 5–19, Aug. 21, Sept. 4–18, Oct. 2, 16, 30–Nov. 13, Dec. 4, 11, 25, 1770; Jan. 1, 22–Feb. 26, Mar. 12–26, Apr. 9, 16, 30–May 28, June 11–25, July 9–Aug. 13, 27, Dec. 3, 1771; Jan. 14, Feb. 4, 25, Mar. 3, 17–Sept. 15, 29–Dec. 29, 1772; Jan. 5–Feb. 2, 16–Mar. 2, 16–May 4, 18–Sept. 28, Dec. 21, 28, 1773; Jan. 25–Feb. 22, Mar. 22–Apr. 12, 26, May 17, 31, June 14–28, July 19–Aug. 2, 16–30, Sept. 13, 20, Oct. 4, 18–Nov. 8, 22–Dec. 6, 20, 27, 1774; Jan. 10, 17, 31–Mar. 21, Apr. 4–18, May 2, 1775.
Harvard has Nov. 22, 1768; Aug. 15, 29–Oct. 24, Nov. 21, Dec. 5, 12, 26, 1769; Feb. 5–Apr. 16, 30–May 14, 28, June 4, 18–July 30, Aug. 13–Dec. 31, 1771; Jan. 7–Dec. 29, 1772; Jan. 5–19, Feb. 2, 9, 1773; May 17, Aug. 30, Sept. 6, Oct. 25, 1774–May 2, 1775.
N. Y. State Lib. has Nov. 29, 1768; Jan. 24, Feb. 21, Mar. 7, 21, Apr. 4, 18, May 2, 16, 30–June 13, 27, July 25–Sept. 5, 19–Dec. 26, 1769; Jan. 2–May 15, 29, July 3, 24, Aug. 21, Oct. 30, 1770; Jan. 1–Feb. 19, Mar. 5–Aug. 6, 20, Sept. 24, Oct. 15–29, Nov. 19–Dec. 3, 17, 31, 1771; Jan. 14–28, Feb. 11, 18, Mar. 3, 10, 31–Apr. 28, May 12, 19, June 2–July 7, 21–Dec. 1, 15, 29, 1772; Jan. 19, 1773–May 2, 1775.
Boston Pub. Lib. has Jan. 3–24, Feb. 7, 14, 28–Mar. 21, Apr. 11, 18, May 2, 30, June 6, 20, July 18, Sept. 5, 19, Oct. 17, 31, Nov. 14, 28, Dec. 12, 26, 1769; Jan. 9, 23–Feb. 6, 20–Mar. 6, 20–May 15, 29–June 12, 26–July 10, 24–Dec. 25, 1770; Jan. 1–22, Feb. 5, 12, 26–July 2, 16–Dec. 31, 1771; Feb. 4, Aug. 4–Dec. 29, 1772; Jan. 5–June 29, July 27, Aug. 24, Sept. 7, 21, Oct. 5, 19, Nov. 2, 9, 30, Dec. 7, 21, 1773; Feb. 1, 22, Mar. 15, Aug. 16, 30, Sept. 6, 20, Oct. 25, Nov. 1–Dec. 27, 1774; Jan. 10, 17, Feb. 7–May 2, 1775.
Portland Pub. Lib. has May 3, 1774–May 2, 1775.
Univ. of Mich. (Clements) has Nov. 29, 1768; Apr. 11, Aug. 8, 22, Sept. 5, 19, Oct. 3–Nov. 7, 28–Dec. 26, 1769; Jan. 2, 9, 23–Feb. 20, Mar. 13, May 1, 15, Nov. 27, Dec. 25, 1770; Mar. 5, Apr. 9, 23–May 7, 21–June 11, 25–July 16, 30, Aug. 6, 20, Sept. 10, 17, 1771; July 21, 1772; Jan. 26, Feb. 2, Mar. 16, Apr. 6, 27, May 18–June 1, July 20, Aug. 17, 31, Sept. 7, Oct. 5, 12, Nov. 16–30, Dec. 14, 1773; Jan. 4–Apr. 19, May 3–June 14, 28–Aug. 16, Sept. 6–27, Oct. 11–Dec. 27, 1774; Jan. 3, 17–31, Feb. 14–Mar. 14, 28–May 2, 1775.
Mass. State Lib. has Jan. 31–May 2, 1775.
Duke Univ. has June 5, 12, 1770; Jan. 15, May 7, 28, June 11, July 2, 16, 30, 1771; Mar. 3, Aug. 4, Sept. 8, Oct. 6–20, Dec. 15, 22, 1772; Jan. 5, 19,

Feb. 16, Mar. 16, Apr. 6, 27, May 18, June 1–July 27, Aug. 10, 31, Sept. 7, 21, 28, Dec. 28, 1773; Jan. 25, Feb. 15, Dec. 6, 1774; Apr. 4, 1775.
Hist. Soc. Penn. has Aug. 23, 30, Sept. 13–27, Dec. 27, 1768; Mar. 17, 1772.
Western Reserve Hist. Soc. has Apr. 12, Oct. 25, Nov. 8, Dec. 6, 1774; Mar. 21, 1775.
Chicago Hist. Soc. has July 31, Aug. 7, 1770.

[Salem] **Essex Register,** 1807–1820+.

Semi-weekly. A continuation of the "Salem Register." The first issue of "The Essex Register" was that of July 23, 1807, new series, no. 1, whole no. 749, published by H[aven] Pool & W[arwick] Palfray, Jr., assisted by S. Cleveland Blydon. With the issue of Jan. 6, 1808, Blydon's name was withdrawn, and the paper published by Pool & Palfray. Pool died June 28, 1811, and beginning with the issue of July 1, 1811, the paper was published by Warwick Palfray, Jun., although his name did not appear in the imprint until the issue of Aug. 31, 1811. Continued by him until after 1820. Rev. William Bentley was a frequent contributor to the paper and in his printed "Diary" may be found many references to it.

Am. Antiq. Soc., Essex Inst., and Lib. Congress have July 23, 1807–Dec. 30, 1820.
N. Y. Hist. Soc. has July 23, 1807–Dec. 29, 1819.
Boston Pub. Lib. has July 27, 1807–Dec. 29, 1810; Jan. 2–Apr. 27, May 7, 25, 29, June 15, 22, July 10, 17, 31, Sept. 18, 21, 28, Oct. 8, 16, 23, Nov. 6–13, 20, 23, Dec. 11, 21, 28, 1811; Apr. 25, 29, May 5, 13, 20–Nov. 4, 21, Dec. 2–30, 1812; Jan. 2, 1813–Dec. 21, 1816, fair; Jan. 1, 1817–Dec. 25, 1819.
Harvard has July 23–Nov. 30, 1807; June 1–Dec. 31, 1808; Nov. 3, 1810–Oct. 29, 1814; Jan. 4–Dec. 30, 1815; Oct. 29, 1817; Dec. 4, 1819; Feb. 9–Mar. 1, May 3–Sept. 27, 1820.
Chicago Hist. Soc. has Aug. 6, 1807–Jan. 27, 1810, fair; Mar. 20–Apr. 28, 1813.
Mass. Hist. Soc. has Apr. 4, 1812; May 22, June 12, July 3–Dec. 18, 1813, fair; Jan. 8–Dec. 31, 1814; Jan. 4–Sept. 27, 1815, fair; Oct. 7, 28, Nov. 29, Dec. 6, 1815, Sept. 10, 1817; Jan. 5, 8, 1820.
N. Y. State Lib. has Aug. 2, Oct. 7, 1809; Jan. 5–Dec. 28, 1811; Jan. 18, Aug. 22, Oct. 3, 14, 1812; Apr. 9, 1814; Feb. 4, 1815; June 8, July 6, Dec. 11, 1816; Mar. 15, May 10, 1817; Feb. 7, July 18, Aug. 12, 29, Sept. 2, 9, 19, 1818; Feb. 12, May 27, 1820.
Wis. Hist. Soc. has Dec. 21, 1808; Mar. 30, 1816; Dec. 19, 1818; Jan. 2, 1819–Jan. 5, 1820.
Boston Athenæum has Aug. 13, Sept. 21, 1808; Apr. 26–May 2, 13–31, Aug. 19, Sept. 9, 20, 1809; Jan. 23, Feb. 13, 1811; June 6, Dec. 2, 1812; Oct. 4, 12, 1814; Aug. 2, Sept. 6–13, 1815; June 5, 8, 15, Nov. 20, 1816; Feb. 1, May 14, June 11, 14, 1817; May 23, Sept. 5, Oct. 28, 31, 1818; May 8, June 2, 1819; May 17, 1820.

MASSACHUSETTS 397

Univ. of Mich. (Clements) has Feb. 16, 20, Mar. 5, 9, Apr. 9, 20, 27, 30, June 1, July 16, Oct. 29, 1808; Jan. 4–21, Feb. 22, 1809; June 12, July 20, Nov. 9, 1811; Feb. 8, 22, Mar. 4, 7, 21, 28, Apr. 4–15, June 10, July 18, Sept. 9, 1812; Apr. 2, 1814; Sept. 18, Oct. 2–20, 27, Dec. 1, 18, 22, 1819; Jan. 5–Dec. 30, 1820, fair.
Me. Hist. Soc. has Jan. 16, 1808–Nov. 11, 1809, fair.
Western Reserve Hist. Soc. has Jan. 2–Nov. 30, 1811, fair; Mar. 29, Dec. 13, 1815; Jan. 3–Dec. 11, 1816, fair; Dec. 23, 1818; Apr. 28, May 1, 1819; Jan. 5, Feb. 12, 26, 1820.
Portland Pub. Lib. has Jan. 2–Dec. 28, 1811.
N. Y. Pub. Lib. has Mar. 14, 1810; Jan. 23–Feb. 20, May 7–June 1, 12–July 6, 17, 1811; Mar. 24, 1819.
Peabody Coll., Nashville, Tenn., has Aug. 28, 1819–Sept. 20, 1820.

[Salem] Friend, 1807.

Weekly. Established Jan. 3, 1807, by Stephen C. Blyth & Haven Pool, with the title of "The Friend." With the issue of Feb. 7, 1807, the imprint was changed to "Editor-Stephen C. Blyth. Printed and published by Haven Pool." Blyth had his name changed by legislative act, and with the issue of May 2, 1807, the name of S. Cleveland Blydon appeared in the imprint as Editor. Discontinued with the issue of July 18, 1807, vol. 1, no. 29, when the paper was sold out to the "Salem Register."

Essex Inst. has Jan. 3, 17–July 18, 1807.
Harvard has Jan. 3, 17–Apr. 18, May 2, 16–June 27, July 11, 1807.
Am. Antiq. Soc. has Jan. 3, 17–Mar. 14, 28, Apr. 25, May 9–June 6, 20, 27, July 11, 1807.
Western Reserve Hist. Soc. has June 6, 1807.
Boston Pub. Lib. has July 18, 1807.

Salem Gazette, 1774–1775.

Weekly. Established July 1, 1774, by E[zekiel] Russell, with the title of "The Salem Gazette, and Newbury and Marblehead Advertiser." There was also a prospectus issue, unnumbered, dated June 24, 1774. With the issue of Dec. 9, 1774, the first "and" in the title was changed to "or." The last issue located is that of Apr. 21, 1775, no. 43.

British Museum has July 1, 1774–Apr. 21, 1775.
Essex Inst. has June 24, July 1–Sept. 2, 16, 1774–Apr. 14, 1775.
Mass. Hist. Soc. has July 15, 29, Aug. 12–Sept. 2, 16–30, Nov. 18, Dec. 23, 30, 1774; Jan. 20, 27, Feb. 10–24, 1775.
Boston Pub. Lib. has June 24–July 8, 29, Aug. 19, Dec. 19, 1774.
Am. Antiq. Soc. has Aug. 30, Sept. 16, Oct. 14, Nov. 4, 18, 1774.
Lib. Congress has Feb. 17, Mar. 3, 1775.

Salem Gazette, 1781.

Weekly. Established Jan. 2, 1781, by Mary Crouch and Company, with the title of "The Salem Gazette, and General Advertiser." There was also a sheet of "Proposals," dated Dec. 6, 1780. The issue of Sept. 4, 1781, vol. 1, no. 36, announced the discontinuance of the paper.

Boston Athenæum has Jan. 2–Sept. 4, 1781.
Essex Inst. has Jan. 2–Apr. 24, May 8, 15, 29, June 5, 19–July 3, 24, Aug. 14–Sept. 4, 1781; also "Proposals" of Dec. 6, 1780.
Lib. Congress has Jan. 2–June 5, 19–July 17, 1781.
Mass. Hist. Soc. has Jan. 2, 16, 23, Mar. 13, 27, Apr. 17, 24, June 26, July 3, Aug. 7, 21, 1781.
Am. Antiq. Soc. has Feb. 6, May 1–15, July 17, Aug. 7, 14, 1781.
Yale has Feb. 27, Mar. 6, 1781.
N. Y. State Lib. has Aug. 7, 1781.

Salem Gazette, 1781–1785.

Weekly. Established Oct. 18, 1781, by Samuel Hall, with the title of "The Salem Gazette." Discontinued at Salem with the issue of Nov. 22, 1785, vol. 5, no. 215, after which it was removed to Boston, and continued as "The Massachusetts Gazette." See under Boston.

Am. Antiq. Soc., Boston Athenæum, Mass. Hist. Soc., Harvard, Essex Inst., N. Y. Pub. Lib., Lib. Congress, Wis. Hist. Soc., and Univ. of Mich. (Clements) have Oct. 18, 1781–Nov. 22, 1785.
Boston Pub. Lib. has Oct. 18, 1781–Nov. 22, 1785, fair.
Yale has Oct. 25, 1781–Dec. 25, 1783; Apr. 8, 1784–Nov. 22, 1785.
N. Y. Hist. Soc. has Oct. 18, 1781–Nov. 15, 1785, fair.
N. Y. State Lib. has Jan. 3, 10, 24–Feb. 14, Mar. 14–Apr. 4, 18, May 30, 1782–Nov. 22, 1785.
Dartmouth has July 18, 1782–Nov. 22, 1785.
Peabody Coll., Nashville, Tenn., has Oct. 18, 1781–Apr. 1, 1784.
Newberry Lib. has Oct. 17, 1782–Oct. 16, 1783.
Detroit Pub. Lib. has Oct. 17, 1782–Oct. 16, 1783.
Wesleyan Univ. has Apr. 1, 1784–Nov. 22, 1785.
Rutgers Univ. has Jan. 24, May 30, Sept. 5, Nov. 7, 21, 29, Dec. 5, 19, 26, 1782; Jan. 2–Feb. 6, May 8–22, June 5–Aug. 14, Oct. 2–16, 1783; Jan. 8, 1784.
Duke Univ. has Mar. 25, Apr. 1, Nov. 16, 1784; Jan. 4–Oct. 25, 1785.
Univ. of Minn. has Nov. 15, 22, Dec. 14–27, 1781.

Salem Gazette, 1790–1820+.

Weekly and semi-weekly. A continuation of "The Salem Mercury." The first issue with the change of title was that of Jan. 5, 1790, which was called "The

American Eagle," no. 1. The next issue was called "The Salem Gazette," Jan. 12, 1790, "number 2, in 1790," published by Thomas C. Cushing, and this was henceforth the title. With the issue of Jan. 4, 1791, the early system of numbering was resumed, that issue being numbered vol. 5, no. 221. With the issue of Oct. 21, 1794, the paper was published by William Carlton. With the issue of June 3, 1796, it was published semi-weekly. With the issue of July 25, 1797, it was again published by Thomas C. Cushing. The word "The" in the title was omitted beginning with the issue of Jan. 3, 1806, but was restored with the issue of Jan. 1, 1818. The paper was continued by Cushing until after 1820.

Am. Antiq. Soc., Harvard, Essex Inst., and Lib. Congress have Jan. 5, 1790–Dec. 29, 1820.

Boston Athenæum has Jan. 5, 1790–Dec. 30, 1800; Jan. 2, 23, 1801–Dec. 28, 1810; Jan. 3, 1812–Dec. 29, 1820.

Mass. Hist. Soc. has Jan. 5, 1790–Dec. 27, 1791; Jan. 17–Feb. 21, Mar. 6, 13, Apr. 17, 24, May 8–22, July 17, 31, Sept. 4, 18–Oct. 2, Dec. 4, 1792; Jan. 8, Feb. 26, Mar. 3, 1793; Apr. 2, 1793–Dec. 29, 1820, fair.

Yale has Nov. 20–Dec. 25, 1792; Jan. 1–Aug. 27, Nov. 26–Dec. 10, 1793; Feb. 11, 1794–Dec. 29, 1820.

Boston Pub. Lib. has Jan. 26, Feb. 23, Apr. 6, 13, Sept. 21, 28, Dec. 28, 1790; Jan. 18, Dec. 6, 1791; Jan. 10, Feb. 28, Mar. 13–Apr. 3, 17, May 8, 15, 1792; Feb. 19, 26, 1793; Jan. 14, 21, Feb. 11, 25–Mar. 18, July 8, Oct. 28, 1794; Jan. 6, 27, Feb. 17, Mar. 3, 31–Apr. 14, 28, June 16, July 28, Aug. 11, 18, Nov. 10–24, Dec. 8, 22, 1795; Jan. 5, Feb. 23, Mar. 1, May 17, 31, June 3–10, 24, 28, July 22, Aug. 2, 5, Sept. 20–27, Oct. 14, 21, Nov. 1–11, 22, Dec. 2, 9–20, 30, 1796; Jan. 3, 1797–Dec. 29, 1820.

N. Y. Hist. Soc. has Nov. 16, 1790; Jan. 4, 1791–Dec. 31, 1799; Jan. 2–Dec. 29, 1801; July 2, 9, Sept. 3–14, 24–Oct. 1, 8, 1802; Jan. 1–Dec. 31, 1805; Jan. 3, Dec. 16, 30, 1806; July 17, Oct. 9, 1807; Mar. 4, Sept. 17, 1808–Dec. 29, 1809; Jan. 5, 1813–Dec. 30, 1814; Jan. 1–Dec. 31, 1819, fair; Jan. 4–Dec. 29, 1820.

Univ. of Mich. (Clements) has Jan. 12–Dec. 14, 1790, fair; Jan. 3–Dec. 18, 1792, fair; Feb. 25, Mar. 11, 18, Aug. 5, 1794; May 19, 1795; June 30, July 7, 14, 18, 1797; Dec. 27, 1799; Nov. 11, 25, 1800; Apr. 3, Sept. 25, 1801; Sept. 2, Dec. 13, 1803; Jan. 1–Dec. 31, 1805; Jan. 17, May 9, 1806–Dec. 8, 1807, fair; Jan. 12, 1808–Nov. 12, 1816, scattering file; Jan. 3–Dec. 26, 1817, fair; May 1–29, Dec. 8, 1818; Jan. 26, Nov. 26, 1819; May 16–Dec. 29, 1820, fair.

Duke Univ. has Jan. 12, 1790–Dec. 13, 1791, fair; Dec. 4, 1792; Jan. 8, 1793–Dec. 30, 1794, fair; Dec. 8, 1797; Aug. 20–Dec. 20, 1799, fair; Jan. 28–Mar. 4, 1800; Jan. 5, 1808–Dec. 29, 1815; Mar. 12, 22, Apr. 19, 1816; Jan. 14, Apr. 8, 1817; Feb. 3, 1818; Aug. 10, Sept. 3, 1819; Apr. 14, 18, 1820.

N. Y. Pub. Lib. has Jan. 5, 1790–Dec. 27, 1791; Jan. 17, Apr. 24, Oct. 16, Dec. 11, 18, 1792; Jan. 1, 1793–Dec. 29, 1797; Mar. 20–Dec. 25, 1798, fair; Jan. 1–Dec. 31, 1799; Jan. 7–July 8, fair, Sept. 12, Nov. 28, 1800; Feb. 24,

1801; Apr. 6, 1802; Jan. 3, Aug. 17, Nov. 19, 1804; Jan. 22, Mar. 8, Aug. 30, Sept. 10, Nov. 8, 22–28, 1805; Jan. 17, 1806; May 8, 1807; June 27, Oct. 13, 1809; Sept. 20, 1811; Sept. 8, 18, 1812; July 30, Aug. 20, 1813; Sept. 16, 1814; May 9, July 7, 1815.

N. Y. State Lib. has Jan. 31, 1792; Jan. 1, 1793–May 26, Dec. 8, 1795; June 28, July 26–Dec. 27, 1796, fair; Jan. 3, 1797–Dec. 31, 1799; Feb. 18, 1800; Jan. 4–Dec. 30, 1803, fair; Oct. 10–Dec. 29, 1820.

Wis. Hist. Soc. has Jan. 5–Dec. 28, 1790; Jan. 11–Aug. 2, 1791, fair; Jan. 3–Dec. 25, 1792; June 25, Dec. 31, 1793; Jan. 14, Dec. 9, 1794; Jan. 6–Dec. 29, 1795; May 17, 1796; Jan. 3–Dec. 29, 1797; Jan. 16, 26, May 4, 15, Oct. 26–Nov. 9, Dec. 14–29, 1798; Jan. 8–Dec. 13, 1799; Jan. 10–Dec. 29, 1812, fair.

Peabody Coll., Nashville, Tenn., has Mar. 6, 1792–Dec. 30, 1794; Jan. 3–Dec. 30, 1800; Jan. 1, 1802–Dec. 26, 1806; Jan. 1, 1808–Dec. 29, 1809; Oct. 6–Dec. 29, 1820.

Me. Hist. Soc. has Jan. 2, 1801–Apr. 9, 1805.

Amherst Coll. has Jan. 5–Apr. 6, 1790.

Bowdoin has Jan. 4–Dec. 27, 1803.

Tenn. Hist. Soc. has Jan. 2–Dec. 29, 1807.

Woburn Pub. Lib. has Jan. 1–Dec. 31, 1811.

Phil. Lib. Co. has Oct. 8, 15, 1793; Nov. 3, 17–Dec. 1, 1795; Jan. 5, 19, 26, Feb. 23, Mar. 8, 15, Apr. 5, 12, May 17, 24, June 8, 1796.

Many libraries have single or scattering issues.

[Salem] **Impartial Register,** 1800–1801.

Semi-weekly. Established May 12, 1800, by William Carlton, with the title of "The Impartial Register." With the issue of July 31, 1800, the title was changed to "The Salem Impartial Register." The last issue with this title was that of Dec. 31, 1801, vol. 2, no. 172, after which the title was changed to "The Salem Register," which see.

Am. Antiq. Soc., Harvard, and Essex Inst. have May 12, 1800–Dec. 31, 1801.
Boston Pub. Lib. has June 23, Sept. 18, 1800–Dec. 31, 1801.
Boston Athenæum has May 12–Dec. 29,.1800; Feb. 5, 26, 1801.
Lib. Congress has June 19, Sept. 25, 29, Nov. 10, Dec. 15, 25, 29, 1800; Jan. 1–Nov. 2, 1801.
N. Y. Pub. Lib. has Sept. 25, Nov. 3, Dec. 11, 22, 1800; Oct. 8, 15, Nov. 16, 1801.
Univ. of Mich. (Clements) has Jan. 5, 12, 29, Mar. 5, 9, May 25, Aug. 3, 1801.
Wis. Hist. Soc. has Nov. 24, Dec. 8, 11, 1800.
N. Y. State Lib. has June 18, Oct. 5, Dec. 21, 1801.
N. Y. Hist. Soc. has Feb. 26, Oct. 26, 1801.
Long Id. Hist. Soc. has Mar. 19, Aug. 6, 1801.
Conn. Hist. Soc. has June 9, 1800.
Mass. Hist. Soc. has June 9, 1801.
Dartmouth has Dec. 28, 1801.

Salem Mercury, 1786–1789.

Weekly. Established Oct. 14, 1786, by Dabney and Cushing [John Dabney and Thomas C. Cushing], with the title of "The Salem Mercury: Political, Commercial, and Moral." With the issue of Apr. 15, 1788, the title was shortened to "The Salem Mercury." The partnership was dissolved, the issues of Oct. 13–27, 1789, bore no publisher's name in the imprint, and beginning with the issue of Nov. 3, 1789, the publisher's name was given as Thomas C. Cushing. The last issue with the title of "The Salem Mercury" was that of Dec. 29, 1789, vol. 3, no. 168, after which the title was changed to "The Salem Gazette." See under Salem Gazette, 1790–1820.

Am. Antiq. Soc., Boston Athenæum, Harvard, Essex Inst., and Lib. Congress have Oct. 14, 1786–Dec. 29, 1789.

Mass. Hist. Soc. has Oct. 14, 28, Nov. 4, 18, Dec. 16–30, 1786; Jan. 6, 1787–Dec. 29, 1789.

N. Y. Pub. Lib. has Oct. 14–Dec. 30, 1786; Jan. 6–June 12, 26–Dec. 11, 25, 1787; Jan. 1–Feb. 12, Apr. 1–Aug. 12, 26–Dec. 23, 1788; Jan. 13–Feb. 24, Mar. 10–24, Apr. 7–Dec. 29, 1789.

Yale has Oct. 14, 28, 1786–Dec. 25, 1787; Jan. 1–July 8, 22–Oct. 7, 21–Dec. 16, 30, 1788; Jan. 6, 13, 27–Apr. 14, 28–June 30, July 14–Oct. 13, Nov. 3, 10, 24, Dec. 8–29, 1789.

N. Y. State Lib. has Dec. 2, 16–30, 1786; Jan. 6–Apr. 21, May 5, 22, 29, July 17, 31, Aug. 14, 21, Sept. 4–Nov. 20, Dec. 4–25, 1787; Jan. 1–Dec. 30, 1788; Jan. 6, 20, Feb. 10–24, Apr. 14, 28, May 5, 19, 26, June 23–July 7, 21, Aug. 18–Sept. 29, Oct. 13, 27–Dec. 8, 1789.

Boston Pub. Lib. has Oct. 14–Dec. 30, 1786; Jan. 6–20, Feb. 10, 17, Mar. 10, 24–Apr. 21, May 5, 15–June 5, 19–July 10, 31–Aug. 21, Sept. 4–18, Oct. 2, 9, 23–Nov. 20, Dec. 4, 25, 1787; Feb. 19, Mar. 4, 11, Apr. 29, July 22, Oct. 7, 14, 1788; Jan. 13–Mar. 3, Apr. 7–May 12, 26–Nov. 17, Dec. 15–29, 1789.

N. Y. Hist. Soc. has May 15, 1787; Aug. 26, 1788; Jan. 6–Dec. 29, 1789.

Duke Univ. has Dec. 16, 1786; Apr. 22, Nov. 4, 1788; Jan. 27, May 5, June 3, 30–Dec. 29, 1789, fair.

Univ. of Mich. (Clements) has Nov. 13, 1787; Jan. 15, 29–Apr. 22, May 6–Dec. 16, 1788.

Amherst Coll. has May 19–Dec. 29, 1789.

Salem Register, 1802–1807.

Semi-weekly. A continuation, without change of volume numbering, of "The Salem Impartial Register." The first issue with the title of "The Salem Register" was that of Jan. 4, 1802, vol. 3, no. 173, published by William Carlton. The word "The" was omitted from the title with the issue of Jan. 3, 1803. William Carlton died July 24, 1805, no paper was issued July 29, and with the issue of Aug. 1, 1805, the paper was published for his widow, Elizabeth Carlton. She died Aug. 25, 1805, and with the issue of Sept. 2, 1805, the paper was published for the Proprietors. The last issue with the title of "Salem Register" was that of July 16, 1807, vol. 8, no. 56, whole no. 748, after which it was continued as the "Essex Register," which see.

Am. Antiq. Soc., Essex Inst., and Harvard have Jan. 4, 1802–July 16, 1807.
Boston Pub. Lib. has Jan. 4, 1802–Dec. 29, 1803; Jan. 3, 1805–July 13, 1807.
Lib. Congress has Feb. 18, Apr. 12, 19, May 10, 20, Sept. 27, 1802; Jan. 6, 1803–July 16, 1807.
Hist. Soc. Penn. has Feb. 15, 1802–Dec. 22, 1803.
N. Y. State Lib. has Jan. 4–Dec. 30, 1802; Aug. 8–Dec. 30, 1805.
N. Y. Hist. Soc. has Jan. 3, 1805–July 16, 1807.
Univ. of Mich. (Clements) has Jan. 28, Feb. 18, 1805; Mar. 20, 1806–Apr. 9, 1807, fair.
British Museum has Jan. 2, 1804–Dec. 30, 1805.
Yale has Jan. 2, 1804–June 20, 1805; Jan. 23, 1806.
Boston Athenæum has Apr. 29, 1805–Nov. 6, 1806.
Wis. Hist. Soc. has Aug. 16, 19, Nov. 15, Dec. 23–30, 1802; Jan. 3, 27, Feb. 17, Aug. 11–18, 25, Sept. 1, 8, 22, 1803; Jan. 3–June 27, 1805.
N. Y. Pub. Lib. has Oct. 18, 21, Nov. 11, 1802; Jan. 6, Nov. 7, 1803; May 7, 1804; Jan. 12, 1807.
Chicago Hist. Soc. has Dec. 29, 1803; May 17, Nov. 12, 15, 1804; Jan. 21–31, Apr. 4, June 6, 13, 20, Sept. 12, Oct. 24, 31, Nov. 4–18, 1805; Mar. 27–Apr. 7, 1806; Feb. 9, Mar. 2, 30, May 11, 1807.
Duke Univ. has Jan. 26, 30, 1804.
Western Reserve Hist. Soc. has Sept. 16, Oct. 7, 21, Nov. 4, 1805.
Dartmouth has Feb. 28, 1805; Mar. 31, 1806.

[Salem] **Weekly Visitant,** 1806.

Weekly. Established Jan. 1, 1806, by Haven Pool, with the title of "The Weekly Visitant." It was ostensibly a literary periodical, of octavo size and eight pages to a number; but since it contained a certain amount of current news, as well as marriage and death notices, it might possibly be included as a newspaper. The last issue was that of Dec. 27, 1806, vol. 1, no. 52, when the establishment was sold out to a group of proprietors, who began publishing a newspaper called "The Friend."

Am. Antiq. Soc., Boston Athenæum, and Essex Inst. have Jan. 1–Dec. 27, 1806.
Brown Univ. has Jan. 8–Mar. 8, 22, 29, Apr. 12, 26–May 31, June 14–Aug. 2, 16, 23, Sept. 6. 20, Oct. 4–Nov. 1, 15–Dec. 13, 1806.
Catholic Univ., Washington, has Jan. 1–June 21, 1806.
Huntington Lib. has Feb. 1, 1806.

[Springfield] **American Intelligencer,** see **West Springfield.**

[Springfield] Federal Spy, 1792–1805.

Weekly. Established Dec. 19, 1792, by James R. Hutchins, with the title of "The Federal Spy." With the issue of Jan. 29, 1793, the title was enlarged to "The Federal Spy and Springfield Advertiser," and with Dec. 24, 1793, to "The Federal Spy and Springfield Weekly Advertiser." With the issue of Dec. 2, 1794, Hutchins disposed of the paper to John W. Hooker and Francis Stebbins, who published it under the firm name of J. W. Hooker and F. Stebbins, and who shortened the title to "The Federal Spy." The partnership was dissolved and the paper published by Francis Stebbins with the issue of June 7, 1796. With the issue of Oct. 1, 1799, Stebbins disposed of the paper to Timothy Ashley. At some date between April and June, 1800, Ashley admitted Henry Brewer to partnership under the firm name of Ashley and Brewer. The partnership was dissolved and with the issue of Mar. 8, 1803, the paper was published by Henry Brewer, and the title shortened to "Federal Spy." The title reverted to "The Federal Spy" with the issue of July 19, 1803. At some time between July 30 and Sept. 10, 1805, the paper was transferred to Luther Baker. The last issue was that of Dec. 31, 1805, vol. 14, no. 2. The paper was then bought by Thomas Dickman who continued it, but changed the name to the "Hampshire Federalist," which see.

Am. Antiq. Soc. has Dec. 19, 1792–Dec. 31, 1793; Jan. 7–28, Feb. 11–Mar. 25, Apr. 8–Oct. 28, Dec. 30, 1794; Feb. 18, Mar. 10, Apr. 14, 28, May 5, 26, June 16, 23, July 14, 21, Aug. 4, 25, Sept. 22, Oct. 13, Nov. 24, 1795; May 17, 31–June 14, July 5–19, Aug. 9–23, Sept. 6–Oct. 4, 25–Nov. 15, Dec. 6, 13, 1796; Mar. 21, Nov. 7, 27, Dec. 11, 1797; Feb. 26, July 10, 31, Aug. 14, 21, Oct. 2, Dec. 18, 1798; June 11, 18, July 16, Aug. 6, Nov. 19, Dec. 10–24, 1799; Jan. 7, 14, 28, Feb. 24, Mar. 24, Apr. 28, July 21, Oct. 27, 1800; Feb. 24, Mar. 3, Apr. 14, July 7, Aug. 11, 25, 1801; Jan. 19, Feb. 9, Mar. 9, Apr. 20, June 1, Aug. 31, Sept. 14, 21, Oct. 19, 26, Nov. 9, 16, Dec. 30, 1802; Jan. 3, Feb. 7, 14, Mar. 15, Aug. 9–Sept. 6, Oct. 4, 1803; Mar. 13, 20, 1804; Feb. 19, Apr. 16, Sept. 10–24, Nov. 5, 19, 26, 1805.

Boston Pub. Lib. has Dec. 19, 1792; Jan. 1–22, Feb. 19–Mar. 12, 26–Apr. 9, 23, May 14, 28, June 11, 18, July 23, Aug. 20, Oct. 22, Nov. 26, Dec. 24, 1793; Jan. 7–28, Feb. 18–Mar. 11, 25–May 6, 20, June 3, 10, July 8, Oct. 14, 28, 1794; Jan. 22, 1798; Sept. 22, 1800; June 16, 1801; July 6, 1802; Apr. 23, 30, May 14, Aug. 13, 1805.

Springfield City Lib. has Feb. 12, July 30, Sept. 10, 17, 1793; Feb. 25, Mar. 11, June 3, Sept. 16, 1794; May 1, 1798; Sept. 3, 17–Oct. 1, 15–29, Nov. 12–Dec. 3, 1799; July 21, Aug. 4, 11, Sept. 8–22, 1800; Dec. 29, 1801; Jan. 5–Apr. 13, 27–Dec. 13, 1802; Apr. 26–June 21, July 12–26, Sept. 20–Nov. 8, 1803; Jan. 3, 10, 24, Feb. 21, Mar. 6–July 24, Aug. 7–Sept. 18, Oct. 23–Nov. 20, Dec. 11, 1804; June 11, 18, July 23, Sept. 17–Oct. 29, Nov. 12, 26, Dec. 3, 1805.

N. Y. Hist. Soc. has May 26, June 30, 1795; Jan. 5, Mar. 22, Aug. 16, 30, Sept.

27–Oct. 18, Nov. 1, 8, 22, Dec. 27, 1796; Jan. 17–31, Feb. 21, Mar. 14, Apr. 4, 11, Oct. 24, 1797; Jan. 8, Feb. 19, Dec. 31, 1799; Oct. 27, Nov. 24–Dec. 29, 1801; Jan. 5–Oct. 12, Nov. 16, 23, Dec. 20, 1802; Jan. 3, Mar. 15, 22, 1803; Feb. 12, Dec. 31, 1805.

Harvard has Feb. 25–Mar. 17, Apr. 14, May 26, June 16–30, July 21, Aug. 11, Dec. 22, 1795; Feb. 23, Apr. 26, May 3, 17, June 7, 28, July 12, 27–Aug. 16, Sept. 20–Oct. 4, 25–Nov. 15, 1796; Jan. 3, 31, Feb. 14, Mar. 7, May 2, 1797; Jan. 8, 1798; Nov. 26, 1799; June 30, July 7, 21–Aug. 11, Sept. 8–Dec. 30, 1800; Jan. 6, 1801–Dec. 27, 1802, fair; Jan. 3–Mar. 22, Apr. 5, May 10–June 21, July 5, 12, Aug. 16, Sept. 13, 20, Oct. 4, 18–Nov. 15, Dec. 6–27, 1803; Jan. 3–Feb. 14, 28, Mar. 13, 27, Apr. 10–May 8, 22, 29, June 26–Aug. 7, Sept. 4, 11, Oct. 9–23, Nov. 6–20, 1804.

Conn. Valley Hist. Soc., Springfield, has Jan. 22, Apr. 16, 1793; Apr. 1, 29, Oct. 14, 1794; Aug. 13, Sept. 24, 1799; June 16, 30, Dec. 23, 1800; Feb. 3, Mar. 31, Apr. 7, July 14, Sept. 29, 1801; Jan. 19, Mar. 9, Apr. 6, 1802.

Univ. of Ill. has Apr. 30, 1799; Apr. 28, June 23, July 7, Aug. 25, Sept. 1–22, Oct. 27–Nov. 17, Dec. 8, 22, 1801; Feb. 16, Mar. 9, 23, Apr. 6, May 11, July 6–27, Aug. 24, 31, Sept. 21, Oct. 12, Nov. 16, 23, Dec. 13, 20, 1802; Jan. 24, Feb. 7, Mar. 29, Aug. 9, Sept. 13, Nov. 15, 1803; June 5, July 10, 1804; Feb. 19, 1805.

Lib. Congress has Apr. 2, Dec. 3, 1793; Mar. 31, Sept. 29, Oct. 6, 20, 1795; Apr. 25, 1797; Aug. 27, Dec. 31, 1799; May 4, 1802.

N. Y. Pub. Lib. has Dec. 9, 1794; July 21, Nov. 17, 1795; June 7, 1796; Mar. 12, June 25, 1799.

Dedham Hist. Soc. has Sept. 22, 1801; Mar. 29, Aug. 23, 1803.

Univ. of Mich. (Clements) has May 6, 1794; Nov. 24, 1795.

Conn. Hist. Soc. has Dec. 31, 1799; Jan. 7, 1800.

Pocumtuck Valley Mem. Assoc., Deerfield, has Sept. 22, 1801; Mar. 29, Aug. 23, 1803.

Essex Inst. has Feb. 25, 1795.

Phil. Lib. Co. has Oct. 27, 1795.

New Haven Colony Hist. Soc. has Dec. 31, 1799.

Kansas City Pub. Lib. has Dec. 31, 1799.

Mass. State Lib. has Jan. 7, 1800.

Long Id. Hist. Soc. has Dec. 30, 1800.

Duke Univ. has May 15, 1805.

[Springfield] **Hampden Federalist**, 1812–1820+.

Weekly. A continuation, without change of volume numbering, of the "Hampshire Federalist." The first issue of the "Hampden Federalist" was that of July 30, 1812, vol. 7, no. 31, published by Thomas Dickman. With the issue of Apr. 28, 1819, the title was changed to "Hampden Federalist & Public Journal." With the issue of Oct. 6, 1819, Dickman transferred the paper to A[braham] G. Tannatt & Co., who continued it until after 1820. The Northampton "Hampshire Gazette" of Oct. 19, 1819, stated that the editorial department was to be in charge of F[rederick] A. Packard.

> Springfield City Lib. has Aug. 6, 20, Sept. 3–17, Oct. 1, 15–Nov. 19, Dec. 3, 10, 1812; Mar. 18–Apr. 1, 15, 22, May 27, June 24, July 8, 22, Aug. 12, Sept. 16, Oct. 14, 21, Nov. 4, 11, Dec. 23, 1813; Jan. 6, 1814–Dec. 26, 1816; Jan. 2–July 24, Aug. 7–Oct. 16, 30–Dec. 25, 1817; Jan. 1, 1818–Dec. 27, 1820.
> Am. Antiq. Soc. has Sept. 10, 1812; Jan. 21–Feb. 11, Apr. 8, May 6, June 3, 10, July 29, Sept. 30, Dec. 23, 1813; Jan. 27, Mar. 17, Apr. 7, 28, May 19, 26, June 16, Dec. 8–22, 1814; May 4, 25, June 1, July 6, 27, Aug. 3, 31, Sept. 7, 21, 28, Oct. 12, 26, Dec. 7, 21, 1815; Jan. 18, Mar. 28, Apr. 11, June 20, July 25, Aug. 29, Dec. 19, 1816; Jan. 2, May 1, July 3, 10, 31, 1817; Jan. 8–22, Feb. 5, 19, Mar. 12, 26–Apr. 30, May 14–June 25, July 9–Aug. 13, 27–Oct. 8, 29, Nov. 12–Dec. 3, 17–31, 1818; Jan. 7, 14, 28–Feb. 18, Mar. 4–31, Apr. 14–June 9, 23–Aug. 11, 25, Sept. 8–Oct. 20, Nov. 3–24, Dec. 8, 1819; Feb. 2, 9, Apr. 26, Sept. 13, 1820.
> N. Y. Hist. Soc. has Jan. 3, 1813; Aug. 4, 1814; Oct. 5, 1815; July 18, 1816; Jan. 16, 1817; Mar. 18, Oct. 6–27, Nov. 10–24, Dec. 8, 15, 29, 1819; Jan. 5–Dec. 27, 1820.
> Wis. Hist. Soc. has Sept. 12–Dec. 26, 1816; Jan. 2–June 19, Sept. 25–Nov. 6, 27–Dec. 25, 1817; Jan. 1–Oct. 22, Dec. 17, 1818.
> Univ. of Mich. (Clements) has Jan. 7, Mar. 11, 1813; Apr. 7, Dec. 1, 29, 1814; Mar. 9, Sept. 7, Nov. 30, 1815; July 18, 1816; May 7, Nov. 26, 1818.
> Lib. Congress has July 25, Aug. 29, Dec. 26, 1816; June 5, Sept. 18, 1817; Nov. 12, 26, 1818.
> Pocumtuck Valley Mem. Assoc., Deerfield, has Dec. 31, 1812; Jan. 21, Apr. 8, Nov. 25, 1813; Oct. 6, 1814; Aug. 11, 1819.
> Greenfield Gazette Office has Apr. 7, 1814; May 9, 1816.
> Conn. Valley Hist. Soc. has May 25, June 8, Aug. 17, 1815; Oct. 27, 1819; Aug. 30, 1820.
> Ky. State Hist. Soc. has Oct. 30, 1817.
> Chicago Hist. Soc. has May 28, 1818.
> Essex Inst. has July 21, 1819.

[Springfield] **Hampden Patriot,** 1818–1820+.

Weekly. Established Dec. 31, 1818, by Ira Daniels, with the title of "Hampden Patriot." Continued after 1820.

> Springfield City Lib. has Dec. 31, 1818–Dec. 27, 1819; Jan. 5–Feb. 9, 23–Apr. 27, May 24, June 14–28, July 12–Dec. 29, 1820.
> Am. Antiq. Soc. has Jan. 21, May 27, Sept. 16, 1819; May 10, June 28, Oct. 25, 1820.
> Conn. Valley Hist. Soc. has Dec. 31, 1818; Aug. 5, 1819.
> N. Y. Pub. Lib. has Mar. 8, Apr. 5, 1820.
> Rutgers Univ. has Oct. 25, 1820.

[Springfield] **Hampshire and Berkshire Chronicle,** see **Hampshire Chronicle.**

[Springfield] **Hampshire Chronicle,** 1787–1796.

Weekly. Established Mar. 6, 1787, by John Russell, with the title of "The Hampshire Chronicle." In May, 1787, Russell took Zephaniah Webster into partnership under the firm name of Russell and Webster. With the issue of Oct. 9, 1787, the partnership was dissolved and the paper published by Zephaniah Webster. Webster sold out, and with the issue of Jan. 1, 1788, the paper was published by Weld and Thomas [Ezra W. Weld and Isaiah Thomas]. With the issue of Sept. 10, 1788, it was published by Ezra Waldo Weld. With the issue of Oct. 26, 1791, the title was changed to "Hampshire and Berkshire Chronicle." Weld sold out, and with the issue of Jan. 1, 1793, the paper was published by Edward Gray. It was discontinued with the issue of Sept. 6, 1796, vol. 9, no. 37, when Gray transferred his establishment to Francis Stebbins, of "The Federal Spy."

Am. Antiq. Soc. has Mar. 6, 13, Apr. 3, 17, May 1, 8, 29, June 5, 19, July 17, Aug. 7–28, Oct. 9–Nov. 27, Dec. 11–25, 1787; Jan. 1–Feb. 13, 27–Mar. 12, 26, Apr. 9–May 7, 21–July 9, 23, 30, Aug. 13–Oct. 29, Nov. 19, 26, Dec. 10, 31, 1788; Jan. 7, 14, 28, Feb. 18–Mar. 4, Apr. 8–May 13, 27, Aug. 12, 26–Oct. 14, Nov. 4, 18–Dec. 30, 1789; Jan. 20–Mar. 3, 17–June 30, July 14–Nov. 3, 17–Dec. 29, 1790; Jan. 5, 19, Feb. 9–Mar. 2, 16, Apr. 6–May 25, June 8, 22–Aug. 31, Sept. 14–Oct. 19, Nov. 2–16, 30–Dec. 28, 1791; Jan. 4–18, Feb. 8–22, Mar. 7, 28–Apr. 11, 25–May 9, 23–Oct. 24, Nov. 7–21, Dec. 12, 19, 1792; Jan. 1, 8, 22, Feb. 5, 26, Mar. 12–May 14, July 23, Aug. 6, Oct. 1, 29, Nov. 26, Dec. 3, 31, 1793; Jan. 14, Feb. 11, Mar. 11–25, Apr. 15–May 6, June 3, July 8, Oct. 28, Nov. 4, 25, Dec. 2, 1794; Feb. 2–Mar. 2, 16, Apr. 13, 27, May 11, 18, June 15, July 6–Aug. 3, 17–31, Sept. 7, Oct. 19, Nov. 9–30, 1795; Jan. 11, Feb. 23, Mar. 1, 29, Apr. 26, May 3, 17, June 7, 21–July 5, 26, Aug. 2, 23, Sept. 6, 1796.

Easthampton Pub. Lib. has July 17, 24, Aug. 7, 14, 28, Sept. 4, 18, 25, Oct. 9–Nov. 13, Dec. 4–25, 1787; Jan. 1–30, Feb. 13–Mar. 5, 1788.

Springfield City Lib. has Mar. 20, 1787; June 25, July 16–Aug. 20, Sept. 17–Oct. 22, Nov. 5, 12, Dec. 3–31, 1788; Jan. 7–Feb. 25, Mar. 11, Apr. 29, May 13, 20, July 29–Aug. 12, 26–Sept. 16, 30–Nov. 4, 18, Dec. 2, 9, 23, 30, 1789; Jan. 6, 20, Feb. 3, 17, 24, Mar. 17, Apr. 14, 21, May 5–June 23, July 14–Aug. 4, 18–Sept. 8, 22, 29, Nov. 17, 24, Dec. 8–29, 1790; Jan. 5–Sept. 7, 21, 1791.

Conn. Valley Hist. Soc. has Mar. 6, 12, 1787; Jan. 1, 30, 1788; Sept. 1, 1790; Jan. 13, Sept. 7, 21–Nov. 2, 16, 1791.

Mass. Hist. Soc. has Sept. 25, 1787; Dec. 28, 1791; Jan. 18, 25, Feb. 15, 29–Mar. 21, Apr. 4, 1792.

Boston Pub. Lib. has Sept. 10, 17, 1788; Sept. 23, Oct. 14, 1789; July 6, Aug. 10, Dec. 21, 1791; Mar. 26, May 7, 1793; Mar. 18, 1794; Feb. 23, 1795.

Harvard has Oct. 17, 1792; Mar. 2–16, Apr. 13, 20, May 11, June 1, 22, July

20, Aug. 3, Nov. 23, Dec. 28, 1795; Jan. 4, Feb. 16, 23, May 3–17, 31–June 21, July 12, 26–Aug. 9, 30, 1796.
Lib. Congress has Oct. 16, 1787; June 18, 1788; May 13, June 17, Aug. 5, 1789; Feb. 17, 1790; May 11, July 20, Sept. 7, Nov. 9, 1795; July 26, 1796.
Wis. Hist. Soc. has Apr. 6, 1791; Mar. 23, Sept. 14, 1795.
N. Y. Hist. Soc. has Sept. 25, 1787; Mar. 5, 1788.
N. Y. Pub. Lib. has May 17, Aug. 23, 1796.
Univ. of Mich. (Clements) has Jan. 15, 1788.
Phil. Lib. Co. has Oct. 22, 1793.

[Springfield] Hampshire Federalist, 1806–1812.

Weekly. Established Jan. 7, 1806, by Thomas Dickman, who purchased the "Federal Spy" and started the "Hampshire Federalist" with a new volume numbering. The last issue with this title was that of July 23, 1812, vol. 7, no. 30, after which it was changed to "Hampden Federalist," which see.

Springfield City Lib. has Jan. 7, 1806–Dec. 26, 1811; Jan. 9, 23–Feb. 6, 20–Mar. 5, 26, Apr. 9–23, May 7, 21, Apr. 30, May 28–July 23, 1812.
Boston Pub. Lib. has Jan. 7, 1806–Dec. 28, 1809.
Am. Antiq. Soc. has Jan. 7, 1806–Dec. 31, 1807; Feb. 4, 11, May 12, June 2, Sept. 1–15, 29, Oct. 6, 20–Nov. 10, Dec. 1–15, 1808; Jan. 5, 12, 26, Feb. 2, 23, Mar. 16–Apr. 13, 27, May 4, June 29–July 27, Aug. 17–Sept. 28, Oct. 12, 26, Nov. 9, 16, 1809; Jan. 11, 1810–Dec. 26, 1811; Jan. 9–23, Feb. 6–27, Mar. 19–Apr. 2, 23–May 7, 21–July 2, 16, 1812.
Lib. Congress has Jan. 14–Dec. 31, 1806; Feb. 11, July 9, 30, 1807; Jan. 5–Dec. 28, 1809; Apr. 5, 12, May 17, July 5, 19, 26, Sept. 27, 1810; Jan. 3–Dec. 26, 1811.
Forbes Lib., Northampton, has Jan. 21–Apr. 8, 29, May 6, Oct. 1, 1807; Jan. 7, 1808–Dec. 27, 1810; Feb. 28–Dec. 26, 1811.
N. Y. Hist. Soc. has Sept. 30, 1806; Jan. 21–Mar. 4, 18, Apr. 8, May 14, June 25, July 2, 23, Oct. 8–Dec. 31, 1807; Jan. 21–Aug. 4, 18–Sept. 1, 29, Nov. 3–24, Dec. 8–29, 1808; June 1, 1809; Oct. 31, 1811; May 28, 1812.
Harvard has Jan. 7, Feb. 11, 18, Apr. 22, 29, June 10–July 8, 29–Aug. 12, 26, Sept. 9, 16, 30, Oct. 7, 1806; Jan. 7, Oct. 8, 1807.
Essex Inst. has Apr. 1, July 15, 1806; Oct. 20, 27, 1808; Dec. 28, 1809.
Univ. of Mich. (Clements) has Mar. 7, 21, Apr. 11, 25, May 23, June 6, 13, July 4, 18, Aug. 1, 15, 22, Nov. 14, Dec. 19, 1811.
Conn. Valley Hist. Soc., Springfield, has Sept. 15, 1808; Feb. 23, 1809; Oct. 13, 1810; Jan. 9, 1812.
Univ. of Ill. has Feb. 11, 1806.
Wis. Hist. Soc. has Dec. 17, 1806; Dec. 22, 1808.
Pocumtuck Valley Mem. Assoc., Deerfield, has June 18, 1807.
N. Y. State Lib. has Oct. 17, 1811.
Yale has July 13, 1811.

[Springfield] Hampshire Herald, 1784–1786.

Weekly. A continuation, without change of numbering, of the "Massachusetts Gazette." The first issue with the title of "The Hampshire Herald; or, the Weekly Advertiser" was that of July 27, 1784, vol. 3, no. 116, published by Brooks and Russell [――― Brooks and John Russell]. With the issue of June 21, 1785, the partnership was dissolved and John Russell assumed sole proprietorship. In September, 1785, Russell admitted Gad Stebbins to partnership, under the firm name of Stebbins and Russell. The title of the paper was shortened to "The Hampshire Herald" with the issue of either Nov. 1, 8, or 15, 1785. With the issue of Aug. 1, 1786, the size of the paper was much reduced, because of the effects of the newspaper tax, and the title was shortened to "Hampshire Herald." The paper was discontinued with the issue of Sept. 26, 1786, vol. 5, no. 229.

> Am. Antiq. Soc. has July 27–Dec. 28, 1784; Jan. 4–July 5, 19, Aug. 9, 23–Sept. 6, Oct. 4, Nov. 15, 22, 1785; Jan. 3, 17–Feb. 14, Mar. 7–May 2, 23–Aug. 1, 15, 29–Sept. 26, 1786.
> Easthampton Pub. Lib. has Sept. 7, 1784–Mar. 22, 1785.
> Duke Univ. has July 27, Aug. 3, 24, Sept. 7, Oct. 12–Dec. 28, 1784; Jan. 4–18, Feb. 8, 22–Mar. 22, Apr. 5–19, May 3, 10, 24, 31, July 5, 1785.
> Boston Pub. Lib. has Aug. 31, Oct. 12, Nov. 30, Dec. 21, 28, 1784; Mar. 1, 22, July 5, Oct. 25, 1785; May 29, Aug. 29, 1786.
> Mass. Hist. Soc. has Sept. 21, Oct. 5, 1784; Jan. 4, 18, 25, Mar. 15, 29, Apr. 12, 1785; Sept. 26, 1786.
> Lib. Congress has Aug. 10, 1784; Aug. 9, 1785; Aug. 1, 1786.
> Conn. Valley Hist. Soc. has Nov. 2, 1784; Dec. 13, 1785.
> Pocumtuck Valley Mem. Assoc., Deerfield, has Dec. 21, 1784; Nov. 29, 1785.
> Springfield City Lib. has Oct. 18, 1785; Aug. 15, 1786.
> N. Y. Hist. Soc. has Sept. 5, 19, 1786.
> Minn. Hist. Soc. has Mar. 28, 1786.
> N. Y. Pub. Lib. has Sept. 19, 1786.

[Springfield] Massachusetts Gazette, 1782–1784.

Weekly. Established May 14, 1782, by Babcock and Haswell [Elisha Babcock and Anthony Haswell] with the title of "The Massachusetts Gazette, or the Springfield and Northampton Weekly Advertiser." With the issue of Aug. 13, 1782, the title was shortened to "The Massachusetts Gazette, or the General Advertiser." The partnership was dissolved and with the issue of May 13, 1783, the paper was published by Elisha Babcock. With the issue of Sept. 9, 1783, the title was changed to "The Massachusetts Gazette, or General Advertiser." With the issue of May 11, 1784, Babcock sold out to Brooks and Russell [――― Brooks and John Russell] who made a slight change in the punctuation of the title, to "The Massachusetts Gazette: or, General Advertiser." The last issue was that of July 20, 1784, vol. 3, no. 115, after which the title was changed to "The Hampshire Herald," which see.

Conn. Valley Hist. Soc., Springfield, has May 14, 1782–May 4, 1784.

Am. Antiq. Soc. has Proposals (May 1782); May 14–Dec. 31, 1782; Jan. 7–Feb. 18, Mar. 4–Aug. 19, Sept. 16–Oct. 21, Nov. 4, 11, 25, Dec. 9–30, 1783; Jan. 6, 20, 27, Feb. 10, 24–Mar. 9, 23, Apr. 6, 27, May 18, June 1, 22–July 20, 1784.

Lib. Congress has May 14–Dec. 31, 1782; Jan. 7–May 6, Oct. 7–Nov. 11, 1783; Jan. 13, 1784.

Boston Pub. Lib. has May 14, June 4, July 9, Sept. 24, Dec. 24, 1782; Apr. 8, May 6, June 10, 1783; Apr. 27, 1784.

Mass. Hist. Soc. has July 16, Sept. 3, 17–Oct. 15, 1782; May 20, Sept. 9, Dec. 23, 1783; Mar. 23, Apr. 20, 27, 1784.

N. Y. Hist. Soc. has Oct. 29, Nov. 12, Dec. 3, 1782; Apr. 22, Dec. 30, 1783; Mar. 2–23, Apr. 6, 27, May 11–25, June 22, 1784.

N. Y. Pub. Lib. has Apr. 22, 1783; May 11, 25, 1784.

Harvard has July 22, Aug. 19, Sept. 9, 1783.

Conn. State Lib. has Mar. 23, June 8, 1784.

Pocumtuck Valley Mem. Assoc., Deerfield, has Aug. 20, Oct. 29, 1782; Jan. 7, 1783.

[Springfield] **Republican Spy,** 1803–1804.

Weekly. Established June 14, 1803, by Timothy Ashley, with the title of "The Republican Spy." With the issue of Nov. 8, 1803, the title was changed to "Republican Spy." With the issue of June 11, 1804, vol. 2, no. 53, the paper was discontinued at Springfield and removed to Northampton. See under Northampton.

Conn. Valley Hist. Soc., Springfield, has June 14, 1803–June 11, 1804.

Harvard has June 21–July 12, 26, Aug. 9–23, Sept. 13, 27–Oct. 18, Nov. 1, 8, 1803; Jan. 10, 17, Feb. 7–28, Mar. 13, 27, Apr. 2, 16, 23, May 21, June 4, 1804.

Am. Antiq. Soc. has June 14, July 19, Aug. 2, 16, 30, Oct. 4, Nov. 1, 15, Dec. 6–20, 1803; Jan. 3–Feb. 14, Mar. 13, Apr. 16–May 7, June 11, 1804.

Lib. Congress has Aug. 30, Sept. 10, Oct. 4, 18–Nov. 8, 22, 1803; Jan. 3, 17, 1804.

N. Y. Pub. Lib. has June 14, 1803.

[Stockbridge] **Andrews's Western Star,** see **Western Star.**

[Stockbridge] **Berkshire Herald,** 1814–1815.

Weekly. A continuation, without change of volume numbering, of the "Farmer's Herald." The earliest issue located with the title of "Berkshire Herald" is that of Dec. 22, 1814, vol. 7, no. 23, whole no. 335, published by Milo Smith

& Co., and the change of title was made early in December, 1814. With the issue of Aug. 3, 1815, the partnership was dissolved, and the paper was printed for the Proprietors. With the issue of Sept. 21, 1815, it was printed for the Proprietors by Matthew Van Yorx. The last issue with the title of "Berkshire Herald" was that of Nov. 23, 1815, vol. 8, no. 19, when the paper was consolidated with "The Berkshire Reporter" of Pittsfield, which was removed to Stockbridge and continued as the "Berkshire Star."

Am. Antiq. Soc. has Jan. 5–Nov. 23, 1815.
Boston Pub. Lib. has Dec. 22, 29, 1814.
Berkshire Athenæum, Pittsfield, has July 6–20, 1815.

[Stockbridge] **Berkshire Star,** 1815–1820+.

Weekly. A continuation, without change of volume numbering, of "The Berkshire Reporter" of Pittsfield, which was removed to Stockbridge, consolidated with the "Berkshire Herald" of that town, and continued as the "Berkshire Star." The first issue of the "Berkshire Star" was that of Nov. 30, 1815, vol. 26, no. 1352, printed by Milo Smith, for R[ichard] H. Ashley. With the issue of Jan. 18, 1816, it was published by R. H. Ashley & Co. Ashley tried to sell out his interest in 1817, and beginning with the issue of Aug. 14, 1817, the imprint with his name was omitted. The firm was dissolved on Sept. 1, 1817, the advertisement being signed by R. H. Ashley and Charles Webster, and with the issue of Sept. 18, 1817, the imprint became "published by Charles Webster." It was so continued until after 1820.

Am. Antiq. Soc. has Nov. 30, 1815–Dec. 25, 1817; Apr. 22–May 6, July 29, Aug. 5, 1819; Mar. 2, 16–30, 1820.
Berkshire Athenaeum, Pittsfield, has Nov. 30–Dec. 28, 1815; Jan. 4–Mar. 21, Apr. 4, 11, 25–May 30, June 13–Dec. 12, 26, 1816; Jan. 2, 1817–Dec. 28, 1820.
Lib. Congress has Nov. 30, Dec. 7, 1815; Jan. 2–16, 1817; Aug. 27, 1818; Aug. 12, 1819; Jan. 6–Dec. 28, 1820.
Mrs. Raymond L. Buell, Richmond, Mass., has Mar. 25, 1819; Mar. 23–June 29, July 20–Dec. 28, 1820.
Univ. of Mich. (Clements) has Mar. 14, Oct. 31, 1816; Jan. 21, 1819.
Paducah, Ky. Pub. Lib. has June 6, 1816.
Western Reserve Hist. Soc. has Aug. 7, 1817.
Stockbridge Pub. Lib. has Feb. 19, 1818.
Mass. Hist. Soc. has Oct. 1, 1818.
Wis. Hist. Soc. has Dec. 10, 1818.

[Stockbridge] **Farmer's Herald,** 1808–1814.

Weekly. Established July 30, 1808, judging from the date of the earliest issue located, that of Oct. 1, 1808, vol. 1, no. 10, "The Farmer's Herald," published "for the Proprietors." The issue of Jan. 28, 1809, is the same. The next issue located, that of Aug. 26, 1809, vol. 2, no. 57, was printed by Edward P. Seymour, and so to the last issue located, that of Nov. 24, 1814, vol. 7, no. 19. In December, 1814, probably on Dec. 1, the title, without change of volume numbering, was changed to "Berkshire Herald," which see.

Am. Antiq. Soc. has Oct. 1, 1808; Jan. 28, Aug. 26, 1809; Jan. 13, Mar. 31, Apr. 28, July 14, 28, Sept. 22, Oct. 6-20, 1810; Jan. 5, Feb. 9, Mar. 2, 16, Apr. 6-20, May 4, 18, Aug. 17, Oct. 26-Nov. 9, 1811.
Boston Pub. Lib. has May 2, 1812-Oct. 13, Nov. 3, 24, Dec. 22, 29, 1814.
Stockbridge Pub. Lib. had Oct. 6, 20, 27, 1810; Dec. 28, 1811; Jan. 14, Mar. 11, Nov. 11, 1813, but these issues were discarded by one of the trustees.
Trinity Coll., Hartford, has Aug. 25, 1810; Jan. 26, 1811.
Univ. of Mich. (Clements) has Nov. 2, 1811; July 8, 1813.
Wis. Hist. Soc. has Nov. 12, 19, 1808.
N. Y. Hist. Soc. has Nov. 25, 1809.
Mrs. Raymond L. Buell, Richmond, Mass., has Sept. 7, 14, 1811.
Forbes Lib., Northampton, has Nov. 25, 1813.

[Stockbridge] **Political Atlas**, 1807.

Weekly. Established Feb. 14, 1807, by Cornelius Sturtevant, Jun., with the title of "The Political Atlas." The last issue located is that of Dec. 12, 1807, vol. 1, no. 44.

Am. Antiq. Soc. has Feb. 14, 28, Mar. 7, 28, Apr. 18, May 2, 23, July 4, 1807.
Harvard has Feb. 14-28, Mar. 14-28, May 2, 30, June 13, 1807.
Stockbridge Pub. Lib. has Oct. 10, 1807.
N. Y. Hist. Soc. has Dec. 12, 1807.

[Stockbridge] **Western Star**, 1789-1806.

Weekly. Established Dec. 1, 1789, by Loring Andrews, with the title of "The Western Star." The word "The" was removed from the title with the issue of Mar. 27, 1792. With the issue of June 17, 1794, the title was changed to "Andrews's Western Star." With the issue of Feb. 27, 1797, Andrews conveyed the paper to Rosseter & Willard [Benjamin Rosseter and Heman Willard] who changed the title back to "The Western Star." With the issue of Aug. 7, 1798, the partnership was dissolved and the paper published by Benjamin Rosseter. With the issue of Aug. 19, 1799, Rosseter sold out the paper to a group of proprietors, and it was printed by H[eman] Willard, for Horatio Jones & Co. With the issue of Aug. 31, 1801, it was published by H. Willard & Co., and with the issue of Aug. 21, 1802, by H. Willard. The last issue located with title of "The Western Star" is that of Nov. 8, 1806, vol. 17, no. 52, whole no. 880. In January, 1807, the paper was removed to Pittsfield and continued without change of volume numbering, under the title of "The Berkshire Reporter." See under Pittsfield.

Harvard has Dec. 1, 1789–Dec. 26, 1796; Jan. 2–Apr. 24, May 29–July 17, Sept. 11, 18, Oct. 9, Nov. 6–Dec. 25, 1797; Jan. 8–22, Feb. 5, 12, 26–Mar. 12, Apr. 23, May 7–June 4, 26, July 31, Aug. 21, Sept. 4, Oct. 2, 23, 30, Nov. 13, 1798; Feb. 5–19, Mar. 4, Apr. 29–May 20, June 3–17, July 29, Aug. 12–26, Sept. 9–23, Oct. 8, 22, 1799; Mar. 25, June 9, July 7, Aug. 11–25, Sept. 8, Oct. 13, Nov. 17, 24, Dec. 8–29, 1800; Jan. 5–26, Feb. 23, Mar. 9–30, Apr. 13–June 1, 15–July 13, 27–Aug. 10, 24–Sept. 7, 28–Oct. 17, 31, Nov. 7, 21–Dec. 26, 1801; Jan. 2–23, Feb. 6, 13, 27–May 1, 22–Aug. 14, 28–Oct. 16, Nov. 6–Dec. 25, 1802; Jan. 1–22, Feb. 5–26, Mar. 12, 26, Apr. 2, 16, 30, May 14–July 2, 16–Sept. 3, 17–Dec. 31, 1803; Jan. 7, 21, Feb. 4–Mar. 3, 17–31, Apr. 14–May 5, 19–June 2, 23–July 7, 21–Aug. 18, Sept. 1, 8, 22, Oct. 6, 20, Nov. 3–Dec. 1, 15, 29, 1804; Jan. 19, Feb. 2, 16, Aug. 10, Oct. 19, 1805.

Am. Antiq. Soc. has Dec. 15, 1789–Dec. 28, 1790; Jan. 4–June 7, 21–July 5, 19, Aug. 2–Sept. 20, Oct. 4, 11, 25, Nov. 8, 15, 29–Dec. 13, 27, 1791; Jan. 3–Mar. 6, 20–Apr. 3, May 1–22, June 5, 12, 26–Aug. 21, Sept. 4–Nov. 6, 20–Dec. 4, 18, 25, 1792; Jan. 1, 15–Mar. 5, 26–Apr. 9, May 7–21, June 4, Oct. 22, Dec. 24, 1793; Jan. 14, Feb. 4, 18–Mar. 11, 25, Apr. 15–May 6, 20, June 17, July 1–22, Aug. 5–19, Sept. 9, 16, Oct. 7–Dec. 30, 1794; Jan. 6, 20, 27, Feb. 10, 24–Mar. 24, Apr. 14–May 12, 26, June 9–Sept. 15, 29–Oct. 13, Nov. 3–Dec. 29, 1795; Jan. 5–Dec. 26, 1796; Jan. 2–May 15, June 5, 26, July 10, 17, 31–Aug. 21, Sept. 11–25, Oct. 9–23, Nov. 6, 20–Dec. 4, 25, 1797; Jan. 1–Feb. 5, 19, Mar. 12, Apr. 9, 23, May 7–28, June 18, July 3, 24, Sept. 11, Oct. 30, Nov. 27–Dec. 18, 1798; Jan. 15, Feb. 19, July 8, Sept. 30, 1799; Mar. 18, Nov. 10, 1800; Jan. 12–Mar. 16, Apr. 6, 27–June 29, July 13, Aug. 3–Sept. 7, 21–Oct. 17, 31, Nov. 14–Dec. 19, 1801; Jan. 2–16, 30, Feb. 6, June 12–26, Aug. 7, 14, Sept. 11, Oct. 2, 9, 23, Nov. 6, Dec. 11, 1802; Jan. 22–Feb. 26, Mar. 12–Apr. 2, June 25, Aug. 20, Sept. 3–Dec. 31, 1803; Jan. 7–Mar. 3, 17–Sept. 15, 29–Nov. 17, 1804; Feb. 9, Apr. 13, July 20, Nov. 2, 1805; July 26, Oct. 4, 11, Nov. 8, 1806.

Boston Pub. Lib. has Dec. 15, 22, 1789; Jan. 5, 12, Feb. 16–Apr. 6, 27–July 27, Aug. 10–Nov. 2, 16–Dec. 28, 1790; Jan. 4–Feb. 1, 22–Mar. 29, Apr. 12, 19, May 10–24, 1791; Jan. 3, 1792; May 6, Dec. 23, 1794; Mar. 17, 24, June 30, July 21, 28, Aug. 18–Sept. 1, 1795; May 17–31, July 12, 19, Aug. 9, 16, Sept. 5–19, Oct. 17–31, Nov. 21, 28, Dec. 12, 26, 1796; Jan. 2, 23–Feb. 20, Mar. 6, 20, 27, Apr. 17, 24, May 15, Oct. 16, 1797.

Boston Athenæum has Jan. 10–31, Mar. 20, 27, June 26, July 2, 1792; Nov. 10, Dec. 1, 29, 1795; Jan. 12–Feb. 9, Mar. 1, 15–29, Apr. 19–June 21, 1796.

N. Y. State Lib. has Oct. 27, 1800–Aug. 1, 1802.

Berkshire Athenaeum, Pittsfield, has Jan. 19, May 4, 11, 25, June 29, Sept. 21, Oct. 26, Nov. 2, 1790; Mar. 1, May 3, June 21, 28, July 12, 19, Aug. 2, 16,

MASSACHUSETTS 413

Nov. 8, 1791; Jan. 29, 1793; Nov. 4, 1794; Mar. 17, Nov. 24, 1795; July 24, 1798; Jan. 1, Dec. 31, 1799; Jan. 7, Mar. 4, 1800; Aug. 24, 1801; July 12, 19, 1806.
N. Y. Hist. Soc. has Oct. 12–Nov. 2, 16, 23, 1790; Jan. 11, 1791; Nov. 26, 1793; May 28, 1798; Mar. 25, June 29, Aug. 19, 26, 1799; Mar. 18, 25, Apr. 15–June 2, 16, 23, Aug. 4, 1800; May 4, 1801; Mar. 20, 1802.
Stockbridge Pub. Lib. has Dec. 21, 1800; Jan. 9, Feb. 13, Aug. 10, 31, Nov. 28, 1801; Oct. 1, 1803; Jan. 14, Mar. 17, 1804; Sept. 18, 1806. Eighteen issues previously owned were discarded by order of one of the trustees.
N. Y. Pub. Lib. has Nov. 1, 1791; Jan. 17, Sept. 25, 1792; Mar. 5, 1793; July 15, Sept. 9, 30, 1794; Apr. 7–21, May 5, 1795; Dec. 5, 1796; Sept. 30, 1799.
Western Reserve Hist. Soc. has May 22, June 19, Sept. 11, Oct. 23, 1797; Oct. 23, 1798; July 15, 1799; July 28, Aug. 18, 1800; Jan. 12, Feb. 2, 9, 23, Apr. 13, June 1, 1801; Oct. 1, 1803.
Yale has Dec. 24, 1799; Jan. 7–May 13, 26–July 14, 1800.
Wis. Hist. Soc. has July 31, 1792; Dec. 9, 23, 1794; Mar. 24, Sept. 15, 22, Dec. 13, 1795.
Troy Pub. Lib. has Dec. 5, 1800; Apr. 20, 1801; Sept. 4, 1802; Apr. 30, 1803; Jan. 21, July 14, Sept. 1, 1804.
Lib. Congress has May 4, 1790; Nov. 29, 1791; Nov. 24, 1795; Dec. 31, 1799.
Conn. Hist. Soc. has Jan. 15, 1798; Dec. 31, 1799; Jan. 7, 1800; Aug. 17, 1801.
Univ. of Mich. (Clements) has Oct. 5, 1801; Mar. 6, 1802; Oct. 27, 1804.
Duke Univ. has Dec. 6, 13, 1791.
Mass. Hist. Soc. has Feb. 21, Mar. 13, 1792.
Pocumtuck Valley Mem. Assoc., Deerfield, has Aug. 20, 1793; Feb. 13, 1802.
Univ. of Ill. has Mar. 6, 1802; June 9, 1804.
Long Id. Hist. Soc. has Jan. 12, 1801.
Univ. of Pittsburgh has Nov. 27, 1802.
Colgate Univ. has Oct. 27, 1804.

[Watertown] **Boston Gazette**, 1775–1776, see under **Boston**.

[West Springfield] **American Intelligencer**, 1795–1797.

Weekly. Established Aug. 18, 1795, by Richard Davison, with the title of "American Intelligencer." With the issue of Oct. 4, 1796, Davison transferred the paper to Edward Gray. The last issue located is that of Nov. 28, 1797, vol. 3, no. 120.

Am. Antiq. Soc. has Aug. 25, Sept. 15, 22, Oct. 6, Nov. 17, 24, 1795; Apr. 14, June 7, 14, 28, July 5, Sept. 20, Oct. 4, 18–Nov. 22, Dec. 6, 27, 1796; Jan. 10, 17, 31, Feb. 21, Mar. 7, Apr. 4, 18, 25, June 6, 13, 27, July 18, Aug. 1, 22, Sept. 12–Oct. 10, 24, Nov. 14–28, 1797.
Harvard has Feb. 23, Mar. 15, Apr. 26–May 10, June 28, July 12, 26, Aug. 9–

30, Sept. 13–Oct. 11, 25–Nov. 8, Dec. 6–27, 1796; Jan. 10–Mar. 7, 21, Apr. 4–25, May 30–June 27, July 11, Sept. 5, Oct. 3, 10, Nov. 7, 14, 1797.
Conn. Valley Hist. Soc., Springfield, has Sept. 29, Dec. 8, 1795; Mar. 8, May 10, 24, June 21, Aug. 9, Sept. 20, Nov. 29, Dec. 27, 1796; Apr. 11, May 2, 16, June 13–27, July 25, Sept. 12, 19, Oct. 3, 1797.
N. Y. Pub. Lib. has Sept. 8, 1795; Mar. 29, 1796.
Boston Pub. Lib. has Sept. 22, 1795.

[Worcester] **American Herald,** 1788–1789.

Weekly. A continuation of the "American Herald" of Boston. The paper was removed to Worcester, and established there with the issue of Aug. 21, 1788, vol. 8, no. 368, "The American Herald; and the Worcester Recorder," published by Edward Eveleth Powars. The last issue located, and probably the last published, was that of Oct. 8, 1789, vol. 8, no. 424.

Am. Antiq. Soc. has Aug. 21, 1788–Oct. 8, 1789.
Duke Univ. has Oct. 16, 1788; June 25, Oct. 8, 1789.
Boston Pub. Lib. has July 23, Oct. 8, 1789.

[Worcester] **Haswell's Massachusetts Spy,** see **Massachusetts Spy.**

[Worcester] **Independent Gazetteer,** 1800–1801.

Weekly. Established Jan. 7, 1800, by Mower & Greenleaf [Nahum Mower and Daniel Greenleaf] with the title of "The Independent Gazetteer." With the issue of Oct. 7, 1800, the partnership was dissolved and the paper published by Daniel Greenleaf. It was discontinued with the issue of Dec. 29, 1801, vol. 2, no. 104.

Am. Antiq. Soc. has Jan. 7–June 10, 24–Oct. 28, Nov. 11–Dec. 2, 16–30, 1800; Jan. 6–Dec. 29, 1801.
Conn. Hist. Soc. has Jan. 7, 1800–Aug. 11, 1801, fair; Sept. 8, 1801.
Harvard has Jan. 7, Aug. 5, 12, 26, Sept. 16, Dec. 30, 1800; Feb. 3, 10, 24, Mar. 24, May 26, Sept. 1, 8, 22, Oct. 27–Dec. 29, 1801.
Lib. Congress has Feb. 11, Nov. 18, 1800; Feb. 3, Mar. 17, Apr. 7, 1801.
N. Y. Hist. Soc. has Mar. 25, Apr. 22, 1800; June 9, 16, 1801.
N. Y. Pub. Lib. has Apr. 22, May 13, July 1, Oct. 7, 1800.
Yale has Jan. 20, May 19, June 23, 1801.
Univ. of Mich. (Clements) has Apr. 7, June 2, Sept. 29, 1801.
Wis. Hist. Soc. has Nov. 11, 1800.

Worcester Magazine, see [Worcester] **Massachusetts Spy.**

[Worcester] **Massachusetts Herald,** 1783.

Weekly. Established Sept. 6, 1783, by Isaiah Thomas, with the title of "The Massachusetts Herald: Or, Worcester Journal." It was of quarto size, and was largely an abridged edition of Thomas's other paper, the "Massachusetts Spy." It was discontinued with the issue of Sept. 27, 1783, vol. 1, no. 4.

Am. Antiq. Soc. has Sept. 6–27, 1783.
Mass. Hist. Soc. has Sept. 20, 1783.
Duke Univ. has Sept. 20, 1783.

[Worcester] **Massachusetts Spy**, 1775–1820+.

Weekly. A continuation of "The Massachusetts Spy" published at Boston. The first issue published at Worcester was that of May 3, 1775, vol. 5, no. 219, "The Massachusetts Spy Or, American Oracle of Liberty," published by Isaiah Thomas. Upon the copy of this issue owned by the American Antiquarian Society, Thomas has written "This News-paper is the first Thing ever printed in Worcester — Isaiah Thomas." With the issue of Aug. 16, 1775, the title was changed to "Thomas's Massachusetts Spy Or, American Oracle of Liberty." There were no issues published on Feb. 23, Mar. 8 to Apr. 5, or Apr. 19, 1776. Thomas relinquished publication on lease with the issue of May 31, 1776, and after an interval of two weeks, it was published by W[illiam] Stearns and D[aniel] Bigelow, who changed the title back to "The Massachusetts Spy Or, American Oracle of Liberty." There were various slight changes in the punctuation and arrangement of the title during the following year. With the issue of Aug. 14, 1777, the paper was published on lease from Thomas by Anthony Haswell, who changed the title to "Haswell's Massachusetts Spy Or American Oracle of Liberty." During his management of nearly a year, Haswell continually altered the title, sometimes omitting his name and sometimes inserting it. With the issue of June 25, 1778, Isaiah Thomas resumed the proprietorship, changing the title to "Thomas's Massachusetts Spy Or, American Oracle of Liberty." With the issue of May 24, 1781, the title was changed to "Thomas's Massachusetts Spy Or, The Worcester Gazette." With the issues of Apr. 11, 1782, Mar. 11, 1784, and Jan. 6, 1785, there were slight changes in the title. With the issue of Mar. 30, 1786, vol. 16, no. 782, Thomas discontinued the publication as a newspaper, because of the state tax on advertisements, and established "The Worcester Magazine," in April, 1786. This was published weekly, octavo in size and paged. Although a magazine in name, it continued the same kind of news as had been printed in the newspaper, current intelligence, death and marriage notices, and advertisements, which being in a magazine were not subject to tax. The magazine was continued through March, 1788, vol. 4, no. 26, comprising four volumes, each with a title-page. The tax was taken off in March, 1788, and on Apr. 3, 1788, Thomas revived the newspaper with the title of "Thomas's Massachusetts Spy: Or, The Worcester Gazette," vol. 17, no. 783. With the issue of Jan. 5, 1792, he admitted Leonard Worcester into partnership, the paper being published by Isaiah Thomas and Leonard Worcester. With the issue of Mar. 6, 1799, it was printed by Isaiah Thomas, Jun., for Isaiah Thomas and Son, but with the issue of June 10, 1801, Isaiah Thomas, Jun., became sole publisher. With the issue of Mar. 12, 1806, Isaac Sturtevant became associated with Thomas, and the paper was printed by him for Isaiah Thomas, Jun. With the issue of Oct. 17, 1810, James Elliot became the publisher, and the paper was printed by Isaac Sturtevant for James Elliot, the title being changed to "The Massachusetts Spy, or Worcester Gazette." With the issue of Feb. 27, 1811, Isaiah Thomas, Jun., took the paper back, which was then printed by Isaac Sturtevant for Isaiah Thomas, Jun., changing the title to "Thomas's Massachusetts Spy, or Worcester Gazette." With the issue of Aug. 12, 1812, Isaac Sturtevant became sole publisher. With the issue of Oct. 26, 1814, William Manning became publisher. With the issue of Oct. 27, 1819, George A. Trumbull was admitted to partnership and the paper published by Manning & Trumbull. It was so continued until after 1820.

Am. Antiq. Soc. has May 3, 1775–Dec. 27, 1820.
Mass. Hist. Soc. has May 3–Dec. 29, 1775; Jan. 5–Feb. 16, Mar. 1, Apr. 12, 26, May 3, 17–31, June 21–Aug. 28, Sept. 11, 25–Dec. 26, 1776; Jan. 2–16, Feb. 6, 27, Mar. 27, Apr. 3, 17, May 2, 29, Aug. 4, Sept. 4, 11, 25, Oct. 9, Nov. 21–Dec. 19, 1777; Jan. 1, 1778–Dec. 27, 1820.
Boston Athenæum has Sept. 2, 9, 23, 1779; May 25, June 15, 1780–Apr. 10, 1783; Sept. 11, 1783–Mar. 30, 1786; Apr. 3, 1788–Mar. 29, 1820.
Boston Pub. Lib. has May 3–Dec. 29, 1775; Jan. 5–Feb. 16, Apr. 12–May 31, June 21, July 5, 17, Aug. 21, 28, Sept. 11, 1776; July 24, Aug. 21, Sept. 25, Dec. 25, 1777; Jan. 1, Apr. 30, June 5, 25–Aug. 13, Sept. 3–Dec. 31, 1778; Jan. 7, 1779–Dec. 28, 1780, fair; Jan. 4, 11, 25, Feb. 1, May 10, 24, 31, Nov. 8, 1781; Jan. 3, 1782–Dec. 31, 1789; Jan. 7–Apr. 29, May 20, July 15, Aug. 5, 12, Sept. 2, Oct. 14–Dec. 30, 1790; Jan. 13, 1791–Dec. 29, 1813; Jan. 5–Mar. 30, July 6, 1814–Dec. 27, 1820.
Lib. Congress has May 3–Dec. 29, 1775; Jan. 5–Feb. 16, Apr. 12, 26, May 3, 18, 31, July 5, 24, 1776; Feb. 12, Apr. 2–16; May 14, 28, June 11, July 9, 23, Aug. 6, 13, 27, Sept. 10, 24–Nov. 5, 19, Dec. 3, 10, 31, 1778; Jan. 7, 21, Feb. 4, 25, Mar. 4, 18–June 10, July 1, 15–Sept. 16, 30–Oct. 28, Nov. 18–Dec. 10, 1779; Feb. 10, Mar. 23, Apr. 13, 20, May 11, 25, June 29, July 21, 27, Aug. 3, Dec. 6, 1780; Apr. 5, May 24, 31, July 12, 26–Aug. 16, Sept. 6–27, Dec. 20, 1781; Jan. 3–Nov. 21, 1782; Feb. 13–Apr. 24, May 16–June 12, July 10–Sept. 11, Oct. 9–23, Dec. 10, 18, 1783; Jan. 1, 1784–Dec. 28, 1808; Feb. 29–May 31, June 14, Oct. 18–Nov. 2, 29, Dec. 13, 27, 1809; Jan. 3, 1810–Dec. 29, 1819; Feb. 23–Mar. 8, 22, June 21, July 4, Aug. 2, 9, 23–Sept. 6, 20, Nov. 15, Dec. 13, 20, 1820.
Am. Philos. Soc. has Apr. 3, 1788–Dec. 27, 1820.
Wis. Hist. Soc. has Mar. 2, May 3, Aug. 30, Nov. 3, Dec. 1, 1775; July 17, Dec. 4, 1776; Apr. 1, Oct. 21, 1779; Apr. 13, 1780–Apr. 4, 1782; Jan. 8, 1784–June 16, 1785; July 24, 1788–Dec. 26, 1804, fair; Mar. 6–20, Apr. 3, 17–May 1, 22–June 5, 26, July 10, 17, Aug. 7–28, Sept. 25, Oct. 9, 16, Dec. 4, 1805; Jan. 1, 15–Mar. 5, 26, Apr. 23, 30, May 14, 21, July 9, Aug. 6, 13, 27,

MASSACHUSETTS 417

Sept. 10, Oct. 15, 29, Nov. 5, Dec. 10, 24, 31, 1806; Jan. 7–Dec. 30, 1807; Apr. 20, 27, May 18, June 15, Aug. 24, Sept. 7, Oct. 5, Nov. 2, 16, 23, Dec. 7, 21, 1808; Jan. 4, 1809–Dec. 27, 1820.
British Museum has Jan. 1, 1784–Jan. 5, 1786; Apr. 3, 1788–Feb. 25, 1795; Mar. 30, 1796–Dec. 27, 1820.
Worc. Pub. Lib. has May 3, Dec. 1, 1775; Jan. 5, 12, June 28–Aug. 28, Sept. 11, Oct. 16, 1776; Jan. 23, 30, May 29, 1777; Oct. 8, Nov. 28, 1778; Apr. 29, July 22, Sept. 16, 1779; July 27, Nov. 30, 1780; Mar. 1, 1781; July 4, Aug. 15, 1782; Feb. 27, Mar. 13, Apr. 3, 24, May 22, 29, July 10, 17, 1783; Jan. 1–Dec. 30, 1784; Jan. 6–20, Feb. 3–24, Mar. 17–31, Apr. 21–June 16, Dec. 8, 1785; Nov. 13, 1788–Dec. 15, 1791, fair; Jan. 5, 1792–Dec. 27, 1820.
Dartmouth has Jan. 12, 26, Feb. 2, 1776; Feb. 26, 1784–Mar. 23, 1786, fair; Apr. 3, 1788–Dec. 30, 1790, fair; Jan. 6, 1791–Dec. 26, 1793; Jan. 6, 1796–Dec. 28, 1808; Jan. 3, 1810–Dec. 29, 1819.
N. Y. Hist. Soc. has Sept. 10, Nov. 19, 1778; Jan. 7, Feb. 4, 1779; Mar. 7, 1782; Jan. 1–Dec. 30, 1784; Aug. 4, 1785–Mar. 30, 1786; Apr. 3, 1788–Dec. 30, 1790, fair; Jan. 6, 1791–Dec. 27, 1820.
N. Y. State Lib. has May 31, June 28, July 12, Aug. 16, Sept. 29, Oct. 6, Nov. 17, Dec. 1, 8, 22, 29, 1775; Jan. 5, 12, Feb. 16, June 28, July 5, 17, 1776; Mar. 27, 1777; Mar. 12, Oct. 1, Dec. 17, 1778; Jan. 21, July 22, 29, Aug. 12, 19, Sept. 2–Oct. 28, Nov. 11, 18, Dec. 16, 1779; Mar. 2, 23, Nov. 23, Dec. 14, 1780; Jan. 25–Mar. 8, May 24–Dec. 27, 1781; Jan. 3–May 30, June 20, Sept. 12, 19, Oct. 10, 31, 1782; Jan. 2, 9, May 1, Dec. 10, 1783; Jan. 1, 1784–Dec. 25, 1788; Apr. 9, 1789–Dec. 28, 1808, fair.
N. Y. Pub. Lib. has May 3, 17, June 7, 21–Aug. 9, Sept. 29, Oct. 13–Dec. 29, 1775; Jan. 5–Feb. 2, 16, Apr. 26, Sept. 18, Dec. 4, 19, 1776; Apr. 17, Oct. 23, 30, 1777; Jan. 29, Feb. 5, 19, Mar. 5, 12, 26, Apr. 2, 16–30, May 14, 28–June 11, July 2–23, Oct. 8, 22, Nov. 5, Dec. 10, 31, 1778; Feb. 4, Apr. 15, 22, June 10, 24–July 8, 29, Aug. 5, 19, 26, Oct. 7–Nov. 5, 18, 1779; Aug. 3, 1780; Jan. 4, 1781–Dec. 26, 1782; Apr. 17, 24, June 26, Aug. 21, Oct. 16, 1783; Jan. 1, Mar. 18, Apr. 22, 29, May 27–June 17, July 1–15, 29–Aug. 19, Sept. 2, 23, 30, Oct. 14, Nov. 4, 18, 24, 1784; Jan. 13–Mar. 3, 17, Apr. 21, 28, May 12, 19, June 16, 23, July 7, 14, 28, Sept. 29, Nov. 17, Dec. 8, 29, 1785; Feb. 2, 1786; Apr. 3, 1788–Dec. 31, 1800, fair; June 10, 24, 1801; Mar. 3, 1802–Dec. 28, 1803, fair; Mar. 7–28, 1804.
Yale has Mar. 3–Nov. 10, 1785, fair; Apr. 3, May 22, July 3–17, Aug. 21, Oct. 2, 30–Dec. 18, 1788; Jan. 8–Mar. 19, Apr. 9, July 30–Aug. 20, 1789; Mar. 4, 1790–Dec. 29, 1791, fair; Mar. 1, 1792–May 13, 1795; May 25–Dec. 21, 1796; Mar. 1, 1797–Feb. 26, 1800; Jan. 7, 1801–Dec. 29, 1802; Mar. 6, 1805–Feb. 12, May 7, 1806; Jan. 7, 1807–Feb. 23, 1820.
Mass. State Lib. has Jan. 6, 1785–Dec. 31, 1789; Jan. 12, 1792–Dec. 2, 1805; Mar. 1, 1809–Feb. 24, 1813; Mar. 2, 1814–Dec. 22, 1819.
Harvard has May 3, 1775; Jan. 1, 1776; Oct. 8, 1778; Dec. 16, 1779; Oct. 1, 1789; Jan. 6, 23, May 5, June 16, 23, July 7, 28, Sept. 1, 22, 29, 1791; Jan. 19,

Apr. 5, May 24, July 26, Aug. 23, Nov. 15–28, Dec. 13, 1792; Jan. 3, 1793–Dec. 31, 1794; Feb. 11, 1795–Feb. 20, 1799, scattering issues; Apr. 10, 1799–Dec. 28, 1808, fair; Jan. 4, 11, May 24, 1809.

Worc. Hist. Soc. has Mar. 4, 1795–Dec. 28, 1796; Dec. 5, 1804–Dec. 25, 1805; Jan. 29–Dec. 24, 1806; Jan. 15, 1812–Dec. 29, 1813; Dec. 7, 1814–Jan. 22, 1817.

Univ. of Mich. (Clements) has June 21, 28, July 19, Aug. 16, 23, Oct. 20, Nov. 17–Dec. 15, 29, 1775; Jan. 5, May 3, Oct. 9, Nov. 13, 1776; Apr. 3, 24, Sept. 4, 1777; Mar. 18, Oct. 7, 1779; July 26, Aug. 2, Sept. 6, 1781; Jan. 10, 17, Mar. 7–28, Apr. 11, 18, May 2, 16, 1782; Feb. 6, Apr. 17, 24, May 29, Aug. 14, Nov. 27, Dec. 10, 25, 1783; Jan. 1–Feb. 12, Apr. 14, 1784–Dec. 29, 1785, fair; May 8, 1788–Oct. 29, 1789, fair; May 27, June 3, Aug. 5, Sept. 30, 1790; Feb. 24, June 23, Oct. 20, Nov. 24, 1791; Jan. 26–Dec. 27, 1792, fair; Jan. 3, 1793–Dec. 31, 1794; Jan. 7, 1795–Dec. 30, 1801, fair; Jan. 6, 1802–Aug. 31, 1814, scattering issues; Mar. 1, 1815–Apr. 17, 1816; Jan. 8, Mar. 5, 1817–Feb. 24, 1819.

Conn. Hist. Soc. has Jan. 1, 1784–June 16, 1785; Jan. 21, 1790–Dec. 29, 1791.

Univ. of Chicago has May 3, 1775–July 5, 1792, a few scattering issues; Jan. 3, 1793–Nov. 30, 1796, fair; Nov. 7, 1798; Aug. 21, 1799; June 18–Dec. 17, 1800, scattering.

Columbia Univ. has Jan. 9, 1783–Dec. 30, 1784.

Univ. of Ill. has Aug. 4, 1785–Mar. 30, 1786; Mar. 12, June 18, July 9, 1789; Feb. 11, 1790–Oct. 18, 1792, fair; Aug. 22, 1804; May 29, 1805.

Concord, Mass., Pub. Lib. has Apr. 4, 1793–Feb. 25, 1795.

Mrs. Raymond L. Buell, Richmond, Mass., has Mar. 27, 1794–Feb. 24, 1796.

Detroit Pub. Lib. has Mar. 7, 1804–Feb. 26, 1806; Oct. 26, 1814–Dec. 27, 1815.

Newberry Lib. has Mar. 6, 1811–Feb. 26, 1812.

Univ. of Texas has Jan. 7, 1818–Feb. 24, 1819.

Duke Univ. has July 5, 1775–Sept. 10, 1800, a few scattering issues; Jan. 14–Dec. 30, 1801; Jan. 6, Apr. 14, June 30, 1802; Apr. 20, 1803; Jan. 9–Nov. 20, 1805; Sept. 8, Dec. 8, 1819.

Western Reserve Hist. Soc. has May 3, Nov. 17, 1775; July 17, 1776; May 6, 1789; Nov. 18, 1801–Dec. 28, 1802, fair; Nov. 11, 1807–Sept. 20, 1820, a few scattering issues.

Many libraries have single or a few scattering issues.

[Worcester] National Aegis, 1801–1820+.

Weekly. Established Dec. 2, 1801, with the title of "The National Aegis," edited by "Hector Ironside" [Francis Blake] and published by Robert Johnson. With the issue of Dec. 30, 1801, Sewall Goodridge replaced Johnson as publisher. With the issue of June 1, 1803, the editor's name was omitted from the imprint, the paper was published by Sewall Goodridge solely, and the title was slightly altered to "National Aegis." In a manuscript account of Worcester newspapers by William Lincoln, in the American Antiquarian Society, it is stated that Francis Blake was editor until March, 1804, when he was succeeded by Edward Bangs, who retired June 12, 1805. With the issue of Oct. 23, 1805, the paper was transferred to Samuel Cotting. Immediately after the issue of Dec. 11, 1805, vol. 5, no. 211, the former editor, Francis Blake, attached most of the printing apparatus, and it was not until Feb. 19, 1806, vol. 5, no. 212, that the paper was again able to make its appearance, when it was "Published by the Proprietors." With the issue of Mar. 12, 1806, it appeared in new type and with the title "The National Aegis." With the issue of May 21, 1806, the name of Samuel Cotting appears in the imprint as publisher.

On July 6, 1806, Cotting broke up the forms of the next issue, took away some of the printing apparatus, and began printing on July 9, on a new press in another office, a paper which he called "The National Aegis," continuing the numbering of the regular paper. The proprietors of the regular Aegis were unable to publish a full sized issue on July 9, 1806, and brought out a single-page, or broadside, with the heading of "The National Aegis," published under the direction of a committee of the proprietors. The next issue, July 16, was "Printed for the Proprietors." Cotting, with his issue of July 16, changed his title to "National Aegis." There were therefore two papers published, both with the same volume numbering, one called "The National Aegis," printed for the Proprietors, and the other called "National Aegis," published by Samuel Cotting. During this period Levi Lincoln was evidently editor of "The National Aegis," having succeeded Samuel Brazer in that capacity, although the exact time of the change of editorship is not certain. The Republicans of Worcester County met, Sept. 4, 1806, and resolved that the "Trustees' Aegis" was the genuine paper and that Cotting's paper was spurious. Cotting's "National Aegis" survived this vote only a few weeks and was discontinued with the issue of Dec. 3, 1806 (see "The National Aegis" of Dec. 17, 1806), but was revived with the issue of Feb. 18, 1807, and finally discontinued with the issue of Apr. 15, 1807, vol. 6, no. 290. "The National Aegis" continued on, and with the issue of Dec. 31, 1806, was printed for the Proprietors by Samuel Nutting. In a collection of original documents relating to the Aegis, owned by the American Antiquarian Society, is a bill against the paper made out by Samuel Nutting, dated Jan. 30, 1807, in which he charges for printing the paper beginning with Aug. 10, 1806, and with editing it from Nov. 5, 1806. With the issue of Mar. 11, 1807, the paper was printed and published by Henry Rogers. C. C. Baldwin, in his "Diary," p. 299, states that Edward D. Bangs was the real editor (referring to the period subsequent to 1813), with Rogers as publisher and nominal editor. The paper was so continued until after 1820.

Am. Antiq. Soc. has Dec. 2, 1801–Dec. 27, 1820; also July 9–23, Sept. 3, 1806; Apr. 15, 1807, of Cotting's "National Aegis."

Boston Pub. Lib. has Dec. 2, 1801–Nov. 20, 1805; Jan. 6–27, Feb. 10, 24, Mar. 2, 16, 23, Apr. 6, 27–May 18, June 15–Aug. 10, 24, 31, Sept. 14, 28,

Oct. 12–Nov. 2, 16, Dec. 7, 21, 28, 1808; Jan. 18, 1809–Dec. 25, 1811; Jan. 1–Mar. 4, 18–Apr. 8, 22, May 6, June 10–Oct. 14, 28, Nov. 4, 18, 25, Dec. 9–30, 1812; Jan. 6, 1813–Dec. 27, 1820, fair.

Boston Athenæum has Dec. 2, 1801–Dec. 11, 1805; Feb. 19, 1806–Dec. 25, 1811; Jan. 1, 15, 22, Feb. 12, Mar. 4, 18, Apr. 15–29, May 27, June 10, July 7, 15, Aug. 19, Sept. 2, 9, 30, Dec. 2, 1812; July 14, 28, Aug. 11, Sept. 22, Oct. 13, 27, 1813; Jan. 19–Feb. 2, Apr. 13, June 29, July 13–Dec. 28, 1814; Jan. 5, 18–Feb. 8, 22, Mar. 22, May 31, July 12, 26, Aug. 2, Sept. 6, Oct. 11, Nov. 22, Dec. 6–20, 1815; Jan. 10–24, Feb. 7–21, Mar. 6–27, Apr. 17, 24, May 8–July 10, Aug. 28, Sept. 25, Oct. 16, Dec. 11, 18, 1816; Jan. 29, Oct. 15, 1817; Sept. 9, 1818; Aug. 11, Dec. 8, 1819; Jan. 19, Sept. 27, Nov. 15–29, 1820.

Dartmouth has Dec. 9, 1801–Dec. 26, 1804; Jan. 2–Nov. 27, 1805, fair; Mar. 12, 26, Apr. 2, 16, 23, May 28, June 11–25, July 9–Aug. 13, Sept. 3, Oct. 1–Dec. 31, 1806; Jan. 14, 1807–Dec. 30, 1812; Jan. 6, 1813–Dec. 27, 1820, fair.

Worc. Pub. Lib. has Dec. 2, 1801–Dec. 29, 1802; Jan. 5, 1803–Dec. 26, 1804, fair; Jan. 2, 1805–Dec. 27, 1809; Jan. 3–May 2, 23, June 6, 13, 27, July 11, Oct. 10, 24–Nov. 7, 21, Dec. 19, 1810; Jan. 30, Feb. 6, 27, Mar. 6, 20–Apr. 17, May 1, July 17, 24, Aug. 7, 14, 28, Sept. 11, 25, Nov. 13–Dec. 4, 18, 25, 1811; Jan. 1, 1812.

Lib. Congress has Dec. 2, 1801–Dec. 29, 1802; Jan. 5, 1803–Dec. 30, 1807, fair, including also the "Cotting" file of July 9, 1806–Apr. 15, 1807; Mar. 2, 1808–Oct. 25, 1809, fair; Feb. 14, 28, May 16, Aug. 8, 22, Oct. 10, 1810; Feb. 6, Mar. 6, Apr. 3, Aug. 14, 1811; July 1, 1812; June 30, Sept. 22, Nov. 3, 1813; Sept. 28, 1814; Dec. 13, 1815; July 3, 24, Aug. 21, Sept. 25–Dec. 25, 1816; Mar. 26, Sept. 17, 1817; July 29, 1818; Jan. 6, 1819–Dec. 27, 1820.

Patten Lib., Bath, Me., has Mar. 23, 1808–Dec. 25, 1816.

Trinity Coll., Hartford, has July 13, 1803–Dec. 31, 1806, fair; Jan. 14, Feb. 4, 18–Mar. 11, 25–May 13, June 17, Sept. 2, 1807; Nov. 8, 15, 1809; Nov. 6, 1811; Sept. 23, 1812.

Harvard has Dec. 9, 30, 1801; Mar. 13, Apr. 10, May 22, 29, 1805; June 4, 11, Aug. 7, Dec. 11, 1806; Jan. 7, 14, Mar. 4–18, Apr. 1, 29, May 27, June 3, July 15, 22, Sept. 16, 30, Nov. 11, 1807; July 27, Aug. 3, 17, 31, Nov. 9–23, Dec. 21, 1808.

N. Y. Hist. Soc. has Dec. 2, 1801–May 25, 1803; Oct. 12, 1803; Apr. 4, 1804; Sept. 18, 1805; Dec. 16, 1807; Apr. 20, May 25, June 8, July 13, 27–Aug. 24, 1808; Jan. 11, Feb. 15, Apr. 12, May 17, June 28, 1809; July 1, 1812; Oct. 20, 1813; Sept. 6, 1815; June 30, Oct. 13, 1819.

Univ. of Mich. (Clements) has Dec. 16, 1801–Nov. 30, 1803, fair; Jan. 18–Feb. 1, June 6, July 18, Sept. 12, Oct. 3, 1804; Jan. 9–Dec. 4, 1805, fair; Feb. 19–Mar. 26, Apr. 9, 23–July 16, 30, Aug. 13, Sept. 3, Oct. 1, 15, Nov. 12–26, 1806; Jan. 7, Feb. 4, Mar. 4, 18, Apr. 22, May 13, June 17, 24, July 22, Aug. 26, Sept. 16, Oct. 7, 14, Nov. 18, 25, 1807; Mar. 16, 30, Apr. 20, 27,

May 18, June 1, 8, 22–July 6, Sept. 7, 1808; Jan. 18, Feb. 8, Mar. 8–22, May 31, June 21, 1809; Jan. 2, July 3, 1811; Jan. 8, Mar. 18, Apr. 29, May 13, June 24, 1812; Dec. 1, 1813; Aug. 7, Sept. 18, 1816; Aug. 26, 1818; July 28, 1819; Mar. 8, 1820.

Yale has Jan. 6, 1802–Dec. 11, 1805; July 9, 30, Sept. 3, 1806; May 13, June 24, Oct. 7, 1807; June 22–July 6, 1808.

Essex Inst. has May 26, 1802–Apr. 18, 1804, fair.

Bowdoin has Nov. 30, 1803–Nov. 21, 1804.

N. Y. State Lib. has Jan. 5–Dec. 28, 1803, fair; Jan. 4–Feb. 1, 15–Apr. 4, 18, 25, May 23, June 13, 27–July 25, Sept. 12–Nov. 14, 28–Dec. 26, 1804; Jan. 2–Dec. 11, 1805; Mar. 5–Nov. 19, 1806, fair; Mar. 11, 18, 1807; May 4, 18, Aug. 3, 1808; Mar. 14, Aug. 15, Oct. 17, 24, Nov. 14, Dec. 12, 1810; Feb. 27, 1811; Jan. 22, June 3, 1812; Oct. 20, 1813; Jan. 5, 19, Mar. 16, July 13, 20, 1814; Aug. 9, 1815.

Conn. Hist. Soc. has June 15, Aug. 24, 1803; Feb. 27, 1805; Jan. 31–Oct. 3, 1810; Dec. 25, 1811–Dec. 30, 1812.

Duke Univ. has Dec. 9, 1801–Dec. 29, 1802, fair; Sept. 7, 1808; Apr. 17, 1816.

Mass. Hist. Soc. has Dec. 2, 1801; Mar. 10, Apr. 14, 1802; Feb. 2, Apr. 6, 13, Dec. 28, 1803; Feb. 8, Mar. 7, 14, Aug. 22, Dec. 19, 1804; Jan. 9, July 3, 31, 1805; Mar. 5, Nov. 12, 1806.

N. Y. Pub. Lib. has May 5–July 21, Aug. 18, 1802; Jan. 26, Feb. 2, 23, Apr. 20, May 4, 25, June 1, 15, 1803; Apr. 1, 1807; Mar. 29, 1809; Aug. 19, 26, Dec. 16, 1812.

[Worcester] **Scorpion**, 1809.

Weekly. Established July 26, 1809, with the title of "The Scorpion," printed "for the Editors." It was a scurrilous paper, without current news, and produced solely to attack the proprietors of "The National Aegis" and other Worcester Democrats. It was of quarto size, and according to a manuscript note in the issue of Aug. 9, owned by the American Antiquarian Society, only three issues were published.

Am. Antiq. Soc. has July 26, Aug. 2, 9, 1809.

[Worcester] **Thomas's Massachusetts Spy**, see **Massachusetts Spy**.

MICHIGAN

Detroit Gazette, 1817–1820+.

Weekly. Established July 25, 1817, by Sheldon & Reed [John P. Sheldon and Ebenezer Reed], with the title of "Detroit Gazette." Continued by them until after 1820.

The Univ. of Michigan Library in 1919–24 reproduced the "Detroit Gazette" in photostat from 1817 to 1830, which set is to be found in the following libraries: — Univ. of Mich. (Clements), W. L. Clements Estate, Grand Rapids Pub. Lib., Am. Antiq. Soc., N. Y. Pub. Lib., N. Y. Hist. Soc., Lib. Congress, Newberry Lib., Univ. of Illinois, Missouri Hist. Soc., Wis. Hist. Soc., Minn. Hist. Soc., and Univ. of Texas.

Detroit Pub. Lib. has July 25, 1817–Dec. 29, 1820.
Wis. Hist. Soc. has Apr. 24, June 26, Nov. 7, 13, Dec. 11, 1818; Jan. 8, 15, Mar. 5, May 7, July 23, 1819–Dec. 29, 1820.
Lib. Congress has Jan. 1, 1819–Dec. 22, 1820.
Mich. State Lib. has Jan. 28–Dec. 29, 1820.
Am. Antiq. Soc. has Jan. 9, Apr. 24, May 8, 1818; Apr. 30, May 28, July 9, Nov. 19, 1819; Jan. 7–21, 1820.
N. Y. State Lib. has Dec. 24, 1819; Dec. 15, 22, 1820.
N. Y. Hist. Soc. has Aug. 11, 18, 1820.
N. Y. Pub. Lib. has Nov. 13, 1818.

[Detroit] Michigan Essay, 1809.

Weekly. Established Aug. 31, 1809, printed and published by James M. Miller, with the title of "Michigan Essay; or, the Impartial Observer." For the part taken by Father Richard in the establishing of the press, see P. J. Foik, "Pioneer Catholic Journalism," 1930, and D. C. McMurtrie, "Early Printing in Michigan," 1931. Silas Farmer, in his "History of Detroit," 1884, vol. 1, p. 670, stated that five copies of this paper had been discovered, all of the initial issue. The copy in the American Antiquarian Society has written upon it: "Utica, N. Y., Aug. 3, 1810. Mr. Thomas; Sir, I send you this paper printed by a friend of mine to insert in your 'History of Printing.' If he sees your advertisement, he will send you more, perhaps of a later date. Your ob't Serv't, C. S. McConnell."

S. R. Brown, in his "View of the Campaigns of the North-western Army," 1814, p. 156, refers to this paper and says that Miller "did not meet with sufficient encouragement to continue it beyond the third number." Mr. C. M. Burton in 1909 made a photographic fac-simile of this initial issue, in an edition of a thousand copies, in connection with the Detroit Centenary Celebration, which fac-simile is in most large libraries.

Am. Antiq. Soc. has Aug. 31, 1809.
Detroit Pub. Lib. has Aug. 31, 1809.

MISSISSIPPI

Fort Stoddert, see under **Alabama**.

Huntsville, see under **Alabama**.

Monticello Republican, 1820.

Weekly. Established Mar. 25, 1820, according to the only issue located, that of Apr. 1, 1820, vol. 1, no. 2, published by William Evens, with the title of "Monticello Republican." Evens printed proposals for this paper in the Natchez "Mississippi State Gazette" of Jan. 22, 1820, stating that it would begin in March.

Duke Univ. has Apr. 1, 1820.

[Natchez] Constitutional Conservator, 1802–1803.

Weekly. Established in October, 1802, judging from the date of the first and only issue located, that of Apr. 16, 1803, vol. 1, no. 27, published by John Wade, with the title of "The Constitutional Conservator." The "Natchez Conservator" of Jan. 8, 1803, is quoted in the Georgia "Augusta Herald" of Mar. 9, 1803.

Harvard has Apr. 16, 1803.

Natchez Gazette, 1808.

Weekly and semi-weekly. A continuation, without change of volume numbering, of the "Mississippi Herald & Natchez Gazette." The first issue with the title of "Natchez Gazette" was that of Jan. 7, 1808, vol. 7, no. 1, whole number 313, published by Andrew Marschalk. In July, 1808, the paper became a semi-weekly, the size being reduced to quarto. With the issue of Sept. 14, 1808, the title was changed to "The Natchez Gazette" and the size was enlarged to folio, the two semi-weekly issues consisting of four pages and two respectively. The last regular issue was that of Nov. 16, 1808, vol. 7, no. 62, after which Marschalk issued a final supplement, Nov. 19, 1808, in which he wrote his "Valedictory" and reprinted nine editorials from other papers dunning delinquent subscribers.

Am. Antiq. Soc. has Jan. 7, Feb. 18, Mar. 24, Apr. 7, May 12, June 9, 16 suppl., Aug. 5, 10, 17, 26, 31 and suppl., Sept. 2–14, Oct. 21, Nov. 16, 19 suppl., 1808.
Miss. Dept. of Archives has Jan. 14, Aug. 31, 1808.
William M. Drake, Church Hill, Miss., has Apr. 28, 1808.

Natchez Gazette, 1811–1813.

Weekly. Established June 20, 1811, by David M'Keehan, with the title of

"The Natchez Gazette, and Mississippi General Advertiser." At some time between May 1812 and July 1813, the publishing firm became M'Keehan & M'Curdy [David M'Keehan and James M'Curdy] and the title was shortened to "The Natchez Gazette." The last issue located is that of July 28, 1813, vol. 3, no. 7.

> Am. Antiq. Soc. has June 20–July 4, Aug. 1, 15, 22, Sept. 5–26, Oct. 10–31, Nov. 14, Dec. 26, 1811; Jan. 9–Feb. 13, Mar. 5, 26, Apr. 2, May 7, 1812; July 28, 1813.
> Hist. Soc. Penn. has Aug. 8, 1811.
> Lib. Congress has Feb. 6, 1812.

[Natchez] Green's Impartial Observer, 1800–1801.

Weekly. Established May 5, 1800, by J[ames] Green, with the title of "Green's Impartial Observer." The last issue located is that of Apr. 4, 1801, vol. 1, no. 23. See also under Natchez "Intelligencer," 1801. The Natchez "Time's Tablet" of Sept. 28, 1833 (copy in Am. Antiq. Soc.) advertises for early Natchez newspapers, among them the Observer, printed by James Green.

> Univ. of Chicago has May 5–Sept. 20, Oct. 18, Nov. 29, Dec. 13, 1800; Jan. 24, Feb. 21, Apr. 4, 1801.
> Lib. Congress has Jan. 24, Feb. 21, 1801.

[Natchez] Independent Press, 1819.

Weekly. Established Mar. 24, 1819, by Peter Isler, with the title of "The Independent Press." The last issue located is that of May 19, 1819, vol. 1, no. 9, although a copy for July 14, 1819, is referred to in the "Savannah Museum" of Aug. 24, 1819. Isler proposed to publish a paper at Monticello, Miss., to be called "The Rights of the People," according to his advertisement in the "Mississippi State Gazette" of Nov. 4, 1820, but there is no evidence to show that it was established.

> Lib. Congress has Mar. 24–Apr. 21, May 19, 1819.
> Am. Antiq. Soc. has May 12, 1819.

[Natchez] Intelligencer, 1801.

Weekly. Established Aug. 11, 1801, judging from the date of the earliest issue located, that of Oct. 6, 1801, vol. 1, no. 9, published by D[arius] Moffett & Co., with the title of "The Intelligencer." The last issue located is that of Dec. 8, 1801, vol. 1, no. 17. Andrew Marschalk, in a letter written in 1837 ("Proceedings of Miss. Press Assoc.," 1885, p. 225), states, "About March or April 1800, a Mr. Green, from Baltimore, brought a press to Natchez. I do not recollect the title of his paper; it ceased while I was at the North, and the press fell into the hands of James Ferrell, who with one Moffatt, published a paper for a short time."

Harvard has Oct. 6, 13, Dec. 1, 8, 1801.

Natchez Intelligencer, 1815.

Weekly. No copy of this paper has been located. James M'Curdy advertised in the "Mississippi Republican" of May 24, 1815, that within a few weeks, probably in August, he would commence the publication of a newspaper. The "Washington Republican" of Oct. 28, 1815, records the death, on Oct. 27, of James M'Curdy, editor of "The Natchez Intelligencer." On Nov. 17, 1815, the "Washington Republican" took over the unexpired subscriptions to "The Natchez Intelligencer," and made the title of that paper part of its own title.

[Natchez] Mississippi Gazette, 1799–1801.

Weekly. This paper was established by Benjamin M. Stokes late in the year 1799. Andrew Marschalk, the pioneer Mississippi printer, writing in 1837 (printed in "Proceedings of Miss. Press Assoc.," 1885, p. 225), relates his recollections of the beginnings of printing in Mississippi and says that he sold a printing-press "to Ben. M. Stokes, and he commenced in Natchez, and continued some time, the Mississippi Gazette, on a foolscap sheet. This was some time in the summer of 1799; but he soon failed." Gov. Winthrop Sargent, in writing to Timothy Pickering, Feb. 10, 1800, said "I take leave to send you the Mississippi Gazette, and shall so continue to do." ("Miss. Territorial Archives," 1905, vol. 1, p. 207.) A quotation from the "Mississippi Gazette" of Mar. 22, 1800, appeared in the Boston "Columbian Centinel" of May 31, 1800, and further quotations in the Knoxville "Impartial Observer" of Apr. 30, 1800, and in the "Winchester (Va.) Gazette" of May 21, 1800. Stokes presumably was the sole printer of the paper up to February 1801, since in the Natchez "Green's Impartial Observer" of Feb. 21, 1801, he advertised that he had "now in press" a pamphlet Petition to Congress. It must have been soon afterwards that he formed a partnership with R[————] T. Sackett. Benjamin M. Stokes, presumably the printer later at Natchez, married at Cincinnati Prudence Cadwell on Aug. 8 (Cincinnati "Western Spy," Aug. 13, 1799).

The earliest issue located is that of Oct. 13, 1801, vol. 2, no. 7, entitled "The Mississippi Gazette," and published by B. M. Stokes. The volume numbering would carry the date of establishment back to September 1800, which would indicate a previous hiatus in numbering or suspension of publication. It is in this issue of Oct. 13, 1801, that B. M. Stokes and R. T. Sackett announce that they have dissolved partnership as printers, and R. T. Sackett states that he is relinquishing his share in the conduct of the paper "from his dislike of the climate of this country." He evidently did not leave the State, since in the issue of Nov. 10, 1801 (misprint of "September" in the imprint), vol. 2, no. 8, Benjamin M. Stokes announces that he has disposed of the paper to Sackett & [————] Wallace, who appear in the imprint as the publishers. They are given as the publishers of the succeeding issues of Nov. 24, 1801, vol. 2, no. 9, and Dec. 1, 1801, vol. 2, no. 10, which latter issue is the last located.

Harvard has Oct. 13, Nov. 10, 24, Dec. 1, 1801.

[Natchez] Mississippi Gazette, 1811.

There are references to a paper with the title of "The Mississippi Gazette," of Natchez, in the "Natchez Gazette" of June 27, July 4, Aug. 15, Oct. 17 and 24, 1811. The last reference implies that John Shaw was the editor. The paper is also noted in the Natchez "Weekly Chronicle" of Jan. 21, 1811. Possibly it was the "Gazette" published by William O. Winston, who sold his paper to P. Isler, who established the "Mississippi Republican" in April, 1812. No copy of the paper has been located.

[Natchez] Missisippi Herald, 1802–1807.

Weekly and semi-weekly. Established July 27, 1802, judging from the date of the earliest issue located, that of Aug. 10, 1802, vol. 1, no. 3, published by Andrew Marschalk, with the title of "Missisippi Herald." Marschalk, in a letter written in 1837, says: "I arrived from Philadelphia the last of July, 1802, and commenced the Mississippi Herald, I think the 26th of July, the same year" ("Proceedings of Miss. Press Assoc.," 1885, p. 225.) At some time between June 4 and July 18, 1803, the title was changed to "Missisippi Herald, and Natchez Repository," and the paper enlarged to eight pages, small folio. At some time between this date and Sept. 19, 1803, the title was changed to "Missisippi Herald, and Natchez City Gazette." With the first issue in February, 1804, the paper became a semi-weekly of four pages, and the spelling of the first word in the title was changed to "Mississippi." With the issue of Aug. 31, 1804, the paper reverted to a weekly issue, the size was changed to large folio, and the title was altered to "Missisippi Herald & Natchez Gazette." The spelling of "Missisippi" in the title was dependent upon the width of the page, which did not admit of even another letter, as the word was spelled "Mississippi" elsewhere in the paper and also in the title of "Extra" issues. From Sept. 2, 1806, to Aug. 25, 1807, the spelling was "Misissippi." The last issue with the title of "Missisippi Herald & Nachez Gazette" was that of Dec. 31, 1807, vol. 6, no. 52, whole no. 312, after which the title was changed to "Natchez Gazette," which see.

Am. Antiq. Soc. has July 18, Sept. 19, 1803; Jan. 21, May 19–30, Aug. 7, 10, 31, Sept. 21, Oct. 19–Nov. 29, Dec. 21, 1804; Apr. 20 extra, May 11 extra, July 26, Aug. 9, 30, Oct. 1–22, 1805; Jan. 22, Feb. 25, June 10, 24, July 1, 15, Aug. 5–19, Sept. 2–Nov. 25, Dec. 9–30, 1806; Jan. 13–Apr. 22, May 6–20, June 10–July 29, Aug. 25–Sept. 15, Oct. 14, Nov. 13, 19, Dec. 3–31, 1807.

Yale has Aug. 1, 1804–Dec. 10, 1805.

R. Percy Stewart, Natchez, has Nov. 14, 1803; July 20, 1804; Feb. 7, 1806–Dec. 31, 1807.

Harvard has Oct. 31, Nov. 14, 1803; Jan. 21, Apr. 26, May 19–30, June 15, 26, 29, Oct. 5, 19–Nov. 2, 1804; Feb. 1, Oct. 8, 22, 1805; Feb. 4, 18, Mar. 18, 25, Sept. 23, 1806; Oct. 21, Nov. 26, Dec. 24, 1807.

Miss. Dept. of Archives has Apr. 15, 29, May 13–June 3, Dec. 23, 1806; Feb. 4, June 10, 1807.

William M. Drake, Church Hill, Miss., has June 10, July 22, Sept. 2, 1806; Dec. 17, 1807.

Duke Univ. has Sept. 23, Oct. 28, 1806; May 20, June 17, July 8–22, Sept. 12, Dec. 10, 17, 1807.

N. Y. Hist. Soc. has Aug. 10, 17, 1802.

Univ. of Chicago has Feb. 13, July 6–13, 1804.

Lib. Congress has Sept. 28, 1802; Mar. 25, Apr. 22, 1807.

Phil. Lib. Co. has Feb. 19, 1803.

William Nelson had May 28, 1803 (reproduced in "N. J. Archives," ser. 1, vol. 19, p. xxi).

Univ. of Texas has photostat of Nov. 21, 1805.

[Natchez] **Mississippi Messenger,** 1804–1808.

Weekly. Established Sept. 7, 1804, by Timothy & Samuel Terrell, with the title of "The Mississippi Messenger." With the issue of July 8, 1806, Timothy Terrell withdrew and the paper was published by Samuel Terrell. With the issue of May 26, 1807, the publishing firm became John Shaw & Timothy Terrell. The last issue located is that of Aug. 11, 1808, vol. 5, no. 206.

Miss. Dept. of Archives has Sept. 6–Oct. 29, Nov. 12, 26, Dec. 3, 1805; Jan. 7, 21, 28, Feb. 11, 25–Aug. 19, Sept. 2, 16–Nov. 25, Dec. 9–23, 1806; Jan. 6–Feb. 4, 17, Mar. 17–Apr. 14, May 5, 19–June 9, 23–Dec. 10, 1807; Jan. 21–Feb. 11, 25, Mar. 17–Apr. 14, May 12, 26–Aug. 11, 1808.

Am. Antiq. Soc. has Sept. 7, Oct. 12–Nov. 30, 1804; Jan. 18, 25, Feb. 8, Mar. 15, 29, Apr. 26, June 7, July 19, Aug. 16, 30, Sept. 6, Oct. 29, Nov. 5, 1805; June 2, 16, July 7, 14, Sept. 22, Nov. 26, 1807; Mar. 24, July 7, 1808.

Lib. Congress has Apr. 28, June 23, Aug. 18, Nov. 12, 1807.

Harvard has June 9, 1807.

[Natchez] **Mississippi Republican,** 1812–1820+.

Weekly and semi-weekly. Established Apr. 8, 1812, judging from the date of the earliest issue located, that of Apr. 29, 1812, vol. 1, no. 4, published by P[eter] Isler, with the title of "Mississippi Republican." P. Isler writes the Secretary of State, May 5, 1812, stating that he has "purchased the establishment from which Mr. Winston's Gaz. has heretofore issued," and requesting that he may have the privilege of publishing federal laws, previously given to William O. Winston

(C. E. Carter, "Territorial Papers," vol. 6, p. 289). With the issue of Dec. 1, 1813, Isler admitted James M'Curdy to partnership, and the paper was published by P. Isler and J. M'Curdy. At some time between Mar. 8 and May 24, 1815, M'Curdy withdrew, and the paper was again published by P. Isler. With the issue of Jan. 21, 1818, Isler transferred the paper to Richard C. Langdon. It was changed to a semi-weekly with the issue of Oct. 13, 1818, but reverted to a weekly with the issue of Jan. 12, 1819. With the issue of Nov. 14, 1820, the paper was purchased and published by William Evens & Co. [William Evens and J―――― W. Foote]. It was so continued until after 1820.

Miss. Dept. of Archives has Apr. 28, Oct. 27, Nov. 3, 24, Dec. 1, 15-29, 1813; Jan. 5-Dec. 21, 1814, fair; Jan. 18, Feb. 1, Mar. 1, July 26, 1815; May 28, June 18, July 2, Aug. 13-27, Sept. 10-Oct. 1, 1817; Jan. 14, 1818-Dec. 12, 1820.

Lib. Congress has Feb. 9, Mar. 2-Apr. 27, May 11-June 1, 15, 22, July 20-Aug. 3, 17-Dec. 28, 1819; Jan. 4-18, Feb. 1-May 16, 30, June 6, July 4-18, Aug. 1, 8, 22-Oct. 31, Nov. 14, 28, Dec. 5, 19, 26, 1820.

Am. Antiq. Soc. has Apr. 29, May 20, 1812; Oct. 20, 1813; Jan. 26, 1814; Mar. 1, May 24, 1815; Apr. 9, 1818; Mar. 23, 1819.

Univ. of Chicago has July 23, 1818.

[Natchez] **Mississippi State Gazette,** 1818-1820+.

Weekly and semi-weekly. A continuation, without change of numbering, of "The Washington Republican and Natchez Intelligencer." The first issue with the new title of "The Mississippi State Gazette" was that of Jan. 3, 1818, vol. 6, no. 1, published by Andrew Marschalk. With the issue of July 4, 1818, Marschalk admitted William Evens to partnership, and the paper was published by Marschalk & Evens. With the issue of Sept. 9, 1818, the paper became a semi-weekly, but reverted to a weekly with the issue of July 3, 1819. The paper was suspended with the issue of Sept. 4, 1819, but resumed publication on Dec. 4, 1819. With the issue of Jan. 1, 1820, Evens withdrew and Andrew Marschalk appeared as sole publisher. Continued until after 1820. Evens proposed in "The Mississippi State Gazette" of Jan. 22, 1820, to publish a newspaper at Monticello, Miss., to be called the "Monticello Republican," and to begin in March 1820; but he did not succeed in establishing it, and in November, 1820, purchased the "Mississippi Republican" of Natchez.

Miss. Dept. of Archives has Jan. 3, 1818-Dec. 30, 1820.

R. Percy Stewart, Natchez, has Jan. 3, 1818-Dec. 25, 1819; Apr. 8, May 6, 1820.

Lib. Congress has June 6-20, July 4-25, 1818; Jan. 2, 1819-Dec. 30, 1820, fair.

Am. Antiq. Soc. has May 2, Sept. 5, 19-Dec. 23, 1818; Mar. 6, Aug. 14, 1819; Jan. 8, 22, 29, Mar. 4, 11, Apr. 8-May 27, June 10, Sept. 30, Oct. 28, Nov. 4, 25-Dec. 9, 23, 1820.

N. Y. Hist. Soc. has Oct. 3, 1818; Jan. 22, 29, Apr. 8–May 13, 27, Nov. 4, 25, Dec. 23, 1820.
Univ. of Chicago has July 11, 25, 1818.

[Natchez] **Mississippian**, 1808–1811.

Weekly. Established Dec. 1, 1808, judging from the date of the earliest perfect issue located, that of Dec. 22, 1808, vol. 1, no. 4, printed by John Shaw, with the title of "The Mississippian." The last issue located is that of Sept. 10, 1810, vol. 2, no. 80. The paper is quoted in the "Muskingum Messenger" of Zanesville, Ohio, of Feb. 20, 1811.

Am. Antiq. Soc. has Dec. 8 (imperfect), 22, 29, 1808; Jan. 19, Feb. 2, Mar. 9–23, May 1, 15, 29, June 5, Aug. 14, 1809; May 14, June 4, Aug. 20, 27, Sept. 10, 1810.
Lib. Congress has Dec. 29, 1808.

[Natchez] **Washington Republican**, 1815–1817.

Weekly. A continuation, without change of volume numbering, of the "Washington Republican," published at Washington, Miss., by Andrew Marschalk. The first issue printed at Natchez was that of Nov. 17, 1815, vol. 3, no. 30, published by Andrew Marschalk, with the title of "Washington Republican and Natchez Intelligencer." Marschalk had just purchased "The Natchez Intelligencer" and stated that his new paper would be delivered to patrons of the former publication, to fill out the terms of their subscription. With the issue of Mar. 27, 1816, the title was slightly changed to "The Washington Republican and Natchez Intelligencer." The last issue with this title was that of Dec. 27, 1817, vol. 5, no. 29, after which the title was changed to "The Mississippi State Gazette," which see.

Miss. Dept. of Archives has Nov. 17, 1815–Dec. 27, 1817.
Am. Antiq. Soc. has Apr. 24–May 22, July 3–Aug. 21, Sept. 4, 11, 1816; Jan. 1, 15, 22, Mar. 5, 19–Apr. 16, June 14, 1817.
Univ. of Mich. (Clements) has July 31, Sept. 11, 1816.

[Natchez] **Weekly Chronicle**, 1808–1812.

Weekly. Established July 6, 1808, by John W. Winn & Co., with the title of "The Weekly Chronicle." The last issue located is that of Apr. 8, 1811, vol. 3, no. 40, whole no. 144. The paper is quoted in the Cincinnati "Liberty Hall" of July 18, 1811, and Nov. 3, 1812.

Miss. Dept. of Archives has July 6, 1808–July 2, 1810.
Am. Antiq. Soc. has July 6–Aug. 3, 17, 31, Sept. 7, Oct. 12–Nov. 2, 16, Dec. 14–28, 1808; Jan. 11, 25, Feb. 22–Apr. 5, May 6, 13, June 3, 17, 1809; May 28,

June 25–July 16, Aug. 13, 27, Sept. 10, Oct. 8, Nov. 5, 12, Dec. 31, 1810; Jan. 7, 21, 28, Feb. 11–Mar. 4, Apr. 8, 1811.
U. S. Dept. of State, Bureau of Rolls, has Aug. 6, 1810.
N. Y. Hist. Soc. has Jan. 21, 1811.

Port-Gibson Correspondent, 1818–1820+.

Weekly. Established in November, 1818, judging from the date of the earliest issue located, that of Mar. 27, 1819, vol. 1, no. 20, published by James Hughes, with the title of "The Port-Gibson Correspondent." The Natchez "Mississippi State Gazette" of Nov. 18, 1818, records the receipt of the first issue of the "Port-Gibson Correspondent," published at Port Gibson by James Hughes. With the issue of Nov. 11, 1820, the word "The" was omitted from the title. Continued until after 1820.

Lib. Congress has Mar. 27–May 15, July 24, Aug. 28, Sept. 4, 18–Oct. 2, 23–Nov. 6, 20, Dec. 4–25, 1819; Jan. 1, Feb. 19, Mar. 25, Apr. 8, 29, May 6, 20, June 10–24, July 15–29, Aug. 12, Sept. 2, 16–Oct. 28, Nov. 11, 27, Dec. 2, 23, 1820.

St. Stephens, see under **Alabama.**

Washington Republican, 1813–1815.

Weekly. Established at Washington, Miss., then the capitol of Mississippi Territory, six miles east of Natchez, Apr. 13, 1813, by Andrew Marschalk, with the title of "Washington Republican." With the issue of Oct. 13, 1813, Marschalk joined partnership with Thomas Eastin and the paper was published by Marschalk & Eastin. With the issue of Apr. 27, 1814, the partnership was dissolved and the paper again published by Andrew Marschalk. The last issue at Washington was that of Nov. 11, 1815, vol. 3, no. 29, after which the paper was removed to Natchez and continued by Marschalk without change of volume numbering.

Miss. Dept. of Archives has Apr. 13, 1813–Nov. 11, 1815.
Lib. Congress has Mar. 29, 1815.

MISSOURI

[Boon's Lick] Missouri Intelligencer, see under Franklin.

[Franklin] Missouri Intelligencer, 1819–1820+.

Weekly. Established Apr. 23, 1819, by Patten & Holladay [Nathaniel Patten and Benjamin Holladay, corrected to Holliday with the second issue], with the title of "Missouri Intelligencer, and Boon's Lick Advertiser." Franklin was the county seat of Howard County, and the most populous town in what was called the "Boon's Lick country." The printed broadside "Proposals" was dated Feb. 11, 1819, and signed by N. Patten, Jr. With the issue of Nov. 5, 1819, the title was shortened to "Missouri Intelligencer." The partnership was dissolved on June 17, 1820, and Holliday nominally continued as publisher, but Patten evidently continued to print the paper (see "Missouri Historical Review," 1915, vol. 9, p. 141; vol. 13, p. 365). The paper was continued until after 1820.

National Archives, State Dep't Papers, has "Proposals," Feb. 11, 1819, with letter from Patten of Mar. 24 (Photostats in Lib. Congress and Am. Antiq. Soc.).

State Hist. Soc. of Mo., Columbia, has Apr. 23–June 11, 25–Sept. 3, 17–Oct. 1, 15, Nov. 5–Dec. 17, 31, 1819; Jan. 7, 21–Apr. 22, May 6–July 1, 22–Oct. 14, Nov. 4–18, Dec. 9, 18, 1820.

Long Id. Hist. Soc. has June 11, 1819.

Muskingum Co. Pioneer & Hist. Soc., Zanesville, Ohio, has Feb. 4, 1820.

[Jackson] Independent Patriot, 1820+.

Weekly. Established Nov. 25, 1820, judging from the date of the first issue located, that of Dec. 23, 1820, vol. 1, no. 5, published by Stephen Remington & Co. [Stephen Remington and James Russell], with the title of "Independent Patriot." Continued until after 1820.

Lib. Congress has Dec. 23, 30, 1820.

[Jackson] Missouri Herald, 1819–1820.

Weekly. Established June 25, 1819, judging from the advertisements and date of the first issue located, that of Aug. 13, 1819, vol. 1, no. 8, published by T[ubal] E. Strange, with the title of "Missouri Herald." The "National Intelligencer" of July 28, 1819, states that the first number appeared on June 25, 1819. The prospectus, signed by T. E. Strange, is published in the "Edwardsville [Ill.] Spectator" of June 5, 1819. With the issue of Apr. 8, 1820, Strange took Zenas Priest into partnership under the firm name of T. E. Strange & Co. The last issue located is that of Aug. 26, 1820, vol. 2, no. 4. In the National Archives,

State Dep't Papers, is a letter from Stephen Remington, dated Nov. 2, 1820, stating that he had purchased the "Missouri Herald" from Strange and changed the title to "Independent Patriot."

Lib. Congress has Aug. 13–Oct. 2, Dec. 11, 1819; Jan. 29–May 13, 27–Aug. 5, 19, 26, 1820.

[St. Charles] Missourian, 1820+.

Weekly. Established June 24, 1820, by Robert M'Cloud, with the title of "The Missourian." Continued until after 1820.

Lib. Congress has June 24–Aug. 26, Dec. 23, 1820.
N. Y. State Lib. has July 29, Aug. 12, Nov. 11, 1820.

[St. Louis] Emigrant, 1817–1818.

Weekly. A broadside prospectus for publishing a weekly newspaper, to be called "The Emigrant and General Advertiser," was published by Sergeant Hall, dated Mar. 10, 1817. The first issue of May 17, 1817, is quoted in the "Missouri Gazette" of July 26, 1817. There are constant references to the "Emigrant" and its editor, Sergeant Hall, in the "Missouri Gazette" in 1817 and 1818, always specifically terming it the "Emigrant." There is nothing to show that its title was ever the "Western Emigrant." No copies have been located. It was discontinued in August 1818 (see "Missouri Gazette" of Aug. 8, 1818), to be succeeded, without change of volume numbering, by the "St. Louis Enquirer." According to a letter of Jan. 30, 1818 (see printed "Calendar of Miscellaneous Letters received by the Department of State," 1897, p. 396), S. Hall was authorized to print U. S. Laws in his "Emigrant and General Advertiser." In the National Archives, State Dep't Papers, is a letter of Jan. 12, 1819, stating that Hall's paper had been transferred to Henry and Maury, who "now conduct the paper under the title of 'The St. Louis Enquirer.'"

Ind. State Lib. has Prospectus of Mar. 10, 1817 (photostat in Am. Antiq. Soc.).

St. Louis Enquirer, 1818–1820+.

Weekly and semi-weekly. Established as a weekly in August 1818, succeeding, without change of volume numbering, "The Emigrant and General Advertiser." The earliest issue located is that of Mar. 17, 1819, vol. 2, no. 42, published by Isaac N. Henry & Co. J. T. Scharf, in his "History of St. Louis," 1883, vol. 1, p. 905, says that the proprietors were Isaac N. Henry and Evarist Maury, with Thomas H. Benton as editor. J. Q. Adams, in his "Memoirs," vol. 5, p. 327, writing under date of Mar. 10, 1821, refers to "the St. Louis Enquirer, a Missouri newspaper, of which Benton is half owner and was editor." The firm name of Henry and Maury appears on a Sermon by Salmon Giddings, printed at St. Louis in 1818. A publisher's advertisement in the "St. Louis Enquirer," dated Apr. 21,

1819, states that the paper "has been before the public for eight months," which would date the change of title back to August 1818. With the issue of Sept. 4, 1819, the paper was published semi-weekly, and a weekly country edition was also published, without heading and with few advertisements. The paper reverted to its regular weekly issue on Sept. 3, 1820. It was continued until after 1820.

    Lib. Congress has Mar. 17, 31–June 30, July 14–Sept. 1, Dec. 29, 1819; May 10–Dec. 30, 1820; also Sept. 8–Oct. 13, 27–Nov. 17, Dec. 1–24, 1819; Jan. 12, 19, Feb. 2, 16, Mar. 1–29, Apr. 12–May. 10, June 28, July 5, 19, 26, Aug. 9–30, 1820, of the country edition.
    Mo. Hist. Soc., St. Louis, has Sept. 1, 1819–Aug. 30, 1820.
    St. Louis Mercantile Lib. has Oct. 13, 20, 23, Nov. 6, 10, 27, Dec. 1, 4, 11, 18, 22, 29, 1819; Jan. 5, 8, 12, Feb. 12, 27, Mar. 4, 18, 25, 29, Apr. 12, 15, June 7, Oct. 7, 21, 1820.
    Wis. Hist. Soc. has Sept. 25, 29, Oct. 2, 6, Nov. 13, 17, Dec. 29, 1819; Aug. 26, 1820.
    Am. Antiq. Soc. has May 19, 1819.
    Univ. of Ill. has Aug. 4, 1819.
    Univ. of Ga. has Jan. 15–26, 1820.

[St. Louis] **Louisiana Gazette**, see **Missouri Gazette**.

[St. Louis] **Missouri Gazette**, 1808–1820+.

Weekly. Established July 12, 1808, by Joseph Charless, judging from the date of the earliest issue located, that of July 26, 1808, vol. 1, no. 3, entitled "Missouri Gazette." Charless also issued a Prospectus, undated, announcing the paper. Jacob Hinkle, although his name did not appear in the imprint, assisted Charless in printing the paper, but soon absconded, according to Charless' statement in the issue of Nov. 23, 1808. With the issue of Nov. 30, 1809, the title was changed to "Louisiana Gazette," in order to give the name a general rather than a local significance; but with the issue of July 18, 1812, after Congress had created Missouri Territory, the title was changed back to "Missouri Gazette." With the issue of Feb. 26, 1814, the title was changed to "Missouri Gazette & Illinois Advertiser." With the issue of July 15, 1815, the title was shortened to "Missouri Gazette," although the longer title was retained at the head of the first column. With the issue of May 8, 1818, the title reverted to "Missouri Gazette & Illinois Advertiser," and with that of July 10, 1818, was changed to "Missouri Gazette & Public Advertiser." With the issue of Sept. 20, 1820, Charless transferred the paper to James C. Cummins, who continued it until after 1820. Beginning with Sept. 11, 1819, a "Mercantile Paper or Gazette Extra" was published on Saturday, in addition to the regular weekly Wednesday issue, and was continued until Jan. 15, 1820. It bore the same title as the regular paper, but had no volume numbering.

The Missouri Historical Society in 1932 reproduced this newspaper in photostat from July 26, 1808, to Dec. 25, 1818. The following libraries ordered the set: — Lib. Congress, N. Y. Pub. Lib., Newberry Lib., Wis. Hist. Soc., Univ. of Mich. (Clements), Minn. Hist. Soc., Univ. of Texas, Huntington Lib., State Hist. Soc. of Mo., and Mo. Hist. Soc. The Am. Antiq. Soc. ordered all photostats missing in its file.

Mo. Hist. Soc., St. Louis, has July 26, 1808–Dec. 27, 1820; also Prospectus.
Am. Antiq. Soc. has Mar. 22, May 24, Oct. 26, Nov. 16–30, Dec. 23, 1809; Jan. 18, Mar. 8, 22, Apr. 12, May 3, 24–June 14, July 5–Nov. 28, 1810; Jan. 2, 1811–Feb. 13, 1818; May 26, June 2, 1819; Apr. 12, July 26, 1820.
Lib. Congress has Jan. 1, 1819–Dec. 20, 1820.
Wis. Hist. Soc. has July 26, Oct. 5, 1808.
Pocumtuck Valley Mem. Lib., Deerfield, Mass., has July 26, 1808; Oct. 4, 1809.
Chicago Hist. Soc. has July 5, 1809.
N. Y. Pub. Lib. has Oct. 4, 1809.
St. Louis Mercantile Lib. has July 10, 1810, extra; Feb. 22, 1817.
Univ. of Ill. has Jan. 16, 1818.
N. Y. State Lib. has Mar. 17–31, Apr. 14, May 26–June 16, 1819.

[St. Louis] Western Journal, 1815–1817.

Joshua Norvell, under date of Mar. 2, 1815, advertised from St. Louis in the "Missouri Gazette" of Mar. 4, 1815, that subscription papers for the "Western Journal" should be returned to him, as he planned to "commence its publication very shortly." There are quotations from the "Western Journal" in the "Missouri Gazette" of June 24, Sept. 9, 30, 1815, and Sept. 28, 1816. No copy located. The "Missouri Gazette" of Aug. 18, 1819, gives an account of this paper, which was succeeded early in 1817 by the "Emigrant."

NEW HAMPSHIRE

[Amherst] Farmer's Cabinet, 1802–1820+.

Weekly. Established Nov. 11, 1802, by Joseph Cushing, with the title of "The Farmer's Cabinet." With the issue of Oct. 17, 1809, Cushing transferred the paper to Richard Boylston, who altered the title to "Farmer's Cabinet." Continued by him until after 1820.

Amherst Pub. Lib. has Nov. 11, 1802–Dec. 30, 1820.
N. H. Hist. Soc. has Nov. 11, 1802–Dec. 27, 1808; Jan. 3–Apr. 29, Sept. 12–Oct. 17, 31–Dec. 26, 1809; Jan. 2, 1810–Dec. 30, 1820.
Dartmouth has Nov. 11, 1802–Dec. 27, 1808; Jan. 2, 1810–Dec. 30, 1820.
Am. Antiq. Soc. has Dec. 30, 1802; Jan. 20, 1803–Dec. 25, 1804, fair; Jan. 1, 1805–Dec. 29, 1807; Jan. 5–Dec. 27, 1808, fair; Jan. 3, 1809–Dec. 30, 1820.
Harvard has Nov. 18, 1802; Jan. 13, 1803–Nov. 10, 1807, fair; June 7, July 26, Aug. 16, 30, Sept. 20–Nov. 1, 22–Dec. 27, 1808; Jan. 3, 1809.
Univ. of Mich. (Clements) has Feb. 28, 1809; Jan. 30, 1810–Dec. 30, 1820, fair.
Duke Univ. has Sept. 25, Dec. 11, 18, 1804; Jan. 1, 1805–Dec. 22, 1807, fair; Jan. 12, Feb. 23, July 12, Nov. 8, 29, Dec. 6, 1808; Jan. 2, 16–Feb. 13, 27–Mar. 13, Apr. 17, June 19, July 3, Aug. 14, 21, Sept. 11, Oct. 30, 1810; Jan. 15, Feb. 5, 12, 26–Mar. 19, Apr. 16, 30, May 7, July 9, Aug. 27, Sept. 17–Oct. 8, 22, Nov. 5, 26, 1811; Jan. 20, Mar. 2, 9, Oct. 5, 1812–Dec. 30, 1820.
Lib. Congress has Aug. 11, 1803; Dec. 4–18, 1804; Jan. 1–Dec. 24, 1805, fair; Jan. 14, Sept. 30, Oct. 14, Nov. 4, 1806; Jan. 6–Dec. 1, 1807, fair; Mar. 8, Apr. 12, June 14, July 26, Sept. 18, 27, 1808; Mar. 21, June 6, 20, 1809; Sept. 11, 25, Oct. 9, Nov. 6–Dec. 18, 1810; Jan. 1, 8, 22–Mar. 12, Apr. 2, 9, May 28, June 25, July 9, 23, 30, Sept. 10, Nov. 5–19, 1811; June 15, Nov. 9, 1812; June 19, Nov. 1, 8, 22, 1813; Jan. 3–Dec. 12, 1814, fair; Jan. 2–Feb. 6, Apr. 8, 15, May 27, June 10–24, July 8, 22, 29, Sept. 9–23, Oct. 7, 21–Nov. 25, Dec. 23, 1815; Jan. 6, 1816–Dec. 30, 1820.
Yale has Oct. 23, 1810–Nov. 26, 1811, fair; Jan. 13–Dec. 21, 1812; Feb. 15, 1813–Dec. 5, 1814, fair; Mar. 11, 25, Apr. 1, 29, May 20, June 10, July 8, Oct. 21, Nov. 11, 1815–Nov. 29, 1817; Jan. 24–Dec. 26, 1818, fair; Dec. 11, 1819; Jan. 15–Dec. 30, 1820.
Boston Pub. Lib. has July 14, 1803–Oct. 3, 1809.
Mass. Hist. Soc. has Nov. 25, 1802–Oct. 27, 1803; Mar. 3, May 5, 1807–Apr. 26, 1808, fair; Oct. 25, Dec. 13, 1808; Nov. 27, Dec. 11, 1819; Dec. 30, 1820.
N. Y. Hist. Soc. has Jan. 23, Apr. 9, 1805; June 24, 1806; Jan. 27, June 23, Aug. 11, 18, 1807; Feb. 23, June 21, Oct. 11, 1808; Jan. 31, Oct. 10, 1809; June 12, 19, 1810; Apr. 6, May 4, June 8, 15, Sept. 28, Nov. 9, 30, 1812; June 13, July 5, Sept. 6, Nov. 22, 1813; May 16, June 6, 13, July 4, 11, 25–

Aug. 8, 22, 29, Oct. 24, 1814; Jan. 16, Mar. 6–18, May 6, 1815; June 29, 1816; Dec. 27, 1817; Jan. 30, 1819.

N. Y. State Lib. has Aug. 18, 25, 1803; Feb. 12, Dec. 31, 1805; Sept. 9, 23, Oct. 21, Nov. 4, 11, Dec. 2, 9, 1806; Feb. 10, Mar. 17–31, Apr. 14–May 5, 26, June 16, July 21, Aug. 4, Sept. 8, Oct. 6, Nov. 3, 17–Dec. 8, 22, 1807; Jan. 19, 1808; May 30, Aug. 8, 1809; June 18, 1811; Mar. 2, 1812; Jan. 16, 1815–Dec. 28, 1816; July 26, 1817; Aug. 8, 22, Sept. 26, Oct. 10–24, 1817; Feb. 7, 1819.

Essex Inst. has Nov. 18, 1802–Sept. 8, 1803; Nov. 6, 1804; Sept. 1, 1807; Sept. 6, Dec. 20, 27, 1808; Nov. 14, 1809; June 19, 1810; Apr. 29, 1815; June 1, 1816; July 5, Oct. 25, Dec. 27, 1817; Jan. 3, July 4, 18, 25, Aug. 8, 22, 1818; Nov. 6, 1819.

Ohio Arch. & Hist. Soc. has May 14, 1805; Jan. 24, Dec. 19, 1809; Feb. 6, 13, Mar. 13, 1810; Feb. 26, Mar. 19, 1811; Apr. 11, 25, May 9, 1814; Jan. 30, Oct. 14, 28, 1815; Jan. 6, Oct. 12, 1816; Sept. 13, 20, 1817; Jan. 17, Feb. 28, Apr. 25, May 9, 16, June 27, Aug. 1, 8, Sept. 26, Oct. 24, Dec. 12, 26, 1818; Aug. 14, Nov. 6, 1819; Feb. 26, Aug. 19, 1820.

Manchester, N. H., City Lib. has Apr. 12–Dec. 20, 1808.

Boston Athenæum has Mar. 24, Dec. 8, 1807; July 26, Aug. 9, 1808; May 9–23, 1809; May 24, 1813; Feb. 28, 1818.

N. Y. Pub. Lib. has July 7, 1807; June 20, Oct. 17, 1809; Dec. 14, 1812; Feb. 8, 15, Mar. 15, 1813; May 25, 1816; Apr. 11, 1818; Oct. 30, 1819.

Wis. Hist. Soc. has July 16, 1811; Dec. 12, 1818.

[Amherst] Hillsboro' Telegraph, 1820+.

Weekly. Established Jan. 1, 1820, by Elijah Mansur, with the title of "Hillsboro' Telegraph." So continued until after 1820.

N. H. Hist. Soc. has Jan. 1–Apr. 8, 22–Oct. 21, Nov. 4–Dec. 30, 1820.
Dartmouth has Jan. 1, 15, Mar. 18, Apr. 15, May 27, June 3, July 1, 15, Sept. 2, 9, Dec. 9, 30, 1820.
Boston Athenæum has Jan. 1, 22, 29, 1820.
Am. Antiq. Soc. has Mar. 18, Sept. 23, 1820.
Essex Inst. has Sept. 2, 1820.
Lib. Congress has Sept. 23, 1820.
York Inst., Saco, has Dec. 23, 1820.

Amherst Journal, 1795–1796.

Weekly. Established Jan. 16, 1795, by Nathaniel Coverly with the title of "The Amherst Journal, and the New-Hampshire Advertiser." With the issue of Apr. 24, 1795, Coverly admitted his son Nathaniel to partnership, the firm being known as Nathaniel Coverly and Son. The paper was discontinued with the issue of Jan. 9, 1796, vol. 1, no. 52, to be succeeded by the "Village Messenger."

NEW HAMPSHIRE 437

N. H. Hist. Soc. has Jan. 16–May 29, Aug. 14, 1795; Jan. 2, 1796.
Dartmouth has Feb. 6–20, Mar. 13, 20, Apr. 3–17, May 22–June 26, Aug. 28–Dec. 26, 1795.
Am. Antiq. Soc. has Apr. 10, 24, May 1, 8, June 12, July 17–Aug. 14, Dec. 12, 1795.
Harvard has Mar. 13, 20, May 15–29, June 12, Aug. 7–21, 1795.
Lib. Congress has May 1, 1795.
Amherst Pub. Lib. has Jan. 2, 9, 1796.

[Amherst] **Village Messenger,** 1796–1801.

Weekly. Established Jan. 9, 1796, by Biglow and Cushing [William Biglow and Samuel Cushing], with the title of "Village Messenger." The firm was dissolved with the issue of July 12, 1796, and the paper published by Samuel Cushing. With the issue of Apr. 18, 1797, Cushing transferred the paper to Samuel Preston, who continued to publish it until its discontinuance with the issue of Dec. 5, 1801, vol. 6, no. 50.

Amherst Pub. Lib. has Jan. 9, 1796–Nov. 28, 1801.
Am. Antiq. Soc. has Feb. 9, Apr. 6, May 3, 10, 24, June 21, 28, Sept. 13, 27, Oct. 11–25, Nov. 8–22, Dec. 6–27, 1796; Jan. 31, Feb. 7, 28–Apr. 4, 18–June 10, 24–Aug. 19, Sept. 2–Nov. 11, Dec. 9, 1797; Jan. 13–Apr. 7, 28–May 19, June 2–16, 30, July 21, Aug. 4, 11, 25–Nov. 3, 17–Dec. 29, 1798; Jan. 12, 19, Feb. 16, 23, Mar. 23–Apr. 13, June 1, 15, 29–Dec. 28, 1799; Jan. 4–Dec. 27, 1800; Jan. 3–Aug. 22, Sept. 5–Oct. 31, 1801.
Harvard has Feb. 9, Mar. 1, 8, 29, 1796; May 27, June 10, July 8, 15, 22, Aug. 12, Sept. 9, 23, Oct. 7, Dec. 16, 1797; Apr. 21, Sept. 1–22, Oct. 13, Nov. 3, 17, 24, 1798; Mar. 9, May 25, June 8, 15, July 27–Aug. 10, 24–Sept. 7, Oct. 12, 19, Nov. 2, 9, 23, 30, Dec. 21, 28, 1799; Jan. 25, Feb. 1, Mar. 1–15, Apr. 5, 12, May 24, Sept. 20, 27, Nov. 15, 22, Dec. 20, 1800; Jan. 17, 31–Feb. 14, Mar. 7, 14, Apr. 11, May 2, 16–30, June 13–27, July 18, Aug. 1–15, 29–Sept. 19, Oct. 3, 31, Nov. 21–Dec. 5, 1801.
Boston Pub. Lib. has May 24, June 28, Sept. 13, Dec. 13, 20, 1796; Feb. 28–Mar. 14, 28, Apr. 18, May 2, 16, June 3, 10, July 1–29, Aug. 12, 19, Sept. 2–Oct. 21, 1797; Feb. 10–24, Mar. 10–24, Apr. 7, 21, 28, July 7, Sept. 8, 22, Nov. 24, 1798; Jan. 19, 1799; Mar. 7, 28, 1801.
N. H. Hist. Soc. has May 31, Nov. 22, 1796; Mar. 7, May 13, July 22, Oct. 14, 1797; Feb. 10–24, Mar. 24, May 19, June 23, July 7, Aug. 11, Nov. 24, 1798; Feb. 23, Apr. 20, May 18, Nov. 16, 1799; Jan. 11, 25–Feb. 8, Mar. 8, 15, Apr. 5, 12, 26–May 17, 31–Aug. 23, Sept. 6–Dec. 20, 1800; Jan. 31, Feb. 14, 28–Mar. 14, Apr. 11, 18, May 2–June 6, 20–July 4, 25, Sept. 26, Oct. 3, 1801.
N. Y. Hist. Soc. has Jan. 9–Feb. 23, Mar. 8–22, Apr. 12, 1796; Apr. 28, July 28, Aug. 4, 1798; July 5, 13, 27, Oct. 4, Dec. 6, 1800.
N. Y. Pub. Lib. has Feb. 17, Apr. 7, June 9, Oct. 27, 1798; Jan. 18, July 26, Aug. 9, 23, Dec. 13, 1800; June 6, 1801.

Lib. Congress has Aug. 12, 1797; Jan. 11, 18, May 17, 31, Oct. 11, Nov. 15, 1800; Jan. 3, 1801.
Univ. of Mich. (Clements) has Aug. 17, Sept. 14, Oct. 5–19, Nov. 23, 1799; Mar. 29, 1800.
Wilton, N. H., Free Lib. has Oct. 7, 1797; Oct. 4, 1800.
Dartmouth has July 28, 1798.
N. Y. State Lib. has June 15, 1799; Dec. 27, 1800.
Long Id. Hist. Soc. has Jan. 24, 1801.
Duke Univ. has June 20, 1801.

[Concord] **American Patriot,** 1808–1809.

Weekly. Established Oct. 18, 1808, by William Hoit, Jun., with the title of "American Patriot." The last issue with this title was that of Apr. 11, 1809, vol. 1, no. 26, after which the paper was transferred to Isaac Hill and the title changed to "New-Hampshire Patriot," which see.

Dartmouth has Oct. 18, 1808–Apr. 11, 1809.
N. H. Hist. Soc. has Oct. 18–Nov. 22, Dec. 6–20, 1808; Jan. 3, 24–Feb. 21, Mar. 7, 21–Apr. 4, 1809.
Am. Antiq. Soc. has Oct. 18, Nov. 15, Dec. 13, 27, 1808; Jan. 3–Mar. 28, 1809.
Boston Athenæum has Oct. 25, Nov. 1, Dec. 6, 1808; Jan. 31–Feb. 21, Mar. 7, 1809.
Harvard has Oct. 25, Nov. 15, 22, Dec. 6, 27, 1808.
Lib. Congress has Nov. 8, Dec. 13, 1808; Jan. 3–Feb. 28, Mar. 14, 21, Apr. 4, 1809.
Univ. of Mich. (Clements) has Jan. 31–Feb. 21, 1809.
N. Y. State Lib. has Feb. 14, 21, Mar. 7, 1809.
Concord, N. H., Pub. Lib. has Jan. 24, 1809.

[Concord] **American Republican Gazette,** see **Republican Gazette.**

[Concord] **Courier of New Hampshire,** 1794–1805.

Weekly. A continuation, without change of volume numbering, of "Hough's Concord Herald," the first issue with the title of "Courier of New Hampshire" being that of Feb. 13, 1794, vol. 5, no. 1, whole no. 209, published by George Hough. It was so continued until Oct. 30, 1805, vol. 16, no. 44, with which issue it was discontinued.

N. H. Hist. Soc. has Feb. 13, 1794–Oct. 30, 1805.
Am. Antiq. Soc. has Feb. 13–Dec. 27, 1794; Jan. 3–31, June 13, July 4, 11, 25–Sept. 5, 26, Oct. 10, 24, 1795; Jan. 11, Feb. 15–Dec. 27, 1796; Jan. 3–Feb. 28, Mar. 14, 28–Apr. 18, May 2–16, Aug. 1, Sept. 12, Oct. 3, 10, 24, Nov. 21, 28, Dec. 26, 1797; Jan. 2, 9, 23–Feb. 13, 27, Mar. 6, 27, Apr. 3,

NEW HAMPSHIRE 439

10, May 15, July 3–17, Aug. 7, Sept. 4, 18–Dec. 1, 22, 1798; Jan. 19, Feb. 2, 1799–Oct. 30, 1805.
Harvard has Feb. 14, May 23, June 6, 27, July 4, Aug. 1, 29, 1795; Mar. 7, 28, June 14–28, July 19, 26, Aug. 9, 23–Sept. 6, 30, Oct. 11, 18, Nov. 8–Dec. 20, 1796; Jan. 3, 17, 31, Feb. 14, 21, Mar. 14–Apr. 18, July 4, Aug. 29, Oct. 24, Nov. 14–28, Dec. 12, 26, 1797; Jan. 2–16, 30, Feb. 6, Mar. 20, Apr. 3, 10, 24, May 1, June 5, July 17, 24, Aug. 21, Sept. 4, Nov. 17, Dec. 1, 1798; Feb. 16, Mar. 2, May 4, July 20, Aug. 17–Oct. 5, 1799; May 31, June 28, Aug. 30, Oct. 4, 18, Nov. 22, 29, Dec. 19, 1800; Jan. 2, Feb. 13–Apr. 2, 16–30, May 14, 28, June 18, July 2, 9, 30, Aug. 6, 27, Sept. 17–Oct. 1, 22, 29, Nov. 19, Dec. 8, 1801; Jan. 21, 28, Feb. 25, Mar. 25–Apr. 8, June 17, 24, July 15–Aug. 5, 19–Sept. 2, 16, 23, Oct. 7–21, Nov. 4–18, Dec. 9, 23, 30, 1802; Jan. 6, 20, Feb. 3, 17, Mar. 3–Apr. 14, 28–May 12, 26, June 9, 23–Aug. 25, Sept. 8, 15, 29–Oct. 12, 26, Nov. 9–Dec. 7, 1803; Jan. 4, 11, 25–Feb. 8, 22, Mar. 14, Apr. 4–May 2, 16–30, June 20, July 4–Aug. 1, 15, 29, Oct. 3, 10, Nov. 7, 14, 28, Dec. 12, 26, 1804; Jan. 2–Feb. 13, July 17, 31, Sept. 18, 25, 1805.
Lib. Congress has Feb. 13, 27–Mar. 20, Apr. 3–17, May 1–June 5, 19–Sept. 4, 18, Oct. 2, Nov. 1–15, 29, 1794; Feb. 7–July 4, 18–Dec. 26, 1795; Jan. 2–Feb. 1, 22, Mar. 7, June 28, July 12, Sept. 6, 20, Oct. 11, 25, Nov. 8, Dec. 6, 1796; Jan. 3–17, 31, Aug. 22, 1797; Feb. 6–Dec. 29, 1798; Jan. 5–Feb. 9, Mar. 23, Aug. 3, Nov. 2, Dec. 14, 28, 1799; Jan. 4, 11, Feb. 22, Apr. 5, 19, Sept. 13, 1800; May 7, June 4, Oct. 29, 1801; June 17, July 8, Nov. 11, 24, Dec. 2, 13, 1802; Jan. 13, 27, Feb. 3, 17–Mar. 3, May 19, Aug. 11, 18, Sept. 8, 15, Oct. 5, Dec. 14, 1803; Mar. 14, 21, May 23, July 25, Aug. 22, Sept. 19, Oct. 3, Dec. 26, 1804; Jan. 2, 23, June 12, 1805.
Boston Pub. Lib. has Mar. 27–Apr. 17, May 8, 1798–Jan. 9, 1801; Apr. 28, 1803–Feb. 6, 1805.
Concord Pub. Lib. has July 3, 1794; Sept. 19, 1795; Feb. 29, Aug. 23, 1796; June 27, July 4, 1797; Mar. 20, May 29, 1798; Jan. 11, Feb. 1, 8, Apr. 26, 1800; Jan. 16, Nov. 12, 19, Dec. 3, 31, 1801; Jan. 21, Feb. 18, Aug. 19, Sept. 9, 30, 1802; May 30, Oct. 24, 31, Dec. 5, 1804.
Boston Athenæum has Dec. 27, 1794; Jan. 3, 1795; Dec. 13, 1796; June 13, 1797; June 12, 19, Nov. 17–Dec. 8, 1798; June 7, 14, Nov. 22, 29, 1800; Jan. 7, 1802–July 7, 1803; July 11, 25, 1804.
Dartmouth has Feb. 13–Mar. 13, 27, Sept. 11, 1794; May 2, 16, 23, June 20, Aug. 15–Sept. 5, Oct. 3, 10, Nov. 21–Dec. 26, 1795; June 12, Sept. 29, Nov. 24–Dec. 8, 22, 1798; Jan. 25, 1800; Dec. 28, 1801; July 15, Oct. 21–Nov. 4, 24, 1802; Dec. 14, 1803.
N. Y. Pub. Lib. has Apr. 10, May 8, 29, June 5, Aug. 14, 21, 1794; Oct. 27–Nov. 10, Dec. 1, 1798; Sept. 13, Nov. 22, 1800; June 2, 1803.
N. Y. Hist. Soc. has Jan. 11, 18, Feb. 1–29, Apr. 11, 18, May 2–July 12, 26–Aug. 9, 30, Sept. 6, 20, Oct. 25, Nov. 1, 15–29, 1796; July 17, Aug. 7–21, 1798; Dec. 19, 1800; June 20, July 4, 11, Aug. 8, 1804; Apr. 17, June 12, 1805.

Univ. of Mich. (Clements) has June 12, 1794; Aug. 8, 15, 1795; May 30, June 14, 21, 1796; June 15, 1799; June 18, 1801; Jan. 7, May 20, July 1, 1802; Sept. 1, 1803; Jan. 30, Oct. 2, 1805.
Phil. Lib. Co. has Oct. 17, 24, 1795; Jan. 11, 18, 1796.
Mass. Hist. Soc. has Feb. 29, 1797.
Western Reserve Hist. Soc. has Aug. 16, 1800.
Duke Univ. has Dec. 19, 1800.
Long Id. Hist. Soc. has Apr. 11, 1804.
York Inst., Saco, has June 13, 1804.

[Concord] **Federal Mirror**, see **Mirrour**.

Concord Gazette, 1806–1819.

Weekly. Established July 12, 1806, by Hoit & Tuttle [William Hoit, Jr. and Jesse C. Tuttle], with the title of "Concord Gazette." Hoit with the issue of Sept. 27, 1806, spelled his name Hoyt in the imprint. The paper was discontinued with the issue of Feb. 17, 1807, vol. 1, no. 32. It was reestablished June 9, 1807, by J. C. Tuttle, with a new volume numbering and with the title of "The Concord Gazette." With the issue of June 6, 1809, the title was shortened to "Concord Gazette." With the issue of Jan. 4, 1814, the full name of the publisher, Jesse C. Tuttle, was given in the imprint, which was changed with the issue of Aug. 16, 1814, to "Printed by Jesse C. Tuttle for the Proprietors." With the issue of Apr. 11, 1815, the paper was transferred to William S. Spear & Co. With the issue of Apr. 9, 1816, the partnership was dissolved and the paper was published by William S. Spear. With the issue of July 8, 1817, the paper was transferred to Joseph C. Spear. With the issue of Feb. 9, 1819, Spear formed a partnership with Abijah W. Thayer, and the paper was published by Spear and Thayer, but within a few weeks, at some time between Mar. 20 and Apr. 3, 1819, it was again published by Joseph C. Spear. It was discontinued with the issue of May 8, 1819, judging from an "obituary" notice in the New Hampshire Patriot of May 18, 1819. The last issue located is that of May 1, 1819, vol. 12, no. 48.

N. H. Hist. Soc. has July 19–Aug. 16, 30–Sept. 20, Dec. 27, 1806; Jan. 3, 20, Feb. 3, 17, June 9, 30–Dec. 29, 1807; Jan. 5–19, Feb. 2–May 19, 31–July 26, Aug. 23, 30, Oct. 11, 18, Nov. 1, 8, 1808; Jan. 3, 17, Mar. 28, July 4, 11, Oct. 17, 1809; Mar. 6, Apr. 3, 10, 24–May 29, July 31, Sept. 4, 18–Oct. 23, Nov. 6, Dec. 18, 1810; Feb. 26–Mar. 9, May 21, June 4, 18, 1811; Mar. 7, 24, Apr. 28–May 19, June 9, 16, July 7, Aug. 18, Sept. 1–15, 29–Nov. 10, 24, Dec. 1, 22, 1812; Jan. 5–Mar. 6, 23, 30, Apr. 13–27, Aug. 10, 31, Dec. 21, 28, 1813; Jan. 4–Dec. 27, 1814, complete; Jan. 3–Apr. 25, May 9–June 13, 27–July 18, Aug. 1–Dec. 26, 1815; Jan. 2–Nov. 5, Dec. 31, 1816; Mar. 4, 6, 27, June 17, July 1, 8, 22, Aug. 5, 19, Oct. 7, Nov. 4, Dec. 9, 1817; Mar. 3,

NEW HAMPSHIRE 441

24–May 5, 19–June 2, 16–Aug. 18, Sept. 1–29, Oct. 13–Nov. 24, Dec. 8–29, 1818; Jan. 5, 19, Feb. 2–16, Mar. 6, 13, Apr. 17, 24, 1819.

Boston Athenæum has Nov. 29, 1808; Jan. 10, May 23, June 13, 1809; Feb. 6–Mar. 13, 27, Apr. 3, May 1, 8, June 12–26, 1810; June 18, 1811; Mar. 3, Apr. 7, June 9, 16, Sept. 22, Oct. 13, 27, 31, Nov. 17, Dec. 15, 1812; Jan. 12–Feb. 9, 23, Mar. 2, Apr. 13, Aug. 17, 24, Oct. 12, Dec. 21, 28, 1813; Jan. 4, 1814–Apr. 8, 1817, fair; Apr. 22–May 6, 20, 27, July 15, 1817; Feb. 3–17, Mar. 17, 24, May 5, June 9, 23, July 14, Aug. 4, 18, Sept. 8–22, Oct. 13, Nov. 10–24, Dec. 8, 15, 1818; Jan. 5, 26, Feb. 9–27, Apr. 3, May 1, 1819.

Am. Antiq. Soc. has July 26, Aug. 2, Sept. 13, 20, Dec. 20, 27, 1806; June 30, Sept. 1, 8, 22, 29, Nov. 10, Dec. 22, 1807; Feb. 16, Mar. 15, 29, May 3–17, July 12, Aug. 16, 23, Oct. 4–25, Nov. 8, Dec. 6, 1808; Jan. 10, 24–Feb. 7, 28–Mar. 14, July 18, Sept. 26, 1809; Jan. 2, May 1–15, June 12, 19, July 17, Aug. 14, Sept. 4, Oct. 30, Dec. 18, 1810; Jan. 8, Feb. 5–Mar. 9, Apr. 9, June 11, 18, Sept. 10, Oct. 8, 15, 29, Nov. 12–Dec. 31, 1811; Jan. 7–Feb. 11, Apr. 7, 14, May 12–26, June 16, July 7, 21, Sept. 8, Oct. 6, 20, 27, Nov. 24, Dec. 8, 22, 29, 1812; Jan. 5–19, Feb. 2, 16, 23, Mar. 6, 30, Apr. 13, Sept. 7, Dec. 6, 1813; Feb. 15, Apr. 12–May 10, Aug. 2, 9, Sept. 13–Dec. 27, 1814; Jan. 3, 17–Apr. 11, 25, May 9–June 6, 27, July 4, 25–Dec. 26, 1815; Jan. 2–16, 30–Mar. 19, June 11, July 23, 1816; Apr. 14, 21, June 16, 30, July 14, Aug. 4, Sept. 22, 29, Oct. 13–27, Dec. 15, 1818; Feb. 20, 1819.

Boston Pub. Lib. has Apr. 26, May 24, Aug. 2–30, Sept. 13, 20, 1808; Mar. 21, Apr. 4, 25, Aug. 8, 1809; Mar. 5, 1811; May 16, 30, June 13, July 11, Aug. 22, 29, Sept. 12, 26, Oct. 10–Nov. 14, 1815; Apr. 2–May 14, 28–Aug. 6, Sept. 3–17, Oct. 8, 1816; Sept. 8, 15, 1818.

N. Y. Hist. Soc. has Jan. 3, June 6, 1809–May 28, 1811; Sept. 1, 1812; Dec. 21, 1813–Dec. 13, 1814; Aug. 6, Sept. 3, 10, Oct. 8, Dec. 10, 1816; Jan. 7, 14, 28, Feb. 18–Mar. 4, 18, Dec. 16, 1817; May 26, 1818.

Lib. Congress has June 9–30, Oct. 6, 1807; Apr. 5–Dec. 20, 1808; June 3, 1812; June 27, 1813; Aug. 27, Oct. 11–25, Nov. 8–22, Dec. 13–27, 1814; Jan. 17–Dec. 26, 1815, fair; Feb. 20, 1816; June 30, 1818.

N. Y. State Library has July 7–21, Aug. 11, Sept. 1–29, 1807; Jan. 5–May 10, 1808; Feb. 11, 1812; Oct. 4–Nov. 15, 1814; May 30, 1815; Feb. 6, Apr. 30, 1816.

Harvard has Aug. 2, 23, Sept. 27, Nov. 1, 29, Dec. 6, 1806; Apr. 19, June 14, Aug. 2, 16, 23, Sept. 20, Oct. 11–25, Nov. 22, Dec. 6, 13, 27, 1808; Jan. 3, 1809.

Ohio Hist. & Phil. Soc. has Nov. 15, 1814–June 6, 1815.

Concord Pub. Lib. has June 9, 1807; June 27, 1809; Oct. 29, 1810; June 11, 1811; Aug. 4, Nov. 24, 1812; June 11, Aug. 13, 1816; Sept. 1, 1818.

Dartmouth has Aug. 2, Nov. 8, 1808; Mar. 28, 1809; Nov. 10, 1812; Jan. 26, 1813; Nov. 22, 1814; Nov. 7–21, Dec. 26, 1815.

Western Reserve Hist. Soc. has June 11, 1811; Apr. 14, 1812; Mar. 29–Apr. 12, 1814.

Univ. of Mich. (Clements) has Mar. 5, 1811.
Duke Univ. has Oct. 13, 1818.
Wis. Hist. Soc. has Dec. 15, 1818.

Concord Herald, 1790–1794.

Weekly. Established Jan. 6, 1790, by George Hough, with the title of "The Concord Herald, and Newhampshire Intelligencer." With the issue of Jan. 19, 1791, the title was changed to "Hough's Concord Herald," the first word being in much smaller type than the rest of the title, but with the issue of Mar. 9, 1791, the title reverted to "Concord Herald." With the issue of July 4, 1792, the publishing firm became George Hough and Elijah Russell, but with the issue of Aug. 25, 1792, Russell's name was dropped and the paper was again published by George Hough. With the issue of Sept. 8, 1792, the title as before was altered to "Hough's Concord Herald." The last numbered issue was that of Jan. 30, 1794, vol. 4, no. 52, whole no. 208, after which a single page issue was published "Gratis," Feb. 6, 1794, and then the title was changed to "Courier of New Hampshire," Feb. 13, 1794, vol. 5, no. 1, whole no. 209, which see.

N. H. Hist. Soc. has Jan. 13, 27–May 4, 18–June 15, 29–Dec. 28, 1790; Jan. 4–Feb. 16, Mar. 9, 1791–Dec. 27, 1792; Jan. 3–31, Feb. 21–Apr. 25, 1793.

Am. Antiq. Soc. has Jan. 6, 13, 27–May 4, 18–June 15, 29–Dec. 28, 1790; Jan. 4–Feb. 16, Mar. 2, 16–30, Apr. 13, 20, May 11, June 29, July 27, Aug. 10–31, Sept. 28–Oct. 12, Nov. 9–23, Dec. 7, 1791; Jan. 18, Feb. 1–15, 29, Mar. 14–Apr. 4, 25, May 9, 23–June 6, 27–July 25, Aug. 11, 18, Sept. 8, 22–Dec. 6, 27, 1792; Jan. 3–17, Feb. 7–21, Mar. 7–Apr. 18, May 2–16, Aug. 8, Dec. 19, 1793.

Lib. Congress has Mar. 3, 27, Apr. 13–May 4, June 1, 15, 29–July 27, Aug. 17–Sept. 14, 28, Oct. 5, 19, 26, Nov. 9, 16, 1790; Feb. 16, Mar. 30, Aug. 10, 1791; May 9–Dec. 27, 1792; Jan. 3–Aug. 1, 15–Dec. 26, 1793; Jan. 2–30, 1794.

Dartmouth has Oct. 26, 1790; Sept. 7, 1791–May 30, 1792, fair; Oct. 25, 1792–Dec. 5, 1793; Jan. 2–Feb. 6, 1794.

Concord Pub. Lib. has Jan. 13, Feb. 24, Mar. 16, Apr. 6, Nov. 9, 23, Dec. 28, 1790; May 16, 1792; Jan. 27, Aug. 29, 1793.

N. Y. State Lib. has Feb. 17, 24, June 8, Nov. 30, 1790; Mar. 9–Dec. 14, 1791.

N. Y. Hist. Soc. has Mar. 16, 30, 1790; Feb. 9, 1791; Feb. 14, 1793–Feb. 6, 1794.

Boston Athenæum has Apr. 6, May 25, June 1, 15, July 6, Sept. 14, 1790; Jan. 26–Feb. 9, June 1–15, Aug. 31, Sept. 14, 1791; Jan. 18, Feb. 1, 15, 22, Oct. 25, 1792; Apr. 11, July 18, 1793.

Univ. of Mich. (Clements) has June 15, July 13, Aug. 24–Sept. 7, 21, 28, 1790; June 6, July 25, Aug. 11, Sept. 29, 1792.

Harvard has May 16, June 6–27, 1792.

Mass. Hist. Soc. has Mar. 14, Dec. 6, 1792.
Western Reserve Hist. Soc. has Feb. 29, 1792.
N. Y. Pub. Lib. has July 11, 1792.

[Concord] Hough's Concord Herald, see Concord Herald.

[Concord] Mirror, see Mirrour.

[Concord] Mirrour, 1792–1799.

Weekly. Established presumably on Oct. 29, 1792, by Elijah Russell, with the title of "The Mirrour," as the issue of Nov. 5, is numbered vol. 1, no. 2. There was, however, a number published Sept. 6, 1792, numbering vol. 1, no. 1, but this was evidently a prospectus number. There was also an "Extra" published on Oct. 31, 1792. With the issue of Oct. 24, 1794, Russell took Moses Davis into partnership and the paper was published by Elijah Russell and Moses Davis, which firm name with the issue of Mar. 27, 1795, was abbreviated to Russell and Davis. With the issue of Apr. 10, 1795, the title was changed to "The Federal Mirror." The last issue with this title was that of Nov. 15, 1796, vol. 5, no. 212. On Nov. 22, 1796, Russell retired and Moses Davis began a paper with the new title of "Republican Gazetteer," continuing the advertisements from "The Federal Mirror," but starting a new volume numbering. For this paper, see under "Republican Gazetteer." On Apr. 11, 1797, the title was again changed to "The New Star," which see. On Oct. 10, 1797, Russel and Davis [Elijah Russel, who had in the meantime entered the firm and spelled his name Russel, and Moses Davis] changed the title back to "The Mirror," and installed the old volume numbering, this issue being vol. 5, no. 259. With the issue of Nov. 7, 1797, the partnership was dissolved and the paper published by Moses Davis. The last issue located is that of Sept. 2, 1799, vol. 7, no. 357, and this must have been about the last issue published, as Davis had removed to Hanover and established the "Dartmouth Gazette," Aug. 27, 1799.

N. H. Hist. Soc. has Sept. 6, Nov. 5, 19, 26, Dec. 10–31, 1792; Jan. 14–June 10, 24, July 1, 22, 29, Aug. 12–26, Oct. 7, 21, Nov. 4–18, Dec. 9–23, 1793; Jan. 6, 13, Feb. 10–Mar. 3, Apr. 21–Nov. 7, 21, Dec. 5–26, 1794; Jan. 2– Aug. 14, Sept. 4–Oct. 9, Nov. 3, Dec. 4, 11, 25, 1795; Jan. 1, Feb. 2–23, Mar. 29, May 10, 31, June 14–28, July 12, 26, Aug. 16, 23, Sept. 6, 27, Oct. 4, 18–Nov. 8, 1796; Oct. 10, 24, Nov. 21–Dec. 4, 19, 26, 1797; Jan. 9, 16, 30–June 12, 26, July 10–31, Aug. 28, Sept. 4, Oct. 8, 15, 29, Nov. 26, Dec. 10, 24, 31, 1798; Jan. 7, Feb. 11, 25–Mar. 11, Apr. 1, 22, May 6, 13, June 24, July 8, 1799.

Am. Antiq. Soc. has Oct. 31, Nov. 12, 26–Dec. 31, 1792; Jan. 7, 14, 28– Feb. 18, Mar. 4–Apr. 15, 29–May 20, 1793; May 12, Aug. 18, 1794; Feb. 20, Mar. 27, Apr. 24, May 1, July 3, Aug. 7–28, Oct. 23, 30, 1795; Feb. 16, May 17, June 28, July 12, 19, Sept. 6, 13, Oct. 18, Nov. 1, 15, 1796; Oct. 17,

24, Nov. 21–Dec. 19, 1797; Jan. 9–June 19, July 10–Aug. 7, 28–Sept. 11, 25, Oct. 8–22, Nov. 26, Dec. 3–17, 31, 1798; Jan. 7, 28, Feb. 11–Apr. 8, 22–June 24, Aug. 5, 26, Sept. 2, 1799.

Harvard has Mar. 13, May 15, 1795; May 3, July 26–Aug. 9, 23–Sept. 6, 20, 27–Oct. 18, Nov. 1, 1796; Oct. 10, 24, 31, Nov. 28–Dec. 26, 1797; Jan. 2, 30–Feb. 13, 27, Mar. 13, 20, Apr. 10, 15, May 8, June 12, July 3, 17, 31, Aug. 21–Sept. 11, Oct. 22–Dec. 3, 1798; Jan. 14, Mar. 18, Apr. 29–May 13, June 10, July 8, 15, 29–Sept. 2, 1799.

N. Y. Hist. Soc. has Nov. 19–Dec. 3, 1792; July 29, 1793; Feb. 3, Mar. 10, May 19–June 2, 16–Aug. 25, Sept. 8, 15, Oct. 17, 31, Nov. 7, 1794; July 5, 1796; Apr. 8, 1799.

Concord Pub. Lib. has Nov. 5, Dec. 10, 24, 31, 1792; Jan. 21, 28, Mar. 25–Apr. 15, May 6, 27–June 10, 24–July 15, 1793; Sept. 4, Oct. 16, 1795; June 21, 1796; Nov. 28, 1797; Feb. 11, 1799.

Lib. Congress has Nov. 26, 1792; Apr. 22, May 6, June 10, 17, 1793; Jan. 13, June 23, 1794; June 12, Sept. 4, 1795; Aug. 16, Sept. 13, 1796; June 12, Oct. 1, Nov. 19, Dec. 31, 1798; Jan. 7, 1799.

N. Y. State Lib. has Dec. 26, 1794; Jan. 2, 23, Feb. 6, Mar. 20, Apr. 3, 17, May 15–29, Aug. 7, Sept. 11–25, 1795; Feb. 11, 1799.

Boston Athenæum has Sept. 6, 1792; June 10, 17, July 1, 1793; Jan. 2, May 15, Aug. 14, 1795; June 14, 1796; June 19, 1798.

N. Y. Pub. Lib. has May 6, 1793; Oct. 17, 1794.

Duke Univ. has Mar. 6, 1798; Feb. 11, 1799.

Dartmouth has Nov. 4, 1793.

Essex Inst. has Nov. 18, 1793; July 17, 1795.

Wis. Hist. Soc. has Feb. 20, 1795.

Phil. Lib. Co. has June 21, 1796.

Me. Hist. Soc. has May 6, 1799.

[Concord] **New-Hampshire Patriot**, 1809–1820+.

Weekly. A continuation, without change of numbering, of the "American Patriot." The first issue with the title of "New-Hampshire Patriot" was that of Apr. 18, 1809, no. 1, new series, whole no. 27, published by Isaac Hill. With the issue of Apr. 16, 1811, Isaac Hill took his brother Walter into partnership and the paper was published by I. & W. R. Hill. The firm name was changed in the imprint to Isaac & W. R. Hill with the issue of May 31, 1814. With the issue of Aug. 29, 1815, W. R. Hill withdrew because of ill health and the paper was again published by Isaac Hill as sole proprietor. With the issue of Jan. 5, 1819, Hill took Jacob B. Moore into partnership, the firm name for this issue being Jacob B. Moore & Co., which was changed, however, with the issue of Jan. 12, 1819, to Hill & Moore. A new series volume numbering was also begun. With the issue of Feb. 2, 1819, the title was enlarged to "New-Hampshire Patriot & State Gazette." So continued until after 1820.

NEW HAMPSHIRE   445

N. H. Hist. Soc., Dartmouth, Am. Antiq. Soc., N. Y. State Lib., and Wis. Hist. Soc. have Apr. 18, 1809–Dec. 26, 1820.
Boston Athenæum has May 9, 1809–Dec. 26, 1820.
Concord Pub. Lib. has Apr. 25, 1809–Dec. 28, 1819.
Minn. Hist. Soc. has Sept. 12, Oct. 24, Dec. 19, 1809; Jan. 23, 1810–Dec. 26, 1820.
Lib. Congress has Apr. 18, 1809–Dec. 26, 1815, fair; Jan. 2, 1816–Dec. 26, 1820.
N. Y. Hist. Soc. has Apr. 18, 1809–Dec. 29, 1818; Jan. 5–Mar. 9, Apr. 6, 13, May 25, June 15–July 20, Aug. 3, 17–31, Sept. 14–28, Oct. 12, Dec. 7, 14, 28, 1819; Jan. 11, 25, Feb. 8, Mar. 14, Apr. 18, June 13, 27, July 18, Aug. 1, 15, Nov. 14, Dec. 12, 1820.
Essex Inst. has Jan. 1, 1811–Dec. 30, 1817.
Univ. of Mich. (Clements) has May 9, Sept. 12, 26, Nov. 28–Dec. 26, 1809; Jan. 16, 1810–Dec. 26, 1820, fair.
Boston Pub. Lib. has Oct. 31, 1812–June 13, 1815; Sept. 12, 19, Oct. 10, 24, Nov. 28, 1815; Feb. 13, Apr. 23, Sept. 3, 24, Oct. 1, Nov. 2, 12, 26, Dec. 3, 1816; Sept. 8, 1818; July 27, 1819; Dec. 19, 1820.
Manchester (N. H.) City Lib. has Jan. 5, 1813–Dec. 26, 1820.
Duke Univ. has Jan. 15, 1811–Aug. 13, 1816, fair.
Mass. Hist. Soc. has Jan. 3, 1815–Dec. 30, 1817, fair; Jan. 6, 1818–Dec. 28, 1819; May 2, July 11, 1820.
Harvard has Dec. 6, 1815–July 14, 1818.
Yale has Oct. 17, 1809–Dec. 31, 1811; Jan. 7, 1812–Dec. 28, 1813, scattering issues; Mar. 5, 1814–Dec. 31, 1816, fair; Apr. 29, Aug. 19, Sept. 23, 1817; Jan. 6, Feb. 10–24, Apr. 7, May 26, June 30, July 7, Oct. 27, Dec. 8, 1818; Jan. 5, 1819–Oct. 3, 1820, scattering file.
Chicago Hist. Soc. has Dec. 5, 1809–July 28, 1812, fair.
N. Y. Pub. Lib. has Dec. 26, 1809; July 3, 31, Nov. 27, Dec. 11, 1810; May 28, Sept. 10, Nov. 19, Dec. 10, 1811; Jan. 21, 1812; Jan. 7, 1817–Dec. 22, 1818, fair.
Me. Hist. Soc. has Feb. 20, 1810; Dec. 12, 1815; Dec. 23, 1817; Jan. 5–Dec. 14, 1819.
Western Reserve Hist. Soc. has Aug. 6, 1811; Oct. 13, 1812–Nov. 15, 1814, scattering file; Oct. 17, 1815; Dec. 23, 1816; Apr. 22, June 24, July 1, 15, 29, 1817; June 23–July 7, 28, Aug. 11, Sept. 29, 1818.

[Concord] New Star, 1797.

Weekly. Established Apr. 11, 1797, by Russel & Davis [Elijah Russel and Moses Davis], with the title of "The New Star," supplanting "Russel & Davis' Republican Gazetteer" and continuing the advertisements from that paper. It was of small octavo size, each issue consisting of sixteen pages or two parts of eight pages each. It was discontinued with the issue of Oct. 3, 1797, no. 26. On Oct. 10, 1797, Russel and Davis brought out the paper in folio size with its former title of "The Mirror," because of "the decided disapprobation of a large majority of our patrons to it book wise." See under "Mirror."

N. H. Hist. Soc. has Apr. 11–Oct. 3, 1797.
Am. Antiq. Soc. has June 10, 13, 27–Oct. 3, 1797.
Harvard has Apr. 11, 18, July 4, 11, Aug. 15, 29, Sept. 26, 1797.
N. Y. Pub. Lib. has Apr. 25–June 13, 1797.
N. H. State Lib. has July 11–Sept. 19, 1797.

Concord Observer, 1819–1820+.

Weekly. Established Jan. 4, 1819, by George Hough, with the title of "Concord Observer." So continued until after 1820.

N. H. Hist. Soc., Dartmouth, Am. Antiq. Soc., N. Y. Hist. Soc., N. Y. State Lib., and Univ. of Mich. (Clements) have Jan. 4, 1819–Dec. 25, 1820.
Lib. Congress has Jan. 4, 1819–Dec. 18, 1820.
Duke Univ. has Jan. 11–Dec. 27, 1819.
Yale has Jan. 4–Dec. 13, 1819; Sept. 11, Dec. 4, 18, 25, 1820.
Boston Athenæum has Mar. 1, May 10, July 26, Sept. 27, Nov. 15, 29, Dec. 6, 20, 1819; Mar. 6, 20, May 15, July 17, 31, Aug. 21, Sept. 4, 11, 25, Oct. 9, Nov. 6, 13, Dec. 11, 25, 1820.

[Concord] Republican Gazette, 1801–1803.

Weekly. Established Feb. 5, 1801, by Elijah Russell, with the title of "Republican Gazette." With the issue of Apr. 16, 1801, Russell's name was omitted from the imprint, but with the issue of Oct. 1, 1801, it appeared at the head of the local column on the third page, and on Oct. 22, 1801, was restored to the imprint. With the issue of Aug. 10, 1802, the title was changed to "The American Republican Gazette," without change of numbering, "by Citizen Newschool, Esquire," and printed by E. Russell for the Proprietor. With the issue of either Oct. 19 or 26, 1802, the proprietor's name was omitted and the paper was printed by E. Russell. The last issue located is that of Apr. 28, 1803, vol. 3, no. 116. The Portsmouth "United States Oracle" of May 14, 1803, states that Russell, editor of "Concord Republican," has absconded, jumping his bond after arrest. He died suddenly at Washington, Vt., May 28, 1803 (Portsmouth "New Hampshire Gazette," June 7, 1803).

Harvard has Feb. 5–19, Mar. 5–Apr. 16, May 7–June 11, 25, July 23, Aug. 6, 20–Nov. 12, 25, Dec. 3, 17–30, 1801; Jan. 5–19, Feb. 2–Mar. 2, 23–Apr. 20, May 4, June 8–22, July 13, Aug. 3–24, Sept. 6, Oct. 5, 12, 26, Nov. 2, 23, 30, Dec. 16, 23, 1802; Jan. 6, 13, 27, Feb. 3, 17–Mar. 31, Apr. 21, 28, 1803.
N. H. Hist. Soc. has Feb. 12, Apr. 2, 16, 30, May 7, 28, June 11–25, July 23–Aug. 20, Sept. 3, 17–Nov. 19, Dec. 3, 1801; Feb. 16, Mar. 30, June 22–Aug.

21, Oct. 5, 12, 26–Nov. 30, Dec. 7, 16, 1802; Jan. 6–Feb. 24, Mar. 10, 31–Apr. 14, 1803.
Am. Antiq. Soc. has Apr. 16, June 25, July 16, Oct. 22, 1801; Apr. 21, 1803.
N. Y. Hist. Soc. has Feb. 19, 1801; Feb. 16, Dec. 7, 1802.
Dartmouth has Oct. 15, 1801; Dec. 30, 1802; Mar. 3, 1803.
Concord Pub. Lib. has May 25, Nov. 16, 1802; Apr. 28, 1803.
Lib. Congress has Mar. 5, 1801.
Me. Hist. Soc. has Jan. 13, 1803.

[Concord] **Republican Gazetteer,** 1796–1797.

Weekly. Established Nov. 22, 1796, by Moses Davis, with the title of "Republican Gazetteer." It supplanted the "Federal Mirror," and advertisements were continued from that paper. With the issue of Jan. 24, 1797, Elijah Russel entered the firm, the paper was published by Russel and Davis, and the title was changed to "Russel & Davis' Republican Gazetteer." The last issue with this title was that of Apr. 4, 1797, vol. 1, no. 20, after which the title was changed to "The New Star," which see.

Harvard has Nov. 22, 29, Dec. 13, 1796; Jan. 24, 31, Feb. 28, Mar. 21, 28, 1797.
N. H. Hist. Soc. has Nov. 29, 1796; Jan. 3, 24, Feb. 28–Mar. 14, 1797.
Am. Antiq. Soc. has Dec. 13, 1796; Jan. 31, Mar. 7–Apr. 4, 1797.
N. Y. Hist. Soc. has Jan. 17, Mar. 28, 1797.

[Concord] **Russel & Davis' Republican Gazetteer,** see **Republican Gazetteer.**

[Dover] **Phenix,** see **Phoenix.**

[Dover] **Phoenix,** 1792–1795.

Weekly. A continuation, without change of numbering, of "The Political Repository," the office of which paper was burned Jan. 14, 1792. The earliest issue located with the new title of "The Phoenix" is that of Feb. 8, 1792, vol. 2, no. 81, published by Eliphalet Ladd. Judging by the volume numbering, the new paper was begun on Jan. 25, 1792, after a lapse of one issue following the fire. Timothy Alden, in his "Century Sermon," 1801, states that it was begun Jan. 23, 1792. With the issue of either Apr. 4 or 11, 1792, the spelling of the title was changed to "The Phenix." At some time between September and November, 1793, Ladd admitted George S. Homans to the firm, and the paper was published by E. Ladd and G. S. Homans. In March, 1794, Ladd's brother-in-law, Samuel Bragg, Jr., became publisher. The last issue located is that of Aug. 22, 1795, vol. 6, no. 7, and it was evidently discontinued with the issue of Aug. 29, 1795, to be succeeded by "The Sun," which see.

Am. Antiq. Soc. has Feb. 8, Mar. 28, Aug. 2, Sept. 26–Nov. 7, Dec. 5, 19, 26, 1792; Jan. 5, 12, Mar. 9–Apr. 20, May 18, 25, Sept. 14, Nov. 30, Dec. 7, 21,

1793; May 17, Aug. 9, Dec. 13, 1794; Feb. 7, Apr. 11, 25, May 2, June 27, July 25, Aug. 15, 22, 1795.
Boston Athenæum has Mar. 14, 28, Apr. 11, July 12, 1792; Apr. 13, May 25, 1793; Apr. 12, 1794; Feb. 21, May 16, Aug. 8, 1795.
N. H. Hist. Soc. has Dec. 26, 1792; Jan. 26, Feb. 23, Mar. 9, Apr. 27, 1793.
Dover Pub. Lib. has Aug. 15, 29, 1792; Mar. 9, 1793.
Lib. Congress has Aug. 2, 29, 1792.
Wis. Hist. Soc. has Aug. 2, 1792; Dec. 6, 1794.
Conway, N. H., Pub. Lib. has July 19, 1792.
N. Y. Pub. Lib. has Aug. 15, 1792.
Mass. Hist. Soc. has Jan. 5, 1793.
N. Y. Hist. Soc. has Mar. 2, 1793.
Pejepscot Hist. Soc., Brunswick, Me., has July 11, 1795.

[Dover] **Political and Sentimental Repository**, 1790–1792.

Weekly. Established July 15, 1790, judging from the date of the earliest issue located, that of July 29, 1790, vol. 1, no. 3, published by Eliphalet Ladd, with the title of "Political and Sentimental Repository, or Strafford Recorder." At some time between Jan. 6 and June 9, 1791, the title was changed to "The Political Repository, or Strafford Recorder." The last issue located is that of Jan. 4, 1792, vol. 2, no. 77. Ladd's office was burned Jan. 14, 1792 (J. W. Moore "Moore's Historical, Biographical, and Miscellaneous Gatherings," 1886, p. 521), and when he started the paper again, he changed the title to "The Phoenix," which see.

Am. Antiq. Soc. has July 29–Sept. 2, 23–Oct. 14, 28, Nov. 18–Dec. 16, 1790; Jan. 6, July 20, Nov. 16, Dec. 7, 1791; Jan. 4, 1792.
Boston Athenæum has Oct. 28, 1790; June 23, Aug. 17, Sept. 21, Oct. 19–Nov. 2, 23, 1791.
Harvard has June 9, Sept. 21, 1791.

[Dover] **Political Repository**, see **Political and Sentimental Repository**.

[Dover] **Strafford Register**, 1818–1820+.

Weekly. A continuation, without change of volume numbering, of "The Dover Sun." The earliest issue with the title of "Strafford Register," was that of Aug. 25, 1818, vol. 7, no. 7 (error in numbering for vol. 7, no. 8), published by John Mann. The paper was continued until after 1820.

Dover Pub. Lib. has Aug. 25–Sept. 6, 22, 1817–June 29, Aug. 24, 1819; Feb. 15, 22, Mar. 27, June 6, 1820.
N. H. Hist. Soc. has Oct. 20, Nov. 10, 1818; Feb. 9, Aug. 10, 17, Dec. 21, 28, 1819; Jan. 4, May 16, July 4–Dec. 26, 1820.

Boston Athenæum has Dec. 8, 1818; Jan. 12, 26, Mar. 2, 30, June 8, Sept. 21, Oct. 5, 1819; July 25, Sept. 19, Oct. 17, Nov. 7, 1820.
Am. Antiq. Soc. has Aug. 25, Sept. 1, 1818; Jan. 26, Aug. 3, Dec. 21, 1819.
Dartmouth has Oct. 19, 1819.

[Dover] Sun, 1795–1818.

Weekly. Established Sept. 5, 1795, by Samuel Bragg, Jr., with the title of "The Sun," succeeding his other paper, "The Phenix." With the issue of Nov. 18 or 25, 1795, the title was changed to "The Sun. Dover Gazette, and County Advertiser." The printing-office was burned out on Dec. 25, 1810, and it was not until January, 1811, that the paper was again published. Samuel Bragg, Jr., died Dec. 8, 1811, and his father Samuel Bragg took over the establishment. With the issue of July 4, 1812, John Mann became the publisher, and changed the title to "Dover Sun," with a new volume numbering. With the issue of Dec. 3, 1814, the title was changed to "The Dover Sun." The last issue was that of Aug. 18, 1818, vol. 7, no. 7, after which the title became "Strafford Register," which see.

Dover Pub. Lib. has May 4, Oct. 26, 1796; Feb. 22, 1797; Jan. 24, Mar. 14, Apr. 11, 25, May 9, 23, 30, June 20–July 11, 25, Aug. 8, 15, 29–Sept. 26, Oct. 10, 24, 1798; May 29, Oct. 2, Dec. 11–25, 1799; Jan. 8, 22, 1800–Nov. 7, 1807, fair; Apr. 16, July 16, Sept. 10, 1808; Feb. 18, 1809–Dec. 1, 1810, fair; July 23, Dec. 11, 1811; Jan. 2, 1813–Dec. 10, 1814, fair; Jan. 14–Feb. 18, Mar. 4, 18, Apr. 15, May 13, 27, June 10, July 15, 22, Aug. 5, Sept. 9, 23, Oct. 7–21, Nov. 18, 25, Dec. 9, 30, 1815; Jan. 6, Feb. 17, Mar. 9, 23, Apr. 6, May 4, June 22, July 6, 30, Aug. 6, Sept. 3, 24, Nov. 5, Dec. 10, 1816; Jan. 7–21, Feb. 4–Mar. 11, 25–July 1, Oct. 21, Dec. 20, 1817; Jan. 6, 20, Feb. 10, 17, Mar. 3, 10, Apr. 7, July 7–Aug. 18, 1818.

Am. Antiq. Soc. has Oct. 10, Nov. 11, Dec. 2, 1795; May 18, June 29, Sept. 14, 28, Oct. 12–Nov. 2, 16, 23, 1796; Feb. 1–Mar. 1, Apr. 5, 12, May 17, 24, June 28, July 12, 26, Aug. 30, Sept. 13–Oct. 4, 25, Nov. 8–22, Dec. 6, 20, 27, 1797; Jan. 3, 17–July 18, Sept. 12, Oct. 31–Nov. 28, Dec. 12–26, 1798; Jan. 9–23, Feb. 6–20, Mar. 6, 27, May 29, 1799; Apr. 23, May 28, 1800; Apr. 15, 1801; Nov. 6, 20, 1802; Jan. 29, Mar. 12, July 9, Aug. 27, Oct. 1, 1803; Jan. 7–Apr. 14, 28–May 19, June 9–July 21, Aug. 4–18, Sept. 22–Oct. 27, Nov. 17, Dec. 15, 1804; Mar. 2, 16–June 15, 29–Sept. 21, Oct. 5–Dec. 28, 1805; Jan. 4–Feb. 1, 15–Apr. 5, 19–June 14, 28, July 5, 19, Aug. 2, 16–30, Sept. 20, Oct. 4, Nov. 1, 8, 22, Dec. 27, 1806; Jan. 31, Feb. 21–Mar. 21, Apr. 25–May 9, 23, June 20, 27, July 25, Aug. 15, 29, Sept. 12, 19, Oct. 10, 31, Nov. 14, 28, 1807; Mar. 26–Apr. 9, May 7, 21, June 4, 11, July 16, 23, Aug. 6, Sept. 3–24, Dec. 3, 10, 1808; Apr. 7, Sept. 22, 1810; Dec. 28, 1811; Feb. 1, July 11, 1812; Jan. 23, May 22, 1813; Sept. 3, 10, Oct. 15, Dec. 3, 1814; Apr. 29, July 8, Aug. 5–19, Sept. 9, 23–Oct. 28, Nov. 11, 25–Dec. 30,

1815; Jan. 6–May 25, June 29–Oct. 29, Nov. 12–Dec. 31, 1816; Jan. 14–28, Feb. 18, 1817; Mar. 31, May 5, Aug. 4, 1818.

N. H. Hist. Soc. has May 17, 1797; May 30, Oct. 10, 1798; Jan. 8–Dec. 31, 1800, fair; Feb. 6, 13, Mar. 20–Apr. 17, May 15, June 12, 1802; Jan. 22, 1803–Dec. 21, 1805, fair; Jan. 4, 1806; Jan. 17–Dec. 26, 1807, fair; Jan. 28, July 8, 15, Dec. 30, 1809; Jan. 6–Dec. 22, 1810, fair; July 23, 1811; Dec. 5, 1812; Jan. 2–Mar. 6, Apr. 3–Dec. 25, 1813; Feb. 19, Mar. 5–June 18, July 2–Dec. 31, 1814; Jan. 27–Dec. 31, 1816; June 3, 1817; May 12, 1818.

Harvard has May 18, June 1, 15–July 13, Aug. 3, 10, 24–Dec. 28, 1796; Jan. 4–Feb. 15, Mar. 1, 8, 22–Apr. 5, June 7–21, July 12, Sept. 13, Oct. 4, Nov. 22, Dec. 6–20, 1797; Jan. 3, 10, Feb. 14–28, Mar. 21, Apr. 11–25, May 9, 30, July 4, Aug. 22, Sept. 12, 19, Oct. 3, 10, 31, Nov. 14, 21, Dec. 5, 12, 26, 1798; Feb. 6–Mar. 6, 20, Apr. 10, 24–May 15, June 19, July 31, Aug. 7, 21, Sept. 11–Oct. 2, 16, Nov. 6, 13, Dec. 4, 25, 1799; Jan. 15–May 21, June 11–Oct. 1, Nov. 12, Dec. 24, 1800; Jan. 14, Feb. 11, 25, Mar. 18, 25, Apr. 8, 29–May 27, June 10, July 1, 15–29, Aug. 26–Sept. 23, Oct. 7, 17, 24, Nov. 7–21, Dec. 5, 12, 26, 1801; Jan. 2–Feb. 13, Mar. 6–20, Apr. 10, 17, May 1–July 10, 24, Aug. 7–Oct. 23, Nov. 13, 20, Dec. 4, 25, 1802; Jan. 1–Feb. 26, Mar. 12, 19, Apr. 2–May 28, July 9, 16, 30, Aug. 20–Nov. 12, Dec. 3–31, 1803; Jan. 14–Mar. 3, 17–31, Apr. 28, May 12–26, June 23–Aug. 18, Sept. 1–Oct. 6, 20–Dec. 15, 29, 1804; Jan. 5, 19, Feb. 16, 23, Mar. 9, 23–May 4, June 1, 8, 29, July 6, 20–Sept. 7, 21, 28, Oct. 19, Nov. 2–23, Dec. 7–21, 1805; Jan. 4, 11, Feb. 1–22, Sept. 20–Oct. 11, 1806.

Boston Athenæum has Feb. 17, Apr. 6, 13, May 4, June 22, Aug. 31–Sept. 14, 1796; Mar. 1, 15, May 3, 1797; Feb. 28, Sept. 5, 12, 1798; Feb. 27, Sept. 11, 1799; Feb. 26, Apr. 23, 1800; Sept. 6, 1806; Sept. 5, 1807; May 6, 1809; July 18, 1812; July 30, Aug. 20, Oct. 1, 8, 1814; Feb. 25, July 1, 1815; Mar. 9, 1816; Jan. 21, Mar. 4, Apr. 1, May 13, 1817; June 30, 1818.

Western Reserve Hist. Soc. has Jan. 26–Nov. 16, 1805.

Lib. Congress has Mar. 7, 14, Apr. 4, May 2, 9, 23, 30, July 4, 1798; Feb. 4, 18, 1801; Feb. 19, 1803; Mar. 3, 17, 24, Nov. 17, 1804; Mar. 16, 23, Apr. 6, May 4, 25–June 8, Sept. 14, 21, 1805; July 5, 1806; Nov. 21, 1807; Nov. 12, 1808; Mar. 25, Aug. 19, 1809; Apr. 7, 1810; Aug. 19, 1815.

Dartmouth has Apr. 9, May 7, 14, Nov. 19, 1803; Nov. 7, 21, 1807; Jan. 20, July 21, Oct. 6, 1810; Oct. 31, 1812; May 15, 22, Nov. 6, 1813; Oct. 15, Nov. 19–Dec. 3, 1814; Sept. 30, Oct. 14, 1815; Mar. 30, Apr. 13, 20, May 4, 11, July 30, Aug. 27, 1816.

Mass. Hist. Soc. has Feb. 18, Mar. 3–24, 1804; June 4, 1806.

Phil. Lib. Co. has Sept. 12, Nov. 4, 1795; Apr. 13, 20, May 18, 1796.

N. Y. Hist. Soc. has Dec. 24, 1800; Oct. 29, 1803; Dec. 1, 1804; Apr. 6, 1805; Jan. 14, 1809.

N. Y. Pub. Lib. has Mar. 30, 1796.

York Inst., Saco, has Apr. 24, 1799.

Long Id. Hist. Soc. has Apr. 17, 1800.

Dresden Mercury, see under **Hanover.**

[Exeter] American Herald of Liberty, see **Herald of Liberty.**

Exeter Chronicle, 1784.

Weekly. Established June 10, 1784, by Melcher and Osborne [John Melcher and George J. Osborne] with the title of "The Exeter Chronicle, or Weekly Advertiser." The last issue located is that of Dec. 3, 1784, vol. 1, no. 26, and it was probably discontinued with this issue.

Boston Athenæum has June 10–Dec. 3, 1784.
Dartmouth has June 10, 17, July 1–Aug. 26, Sept. 9–Dec. 3, 1784.
Am. Antiq. Soc. has Sept. 2, Nov. 19, 1784.
N. H. Hist. Soc. has Sept. 16, 1784.
N. Y. Hist. Soc. has Nov. 26, 1784.

[Exeter] Constitutionalist, 1810–1814.

Weekly. Established May 21, 1810, by E[phraim] C. Beals, with the title of "The Constitutionalist," and printed at the office of C[harles] Norris & Co. With the issue of Oct. 8, 1810, the title was changed to "Constitutionalist," set up in a decorative heading which included the names of the seventeen states. With the issue of Feb. 5, 1811, Beals transferred the paper to C. Norris & Co. Because of the loss of printing material by fire, Norris discontinued the paper with the issue of June 4, 1811, vol. 2, no. 3. The paper was reestablished by E. C. Beals June 23, 1812, with the title of "Constitutionalist and Weekly Magazine," vol. 2, no. 1. With the issue of Dec. 29, 1812, the paper was published by Joseph G. Folsom, although it was stated in the previous issue that the printing was to be performed by E. C. Beals. With the issue of June 15, 1813, Folsom transferred the paper to Nathaniel Boardman, although the latter's name did not appear in the imprint until the succeeding issue. The paper was discontinued with the issue of June 14, 1814, vol. 3, no. 52.

Exeter Pub. Lib., N. H. Hist. Soc., and Lib. Congress have May 21, 1810–June 14, 1814.
Am. Antiq. Soc. has May 21–Sept. 24, Oct. 15–29, Nov. 5, 26, Dec. 31, 1810; Jan. 7, 14, 29, Feb. 26, Mar. 5–Apr. 2, 23, 30, May 14, 28, 1811; June 23–Dec. 29, 1812; Jan. 5–Aug. 31, Sept. 21–Nov. 2, 16–30, Dec. 21, 28, 1813; Jan. 4, 11, 25–Feb. 15, Mar. 1–Apr. 19, May 24–June 14, 1814.
Boston Athenæum has May 21, 1810–Jan. 14, Feb. 12–Apr. 2, 16–30, May 14–June 4, 1811; June 23, 1812–Feb. 23, Mar. 8, May 11, June 8, 29, July 6, Aug. 17, Sept. 21, 1813; Feb. 8, 22, Mar. 7, 1814.
N. Y. Hist. Soc. has Sept. 17–Oct. 1, 1810; June 23, 1812–June 15, 1813.
Boston Pub. Lib. has June 23, 1812–June 15, 1813.
Colby Coll. has Feb. 23, 1813–Feb. 8, 1814.

Univ. of Mich. (Clements) has May 21, 28, June 11, 18, July 9, Sept. 10, Oct. 29, 1810; Feb. 26, Apr. 2, 1811; June 23–July 7, 21, Aug. 11–Dec. 29, 1812; Mar. 23, July 20, Aug. 17, 1813.
Yale has May 28, June 18, 1810; Mar. 26, 1811; Aug. 11, 18, 1812.
Rutgers Univ. has Apr. 6, May 25, June 8, 1812.
Essex Inst. has Oct. 1, 1810; Mar. 16, 1813.
Minn. Hist. Soc. has July 14, 1812; Apr. 26, 1814.
Dartmouth has May 18, June 15, Aug. 31, 1813.
Duke Univ. has Oct. 19, 1813.
Chicago Hist. Soc. has Jan. 4, 1814.
Mass. State Lib. has May 24, 1814.

Exeter Federal Miscellany, see Ranlet's Federal Miscellany.

[Exeter] Freeman's Oracle, 1786–1789.

Weekly. Established July 1, 1786, by Lamson and Ranlet [John Lamson and Henry Ranlet] with the title of "The Freeman's Oracle, and New-Hampshire Advertiser." With the issue of May 2, 1788, the title was slightly changed to "The Freeman's Oracle; or, New-Hampshire Advertiser," and with the issue of May 9, 1788, a colon replaced the semi-colon in the title. On Aug. 11, 1789, the firm was dissolved and beginning with the succeeding issue the paper was published by John Lamson. The last issue located is that of Nov. 12, 1789, vol. 4, no. 171, and the paper was discontinued with the issue of Dec. 3, 1789, according to the editor's statement in "The New Hampshire Gazetteer" of Dec. 12, 1789.

Boston Athenæum has July 1, 1786–July 14, 1787; Aug. 4, Sept. 22, Dec. 1–28, 1787; Jan. 4–Dec. 20, 1788; Jan. 13–27, Apr. 28, Oct. 7, Nov. 12, 1789.
Am. Antiq. Soc. has Aug. 29–Sept. 12, Oct. 3, 10, Dec. 16, 30, 1786; Jan. 13, 20, Feb. 10, Mar. 3–31, Apr. 28, May 12, 19, June 2, 23, 30, July 14, 28, Aug. 25, Sept. 8, Oct. 20, 27, Nov. 17–Dec. 28, 1787; Jan. 25, Mar. 7, 14, Apr. 25, July 4–18, Aug. 2–Sept. 20, Oct. 4, 1788; Feb. 17, Mar. 3, 17, 24, Apr. 21–May 19, June 23, July 7, 14, Aug. 11, Oct. 7, 1789.
Dartmouth has Jan. 20, 1787; June 27, 1788; Feb. 24, Mar. 31–Apr. 14, 28–May 12, 26, June 9–Aug. 11, Nov. 12, 1789.
N. Y. Hist. Soc. has Feb. 10, June 2, 1789.
Essex Inst. has Feb. 24, Mar. 3, 1787.
Lib. Congress has Sept. 19, 1786.
Western Reserve Hist. Soc. has Nov. 24, 1787.
N. H. Hist. Soc. has Nov. 1, 1788.

[Exeter] Herald of Liberty, 1793–1796.

Weekly. A continuation, without change of volume numbering, of "The New Hampshire Gazetteer." The first issue with the title of "The Herald of Liberty" was that of Feb. 20, 1793, vol. 7, no. 33, published by Henry Ranlet. With the issue of May 14, 1793, the title was changed to "The American Herald of Liberty." With the issue of Jan. 7, 1794, the paper was transferred to Sterns and Winslow [William Sterns, spelled Stearns Apr. 29, 1794, and after, and Samuel Winslow], who abbreviated the title to "American Herald of Liberty." With the issue of Nov. 4, 1794, the firm was dissolved and the paper published by William Stearns, but with the issue of Dec. 6, 1794, it was transferred to Samuel Winslow. At some time between Nov. 25, 1795, and Jan. 6, 1796, the title was changed to "The Herald of Liberty: Or, Exeter Gazette." The last issue located is that of July 12, 1796, vol. 11, no. 2, and the paper was undoubtedly discontinued shortly afterwards.

Dartmouth has Feb. 20–July 2, 16, 23, Aug. 6, 20–Sept. 24, Oct. 8, 1793–Dec. 6, 1794.

N. H. Hist. Soc. has June 11, 1793–May 14, 1795; June 7, 1796.

Am. Antiq. Soc. has Feb. 20, Mar. 6–May 8, June 4–18, Nov. 5, 1793; Jan. 7, May 20, June 24, July 1, Aug. 12, Sept. 9, 1794; Jan. 3, 10, Feb. 7, 21, Apr. 11, 18, July 30, Aug. 6, 27, 1795; Mar. 2, 30, June 21, 1796.

Lib. Congress has Feb. 20–Apr. 3, 17–May 8, 21–June 25, July 9–23, Aug. 27, Oct. 8, 22, 29, 1793; Apr. 1, 8, July 1, Aug. 12, Sept. 3, Oct. 14, 1794; Aug. 13, 1795; Jan. 6, Mar. 2, 1796.

Boston Athenæum has June 4–Sept. 10, Oct. 22–Dec. 10, 1793; July 2, Sept. 3, 10, Oct. 1, Nov. 18, 1795; Feb. 24, June 28, July 12, 1796.

N. Y. Pub. Lib. has Mar. 4, 11, 1794; Jan. 24, 1795.

N. Y. Hist. Soc. has Mar. 13, 1793.

Boston Pub. Lib. has Apr. 10, 1793.

Phil. Lib. Co. has Oct. 15, 1793.

Me. Hist. Soc. has Apr. 25, 1795.

Exeter Journal, 1778–1779.

Weekly. Established Feb. 17, 1778, by Zechariah Fowle, with the title of "The Exeter Journal, or, New Hampshire Gazette." With the issue of May 12, 1778, the title was changed to "The Exeter Journal or, the New-Hampshire Gazette, and Tuesday's General Advertiser." With the issue of June 16, 1778, the title was changed to "New-Hampshire Gazette. Or, State Journal, and General Advertiser." The issues from June 16 to July 14, 1778, were not numbered, but July 21, 1778, was numbered vol. 1, no. 22. From June 16, 1778, to Feb. 16, 1779, vol. 1, no. 52, the paper was printed for both Exeter and Portsmouth, the two being identical except for the imprint, which read Z. Fowle or Zechariah Fowle for the Exeter issues, and D. Fowle or Daniel Fowle for the Portsmouth issues (see also under Portsmouth–New Hampshire Gazette). With the issue of Feb. 23, 1779, no. 53, the identical printing for both towns was abandoned and the title of the Exeter paper was changed to "The Exeter Journal or, the New-Hampshire Gazette, and Tuesday's General Advertiser." The last issue with this title was that of May 25, 1779, no. 66. All these issues from Feb. 23 to May 25, 1779, were totally different from the "New-Hampshire Gazette" printed at Portsmouth. Then, on June 1, 1779, the paper was apparently printed for both Exeter and Portsmouth, with the title of "New-Hampshire Gazette. Or, State Journal, and General Advertiser," vol. 2, no. 67, but without any imprint whatever. This method was followed until Sept. 8, 1781, although issues of Dec. 25, 1779, and Jan. 1, 1780, have been located bearing the Exeter imprints of Zechariah Fowle, also Feb. 26, 1781. All issues, however, from June 1, 1779, to Sept. 8, 1781, are listed in this Bibliography under Portsmouth.

Boston Athenæum has Feb. 24–Apr. 7, 21–June 23, July 7–Sept. 8, 22–Nov. 10, 24–Dec. 29, 1778; Feb. 2–23, Mar. 9–Apr. 6, 20–May 25, 1779.
Lib. Congress has Mar. 31, June 23, July 14–28, Dec. 1, 1778.
Am. Antiq. Soc. has Apr. 7, Aug. 11, 1778; Jan. 12, Feb. 9, 1779.
N. H. Hist. Soc. has Mar. 3, 1778; Mar. 2, 23, 1779.
N. Y. State Lib. has Aug. 25, 1778.

[Exeter] **Lamson's Weekly Visitor,** 1795.

Weekly. Established May 5, 1795, by J[ohn] Lamson, with the title of "Lamson's Weekly Visitor." With the issue of June 2, 1795, the title was changed to "The Weekly Visitor" and with the issue of June 16, 1795, it was changed to "The Weekly Visitor: Or, Exeter Gazette," published by John Lamson. The last issue located is that of Dec. 26, 1795, vol. 1, no. 33.

Harvard has May 5, 19–June 2, 16, July 14, 28, 1795.
Lib. Congress has May 26, June 2, 30–Sept. 8, 22, 29, Oct. 13, 20, Nov. 18–Dec. 12, 26, 1795.
Boston Athenæum has June 9, Sept. 15, 1795.
Am. Antiq. Soc. has July 14, Aug. 25, 1795.
Dartmouth has Sept. 8, 1795.
N. Y. Hist. Soc. has Sept. 8, 1795.
Essex Inst. has Nov. 28, 1795.

[Exeter] **New Hampshire Gazette,** 1776–1777.

Weekly. Established May 22, 1776, by Robert L. Fowle. The initial issue was in the nature of a prospectus, being termed by the editor a "Hand-Bill," and was entitled "A New Hampshire Gazette." It was a single sheet and bore no volume numbering. Another "Hand-Bill" was promised for May 27, although no copy has been located. On June 1, 1776, appeared the first regular issue, entitled "New Hampshire Gazette, or, the Exeter Morning Chronicle." This was numbered vol. 1, no. 3, and referred to the two "Hand-Bills" previously published. This and most of the succeeding issues were single sheets and without the name of publisher in the imprint. With the issue of June 22, 1776, the title was slightly changed to "The New Hampshire Gazette, or, Exeter Morning Chronicle." With the issue of Sept. 7, 1776, the title was changed to "The New-Hampshire [State] Gazette, or, Exeter Circulating Morning Chronicle," and with the issue of Jan. 21, 1777, to "The State Journal or, the New-Hampshire Gazette, and Tuesday's Liberty Advertiser." The last issue located with this title is that of July 15, 1777, no. 61, in which issue the publisher states that the paper will in the future be published by Daniel Fowle, "who proposes to keep the Office open at Exeter, as also at Portsmouth, in case proper Encouragement is given." The "late Publisher" desires that his subscribers will settle their accounts. Robert L. Fowle fled soon afterwards from Exeter, having been suspected as a Tory and accused of aiding in the counterfeiting of paper currency (see N. H. State Papers, vol. 8, and Sabine's Loyalists, vol. 1, p. 432).

Am. Antiq. Soc. has May 22, June 1–29, July 13–Dec. 10, 24, 31, 1776; Jan. 7–Mar. 4, 18, 25, Apr. 8–May 27, June 10, 24, July 1, 1777.

Boston Athenæum has Oct. 12–Dec. 31, 1776; Jan. 14–July 15, 1777.

N. Y. Hist. Soc. has June 1, July 6–Dec. 31, 1776; Jan. 7–21, Feb. 4–Mar. 18, Apr. 1–29, May 27, June 3, 24, 1777.

N. H. Hist. Soc. has June 22–July 13, Aug. 3–Sept. 7, 28–Oct. 29, Nov. 12, 26–Dec. 24, 1776; Jan. 14, Feb. 4–Mar. 18, Apr. 1–29, May 27, June 3, 24, 1777.

Mass. Hist. Soc. has May 22, June 8–July 20, Aug. 3–Sept. 7, 21, Oct. 5, 29, Nov. 12, 19, Dec. 10, 1776; Feb. 4, Mar. 11, 18, May 27, June 17, 1777.

Boston Pub. Lib. has June 1, 22, 29, July 13, Aug. 3, 31, Sept. 14, 21, Oct. 5, 12, 29, Nov. 5, 26, Dec. 3, 1776; Jan. 7, 14, Feb. 4, 18, 25, Mar. 18, 1777.

Lib. Congress has Aug. 10, Oct. 29, 1776; Apr. 1, 15, 22, 1777.

[Exeter] **New-Hampshire Gazette**, 1778–1779, see **Exeter Journal**.

[Exeter] **New Hampshire Gazetteer**, 1789–1793.

Weekly. Established Aug. 18, 1789, by H[enry] Ranlet, with the title of "The New Hampshire Gazetteer." The last issue with this title was that of Feb. 13, 1793, vol. 7, no. 32, after which the name was changed to "The Herald of Liberty," which see.

Dartmouth has Aug. 18–Sept. 5, 19–Nov. 14, Dec. 19, 26, 1789; Jan. 2, 9, 23, 30, Feb. 13, 27–Apr. 30, May 28–June 11, July 2–23, Aug. 13–Sept. 10, 24–Oct. 16, 30–Nov. 20, Dec. 26, 1790; Sept. 2, Oct. 21, 1791; July 18, 27, Aug. 10, 17, 31–Dec. 26, 1792; Jan. 2–Feb. 13, 1793.

Am. Antiq. Soc. has Sept. 5–19, Oct. 3, 10, 31–Nov. 21, Dec. 5–26, 1789; Jan. 2–30, Mar. 6, 13, 27–Apr. 10, 24–May 7, 21, June 4–Aug. 20, Sept. 3, 17–Oct. 30, Nov. 13, 20, Dec. 11, 25, 1790; Apr. 9–30, May 13, 27, June 3, 17–July 1, 29, Sept. 9–23, Oct. 14, 28–Nov. 12, 26, Dec. 17, 24, 1791; Jan. 28, Feb. 4, Mar. 7, 14, 28, Apr. 25–May 9, July 11, 18, Aug. 3–Sept. 28, Oct. 19–Nov. 28, Dec. 12, 19, 1792; Jan. 2, 16–Feb. 13, 1793.

N. H. Hist. Soc. has Dec. 19, 1789; Dec. 4, 1790; Jan. 8–29, Feb. 12, 26, Mar. 12–June 24, July 8–Dec. 31, 1791; Jan. 14–July 18, Aug. 3, 17, 31–Sept. 21, Oct. 12, 19, Nov. 14–Dec. 26, 1792; Jan. 2–Feb. 13, 1793.
Boston Athenæum has Mar. 6, July 23, Sept. 24, 1790; Aug. 5, 12, 1791; Jan. 28, Feb. 4, Sept. 21, Oct. 31, Dec. 12, 1792.
N. Y. Hist. Soc. has Aug. 13, 1790; Aug. 19, 1791; Jan. 2, 1793.
Mass. Hist. Soc. has Dec. 17, 1791; Feb. 4, 1792.
Lib. Congress has Aug. 3, 1792; Jan. 30, 1793.
N. Y. State Lib. has Jan. 29, 1791.
Boston Pub. Lib. has Sept. 9, 1791.
Wis. Hist. Soc. has Apr. 18, 1792.
Univ. of Mich. (Clements) has Jan. 30, 1793.

[Exeter] **New-Hampshire Spy,** 1796–1797.

Weekly. Established Sept. 24, 1796, by Henry Ranlet, with the title of "The New-Hampshire Spy." With the issue of Nov. 19, 1796, the title was abbreviated to "New-Hampshire Spy." The paper was discontinued with the issue of Mar. 18, 1797, vol. 1, no. 26.

Am. Antiq. Soc. has Oct. 1, 15–29, Nov. 12–26, Dec. 3 extra, 17–31, 1796; Feb. 4–Mar. 4, 18, 1797.
Harvard has Sept. 24, Oct. 1, 15, 1796.
N. H. Hist. Soc. has Dec. 3 extra, 24, 1796; Jan. 14, 28, 1797.
Boston Athenæum has Sept. 24, 1796.
York Inst. Saco, has Dec. 3, 1796.

[Exeter] **New-Hampshire State Gazette,** see **New Hampshire Gazette,** 1776–1777.

[Exeter] **Political Banquet,** 1799–1800.

Weekly. A continuation, without change of volume numbering, of "Exeter Federal Miscellany." The first issue located of the paper under its new title of "Political Banquet, and Farmer's Feast," is that of Oct. 8, 1799, vol. 1, no. 45, published by Henry Ranlet. The last issue located is that of Dec. 31, 1799, vol. 2, no. 5. Jacob B. Moore, in "American Quarterly Register" for Nov. 1840, vol. 13, p. 175, says that the paper continued about a year.

Lib. Congress has Oct. 8, 1799.
Am. Antiq. Soc. has Nov. 12, Dec. 31, 1799.

[Exeter] **Ranlet's Federal Miscellany,** 1798–1799.

Weekly. Established Dec. 5, 1798, judging from the date of the earliest issue located, that of Dec. 12, 1798, vol. 1, no. 2, "Ranlet's Federal Miscellany,"

NEW HAMPSHIRE 457

printed by H[enry] Ranlet. With the issue of Jan. 16, 1799, the title was changed to "Exeter Federal Miscellany," printed by Henry Ranlet. The last issue located with this title is that of Sept. 24, 1799, vol. 1, no. 43. Within two weeks, the title was changed to "Political Banquet, and Farmer's Feast," which see.

Harvard has Dec. 12–26, 1798; Jan. 16, Feb. 6, 13, 1799.
Am. Antiq. Soc. has Feb. 13, Apr. 24, May 28, Sept. 24, 1799.
Lib. Congress has Jan. 9, Sept. 3, 1799.
N. Y. Hist. Soc. has Apr. 17, 1799.

[Exeter] State Journal, see New Hampshire Gazette, 1777.

[Exeter] Watchman, 1816–1820+.

Weekly. Established Oct. 1, 1816, by H[enry] A. Ranlet, with the title of "The Watchman." With the issue of Dec. 3, 1816, the title was changed to "Exeter Watchman." With the issue of July 14, 1818, Ranlet transferred the paper to Nathaniel Boardman, who with Aug. 4, 1818, engaged J[ohn] J. Williams as printer. With the issue of Nov. 9, 1819, Boardman brought out the paper, with a new series volume numbering, under the changed title of "Exeter Watchman and Agricultural Repository," the name of the printer being omitted from the imprint. Continued until after 1820. On Feb. 6, 1821, Samuel T. Moses bought the paper, changed the title to "Northern Republican" and restored the original volume numbering, calling that issue vol. 5, no. 14.

Dartmouth has Oct. 1–Dec. 31, 1816; Jan. 7, 21–Mar. 11, 25–Apr. 8, 22, May 7–27, June 10, 24–July 22, Aug. 12–Sept. 23, Oct. 7, 14, 28–Nov. 11, 25–Dec. 30, 1817; Jan. 6–Oct. 6, 20–Dec. 29, 1818; Jan. 5–July 6, Aug. 17, 1819.
Am. Antiq. Soc. has Oct. 1, 8, 22, 29, Nov. 19, 1816; Mar. 25–Apr. 8, 22–May 13, 27–Oct. 28, Nov. 11–25, Dec. 9–30, 1817; May 19, 1818; June 29, July 6, Aug. 10, 17, 1819; Sept. 5, 1820.
N. H. Hist. Soc. has Oct. 15, 1816; Feb. 4, Oct. 21, 1817; Sept. 1, 1818; Mar. 10, Oct. 5, Nov. 9, 1819–Oct. 31, 1820.
Boston Athenæum has Oct. 29, Nov. 19, 1816; Jan. 7, Feb. 11, 18, Mar. 4, Apr. 15, May 20, Sept. 23, Oct. 14, 1817; Mar. 17, May 26, June 23, July 21, 1818; Feb. 23, Mar. 2, Apr. 20, May 18, Aug. 17, Sept. 21, Oct. 19, 1819; Feb. 8, Apr. 25, Aug. 22, 29, 1820.
Harvard has Mar. 11, July 22, 1817; Sept. 12, 1820.
Duke Univ. has May 13, July 22, 1817.
Lib. Congress has Mar. 18, 1817.
Univ. of Ill. has Aug. 26, 1817.
Wis. Hist. Soc. has Dec. 15, 1818.
Me. Hist. Soc. has July 13, 1819.

[Exeter] Weekly Visitor, see Lamson's Weekly Visitor.

Gilmanton Gazette, 1800.

Weekly. Established Aug. 30, 1800, judging by the date of the earliest issue located, that of Dec. 6, 1800, vol. 1, no. 15, published by Leavitt & Clough [Dudley Leavitt and ——— Clough], with the title of "The Gilmanton Gazette: and Farmers' Weekly Magazine." The issue of Dec. 20, 1800, vol. 1, no. 17, is the last located.

N. Y. Hist. Soc. has Dec. 6, 20, 1800.
Lib. Congress has Dec. 13, 1800.
N. H. Hist. Soc. has Dec. 20, 1800.

Gilmanton Rural Museum, 1799–1800.

Weekly. Established Oct. 28, 1799, judging from the date of the earliest issue located, that of Nov. 11, 1799, vol. 1, no. 3, published by Elijah Russell with the title of "Gilmanton Rural Museum." In the issue of Feb. 28, 1800, Russell states: "The Editor has obtained a supply of paper, and will continue the Museum of the present size, if suitably encouraged. The three small numbers are equal to two large ones, consequently this No. is 17. Feb. 28." Timothy Alden, in his "Century Sermon," 1801, says that the paper was published by Russell for six months.

Harvard has Nov. 11, 18, 1799.
N. H. Hist. Soc. has Feb. 28, 1800.

[Greenland] New Hampshire Gazette, 1775, see under Portsmouth.

[Hanover] American, 1816–1817.

Weekly. Established Feb. 7, 1816, by David Watson, Jun., with the title of "The American." The last issue located is that of Apr. 2, 1817, vol. 2, no. 9.

Boston Athenæum has Feb. 7, 1816–Apr. 2, 1817.
Dartmouth has Feb. 7, 21–July 24, Aug. 7–21, Sept. 4–Dec. 25, 1816; Jan. 8, 15, Feb. 5–26, Mar. 19–Apr. 2, 1817.
Wis. Hist. Soc. has Feb. 7, 1816–Feb. 12, 1817.
Am. Antiq. Soc. has Feb. 7, 21, Mar. 20–May 22, June 5, 19–Aug. 21, Sept. 4–Oct. 23, Nov. 6–Dec. 25, 1816; Jan. 1–Mar. 26, 1817.
N. H. Hist. Soc. has Aug. 21, 28, Sept. 11, Oct. 16, 1816; Feb. 5, 1817.
N. Y. Pub. Lib. has Sept. 25, Oct. 2, 1816.

[Hanover] Dartmouth Gazette, 1799–1820.

Weekly. Established Aug. 27, 1799, by Moses Davis, with the title of "Dartmouth Gazette." Davis died July 24, 1808. The issue of July 27 retained his name in the imprint, that of Aug. 3 bore no publisher's name, and that of Aug. 10 was "printed for the Proprietor" by Colburn & Day [———— Colburn and ———— Day]. With the issue of Oct. 19, 1808, the paper was transferred to C[harles] & W[illiam] S. Spear. With the issue of Oct. 31, 1810, Henry Spear was added to the firm, and the paper was published by C., W.S., & H. Spear. Publication was suspended from Apr. 24 to June 5, 1811, and on the latter date the paper was published by Charles Spear. At some time between Oct. 13 and Nov. 17, 1813, the title was changed to "Dartmouth Gazette, and Grafton and Coos Advertiser," but with the issue of Feb. 21, 1816, it reverted to "Dartmouth Gazette." The last issue located is that of Feb. 23, 1820, vol. 20, no. 26, and the paper was discontinued shortly afterwards, as was noted in the first issue of the "Dartmouth Herald" of June 21, 1820.

Dartmouth has Aug. 27, 1799–Dec. 30, 1807; Jan. 6–Oct. 12, Nov. 16, Dec. 14, 1808; Jan. 18, Feb. 15, Mar. 8, Apr. 5, May 31, June 14–July 5, 26, Aug. 2, 23, Sept. 13, Nov. 8, Dec. 13, 27, 1809; Jan. 17, Feb. 7–21, Mar. 7, 14, Apr. 25, July 4, 18, Aug. 2, 8, 22, Sept. 5, 25, Oct. 3, 31, Nov. 14, Dec. 12, 26, 1810; Jan. 2, 16, 23, Feb. 20, Mar. 13, 20, Apr. 17, June 12, July 17, 31, Aug. 14, Sept. 4, 11, Oct. 2, 16–Nov. 6, 20–Dec. 4, 25, 1811; Jan. 1, 8, 29, Feb. 4, 18–Mar. 10, Apr. 28–May 19, June 16–30, July 14, 28–Sept. 15, Dec. 16, 1812; Jan. 5–27, Feb. 3, 24–Mar. 10, 24, 31, Apr. 28, May 12, 26, June 9, 16, 30–July 14, 28, Aug. 11, 25–Sept. 29, Oct. 20, Dec. 8–22, 1813; Jan. 5–19, Feb. 2, 9, 23–Apr. 27, May 11, 25, June 1, 15, July 6–27, Aug. 10–24, Sept. 14, 21, Oct. 26–Nov. 23, Dec. 14–28, 1814; Jan. 4–18, Feb. 1–May 31, June 14–Sept. 27, Oct. 11–Dec. 27, 1815; Jan. 3–Dec. 25, 1816; Jan. 1–22, Feb. 5–Dec. 31, 1817; Jan. 7, 14, 28–May 20, June 3–Oct. 7, 21–Dec. 30, 1818; Jan. 6–27, Feb. 10–Mar. 31, Apr. 14, 21, May 5, 12, 26, June 2, 23, 30, Aug. 25–Sept. 22, Oct. 6–20, Nov. 3, 10, 24, Dec. 1, 8, 1819; Jan. 5, 19, Feb. 9–23, 1820.

Am. Antiq. Soc. has Nov. 18, 1799; Jan. 20, 27, Feb. 17, Apr. 21, May 12–26, June 9–30, July 14, Aug. 11, 25, Sept. 15–Oct. 6, 20, 25, Nov. 15–29, Dec. 20, 1800; Jan. 3, 17, Feb. 21, Mar. 14, 21, Aug. 22, Oct. 17, Nov. 7, Dec. 5, 1801; Feb. 6, 13, 27, Apr. 10, May 22, Aug. 28, Sept. 4, 11, Oct. 30, Nov. 13, 27, 1802; Jan. 1, 22, Feb. 5, 26, May 7, July 23, Aug. 6–Sept. 10, Dec. 2, 16, 1803; Feb. 10, Mar. 9–23, Apr. 27–Dec. 28, 1804; Jan. 4–Aug. 2, 16–Sept. 20, Oct. 4–Nov. 15, Dec. 6, 27, 1805; Jan. 3, 10, 31, Feb. 14, May 7, 28, Apr. 4, 18, May 23, June 6, 20–July 18, Aug. 1–Sept. 12, Oct. 3–Nov. 7, 28–Dec. 19, 1806; Jan. 2–Feb. 6, 20–Mar. 6, 20–Apr. 10, 24, May 8–July 8, Aug. 5–Sept. 23, Oct. 7, 14, 28, Nov. 11–Dec. 2, 23, 30, 1807; Jan. 6, 13, Feb. 10, 17, Mar. 9, Apr. 20, May 11, Aug. 3, 24–Sept. 14, Oct. 5, 1808; Dec. 27, 1809; Feb. 7, Mar. 14, Apr. 25, May 30, July 11, Aug. 1, 15, Sept. 12, Oct. 24, 31, Nov. 21, 28, Dec. 12, 26, 1810; Jan. 23, Feb. 13, 27, Mar. 6, 13, Aug. 14, Sept. 4, 11, Dec. 4, 11, 1811; May 5, 19, June 30, July 14, Sept. 1–15, 29, Oct. 20, 27, Nov. 10, Dec. 9, 30, 1812; Jan. 13, 20, Mar. 10,

31, May 18, July 7, Sept. 1, 8, 29, Dec. 8, 1813; Jan. 5, 26–Feb. 9, Apr. 27, May 25, June 22, 29, July 13, 27, Aug. 10, Sept. 14, Oct. 12–26, Nov. 9, 16, Dec. 14, 1814; Jan. 11, 18, Feb. 1–15, Mar. 8, 15, 29–Apr. 19, May 3, 10, 17–31, June 21, July 5–19, Aug. 9–Sept. 27, Oct. 11, Nov. 1–Dec. 13, 27, 1815; Jan. 10, 24–Feb. 21, Mar. 6–Apr. 10, 24–May 15, June 5, 19–Aug. 7, 21, 28, Sept. 11–Oct. 30, Nov. 13–Dec. 25, 1816; Jan. 1–15, Feb. 19–Mar. 5, 19–Sept. 10, 24, Oct. 8–Nov. 12, 26, Dec. 3, 24, 31, 1817; Jan. 7–May 20, June 17, July 8, 22, 29, Aug. 19, Sept. 30, Oct. 7, 28, Nov. 18, 25, Dec. 16, 30, 1818; Jan. 6–27, Mar. 3, May 12, June 30, July 28, Sept. 8, Oct. 20, Dec. 8–22, 1819; Jan. 5, Feb. 9, 1820.

Harvard has Aug. 27, Sept. 16–Oct. 28, Nov. 11, 25, Dec. 23, 30, 1799; Jan. 13, 27–Mar. 3, 17–May 26, June 9–July 21, Aug. 4–Oct. 20, 25, Nov. 8–Dec. 20, 1800; Mar. 14–Apr. 11, 25–June 20, July 11–25, Aug. 8–Oct. 24, Nov. 21, Dec. 12, 26, 1801; Jan. 2–Mar. 27, Apr. 17–May 1, 15, Oct. 9, 30, Nov. 6, 1802; Jan. 22, Feb. 5, 26, Mar. 5, 19, Aug. 13, Sept. 24, Nov. 11–18, Dec. 9–23, 1803; Jan. 6, Feb. 3, 24, Mar. 9, 30–Apr. 13, May 25, 1804.

Boston Athenæum has Jan. 2, Oct. 21, 1807; May 17, Nov. 8, 1809; Mar. 14, Nov. 21, 1810; Mar. 13, July 3, 31, Aug. 7, 21, Oct. 9, 1811; Oct. 13, 1812; Sept. 1, Oct. 6, 1813; Jan. 12, 1814; Jan. 11, Dec. 20, 1815; Jan. 10, 31, Feb. 14, Mar. 27, June 26, Aug. 28, Sept. 18, Oct. 2, 16–30, Dec. 25, 1816; Jan. 1–22, Mar. 10–Apr. 2, 23, 1817; Mar. 4, July 29, Sept. 16, Oct. 7, Nov. 18, 1818; Feb. 3, 17, 24, May 6, 19, June 16, Oct. 13, Nov. 24, Dec. 8, 22, 1819; Jan. 26, 1820.

N. H. Hist. Soc. has Nov. 15, 1800; Sept. 26, 1801; May 15, 1802; May 21, Sept. 3, 1803; Feb. 10, 1804; Apr. 19, 1805; Sept. 5, Nov. 7, 1806; Nov. 11, Dec. 16, 1807; Jan. 13, 27, Feb. 10, Apr. 13, 1808; Feb. 15, Sept. 20, 1809; July 11, Oct. 6, Nov. 17, 1810; July 10, 1811; Jan. 12, 26, Mar. 23, Apr. 6, 20, July 20, Oct. 5, 19–Nov. 2, 19, 1814; Oct. 4–25, Nov. 29, 1815; July 2–16, Oct. 8, Nov. 12, Dec. 3, 1817; Feb. 11, Mar. 25, Sept. 30, 1818; Feb. 9, 1820.

N. Y. Hist. Soc. has Dec. 27, 1800; Feb. 21–Mar. 21, Apr. 4–May 9, 23–June 27, Aug. 1, 15–Sept. 26, Oct. 10, 1801–Dec. 25, 1802; Jan. 1–Mar. 5, 19–Sept. 24, Oct. 8–29, 1803; Jan. 6–27, Feb. 10, 17, Mar. 2–June 15, 29, July 6, Aug. 3–17, 31, Sept. 7, 1804; Jan. 25, Feb. 15, June 14, July 19, 1805; Feb. 1, 1809.

Boston Pub. Lib. has Mar. 13, Sept. 16–30, Oct. 14–28, Nov. 18–Dec. 16, 1807; Jan. 13, Feb. 3–Mar. 9, Apr. 6–Dec. 28, 1808; Jan. 4, 11, Feb. 1–June 28, Aug. 9, 23, 30, Sept. 13, 20, Oct. 4–25, 1809; Jan. 3, Mar. 14, 28, Apr. 4, 1810; Jan. 16, Feb. 27, Apr. 10, 17, Aug. 7, 1811; Aug. 25, 1813; Oct. 9, 1816.

Lib. Congress has Apr. 21, July 14, 1800; Aug. 14, Sept. 11, 1802; Aug. 20–Sept. 3, 1803; Mar. 9, July 13, Aug. 10, 1804; Apr. 26, Sept. 27, 1805; Feb. 28, June 20, Nov. 7, Dec. 5, 12, 1806; Jan. 2, 16–Mar. 6, 27, Apr. 17, May 1, 15, 29, June 17, Sept. 2, 9, 30, Oct. 14, 28–Dec. 2, 1807; Feb. 3,

May 11, 18, Dec. 28, 1808; Oct. 11, 25, 1815; May 1, Aug. 7, 1816; Jan. 15, Mar. 26, 1817; July 22, Dec. 2, 9, 1818; Apr. 28, 1819.
Univ. of Mich. (Clements) has Aug. 23, 1805; May 15, Aug. 19, Sept. 2, Oct. 28, 1807; Feb. 21, 1816; Feb. 25, Sept. 30, 1818.
Danbury Ct., Lib. has Sept. 1, 1812; Aug. 23, Sept. 13, 1815; Aug. 14, 21, Sept. 4, 1816.
Troy Pub. Lib. has June 20, July 11, 25, Oct. 17, 1801; Feb. 27, 1802.
Univ. of Ill. has Mar. 9, Oct. 19, 1804; June 21, Aug. 2, 1805.
Buffalo Pub. Lib. has Mar. 24, 1800.
Cheshire Co. Hist. Soc., Keene, has Dec. 12, 1801.
Me. Hist. Soc. has July 26, 1804.
Duke Univ. has Aug. 22, 1806.
Wis. Hist. Soc. has Dec. 16, 1818.

[Hanover] **Dartmouth Herald,** 1820+.

Weekly. Established June 21, 1820, by Bannister & Thurston [Ridley Bannister and Lyman Thurston], with the title of "Dartmouth Herald." So continued until after 1820.

Dartmouth has June 21–Dec. 27, 1820.
N. H. Hist. Soc. has June 21–July 26, Sept. 6, Oct. 11, Nov. 8, 15, 1820.
Am. Antiq. Soc. has July 5, 19–Aug. 2, Sept. 6, 20–Oct. 11, Nov. 8, 15, 1820.
Boston Athenæum has Dec. 6, 1820.

[Hanover] **Dresden Mercury,** 1779.

Weekly. Established May 4, 1779, judging from the date of the earliest issue located, that of July 13, 1779, no. 11, published by Judah Padock [Spooner] & Alden Spooner, with the title of "The Dresden Mercury, and the Universal Intelligencer." The paper was printed at Dresden "in the South End of Dartmouth College." Dresden was a name given from 1778 to 1784 to a town comprising chiefly that part of the town of Hanover in the vicinity of Dartmouth College. Although, as one of the towns in the New Hampshire Grants, Dresden belonged at one time to the jurisdiction of Vermont, it later sought incorporation with New Hampshire and its territory is wholly within the limits of New Hampshire today. Major John Hawkins, who visited Hanover in 1779, records in his Journal, "This day I had the perusal of the 1st No. of the Dresden Mercury, dated May 4th." (Original diary in Hist. Soc. Penn.). The last issue located is that of Sept. 27, 1779, no. 22.

N. Y. Pub. Lib. has July 13, 1779.
Am. Antiq. Soc. has Aug. 3, 9, 1779.
Arthur H. Keyes, Rutland, Vt., has Sept. 13, 1779.
Dartmouth has Sept. 27, 1779.

[Hanover] Eagle, 1793–1799.

Weekly. Established July 22, 1793, by Josiah Dunham, with the title of "The Eagle: or, Dartmouth Centinel." With the issue of Mar. 2, 1795, the paper was edited by Josiah Dunham and printed by John M. Dunham. With the issue of Apr. 6, 1795, Josiah Dunham disposed of the paper to John M. Dunham and Benjamin True, being thenceforth engaged by them as editor, and the paper was edited by Josiah Dunham and printed by Dunham and True. With the issue of June 6, 1796, it was printed and published by Dunham and True. The partnership was dissolved and with the issue of Mar. 20, 1797, the paper was published by Benjamin True. In July 1798, the title was changed to "The Eagle." The last issue located is that of June 1, 1799, vol. 6, no. 45, and the paper was discontinued soon afterwards. Timothy Alden, in his "Century Sermon," 1801, states that after July 24, 1798, it was published by Benjamin True, but under the superintendence of Moses Fiske, until the first week in June, 1799, when it was discontinued.

Am. Antiq. Soc. has July 22, 29, Aug. 19–Dec. 30, 1793; Jan. 6–Dec. 8, 22, 29, 1794; Jan. 5–Dec. 28, 1795; Jan. 4–Apr. 25, May 9–Aug. 29, Oct. 10–31, Nov. 21–Dec. 5, 19, 26, 1796; Jan. 2, 16, 1797; May 7, Aug. 7, Oct. 9, Nov. 13, Dec. 4, 18, 1798; Jan. 1–22, Feb. 26, Mar. 12, 19, 1799.

Boston Pub. Lib. has Aug. 19, Nov. 18–Dec. 9, 1793; Jan. 20, 27, Feb. 3, Mar. 3, 17–Apr. 21, May 12–26, Aug. 4, 11, Sept. 22, 29, Oct. 13, 20, Nov. 3, Dec. 22, 1794; Jan. 5, Feb. 9–Mar. 2, 16, May 4, 11, June 22, July 6, 13, 27, Aug. 17, 27, Nov. 23, Dec. 7, 28, 1795; May 16–30, June 13, July 4, 18, Aug. 15, 29, 1796.

Harvard has Aug. 19, 1793; Jan. 6, 1794; Feb. 16, Mar. 23, June 8, 29, July 6, 1795; Feb. 8, 15, May 9, Aug. 1, 1796; Mar. 27, May 29, June 5, July 10, 31, Sept. 18, 25, Oct. 16, Nov. 13, 1797; Mar. 5, 26, Apr. 9, 23, May 7, 14, June 4, 11, 25, July 2, 31, Aug. 14, 28, Sept. 11, Oct. 16, 23, Dec. 25, 1798; Jan. 1–15, Feb. 12, 26, Mar. 12–Apr. 2, June 1, 1799.

Dartmouth has July 22, Oct. 28, 1793; Jan. 6, Apr. 7, 1794; July 13–27, Oct. 5–26, 1795; July 11, Aug. 8, 1796; May 15, 29, July 24, Aug. 21, Sept. 4, Oct. 23, Dec. 25, 1797.

N. Y. Pub. Lib. has Sept. 16, 23, Oct. 14, 1793; Sept. 8, 29, Oct. 13, 27, 1794; Jan. 12, 1795; Apr. 18, Nov. 7, Dec. 12, 1796; Apr. 24, 1797.

N. H. Hist. Soc. has May 4, July 13, 1795; Apr. 4, 25, 1796; Oct. 9, 16, 1798; Apr. 2, 1799.

Boston Athenæum has July 29, 1793; Feb. 1, Nov. 7, 1796.

Lib. Congress has Sept. 29, 1794; June 8, 1795.

York Institute, Saco, has June 1, 1795.

Long Id. Hist. Soc. has Feb. 8, 1796.

NEW HAMPSHIRE

[Haverhill] Advertiser, 1810.

Weekly. Established May 24, 1810, judging from the earliest issue located, that of June 7, 1810, vol. 1, no. 3, published by T[heophilus] L. Houghton, and entitled "The Advertiser." It was of quarto size. The last issue located is that of July 19, 1810, vol. 1, no. 9.

Am. Antiq. Soc. has June 7, July 19, 1810.
Dartmouth has June 28, 1810.

[Haverhill] Coos Courier, 1808–1810.

Weekly. Established Apr. 21, 1808, by Theophilus L. Houghton, with the title of "Coos Courier." The last issue located is that of Mar. 15, 1810, vol. 2, no. 45.

Dartmouth has Aug. 18–Nov. 17, Dec. 1–22, 1808; Jan. 5–Mar. 30, Apr. 13–27, Nov. 23, 1809.
Am. Antiq. Soc. has Apr. 21, July 7, 1808; July 13, 1809; Mar. 8, 15, 1810.
Boston Athenæum has Sept. 15, 1808; Mar. 8, 1810.
N. H. Hist. Soc. has Dec. 15, 1808; Feb. 1, 8, 1810.
Essex Inst. has Oct. 11, 1808.
N. Y. Hist. Soc. has Feb. 2, 1809.

[Haverhill] Grafton & Coos Intelligencer, 1820+.

Weekly. Established Nov. 30, 1820, with the title of "The Grafton & Coos Intelligencer." This issue is numbered vol. 1, no. 1, whole no. 52, evidently a continuation of "The New Hampshire Intelligencer" established in November 1819. No name of publisher is given, but the proprietor was Sylvester T. Goss, who was given as publisher of the issue of Dec. 13, 1820. The paper was continued after 1820, and in 1821 had its title changed to the "New Hampshire Intelligencer."

Dartmouth has Nov. 30, 1820.
Am. Antiq. Soc. has Dec. 6, 13, 1820.
N. Y. Pub. Lib. has Dec. 20, 1820.
N. H. Hist. Soc. has Dec. 27, 1820.

[Haverhill] Grafton Minerva, 1796–1797.

Weekly. Established Mar. 3, 1796, judging from the date of the earliest issue located, that of Mar. 24, 1796, vol. 1, no. 4, published by Nathaniel Coverly and Son, with the title of "The Grafton Minerva, and Haverhill Weekly Bud." At some time between Apr. 7 and May 12, 1796, the paper was published by Nathaniel Coverly alone. The last issue located is that of Jan. 23, 1797, vol. 1, no. 46. The son was probably Nathaniel, Jun'r, as he established "The Orange Nightingale" at Newbury, Vt., May 12, 1796.

Phil. Lib. Co. has Mar. 24, 31, May 12, 26–June 30, July 14, 28, 1796.
Harvard has May 19, June 16–30, July 14, Aug. 18, 1796; Jan. 12, 23, 1797.

[Haverhill] **New Hampshire Intelligencer**, 1819–1820.

Weekly. According to Hamilton Child's "Gazetteer of Grafton County," 1886, p. 112(35), "The New Hampshire Intelligencer" was established in November, 1819, by Sylvester T. Goss. No copy located. It was succeeded in November, 1820, by "The Grafton & Coos Intelligencer," which see.

[Keene] **Cheshire Advertiser**, 1792.

Weekly. Established Jan. 5, 1792, judging from the date of the earliest issue located, that of Jan. 19, 1792, vol. 1, no. 3, published by James D. Griffith, with the title of "The Cheshire Advertiser." The name of the publisher was given in the imprint early in February as James Davenport Griffith. The last issue located is that of Dec. 6, 1792, vol. 1, no. 48.

Am. Antiq. Soc. has Jan. 19, 26, Feb. 16, 23, Mar. 8, 22, Apr. 4, Sept. 20, Dec. 6, 1792.

[Keene] **Columbian Informer**, 1793–1795.

Weekly. Established Apr. 4, 1793, judging from the date of the earliest issue located, that of Apr. 18, 1793, vol. 1, no. 3, published by Henry Blake & Co., and entitled "The Columbian Informer; Or, Cheshire Journal." Henry Blake died Mar. 9, 1795, and thenceforth the name of the publisher was omitted from the imprint. In the issue of Mar. 24, 1795, W[illiam] W. Blake as "surviving partner," advertises that old debts due the firm should be paid to him. The last issue located is that of July 21, 1795, vol. 3, no. 17, and the paper was undoubtedly discontinued in August.

Dartmouth has Aug. 14–Oct. 16, Nov. 27, 1793; Feb. 19, June 24–Aug. 26, Sept. 9–Dec. 30, 1794; Jan. 6–Mar. 3, 17–Apr. 21, 1795.
N. Y. Pub. Lib. has Apr. 18, July 10, Aug. 7, Oct. 2, 1793; Oct. 28, Nov. 4, 25, Dec. 2, 1794; Jan. 13, Feb. 17, June 30, 1795.
Am. Antiq. Soc. has Aug. 14, Nov. 6, Dec. 11, 25, 1793; Apr. 15, May 13, June 17, Dec. 9, 1794; Jan. 13–Feb. 17, Mar. 31, Apr. 7, 1795.
Keene Pub. Lib. has Jan. 15–Mar. 18, Apr. 1, 15–May 6, June 3–17, Sept. 23–Nov. 11, Dec. 23, 30, 1794.
Lib. Congress has June 6, 1793; July 29, 1794; Feb. 3, Mar. 3, 31, May 26, June 16, 1795.
N. Y. Hist. Soc. has Sept. 25, 1793.

Pocumtuck Valley Mem. Assoc., Deerfield, has Apr. 29, 1794.
Dublin, N. H., Hist. Soc. has Sept. 16, 1794.
Alice M. Gowing, Dublin, N. H., has Oct. 14, 28, 1794.
Esther Chatterton, Acworth, N. H., had July 21, 1795, but not found by her heirs.

[Keene] **New-Hampshire Recorder,** 1787–1791.

Weekly. Established Aug. 7, 1787, judging from the date of the earliest issue located, that of Aug. 21, 1787, vol. 1, no. 3, published by James D. Griffith, with the title of "The New-Hampshire Recorder, and the Weekly Advertiser." After December, 1787, the name of the publisher was generally given in the imprint as James Davenport Griffith. The issues from Mar. 25 to Apr. 8, 1788, were published in small folio because of the scarcity of paper, the title being abbreviated to "The New-Hampshire Recorder." With the issue of Apr. 15, 1788, however, the regular title was resumed. On account of scarcity of paper, there were no issues published from Nov. 27, 1789, vol. 2, no. 52, to Mar. 18, 1790, vol. 3, no. 1, with the exception of a half-sheet following Nov. 27, 1789, and also numbered vol. 3, no. 1. The paper was discontinued with the issue of Mar 3, 1791, vol. 3, no. 39.

Am. Antiq. Soc. has Aug. 21–Sept. 18, Oct. 16, 23, Nov. 6, 13, 27, 1787; Jan. 1, Feb. 5, 19–Mar. 4, 25, Apr. 8, 15, June 3, 24, July 1, Aug. 5, 12, Sept. 9–Oct. 7, Nov. 11, 18, Dec. 23, 30, 1788; Jan. 6, 13, 27–Feb. 12, Mar. 5–19, Apr. 3, May 14, 21, Aug. 20–Oct. 15, 29, Nov. 5, 27, 1789; Mar. 18–Apr. 22, May 6–27, July 22–Oct. 7, 21, Nov. 24, Dec. 9, 1790; Jan. 6, 1791.
Keene Pub. Lib. has Sept. 9, 1788–Nov. 27, 1789; Mar. 18, 1790–Feb. 24, 1791.
Lib. Congress has Sept. 25, Oct. 16–30, Nov. 13–Dec. 18, 1787; Jan. 8–Feb. 5, July 1, 15, Oct. 7–21, 1788; Feb. 26–Mar. 19, Nov. 5, 1789.
N. H. Hist. Soc. has Dec. 25, 1787.
Essex Inst. has Mar. 25, 1788.
Cheshire Co. Hist. Soc., Keene, has Mar. 25, 1788.
Springfield, Mass., City Lib. has Sept. 30, 1788.

[Keene] **New Hampshire Sentinel,** 1799–1820+.

Weekly. Established Mar. 23, 1799, by John Prentiss, with the title of "New-hampshire Sentinel." With the issue of Apr. 24, 1819, John Prentiss admitted his brother George to the firm and the paper was published by John & George W. Prentiss. It was so continued until after 1820.

Keene Pub. Lib. has Mar. 23, 1799–Dec. 31, 1808; Jan. 7–Feb. 25, Mar. 11–May 27, July 1–Sept. 9, 30–Nov. 18, Dec. 2, 9, 23, 30, 1809; Jan. 6–27, Feb. 10–Apr. 28, June 23, Aug. 4–18, Sept. 15–29, Oct. 13–27, Nov. 10–Dec. 29, 1810; Jan. 5, 12, 26, Feb. 2, 16–Mar. 9, June 15, 22, Aug. 10,

Oct. 19, Nov. 2, 30, Dec. 7, 1811; Jan. 4, 18, Feb. 1–Apr. 4, 18–Sept. 26, Nov. 21, Dec. 5–19, 1812; Jan. 2, 1813–Dec. 30, 1820.

Dartmouth has Mar. 23–Apr. 27, May 11–June 8, 29–July 20, Aug. 17, 31–Sept. 21, Oct. 5–26, Nov. 9, 23, Dec. 7–28, 1799; Jan. 11–25, Feb. 8–June 21, July 5–26, Aug. 9, 23–Sept. 20, Oct. 4–Nov. 15, 29, Dec. 6, 20, 27, 1800; Jan. 3, 17–Apr. 6, 25, May 2, 16, 23, June 6–Nov. 14, Dec. 5, 19, 26, 1801; Jan. 2–June 26, July 10–31, Aug. 14–Oct. 23, Nov. 6–Dec. 4, 25, 1802; Jan. 1–Apr. 23, May 7, 21, June 4, 11, 25, July 9–Aug. 20, Sept. 10–Dec. 31, 1803; Jan. 7, 14, 28, Feb. 11–25, Mar. 24–Apr. 14, 28, May 5, 19–June 16, 30, July 14–Sept. 15, 29, Oct. 6, 20, 27, Nov. 10, 17, Dec. 1, 15–29, 1804; Jan. 19–Feb. 16, Mar. 2–23, Apr. 6, 20, 27, May 11–June 8, 29–July 13, 27–Sept. 21, Oct. 5, 19–Nov. 23, Dec. 14–28, 1805; Jan. 4–Mar. 1, 15–May 17, 31–Aug. 9, 23–Oct. 11, Nov. 1–22, Dec. 6–27, 1806; Jan. 3, 10, 24–Sept. 12, 26–Dec. 26, 1807; Jan. 2–Mar. 12, 26–July 23, Aug. 6–Dec. 31, 1808; Jan. 7, 1809–Dec. 30, 1820.

Lib. Congress has Apr. 13, May 4, Oct. 12, Dec. 7, 28, 1799; Mar. 15, May 17, 31, Aug. 23–Sept. 27, Oct. 11–Nov. 29, Dec. 13–27, 1800; Jan. 3–31, Feb. 14–Mar. 7, 21, Aug. 29, Nov. 7, Dec. 5, 1801; Sept. 11, 1802; Dec. 17, 1803; June 23, July 28–Aug. 11, Sept. 1, 15, 29, Nov. 3, Dec. 29, 1804; Feb. 16, June 8, July 13–27, Aug. 17–Sept. 7, 21–Oct. 5, Nov. 30, Dec. 21, 1805; Mar. 29, Apr. 5, May 3, 17, June 21–July 12, Aug. 16, 23, Sept. 13, 27, Oct. 18, 1806; Mar. 26, May 7, July 30, 1808; Mar. 24, 1810–Mar. 30, 1816; Sept. 28, Nov. 23, 1816; Oct. 4, 1817; Aug. 29, Nov. 14, 1818; Jan. 9, 1819–Dec. 30, 1820.

N. H. Hist. Soc. has Mar. 23, Aug. 31, Oct. 19, 1799; Sept. 27, 1800; Sept. 19, 1801; Oct. 29, 1803; Mar. 24, Sept. 1, 1804–Nov. 16, 1805; Apr. 18–May 2, 16, 30, June 13, July 11, Aug. 22, Sept. 12, 19, Dec. 5–19, 1807; Jan. 2–Apr. 16, May 7, June 25, Sept. 24–Oct. 8, 1808; Apr. 21, May 12, 1810; May 25, June 1, July 6, 1811; Feb. 22–Mar. 14, May 9, 1812–Dec. 28, 1816; Jan. 11–Mar. 21, Apr. 11 May 10, 24–July 26, Aug. 9–Oct. 11, Nov. 1–Dec. 6, 1817; Mar. 7, 14, Apr. 4, Dec. 19, 1818; Jan. 2, 9, Feb. 6, Mar. 6–July 10, Aug. 21–Sept. 25, Oct. 9–Dec. 25, 1819; Jan. 1–Dec. 30, 1820.

Am. Antiq. Soc. has Mar. 23–Dec. 28, 1799; Jan. 4–Mar. 15, May 3, Oct. 25, Nov. 29, 1800; Mar. 7, 21, 28, Apr. 11–May 2, 16–Aug. 29, Sept. 12–Oct. 31, Nov. 14–Dec. 26, 1801; Jan. 2–Mar. 6, June 26, Nov. 13, 1802; July 30, Nov. 5, 1803; Mar. 17, 24, Apr. 21, June 30, Aug. 4, 11, Sept. 1, 15, Nov. 17–Dec. 1, 1804; Mar. 16, 23, Apr. 13, July 6, Aug. 31, 1805; July 12, 19, Aug. 9, Oct. 25, 1806; Jan. 3, Feb. 7, Apr. 11, June 13, Aug. 22, Sept. 19, Oct. 24, 1807; Jan. 9, Feb. 6, Mar. 26, Apr. 2, May 21, June 11, 25, July 2, 16, Aug. 20, Sept. 24, Oct. 1, 15–29, Nov. 26–Dec. 10, 1808; Jan. 7, Mar. 4, Apr. 29, May 20, 27, June 17, July 15, Aug. 19, Sept. 9–23, 1809; Jan. 13, Mar. 3, Apr. 21, May 12, 19, June 2, July 7, 28, Aug. 18, Sept. 8, 22, Nov. 10, Dec. 15–29, 1810; Jan. 12, 19, Feb. 9, 16, Mar. 9, Apr. 6, 20, 27, May 25, June 8, 22, July 6, Aug. 3, 17–31, Sept. 14–Oct. 12, 26–Nov. 9, 23–Dec. 7, 21, 28,

NEW HAMPSHIRE 467

1811; Jan. 4, 11, 25–Feb. 8, 29, Mar. 14, 28–Apr. 18, May 2–June 6, 20, July 4, 11, 25, Aug. 1, 15–29, Sept. 12, 26–Oct. 24, Nov. 21–Dec. 26, 1812; Jan. 30, May 29, June 19–Dec. 25, 1813; Jan. 1–Mar. 26, Apr. 9–30, May 14–Aug. 6, 13, 27, Sept. 17, Oct. 8, 1814; Jan. 7–28, Feb. 11, 25–Mar. 18, Apr. 1–May 20, June 3, 10, July 1–Aug. 5, 19–Dec. 23, 1815; Jan. 6–20, Feb. 3–17, Mar. 3–16, Apr. 13, May 4, 18, June 22–July 6, 20, 27, Aug. 10, 31, Sept. 7, 21, Oct. 12, 19, Nov. 2, 9, 23, Dec. 7, 1816; Apr. 26, May 24, June 6, 21–July 19, Aug. 16, Oct. 4, 1817; Jan. 31, Feb. 28, Mar. 21, Apr. 4, 11, May 2–June 6, 27, Aug. 8, 29, Oct. 10, 17, Nov. 14–Dec. 26, 1818; Jan. 2–June 5, 26–Dec. 25, 1819; Jan. 1–Aug. 5, 19–Dec. 2, 16–30, 1820.
Harvard has Apr. 6, 1799–Mar. 23, 1805, fair; Oct. 19, Nov. 9, Dec. 14, 1805; Jan. 18, Feb. 1–15, Apr. 5, 1806; Apr. 25, Aug. 1, 22, Oct. 10, 24, 1807; Aug. 13, 1808.
N. Y. Hist. Soc. has Apr. 6, 1799; Dec. 20, 1800; May 9, 1801; Apr. 6, 1805; Jan. 28, 1809; Aug. 13, 27–Oct. 1, 15–Nov. 19, Dec. 3–17, 31, 1814; Apr. 6, 13, 27–June 8, July 13–Sept. 21, Oct. 5, Dec. 21, 28, 1816; Jan. 4, 1817–July 4, 1818.
Essex Inst. has June 13, 1801; June 7, 1806; Oct. 12, 1816; Mar. 21, 1818–Dec. 30, 1820, fair.
Univ. of Ill. has June 9, Sept. 1, 29–Oct. 13, Nov. 10, Dec. 29, 1804; Jan. 26, June 15, 29, Sept. 7, 21, Oct. 5, 26, 1805; Feb. 22, Mar. 22, Apr. 5, 1806; Jan. 3, June 13, 1807.
Boston Athenæum has Mar. 2, 1805; May 20, 1809; Mar. 5, 1814; Feb. 10, June 22, 1816; Dec. 4, 25, 1819; Jan. 1, Apr. 15, Nov. 4, 25, 1820.
Alice M. Gowing, Dublin, N. H., has Sept. 27, 1799; Sept. 18, 1802; Oct. 15, 1803.
Univ. of Mich. (Clements) has Apr. 6, Oct. 5, 12, 26, Dec. 7, 1811; Jan. 11, May 2, 23, 30, 1812; Sept. 30, 1815; Aug. 10, 1816; Jan. 22, 1820.
Dublin, N. H. Hist. Soc. has Dec. 7, 1805; Apr. 1, 1820.
Boston Pub. Lib. has Oct. 29, 1803.
Me. Hist. Soc. has Mar. 18, 1809.
Wis. Hist. Soc. has Dec. 19, 1818.

[**Keene**] **Rising Sun**, 1795–1798.

Weekly. Established Aug. 11, 1795, by Cornelius Sturtevant, Jun. & Co., with the title of "The Rising Sun." The partners in the firm were Abijah Wilder and Elias Sturtevant (Griffin, History of Keene, p. 300). With the issue of Apr. 7, 1798, the paper was transferred to Elijah Cooper. The last issue located is that of June 23, 1798, vol. 3, no. 46.

N. Y. Hist. Soc. has Sept. 15, 1795–Feb. 24, 1798.
Cheshire Co. Hist. Soc., Keene, has Sept. 8, Oct. 6–Dec. 29, 1795; Jan. 5–19, Feb. 9, 16, Mar. 8, 22–Apr. 12, 26–June 21, July 12–Dec. 20, 1796; Jan. 3–Feb. 14, Mar. 7–Apr. 18, 1797.

Am. Antiq. Soc. has Aug. 11, 1795; Feb. 16, Mar. 29, May 10, 31, June 21, 28, July 5, 19, Aug. 2, 23, Sept. 6, 20, Oct. 11, Nov. 1–15, 29–Dec. 13, 1796; Feb. 14, 21, Mar. 7–21, Apr. 18, May 2–16, July 11, Aug. 12, Sept. 9–23, Oct. 7–21, Nov. 4, 11, Dec. 23, 1797; Jan. 13, 20, Feb. 3, 10, Mar. 17–31, Apr. 14, 28, May 12, 19, 1798.
Harvard has Mar. 8, 15, Nov. 15, 22, Dec. 27, 1796; Jan. 3, 17–Feb. 21, Mar. 28, Apr. 4, 18, May 23, June 5, 27, July 4, Aug. 1, 12, 19, Sept. 16, Oct. 7, 21, Nov. 11, Dec. 9, 16, 30, 1797; Jan. 6–20, Feb. 10–24, 1798.
Lib. Congress has Apr. 12, June 28, 1796; Feb. 17, 1798.
Keene Pub. Lib. has Jan. 26, 1796.
N. H. Hist. Soc. has June 23, 1798.

[Portsmouth] Federal Observer, 1798–1800.

Weekly. Established Nov. 22, 1798, by Treadwell & Hart [William Treadwell and Samuel G. Hart] with the title of "Federal Observer." With the issue of Aug. 1, 1799, the firm was dissolved and the paper published by W. Treadwell. With the issue of May 22, 1800, it was published by W. Treadwell & Co. The last issue located is that of May 29, 1800, vol. 2, no. 80. Timothy Alden, in his "Century Sermon," says that it was discontinued June 12, 1800.

Boston Athenæum has Nov. 22, 1798–May 29, 1800.
N. H. Hist. Soc. has Nov. 29, 1798–Feb. 21, July 11, Aug. 8, Sept. 5, 12, 26, 1799.
Am. Antiq. Soc. has Dec. 27, 1798; Jan. 3, 17, Apr. 18, Aug. 8, 1799.
Lib. Congress has Nov. 29, Dec. 20, 1798.
Harvard has Mar. 7, 1799.
N. Y. Pub. Lib. has Jan. 24, 1800.

[Portsmouth] Fowle's New-Hampshire Gazette, see New-Hampshire Gazette.

[Portsmouth] Freeman's Journal, 1776–1778.

Weekly. Established May 25, 1776, with the title of "The Freeman's Journal, or New-Hampshire Gazette," printed by Benjamin Dearborn. With the issue of Dec. 31, 1776, Dearborn states that he has transferred the paper to Daniel Fowle, although the latter's name did not appear in the imprint until Jan. 13, 1778. The last issue with this title was that of June 9, 1778, vol. 2, no. 52. Fowle then changed the title to "New-Hampshire Gazette. Or, State Journal." See under "New-Hampshire Gazette."

Mass. Hist. Soc. has May 25, 1776–Nov. 29, 1777; Mar. 24–June 9, 1778.
N. Y. Hist. Soc. has May 25, 1776–May 3, 1777; Aug. 9, 1777; Mar. 31, 1778.
N. H. Hist. Soc. has May 25–Oct. 12, 22–Dec. 3, 17–31, 1776; Jan. 7–May 3, 24, 31, July 19, Aug. 9, Sept. 20, 1777; Mar. 31, 1778.

Am. Antiq. Soc. has Aug. 3, 10, Oct. 12, 22, 29, Nov. 12, Dec. 10, 1776; Jan. 14, Feb. 18–Apr. 19, May 3, 17–June 7, 28, Sept. 13, Nov. 8, 1777; Mar. 31, 1778.
Lib. Congress has Nov. 19, Dec. 10, 1776; Feb. 4, Mar. 4, 8, June 28, Aug. 16, 23, 1777; Jan. 6, 13, Mar. 3, 10, June 2, 1778.
Univ. of Mich. (Clements) has June 15, 29, July 13–27, Aug. 31, Oct. 12, Nov. 12, 1776; Apr. 5, 1777.
Boston Athenæum has Oct. 4, 11, Nov. 1, 8, 29, 1777; Jan. 27, Feb. 10, Mar. 24, Apr. 21, 1778.
Wis. Hist. Soc. has July 20, Nov. 5, 1776; Jan. 7, Mar. 15, July 12, 1777.
Dartmouth has June 14, Sept. 27, 1777; Jan. 30, 1778.
N. Y. State Lib. has Feb. 25, 1777.
N. Y. Pub. Lib. has Feb. 3, 1778.
Yale has Mar. 31, 1778.

[Portsmouth] **Herald of Gospel Liberty**, 1808–1810, 1814–1815.

Bi-weekly. Established Sept. 1, 1808, by Elias Smith, with the title of "Herald of Gospel Liberty." It was of quarto size, with pagination, and was issued fortnightly. It carried almost no current news, with the exception of religious intelligence, and was more of a magazine than a newspaper. It would not have been included in this Bibliography had it not been for the following statement by the editor in his prefatory address: "A religious Newspaper, is almost a new thing under the sun; I know not but this is the first ever published to the world." The last issue published at Portsmouth was that of Apr. 13, 1810, vol. 1, no. 43, after which the paper was removed to Portland, Me., and later to Philadelphia. It was again published at Portsmouth, beginning with the issue of Feb. 4, 1814, vol. 6, no. 12. It was suspended from Dec. 9, 1814, to Feb. 3, 1815, and from Sept. 29 to Dec. 22, 1815. This latter issue, vol. 7, no. 26, was the last published in newspaper form, although there was an Extra on Mar. 8, 1816, vol. 7, no. 26. In August 1816 it was continued in Boston as an octavo magazine.

Am. Antiq. Soc. has Sept. 1, 1808–Apr. 13, 1810; Feb. 4, 1814–Dec. 22, 1815; Mar. 8, 1816.
N. H. Hist. Soc., Wesleyan Univ., and Chicago Theol. Sem. have Sept. 1, 1808–Apr. 13, 1810; Feb. 4, 1814–Dec. 22, 1815.
Antioch Coll. has Sept. 1, 1808–Apr. 13, 1810; Feb. 4, 1814–Sept. 29, 1815.
N. H. State Lib. has Sept. 1, 1808–Apr. 13, 1810; Feb. 4, 1814–Mar. 3, 1815.
Lib. Congress has Sept. 1, 1808–Apr. 13, 1810; Feb. 4, 18, June 10–July 8, Sept. 6, 16, Nov. 25, Dec. 9, 1814; Feb. 17, Mar. 31, Apr. 28, June 9, 23, 1815.
Congregational Lib. of Boston has Sept. 1, 1808–Apr. 13, 1810; Feb. 4–July 22, 1814.
N. Y. Hist. Soc. has Sept. 1, 1808–Apr. 13, 1810; Feb. 18, 1814.

Mass. Hist. Soc., Hist. Soc. Penn., Juniata Coll., Penn. State Lib., and Presbyterian Theol. Sem., Chicago, have Sept. 1, 1808–Apr. 13, 1810.
Me. Hist. Soc. has Sept. 1, 1808–Sept. 15, 1809.
Boston Pub. Lib. has Sept. 1, 1808–Aug. 4, 1809; Jan. 5, Mar. 16, 1810.
Univ. of Mich. (Clements) has Sept. 1, 15, Nov. 10, Dec. 8, 22, 1808; Jan. 5, 19, Mar. 2–31, May 12, 26, June 23–July 21, Sept. 29–Dec. 22, 1809; Jan. 5, 19, Mar. 2–Apr. 13, 1810.
N. Y. Pub. Lib. has July 21–Oct. 13, 1809.
Defiance Coll., Defiance, Ohio, has Sept. 15–Dec. 22, 1809.
Presbyterian Hist. Soc. has Feb. 4–Oct. 7, 1814, fair.

[Portsmouth] Intelligencer, 1806–1817.

Weekly. Established Dec. 4, 1806, by Samuel Whidden, with the title of "The Intelligencer." With the issue of Jan. 7, 1813, the title was changed to "Intelligencer." The last issue was that of May 15, 1817, vol. 11, no. 562, it being succeeded, the following week, by "The Oracle of New-Hampshire," which see.

N. H. Hist. Soc. has Sept. 6, 1810; Jan. 30, Mar. 5, Oct. 22, Nov. 26, Dec. 10–31, 1812; Jan. 7, 21–Apr. 1, 15–Sept. 2, 16–Nov. 4, 25–Dec. 9, 1813; Jan. 5, Feb. 2, 16–Mar. 30, Apr. 13–July 13, 27, Aug. 3, 24, Sept. 7, 14, Oct. 5–Dec. 28, 1815; Jan. 4, 1816–May 15, 1817.
Am. Antiq. Soc. has Dec. 4, 18, 1806; Jan. 1, Mar. 19, Oct. 29, 1807; Aug. 4, 1808; June 7, 21, 1810; Mar. 5, Apr. 2, 1812; Sept. 23, 1813; Oct. 26–Dec. 28, 1815.
Boston Athenæum has May 25, 1809; Mar. 8, Aug. 23, 1810; Feb. 28, 1811; July 15, Oct. 7, 1813; Feb. 10, Apr. 21, May 19, Aug. 11, 18, Sept. 1, 8, Oct. 20, 1814; Feb. 9, 23, June 29, 1815; Feb. 1, 15, Mar. 14, Sept. 26–Oct. 24, Nov. 7, 1816; Jan. 9–23, Feb. 13, Mar. 6, 20, Apr. 10, 1817.
Lib. Congress has Jan. 4, 1816–May 1, 1817.
Newberry Lib. has July 29–Aug. 19, Sept. 2, 16–Nov. 4, 25, Dec. 9–30, 1813; Jan. 6, 13, 27–June 23, July 7–Oct. 27, Nov. 10–Dec. 1, 15–29, 1814; Jan. 5–Apr. 20, May 4–Aug. 3, 17–Dec. 6, 21, 1815; Jan. 4, 18, 25, Feb. 1, 15–June 6, 20–Oct. 17, 31–Dec. 12, 26, 1816; Jan. 9, Apr. 17, 1817.
N. Y. Hist. Soc. has Nov. 3, 1808; Jan. 5, 1809; Aug. 8, 1816.
Harvard has Dec. 11, 1806.
Pocumtuck Valley Mem. Lib., Deerfield, Mass., has Apr. 9, 1807.

Portsmouth Mercury, 1765–1767.

Weekly. Established Jan. 21, 1765, by Thomas Furber, with the title of "The Portsmouth Mercury, and Weekly Advertiser." With the issue of Apr. 8, 1765, Furber admitted Ezekiel Russell to partnership and the paper was published by Furber & Russell. The last issue located is that of Sept. 29, 1766, vol. 2, no. 89. Furber & Russell were printing at Portsmouth well into 1767. Timothy

NEW HAMPSHIRE 471

Alden's "Century Sermon," 1801, states that the newspaper was published from 1765 to 1767.

British Museum has Jan. 21–Dec. 16, 1765.
Mass. Hist. Soc. has Jan. 21, Mar. 18, July 15, Sept. 16, 23, Oct. 7–28, Nov. 18–Dec. 23, 1765; Jan. 20, Apr. 21, May 5, Sept. 1, 8, 1766.
Am. Antiq. Soc. has Jan. 21, Mar. 11, 1765; Feb. 17, 24, Mar. 24–Apr. 14, 28–May 19, June 2, 9, 30, Sept. 22, 29, 1766.
Yale has Sept. 2, 23, Oct. 7, 14, 28, Nov. 13–Dec. 2, 16–30, 1765; Jan. 27, Feb. 10, 17, 1766.
Univ. of Mich. (Clements) has Jan. 21, 1765.
Lib. Congress has Nov. 13, 1765, Extra; Sept. 8, 1766.
N. H. Hist. Soc. has Nov. 13, 1765, Extra.

[Portsmouth] **New-Hampshire Gazette**, 1756–1820+.

Weekly. Established Oct. 7, 1756, by Daniel Fowle, with the title of "The New-Hampshire Gazette." It was of quarto size, but was enlarged to folio with the issue of Jan. 7, 1757. With the issue of Mar. 11, 1763, the title was changed to "The New-Hampshire Gazette, and Historical Chronicle." With the issue of Sept. 7, 1764, Daniel admitted his nephew Robert L. Fowle to a share in the management, and the paper was printed by Daniel & Robert Fowle. With the issue of Apr. 23, 1773, it was printed by Daniel Fowle alone (Robert Fowle alludes to his withdrawal from the firm and his removal from the Colony, in "The New-Hampshire Gazette," of Exeter, for June 1, 1776). In the issue of June 9, 1775, Daniel Fowle "takes leave of his customers," and his name disappeared from the imprint. The issues of Oct. 3 and Oct. 17, 1775, were issued in shortened size with the abbreviated title of "The New-Hampshire Gazette." There was no issue for Oct. 24, 1775, and the issue of Nov. 2, 1775, was printed "with great difficulty" because of the threatened British attack on Portsmouth. In this issue it was stated that the printing press "is removed to Greenland, about six miles from Portsmouth." None of the Greenland issues bore any imprint. The issue of Dec. 5, 1775, states that the press "is now again removed from Greenland to Portsmouth," and the issue of Dec. 12 carries the Portsmouth imprint of D. Fowle. It was so published up to the issue of Jan. 9, 1776, no. 1001, in which issue was published a communication strongly attacking independency. The paper was presumably suspended with this issue, although Fowle in the "Freeman's Journal" of Dec. 24, 1776, states that he published the paper "till the beginning of February last." On Jan. 17, 1776, the New Hampshire House of Representatives "Voted that Daniel Fowle Esq' the Supposed Printer of said Paper be forthwith Sent for and ordered to Appear before this house and give an account of the Author of said Piece, and further to answer for his Printing said piece" (N. H. State Papers, vol. 8, p. 24).

On May 25, 1776, a paper was established at Portsmouth with the title of "The Freeman's Journal, or New-Hampshire Gazette," vol. 1, no. 1, printed by Benjamin Dearborn. It was later transferred to Daniel Fowle, who continued it under that title through the issue of June 9, 1778, vol. 2, no. 52. For an account of this paper, see under "Freeman's Journal."

On June 16, 1778, Daniel Fowle and his brother Zechariah began to print a paper for both Portsmouth and Exeter, the only difference being the imprint, which read Portsmouth, Printed by D. (or Daniel) Fowle, or Exeter, Printed by Z. (or Zechariah) Fowle. Sometimes the imprint was omitted, which makes it difficult to distinguish the issues. The paper was entitled "New-Hampshire Gazette. Or, State Journal, and General Advertiser." It bore no volume numbering. Beginning with July 21, 1778, vol. 1, no. 22, the Exeter issues started a volume numbering, and with Sept. 15, 1778, vol. 1, no. 30, the Portsmouth issues did likewise, but continuing the numbering begun by Zechariah Fowle for the "Exeter Journal." The last issue thus published for both towns was that of Feb. 16, 1779, vol. 1, no. 52. For the Exeter issues, see under "Exeter Journal."

The issue of Feb. 23, 1779, vol. 2, no. 53, entitled "New-Hampshire Gazette. Or, State Journal, and General Advertiser" was therefore published by D. Fowle solely for Portsmouth. This was continued until May 25, 1779, vol. 2, no. 66. On June 1, 1779, vol. 2, no. 67, the paper was apparently again printed for both Portsmouth and Exeter, without any imprint whatever (see also under "Exeter Journal"). With the issue of Oct. 5, 1779, a volume numbering was adopted, vol. 23, no. 2196, made to harmonize with the year of the establishment of the "New-Hampshire Gazette" in 1756, the volume being correct, but the numbering one thousand too much, as it should have been no. 1196. The issue of Jan. 15, 1780 was numbered 22010, instead of 2210, which error was not corrected until Apr. 15, 1780, no. 2225. With the issue of May 13, 1780, no. 1229, the error in the first figure was corrected and the numbering at last straightened out. The Portsmouth issues bore no imprint until Feb. 12, 1781, when it began to be given as "Portsmouth: Printed by Daniel Fowle." There were occasional slight changes in the punctuation of the title in 1779–1781, also abbreviations for want of space to "New-Hampshire Gazette." Throughout 1779–1781 there were frequent references to printing offices respectively at Portsmouth and at Exeter. For instance, the issue of Apr. 16, 1781, which was statedly printed at Portsmouth, referred to an advertisement which was to be "inserted in the New Hampshire Gazette, printed at Exeter." This double printing for Portsmouth and Exeter was given up in the issue of Sept. 3, 1781.

In the issue of Sept. 8, 1781, it is stated, "As there is but one Gazette to be printed in this State for the future, (by request of Authority) which 'tis probable will be in this town, it being thought most convenient for the Public in general: Therefore, those who have been customers previous to this notice, for the New-Hampshire Gazette printed at Exeter, or in Portsmouth, are most earnestly requested to make immediate payment at the respective Printing Offices." With this issue Fowle omitted his name from the imprint and changed the title to "The New-Hampshire Gazette, and General Advertiser." The paper was without printer's name until the issue of Aug. 28, 1784, when the name of Robert

Gerrish was given as printer. The issues of Sept. 4 to Dec. 10, 1784, carried no printer's name. The issue of Dec. 17, 1784, was printed and published by Daniel Fowle. It is probable that Fowle took Robert Gerrish into partnership during this period of 1781-1784. Fowle & Gerrish were paid by the State for printing by a vote of Jan. 15, 1782 (see "N. H. State Papers," vol. 8, p. 928). When Robert Gerrish established "The New-Hampshire Mercury" Dec. 24, 1784, he stated that he would publish that paper "in the manner and at the price he lately did the New-Hampshire Gazette."

With the issue of Dec. 24, 1784, the title was changed to "Fowle's New-Hampshire Gazette, and General Advertiser," printed by Melcher and Osborne [John Melcher and George Jerry Osborne, Jun.]. With the issue of Jan. 21, 1785, the New Hampshire seal was made part of the title, which included the word "The" before "General Advertiser." The printing firm was dissolved with the issue of Jan. 27, 1786, and the paper was published by John Melcher. Daniel Fowle retained the proprietorship of the paper up to the time of his death, which occurred June 8, 1787.

With the issue of June 9, 1787, the title of the paper was changed to "The New-Hampshire Gazette, and General Advertiser," the word "the" being inserted after "and" with the issue of June 16, 1787. With the issue of Apr. 16, 1793, the title was shortened to "The New Hampshire Gazette." With the issue of Feb. 9, 1802, Melcher sold the paper to Nathaniel S. & W[ashington] Peirce. With the issue of Apr. 24, 1804, Benjamin Hill was admitted to the firm, and the paper was published by Peirce, Hill & Peirce. With the issue of Mar. 26, 1805, the title was altered to "New-Hampshire Gazette." With the issue of Apr. 23, 1805, the firm was dissolved and the paper published by Peirce & Gardner [Nathaniel S. Peirce and Samuel Gardner]. This firm was dissolved on Apr. 17, 1809, and with the issue of Apr. 18, the imprint became "Published for the Proprietors," changed with the issue of May 23, 1809, to "Published for the Proprietor." With the issue of June 27, 1809, the paper was published by W[illiam] Weeks, who, with the issue of Dec. 14, 1813, transferred it to Beck & Foster [Gideon Beck and Daniel C. Foster]. It was so continued until after 1820.

Portsmouth Athenaeum has Oct. 7, 21, 1756–Dec. 28, 1764; Jan. 3, 1766–Dec. 29, 1769; Feb. 9, Mar. 2, 1770–Oct. 10, 1775; Sept. 21, 1779; July 22, 1780; Mar. 19, 1781–Dec. 21, 1782; Jan. 3, 1784–Dec. 28, 1819.

Mass. Hist. Soc. has Oct. 7, 1756–Jan. 9, 1776, fine file; June 16–Sept. 22, 1778; Feb. 2, Mar. 16, 23, May 25, June 8, 15, 29, Aug. 17, Oct. 5, 12, Nov. 23, 1779; Jan. 22, Sept. 30, Oct. 21, Nov. 27, 1780; Feb. 12, Mar. 19, 26, Apr. 23, June 11, Aug. 20, 27, Oct. 6, 20, 27–Nov. 10, 24, Dec. 8, 15, 1781; Jan. 5, 19, Mar. 16, 23, Apr. 13, June 1, Aug. 31, Oct. 5, Nov. 3, 10, Dec. 28, 1782; Jan. 11, Apr. 12, May 10, Aug. 30, Sept. 20, 1783; Mar. 27, 1784–Mar. 24, 1787; June 16, 23, 1787; June 26, 1788; Aug. 27, 1789; Sept. 30, 1790; Oct. 20, 27, 1791; Feb. 1, 8, Mar. 7–28, 1792; Jan. 9, May 28, July 23, Aug. 27, Sept. 3, 1799; Jan. 8, June 24, 1800.

N. H. Hist. Soc. has Nov. 18, 1757; May 26, Oct. 6, 13, Nov. 3, 1758; Feb. 23, Mar. 9, Aug. 17, Sept. 7, 1759; Jan. 11–25, May 23, July 4, 1760; Mar. 26, Dec. 24, 1762; Mar. 11, 1763; June 1, 1764; Jan. 4–July 19, Aug. 2, 23–Dec. 27, 1765; Mar. 14–Dec. 26, 1766; Jan. 23, Mar. 20, July 17, Oct. 16, Nov. 13, Dec. 18, 1767; Jan. 22, June 24, Aug. 5, Sept. 30, Oct. 14, 1768; June 2, Aug. 18, 1769; Jan. 5–June 22, July 6–Sept. 28, Nov. 23, Dec. 21, 1770; Feb. 1–15, Nov. 29, Dec. 13, 20, 1771; Jan. 3–Dec. 25, 1772, fair; Mar. 19, Aug. 20, 1773–May 26, 1775; July 4, 18, 25, Aug. 15, 29, Sept. 26, Nov. 2, 8, 1775; Jan. 9, 1776; June 16, 1778–Apr. 24, 1784, good; May 22, 1784; Jan. 7, 1785–Dec. 30, 1789, fair; Jan. 6, 1790–Dec. 26, 1820.

Am. Antiq. Soc. has Dec. 2, 1757; Apr. 13–28, June 16–Aug. 4, 25–Sept. 22, Oct. 13–Dec. 15, 1758; May 11, 1759; Jan. 9, Mar. 6, 20, May 8, July 31, Aug. 28, Sept. 4, Nov. 6, 27–Dec. 11, 25, 1761; Jan. 15–Apr. 30, May 14, 21, June 4, 18–Aug. 6, Oct. 1, 1762; Jan. 21–Mar. 4, 1763; Apr. 12, 19, June 28, July 12, Aug. 16, Oct. 18, 31, 1765; Apr. 14, May 1, 9, 22, June 13–27, July 11, 25–Aug. 22, Sept. 4–Dec. 26, 1766; Jan. 2–Apr. 17, May 8–22, June 5–Aug. 28, Oct. 2, 1767; Dec. 7, 1770; Jan. 4, Aug. 23, 1771; Aug. 7, 1772; Aug. 20, Sept. 10, 1773; Mar. 18, Apr. 29, May 6, 20, 27, June 17, July 8, 29, Sept. 9, 16, Oct. 14, 21, Nov. 11, Dec. 16, 1774; Jan. 20, Feb. 3, Mar. 24, Apr. 28, May 5, 26, June 2, July 11, 25, Aug. 15, 1775; July 14, Aug. 25, Sept. 2, 8, 22, Oct. 13–Nov. 17, 1778; May 25, Aug. 3–17, 31, Oct. 26, Nov. 9, 23, 1779; Mar. 4, 18, June 3, 1780–Dec. 28, 1782; Jan. 18, Feb. 1–22, Mar. 15–May 31, June 21–July 19, Aug. 2, 23, 30, Sept. 27–Nov. 8, 22, Dec. 20, 1783; Jan. 3–17, Feb. 7–Mar. 20, Apr. 3–July 31, Aug. 21, Oct. 9, Nov. 4, 11, Dec. 10, 1784; Jan. 7, Feb. 25, Mar. 4, 18, 25, Apr. 22, 29, May 20, 27, June 10, July 1, 8, 29, Aug. 12–26, Sept. 23, Oct. 14, 28, Nov. 11, 18, Dec. 23, 30, 1785; Jan. 13–Feb. 18, Mar. 4–June 1, 15, 29–July 27, Aug. 10–Nov. 11, Dec. 2, 16–30, 1786; Jan. 6–20, Feb. 3, 17–Mar. 3, 17, 24, Apr. 7–21, May 5–June 9, 23, July 7–Aug. 4, 18–Sept. 15, Oct. 13–Nov. 16, Dec. 12, 1787; Jan. 16, 23, Feb. 6–Mar. 19, Apr. 2, 9, 23, May 15, 22, June 5, 19–July 31, Aug. 14, 28, Sept. 4, 18, Oct. 2, 9, 30, Nov. 6, 27–Dec. 17, 31, 1788; Jan. 7, 21, Feb. 4, 18, 25, Mar. 18–Apr. 1, 22–May 28, June 11, 25, July 30, Aug. 27–Sept. 24, Oct. 8, 29, Nov. 11, Dec. 2–30, 1789; Jan. 6, 1790–Dec. 28, 1793, fair; Jan. 4, 1794–Dec. 29, 1812; Jan. 5–Feb. 9, Mar. 2–30, Apr. 13, 27, May 18–June 1, 15–Aug. 31, Sept. 14, Oct. 5–26, Nov. 9–Dec. 28, 1813; Jan. 4, 1814–Dec. 26, 1820.

Lib. Congress has Oct. 19–Nov. 16, Dec. 7–29, 1759; Jan. 4–Mar. 7, Apr. 3–25, May 30–June 13, July 11–Aug. 29, Sept. 12, 1760; July 15, Aug. 20, Sept. 17, 1762; Mar. 4, Aug. 12, Nov. 4, 18, Dec. 2, 16, 1763; Feb. 3, Mar. 16–Sept. 14, 1764; Oct. 4, 1765; Jan. 10, 17, Mar. 28–June 20, July 4–Sept. 5, 19–Oct. 3, 17–Dec. 19, 1766; Jan. 30, Feb. 6, Apr. 10, May 8, Nov. 27, 1767; Jan. 1, 1768–June 9, 1775, fair; Dec. 5, 1775; Apr. 6, Aug. 17, 1779; May 13, June 24, July 1–Aug. 5, 26, Sept. 9, 23, 30, Oct. 14, 1780; Jan. 1, 1781–Dec. 27, 1783, fair; Mar. 27, 1784; Jan. 21, Feb. 4, 11, 25–

NEW HAMPSHIRE 475

Mar. 11, July 8, 29–Aug. 19, Sept. 2, 16, 23, Oct. 14, 28, 1785; Jan. 6, Oct. 5, 1786; Jan. 27, Feb. 3, 24, Mar. 24, June 2–16, July 14, Aug. 18, Sept. 1, 22, Oct. 6–27, Nov. 9–21, Dec. 5–26, 1787; Jan. 2, 9, 23–Mar. 19, 26, July 3, Aug. 21, 1788; Feb. 11, Apr. 29, May 6, June 11, Aug. 6, Sept. 3, 17, 24, Oct. 8, 15, 29–Dec. 30, 1789; Jan. 6, 13, 27, Feb. 10, Mar. 17, 31–July 29, Aug. 12–Dec. 18, 1790; Jan. 15, Mar. 12–Apr. 16, 30–July 7, 21–Sept. 22, Oct. 6–27, Nov. 30–Dec. 28, 1791; Jan. 4, Feb. 1–Nov. 1, 21–Dec. 26, 1792; Feb. 27, Mar. 13, 19, Apr. 2–30, May 14, 21, June 4, 11, 25–July 9, 23, Aug. 6, 20, Oct. 22–Nov. 5, 30, Dec. 28, 1793; Jan. 11, Feb. 1, 15, 1794; Feb. 10, Mar. 24–June 30, July 14–Oct. 27, Nov. 10–Dec. 15, 1795; Jan. 2, 1796–Dec. 19, 1798, fair; Jan. 2, 9, 30, Feb. 13–Mar. 13, Apr. 3, 10, 23, May 7–June 11, 25, July 9–23, Aug. 6, 20, Sept. 3–17, Oct. 1, 8, 23, Nov. 6– 20, Dec. 4, 1799; Jan. 29–Feb. 12, 26, Mar. 12–26, Apr. 16–29, May 20– June 3, 17, 24, July 15, 22, Aug. 5–19, Sept. 2, 30, Oct. 21, 28, Nov. 11–25, Dec. 16, 1800; Jan. 6–Dec. 22, 1801; Jan. 19, Feb. 9–23, Mar. 16, 30– Apr. 13, Sept. 14, 21, Oct. 12, 19, Nov. 2–23, Dec. 7, 21, 28, 1802; Jan. 25, Feb. 8, 15, Mar. 8, Apr. 12, 19, May 31, July 19, Aug. 2, 16, 1803; Feb. 21, 1804–Dec. 29, 1807; Mar. 22, May 3, 17–31, June 14, 28, July 12, Aug. 16– Sept. 6, Oct. 11, 1808; Jan. 3, 1809–Dec. 24, 1811; Jan. 7–Apr. 7, July 7, Aug. 13, Sept. 1–Oct. 13, 27–Dec. 29, 1812; Jan. 5, 1813–Dec. 26, 1820, fair.
Dartmouth has June 15, 1759 (Postscript); Dec. 25, 1761; Jan. 15, 1762; Oct. 25, 1765; Aug. 12, 1768; May 22, 1772; Feb. 4, July 22, 1774; Apr. 21, Dec. 12, 1775; June 14, July 26, Sept. 27, 1777; Jan. 20, 1778; Aug. 5, 1780; Jan. 29–Dec. 29, 1781, fair; Feb. 9, 16, Mar. 2–23, Apr. 6, 20, 27, May 11, 25, June 1, Sept. 21, 1782; June 14, 1783; Jan. 3, 10, Feb. 21, May 8, Oct. 21, Dec. 10, 24, 31, 1784; Jan. 7, 1785–Dec. 29, 1795, fair; Jan. 2, 1796–Dec. 29, 1801; Jan. 12, 1802–Dec. 26, 1820, fair.
N. Y. Hist. Soc. has Aug. 4, 18, 1758; Jan. 2–23, Feb. 6–20, Mar. 6, Apr. 3, 24, May 1, 15, 22, June 5–26, July 10, 17, Aug. 28–Sept. 11, 25, Oct. 9, 30, Nov. 20–Dec. 4, 1767; Jan. 22, Apr. 22, 1768; Feb. 16, 23, Apr. 20, June 1, 1770; Jan. 25, Feb. 1, 15, Apr. 12, Oct. 4, 1771–Aug. 15, 1775; Nov. 2, 8, 1775; Jan. 9, 1776; June 16, 1778–Dec. 25, 1779; Jan. 1, 22–Feb. 5, 19, Mar. 4–Apr. 22, May 6–20, June 10, 17, July 29, Aug. 5, Sept. 9, 1780; Feb. 5– 19, Apr. 9, 16, May 7–June 25, July 9–23, Aug. 6, 11, 25–Nov. 3, Dec. 8, 1781; Jan. 5, 1782–Dec. 20, 1783, fair; Jan. 10–24, Feb. 14, June 5, 19, Oct. 21, Nov. 18, Dec. 3, 1784; Feb. 18, Mar. 25–Apr. 22, May 13–27, June 10, July 1–Aug. 26, Sept. 16–Oct. 14, 28–Nov. 18, Dec. 16, 30, 1785; Jan. 13, 27–Feb. 25, Mar. 11–Apr. 27, May 11, 25, June 15, 29, July 13–27, Aug. 10, 31, Sept. 14, 21, Dec. 9–30, 1786; Feb. 3, Mar. 24, Apr. 14, Aug. 25, Dec. 12, 26, 1787; June 26, 1788; May 21, Oct. 22, Dec. 9, 16, 1789; May 12, Oct. 21, 1790; Mar. 26, Sept. 22, Oct. 20, 1791; Apr. 25, July 19, Nov. 1, 1792; Sept. 10–Dec. 28, 1793; Jan. 4, Mar. 1, 1794–Dec. 29, 1795; Apr. 9, 1796; Dec. 21, 1797; Apr. 11, July 3, 1798; Sept. 1, 1801; Feb. 16, May 11, June 22, July 13, 20, Oct. 19, Nov. 30, Dec. 28, 1802; Jan. 11, 18, Apr. 26,

May 10, 24–June 7, 21–July 26, Aug. 16, 30, Nov. 29, 1803; Feb. 28, Mar. 6, 29, July 10, 17, Sept. 18, 1804; Jan. 1, 15, 29, Feb. 12, Mar. 19, May 7, June 11, 25, July 2, 23, Nov. 5, Dec. 10–24, 1805; Mar. 25, Sept. 23, Nov. 18, Dec. 30, 1806; Mar. 3, Apr. 7, 1807; Jan. 12, Oct. 11, 1808; Jan. 24, 1809; May 5, 12, June 2, 16, 23, July 14, Aug. 11, 1812; May 11, Dec. 14–28, 1813; Jan. 4, 1814–Dec. 26, 1820.

Boston Athenæum has May 15, Aug. 14, 1772; May 20, Oct. 21, Dec. 9, 1774; Jan. 13, 20, Feb. 3–17, Apr. 14, July 18, 25–Aug. 15, Sept. 12, 26, Nov. 8, 1775; Jan. 9, 1776; Jan. 4, 1783–Jan. 10, 1784; Dec. 10, 1784–Aug. 17, 1786, fair; Oct. 26, Nov. 11, Dec. 16, 1786; Feb. 24, Mar. 31, Apr. 25, June 30, July 28, Sept. 8, Nov. 28, Dec. 26, 1787; Jan. 2–Dec. 24, 1788; Mar. 18, 1789; Feb. 24, 1790–Sept. 27, 1792; Oct. 11, 25, 31, Nov. 21, Dec. 12, 1792; Feb. 6, Apr. 9, June 11, Sept. 24, Dec. 7–28, 1793; Jan. 4, Feb. 1, 1794–Dec. 26, 1820.

Harvard has July 4, 1766; Sept. 3, 1789–Jan. 29, 1791; June 16, 23, July 28, 1791; May 17, 1792; Feb. 17, 24, Mar. 10, Apr. 7, June 16, July 28, 1795; Jan. 2, Feb. 27, Apr. 2, 23, May 28, June 25, July 9, 23, 30, Aug. 27, Sept. 3, 17, 24, Oct. 8, 22, Nov. 12, 26, Dec. 3–17, 31, 1796; Jan. 7–Feb. 25, Mar. 11–25, Apr. 8, 22, June 13, Aug. 22, Oct. 25, Nov. 1, 8, 22, 29, Dec. 13, 20, 1797; Jan. 10, 17, Feb. 14, Mar. 28, Apr. 18, May 8, 15, June 19, July 3, 10, 24, Sept. 18, Nov. 7, 1798; Mar. 13, Aug. 13, Oct. 16, 1799; Feb. 12, 1800–Dec. 1, 1807, fair; June 28, Aug. 2, 9, 23, Sept. 20, Nov. 22, 29, Dec. 20, 1808; Dec. 4, 1810–Nov. 24, 1812.

Yale has Sept. 5, 1760; May 24, July 12, Aug. 16–Sept. 27, Oct. 11–Nov. 15, 29, Dec. 13–27, 1765; Jan. 17–Feb. 7, 21, Mar. 14, 28, Apr. 4, Sept. 4, Nov. 7, 14, 1766; Feb. 2, 1779; May 28, 1796; Jan. 3, 31, Mar. 7, 1798; June 18, Dec. 28, 1799; Jan. 1–Dec. 30, 1800; Apr. 6, 1802; Jan. 25, 1803–May 6, 1806; Jan. 20, 1807–Sept. 12, 1809, scattering file; Jan. 14, 28, 1812.

N. Y. State Lib. has May 16, 1766; June 10, 1774; June 1, 1779; May 14, 21, July 2, 1793; July 15, 1794; May 21, June 25, July 2, Aug. 6, 13, Sept. 3, 10, 24, Oct. 8–22, Nov. 19–Dec. 3, 1796; Jan. 14–Dec. 21, 1797, fair; Jan. 3, 1798–Dec. 4, 1799; Jan. 17, 31, Apr. 10, May 15, 22, June 19, July 24, Sept. 4, 25, Oct. 16, Nov. 20, Dec. 18, 1804; Jan. 22, 1805–Dec. 23, 1806, fair; Mar. 17, 24, Oct. 20, 27, Dec. 22, 29, 1807; Jan. 5–Dec. 27, 1808; Jan. 24, Mar. 21, Apr. 11–Nov. 21, 1809; Jan. 23, Sept. 25, 1810; Mar. 19, June 4, Nov. 12, Dec. 24, 31, 1811; Jan. 7, 1812; Jan. 19, 26, 1813; Jan. 5, 1819–Dec. 26, 1820.

N. Y. Pub. Lib. has Dec. 10–24, 1756; May 16, June 30, Aug. 8, Nov. 7, 14, 1766; Mar. 16, June 8, Nov. 9, 1770; Oct. 18, 1771; Feb. 3, 1778; Aug. 3, 1779; July 16, 1781; June 21–July 5, 1783; Sept. 2–30, Nov. 4, 1785; Oct. 27, 1787; Jan. 30, Feb. 6, Mar. 5, Apr. 9, 16, 30, May 29, July 31, Sept. 18, Oct. 30, 1788; Apr. 29, Oct. 29, 1789; Feb. 10–Dec. 29, 1795, fair; Jan. 7, 1797–Dec. 15, 1801, scattering file; Jan. 31, Apr. 11, 1809; Nov. 12, Dec. 31, 1816.

Wis. Hist. Soc. has Oct. 13, 1758; Apr. 10, June 5, July 10, 1761; Apr. 19, June 1, Aug. 24, Sept. 21, 1764; Nov. 30, Dec. 28, 1770; June 5, 1772; Apr.

22, 29, Sept. 16, 30, Oct. 14, 21, Nov. 11–25, 1774; May 8, Sept. 11, 1784–Nov. 2, 1786; Jan. 27, Apr. 7, July 14, Dec. 1, 1795; Nov. 19, 1796; Dec. 15, 1818.
Univ. of Chicago has Feb. 20, Apr. 9, 1796–July 10, Aug. 28, 1798.
Univ. of Mich. (Clements) has Mar. 16, 1759; Mar. 28, Oct. 24, Nov. 7, 14, Dec. 26, 1760; Jan. 2, 9, July 31, Sept. 18, 1761; Jan. 1, Aug. 7, 1762; Mar. 11, 1763; Feb. 3, May 4, Aug. 17, 31, 1764; Mar. 15, June 7, 1765; May 22, 1766; Jan. 2–23, Mar. 13, 20, Oct. 2, 31, Dec. 24, 1767; Jan. 1, 1768.
Boston Pub. Lib. has Feb. 5, Mar. 5, 12, July 2, 1762; Jan. 7, 1763; Sept. 23, 1774; Oct. 19, 1779; Apr. 9, 1781; Sept. 24, Oct. 1, 1789; Nov. 13, 1790; July 21, 1791; Apr. 26, May 3, 1794; Mar. 20, 1799; Aug. 14, 1804; Nov. 10, 1807; May 12, 1812; Sept. 13, 1814; Oct. 21, 1817.
Essex Inst. has Oct. 2, 1761; Apr. 19, 1765; Mar. 24, Sept. 5, 1775; Dec. 1, 1781; Aug. 7, 1784.
Phil. Lib. Co. has Oct. 18, Nov. 15, 1765; Oct. 15, 1793; July 23, 30, 1796.
Rutgers Univ. has Dec. 20, 1808–Dec. 26, 1809.
Newberry Lib. has Dec. 10, 1816–Dec. 29, 1818, fair.
Several libraries have single or a few scattering issues.

[Portsmouth] **New-Hampshire Mercury**, 1784–1788.

Weekly. Established Dec. 24, 1784, by Robert Gerrish, with the title of "The New-Hampshire Mercury, and General Advertiser." With the issue of Feb. 24, 1785, there was a change in the set-up of the title, and the word "The" was inserted before "General." This was henceforth the title except for the issues of Mar. 1, and Oct. 18, 1786, which were of smaller size because of shortage of paper, and bore the abbreviated title of "The New-Hampshire Mercury." The last issue located is that of Mar. 12, 1788, vol. 4, no. 167.

Am. Antiq. Soc. has Dec. 24, 1784–Mar. 12, 1788.
N. H. Hist. Soc. has Dec. 24, 31, 1784; Jan. 7, 21–Feb. 16, Mar. 2–Apr. 12, 26, May 17, 31, June 7–July 5, 19, 26, Aug. 9–Oct. 4, 18–Dec. 27, 1785; Jan. 3–Feb. 22, Mar. 8–22, Apr. 5, 19, 26, May 17–June 7, 21–July 26, Aug. 16, 23, Sept. 6–Oct. 25, Nov. 22–Dec. 6, 20, 27, 1786; Jan. 10, 17, 31–Mar. 7, 28–Apr. 18, May 10, June 7, 14, July 5, 12, Aug. 2–Sept. 13, Oct. 4, 11, 25, Nov. 9–23, Dec. 4–18, 1787; Jan. 2, 23–Feb. 6, 27, 1788.
N. Y. Pub. Lib. has Jan. 14–25, Feb. 8–Apr. 12, May 3–24, June 7–Oct. 11, 25–Dec. 20, 1785; Jan. 10–Feb. 15, Mar. 1–May 17, 31–Dec. 27, 1786; Jan. 10–Mar. 28, 1787.
Boston Athenæum has Mar. 29, May 24, June 7–21, July 12, Aug. 30, Oct. 4, Nov. 1, 1785; Jan. 10, Feb. 1, 15, Mar. 1, 15, Apr. 19, May 31, July 26–Aug. 9, 30, Sept. 6, 20–Oct. 4, Nov. 15, 29, Dec. 6, 1786; Feb. 7–21, Mar. 14, 21, Apr. 25, May 10–24, June 21–July 5, 19–Sept. 6, Oct. 18, 1787.
Mass. Hist. Soc. has Jan. 7, Feb. 24–Mar. 8, 22–Apr. 12, 26–Sept. 27, Oct. 18–

Nov. 8, 29–Dec. 27, 1785; Feb. 8–Mar. 8, 29, Apr. 12–May 3, 24, June 14, 21, July 12–Sept. 6, Oct. 25–Nov. 22, 1786; Jan. 3–Feb. 7, 1787.
Lib. Congress has Dec. 31, 1784; Mar. 2–29, Apr. 26, May 3, June 7–21, Sept. 20, 1785; Jan. 3, Feb. 1, 8, 22, Mar. 8, 15, Aug. 9, 30, Sept. 20, 27, Nov. 1, 29, Dec. 20, 27, 1786; Feb. 7–28, Mar. 21, 28, Apr. 18, 25, May 31, July 5, Aug. 9, Oct. 4, Dec. 26, 1787; Jan. 30, Feb. 20, 27, 1788.
Me. Hist. Soc. has May 17, July 12, 1785; Mar. 7, 1787.
Univ. of Ill. has Dec. 13, 27, 1786; May 24, 1787.
N. Y. Hist. Soc. has Mar. 22, 1785; Apr. 5, 1786.
Essex Inst. has Jan. 14, 1785.
Boston Pub. Lib. has Sept. 13, 1785.
Dartmouth has Dec. 13, 20, 1785; May 3, 1786.
Harvard has Aug. 2, 1786.

[Portsmouth] **New-Hampshire Spy,** 1786–1793.

Semi-weekly and weekly. Established Oct. 24, 1786, by George Jerry Osborne, Jun., with the title of "New-Hampshire Spy." The paper was of small folio size, published semi-weekly and the pages were numbered. With the issue of Jan. 23, 1787, the title was slightly changed to "The New-Hampshire Spy." With the issue of Mar. 6, 1789, the title was changed to "Osborne's New-Hampshire Spy." With the issue of Nov. 12, 1791, George admitted John Osborne to partnership, and the paper was published by George and John Osborne, and the title changed to "Osbornes' New-Hampshire Spy." With the issue of May 30, 1792, the partnership was dissolved and the paper published by John Osborne, and the title reverted to "Osborne's New-Hampshire Spy." With the issue of Sept. 1, 1792, the size of the paper was enlarged, publication was changed to weekly and the spelling of the title was slightly changed to "Osborne's Newhampshire Spy." The paper was discontinued with the issue of Mar. 2, 1793, vol. 13, no. 12.

Lib. Congress has Oct. 24, 1786–Dec. 25, 1787; Jan. 1, 4, 15, 22, 25, Mar. 7, 14–25, Apr. 1, 4, 11–May 2, 10–June 14, 21–Sept. 23, 30–Nov. 7, 14–Dec. 9, 16–30, 1788; Jan. 13, Feb. 3, 10, 14, Apr. 17, 24, May 4, 23, 1789; Sept. 1, 1790; June 4, July 27, Aug. 31, Sept. 10–28, Oct. 5–12, 29, Nov. 2, 9–16, 23–30, Dec. 17, 21, 28, 1791; Jan. 14, 23, Feb. 1, 11–29, Mar. 7, 14–22, 28, 31, Apr. 11, 14, 21, 25, May 2–9, 19, 30, June 2, 13, 20, 23, July 25, Aug. 1, 4, 11, 18, Nov. 24, 1792; Jan. 5, Feb. 9, Mar. 2, 1793.
Am. Antiq. Soc. has Nov. 10, 14, Dec. 19, 1786; Jan. 2–Apr. 20, May 5, June 12, 26, July 3, 7, 17, 21, Aug. 14, Sept. 11, 29, Oct. 2, 9–Nov. 6, 13–23, 30, Dec. 7, 15, 1787; Jan. 1, 8, 15, 18, Feb. 1, 8–15, 22–Mar. 4, 11, 18–Apr. 8, 22, 29, May 10, 17, 27, June 7, 14, 17, 24, 28, July 5, 12, 22, Aug. 2, 12–19, Sept. 2, 6, 13, 20, 27, Oct. 4–18, 28–Nov. 11, 18–Dec. 5, 12, 16, 23, 26, 1788; Jan. 6–Feb. 3, 10–20, 27, Mar. 6–June 16, 23–30, July 7, 11, 25, Aug. 1–11, 18, 29–Sept. 5, 12–19, 29, Oct. 6, 10, 20, 31, Nov. 13, 20–Dec. 1, 25, 1789; Jan. 23, 27, Feb. 3, 10–24, Mar. 3–17, Apr. 3, 7, 14, 21, 28, May 5–22, 29–

June 12, 19, 26, 30, July 7, 14, 28, Aug. 4–11, 18, 25, Sept. 1, 15, 22–Nov. 6, 13, 24, Dec. 1–8, 15, 22, 1790; Jan. 1, 5, 12–19, Feb. 9, 19, Mar. 5, 16, 19, 30, Apr. 6, 9, 20, May 4, 11, 14, 25, June 1, 8–15, July 13, 16, 23, 27, Aug. 3–13, 20, 31, Sept. 7, 14, 21, Oct. 1, 8, 19, 22, 29, Nov. 30, 1791; Jan. 14, 18, Feb. 4, 11–22, 29, Mar. 3, 10, 17–24, 31, Apr. 7–14, 21–28, May 5, 16, 23–June 2, 20, 27, 30, July 10, 14, 25–Aug. 4, 11, 22, 25, Sept. 8, 29–Oct. 13, 27, Nov. 10, 17, Dec. 1, 29, 1792; Jan. 5, Feb. 16, 1793.

N. Y. Hist. Soc. has Jan. 2, 1788–Mar. 2, 1793, fair.

N. H. Hist. Soc. has Apr. 20, 24, June 19, 23, 1787; July 22, Nov. 21, 25, Dec. 26, 1788; Jan. 6–Dec. 18, 1789, fair; Jan. 1, Feb. 6, Mar. 3–17, 27–Apr. 3, May 5, 8, 15, 19, June 9–23, July 7, 14, 24–31, Aug. 7–14, 25, 28, Sept. 4–22, Oct. 27, Dec. 1, 29, 1790; Jan. 12, 19–30, Feb. 5–16, 23, 26, Mar. 5, 16–23, 30, Apr. 2, 9–16, 23, 30–May 14, 21, 28–June 11, 22, 29, July 27, Aug. 3–Dec. 31, 1791; Jan. 4–21, 28–June 13, 20–July 10, 18–Aug. 18, 25, Sept. 1, 8, 22, 29, Oct. 13, Nov. 3–17, Dec. 1–29, 1792; Jan. 12, Feb. 16–Mar. 2, 1793.

Wis. Hist. Soc. has Oct. 27, 1786–Oct. 2, 1787; Dec. 4, 1787.

Dartmouth has Nov. 7, 14, 1786; Jan. 12–Feb. 2, 9, 27–Mar. 13, 20, 23, Apr. 20, 1787; Jan. 15, 18, 25, Feb. 5, 11, May 10–17, 27–June 7, 28, July 5, 12, 15, 22, Aug. 5, Oct. 14, Nov. 18–28, Dec. 5, 12, 16, 1788; Feb. 14, 17, 24, Mar. 27–Apr. 17, May 26, June 6–23, July 11–18, 25–Aug. 18, 1789; May 1, 8, 22, June 2, 16, 23–July 28, Aug. 4, 11, Sept. 18, Oct. 23, Dec. 1–8, 1790; Feb. 26, Apr. 16–Aug. 31, Oct. 29, Nov. 5, 26–Dec. 3, 10, 14, 21, 1791; Apr. 4, 11, 14, May 16, July 21, 28–Aug. 8, 15, 1792.

Harvard has Jan. 2, 19–30, Feb. 6, 20, Mar. 2, 6, 30, Apr. 10–17, May 1, June 9, 30, July 3, 14, Aug. 18–25, Nov. 9–30, Dec. 7–18, 28, 1787; Jan. 1, 4, 11–18, 25, Feb. 15, 22, Mar. 11, 18–Apr. 11, 22–May 6, 13, 24, June 7, 17, 24, 28, July 22, Aug. 9–19, 1788.

Mass. Hist. Soc. has Jan. 5, 30, Feb. 6, 23, 1787; June 24, 28, 1788; Feb. 11, Mar. 10, 24, 28, 1792.

Boston Athenæum has Aug. 16, Oct. 25, Nov. 1, 4, Dec. 12, 1788; Jan. 6, May 1, June 27, Sept. 8, 1789; Jan. 6, Feb. 3, 24, Mar. 24, May 1, 29, June 9, 26, 30, Aug. 25, 1790; Jan. 1, Feb. 9, Mar. 23, May 4, July 30, Aug. 24, 27, Sept. 3, Dec. 21–28, 1791; Feb. 25, May 9, June 23, Aug. 8, 1792.

N. Y. Pub. Lib. has Oct. 27–Dec. 29, 1786; Apr. 6, 1787; Nov. 1, 1788; May 9, 1789; Mar. 17, 31, 1792; Jan. 5, 1793.

N. Y. State Lib. has Oct. 21, 1788; Aug. 3–27, Oct. 8, 1791.

Boston Pub. Lib. has Nov. 20, 1787; Feb. 22, Mar. 28, 1788; Mar. 16, Aug. 10, 1791.

Univ. of Mich. (Clements) has Feb. 18, 1792.

Portsmouth Oracle, 1803–1820+.

Weekly. A continuation, without change of numbering, of the "United States Oracle, and Portsmouth Advertiser," the first issue with the title of "Portsmouth

Oracle" being that of Oct. 22, 1803, vol. 14, no. 3, published on Saturday by William & Daniel Treadwell. For the country edition of the paper, published on Tuesday, see under "Oracle Post." With the issue of Oct. 19, 1805, the Treadwells sold out the paper to Samuel Larkin, and it was printed by William Treadwell, for the Proprietor. With the issue of May 3, 1806, William Treadwell purchased the paper from Larkin, and it was published by William Treadwell. With the issue of Sept. 25, 1813, the paper was purchased and published by Charles Turell. With the issue of Jan. 6, 1816, the title was altered to "The Portsmouth Oracle." It was so continued until after 1820.

N. H. Hist. Soc. has Oct. 22, 1803–Dec. 30, 1820.

Boston Athenæum has Dec. 10, 1803; Jan. 7, 1804–Dec. 30, 1820.

Mass. Hist. Soc. has Oct. 22, 1803–Dec. 29, 1804; Feb. 9, July 6, Sept. 21, Nov. 30, Dec. 21, 1805; Jan. 4, 1806–Dec. 30, 1820.

Dartmouth has Oct. 29, Nov. 8–Dec. 31, 1803; Jan. 7–Nov. 10, 24, Dec. 1, 22, 1804; Feb. 23, Mar. 23, Apr. 20, May 4, 25–Dec. 21, 1805; May 17, 1806–Dec. 31, 1814, fair; Jan. 7, 1815–Dec. 30, 1820.

Am. Antiq. Soc. has Dec. 10, 1803–Dec. 28, 1805; Jan. 4–May 10, June 14, July 19, 26, Oct. 4, 25, Nov. 1, 22, Dec. 13, 27, 1806; Jan. 17, Feb. 7, Mar. 7, 28, Apr. 11, May 2, 9, June 20, Sept. 5, 19, Oct. 3–Nov. 7, 21–Dec. 26, 1807; Jan. 2, 1808–Dec. 15, 1810; Mar. 9, 23, Apr. 20, May 25, June 15, 29, Aug. 3, 17, Oct. 19, Nov. 30, 1811; Jan. 4, 1812–Dec. 25, 1813; Jan. 1, 1814–Dec. 21, 1816, fair; Feb. 1, Mar. 29, Apr. 12, 26, May 10, July 19, 26, Aug. 30, Sept. 6, 27, Nov. 22, Dec. 13, 27, 1817; Jan. 3, 1818–Dec. 25, 1819, fair; Jan. 29, May 13, 20, Dec. 2, 9, 1820.

Lib. Congress has Dec. 10, 1803; Mar. 17, July 21, 1804; Jan. 5, 1805–Oct. 5, 1811; Jan. 4, 1812–Dec. 30, 1815; Jan. 13, 27, Feb. 10, Mar. 9, May 11, June 8–22, July 6, Aug. 3–17, 31, Sept. 21, 28, Oct. 12, 26, Nov. 9, 16, 30, Dec. 21, 1816; Feb. 15–Mar. 22, Apr. 5–19, May 10, 17, June 21–Aug. 9, Nov. 15, 1817; Jan. 10–24, Feb. 14, Mar. 7, May 16, Aug. 1–15, Oct. 24, 1818; July 17, 1819–Dec. 30, 1820.

N. Y. Hist. Soc. has Oct. 22, 1803–Jan. 14, 1809; Sept. 25, 1813–Dec. 31, 1814; Jan. 17, Mar. 7, 1818.

Yale has Oct. 22, 1803; Jan. 14, Feb. 25, 1804–Dec. 30, 1809.

York Inst., Saco, has Feb. 28, 1807–Dec. 26, 1812, Mar. 27, 1813–Dec. 27, 1817.

Harvard has Oct. 22, 1803–Dec. 5, 1807, fair; June 18, Aug. 6–27, Sept. 17–Oct. 1, 29, Nov. 5, 19–Dec. 10, 24, 1808.

Essex Inst. has Oct. 14, 1809; Dec. 24, 1814; Jan. 7–Dec. 30, 1815; Apr. 6–20, 1816; Jan. 4–Dec. 27, 1817; Jan. 2, 1819–Dec. 30, 1820.

N. Y. State Lib. has Nov. 26, Dec. 3, 1803; Jan. 14, 21, Mar. 10, 24, July 7, 21, Aug. 4, 25, Sept. 8, 22, 1804; Mar. 2, 16, 23, June 29–Aug. 31, Oct. 5, Nov. 2–23, Dec. 7, 1805; Feb. 22–Apr. 12, June 14, July 12, Oct. 11, Nov. 15, 1806; Feb. 7, Mar. 7, May 2, Sept. 19, Nov. 21–Dec. 5, 1807; Feb. 27, Aug. 27–Dec. 31, 1808; Jan. 7, Feb. 4–May 20, June 3–17, July 1, Dec. 29, 1809; Jan. 13, 27, Feb. 17–Mar. 3, 17–June 9, Dec. 1, 1810.

Boston Pub. Lib. has Oct. 19, 1811; July 17, 31, Oct. 2, Nov. 6, 1813; Mar. 12, Aug. 16, 1814; July 8, 29, Sept. 30–Oct. 21, Nov. 4–Dec. 2, 1815; Jan. 27– Feb. 10, 24–Mar. 9, 23, June 8, 15, 29–Aug. 17, Sept. 7, Nov. 23, Dec. 14, 21, 1816; Jan. 4–25, Feb. 8–Mar. 29, Apr. 12, May 3, 31, June 7, July 19, 26, Sept. 5, 27, Oct. 18, 25, Nov. 8–29, 1817; Jan. 10, Mar. 7, 21, May 23, June 6, 27–July 11, Aug. 8, 22, Oct. 10, Dec. 5, 1818; Jan. 2, 30, Feb. 13– Mar. 20, Apr. 17, 24, May 8, 15, 29–July 24, Aug. 7, 21–Sept. 18, Nov. 20, 27, Dec. 11, 18, 1819; Mar. 11, 18, Apr. 22–May 6, 20, June 3, 10, 24, Aug. 5, Nov. 4, 1820.

Me. Hist. Soc. has Feb. 3–Dec. 29, 1810; Feb. 2, 1811–Dec. 26, 1812, fair.

Portland Pub. Lib. has Oct. 10, 1807–Aug. 12, 1809.

Duke Univ. has Feb. 27, Mar. 19, May 7, 14, June 11, July 30, 1808–Sept. 15, 1810, fair; Feb. 5, 1814; Feb. 4, Aug. 5, 1815.

N. Y. Pub. Lib. has Dec. 3, 1803; Dec. 19, 1807; Jan. 18, Apr. 25, May 9, 1812; Sept. 4, 1813; Feb. 12, 1814; Jan. 21, 1815; Jan. 13, Dec. 28, 1816; Feb. 8, May 3, 1817; Sept. 19, 1818; Jan. 2–Dec. 25, 1819.

Univ. of Mich. (Clements) has Aug. 11, Nov. 17, 1810; Aug. 3, 1811; Feb. 15– Dec. 26, 1812, fair; Mar. 20, Apr. 10, May 29, Sept. 4, Oct. 9, Nov. 6, 1813; June 25, 1814; Jan. 21, Feb. 4, 25, Sept. 23, 1815; Jan. 6, Sept. 21, Oct. 5, 1816; Jan. 25, Mar. 15, 29, 1817; Feb. 7, 28, Mar. 21, 1818; Sept. 18, 25, Dec. 11, 1819; May 20, Oct. 21, 1820.

[Portsmouth] Oracle of New-Hampshire, 1817.

Weekly. Established May 22, 1817, by Samuel Whidden, with the title of "The Oracle of New-Hampshire." The paper was issued without any volume numbering. The last issue located is that of Sept. 11, 1817.

N. H. Hist. Soc. has May 22–Sept. 11, 1817.
Boston Athenæum has June 5–26, 1817.

[Portsmouth] Oracle of the Day, 1793–1799.

Semi-weekly and weekly. Established June 4, 1793, by Charles Peirce, with the title of "The Oracle of the Day," published semi-weekly. With the issue of Jan. 2, 1796, the size of the sheet was enlarged and the paper was published weekly. The last issue with this title was that of Dec. 28, 1799, vol. 10, no. 11, after which the title was altered to "The United States Oracle of the Day," which see.

N. H. Hist. Soc. has June 4, 1793–Dec. 28, 1799.
Am. Antiq. Soc. has June 22, July 16, 23–Aug. 6, 13–20, Oct. 1, 1793; Jan. 8, Feb. 12, Mar. 19, 1794–Dec. 28, 1799.
Dartmouth has May 3, 1794–Dec. 28, 1799.
Mass. Hist. Soc. has June 8, July 30, Aug. 17, 1793; Jan. 1, 1794–Dec. 28, 1799, fair.

Yale has Jan. 9, 1796–Dec. 21, 1799.

Lib. Congress has Jan. 4, July 5, 26, Aug. 2, Oct. 11, 14, 25, 29, Nov. 29, 1794; Jan. 7, Feb. 28, Apr. 11, 21, May 16, June 20, 27, July 11, 14, 25, Aug. 11, 15, 25, Oct. 31, Nov. 21, 28, 1795; Jan. 2, June 23, July 7, 21, Aug. 11, Sept. 8–29, Oct. 13, 19, Nov. 2, 23, 1796–Dec. 29, 1798; Jan. 5, 12, 26, Feb. 16, 23, Mar. 9, 23, Apr. 6, 13, May 18–June 22, Aug. 31, Oct. 5, Nov. 16, Dec. 7, 28, 1799.

Harvard has Feb. 14, 18, Mar. 11, 14, May 19, June 6–20, July 14, 28, Aug. 15, 18, Sept. 5, 8, Oct. 17, Nov. 14, Dec. 23–30, 1795; Jan. 2, Feb. 24, Mar. 2, 16, May 5, 19, June 2, 23, July 7–Aug. 25, Sept. 8, 22, Oct. 6, 13, 26–Nov. 9, 23, Dec. 7, 14, 28, 1796; Jan. 11, Feb. 22, Mar. 1, 15–Apr. 27, May 27, June 24, July 15, Sept. 16, 30, 1797; Jan. 6, 13, May 19–June 2, 16, Aug. 19, Oct. 14–28, Nov. 18, Dec. 16, 23, 1798; Oct. 26, 1799.

Boston Athenæum has Jan. 27, Feb. 3, Apr. 13–May 5, 26, July 7–21, Aug. 14, Sept. 1–Nov. 16, 1796; Jan. 4, 1797–Dec. 28, 1799.

N. Y. State Lib. has Mar. 3, 24, Apr. 7, 28, May 26–June 9, July 21–Aug. 11, Sept. 8–Dec. 22, 1798.

Phil. Lib. Co. has Nov. 4, 21–Dec. 2, 1795; Jan. 2, June 2, 1796; Sept. 22, 1798.

N. Y. Pub. Lib. has Aug. 12, 1794; Aug. 5, Oct. 7, Dec. 2, 1797; Sept. 29, Nov. 24, 1798.

Duke Univ. has July 27, Aug. 3, 17, 24, Sept. 14, Oct. 26, Nov. 30, 1799.

Essex Inst. has July 28, Oct. 6, 1798; Aug. 24, 31, 1799.

Univ. of Mich. (Clements) has Jan. 5, 26, Feb. 16, Aug. 31, 1799.

Hist. Soc. Penn. has Sept. 24, 1793.

Wis. Hist. Soc. has Dec. 24, 1794.

[Portsmouth] Oracle Post, 1803–1805.

Weekly. The country edition published on Tuesday, of the "Portsmouth Oracle" which was published on Saturday. It was a continuation of the "United States Oracle, For the Country," the first issue with the title of "Oracle Post" being that of Oct. 25, 1803, vol. 14, no. 3, published by William & Daniel Treadwell. The last issue of the country edition was that of June 18, 1805, vol. 16, no. 38, and the advertisement of the paper as a country edition disappeared from the "Portsmouth Oracle," in the issue of June 29, 1805.

N. H. Hist. Soc. has Oct. 25–Dec. 27, 1803; Mar. 6, Nov. 13, 1804; Jan. 1–Mar. 5, 19–June 18, 1805.

Am. Antiq. Soc. has Oct. 25–Dec. 27, 1803; Jan. 3, Sept. 25, 1804; Jan. 8–June 18, 1805.

Boston Athenæum has Nov. 1, 1803; July 10, 31, 1804–Apr. 2, 1805.

Yale has Nov. 1, 1803–Feb. 21, 1804.

Dartmouth has Apr. 26, July 12, Nov. 1, 29–Dec. 20, 1803; Jan. 3–May 1, 15–June 12, 26, July 31, Aug. 7, 21–Sept. 25, Oct. 30–Nov. 20, Dec. 4–25, 1804; Jan. 1–15, Feb. 5, 12, 26–Mar. 19, Apr. 2–23, May 14–28, 1805.

Lib. Congress has May 8, Sept. 25, Oct. 2, Nov. 13, 1804; Jan. 29, Apr. 30, June 18, 1805.
Harvard has Nov. 8, 1803; Feb. 21, 1804.

[Portsmouth] Osborne's New-Hampshire Spy, see **New-Hampshire Spy.**

[Portsmouth] People's Advocate, 1816–1817.

Weekly. Established Sept. 24, 1816, with the title of "The People's Advocate." The paper was of quarto size, and primarily an electioneering sheet without current news. The first two issues, published on Sept. 24 and Oct. 5, bore no publisher's name, but the issue of Oct. 15, 1816, was printed by W[illiam] Weeks and "published for the editors." With the issue of Oct. 29, 1816, vol. 1, no. 5, the size of the paper was enlarged to folio. The issue of Nov. 19, 1816, began a new series, with a new volume numbering. It now became a regular newspaper, and was published by W. Weeks & D[aniel] P. Drown. It was discontinued with the issue of May 17, 1817, vol. 1, no. 26. Jacob B. Moore, in "American Quarterly Register" for Nov. 1840, vol. 13, p. 180, states that the paper was edited by Estwicke Evans.

N. H. Hist. Soc. has Sept. 24, Oct. 5, 22, Nov. 19, 1816–Mar. 22, Apr. 26, May 10, 1817.
Boston Athenæum has Sept. 24–Oct. 29, Nov. 19, 30, Dec. 14, 21, 1816; Jan. 4–Apr. 19, May 3, 17, 1817.
Am. Antiq. Soc. has Sept. 24, Oct. 15, 29, Nov. 19, Dec. 14–28, 1816; Jan. 4, Feb. 22, Mar. 1–15, Apr. 19, 1817.
Lib. Congress has Oct. 29, Nov. 19, Dec. 21, 1816.
N. Y. Hist. Soc. has Oct. 5, 29, 1816.
N. Y. Pub. Lib. has Oct. 22, 1816.
Univ. of Mich. (Clements) has Mar. 15, 1817.

[Portsmouth] Political Star, 1804.

Weekly. Established June 28, 1804, with the title of "Political Star," published by J. Whitelock, for M. J. de Rochemont [John Whitelock for Maximilian John de Rochemont]. The last issue located is that of Nov. 8, 1804, vol. 1, no. 20.

N. Y. Hist. Soc. has June 28–Nov. 8, 1804.
Harvard has June 28–July 26, Aug. 9, 16, 30–Sept. 20, Oct. 4, 11, 25, 1804.
N. H. Hist. Soc. has July 26–Aug. 23, Sept. 6, 20, Oct. 4, 11, 25, 1804.
Am. Antiq. Soc. has July 5, 12, Aug. 30, Sept. 20, Nov. 8, 1804.
Lib. Congress has Sept. 20, 1804.

[Portsmouth] Republican Ledger, 1799–1803.

Weekly. Established Aug. 29, 1799, judging from the issue of Sept. 19, 1799, vol. 1, no. 4, published by George Jerry Osborne, Jun., with the title of "The

Republican Ledger." Osborne died June 2, 1800, and from June 10 to Aug. 5, the imprint bore no publisher's name. With the issue of Aug. 12, 1800, the names of Nutting & Whitelock [Samuel Nutting and John Whitelock] appeared as publishers. With the issue of Nov. 24, 1801, the title was changed to "Republican Ledger, and Portsmouth Price Current." The partnership was dissolved, and with the issue of Apr. 27, 1802, the paper was published by S. Nutting. The last issue located is that of Dec. 20, 1803, vol. 5, no. 17. Farmer and Moore, in their "Gazetteer of New Hampshire," 1823, p. 276, state that it was discontinued with the issue of Dec. 27, 1803.

Dartmouth has Sept. 19, 26, Oct. 23, Nov. 6–Dec. 25, 1799; Jan. 1, 15–Feb. 26, Mar. 12–June 18, July 1–Oct. 29, Nov. 18–Dec. 30, 1800; Jan. 6–Feb. 17, Mar. 3–Dec. 29, 1801; Jan. 5–Feb. 2, 16, 23, 1802; Jan. 4–Mar. 29, Apr. 12–Aug. 16, 30–Oct. 25, Nov. 8–Dec. 20, 1803.

Harvard has June 17, July 29, Aug. 5, 19, 26, Sept. 9, 23–Oct. 21, Nov. 11, 25, Dec. 23, 30, 1800; Jan. 20, Feb. 10, 17, Mar. 17, 31–Apr. 21, May 5, 12, 26, June 2, July 7, 14, Aug. 4, 18, Sept. 1, 15, 22, Nov. 3, 17, Dec. 8–29, 1801; Jan. 5, 12, 26, Feb. 2, 16–Mar. 2, 16–30, Apr. 20–May 4, 18, 25, June 8–Aug. 17, Sept. 7–Nov. 2, 16–30, Dec. 14, 1802; Jan. 11–Feb. 15, Mar. 1–29, Apr. 12–May 31, June 14, 21, July 5–Aug. 2, 23–Sept. 13, Oct. 4, 1803.

Am. Antiq. Soc. has Dec. 18, 1799; Sept. 16, Oct. 7, Nov. 4, 18, Dec. 9, 16, 1800; Jan. 6, 27, Feb. 17, Mar. 3–24, Apr. 6, 14, May 5–19, June 2, 23, July 7, 21, 28, Aug. 11, 25, Sept. 1, 15, 29, Oct. 13–Nov. 2, 17–Dec. 8, 1801; Jan. 12, Feb. 2, Mar. 2–16, Apr. 6, May 4–18, June 1, 15–July 6, 27, Aug. 10, 24, 31, Sept. 21, 28, Oct. 19, Nov. 2, 9, 23–Dec. 14, 1802; Jan. 18–Mar. 8, 29, Apr. 12–May 17, June 7–July 5, 19–Aug. 16, 30, Sept. 13–Oct. 4, 1803.

N. H. Hist. Soc. has June 10, Oct. 14, 1800; Aug. 4, 18–Nov. 2, 17–Dec. 29, 1801; Jan. 5–Mar. 9, 23–Apr. 6, June 15, July 20, Aug. 10, Sept. 14, Oct. 2–Nov. 17, Dec. 7, 21, 1802; Jan. 4–Feb. 22, Mar. 29, Apr. 19–May 24, June 14–Aug. 2, Sept. 13, Oct. 4, 25–Nov. 8, 29, 1803.

Boston Athenæum has Feb. 19–Apr. 16, 30–May 27, June 3–July 1, 15–29, Aug. 12–26, 1800; Apr. 28, Oct. 13, 20, 1801; Feb. 2, 1802.

Lib. Congress has July 15, Aug. 5, 19, Oct. 29, 1800; Mar. 17, 31, Apr. 21, 1801; Feb. 16, 23, Mar. 9–23, May 25, 1802; Feb. 15, Mar. 1, 22, Apr. 12, 26, May 24, 31, June 14, 21, 1803.

N. Y. Hist. Soc. has Jan. 1, Sept. 23, 1800; Feb. 17, Aug. 11, Nov. 2, 10, 1801; Jan. 11, 1803.

Univ. of Mich. (Clements) has June 2, 1801.

Essex Inst. has Mar. 9, 1802.

[Portsmouth] United States Oracle, 1800–1803.

Weekly. A continuation, without change of numbering, of "The Oracle of the Day," the first issue with the title of "The United States Oracle of the Day" being that of Jan. 4, 1800, vol. 10, no. 12, published by Charles Peirce. With the issue of July 4, 1801, Peirce transferred the paper to William Treadwell, & Co. [William and Jacob Treadwell]. With the issue of Oct. 17, 1801, the title was altered to "United States Oracle, and Portsmouth Advertiser." In the issue of Mar. 27, 1802, it was announced that beginning with Mar. 30, 1802, a country edition of the paper would be published, entitled "United States Oracle, (For the Country)." This was published on Tuesday, whereas the town edition appeared on Saturday, and both editions bore the same volume numbering. With the issue of Dec. 11, 1802, the firm of William Treadwell & Co. was dissolved, and the paper was published by William & Daniel Treadwell. The last issue with the title of "United States Oracle, and Portsmouth Advertiser" was that of Oct. 15, 1803, vol. 14, no. 2, after which the title was changed to "Portsmouth Oracle," which see. The "United States Oracle, For the Country" was also given up in favor of the "Oracle Post," the last issue being that of Oct. 18, 1803, vol. 14, no. 2. For continuation of this country edition, see under "Oracle Post."

N. H. Hist. Soc. has Jan. 4, 1800–Oct. 15, 1803; also Apr. 13–Aug. 17, 31–Dec. 21, 1802; Jan. 25–Oct. 18, 1803, of country issue.

Mass. Hist. Soc. has Jan. 4, 1800–Feb. 28, Apr. 11, 1801–Oct. 15, 1803.

N. Y. Hist. Soc. has Jan. 18, 1800–Oct. 15, 1803.

Dartmouth has Jan. 4, 1800–Dec. 26, 1801; Jan. 2, 1802–Oct. 11, 1803, fair.

Yale has Jan. 3, 1801–Apr. 3, 1802; Sept. 17, Oct. 1–15, 1803; also Apr. 13, 1802–Sept. 13, 20, 1803 of country issue.

Am. Antiq. Soc. has Jan. 4, 1800–Dec. 26, 1801; Jan. 23–Apr. 3, 17–May 8, 22–Aug. 28, Sept. 11–Dec. 11, 25, 1802; Jan. 1–15, Sept. 24, 1803; also June 8, 29–July 27, Aug. 10–Oct. 26, Nov. 9–Dec. 21, 1802; Jan. 25–June 7, 21–Oct. 18, 1803 of country issue.

Harvard has May 17, Aug. 23, Nov. 1, Dec. 20, 1800; Jan. 17–Dec. 26, 1801, fair; Jan. 9, 1802–Oct. 15, 1803, fair.

Boston Athenæum has Jan. 4, 1800–Mar. 20, July 17–Dec. 25, 1802; Jan. 1–15, Apr. 30, July 2, 1803.

Lib. Congress has Jan. 4–Dec. 20, 1800; Jan. 3–Sept. 26, Oct. 17, Nov. 28, 1801; Feb. 20, Mar. 13, Sept. 25, 1802; Jan. 7, 15, June 18, 1803; also July 6, 13, 27, Aug. 31, 1802, Feb. 8, May 10–24, July 19, 26, Sept. 6, Oct. 11, 18, 1803 of country issue.

N. Y. Pub. Lib. has Jan. 17, Sept. 12, 26, Oct. 31, Nov. 28, 1801; Feb. 27, Mar. 13–Apr. 24, May 29, Aug. 21, Oct. 23, 30, 1802; Mar. 12, 21, 26, Apr. 2, June 18, July 30, Aug. 13, Sept. 17, 1803.

Wis. Hist. Soc. has Jan. 4–25, Feb. 22, Mar. 1, July 5, 26, Aug. 2, 16, 23, Sept. 6, 27, Oct. 11, Nov. 22, Dec. 6, 20, 1800.

N. Y. State Lib. has Feb. 15, Mar. 8, 29, 1800; June 13, 1801; Aug. 14, 21, Oct. 16, Dec. 25, 1802; Jan. 15, 22, Feb. 12, Apr. 2, 1803.

Duke Univ. has Feb. 1, 1800; Mar. 6, 1802; also May 25, 1802 of country issue.

Essex Inst. has Mar. 15, 22, July 5, 1800.

Me. Hist. Soc. has Feb. 15, 1800; Feb. 28, 1801.

Mass. State Lib. has Apr. 19, 1800; Feb. 6, 1802.
Univ. of Mich. (Clements) has Jan. 4, 1800.

[Portsmouth] War Journal, 1813.

Weekly. Established Mar. 12, 1813, by Beck & Foster [Gideon Beck and Daniel C. Foster], with the title of "War Journal." It was discontinued with the issue of Dec. 10, 1813, vol. 1, no. 40. Beck & Foster became publishers of the "New Hampshire Gazette," Dec. 14, 1813.

N. H. Hist. Soc. has Mar. 12–Sept. 10, 24–Dec. 10, 1813.
Am. Antiq. Soc. has Mar. 19, Apr. 30, May 14, June 11, July 2, 9, Aug. 6, 13, 27, Sept. 10, Oct. 8, Nov. 5, 1813.
Boston Athenæum has Apr. 30, May 21, July 2, 1813.

[Walpole] Democratic Republican, 1812–1813.

Weekly. Established July 4, 1812, by Folsom & Pool [Benjamin Folsom and Henry Pool], with the title of "Democratic Republican." It was discontinued with the issue of July 5, 1813, vol. 1, no. 52.

Boston Athenæum has July 4, 1812–Feb. 22, Mar. 8–Apr. 12, 26–July 5, 1813.
N. Y. Hist. Soc. has July 4–Aug. 17, 31–Nov. 9, 23–Dec. 7, 21, 1812.
Am. Antiq. Soc. has July 4, 18, 27, Aug. 17, Dec. 7, 1812; Jan. 18, 25, Feb. 1, 22, May 17, June 7, 14, 1813.
Cheshire Co. Hist. Soc., Keene, has July 18, Aug. 3, 17, Sept. 28, Nov. 16, 30, 1812.
N. H. Hist. Soc. has Nov. 23, 1812; Jan. 18, Mar. 1–15, 1813.
Lib. Congress has Sept. 7, 21, 1812.
Duke Univ. has Aug. 17, 1812.
N. Y. Pub. Lib. has Dec. 28, 1812.

[Walpole] Farmer's Museum, see Farmer's Weekly Museum.

[Walpole] Farmer's Weekly Museum, 1797–1810.

Weekly. A continuation, without change of volume numbering, of "The Newhampshire and Vermont Journal." The first issue with the title of "The Farmer's Weekly Museum: Newhampshire and Vermont Journal," was that of Apr. 4, 1797, vol. 5, no. 209, printed by David Carlisle, Jun. (the "Jun." was omitted with the issue of Dec. 11, 1797, following the death of the printer's father). The paper was edited by Joseph Dennie, although his name was not given in the imprint. With the issue of Feb. 20, 1798, Isaiah Thomas resumed the proprietorship, Dennie continuing as editor. The imprint read "Printed by David Carlisle for Isaiah Thomas," changed with the issue of Mar. 6, 1798, to "Printed for Isaiah Thomas." With the issue of May 29, 1798, Isaiah Thomas admitted Alexander Thomas to the firm, and the paper was Printed by David Carlisle for Thomas & Thomas. Alexander Thomas conducted the paper, although Joseph Dennie continued to contribute (see J. T. Buckingham "Specimens of Newspaper Literature," vol. 2, p. 181). With the issue of Apr. 1, 1799, the title was changed to "Farmer's Museum, or Lay Preacher's Gazette," and with that of Feb. 17, 1800, to "Farmer's Museum, or Literary Gazette." With the issue of May 12, 1801, the printer's name in the imprint was changed to Thomas Carlisle, and with that of May 19, 1801, to David & Thomas Carlisle. With the issue of Oct. 6, 1801, Thomas & Thomas disposed of the paper to David Newhall, whose name appeared as publisher. With the issue of Oct. 4, 1803, the paper was published by David Newhall for Thomas & Thomas, and with that of Oct. 11, 1803, it was again published by Thomas & Thomas. With the issue of Sept. 15, 1804, the title was shortened to "The Farmer's Museum," and the paper was printed by Geo. W. Nichols, for Thomas & Thomas. The printer's name was omitted with the issue of Feb. 20, 1807. The paper was suspended with the issue of Mar. 27, 1807, vol. 15, no. 2. It was resumed with the issue of Oct. 24, 1808, entitled "Farmer's Museum," vol. 15, no. 1, published by Thomas & Thomas and Cheever Felch. Alexander Thomas died July 2, 1809, and with the issue of July 24, 1809, the paper was published and printed by Cheever Felch. It was discontinued with the issue of Oct. 15, 1810, vol. 16, no. 52.

Am. Antiq. Soc. has Apr. 4, 1797–Dec. 28, 1802; Jan. 4, 18, Feb. 1–22, Mar. 8–Apr. 5, 19–May 10, 24, 31, July 26, Aug. 30, Oct. 4, 18, Dec. 27, 1803; Jan. 28, Feb. 18, Mar. 10, 1804–Oct. 15, 1810.

N. H. Hist. Soc. has Apr. 4, 1797–Dec. 29, 1801; Jan. 5–Apr. 27, May 11, 18, June 1–Dec. 28, 1802; Jan. 4, 18–Feb. 22, Mar. 8–June 7, 21, July 5–Aug. 5, 23–Nov. 15, 29–Dec. 27, 1803; Jan. 7–Mar. 19, June 2–Dec. 29, 1804; Jan. 5–Apr. 13, 27–Oct. 12, 26–Dec. 27, 1805; Jan. 3–31, Feb. 14–July 11, Aug. 1–Nov. 14, 28, Dec. 19, 26, 1806; Jan. 2–Mar. 27, 1807; Oct. 24, Nov. 7–28, Dec. 12–26, 1808; Jan. 2–Feb. 16, 26–Apr. 17, May 1–July 24, Aug. 21–Sept. 25, Oct. 9, 23, Nov. 6–Dec. 11, 25, 1809; Jan. 8–Feb. 5, 19, 26, Mar. 12, 26–Apr. 16, 30–Oct. 8, 1810.

Conn. Hist. Soc. has Aug. 28, 1797–Oct. 19, 1805.

Lib. Congress has Apr. 4, 1797–Dec. 31, 1803; Mar. 17, June 16, July 21, Aug. 4–Dec. 29, 1804; Jan. 19, Feb. 23, Mar. 23, Aug. 3, Sept. 7, 1805; Jan. 10, May 23, Sept. 12, 19, Oct. 24, 1806; May 28, 1810.

Harvard has Apr. 4, 1797–June 16, 1800; July 21, Aug. 25, Oct. 13, Nov. 10, 17, Dec. 15, 1800; Jan. 12, 1801–June 23, 1804, fair; Sept. 8, Oct. 13, Nov. 17–Dec. 8, 22, 1804; Feb. 2, Mar. 9, 30, Apr. 20, May 18, June 1, 1805; Jan. 31, Feb. 7, Mar. 14, 28, Apr. 4, May 9, 16, 30–June 20, Aug. 8, Sept. 19, 1806.

Dartmouth has Apr. 4, 1797–Dec. 29, 1801; Jan. 5, 12, 26, Feb. 15, 23, Mar. 9, 23–Apr. 6, 1802; Jan. 4, 18, 25, Apr. 26, May 3, Dec. 27, 1803; May 19, June 2–23, July 14, Aug. 4, 11, Sept. 8–22, Oct. 6, 13, 27–Nov. 10, 31,

Dec. 15–29, 1804; Jan. 5–Feb. 23, Mar. 9–30, Apr. 13, July 6, Aug. 17, 24, 1805.
Boston Pub. Lib. has Apr. 4, 1797–June 29, 1802; Mar. 22, 1803; Apr. 28–May 12, June 2, 16–July 14, Aug. 4–18, Sept. 1–Dec. 29, 1804; Jan. 26–Feb. 16, May 4–18, June 1–July 27, 1805; Jan. 31, 1806; Feb. 13, Mar. 6, 20, 1807.
Univ. of Mich. (Clements) has Apr. 4, 1797–Dec. 30, 1799; Jan. 6, 1800–Dec. 14, 1802, fair; Apr. 26, 1803; Nov. 24, 1804; Apr. 6–June 22, July 6–20, Aug. 3–Dec. 27, 1805; Jan. 3–31, Feb. 14–May 9, 23, June 13–Sept. 26, 1806.
N. Y. State Lib. has Apr. 4, 1797–Oct. 6, 1801; Feb. 15, June 22, July 6, Aug. 3, 10, Sept. 14, Oct. 5, 12, 1802; Feb. 11, 1804; Mar. 30, July 13, Aug. 17, 24, 1805; Oct. 24, 1806; Oct. 24, Nov. 28, 1808; Aug. 21, 1809; Mar. 12, Apr. 30, May 14, July 9, 23, 30, Sept. 10, 24, 1810.
N. Y. Hist. Soc. has Apr. 4, 1797–Sept. 15, 1801; Jan. 19, Dec. 28, 1802; Feb. 9, Apr. 6, Aug. 24, 1805; Jan. 23, 30, 1809.
Mass. Hist. Soc. has Oct. 9, 1797–July 7, 1801; Nov. 30, 1802; Apr. 7, July 14, 1804; May 23, Oct. 3, Nov. 14, Dec. 19, 1806; Feb. 27, 1807.
Wis. Hist. Soc. has Apr. 4, 1797–Apr. 7, 1801.
Md. Hist. Soc. has Apr. 4, 1797–Sept. 1, 1800.
Boston Athenæum has Apr. 4, 1797–Apr. 14, 1800; Oct. 1–15, 1810.
N. Y. Pub. Lib. has Apr. 4, 1797–Mar. 18, 1799; Jan. 6–Mar. 31, June 16, 23, Aug. 6, 25, Nov. 3, Dec. 1, 1800.
Essex Inst. has Apr. 4, 1797–Dec. 30, 1799.
Phil. Lib. Co. has Apr. 11, 1797–Mar. 27, 1798; Apr. 1–Oct. 21, 1799.
Yale has Apr. 4, 1797–Sept. 2, 1799, fair; Jan. 6, 20, 27, May 12, June 2, 9, Sept. 22, 29, Dec. 8, 1800; Jan. 5, Oct. 13, 1801; Oct. 5, 1802.
Univ. of Minn. has July 3, 1797–July 3, 1798.
New Haven Col. Hist. Soc. has Jan. 2, 1798–Dec. 9, 1799, fair.
Walpole Pub. Lib. has Feb. 13, Apr. 3, 1798; Jan. 7, 1799; Jan. 6–Mar. 24, Apr. 21–Dec. 29, 1800; Jan. 12–Mar. 17, 1801; June 15, Aug. 24–Nov. 16, 1802; Nov. 12, 1806; Nov. 28–Dec. 12, 1808; Jan. 9, Feb. 20, 27, Mar. 13, Aug. 28, Sept. 11, 25, 1809.
Martin Memorial Lib., York, Pa., has Mar. 20, 1798–Dec. 30, 1799.
Minn. Hist. Soc. has Dec. 11, 1797; Feb. 27, May 29, June 12, July 10–31, Aug. 13–Sept. 17, Oct. 1, 15–29, Nov. 19, 26, Dec. 10, 24, 31, 1798; Jan. 14, Feb. 4, Mar. 18, Apr. 15, May 6, Aug. 5, Sept. 23, Oct. 7, 21, Dec. 2, 30, 1799; Jan. 20, Mar. 3, 31, 1800; Jan. 19, Feb. 24, Mar. 17, 31, May 5, 19, 26, June 9, Sept. 29–Oct. 13, Nov. 3–Dec. 22, 1801.
Arkansas Hist. Comm. has Apr. 11, 1797; Apr. 1, 1799–May 5, 1800, fair.
Duke Univ. has Feb. 6, May 1, 1798; Feb. 3, 1800; Feb. 13, 1807.

[Walpole] **New Hampshire and Vermont Journal**, see **New Hampshire Journal**.

[Walpole] **New Hampshire Journal,** 1793–1797.

Weekly. Established Apr. 11, 1793, by Isaiah Thomas and David Carlisle, Jun., with the title of "The New Hampshire Journal: Or, The Farmer's Weekly Museum." With the issue of Apr. 11, 1794, the title was changed to "The Newhampshire and Vermont Journal: Or, The Farmer's Weekly Museum." With the issue of Apr. 5, 1796, Thomas retired from the firm, and the paper was printed by David Carlisle, Jun. Joseph Dennie became the editor, although his name was not given in the imprint (see J. T. Buckingham, "Specimens of Newspaper Literature," vol. 1, p. 175). The last issue with the above title was that of Mar. 28, 1797, vol. 4, no. 208, after which the title was changed to "The Farmer's Weekly Museum: Newhampshire and Vermont Journal," which see.

Am. Antiq. Soc. has Apr. 11, 1793–Mar. 28, 1797.
Boston Pub. Lib. has Apr. 25, May 9, 16, Sept. 20, Nov. 1, 15, Dec. 6, 20, 1793; Jan. 31, Feb. 21, 28, Apr. 11, 1794–Mar. 28, 1797.
N. Y. Hist. Soc. has Apr. 11, 1793–Apr. 4, 1794; Nov. 24, 1795; Nov. 15, 1796–Mar. 28, 1797.
N. H. Hist. Soc. has Apr. 11, May 2, 9, 30, June 6, 20–July 12, 26–Sept. 6, 20, Oct. 4–Nov. 15, 29–Dec. 27, 1793; Jan. 3, 10, 24, Feb. 14–Mar. 28, May 9, 16, June 6, 27, July 4, Sept. 19, Oct. 10, Dec. 16, 30, 1794; Feb. 17, Apr. 7, May 19–June 2, Sept. 15, Oct. 27, Nov. 17, 1795; Apr. 5–19, May 3, 31, June 7, 21–July 5, 19, Sept. 13, 20, Oct. 4–Nov. 22, Dec. 6–27, 1796; Jan. 3, 10, 24–Mar. 28, 1797.
Walpole Pub. Lib. has Apr. 11, 1793–Apr. 4, 1794.
Md. Hist. Soc. has Apr. 12, 1796–Mar. 28, 1797.
Mass. Hist. Soc. has Oct. 4, 1796–Mar. 7, 1797.
Boston Athenæum has Nov. 1, 1796–Mar. 28, 1797.
Harvard has Feb. 17–Mar. 10, Apr. 7, 14, May 19, June 16, 23, 1795; Mar. 8, 15, Apr. 5, May 10, June 21, July 5, Aug. 30, Sept. 27, Oct. 11–Dec. 27, 1796; Jan. 3–Mar. 28, 1797.
Lib. Congress has May 2, June 27, 1793; June 28, Oct. 11–Nov. 8, 29, Dec. 20, 1796; Jan. 10, Feb. 14–Mar. 28, 1797.
N. Y. Pub. Lib. has June 13, July 12, Aug. 9, 1793; Aug. 22, Sept. 19, Oct. 3, 10, 1794; Feb. 3, Oct. 13, 1795; Feb. 21–Mar. 28, 1797.
N. Y. State Lib. has Jan. 31–Mar. 28, 1797.
Conn. Hist. Soc. has Nov. 24, 1795; Nov. 1, 22, 1796; Jan. 31, Feb. 21, Mar. 7, 21, 1797.
Univ. of Mich. (Clements) has Oct. 10, 1794.
Yale has Mar. 14–28, 1797.

[Walpole] **Political Observatory,** 1803–1809.

Weekly. Established Nov. 19, 1803, with the title of "Political Observatory," printed for the Proprietors by David Newhall. With the issue of Apr. 13, 1805, it was printed for the Proprietors by N. Charter & S. Hale [Nathaniel Charter and Salma Hale, according to a statement in the issue of May 11, 1805]. Stanley Griswold was editor of the paper from its commencement until May 1805. With the issue of June 5, 1807, the printing firm became Nichols & Hale [George W. Nichols and Salma Hale]. With the issue of May 16, 1808, the paper was published by George W. Nichols. It was discontinued with the issue of Mar. 20, 1809, vol. 6, no. 279. Mr. C. C. Wilber informs me that in the records of the Court of Common Pleas, Cheshire SS. September term, 1810, Amasa Allen, Jonathan Royce, Thomas C. Drew and Alexander Watkins of Walpole, David Hale of Alstead, and Nathaniel Charter, printer of Richmond, Va., brought a suit calling themselves "late partners under the firm of the Proprietors of the Political Observatory."

Dartmouth has Nov. 19, 1803–Dec. 29, 1807; Jan. 5–June 20, July 4, 25, Aug. 1, 22, 29, Sept. 12, 19, Oct. 10, Nov. 14–Dec. 26, 1808; Jan. 2, 9, Feb. 13, 27, Mar. 4, 13, 1809.

Am. Antiq. Soc. has Nov. 19, 1803–Dec. 27, 1805; Jan. 3–Feb. 28, Mar. 14, 21, Apr. 4, 11, May 16–30, June 13, 27, July 11, Oct. 31, Nov. 7, Dec. 5, 26, 1806; Apr. 3, 10, 24, May 15, 22, June 26, July 3, Aug. 24, Sept. 28, Oct. 12, Nov. 9, 1807; Apr. 11, June 13, Aug. 22, 29, Oct. 17, 31, Nov. 7, 28, Dec. 12, 26, 1808; Jan. 2, Feb. 20, Mar. 4, 13, 1809.

N. H. Hist. Soc. has Nov. 19, 1803–Dec. 6, 1805; Dec. 27, 1805; Jan. 10, 17, 31–Feb. 28, Mar. 14–June 27, July 18, Aug. 1–Sept. 19, Oct. 3, 24, Dec. 5, 12, 26, 1806; Jan. 1–Mar. 27, Apr. 10, 24, Oct. 19, 1807; Jan. 25, Apr. 18, July 11, Sept. 26, Oct. 17, Nov. 21, Dec. 19, 26, 1808; Jan. 9, 1809.

Harvard has Dec. 17, 1803–Nov. 16, 1807, fair; Aug. 8–29, Sept. 26–Oct. 10, 24, Nov. 28–Dec. 26, 1808.

Lib. Congress has Nov. 19, 1803–Nov. 29, 1805, fair; Jan. 31, Feb. 21, 1806; Apr. 17–May 22, June 5, 19–July 3, Sept. 21, Dec. 1, 1807; Nov. 21, 1808.

Boston Athenæum has Nov. 19–Dec. 21, 1803; Jan. 21, Feb. 4, Mar. 3, 17–Apr. 28, May 12, 19, June 2, 1804–Nov. 9, 1805.

N. Y. Hist. Soc. has Dec. 22, 29, 1804; Jan. 5, 19, Mar. 2, 23–Apr. 27, June 1–22, July 6, 13, 27–Aug. 17, 31–Nov. 2, Dec. 20, 1805; Jan. 3, 10, 24–Feb. 7, 21–Mar. 7, Apr. 4–May 2, 30–June 27, Aug. 15–29, Sept. 12, Oct. 10, Nov. 14, 21, Dec. 5, 26, 1806; Jan. 2, 16, Feb. 13–27, Mar. 13, 20, Apr. 10, 24–May 15, June 12–26, Aug. 3, 24, 31, Sept. 21–Oct. 19, Nov. 2–Dec. 1, 15–29, 1807; Jan. 5, 25–Mar. 28, Apr. 18, May 2, 9, 1808.

Conn. Hist. Soc. has Nov. 19, Dec. 3, 10, 24, 31, 1803; Jan. 7–28, Feb. 11–Mar. 3, May 12, 19, June 9, 23, Aug. 18, Nov. 10, Dec. 1, 8, 22, 29, 1804; Jan. 5, June 8, 22, Aug. 31, Sept. 7, Oct. 12, 1805.

N. Y. State Lib. has June 16, 23, July 14–Aug. 4, 25, Sept. 1, 1804; Mar. 16, 1805; Jan. 2, 30–Apr. 10, 24, 1807.

Univ. of Mich. (Clements) has Dec. 3, 1803; Feb. 18–Apr. 28, May 12, 1804; Feb. 16, Aug. 17, 31, 1805; May 16, June 27, 1806.

Univ. of Ill. has Mar. 24, Apr. 28, Nov. 24, 1804; Jan. 24, 1806.
Yale has Mar. 3, 17, 1804.
Me. Hist. Soc. has June 22, 1805.
Duke Univ. has July 13, 1805.
Boston Pub. Lib. has Aug. 24, 1805.
Cheshire Co. Hist. Soc., Keene, has Sept. 28, 1807.

NEW JERSEY

[Bridgeton] **Apollo, 1804.**

Weekly. Established May 17, 1804, judging from the earliest issue located, that of June 21, 1804, vol. 1, no. 6, published by John Westcott, Jun., at "Bridge-Town (West) New-Jersey," with the title of "The Apollo, and Bridgetown Weekly Miscellany." The paper was discontinued with the issue of Dec. 6, 1804, vol. 1, no. 26.

> Harvard has June 21, 28, July 12–Aug. 1, 15, 22, Sept. 5–19, Oct. 3, 17, Nov. 5–20, 1804.
> Cumberland Co. Hist. Soc., Bridgeton, has Dec. 6, 1804.

[Bridgeton] **Argus, 1795–1796.**

Weekly. Established Oct. 1, 1795, judging from the date of the earliest issue located, that of Nov. 5, 1795, no. 6, published by M'Kenzie and Westcott [Alexander M'Kenzie and James D. Westcott], with the title of "The Argus; and New-Jersey Centinel." With the issue of Oct. 13, 1796, the firm was dissolved and the paper published by Alexander M'Kenzie. The last issue located is that of Nov. 10, 1796, no. 57.

> Harvard has Nov. 5–27, Dec. 17, 31, 1795; Jan. 7, Apr. 29, June 9–23, July 7, 14, 28–Aug. 25, Sept. 8, 15, 29, Oct. 13, 20, Nov. 3, 10, 1796.
> Cumberland Co. Hist. Soc., Bridgeton, has Nov. 5, Dec. 10, 17, 31, 1795; Jan. 7–21, Feb. 4, 18, Mar. 3–17, 1796.
> N. Y. Pub. Lib. has Dec. 3, 1795.
> Brearly Masonic Lodge, Bridgeton, has Dec. 24, 1795.

[Bridgeton] **East-Jersey Republican, 1816.**

Weekly. Established Apr. 10, 1816, judging from the earliest issue located, that of May 22, 1816, vol. 1, no. 7, published by Nathaniel L. Combes, with the title of "East-Jersey Republican." The last issue located is that of July 3, 1816, vol. 1, no. 13.

> Lib. Congress has May 22, June 5, 26, July 3, 1816.

[Bridgeton] **Plain Dealer, 1775–1776.**

Weekly. Established Dec. 25, 1775, and continued in eight weekly numbers, to Feb. 12, 1776, under the title of "The Plain Dealer." These issues were not printed, but consisted of weekly papers on various topics, written out in manuscript and posted up in Matthew Potter's tavern at Bridgeton. They were contributed by members of a literary association at Bridgeton and were in essay

NEW JERSEY 493

form, somewhat after the style of the "Spectator." They were first printed from a contemporaneous copy in manuscript, in 1894, in a quarto pamphlet of thirty-nine pages, with an introduction and notes by William Nelson, the sub-title being "The First Newspaper in New Jersey." Chiefly because of this title, and not because of its contents, which had no current news or other newspaper features, the "Plain Dealer" is included in this bibliography.

Nearly all of the larger libraries of the country have the 1894 pamphlet, of which 100 copies were printed. The original manuscript file of eight numbers is in the Rutgers University Library.

[Bridgeton] Washington Whig, 1815-1820+.

Weekly. Established July 24, 1815, by Peter Hay, with the title of "Washington Whig." Elmer, in his "History of Cumberland County," 1869, p. 57, says that it was established in 1815 by the Washington Whig Society, with Peter Hay as publisher. With the issue of Jan. 20, 1817, William Schultz became the publisher. With the issue of May 4, 1818, the title was slightly altered to "The Washington Whig." The paper was continued until after 1820, although with the issue of Jan. 1, 1821, the paper was purchased by John Clarke & Co., who started a new series of volume numbering and changed the title to "Washington Whig."

Cumberland Co. Hist. Soc., Bridgeton, has July 24, 1815-Dec. 25, 1820.
Lib. Congress has Jan. 12-Feb. 9, 23-Dec. 27, 1819; Jan. 3-Feb. 21, Mar. 6, 13, Apr. 3-May 1, 15-July 3, 17, 31, Aug. 21-Dec. 11, 1820.
N. J. Hist. Soc. has Aug. 25, 1817.
Morristown Lib. has Sept. 1, 1817.

Burlington Advertiser, 1790-1791.

Weekly. Established Apr. 13, 1790, by I[saac] Neale and D[aniel] Lawrence, with the title of "The Burlington Advertiser, or Agricultural and Political Intelligencer." With the issue of Apr. 12, 1791, Lawrence retired and the paper was published by Isaac Neale. It was discontinued with the issue of Dec. 13, 1791, vol. 2, no. 88.

N. Y. Pub. Lib. has Apr. 13, 1790-Dec. 13, 1791.
Am. Antiq. Soc. has June 15-29, July 13, 20, 1790; Feb. 15, 1791.
Harvard has Aug. 2, Sept. 13, 27, 1791.

[Burlington] New-Jersey Gazette, 1777-1778.

Weekly. Established Dec. 5, 1777, by Isaac Collins, with the title of "The New-Jersey Gazette." The last issue printed at Burlington was that of Feb. 25, 1778, vol. 1, no. 13, after which Collins removed the paper to Trenton. In the N. Y. Public Library file is included the manuscript Proposals for establishing the paper.

Am. Antiq. Soc., N. J. Hist. Soc., N. J. State Lib., Princeton, N. Y. Hist. Soc., N. Y. Pub. Lib., Hist. Soc. Penn., Penn. State Lib., and Lib. Congress have Dec. 5, 1777–Feb. 25, 1778.
Rutgers Univ. has Dec. 10–24, 1777; Jan. 7, 21–Feb. 25, 1778.
Wis. Hist. Soc. has Dec. 5, 1777.

[Burlington] **Rural Visiter**, 1810–1811.

Weekly. Established July 30, 1810, by D[avid] Allinson, with the title of "The Rural Visiter." The paper was of quarto size, with numbered pages and four pages to the issue. Although of magazine form, it could be considered as a newspaper, since it included current news, death notices and advertisements. Beginning with Oct. 13, 1810, an issue of eight pages was published every two weeks, the intervening issues consisting of four pages. Beginning with Feb. 4, 1811, all the issues consisted of eight pages, but the last two pages, which included advertisements, were unpaged. With the issue of Feb. 11, 1811, David Allinson took his brother John C. Allinson into partnership, the firm name being D. Allinson & Co. With the issue of May 6, 1811, the size of the paper was reduced to four pages, all numbered. The final issue was that of July 22, 1811, vol. 1, no. 52, consisting of eight pages and including an Index. The volume was provided with the title-page.

Am. Antiq. Soc., N. J. Hist. Soc., N. J. State Lib., N. Y. Pub. Lib., Princeton, Rutgers, Vineland Hist. Soc., Monmouth Co. Hist. Assoc., Conn. Hist. Soc., N. Y. Hist. Soc., Hist. Soc. Penn., Lib. Congress, Brown, Trinity, Yale, Watkinson Lib., Haverford Coll., Juniata Coll., Swarthmore Coll., Univ. of Penn., Grosvenor Lib., Buffalo, Univ. of Ill., Univ. of Mich. (Clements), and Univ. of Minn. have July 30, 1810–July 22, 1811.
New Haven Col. Hist. Soc. has July 30, 1810–July 22, 1811, fair.
N. Y. Pub. Lib. has Jan. 28, Feb. 18, 1811.
Duke Univ. has Jan. 28, Feb. 18, 1811.

[Camden] **Gloucester Farmer**, 1818–1820.

Weekly. Removed from Woodbury to Camden in 1818. The earliest Camden issue located is that of Jan. 7, 1819, vol. 2, no. 97, published by John A. Crane, with the title of "Gloucester Farmer." Crane continued its publication until Dec. 20, 1820, when it was united with the "Columbian Herald" at Woodbury, under the title of "The Herald and Gloucester Farmer."

N. J. Hist. Soc. has Jan. 7, 28, Feb. 25, Mar. 11, July 28, Oct. 19, Nov. 2, 1819.

NEW JERSEY 495

[Chatham] **New-Jersey Journal,** 1779–1783.

Weekly. Established Feb. 16, 1779, by Shepard Kollock, with the title of "The New-Jersey Journal." The last issue located is that of Nov. 12, 1783, vol. 5, no. 248, in which it is announced that the paper would be discontinued "at the evacuation of New-York," to be succeeded by the "New-York Gazetteer and Country Journal." Evidently this was the last, or next to the last, issue, since New York was evacuated on Nov. 25, 1783.

> N. Y. Hist. Soc. has Feb. 16, Mar. 23, 30, Apr. 13–May 18, June 8, 22, July 20, Sept. 7, 21, Oct. 5–Nov. 2, 16, 30, Dec. 14, 21, 1779; Jan. 25, Feb. 2, Mar. 29–Apr. 12, 26–May 31, June 14, 21, July 5, 12, 26–Aug. 9, 23, Sept. 6–20, Oct. 11, 25–Nov. 15, Dec. 27, 1780; Jan. 3–17, 31, Feb. 21–Aug. 15, 29–Sept. 26, Oct. 10, 17, 31, Nov. 14–28, Dec. 12–26, 1781; Jan. 9, 16, 30–May 15, 29–July 3, 17–Aug. 28, Sept. 11–Oct. 30, 1782; Jan. 1, 15, Feb. 26, Mar. 5, Apr. 9, May 7–21, July 2, 9, 23, 30, Sept. 17, Nov. 5, 1783.
> N. J. Hist. Soc. has Feb. 23, 1779; Jan. 11–Feb. 16, Mar. 1–15, 29–June 21, July 12–Aug. 9, 23–Nov. 8, Dec. 6–27, 1780; Jan. 3–24, Feb. 21–Dec. 26, 1781; Jan. 2, 9, 23–Dec. 25, 1782; Jan. 1–Sept. 10, 1783.
> Am. Antiq. Soc. has Apr. 27, June 15, 1779; Mar. 22, June 21, 1780; Jan. 24, Apr. 11, May 16, 23, June 20, July 11, 18, Aug. 1, 15, 22, Sept. 19–Oct. 31, Nov. 14–Dec. 26, 1781; Jan. 2, 9, 23–July 10, 24–Oct. 2, 16–Dec. 18, 1782; Jan. 1–Apr. 16, 30–May 28, June 11, July 2–Aug. 13, 27–Oct. 1, 22, Nov. 12, 1783.
> Mass. Hist. Soc. has May 16, Sept. 19, Nov. 28, 1781; Mar. 6, 20, Apr. 3, 24–May 8, June 5, 12, Aug. 21, Oct. 23, Nov. 6, 1782; Apr. 2, 1783.
> Hist. Soc. Penn. has Jan. 18, Feb. 9, 1780; Feb. 28–Apr. 18, May 2, 9, June 27, July 4, Aug. 1, Sept. 12, 26, Oct. 17, 31, 1781; Apr. 17, 1782.
> Morristown Nat. Park Museum has Sept. 20, 1780; June 20, Aug. 8, Oct. 3, 17, 31, Nov. 7, 1781.
> Lib. Congress has Feb. 6, 27, Mar. 20, Apr. 10, Aug. 28, Sept. 11, 18, Nov. 27, 1782; Jan. 1, Mar. 12, 26, Apr. 9, 1783.
> Amer. Philos. Soc. has Oct. 19, Dec. 21, 1779; Oct. 11, 1780.
> Morristown Lib. has Dec. 7, 1779; Aug. 1, 8, 1781.
> British Museum has Nov. 22–Dec. 27, 1780.
> N. Y. Pub. Lib. has Sept. 13, 1780.
> Wis. Hist. Soc. has Apr. 11, 1781.
> N. J. State Lib. has Apr. 16, 1783.

[Elizabeth Town] **Essex Patriot,** 1812–1813.

Weekly. Established Dec. 1, 1812, by G. L. Austin & Co. [Galen L. Austin and Lewis Deare], with the title of "Essex Patriot." The printing office was detroyed by fire on Oct. 20, 1813, and there is some evidence to show that the next few issues were printed at New Brunswick (see "Proc. N. J. Hist. Soc.,"

1923, ser. 4, vol. 8, p. 216). The firm of G. L. Austin & Co. was dissolved Nov. 10, 1813, and thereafter the paper was published by Russel Canfield. The last issue located is that of Dec. 21, 1813, vol. 2, no. 4.

N. J. Hist. Soc. has Dec. 1, 1812; Mar. 9, Nov. 23, Dec. 14, 21, 1813.
Yale has Jan. 12, 1813.

[Elizabeth Town] Federal Republican, 1803.

Weekly. Established late in January 1803, judging from the first and only issue located, that of June 21, 1803, vol. 1, no. 22, published by John Woods, with the title of "Federal Republican." It was not long continued, since in the "New Jersey Journal," under date of Mar. 5, 1804, John Woods advertises that he is "about to remove out of this State," and refers to the recent discontinuance of his paper, the "Federal Republican."

Am. Antiq. Soc. has June 21, 1803.

Elizabeth-Town Gazette, 1818–1820+.

Weekly. Established Sept. 8, 1818, by J[ames] & E[dward] Sanderson, with the title of "Elizabeth-Town Gazette." It was so continued until after 1820.

Rutgers Univ. has Sept. 8, 1818–Dec. 26, 1820.
N. J. Hist. Soc. has Sept. 14, Oct. 12, Dec. 28, 1819; Jan. 11, Apr. 4, Aug. 22, Sept. 5, Oct. 17, 1820.
Am. Antiq. Soc. has Sept. 15, Oct. 20, 27, 1818; Jan. 26, 1819; Nov. 7, 1820.

[Elizabeth Town] New-Jersey Journal, 1786–1820+.

Weekly. A continuation, without change of numbering, of "The Political Intelligencer and New-Jersey Advertiser." The first issue with the new title of "The New-Jersey Journal, and Political Intelligencer" was that of May 10, 1786, no. 134, published by Shepard Kollock. With the issue of June 13, 1792, the title was shortened to "The New-Jersey Journal." In the issue of Jan. 2, 1798, a semi-weekly publication was announced, and a new volume numbering was begun with this issue. But the project fell through, and with the succeeding issue, that of Jan. 9, 1798, the former volume numbering was resumed. With the issue of Aug. 21, 1798, the title was shortened to "New-Jersey Journal." With the issue of Sept. 8, 1818, Kollock disposed of the paper to P[eter] Chatterton, who continued publishing it until after 1820.

N. J. Hist. Soc. has May 10, 1786–Dec. 26, 1809; Jan. 2–May 8, 29, June 5, July 3, 17–Aug. 7, 21, Sept. 4–18, Oct. 9, 23, Nov. 13–Dec. 25, 1810; Jan. 1–July 9, 30, Aug. 13–27, Sept. 10, 1811–Dec. 22, 1814; Jan. 10–31, Feb. 21, Mar. 14–June 6, 20–July 18, Aug. 1–Oct. 17, Nov. 7–Dec. 26, 1815; Jan. 2,

New Jersey

23, Feb. 20, Mar. 5-19, Apr. 2, 16-30, May 14-June 4, 25-Aug. 27, Sept. 10-Dec. 10, 24, 1816-Dec. 26, 1820.

Am. Antiq. Soc. has May 10, Aug. 2-16, Nov. 22, Dec. 6, 1786; Jan. 10-Feb. 14, 28-June 13, 27-Aug. 22, Sept. 5, 19-Dec. 26, 1787; Jan. 2-Oct. 1, 22-Dec. 3, 17, 24, 1788; Jan. 7-Feb. 4, 18-Mar. 18, Apr. 1-May 13, 27-July 29, Aug. 19-Sept. 23, Oct. 7-Nov. 11, 25-Dec. 16, 30, 1789; Jan. 13, 20, Feb. 17, Mar. 3, 10, 31, Apr. 28-May 12, 26-July 28, Aug. 18, Sept. 8, 15, Oct. 6-20, Nov. 3, 17-Dec. 8, 29, 1790; Jan. 5, Feb. 16-Dec. 28, 1791; Jan. 4-June 27, July 11-Dec. 26, 1792; Jan. 2-May 22, June 5, 12, 1793; Jan. 1-Dec. 31, 1794; Jan. 28, Apr. 8, May 6, 13, July 8, 22, Aug. 12-Sept. 2, Nov. 11, 25, Dec. 30, 1795; Mar. 2, 9, June 8, 15, 29, July 13, Sept. 14, Oct. 19, 26, Nov. 16, 30, 1796; Jan. 4, 25, Feb. 8-Mar. 22, Apr. 5-May 3, 17, June 21, July 5, 12, 26-Aug. 30, Sept. 13, Oct. 4, Nov. 1-15, 29, Dec. 5, 19, 1797; Jan. 16, 23, Feb. 27-Mar. 20, Apr. 24, May 1, 15-June 5, Aug. 28, Sept. 18, Oct. 9-30, Nov. 13, Dec. 4, 11, 25, 1798; Jan. 1, 15-29, Feb. 12, Mar. 5, Apr. 2, May 7, June 18, Aug. 13, Dec. 31, 1799; Mar. 25, Apr. 22, July 22, Dec. 2, 1800; Dec. 28, 1802; Mar. 1, May 3, Aug. 9, Sept. 13, 1803; Jan. 24, 1804; Aug. 25, Sept. 22, Oct. 6-27, Nov. 3, Dec. 8, 15, 1807; Feb. 28, Nov. 21, 28, 1809; Jan. 2, Feb. 20, Mar. 13, Apr. 3, May 29, July 24, 1810; Jan. 1-May 14, 28-July 9, 30, Aug. 6, Oct. 1, 15-Nov. 5, 19-Dec. 10, 1811; Jan. 21-Feb. 11, 25-June 9, 30-Dec. 29, 1812; Jan. 19, Feb. 9, 16, Mar. 2-16, 30-Aug. 24, Sept. 14, 21, Oct. 5-19, Nov. 2-16, Dec. 7, 1813; June 29, 1819.

Lib. Congress has Oct. 4, 1786; June 27-July 11, 25, Aug. 15-29, Oct. 3, Nov. 7-Dec. 12, 26, 1787; Jan. 2, 30, Feb. 13, 20, 1788; Jan. 14-Feb. 4, Mar. 4-Dec. 30, 1789; Jan. 6-Aug. 11, Sept. 8-Oct. 6, 27-Dec. 29, 1790; Jan. 5-26, Mar. 23-May 18, June 1-Dec. 28, 1791; Jan. 4-Dec. 26, 1792; Jan. 2-Aug. 28, Sept. 11-Dec. 11, 25, 1793; Aug. 26, 1795; Oct. 5, 1796; Dec. 24, 1799; May 12, 1801; Aug. 18, Oct. 6, 1807.

N. J. State Lib. has Oct. 18, Nov. 22-Dec. 27, 1786; Jan. 3-24, Feb. 14-Apr. 25, May 9-June 27, July 11, 25-Sept. 5, 19, Oct. 3-17, 31-Dec. 6, 1787; Jan. 2-30, Feb. 13, 20, Mar. 5, Apr. 2, May 7, 14, June 4, July 9-Aug. 20, Sept. 17, 24, Oct. 15, Nov. 5, 12, 1788; Jan. 14, Feb. 18, May 13, 27, June 24-July 22, Aug. 5-26, Sept. 9-23, Oct. 14-Nov. 4, 18-Dec. 2, 16-30, 1789; Jan. 6, 13, 27, Feb. 3, 17-Mar. 17, 1790; Jan. 4-Apr. 18, May 2-23, June 6-Dec. 26, 1792; Jan. 9-23, Feb. 6-May 15, 29-Dec. 25, 1793; Sept. 10, 1794; Apr. 29, 1795.

Rutgers Univ. has Nov. 8, 1786-Sept. 5, 1787; Sept. 19, 26, Oct. 10, 17, Nov. 14, Dec. 12, 1787; June 18, 25, July 2, 25, Aug. 6, Sept. 3, 1788; Feb. 4, July 15, 1789; Jan. 27, Mar. 3-17, Apr. 28, May 5, 26, Aug. 11, 1790; Mar. 9-Apr. 13, May 4-18, June 8-22, 1791; Jan. 15, 22, Feb. 22, Apr. 2, 23, May 14, June 25, July 9-23, Aug. 6, 27, Sept. 3, Nov. 5-19, Dec. 10-24, 1794; May 6, July 15, Sept. 16, Oct. 14, Nov. 4, 11, Dec. 9, 1795; Jan. 6, 1796-Dec. 26, 1797; Jan. 29-Aug. 6, 1805; Nov. 21, 1809; June 19, Sept. 25, 1810; Apr. 16,

Oct. 15, 1811; Jan. 21, 1812; Feb. 21, 1815; Jan. 30, 1816; Apr. 13, 1819; Apr. 18, 1820.
Hist. Soc. Penn. has Aug. 1, 1787–Mar. 24, 1790.
Harvard has June 22–July 20, Sept. 28, Nov. 17, 23, 1791; Feb. 25–Mar. 11, May 27, June 17–July 8, 22, Aug. 5, 19, Nov. 25, 1795; Jan. 20, Apr. 6, 13, May 18, June 1, 29, July 6, 20–Sept. 21, Oct. 12–Dec. 28, 1796; Jan. 4–Mar. 29, Apr. 12–May 3, 24–June 14, 28–July 12, Sept. 6, 20–Oct. 4, 25–Nov. 8, 22, 29, Dec. 12, 19, 1797; Jan. 9, 16, 30–Feb. 13, Mar. 6, 13, 27, Apr. 3, 17, May 1, 15–June 5, 19, 26, July 10, 17, Sept. 11, Oct. 2, 23, 30, Nov. 13–27, Dec. 11, 18, 1798; Jan. 1, Feb. 19–Mar. 12, 26, Apr. 9, 23–May 7, 21–June 4, 18, July 30, Aug. 6, 20, Sept. 3, 10, 24, Oct. 15–Dec. 3, 17, 1799; Jan. 14, 21, Feb. 4, 18, 25, Mar. 11, 25, Apr. 8–22, May 6–27, June 17, July 1, 8, 22, 29, Aug. 12, 26–Oct. 7, 21–Nov. 4, 25, Dec. 9, 1800; Jan. 6–27, Feb. 17, Mar. 3, 17–Apr. 7, 21–June 2, 16, 30, July 28, Aug. 4–Sept. 15, Oct. 6, 27–Nov. 17, Dec. 1, 8, 29, 1801; Feb. 2, Aug. 24, Dec. 28, 1802; June 14, Sept. 6, 13, 27–Oct. 11, 25–Nov. 8, 22–Dec. 27, 1803; Jan. 3, 17, Feb. 7–21, Mar. 13, 20, Apr. 3, 10, May 1–15, June 19, 26, July 17, Aug. 7, 14, Nov. 6, Dec. 11, 1804; Jan. 22–Feb. 12, Mar. 5, 19, Apr. 2, 16–May 14, June 4–July 9, 23, 30, Sept. 8–22, Nov. 5, 26, Dec. 3, 1805; Jan. 21, Feb. 11, 18, Aug. 5, Nov. 18, 1806; Nov. 3, 1807; Sept. 27, 1808.
Vineland, N. J., Hist. Soc. has Jan. 14, 21, Feb. 4, Apr. 1, 15, 22, July 1, Aug. 26–Sept. 23, Oct. 7, 28, 1789; Apr. 6, 1791–June 5, 1793, fair.
Princeton has Feb. 2, 1791–Mar. 20, 1793; Feb. 18, Mar. 25, 1795.
N. Y. Pub. Lib. has Dec. 29, 1790; Oct. 29, 1794; July 27, 1796; Mar. 30–Apr. 13, 1813; Feb. 1–Dec. 13, 1814; Jan. 7, 1817–Dec. 29, 1818.
Wis. Hist. Soc. has Feb. 1–Nov. 29, 1797; July 24, 1810; Dec. 15, 1818.
Elizabeth Pub. Lib. has Oct. 12, 1802; Mar. 29, June 14, Sept. 20, Nov. 1, 22, 1803; Feb. 21, Mar. 13, Apr. 3, June 5, 1804; Jan. 1–15, May 14, 21, July 2, 1805; July 17, 24, 1810.
N. Y. Hist. Soc. has Dec. 24, 1799; July 22, Sept. 9, 1800; Mar. 12, June 11, 1816; Mar. 4, 1817; May 26, June 2, Aug. 18, 1818.
Morristown Nat. Park Museum has Dec. 14, 1791; Sept. 23, 1795; Sept. 28, 1796; Dec. 24, 31, 1799; Jan. 7, May 20, 1800; Mar. 12, 1811.
Boston Pub. Lib. has Feb. 7, Mar. 21, 1787; Dec. 12, 1792; Jan. 28, 1795.
Long Id. Hist. Soc. has Dec. 23, 1800; Mar. 17, 1801; Sept. 21, Oct. 26, Nov. 30, 1802.
Mass. Hist. Soc. has July 22, 1795.
Williams Coll. has Dec. 24, 31, 1799.
Univ. of Texas has Mar. 15, 1803.
Univ. of Ill. has May 15, Sept. 25, 1804.
Yale has May 12, July 28, 1812.
Morristown Lib. has June 1, 1819.

NEW JERSEY

[Elizabeth Town] Political Intelligencer, 1785–1786.

Weekly. Removed from New Brunswick to Elizabethtown without change of title or numbering. The first issue at Elizabethtown was that of Apr. 20, 1785, vol. 1, no. 79, published by Shepard Kollock, with the title of "The Political Intelligencer. And New-Jersey Advertiser." The last issue with this title was that of May 3, 1786, vol. 3, no. 133, after which the title was changed to "The New-Jersey Journal and Political Intelligencer," which see.

N. J. Hist. Soc. has Apr. 20, May 11, 1785–May 3, 1786.
Rutgers Univ. has Oct. 5, 12, 1785.
Am. Antiq. Soc. has Nov. 2, 1785; Apr. 19, 1786.
N. J. State Lib. has Feb. 1, 22, 1786.

[Freehold] Monmouth Star, 1819–1820+.

Weekly. Established Nov. 2, 1819, judging from the date of the earliest issue located, that of Dec. 21, 1819, vol. 1, no. 8, published by H[———] Jones, with the title of "Monmouth Star." At some time between Mar. 29 and June 12, 1820, the paper was transferred, being published for West Deklyn, who continued it until after 1820.

N. J. Hist. Soc. has Dec. 21, 1819; Feb. 2, Mar. 8, 22, June 12, 26, July 3, 24, Nov. 6, 1820.
Monmouth Co. Hist. Assoc., Freehold, has Aug. 7, 1820.

[Freehold] Spirit of Washington, 1814–1815.

Weekly. Established May 16, 1814, judging from the date of the first issue located, that of June 20, 1814, vol. 1, no. 6, published by John K. Joline, with the title of "Spirit of Washington." The last issue located is that of Feb. 20, 1815, vol. 1, no. 40. In March 1815 the paper was removed to Mount Holly, N. J., where it was continued, with the same title and without change of volume numbering.

Am. Antiq. Soc. has June 20, 1814.
Monmouth Co. Hist. Assoc., Freehold, has Aug. 22, Nov. 28, 1814.
N. J. Hist. Soc. has Feb. 20, 1815.

Freneau, see Mount Pleasant.

[Hackensack] Impartial Register, 1804–1805.

Weekly. Established in August 1804, judging from a reference in the Trenton "True American" of Aug. 27, 1804, which mentions "The Impartial Register," commenced at Hackensack by Blauvelt & Crissy [Thomas T. Blauvelt and James Crissy]. The only copy located is that of May 15, 1805, vol. 1, no. 35, published by Thomas T. Blauvelt, with the title of "The Impartial Register." In the "Centinel of Freedom," July 2, 1805, is a reference to the marriage of Thomas T. Blauvelt, editor of the "Impartial Register" of Hackensack, to Mary Terhewn, on June 9, 1805.

Harvard has May 15, 1805.

Monmouth, see Mount Pleasant.

Morris-Town Gazette, 1784–1785.

The fact of the establishment of a paper at Morristown in this year is known through an entry in the diary of Joseph Lewis, of Morristown, under date of June 30, 1784: "This day David Cree printed the first newspaper that was ever printed in Morristown" (Transcript of original diary in library of N. J. Historical Society). In the Springfield "Morning Herald and Weekly Advertiser" of Apr. 27, 1785, David Cree, the publisher, advertises for payments due to the "Morris-Town Gazette and New-Jersey Advertiser" published recently by Cree — at least this is the probable title made up from the advertisement, which is mutilated. Cree removed apparently in 1785 to Springfield which was about ten miles from Morristown.

[Morristown] Genius of Liberty, 1798–1811.

Weekly. Established May 24, 1798, by Jacob Mann, with the title of "The Genius of Liberty." It continued the advertisements from the "Morris County Gazette," but adopted a new volume numbering. With the issue of Apr. 30, 1801, Mann transferred the paper to Henry P. Russell. In 1806, at some time between Mar. 6 and Oct. 16, the title was enlarged to "The Genius of Liberty, and Morris Advertiser," but it reverted to "The Genius of Liberty" within a year or two, probably in 1808. In 1808, the paper was transferred to Charles Russell, according to a statement in the "Centinel of Freedom," Newark, Nov. 15, 1808, which said that the paper had "recently been disposed of by the former proprietor, to Mr. Charles Russell." The issues which have been located for 1809 are published by Charles Russell, but those of 1810 and 1811 are published by Henry P. Russell. With the issue of Aug. 7, 1810, the size of the paper was reduced to quarto. The paper was discontinued with the issue of July 30, 1811, no. 689, as was shown from a nearly complete file in the Morristown Public Library which was destroyed by fire in February 1914. The paper was immediately succeeded by the "Morris-Town Herald."

Harvard has May 24, June 7, 14, July 5, 12, Aug. 9, Nov. 22, 1798; Jan. 10, Feb. 21, Mar. 7, July 25, Nov. 7, 28, 1799; Jan. 30, Mar. 6, 13, June 26, July 17, Aug. 14, 28, Sept. 18, Oct. 9, 23, Nov. 13, 20, Dec. 11, 1800; Jan. 1, 22, Mar. 19–Apr. 16, May 7, 21, June 4, 18, 25, July 9–30, Aug. 27, Sept. 3,

10, Oct. 8, Nov. 6, 13, Dec. 25, 1801; Jan. 1, June 4–July 9, Nov. 5, 1802; Jan. 28, Feb. 4, Mar. 18, Apr. 15, May 27, June 10, 17, July 1–Aug. 12, Sept. 9–23, Oct. 7–28, Dec. 30, 1803; Feb. 3, 17, Mar. 9, 16, Apr. 20–May 4, June 1, 28, July 5, 26, Aug. 2, Sept. 13, Nov. 1–15, Dec. 20, 1804; Jan. 3, 17–Feb. 7, 21, Mar. 7–28, July 25, 1805.
N. Y. Pub. Lib. has May 24, 1798–Apr. 2, 1801.
N. J. Hist. Soc. has Sept. 6, 1798; Feb. 28, Mar. 14, 1799; Oct. 9, 23, Dec. 11–25, 1800; Jan. 1–Apr. 16, 30–Sept. 17, Oct. 1–16, Nov. 6, 13, 27, Dec. 11, 1801; Jan. 1, 15, May 28, 1802–May 6, 1803; May 23, June 13–July 11, 25, Aug. 8–Oct. 3, 1809; Mar. 5, 1811.
Am. Antiq. Soc. has May 24, June 14, Oct. 25, Dec. 20, 1798; Jan. 10, Apr. 25, Aug. 1, Sept. 12, 1799; Apr. 10, 24, June 5, 1800; June 18, 1801; Mar. 9, 1804; Apr. 11, 1805; Feb. 27, Oct. 16, Nov. 27, 1806; June 12, 26, Aug. 7, Sept. 11, 1810; Jan. 22, 1811.
Lib. Congress has May 24–June 21, July 5, 26, Aug. 9, 16, Sept. 20, Oct. 18, Nov. 1, 15, 1798; Dec. 18, 1800; Feb. 5, 26, 1801; June 17, 1803; Dec. 13, 1808.
Morristown Nat. Park Museum has May 24, 1798; Jan. 3, 1799; Apr. 10, July 10, 31, 1800; Sept. 5, 1805.
Long Id. Hist. Soc. has Aug. 23, Sept. 20, Nov. 22, 1798; July 30, 1801.
Morristown Lib. has July 9, Sept. 10, Oct. 29, 1807; Nov. 24, 1808; July 11, 1809.
Troy Pub. Lib. has Nov. 1, 15, 1798.
Phil. Lib. Co. has July 19, 1798.
Williams Coll. has Dec. 26, 1799.
Rutgers Univ. has Oct. 9, 1800.
Wis. Hist. Soc. has May 30, 1808.
N. Y. State Lib. has Jan. 10, 1809.

Morris-Town Herald, 1811–1814, 1816–1817.

Weekly. Established Aug. 6, 1811, by Henry P. Russell, with the title of "Morris-Town Herald." It was of quarto size, but was enlarged to folio with the issue of Oct. 28, 1812. It was suspended with the issue of Oct. 27, 1814, no. 169, to be followed by "The Memorandum," which see, but was resumed with the issue of May 9, 1816, no. 170. It was discontinued by Russell with the issue of Sept. 25, 1817, no. 242. A nearly complete file was owned by the Morristown Public Library, destroyed by fire in February 1914, from which the above facts were taken (letter from F. A. Canfield to editor, Mar. 10, 1917).

Morristown Lib. has Jan. 7, 1812; Apr. 3, 1813.
N. J. Hist. Soc. has Dec. 30, 1812; Mar. 4, Oct. 21, Nov. 25, 1813; Jan. 13, 20, Apr. 14, 1814.
Am. Antiq. Soc. has Sept. 2, 1812.

[Morristown] **Memorandum,** 1815–1816.

Weekly. Established Dec. 21, 1815, by Henry P. Russell, with the title of "The Memorandum." It probably was discontinued with the issue of May 2, 1816, no. 20, as the "Morris-Town Herald" resumed publication on May 9, 1816.

The Morristown Public Library had a file, lost in the fire of February, 1914, which lacked only nos. 1, 2, 8 and 20 (letter from F. A. Canfield).

N. J. Hist. Soc has Mar. 21, 1816.

[Morristown] **Morris County Gazette,** 1797–1798.

Weekly. Established May 24, 1797, by E[lijah] Cooper & Co., with the title of "Morris County Gazette." The "History of Morris County," 1882, states that Caleb Russell was the prime mover in the enterprise, having secured the services of Elijah Cooper, a practical printer, to attend to the details of the business. With the issue of Aug. 9, 1797, it was published by Elijah Cooper alone. In November, 1797, Cooper withdrew and the paper was published by Caleb Russell. With the issue of Jan. 2, 1798, it was published by Jacob Mann, and was so continued until May 15, 1798, vol. 1, no. 52, without any mention of discontinuation. The "History of Morris County" states that the last number appeared on May 15, 1798. Mann established "The Genius of Liberty," as its successor, on May 24, 1798.

N. J. Hist. Soc. has May 24–June 28, July 12, 26–Aug. 9, Sept. 6, Oct. 4–Nov. 8, 1797.

Lib. Congress has Dec. 6, 1797; Mar. 6, 20–Apr. 17, May 1–15, 1798.

Harvard has Dec. 27, 1797; Jan. 2, 9, Feb. 6, 20–Mar. 20, Apr. 10, 24, May 1, 1798.

Am. Antiq. Soc. has June 14, 28, Oct. 4–18, Nov. 1, 8, 1797; Jan. 2, 9, 23, Feb. 13, 27, Apr. 10, 1798.

[Morristown] **Palladium of Liberty,** 1808–1820+.

Weekly. Established Mar. 31, 1808, by Jacob Mann, with the title of "Palladium of Liberty." The title was slightly changed to "The Palladium of Liberty," with the issue of Sept. 2, 1813, but reverted to "Palladium of Liberty" in October 1816. The paper was continued by Mann until after 1820. A nearly complete file was in the Morristown Public Library, which was destroyed by fire in February 1914.

N. J. Hist. Soc. has May 5–June 13, 27–July 11, Sept. 5–Oct. 24, 1808; June 13, 27, July 5, 11, 25, Aug. 8–29, Sept. 5, 19, 1809; Mar. 27, 1810–Mar. 22, 1815; June 14, Dec. 21, 1815; Jan. 4, Oct. 10–31, Nov. 28, Dec. 5, 1816; Jan. 1, 16, 30–Feb. 27, Mar. 20–Apr. 3, May 1, 8, June 5–26, Aug. 7, 14, 1817; Sept. 17–Oct. 1, 15, 1818; Oct. 14, 1819–Dec. 28, 1820.

Morristown Lib. has Apr. 23, 1811; June 25, 1812; Jan. 18, 25, Feb. 8, 22, 1816; Apr. 3, 1817–Dec. 28, 1820.
Rutgers Univ. has Mar. 27, 1810–Mar. 19, 1811; Feb. 5, 12, 26, Mar. 5, May 28, June 11, 25–July 16, Aug. 13, Sept. 3–Oct. 7, 22, Nov. 12, 1818; Mar. 11–Apr. 1, 22–May 6, 27, 1819; Sept. 14, Dec. 21, 1820..
Am. Antiq. Soc. has May 9, 1808; Feb. 28, Dec. 26, 1809; Feb. 27, June 12, 1810; Sept. 26, 1816; Aug. 7, Nov. 6, 1817.
Morristown Nat. Park Museum has Mar. 31, June 13, 1808; Apr. 30, 1811; Aug. 25, 1814.
Boston Athenæum has Oct. 10, 1808; Apr. 25, May 23, 1809.
Harvard has Oct. 3, Nov. 15, 1808.
East Hampton, N. Y., Free Lib. has Apr. 18, 1809.
N. Y. Pub. Lib. has Feb. 18, 1813; July 2, 1818.
Univ. of Mich. (Clements) has May 30, 1809.
Buffalo Hist. Soc. has July 11, 1809.

[Mount Holly] Burlington Mirror, 1818–1819.

Weekly. Established Sept. 16, 1818, by Nathan Palmer & Son [Nathan and Strange N. Palmer] with the title of "The Burlington Mirror." The last issue with this title was that of Sept. 8, 1819, vol. 1, no. 52, after which the title was changed to "The New-Jersey Mirror and Burlington County Advertiser," which see.

Rutgers Univ. and Hist. Soc. Penn. have Sept. 16, 1818–Sept. 8, 1819.
New Jersey Mirror office, Mount Holly, has Sept. 16, Oct. 14, 1818–Sept. 8, 1819.

[Mount Holly] New-Jersey Mirror, 1819–1820+.

Weekly. A continuation, without change of volume numbering, of "The Burlington Mirror." The first issue with the title of "The New-Jersey Mirror and Burlington County Advertiser" was that of Sept. 15, 1819, vol. 2, no. 1, published by Nathan Palmer & Son [Nathan and Strange N. Palmer]. The paper was continued by them until after 1820.

N. J. Hist. Soc. and Rutgers Univ. have Sept. 15, 1819–Dec. 27, 1820.
New Jersey Mirror office has Sept. 15, Oct. 13, 1819–Dec. 27, 1820.

[Mount Holly] Spirit of Washington, 1815.

Weekly. A continuation, without change of volume numbering, of the paper of the same name, published at Freehold, N. J. It was removed to Mount Holly in March 1815, according to the earliest and only issue located, that of Mar. 25, 1815, vol. 1, no. 42, published by John K. Joline, with the title of "Spirit of Washington."

N. J. Hist. Soc. has Mar. 25, 1815.

[Mount Pleasant] Jersey Chronicle, 1795–1796.

Weekly. Established May 2, 1795, by Philip Freneau, with the title of "Jersey Chronicle," published at "Mount-Pleasant, near Middletown-Point, Monmouth, N. Jersey." The local news appeared under the heading of Monmouth, although Monmouth was the name of the county. The paper contained eight pages and was of square octavo size, but with the issue of May 16, 1795, was increased in size to quarto. It was discontinued with the issue of Apr. 30, 1796, vol. 1, no. 52. The village of Mount Pleasant has been called Freneau since 1890.

Freneau had previously planned a paper at Mount Pleasant to be called "The Monmouth Gazette, and East-Jersey Intelligencer," which, however, was not established. He issued a prospectus, dated July 4, 1794, a copy of which is owned by the Monmouth Co. Hist. Assoc. (see "American Literature," vol. 6, p. 332).

N. Y. Hist. Soc. has May 2–Oct. 24, Nov. 7, 1795–Apr. 30, 1796.
Monmouth Co. Hist. Assoc., Freehold, N. J., has May 9, 1795–Apr. 30, 1796.
Harvard has Mar. 5, 9, 26, Apr. 9–23, 1796.
Am. Antiq. Soc. has Oct. 31, Dec. 12, 1795; Apr. 2, 1796.
N. J. Hist. Soc. has June 20, 1795.
Wis. Hist. Soc. has Oct. 24, 1795.

[New Brunswick] Arnett's Brunswick Advertiser, 1793.

Weekly. Established Nov. 5, 1793, judging from the first and only issue located, that of Nov. 12, 1793, vol. 1, no. 2, published by Shelly Arnett, with the title of "Arnett's Brunswick Advertiser." Arnett started his paper immediately after the dissolution of his partnership with Blauvelt, with whom he had published "The Guardian." The title was later changed to "Arnett's New-Jersey Federalist," which see.

Harvard has Nov. 12, 1793.

[New Brunswick] Arnett's New-Jersey Federalist, 1793–1795.

Weekly. A continuation, without change of volume numbering, of "Arnett's Brunswick Advertiser," the change of title having occurred sometime between November 1793 and December 1794. The earliest issue located is that of Dec. 25, 1794, vol. 2, no. 60, published by Shelly Arnett, with the title of "Arnett's New-Jersey Federalist." The last issue of Arnett's paper was undoubtedly that of Mar. 5, 1795, vol. 2, no. 70, and with the succeeding issue it was purchased by George F. Hopkins, who changed the title to "The New-Jersey Federalist," which see.

Rutgers Univ. has Dec. 25, 1794; Feb. 26, 1795.
Harvard has Feb. 26, 1795.

[New Brunswick] **Brunswick Gazette,** 1787–1792.

Weekly. A continuation, without change of volume numbering, of "The New-Brunswick Gazette." The earliest issue located with the new title of "The Brunswick Gazette, and Weekly Monitor," is that of July 3, 1787, vol. 1, no. 40, published by Shelly Arnett. With the issue of June 16, 1789, the title was shortened to "The Brunswick Gazette." With the issue of Nov. 10, 1789, the paper was transferred to Abraham Blauvelt. With the issue of Mar. 13, 1792, the title was slightly changed to "The Brunswic Gazette." The paper was discontinued with the issue of Oct. 30, 1792, no. 318, to be succeeded by "The Guardian."

N. J. Hist. Soc. has July 3, 1787–Apr. 14, 1789; Mar. 23, Sept. 7, 1790; Sept. 11, 25, 1792.
Rutgers Univ. has June 2–Nov. 17, 1789; Aug. 17, 1790–May 10, June 7, 1791; Mar. 20, May 1, 29, June 5, 1792.
Margaret L. Terhune, Matawan, N. J., has June 28, 1791–July 17, 1792.
Am. Antiq. Soc. has Aug. 18, 1789; Aug. 3–17, Sept. 7, Oct. 5, Nov. 30, Dec. 21, 1790; Feb. 1, 8, Mar. 29, Apr. 12–May 3, 17, June 7, 28–July 19, Aug. 16–30, Oct. 4, 18, Nov. 1, 1791; Jan. 3, 17–31, Feb. 14, 28–Mar. 13, May 8–22, June 5–19, Aug. 7, 1792.
Lib. Congress has June 21, 28, July 12–Nov. 22, Dec. 6, 1791–Apr. 24, 1792.
Hist. Soc. Penn. has Aug. 7–Oct. 30, 1792.
N. Y. Hist. Soc. has July 17, 1787; Apr. 21, June 16, 1789; May 4, 25, July 6, 1790.
Harvard has Mar. 29, June 21, July 5–26, Sept. 27, 1791.
N. Y. Pub. Lib. has Oct. 23, 1787.
Princeton has May 1, 1792.

[New Brunswick] **Fredonian,** 1811–1820+.

Weekly. Established Apr. 17, 1811, by D[avid] & J[ames] Fitz Randolph, with the title of "The Fredonian." With the issue of May 2, 1816, the partnership was dissolved and the paper published by D. Fitz Randolph. It was so continued until after 1820.

Rutgers Univ. has June 26–July 31, Aug. 14–Sept. 4, 18, 1811–Nov. 26, 1812; Feb. 18, Apr. 15, 22, May 13–27, July 15, Oct. 7–Nov. 11, 25, Dec. 23, 30, 1813; Jan. 6–May 19, June 2, 16–July 21, Aug. 4, 11, Sept. 15, 29, Oct. 20, Nov. 3, 10, 24, Dec. 22, 1814; Jan. 5, Feb. 2, 9, 23, Mar. 2, 30–May 4, 18, 25, June 8, 29, July 6, 27–Aug. 24, Sept. 7, Oct. 12, 19, Nov. 9, 16, 1815; Jan. 25, Feb. 22, Mar. 8, 21–May 2, 16, June 6, 27–July 25, Aug. 29, Sept. 12, Oct. 3–31, Nov. 14, 21, Dec. 12–26, 1816; Jan. 2–Mar. 27, Apr. 24–May 15, 29, June 12–July 3, 17, 24, Aug. 21, Sept. 18, Oct. 2–Nov. 6, 20, Dec. 11, 18, 1817; Jan. 1–Nov. 12, 26–Dec. 17, 31, 1818; Jan. 7–Oct. 7, 21–Dec. 16, 30, 1819; Jan. 6–Aug. 10, 24–Dec. 28, 1820.
Lib. Congress has Mar. 10, 1814; Aug. 8, 1816; Jan. 7–Nov. 25, Dec. 9–30,

1819; Jan. 6–Apr. 27, May 11–June 22, July 6–Oct. 26, Nov. 9, 16, 1820.
N. J. Hist. Soc. has June 29, 1815; Feb. 13, Aug. 21, 1817; July 16, Aug. 6, 20, 1818; June 3, 1819; Jan. 20, Mar. 9, 1820.
Am. Antiq. Soc. has Apr. 24, 1811; Dec. 9, 1813; May 14, 1818; June 10, 1819.
Mass. Hist. Soc. has Dec. 2, 1813.
New Haven Col. Hist. Soc. has Feb. 9, 1815.

New-Brunswick Gazette, 1786.

Weekly. Established Oct. 5, 1786, by Shelly Arnett, with the title of "The New-Brunswick Gazette, and Weekly Monitor." Within a few months the title was changed to "The Brunswick Gazette, and Weekly Monitor," which see.

N. J. Hist. Soc. has Oct. 5, 1786.

[New Brunswick] Genius of Liberty, 1795–1796.

Weekly. A continuation, without change of volume numbering, of "The New-Jersey Federalist." Judging from an advertisement in the issue of Jan. 22, 1795, the first issue with the new title of "Genius of Liberty, & New-Brunswick Advertiser" was that of June 11, 1795, no. 84, published by George F. Hopkins. In October 1795, the title was altered to "Genius of Liberty, & New-Jersey Advertiser." The last issue located is that of Feb. 22, 1796, no. 121. Hopkins went to New York, where he participated in the publication of "The Minerva," May 2, 1796.

Harvard has June 22, Aug. 24, Sept. 14, Dec. 21, 1795; Jan. 11, Feb. 22, 1796.
Am. Antiq. Soc. has Aug. 10, 17, 31, Oct. 5, Nov. 9, 16, 1795.
Rutgers Univ. has Oct. 26, 1795.

[New Brunswick] Guardian, 1792–1816.

Weekly. Established Nov. 7, 1792, by Arnett and Blauvelt [Shelly Arnett and Abraham Blauvelt], with the title of "The Guardian; or, New-Brunswick Advertiser." With the issue of Nov. 5, 1793, the firm was dissolved and the paper published by Abraham Blauvelt. With the issue of Nov. 24, 1795, the word "The" was omitted from the title. With the issue of Oct. 20, 1814, Blauvelt disposed of the paper to G[alen] L. Austin, but with the issue of May 18, 1815, bought it back from Austin's family, and continued its publication presumably to the issue of Apr. 11, 1816, vol. 24, no. 26. The New Brunswick "Times," in its issue of Apr. 11, 1816, announced that they had purchased from Mr. Blauvelt the entire establishment of "The Guardian," which after that date would be "blended" with "The Times."

Rutgers Univ. has Nov. 7, 1792–Oct. 23, 1798; May 28, 1799; Jan. 7, Oct. 22, 1800; Mar. 27, 1801; Nov. 5, 1801–Nov. 26, 1807; Mar. 3, 1808; July 13,

NEW JERSEY 507

1809; June 13, Aug. 1, 1811; July 30, 1812; Oct. 20, 27, 1814; Mar. 16, Apr. 6, May 18, Sept. 14, 1815; Feb. 22, 1816.
Lib. Congress has June 30, 1795; Oct. 30–Dec. 25, 1798; Jan. 8–May 28, June 11–July 9, 23–Dec. 31, 1799; Jan. 7–June 10, 24–Dec. 24, 1800; Jan. 1–8, 22–Aug. 6, 20–Oct. 22, 1801; June 2, 1803; Sept. 1, 1808; Oct. 18, 1810–Oct. 7, 1813.
Hist. Soc. Penn. has Nov. 7, 1792–Sept. 23, 1794.
New Brunswick Pub. Lib. has Nov. 5, 1801–Oct. 18, 1804.
Harvard has Mar. 17, May 12–June 2, 16, 23, July 21, Aug. 4, 18, 25, Sept. 15, Oct. 13, 1795; Jan. 12, Apr. 26–May 10, June 21, 28, July 12–Aug. 9, 23, 30, Sept. 20, Oct. 18–Nov. 8, 22–Dec. 20, 1796; Jan. 10–Feb. 28, Mar. 14–May 3, 23, July 11, Sept. 5, Oct. 24, Nov. 7, 14, Dec. 5, 1797; Apr. 10, 24, May 8, 22, 29, June 26, July 3, 17, 31–Aug. 14, Sept. 11, Oct. 23, Nov. 6–27, Dec. 11, 1798; Jan. 1–22, Feb. 19, Mar. 5–19, Apr. 9, 16, May 7–21, June 4, July 30, Aug. 6, 20, Sept. 3–Oct. 1, 22, Nov. 12, 26, Dec. 17, 1799; Jan. 14–Feb. 4, 18, Mar. 18, 25, Apr. 8–May 6, 20, June 10–24, July 29–Aug. 26, Sept. 10–Oct. 15, 29–Nov. 19, Dec. 3–17, 1800; Jan. 22–Feb. 5, 26–Mar. 12, 26, Apr. 9–30, May 14–June 18, July 2, 16–Sept. 17, Oct. 1, 29–Dec. 3, 17, 31, 1801; Jan. 14, Mar. 25, 1802; Oct. 13, 27, 1803; May 31, Sept. 6, Oct. 18, 1804; Aug. 6, Sept. 3, 1807.
Am. Antiq. Soc. has Nov. 14, 21, 1792; May 1, 1793; Oct. 27, 1795; Nov. 1, 8, Dec. 13, 1796; Apr. 25, June 6, July 18, Aug. 1–Sept. 5, 19–Oct. 3, 17, 24, Nov. 7–Dec. 5, 19, 1797; Jan. 2, 16–Feb. 6, 20, 27, May 8, 15, 29, July 3, 24, Aug. 21, Nov. 27, Dec. 11, 1798; Jan. 8, 29, June 25, Oct. 1, 1799; May 20, June 10, July 15, 1800; May 4, 19, 1803; Mar. 1, July 26, 1804; Nov. 21, 1805; June 5, Aug. 21, 28, Nov. 6–20, 1806; Jan. 8, 15, Feb. 5, 1807.
Univ. of Mich. (Clements) has Nov. 28–Dec. 26, 1792; Jan. 2–Feb. 13, 27, Mar. 20, Apr. 3–17, 1793.
N. J. Hist. Soc. has Feb. 27, Aug. 14, 1793; Dec. 30, 1794; July 11, 1797; Dec. 24, 1799; July 20, 1809; Dec. 20, 1813; Nov. 24, Dec. 29, 1814; Apr. 13, Nov. 16, 1815.
Monmouth Co. Hist. Assoc., Freehold, has Mar. 24, 1795; May 10, 1796; Dec. 24, 1799; Jan. 17, 1811; Dec. 14, 1814.
Phil. Lib. Co. has Oct. 2, 16, 23, 1793.
N. Y. Pub. Lib. has July 18, 1805; Apr. 2, 1812.
Princeton has Oct. 4, 1810.
Wesleyan Univ. has Feb. 9, 1815.

[New Brunswick] New-Jersey Federalist, 1795.

Weekly. A continuation, without change of volume numbering of "Arnett's New-Jersey Federalist." The first issue with the new title of "The New-Jersey Federalist" was that of Mar. 12, 1795, vol, 2, no. 71, published by George F.

Hopkins. Apparently the last issue with this title was that of June 4, 1795, after which the title was changed to "Genius of Liberty," which see.

Harvard has Mar. 12, Apr. 2, 23, 1795.
Am. Antiq. Soc. has May 7, 1795.

[New Brunswick] **Political Intelligencer,** 1783–1785.

Weekly. Established Oct. 14, 1783, by Kollock and Arnett [Shepard Kollock and Shelly Arnett], with the title of "The Political Intelligencer. And New-Jersey Advertiser." With the issue of July 13, 1784, the partnership was dissolved and Shepard Kollock became sole proprietor. The last issue printed at New Brunswick was that of Apr. 5, 1785, no. 78, and upon Apr. 20, it was removed to Elizabethtown.

N. J. Hist. Soc. has Oct. 14, 1783–Apr. 5, 1785.
N. Y. Hist. Soc. has June 8, Sept. 14, 1784; Jan. 4, Mar. 22, 1785.
Am. Antiq. Soc. has Oct. 21, Nov. 4, 11, 1783.
Rutgers Univ. has Dec. 2, 1783; Sept. 21, 1784.
Lib. Congress has Oct. 26, 1784.

[New Brunswick] **Republican Herald,** 1810.

Weekly. Established Jan. 17, 1810, judging from the earliest issue located, that of Feb. 7, 1810, vol. 1, no. 4, published by Isaac Arnett Kollock & Co., with the title of "Republican Herald." The last issue located is that of Feb. 14, 1810, vol. 1, no. 5.

Am. Antiq. Soc. has Feb. 7, 14, 1810.

[New Brunswick] **Times,** 1815–1820+.

Weekly. Established June 1, 1815, by Deare & Myer [Lewis Deare and William Myer], with the title of "The Times: and New-Brunswick General Advertiser." On May 31, 1817, judging from an advertisement in the issue of Sept. 11, 1817, this firm was dissolved, and the paper published by William Myer. With the issue of Oct. 8, 1818, the title was slightly changed to "The Times, & New-Brunswick Advertiser." The paper was continued by Myer until after 1820.

Rutgers Univ. has June 1, 1815–May 22, 1817; Oct. 2, Nov. 13, 1817; Apr. 2, 1818; May 28, 1818–Dec. 28, 1820.
N. J. Hist. Soc. has Jan. 23, Feb. 27, Sept. 11, 1817; Apr. 23, July 9, Nov. 12, 1818; Dec. 21, 1820.
Am. Antiq. Soc. has July 20, 1815; Apr. 18, Dec. 26, 1816; July 16, Oct. 8, Dec. 24, 1818; Apr. 8, 22, 1819.
Wis. Hist. Soc. has June 8, 1815.
N. Y. Pub. Lib. has Dec. 3, 1818.
Lib. Congress has Oct. 28, 1819.

[Newark] **Centinel of Freedom**, 1796–1820+.

Weekly. Established Oct. 5, 1796, by Daniel Dodge & Co., with the title of "The Centinel of Freedom." With the issue of Oct. 4, 1797, the firm name was changed to Aaron Pennington & Daniel Dodge. The paper was sold to Jabez Parkhurst & Samuel Pennington with the issue of Oct. 1, 1799, but with the issue of Dec. 31, 1799, Parkhurst retired and the paper was published by Samuel Pennington & Stephen Gould. This firm was dissolved with the issue of May 3, 1803, and the paper published by Samuel Pennington. With the issue of Nov. 22, 1803, he transferred it to Tuttle & Pike [William Tuttle and John Pike], changed with the issue of Aug. 14, 1804, to W. Tuttle & Co. The firm was dissolved and the paper published by Wm. Tuttle with the issue of Aug. 2, 1808. The printing-office was damaged by fire on Mar. 20, 1809, resulting in no issue on Mar. 21 and resumption on Mar. 28. With the issue of Sept. 14, 1813, William Tuttle disposed of a half interest to his brother John, and the paper was published by John Tuttle & Co., and was so continued until after 1820.

N. J. Hist. Soc. has Oct. 5, 1796–Dec. 26, 1820.

Am. Antiq. Soc. has Oct. 5–Dec. 14, 1796; Jan. 4, 1797–Dec. 25, 1798; Jan. 1– Sept. 24, Oct. 1, 15, Nov. 12, Dec. 17, 31, 1799; Jan. 7, 1800–Dec. 26, 1820, with only a few issues missing.

Lib. Congress has Nov. 2–30, 1796; Jan. 25, Feb. 8–22, Mar. 8, Apr. 5, June 28, Aug. 30, Sept. 6, Nov. 8, 15, 29, Dec. 19, 26, 1797; Jan. 2–30, Feb. 20–Mar. 6, 20, Apr. 10, 17, May 1–15, 29, July 3, 17, 31, Sept. 4, 18, Oct. 30, Nov. 20, Dec. 25, 1798; Jan. 15, 22, Feb. 5, 19, Mar. 5, 19, 26, Apr. 16–30, May 14– June 11, 25, July 9–Aug. 6, 20, Sept. 10, Dec. 31, 1799; Apr. 22, 29, May 13, 27,˙June 17, Oct. 21, Nov. 11, Dec. 2, 1800; Mar. 10, July 14, 28, Aug. 18, 1801; May 11, 1802; Apr. 12, July 19, Aug. 2, 9, Oct. 25, 1803; Jan. 17, Feb. 28, Mar. 13, 1804; Apr. 23, 1805; Jan. 21, Mar. 4, Oct. 14, 1806; Apr. 7, 14, July 21, 1807; June 21, Oct. 4, Dec. 13, 1808; Apr. 11, 18, May 9, 23, July 18, 1809; Jan. 30, Feb. 6, 20–Mar. 20, Apr. 10–May 1, 15–June 19, July 3, 10, 31–Oct. 2, 16, 30, Nov. 13, 27, Dec. 18, 25, 1810; Jan. 1–Feb. 12, Mar. 5–May 7, 21–June 18, July 16–Aug. 13, Sept. 10–24, Oct. 8, 15, 29, Nov. 19, 26, Dec. 10, 24, 31, 1811; Jan. 7–Mar. 24, Apr. 7–June 30, July 14– Aug. 18, Sept. 22, Oct. 13, Dec. 8, 1812; Jan. 19, Mar. 16, 30–Apr. 27, June 1, July 20, Aug. 24, 31, Sept. 12, 19, Nov. 9, 23, 1813; Jan. 18, Feb. 1, 8, Mar. 1, 8, Apr. 26, May 10, 31, June 28, July 5, 12, Aug. 2, 16, Sept. 13– Nov. 1, Dec. 6, 13, 1814; Jan. 10, Mar. 28, Aug. 29, Oct. 10, 17, 1815; Jan. 30, Feb. 6, Mar. 19, June 18, July 23, Aug. 20, 1816; Feb. 3, 10, Mar. 10, Apr. 7–May 12, 26, June 9, July 28, Sept. 1, Oct. 20, Nov. 10, 17, Dec. 1– 29, 1818; Jan. 5–Mar. 9, 23, 30, Apr. 13, May 11, 18, June 8–29, Aug. 10, Nov. 30–Dec. 14, 1819; Jan. 4, Feb. 1, 22, Mar. 7–28, Apr. 25–Aug. 29, Sept. 12–26, Oct. 10, 24, Nov. 7–28, Dec. 12, 26, 1820.

N. Y. Pub. Lib. has Oct. 5–Dec. 7, 1796; Jan. 4, 1797–Sept. 24, 1799, fair; Mar. 4, 1800; Jan. 6, 1801–May 4, 1802.

Princeton has (on deposit) Oct. 12, 1796–Sept. 22, 1801, fair.
N. Y. Hist. Soc. has Feb. 1, 1797; Dec. 17, 1799; Jan. 7, 21–Feb. 18, Apr. 1, 15–May 6, July 1–22, Aug. 5–26, Sept. 9–30, Oct. 21, Nov. 11–Dec. 23, 1800; Jan. 6–20, Feb. 3–Sept. 22, 1801; Jan. 2, 1810–Dec. 31, 1811; Sept. 13, 1814; Jan. 3–Dec. 26, 1815; Apr. 23, May 14, 1816; Sept. 15, 1818; Jan. 19, 1819.
Harvard has Oct. 12–Dec. 14, 28, 1796; Jan. 11–May 3, 24, 31, June 14–July 12, Sept. 13–Oct. 11, Nov. 15, 22, Dec. 12, 1797; Jan. 2, 16, 23, Feb. 6, 27–Mar. 13, Apr. 3, 10, 24, May 1, June 5, July 10, Aug. 21, Sept. 18, Oct. 23, 30, Dec. 11, 1798; Feb. 19, 1799; Aug. 26, Sept. 16, Oct. 7, 29, 1800; Jan. 13, 20, Feb. 10, 17, Apr. 7, 28, May 19–June 9, 23–July 21, Aug. 11, 18, Sept. 8–22, Oct. 6, 20, 27, Nov. 16, Dec. 8, 15, 1801; Jan. 4, 18, Apr. 5, 26, May 17–June 14, 28, July 6, 19, Aug. 2, 16–Sept. 13, 27–Oct. 12, 25, Nov. 29, 1803; May 8, 15, July 17, 24, Aug. 7, 22, Sept. 4, 18, Oct. 2, 9, Nov. 6, 20, 1804; Jan. 8, 22, Feb. 5–19, Mar. 12–26, Apr. 9–30, May 21, 29, June 11, July 2, 9, Aug. 13–27, Sept. 10–24, Oct. 8, 22–Nov. 26, Dec. 17, 31, 1805; Jan. 7–Feb. 11, 25, Mar. 4, 25, Apr. 1, May 13, July 29, 1806.
Rutgers Univ. has Mar. 29, May 3, 10, 1797; Mar. 13–Sept. 18, 1798, fair; Aug. 20, 1799; Jan. 6, 1807–Sept. 13, 1808; Sept. 26, 1809–Aug. 14, 1810; June 18, Oct. 8, 1811; Mar. 17, 31, June 16–July 14, Aug. 18, Nov. 10, 1812; Mar. 16, 23, June 15, Sept. 21, 1813–Sept. 10, Oct. 8, 1816; Sept. 15, 1818–Sept. 7, 1819; Jan. 11, Nov. 21, 1820.
Morristown Nat. Park Museum has June 12, 1798; July 9, Dec. 24, 1799; Aug. 5, 1800; Nov. 24, 1807.
N. J. State Lib. has July 12, 1797; Nov. 27, 1798.
Duke Univ. has May 1, 8, 1798; Aug. 6, 1799.
Mass. Hist. Soc. has Mar. 3, Dec. 29, 1812.
Williams Coll. has Dec. 24, 1799.
Long Id. Hist. Soc. has Nov. 25, 1800.
N. Y. State Lib. has June 12, 1810.
Morristown Lib. has Oct. 20, 1812.
Wis. Hist. Soc. has Nov. 3, 1818.

Newark Gazette, 1797–1804.

Weekly. A continuation of "Woods's Newark Gazette and New-Jersey Advertiser," but with a new volume numbering. The first issue, that of Nov. 8, 1797, bore the title of "Newark Gazette and New-Jersey Advertiser" and was printed by John Woods for the Proprietors. With the issue of Feb. 6, 1798, it was printed by John H. Williams for the Proprietors. With the issue of May 7, 1799, it was bought and published by Jacob Halsey, who changed the title with the issue of May 21, 1799, to "The Newark Gazette." With the issue of May 19, 1801, the paper was transferred to John Wallis. With the issue of June 5, 1804, the title was changed to "Newark Gazette and Federal Republican." The last issue located is that of Dec. 4, 1804, vol. 8, no. 3. In the "Centinel of Freedom" of

Jan. 1, 1805, is to be found this statement: "The Newark Gazette expired on Tuesday [Dec. 25, 1804] of a decline which it bore with Christian fortitude. . . . Scarcely had it given up the ghost . . . ere it had been born again. Like the Phoenix of the East, the Republican Herald arose out of the corrupted remains of the Newark Gazette."

Rutgers Univ. has Nov. 8, 1797–Dec. 4, 1804.
N. J. Hist. Soc. has Nov. 15, 1797–June 16, 1801.
Harvard has Nov. 8–Dec. 19, 1797; Jan. 2, 9, 30, Feb. 13, 27, Mar. 6, Apr. 3, 24, May 1, 15–29, June 19, July 17, Sept. 4–18, Nov. 6, 13, 1798; Jan. 15, 22, Feb. 19–Mar. 5, 26, Apr. 2, 16, May 21, June 18, Aug. 20, Sept. 17, Oct. 1–15, 29, 1799; Mar. 25, Apr. 8, May 6, 27, June 10, 17, July 29–Aug. 19, Sept. 16, 1800; Jan. 27, 1801.
Am. Antiq. Soc. has Dec. 5, 19, 26, 1797; Jan. 2–Feb. 20, Mar. 6–20, Apr. 3, 10, 24, May 8, 22, 29, June 26, July 10–24, Oct. 2, 23, Nov. 6, 20–Dec. 4, 1798; Jan. 8–Mar. 19, Apr. 16, 23, May 14–June 4, 18–July 2, 16–Aug. 6, 27, Sept. 17, Nov. 12, 26, Dec. 17, 1799; May 27, 1800; Mar. 20, 1804.
Princeton has (on deposit) Nov. 8, 1797; Mar. 20–Nov. 20, 1798, fair.
Colgate Univ., Hamilton, has July 10, 31, Oct. 2, 30, 1804.
Lib. Congress has Sept. 25, 1798; Nov. 4, 1800.
Long Id. Hist. Soc. has Feb. 10, 1801.

Newark Messenger, 1817–1818.

Weekly. Established Oct. 10, 1817, with the title of "The Newark Messenger," edited by William Ward and printed by Peter Conover. The firm was dissolved with the issue of Sept. 15, 1818, and the paper published by William Ward. With the issue of Oct. 23, 1818, it was printed and published by V[———] R. Paine, Mr. Ward continuing as editor. The last issue located is that of Nov. 20, 1818, vol. 2, no. 6, and the paper was evidently soon after discontinued, to be succeeded by "The Newark Patriot."

N. J. Hist. Soc. has Oct. 10–Dec. 5, 26, 1817; Jan. 9, 16, 30, Feb. 13, 20, Mar. 6–Apr. 17, May 1–29, June 19, 26, July 10, 17, Aug. 7, 14, Oct. 9, Nov. 20, 1818.
Plainfield, N. J., Pub. Lib. has Oct. 31–Nov. 21, Dec. 5, 12, 26, 1817; Jan. 9–30, Feb. 20–Apr. 3, 17–Nov. 6, 1818.
Am. Antiq. Soc. has Apr. 10, 1818.

[Newark] Modern Spectator, 1807–1808.

Weekly. Established Nov. 27, 1807, by Kollock & Gould [Isaac Arnett Kollock and Elias B. Gould], with the title of "The Modern Spectator." It was published in magazine form, of quarto size and with pagination, but because of its current local news, death notices and advertisements, it might be regarded as a newspaper. In December 1807, E. B. Gould became sole publisher. It was discontinued with the issue of Nov. 25, 1808, vol. 1, no. 46.

N. J. Hist. Soc. has Nov. 27, 1807–Nov. 25, 1808.

[Newark] **New-Jersey Eagle,** 1820+.

Weekly. Established Mar. 3, 1820, with the title of "New-Jersey Eagle, and Newark, Orange, and Bloomfield Early Intelligencer," printed and published by Edward M. Murden and edited by Joseph T. Murden. With the issue of Nov. 3, 1820, the title was abbreviated to "New-Jersey Eagle" and the paper was edited by William B. Kinney and printed by J[acob] Johnson. Continued until after 1820.

N. J. Hist. Soc. has Mar. 3–Dec. 29, 1820.

[Newark] **New-Jersey Telescope,** 1808–1809.

Semi-weekly and weekly. Established as a semi-weekly Nov. 4, 1808, with the title of "New-Jersey Telescope," printed for the Proprietor by William W. Vermilye. With the issue of May 5, 1809, the paper was published by Thomas T. Blauvelt. With the issue of Nov. 7, 1809, vol. 2, no. 1, the paper became a weekly. This issue is the last located. The press and types were sold in Newark by William Tuttle, according to an advertisement in the "Centinel of Freedom," Feb. 27, 1810.

Rutgers has Nov. 4, 1808–Oct. 27, 1809.
Am. Antiq. Soc. has Nov. 4, 1808–May 2, Oct. 31, Nov. 7, 1809.
N. J. Hist. Soc. has Nov. 8, 1808–Mar. 28, May 12–23, 1809.
Harvard has Nov. 18, 1808.

[Newark] **New-York Gazette,** 1776.

Weekly. First printed at Newark by Hugh Gaine on Sept. 21, 1776, with the title of "The New-York Gazette; and the Weekly Mercury," no. 1301. Hugh Gaine, the publisher of "The New-York Gazette," immediately prior to the British occupation of New York, removed presses and type to Newark, N. J., and there, on Sept. 21, 1776, issued his paper, with the above title. The imprint was "Printed by Hugh Gaine, at Newark, in East New-Jersey," and the size of the paper was one leaf, folio. This was followed by issues on Sept. 28, Oct. 5, 12, 19, 26, and Nov. 2, 1776, these six issues consisting of two leaves, quarto. The issue for Oct. 12 announces that "This paper has now been published in this town four weeks, and sent to the customers, that could be found, as usual." The last Newark issue was that of Nov. 2, 1776, no. 1307. Gaine then returned to New York. In the meantime Gaine's New York office, under the inspection of the British authorities, had been used for the publication of a paper with the same title, and the same volume numbering, nos. 1301-1307, but issued weekly from Sept. 30 to Nov. 11. The issue of Sept. 30 allowed Gaine's name to remain in the imprint, but the subsequent issues omitted it. The Newark issues were evidently edited and printed in Newark, since the type of the heading differs from the New York issues, and the news and advertisements were expressly intended for New Jersey. A full discussion of the subject is given in Ford's "Journals of Hugh Gaine," vol. 1, pp. 54-58.

N. Y. Pub. Lib. has the Newark issues, Sept. 21-Nov. 2, 1776.
Am. Antiq. Soc. and N. Y. Hist. Soc. have Sept. 28, 1776.

Newark Patriot, 1819.

Weekly. Established Jan. 1, 1819, by Pares & Son [ ], with the title of "The Newark Patriot and New Jersey General Advertiser." The last issue located is that of Apr. 2, 1819, vol. 1, no. 14.

Plainfield, N. J., Pub. Lib. has Jan. 1-Apr. 2, 1819.

[Newark] Republican Herald, 1804-1805.

Weekly. Established Dec. 25, 1804, by David C. Baldwin, with the title of "Republican Herald." It was discontinued in March, 1805, according to the following statement in the "Centinel of Freedom" of Apr. 2, 1805: "The Republican Herald, of this town, which was commenced about the beginning of the present year, was discontinued week before last."

N. J. Hist. Soc. has Dec. 25, 1804.

[Newark] Woods's Newark Gazette, 1791-1797.

Weekly. Established May 19, 1791, by John Woods, with the title of "Woods's Newark Gazette." With the issue of Feb. 14, 1793, the title was changed to "Woods's Newark Gazette and Paterson Advertiser." In a Supplement to the issue of Jan. 22, 1794, Woods issued "Proposals" for publishing the paper semi-weekly, but the plan did not meet with support, so was given up. With the issue of May 13, 1795, the title was changed to "Woods's Newark Gazette and New-Jersey Advertiser." The last issue with this title was that of Nov. 1, 1797, vol. 7, no. 26, when Woods sold out to Proprietors who started a new volume numbering and adopted the new title of "Newark Gazette and New-Jersey Advertiser," which see.

N. J. Hist. Soc. has May 19, 1791-Nov. 1, 1797.
Am. Antiq. Soc. has June 16, 23, July 7, 28, Aug. 4, 18, Sept. 1, 15, 1791; Jan. 26-Feb. 9, May 10, 31, Aug. 23, Oct. 4, Nov. 15, Dec. 13, 19, 1792; Feb. 7, Apr. 24, May 15, July 3, Aug. 7, Oct. 2-Dec. 25, 1793; Jan. 1-July 2, 16-Dec. 31, 1794; Jan. 7-Apr. 1, 22, 29, May 13, 20, June 3-Sept. 9, Nov. 4,

1795; May 11–Sept. 28, Oct. 12–Nov. 2, 16, 23, Dec. 14–28, 1796; Jan. 4, 18–May 10, 24–June 7, July 5, Oct. 25, 1797.

Lib. Congress has Oct. 2, 1793; Mar. 12–Apr. 30, May 14–July 2, 16–Aug. 6, 20–Sept. 3, Oct. 29, 1794; Nov. 11, 1795; May 11, 25, June 8, 29, July 6, 20–Aug. 31, Sept. 14–Dec. 7, 1796; Jan. 4, 18, 25, Feb. 8, 15, 1797.

Harvard has June 16, July 7, 28, Nov. 24, 1791; Mar. 4, 25, May 27, June 10–July 8, 22, Aug. 5, Sept. 9, Nov. 18, 1795; Mar. 16–Apr. 6, May 4, 11, 25, June 29, July 6, 20–Aug. 10, 24–Sept. 21, Oct. 12–Dec. 28, 1796; Jan. 11–25, Feb. 8–Mar. 1, 15–Apr. 26, May 24–June 14, 28, July 12, Aug. 16, 30, Oct. 4–Nov. 1, 1797.

Phil. Lib. Co. has Oct. 2, 16, 23, 1793; Oct. 28–Nov. 11, 25, Dec. 9, 1795; Jan. 13, 27, Mar. 16, 23, Apr. 6, 13, 27, May 11, 25–June 29, July 13–Aug. 17, 1796.

N. Y. Pub. Lib. has Dec. 4, 1793; May 21, Oct. 8, 1794.

Wis. Hist. Soc. has Aug. 2, 1792; Apr. 1, 1795.

Rutgers Univ. has Oct. 29, 1794.

Princeton has Sept. 23, Oct. 7, 1795.

N. J. State Lib. has July 12, 1797.

[Newton] Farmers Journal, 1796–1798.

Weekly. Established Jan. 8, 1796, judging from the earliest issue located, that of Feb. 5, 1796, vol. 1, no. 5, published by Eliot Hopkins and William Hurtin, with the title of "The Farmers Journal, and Newton Advertiser." Early in 1797, the firm name was changed to Eliot Hopkins, & Co. At some time between Jan. 31 and May 16, 1798, the title was changed to "Farmer's Journal, & Newton Advertiser," and the firm name to E[liot] Hopkins & P[———] Smith. The last issue located is that of Oct. 17, 1798, vol. 3, no. 140.

Harvard has Dec. 16, 1796; Mar. 17, May 19, 26, June 23–July 7, Sept. 15, 22, Nov. 1, 1797; May 16, 23, Oct. 17, 1798.

N. J. Hist. Soc. has Feb. 5, 1796; Jan. 31, 1798.

Elmer T. Hutchinson, Elizabeth, N. J., has Feb. 5, 1796.

[Newton] Sussex Register, 1813–1820+.

Weekly. Established July 6, 1813, judging from the issue of Sept. 7, 1813, vol. 1, no. 10, published by John H. Hall, with the title of "Sussex Register." It was so continued until after 1820.

Sussex Register office has Sept. 7, 1813–Dec. 18, 1820.

N. J. Hist. Soc. has Jan. 30, July 31, Sept. 11, 1815; May 27, 1816; July 20, Dec. 28, 1818; Mar. 29, June 28, Sept. 13, 27, Oct. 18, 1819; July 24, Aug. 21, 1820.

Am. Antiq. Soc. has July 4, 1814.

N. Y. Hist. Soc. has Aug. 10, 1818.

NEW JERSEY 515

[Paterson] Bee, 1815–1816.

Weekly. Established Nov. 7, 1815, judging from the earliest issue located, that of Jan. 23, 1816, vol. 1, no. 12, published by Peter Conover, with the title of "The Bee and Paterson Advertiser." With the issue of July 2, 1816, Conover formed a partnership with Peter Haring, and the paper was published by Conover and Haring. The issue of July 2, 1816, vol. 1, no. 34, is the last located. The paper is quoted in the Norfolk, Va., "American Beacon" of Dec. 9, 1816.

N. Y. Hist. Soc. has Jan. 23, Mar. 26, July 2, 1816.

[Paterson] Bergen Express, 1817–1819.

Weekly. Established in June 1817, judging from the earliest issue located, that of Apr. 29, 1818, vol. 1, no. 47, published by H[———] Jones, with the title of "Bergen Express, and Paterson Advertiser." The last issue located, that of Aug. 25, 1819, vol. 3, no. 12, states that with the following issue the paper would be discontinued.

N. J. Hist. Soc. has Apr. 29, 1818.
N. Y. Hist. Soc. has May 13, Nov. 4, 1818; May 5, 12, 1819.
Lib. Congress has Aug. 25, 1819.

[Perth Amboy] New-Jersey Gazette, 1819.

Weekly. Established Feb. 4, 1819, by J[oseph] T. Murden & Co., with the title of "New-Jersey Gazette, and Perth-Amboy Commercial Advertiser."

Mrs. Lucien B. Horton, Fort Lauderdale, Fla., has Feb. 4, 1819–July 27, 1820, to be given to N. J. Hist. Soc.
Am. Antiq. Soc. has July 1, 1819.

Princeton Packet, 1786–1787.

Weekly. Established June 22, 1786, by James Tod, with the title of "The Princeton Packet, and the General Advertiser." The last issue located is that of June 28, 1787, vol. 2, no. 54. Tod left Princeton in November, 1787 (letter from Prof. V. L. Collins of Princeton) to take charge of Erasmus Hall at Flatbush, Long Island.

H. E. Pickersgill, Perth Amboy, had June 22, 1786, which he intended to give to the Princeton Library, but since his death the paper has not been found.
N. J. Hist. Soc. has Aug. 10, 1786; Mar. 22, June 28, 1787.
Princeton has Oct. 5, 1786; Jan. 11, Feb. 22, Apr. 26, 1787.
Rutgers Univ. has Dec. 14, 1786; Mar. 29, 1787.
Minn. Hist. Soc. has Mar. 8, 1787.

Salem Messenger, 1819–1820+.

Weekly. Established Sept. 18, 1819, by Elijah Brooks, with the title of "Salem Messenger." It was so continued until after 1820.

Salem Co. Hist. Soc., Salem, has Sept. 18, 1819–Dec. 27, 1820.
N. J. Hist. Soc. has Nov. 17, Dec. 8, 1819; Oct. 25, Dec. 20, 1820.
Am. Antiq. Soc. has Dec. 29, 1819; Apr. 26, 1820.
Atlantic City Pub. Lib. has May 10, 1820.

[Salem] Observer, 1798–1799.

Weekly. Established in December 1798, judging from the date of the first and only issue located, that of May 4, 1799, vol. 1, no. 19, published by Black & North [William Black and Marcus(?) North], with the title of "The Observer." The Salem "National Standard" of June 6, 1860, notes a file at that time owned by a Mr. John Bailey, containing nos. 19–32, and states that but 36 numbers were published, after which the publisher announced his intention to remove to Dover, Del. Black did establish "The Friend of the People" at Dover in September 1799.

Camden Co. Hist. Soc., Camden, has May 4, 1799.

[Salem] West-Jersey Gazette, 1817–1819.

Weekly. Established Aug. 13, 1817, judging from the date of the earliest issue located, that of Aug. 20, 1817, vol. 1, no. 2, published by I[saac] A. Kollock, with the title of "West-Jersey Gazette." In August 1818, the title was changed to "West-Jersey Gazette, and Salem and Gloucester Advertiser," the publisher's name appearing as Isaac A. Kollock. The last issue located is that of Jan. 13, 1819, vol. 2, no. 75.

N. J. Hist. Soc. has Mar. 25, Apr. 22, May 20, June 3, July 15, Aug. 12, 1818; Jan. 13, 1819.
Rutgers Univ. has Aug. 20, 1817.
Salem Co. Hist. Soc. has Mar. 4, 1818.

[Somerville] New Jersey Intelligencer, 1815.

Weekly. Published at Somerville in 1815 by John C. Kelley, with the title of "New Jersey Intelligencer." Issues of Mar. 8 and June 8, 1815, were noted in the "Somerset County Historical Quarterly," vol. 1, p. 144, and vol. 8, p. 75, but are not now to be located. A receipt for payment of subscription to Sept. 6, 1815, is owned by the Rutgers Library.

[Springfield] Morning Herald, 1785.

Weekly. Published at Springfield by David Cree, with the title of "The Morning Herald and Weekly Advertiser." Since the only issue located, that of

Apr. 27, 1785, is mutilated and has the volume numbering torn off, the date of establishment cannot be determined. Cree had recently removed from Morristown, which was about ten miles from Springfield. In the "New-York Gazetteer" of Mar. 17, 1786, was printed this advertisement: "To be Sold, on Wednesday the fifth of April, at Springfield, New-Jersey, Sundry Printing Materials, Formerly belonging to David Cree, distrained for Rent. M. Denman."

N. J. Hist. Soc. has Apr. 27, 1785.

[Trenton] **Federal Post,** 1788–1789.

Weekly and semi-weekly. A continuation, without change of volume numbering, of "The Trenton Weekly Mercury." The change of title probably came in May 1788, but the earliest issue located is that of Aug. 5, 1788, vol. 2, no. 13, published by Frederick C. Quequelle and George M. Wilson, with the title of "The Federal Post; or, the Trenton Weekly Mercury." With the issue of Sept. 23, 1788, the title was shortened to "The Federal Post," and in the issue of Oct. 3, 1788, it was announced that it would be published semi-weekly. The next issue appeared on Oct. 7, but the next on Oct. 14, and publication was henceforth weekly. With the issue of Nov. 11, 1788, the paper was published by Frederick C. Quequelle. The last issue located is that of Jan. 27, 1789 (misprinted 1788), vol. 2, no. 33, which erroneously bore the same volume numbering as that of the preceding issue located, Dec. 23, 1788, vol. 2, no. 33.

N. J. State Lib. has Aug. 5–Sept. 9, 30–Dec. 23, 1788; Jan. 27, 1789.
N. J. Hist. Soc. has Sept. 23, 1788.

[Trenton] **Federalist,** 1798–1820+.

Weekly. Established July 9, 1798, by G[ershom] Craft & W[illiam] Black, with the title of "The Federalist; or New-Jersey Gazette." With the issue of July 23, 1798, the firm was dissolved and the paper published by G[ershom] Craft. The last issue with this title was that of June 30, 1800, vol. 2, no. 104, after which it was united with the "New-Jersey State Gazette," continuing its own leading title, but adopting the latter paper's numbering. The first issue, therefore, of "The Federalist & New-Jersey State Gazette" was that of July 8, 1800, vol. 2, no. 71, published by Sherman, Mershon, Thomas & Craft [George Sherman, John Mershon, Isaiah Thomas and Gershom Craft]. The firm name was changed to Sherman, Mershon & Thomas with the issue of Sept. 23, 1800, which firm in turn was dissolved and the paper published by Sherman & Mershon with the issue of Dec. 29, 1801. The title was changed to "Trenton Federalist" with the issue of May 11, 1802. John Mershon died Dec. 17, 1806, and with the issue of Dec. 22, 1806, the paper was published by George Sherman. It was so continued until after 1820.

N. J. State Lib. has July 9, 1798–Dec. 25, 1820.

Am. Antiq. Soc. has Sept. 17, Nov. 5, 19, 26, Dec. 10–24, 1798; Jan. 14, 21, Feb. 25, Dec. 23, 1799; Jan. 6, Mar. 3, 10, Dec. 2, 9, 23, 1800; Jan. 5–Mar. 16, Apr. 20–May 11, Sept. 6, 1802–Oct. 28, 1805; Aug. 4, 1806–Dec. 25, 1820.

N. J. Hist. Soc. has July 9, 1798; Apr. 15, July 22, Aug. 26, Dec. 30, 1799; Jan. 7, 21, Mar. 31, June 3, Sept. 30, 1800; July 19, Oct. 4, Nov. 29, 1802; Jan. 10, 1803–Dec. 28, 1812; Jan. 2, 1815–Dec. 30, 1816; Apr. 7, July 14, Aug. 4, 1817; Mar. 16, Apr. 13, 20, May 18, Aug. 17, 24, 1818; Mar. 8, May 10, Dec. 27, 1819; Feb. 14, July 3, Aug. 14, 1820.

Lib. Congress has Aug. 6, 13, Sept. 3–Oct. 1, 15–Nov. 26, Dec. 10–31, 1798; Jan. 7, 21–Mar. 11, 25, Apr. 1, 15–May 13, 27, June 10–24, July 15–Aug. 19, Sept. 9–Nov. 4, 25–Dec. 30, 1799; Jan. 6–Apr. 14, 28–June 30, Oct. 21, Nov. 25, 1800; Sept. 15, 1806; Jan. 5, 1807–Dec. 28, 1812; Aug. 23, 1814; Jan. 6, 1817–Dec. 28, 1818; May 10, 17, 1819.

N. Y. Hist. Soc. has Aug. 6, 27, Sept. 10–24, Oct. 29–Dec. 10, 1798; Jan. 14, 21, Feb. 25, Apr. 22, May 6, 20, 27, June 10–24, July 15, 22, Sept. 9–23, Oct. 14, 21, Nov. 11–Dec. 2, 16–30, 1799; Jan. 6–27, Feb. 10, Mar. 3, 10, Apr. 21, May 5, 12, 26, June 2, 23, 1800; Jan. 19–Feb. 9, 23–Mar. 9, 23–June 8, 22–July 27, Aug. 10–24, Sept. 7–21, Oct. 5–Dec. 28, 1807; Jan. 4–Mar. 21, Apr. 4–Sept. 5, 19, 26, Oct. 10–Nov. 14, Dec. 5, 1808; July 17, 24, 1809; Oct. 8, 1810; June 3, July 15, Aug. 26, 1811; Jan. 30, Feb. 24, Apr. 20, June 29, July 6, 1812; Sept. 27, 1813; Feb. 21, Apr. 11, May 2, July 4, Sept. 20, Nov. 14, 21, 1814; Jan. 16, Mar. 20, June 12, Sept. 25, 1815; Jan. 22, Feb. 12, June 10, 17, Sept. 16, Dec. 9, 1816; Feb. 24, Dec. 1, 1817; Jan. 19, June 1, Aug. 10, 17, Oct. 5, 1818; Aug. 28, 1820.

Carnegie Lib., Pittsburgh, has July 9, 1798–July 1, 1799.

Harvard has Feb. 25, Apr. 8, 1799; Jan. 13, Apr. 21, 28, May 26–June 9, 23, Sept. 2, 1800; Mar. 3–Apr. 21, May 5–June 9, 23, July 21, Aug. 11–25, Sept. 29, Oct. 20, 27, Nov. 10–Dec. 1, 15, 1801; May 18, June 29, Sept. 20, 1802; Mar. 21, Apr. 18, June 27, Sept. 19, Oct. 10, Nov. 14, 1803; Jan. 30, Feb. 20, Mar. 12, 1804.

Trenton Public Library has Nov. 5, Dec. 10–31, 1798; Jan. 7, Feb. 4, 25–Mar. 18, Apr. 29–Aug. 5, 19–Dec. 16, 1799; Jan. 20–Apr. 14, 28–June 30, July 8, 22–Sept. 9, 23, Oct. 21, 1800; Mar. 10, Sept. 15, 1801; Dec. 15, 1806; Jan. 26, July 27, 1807; Apr. 9, July 16, 1810; June 10, July 8, Aug. 5, 1811; Aug. 16, 1813; Oct. 31, 1814; Mar. 6–27, 1815; Jan. 6, 1817–Dec. 28, 1818; Mar. 8, 1819; Apr. 24, 1820.

Rutgers Univ. has Apr. 15, 22, 1799; Sept. 23, 1800; Dec. 1, 1801; Feb. 9, Sept. 6, 1802; Jan. 9, July 23, Dec. 31, 1804; July 22, 1805; Jan. 20, 1806; Mar. 2, Dec. 14, 1807; Apr. 11, July 11, 1808; July 9, Oct. 15, Nov. 19, 1810; June 29, Dec. 7, 1812; Apr. 12, Dec. 27, 1813; Jan. 17, Sept. 20, 1814; Jan. 8, Feb. 19, Sept. 23, 1816; July 14, 1817; Aug. 24, 1818; Jan. 10, Dec. 18, 1820.

N. Y. Pub. Lib. has Feb. 11, 1799; July 29, 1800; May 5, 1801; Nov. 11, 1811; Oct. 12, 1812.

NEW JERSEY 519

Camden Co. Hist. Soc., Camden, has Feb. 7, 1814; July 29, 1816.
Phil. Lib. Co. has July 16, 1798.
Washington Headquarters, Morristown, N. J., has Aug. 13, 1798.
Conn. Hist. Soc. has Dec. 23, 1799.
Adriance Lib., Poughkeepsie, has Sept. 9, 1800.
Monmouth Co. Hist. Assoc., Freehold, N. J., has Aug. 18, 1801.
Wis. Hist. Soc. has Sept. 8, 1801; Dec. 7, 1818.
Univ. of Texas has Dec. 5, 1803.
Cornell Univ. has Sept. 28, 1807.
N. Y. State Lib. has July 29, 1811.
Princeton has Jan. 27, 1817; Jan. 11, 1819.

Trenton Mercury, 1787–1788.

Weekly. Established May 12, 1787, with the title of "The Trenton Mercury, and Weekly Advertiser," published by Frederick Quequelle and James Prange. With the issue of May 22, 1787, vol. 1, no. 2, the title was slightly changed to "The Trenton Mercury and the Weekly Advertiser," and the publishing firm to Frederick C. Quequelle and George M. Wilson. With the issue of Oct. 30, 1787, the title was changed to "The Trenton Weekly Mercury." The last issue located with this title is that of Jan. 22, 1788, vol. 1, no. 38. Within six months, probably in May 1788, the title was changed to "The Federal Post; or, the Trenton Weekly Mercury," which see.

Hist. Soc. Western Penn., Pittsburgh, has May 12–Oct. 2, 23–Dec. 25, 1787.
Am. Antiq. Soc. has May 12, Sept. 25, Oct. 9, 1787; Jan. 22, 1788.

[Trenton] Miscellany, 1805.

Weekly. Established June 10, 1805, by James Oram, with the title of "The Miscellany." It was a quarto of eight numbered pages, and was a magazine in nature, but since it included current news, and marriage and death records, it is included in this Bibliography. The last issue located is that of Dec. 2, 1805, vol. 1, no. 26.

Phil. Lib. Co. has June 10–Dec. 2, 1805.
Princeton has June 10, 17, July 1–22, Aug. 12, 19, Sept. 2–16, 30–Oct. 14, Nov. 4–18, 1805.
Trenton Pub. Lib. has June 10, 1805.
N. J. Hist. Soc. has Sept. 2, 1805.

[Trenton] New-Jersey Gazette, 1778–1786.

Weekly. Removed from Burlington by the publisher, Isaac Collins, and established at Trenton under the name of "The New-Jersey Gazette," with the issue of Mar. 4, 1778, vol. 1, no. 14. There were no issues upon July 7, 14, 21, 1779, and the paper was suspended with the issue of July 16, 1783, vol. 6, no. 290. Collins printed an interesting prospectus, on Dec. 2, 1783, announcing the revival of his paper, and resumed publication with the issue of Dec. 9, 1783, vol. 7, no. 291. It was finally discontinued with the issue of Nov. 27, 1786, vol. 9, no. 446.

N. J. State Lib., Rutgers Univ., N. Y. Hist. Soc., and Hist. Soc. Penn., have Mar. 4, 1778–Nov. 27, 1786.

Lib. Congress has Mar. 4, 1778–Dec. 27, 1784; Mar. 7–Dec. 26, 1785; Jan. 9–Mar. 28, May 8–July 3, 17–Aug. 7, 21–Sept. 11, 25–Nov. 27, 1786.

Princeton has Mar. 4, 1778–July 16, Dec. 16–30, 1783; Jan. 6–20, Apr. 13–July 12, 26–Dec. 27, 1784; Jan. 3–Apr. 11, 25–Nov. 21, Dec. 5, 1785–Nov. 27, 1786.

N. J. Hist. Soc. has Mar. 4, 1778–July 16, 1783; Dec. 9, 1783–Nov. 27, 1786.

N. Y. Pub. Lib. has Mar. 4, 1778–July 16, 1783; Jan. 24, Feb. 7–Mar. 28, Apr. 18–June 13, 27–July 11, Aug. 8, 22–Sept. 5, Dec. 12, 19, 1785; Jan. 2, 16, Feb. 27, Mar. 12, 27, Apr. 10–May 8, 29, 1786.

Am. Antiq. Soc. has Mar. 4–18, Apr. 1–Dec. 16, 31, 1778; Jan. 6, 20, 27, Mar. 3, 31, Apr. 7, June 16, 30, Aug. 11, 25, Sept. 1, 22, Nov. 10, Dec. 1, 1779; Jan. 5, 19–Feb. 16, Mar. 1–Nov. 1, 22–Dec. 20, 1780; Jan. 10, Mar. 14, June 13, Aug. 1, 8, Sept. 19, Oct. 3, 10, 24–Nov. 7, 28–Dec. 12, 26, 1781; Jan. 2, 16, 30, Feb. 6–20, Mar. 6–27, Apr. 10, 24–May 8, 22–July 10, 31–Sept. 11, 25–Oct. 9, 23, Nov. 6–27, 1782; Jan. 8, 15, Feb. 12, 26, Mar. 12, Apr. 2, 30, May 7, June 11–July 16, Dec. 9, 16, 1783; prospectus of Dec. 2, 1783; Aug. 9–Dec. 27, 1784; Jan. 3–June 27, Aug. 1–Sept. 12, 26–Dec. 26, 1785; Jan. 2–June 19, July 3–31, Aug. 21–Oct. 30, Nov. 13, 27, 1786.

Univ. of Mich. (Clements) has Apr. 29, May 20–June 24, July 8–Dec. 31, 1778; Feb. 10–Mar. 10, 24–May 12, June 9–30, Aug. 18, Sept. 1–22, Oct. 6, 20, 27, Nov. 10, Dec. 15–29, 1779; Jan. 19, Feb. 9, 16, Mar. 8–Apr. 5, May 10–24, Aug. 16–30, Oct. 4, 11, Nov. 8, 29, Dec. 6, 1780; Jan. 24, Feb. 14–28, Mar. 14, 21, Apr. 11, May 9, 16, 30–June 13, July 4, 11, 25, Aug. 8, 22, Sept. 5, 19, Oct. 3, 24, Nov. 7, Dec. 5, 1781; Jan. 2, 16, 23, Mar. 13, Apr. 3, 10, May 22–June 5, 19–July 3, 24, 31, Aug. 21–Sept. 25, Oct. 16, 23, Nov. 13, 27, Dec. 4, 18, 1782; Jan. 1–29, Feb. 26, Apr. 2–16, 1783.

Chicago Hist. Soc. has Jan. 12–Dec. 20, 1780.

Carnegie Lib., Pittsburgh, has Jan. 2–Nov. 27, 1786.

Mass. Hist. Soc. has Nov. 10, 1779; Nov. 7, 28, 1781; Feb. 13, Mar. 13, Apr. 10, 17, May 1, 8, June 12, July 10, 1782.

Wis. Hist. Soc. has Apr. 8, 29–May 13, 27, June 24, Aug. 5, Sept. 30–Oct. 14, Dec. 16, 23, 1778; Sept. 28, 1779; Sept. 6, 13, 1780.

Amer. Philos. Soc. has June 17, July 29, Aug. 26, Oct. 14, Nov. 4, 1778; Mar. 10, June 2, Nov. 24, 1779.

N. Y. State Lib. has Apr. 29, July 29, 1778; May 12, Aug. 11, 25, 1779.

Monmouth Co. Hist. Assoc., Freehold, has June 30, 1779; June 14, 1780; May 22, 1782.

NEW JERSEY

Morristown Nat. Park Museum has June 7–21, 1780.
Harvard has Oct. 14, 1778.
British Museum has Nov. 22, Dec. 6, 1780.
Duke Univ. has Nov. 14, 1781; Jan. 2, 1786.
Camden Co. Hist. Soc., Camden, has Mar. 4, 1778.
Trenton Pub. Lib. has Oct. 31, 1781.
Boston Pub. Lib. has July 12, 1784.

[Trenton] **New-Jersey State Gazette**, 1792–1796.

Weekly. Established Sept. 12, 1792, by Matthias Day and Co., with the title of "New-Jersey State Gazette." With the issue of Mar. 20, 1793, the firm name became Day and Hopkins [Matthias Day and George F. Hopkins]. The partnership was dissolved and the paper printed by Matthias Day with the issue of Feb. 26, 1794. The last issue with this title was that of July 5, 1796, vol. 4, no. 44, after which the title was changed to "The State Gazette, & New-Jersey Advertiser," which see.

N. J. Hist. Soc. has Sept. 12, 1792–July 5, 1796.
N. Y. Hist. Soc. has May 7, 1794–July 5, 1796.
Am. Antiq. Soc. has Sept. 19–Oct. 10, Nov. 7, 14, 28–Dec. 19, 1792; Jan. 23–Feb. 6, 20, 27, Mar. 20, 27, Apr. 10, 17, May 8–22, June 12, July 24, Aug. 7, 14, Nov. 27, Dec. 4, 25, 1793; July 9, 30, Sept. 10, 17, Oct. 8, Dec. 16, 30, 1794; Mar. 3, 17, Apr. 7, 21, May 5, June 23, July 21, Aug. 4, 11, 25, Sept. 1, 15, Oct. 6, Nov. 3, 24, Dec. 8, 1795; May 24–June 14, 1796.
Lib. Congress has Feb. 17–Apr. 14, 28, May 12–Aug. 11, Oct. 13, 1795; Jan. 19–May 17, June 7–July 5, 1796.
Rutgers Univ. has Feb. 17, Mar. 10–Apr. 7, May 31, Sept. 8–Dec. 29, 1795; Jan. 5, 12, 1796.
Harvard has Sept. 17, 1794; Mar. 3, 17, June 16, 23, July 21, Oct. 13, Dec. 29, 1795; Jan. 12, Mar. 8, 22, 29, Apr. 26, May 3, 17, 31, 1796.
Phil. Lib. Co. has Dec. 1, 8, 1795; Jan. 19, 1796.
N. Y. Pub. Lib. has Sept. 4, 1793.
Boston Pub. Lib. has Dec. 30, 1794.
Morristown Lib. has Mar. 1, 1796.

[Trenton] **New-Jersey State Gazette**, 1799–1800.

Weekly. Established Mar. 5, 1799, by Sherman & Mershon [George Sherman and John Mershon], with the title of "New-Jersey State Gazette." The paper was really a continuation of "The State Gazette, & New-Jersey Advertiser," although it began a new volume numbering and had a different title. With the issue of Mar. 26, 1799, Isaiah Thomas, nephew of Isaiah Thomas of Worcester, was admitted to the firm and the paper published by Sherman, Mershon & Thomas. The last issue with this title was that of July 1, 1800, vol. 2, no. 70, after which the paper was united with "The Federalist; New-Jersey Gazette." It continued its own volume numbering, but changed its title to "The Federalist & New-Jersey State Gazette." See under "Federalist."

N. J. State Lib. has Mar. 5, 1799–July 1, 1800.
N. Y. Pub. Lib. has Mar. 5, July 2, 1799; Feb. 18, Mar. 11, 18, Apr. 1, June 24, 1800.
Hist. Soc. Penn. has June 25, July 2, Dec. 24, 1799.
Lib. Congress has Dec. 3, 1799; Jan. 21, 1800.
Conn. Hist. Soc. has Dec. 24, 31, 1799; Jan. 14, 1800.
Harvard has Apr. 9, 1799.
Am. Antiq. Soc. has Dec. 10, 1799.
Williams Coll. has Dec. 31, 1799.
Monmouth Co. Hist. Assoc., Freehold, has Dec. 31, 1799.
N. J. Hist. Soc. and Princeton have Jan. 21, 1800.

[Trenton] State Gazette, 1796–1799.

Weekly. A continuation, without change of volume numbering, of the "New-Jersey State Gazette." The first issue with the new title of "The State Gazette, & New-Jersey Advertiser" was that of July 12, 1796, vol. 4, no. 45, published by Matthias Day. It was so continued until the issue of Feb. 26, 1799, vol. 7, no. 26. Day then sold out to Sherman & Mershon, who began a paper with new numbering and with the title of "New-Jersey State Gazette," which see.

N. J. Hist. Soc. has July 12, 1796–Feb. 26, 1799.
Rutgers Univ. has Oct. 4, 1796–Aug. 1, 1797; Nov. 14, 1797–Aug. 14, 1798; Sept. 11–Nov. 6, 1798.
N. Y. Hist. Soc. has July 12, 1796–Oct. 17, 1797.
N. J. State Lib. has Jan. 3, 1797–July 3, 1798.
Am. Antiq. Soc. has July 19, Oct. 18–Nov. 22, Dec. 13, 27, 1796; Jan. 3, 24–Feb. 14, 28–Mar. 14, Apr. 11, 25, May 9, 30, June 27, July 11–Aug. 29, Sept. 12, 19, Oct. 17, 24, Nov. 14, 21, Dec. 5, 19, 26, 1797; Jan. 9, 23–Feb. 13, 27–Mar. 13, Apr. 3, 24–May 29, June 26, July 3, 24, Sept. 4, 11, Oct. 16, 23, Nov. 27, Dec. 11, 18, 1798; Jan. 15, 29, Feb. 5–19, 1799.
Harvard has July 19–Sept. 20, Oct. 11–Nov. 1, 22–Dec. 6, 27, 1796; Jan. 3–Mar. 21, Apr. 4, 11, 25, May 2, 23–June 13, July 4, Sept. 5, 19–Oct. 3, 17, Nov. 7, 14, 28–Dec. 12, 1797; Jan. 16–Feb. 13, Mar. 13, Apr. 3, 17, May 1–22, June 5, 26, July 3, Aug. 28–Sept. 11, Oct. 23, 30, Nov. 13, 27, Dec. 18, 1798.
Lib. Congress has Aug. 2–30, Sept. 27, 1796.
N. Y. Pub. Lib. has Mar. 13, 27, Apr. 24, July 3, 1798.
Morristown Nat. Park Museum has Jan. 3, 1797.
Morristown Lib. has Feb. 20, 1798.
Phil. Lib. Co. has July 17, 1798.

Princeton has Sept. 25, 1798.
Hist. Soc. Penn. has Dec. 4, 1798.

[Trenton] **True American**, 1801–1820+.

Weekly. Established Mar. 10, 1801, by Matthias Day and Jacob Mann, with the title of "The True American." With the issue of June 23, 1801, James J. Wilson was added to the firm, the name of which became Day, Mann, and Wilson. With the issue of Nov. 3, 1801, Day retired and the paper was published by Jacob Mann and James J. Wilson. Mann sold out his share, with the issue of Feb. 9, 1802, to Lewis Blackwell, and the publishers became Wilson & Blackwell. With the issue of May 14, 1804, the partnership was dissolved, and James J. Wilson became sole publisher. With the issue of Nov. 25, 1805, Silas Halsey, Jr., was admitted to partnership and the firm became Wilson & Halsey. With the issue of July 4, 1808, Halsey withdrew and James J. Wilson again became sole publisher. The paper was continued by him until after 1820.

N. J. State Lib. has Mar. 10, 1801–Dec. 30, 1820.

Am. Antiq. Soc. has May 19, June 23–Dec. 29, 1801; Jan. 5–Mar. 30, May 11–July 26, Aug. 9–Nov. 8, 22–Dec. 27, 1802; Jan. 3–Feb. 21, Mar. 7–21, Apr. 4–Aug. 8, 22, 29, Sept. 12–Oct. 24, Nov. 7–Dec. 26, 1803; Jan. 2–Feb. 6, 20, 27, Mar. 19–Apr. 9, 23–May 14, 28, June 18–Dec. 31, 1804; Jan. 7–June 3, 17–Aug. 19, Sept. 2–Dec. 23, 1805; Jan. 6–Feb. 3, 17, 24, 1806; Jan. 5, Feb. 23–Mar. 9, Apr. 13, June 1–15, 1807; May 16, Aug. 29, Sept. 19, 1808; Feb. 13–Mar. 6, July 24, Aug. 28, Oct. 2, Dec. 4, 1809; Jan. 29, Feb. 5, 26–Mar. 12, June 4, July 2–16, Aug. 13, 27, Sept. 3, Oct. 15, 29, 1810; Jan. 7, 14, Feb. 11, Mar. 11, Apr. 8, 22, 29, May 13, June 3, July 29, Sept. 16, 23, Oct. 7, Nov. 11, 18, Dec. 9, 30, 1811; Jan. 13, 27–Feb. 24, Mar. 9, 23, Apr. 13, 27, May 18, June 15, July 6–27, Aug. 24, Sept. 15, Oct. 5, 12, Dec. 21, 28, 1812; Jan. 18, Feb. 22, Mar. 15, Apr. 19, May 17, July 12, 26, Aug. 2, 23, 30, Sept. 13, Oct. 11, Nov. 8, Dec. 6, 20, 1813; Mar. 7–21, Apr. 4, May 9, 30, June 27, July 25, Aug. 2, 16, 30, Sept. 6, 26, Oct. 3, 10, 31, Nov. 7, Dec. 5, 19, 1814; Jan. 2, July 10, Aug. 28–Sept. 11, Oct. 9, Dec. 4, 11, 1815; Jan. 22, Feb. 26, July 29, Dec. 16, 1816; Mar. 9, 1818; Nov. 29, 1819.

Princeton has Mar. 17, 1801–Mar. 30, 1802; May 11, 1802–Jan. 16, Apr. 2–16, May 28, June 11, 25, July 2, 9, 30, Aug. 27, Sept. 17, Oct. 22, Nov. 5, 19, 1804; Jan. 7, 1805–Dec. 29, 1806, fair; Feb. 23–Dec. 21, 1807, fair; Jan. 1, 22, 29, Mar. 19, Apr. 9–30, Aug. 13, Sept. 10, Oct. 29–Nov. 12, 1810; Jan. 14, Feb. 4, 11, Mar. 11, Apr. 29, May 13, 20, June 24, July 22, Aug. 5, Sept. 23, Nov. 11–25, Dec. 16, 23, 1811; Jan. 25, Feb. 1, 21, Mar. 1–15, 29, Apr. 5, 19, May 10, 24–June 14, July 19–Aug. 2, Sept. 6, 20, Oct. 4–18, Nov. 15–29, 1819; Mar. 13, 1820.

Lib. Congress has Apr. 7, 1801; Oct. 24, 1803; Dec. 23, 1805; June 30–July 14, 1806; Mar. 30, Apr. 6, June 22, July 20, Aug. 31, Sept. 28, Nov. 16, 23, 1807; Jan. 4, 1808; Dec. 25, 1809; Aug. 20, Oct. 1, 15, Nov. 26, 1810; Feb. 4,

Mar. 4, 18, Apr. 1, 22–May 6, 20, June 3, Aug. 5–19, 1811; Feb. 24, Mar. 2, Apr. 27, Nov. 16–30, 1812; Mar. 1, 8, May 24, Aug. 9, Oct. 18, 1813; Jan. 3, Feb. 7, 14, May 16, June 16, Oct. 3, Dec. 5, 12, 1814; June 5, Sept. 18, 1815; Jan. 8, 15, 25, 1816; Mar. 9, Apr. 6, Sept. 21, 1818; Jan. 4, 1819–Dec. 30, 1820.

N. J. Hist. Soc. has Aug. 25, 1801; Feb. 23, July 19, Nov. 29, 1802; July 18, Nov. 7, 21, Dec. 12, 1803; Jan. 23, Feb. 20, Mar. 19, Apr. 30, Aug. 6, Sept. 10, 17, Nov. 26–Dec. 17, 1804; Jan. 7–21, Feb. 4, 11, Mar. 11, Apr. 1, 15–May 20, June 3, 10, July 8, 15, Oct. 7–28, 1805; Feb. 10, Mar. 17, Aug. 6, 1806; Feb. 1, 1808; Jan. 13, May 11, 25, June 15, July 6, Aug. 10, Nov. 9, 16, Dec. 21, 1812; Jan. 11, Apr. 19, 26, June 14, Aug. 23, 1813; Jan. 3, 17, 31, Feb. 28, Mar. 7, Apr. 4–18, Oct. 3, 17, 1814; Feb. 6, 27, Mar. 20, Aug. 28, Sept. 25, 1815; Jan. 8, 1816; Aug. 11, 1817; June 8, Aug. 3, 24, Sept. 7, 1818; Apr. 12, Dec. 6, 20, 1819; Feb. 11, 21, May 22, 1820.

N. Y. Pub. Lib. has Mar. 7, 1803–Dec. 17, 1804; Jan. 7, 14, 28–Feb. 11, 25, Apr. 29, Sept. 23, Oct. 21, Nov. 11, 18, 1805; Feb. 3, 24, Mar. 17, May 5, June 16–30, July 21, Aug. 18, Sept. 15, Oct. 6, 13, Nov. 17, 24, 1806; Jan. 5, 19, Feb. 23, Mar. 9, 1807; Sept. 4, 1809; July 20, 1812.

Harvard has Mar. 10, 17, 31, Apr. 7, 21, May 12, 26, June 16–30, July 14, 28–Aug. 18, Sept. 8–Oct. 6, Nov. 3–Dec. 29, 1801; Jan. 5–19, Feb. 2–Mar. 2, 23–Apr. 13, May 4, 11, 25, June 1, 14–Aug. 2, 23, 30, Sept. 20, Nov. 15, 29, Dec. 20, 27, 1802; Jan. 17, 31, Mar. 28, Apr. 11, May 2, June 6, July 4–25, Aug. 8–22, Sept. 5, 26, 1803; Feb. 6, Mar. 19, May 7, 14, Aug. 13, Sept. 10, 1804; Feb. 18–Apr. 1, 22, 29, May 13–June 10, 24–July 8, 22, 29, Aug. 12, Sept. 2, 9, 30, Oct. 14, Nov. 4, 11, Dec. 2, 16–30, 1805; Jan. 13, 27–Apr. 21, May 12–June 23, Aug. 18–Sept. 8, 22, 29, Oct. 13, Nov. 10, Dec. 22, 1806; Mar. 9, 23–Apr. 13, 27, May 4, June 1, 8, 22–July 6, 20, 27, Aug. 17, 31, Sept. 14, 28, Oct. 26, Nov. 9, 23, Dec. 14, 1807; Oct. 3, Nov. 7, 21, Dec. 12, 19, 1808.

N. Y. Hist. Soc. has Feb. 3, 1806; Oct. 17, 1808; Apr. 17, Aug. 7, 1809; June 25, July 16, Aug. 13, Sept. 3, 24, Dec. 10, 1810; Mar. 18, Oct. 28, Nov. 4, 1811; Oct. 26, 1812; Feb. 21, 28, Mar. 28, Apr. 4, 25, May 23, July 4, 11, Oct. 3–24, Nov. 14, 1814; Jan. 1, Feb. 27, Mar. 20, May 22, June 19, July 3, 10, 24, 31, Sept. 4, Oct. 30, Dec. 4–25, 1815; Aug. 26, Feb. 8, Apr. 26, May 3, 1819; Jan. 24–Dec. 30, 1820.

Univ. of Ill. has Oct. 24, 1803; Oct. 29, 1804; Oct. 14, Dec. 23, 30, 1805; Feb. 17, Mar. 17, Apr. 14, 21, 1806; May 8–Dec. 9, 1820, fair.

Rutgers Univ. has Sept. 26, 1803; Jan. 30, 1804; July 22, 1805; May 5, June 2, 9, 1806; July 9, Sept. 24, Nov. 12, Dec. 3, 1810; Apr. 8, 1811; May 25, 1812; Mar. 1, July 26, Sept. 6, Dec. 13, 1813; Jan. 13, 31, Oct. 24, Nov. 7, 21, 1814; Dec. 4, 1815; July 1, 1816; May 26, 1817; Jan. 6, Mar. 16, 1818.

Trenton Pub. Lib. has May 26, 1801; Feb. 9, 1802; Oct. 3, 1803; Dec. 10, 1804; Feb. 24, 1806; Dec. 14, 1807; Mar. 28, Nov. 7, 1808; Feb. 27, May 8, 15, 1809; Feb. 18, Aug. 19, 1811; Apr. 12, 1813; Jan. 30, Feb. 20, 1815.

N. Y. State Lib. has Jan. 18, 1808; July 3, 1809; May 21, June 11, 1810; Apr. 8, Dec. 2, 9, 1811; Feb. 17, June 15, 22, July 6, Aug. 10, Oct. 19, 26, Nov. 16, Dec. 14, 1812; June 21, 1813.
Morristown Nat. Park Museum has Sept. 8, 1801; Feb. 27, 1804; Dec. 30, 1805; Dec. 22, 1806; July 27, 1807; Feb. 5, Oct. 29, 1810; Feb. 22, Aug. 15, 1818.
Monmouth Co. Hist. Soc., Freehold, has Sept. 3, 1810; Nov. 18, 1816; Aug. 14, 1820.
Univ. of Texas has June 13, 1803.
Atlantic City Pub. Lib. has July 28, 1806.
Hist. Soc. Penn. has July 11, 1808.
Jersey City Pub. Lib. has May 23, 1810.
Morristown Lib. has Apr. 10, 1815.
Wis. Hist. Soc. has Dec. 7, 1818.

Trenton Weekly Mercury. See **Trenton Mercury.**

[Woodbridge] Constitutional Courant, 1765.

The only issue was that of Sept. 21, 1765, "Numb. I," with the title of "The Constitutional Courant" and the imprint "Printed by Andrew Marvel, at the Sign of the Bribe refused, on Constitution Hill, North-America." Although issued in the form of a newspaper, it was really a political manifesto, consisting of essays against the Stamp Act. In the heading at the top of the first page was a snake device, with the motto above it, "Join or Die."

This paper was printed by William Goddard at Woodbridge on James Parker's printing-press. Isaiah Thomas, in his "History of Printing," 1810, pp. 322–323, gives a long description of the paper and states: "Only one number of the Constitutional Gazette was published; a continuance of it was never intended. It was printed by William Goddard, at Parker's printing house at Burlington — Goddard having previously obtained Parker's permission occasionally to use his press." Thomas also states that the edition was secretly forwarded to New York, where it was sold by a hawker named Samuel Sweeney, and says that he thinks it was reprinted both at New York and Boston. Goddard helped Thomas greatly in the preparation of his History, but Thomas here evidently relied too much on memory, and so made errors which have caused confusion for many later writers. A letter from William Goddard himself, in the Thomas Papers in the American Antiquarian Society and here noticed for the first time, corrects these discrepancies. Writing to Thomas under the date of Apr. 22, 1811, Goddard makes certain criticisms of the "History of Printing," and referring specifically to pp. 322–323, says: "Instead of *Constitutional Gazette*, it should be *Constitutional Courant*, in three places. It was printed at Woodbridge, and the Impression sent, by Express, to New York, where the sale was rapid and extensive. The Government was alarmed at the patriotic Fervor it produced. It was sold by *Laurence* Sweeny." This is first-hand testimony from the author of the paper, and explains why the errors were corrected in the 1874 edition of Thomas's History.

There are at least three different forms of this paper: (A) A sheet printed on both sides, the snake device with no border lines, and the imprint at the bottom of the third column of the second page. Copies in N. Y. Hist. Soc., N. Y. Soc. Lib., N. Y. Pub. Lib., Hist. Soc. Penn., Phil. Lib. Co., British Museum, and Public Record Office at London. (B) A sheet printed on both sides, the snake device within border lines, and the imprint in a single line across the bottom of the second page. Copies in Boston Athenæum, Mass. Hist. Soc., Harvard, and Yale. (C) A broadside printed on one side only, without the snake device, the imprint at the end of the third column, and omitting two articles contained in the other editions. Copies in Phil. Lib. Co., Amer. Philos. Soc., and Harvard. The varying copies may have been printed at either New York, Philadelphia or Boston, but there seems to be no way of confirming this point, so they are all here grouped under Woodbridge, the original place of publication. For an excellent paper on the Constitutional Courant, by Albert Matthews, see Publications of Colonial Society of Mass., vol. 11, pp. 421–453.

[Woodbury] **Columbian Herald**, 1819–1820+.

Weekly. Established Sept. 23, 1819, by Philip J. Gray & Co., with the title of "Columbian Herald." With the issue of Feb. 17, 1820, Philip J. Gray became sole publisher. With the issue of Dec. 20, 1820, the title was changed to "The Herald and Gloucester Farmer." Continued after 1820.

Camden Co. Hist. Soc., Camden, has Sept. 23, 1819–Dec. 27, 1820.
Gloucester Co. Hist. Soc., Woodbury, has Mar. 8, 1820.
N. J. Hist. Soc. has Nov. 29, 1820.

[Woodbury] **Gloucester Farmer**, 1817–1818.

Weekly. Established Jan. 1, 1817, by John A. Crane, with the title of "Gloucester Farmer." The Elizabethtown "New Jersey Journal" of Jan. 28, 1817, states: "John A. Crane, editor of the Gloucester Farmer, Woodbury, has been severely beaten by a number of persons, for a publication in that paper." This journal was removed from Woodbury to Camden in 1818. See under Camden.

Am. Antiq. Soc. has Jan. 1, 1817.
Gloucester Co. Hist. Soc., Woodbury, has Feb. 5, 26, 1817.

[Woodbury] **Herald**, 1820. See **Columbian Herald**.

NEW YORK

Albany Advertiser, 1815–1817.

Semi-weekly. Established Sept. 27, 1815, with the title of "The Albany Advertiser," published by John W. Walker, for Theodore Dwight. It was the semi-weekly edition of "The Albany Daily Advertiser." With the issue of Mar. 22, 1817, no. 156, it was discontinued under this title. Dwight sold his entire plant to "The Albany Gazette," yet considered that his semi-weekly edition was continued at New York by the "New-York Advertiser," which he established Mar. 26, 1817.

Am. Antiq. Soc. has Sept. 30–Oct. 11, 21, Dec. 16–30, 1815–Mar. 22, 1817.
N. Y. State Lib. has Oct. 11, 21, Nov. 11, 1815–Mar. 22, 1817.
Yale has Oct. 21, 1815–Jan. 20, 1817.
Lib. Congress has Dec. 16, 1815–Mar. 22, 1817.
N. Y. Hist. Soc. has Dec. 16, 27, 1815; Jan. 3, 17, 21, 27–Feb. 17, 24–Mar. 2, 9–20, 27, Apr. 3, 10–24, May 4–18, 25, June 1–15, 22, July 3–17, 27–Aug. 4, 21, 24, 31, Sept. 18, 28, Oct. 9–26, Nov. 6, 16, Dec. 11, 18, 28, 1816; Jan. 1, 11, 15, 29–Feb. 5, 15–26, Mar. 5–12, 1817.
Univ. of Chicago has Mar. 8, 12, 19, 22, 1817.
Wis. Hist. Soc. has Feb. 5, 1817.

Albany Argus, 1813–1820+.

Semi-weekly. Established Jan. 26, 1813, by J[esse] Buel, with the title of "The Albany Argus." It was so continued until after 1820. Under date of Oct. 15, 1820, Buel called for payment of accounts, styling himself "late editor of the Argus," but stating that he would "give his personal attention to the business until February." With the issue of Mar. 2, 1821, the imprint changed to Cantine & Leake [Moses I. Cantine and Isaac Q. Leake].

N. Y. State Lib. has Jan. 29, 1813–Dec. 29, 1815; Jan. 2, 23–Mar. 29, Apr. 12, 30, May 21–July 5, Sept. 10, 17, 20, 27, Oct. 4–11, 22, 29, Nov. 1, 12–19, Dec. 31, 1816; Jan. 7, 1817–Dec. 29, 1820.
N. Y. Pub. Lib. has Jan. 26, 1813–Jan. 21, Apr. 8, 1814; Jan. 24–July 14, 1815; Jan. 5, 12–30, Feb. 6, 9, 16–Apr. 12, 23, 30–June 25, July 2–Dec. 31, 1816; Jan. 12, Apr. 20, 30, May 11, 21, 25, June 15, Dec. 31, 1819; Jan. 11, Feb. 8, Mar. 7, 10, 24, 28, Apr. 28, May 2, 9, 16, 23, June 2, 6, 19, July 25, Aug. 8, 15, 22, Sept. 1, 5, 12, 19, 1820.
Am. Antiq. Soc. has Jan. 29, Feb. 5, 12, 16, Mar. 12, 16, 23, Apr. 20, 27, May 4, 14, 21, June 1, 22, July 2, 6, 13, 23, Aug. 6, 31, Sept. 3, 10, 28, 31, Oct. 5, 12, Nov. 5, 16, 30, Dec. 14, 31, 1813; Jan. 18, 1814–Sept. 27, 1816; Nov. 1, Dec. 20, 1816; Jan. 17, 21, Apr. 22, 25, May 2, 23, June 6, 20, 24, July 1, 4, Oct. 7, 10, Nov. 4, 7, 14, 18, 25, 1817; Jan. 16–27, Feb. 3, 10, Mar. 20–

Apr. 21, 28, May 1, 15, June 9, 12, 19, 23, Aug. 18, Sept. 15, 29, Oct. 2–Dec. 1, 8–29, 1818; Jan. 5, 8, 29, Feb. 23, Mar. 2, Aug. 24, Nov. 5, 1819; Feb. 8, 11, Mar. 14, May 12, June 9, Oct. 6, 1820.

Lib. Congress has Nov. 4–Dec. 30, 1814; Jan. 3–June 27, July 28, Oct. 3, Nov. 10, 28, Dec. 8, 26, 1815; Jan. 2, 26, Feb. 13, 16, Mar. 12, Apr. 5, 23, May 24, 31, Aug. 9, 1816; Oct. 21–28, Nov. 4, Dec. 2, 16–30, 1817; Jan. 2–30, Feb. 6–Apr. 28, June 2–July 31, Aug. 28, Sept. 4–15, 22–Oct. 9, 1818; Jan. 1, 1819–Dec. 29, 1820.

N. Y. Hist. Soc. has May 21, June 4–11, 18, 25, Aug. 31, 1813; Jan. 4, Apr. 26, Aug. 9, 19, 1814; May 5, July 14, 25, 1815; Dec. 6–13, 20–31, 1816; Apr. 15, 22–May 6, 13, 1817; Sept. 22, 1818; June 29–July 16, 27–Sept. 17, 24–Oct. 5, 26–Nov. 3, Dec. 7–24, 31, 1819; Jan. 18–Dec. 26, 1820.

Long Id. Hist. Soc. has July 14, 1818–Aug. 6, 1819.

Newberry Lib. has Apr. 20, Aug. 27, Sept. 7, 14, Oct. 1, 5, 1813; Jan. 21–Feb. 1; 8, May 20, 27–June 10, 17, 24, July 5, 12, 19, 26–Aug. 16, 23, 30–Sept. 23, Oct. 14–28, Nov. 4, 8, 18, 29, Dec. 2, 9–20, 27, 30, 1814; Jan. 3, 6, 13, 17, 1815.

Minn. Hist. Soc. has Aug. 8, 1815–Mar. 1, 1816, fair.

Duke Univ. has Feb. 4, 25–Mar. 4, 11, June 24, Aug. 12–19, Sept. 9, 16, Oct. 18, Nov. 25–Dec. 9, 1814; Jan. 3–10, 20, May 19, 23, 1815.

Skaneateles Lib. has Aug. 24, Nov. 30, Dec. 7, 1813; Jan. 7, 25, 28, 1814; Nov. 13, 1815; Feb. 2, Mar. 1, May 3, 14, 17, June 11, 1816; Aug. 24, 1818.

Oneida Hist. Soc., Utica, has Aug. 2, 1814; Mar. 7, 11, Dec. 30, 1817; Apr. 21, Nov. 13, 1818.

Univ. of Rochester has Sept. 2, 1814; Nov. 20, 1818; Jan. 15, Feb. 9, 12, 19, Mar. 2–16, 30, Apr. 2, 16, 27, June 8, 1819.

Cornell Univ. has Sept. 23, Nov. 15, Dec. 16, 30, 1814; Sept. 8, 1815.

Mass. Hist. Soc. has Apr. 15, 1814; Sept. 15, 1818.

Chicago Hist. Soc. has Aug. 8, 1817.

Western Reserve Hist. Soc. has Mar. 17, Apr. 10, 1818.

Univ. of Chicago has Nov. 3, 1818.

[Albany] **Balance,** 1809–1811.

Semi-weekly and weekly. Established as a semi-weekly Jan. 4, 1809, by Croswell & Frary [Harry Croswell and Jonathan Frary], with the title of "The Balance, and New-York State Journal." It succeeded at Albany the "Republican Crisis," and was a continuation of "The Balance" published at Hudson, except that it was enlarged to folio and adopted a new series volume numbering. With the issue of Jan. 2, 1810, the word "and" in the title was changed to "&." With the issue of July 3, 1810, the partnership was dissolved and the paper published by Harry Croswell. With the issue of Jan. 1, 1811, the title was changed to "The Balance, & State Journal," the publication to weekly, a new volume numbering was adopted, and the size was altered to quarto, with eight pages to the issue and pagination. The paper was discontinued with the issue of Dec. 24, 1811, vol. 1, new series, no. 52.

Am. Antiq. Soc., N. Y. State Lib., and Wis. Hist. Soc. have Jan. 4, 1809–Dec. 24, 1811.

N. Y. Hist. Soc. has Jan. 7–Dec. 25, 1809; Jan. 2–Dec. 25, 1810, fair; Jan. 1–Dec. 24, 1811.

Dartmouth has Jan. 11–Dec. 29, 1809, fair; Jan. 2, 1810–Dec. 24, 1811.

Lib. Congress has Jan. 4–Dec. 29, 1809; Jan. 19, 26, Feb. 23–Mar. 9, 16–23, Apr. 6, 10, 17–24, May 1–11, 22, 25, June 1, 5, 12–19, 29, July 3, 6, 13, 20, 24, 31, Aug. 17, 28–Sept. 11, 18–25, Oct. 2, 5, 23, 30, Nov. 9–16, 23, 30, 1810; Jan. 1–Dec. 10, 24, 1811.

Schoharie Co. Hist. Soc. has Jan. 4–Dec. 29, 1809.

Cornell Univ. has Jan. 11–Dec. 29, 1809, fair.

Trinity Coll., Hartford, has Feb. 8, 14–21, Mar. 14, 17, 31, Apr. 14, May 30, July 25, Nov. 3, Dec. 29, 1809; Jan. 12, 16, 23, 1810; Jan. 1–Dec. 24, 1811.

Rutgers Univ. has Jan. 2, 1810–Dec. 24, 1811.

Hist. Soc. Penn., New Haven Col. Hist. Soc., Union Coll., Adriance Lib. of Poughkeepsie, and Detroit Pub. Lib. have Jan. 1–Dec. 24, 1811.

Univ. of Mich. (Clements) has Jan. 14, Feb. 8, Mar. 17, 21, 31, Apr. 4, 7, Aug. 22, Sept. 19, 29, Oct. 17, 20, 27, 1809; June 4, 1811.

N. Y. Pub. Lib. has Feb. 13, 1810.

Albany Centinel, 1797–1806.

Semi-weekly. Established July 4, 1797, by Loring Andrews and Co. (the co-partners were Isaiah Thomas, Ebenezer T. Andrews and Obadiah Penniman, who operated the Albany Bookstore), with the title of "The Albany Centinel." With the issue of Oct. 5, 1798, the firm was dissolved and the paper published by Loring Andrews. With the issue of July 7, 1801, the paper was purchased and published by Whiting & Leavenworth [Daniel Whiting and David Leavenworth]. With the issue of Apr. 9, 1802, Samuel Whiting was admitted to the firm, which became Whiting, Leavenworth and Whiting. With the issue of Apr. 1, 1803, Leavenworth withdrew and the paper was printed by Asa H. Center, for Daniel & Samuel Whiting. With the issue of Sept. 20, 1803, Eleazer F. Backus was admitted to the firm, and the paper was printed by Asa H. Center, for Whiting, Backus & Whiting. In October, 1804, Center's name disappeared from the imprint, and the paper was published by Whiting, Backus & Whiting. With the issue of May 24, 1805, it was printed by William Tucker, for Whiting, Backus & Whiting. With the issue of Mar. 4, 1806, the firm name was changed to Backus & Whiting, Daniel Whiting having withdrawn. On Nov. 10, 1806, the last issue being vol. 10, no. 37 (Munsell, "Typographical Miscellany," p. 103), the paper was sold to Isaac Mitchell, who established in its place the "Republican Crisis."

Harvard has July 4, 1797–Dec. 29, 1801; Jan. 1–8, 15–Feb. 2, 9–19, 26–Aug. 20,

27–Dec. 17, 28, 31, 1802; Jan. 4–Feb. 18, 25, Mar. 1, 11–18, 25–Apr. 5, 12, 15, 22–May 3, 10–20, 27–June 24, July 1–15, 22, 29, Aug. 2, 5, 16, 23–Sept. 16, 23–Oct. 7, 14–Dec. 30, 1803; Jan. 3–31, Feb. 7–Mar. 2, 9–May 1, 8, 15, 22–June 1, 19, 22, 29, July 6–17, 24–Oct. 2, 16–Nov. 30, Dec. 7–28, 1804; Jan. 1–22, Feb. 1–Apr. 12, 19–June 7, 14, Nov. 1, 1805; Jan. 14–21, 28, May 23, 29, Aug. 5, Oct. 31, 1806.

Am. Antiq. Soc. has July 4–Sept. 1, 8–Dec. 12, 19–26, 1797; Jan. 2–Feb. 23, Mar. 2–June 12, 19–July 3, 10–17, 24–Aug. 10, 17–Oct. 23, 30–Dec. 7, 14–28, 1798; Jan. 1–Mar. 5, 12–May 21, 28–July 9, 16–Aug. 30, Sept. 6–Oct. 8, 15–Nov. 1, 8–Dec. 31, 1799; Jan. 3–Feb. 18, 25–May 13, 20–30, June 6–24, July 1, 4, 15–Aug. 19, 26–Oct. 14, 21–Dec. 30, 1800; Jan. 2–20, 27–Feb. 27, Mar. 6–Apr. 17, 24–June 12, 19–July 3, 10, Aug. 18, Dec. 4, 1801; Jan. 19, 22, 29, Feb. 2, 12, 16, 23, 26, Mar. 12, 23, 26, June 15, Aug. 6, 1802; Feb. 4, 18, 25, Mar. 1, 4, Apr. 5, July 5–Oct. 4, 11–Dec. 30, 1803; May 1, 1804; Jan. 29, Apr. 5, 12, 16, May 10, 17, July 9, 16–Sept. 17, 24–Nov. 5, 1805; Feb. 7, 11, 21–Apr. 29, May 9–16, 27–June 20, 1806.

Troy Pub. Lib. has Dec. 8, 1801–Mar. 30, 1804.

N. Y. Hist. Soc. has July 4, 14–21, Aug. 15, 29, Sept. 15, 22, Dec. 8, 19, 1797; Jan. 2, 5, 16, 19, Feb. 2, Mar. 6, 9, Apr. 13, 17, 27, May 18, June 29, July 3, 24, 27, Aug. 7, 10, 17, Sept. 21–28, Dec. 4, 25, 1798; Jan. 11, Feb. 22, 26, Mar. 19, 26–Apr. 2, 23–30, Aug. 27, Nov. 8, 15, 29, Dec. 10–17, 31, 1799; Jan. 3–17, 24, 31, Feb. 7–25, Mar. 4, 14, 21, 28, Apr. 4, 8, 15, May 16, 27, 30, June 6, 10, 17, 20, July 1, 8, 18, Aug. 8, 15, 22, Sept. 5–16, Oct. 3, 17, 24, 31, Nov. 7–14, 25, Dec. 2, 9, 23–30, 1800; Jan. 16–23, 30–Feb. 6, 20–Mar. 3, 10, 13, 24, 27, Apr. 10, 17, 24–May 1, 15, 26–June 2, 12, July 3, 14, 21, 31, Aug. 11, 18–25, Sept. 1–22, Oct. 2, 6, 13–20, 27, 30, Nov. 10, 17, Dec. 1, 8, 11, 18–29, 1801; Jan. 29, Mar. 9, Sept. 3, Oct. 15, Nov. 2, 12, Dec. 4, 7, 1802; Jan. 14, Feb. 4–15, 25, Mar. 1, 15, Apr. 1, 5, 12, 26, May 3, 10, 31, June 3, 10, 28, July 8–26, Aug. 2–9, 15, Sept. 9, 27, Oct. 4, 7, Nov. 18, 25, Dec. 9, 20–30, 1803; Jan. 3, 6, 17, Feb. 3, Mar. 16, 23, Apr. 17, 20, 27, May 4, 11, July 10–20, 31–Aug. 21, Sept. 7–14, Nov. 2, 13, 23, 27, Dec. 7, 14, 1804; Jan. 8, Feb. 12, Mar. 1, 12, 29–Apr. 5, 23, 30, May 3, Dec. 3, 10, 13, 1805; Feb. 4, Apr. 1, 8–18, May 2–9, June 13, 17, July 4, Aug. 29, 1806.

N. Y. State Lib. has July 14, 1797; Apr. 3, June 12, July 3, Nov. 6, 1798; July 5, 9, 16, 19, 30, Aug. 2, 23, 27, Oct. 15, 1799; Jan. 14, 17, Feb. 21, 28, Mar. 18–June 24, July 11, 18, 22, 29, 1800; June 16, Aug. 11, 18, 25, 28, Dec. 4, 25, 1801; Jan. 8, Dec. 7, 24, 28, 1802; Feb. 25, Mar. 1–8, 15, Apr. 19, 22, May 3, 13, 17, 27, June 3, 24, July 1, 8, Aug. 16, 23, 30–Sept. 9, 23, 30, Oct. 4, Nov. 8, 29, Dec. 2, 6, 1803; Apr. 20, May 1, 15, July 17, Aug. 10, 1804; Feb. 5, July 5, 1805–Sept. 9, 1806.

Rochester Hist. Soc. has June 24, 1798–June 28, 1799.

Boston Pub. Lib. has July 18, Aug. 4–22, 29, Sept. 1, 8–Oct. 3, 10–31, Nov. 7, 14, 17, 28, Dec. 8, 19–26, 1797; Jan. 5–16, 30–Feb. 13, 20, 23, Mar. 2–20, 27–Apr. 3, 10, 24, May 1–15, 22, June 26, July 3, 10, 13, Sept. 11, 28, Oct. 5,

19, 23, 30, Nov. 2, 20, 27, Dec. 4-14, 21, 25, 1798; Jan. 4-18, 29, Feb. 5, 15-22, Mar. 5, 15, 26, Aug. 9, 1799; Apr. 11, 15, June 6, 1800.
Lib. Congress has Nov. 28, 1797; Oct. 22-29, Nov. 8, 12, 1799; Jan. 17, Feb. 25, Mar. 28-Apr. 8, June 6, Aug. 8, Oct. 7, Dec. 16, 23, 1800; Jan. 22, July 12, Sept. 24, 1805.
N. Y. Pub. Lib. has Dec. 12, 1797; May 4, June 15, 19, July 13-31, Aug. 7, 10, 17, 31, Sept. 21, 25, Oct. 12, Nov. 20, 23, Dec. 5, 18, 21, 1798; Jan. 11-29, Feb. 26, Mar. 15, July 9, 1799; Nov. 21, 1800; Suppl. of Mar. 31, 1804; Apr. 10, 1804; Aug. 22, Oct. 24, 1806.
Wis. Hist. Soc. has Jan. 17-Dec. 30, 1800, fair; July 30, 1802; Oct. 2, 1804; July 5, 1805.
Univ. of Rochester has Feb. 5, 9, Mar. 9, Apr. 2, June 1, 11, 22, 25, July 6, 27, Aug. 17, 1802.
Univ. of Ill. has Feb. 26, 1802; Feb. 28, Sept. 11, 25, Oct. 23, 1804.
Long Id. Hist. Soc. has Dec. 25, 1804.
Univ. of Pittsburgh has Feb. 20, 1798.
Univ. of Mich. (Clements) has Dec. 25, 1798.
Otsego Co. Hist. Soc., Cooperstown, has Nov. 29, 1799.
Buffalo Hist. Soc. has Dec. 31, 1799.
Yale has July 15, 1800.
Detroit Pub. Lib. has Dec. 6, 1803.

Albany Chronicle, 1796-1798.

Weekly. Established Sept. 12, 1796, by John M'Donald, with the title of "The Albany Chronicle." The printing-office was destroyed by fire Nov. 2, 1796, and the paper was consequently suspended. It was resumed on Jan. 2, 1797, with which issue M'Donald took Robert Moffitt into partnership, under the firm name of John M'Donald & Co. On Feb. 13, 1797, Moffitt announced that because of his poor health, he was no longer a partner (see "Albany Gazette" Mar. 13, 1797); and in June, 1797 he removed to Lansingburgh. With the issue of Aug. 28, 1797, the title was changed to "Albany Chronicle: or, Journal of the Times," edited by John M'Donald, and printed by J[oseph] Fry and H[enry] C. Southwick. In February or March, 1798, Joseph Fry became sole proprietor and publisher. The last issue located is that of Apr. 9, 1798, vol. 2, no. 75.

Harvard has Sept. 12, 26-Oct. 17, 1796; Jan. 2-30, Feb. 13-Mar. 6, 20-Apr. 10, 24, June 19, Dec. 11, 1797; Jan. 15, Apr. 2, 1798.
Am. Antiq. Soc. has Sept. 19, 1796; Jan. 30-Mar. 13, 27, Apr. 10, 17, May 8, June 5, Aug. 7, Oct. 16, 1797; Jan. 29, Mar. 26-Apr. 9, 1798.
N. Y. Hist. Soc. has Jan. 9, 16, Mar. 13-Aug. 7, 21, Sept. 4-Oct. 30, Nov. 13, 27, 1797; Jan. 1-15, 1798.
Troy Pub. Lib. has Feb. 20-Oct. 2, 1797.
N. Y. State Lib. has Apr. 24, 1797.

Albany Daily Advertiser, 1815–1817.

Daily. Established Sept. 25, 1815, with the title of "The Albany Daily Advertiser," published by John W. Walker, for Theodore Dwight. With the issue of Mar. 24, 1817, no. 464, it was discontinued under this name and was consolidated with "The Albany Gazette."

N. Y. State Lib. has Sept. 25–Dec. 30, 1815; Jan. 1–Apr. 22, 29, 30, May 2–6, 8, 15, 16, 20–22, 27–June 21, July 1–4, 8, 13, 17, 19, 23, 25, 26, 29–Aug. 30, Oct. 31–Dec. 31, 1816; Jan. 1, 6, 13–15, 25, 31, Feb. 1–4, 6, 12, 19–Mar. 24, 1817.
Wis. Hist. Soc. has Feb. 2–July 9, 1816.
Am. Antiq. Soc. has Mar. 11, July 23, Aug. 29, Nov. 18–20, 1816; Jan. 1, 13, 15, 31, 1817.
Oneida Hist. Soc., Utica, has Jan. 31, 1816.
N. Y. Hist. Soc. has Mar. 11, 1816.

[Albany] Federal Herald, 1788.

Weekly. Established Feb. 11, 1788, judging from the earliest issue located, that of Feb. 25, 1788, vol. 1, no. 3, entitled "The Federal Herald," printed by Claxton & Babcock [Thomas Claxton and John Babcock]. With the issue of Apr. 7, 1788, the firm was dissolved and the paper printed by J. Babcock & Co. The last issue published at Albany was that of Apr. 14, 1788, vol. 1, no. 10, after which the paper was removed to Lansingburgh and there continued, without change of title or volume numbering. Thomas Claxton became doorkeeper of the U. S. House of Representatives in 1789.

Am. Antiq. Soc. has Feb. 25, Mar. 3, 17, 31, Apr. 7, 1788.
N. Y. State Lib. has Mar. 3, 1788.
Schenectady Co. Hist. Soc. has Mar. 24, 1788.

Albany Gazette, 1771–1772.

Weekly. Established Nov. 25, 1771, by Alexander and James Robertson, with the title of "The Albany Gazette." The last issue located is that of Aug. 3, 1772.

Mass. Hist. Soc. has Dec. 2, 16, 30, 1771; Jan. 27, Feb. 3, 17, Mar. 2, June 1, 22, 29, July 27, Aug. 3, 1772.
Am. Antiq. Soc. has Nov. 25, 1771.
Lib. Congress has Feb. 24, 1772.

Albany Gazette, 1784–1820+.

Weekly, semi-weekly and daily. Established May 28, 1784, by Charles R. Webster, with the title of "The Albany Gazette." Joel Munsell, in his "Typographical Miscellany," 1850, p. 95, so states from having seen a complete early file in the N. Y. State Library, which, however, was destroyed in the fire of 1911. The earliest issue located is that of June 10, 1784, vol. 1, no. 3. On May 25, 1789, it changed from a weekly to a semi-weekly, and the imprint became Charles R. and George Webster. The plant suffered a serious fire on Nov. 17, 1793 (see "Albany Register" of Nov. 18), but apparently continued regular publication. With the issue of May 19, 1806, the Websters admitted their nephew, Elisha W. Skinner, to partnership, the paper being published by Websters and Skinner. In 1811, at some time between Sept. 5 and Nov. 4, Elisha's brothers, Hezekiah and Daniel, were admitted and the firm name became Websters and Skinners. With the issue of Mar. 25, 1817, no. 465, the paper was consolidated with "The Albany Daily Advertiser," was printed by Theodore V. W. Gould, published by William L. Stone for Websters, Skinners, & Co., changed its title to "The Albany Gazette & Daily Advertiser," adopted the volume numbering of the Advertiser, and became a daily. A semi-weekly, edition, however, was also issued, beginning with Mar. 27, 1817, entitled "The Albany Gazette, for the Country," and continuing the volume numbering of the old Albany Gazette; with the issue of Mar. 31, 1817, the words "for the Country" were omitted. With the issue of the daily of May 27, 1818, and the semi-weekly of May 28, 1818, Stone withdrew and the paper was published for Websters & Skinners, and printed by T. V. W. Gould. With the issue of July 26, 1819, for both papers, Gould's name disappeared from the imprint. With the issue of the daily of July 27, 1819, and of the semi-weekly of Aug. 5, 1819, it was published by Websters & Skinners. So continued until after 1820.

Am. Antiq. Soc. has June 16, 30, July 7, 21, 28, Aug. 11, 1785; Jan. 12–26, Feb. 9, Mar. 2, Aug. 17, 24, Sept. 7, 14, 28–Dec. 28, 1786; Jan. 4–Feb. 15, Mar. 1–Apr. 19, May 3–June 14, 28, July 12, 19, Aug. 2, 23, Sept. 6, Oct. 4–Dec. 20, 1787; Jan. 3–17, 31, Feb. 7, 21, Mar. 13, 27, May 15, June 12, July 3, 17, Aug. 7, Oct. 2, Dec. 26, 1788; Jan. 9, 23–Feb. 6, Mar. 13, Apr. 24, June 11, 15, July 6, Aug. 10, 13, Sept. 21, 28–Oct. 5, 15–22, 29, Nov. 12, 23, Dec. 10–17, 1789; Jan. 18, Mar. 22, Apr. 8, 19, 26, May 3, 10, 17, 24, June 3, 24, July 12, 15, 22, Aug. 5, 9, 30, Sept. 13, 23, Oct. 25, Nov. 4, 8, 18, 25, Dec. 9, 1790; Jan. 6, 31, Feb. 3, 24, Mar. 31, Apr. 11, 14 May 2, 5, 26, June 9, 16–30, July 14, 25, 28, Aug. 4, 11, 18, 25, Sept. 22, 29, Oct. 10, 13, Nov. 3, 7, 14, Dec. 1–8, 1791; Jan. 12, 26, Feb. 23, Mar. 5, 22, 29, Apr. 9–16, May 3, 10, 24, 31–June 14, 21–28, July 5, 12, 19, 23, Aug. 2, 6, 20, Sept. 3, 10, 17, 20, 27, Oct. 4, 11, 15, Nov. 1–8, 15–22, Dec. 3–10, 27, 1792; Jan. 3, 10–24, Feb. 7–14, 21, Mar. 4, 14, 21–28, Apr. 4–18, 25, 29, May 6, June 6, Aug. 5, 12, 19, Sept. 12, 19, Oct. 31, Nov. 14, 1793; Jan. 9, 20, 30, Feb. 6, May 15, Oct. 23, Dec. 11, 19, 1794; Jan. 12, 30, Feb. 9–20, 27, Mar. 2, 6, 20, 27, Apr. 3, 17, 20, 27, June 8–22, July 6–Sept. 26, Oct. 2–Dec. 28, 1795; Jan. 1–Mar. 21, 28–May 6, 13–20, 27–Sept. 30, Oct. 7–21, 31, Nov. 7, Dec. 2, 5, 19, 1796; Jan. 9, 20, 23, 30–Feb. 6, 13, 20–Apr. 28, May 5, 12, June 2, 9, 23, 30, July 21, 24, 31, Aug. 4, 7, 14–21, Sept. 8, 15–29, Oct. 6–16, 27, 30, Nov. 17, Dec. 11–22,

1797; Jan. 5–22, 29–Feb. 5, 12–19, 26, Mar. 5, 16–Apr. 2, 13, 16, 30, May 7–14, 25, 28, June 4, 8, 18, 22, July 9, 23, Aug. 17, 27, Sept. 7, Oct. 15, 29, Nov. 5, 9, 16, 19, 26, 30, Dec. 24, 1798; Jan. 11, 18–25, Feb. 1, Mar. 1, 8, 22–29, Apr. 5, May 10, 13, 20, June 10, 21–28, July 5–12, Sept. 2, 26, Nov. 14, 18, 28, Dec. 2, 16–23, 30, 1799; Jan. 13, 23, Feb. 6–17, Mar. 3, 13–Apr. 14, May 12, 29, June 2, 30–July 7, 28, Aug. 14, Oct. 6, 30, Dec. 18, 25, 1800; Jan. 5, 26, Feb. 19, 23, Mar. 5, 23, 30, Apr. 9, 16, 23, 27, May 4–14, June 4, Aug. 13, 17, 24–Sept. 3, 24–Oct. 1, 8, 29, Nov. 30, Dec. 17, 1801; Jan. 7, 11, 25, Feb. 1, 8, 18, Mar. 4, 22–29, Apr. 5, 12, 22–29, May 13, 20, 27–June 7, 21, July 8, 15, 19, 29, Aug. 23, 30, Sept. 6, 9, 16, 20, Oct. 11, 21, 28, Nov. 8, 18–Dec. 6, 13, 23, 30, 1802; Jan. 10, 20, 31, Feb. 14, 21, 28–Mar. 14, Apr. 14, 21, 25, May 2, 9, 12, June 2, 6, 23, 30, July 7, 11, 21, 28, Aug. 15, 22–Sept. 12, 22, 29, Oct. 20, Nov. 3, 21, Dec. 1, 19, 1803; Apr. 4, 1805; Dec. 1, 8, 1806; Sept. 3, 1807; Feb. 8, June 7, 14, July 12, 16, 26, Sept. 20, 1810; Feb. 21, 28, Mar. 14, 18, July 15, Aug. 12, Nov. 4, 1811; Oct. 8, 22, Nov. 30, Dec. 14, 1812; Jan. 14, 18, Feb. 1, 4, 11–18, Mar. 11, Apr. 26, 29, May 3, 13, June 28, July 29–Aug. 12, Oct. 28, Nov. 1, 8, Dec. 6, 1813; Jan. 17, Nov. 17, 24, Dec. 8, 1814; Jan. 30, Feb. 23, 1815; Oct. 7, Dec. 23, 1816; Feb. 24, Mar. 27, 31, 1817–Sept. 24, 1818; Jan. 27, Feb. 25, Apr. 15, Aug. 9, 25, Dec. 2, 25, 1819; Mar. 2, 18, May 1, 31, Nov. 15, 1820.

N. Y. Hist. Soc. has Nov. 4, 1784; Aug. 6, 24, 1789; May 10, June 21, July 8, Aug. 9, 23, 30, Sept. 16, Nov. 1, Dec. 16, 1790; Jan. 10, 13, 17, 27, Feb. 3, 7, 17, Apr. 14, 21, 28, May 2, 9, 12, 30, June 2, Sept. 8, 19, 1791; Mar. 26, 1792; Apr. 11, 1793; May 26, 1797; Jan. 1, Apr. 13, 16, 27, May 11, 28, June 8, July 6, 9, Aug. 3–13, Nov. 12, Dec. 3–10, 17, 1798; Feb. 8, Nov. 11, 14, Dec. 9, 16, 23, 30, 1799; Jan. 2, 6, Feb. 27, Mar. 24, 27, Apr. 7, May 15, June 19, 23, Aug. 14, Oct. 16, 1800; Jan. 1, 5, Mar. 16, Apr. 20, 30, June 4, 8, 25, July 9, Aug. 13–Sept. 3, Nov. 2, 26, Dec. 14, 17, 1801; Jan. 25, Feb. 11, 18, 22, June 10, July 12, Sept. 30, Oct. 7, Dec. 13, 1802; Jan. 17, 31, Feb. 7, 14, 21, Mar. 3, 21, May 26, July 12, 18, 28, Aug. 1, 25, Sept. 1, 8, Oct. 3, 31, Dec. 19, 1803; Jan. 2, Feb. 2, Mar. 5, 29, Apr. 12–19, 26, May 10, June 4, July 9, 16–23, 30, Aug. 2, Sept. 6, 13, Oct. 25, Nov. 1, 15, 26, 29, Dec. 6, 10, 17, 24, 1804; Jan. 17, Mar. 4, Apr. 15, 22–May 2, 9, 13, 23, June 6, 17–24, Aug. 1, 29, Sept. 16, Dec. 12, 19, 23, 1805; May 1, 12, 29, June 12, 16, 23, 26, July 31, Aug. 4, Sept. 15, 25, Oct. 16, Nov. 6, Dec. 25, 1806; Jan. 22, Feb. 23, Mar. 2, 23, 26, Apr. 9, 20, 23, 30, May 11, 21, 25, June 4, 29, July 9, 30, Aug. 10, 1807; Jan. 11–18, Feb. 1, 11, 25, 29–Mar. 7, 31, Apr. 4, 14, May 5, 12, June 6–13, July 4, 14, 18, Aug. 1, 4, 11, Sept. 15, Oct. 3, 6, 20, 24, 1808; Mar. 27, 1809; Feb. 5, 19–26, Dec. 17, 1810; Nov. 11, Dec. 2, 19, 1811; Jan. 2, June 18–29, July 9–27, Aug. 10, 17, 24, 31, Sept. 24, 28, Oct. 5, 12, 19–Dec. 31, 1812; Jan. 4, 7, 18, 28, Feb. 1–8, Mar. 15–22, 29, Apr. 5, 8, 15–May 13, 24–31, June 7–July 8, 15–22, 29–Oct. 21, 28–Dec. 30, 1813; Feb. 3, Mar. 10, Apr. 4, 7, 14, 18, May 2, 9, June 27, July 4, 7, Sept. 26, Oct. 6, 10, 20, Nov. 10–17, 28, Dec. 1, 5, 19–26, 1814; Mar. 6,

NEW YORK 535

13, 23–Apr. 6, 13, May 1–8, 29, June 15, 26–July 3, 13–24, Aug. 3, 21, 30, Sept. 7, Oct. 23, 26, 1815; June 17, Aug. 8, Sept. 12, 19, 1816; Jan. 3, 1819–Nov. 3, 1820. Also Apr. 22, Nov. 10, 1817; Jan. 7–10, Mar. 17, June 2, Nov. 11, 1818; Oct. 15, 1819 of the Daily.

N. Y. State Lib. has Sept. 15, Dec. 1, 1785; June 15, 29, Aug. 31, Sept. 14, 1786; Aug. 2, Oct. 18, Nov. 1, 29, Dec. 6, 1787; Feb. 27, 1789; Apr. 5, Oct. 14, 1790; Jan. 3, 1791; June 12, July 10, Aug. 3, 14, 21, 24, Oct. 16, 23–30, Dec. 18, 21, 28, 1795; Feb. 15, 26, Mar. 4, 18, Apr. 11, May 7, June 13, 27, Aug. 8, Sept. 30, 1796; Sept. 22, Nov. 6, 1797; Feb. 2, Mar. 19, Apr. 9, 17, 27, May 4, 14, 25, Sept. 3, Oct. 29, Nov. 9, 1798; Mar. 1, 22, Apr. 22, June 7, 10, 17, July 8, 12, Oct. 14, Dec. 23, 1799; Nov. 10, 1800; Aug. 13–20, Oct. 22, 1801; Oct. 18, 1802; Feb. 21, June 2, July 21, 1803; May 3, 1804–May 16, Sept. 12, 1805; Jan. 27, 1806; Apr. 20, Nov. 12, 1807; July 14, Oct. 27, Nov. 14, 1808; Mar. 2, June 8, Sept. 25, Nov. 6, 1809; Jan. 1, Feb. 26, Apr. 23, Sept. 6, 17, Dec. 17, 1810; Mar. 25, May 23–June 3, 13, 17, July 1, 8, 15, 18, 29, Aug. 26, 29, Sept. 5, 1811; Mar. 23, 30, Apr. 16, 20, 27, 30, May 28, June 25, July 16, Aug. 3–10, Sept. 21, Oct. 8–Nov. 30, Dec. 14, 21, 1812; Jan. 4–25, Feb. 1–Mar. 25, Apr. 1, 12–May 6, 13–June 7, 14, 21–July 22, 29, Aug. 5–19, 26, Sept. 2, 6, 13–Oct. 14, 25, 28, Nov. 8, 15–Dec. 2, 20, 30, 1813; Jan. 3, Mar. 7, Apr. 18, May 2, 12–19, 26, 30, June 2–13, Aug. 11, 15, 29, Sept. 1, 5, 12–Oct. 20, 31, Nov. 3–17, 24, Dec. 5–26, 1814; Jan. 2–Feb. 23, Apr. 27, July 27, 1815; May 6, July 15, 1816; Mar. 27, 1817–May 28, 1818; Mar. 25, 1819–Dec. 29, 1820. Also Mar. 25, 1817–Dec. 29, 1820 of the Daily.

Harvard has July 22, 1790; July 14, Nov. 10, 14, 1791; Feb. 20, 23, Mar. 2, May 29, June 19, 22, Sept. 21, 26, Oct. 26, 30, Nov. 6, 20, 27, 30, Dec. 11–18, 1795; Jan. 1, 15–22, 29, Feb. 5, 12–19, 26–Apr. 1, 8–15, May 2–9, June 17–July 22, 29, Aug. 5–15, 22, 26, Sept. 5, 12–19, 30–Oct. 14, 21–31, Nov. 7, 11, 18, 21, 28, Dec. 2, 19–30, 1796; Jan. 6, 13, 16, 23–Feb. 6, 13–20, 27–Mar. 27, Apr. 3–24, May 1, 12–June 2, 12–19, 30, July 7, 14, Aug. 14–28, Sept. 4, 8, 15, 18, 25–Oct. 13, 20, 27, Nov. 6–17, Dec. 8, 1797; Feb. 19, Mar. 5, 12–26, Apr. 6–13, May 7, 28, June 4, 15, 18, July 20, 30, Aug. 10–17, Sept. 7, Oct. 15, 19, 29, Nov. 2, 9, 23, 26, 1798; Jan. 14–21, July 22, 29, Aug. 9, 27, 30, 1799; Feb. 3, June 19, 23, 1800; May 14, 21, Dec. 14, 31, 1801; Jan. 11–Feb. 18, 25–Mar. 11, 18–Apr. 1, 8–15, 22–July 1, 12–Aug. 19, 31–Sept. 23, Oct. 4, 7, 14–21, Nov. 1, 4, 15, 22, Dec. 9, 16, 1802; Jan. 6, 13, 27, Feb. 3, 10, 21, Mar. 7, 14, 21, 31, Apr. 28–May 23, 30, June 6, 13–30, July 7–Aug. 8, 22–Dec. 1, 8–22, 29, 1803; Jan. 2, 9–Feb. 13, 23–Apr. 12, 19–May 7, 14, 17, 24, 31, June 18, 21, 28–July 12, 19–Aug. 13, 20, 23, 30–Sept. 6, 13–Nov. 19, 26–Dec. 13, 20–31, 1804; Jan. 3–21, 31, Feb. 4, 11–Apr. 11, 18, 22, 29–May 27, June 6, 13, Dec. 12, 30, 1805; Apr. 7, Dec. 29, 1806; May 18, Nov. 30, 1807; July 20, 1812.

Lib. Congress has Feb. 13, 27, Mar. 12, 26, Apr. 16, May 7, July 30, Aug. 2, 9, 23, Sept. 10, 1792; Sept. 12, 1793; Oct. 30, Nov. 3, 17, 24, 1794; Jan. 30,

Feb. 6–16, Mar. 6, 13–23, Oct. 16, 1795; June 9–16, 1797; Mar. 30, 1798; Mar. 4, May 10, Nov. 21, Dec. 26, 1799; Feb. 24, Mar. 10, Apr. 24, May 19, June 9, 1800; Nov. 11, 1802; Apr. 7, July 21, 1803; Dec. 6, 1813; Oct. 1, 1817–Mar. 24, 1818; Apr. 29, 1819.

N. Y. Pub. Lib. has Sept. 20, Dec. 30, 1790; Sept. 19, 1791; Oct. 16, 1794–Dec. 25, 1795; May 2, Oct. 10, 1796; Mar. 13, 1797; Apr. 23, 1798; May 25, 1807–May 19, 1808; Aug. 24, 1809; June 4, Aug. 24, 1812; Mar. 30–Dec. 31, 1818; Jan. 4–Mar. 22, Apr. 8–15, May 13, June 3, July 12, Aug. 9, 26, Dec. 2, 13, 1819; Jan. 6, Feb. 17, Mar. 2, 13, 20, May 4, 22, June 8, 22, July 13, 21, Sept. 19, Oct. 3, 17–24, Nov. 7, 10, 21, Dec. 5, 19–26, 1820.

Wis. Hist. Soc. has Dec. 30, 1799; Mar. 13, 20, 24, Apr. 24–May 5, 12, 15, 22, 29–June 5, 12–July 7, 17, 24–31, Aug. 28, Sept. 11, 29–Oct. 9, 16, 27, Nov. 17, 27, Dec. 15, 1800; Sept. 19, 1808; Mar. 27, 1817–May 28, 1818; Dec. 10, 1818.

Schoharie Co. Hist. Soc. has Jan. 6, 1812–Dec. 27, 1813.

Trinity Coll., Hartford, has Jan. 14, 17, Mar. 14, Apr. 22, June 17, 27–July 8, Aug. 5, Sept. 23, 26, Oct. 24, 31, Nov. 28–Dec. 5, 19, 1805; Oct. 16, 1806; Jan. 12, 22–29, Feb. 19, July 20, Aug. 10, Oct. 1, 1807; Jan. 4, Feb. 16, June 12, 16, Nov. 16, 1808; Jan. 29, Mar. 19, 1810; Jan. 24, 1811; Sept. 29, 1814. Also Mar. 26–Sept. 24, 1818, of the Daily.

Oneida Hist. Soc., Utica, has Feb. 17, Mar. 19, June 1, 15–25; July 27, 30, Aug. 13, 17, Sept. 21, Dec. 3, 1812; Feb. 4, 25, Mar. 22, June 14, July 5, Oct. 18, 1813; Jan. 13, 20, Feb. 28, Mar. 3, 17, Apr. 21, May 2–12, 19–26, June 16–23, July 4–14, 21, 25, Aug. 4, 8, 18, 22, Sept. 22, 29, Oct. 24, Nov. 7, 10, 21–28, Dec. 12, 22, 1814; Jan. 2, 9, Feb. 9, 20, Mar. 20, Apr. 13–24, May 1, 29, June 8–19, July 13, 20, 24, Aug. 21, 28, Sept. 11, 14, 21, 25, Oct. 26, Nov. 2–16, 23, Dec. 7, 18, 25, 1815; Jan. 11–18, Aug. 15, 1816; Aug. 25, 1817; Jan. 31, June 1, Sept. 22, 1820.

Buffalo Hist. Soc. has May 5–Dec. 26, 1794.

Phil. Lib. Co. has Oct. 30, Nov. 13, 16, 23, Dec. 4, 1795; Jan. 22, Mar. 14–Apr. 8, 15–29, May 16, 27–June 6, 17, 24, 27, July 15, 18, Aug. 5, 8, 19, 1796.

Mass. Hist. Soc. has Nov. 16, 23, 1786; Jan. 25, Feb. 1, 15, Mar. 15, 1787.

Univ. of Ill. has Dec. 1, 1803; June 7–July 9, Sept. 13, Oct. 11, 22, Nov. 5, Dec. 3, 1804; Mar. 27, 31, 1806; July 9, 1807.

Univ. of Rochester has Sept. 18, 1794; Aug. 7, 1797; Feb. 7, July 10, Sept. 5, 12, Oct. 3, 31, Nov. 21, 1820.

Mrs. Charles E. Lansing, Albany, has June 10, Oct. 21, 1784; Jan. 14, 1785; July 26, 1787; Jan. 24, 1788.

Univ. of Mich. (Clements) has Jan. 30, Feb. 13, 20, 27, 1797; Apr. 10, 1800; Aug. 5, 1813.

Univ. of Pittsburgh has Apr. 2, 1792; Aug. 7, 1797; Feb. 23, 1801; Dec. 9, 1811; Aug. 13, 1819.

Western Reserve Hist. Soc. has Sept. 20, 1792; Feb. 6, 1797; Feb. 19, Mar. 30, 1818.

Syracuse Univ. has Oct. 30, Dec. 4, 1795; Mar. 12, 1801.

Walter S. Nicoll, Albany, has Feb. 2, 1786.
Schenectady Co. Hist. Soc. has Aug. 25, 1794.
N. Y. State Hist. Assoc. has Oct. 30, 1797.
Dartmouth has Nov. 4, 1805.
Boston Pub. Lib. has Feb. 28, 1809.
Rutgers Univ. has Oct. 5, 1809.
Hist. Soc. Penn. has Mar. 11, 1813.
Alonzo P. Walton, Schenectady, has Dec. 9, 1813.
Wesleyan Univ. has Sept. 19, 1814.
Yale has Sept. 1, 1818.

[Albany] **Geographical & Military Museum, 1814.**

Weekly. Established Feb. 28, 1814, by S[amuel] R. Brown, with the title of "Geographical & Military Museum." It was of quarto size, with pagination and eight pages to the issue. The last issue located is that of June 6, 1814, vol. 1, no. 15.

N. Y. State Lib. has Feb. 28–June 6, 1814.
Am. Antiq. Soc. has Feb. 28–Apr. 18, May 2, 16–June 6, 1814.
Ohio Arch. & Hist. Soc. has Feb. 28, Mar. 7, 21–May 2, 16–June 6, 1814.
N. Y. Hist. Soc. has Feb. 28, Mar. 28, Apr. 25–June 6, 1814.
Wis. Hist. Soc. has Mar. 28–Apr. 18, May 2, June 6, 1814.
Lib. Congress has Mar. 28, Apr. 18–May 23, 1814.

[Albany] **Guardian, 1807–1808.**

Weekly. Established Nov. 21, 1807, by Van Benthuysen & Wood [Obadiah R. Van Benthuysen and William Wood], with the title of "The Guardian." It was of quarto size, and with pagination. Although a magazine in appearance, it could be regarded as a newspaper, as it contained current news, death notices and advertisements. It was discontinued with the issue of Nov. 12, 1808, vol. 1, no. 52.

Am. Antiq. Soc. has Nov. 21, 1807–Nov. 12, 1808.
N. Y. Hist. Soc. has Nov. 21, 1807–Jan. 23, Feb. 6–Nov. 12, 1808.
Univ. of Mich. (Clements) has Nov. 28–Dec. 26, 1807; Jan. 2–Apr. 30, May 14–July 16, 30–Sept. 3, 17–Oct. 29, 1808.
Conn. Hist. Soc. has Apr. 23–Nov. 12, 1808.

Albany Journal, 1788–1789.

Semi-weekly and weekly. Established as a semi-weekly Jan. 26, 1788, by Charles R. and George Webster, & Co., with the title of "The Albany Journal: or, the Montgomery, Washington and Columbia Intelligencer." It was the intention to publish it twice a week during the session of the legislature, but with the issue of Mar. 31, 1788, and thenceforth, it was published weekly. It was of quarto size, and was issued in connection with "The Albany Gazette." The last issue located is that of May 11, 1789, vol. 2, no. 77, and in that month it was discontinued, as the Gazette was changed to a semi-weekly on May 25, 1789.

> N. Y. State Lib. has Feb. 2, 9, 11, 18, 23, Mar. 3, 8, 15, 17, May 12, June 16, 23, July 7, 21, Aug. 4, Oct. 20, Nov. 3, Dec. 22, 1788; Feb. 16, Mar. 2, 30–May 11, 1789.
> Am. Antiq. Soc. has Feb. 2, 4, 9, 23, Mar. 10, 15, June 16, July 14, 21, Aug. 4, 18, 25, Sept. 8, 15, 29, Dec. 8, 1788; Jan. 26, Apr. 13–27, 1789.
> N. Y. Pub. Lib. has Aug. 4, 1788.

[Albany] New-York Gazetteer, 1782–1784.

Weekly. Established June 3, 1782, judging from the earliest issue located, that of July 15, 1782, vol. 1, no. 7, published by Balentine and Webster [Solomon Balentine and Charles R. Webster], with the title of "The New-York Gazetteer, or, Northern Intelligencer." With the issue of Aug. 4, 1783, the partnership was dissolved and the paper published by Solomon Balentine. The last issue located is that of May 1, 1784, vol. 2, no. 101, and the paper was discontinued immediately thereafter. J. Munsell, in his "Typographical Miscellany," p. 225, says "The office file of this paper was in Mr. Webster's possession until it was destroyed by the great fire of 1793."

> Am. Antiq. Soc. has July 15, Aug. 19–Nov. 4, 18–Dec. 30, 1782; Jan. 13, 27, Feb. 3, 17, Mar. 3, Apr. 7, May 19, 26, June 9, 30, July 14, Aug. 4, Sept. 1, 8, 22–Oct. 6, 20–Nov. 3, 24, Dec. 22, 1783; Mar. 13, May 1, 1784.
> N. Y. State Lib. has Dec. 23, 30, 1782; Jan. 6, 13, 27–Mar. 10, 1783.
> Mass. Hist. Soc. has Aug. 19, Sept. 9, Dec. 23, 1782.
> N. Y. Pub. Lib. has Aug. 19, 1782.
> Lib. Congress has Apr. 7, 1783.
> N. Y. Hist. Soc. and Univ. of Mich. (Clements) have Oct. 20, 1783.

[Albany] New-York Statesman, 1820+.

Semi-weekly. Established May 16, 1820, with the title of "The New-York Statesman," printed for the Proprietor, by E. & E. Hosford [Elijah and Elisha Hosford]. The announcement is signed by Nathaniel H. Carter, as Proprietor, and states that the paper succeeds "The Albany Register." So continued until after 1820.

> N. Y. Hist. Soc., and Troy Pub. Lib. have May 16–Dec. 29, 1820.
> Lib. Congress has May 16–June 9, 16–Sept. 19, 26–Oct. 17, 27, Nov. 7–21, 28–Dec. 22, 1820.
> Am. Antiq. Soc. has May 16–June 2, July 4–Aug. 15, 22–Sept. 22, 29–Oct. 27, Nov. 3–Dec. 19, 26, 29, 1820.

N. Y. State Lib. has May 19-June 9, Nov. 21, 1820.
Univ. of Rochester has Aug. 1, 1820.

[Albany] **Plough Boy,** 1819–1820+.

Weekly. Established June 5, 1819, with the title of "The Plough Boy," edited by Henry Homespun, Jr. (pseudonym of Solomon Southwick), and printed for the editor by John O. Cole. It was of quarto size, eight pages to the issue, with pagination and a title-page. With the issue of Jan. 22, 1820, the title was changed to "The Plough Boy. And Journal of the Board of Agriculture," and the name of Solomon Southwick replaced that of Henry Homespun, Jr., in the imprint. So continued until after 1820.

Am. Antiq. Soc., N. Y. State Lib., N. Y. Pub. Lib., N. Y. Hist. Soc., Yale, Penn. State Lib., Lib. Congress, Boston Pub. Lib., Harvard, Rutgers Univ., Columbia Univ., John Crerar Lib., Newberry Lib., Univ. of Chicago, Univ. of Penn., Univ. of Vt., Ind. State Lib., La. State Univ., Wis. Hist. Soc., Minn. Hist. Soc., and Univ. of Texas have June 5, 1819–Dec. 30, 1820. Many libraries have imperfect files.

Albany Register, 1788–1820+.

Weekly and semi-weekly. Established as a weekly in October, 1788, judging from the date of the earliest issue located, that of Apr. 6, 1789, vol. 1, no. 26, published by Robert Barber & Co., with the title of "The Albany Register." At some time between May 23 and June 13, 1791, Robert Barber retired and the paper was published by John Barber. At some time between Sept. 24 and Oct. 22, 1792, Solomon Southwick was admitted to partnership, and the paper was published by John Barber and Solomon Southwick. With the issue of July 10, 1795, it was published semi-weekly. With the issue of Sept. 5, 1800, the partnership was dissolved and the paper published by John Barber. Barber died July 10, 1808, and with the issue of July 19, 1808, it was "printed by Solomon Allen, Jun., for the Proprietor, successor of John Barber;" Solomon Southwick signed the announcement as editor. In November, 1809, this was changed to Solomon Allen, Jun., for S. Southwick. With the issue of May 4, 1810, the "Jun." was omitted after Allen's name. With the issue of May 1, 1812, Allen retired, and the paper was printed by H. C. Southwick, for S. Southwick, changed with the issue of Oct. 28, 1814, to Henry C. Southwick, for Solomon Southwick. With the issue of July 2, 1816, Solomon Southwick's name appeared in the imprint as sole publisher. Because of financial trouble, Southwick suspended publication with the issue of May 13, 1817. The paper was revived July 4, 1817 by Israel W. Clark. With the issue of Oct. 1, 1819, the imprint was changed to "Printed by Jeremiah Tryon, for the Proprietors," but with the issue of May 9, 1820, Tryon's name was omitted and the imprint became "For the Proprietors." The paper was suspended with the issue of May 12, 1820, vol. 32, no. 24, being succeeded by "The New-York Statesman," but was revived in 1821.

N. Y. State Library has May 11, Sept. 14, 1789; Feb. 1, Mar. 1, 22, Apr. 19, 1790; Jan. 6, 27, 31, Feb. 3, 1791; Jan. 30, Apr. 16, 1792; May 13, 1793–Dec. 29, 1794; May 11, June 15, July 17–Nov. 2, 16, 20, 27, Dec. 11, 21, 1795; Jan. 1, 8, May 2, 27–Oct. 31, Nov. 28, Dec. 5, 12–23, 30, 1796; Jan. 2, 13, 16, Feb. 24, June 16, Oct. 13–Dec. 29, 1797; Jan. 1–Oct. 9, 19, 1798; Mar. 15, 1799; May 23–Dec. 30, 1800; Jan. 2–Oct. 9, Nov. 10, 17, 1801; Jan. 15–May 14, June 1, Dec. 3, 1802; Jan. 7, Apr. 5, 19, May 3, Sept. 20, 30, Oct. 1, 21, Nov. 4, 8, 15–22, 1803; Jan. 20, Feb. 7, 17, June 8, 1804–Sept. 9, 1806; Oct. 10, 1806–Dec. 30, 1808; Jan. 6, 10, 17–24, Feb. 7, 14, 21, Mar. 10, 14, 28, Apr. 4, 21, May 9, 26, June 20, 23, July 14, Sept. 22, Oct. 6, 17–31, Nov. 21, 1809–Dec. 31, 1811; Jan. 3–May 1, 8, 15–Aug. 28, Sept. 4, 25, Oct. 2–9, 16–27, Nov. 3, 9, Dec. 15, 25, 29, 1812; Jan. 1, Feb. 5, 12, Apr. 6, 9, 16, 20, May 18, 28, June 8, 18, 29, July 2, 13, 20–30, Aug. 6, Oct. 5, 8, 15, 21, 26, Nov. 19, 26, Dec. 17, 28, 31, 1813; Jan. 4–Feb. 11, 18, Mar. 25–Apr. 8, 19, 22, May 3–10, 17, July 15, 26, Aug. 5–16, 23, Sept. 13, 23–Oct. 4, 14, Nov. 8, 18, 25, Dec. 6, 30, 1814; Jan. 10–17, 27, Feb. 3, 7, 17, 24, 28, Apr. 18, May 2, 5, 12, 30–June 6, 16–23, July 3, 7, Aug. 11, 16, 22, 29, Sept. 19, Oct. 27, 31, Nov. 7, 28, Dec. 1, 5, 1815; Jan. 2–Dec. 31, 1816; Jan. 21, Feb. 21, 25, Mar. 4, Apr. 1, July 4, 1817; Feb. 26, Mar. 12–May 18, June 8, 29, July 16–Dec. 31, 1819; Jan. 4–28, Mar. 31, Apr. 7–14, 21, May 9, 12, 1820.

Am. Antiq. Soc. has Apr. 6, 1789; May 3, 10, 1790; Mar. 28, Apr. 18, May 9, 16, June 27–Aug. 8, 29, Sept. 19, 26, Oct. 10, 17, 1791; Jan. 16, 30, Feb. 13, 20, Mar. 5, 26, Apr. 2, July 16, Aug. 6, 20, Sept. 17, Dec. 10, 1792; Jan. 7, Feb. 11, Mar. 18, Apr. 15, 29, May 6, July 29, Aug. 5, Oct. 28, 1793; Jan. 13, Feb. 10, 17, Apr. 21, Sept. 15, 1794; Jan. 12, 19, Feb. 2, Mar. 2, 30, Apr. 20, June 15, July 6, Aug. 3, 28, Sept. 28, 1795; May 27, Nov. 21, Dec. 5, 9, 1796; Feb. 20, Apr. 10, June 12, 26, Aug. 14, 21, 1797; Jan. 22, Apr. 27, June 8, 11, 22, 25, Oct. 1–8, Nov. 5, Dec. 14, 24, 1798; Jan. 4, Mar. 22, June 10, 28, Dec. 6, 1799; Mar. 21, Apr. 11, 15, May 27, 30, Aug. 19, Oct. 10–Dec. 30, 1800; Jan. 2, 1801–Dec. 31, 1802; Jan. 4–May 20, 27–Oct. 7, 28, Nov. 18, 22, Dec. 9–30, 1803; Jan. 6–17, 24, 27, Feb. 3, 7, 14, 28–Mar. 23, 30–Apr. 10, 17–May 4, 11–Aug. 10, 17–Sept. 25, Oct. 5–16, Nov. 13–30, Dec. 14–28, 1804; Jan. 1–25, Feb. 1–Mar. 12, 19–Apr. 23, 30–May 28, June 4–Aug. 9, 16–Oct. 8–18, Nov. 15, Dec. 6, 10, 13, 31, 1805; Feb. 21, May 30, Aug. 26, Oct. 17, 1806–Dec. 30, 1808; Jan. 20, Feb. 14, June 6, 13, Oct. 20, 27, Nov. 10–24, Dec. 1–29, 1809; Jan. 2–26, Feb. 2–June 29, July 6–Aug. 3, 10–Dec. 28, 1810; Jan. 8–Mar. 15, 22–Apr. 9, 19, 23, 30, May 3, 10, 14, 21, 24, 31–Sept. 27, Oct. 4–Nov. 5, 22, Dec. 6, 13–27, 1811; Jan. 3–28, Feb. 4–Apr. 14, 24, May 5, 12, 19, 22, 29–July 7, 14–Aug. 4, 14, 25, 28, Sept. 4–15, 25–Oct. 9, 23, 27, Nov. 3, 20, Dec. 1, 4, 1812; Jan. 1–Dec. 31, 1813; Jan. 18, 25, 28, Feb. 4, 18, 25, Mar. 11, 22, 25, Apr. 15, Aug. 5, Sept. 20, Nov. 25,

NEW YORK 541

Dec. 2-9, 1814; Jan. 3-Dec. 29, 1815; Jan. 2, 5, 12, Feb. 2, 6, 13, Mar. 19, Apr. 12, 16, May 3, 17, June 18, July 26, Aug. 27, Dec. 6, 1816; Jan. 3- May 13, 1817; Sept. 4, 18, 1818; Aug. 10, Oct. 12, 15, Nov. 30, Dec. 3, 1819; Jan. 4-Apr. 28, May 5-12, 1820.
Harvard has June 13, 27, July 4, Sept. 19, 26, Nov. 7, 1791; Oct. 22, 1792; Sept. 2, 30, Oct. 7, 1793; Jan. 27, Feb. 10, June 2, 1794; Feb. 23, Mar. 9, May 25, Aug. 3, Nov. 6, 16, Dec. 18, 21, 1795; Feb. 29, Mar. 7, 14, 28, Apr. 1, 4, 22, 29-May 13, 20, 23, June 20, 27, July 11, Aug. 1-15, Sept. 16, 23, Oct. 7-17, 24, Nov. 28, Dec. 12, 19, 26, 30, 1796; Jan. 2-16, Feb. 6, 17- Mar. 10, 17-27, Apr. 3-10, 21, 24, May 12, June 12, 19, 23, Aug. 11, 14, 21, Sept. 11, 22, 29, Oct. 16, Nov. 3, 13, 1797; Jan. 5, Mar. 2, 19, June 29, July 2, 9, Sept. 3, 1798; Aug. 22, Sept. 2, 30, Nov. 7, 14, 18, Dec. 19, 1800; Jan. 2, 16, 30, Feb. 24, Mar. 6, 17, 20, 31, Apr. 7, 14, 24, May 5, 8, 15, 19, July 14, Aug. 7, 11, 18, 25, 28, Sept. 8, 15, 18, Oct. 6, Dec. 1, 8, 18, 22, 29, 1801; Jan. 12, Feb. 9, Mar. 2, 16, 30, Apr. 2, 6, May 4, 7, 14, 25, June 15, 22, 29, July 6, 13, 20, 27, Aug. 3-13, 24, Sept. 3, 14, 21, 28, Oct. 5, 12, 19, 26, Nov. 2, 9-16, 23-30, Dec. 7-31, 1802; Jan. 4-Feb. 4, 15-22, May 1, 11, 15, 22-Apr. 19, 26-May 20, 27, 31, June 7, 10, 17-24, July 1, 5, 12, 15, 26- Sept. 20, 27-Oct. 18, 25-Nov. 1, 1803; Feb. 3, 10, 21, Mar. 20, 23, Apr. 3, 17-27, May 4, 8, 18, 22, 29, June 1, 19-29, July 6, 10, 17-24, 31-Aug. 10, 24, 28, Sept. 11, 21-Oct. 12, 26, 30, Nov. 6-23, Dec. 4-28, 1804; Jan. 4, 22, 29, Feb. 1, 15, Mar. 1, 12-26, Apr. 26, 30, May 7, 14, 17, 31-June 21, 28, July 16-22, 30-Oct. 8, 15-Nov. 15, 26, Dec. 3, 10-17, 27, 31, 1805; Jan. 10, 14, 21, 28-Mar. 4, 11-Apr. 18, 25, 29, May 6, 13-June 6, 17-24, July 4, 8, 18-Aug. 8, 15, 19, 26, Sept. 2, 9-30, Oct. 10, 14, 24, 28, Nov. 4, 11-Dec. 2, 9-23, 30, 1806; Jan. 2-Dec. 4, 1807, fair; Jan. 29, Feb. 9, Mar. 4, July 19, 22, 29, Aug. 5-26, Sept. 2, 9, 23, 30-Oct. 11, 21-Nov. 1, 8-15, 22, 29, Dec. 9, 16, 23-30, 1808; Nov. 6, 1810; Apr. 2, June 25, July 5, 12, 19-Aug. 9, 16, 20, Sept. 10, 17-27, Oct. 4, 18, 22, Nov. 8, 19, 22, Dec. 3, 10, 17, 24, 1811; Jan. 3-10, 21, 28, 31, Feb. 7, 11, Mar. 6, 10, 17, Apr. 14, May 22, June 5, 19, 23, July 21, 31, Aug. 7, 14, 25, 28, Sept. 4, 29, Oct. 9, 13, 1812.
N. Y. Pub. Lib. has July 27, 1789; Oct. 19-29, Nov. 12, 19-Dec. 31, 1798; Jan. 7-Feb. 11, 18, Apr. 19, 26, May 3, 10, 17, June 28, July 8, 19, Aug. 19- 26, Sept. 6, 10, 24, Oct. 11, Nov. 1-15, 22-Dec. 13, 20-31, 1799; Jan. 3-14, 24, 31, Feb. 7, 11, 18-28, Mar. 11, 14, 21, 25, Apr. 1, 8-29, May 9-June 24, July 1-Aug. 1, 1800; Nov. 6, 1801; Jan. 29, July 13, 17, Aug. 3- Sept. 7, 14-Oct. 12, 22-Nov. 12, 19-Dec. 3, 10, 14, 21-28, 1802; Jan. 4, 1803; July 22-29, Aug. 8-26, Sept. 2-9, 19, 30, Oct. 7-14, 21-Nov. 21, Dec. 5, 12-23, 30, 1806; Feb. 23, Mar. 18-May 6, 13-June 7, 1808; Feb. 7, 1809; June 25, July 16, Sept. 6, 27, Oct. 8-Nov. 5, 12-26, Dec. 6-13, 27, 31, 1811; Jan. 3, 10-21, 28, Feb. 4-14, 21-Mar. 24, 31-June 30, July 7-Dec. 1, 8-29, 1812; Jan. 1-Feb. 6, 12-23, Mar. 2-Apr. 13, 20-June 22, 29-Dec. 31, 1813; Jan. 4-17, 24-Nov. 11, 18-Dec. 30, 1814; June 30, 1818.
Queens Borough Pub. Lib., Jamaica, N. Y., has Oct. 22, 1798-Oct. 8, 1799.

N. Y. Hist. Soc. has Nov. 29, 1790; Aug. 4, 1794; Mar. 8, Oct. 22, 1799; Oct. 14, 1800–Oct. 6, 1801; Jan. 29, 1802; June 21, Aug. 2, Sept. 23, Nov. 4, Dec. 27, 1803; July 16–23, Aug. 23, Sept. 6, 13, 17, 27–Oct. 8, 1805; Sept. 5, 1806; Feb. 19, Mar. 19, Apr. 13, 1807; Jan. 15, 19, Mar. 4, 15, 18, 29, Apr. 8, 19, June 17, 21, July 15, Aug. 30, Nov. 11, Dec. 2, 6, 20, 23, 1808; Feb. 24, 1809; Jan. 2, 23, 26, Feb. 6, 9, Mar. 13, May 29, June 19, July 10, Aug. 31, Sept. 4, Dec. 11, 25, 1810; Feb. 5, 1811; Aug. 25, 28, Oct. 20, Nov. 13, 1812; Jan. 26, Feb. 9, Mar. 16, 30, June 8, 1813; Apr. 8, Oct. 14, 1814; June 23, July 28, 1815; May 28, Dec. 16, 1816; Feb. 28, Apr. 29, 1817; Dec. 21–31, 1819; Jan. 4–Apr. 28, May 12, 1820.

Lib. Congress has Dec. 31, 1792; May 6, 1799; Apr. 8, 11, 18, 25–June 10, 20–July 11, 18, 25, Aug. 5–12, 22–Sept. 5, 12–19, 26, Oct. 10, 21, Nov. 4, 7, 18, Dec. 5–16, 26, 1800; Mar. 13, June 2, Nov. 6, 1801; Feb. 16, Apr. 2, 13, 16, 27, May 14, Aug. 10–Sept. 3, 21, Oct. 1, 15, 1802; Jan. 13, 1804; Mar. 16, 19, July 17, Sept. 1–11, 29, Oct. 16, Dec. 1, 4, 11–18, 25, 29, 1807; Jan. 1–Aug. 5, 1808, fair; Oct. 25, Nov. 11, 18, 22, 1808; Mar. 21, June 6, 16, 1809; Feb. 13, 1810; Jan. 21, Apr. 21, May 1, June 26, 1812; July 30, 1813; Aug. 30, 1814; Feb. 28, June 20, 30, July 7, 1815; Mar. 15, 22, Apr. 5, 12, 23, Aug. 9, 13, 1816; Mar. 11, 25, 28, Apr. 11, 15, 1817; Feb. 9, Apr. 6, May 14, 18, June 1, 4, 8, Oct. 15, 22, Nov. 19, 1819.

Union Coll. has Jan. 3, 1806–Dec. 30, 1808; Jan. 16–Dec. 18, 1810.

Yale has July 30, 1792; Oct. 10, 1806–Dec. 30, 1808.

Univ. of Rochester has Feb. 22, July 26, Aug. 2, 9, Oct. 18, Nov. 25, Dec. 6, 1790; Feb. 14, Mar. 21, May 23, July 4, Oct. 10, 1791; May 7, 1792; Apr. 27, 1798; May 21, June 8, 22, 1802; Apr. 21, 24, May 5, 12, 19, 26, June 2, 9, 12, 23–July 3, 14, 24, 31, Aug. 4, 11–21, 28, Sept. 4, Oct. 20, 27–Nov. 6, 18, 20, Dec. 11, 29, 1812; Jan. 1, 8, 19, 22, Feb. 2, 9, 23, Mar. 12, 19–Apr. 23, June 1, 22, Aug. 6, 10, 31, Sept. 7, 10, 17–28, Oct. 15, Nov. 5, 1813; Jan. 4, 18–28, Feb. 22, 25, Mar. 11, 15, Apr. 5, 12, 22, 26, May 3, 6, June 14, Sept. 27–Oct. 4, 18, 28, Nov. 15, 18, 29, Dec. 6, 30, 1814; July 14, Aug. 28, 1818; Jan. 26, 29, Feb. 16, Apr. 2, 1819.

Univ. of Mich. (Clements) has Feb. 10, Aug. 4, Sept. 1, 1801; Jan. 15, Feb. 23, June 8, 1802; May 17, June 17, Sept. 16, 1803; Apr. 7, 14–May 29, June 5–30, July 7–Aug. 11, 21, Sept. 1–22, 29–Oct. 30, Nov. 6, 10, 17, 24, Dec. 11–29, 1812; Jan. 8, 15, Mar. 2, Apr. 2, 6, 20, May 7, 21–June 1, 11–16, 30–Aug. 6, 24, 31–Sept. 7, Oct. 8, Nov. 16, Dec. 14, 21, 31, 1813; Jan. 4–14, 21–June 3, 10, 21–28, July 5–Sept. 30, 1814; Mar. 21, 24, Apr. 4–May 16, Aug. 1–Sept. 26, Oct. 3–Nov. 3, 14–Dec. 1, 8, 1815; Oct. 8–Nov. 1, 1816.

Wis. Hist. Soc. has Dec. 31, 1799; Feb. 21, 28–Mar. 11, 20, 28, Apr. 8, 22–29, May 9, 23, 30, June 6, 10, 17–July 15, 22–Aug. 8, 15–Sept. 5, 12–23, 30–Oct. 21, 28–Dec. 2, 12, 23–30, 1800; Apr. 13, 1802; Jan. 4–Dec. 30, 1814; Dec. 4, 1818.

Minn. Hist. Soc. has Oct. 11, 1803–Oct. 2, 1804; July 12–Dec. 31, 1811; Jan. 10–Apr. 17, Sept. 4, 15–Dec. 8, 1812.

Buffalo Hist. Soc. has Jan. 6, May 12, June 9–Dec. 29, 1794.
Duke Univ. has Apr. 21, 24, May 15–22, July 14, Nov. 20–Dec. 4, 15–29, 1801; Jan. 1, 5, 12–19, Mar. 26, Apr. 2, 20–30, May 7, 14, June 4–18, July 13, 27, 30, Aug. 6–13, 1802; June 10, 1803; Jan. 13, Feb. 14, Mar. 6, Apr. 10, 27, June 5–12, July 10, 27, Aug. 24, Oct. 9, 1804; Jan. 18, Feb. 15, June 7, Aug. 2, 1805; June 17, 1808; Dec. 22, 1809; Mar. 1, 8, 22, 26, May 3, 31, June 28, July 2, 16, Oct. 18, Nov. 5, 1811; Jan. 21, 24, Feb. 28, Mar. 17, 31, Apr. 3, 10, May 5, 19, 29, June 9, 16, 19, Aug. 25, Nov. 20, 1812; Jan. 1, 8–19, Feb. 5–12, 23, Mar. 9, 16, 19, Apr. 2, 9–20, 30, May 7–14, 25–June 1, 8, 11, 22–29, 1813.
Univ. of Ill. has Jan. 9, 1801; June 15, July 27, Dec. 10, 1802; Dec. 6, 13, 1803; Jan. 6, 27, Mar. 6, 20, 30, May 1, 25, June 1, 12, Nov. 9, Dec. 4, 7, 21–28, 1804; Jan. 11, 15, 25–Feb. 3, Apr. 30, May 10, 28, June 4, 7, 25, Aug. 13, 1805.
Skaneateles Lib. Assoc. has Oct. 14–Dec. 30, 1808.
Troy Pub. Lib. has Jan. 7–May 12, 1820.
Long Id. Hist. Soc. has Nov. 21, 1800; July 28, 1801; May 8, 1810; Apr. 30, 1811; Mar. 2, Apr. 20–June 4, 18–July 5, 13–23, 30, Aug. 6, 1819.
Louisville Pub. Lib. has Sept. 9, 16, 23, Oct. 7, 11, 18, Dec. 13, 16, 30, 1814; Feb. 3, 10, Mar. 17, 1815.
Oneida Hist. Soc. has June 14, 1814; Dec. 31, 1816; Jan. 19, 1819; Feb. 25, 29, Mar. 3, 31, Apr. 18, May 2, 1820.
Mass. Hist. Soc. has Mar. 24, 27, July 14, 1812.
Phil. Lib. Co. has Sept. 16, 1793; Aug. 31, 1798.
Univ. of Pittsburgh has Nov. 18, 1793; Dec. 23, 1800.
Cornell Univ. has June 7, 1799; Nov. 28, 1809; Apr. 7, 1820.
Boston Pub. Lib. has Sept. 15, 1807; May 14, 1813.
Schenectady Co. Hist. Soc. has Oct. 13, 17, 1809; May 8–15, 1810.
Senate House, Kingston, N. Y., has Sept. 1, 1801.
Cayuga Co. Hist. Soc., Auburn, has Mar. 29, 1814.

Albany Republican, 1812.

Weekly. Established Apr. 11, 1812, by Samuel R. Brown, with the title of "The Albany Republican." It was discontinued with the issue of July 21, 1812, vol. 1, no. 16.

N. Y. Pub. Lib. has Apr. 11–July 14, 1812.
N. Y. State Lib. has Apr. 11, 22, May 6–June 10, July 7–21, 1812.
Am. Antiq. Soc. has Apr. 11–29, June 3, July 1, 14, 21, 1812.

[Albany] Republican Crisis, 1806–1808.

Semi-weekly. Established Nov. 11, 1806, by Isaac Mitchell, with the title of "Republican Crisis." It succeeded "The Albany Centinel" and continued the advertisements in that paper, although starting a new volume numbering. With the issue of Nov. 10, 1807, it was printed by William Tucker, for the Proprietors. The Hudson "Bee" of Nov. 17, 1807, refers to Mitchell's valedictory, and says that the paper remains in the hands of the proprietors, Backus & Whiting. The N. Y. State Library has a receipt of Dec. 18, 1807, for two years subscription, signed by John L. Tiffany for Backus & Whiting. This was evidently Eleazer Backus and Samuel Whiting, who had previously published the "Albany Centinel." In January, 1808, this was changed to Printed by William Tucker, for Harry Croswell & Co. With the issue of Aug. 2, 1808, it was printed by William Tucker for Croswell & Frary [Harry Croswell and Jonathan Frary]. The paper was discontinued with the issue of Dec. 27, 1808, vol. 2, no. 119, being succeeded by "The Balance."

Harvard has Nov. 11, 14, 21–Dec. 5, 12, 19–30, 1806; Jan. 2–22, 29, Feb. 2, 16–23, Mar. 9, 12, 19–26, Apr. 2, 6, 13, 16, 27, 30, May 7, 22, 29, June 2–9, 19, 23, 30–July 10, 21, 28, Aug. 4, 18, 25–Sept. 8, 15–Oct. 13, 20–Nov. 3, 10–17, 27, Dec. 1, 1807; June 24, July 22–29, Aug. 12, 19–26, Sept. 9, 16–23, 30–Oct. 7, 14, 25, 28, Nov. 8–18, Dec. 2–13, 23, 27, 1808.

Am. Antiq. Soc. has Nov. 11, 18, 25, 1806; Jan. 9, 19, 22, Mar. 9, Apr. 2, 6, 16, June 19, July 14, 1807; Jan. 29, Apr. 1, Sept. 9, Nov. 22, 1808.

Univ. of Ill. has Jan. 6, 19, 26, June 30, Oct. 23, 1807.

Lib. Congress has Mar. 19, Apr. 9, Aug. 7, 1807; Jan. 15, 1808.

N. Y. Hist. Soc. has Apr. 23, June 5, 1807.

N. Y. Soc. Lib. has Jan. 29, Dec. 27, 1808.

Hist. Soc. Penn. has Mar. 12, 1807.

N. Y. State Lib. has July 31, 1807; June 7, July 8, 1808.

Angelica Republican, 1820+.

Weekly. Established Oct. 3, 1820, judging from the date of the earliest issue located, that of Nov. 14, 1820, vol. 1, no. 7, published by Franklin Coudery, with the title of "The Angelica Republican." The prospectus, reprinted in the issue of Nov. 14, is dated Oct. 3. It was so continued until after 1820.

Am. Antiq. Soc. has Nov. 14, Dec. 5, 12, 1820.

[Athens] Monitor, 1805–1806.

Weekly. Established Dec. 21, 1805, judging from the first and only issue located, that of Feb. 8, 1806, vol. 1, no. 8, published by Joseph Tennery, with the title of "Monitor."

N. Y. State Lib. has Feb. 8, 1806.

[Auburn] Advocate of the People, 1816–1818.

Weekly. Established Sept. 18, 1816, by H[enry] C. Southwick, with the title of "The Advocate of the People." It was discontinued by him with the issue of Mar. 11, 1818, vol. 2, no. 78.

> Cayuga Co. Hist. Soc., Auburn, has Sept. 18, Oct. 30, 1816–Mar. 11, 1818.
> Am. Antiq. Soc. has Sept. 18–Oct. 9, 30, Nov. 27, 1816; July 9–23, 1817.
> Wis. Hist. Soc. has Oct. 2, 1816.
> N. Y. State Lib. has Apr. 29, 1817.

[**Auburn**] **Castigator**, 1819–1820+.

Weekly. The earliest known issue is that of June 23, 1819, second series, No. 1, entitled "The Castigator," by Captain Caleb Cudgel, Esquire, and Company, printed by James M. Miller. The numbering would imply an earlier publication. Although somewhat of a magazine in nature, it carried advertisements, death and marriage notices, and news quotations. Before 1823 it was removed to Ithaca (Jan. 1–Mar. 29, 1823 in Cornell Lib. Assoc.). J. M. Miller, in the issue of Jan. 1, 1823, states "In commencing the fifth series of the Castigator in Ithaca, it would be well to mention that it was formerly printed in Auburn by the same 'Genius' who now conducts it."

> N. Y. State Lib. has June 23, 30, 1819.

[**Auburn**] **Cayuga Patriot**, 1814–1820+.

Weekly. Established Oct. 19, 1814, by J[ames] G. Hathaway, with the title of "The Cayuga Patriot." The paper was of quarto size, paged and eight pages to the issue. Hathaway was soon succeeded early in 1815, and certainly before Apr. 26, 1815, by Samuel R. Brown (see also Follett, "History of Press in Western New York," p. 68). Early in 1816 Brown disposed of the paper to James Beardslee, who changed the size to a folio of four pages. The last issue located published by Beardslee is that of Sept. 3, 1817, and the next known issue is that of Dec. 9, 1818, published by D[avid] Rumsey. The change presumably came in 1818, as James Beardslee & Co., and later David Rumsey printed pamphlets at Auburn in that year. Rumsey sold out in 1819 to U[lysses] F. Doubleday, who continued the paper until after 1820.

> Am. Antiq. Soc. has Nov. 2, 1814; Apr. 26, 1815; Mar. 13, 27, Apr. 17, 30, June 19, Sept. 4, 1816; Jan. 13, Apr. 28, 1819.
> Cayuga Co. Hist. Soc., Auburn, has Dec. 14, 1814; May 31, 1815; Apr. 2, Sept. 3, 1817; Sept. 1, 1819; Aug. 2, Sept. 6, 13, 27, Oct. 18–Nov. 15, Dec. 13–27, 1820.
> N. Y. State Lib. has May 10, 1815; June 5, 1816.
> Wis. Hist. Soc. has Oct. 26, 1814.
> N. Y. Pub. Lib. has Nov. 9, 1814.
> Harvard has Dec. 7, 1814.
> H. Armour Smith, Yonkers, has Jan. 4, 1815.

Wesleyan Univ. has May 17, 1815.
Skaneateles Lib. has Dec. 9, 16, 1818.
N. Y. Hist. Soc. has Aug. 18, 1819.

[Auburn] Cayuga Republican, 1819–1820+.

Weekly. Established Mar. 24, 1819, by Augustus Buckingham, with the title of "Cayuga Republican," succeeding the "Auburn Gazette." With the issue of June 30, 1819, it was published by Frederick Prince, and was so continued until after 1820. It has been stated (Cayuga Co. Hist. Soc. Coll., vii. 61) that these were but nominal publishers, and that Thomas M. Skinner was the sole owner and publisher.

Cayuga Co. Hist. Soc., Auburn, has Mar. 24, 1819–Dec. 27, 1820.

[Auburn] Cayuga Tocsin, 1813–1814.

Weekly. Removed from Union Springs in 1813. The earliest Auburn issue located is that of June 2, 1813, vol. 2, no. 75, entitled "The Cayuga Tocsin" and published by R[oyall] T. Chamberlain. The last issue located is that of July 13, 1814, vol. 3, no. 133.

Harvard has June 2–30, Aug. 4, 18, Sept. 1, 15, Oct. 13, 20, Nov. 3, 17, Dec. 1, 8, 1813; Mar. 16–30, Apr. 12, June 8, 1814.
Am. Antiq. Soc. has Oct. 13, 1813; Jan. 19, 26, Mar. 2, July 6, 1814.
Wesleyan Univ. has July 13, 1814.

Auburn Gazette, 1816–1819.

Weekly. Established June 12, 1816, by Skinner & Crosby [Thomas M. Skinner and William Crosby], with the title of "Auburn Gazette." Crosby died Dec. 27, 1817, and with the issue of Dec. 31, 1817, the paper was published by Thomas M. Skinner. With the issue of Mar. 17, 1819, vol. 3, no. 41, it was discontinued, to be succeeded by the "Cayuga Republican."

Cayuga Co. Hist. Soc., Auburn, has June 12, 1816–Mar. 17, 1819.
N. Y. State Lib. has Aug. 6, 1817.
Am. Antiq. Soc. has May 6, 1818.

[Auburn] Western Federalist, 1809–1816.

Weekly. Established in May 1809, judging from the date of the earliest issue located, that of Jan. 17, 1810, vol. 1, no. 35, published under the title of "The Western Federalist" by H[enry] & J[ames] Pace. The last issue located is that of Jan. 10, 1816, vol. 7, no. 345.

Cayuga Co. Hist. Soc., Auburn, has Jan. 31, July 11, 1810; June 5, 1811–Apr. 28, May 26, 1813.
N. Y. State Lib. has Jan. 17, Mar. 7, 1810; Sept. 11, 1811.
N. Y. Pub. Lib. has Jan. 10, 1816.

Aurora Gazette, 1805–1809.

Weekly. Established June 19, 1805, judging from the date of the earliest issue located, that of July 17, 1805, vol. 1, no. 5, published by Henry Pace, with the title of "The Aurora Gazette." The last issue located, published by Pace, is that of June 17, 1808, vol. 3, no. 146. Pace removed to Auburn in May 1809 to establish "The Western Federalist."

Lib. Congress has Oct. 7, Nov. 27, 1805; Jan. 8, 22–Apr. 1, May 6, 1808.
Univ. of Ill. has Aug. 7, 21, 1805; Apr. 30, 1806.
Am. Antiq. Soc. has Nov. 13, 1805.
Wells Coll., Aurora, has Feb. 12, 1806; May 6, 1807; June 17, 1808.
N. Y. State Lib. has June 10, 1807; June 17, 1808.
Cayuga Co. Hist. Soc., Auburn, has July 17, 1805; Apr. 15, 1807.

[Ballston Spa] Advertiser, 1810–1811, see under Saratoga Advertiser.

[Ballston Spa] Aurora Borealis, 1809–1810, see under Saratoga Advertiser.

[Ballston Spa] Independent American, 1808–1818.

Weekly. Established Sept. 27, 1808, by William Child, with the title of "The Independent American." With the issue of July 10, 1810, the paper was published by Comstock & Bates [James Comstock and Isaac Bates] for Wm. Child. Comstock dissolved partnership with Bates, and with the issue of Oct. 9, 1810, it was published by James Comstock for Wm. Child. With June 18, 1811, James Comstock became sole publisher. With the issue of Oct. 8, 1811, the initial "The" was dropped. The last issue is that of May 16, 1818, vol. 10, no. 34. On May 13, 1818, Comstock established "The People's Watch-Tower" in its stead.

N. Y. State Lib. has Sept. 27, 1808–May 6, 1818.
William Rooney, Esq., Ballston Spa, has in his custody Sept. 21, 1813–Sept. 14, 1814.
N. Y. Hist. Soc. has Feb. 28, 1809; Apr. 3, 1810; Dec. 15, 1812; Dec. 7, 1814; Apr. 29, 1818.
Am. Antiq. Soc. has Apr. 24, Oct. 9, Nov. 6, 1810; Apr. 30, May 28, July 23, 30, 1811; Dec. 14, 1813.
Univ. of Mich. (Clements) has July 30, 1811.

[Ballston Spa] People's Watch-Tower, 1818–1820.

Weekly. Established May 13, 1818, by J[ames] Comstock, with the title of "The People's Watch-Tower." It was discontinued in October, 1820, when H. G. Spafford bought the paper and established the "Saratoga Farmer" in its place.

N. Y. State Lib. has May 13, Oct. 21, 1818; Aug. 19, 1819.
N. Y. Hist. Soc. has Apr. 7, June 16, 1819.
Minn. Hist. Soc. has Apr. 7, 1819.
Am. Antiq. Soc. has Apr. 5, 1820.

[Ballston Spa] Republican Telescope, 1801–1802.

Weekly. Established Mar. 5, 1801, judging from the first issue located, that of Apr. 16, 1801, vol. 1, no. 7, published by William Child, with the title of "Republican Telescope." It was in existence as late as September, 1802, according to a statement in "The Troy Gazette" of Sept. 15, 1802.

Troy Pub. Lib. has Apr. 16, 1801.
Lib. Congress has Apr. 23, 1801.

[Ballston Spa] Rural Visiter, 1812.

Weekly. Established Apr. 7, 1812, with the title of "The Rural Visiter, and Saratoga Advertiser," published by John Howe, for the Proprietor [Samuel R. Brown]. It was of quarto size. The last issue located is that of June 23, 1812, vol. 1, no. 12, and on Aug. 19, 1812, the paper was replaced by the "Saratoga Patriot."

Am. Antiq. Soc. has May 5, June 23, 1812.

[Ballston Spa] Saratoga Advertiser, 1804–1812.

Weekly. Established Nov. 12, 1804, by J. Swaine and D. C. Miller [John Swaine and David C. Miller], with the title of "The Saratoga Advertiser." With the issue of Dec. 31, 1804, T——— White and William Child replaced Swaine in the firm, which became T. White, W. Child & D. C. Miller. With the issue of Mar. 25, 1805, D. C. Miller became sole proprietor. In May, 1808, a partnership was formed with Isaac Riggs, and the paper was published by Miller & Riggs. This firm was dissolved with the issue of Dec. 12, 1808, and David C. Miller became sole publisher. Samuel R. Brown purchased a half interest, and with the issue of Sept. 4, 1809, the paper was published by Miller & Brown. With the issue of Nov. 6, 1809, the title was changed to "Aurora Borealis; and, Saratoga Advertiser," and during the same month, the firm name became Brown & Miller. With the issue of Mar. 6, 1810, the front page title heading was discontinued and column headings of "Aurora Borealis" and "Saratoga Advertiser" were printed on the second and fourth pages. With the issue of June 5,

1810, the front page title was restored, being altered to "The Advertiser." With the issue of July 3, 1810, D. C. Miller retired from the firm and the paper was published by Samuel R. Brown. With the issue of Nov. 6, 1810, R[ussell] Prentice was admitted to the firm which was called Brown & Prentice, but with Dec. 11, 1810, the paper was again published by S. R. Brown. With the issue of Oct. 1, 1811, it was printed by James M. Miller, for Samuel R. Brown, editor and proprietor. With the issue of Nov. 5, 1811, the title reverted to "Saratoga Advertiser." In January, 1812, Miller's name was omitted and the paper was printed and published by S. R. Brown. It was discontinued with the issue of Mar. 31, 1812, vol. 8, no. 22.

> Am. Antiq. Soc. has Nov. 12, 19, Dec. 3, 1804; Sept. 26, Oct. 10, 17, Nov. 21–Dec. 5, 19, 26, 1808; Jan. 2, 16, 30–Feb. 27, Mar. 15, 22, June 5, Aug. 28, Sept. 25, Oct. 9, 16, Nov. 6, 14, Dec. 5, 12, 26, 1809; Jan. 2, 16, Feb. 6, 20, Mar. 6, 20, 27, Apr. 30, May 7, 22, June 12–26, July 10–31, Aug. 21–Sept. 25, Nov. 6, 13, 27, Dec. 11, 25, 1810; Jan. 15, Feb. 5–Mar. 12, 26–Apr. 9, 23, May 6, June 11–25, July 9, 30, Aug. 6, Sept. 24–Oct. 29, Nov. 12, 19, Dec. 31, 1811; Jan. 21, Feb. 4–18, Mar. 31, 1812.
>
> N. Y. Hist. Soc. has Dec. 24, 1804–Apr. 1, 1805; May 29, June 5, Aug. 28, 1810.
>
> Harvard has Sept. 25–Oct. 9, 23–Dec. 4, 18, 25, 1810; Jan. 8, Feb. 19, Mar. 12, 26, Apr. 2, 16, 23, June 11, July 2, Aug. 6–20, Sept. 24, Oct. 1, Nov. 5, 26, Dec. 3, 17, 1811; Jan. 28, Feb. 11, 25, Mar. 10, 1812.
>
> Conn. Hist. Soc. has Oct. 16, 23, 1809; Jan. 30, 1810.
>
> Alonzo P. Walton, Schenectady, has Sept. 18, 1809.
>
> Rutgers Univ. has Apr. 30, 1810.
>
> Univ. of Pittsburgh has Dec. 10, 1811.
>
> N. Y. State Hist. Assoc. has Dec. 24, 1811.

[Ballston Spa] Saratoga Courier, 1815–1817.

Weekly. Established Nov. 8, 1815, judging from the earliest issue located, that of Dec. 6, 1815, vol. 1, no. 5, published by Ulysses F. Doubleday, with the title of "Saratoga Courier." The last issue located is that of June 18, 1817, vol. 2, no. 8.

> Am. Antiq. Soc. has Dec. 6, 13, 1815; Jan. 3, 17, 31, Feb. 14, Mar. 6, 13, July 24, 1816; June 18, 1817.

[Ballston Spa] Saratoga Farmer, 1820+.

Weekly. Established by Horatio Gates Spafford in October 1820, with the title of "The Saratoga Farmer," succeeding "The People's Watch-Tower." Spafford, in an advertisement in the "Saratoga Sentinel" of Saratoga Springs for Jan. 23, 1822, states that he was connected with the paper from Oct. 16, 1820 to Oct. 16, 1821.

> N. Y. Hist. Soc. has Jan. 17, 1821, vol. 1, no. 14.

[Ballston Spa] Saratoga Journal, 1814–1818.

Weekly. Established Jan. 11, 1814, judging from the date of the earliest issue located, that of Feb. 1, 1814, vol. 1, no. 4, published for I[saiah] Bunce, with the title of "Saratoga Journal." It succeeded the "Saratoga Patriot," and continued some of its advertisements. Bunce discontinued the paper with the issue of Feb. 11, 1818, vol. 5, no. 6.

Am. Antiq. Soc. has Feb. 1, 8, Apr. 5, 19, July 20, Aug. 31, Sept. 14, 21, Oct. 19, Nov. 23, 30, 1814; Jan. 25, Mar. 22, Oct. 18, Nov. 29, 1815; Jan. 31, Feb. 7, 21, Apr. 3, 24, May 29, June 5, July 31, Oct. 28, 1816.
N. Y. State Lib. has Apr. 26, 1814; July 5, 1815; Oct. 29, 1817; Feb. 11, 1818.
N. Y. Hist. Soc. has Feb. 8, Mar. 8, May 31, 1815; Feb. 21, 1816.
Harvard has Feb. 22, Mar. 15, June 8, 1814.
Minn. Hist. Soc. has Apr. 30, June 18, July 30–Aug. 13, 1817.
Lib. Congress has June 4, 11, 1817.

[Ballston Spa] Saratoga Patriot, 1812–1814.

Weekly. Established Aug. 19, 1812, by Samuel R. Brown, with the title of "Saratoga Patriot." With the issue of July 20, 1813, Brown disposed of the paper to R. Prentice and it was published by Prentice & M'Connell [Russell Prentice and Cephas S. M'Connell]. The last issue located is that of Dec. 28, 1813, vol. 2, no. 20, and it was discontinued with the following issue, to be succeeded on Jan. 11, 1814, by the "Saratoga Journal."

Am. Antiq. Soc. has Sept. 16–Oct. 14, Nov. 25, Dec. 30, 1812; Jan. 13, 26, Mar. 2, 23, July 20, Sept. 7, Oct. 12, Nov. 16, Dec. 28, 1813.
Harvard has Aug. 19, Oct. 14, 1812; Jan. 20, Sept. 14, 1813.
Lib. Congress has Mar. 16, Aug. 24, Oct. 19, 1813.
N. Y. Hist. Soc. has Dec. 9, 1812; June 29, 1813.
N. Y. Pub. Lib. has June 15, 1813.

[Ballston Spa] Saratoga Register, 1798–1800.

Weekly. Established in July, 1798, judging from the date of the earliest issue located, that of Sept. 5, 1798, vol. 1, no. 13, entitled "The Saratoga Register: or, Farmer's Journal," published by Increase & William Child. Sylvester's "History of Saratoga County," p. 100, states that it was established June 14, 1798, and that in April, 1800, the firm was dissolved, William Child becoming sole proprietor. William Child published the first issue of "The Political Magazine" in October 1800 (nos. 1 and 2 in N. Y. State Lib.)

Am. Antiq. Soc. has Sept. 5, Nov. 21, 1798.

[Ballston Spa] Saratoga Republican, 1818–1820+.

Weekly. Established Feb. 18, 1818, judging from the date of the earliest issue located, that of Apr. 8, 1818, vol. 1, no. 8, published by Ulysses F. Doubleday, with the title of "Saratoga Republican." Continued until after 1820.

Am. Antiq. Soc. has Apr. 8, Sept. 9, 1818.
N. Y. State Lib. has May 13, 1818.
Alonzo P. Walton, Schenectady, has Aug. 19, 1818.
Cayuga Co. Hist. Soc., Auburn, has Apr. 28, 1819.

[Batavia] **Cornucopia,** 1809–1811.

Weekly. Established Mar. 24, 1809, judging from the date of the earliest issue located, that of May 12, 1809, vol. 1, no. 8, published by S[amuel] Peek & B[enjamin] Blodget, with the title of "Cornucopia." Peek died Oct. 27, 1811, and the paper was immediately discontinued.

N. Y. State Lib. has May 12, 1809; Jan. 12, 26, Feb. 2, 1810.
Am. Antiq. Soc. has June 2, 9, 29, 1809.

[Batavia] **Genesee Intelligencer,** 1807–1808.

Weekly. Established in the spring of 1807, by Elias Williams, with the title of "Genesee Intelligencer." About July 1, 1807, Benjamin Blodget was taken into partnership, but after thirteen numbers were published by the new firm, Williams disappeared and the paper was discontinued. This account is based on a letter written by Blodgett in 1846 (Follett, "Press of Western New York," p. 71). In February, 1808, judging from the numbering of the issue of May 20, 1808, vol. 1, no. 13, the paper must have been reestablished, this issue published by Williams & Blodget. The last issue located is that of July 15, 1808, vol. 1, no. 21.

N. Y. State Lib. has May 20, July 1, 15, 1808.

[Batavia] **Republican Advocate,** 1811–1820+.

Weekly. Established Nov. 9, 1811, by Benjamin Blodget, with the title of "Republican Advocate." With the issue of July 18, 1812, Blodget altered his name in the imprint to Blodgett. In April, 1815, David C. Miller was admitted to partnership, and the paper published by B. Blodgett & Co. Between 1816 and June 16, 1820, the firm became Miller & Blodgett, who continued until after 1820.

Am. Antiq. Soc. has Nov. 16, 1811; Feb. 22, May 9–23, June 6, July 11, 18, Aug. 8, Sept. 12, Oct. 3, Dec. 1, 30, 1812; July 7, Aug. 25, Oct. 6, 13, 27, 1813; Sept. 3, 24, Nov. 26, Dec. 31, 1814; Feb. 4, Apr. 22, Oct. 7, 1815; Feb. 17, Mar. 16, Apr. 13, May 11, 1816.
Univ. of Ill. has Jan. 28, 1815.
Cayuga Co. Hist. Soc., Auburn, has June 16, 1820.

[Batavia] **Spirit of the Times,** 1819–1820+.

Weekly. Established early in February, 1819, judging from the earliest issue located, that of July 30, 1819, vol. 1, no. 26, published by O[ran] Follett, with the title of "Spirit of the Times." The "National Intelligencer," of Mar. 20, 1819, states that it was established by Follett on Feb. 3. See also notice of paper in "Erie Patriot" of Feb. 20, 1819. Frederick Follett, in his "Press of Western New York," p. 72, states that it was established by Oran Follett on Feb. 3, 1819, and was so continued until after 1820.

Am. Antiq. Soc. has July 30, 1819.
N. Y. Hist. Soc. has Feb. 25, 1820.

[Bath] **Farmers Gazette,** 1816–1817.

Weekly. Established in September, 1816, judging from the first and only issue located, that of July 22, 1817, vol. 1, no. 42, published by David Rumsey, with the title of "Farmers Gazette."

Am. Antiq. Soc. has July 22, 1817.

Bath Gazette, 1796–1798.

Weekly. Established Dec. 21, 1796, judging from the date of the earliest issue located, that of Jan. 5, 1797, vol. 1, no. 3, published by William Kersey and James Edie, with the title of "The Bath Gazette, and Genesee Advertiser." The last issue located is that of Apr. 12, 1798, vol. 2, no. 17.

Harvard has Jan. 5, 19–Feb. 23, Mar. 9–23, 1797.
N. Y. State Lib. has July 6, Oct. 12, Dec. 14, 21, 1797; Jan. 4, 18–Mar. 1, 15, Apr. 5, 12, 1798.
Newberry Lib. has Aug. 3, 1797.
Cornell Univ. has Dec. 21, 1797.

[Bath] **Steuben Patriot,** 1816–1820+.

Weekly. Established Nov. 26, 1816, by B[enjamin] Smead, with the title of "Steuben Patriot." According to a list of New York papers of Jan. 1, 1818, it was published by Benj. Smead & Son with the title of "Steuben and Allegany Patriot" (see list in "Albany Argus," Jan. 6, 1818). Continued until after 1820.

Am. Antiq. Soc. has Nov. 26, Dec. 3, 17, 1816; Mar. 18, 1817.
N. Y. Pub. Lib. has Apr. 22, 1817.

[Bath] **Western Republican,** 1819–1820+.

Weekly. Established Oct. 6, 1819, judging from the date of the earliest issue located, that of Dec. 15, 1819, vol. 1, no. 11, published by Erastus Shepard, with the title of "Western Republican." Continued until after 1820.

N. Y. Soc. Lib. has Dec. 15, 29, 1819; Jan. 12, 1820.

[Binghamton] Broome County Patriot, 1812–1813.

Weekly. Established Nov. 10, 1812, by Chauncey Morgan, with the title of "The Broome County Patriot." It was printed at Chenango-Point, or Binghamton. The name of "Chenango-Point" was given in the imprint, but the publisher's prospectus was dated at Binghamton and at the head of the column of local news were the words "Binghamton Patriot." The paper was discontinued with the issue of May 18, 1813, vol. 1, no. 28, to be succeeded by the "Political Olio."

N. Y. State Lib. has Nov. 10, 1812–May 18, 1813.
Am. Antiq. Soc. has Nov. 17, Dec. 1, 1812.

[Binghamton] Phoenix, 1814–1819.

Weekly. Established in July, 1814, judging from the date of the earliest issue located, that of Dec. 14, 1814, vol. 1, no. 21, published by Tracy Robinson, with the title of "The Phoenix." In the "Oxford Gazette" of Aug. 9, 1814, is a reference to the first two numbers of "The Phoenix," published by Tracy Robinson. In the "Albany Gazette" of Sept. 1, 1817, is a reference to Augustus Morgan, editor of the Binghamton Phoenix. The issue of Sept. 23, 1817, entitled "Binghamton Phœnix," was published by A. Morgan & Co. According to a list of New York papers of Jan. 1, 1818, it was published by A[ugustus] Morgan & Co. (see "Albany Argus," Jan. 6, 1818). It was stated that in 1818 the paper was sold to Anson M. Howard and was discontinued about 1820 (Lawyer's "Binghamton," p. 448). But in the Norfolk (Va.) "American Beacon" of Aug. 17, 1819, is reprinted A. M. Howard's valedictory, stating that the paper was discontinued with the issue of July 15, 1819.

Buffalo Hist. Soc. has Jan. 25, Feb. 15, 1815.
Buffalo Pub. Lib. has Dec. 14, 1814.
Am. Antiq. Soc. has Sept. 23, 1817.

[Binghamton] Political Olio, 1813–1814.

Weekly. Established May 25, 1813, under the title of "Political Olio," succeeding "The Broome County Patriot." The first issue gave no name of publisher, but the issue of June 1 was "printed and published by Augustus Morgan for the proprietors." At some time between June 8 and Aug. 17, 1813, the word "proprietors" was changed to "proprietor." The last issue located is that of Apr. 5, 1814, vol. 1, no. 46. J. B. Wilkinson's "Annals of Binghamton," 1840, p. 230, states that "The Broome County Patriot," but really referring to its successor, the "Political Olio," passed into the hands of Reuben S. Close, and later of Dr. Elihu Ely, and expired before 1815, being purchased by Dr. Tracy Robinson, who established "The Phoenix."

N. Y. State Lib. has May 25–June 8, Aug. 17–31, 1813; Apr. 5, 1814.

[Binghamton] Republican Herald, 1818–1820+.

Weekly. Established in 1818 by Abraham Burrell, who sold out about 1820 to Dorephus Abbey, who continued the paper after 1820 (J. B. Wilkinson "Annals of Binghamton," 1840, p. 230). No copy located.

[Bloomingburgh] Sullivan Whig, 1820+.

Weekly. Established in December, 1820, according to a reference in the Kingston "Craftsman" of Dec. 30, 1820, mentioning the receipt of the first number of the "Sullivan Whig," printed at Bloomingburgh and edited by John Jansen Tappen. The earliest issue located is that of Mar. 13, 1822, vol. 2, no. 65, published by J. J. Tappen, with the title of "Sullivan Whig."

Boston Athenæum has Mar. 13, 1822.

[Brooklyn] Brooklyne Hall Super-Extra Gazette, 1782.

Henry R. Stiles, in his "History of Brooklyn," 1869, vol. 1, p. 323, states that in the summer of 1782 Charles Looseley issued a newspaper or handbill printed upon a sheet of "letter size," and in three columns on one side of the sheet only, called "The Brooklyne Hall Super-Extra Gazette," dated June 8, 1782. Brooklyn Hall was the name of Charles Looseley's King's Head Tavern, a famous headquarters for royalists and English officers. Looseley conducted lotteries, sponsored horse-races, and otherwise sought to amuse the English officers then quartered in New York. He advertised extensively in Robertson's "Royal American Gazette" and in Rivington's "Royal Gazette," heading all his advertisements with the words "Pro Bono Publico." The American Antiquarian Society has a broadside headed "Pro Bono Publico," announcing a three days' race meet to be run at Ascot-Heath, dated May 8, 1781, and printed in New York by A. Robertson. This same heading of "Pro Bono Publico" Looseley carried at the top of his so-called newspaper. Stiles, on p. 443, reproduces the heading of the paper and prints the text. A reading of this shows that it included recent and current news, a letter "To the Editors of the Brooklyne Hall Super-Extra Gazette," and several advertisements. Stiles concludes: — "It has been suggested that the Super-Extra Gazette was the Brooklyn extra of the New York Royal Gazette, issued on some special occasion; our impression, however, is that it was merely a handbill, published by the enterprising Looseley to advertise the lottery which was then drawing at his tavern." The paper bore no volume numbering and it should be remarked that the "Royal Gazette" of June 8, 1782, made no mention of an extra or even of any such publication.

When Stiles saw this unique issue of the paper, it was deposited in the Naval Lyceum in the Brooklyn United States Navy Yard. Inquiry at the Brooklyn Navy Yard in 1917 revealed that the Naval Lyceum was demolished many years ago and that the Naval relics were sent to the Naval Academy at Annapolis. But the broadside could not be found in the library of the Naval Academy and all trace of it has been lost.

[Brooklyn] Courier, see **Long Island Courier.**

Brooklyn Intelligencer, 1807.

Weekly. A continuation, without change of volume numbering, of "The Long-Island Weekly Intelligencer." The earliest issue located with the new title of "The Brooklyn Intelligencer, and Long-Island Advertiser" is that of July 23, 1807, vol. 2, no. 56, published by Robinson & Little [William C. Robinson and William Little]. The change of title probably occurred on July 2. The new paper was a quarto of eight pages. The last issue located is that of Sept. 24, 1807, vol. 2, no. 65. In the following month Little established "The Brooklyn Minerva."

Am. Antiq. Soc. has July 23–Sept. 24, 1807.

[Brooklyn] **Long Island Courier,** 1799–1803.

Weekly. Established July 4, 1799, judging from the date of the earliest issue located, that of July 11, 1799, vol. 1, no. 2, published by Thomas Kirk, with the title of "The Courier, and Long Island Advertiser." With the issue of Aug. 1, 1799, the title was changed to "The Courier, and New-York and Long Island Advertiser," and with the issue of July 3, 1800, to "The Long Island Courier." The paper was suspended with the issue of Jan. 13, 1803, vol. 4, no. 185.

Lib. Congress has July 11–Nov. 21, Dec. 5–26, 1799; Jan. 2–Feb. 13, 27–June 12, 26–July 17, 31–Dec. 31, 1800; Jan. 7–Mar. 25, 1801; June 2–16, 30, 1802–Jan. 13, 1803.
Long Id. Hist. Soc. has Oct. 15, Nov. 5, 19, 1800–Feb. 18, 1801; Apr. 22, Nov. 18, Dec. 9, 16, 1801; Jan. 27–Feb. 10, 24, Mar. 31, Apr. 7, June 16, Oct. 20, 1802.
Am. Antiq. Soc. has July 11, Aug. 29, Sept. 5, 26, 1799; Oct. 15, 29, 1800.
N. Y. Pub. Lib. has Sept. 5, 1799.
East Hampton Free Lib. has June 17, 1801.
Harvard has Aug. 5, 1801; Apr. 28, 1802.

[Brooklyn] **Long Island Star,** 1809–1820+.

Weekly. Established June 8, 1809, by Thomas Kirk, with the title of "The Long Island Star." With the issue of June 7, 1810, the title was slightly altered to "Long-Island Star." With the issue of June 5, 1811, the paper was bought and published by Alden Spooner. With the issue of Dec. 2, 1812, Henry C. Sleight was admitted to partnership, and it was published by Spooner & Sleight; but with the issue of June 2, 1813, the partnership was dissolved, Sleight entered military service and Alden Spooner again became the publisher. Spooner purchased the "New York Columbian" in New York City, and with the issue of Sept. 24, 1817, the Star was published by Erastus Worthington for Alden Spooner. The two then formed a partnership and with the issue of Jan. 7, 1818, it was published by Spooner & Worthington. With the issue of Jan. 6, 1819, the partnership was dissolved, and the paper published by Erastus Worthington. It was so continued until after 1820.

Long Id. Hist. Soc. has June 8, 1809–Dec. 27, 1820.
Am. Antiq. Soc. has June 8, 15, July 6–Oct. 19, Nov. 2–16, 1809; Feb. 15–Mar. 22, Apr. 5–May 31, 1810; Jan. 31, Feb. 21, Mar. 7, 14, July 24, Aug. 21, Sept. 25, 1811; June 3, 1812–May 1, 1816; Jan. 7, 1818–Dec. 29, 1819; Jan. 5–Feb. 2, Apr. 26–May 17, 31, June 21, July 26–Sept. 20, Oct. 11, 18, Nov. 8, 22–Dec. 6, 27, 1820.
N. Y. Hist. Soc. has June 8–Dec. 7, 21, 28, 1809; Jan. 4–May 10, 24–June 14, 28, July 19, 26, Aug. 9–Sept. 27, Oct. 11–Dec. 27, 1810; Jan. 3–May 2, 16–July 3, 24–Nov. 13, 27–Dec. 11, 1811; Nov. 4, 25, Dec. 2, 16, 30, 1812; Jan. 13–27, Feb. 10–Apr. 7, 21, May 12, 19, June 2–July 28, Aug. 11–Oct. 13, 27–Dec. 29, 1813; Jan. 5–19, Feb. 2, 9, 23–Mar. 9, 23, 30, Apr. 13–June 15, 29–July 27, Aug. 10, 17, 31–Oct. 5, 19, Nov. 2, 16, 23, Dec. 7, 1814; Aug. 23–Sept. 27, Oct. 11–Dec. 27, 1815; Jan. 3–Nov. 13, Dec. 4–25, 1816; Jan. 1–Sept. 10, Oct. 17–Nov. 12, 26–Dec. 31, 1817; Jan. 7–Mar. 18, Apr. 22–July 29, Aug. 19–Oct. 7, 21–Nov. 25, Dec. 16–30, 1818; Jan. 20–Feb. 17, Mar. 10–Apr. 21, May 5, 12, 26, June 2, 23–July 21, Aug. 11, 25, Sept. 8–22, Oct. 13, 27–Dec. 29, 1819; Feb. 16–Apr. 19, June 14, July 12, 1820.
N. Y. Pub. Lib. has Sept. 14, 1809; Oct. 23, Nov. 6–27, 1811; Jan. 1–29, Feb. 12–July 1, 15, Dec. 30, 1812; Jan. 6–Aug. 4, 18–Dec. 22, 1813; Jan. 5–Mar. 9, 1814; May 19, 1819.
Lib. Congress has Aug. 28, 1811; Jan. 29, 1812; Mar. 29, 1815–Dec. 29, 1819; Mar. 15, 1820.
Hist. Soc. Penn. has June 15, 1809–May 31, 1810.
Duke Univ. has Apr. 13–July 13, Aug. 3–Dec. 28, 1814; Jan. 6, July 28, Aug. 4, Oct. 6, Dec. 15, 1819.
N. J. Hist. Soc. has Dec. 29, 1813; Mar. 22–Apr. 5, May 17, July 19, Aug. 2, Sept. 27, Nov. 1, Dec. 13, 20, 1815; June 5, July 17, Aug. 7, 1816; Apr. 9, May 7, 1817.
East Hampton Free Lib. has Oct. 19, 1809; July 24, Dec. 4, 1811; Oct. 7, 1812; July 27, 1814; Nov. 1, 1820.
N. Y. State Lib. has July 20, 1809; Apr. 29, 1812; July 27, 1814; Jan. 4, 1815.
Queens Borough Pub. Lib., Jamaica, has Aug. 30, 1810; May 5, 1813.

Smithtown Lib., Long Id., has June 24, 1818.
Univ. of Chicago has Oct. 7, 1818.

[Brooklyn] Long-Island Weekly Intelligencer, 1806–1807.

Weekly. Established July 3, 1806, by Robinson & Little [William C. Robinson and William Little], with the title of "The Long-Island Weekly Intelligencer." The last issue located is that of June 11, 1807, vol. 1, no. 50. In July, 1807, the size was changed from a four-page folio to an eight-page quarto, and the title was changed to "The Brooklyn Intelligencer," which see.

Am. Antiq. Soc. has July 3, 17, 31–Aug. 14, 1806.
Long Id. Hist. Soc. has Sept. 4, Oct. 9–23, 1806; Jan. 29, Feb. 19, Mar. 5, 1807.
N. J. Hist. Soc. has Nov. 27, 1806; June 11, 1807.
East Hampton Free Lib. has Mar. 5, 1807.

Brooklyn Minerva, 1807.

Semi-weekly. Established Oct. 21, 1807, by William Little, with the title of "The Brooklyn Minerva, and Long-Island Advertiser." The last issue located is that of Dec. 9, 1807, vol. 1, no. 15.

Am. Antiq. Soc. has Oct. 21–Dec. 2, 9, 1807.
Long Id. Hist. Soc. has Nov. 7, 1807.

Buffalo Gazette, 1811–1818.

Weekly. Established Oct. 3, 1811, by Smith H. Salisbury & Co., with the title of "Buffalo Gazette." With the issue of Nov. 19, 1811, the firm name was changed to Smith H. & H. A. Salisbury, and with June 1, 1813, to Smith H. Salisbury, Editor. Soon after the issue of Dec. 21, 1813, the British threatened Buffalo, burning the village on Dec. 30. The paper was removed to Harris' Tavern, at what was known as Harris Hill, near Williamsville, and there appeared Jan. 18, 1814. The imprint reads "Printed at Harris' Inn, near Williams' Ville," and an advertisement states that the office was located 100 rods northeast of the village. The last issue at Williamsville was on Mar. 28, 1815, and on Apr. 4, 1815, the paper returned to Buffalo. With the issue of May 9, 1815, it was printed by H. A. Salisbury, for S. H. Salisbury, an advertisement being inserted that the firm of Smith H. and Hezekiah A. Salisbury was dissolved. With the issue of June 20, 1815, the title was changed to "Buffalo Gazette, and Niagara Intelligencer," and the printer's name was omitted, that of the proprietor, S. H. Salisbury, alone being given. With the issue of Oct. 24, 1815, the brothers again formed a partnership and the paper was published by S. H. & H. A. Salisbury. With the issue of Jan. 2, 1816, the title reverted to "Buffalo Gazette." In January, 1818, Smith H. Salisbury sold out his interest to William A. Carpenter, who with Hezekiah A. Salisbury published the paper under the firm name of Carpenter & Salisbury. The last issue with the title "Buffalo Gazette" was that of Apr. 14, 1818, vol. 7, no. 27, after which Carpenter retired and the title was changed to "The Niagara Patriot," which see.

Buffalo Hist. Soc. has Oct. 3, 1811–Apr. 14, 1818, with only 25 issues missing.
Wis. Hist. Soc. has Oct. 19, 1813–Oct. 8, 1816.
Am. Antiq. Soc. has Oct. 29, 1811; June 29, 1813; Oct. 18, 1814.
Ontario Co. Hist. Soc., Canandaigua, has Sept. 2, 16, Nov. 25, 1817; Mar. 24, 1818.
N. Y. Hist. Soc. has Apr. 27, 1813.
Harvard has Aug. 17, Oct. 26, 1813.
Penn. State Lib. has Sept. 5, 1813.
N. Y. State Lib. has Sept. 13, 1814.
Detroit Pub. Lib. has Aug. 11, 1813, extra.

[Buffalo] Niagara Journal, 1815–1820+.

Weekly. Established July 4, 1815, by Day & Stillman [David M. Day and Isaiah Stillman], with the title of "Niagara Journal." In January, 1816, the partnership was dissolved and the paper published by David M. Day. It so continued until after 1820.

Am. Antiq. Soc. has July 4, 18, Aug. 8, 22, Sept. 5–19, Oct. 3–31, Nov. 14–28, Dec. 12, 1815; Feb. 20, Mar. 12, 26, May 14, June 11, 25, 1816; Oct. 28, 1817; May 12, July 28, Aug. 25, Sept. 15, 22, Oct. 20, 27, Nov. 10, Dec. 29 1818; July 6, 1819.
Buffalo Hist. Soc. has Nov. 28, 1815; Nov. 4, 1817; Apr. 13, 1819–Feb. 22, 1820.
N. Y. Pub. Lib. has May 28, June 4, 18, July 2, 16, 1816.

[Buffalo] Niagara Patriot, 1818–1820+.

Weekly. Established Apr. 21, 1818, by Hezekiah A. Salisbury, with the title of "The Niagara Patriot." It succeeded the "Buffalo Gazette" and continued its advertisements, but adopted a new volume numbering. It was so continued until after 1820.

Buffalo Pub. Lib. has Apr. 21–June 9, 23–July 14, 28–Dec. 8, 22, 29, 1818; Jan. 5–Mar. 2, 23, 30, Aug. 24–Oct. 5, 19–Dec. 28, 1819; Jan. 4–Feb. 15, 29–May 16, 30–Dec. 26, 1820.
Buffalo Hist. Soc. has Apr. 28–June 9, 1818.
Ontario Co. Hist. Soc., Canandaigua, has May 26, Dec. 22, 1818.
Univ. of Rochester has May 4, 1819.
Am. Antiq. Soc. has Dec. 17, 1819.
N. Y. Hist. Soc. has Apr. 25, 1820.

NEW YORK

[Caldwell] Lake George Watchman, 1818–1820+.

Weekly. Established Sept. 4, 1818, judging from the date of the earliest issue located, that of Oct. 2, 1818, vol. 1, no. 5, published by T[imothy] Hoskins, with the title of "The Lake George Watchman." So continued until after 1820. The town of Caldwell is now called Lake George.

N. Y. State Lib. has Oct. 30, 1818; Sept. 10, 1819; Mar. 3, 1820.
Harrison K. Bird, New York, has Oct. 2, 1818.
N. Y. Pub. Lib. has Aug. 11, 1820.

Cambridge Gazette, 1803–1804.

Weekly. Established Dec. 7, 1803, judging from the date of the first issue located, that of Mar. 21, 1804, vol. 1, no. 16, published by J[oseph] Tennery, with the title of "Cambridge Gazette."

Am. Antiq. Soc. has Mar. 21, 1804.
Lib. Congress has May 2, 1804.

[Canaan] Columbian Mercury, 1794–1795.

Weekly. Established June 11, 1794, judging from the date of the first and only issue located, that of Oct. 1, 1794, vol. 1, no. 17, published by Elihu Phinney, with the title of "Columbian Mercury, and Canaan Repository of Rural Knowledge." Phinney, in his own handwriting on the margin of the copy of the "Otsego Herald" of June 23, 1810, owned by the American Antiquarian Society, states that the "Columbian Mercury" was published by him at Canaan for nearly a year, and that the office was removed to Otsego, or Cooperstown, Feb. 28, 1795. In the N. Y. State Lib. Report for 1857, p. 68, is recorded the acknowledgement of the gift of the "Columbian Mercury and Canaan Repository," vol. 1, no. 5–8, published by Elihu Phinney, 1794. This file was destroyed in the State Library fire of 1911.

Am. Antiq. Soc. has Oct. 1, 1794.

[Canandaigua] Genesee Messenger, 1806–1810.

Weekly. Established Nov. 25, 1806, by John Abbott Stevens, with the title of "Genesee Messenger." The last issue with this title was that of Nov. 27, 1810, after which it was changed to "Ontario Messenger," which see.

Am. Antiq. Soc. has Nov. 25–Dec. 30, 1806; Jan. 13, 20, Apr. 14, 28, May 19, 26, June 9–30, July 14, Aug. 4–18, Sept. 1–15, 29, Oct. 6, 13, Nov. 24, Dec. 8–22, 1807; Jan. 26, Feb. 9, Mar. 8, Apr. 12, May 24, 31, June 14–28, Aug. 2, 16, 23, Sept. 6, Oct. 4, 18, 25, Nov. 15, 1808; Jan. 3, 17–Mar. 7, Apr. 18, 25, May 16, June 6–27, July 11, 18, Aug. 1, 22, 29, Sept. 12, 19,

Oct. 3, 31–Nov. 14, 28, Dec. 5, 19, 1809; Jan. 2, 16–30, Feb. 20, Mar. 6–27, Apr. 10, May 1–June 5, 19–July 24, Sept. 25, Oct. 9, 16, 1810.

Univ. of Ill. has Mar. 3, 17, Apr. 14–28, June 9, July 14, 28, Sept. 1, Nov. 10, 1807; Feb. 9–Mar. 1, June 7–21, July 19, Oct. 11, 1808; Apr. 11, 18, May 9, 16, July 18, Aug. 22, 1809.

N. Y. State Lib. has Nov. 25, 1806; Feb. 17, Oct. 20, 1807; Apr. 12, Oct. 25, 1808; Mar. 21, Aug. 15, Dec. 12, 1809; Apr. 17, June 26, 1810.

N. Y. Hist. Soc. has Oct. 27–Nov. 24, Dec. 8, 1807; Jan. 12, 26, Feb. 9, Mar. 1, 22, 1808; May 1, 8, 1810.

Cornell Univ. has Dec. 9, 1806; May 8, 1810.

Buffalo Hist. Soc. has Oct. 27, Nov. 3, 1807; Mar. 1, 1808.

Harvard has Mar. 8, Oct. 25, Nov. 8, 1808; Mar. 7, 1809.

Skaneateles Lib. Assoc. has Jan. 9, 1810.

[Canandaigua] **Ontario Freeman,** 1803–1806.

Semi-weekly and weekly. Established in December, 1803, judging from the earliest issue located, that of Dec. 29, 1803, vol. 1, no. 6, published in quarto size, semi-weekly, by Silvester Tiffany, with the title of "Ontario Freeman." In the Ovid "Bee" of June 27, 1855, a list of early New York newspapers includes the "Ontario Freeman" of Dec. 8, 1803, published by Silvester Tiffany. In the Canandaigua "Western Repository" of Apr. 17, 1804, is a reference to the reported suspension of the "Ontario Freeman;" and it was apparently suspended in October, 1804, since it was editorially announced on June 4, 1805, that the paper was being resumed after a suspension of seven months. This issue of June 4, 1805, is entitled "Ontario Freeman," vol. 2, no. 2, total no. 55, published weekly by John A. Stevens and enlarged to folio size. The last issue located is that of Aug. 6, 1805, vol. 2, no. 11. The Kingston "Plebeian" of June 6, 1806, after quoting from the "Ontario Freeman," states: "After the partial conduct of the late printer, Mr. Tiffany, the proprietor of this paper, took the charge of it to himself." This would imply that Silvester Tiffany had resumed proprietorship of the "Ontario Freeman." It was discontinued in 1806, as the "Genesee Messenger" of Nov. 25, 1806, in the prospectus refers to it as "lately printed." In this prospectus Stevens states that he was only the printer of the "Ontario Freeman," but of the "Genesee Messenger" he was editor as well.

N. Y. State Lib. has Dec. 29, 1803.

Ontario Co. Hist. Soc., Canandaigua, has Feb. 13, 1804.

Univ. of Ill. has May 14, 1804; Aug. 6, 1805.

Harvard has June 4–18, July 2, 1805.

Am. Antiq. Soc. has June 11, July 2, 23, 1805.

[Canandaigua] **Ontario Gazette,** 1799–1803.

Weekly. A continuation of the "Ontario Gazette," begun by Lucius Cary at Geneva in November, 1796. It was removed from Geneva to Canandaigua in

1799, and the earliest issue located is that of July 16, 1799, vol. 3, no. 15, published by Lucius Cary, with the title of "The Ontario Gazette." Between Nov. 5, 1799, and Mar. 31, 1800, the title was changed to "The Ontario Gazette, & Genesee Advertiser;" between Mar. 31 and July 21, 1800, to "The Ontario Gazette, & Geneseo Advertiser;" and between Sept. 14, 1801, and July 13, 1802, to "Ontario Gazette, & Genesee Advertiser." The last issue located is that of Dec. 7, 1802, vol. 6, no. 25. The initial issue of the "Western Repository" of May 3, 1803, states that it was established in place of the "Ontario Gazette," which had been sold by its former owner.

Univ. of Ill. has July 16, 30, Aug. 13, 27, Nov. 5, 1799; Mar. 31, July 21, 28, Sept. 1, Nov. 17, 1800; July 13, 27, Sept. 14, Oct. 12, 19, Nov. 2, 30, Dec. 7, 1802.

Ontario Co. Hist. Soc., Canandaigua, has Sept. 24, 1799.

N. Y. State Lib. has Sept. 7, 1801.

Buffalo Pub. Lib. has Sept. 14, 1801.

[Canandaigua] Ontario Messenger, 1810–1820+.

Weekly. A continuation, without change of volume numbering, of the "Genesee Messenger." The first issue with the new title of "Ontario Messenger" was that of Dec. 4, 1810, vol. 5, no. 211, published by J[ohn] A. Stevens. The paper in 1812, at least, was edited by John C. Spencer (see "Albany Register," Apr. 14, 1812; also "Geneva Gazette," Jan. 15, 1812). With the issue of Nov. 15, 1814, Stevens admitted David M. Day to partnership, under the firm name of Stevens & Day. The partnership was dissolved on June 14, 1815, and the paper published by John A. Stevens. It was so continued until after 1820. The "Geneva Palladium" of Aug. 23, 1820, says that the "Ontario Messenger" was purchased on July 25, 1820, by John C. Spencer, and that in spite of John A. Stevens' assertion that he was the sole proprietor, it was generally believed that Spencer was the editor.

Am. Antiq. Soc. has Dec. 4–25, 1810; Jan. 1–15, Mar. 19, Aug. 13, Oct. 8, 22, 1811; Mar. 24, June 2, 16, 23, Sept. 8, Nov. 10–Dec. 1, 15, 22, 1812; Jan. 12, Feb. 9, 23, Mar. 2, 30, May 4, July 6–27, Aug. 10, Nov. 23, Dec. 28, 1813; Jan. 4, Feb. 1, 15, Mar. 22, May 24, July 26, Aug. 9, Sept. 13, Oct. 11, Nov. 1, 8, 29, Dec. 13, 1814; Jan. 3, Mar. 7, 21, 28, Apr. 25, June 13, Sept. 26, Oct. 10, Nov. 21–Dec. 5, 1815; Jan. 16, Feb. 20–Mar. 5, 19, 26, Apr. 23, 1816; Oct. 20, 1818.

N. Y. State Lib. has Mar. 26, Apr. 9, 1811; Apr. 7, May 5, July 14, Aug. 4, 25, Oct. 6, 27, Nov. 3, Dec. 1, 1812; Feb. 16, 23, Apr. 27, July 13, Aug. 17, Sept. 21, Dec. 28, 1813; Apr. 26, 1814; Jan. 24, Feb. 7–Apr. 18, May 2–16, 30–June 13, 27–Oct. 10, 24–Nov. 14, 1815.

Lib. Congress has Apr. 29, 1817; Jan. 5–Dec. 28, 1819; Jan. 4, 18, Feb. 1–Apr. 11, 25–May 9, 23–Dec. 19, 1820.

Harvard has July 13–27, Aug. 24–Sept. 7, 21, Oct. 26, Nov. 9, Dec. 28, 1813; Mar. 29, Apr. 5, May 24, Oct. 25, Dec. 13, 1814.

Ontario Co. Hist. Soc., Canandaigua, has June 2, 1812; Aug. 10, 1813; May 16, 23, June 20, 1815; Sept. 10, Dec. 10, 1816; Apr. 8, 1817; July 6, 1819.

Cornell Univ. has Jan. 8, Feb. 19, 1811; June 15, 1813; June 11, 1816; Oct. 24, 1820.

N. Y. Pub. Lib. has Nov. 19, 1811; May 26, June 2, July 7, Oct. 27, 1812.

N. Y. Hist. Soc. has June 16, 1812; Aug. 29, 1815; Aug. 31, 1819.

Buffalo Hist. Soc. has Nov. 15, 1814.

Univ. of Ill. has Dec. 13, 1814.

[Canandaigua] Ontario Repository, 1809–1820+.

Weekly. A continuation, without change of volume numbering, of the "Western Repository." The first issue with the new title of "Ontario Repository" was that of Apr. 25, 1809, vol. 7, no. 1, published by James D. Bemis. With the issue of July 23, 1811, the title was altered to "Ontario Repository, and Western Advertiser," but with that of June 1, 1813, reverted to "Ontario Repository." With the issue of Oct. 18, 1814, Nathaniel Beach was admitted to partnership, and the paper was published by Bemis & Beach. With the issue of June 18, 1816, the partnership was dissolved and James D. Bemis became sole proprietor. With the issue of Apr. 13, 1819, Chauncey Morse and Samuel C. Ward were admitted to partnership, and the paper was published by J. D. Bemis & Co. It was so continued until after 1820.

Wood Lib., Canandaigua, has Apr. 25, 1809–Dec. 26, 1820.

Ontario Co. Hist. Soc., Canandaigua, has Mar. 3, Apr. 14, June 9, July 7, Dec. 1, 1812; Jan. 19, 1813–Jan. 5, 1819, fair.

Am. Antiq. Soc. has Nov. 14, 28, 1809; Jan. 23, Feb. 6, Apr. 10, May 22, 29, June 26, July 17, 24, Aug. 7, Nov. 9, 23, 1810; Jan. 22, Feb. 19, 26, Mar. 19, May 14, July 9, 1811; July 6, 20, Dec. 28, 1813; Sept. 22, Dec. 29, 1818; Aug. 3, 1819.

Buffalo Hist. Soc. has Apr. 15, 1817–Apr. 7, 1818; July 7, 14, 1818.

N. Y. State Lib. has Feb. 11, 1806; Mar. 2, 1809; Nov. 5, Dec. 3, 31, 1816; Jan. 5–Feb. 25, 1817; Feb. 16, 1819.

N. Y. Pub. Lib. has July 7, 1812.

Harvard has July 6, 1813.

Wis. Hist. Soc. has Dec. 1, 1818.

N. Y. Hist. Soc. has Apr. 6, 1819.

[Canandaigua] Western Repository, 1803–1809.

Weekly. Established May 3, 1803, with the title of "Western Repository, & Genesee Advertiser," printed by John K. Gould, for the Proprietors. With the issue of Aug. 16, 1803, the title was shortened to "Western Repository," and the firm name became Gould & Post, it being stated that John K. Gould and Russell E. Post had purchased the establishment from the former proprietors. With the issue of Oct. 30, 1804, James D. Bemis replaced Post in the firm, and the paper was published by Gould & Bemis. Gould died Mar. 9, 1808, and with the issue of Mar. 15, 1808, James D. Bemis was the publisher. The last issue with this title was that of Apr. 18, 1809, vol. 6, no. 52, after which the title was changed to "Ontario Repository," which see.

    Wood Lib., Canandaigua, has May 3, 1803–Apr. 16, 1805.
    Ontario Co. Hist. Soc., Canandaigua, has Sept. 13, Dec. 6, 1803; Jan. 6, 1807; Apr. 28, 1807–Apr. 18, 1809.
    Harvard has Aug. 16, 30–Oct. 11, 1803.
    Am. Antiq. Soc. has Nov. 1, 1803; Jan. 24, Feb. 7, Mar. 13, Aug. 7, 1804; Mar. 25, Apr. 9, 1805; Feb. 25, Oct. 21, 1806; Mar. 5, July 21, Dec. 8, 1807.
    Univ. of Ill. has June 28, Dec. 6, 1803; Jan. 22, Feb. 5, May 14, 1805.
    Minn. Hist. Soc. has Apr. 19, May 31–June 14, Aug. 23, Oct. 4, Nov. 29, Dec. 27, 1808.
    N. Y. State Lib. has Aug. 16, Oct. 25, Nov. 29, 1803; June 30, Sept. 29, 1807; Aug. 2, 1808.
    Cayuga Co. Hist. Soc., Auburn, has Nov. 29, 1803.
    Troy Pub. Lib. has Mar. 13, 1804.
    N. Y. Pub. Lib. has Aug. 28, 1804.
    British Museum has Apr. 18, 1809.

[Carmel] **Putnam County Courier,** 1814.

    Weekly. Established in 1814, with the title of "The Putnam County Courier" (French, "Gazetteer of New York," 1860, p. 540). No copy located.

[Catskill] **American Eagle,** 1807–1811.

    Weekly. Established in January, 1807, judging from the date of the earliest issue located, that of Aug. 3, 1808, vol. 2, no. 83, published by Nathan Elliot, with the title of "American Eagle." Early in 1811, Joseph G. Greenman succeeded Elliot as proprietor. The last issue located is that of May 8, 1811, vol. 5, no. 227.

    Wis. Hist. Soc. has Jan. 4, 1809–Dec. 19, 1810.
    Am. Antiq. Soc. has Aug. 3, 1808; Jan. 31, July 11, 25, Aug. 29, Sept. 26, Oct. 24, 1810; Apr. 10, May 8, 1811.

Catskill Emendator, 1813.

    The New York "Columbian" of Dec. 4, 1813, refers to "a new paper started in Catskill by Michael J. Kappel, entitled the Catskill Emendator." No copy located. (See also Munsell, "Typographical Miscellany," p. 120.) This paper was apparently continued as the "Greene & Delaware Washingtonian."

[Catskill] Greene & Delaware Washingtonian, 1814–1816.

Weekly. Judging from the date of the only issue located, that of July 31, 1816, vol. 3, no. 38, printed by Richard Corss, for James Bill, with the title of "Greene & Delaware Washingtonian," this paper must have been established in November, 1813. If so, it was presumably a continuation of the "Catskill Emendator," without change of volume numbering. French, in his "Historical Gazeteer," 1860, p. 330, says that this paper was commenced at Catskill in 1814 by Michael J. Kappel. The issue of July 31, 1816, was the last, since therein it was announced that it would be succeeded by the "Middle District Gazette."

Am. Antiq. Soc. has July 31, 1816.

[Catskill] Middle District Gazette, 1816.

No copy located. In the last issue of the "Greene & Delaware Washingtonian," for July 31, 1816, it is announced that the paper would be succeeded by the "Middle District Gazette," to be published by William L. Stone. In the "Albany Advertiser" of Aug. 1, 1816, is printed the prospectus of the "Middle District Gazette."

Catskill Packet, 1792–1799.

Weekly. Established Aug. 6, 1792, by M[ackay] Croswell, & Co., with the title of "Catskill Packet." J. D. Pinckney, in his "Reminiscences of Catskill," 1868, p. 36, says that Mackay Croswell's partner was Thomas O. Croswell, who retired at the end of the first or second year. On Jan. 7, 1793, the name of Mackay Croswell appeared alone in the imprint, but on Jan. 14, 1793, it reverted to Mackay Croswell, & Co., shortened to M. Croswell, & Co., with the issue of Aug. 13, 1793. With the issue of Aug. 9, 1794, the title was altered to "Catskill Packet, & Western Mail." With the issue of Jan. 11, 1796, the name of Mackay Croswell appeared alone in the imprint. With the issue of Jan. 7, 1797, the title was shortened to "The Catskill Packet." With the issue of Jan. 6, 1798, the title was changed to "The Packet." The paper was suspended with Dec. 29, 1798, vol. 6, no. 52, but was resumed with the issue of Mar. 9, 1799, vol. 7, no. 1, when it was still entitled "The Packet." It was discontinued with the issue of Aug. 29, 1799, vol. 7, no. 26.

Greene Co. Hist. Soc., Coxsackie, N. Y., has Aug. 6, 1792–Dec. 30, 1797; Mar. 9–Aug. 29, 1799.
Yale has Aug. 6, 1792–Dec. 30, 1797.
N. Y. Hist. Soc. has Aug. 6, 1792–July 29, 1793; Oct. 11, 25, 1794; Sept. 26, 1795.

Am. Antiq. Soc. has Aug. 13, 20, Sept. 3–Oct. 1, 15–29, Dec. 3, 10, 31, 1792; Jan. 7, 21, 28, Feb. 11, Mar. 11, 18, Apr. 1, May 13, 20, June 3, 1793; Mar. 11, Aug. 9, 1794–Dec. 26, 1795; Jan. 2, Aug. 22, 29, 1796.
N. Y. State Lib. has July 15, 1793; Aug. 9, 1794–Dec. 26, 1795; Jan. 6–Dec. 29, 1798.
Harvard has May 23, 1795.
N. Y. Pub. Lib. has June 27, 1796.

Catskill Recorder, 1804–1820+.

Weekly. Established May 14, 1804, by Mackay Croswell, with the title of "Catskill Recorder." It was really a continuation of the "Western Constellation," although it adopted a new volume numbering. With the issue of Feb. 15, 1815, the name in the imprint was changed to M. Croswell, and with that of May 7, 1817, to M. Croswell, & Son. With the issue of May 3, 1820, the firm was dissolved and the paper was published by E[dwin] Croswell, son of Mackay Croswell. Continued until after 1820.

Greene Co. Hist. Soc., Coxsackie, has May 14, 1804–Oct. 9, 1811; Nov. 21, Dec. 4–25, 1811; Jan. 1, 15, 22, Feb. 12, Mar. 11, Apr. 15, 29, May 6, June 3–24, Aug. 12, Oct. 28, 1812; June 2, 1813; May 4, 1814–May 1, 1816; May 7, 1817–Dec. 27, 1820.
N. Y. Hist. Soc. has Aug. 19–Nov. 25, Dec. 23, 30, 1805; Jan. 6–Mar. 10, 24–Apr. 21, May 5–26, June 9, 30–July 14, Aug. 4–25, 1806.
Am. Antiq. Soc. has Apr. 7, 21, May 5, 1807; Feb. 9, Apr. 27, 1808; Aug. 15, 1810; Mar. 27, 1811; Dec. 29, 1813; May 21, June 11, July 9, 23, Sept. 24, 1817; Mar. 25, Oct. 21, 1818–Sept. 6, 1820.
Buffalo Pub. Lib. has May 7, 1817–Apr. 29, 1818.
Harvard has July 2–16, Sept. 10, Oct. 8, 29, Nov. 5, Dec. 3, 24, 31, 1804; Jan. 7, 14, 28, 1805.
Univ. of Rochester has Dec. 2, 9, 1818; Jan. 13, Feb. 3, 10, 24–Mar. 17, Apr. 21, May 19, Dec. 15, 1819; Jan. 26, Mar. 1, 22, Apr. 5, May 31, June 28, July 19, Aug. 9, 23, Oct. 18, Dec. 6, 1820.
N. Y. State Lib. has Mar. 24, Apr. 7, 1807; July 20, 1808; July 15, Nov. 18, 1812; July 13, 1814.
East Hampton Free Lib. has Nov. 11, 1805.
Duke Univ. has May 5, June 30, 1819.
Mass. Hist. Soc. has Nov. 24, 1819.
Western Reserve Hist. Soc. has Jan. 19, 1820.

[Catskill] Western Constellation, 1800–1804.

Weekly. Established May 26, 1800, by Mackay and Harry Croswell, with the title of "Western Constellation." With the issue of Apr. 6, 1801, the firm was dissolved, and the paper published by Mackay Croswell. The last issue located is that of Apr. 9, 1804, vol. 4, no. 204.

    Greene Co. Hist. Soc., Coxsackie, has May 26, 1800–Apr. 13, 1801.
    N. Y. State Lib. has May 24, 1802–May 14, 1803.
    Harvard has Dec. 29, 1800; Feb. 2, 16, Aug. 17, Sept. 28–Oct. 19, Nov. 9–23, 1801; Jan. 4–Feb. 22, Mar. 1–June 14, 28, July 12–26, Aug. 23, Sept. 27, Oct. 18, 25, Nov. 6, 1802; Jan. 15, 29–Feb. 12, Mar. 12, 19, Apr. 2, May 14–June 11, July 18, Aug. 8, 22, Oct. 17–31, 1803; Apr. 9, 1804.
    Am. Antiq. Soc. has Oct. 4, 1800; Nov. 30, 1801.

[Cazenovia] Pilot, 1808–1820+.

    Weekly. Established Aug. 10, 1808, by Baker & Newton [Oran E. Baker and George Newton], with the title of "The Pilot." With the issue of Dec. 20, 1809, the partnership was dissolved and the paper published by Oran E. Baker. It was so continued until after 1820.

    Cazenovia Pub. Lib. has Aug. 10, 1808–Dec. 28, 1820.
    N. Y. Hist. Soc. has Aug. 10, 31–Sept. 14, Oct. 26, Nov. 2, Dec. 7–28, 1808; Jan. 18, 25, Feb. 8–Apr. 19, May 3–24, June 7–19, Aug. 2–Sept. 6, 20–Dec. 20, 1809; Feb. 14, May 16, 1810.
    Am. Antiq. Soc. has Aug. 10, 31, Sept. 7, 28, Oct. 5, Nov. 2, 1808; Feb. 8, Mar. 15, Aug. 23, 1809; Apr. 18, July 11, 25, 1810; Mar. 20, Aug. 28, 1811; Sept. 16, Nov. 11, 1812; Dec. 1, 22, 29, 1813; Jan. 5, 26, Feb. 9, 16, Mar. 2, 1814; May 13, 1818.
    Harvard has Oct. 12, 19, Nov. 9, 30, 1808; May 15, Aug. 21, 28, Sept. 11, 1811.
    N. Y. Pub. Lib. has Apr. 19, 1809.
    N. Y. State Lib. has June 5, 1816.

Chenango Point, see Binghamton, Broome County Patriot.

Cherry-Valley Gazette, 1818–1820+.

    Weekly. Established Oct. 8, 1818, by L. & B. Todd [Lemuel and Bethel Todd], with the title of "Cherry-Valley Gazette." So continued until after 1820.

    Am. Antiq. Soc. has Oct. 8, 1818–Sept. 28, 1819; Oct. 3–Dec. 26, 1820.
    Cherry Valley Lib. and Cherry Valley News have Oct. 8, 1818–Sept. 28, 1819.
    N. Y. State Lib. has Oct. 5, 1819–Sept. 26, 1820.
    N. Y. Pub. Lib. has Apr. 27, May 4, 1819.
    N. Y. Hist. Soc. has May 11, 25, 1819.

[Cherry Valley] Otsego Republican Press, 1812–1813.

    Weekly. Established Aug. 14, 1812, by Clark & Crandal [Israel W. Clark and

Edward B. Crandal], with the title of "Otsego Republican Press." The paper was discontinued with the issue of Aug. 6, 1813, vol. 1, no. 52.

Am. Antiq. Soc. has Aug. 14, 1812–June 11, 1813; Aug. 6, 1813.
N. Y. State Lib. has Aug. 14, 1812; Mar. 26, 1813.

Cooperstown Federalist, 1809–1817.

Weekly. A continuation, without change of volume numbering, of "The Impartial Observer," the first issue with the title of "Cooperstown Federalist" being that of June 3, 1809, vol. 1, no. 33, published by John H. Prentiss. With the issue of Dec. 2, 1809, John Prentiss took his brother Henry into partnership, and the paper was published by J. H. & H. Prentiss. Early in 1813, Henry Prentiss retired from the firm and the paper was published by J. H. Prentiss. The last issue located is that of Apr. 18, 1816, vol. 8, no. 28, and somewhat later, probably in 1817, the title was changed to "The Freeman's Journal," which see.

Otsego Co. Hist. Soc., Cooperstown, has June 3, 1809–Oct. 10, 1812.
N. Y. State Lib. has Aug. 11, 18, Sept. 1, Nov. 24, 1810; Jan. 5, Feb. 16, Mar. 9, Apr. 13–27, May 18, June 8, Sept. 21, Nov. 30, Dec. 7, 28, 1811; Jan. 11, 18, Feb. 15, 22, Mar. 7, 14, Apr. 18, May 16, 30, Nov. 28, Dec. 5, 1812; Mar. 13, June 26, July 3, Aug. 21, 28, 1813.
Am. Antiq. Soc. has Feb. 3, Aug. 11, Sept. 20, 1810; Feb. 23, Mar. 23, Aug. 10, 1811; Feb. 22, 1812; Jan. 29–Feb. 12, 26, 1814.
Univ. of Rochester has June 17, 1809.
N. Y. Pub. Lib. has Sept. 1, 1814.
Colgate Univ. has Feb. 2, 1815.
Lib. Congress has May 4, 1815; Apr. 18, 1816.

[Cooperstown] Freeman's Journal, 1817–1820+.

Weekly. A continuation, without change of volume numbering, of the "Cooperstown Federalist." The change of title probably occurred in 1817, when the paper was published by John H. Prentiss, although the first issue located is that of Nov. 30, 1818, vol. 11, no. 9, published by J[ohn] J. Lappon, with the title of "The Freeman's Journal, and Otsego County Advertiser." With the issue of Oct. 4, 1819, J[ohn] H. Prentiss became the publisher, shortening the title to "The Freeman's Journal," and continued the paper until after 1820.

Otsego Co. Hist. Soc., Cooperstown, has May 24, Oct. 4, 1819–Dec. 25, 1820.
Wis. Hist. Soc. has Nov. 30, 1818; Feb. 28–Dec. 18, 1820.
Am. Antiq. Soc. has July 26, Aug. 2, 1819.

[Cooperstown] Impartial Observer, 1808–1809.

Weekly. Established Oct. 22, 1808, with the title of "The Impartial Observer," published by W. Andrews and printed by J[ohn] H. & H[enry] Prentiss. With the issue of Mar. 25, 1809, William Andrews retired and the paper was printed and published by John H. Prentiss. The last issue with the above title was that of May 27, 1809, vol. 1, no. 32, after which it was changed to "Cooperstown Federalist," which see.

Otsego Co. Hist. Soc., Cooperstown, has Oct. 22, 1808–May 27, 1809.
Am. Antiq. Soc. has Oct. 22, Nov. 5, 26, 1808; Apr. 22, 1809.
Harvard has Oct. 22–Nov. 5, 1808.
Lib. Congress has Dec. 10, 1808.
N. Y. State Lib. has Mar. 11, 1809.

[Cooperstown] **Otsego Herald**, 1795–1820+.

Weekly. Established Apr. 3, 1795, by Elihu Phinney, with the title of "The Otsego Herald; or, Western Advertiser." With the issue of June 12, 1795, the semi-colon in the title was changed to a colon, and with that of Aug. 14, 1795, the initial "The" was omitted. With the issue of Sept. 19, 1805, the title was shortened to "Otsego Herald." On Apr. 3, 1807, the village of Cooperstown was incorporated as Otsego, accordingly with the issue of Apr. 16, 1807, Cooperstown was replaced by Otsego in the imprint. Elihu Phinney died July 12, 1813, and with the issue of July 17, 1813, the paper was published by H. & E. Phinney [Henry and Elihu Phinney, Jr.]. With this issue, moreover, Otsego was changed to Cooperstown in the imprint, the change having been made by the legislature June 12, 1812. With the issue of Aug. 14, 1813, the paper was published by I[srael] W. Clark, for the Proprietors. Clark withdrew, and with the issue of Mar. 26, 1814, the paper was published by H. & E. Phinney, and was so continued until after 1820.

Otsego Co. Hist. Soc., Cooperstown, has Apr. 3, 1795–Dec. 25, 1820.
Harvard has Apr. 3, May 8–22, June 5, 12, 26, July 17, Sept. 4, Oct. 2, 1795; Mar. 17–31, May 19, 26, June 9, 23–July 14, Aug. 4–Sept. 15, 29–Oct. 27, Nov. 10–Dec. 1, 15–29, 1796; Jan. 5, 19, 26, Feb. 9–23, Mar. 9, 16, Nov. 9, 1797; Jan. 11, 1798.
Am. Antiq. Soc. has Mar. 31–Oct. 13, 27–Dec. 29, 1796; Jan. 5–Mar. 23, May 11, 1797; Apr. 26–May 10, June 28, 1798; Feb. 24, 1803–Feb. 16, 1804; June 23, 1810; Mar. 23, 1811; May 30, 1812.
N. Y. State Lib. has Dec. 1, 1796; Mar. 23, 1797; Sept. 11, 1800; Jan. 27, Feb. 10, 1810; Mar. 16, July 13, 1811; Apr. 4, May 23, Aug. 26, Oct. 31, 1812; Feb. 6, June 26, 1813.
N. Y. Pub. Lib. has July 3, 1795; May 19, June 9, 23, 1796.
Troy Pub. Lib. has Jan. 17, 1799; Aug. 28, Oct. 23, 1800; July 9, Nov. 5, 1801.
Lib. Congress has May 1, 1795; Apr. 18, 1816.
N. Y. Hist. Soc. has Feb. 2, Mar. 9, 1797.
Colgate Univ. has Dec. 23, 1802.
Univ. of Pittsburgh has Dec. 14, 1811.

Monmouth Co. Hist. Assoc., Freehold, N. J., has Aug. 8, 1812.
Chicago Hist. Soc. has Apr. 6, 1815.

[Cooperstown] **Watch-Tower**, 1814–1820+.

Weekly. Established Apr. 6, 1814, judging from the date of the earliest issue located, that of May 18, 1814, vol. 1, no. 7, published by I[srael] W. Clark, with the title of "The Watch-Tower." In May, 1817 (see advertisement regarding debts due to Clark in the issue of July 10, 1817), Clark removed to Albany and the paper was published by E[dward] B. Crandal. The issue of July 26, 1819, vol. 6, no. 278, was published by E. B. Crandal. The paper was continued until after 1820.

Am. Antiq. Soc. has May 18, Aug. 18, 1814; Feb. 1, Sept. 26, Oct. 3, 1816; July 10, 24, 1817; July 26, 1819.
N. Y. State Lib. has May 16, 30, June 6, 1816.
H. Armour Smith, Yonkers, has Aug. 10, 1815.

Cortland Republican, 1815–1820+.

Weekly. Established June 30, 1815, by J[ames] Percival, with the title of "Cortland Republican." With the issue of Oct. 7, 1815, the paper was published by Osborn & Campbell [John W. Osborn and David Campbell]. With the issue of Aug. 16, 1816, this was changed to Osborn & Boies [John W. Osborn and Obadiah Boies], but with the issue of Dec. 13, 1816, it reverted to Osborn & Campbell. With the issue of Feb. 7, 1817, the publishers became B. S. & D. Campbell [Benjamin S. and David Campbell], but with the issue of Apr. 22, 1819, D. Campbell became sole publisher and continued the paper until after 1820.

Cortland Free Lib. has June 30, 1815–Dec. 27, 1820.
Phillips Free Lib., Homer, has Mar. 22, 1816; Apr. 25, Aug. 29, 1818; Dec. 9, 1819.
N. Y. Hist. Soc. has Feb. 21, 1817.
Cortland Co. Hist. Soc. has Oct. 18, 1820.

[Delhi] **Delaware Gazette**, 1819–1820+.

Weekly. Established Nov. 18, 1819, by J[ohn] J. Lappon, with the title of "Delaware Gazette." Continued until after 1820.

Cannon Free Lib., Delhi, has Nov. 18, 1819–Dec. 14, 1820.
N. Y. Pub. Lib. has Dec. 9, 1819.

Derne, see under **Manlius**.

[Elizabethtown] **Essex Patriot,** 1817–1818.

Weekly. Established Mar. 25, 1817, judging from the first and only copy located, that of June 10, 1817, vol. 1, no. 12, published by L[ewis] Person, for Oliver Person, with the title of "Essex Patriot." Continued certainly as late as January, 1818 (see "Albany Argus," Jan. 6, 1818).

Am. Antiq. Soc. has June 10, 1817.

[Elizabethtown] **Reveille,** 1812–1816.

Weekly. Established Apr. 22, 1812, by Luther Marsh, with the title of "The Reveille." William Ray was editor of the paper, although without pay, and associated with him was Ezra C. Gross (G. L. Brown, "Pleasant Valley, a history of Elizabethtown," 1905, pp. 233–241). The last issue located is that of Nov. 16, 1814, vol. 3, no. 30. It is included in a list of newspapers published in New York in December, 1815 (see "Albany Argus" of Dec. 26, 1815). Luther Marsh died Mar. 9, 1816, at which time the paper doubtless expired.

Am. Antiq. Soc. has Apr. 22, May 6, 20, July 15, Sept. 2, Nov. 18, 1812.
Harvard has June 3, 24, Oct. 1, Nov. 11, 1812; Nov. 16, 1814.
William King, Crown Point, N. Y., had June 10, 1812, now lost, but photostat in N. Y. State Lib.
Robert L. Hale, Columbia Univ., N. Y., has May 18, 1814, photostat in N. Y. State Lib.
Mrs. Walter S. Brown, Elizabethtown, has Oct. 12, 1814, photostat in N. Y. State Lib.

Elmira, see **Newtown.**

[Fayette] **Seneca Patriot,** 1817–1818.

Established apparently during 1817, after the discontinuance of the "Seneca Patriot" at Ovid. It appears in a list of newspapers of Jan. 1, 1818 ("Albany Argus," Jan. 6, 1818), where the name of G. Hathaway is given as the publisher, a misprint for J[ames] G. Hathaway. No copy located.

[Fishkill] **New-York Packet,** 1777–1783.

Weekly. Removed from New York and established at Fishkill in January, 1777. The first Fishkill issue was undoubtedly that of Jan. 16, 1777, vol. 1, no. 36, but the earliest located is that of Feb. 6, 1777, vol. 1, no. 39, published by Samuel Loudon, with the title of "The New-York Packet, and the American Advertiser." During the six years the paper was printed at Fishkill, the title was occasionally shortened to "The New-York Packet," as scarcity of paper stock reduced the size of the sheet. The last issue published at Fishkill was that of

NEW YORK 571

Aug. 28, 1783, no. 331, and the paper immediately thereafter was removed to New York City, where it was continued on Nov. 13, 1783, without change of volume numbering. See under New York.

N. Y. Hist. Soc. has Feb. 13, May 8, Sept. 11, Oct. 23, 30, Nov. 27, 1777; Apr. 23, May 14, June 11, 25, Aug. 13, Oct. 29, Dec. 10, 1778; Jan. 21–Mar. 18, Apr. 1, 15, 29–May 20, June 3–July 1, 22, 29, Aug. 12, 19, Sept. 9–Oct. 14, 28–Nov. 18, 1779; Jan. 27–Mar. 2, 23–Apr. 27, May 11–25, June 8, 29, Aug. 3–Dec. 28, 1780; Jan. 4–Feb. 8, 22–Oct. 11, 25, Nov. 1, 15–Dec. 27, 1781; Jan. 3–Dec. 26, 1782; Jan. 2–Mar. 20, Apr. 17–May 1, 15–29, June 12, 26–July 24, Aug. 14, 28, 1783.

Am. Antiq. Soc. has July 3, Sept. 4, 1777; July 2, 16–Aug. 20, Sept. 3–24, Oct. 8, Dec. 17, 1778; Apr. 29, May 20, Sept. 2, 16, Oct. 7, 21, 28, Nov. 11, Dec. 16, 1779; June 1, Aug. 24, Sept. 7–Oct. 5, 19, Nov. 2–23, Dec. 21, 28, 1780; Jan. 4, 11, 25, Feb. 8, 15, Mar. 1, 8, Apr. 5–May 3, 24–June 7, 21, July 5–26, Sept. 6, 13, Oct. 11, 18, Nov. 8, 22, Dec. 6–27, 1781; Jan. 3–Feb. 28, Mar. 14–28, Apr. 11–Oct. 10, 24, 31, Nov. 14–Dec. 26, 1782; Jan. 2–Feb. 13, 27, Mar. 27, Apr. 3, 24, May 8, 22–June 5, 26, July 10–31, Aug. 28, 1783.

Lib. Congress has Dec. 4, 1777; Feb. 19–Mar. 19, Apr. 2–23, Mar. 7, 14, 28–June 11, Aug. 13, 20, Oct. 8, 29, Dec. 10, 1778; Nov. 25, Dec. 30, 1779; Sept. 14, Oct. 12–Nov. 2, Dec. 21, 28, 1780; Jan. 11–Feb. 8, Mar. 1, 8, 22, Apr. 12, 26, May 10, June 21, July 5–19, Aug. 30–Oct. 11, 25, Nov. 1, 15, 22, Dec. 6–20, 1781; Jan. 3–Feb. 14, Mar. 14–Apr. 4, May 2–23, June 6–Nov. 7, 21–Dec. 12, 26, 1782; Jan. 23, Feb. 20, 27, 1783.

N. Y. State Lib. has May 15, 1777; Oct. 1, Dec. 10, 1778; Sept. 9, 1779; May 25–June 15, Aug. 24–Oct. 19, Nov. 2, 1780; Jan. 4, Feb. 1, Mar. 1, Apr. 12–May 10, 24–June 21, July 5, 19, Aug. 2, Sept. 6, 13, 27, Oct. 4, 18, Nov 15, 22, Dec. 13–20, 1781; Jan. 3, 17–Feb. 7, 21, Mar. 21, 28, Apr. 11–May 30, June 13–27, July 18–Nov. 7, 21–Dec. 19, 1782; Jan. 9, 16, Feb. 13, Mar. 13, 20, May 15, 22, June 5, 12, July 10, 1783.

Mass. Hist. Soc. has Feb. 6, Mar. 27, Nov. 13, 1777; Aug. 6, Oct. 8, Dec. 10, 1778; Jan. 21, June 3, July 22, Sept. 9, Oct. 7, Dec. 9, 1779; Feb. 3, Mar. 23, June 15, Nov. 23, Dec. 21, 1780; Jan. 11, Mar. 22, May 3, June 21, Sept. 27, Oct. 11, 18, Nov. 8, 22, Dec. 20, 27, 1781; Feb. 7, 21, Mar. 7, 28, Apr. 11–25, May 9–23, June 20, July 4, 11, Oct. 3, 10, Nov. 7, 1782; Apr. 3, July 17, 1783.

N. Y. Pub. Lib. has Mar. 13, 1777; Sept. 24, 1778; June 17, July 1, Dec. 2, 1779; May 11, 1780; Apr. 12, May 10, July 5, Aug. 2, Oct. 11, Nov. 1, 15, 1781; Jan. 10–Feb. 28, Mar. 14, 21, Apr. 11, May 9–30, June 13, July 18, 25, Aug. 8–Sept. 12, 26–Oct. 24, Nov. 14–28, Dec. 12–26, 1782; June 19, 26, July 10–Aug. 28, 1783.

Yale has Jan. 4–Aug. 9, Sept. 6–Nov. 22, Dec. 6–27, 1781; Jan. 3–Mar. 28, Apr. 11–Aug. 29, Sept. 12, 26–Dec. 5, 19, 26, 1782; Jan. 23, 30, Feb. 13, Mar. 13–27, Apr. 10, 24, May 1, 1783.

Adriance Lib., Poughkeepsie, has Feb. 4, May 20, June 17, 24, July 8, Aug. 19, Sept. 2, Oct. 14, 21, Nov. 4, 18, Dec. 2, 9, 1779; May 11–June 1, 15, 1780; Feb. 13, 27, Mar. 13, 20, Apr. 17–June 12, 26, July 3, Aug. 14, 1783.

Western Reserve Hist. Soc. has Jan. 10, 24, Feb. 14–28, Mar. 28, May 2, 23, June 6–27, July 11, 18, Aug. 1, 22, Sept. 12, Oct. 31–Nov. 14, 1782.

Hist. Soc. Penn. has Oct. 1, 1778; July 1, 15, 22, Sept. 23, 1779; Nov. 2, 23, 1780; Dec. 13, 1781; July 4–18, Oct. 3, 10, 24, Dec. 5, 1782; May 1, July 17, 1783.

Amer. Phil. Soc. has Mar. 18, Sept. 2, 16–30, Oct. 14, 21, 1779; Mar. 23, 1780.

Boston Pub. Lib. has Oct. 21, 1779; June 7, July 5, 1781; July 18, 1782; Mar. 27, 1783.

Rutgers Univ. has Jan. 31, Aug. 8, 1782; Jan. 16, 1783.

Wesleyan Univ. has Feb. 19, 1778.

Buffalo Hist. Soc. has July 16, 1778.

Smithtown Lib., Long Id., has May 24, 1781.

Wis. Hist. Soc. has Aug. 2, 1781.

N. J. State Lib. has Feb. 14, 1782.

Schenectady Co. Hist. Soc. has July 11, 1782.

Long Id. Hist. Soc. has Apr. 3, 1783.

Senate House, Kingston, has June 26, 1783.

[Fredonia] **Chautauque Gazette**, 1817–1820+.

Weekly. William A. Carpenter stated in 1847 (see Follett "Press of Western New York," p. 28) that he established this paper the first Tuesday in January [Jan. 7], 1817, and soon after sold it to James Hull. The "Buffalo Gazette" of Jan. 14, 1817, states "We have received two nos. of the Chautauque Gazette, printed at Fredonia, (late Canadaway) by Messrs. Carpenter & Hull." The earliest issue located is that of Mar. 11, 1817, vol. 1, no. 10, printed by Percival & Hull [James Percival and James Hull], with the title of "Chautauque Gazette," which would date the establishment on Jan. 7. The next issue located, that of Dec. 9, 1817, is published by James Hull, who continued the paper until after 1820. The issue of Jan. 13, 1818, refers to William A. Carpenter as a former proprietor.

Barker Lib., Fredonia, has Mar. 11, Dec. 9, 1817; Feb. 10, 1818; July 6, 1819; Jan. 4, 1820.

Prendergast Lib., Jamestown, has May 19, Aug. 10, 1818.

Am. Antiq. Soc. has Jan. 13, 1818; Sept. 5, 1820.

Minn. Hist. Soc. has Aug. 31, 1819.

[Geneva] **Expositor**, 1806–1809.

Weekly. Established Nov. 19, 1806, by James Bogert, with the title of "The Expositor." With the issue of Feb. 3, 1808, the imprint of the publisher was changed to James Bogert, & Co. The last issue was that of June 14, 1809, vol. 4, no. 31, after which the title was changed to "The Geneva Gazette."

Hobart Coll., Geneva, has Nov. 19, 1806–June 14, 1809.
N. Y. State Lib. has Nov. 26, Dec. 10, 31, 1806; Mar. 25, Sept. 9, 1807; June 22, Aug. 3, 31, 1808; Apr. 12, 1809.
Am. Antiq. Soc. has Nov. 19, 26, 1806; Mar. 25, Aug. 12, 1807.
Univ. of Ill. has Jan. 7, June 3, 1807; Mar. 30, 1808.
Harvard has Nov. 26, Dec. 17, 1806.
Ontario Co. Hist. Soc., Canandaigua, has Aug. 31, 1808.

Geneva Gazette, 1809–1820+.

Weekly. Established June 21, 1809, by James Bogert, with the title of "The Geneva Gazette." It succeeded his other paper, "The Expositor," although starting a new volume numbering. With the issue of June 15, 1814, the title was slightly altered to "Geneva Gazette." With the issue of June 21, 1815, William Bogert was admitted to partnership and the paper published by J. & W. Bogert, but with the issue of Oct. 16, 1816, the firm was dissolved and James Bogert again became sole proprietor. He continued the paper until after 1820.

Hobart Coll., Geneva, has June 21, 1809–May 31, July 26, Aug. 2, 1820.
Am. Antiq. Soc. has June 21, 1809; June 27, 1810; June 19, 1811–June 7, 1815; July 26, Aug. 2, 23, Sept. 27, Nov. 1, 1815; Apr. 2, June 25, July 9, 1817; Apr. 15, June 10, July 15, Sept. 16, 1818; Jan. 13, Feb. 10, July 28, Aug. 25, Sept. 29, Oct. 27, Nov. 3, 1819.
N. Y. State Lib. has June 21, Aug. 23, 1809; Feb. 28, 1810; Oct. 9, 1811; July 1, Nov. 11, 1812; July 20, Nov. 16, 1814; Jan. 25, July 19, 1815.
Ontario Co. Hist. Soc., Canandaigua, has Sept. 12, 1810; July 10, 1811; Aug. 25, 1813; Feb. 23, 1814; Mar. 1, 1815.
Lib. Congress has Jan. 15, June 7, 1812.
Cornell Univ. has July 15, 1812.
No. Indiana Hist. Soc., South Bend, has Sept. 2, 1812.
N. Y. Pub. Lib. has Nov. 18, 1812.
Univ. of Ill. has Oct. 12, 1814.
H. Armour Smith, Yonkers, has Apr. 12, 1815.
Oneida Co. Hist. Soc., Utica, has July 31, 1816.
N. Y. Hist. Soc. has Feb. 17, 1819.

[Geneva] Impartial American, 1800–1801.

Weekly. Established in February, 1800, judging from the earliest issue located, that of Oct. 28, 1800, vol. 1, no. 36, published by Ebenezer Eaton, for Eaton, Walker & Co. [Ebenezer Eaton and Thomas Walker], with the title of "Impartial American or, Seneca Museum." In the issue of Feb. 17, 1801, Eaton stated that the editors intended to remove in four weeks to Cayuga Bridge, where they expected to establish a paper to be called the "Western Luminary and Federal Republican." The "Western Luminary" was established by Eaton at Scipio, Mar. 31, 1801.

    N. Y. State Lib. has Oct. 28, Nov. 4, Dec. 16, 1800; Jan. 6, Feb. 17, 1801.
    Conn. Hist. Soc. has Jan. 6, 1801.

[Geneva] Ontario Gazette, 1796–1799.

Weekly. Established Nov. 24, 1796, by Lucius Cary, with the title of "The Ontario Gazette and Western Chronicle." The initial issue is erroneously dated on the first page Oct. 24, 1796. The issues of Sept. 8, 1797, Dec. 25, 1798 and Jan. 8, 1799, vol. 2, no. 109, are entitled "Ontario Gazette," published by Cary. The paper was removed in 1799 to Canandaigua, where it was continued under the same title. E. G. Storke, in 1877, stated that a perfect bound file of the Ontario Gazette from 1797 had been recently destroyed by fire (Cayuga Co. Hist. Soc. Collections, no. 7, p. 57).

    Rochester Pub. Lib. has Nov. 24, 1796.
    Newberry Lib. has Mar. 9, July 7, Aug. 25, 1797.
    Am. Antiq. Soc. has Sept. 8, 1797.
    N. Y. Hist. Soc. has Mar. 20, 1798.
    Troy Pub. Lib. has Dec. 25, 1798; Jan. 8, 1799.

Geneva Palladium, 1816–1820+.

Weekly. Established Jan. 10, 1816, by Young & Crosby [Stephen Young and William Crosby], with the title of "Geneva Palladium." The firm was dissolved in the late Spring of 1816 and the paper published by Stephen Young. He died Sept. 16, 1816, although succeeding issues continued his name in the imprint. With the issue of Jan. 22, 1817, the paper was published by Samuel P. Hull, who continued it until after 1820.

    Am. Antiq. Soc. has Jan. 10–24, Apr. 17, Sept. 25, 1816; Jan. 22, Nov. 26, 1817; Mar. 18, May 27, 1818; Mar. 11, July 28, Oct. 20, Nov. 24, Dec. 1, 22, 1819; Jan. 5, May 24, Aug. 23, 30, Nov. 1, 1820.
    N. Y. State Lib. has Jan. 10, 1816.
    East Hampton Free Lib. has June 16, 1819.

[Glen's Falls] Adviser, 1815.

Weekly. Established Mar. 10, 1815, by L[inus] J. Reynolds, with the title of "The Adviser." The last issue located is that of Apr. 14, 1815, vol. 1, no. 6. The title appears in a list of New York State newspapers published in the "Albany Argus" of Dec. 26, 1815.

Wis. Hist. Soc. has Mar. 10, 1815.
Am. Antiq. Soc. has Apr. 14, 1815.

[Glenn's Falls] **Warren Republican,** 1813.

Weekly. Established June 17, 1813, by John Cunningham, with the title of "The Warren Republican." The last issue located is that of Sept. 9, 1813, vol. 1, no. 13.

Am. Antiq. Soc. has June 24, Sept. 9, 1813.

[Goshen] **Friend of Truth,** 1803.

Weekly. Established Jan. 4, 1803, judging from the only copy located (first leaf only), that of Jan. 25, 1803, vol. 1, no. 4, entitled "Friend of Truth." In the handwriting of J. W. Ruttenber, son of the historian, is written on the paper "Ward M. Gazlay, editor."

Newburgh Lib. has Jan. 25, 1803.

[Goshen] **Hurtin's Goshen Repository,** 1797, see **Goshen Repository.**

[Goshen] **Independent Republican,** 1816–1820+.

Weekly. Removed from Montgomery toward the close of 1816, and there continued under its previous title of "Independent Republican," and without change of volume numbering. The earliest Goshen issue located is that of Dec. 16, 1816, vol. 4, no. 193, published by D[aniel] Macduffee. The issue of Dec. 9, 1817, vol. 5, no. 244, was published by S[amuel] Reynolds. In 1818, James A. Chevee became the publisher and so continued until after 1820.

Port Jervis Lib. has Dec. 16, 1816.
Mrs. Frank Drake, Goshen, has Dec. 9, 1817; Mar. 3, 1819.
Independent Republican Office has Jan. 1–Dec. 31, 1820.
Am. Antiq. Soc. has May 4, 1818.

[Goshen] **Orange County Gazette,** 1805–1818.

Weekly. Established May 22, 1805, by Hurtin & Denton [John G. Hurtin and Gabriel Denton], with the title of "Orange County Gazette." At some time between Mar. 25 and May 20, 1806, the paper was taken over by Gabriel Denton. Between the latter date and Mar. 3, 1807, Elliott Hopkins was admitted to partnership under the firm name of Denton & Hopkins. With the issue of Mar. 31, 1807, the paper was transferred to Elliott Hopkins, who started with this issue a new volume numbering. Between September, 1808, and March, 1809, the title became "Orange County Gazette, and Public Advertiser." Early in 1810, Hopkins admitted John Heron to partnership under the firm name of Hopkins & Heron. In November, 1810, Heron was replaced by Thomas C. Fay, with the firm name of F.. Hopkins & Tho. C. Fay. Fay retired in 1811, and the firm name became Ellio.t Hopkins & Co., changed by July, 1813, to Elliott Hopkins alone. In June, 1814, Hopkins disposed of the paper to Theophilus L. & Abijah O. Houghton. The issue of Aug. 18, 1818, vol. 12, no. 23, the last located, was published for the Proprietor. The paper was removed to Newburgh in October, 1818 (see "Orange County Patriot" of Oct. 13, 1818), at which time T. L. Houghton continued as proprietor, and A. O. Houghton remained in Goshen.

Harvard has May 29, June 5, 19, Aug. 27, 1805.
Am. Antiq. Soc. has May 20, 1806; Aug. 4, 11, 25, Sept. 15, 22, Oct. 13, 1807; Aug. 2, Sept. 6, 1808; June 26, July 24, Dec. 4, 1810; July 13, 1813; Sept. 6, 1814.
Newburgh Lib. has Mar. 25, 1806; Mar. 3, Apr. 28, May 19, 1807; Mar. 28, 1809; Dec. 17, 1816; Aug. 18, 1818.
Mrs. Frank Drake, Goshen, has Aug. 15, 1809.
Univ. of Pittsburgh has Dec. 10, 1811.
N. Y. Hist. Soc. has Apr. 13, 1813.

[Goshen] **Orange County Patriot**, 1809–1820+.

Weekly. Established Feb. 7, 1809, by G[abriel] Denton, with the title of "Orange County Patriot, or the Spirit of Seventy-Six." With the issue of May 9, 1809, the paper was transferred to T[imothy] B. Crowell, who altered the punctuation of the title to "Orange County Patriot; or, the Spirit of Seventy-Six." The last issue at Goshen was that of Mar. 19, 1811, vol. 3, no. 7. With the issue of Mar. 26, 1811, the paper was removed to Newburgh, where it was united with the "Newburgh Republican" and a new volume numbering adopted. It was now published by Lewis & Crowell [Eldad Lewis and Timothy B. Crowell]. With the issue of Dec. 24, 1811, the partnership was dissolved, the paper was published by T. B. Crowell, and the former volume numbering was resumed. The issue of Dec. 17, 1811, was vol. 1, no. 39, but that of Dec. 24, 1811, was vol. 3, no. 47. With the issue of May 5, 1812, vol. 4, no. 14, the paper was moved back to Goshen and was continued by Crowell until after 1820.

N. J. Hist. Soc. has Feb. 7, 1809–Dec. 25, 1820.
N. Y. Hist. Soc. has Oct. 24–Nov. 14, Dec. 5, 26, 1809; Jan. 2–Mar. 27, Apr. 10– May 15, July 10, 24, Sept. 11–Oct. 2, 16–Nov. 6, 20–Dec. 25, 1810; Jan. 1, 1811; Apr. 23, 1816.
Am. Antiq. Soc. has Mar. 21, 28, Apr. 11, May 9, 17, 1809; May 8, June 5–19, 1810; Oct. 22, 1816; Apr. 20, 1819.
N. Y. Pub. Lib. has Aug. 30, 1814; June 25, 1816; Jan. 26, 1819.

NEW YORK

[Goshen] Orange Eagle, 1804–1805.

Weekly. Established January 4, 1804, judging from the date of the earliest issue located, that of Feb. 1, 1804, vol. 1, no. 5, published by Wm. A. Carpenter, with the title of "Orange Eagle." The printing-office was completely destroyed by fire on Feb. 17, 1805 (see Poughkeepsie "Political Barometer," Mar. 5, 1805).

Mrs. Frank Drake, Goshen, has Feb. 1, 1804.
N. Y. Pub. Lib. has Mar. 17, 1804, extra, Dec. 8, 1804.
N. Y. State Lib. has Apr. 18, 1804.
Harvard has Oct. 9, 1804.

[Goshen] Orange Farmer, 1820+.

Weekly. Established Feb. 5, 1820, by Williams and Farrand [Samuel Williams and Joseph Farrand], with the title of "Orange Farmer." It was so continued until after 1820.

Am. Antiq. Soc. has Feb. 12, 21, June 5, Sept. 11, Nov. 6, Dec. 11, 1820.
N. Y. Pub. Lib. has Mar. 13, 1820.

[Goshen] Orange Patrol, 1800–1802.

Weekly. Established Jan. 7, 1800, by John G. Hurtin, with the title of "Orange Patrol," succeeding "The Goshen Repository." At some time between Dec. 15, 1801, and Jan. 12, 1802, Gabriel Denton was taken into partnership under the firm name of Hurtin and Denton. The last issue located is that of Apr. 20, 1802, vol. 3, no. 120.

Minn. Hist. Soc. has Jan. 7, 14, 1800; Feb. 10, Apr. 21, July 21, Aug. 4, 25, Sept. 15, 29, Oct. 13, Nov. 3, 10, Dec. 8, 15, 1801; Apr. 20, 1802.
Am. Antiq. Soc. has May 13, 27, June 10, Sept. 30, 1800.
Long Id. Hist. Soc. has Feb. 24, Apr. 7, 1801.
Mrs. Frank Drake, Goshen, has Aug. 4, 11, 1801.
N. Y. Hist. Soc. has Jan. 7, 1800.
Harvard has Feb. 4, 1800.
Morristown, N. J., Nat. Park Museum has Jan. 12, 1802.

Goshen Repository, 1789–1799.

Weekly. Established Jan. 14, 1789, judging from the earliest issue located, that of Mar. 11, 1789, vol. 1, no. 9, published by David Mandeville, with the title of "The Goshen Repository, and Weekly Intelligencer." On Mar. 17, 1789, the firm of David Mandeville and David M. Westcott was established. With the issue of Dec. 27, 1791, a period replaced the comma in the title. With the issue of May 15, 1792, the firm was dissolved and the paper published by David M. Westcott. At some time between Dec. 15, 1795, and Jan. 26, 1796, the paper was transferred to John G. Hurtin. With the issue of Jan. 3, 1797, the publisher became William Hurtin, Jun., and the title was changed to "Hurtin's Goshen Repository, and Weekly Intelligencer." William Hurtin, Jun., died Mar. 5, 1797, in his 23rd year, and with the issue of Mar. 14, 1797, the title reverted to "The Goshen Repository, and Weekly Intelligencer," published by William Hurtin. Early in 1798, the title was shortened to "The Goshen Repository" and the publishing firm became John G. & William Hurtin. With the issue of Apr. 3, 1798, John G. Hurtin became sole proprietor, but on Jan. 8, 1799, the firm name again became John G. & William Hurtin. The paper was discontinued with the issue of Dec. 31, 1799, vol. 11, no. 570, being succeeded by the "Orange Patrol."

Alfred O. Nicoll, Washingtonville, N. Y., has Mar. 29, 1791–Mar. 20, 1792; Feb. 12, 1793–Sept. 29, 1795; May 24–Dec. 27, 1796.

Am. Antiq. Soc. has Mar. 11, 24, 1789; Nov. 16–30, 1790; Oct. 4, 18, Nov. 15, 1791; Mar. 27–Dec. 25, 1792; Jan. 1–Feb. 5, Sept. 17, Oct. 22, Nov. 12, Dec. 3, 1793; Oct. 14, 1794; Feb. 17, June 30, 1795; Jan. 3–Dec. 26, 1797; Oct. 23, 1798; Feb. 12, 1799.

Minn. Hist. Soc. has July 2, 16–30, Aug. 20, 27, Sept. 10–Oct. 1, 15–29, Nov. 12–26, Dec. 17–31, 1793; Jan. 7, 14, 28–Feb. 25, Mar. 11–Apr. 1, 15–May 6, 27, June 3, 17–July 22, Aug. 5, 12, 26–Sept. 23, Oct. 7–Nov. 18, Dec. 2, 9, 23, 1794; Jan. 6–Mar. 17, 31–May 20, June 16–July 7, Aug. 8, Sept. 22, Nov. 24, Dec. 1, 1795; Jan. 26, Apr. 26, Aug. 16, 23, Sept. 6, Oct. 4, 1796; Feb. 21, June 6, Aug. 29, Oct. 3, 1797; Feb. 27, Oct. 16–Nov. 27, Dec. 11–25, 1798; Jan. 1–Feb. 26, Mar. 12–26, Apr. 9–May 7, 21–June 4, 18–July 9, 30–Sept. 24, Oct. 15–31, Nov. 12, 19, Dec. 3–31, 1799.

N. Y. Hist. Soc. has Apr. 28, June 23, Aug. 11, Oct. 20, Dec. 8, 1789; July 6, Dec. 21, 1790; Jan. 4, 1791; June 5, 26, Sept. 25, 1792; Oct. 15, Nov. 12, 1793; Mar. 4, Apr. 1, Sept. 9, Oct. 28, Nov. 18, 1794; Sept. 15, 1795; June 13, 1797; Dec. 31, 1799.

Harvard has Apr. 12, 1796; Mar. 21, May 23, 30, June 20, July 11, Aug. 29, Sept. 12–26, Oct. 10–31, Nov. 14, Dec. 5, 19, 1797; Mar. 6, 13, 27–Apr. 10, 24–June 19, July 10, Aug. 21–Sept. 4, Oct. 30, Nov. 20, Dec. 4, 25, 1798.

Newburgh Lib. has Nov. 10, 17, 1789; July 13, 1790; May 15, 1792; Dec. 3, 1793; Oct. 21, 1794.

N. Y. State Lib. has Dec. 18, 1792; Jan. 15, 1793; Mar. 31, 1795.

Mrs. Frank Drake, Goshen, has Sept. 26, 1797; Dec. 31, 1799.

N. Y. Pub. Lib. has Mar. 31, 1789; Dec. 15, 1795.

H. B. Bruyn, N. Y. City, has Dec. 22, 1789 (photo in N. Y. Pub. Lib.).

Port Jervis Lib. has Aug. 12, 1794.

Yale has Sept. 18, 1798.

[Hamilton] Allegany Mercury, 1818–1819.

Weekly. Established at Hamilton (now Olean), in Cattaraugus County, by

NEW YORK 579

Benjamin F. Smead and succeeded by the "Hamilton Recorder" ("History of Cattaraugus County," 1879, p. 66). No copy located.

Hamilton Gazette, 1816.

Weekly. Established May 16, 1816, judging from the first and only copy located, that of May 23, 1816, vol. 1, no. 2, published by L[inus] J. Reynolds, with the title of "Hamilton Gazette." This paper was published at Hamilton, Madison County.

Am. Antiq. Soc. has May 23, 1816.

[Hamilton] Madison Gazette, 1817–1818.

Weekly. Included in a list of New York papers of Jan. 1, 1818 (printed in "Albany Argus," Jan. 6, 1818), as published by John B. Johnson & Son. No copy located. See under Morrisville.

Hamilton Recorder, 1817–1820+.

A paper with the title of "Hamilton Recorder" is stated to have been established at Hamilton, in Madison County, in 1817, by John G. Stower and Peter B. Havens, which in 1819 passed into the hands of Stower & Williams and was continued until after 1820 (J. H. French, "Gazetteer of State of New York," 1860, p. 389), but no copies have been located. The "Hamilton Recorder" was established at Hamilton, in Madison County, on July 2, 1822, by John C. Johnson, a file of which is in the Colgate Hist. Collection in Colgate Univ. Lib.

Hamilton Recorder, 1819–1820.

Weekly. Established June 11, 1819, by Coudery & Smead [Franklin Coudery and Benjamin Franklin Smead], with the title of "Hamilton Recorder." It was printed at the village of Hamilton, an early name for Olean, in Cattaraugus County. In February or March 1820, the name of Coudery & Smead disappeared from the imprint, and no publisher's name was given, which was the same in the last issue located, that of May 13, 1820, vol. 1, no. 49.

Am. Antiq. Soc. has June 11, July 16, Aug. 28, Oct. 2, 1819; Feb. 5, Mar. 25, May 13, 1820.
Wis. Hist. Soc. has June 11, 1819.
Lib. Congress has June 25, 1819.

[Herkimer] American, 1810–1820+.

Weekly. Established Jan. 4, 1810, by J. H. & H. Prentiss [John H. and Henry Prentiss], with the title of "The American." William L. Stone, Jr., in the memoir of his father published in the "Life and Times of Red Jacket," 1866, p. 11, states

that the "American" was conducted by Col. John H. Prentiss personally for a
few weeks, but was then left in charge of his brother, who was not particularly
successful as a publisher and who finally in 1813 was succeeded by Mr. Stone.
The known issues of the paper show that in 1812 J. H. Prentiss became sole
publisher, but late in 1813 sold out to William L. Stone. Between June and
September 1814, the title was changed to "Herkimer American." With the issue
of Mar. 9, 1815, Stone sold out to Edward P. Seymour, who continued the paper
until after 1820.

> N. Y. State Lib. has Jan. 4, 18–Feb. 1, 22–Mar. 8, 22, Apr. 5, 26, May 17–
> July 12, Aug. 9, 30, 1810; Feb. 7, Apr. 4, 11, May 9, June 6, Dec. 26, 1811;
> Jan. 2, Aug. 6, 1812; July 29, 1813; Apr. 21–May 5, 26, Sept. 15, 29, 1814;
> Mar. 9, 1815; Feb. 22, 29, Mar. 14, May 9, 23, June 6, Aug. 1, 15, 22, 1816.
> Am. Antiq. Soc. has Feb. 8, 22, Mar. 15, Apr. 5, 12, May 3, June 28–July 12,
> 26, Sept. 20, Oct. 11, 18, 1810; Feb. 21–Mar. 21, May 2, 16, Nov. 7, 1811;
> Dec. 30, 1813; Jan. 5, 1815.
> Lib. Congress has Dec. 29, 1814; Jan. 5, 1815.
> Univ. of Rochester has May 7, 1818.

[Herkimer] Bunker-Hill, 1809–1810.

Weekly. Established Nov. 16, 1809, by Holt & Phinney [David Holt and
George G. Phinney], with the title of "Bunker-Hill." It succeeded the "Herkimer
Herald," continuing its advertisements, but adopting a new volume numbering.
On May 3, 1810, Holt retired and Geo. Gordon Phinney became sole publisher.
It was succeeded in September, 1810, by the "Herkimer Intelligencer," which
see.

> Am. Antiq. Soc. has Nov. 30, Dec. 7, 21, 1809; Jan. 4, 18–Feb. 1, 15, 22,
> Mar. 15, 29, Apr. 5, 19, 26, May 10, June 14, 28–July 12, 26, Aug. 2, 1810.

[Herkimer] Farmer's Monitor, 1805–1807.

Weekly. Established Jan. 29, 1805, by D. Holt and J. B. Robbins [David
Holt and James B. Robbins], with the title of "The Farmer's Monitor." It succeeded the "Telescope," continuing its advertisements, but adopting a new volume numbering. With the issue of Nov. 12, 1805, the firm was dissolved and
David Holt became sole publisher. The paper was discontinued with the issue
of May 19, 1807, vol. 3, no. 115.

> Am. Antiq. Soc. has Jan. 29, Feb. 5, 19, Mar. 5, July 30, Aug. 27, Sept. 17,
> Nov. 5, 19, 26, 1805; Apr. 5, May 13–27, June 10, 24, July 8, 15, Aug. 19,
> Sept. 23, Dec. 16, 30, 1806; Jan. 13, 20, Feb. 17–Mar. 31, Apr. 14, 21, May 19,
> 1807.
> Harvard has Feb. 5, 12, Mar. 5, 26, May 28, June 11, 1805.
> Univ. of Ill. has Feb. 11, 1806.

N. Y. Hist. Soc. has Jan. 20, 1807.
N. Y. State Lib. has Feb. 3, 24, Mar. 10, 1807.

Herkimer Herald, 1808–1809.

Weekly. Established July 19, 1808, by George G. Phinney, with the title of "Herkimer Herald." It succeeded the "Pelican," continuing its advertisements, but adopting a new volume numbering. In November, 1809, it was succeeded by a paper called "Bunker-Hill," which see.

Am. Antiq. Soc. has July 26–Aug. 16, Sept. 13, 1808; Nov. 2, 1809.
N. Y. Pub. Lib. has Aug. 16, 1808.

[Herkimer] Honest American, 1811–1812.

Weekly. Established Aug. 22, 1811, by Geo. Gordon Phinney, with the title of "The Honest American." It succeeded the "Herkimer Intelligencer," continuing its advertisements, but adopting a new volume numbering. At some time between May 21 and July 9, 1812, the size of the paper was reduced to quarto. With the issue of Sept. 10, 1812, the paper was transferred to Benjamin Cory, who enlarged it to folio and started a new volume numbering. The last issue located is that of Sept. 17, 1812, vol. 1, no. 2.

Am. Antiq. Soc. has Sept. 12, Oct. 3, 24, 31, Nov. 14–28, Dec. 12, 1811; Jan. 9–30, Feb. 27, May 14, July 9, 16, Sept. 10, 17, 1812.
Harvard has Sept. 12, 1811.
Univ. of Mich. (Clements) has Jan. 2, 1812.

Herkimer Intelligencer, 1810–1811.

Weekly. Established September 13, 1810, judging from the earliest issue located, that of Nov. 22, 1810, vol. 1, no. 11, published by Benjamin Cory, with the title of "Herkimer Intelligencer." It succeeded "Bunker-Hill," continuing its advertisements, but adopting a new volume numbering. It was succeeded in August, 1811, by "The Honest American," which see.

N. Y. State Lib. has Nov. 22, 1810; May 23, 1811.
Am. Antiq. Soc. has Apr. 4, 1811.

[Herkimer] Pelican, 1806–1808.

Weekly. Established about the first of September, 1806, judging from the date of the earliest issue located, that of June 8, 1807, vol. 1, no. 41, published by Benjamin Cory, with the title of "Pelican." The last issue located is that of June 20, 1808, vol. 2, no. 95. It was succeeded in July 1808, by the "Herkimer Herald," which see.

Am. Antiq. Soc. has June 22, July 6, Sept. 14, 21, 1807.

N. Y. State Lib. has June 8, 1807; June 20, 1808.
N. Y. Hist. Soc. has July 20, 1807.

[Herkimer] Telescope, 1801–1805.

Weekly. Established June 8, 1801, judging from the earliest issue located, that of July 27, 1801, vol. 1, no. 8, published by Phinney & Cory [Elihu Phinney and Benjamin Cory], with the title of the "Herkimer Telescope." By 1804 Cory had become sole publisher. The last issue located is that of Nov. 12, 1804, vol. 3, no. 177. The paper was sold by Cory in January, 1805, to Holt & Robbins, who established "The Farmer's Monitor" in its stead.

Conn. Hist. Soc. has July 27, 1801.
Univ. of Ill. has June 18, July 2, Nov. 12, 1804.

[Homer] Cortland Courier, 1811–1812.

Weekly. Established in March, 1811, judging from the date of the earliest issue located, that of June 26, 1811, vol. 1, no. 15, published by James Percival, with the title of "Cortland Courier." Both of the other issues located, Nov. 13, 1811, and July 22, 1812 (vol. 2, no. 71), were published by James Percival. The paper was succeeded in November, 1812, by the "Farmers' Journal," which see.

Phillips Free Lib., Homer, has June 26, 1811.
N. Y. Hist. Soc. has Nov. 13, 1811.
Lib. Congress has July 22, 1812.

[Homer] Cortland Repository, 1813–1820+.

Weekly. Established Dec. 8, 1813, with the title of "Cortland Repository," printed by John W. Osborn for Jesse Searl. Searl & Osborn were printing at Homer in 1814–1815, succeeded in 1816 by Jesse Searl. The title appears in the list of New York newspapers published in the "Albany Argus" of Jan. 6, 1818, as published by J. Searl. Munsell, "Typographical Miscellany," p. 141, says that the paper was discontinued by Jesse Searl May 7, 1819, but this was either an error, or the paper was soon revived, as the issue of Jan. 14, 1820, states that Benjamin B. Drake had become a partner under the firm name of Searl & Drake. This firm continued until after 1820.

Am. Antiq. Soc. has Dec. 15, 1813.
Cortland Co. Hist. Soc., Cortland, has July 21, 1814; Sept. 26, 1818; Jan. 14, Aug. 18, Nov. 24, 1820.
Cortland Free Lib. has Oct. 20, 1814.

[Homer] Cortland Weekly Museum, 1819.

There is a quotation from the "Cortland Weekly Museum," in the "Cherry-Valley Gazette" of May 25, 1819. No copy located.

[Homer] Farmers' Journal, 1812–1813.

Weekly. Established Nov. 4, 1812, with the title of "Farmers' Journal," printed by Thomas Webb, for Hastings R. Bender. It succeeded the "Cortland Courier," continuing its advertisements, but adopting a new volume numbering. In December, 1812, it was printed by John W. Osborn, for Hastings R. Bender. It was succeeded in December, 1813, by the "Cortland Repository," which see.

Am. Antiq. Soc. has Nov. 11, Dec. 30, 1812; Jan. 13, 1813.

[Homer] Western Courier, 1820+.

Weekly. Established in October, 1820, judging from the date of the earliest issue located, that of July 17, 1821, vol. 1, no. 39, published by Roberts & Hull [Elijah J. Roberts and D———— G. Hull]. The "Saratoga Sentinel" of Nov. 8, 1820, records the receipt of the first issue, published by Roberts & Hull.

Am. Antiq. Soc. has July 17, 1821.

[Hudson] Balance, 1801–1808.

Weekly. Established May 21, 1801, by Sampson, Chittenden & Croswell [Ezra Sampson, George Chittenden and Harry Croswell], with the title of "The Balance, and Columbian Repository." With the issue of Jan. 5, 1802, the size of the paper was reduced from folio to quarto, with eight pages to the issue, and a new volume numbering was adopted. With the issue of Jan. 4, 1803, all advertisements were excluded from the regular paper, which comprised eight pages, and were printed separately in a sheet entitled "Balance Advertiser." This was of quarto size until April, 1803, after which it was generally a folio sheet. With the issue of Jan. 3, 1804, the firm was dissolved and the paper published by Harry Croswell. With the issue of Jan. 5, 1808, the title was shortened to "The Balance," and a partnership was formed with Jonathan Frary, the firm being called Croswell & Frary. With this issue, moreover, the extra advertising sheet was discontinued, and the paper issued as an eight page quarto, with the two outside leaves unnumbered and entitled "Balance Advertiser," and the two inside leaves numbered and entitled "The Balance." With the issue of Nov. 15, 1808, the paper was published by F[rancis] Stebbins, for Croswell & Frary. It was discontinued with the issue of Dec. 27, 1808, vol. 7, no. 52. It was succeeded at Hudson by the "Northern Whig," whereas Croswell & Frary went to Albany to establish "The Balance, and New-York State Journal." Title-pages and indexes were provided for the paper from vol. 1 to vol. 7, 1802–1808.

Am. Antiq. Soc., Lib. Congress, N. Y. Hist. Soc., and Yale have May 21, 1801–Dec. 27, 1808.

N. Y. State Lib. has Aug. 13, Oct. 15–Dec. 31, 1801; Jan. 5, 1802–Dec. 27, 1808.

N. Y. Pub. Lib., Cornell Univ., Dartmouth, Trinity Coll., New Haven Col. Hist. Soc., Detroit Pub. Lib., and Brit. Museum have Jan. 5, 1802–Dec. 27, 1808.
Wis. Hist. Soc. has May 21, 1801–June 28, 1808.
Adriance Lib., Poughkeepsie has Jan. 5, 1802–Mar. 29, 1808.
Univ. of Minn. has Jan. 5, 1802–Feb. 2, 1808.
Hist. Soc. Penn. has Jan. 5, 1802–Dec. 29, 1807.
Boston Pub. Lib. and San Francisco Pub. Lib. have Jan. 5, 1802–Dec. 25, 1804; Jan. 7, 1806–Dec. 27, 1808.
Boston Athenæum has Jan. 5, 1802–Dec. 30, 1806.
Brooklyn Pub. Lib. has Jan. 5–Dec. 28, 1802; Jan. 3, 1804–Dec. 30, 1806; Jan. 12–Dec. 13, 1808, fair.
Wyoming, Pa., Hist. Soc. has Feb. 8, 1803–July 5, 1808.
Univ. of Texas has Jan. 5, 1802–Dec. 27, 1803; Jan. 1, 1805–Dec. 27, 1808.
Harvard has Oct. 22, 1801–Dec. 24, 1805, fair.
Duke Univ. has Jan. 5, 1802–Dec. 29, 1807, fair.
Rutgers Univ. has Jan. 5, 1802–Dec. 22, 1807, fair.
Mass. Hist. Soc. has Jan. 5, 1802–Dec. 26, 1803; Jan. 7, 1806–Dec. 29, 1807.
Columbia Co. Hist. Soc., Kinderhook, has Nov. 12, 1801; Jan. 5, 1802–Dec. 25, 1804; Jan. 7–Dec. 30, 1806; Feb. 16, Apr. 19, May 3, 1808.
Univ. of Chicago has Jan. 12–Nov. 30, 1802; Jan. 5, 1803–Dec. 18, 1804; Jan. 7–Dec. 30, 1806.
Western Reserve Hist. Soc. has Jan. 4, 1803–Dec. 25, 1804; Jan. 7–Dec. 30, 1806; Apr. 7, 1807–Mar. 22, 1808.
Brown Univ. has Jan. 5, 1802–Dec. 25, 1804; July 29, 1806; Nov. 3, 1807; June 21, 1808.
Univ. of Mich. (Clements) has Jan. 5, 1802–Dec. 25, 1804.
Chicago Hist. Soc. has Jan. 5, 1802–Dec. 25, 1804.
D.A.R. Lib., Hudson, has Jan. 5, 1802–Dec. 27, 1803.
Ohio Hist. & Phil. Soc. has Jan. 5, 1802–Dec. 27, 1803.
Princeton has Jan. 19, 1802–Dec. 27, 1803.
Case Memorial Lib., Hartford, has Jan. 4, 1803–Dec. 24, 1805.
Troy Pub. Lib. has Jan. 5–Dec. 28, 1802; Jan. 7–Dec. 30, 1806.
Grosvenor Lib., Buffalo, has Jan. 4–Dec. 27, 1803; Jan. 6–Dec. 29, 1807.
H. Armour Smith, Yonkers, has Jan. 5–Dec. 28, 1802; Jan. 6–Dec. 29, 1807.
Watkinson Lib., Hartford, has Jan. 3, 1804–Dec. 24, 1805.
Union Coll. has Jan. 5–Dec. 28, 1802.
East Hampton Free Lib. has Jan. 5–Dec. 28, 1802.
Cayuga Co. Hist. Soc., Auburn, has Feb. 23–Dec. 28, 1802.
Me. Hist. Soc. has May 3–Dec. 27, 1803.
Phil. Lib. Co. has Jan. 6, 1807–Dec. 27, 1808.
Many libraries have scattering issues.
Of the "Balance Advertiser," Harvard has Jan. 18, 1803–Dec. 17, 1805, scattering file; and most of the 1808 files contain the advertising pages.

[Hudson] **Balance Advertiser,** 1803–1808, see under **Balance.**

[Hudson] **Bee,** 1802–1820+.

Weekly. Established Aug. 17, 1802, by Charles Holt, with the title of "The Bee." Holt went to New York to establish "The Columbian;" and "The Bee," with the issue of Oct. 17, 1809, was published by Henry Halland for Charles Holt. In May, 1810, Halland's name was omitted from the imprint, the paper being published for Charles Holt. With the issue of Aug. 10, 1810, it was purchased and published by Samuel W. Clark, who adopted a new volume numbering. With the issue of Aug. 2, 1814, a new form of title was printed, "The Hudson Bee," but with the word "Hudson" in much smaller type. Clark sold the paper Dec. 26, 1820, to John W. Dutcher, who continued it in 1821.

Am. Antiq. Soc. has Aug. 17, 1802–Aug. 20, 1805; Sept. 3–Oct. 15, 29–Nov. 26, Dec. 3, 24, 31, 1805; Apr. 22, May 13, 27, July 8, 15, Aug. 5–19, Sept. 2, 16, Oct. 14, 28, Dec. 2–30, 1806; Jan. 6–27, Feb. 10, 24, Mar. 3–17, 31–May 19, June 2–Aug. 4, 18, 25, Sept. 8–22, Oct. 6–Nov. 17, Dec. 1, 22, 29, 1807; Jan. 5, Feb. 9–Apr. 19, May 3–June 21, July 19, 26, Aug. 2, 16, 23, Sept. 6, 13, 27, Oct. 11–25, Dec. 20, 1808; Jan. 3, 10, 24–Mar. 21, Apr. 4–May 16, June 6, 13, 27–Aug. 1, 22, 29, Sept. 19–Oct. 24, Dec. 5–26, 1809; Jan. 2, 9, 23, 30, Feb. 20–Mar. 6, 20, Apr. 3, 17, 24, May 15, June 8–July 20, Aug. 10–Sept. 14, Oct. 5–Nov. 2, 23, Dec. 7–21, 1810; Jan. 4, 18, 25, Feb. 8–Mar. 29, Apr. 26–May 10, 31, June 7, 28, July 12, 26, Aug. 2, 16, 23, Sept. 6–20, Oct. 1, 22, 29, Nov. 19, Dec. 10, 24, 1811; Jan. 7, 21–Feb. 18, Mar. 3, 17, Apr. 7, 21–May 5, 19–June 30, July 7–21, Aug. 11, Sept. 1–29, Oct. 13, Nov. 3, 10, 24, 1812; Jan. 19, Mar. 2, 16, 23, May 4, 11, Oct. 12, Dec. 7, 21, 1813; Jan. 4, 25, Mar. 8, May 10, 31, June 14–July 12, Aug. 9, 16, Sept. 6–27, Oct. 11, 18, Nov. 15, Dec. 6–20, 1814; Jan. 17, Feb. 21–Mar. 21, Apr. 4, 25, May 2, 30, June 13, Aug. 22, Sept. 19, Oct. 10, 17, Nov. 7–28, Dec. 19, 26, 1815; Jan. 2, 23–Feb. 27, Mar. 12–Apr. 2, 16, May 7, June 11, 25, July 23, Aug. 6, Nov. 19, 1816; Feb. 18, Mar. 11, Apr. 8, Nov. 25, 1817; Feb. 24, June 23, 30, Oct. 13, 27, Dec. 22, 1818; Jan. 5, 19–Feb. 2, 16–Mar. 23, May 4, July 6, Nov. 2, Dec. 21, 28, 1819; Jan. 11, Feb. 1, May 9, June 13, 27, July 11, Aug. 29, Dec. 19, 1820.

Harvard has Aug. 17, 24, Sept. 21–Oct. 12, Nov. 16, 30, Dec. 21, 28, 1802; Jan. 11, 18, Feb. 8, Mar. 8, 22, 29, May 24, June 7–21, July 5–Aug. 2, 23–Sept. 6, 20, 27, Oct. 11, 25, 1803; Feb. 14–Mar. 6, May 15, June 26, July 3, 24–Aug. 7, 28, Oct. 2, 1804; Jan. 1, 8, 22–Feb. 5, 19–Apr. 2, 16, May 7, 21, June 4, July 9, 16, Sept. 24, Nov. 12–26, Dec. 24, 1805; Feb. 4, 11, Mar. 11, Apr. 29, July 22, Aug. 5, 12, Sept. 2, 9, 30, Nov. 25, Dec. 9, 23, 30, 1806; Jan. 27–Feb. 10, 24, Mar. 10, 17, Apr. 21–May 5, 26, July 21, Sept. 1, 15–29, Oct. 20–Nov. 3, 1807; May 17, Aug. 2, 9, Sept. 13, 27, Oct. 11, 18, Dec. 6–20, 1808.

Columbia Co. Hist. Soc., Kinderhook, has May 24, 1808; May 30, 1809; Aug. 10, 17, 31, Sept. 14–Oct. 12, Nov. 9–Dec. 14, 1810; Jan. 4–25, Feb. 8–Mar. 1, 29, Apr. 5, 19, May 3, 31, June 7, 21, July 5, 19, Aug. 9, 23, Sept. 24, Nov. 19, 1811; July 7, 14, 1812; Jan. 11, Mar. 1, Apr. 26, May 24–June 28, July 12, Aug. 23, Sept. 20, 27, Oct. 25–Nov. 22, Dec. 13, 27, 1814; Jan. 10, 1815–Dec. 30, 1817, fair; Nov. 10, 1818; Jan. 5–Dec. 28, 1819; Jan. 4–July 18, Aug. 1, 8, Dec. 26, 1820.

Rochester Hist. Soc. has June 15, 1810–May 12, 1812.

N. Y. Hist. Soc. has Aug. 17–31, Sept. 21–Nov. 30, Dec. 14–28, 1802; Jan. 11–Feb. 8, Mar. 1–15, 29, Apr. 5, 19, 26, May 17–June 14, 28–Aug. 30, Sept. 13–Dec. 27, 1803; Jan. 3–May 22, June 5, 26–July 10, Aug. 14–Dec. 11, 25, 1804; Jan. 8–Feb. 26, Mar. 19, Apr. 2, 9, 30, May 14–June 11, 25–July 13, 1805; May 5, July 21, Oct. 13, 20, Nov. 17, 1807; May 24, June 14, 1808; Feb. 7, 28, Mar. 14, May 9, June 13, 27, July 11–Aug. 1, Sept. 19, 26, Oct. 17, 1809; Jan. 30, Feb. 27, Apr. 3, June 15–July 6, Oct. 19, 26, Dec. 7, 21, 1810; Jan. 4, 25, Feb. 22, Mar. 8, 1811; May 31, June 14, 1814; Oct. 31, 1815.

Yale has Aug. 17, 1802–July 5, 1803.

N. Y. State Lib. has July 17, 1804; Aug. 6, 1805; July 7, 1807; Dec. 13, 1808; Mar. 7, Apr. 18, 1809; Apr. 19, 1811; May 12, 19, July 14, Sept. 29, 1812; Mar. 16, 1813; Sept. 19, Oct. 10, Dec. 19, 1815; Jan. 19, Mar. 16, 23, 1819; Jan. 4–Dec. 26, 1820.

Lib. Congress has Aug. 24–Sept. 28, Oct. 26, 1802; Jan. 4–Dec. 6, 27, 1803; Feb. 7, Sept. 18, 1804; Jan. 5, 1808; June 22, 1810; Apr. 20, 27, May 11, 1813; June 27, 1815; Aug. 13, 20, Dec. 17, 24, 1816.

Mass. Hist. Soc. has Jan. 18, Sept. 27, 1803; Feb. 21–Mar. 13, Oct. 9, 1804; Mar. 5, Nov. 5, 1805; Dec. 16, 1806; Apr. 28, May 12, July 14, 21, Sept. 15, Oct. 6, 1807; Mar. 15, May 31, June 7, 21, July 26, Sept. 27, 1808.

New London Co. Hist. Soc. has Aug. 24, 31, Oct. 5–Dec. 28, 1802.

Shelton, Conn., Pub. Lib. has June 30, 1812; Jan. 19, 1813.

N. Y. Pub. Lib. has Dec. 12, 1815; Feb. 11; 1817.

Univ. of Ill. has Feb. 11, 1806.

Newberry Lib. has May 10, 1808.

Bridgeport Sci. Hist. Soc. has Dec. 15, 1812.

Ontario Co. Hist. Soc., Canandaigua, has May 4, 1813.

Rutgers Univ. has Sept. 27, 1814.

[Hudson] **Columbia Republican**, 1820+.

Weekly. Established Sept. 12, 1820, judging from the earliest issue located, that of Nov. 7, 1820, vol. 1, no. 9, published by Solomon Wilbur, Jun., with the title of "The Columbia Republican." Continued until after 1820.

D.A.R. Lib., Hudson, has Nov. 7–Dec. 26, 1820.

Hudson Gazette, 1792–1803.

Weekly. A continuation, without change of volume numbering, of "The Hudson Weekly Gazette." The change of title occurred probably in January, 1792, but the earliest issue located with the new title is that of Mar. 15, 1792, vol. 8, no. 363, published by Ashbel Stoddard, with the title of "Hudson Gazette." Continued by Stoddard until December 27, 1803, vol. 19, no. 978, when the establishment was sold out to the proprietors of "The Balance." An "obituary" regarding its decease, was published in "The Bee" of Jan. 3, 1804.

> Am. Antiq. Soc. has Mar. 15, May 31, July 19, Aug. 16, Sept. 20, 1792; Jan. 10, Feb. 7, 28, Mar. 7, 28, July 25, Nov. 14, 1793; Feb. 20, May 15, 1794; July 16, 23, 1795; June 23, Sept. 15, 1796; June 12, 1798; Jan. 1, 8, 22, 29, Feb. 12, 26–Apr. 30, May 14–Sept. 17, Oct. 8–Dec. 31, 1799; Feb. 10, 1801– Mar. 16, 1802; Nov. 30, 1802; Jan. 11–Dec. 27, 1803.
> Harvard has June 16, 30, Sept. 22, 1791; July 5, 1792; Dec. 5, 1793; Mar. 26, Apr. 16, May 7, June 4–18, July 2, 23, 30, Aug. 20, Sept. 10, Nov. 12, Dec. 31, 1795; Feb. 25, Apr. 14, 21, May 26, June 2, 16, 23, July 14, 1796; Jan. 2, 23, 30, Feb. 13, 27–Mar. 20, Apr. 3, May 22, June 13–27, July 11, Aug. 15–Sept. 5, 19–Oct. 24, Nov. 7, 14, 1797; Jan. 23, Feb. 13–Mar. 13, 27, Apr. 24, May 15–29, June 12–July 17, 31, Sept. 11, Oct. 31, Dec. 11, 1798; Jan. 1, 8, Feb. 19, 1799; Mar. 3–31, Apr. 14, May 5–June 16, July 7–Aug. 11, 25, Sept. 15–29, Oct. 27–Nov. 10, 24–Dec. 22, 1801; Jan. 5–19, Oct. 26– Dec. 28, 1802; Jan. 4–Feb. 8, 22, 29, Mar. 8–May 3, 17–June 7, 1803.
> Mass. Hist. Soc. has Feb. 10–Dec. 29, 1801, fair.
> N. Y. Pub. Lib. has Sept. 13, 1792; July 18, 1793; Nov. 28, 1796; May 19, 1801; Mar. 16, 1802.
> Wis. Hist. Soc. has Jan. 22, Mar. 12, Aug. 27, Sept. 10, 1795; Oct. 22, 1799.
> Phil. Lib. Co. has Nov. 5, 26, 1795; Apr. 7–21, May 26, June 2, 23, July 14, 1796.
> N. Y. Hist. Soc. has Feb. 18, 1796; Oct. 22, 1799; Sept. 28, Oct. 5, 1802.
> Lib. Congress has Mar. 24, Apr. 28, May 12, July 21, 1801.
> Cayuga Co. Hist. Soc., Auburn, has Sept. 29, 1796.
> N. Y. State Lib. has Oct. 10, 1797; Feb. 17, Apr. 7, 14, 28, June 16, 23, July 14, 21, Aug. 11, Sept. 15, 22, Oct. 15, 22, 1801. They had a complete file, 1792–1803, which was destroyed in the Capitol fire of 1911.

[Hudson] Northern Whig, 1809–1820+.

Weekly. Established Jan. 3, 1809, by Francis Stebbins, with the title of "Northern Whig." It succeeded "The Balance," continuing its advertisements, but adopting a new volume numbering. With the issue of Jan. 3, 1815, Stebbins disposed of the paper to William L. Stone. With the issue of Mar. 11, 1817, Richard L. Corss was admitted to partnership, and the paper was published by Stone & Corss, although Stone himself became engaged in publishing at

Albany. With the issue of Aug. 31, 1819, Corss became the publisher and continued the paper until after 1820.

N. Y. Hist. Soc. has Jan. 3, 1809–Dec. 27, 1814; July 4, 1815.
N. Y. State Lib. has Jan. 3, 1815–Dec. 23, 1817; Nov. 14, 1820. They had a file, 1811–1823, which was destroyed in the Capitol fire of 1911.
D.A.R. Lib., Hudson, has Jan. 7, 1817–Dec. 15, 1818.
British Museum has Dec. 31, 1817–Dec. 26, 1820.
Am. Antiq. Soc. has Dec. 12, 1809; Apr. 12, 26, May 11, June 8, July 13, 1810; Mar. 1, July 12, 1811; July 20, Aug. 3, 1812; Jan. 3–17, 31–Feb. 14, Mar. 7–21, Apr. 11–June 6, 27, July 18–Aug. 1, 15–Sept. 19, Oct. 17–Nov. 7, 21–Dec. 26, 1815; Jan. 2, 16–Mar. 26, Apr. 30, May 7, 21, June 4, 18–Aug. 6, 20–Sept. 3, 17, Oct. 15, 22, Nov. 5–26, Dec. 10, 24, 1816; Sept. 5, 1820.
Univ. of Rochester has Nov. 3, Dec. 8, 29, 1818; Mar. 2, Apr. 13, 27, May 4, Sept. 14, 1819; Jan. 25, Feb. 22–Apr. 4, 18, May 2, 16, 30–June 27, July 25–Aug. 8, 1820.
Columbia Co. Hist. Soc., Kinderhook, has July 18, 1815; Aug. 4, 1818.
Univ. of Pittsburgh has Nov. 25, 1811.
Wesleyan Univ. has May 3, 1814.
Ontario Co. Hist. Soc., Canandaigua, has June 18, 1816.
Wis. Hist. Soc. has Dec. 8, 1818.

[Hudson] Republican Fountain, 1806–1807.

Weekly. Established Nov. 27, 1806, judging from the date of the earliest issue located, that of Jan. 22, 1807, vol. 1, no. 9, published by Sylvester Roberts and Co., with the title of "Republican Fountain." It was discontinued in May or June, 1807 (see Albany "Republican Crisis," June 19, 1807).

N. Y. State Lib. has Jan. 22, Feb. 5, 26, Mar. 12, 26, 1807.
Harvard has Feb. 19, 1807.

[Hudson] Wasp, 1802–1803.

Established July 7, 1802, with the title of "The Wasp," printed by Harry Croswell, for the Editor, "Robert Rusticoat." Undoubtedly Croswell was the editor, issuing it from his office to combat "The Bee." It was of quarto size, and was published occasionally, the exact dates of its twelve numberings being July 7 [8], 17, 31, Aug. 12, 23, 30, Sept. 9, 23, Oct. 14, Nov. 2, 25, 1802, and Jan. 26, 1803, vol. 1, no. 12, which was the last number. A second edition was printed of the first three numbers.

Am. Antiq. Soc. and N. Y. Hist. Soc. have July 7, 1802–Jan. 26, 1803.
Conn. Hist. Soc. has July 8, 1802–Jan. 26, 1803.
Hist. Soc. Penn. has July 31, 1802–Jan. 26, 1803.
Dartmouth has July 8–Aug. 12, 30, Sept. 9, Oct. 14, Nov. 2, 1802.

Univ. of Chicago has Aug. 12–30, Sept. 23, 1802–Jan. 26, 1803.
Rutgers Univ. has Aug. 12–30, Sept. 23, 1802.
N. Y. Pub. Lib. has Aug. 12, Sept. 9, 1802; Jan. 26, 1803.
Harvard has Oct. 14, Nov. 2, 25, 1802; Jan. 26, 1803.
Mass. Hist. Soc. has Sept. 23, 1802.
Long Id. Hist. Soc. has Oct. 14, 1802.

Hudson Weekly Gazette, 1785–1792.

Weekly. Established Apr. 7, 1785, by Webster and Stoddard [Charles R. Webster and Ashbel Stoddard], with the title of "The Hudson Weekly Gazette." In April, 1786, Webster withdrew and Ashbel Stoddard became sole publisher. At some time between Nov. 17, 1791, and Mar. 15, 1792, the title was changed to "Hudson Gazette," which see.

Am. Antiq. Soc. has Apr. 7, 1785 (facsim.); May 18–June 1, 15–29, Aug. 3, 17, Sept. 7–Oct. 5, 19, 26, Nov. 9, 16, 30–Dec. 14, 28, 1786; Jan. 4–25, Feb. 8, 22, Mar. 29, Apr. 5, 26, May 10, 31, June 14, 28, July 5, Aug. 2, 16, Sept. 20–Oct. 4, 25, Nov. 8, 15, Dec. 6–20, 1787; Jan. 3–Feb. 7, 21, Mar. 13, 20, Apr. 3–22, May 13–27, June 17, 24, July 8, Aug. 5–Sept. 9, 23, 30, Oct. 14, 21, Nov. 25, 1788; Jan. 20, Feb. 17, 24, Mar. 17, Apr. 7–28, July 6, 13, Sept. 3–17, Oct. 29, Dec. 17, 1789; Jan. 14, Feb. 18, Apr. 8, 29, June 3, Aug. 5, Sept. 30, Oct. 14, 28, Nov. 11–25, Dec. 30, 1790; Feb. 17, Apr. 7, 21, Nov. 10, 1791.
N. Y. State Lib. has Apr. 5, 1787–Mar. 27, 1788; Apr. 28, 1789. They had a complete file, 1785–1792, which was destroyed in the Capitol fire of 1911.
Harvard has June 16, 30, Sept. 22, 1791.
N. Y. Hist. Soc. has Dec. 10, 1789; Apr. 28, 1791.
Schenectady Co. Hist. Soc. has Nov. 9, 1786.
Mass. Hist. Soc. has Nov. 8, 1787.
H. B. Frankenfield, Phila., has May 6, 1788.
Boston Pub. Lib. has Sept. 2, 1788.
N. Y. Pub. Lib. has Dec. 17, 1789.
Columbia Co. Hist. Soc., Kinderhook, has Sept. 8, 1791.

[Ithaca] American Journal, 1817–1820+.

Weekly. Established Aug. 20, 1817, by Mack and Shepard [Ebenezer Mack and Erastus Shepard], with the title of "American Journal." In the Newtown "Telegraph" of Sept. 9, 1817, it is stated that "The Ithaca Gazette has been discontinued and a new paper entitled the American Journal established in its stead, edited by Ebenezer Mack, and Benjamin [error for Erastus] Shepard, one of the former editors of the Gazette." In the Tompkins County record of mortgages, Erastus Shepard is mentioned several times from August, 1817, to May, 1818, as one of the publishers; and the prospectus of the "American

Journal" gives Ebenezer Mack and Erastus Shepard as the founders of the paper. Early in 1819 the paper was transferred to Mack & Searing [Ebenezer Mack and Augustin P. Searing]. On Nov. 10, 1819, this firm was dissolved and E. Mack became sole publisher. With the issue of June 21, 1820, Mack and Searing again became the publishers and so continued the paper until after 1820.

Am. Antiq. Soc. has Aug. 20, 27, 1817; June 23, July 14, 28, Aug. 11, Sept. 8, 22, 29, Nov. 24, 1819; Feb. 9, 16, Mar. 22, June 28, July 5, Aug. 9, 30, Sept. 13, 27, Oct. 18, 25, Dec. 6, 1820.
Cornell Univ. has Aug. 18, 1819–Dec. 27, 1820.
Cornell Free Lib., Ithaca, has Oct. 15, 1817.
N. Y. State Lib. has Aug. 11, 1819.
Univ. of Rochester has Aug. 2, 1820.

Ithaca Gazette, 1816–1817.

Weekly. Established in August, 1816, judging from the first and only copy located, that of June 5, 1817, vol. 1, no. 42, published by Benjamin, Reed & Shepard [Joseph Benjamin, Ebenezer Reed and Erastus Shepard], with the title of "Ithaca Gazette, and Religious Intelligencer." The paper is mentioned from late in 1816 to August 1817 in the Tompkins County Court record of mortgages (information given by C. H. Hull), where Erastus Shepard is recorded as one of the printers. Ebenezer Mack, in the "American Journal" of Nov. 15, 1820, says "Mr. Shepard, when I came to this place, was one of three proprietors of the Ithaca Gazette." In the issue of Dec. 27, 1820, Mack states that Joseph Benjamin was another of the proprietors. According to an article in "The Telegraph," of Newtown, of Sept. 9, 1817, the "Ithaca Gazette" was succeeded by the "American Journal" in August 1817.

Cornell Univ. has June 5, 1817.

[Ithaca] Republican Chronicle, 1820+.

Weekly. Established Sept. 6, 1820, by Spencer & Stockton [David D. Spencer and Henry R. Stockton], with the title of "Republican Chronicle." It was so continued after 1820.

Cornell Free Lib., Ithaca, has Sept. 6–Dec. 27, 1820.

[Ithaca] Seneca Republican, 1815–1816.

Weekly. Established Sept. 23, 1815, judging from the only issue located, that of Oct. 21, 1815, vol. 1, no. 5, published by J[onathan] Ingersoll, Jr., with the title of "The Seneca Republican." It is listed as the "Republican" among the New York newspapers of December, 1815, published in the "Albany Argus" of Dec. 26, 1815. In the "Utica Patriot" of Feb. 20, 1816, is the record of the marriage at Ithaca of "Jonathan Ingersoll, Jun., Esq., editor of the Seneca Republican" to Eliza Chapman. Copies of the paper in 1815 and 1816 are noted in an article in the "Ithaca Journal" of Mar. 11, 1889.

Am. Antiq. Soc. has Oct. 21, 1815.

Johnstown Gazette, 1795–1798.

Weekly. Established July 15, 1795, by Jacob Dockstader, with the title of "The Johnstown Gazette." In 1798, apparently in October, the paper was transferred to Holden & Smith [David Holden and James Smith]. The last issue located is that of Nov. 28, 1798, vol. 3, no. 177.

N. Y. Pub. Lib. has July 15, 1795.
Am. Antiq. Soc. has Oct. 5, 1796.
Johnstown Hist. Soc. has Apr. 19, 1797.
Harvard has Oct. 11, 1797; Nov. 28, 1798.

[Johnstown] Montgomery Intelligencer, 1805–1807.

Weekly. Established in February, 1805, by William Child, with the title of "Montgomery Intelligencer." With the issue of June 9, 1806, vol. 2, no. 68, Child transferred the paper to James B. Robbins, who adopted a new volume numbering. Immediately after the State election of April, 1807, the paper was discontinued (see "Republican Crisis," of Albany, of June 19, 1807).

Am. Antiq. Soc. has June 9, 16, July 7, Aug. 4, 1806.

[Johnstown] Montgomery Monitor, 1809–1820+.

Weekly. Established Nov. 22, 1809, judging from the date of the earliest issue located, that of Dec. 6, 1809, vol. 1, no. 3, published by Miller & Brown [David C. Miller and Samuel R. Brown], with the title of "Montgomery Monitor." Miller and Brown also published "The Saratoga Advertiser" at Ballston Spa, and announced in that paper, Oct. 16, 1809, that they were about to establish a paper in Montgomery County. Before the end of December, 1809, Brown retired and the paper was published by D. C. Miller. With the issue of Dec. 12, 1810, Miller transferred the paper to R[ussell] Prentice & J[acob] D. Felthousen. With the issue of May 8, 1811, the firm was dissolved and the paper published by R. Prentice. As late as June 21, 1814, Prentice was still the publisher. The issue of Jan. 3, 1815, was published by Prentice & King [Russell Prentice and Sylvester King], but from November, 1815, at least, Sylvester King was the publisher (see also "Albany Argus," Jan. 6, 1818). The "Schenectady Cabinet" of Apr. 8, 1818, announced that the "Monitor" had recently been transferred to Duncan McDonald. In 1820 Horatio G. Spafford became editor of the "Monitor" (Munsell, "Typographical Miscellany," 1850, p. 145).

N. Y. State Lib. has Dec. 6, 13, 1809; Mar. 7, 1810; Feb. 13, Aug. 6, Nov. 26, Dec. 24, 1811; Mar. 3, 10, Oct. 13, 1812; Jan. 26, 1813; Feb. 22, June 21, 1814; Nov. 29, 1815; Feb. 7, June 12, 1816; May 14, Nov. 5, 1817.

Am. Antiq. Soc. has Dec. 27, 1809; Jan. 24, 31, Dec. 12, 19, 1810; Mar. 20, 1811; Feb. 4, 1812; May 18, 1813; Feb. 15, 22, 1814.

Harvard has Dec. 12, 1810; Jan. 23, Feb. 6–20, Apr. 17, May 8–22, June 5, 12, 26, July 3, 17, 1811; Jan. 28, 1812.

N. Y. Pub. Lib. has Jan. 3, 1815.

[Johnstown] **Montgomery Republican**, 1806–1820+.

Weekly. Established in August, 1806, judging from the volume numbering of later issues, and by a mention of the receipt of the first issue in the New York "Morning Chronicle" of Aug. 12, 1806. It was established by William Child, who was succeeded in 1808 by A. Taylor [probably Abraham Taylor, who was publishing the Watertown "Hemisphere" in January 1810]. Before January, 1810, Taylor was succeeded by Asa Child. The printing office was destroyed by fire Oct. 9, 1812 (see Johnstown "Montgomery Monitor," Oct. 13, 1812), but judging from the volume numbering, this did not affect continuous publication. Child continued the paper until after 1820.

Am. Antiq. Soc. has Jan. 24, Mar. 14, July 24, Sept. 18, Oct. 23, 1810; Mar. 9, Aug. 3, 1813; Jan. 25, 1814.

N. Y. State Lib. has May 2, 1809; May 22, 1810; May 3, 1814; Jan. 3, 1815; May 29, 1816.

N. Y. Pub. Lib. has May 5, 1812.

[Kingston] **Craftsman**, 1820+.

Weekly. Established Mar. 29, 1820, by Benjamin G. Jansen, with the title of "The Craftsman." Continued until after 1820.

N. Y. Pub. Lib. and Kingston City Lib. have Mar. 29–Dec. 30, 1820.

Am. Antiq. Soc. has Apr. 12, 1820.

[Kingston] **Farmer's Register**, 1792–1793.

Weekly. Established Sept. 29, 1792, by Nicholas Power and William Copp, with the title of "The Farmer's Register." It was discontinued with the issue of Sept. 21, 1793, vol. 1, no. 52, and succeeded by the "Rising Sun."

Am. Antiq. Soc. has Oct. 6–Nov. 10, 1792.

N. Y. Hist. Soc. has Apr. 6–Sept. 14, 1793.

N. J. Hist. Soc. has June 15, 1793.

[Kingston] **New York Journal**, 1777.

Weekly. A continuation, without change of volume numbering, of Holt's

"New York Journal," which was suspended at New York City in August, 1776, because of the occupation of the city by the British. The paper was removed to Kingston, where it was revived with the issue of July 7, 1777, no. 1757, published by John Holt, with the title of "The New-York Journal, and the General Advertiser." The last Kingston issue was that of Oct. 13, 1777, no. 1771, and four days later the town was burned by the British. The paper was then removed to Poughkeepsie, where it was revived May 11, 1778. See under Poughkeepsie.

N. Y. Pub. Lib. has July 7–Oct. 6, 1777.
N. Y. Hist. Soc. has July 7, 28, Aug. 18, Sept. 8–Oct. 13, 1777.
Lib. Congress has Aug. 25–Sept. 15, 29, Oct. 6, 1777.
Phil. Lib. Co. has Aug. 11, 1777.

[Kingston] **Plebeian**, 1803–1815.

Weekly. Established June 29, 1803, judging from the date of the earliest issue located, that of Aug. 3, 1803, vol. 1, no. 6, published by Buel & Mitchell [Jesse Buel and Isaac Mitchell], with the title of "Plebeian." With the issue of June 24, 1805, the partnership was dissolved and the paper published by J. Buel. With the issue of Jan. 19, 1813, Buel removed to Albany, and the paper was published by Daniel MacDuffee, for the Proprietor. With the issue of July 26, 1814, the paper was purchased and published by John Tappen. The last issue with the title of "Plebeian" was that of July 25, 1815, vol. 12, no. 631, after which it was changed to "Ulster Plebeian," which see.

Harvard has Aug. 3, 31, Sept. 14, 21, Oct. 5, 19, 26, 1803; Jan. 25–Feb. 15, Mar. 14, 21, Apr. 18, June 20, July 25, Aug. 1, 22, 29, Sept. 12, 26–Oct. 10, Nov. 12, Dec. 3, 31, 1804; Jan. 7, 14, 28–Mar. 18, Apr. 1, 8, May 20–June 3, 17, July 1, 15, Aug. 12, 19, Sept. 2–Nov. 1, 22–Dec. 27, 1805; Jan. 3–Feb. 7, 21, 28, Mar. 14, Apr. 11–May 2, 16–30, June 13–July 4, 18, Aug. 8–29, Oct. 10–Nov. 7, 21, Dec. 5–26, 1806; Jan. 9, 16, Feb. 6–20, Mar. 6, 20, 27, May 15, 29, June 5, 19–July 17, Aug. 28–Sept. 29, Oct. 20, 27, 1807; Sept. 27, 1808.

Am. Antiq. Soc. has Feb. 8, Sept. 26, Oct. 3, 1804; Jan. 28, Feb. 11, 18, Mar. 18, Apr. 15, May 13, June 10, July 11, Aug. 19, 26, Oct. 14–Nov. 1, 15, 22, 1805; Jan. 2, Feb. 21, May 23–June 13, 27, July 4, Aug. 1–15, 29, Oct. 10, 24, Nov. 7, 1806; Jan. 9, 16, Feb. 27, Mar. 6, 20, 27, Apr. 10, 24, May 15–June 5, 19, July 3–24, Aug. 7–Sept. 4, 18, 25, Dec. 8, 16, 1807; Jan. 5, 12, Feb. 16, Mar. 1, 8, 22, Apr. 19, May 3, 31, June 21–July 5, 26–Aug. 9, 23–Sept. 13, 27–Oct. 25, Nov. 8, 22, Dec. 20, 27, 1808; Jan. 3–31, Feb. 14–Apr. 4, May 2, 16, 23, June 27, July 18–Aug. 1, 22, Sept. 5, Nov. 7, 14, 28–Dec. 19, 1809; Jan. 2–16, 30, Feb. 6, 20, Mar. 20–Apr. 17, May 1, 8, 22, June 5–July 3, 17, 24, Aug. 7, 14, Sept. 11–25, Oct. 9, 23–Nov. 6, 27–Dec. 18, 1810; Jan. 1, 8, 22, 29, Feb. 26, Mar. 12, 19, Apr. 2–16, 30, May 14, June 25, July 9, 30, Aug. 27, Sept. 10–24, Oct. 8–22, Nov. 12, 19, Dec. 17, 1811; Jan. 7, 21, 28,

Feb. 11, Mar. 3, 17, 31, Apr. 14, May 5, 12, June 23, July 14, 28, Aug. 4, 25–Sept. 8, Oct. 20–Nov. 10, 24, Dec. 8, 29, 1812; Jan. 19, 26, Feb. 9, 23–Mar. 9, 23, June 1, 29, Aug. 31, Oct. 5, 12, Nov. 3, 16, Dec. 28, 1813; Feb. 1, 15, Mar. 29, Aug. 23, 1814; May 16, June 27, 1815.

N. Y. Hist. Soc. has Nov. 26, 1804; May 24, 31, June 21–Dec. 27, 1808; Jan. 3–June 13, July 11, 1809–May 8, 1810; Aug. 2, 1814–July 25, 1815.

Rutgers Univ. has Feb. 9, 1813–July 19, 1814.

Senate House, Kingston, has Mar. 3, Dec. 22, 1812; Feb. 23, 1813; Mar. 21, 28, 1815. They also supposedly have the following issues from the Rev. R. R. Hoes collection: — Jan. 17–Feb. 14, Mar. 14–28, May 2–16, July 11, Nov. 24, Dec. 12, 1806; Feb. 27, Oct. 20, Dec. 8, 22, 1807; Feb. 2, 9, May 3, Aug. 2, Oct. 18, 1808; May 9, June 20, 27, Nov. 24, 1809; Feb. 6, June 5, 1810; Feb. 19, May 7, 21, Oct. 29, Dec. 10, 24, 31, 1811; Feb. 25, Mar. 10, 24, July 21, 1812; Dec. 14, 1813.

N. Y. State Lib. has Nov. 14, Dec. 5, 26, 1806; Mar. 13, Apr. 10, 1807; Jan. 23, Mar. 6, Apr. 24, 1810; Apr. 2, 30, 1811; Aug. 11, 25, Sept. 15, 29, Oct. 13–27, 1812; Apr. 20, 1813.

H. B. Bruyn, N. Y. City, has Oct. 19, 1803; Apr. 7, 21, 28, May 19, 1812 (photos in N. Y. Pub. Lib.).

Lib. Congress has June 27, Aug. 29, Sept. 19, 1809; Sept. 14, 1813.

Univ. of Ill. has Feb. 8, 1804; Mar. 14, 1806.

Univ. of Pittsburgh has Dec. 10, 17, 1811.

Duke Univ. has June 6, 1806.

[Kingston] Rising Sun, 1793–1798.

Weekly. Established Sept. 28, 1793, by William Copp and Samuel Freer, with the title of "Rising Sun." It succeeded "The Farmer's Register," and the initial issue announced the dissolution of the firm of Power and Copp, who had published that paper. The paper was discontinued with the issue of Apr. 28, 1798, vol. 5, no. 240, and was succeeded on May 5, 1798, by the "Ulster County Gazette." William Copp died in New York Sept. 3, 1798.

N. J. Hist. Soc. has Sept. 28–Oct. 12, 26, Nov. 16, 30, Dec. 14–28, 1793; Jan. 11, 18, Mar. 8, Apr. 12, 26, May 24, June 7, July 27, Aug. 15, 22, Sept. 5, Oct. 3–Nov. 7, Dec. 5, 19, 1794; Jan. 2, 23, Feb. 27, Mar. 13, 27, Apr. 10, 17, July 10, 1795; Feb. 24, 1798.

Am. Antiq. Soc. has Dec. 14, 28, 1793; Jan. 4–25, Feb. 8–Mar. 1, 15–29, Apr. 12–May 31, June 14–26, July 18–Sept. 19, Oct. 17, 1794; Mar. 24, 1798.

Senate House, Kingston, has Feb. 1, Mar. 8–Aug. 15, 29, 1794; July 31, Aug. 7, 1795; Sept. 30, 1796; Jan. 20–Feb. 24, Mar. 24, 31, May 6, 20, June 3–July 22, Aug. 5–Sept. 9, 23–Nov. 11, 25–Dec. 30, 1797; Jan. 6, Feb. 10, 17, Mar. 10, 17, Apr. 7–28, 1798.

N. Y. Pub. Lib. has Dec. 7, 1793; Feb. 15, 22, 1794; Aug. 7, 1795, suppl.; Dec. 2, 9, 1797; Feb. 24, 1798.

N. Y. Hist. Soc. has Dec. 28, 1793; Sept. 19, 1794; July 3, Sept. 18, 1795; May 27, 1796; Jan. 13, 1798.
N. Y. State Lib. has Nov. 30, 1793.
Univ. of Pittsburgh has Mar. 18, 1796.
Lib. Congress has Feb. 24, 1797.

[Kingston] **Ulster and Delaware Gazette,** 1798. See **Ulster County Gazette.**

[Kingston] **Ulster County Gazette,** 1798–1803.

Weekly. Established May 5, 1798, judging from the date of the earliest issue seen, that of May 12, 1798, vol. 1, no. 2, published by Samuel Freer and Son, with the title of "Ulster County Gazette." The next two issues located, those of June 30, 1798, no. 9, and Sept. 15, 1798, no. 20, were entitled "Ulster and Delaware Gazette" and were published by Samuel Freer. The issue of May 4, 1799, vol. 2, no. 53, was again called "Ulster County Gazette" and published by Samuel Freer and Son. The issue of May 10, 1800, vol. 2, no. 106, is the last located with this publisher. The next issue located is that of Dec. 19, 1801, published by Samuel S. Freer, with the title of "Ulster County Gazette," the same as three issues in 1803. The last issue located with this title is that of Apr. 30, 1803, vol. 3, no. 261. Between that date and August, 1803, the title was changed to "Ulster Gazette," which see.

The "Ulster County Gazette" has become famous because of the fact that the issue of Jan. 4, 1800, vol. 2, no. 88, containing the news of the death of Washington, has been reproduced so many times that hundreds of thousands of copies are now scattered over the country. R. W. G. Vail, in "The Ulster County Gazette and its Illegitimate Offspring" (N. Y. Public Library Bulletin, April, 1930, also reprint) described 64 varying reprints or facsimiles, and in the last few years several more variations have been discovered. Late in 1930 the Library of Congress acquired an original of the famous issue of Jan. 4, 1800, which caused Mr. Vail to bring out a Supplement entitled "The Ulster County Gazette Found at Last" (N. Y. Pub. Lib. Bulletin, April 1931, also reprint) and photographically reproducing all four pages of the newspaper. In 1938 the American Antiquarian Society acquired an original issue, and hence there are two now located. There are many variations in wording and printing to distinguish the original from the facsimiles. One is that the first line in the last column on the first page of the original reads — "Command the town; and notwithstanding," which does not appear in any known facsimile.

Senate House, Kingston, has May 12, Sept. 15, 1798; May 11, Oct. 12, 19, 26, Nov. 2, 1799; and presumably May 10, 1800, obtained in 1930 from the Rev. R. R. Hoes collection.
N. Y. State Lib. has June 30, 1798; Apr. 26, 1800 (2nd leaf); Apr. 16, 30, 1803.
N. Y. Hist. Soc. has May 4, 1799; Apr. 26, 1800; Dec. 19, 1801.
Lib. Congress has Dec. 28, 1799; Jan. 4 (original), 11, 1800.

Am. Antiq. Soc. has Jan. 4, 1800 (original); July 24, 1802; Feb. 5, 1803.
Harold D. VanDerlyn, Yonkers, has Dec. 28, 1799.
Daniel J. Kelly, Jr., South Bend, Ind., has May 8, July 31, 1802.
Harvard has Dec. 4, 1802.

[Kingston] **Ulster Gazette,** 1803–1820+.

Weekly. A continuation, without change of volume numbering, of the "Ulster County Gazette." The earliest issue located is that of Aug. 13, 1803, vol. 6, no. 276, published by Samuel S. Freer, with the title of "Ulster Gazette." At some time between 1815 and 1817, Samuel S. Freer admitted Anthony Freer to partnership, and the paper was published by S. S. & A. Freer. They were the publishers certainly to Oct. 16, 1819, but the issue of Sept. 25, 1820, was published by Samuel S. Freer alone. The paper was continued until after 1820.

Am. Antiq. Soc. has Aug. 13, 1803; Jan. 28, Mar. 10, 17, 1804; Apr. 13, 1805; Feb. 14, Oct. 10, Nov. 28, 1806; Aug. 28, Oct. 23, 1810; July 16, 1811; Sept. 12, 1815.
Troy Pub. Lib. has Feb. 25, Mar. 3, 31, 1804; Feb. 23, 1805; May 30, 1806; Nov. 2, 1807; Sept. 27, Oct. 4, 1808; Feb. 21, 1809; Sept. 10, 1811.
Lib. Congress has May 26, 1804; Oct. 15, 1811; Feb. 16, Dec. 28, 1813; Dec. 6, 1817; May 22, 1819.
N. Y. State Lib. has Feb. 4, Mar. 10, 1804; Feb. 13, 27, 1810; May 23, 1818; Feb. 6, 1819; Oct. 7, 1820.
Wis. Hist. Soc. has Aug. 18, Sept. 22, 1804.
N. Y. Hist. Soc. has Apr. 11, 1809; Oct. 16, 1819.
Univ. of Pittsburgh has Sept. 3, Dec. 17, 1811.
Harvard has Dec. 17, 1803.
Senate House, Kingston, has Aug. 4, 1804.
Univ. of Ill. has Dec. 22, 1804.
N. Y. Pub. Lib. has photo of Apr. 26, 1808.
Augustus H. VanBuren, Kingston, has Sept. 13, 1817.
No. Ind. Hist. Soc., South Bend, Ind., has Sept. 25, 1820.

[Kingston] **Ulster Plebeian,** 1815–1820+.

Weekly. A continuation, without change of volume numbering, of the "Plebeian." The first issue with the title of "Ulster Plebeian" was that of Aug. 1, 1815, vol. 12, no. 632, published by John Tappen. It was continued by Tappen until after 1820.

N. Y. Hist. Soc. has Aug. 1, 1815–July 18, 1818; Nov. 14, 1818; Jan. 30, Sept. 11, 1819; Aug. 5–Dec. 30, 1820.
Am. Antiq. Soc. has Aug. 22, Oct. 10–24, Nov. 7, Dec. 5, 12, 26, 1815; Jan. 2, 16, 30, Mar. 5, 12, Apr. 23, 1816; Nov. 22, 1817; Jan. 23, June 5, July 17, 31, Aug. 21, 1819; June 17, Sept. 9, Oct. 7, Nov. 25, 1820.

Senate House, Kingston, has Mar. 14, 1818; Nov. 11, 1820.
Lib. Congress has Feb. 20, 1816.

Lake George, see Caldwell.

[Lansingburgh] American Spy, 1791–1798.

Weekly. Established Apr. 8, 1791, by Silvester Tiffany, with the title of "American Spy." With the issue of Aug. 3, 1792, William W. Wands was admitted to partnership and the paper was published by Silvester Tiffany and William W. Wands. With the issue of Dec. 21, 1792, the partnership was dissolved, although this was disputed by Tiffany, and William W. Wands became sole publisher. In June, 1797, Wands declined continuing the business and the press was sold to Robert Moffitt & Co., who established "The Northern Budget," continuing the advertisements from the Spy. After a ten weeks interval, however, Charles R. Webster reestablished the "American Spy" and continued it up to the last issue located, that of Feb. 27, 1798, vol. 7, no. 351. The Spy was succeeded in September, 1798, by the "Lansingburgh Gazette."

Troy Pub. Lib. has Apr. 8, 1791–June 6, 1797.
Am. Antiq. Soc. has June 17, July 1, Aug. 26, Sept. 2, Nov. 4, 11, 1791; Jan. 27, June 15, 22, July 6, 20–Aug. 10, Sept. 28–Oct. 26, Nov. 9–23, 1792; Apr. 5, 26, Dec. 31, 1793; Jan. 7, 28, 1794; Feb. 17, Mar. 17, Nov. 10, 1795; Sept. 20, 1796; Feb. 21, Mar. 28, Apr. 11–25, May 16, Sept. 5, 19, 1797; Jan. 2, 1798.
Harvard has Mar. 30, 1792; Feb. 24, Mar. 10, May 5, 26, June 9, 30, July 21, 28, 1795; Jan. 5, Feb. 16, Mar. 1, 29, Apr. 12, May 3, 10, 24, June 21, 28, Aug. 9, Nov. 1–15, 1796; Jan. 10, 24, 31, Feb. 14, Mar. 14, 28, Apr. 11, 18, Nov. 14, 1797; Feb. 6–27, 1798.
N. Y. Pub. Lib. has June 11, 18, 1793; May 19, 1795; Oct. 11, 1796.
Lib. Congress has Dec. 31, 1793; Sept. 15, 1795; Nov. 14, 1797.
N. Y. State Lib. has Oct. 1, 8, 1793.
Buffalo Hist. Soc. has Dec. 2, 16, 1794.
Boston Pub. Lib. has June 15, 1792.
Univ. of Pittsburgh has Jan. 20, 1795.

[Lansingburgh] Farmer's Oracle, 1796–1797.

Weekly. Established Nov. 1, 1796, by Luther Pratt, & Co. [Luther Pratt and Daniel Curtiss, Jun.], with the title of "Farmer's Oracle, and Lansingburgh Weekly Gazette." The issue of Jan. 24, 1797, was probably the last issue, as on Jan. 31, 1797, the paper was removed to Troy, where it continued under the title of "Farmer's Oracle."

N. Y. Hist. Soc. has Nov. 1, 8, Dec. 13, 1796.
Harvard has Nov. 15, 22, 1796.

[Lansingburgh] **Farmers' Register**, 1803–1807.

Weekly. Established Jan. 25, 1803, by Francis Adancourt, with the title of "Farmers' Register." The last issue published at Lansingburgh was that of Nov. 10, 1807, vol. 5, no. 43, and with the next issue the paper was removed to Troy and continued under the same title.

> Harvard has Mar. 1, 15, 22, Apr. 5, 19, 26, May 10–June 21, July 12–Aug. 2, 16–30, Sept. 20–Oct. 11, 25, Nov. 1, 15, 22, Dec. 13, 20, 1803; Jan. 17, 24, Feb. 7–Mar. 6, 27, Apr. 17–May 1, 15–29, June 19, 26, July 17, 31–Aug. 14, 28–Sept. 18, Oct. 2–16, Nov. 6–20, Dec. 4–25, 1804; Jan. 1, 15–29, Feb. 12–Mar. 19, Apr. 9, 23–May 14, 28, June 11, 18, July 9, 16, Aug. 5–Sept. 23, Oct. 1–22, Nov. 5, 19–Dec. 31, 1805; Jan. 14–28, Feb. 11, 18, Apr. 8–22, May 6, 20, 27, June 17, July 8, 22–Aug. 5, 26–Sept. 23, Oct. 7, 28, Nov. 4, 18–Dec. 23, 1806; Jan. 13–Feb. 17, Mar. 13–Apr. 14, 28, May 5, June 16–July 7, 28, Aug. 18, Sept. 8–Oct. 20, Nov. 3, 10, 1807.
> Am. Antiq. Soc. has Nov. 15, 1803; Jan. 24, Mar. 20, July 24, 1804; Oct. 28, Dec. 2, 9, 30, 1806; Jan. 6, 13, June 16, 23, July 7, Aug. 11–25, Sept. 8, 22–Oct. 13, Nov. 10, 1807.
> Univ. of Ill. has June 26, 1804; Jan. 28, 1806; May 5, 1807.
> N. Y. Hist. Soc. has Feb. 8, 1803.
> N. Y. State Lib. has Mar. 24, 1807.

[Lansingburgh] **Federal Herald**, 1788–1790.

Weekly. Removed from Albany and established at Lansingburgh without change of title or volume numbering. The first Lansingburgh issue was that of Apr. 28, 1788, vol. 1, no. 11, published by Babcock & Hickok [John Babcock and Ezra Hickok], with the title of "The Federal Herald." It was continued by this firm until its suspension, with the issue of June 7, 1790, vol. 4, no. 1, total no. 121.

> Am. Antiq. Soc. has Apr. 28, May 5, 19–June 2, 16–30, July 21–Aug. 11, 25–Sept. 8, 22, Oct. 20, Nov. 3, 17, Dec. 29, 1788; Jan. 19, 26, Feb. 16–Mar. 30, Apr. 13–27, June 8, 22, July 6, Aug. 3–31, Sept. 7, 28, Oct. 5, 26–Nov. 16, Dec. 7, 21, 1789; Feb. 1, Mar. 22–Apr. 5, 19–May 24, June 7, 1790.
> Troy Pub. Lib. has May 5–Nov. 10, 1788; Jan. 12, 26, Feb. 2, 23, May 25, 1789–May 17, 1790.
> N. Y. Hist. Soc. has May 26, 1788.
> Univ. of Pittsburgh has May 11, 1789.

Lansingburgh Gazette, 1798–1820+.

Weekly. Established Sept. 18, 1798, by Gardiner Tracy, with the title of "Lansingburgh Gazette." It succeeded the "American Spy," continuing its advertisements, but adopting a new volume numbering. With the issue of Oct. 14,

NEW YORK 599

1806, Luther Bliss was admitted to partnership and the paper was published by Tracy & Bliss, and continued by them until after 1820.

Troy Pub. Lib. has Dec. 4, 1798–Dec. 27, 1814; Jan. 3–Dec. 26, 1815, fair; Mar. 11, May 27, July 8, Oct. 14, 21, 1817; Feb. 9, Apr. 20, July 13, Aug. 17, Sept. 28, Nov. 16, 1819; Jan. 11, Feb. 15, Mar. 14, 28, June 13, Aug. 8, Oct. 10, 31, Nov. 14, Dec. 5, 1820.
N. Y. State Lib. has Nov. 5, 1799; July 15, Nov. 25, Dec. 9, 1800; Feb. 10, 24–Mar. 10, 24, July 14, 1801; Mar. 24, 31, Apr. 21, May 12, 19, July 28, Aug. 4, 25, Sept. 15, Oct. 27–Nov. 9, 23, Dec. 7, 1802; Jan. 18–Feb. 8, Mar. 1–Apr. 26, Aug. 9, Oct. 18, 1803; Jan. 10, 17, 31, Feb. 21, 28, Mar. 27, June 26, July 10, 17, 1804; Jan. 5–Dec. 27, 1808; May 8, 1810; Mar. 5, May 7, 1811–Dec. 28, 1813; Jan. 25, Feb. 8, 22, Mar. 29, Apr. 5, 26–May 10, 24, June 28, July 5, Aug. 9, 23, Sept. 6, 13, Oct. 4, 18, 1814.
Mich. State Lib. has Feb. 21, 1809–Apr. 24, 1810.
N. Y. Hist. Soc. has Mar. 27, 1810; June 4, 1811; Jan. 5, 1813–Dec. 27, 1814.
Am. Antiq. Soc. has Jan. 15, Aug. 27, Sept. 3, Nov. 12, 1799; May 26, 1801; Jan. 13, 1802; Feb. 15, Apr. 5, Sept. 6, 1803; Feb. 26, 1805; Mar. 18, 1806; Sept. 8, Oct. 27, Nov. 17, 1807; Aug. 16, Dec. 20, 1808; Feb. 14, June 6, 1809; Aug. 7, 1810; Apr. 16, May 7, Nov. 5, 1811; Jan. 26, 1813; Dec. 27, 1814; Dec. 16, 1817; Aug. 10, 1819.
Lib. Congress has Apr. 5, May 10, 1803; Jan. 21, 1806; May 23, 1809; June 2, 9, 23, July 7, 21–Nov. 17, 1812; Nov. 23, 1819; Apr. 25, 1820.
Univ. of Ill. has Oct. 2, 16, 1804; Jan. 15, 29, Aug. 13, Sept. 17, 1805; Feb. 4, Mar. 4, 11, 25, Apr. 22, 1806.
Harvard has Sept. 18, 1798; Nov. 23, Dec. 21, 1802; Mar. 22, Aug. 2, 23, 1803; Apr. 10, May 15, 1804.
Rutgers Univ. has Jan. 11, Apr. 19, Aug. 23, Oct. 18, 1814.
Port Jervis Lib. has Apr. 2, 1799; July 6, Aug. 17, 1813.
N. Y. Pub. Lib. has Sept. 24, 1805; Oct. 22, 1816.
Univ. of Pittsburgh has Dec. 10, 17, 1811; Jan. 21, 1812.
Madison Co. Hist. Soc., Oneida, has Feb. 24, 1801.
Long Id. Hist. Soc. has May 1, 1804.
Dartmouth has Apr. 26, 1814.
Univ. of Mich. has July 26, 1814.
Va. Military Inst., Lexington, has Mar. 28, 1815.

[Lansingburgh] Northern Budget, 1797–1798.

Weekly. Established June 20, 1797, by Robert Moffitt & Co., with the title of "The Northern Budget." With the issue of July 11, 1797, the title was altered to "Northern Budget." The last issue published at Lansingburgh was that of May 8, 1798, vol. 1, no. 47, after which the paper was removed to Troy and continued under the same name.

Troy Pub. Lib. has June 27, 1797–May 8, 1798.

N. Y. Hist. Soc. has June 20, Aug. 1–Sept. 5, Oct. 3, 24–Nov. 21, Dec. 5–19, 1797; Jan. 2, 16–30, 1798.

Harvard has June 20, Aug. 8, 22, Sept. 12–Oct. 3, 24, 31, Nov. 14, 28, 1797; Feb. 6, 1798.

Am. Antiq. Soc. has June 27, July 4, Nov. 28, 1797.

[Lansingburgh] Northern Centinel, 1787–1788.

Weekly. Established May 21, 1787, by Claxton & Babcock [Thomas Claxton and John Babcock], with the title of "The Northern Centinel, and Lansingborough Advertiser." With the issue of Oct. 15, 1787, "Lansingborough" in the title was changed to "Lansingburgh," the printers having been led into error through "being strangers here when they first established their business." The last issue located is that of Jan. 15, 1788, vol. 1, no. 35, and the paper was discontinued before the end of January, and removed to Albany where it was established as "The Federal Herald" on Feb. 11, 1788.

Troy Pub. Lib. has May 21, 1787–Jan. 8, 1788.

Am. Antiq. Soc. has May 28 (facsim.), June 4, 11, July 9, 16, Aug. 6, 13, Sept. 10, 24–Oct. 22, Nov. 27, Dec. 11–25, 1787; Jan. 15, 1788.

N. Y. Pub. Lib. has July 9, 1787.

N. Y. State Lib. has Dec. 18, 1787.

Lansingburgh Recorder, 1794–1795.

Semi-weekly and weekly. A continuation, without change of volume numbering, of "Tiffany's Recorder." The first issue with the title of "Lansingburgh Recorder" was that of Dec. 9, 1794, vol. 3, no. 169, published semi-weekly by Gardner & Hill [George Gardner and James Hill], who had purchased the paper from Tiffany. In January, 1795, publication was changed to weekly, and in March, 1795, the title was changed to "The Recorder." In May, 1795, the paper was removed to Troy, where it was continued without change of volume numbering. The last Lansingburgh issue located is that of May 12, 1795, vol. 3, no. 194.

N. Y. Pub. Lib. has Dec. 9, 1794; Apr. 28, 1795.

Harvard has Mar. 10, 24, May 12, 1795.

Am. Antiq. Soc. has Dec. 26, 1794; Feb. 17, 1795.

[Lansingburgh] Tiffany's Recorder, 1793–1794.

Weekly. The earliest issue located, that of June 11, 1793, no. 92, published by Silvester Tiffany, with the title of "Tiffany's Recorder," seems to show that Tiffany established the paper in June, 1793, but continued the volume numbering of the "American Spy," from the conduct of which paper he had been dropped with the issue of Dec. 21, 1792, no. 90. The last issue located with the title of "Tiffany's Recorder" is that of Sept. 23, 1794, no. 158, and in December the title was changed to the "Lansingburgh Recorder," which see.

N. Y. Pub. Lib. has June 11, 1793.
Lib. Congress has July 9, Nov. 5, 1793; Feb. 18, 1794.
Am. Antiq. Soc. has Dec. 31, 1793; May 27, Aug. 19, Sept. 23, 1794.
N. Y. State Lib. has Aug. 12, 1794.
Wis. Hist. Soc. has Aug. 12, 1794.

Levana Gazette, see under **Scipio.**

[Malone] **Franklin Telegraph,** 1820+.

Weekly. Established Aug. 31, 1820, by Francis Burnap, with the title of "Franklin Telegraph."

Wead Lib., Malone, had Sept. 7–Dec. 28, 1820, but not now located.

[Manlius] **Derne Gazette,** 1806–1807.

Established at Manlius by Abraham Romeyn in July, 1806, at which time the effort was made to change the name of the village from Manlius to Derne. It was discontinued in a little over a year. (Munsell, "Typographical Miscellany," pp. 102, 105, and J. V. H. Clark, "Onondaga," vol. 2, p. 222). No copy located. E. Billings advertised in the "Albany Register" of Apr. 19, 1808, proposals for a newspaper at Derne to be entitled "The Western Republican," to commence in June, but it was presumably never established.

[Manlius] **Herald of the Times,** 1808–1809.

Weekly. Established in May, 1808, judging from the date of the earliest issue located, that of July 19, 1808, vol. 1, no. 9, published by Leonard Kellogg, with the title of "Herald of the Times." (J. V. H. Clark, in his "Onondaga," 1849, vol. 2, p. 222, states that it was established May 24, 1808). In 1809, by July 18, the title was changed to "Manlius Times," which see.

N. Y. State Lib. has July 19, 1808.
Univ. of Ill. has Sept. 13, 1808.
Am. Antiq. Soc. has Jan. 31, 1809.

[Manlius] **Onondaga Herald,** 1818–1819.

Weekly. Established Oct. 28, 1818, judging from the date of the only issue located, that of Feb. 24, 1819, vol. 1, no. 18, published by Daniel Clark, with the title of "The Onondaga Herald." J. V. H. Clark, in his "Onondaga," 1849, vol. 2, p. 223, states that it was established by Daniel Clark on Oct. 28, 1818, in continuation of the "Manlius Times."

W. W. Cheney, Manlius, has Feb. 24, 1819, deposited in Seneca Club, Manlius.

[Manlius] Spirit of the Press, 1816–1817.

The Utica "Columbian Gazette" of Jan. 7, 1817, states that "A republican paper, under this title, 'Spirit of the Press,' has been commenced at Manlius, by S. H. Moore." This may have been Southwick H. Moore, printer, who died at New York, Mar. 11, 1818, aged 23 (see "Auburn Gazette," Mar. 18, 1818).

Manlius Times, 1809–1818.

Weekly. A continuation, without change of volume numbering, of the "Herald of the Times." The earliest issue located with the new title is that of July 18, 1809, vol. 2, no. 61, published by Leonard Kellogg, with the title of "Manlius Times;" and judging from the editorial this was the initial issue. At some time between Mar. 8, 1814, and Dec. 13, 1815, Kellogg took James Beardslee into partnership, as on the latter date the firm of Kellogg and Beardslee was dissolved. The notice of dissolution appears in the issue of Jan. 24, 1816, which issue was published by Kellogg & Clark, since Daniel Clark had replaced Beardslee in the firm. Kellogg died May 22, 1817, recorded in the "Auburn Gazette" of May 28, 1817, as of the firm of Kellogg & Clark, publishers of the "Manlius Times." J. V. H. Clark, in his "Onondaga," 1849, vol. 2, p. 223, lists Seneca Hale among the publishers of this paper, and it is possible that he was connected with it in 1817. The list of New York newspapers of Jan. 1, 1818 (Munsell, "Typographical Miscellany," p. 132), gives Clark as the publisher, and the issue of Aug. 26, 1818, was published by D. Clark. The title in 1818 was "The Manlius Times." The last issue located is that of Sept. 23, 1818, vol. 11, no. 19. In Oct. 28, 1818, the paper was succeeded by "The Onondaga Herald."

> Am. Antiq. Soc. has Jan. 9, Apr. 3, May 15, June 19, July 17, 24, Sept. 18, 1810; Mar. 12, 19, June 25, July 30, Aug. 6, 1811; extra Jan. 31, 1818.
> N. Y. Pub. Lib. has July 18, 1809; Sept. 8, 1812; June 29, 1813; Mar. 8, 1814.
> W. W. Cheney, Manlius, has July 18, 1809; Jan. 23, 1816; Aug. 26, 1818.
> Charles E. Barrett, Syracuse, has June 22, Nov. 2, 1813.
> Univ. of Pittsburgh has Sept. 19, 1809.
> N. Y. State Lib. has Dec. 31, 1811.
> Harvard has Apr. 20, 1813.
> Onondaga Hist. Assoc., Syracuse, has May 25, 1813.
> E. E. Clemons, Manlius, has July 27, 1813.
> Buffalo Hist. Soc. has Jan. 4, 1814.
> Rutgers Univ. has Sept. 23, 1818.

New York

[Martinsburgh] Black River Gazette, 1807–1808.

Weekly. Established Mar. 10, 1807, by James B. Robbins, with the title of the "Black River Gazette" and continued a year (see F. B. Hough, "History of Lewis County," 1860, p. 284). No copy located.

[Mayville] Chautauque Eagle, 1819–1820.

Weekly. Established May 15, 1819, by R[obert] I. Curtis, with the title of "The Chautauque Eagle." With the issue of Aug. 10, 1819, the title was shortened to "Chautauque Eagle." The last issue located is that of Apr. 4, 1820, vol. 1, no. 47. Curtis also printed and edited the "Erie Reflector" of Erie, Penn., located about thirty miles from Mayville, which latter paper was discontinued in April, 1820.

Prendergast Lib., Jamestown, N. Y., has May 15, 1819–Apr. 4, 1820.
Am. Antiq. Soc. has July 17, Oct. 5, 1819.

[Montgomery] Independent Republican, 1813–1816.

Weekly. Established Jan. 26, 1813, by Luther Pratt, with the title of "Independent Republican." The last Montgomery issue located is that of Oct. 8, 1816, vol. 4, no. 30. On Oct. 21, 1816, an agreement was signed by which a group of proprietors residing in Goshen purchased the paper and transferred it to Goshen, where it was continued without change of title or volume numbering. The original agreement was in the possession of the late Frank Drake, of Goshen, N. Y. It is printed in the Goshen "Independent Republican" of Jan. 7, 1913, noting the fact that Joshua Conger was editor of the newspaper at Montgomery. For further issues see under Goshen.

Newburgh Lib. has Apr. 13, June 15–Oct. 5, 1813; Jan. 4–Feb. 22, 1814; Aug. 20, 1816.
Am. Antiq. Soc. has Jan. 26, 1813; Nov. 15, 1814; July 30, Aug. 13, 1816.
Mrs. Frank Drake, Goshen, has Oct. 31, 1813; Mar. 21, 1815; Oct. 8, 1816.

[Montgomery] Orange County Republican, 1806, see under Wardsbridge.

[Morrisville] Gazette, see [Morrisville] Madison County Gazette.

[Morrisville] Madison County Advertiser, see [Morrisville] Madison County Gazette.

[Morrisville] Madison County Gazette, 1817–1820+.

Weekly. Established in May, 1817, judging from the issue of Apr. 23, 1818, vol. 1, no. 47, published by John B. Johnson & Son, at Morris Flats, with the title of "Madison County Gazette." The issue of Aug. 18, 1819, vol. 3, no. 16, is entitled "Gazette, & Madison County Advertiser," published at Morrisville by John B. Johnson & Son. The issue of May 3, 1820, vol. 3, no. 153, is entitled "Madison County Advertiser," published by John B. Johnson & Son, the same as the issue of Jan. 24, 1821, vol. 4, no. 191. French, in the "Gazetteer of New York," 1860, p. 389, says that it was established at Peterboro in May, 1817, by John B. Johnson & Son, with the title of "The Gazette and Madison County Advertiser," removed to Morrisville in 1819, and discontinued in 1822. The list of newspapers of Jan. 1, 1818 (Munsell, "Typographical Miscellany," p. 132), records the "Madison Gazette" as published by John B. Johnson & Son at Hamilton.

N. Y. Pub. Lib. has Apr. 23, 1818.
Madison Co. Hist. Soc., Oneida, has Aug. 18, 1819.
Colgate Univ. has May 3, 1820; Jan. 24, 1821.

Moscow Advertiser, see [Moscow] Genesee Farmer.

[Moscow] Genesee Farmer, 1817-1820+.

Weekly. Established Feb. 6, 1817, judging from the earliest issue located, that of Mar. 27, 1817, vol. 1, no. 8, published by H[ezekiah] Ripley, with the title of "Genesee Farmer." The issue of Sept. 11, 1817, is the same. In a record of newspapers of Jan. 1, 1818 (Munsell, "Typographical Miscellany," p. 133), it is listed as the "Genesee Farmer." It is quoted, however, as the "Moscow Advertiser" in the Buffalo "Niagara Journal" of Dec. 14, 1819, and in the "Saratoga Sentinel" of Oct. 18, 1820 and Jan. 24, 1821. Follett, in his "Press of Western New York," p. 62, refers to it as the "Moscow Advertiser and Genesee Farmer" and says that it was conducted by Hezekiah Ripley from 1817 to after 1820. J. H. Smith, in his "History of Livingston County," p. 123, says that soon after the establishment of the paper, Franklin Cowdery "became associated with Mr. Ripley in its publication, at which time the paper was enlarged and its name changed to the 'Moscow Advertiser and Genesee Farmer.' Within the year Mr. Ripley again became its sole publisher, and changed its name to the 'Moscow Advertiser,' under which title he continued it till January 8, 1824." That Cowdery did publish a newspaper in Moscow is shown in a letter which Daniel Munger wrote Dec. 12, 1857 (clipping from the "Detroit Daily Advertiser," found in a scrapbook of Henry O'Reilley in the New York Historical Society), in which he says: "I will state, that while a lad, I served my time as a printer, with my brother-in-law, Franklin Cowdery, probably the best practical printer in the country at that time. When I first knew him in 1817 or 18, he published a paper at Moscow, Livingston County (then Genesee County)."

Am. Antiq. Soc. has Mar. 27, Sept. 11, 1817.

Mount Pleasant Courier, 1799.

Weekly. Established June 19, 1799, according to the only copy located, so dated and numbered vol. 1, no. 1, published by John Patterson, with the title of "The Mount Pleasant Courier."

Mrs. Robert T. Dennis heirs, Ossining, own June 19, 1799 (photostat in N. Y. Pub. Lib.).

[Mount Pleasant] Impartial Gazette, 1800.

Weekly. Established July 15, 1800, judging from the date of the only issue located, that of July 22, 1800, vol. 1, no. 2, published by Russel Canfield, with the title of "Impartial Gazette." Canfield printed at Mount Pleasant in 1800 and 1801.

Conn. Hist. Soc. has July 22, 1800.

Mount Pleasant Register, 1797–1800.

In the manuscript records of the Westchester County Medical Society, there is reference to a resolve of May 8, 1797, ordered to be printed in the Mount Pleasant Register (Otto Hufeland, in the "Quarterly Bulletin of the Westchester County Historical Society," vol. 14, p. 33). In the New York "Weekly Museum" of May 26, 1798, is a record of the marriage of William Durell, "now printer of the Mount Pleasant Register" to Miss Sarah Street on May 16, 1798. In the New York "Time Piece" of Aug. 6, 1798, is the following: "Last Tuesday at Mount Pleasant, (N. Y.) July 24. The editor of this paper was arrested in the name of the President, for re-printing a paragraph from the New Windsor Gazette, supposed to be a libel against the President." In the New York "American Citizen" of Apr. 21, 1800, is a reference to William Durell, "late Editor of the Mount Pleasant Register," who was convicted for having printed in his Register of June 19, 1798, a libellous communication. In the "American Citizen" of Apr. 18, 1800, is a news item that he was sentenced to four months' imprisonment on Apr. 3, 1800. In the Philadelphia "Aurora" of May 2, 1800, there is a further reference to William Durell and the libel case. Durell's fine and imprisonment were remitted by act of the President of the United States. See also references to Durell in "Am. Hist. Assoc. Report" for 1912, p. 121.

No. copy of this paper has been located.

[Mount Pleasant] Westchester Herald, 1818–1820+.

Weekly. Established Jan. 15, 1818, with the title of "Westchester Herald, and Farmers' Register," printed by J[———] A. Cameron, for S[tephen] Addington. According to the imprint, it was published in the town of Mount-Pleasant, but in the village of Sing-Sing. With the issue of Feb. 17, 1818, it was published by Stephen Addington and printed by S[tephen] Marshall. With the issue of Feb. 24, 1818, the title was shortened to "Westchester Herald." With the issue of Oct. 19, 1819, the paper was printed by S. Marshall for the Proprietor [Joshua Brooks]. With the issue of Dec. 28, 1819, it was printed and published by Stephen Marshall and was so continued until after 1820.

Am. Antiq. Soc. has Jan. 15, 1818–Dec. 26, 1820.
N. Y. Hist. Soc. has Jan. 28, 1818–Dec. 26, 1820.
Ossining Hist. Soc., Ossining, has Feb. 17, 1818; Mar. 30, 1819–Dec. 26. 1820, fair.
Lib. Congress has Mar. 31, 1818.
Univ. of Mich. (Clements) has Dec. 21, 1819.

New Hartford, see under **Whitestown Gazette,** 1793.

New-Windsor Gazette, 1797–1799.

Weekly. Established Nov. 14, 1797, judging from the date of the earliest issue located, that of Jan. 16, 1798, vol. 1, no. 10, published by Jacob Schultz & Abraham Lott, with the title of "The New-Windsor Gazette." In 1799 it was discontinued and removed to Newburgh, where it was re-established as "The Orange County Gazette."

Newburgh Free Lib. has Jan. 16, 1798.
Harvard has Aug. 28, 1798.

New-York Advertiser, 1817–1820+.

Semi-weekly. This was the semi-weekly edition of the "New-York Daily Advertiser." Its first issue was that of Mar. 26, 1817, published by John W. Walker for Theodore Dwight, with the title of "New-York Advertiser." In this initial issue it was stated that the paper was a union of "The Albany Advertiser" and the "New-York Courier," but in fact this statement concerned the publishers, Walker and Dwight, rather than the paper, for "The Albany Advertiser" in March, 1817, was absorbed by "The Albany Gazette." With the issue of Aug. 1, 1817, Dwight took Walker into partnership and the firm name became Dwight & Walker. With the issue of July 10, 1818, William B. Townsend was added to the firm, which became Dwight, Townsend & Walker. The paper was so continued until after 1820.

Am. Antiq. Soc. and N. Y. State Lib. have Mar. 26, 1817–Dec. 28, 1820.
Univ. of Chicago has Mar. 26, 1817–Dec. 28, 1820, fair.
Yale has Jan. 13, 1818–Dec. 7, 1820.
N. Y. Hist. Soc. has Mar. 26, Apr. 9, 1817; Mar. 24, May 22, 1818–Aug. 13, 1819; Nov. 30, 1820.

Lib. Congress has Aug. 14, 1818–May 21, June 22, 29, Aug. 3, 10–16, 24, 27, 1819; Jan. 28, Apr. 21, May 5, Sept. 15, Dec. 18, 1820.
Univ. of Rochester has Jan. 22, Feb. 5, 23, 1819.
Wis. Hist. Soc. has Dec. 4, 1818.

[New York] **American,** 1819–1820+.

Semi-weekly and daily. Established Mar. 3, 1819, as a semi-weekly, with the title of "The American." The names of the publishers were not given in the initial issue, which stated that "This Paper will be conducted by an association of young men." Charles King, for many years the editor, stated in his valedictory in the issue of Feb. 13, 1845, that the paper was "started by himself in company with two friends," and their names are given in "The Columbian" of Feb. 17, 1820, as Charles King, James A. Hamilton and Johnston Verplanck. With the issue of Mar. 6, 1819, J[onathan] Seymour was given as printer. After the issue of Mar. 1, 1820, vol. 1, no. 105, the paper was established as a daily, on Mar. 8, 1820, with a new volume numbering, under the title of "The American," printed by J[ohn] M. Elliott, for the Proprietor. The semi-weekly was continued, also with a new volume numbering, as a country edition, on Mar. 11, 1820, with the title of "The American," changed on Mar. 18, 1820 to "The American. (For the Country)." Both editions were continued until after 1820.

N. Y. Hist. Soc. has Mar. 3, 1819–Dec. 30, 1820; also Oct. 4, 7, 14, 21–Nov. 1, 1820, of country paper.
Lib. Congress has Mar. 3, 1819–Dec. 30, 1820.
Am. Antiq. Soc. has Mar. 3, 1819–Mar. 1, July 7, Sept. 6, 8, 30, Oct. 19, 30, 1820; also Mar. 11–May 3, 10, 13, 20, 24, June 3, 10, 17, 24, July 8–Sept. 30, Oct. 7, 25, Nov. 11–Dec. 30, 1820, of country paper.
N. Y. Pub. Lib., Hist. Soc. Penn., Skaneateles (N. Y.) Lib., Wis. Hist. Soc., and British Museum have Mar. 3, 1819–Mar. 1, 1820.
Yale has Mar. 8–Dec. 30, 1820; also May 17–Dec. 30, 1820, of country paper.
N. Y. State Lib. has May 1, 1819; Mar. 8–Dec. 30, 1820; also Aug. 5–Dec. 30, 1820, of country paper.
Dartmouth has Mar. 3–May 3, 15–July 31, Aug. 7–27, Nov. 3–13, 20–Dec. 18, 25, 1819; Jan. 1–Mar. 1, 1820.
Cayuga Co. Hist. Soc., Auburn, has Mar. 15–Dec. 30, 1820, of country paper.
Champaign, Ill., Pub. Lib. has Mar. 11–Nov. 11, 1820, of country paper.
Duke Univ. has Nov. 13–Dec. 30, 1820.
Univ. of Mich. (Clements) has Mar. 31, May 1, June 16, July 17, 1819; Oct. 5, 7, 1820; also Mar. 15, 1820, of country paper.

[New York] **American Chronicle,** 1762.

Weekly. Established Mar. 20, 1762, by Samuel Farley, with the title of "The American Chronicle." With the second issue, that of Mar. 29, the day of publication was changed from Saturday to Monday. On July 8, 1762, a fire nearly destroyed the printing-office, and after a five day delay, the paper was brought out again on July 17. The last issue located is that of July 22, 1762, vol. 1, no. 18.

Harvard has Mar. 20–July 22, 1762.
N. Y. Pub. Lib. has Apr. 5–June 14, 1762.
Md. Hist. Soc. has May 24, June 7, 1762.

[New York] American Citizen, 1800–1810.

Daily. Established Mar. 10, 1800, by D[avid] Denniston, with the title of "American Citizen and General Advertiser." It was virtually a continuation of the "Argus," although it bore a new title and a new volume numbering. With the issue of May 1, 1801, Denniston formed a partnership with James Cheetham, the firm name being D. Denniston and J. Cheetham. With the issue of Sept. 30, 1802, the title was shortened to "American Citizen." The partnership was dissolved and with the issue of Apr. 9, 1803, James Cheetham became sole publisher. Cheetham died Sept. 19, 1810, but his name remained in the imprint until Nov. 13, 1810, with which issue the paper was published by G[arret] C. Tunison for the Proprietor. It was discontinued with the issue of Nov. 19, 1810, vol. 10, no. 4206, to be succeeded by the "New-York Morning Post." From 1800 to 1810, the "Republican Watch-Tower" was issued as a semi-weekly edition of the "American Citizen."

N. Y. Hist. Soc. has Mar. 10, 1800–Nov. 19, 1810, about 95 per cent complete.
Lib. Congress has Mar. 11–Dec. 31, 1800, fair; Feb. 10, Mar. 13, 1801; Apr. 4, 1801–May 31, 1802; Nov. 23, 1803; Jan. 2–Dec. 7, 1804, fair; Jan. 1–Dec. 31, 1805, fair; Jan. 1, 1806–Nov. 19, 1810.
N. Y. Pub. Lib. has Dec. 2, 1800; Jan. 30–Apr. 30, Aug. 25, 1801; May 1, 1802–Apr. 30, 1803; Aug. 22, 1805; July 12, 1806; Jan. 3–Dec. 24, 1807; Sept. 1, 1808–Mar. 2, May 5, 13–15, 20, June 10–14, 1809.
Am. Antiq. Soc. has Oct. 15, 1800; May 9, Aug. 11–15, Sept. 22, Oct. 21, Nov. 3, 9–14, Dec. 18, 21, 1801; Oct. 1, 1802; Aug. 18, Nov. 17, 22, 1803–Dec. 31, 1804, fair; Jan. 9, 14, Feb. 12, Sept. 21, Oct. 22, Nov. 13, 1805; Jan. 4, 1806–Nov. 19, 1810, fair.
N. Y. State Lib. has May 23, 1800–Dec. 30, 1801, fair; Jan. 1–Nov. 19, 1802; May 1–Oct. 31, 1804; May 1, 1805–Dec. 31, 1807; Jan. 4, 1808–Apr. 3, 1809, fair; Nov. 3, 1809–May 3, 1810, fair; Sept. 20, 1810.
Yale has Apr. 22, 1801–Dec. 31, 1804; Jan. 10, Feb. 18, 1809.
Harvard has Apr. 11, 29, May 2, 8, 15, June 10, July 3, 9, 13, 15, 20, 27, Aug. 3, Sept. 12, 17, 1801; Jan. 15, 22, Feb. 6, May 26, June 15, July 8–10, Nov. 22, 1802; Jan. 4, June 27, Aug. 5, Oct. 7, 14, 17, 24, 29, Nov. 2, 1803; Feb. 16, Mar. 6, 20, 22, 1804; Sept. 16, Oct. 21, 23, 25, Nov. 18, 20, 22, Dec. 24, 1805; Dec. 2, 1806; Nov. 25, 1807; Oct. 4, 1808.

Long Id. Hist. Soc. has Apr. 1, July 17, 18, 1800; May 6, 1803; Jan. 27, 1807–Dec. 21, 1808; Oct. 2, 1809; Oct. 23, 1810.

N. Y. Soc. Lib. has June 24, 1809; Jan. 9, Mar. 3, 22, Apr. 10, May 12–Nov. 14, 1810.

Duke Univ. has Jan. 11–Feb. 6, fair, Feb. 25, Mar. 13, 27, Apr. 12, 29, 1802; Sept. 13, 14, Dec. 5, 6, 1804; Nov. 9–29, 1805, fair; May 1, 1806–Dec. 21, 1807, fair; Jan. 4, 1809–Aug. 16, 1810, fair.

Univ. of Mich. (Clements) has Apr. 26, June 6, Nov. 28, 1800; Jan. 13, 1802; Jan. 9, 10, 13, 17, Mar. 1, 3, 14, 16, 19, Apr. 17, May 21, June 6, Aug. 11–13, 18, 1804; Feb. 20, Apr. 1, 2, July 2–Dec. 23, 1806, fair; Apr. 6, 9, 17, 20–22, 29, July 1–Dec. 30, 1807, fair; Mar. 14, 1808; Aug. 22, 1810.

Ohio Arch. & Hist. Soc. has Oct. 20, 1809–Apr. 2, 1810.

Rutgers Univ. has Mar. 25, 1800; Apr. 15, 1808; Jan. 25, Oct. 20, Nov. 9, 11, 1809; Jan. 15, Mar. 12, 1810.

Several libraries have single or a few scattering issues.

[**New York**] **American Minerva**, 1793–1796.

Daily. Established Dec. 9, 1793, by George Bunce & Co. [Bunce and Noah Webster, Jun., who signed the proposals as editor], with the title of "The American Minerva, Patroness of Peace, Commerce, and the Liberal Arts." The original agreement for establishing the paper is in the N. Y. Public Library. The title was slightly changed, with the issue of Dec. 23, 1793, by omitting the initial "The"; with Mar. 19, 1794, by adding the words "And the New-York (Evening) Advertiser"; with Mar. 20, 1794, by being shortened to "American Minerva, and the New-York (Evening) Advertiser"; and with May 6, 1795, by being altered to "American Minerva; an Evening Advertiser." The last issue with this title was that of Apr. 30, 1796, vol. 3, no. 820, and with the issue of May 2, 1796, the partnership of George Bunce and Noah Webster was dissolved, and the title changed to "The Minerva," which see. A semi-weekly edition was also published under the title of "The Herald; a Gazette for the Country," which see.

N. Y. Hist. Soc. has Dec. 9, 1793–Apr. 30, 1796, lacking 54 issues.

N. Y. Pub. Lib. has Dec. 9, 1793–Mar. 18, Oct. 7, 1794; Apr. 23, 30, 1795; Jan. 2–Apr. 30, 1796, fair.

Am. Antiq. Soc. has Dec. 9, 1793–May 23, 1794; May 29–June 4, Sept. 25, 29, 30, Oct. 9, 18, Nov. 17–19, 28, Dec. 11, 1794; Jan. 31, Mar. 12, Apr. 1, 3, May 27, June 6, 9, 11, 18, 22, 27, July 1, 2, 7, 16, 20, 24, 25, Aug. 11, 28, 29, Sept. 21, 23, Oct. 2, 3, Nov. 18, Dec. 29, 31, 1795; Jan. 11, 23, 30, Feb. 6, 15, 17, 23, 25, 29, Mar. 2, 16, 23, Apr. 5, 8, 14–16, 19, 21, 23, 1796.

Boston Athenæum has Mar. 19, 1794–Apr. 30, 1796.

Mass. Hist. Soc. has Dec. 9, 1793–May 31, 1794; July 2, 1795.

Lib. Congress has Dec. 9–31, 1793; Jan. 6–Mar. 18, May 5, 6, 8, 17, Oct. 24, 27, Nov. 4, 1794; Apr. 6–30, 1796.

N. Y. Soc. Lib. has Mar. 19–Dec. 31, 1794; Feb. 12, 1795.
Yale has Mar. 19–May 31, 1794.
Phil. Lib. Co. has Jan. 1–Apr. 30, 1796.
Harvard has Dec. 14, 1793; Jan. 14, Feb. 1, May 17, 21, 1794; Mar. 11, 13, Apr. 11, May 5, June 29, Aug. 11, 24, Oct. 1, 1795; Jan. 13, Feb. 24, Mar. 12, 1796.
Duke Univ. has Dec. 12, 18, 1793; Jan. 29, Feb. 5, Mar. 26, May 3, 5, 9, 10, 1794.
Univ. of Mich. (Clements) has Apr. 6, 7, 9, 1796.
Hist. Soc. Penn. has Apr. 10, 1794; Mar. 4, 1796.
Rutgers Univ. has Feb. 10, 1794.
N. Y. State Lib. has Mar. 5, 1794.
Buffalo Hist. Soc. has June 3, 1794.

[New York] **American Patriot**, 1811–1812, see **Public Advertiser**, 1807–1813.

[New York] **American Price-Current**, 1786.

Weekly. Established May 1, 1786, judging from the date of the earliest issue located, that of June 26, 1786, vol. 1, no. 9, printed by F[rancis] Childs, for Aeneas Lamont, with the title of "The American Price-Current." The paper was advertised in "The Daily Advertiser," May 2, 1786, as published by Francis Childs, but the "Advertiser" of May 9 advertises it as published by Aeneas Lamont. It was evidently replaced in August, 1786, by "The New-York Price-Current," which see.

Lib. Congress has June 26, 1786.

[New York] **Argus**, 1795–1800.

Daily. Established May 11, 1795, by Thomas Greenleaf, with the title of "The Argus, & Greenleaf's New Daily Advertiser." Greenleaf at the same time was publishing "Greenleaf's New York Journal" as a semi-weekly, with the arrangement of the text and advertisements different from the "Argus." With the issue of May 16, 1795, the title was altered to "The Argus, or Greenleaf's New Daily Advertiser," and with Aug. 3, 1796, to "Argus. Greenleaf's New Daily Advertiser." Greenleaf died Sept. 14, 1798, and after a suspension from Sept. 16 to Nov. 4, inclusive, the paper was brought out Nov. 5, 1798, with Ann Greenleaf, his widow, as publisher. David Frothingham, who had been a publisher at Sag Harbor, in 1799 was Mrs. Greenleaf's foreman or manager, but on Nov. 21, 1799, was tried for libel and sentenced to four months imprisonment. The paper was discontinued with the issue of Mar. 8, 1800, no. 1455, when it was sold out to David Denniston, who established the "American Citizen" in its stead.

N. Y. Hist. Soc. has May 11, 1795–Dec. 31, 1798; Jan. 1–May 10, June 19, 1799–Mar. 8, 1800.

Lib. Congress has May 11–Nov. 21, 1795; Apr. 7, 1796–Mar. 7, 1800, fair.

N. Y. Pub. Lib. has May 11–Dec. 31, 1795; Apr. 5, 7, June 1, 1796–Feb. 28, 1797; Sept. 15, 1798.

N. Y. State Lib. has Nov. 25, Dec. 2, 1795–Dec. 29, 1796; Jan. 7, 12, 20, 21, 24, 25, Feb. 8, 10, 14, 15, 17–20, 22, Mar. 2–4, 9–21, 28–30, Apr. 3, 5, 6, 18, 29, May 31, June 1, 5, 6, July 28, Aug. 18, 22, Sept. 6, 15, 29, 1797; Jan. 24, 29–31, Feb. 2–7, 14, 22, 23, Mar. 20–23, 27, 29, Apr. 18, 19, 23, 24, 26–28, May 3, 5, 7, 18, 25, 31, June 2, 6, Aug. 14, Sept. 14, 1798.

Am. Antiq. Soc. has June 12, Aug. 4, 8, 13, 14, 18–21, Sept. 3, 17, 18, 26, Dec. 15, 1795; Feb. 23, Mar. 17, June 9, July 21, Sept. 24, 1796; Jan. 4, 23, Feb. 21, 22, Mar. 4, 6, 20, 27, 29, Apr. 7, 8, May 3–5, 8–15, 17–20, 23, 31, June 5, 6, July 13, 18, Oct. 17, 18, Nov. 16, 28, Dec. 9, 13, 19, 20, 28, 1797; Jan. 20, Feb. 5, Apr. 12, 30, May 8, Aug. 8, Nov. 5, 8, 14, 15, 20, 22, 28, 30, Dec. 3, 5, 14, 21, 28, 1798; Jan. 22, 28, 30, Feb. 4, 15, Mar. 6, Apr. 2, May 21, Nov. 1, 30, 1799.

N. J. Hist. Soc. has June 16–Dec. 19, 1795.

Princeton has Sept. 3, 1795–Dec. 31, 1796.

Hist. Soc. Penn. has July 29, 1795; Jan. 1–Dec. 31, 1796.

Phil. Lib. Co. has Jan. 2, 1797–Sept. 8, 1798; Nov. 5, 1798–Jan. 5, 1799, fair.

Wis. Hist. Soc. has Aug. 31, 1799–Mar. 8, 1800.

Univ. of Mich. (Clements) has May 19, June 12–Nov. 14, 1795, fair; July 27, 1796; June 29, Dec. 29, 1797; Mar. 18, Apr. 30, Sept. 12, Nov. 7, 8, 1799.

Harvard has Aug. 4, 1796; Jan. 25, 1797; Dec. 3–22, 1798; Apr. 6, 1799.

Univ. of Rochester has Jan. 27, 1796.

New-York Aurora, 1807–1809.

Tri-weekly. This paper was the tri-weekly edition of "The Public Advertiser" and was established presumably in January, 1807. The earliest issue located is that of May 26, 1807, published without any title on the front page, imprint or volume numbering, but with the words "New-York Aurora" at the top of the first column on the first and third pages. It continued the same as far as Apr. 6, 1808. The next issue located, that of Apr. 19, 1808, bore a front-page title "The New York Aurora," but without volume numbering, and was stated to be published by Frank, White & Co. [Jacob Frank and George White]. The next issue located, that of June 24, 1808, reverts to the former column title. It was so published until June, 1809, when it was succeeded, as the country edition of "The Public Advertiser," by "The New York Journal," which see.

Harvard has June 2, 6, 13–20, 27, 30, July 17–24, Aug. 5, Sept. 4–18, 25, 30, Oct. 7, 9, 16, 21–Nov. 4, 11, 18, 24, 1807; Feb. 26, Apr. 6, June 24, 27, July 15, 21–Aug. 10, 20–31, Sept. 7, 9, 14, 21, 23, Oct. 3, 22, 26, Nov. 2–7, 16, 18, 25, 30, Dec. 7, 14, 17–21, 29, 31, 1808; June 2, 1809.

Am. Antiq. Soc. has May 26, 1807; Apr. 19, July 18, 22, 1808; Mar. 17, 20, 31, Apr. 3, 5, May 3, 26–June 7, 1809.

[New York] Booksellers' Advertiser, 1813.

Monthly. Established May, 1813, with the title of "The Booksellers' Advertiser, and Spirit of the Literary World," printed by C[harles] Wiley. The paper stated that it would be devoted exclusively to advertisements and that 3000 copies would be distributed, gratis, throughout the United States. This first issue was filled almost entirely with advertisements of books published by Isaac Riley.

Am. Antiq. Soc. has May, 1813.

[New York] Booksellers' Reporter, 1815.

Monthly. The only issue located is that for October, 1815, published by I[saac] Riley, with the title of "Booksellers' Reporter & Literary Advertiser." This issue is without volume numbering, but bears no evidence of having been preceded by any other issue. Although "for the benefit of the trade generally," it contained chiefly advertisements of books published and for sale by I. Riley.

Am. Antiq. Soc. has October, 1815.

[New York] Bowery Republican, 1806.

Proposals for publishing the "Bowery Republican," signed by J[ohn] Swaine, were printed in the "American Citizen" of Aug. 27, 1806, stating that the paper was to be a weekly and would be issued on Aug. 29. It evidently was published, as the opening "Address" to subscribers was reprinted in the "American Citizen" of Sept. 1, 1806. It is also referred to in the New York "Morning Chronicle" of Sept. 1, 1806. No copy of the paper, however, has been located. In the "Republican Watch-Tower" of Sept. 9, 1806, is a statement by the editor of the Bowery Republican regarding the carriers of his paper. An advertisement, dated Nov. 24, appeared in the "American Citizen" of Nov. 24, 1806, stating that, the first quarter having expired, the paper would be issued as a semi-weekly under the title of "Independent Republican," so to begin on Nov. 25, 1806. See under "Independent Republican."

[New York] Bulletin, 1793.

"Le Bulletin" is the title of a French newspaper evidently printed by Louis Jones at New York in 1793, but no copies have been located. Cabon, in his "Un Siècle et Demi de Journalisme en Haïti" (printed in Am. Antiq. Soc. Proc. Apr. 1939, vol. 49, p. 149), in mentioning certain French newspapers in the United States and the conduct of Genet, the French ambassador, says: "Genest de son côté crut bon de se défendre et eut son journal, le Bulletin, imprimé chez Jones à New York." No newspaper is known with the title of "le Bulletin" printed by Jones at New York. Louis Jones printed at New York in 1793 and his name appears as a printer in the New York Directory of 1795. The "Journal des Révolutions" of Sept. 16, 1793, published at New York by Tanguy de la Boissière, cautions the public not "to be deceived by a certain Bulletin which is published here without signature. The society which fabricates it seems to be devoted to falsehood and calumny; nor are we at a loss to find out the writer of these anonymous slanders, for he may be seen at the hotel of the Plenipotentiary Genet." In September, 1793, Genet resided in New York. The article, continuing, refers specifically to the Bulletin of Sept. 6. The New York "Diary" of Sept. 7, 1793, quotes a long article from the "Bulletin" of Sept. 6, 1793, no. 2, following this on Sept. 9 by an English translation.

New-York Chronicle, 1769–1770.

Weekly and semi-weekly. Established May 8, 1769, by Alexander and James Robertson, with the title of "The New-York Chronicle." The paper was of quarto size, eight pages to the issue, and with pagination. With the issue of Nov. 20, 1769, the size was reduced to four pages and with Nov. 23, 1769, it was changed to a semi-weekly. The last issue located is that of Jan. 4, 1770, vol. 1, no. 40. James Parker, in a letter to Benjamin Franklin, dated Feb. 2, 1770, makes a few uncomplimentary references to the editors of the Chronicle, and says "the Paper is now drop'd" (Mass. Hist. Soc. Proc. ser. 2, vol. 16, p. 221).

N. Y. Hist. Soc. has May 8, 1769–Jan. 4, 1770.
N. Y. Soc. Lib. has May 8–Dec. 25, 1769.
Mass. Hist. Soc. has May 8, 29–June 8, 22–Oct. 26, Dec. 25, 1769.
Wis. Hist. Soc. has May 15–Nov. 27, 1769.
N. J. Hist. Soc. has June 15–July 6, Aug. 10, 17, 31, Sept. 21, 1769.
Monmouth Co. Hist. Assoc., Freehold, N. J., has Oct. 5–Dec. 25, 1769.
Rutgers Univ. has May 15, 1769.
N. Y. Pub. Lib. has Aug. 17, 1769.
N. Y. State Lib. has Oct. 12, 1769.

[New York] Chronicle Express, 1802–1804.

Semi-weekly. Established Nov. 25, 1802, with the title of "Chronicle Express," printed for the Proprietor [Peter Irving], by William A. Davis, as the semi-weekly edition of the "Morning Chronicle." With the issue of Jan. 20, 1803, the name of the printer was omitted from the imprint. The last issue located is that of May 21, 1804, no. 156.

N. Y. Hist. Soc. has Nov. 25, 1802–May 7, 1804.
Am. Antiq. Soc. has Nov. 25, 1802–Dec. 29, 1803; Jan. 2, 9, 12, 19, 26–Mar. 1, 8–Apr. 19, 26–May 17, 1804.
Lib. Congress has Nov. 25, 1802–Apr. 30, 1804, fair.
N. Y. Pub. Lib. has Nov. 25, 1802–Jan. 2, 1804.

Harvard has Nov. 25–Dec. 2, 9–30, 1802; Jan. 3–20, 27, 31, Feb. 10–Mar. 10, 17, 28, Apr. 4, 11–18, May 2–23, 30, June 13, 16, 30, July 7, 16–25, Aug. 1–8, 18, 25–Sept. 5, 12–19, 26–Oct. 10, 17–Nov. 7, 14, 17, 24, Dec. 1, 15, 26, 29, 1803; Jan. 2, 12, 19, Feb. 6, 23, Mar. 12, 19, Apr. 19, 30, May 7, 1804.

Trinity Coll., Hartford, has May 19, 1803–May 21, 1804, fair.

Univ. of Mich. (Clements) has Mar. 7, 14–24, 31, Apr. 4, 11–25, May 2, 5, 12–June 9, 16–23, 30–Aug. 4, 11–Sept. 19, 26–Oct. 3, 27–Nov. 14, 28, 1803; Feb. 2–20, Mar. 1, 12, Apr. 2, 12, 19, 1804.

Yale has Mar. 7, May 16, 19, 26, 30, June 9, 23, 30, July 2, 16, 21, Aug. 11, Oct. 27–Nov. 3, 1803; Feb. 16, Mar. 1, 1804.

Long Id. Hist. Soc. has Apr. 14, 1803.

N. Y. State Lib. has Aug. 4, 1803; Mar. 8, 1804.

Mass. Hist. Soc. has Dec. 1, 1803.

[**New York**] **Columbian**, 1809–1820+.

Daily and semi-weekly. Established Nov. 1, 1809, as a daily, by Charles Holt, with the title of "The Columbian." With the issue of July 10, 1815, Baptis Irvine was admitted to partnership, and the paper was printed by Holt & Irvine (N. Y. Hist. Soc. has manuscript agreement of July 1, 1815). With the issue of Aug. 7, 1816, the partnership was dissolved and it was published by B. Irvine. With the issue of Apr. 19, 1817, the title was changed to "The New-York Columbian." With the issue of Sept. 20, 1817, Irvine sold out to Alden Spooner, who, under the name of A. Spooner, continued the paper until after 1820.

A semi-weekly edition was issued for country subscribers, with the title of "The Columbian. (For the Country)," the first issue being that of Dec. 16, 1809, published by Charles Holt. With the issue of July 12, 1815, Holt & Irvine became publishers; with Aug. 14, 1816, B. Irvine was publisher; in April 1817, the title was changed to "The New-York Columbian"; in September, 1817, the paper was transferred to A. Spooner; and with Jan. 1, 1819, the title was changed to "The Columbian, for the Country," and was so continued until after 1820.

N. Y. Hist. Soc. has Nov. 1, 1809–Dec. 30, 1820 of the daily, with only forty issues missing; also Jan. 15, 1810–Dec. 29, 1813; Nov. 19, 1814; Jan. 4, 1815–Oct. 9, 1816; Apr. 23, May 17–28, 1817; Mar. 13, 27, June 16, 23, July 14, 21, 28, Aug. 11, 14, 21, Sept. 4, 1818, of the semi-weekly.

Lib. Congress has Nov. 2, 1809–Oct. 29, 1813; Jan. 7–11, 29–Nov. 9, Dec. 15, 22, 1814; Oct. 4, 25, Dec. 13, 15, 19, 27, 28, 30, 1815; Jan. 2–6, Mar. 6–May 7, 1816; Jan. 2–Sept. 29, 1817; Jan. 2, 1818–Dec. 30, 1820, of the daily; also Apr. 25, 1810; Jan. 4, 1812–Jan. 2, 1813, fair; June 1, Aug. 10, 1814; Dec. 13, 1815; Aug. 14, Dec. 7, 11, 21, 25, 1816; Jan. 8–15, Feb. 5, 26–Mar. 5, 12, 22, 29, Apr. 5, Nov. 14, 1817; May 29, 1818–June 4, July 9, 1819; July 28, 1820, of the semi-weekly.

Yale has Jan. 2, 1810–June 29, 1816; Oct. 17, 1817; Aug. 3, Nov. 8, 1818, of the daily; also Dec. 15, 1810–Dec. 30, 1812, of the semi-weekly.

NEW YORK 615

Am. Antiq. Soc. has Nov. 1–30, Dec. 11, 18, 1809; Mar. 1–Oct. 27, Nov. 1, 17, Dec. 31, 1810; Jan. 2–Nov. 1, 1811, fair; Jan. 21, Feb. 4, 12, 13, 17, Mar. 3, 7, 20–26, Apr. 11, May 5–8, June 1–Dec. 31, 1812; Jan. 2–Dec. 31, 1813; Apr. 26, Dec. 23, 1814; Jan. 23, Mar. 18, Apr. 4, 21, May 27, Aug. 22, Nov. 7, 16, 1815; Jan. 9, Feb. 28, May 15, July 2–Dec. 31, 1816; Sept. 17, 1817; Apr. 23–Dec. 30, 1818, fair; Jan. 2, 1819–Dec. 30, 1820, of the daily; also Dec. 20–30, 1809; Jan. 3, 17–24, 31–Feb. 10, 17, 21, 28, Mar. 3, 10, 17, 21, Apr. 4, 7, 14–25, May 2, 5, July 18, Dec. 5, 15, 1810; Jan. 16, Feb. 23–Mar. 27, May 4, June 5, 12, 26, 29, Aug. 7, Nov. 9, Dec. 28, 1811; Jan. 1–Dec. 30, 1812; Jan. 2, Apr. 24, Oct. 23, Dec. 18, 1813; Jan. 8, May 7, 11, 21, 25, June 1–Oct. 29, Nov. 5–12, 23, 30–Dec. 31, 1814; Nov. 25, 1815; Mar. 16, 30, May 29, June 5, July 3, 6, 13–Sept. 7, 27, Oct. 19, Nov. 6, 16, 27, Dec. 7, 25, 1816; Mar. 12, Apr. 5, May 14, Nov. 14, 18, 25–Dec. 9, 19–30, 1817; Aug. 7, Nov. 24, 1818; Feb. 9, 16–26, Mar. 12, 16, 23, Apr. 6, 9, 20, 27, 30, May 4, 11–18, July 2, 13, 20, 30, Aug. 17, Sept. 17, Oct. 1, 5, 19, 22, 1819; Feb. 18–29, Mar. 10, 31, Apr. 4, May 2, 23–30, July 4, 1820, of the semi-weekly.
N. Y. State Lib. has Nov. 1, 1809–Dec. 31, 1811; Jan. 2–Aug. 21, 29, Sept. 9, 10, 22, 29, Oct. 2, 5, 7, 13, 20–24, 28, Nov. 13, 21–24, 28, 30, Dec. 11, 19, 1812; Jan. 5–Dec. 31, 1813; Apr. 2, 1814; Sept. 13, 14, 27, 29, Oct. 2–4, 9, 10, 17, 24, 28, Nov. 1, 2, 7, 9, 15, 1815; Jan. 27, Apr. 18, June 25, 1816, of the daily; also Aug. 25, 1810; June 11, 1814; Jan. 17, Mar. 15, 1816; Jan. 12, Feb. 5, 9, 1819, of the semi-weekly.
Long Id. Hist. Soc. has Dec. 16, 1809–Dec. 28, 1811; Feb. 1–Aug. 1, 1812; July 2, 1814–Sept. 18, 1818, scattering issues; also Jan. 1, 1819–Dec. 30, 1820, of the semi-weekly.
Wis. Hist. Soc. has Nov. 1, 1809–Apr. 30, 1810, of the daily; also Mar. 8, 12, 22, Apr. 6, 19, May 3, 10, 28, June 11, 1817; Jan. 12, Mar. 2, Apr. 6, 20–27, Aug. 13, 1819; Mar. 10, Apr. 4, 28, 1820, of the semi-weekly.
Newberry Lib. has Nov. 1, 1809–Apr. 30, 1810, daily.
Rochester Pub. Lib. has Sept. 1, 1810–Aug. 28, 1811.
N. Y. Pub. Lib. has Nov. 1, 1810–May 31, June 12, 1811, daily; also June 24, 1812, semi-weekly.
East Hampton Free Lib. has Sept. 2, 1811–Apr. 30, 1812.
Trinity Coll., Hartford, has Apr. 25, 1812–June 28, 1815, fair, semi-weekly.
Hist. Soc. Penn. has Apr. 16, 1814–Dec. 28, 1816, daily.
Many libraries have single or a few scattering issues.

[New York] Columbian Gazette, 1799.

Weekly. Established Apr. 6, 1799, with the title of "Columbian Gazette," printed for J. M. Williams by Hurtin & M'Farlane [Robert M. Hurtin and Monteith M'Farlane]. Williams was an Englishman who wrote under the pseudonym of "Anthony Pasquin," and signed his editorial announcement as

John Mason Williams. The paper was discontinued with the issue of June 22, 1799, vol. 1, no. 12.

> Boston Athenæum has Apr. 6–June 22, 1799.
> Lib. Congress has May 25, June 8, 1799.
> Am. Antiq. Soc. has May 4, 1799.

[New York] Columbian Gazetteer, 1793–1794.

Semi-weekly. Established Aug. 22, 1793, by John Buel, & Co., with the title of "Columbian Gazetteer." With the issue of Aug. 21 (misdated Aug. 23), 1794, the title was changed to "The Columbian Gazetteer," but with Sept. 4, 1794, reverted to "Columbian Gazetteer." It was discontinued with the issue of Nov. 13, 1794, vol. 2, no. 130, having been purchased by Levi Wayland, who established "The New-York Evening Post" in its stead.

> N. Y. Hist. Soc. has Aug. 22–Dec. 30, 1793; Jan. 2–May 8, 15, 22–June 2, 9, 12, 19, 23, 30–July 7, 14–24, 31–Aug. 7, 14–Nov. 3, 10, 13, 1794.
> Mass. Hist. Soc. has Aug. 22–Sept. 19, 26–Dec. 30, 1793; Jan. 2–Mar. 6, Apr. 21–May 8, 18, 22–June 2, 9, 12, 19, 23, 30–July 7, 14, 21, 24, 31–Aug. 7, 14–Oct. 27, Nov. 3, 10, 13, 1794.
> Yale has Aug. 26–Dec. 30, 1793; Jan. 2–23, Feb. 6, 10, 17, 20, 27–Mar. 6, 13–24, Apr. 3–10, 24–May 15, 22–June 2, 9, 12, 19, 23, 30, July 7, 21–Aug. 7, 18, Sept. 1, 8–25, Oct. 23, 1794.
> Am. Antiq. Soc. has Oct. 24, Nov. 15, 25, Dec. 12, 23–30, 1793; Jan. 6–16, 23–30, Feb. 6, 17–27, Mar. 6, 10, 24, 31–Apr. 7, 14–24, May 5–19, 29, June 5, 26, July 10, 14, 21–28, Aug. 7, 25, Sept. 4–Nov. 13, 1794.
> Harvard has Aug. 29, Sept. 9–19, 26–Nov. 18, 25–Dec. 16, 1793; Jan. 6, 13–23, 30, Feb. 13, Mar. 3, 17, 27, Apr. 3, 14, 17, June 12, 1794.
> Lib. Congress has Sept. 8, 18, 22, Nov. 13, 1794.
> Boston Pub. Lib. has Dec. 23, 1793; Apr. 21, 1794.
> Amer. Philos. Soc. has Dec. 26, 1793; Sept. 22, 1794.
> Univ. of Mich. (Clements) has Aug. 7, 1794.

[New York] Columbian Herald, 1807–1808.

Weekly. Established Nov. 7, 1807, judging from the earliest issue located, that of Jan. 2, 1808, vol. 1, no. 9, published by J[ohn] Griswold, Jun., with the title of "The Columbian Herald, and American Repository." It was of large quarto size, eight numbered pages to the issue, and although a magazine in appearance, contained current news. The last issue located is that of Feb. 27, 1808, vol. 1, no. 17.

> Am. Antiq. Soc. has Jan. 2, 9, 16, Feb. 27, 1808.
> N. Y. Hist. Soc. has Jan. 30, 1808.

[New York] **Commercial Advertiser,** 1797–1820+.

Daily. Established Oct. 2, 1797, with the title of "Commercial Advertiser," by Geo. F. Hopkins, whose name alone appeared in the imprint, although Noah Webster, Jun., was associated in the management. The paper succeeded "The Minerva" and continued its advertisements. With the issue of July 1, 1799, the partnership between Webster and Hopkins was dissolved, the latter withdrew, and Webster admitted his nephew, Ebenezer Belden, to partnership, the firm name being E. Belden & Co. With the issue of Nov. 4, 1803, Webster retired and the paper was printed, for the Proprietor [Zachariah Lewis], by J[oseph] Mills. With the issue of Jan. 12, 1804, the title was altered to "New-York Commercial Advertiser." With the issue of Feb. 25, 1805, the imprint became "Printed, by J. Mills, for Z. Lewis." The title reverted to "Commercial Advertiser" with the issue of Oct. 2, 1809. From May 10, to May 14, 1811, there was no imprint, and with the issue of May 15, 1811, the paper was published by Z. Lewis. With the issue of Jan. 13, 1813, Lewis admitted Francis Hall to partnership, the firm name being Lewis & Hall. With the issue of Apr. 11, 1820, Lewis retired and the paper was conducted by William L. Stone and Francis Hall under the firm name of Francis Hall & Co. It was so continued until after 1820. A semi-weekly edition was also published, for which see under "The Spectator."

N. Y. Hist. Soc. has Oct. 2, 1797–Dec. 30, 1820, with only a few issues missing.

N. Y. Soc. Lib. has Jan. 2, 1800–Dec. 30, 1820.

N. Y. Pub. Lib. has Oct. 1, 1798–Apr. 30, 1801; Feb. 24, 1808–Dec. 31, 1814; Jan. 23, Mar. 18, 1816–Dec. 30, 1820.

Lib. Congress has Oct. 2, 1797–Dec. 31, 1798; Jan. 1, 1799–Dec. 31, 1800, fair; Feb. 14, 17, Apr. 11, May 8, Aug. 7, Sept. 7, Nov. 10, 1801; Mar. 26, Apr. 19, 21, Oct. 18, 1802; June 4, July 23, Nov. 7, 1803; Oct. 25, 31, 1805; July 28, 1806; Jan. 6, Apr. 21, July 4, 17, 22, 24, Aug. 7, 8, 29, Sept. 2, Dec. 10, 1807; Jan. 27, Feb. 9, 1808–Dec. 31, 1810; Mar. 21, 1811–Oct. 31, 1812; Aug. 28, Nov. 10, Dec. 1, 1813; May 17, Oct. 28, Nov. 15, Dec. 6, 7, 23, 1814; Dec. 29, 1815; Jan. 3–Mar. 16, Aug. 8, 9, Sept. 26, Dec. 31, 1816; Jan. 2, July 26, Nov. 4–8, 21, 26, Dec. 1, 2, 8–19, 22, 23, 26–31, 1817; Jan. 9–Feb. 27, Apr. 21, July 3, 1818–Dec. 31, 1819; Jan. 5–12, Feb. 29, May 27–Dec. 30, 1820.

Boston Athenæum has Oct. 2, 1797–Dec. 31, 1803.

Harvard has Nov. 2, 9–13, 16, 23, 1797; Jan. 1, 2, 6, 11, Dec. 6, 8, 10–12, 14, 18, 19, 21, 22, 24, 1798; Feb. 6, Mar. 15, 17, 26, 29, June 2, 3, 5, 9, 12, Aug. 23, 25, Sept. 9, 10, 1800; June 12, Aug. 12, Dec. 5, 1801; Feb. 23, May 11, 24, June 3, July 1, 8, 9, Aug. 13–16, 18, 19, 21–25, Nov. 24, 27, 1802; Feb. 25, June 28, 29, July 16, 1803; June 15, 1805–Dec. 5, 1807, fair; Sept. 9, Oct. 17, 1808.

Am. Antiq. Soc. has Dec. 15, 1797; Feb. 20, Mar. 6–14, 23, May 3, Aug. 7, 8, Sept. 15, 20, 28, Oct. 4, 9, 11, 16, 18, 20, 30, Dec. 15, 20, 21, 1798; Jan. 8,

10, 22, 29, Feb. 11, 12, 21, 28, Mar. 1, 2, 4, 19, 21, 26, 27, Apr. 18, 29, June 8, July 5, 29, Sept. 2, 9, 26, Nov. 6, Dec. 27, 31, 1799; Jan. 6, Mar. 1, Apr. 9, 23, May 13, 16, June 5, 20, Aug. 9, 29, Oct. 10, 28, 30, Nov. 1, 11, 1800; Feb. 11, Mar. 2, July 1, 2, 13, 25, 28, 30, Aug. 11, 25, Dec. 1, 1801; Jan. 19, Nov. 20, 1802; Feb. 26, Oct. 27, 1803; June 2, Aug. 21, 29, Sept. 19, 25, Oct. 31, Nov. 6, 14, 16, Dec. 10, 1804; Mar. 8, 1805; Jan. 11, Feb. 21, 22, June 23, Aug. 19, Sept. 11, 1806; Jan. 31, June 24, July 24, Aug. 7, 1807; June 23, 1808; Sept. 22, 1809; May 24–June 11, 29, 30, July 3–19, Aug. 23, Dec. 11, 1810; Feb. 9, June 29, July 13, 16, 19, 26, Aug. 8, Oct. 24–Dec. 31, 1811; Apr. 14, 25, Aug. 11, 13, 29, 1812; May 4, 1813; Apr. 14, Sept. 20, Dec. 23, 1814; Jan. 13, 14, 19, Feb. 21–Dec. 30, 1815, fair; Jan. 2–Feb. 24, Apr. 23, Sept. 5, Dec. 17, 23, 1816; Jan. 3, 4, Mar. 1, Aug. 7, Oct. 23, Nov. 4, 1817; Feb. 28, May 26, 27, 30, June 30, July 21, Dec. 15, 1818; Feb. 18, 19, Apr. 5–7, May 25, July 3, 31, Aug. 10, Oct. 23, 1819; Jan. 19, May 9, 12, July 14, 15, 18, 1820.

Phil. Lib. Co. has Oct. 2, 1797–Dec. 31, 1798.

Univ. of Chicago has Jan. 3–June 28, 1799, fair.

Yale has Jan. 2–Feb. 28, 1804; May 3, Oct. 2, Nov. 2–Dec. 25, 1809; Mar. 31–May 4, 1810; Dec. 1, 7, 8, 1814; Feb. 10, 1815.

Duke Univ. has Feb. 3, Mar. 17, 1800; June 10, July 11, Dec. 20, 1808; Feb. 27, Mar. 8, Apr. 13, 1809–May 23, Aug. 21, 1810.

Univ. of Mich. (Clements) has Oct. 4, 5, 17, 1797; Jan. 1–June 29, July 5, 23, Oct. 24, Nov. 28, 1798; Dec. 13, 1799; June 4, Aug. 23, Sept. 11, 15, 1800; Nov. 7, Dec. 13, 1811; Oct. 14, 1820.

N. Y. State Lib. has July 16, 1803; Apr. 13, 1805; Jan. 28, July 23, 1806; July 7, Dec. 16, 30, 1809; Jan. 11, Apr. 12, 17, 18, 20, 24, 26–30, May 3, 1810; Apr. 13, 1811; Jan. 30, Apr. 28, July 7, 28, Aug. 4, 7, 10, 12, Nov. 19, Dec. 31, 1812; Apr. 27, May 6, June 18, Nov. 12, 1813; Jan. 22, Mar. 15, Nov. 15, 1814; Sept. 2, 1815; Feb. 21, 1816.

[New York] Constitutional Gazette, 1775–1776.

Semi-weekly. Established Aug. 2, 1775, judging from the date of the earliest issue located, that of Aug. 9, 1775, no. 3, printed by John Anderson, with the title of "The Constitutional Gazette." It was a single leaf folio, but with the issue of Aug. 23, 1775, was changed to a quarto of four pages, with July 31, 1776, enlarged to folio, and with Aug. 28, 1776, reduced to quarto. This issue of Aug. 28, 1776, vol. 2, no. 113, is the last located, and the paper must have been soon discontinued, as the British entered New York in September, 1776.

N. Y. Hist. Soc. has Aug. 9–Dec. 30, 1775; Jan. 3–24, 31–June 12, 19–July 31, Aug. 21–28, 1776.

Am. Antiq. Soc. has Sept. 27, Nov. 1, Dec. 20, 1775; Mar. 30, Apr. 6, May 4, 8, 22, Aug. 7, 1776.

Mass. Hist. Soc. has Nov. 4, Dec. 6, 13, 1775; Jan. 31, Apr. 6, May 29, June 5, 19, 22, Aug. 3, 1776.
Lib. Congress has Oct. 21, 1775.
N. Y. Pub. Lib. has May 22, 1776.

[New York] Corrector, 1804.

Semi-weekly. Established Mar. 28, 1804, with the title of "The Corrector," printed by S[tephen] Gould & Co., and edited by "Toby Tickler, Esq." It was of quarto size, paged, and was published primarily in the interest of the Burr faction. The last issue located is that of Apr. 26, 1804, no. 10.

Am. Antiq. Soc., N. Y. Hist. Soc., Lib. Congress, East Hampton Free Lib., Yale, and Boston Athenæum have Mar. 28–Apr. 26, 1804.
Harvard has Mar. 31, Apr. 11, 1804.
Adriance Lib., Poughkeepsie, has Mar. 31, 1804.

[New York] Country Courier, see Courier.

[New York] Courier, 1815–1817.

Daily. Established Jan. 10, 1815, judging from the date of the earliest issue located, that of Jan. 16, 1815, vol. 1, no. 6, published by B[arent] Gardenier, with the title of "Courier, and Mercantile Directory." At some time between this date and May 6, 1815, the title was changed to "New-York Courier," and the publishers to Gardenier & Buell [Barent Gardenier and ———— Buell]. With the issue of May 13, 1815, the partnership was dissolved and the paper published by B. Gardenier (changed to Barent Gardenier with the issue of June 7, 1815). With the issue of Nov. 17, 1815, it was published by Abraham Asten and edited by Barent Gardenier. With the issue of Jan. 10, 1816, Abraham Vosburgh was added to the firm, which became Gardenier, Asten & Co. With the issue of Apr. 10, 1816, it was published by B. Gardenier; with July 2, 1816, it was published by Abraham Vosburgh and edited by Barent Gardenier (the establishment having been assigned to Vosburgh for debts); and with Jan. 22, 1817, Barent Gardenier again assumed control and became sole publisher. With the issue of Feb. 19, 1817, the paper was taken over by Theodore Dwight, although no name was given in the imprint. The last issue with the title of "New-York Courier" was that of Apr. 8, 1817, vol. 3, no. 690, when it was succeeded by the "New-York Daily Advertiser."

A semi-weekly publication was established June 3, 1816, under the title of "The Country Courier," published by Barent Gardenier, as a large octavo of 16 pages to each issue. It experienced the same changes of publishers as the daily, published by Abraham Vosburgh and edited by Barent Gardenier with July 4, 1816, published by Barent Gardenier with Jan. 27, 1817, and by Theodore Dwight with Feb. 20, 1817. The last issue located is that of Mar. 24, 1817, vol. 2, no. 32. Previous to establishing this publication, Gardenier had published "The Examiner," from Oct. 25, 1813, to May 27, 1816, but this was ostensibly a magazine.

> N. Y. Hist. Soc. has May 6, 1815–Apr. 8, 1817, lacking only 14 issues; also June 3, 1816–Mar. 24, 1817 of the semi-weekly.
> N. Y. State Lib. has Apr. 15, 17, 29, May 9, June 28, Dec. 6, 1816.
> Lib. Congress has Jan. 20, June 29, 1816; Jan. 28, 1817.
> Am. Antiq. Soc. has Jan. 16, 1815; and June 3, 1816–Mar. 24, 1817 of the semi-weekly.
> Yale has Feb. 18, 1817.
> Boston Pub. Lib. has June 3–Oct. 17, 1816 of the semi-weekly.

[New York] Daily Advertiser, 1785–1806.

Daily. Established Mar. 1, 1785, judging from the earliest issue located, that of Mar. 16, 1785, no. 14, published by F. Childs and Co., with the title of "The New-York Daily Advertiser." At some time between this date and Apr. 6, 1785, the name of the publisher in the imprint became Francis Childs. With the issue of Sept. 20, 1785, the title was changed to "The Daily Advertiser, Political, Historical, and Commercial"; with Oct. 27, 1785, to "The Daily Advertiser: Political, Historical, and Commercial"; and with Oct. 17, 1787, to "The Daily Advertiser." With the issue of July 2, 1789, John Swaine was admitted to parnership and the paper was published by Francis Childs and John Swaine (changed to Childs and Swaine with June 11, 1792). With the issue of Nov. 13, 1794, the partnership was dissolved and the paper published by Francis Childs. Swaine died Nov. 17, 1794. With the issue of Jan. 25, 1796, Childs transferred his interest to John Morton, who stated in an editorial that he had been principal proprietor for the past year. Morton's name, however, did not appear in the imprint, which was given as "Printed by William Robins, for the Proprietor." With the issue of July 10, 1798, the name of Charles Snowden appeared alone in the imprint; with Jan. 16, 1800, the paper was printed and published for the Proprietor by Robert Wilson; with Feb. 15, 1802, the word "Proprietor" was changed to "Proprietors"; with May 2, 1803, the printer became J[onathan] Seymour; and with Nov. 23, 1803, George Bruce. In 1803 Samuel Bayard, proprietor of the paper, sold it to Henry Pringle, who with his brother, Thomas Pringle, acted as co-editors. Upon Henry Pringle's death, Oct. 26, 1805, the paper reverted to Samuel Bayard. It was discontinued with the issue of Aug. 30, 1806, vol. 22, no. 6233, and was succeeded by "The People's Friend."

> N. Y. Hist. Soc. has May 9, 14, 16, 23, 30, June 17, Nov. 29, Dec. 5, 13, 19, 26, 27, 1785; Jan. 2, 1786–Apr. 20, 1796, fair; Dec. 2, 1796; Jan. 5, 1797–June 30, 1801, good; Aug. 1–Oct. 31, Dec. 1–31, 1801; Jan. 4, 1802– Dec. 31, 1805, good.

Lib. Congress has Apr. 6, Sept. 1, 1785–Dec. 30, 1786; Jan. 1, 3, 25, Feb. 26, Mar. 16, 31, Apr. 7, 9, 11, 12, 17–21, 27, May 3, 4, 8, June 7, 13, 16, 30, July 2, 1787–Dec. 31, 1793; June 17, July 1–Dec. 31, 1794; Jan. 1–June 30, Sept. 1, 14, 23, Oct. 19, Nov. 17, 23, 1795; June 7, July 4, 7, 9, Aug. 3, Oct. 6, 1796; Jan. 17, Feb. 1, Apr. 5, June 13, July 14, 15, 1797; May 1, 1798–Feb. 18, 1804; Feb. 24, 25, Mar. 6–8, 10, 27, July 17, 1804; Nov. 22, 26, 1805.

Boston Athenæum has Apr. 29–Nov. 21, 1799; Jan. 8, 1800–Aug. 30, 1806.

N. Y. Pub. Lib. has Sept. 26, 28, 30, Oct. 3, 4, 17, 27, 1785; Jan. 3–Feb. 28, Aug. 26, 1786–Aug. 29, 1787, fair; Oct. 17, 1787–Mar. 22, 1788, fair; Apr. 10, May 10, July 1, 1788–Dec. 31, 1791; Jan. 28, 31, Feb. 14, May 14, Oct. 29, Nov. 2, 1792; Jan. 1, 1793–Dec. 31, 1795; Mar. 3, 16, July 6, 1798.

Am. Antiq. Soc. has Mar. 16, Apr. 6, July 14, Dec. 29, 1785; Jan. 2, 17, 18, 26, Mar. 1–Aug. 29, Sept. 26, Oct. 2–Dec. 27, 1786, fair; Jan. 6–10, 29, Feb. 1, 19–Sept. 28, Oct. 9, 12, Nov. 17, 29, Dec. 13–31, 1787, fair; Jan. 1, 1788–Dec. 31, 1790; Jan. 1–Dec. 31, 1791, fair; Jan. 2–Mar. 31, Apr. 4, 9, 20, May 8, 10, 15, 19, 22, 29, June 5, 12, 21–23, July 2, 14, 17, 19, 24, 31, Aug. 7, 11, 14, 21, Sept. 17, 25, Oct. 2, 15, 30, Nov. 5–7, 14, 19, 27, Dec. 7, 12, 19, 26, 1792; Jan. 2, 9, 14, 19, 28, Feb. 7, 11, Mar. 11, 18, Apr. 8, 26, 29, May 16, 24, 27, June 3, 10, 17, 22, 24, 26, July 30, 31, Aug. 3, 6, 7, 12, 22, 27, 29, Sept. 2, 4, 6, 8, 10, 14–19, Oct. 11, Nov. 6, 15, 25, Dec. 14, 20, 1793; Jan. 1, 1794–Apr. 30, 1795, fair; May 19, June 3, 4, 8, July 3, 6, 20, 24, Aug. 3, 17, 19, 26, 31, Sept. 15, 16, Oct. 2, Dec. 2, 1795; Jan. 6, 9, 14, Feb. 8, Apr. 4, 25, May 24, July 14, Sept. 2, 13, Nov. 19, 1796; Feb. 23, Mar. 28, Apr. 4, 8, 12, 22, May 1, 3–6, 13, 19, June 5, 6, 16, 27, 28, July 5, 6, 11, 12, Oct. 5, Nov. 13, 23, Dec. 14, 1797; Jan. 5, 16, 22, 24, Feb. 12–16, 20, 21, Apr. 16, May 4, 5, 10, 12, 28, June 26, 30, July 3, 10, Sept. 5, 21, 26, Oct. 1, 2, 19, 23, 27, Nov. 10, 16, 19–23, 30, Dec. 3–5, 15–19, 21, 22, 27, 29, 31, 1798; Jan. 1, 12, 14, 28, 31, Feb. 15, Mar. 4, 8, 25, 28, 29, May 8, June 22, 24, Oct. 2, 10, Nov. 17, Dec. 19–31, 1799; Jan. 1–Dec. 31, 1800, fair; Jan. 6–June 29, July 6–Aug. 8, Sept. 1–30, Nov. 11–24, 1801, fair; June 27, July 14, 1804; Jan. 16, 1805.

Univ. of Mich. (Clements) has May 17, 1785; June 26, 27, 30, 1786; Feb. 1, Apr. 19, July 2, 1787; Jan. 1, 1788–Dec. 31, 1791; Oct. 31, 1792; Jan. 1–June 29, 1793; July 1–Dec. 31, 1794; Feb. 2, Mar. 23, 1795; May 23, June 5, Sept. 8, 22, Nov. 14, 1798; Feb. 18, Mar. 2, May 2, 1799–Oct. 28, 1800, fair; Sept. 14–17, 1801.

N. Y. Soc. Lib. has Sept. 6, 1785; Jan. 1–July 30, 1791; Apr. 5, 1796–Jan. 26, 1798; Mar. 22, July 25, 1798; Sept. 16, 1799–Sept. 27, 1804.

Yale has Apr. 11, 13, 18, Sept. 4, 1786–Dec. 31, 1787; Jan. 26, 28, Feb. 2, 5, 7, Apr. 8, 10, May 24, June 6, 23–26, July 23–Dec. 17, 1788, fair; Jan. 1, 1789–July 16, 1790; Jan. 1, 1791–Dec. 31, 1792.

N. Y. State Lib. has Feb. 24, May 2–9, July 21, Aug. 1, Sept. 10, 1787; Jan. 2–Dec. 27, 1788, fair; Jan. 7, Mar. 20, June 30, July 10, 18, 27, Aug. 8, Sept. 7,

Oct. 2, 10, 1789; Jan. 1, 1790–Dec. 29, 1791, fair; Feb. 11–Mar. 1, June 13, 14, Aug. 20, Sept. 3–25, Oct. 12, Nov. 9–Dec. 24, 1792, fair; Jan. 1, 1793–Dec. 30, 1795, fair; Jan. 2, Nov. 8, 1796; Feb. 15, 1797; June 22, 1799; Oct. 28, 1803; Mar. 5, 1804; July 23–Aug. 30, 1806, fair.

Wis. Hist. Soc. has Jan. 1–Dec. 31, 1788; Jan. 1–Dec. 29, 1790; Jan. 2–Dec. 31, 1792, fair; Jan.–June, 1793, scattering; July–Dec. 1793; May 1–Aug. 31, 1795; Jan. 2–Dec. 30, 1797; June 16, 1802.

H. Armour Smith, Yonkers, has Apr. 12, 23–29, May 4–6, 11, 12, 24, 27, 30, 31, June 7, 17, 18, 22, July 8, 20, Aug. 9, 20, 26, Nov. 10, Dec. 18, 1796; Mar. 9–14, 20, 25, 29, 31, July 7, 14, Oct. 12, 21, 24, 27–31, Nov. 28, 29, Dec. 27–30, 1797; Jan. 25–Feb. 2, 6, Mar. 10, 19, 22, 23, 27–Apr. 3, 11, 12, July 13–16, Aug. 1, 3, 8, 10–13, 20, 25, 27, Oct. 18, Dec. 3, 6, 7, 1798; July 1–Dec. 12, 1799, fair.

Harvard has Aug. 11, 24, 1787; July 11, 1789; June 15, 17, 18, 22, 23, 23, 29, July 1, 4, 7, 12, 14–19, 22, 28, 30, Aug. 1, 2, Sept. 8, 13, 16–19, 27, 30, Oct. 1, 3, Nov. 15, 16, 18, 1791; Mar. 17, May 14, 30, June 1, 2, 5, 7, 14–16, 20, July 4, 10, 13, 14, 21–24, 26, Aug. 1, 28, 30, Oct. 2, Nov. 6, 7, Dec. 3, 26, 1792; Jan. 9, 19, Feb. 7, Mar. 4, Apr. 11, Sept. 5, 6, 11, 13, 23, Oct. 7, Nov. 15, 18, 23, 26, 27, 29, Dec. 2, 7–10, 1793; Jan. 4, 24, Feb. 3, 4, 10, 18, 20, Mar. 3, 7, 21, Apr. 8, 15, 28, May 2, 3, 9, 20, 21, June 2, 11, Aug. 14, 15, Sept. 8, 19, 23, Nov. 29, Dec. 16, 20, 23, 25, 1794; Jan. 2, 10, 13, 16, 19, 28, Feb. 5, 7–10, 12, 13, 16, 27, Mar. 3, 14, 18, 21–24, 26, Apr. 8, 9, 13, June 27, 1795; Feb. 1, May 16, Nov. 7, 1796; Mar. 17, Apr. 3, June 19, Nov. 10, 13, 20, 1797; Jan. 8, Dec. 5–8, 10, 12–17, 19, 21, 22, 1798; Feb. 28, Mar. 4, July 26, Sept. 13, 1799; Feb. 3, Mar. 15, 18, 24, 28, Apr. 2, 3, 7, 11, 18, July 10, 12, 28, Sept. 5, 15, Oct. 17, 24, 31, Nov. 14, 21, Dec. 1, 15, 22, 26, 29, 1800; Jan. 2, 5, 9, 12, 19, 26, Feb. 6, 12, 13, 20, 27, Mar. 8, 10, 19, 23, 24, 27, 30, Apr. 3, 13, 20, 24, 27, May 1, 4, 5, 8, 18, 22, 25, June 1, 12, 15, 19, 26, 29, July 6, 9, 13, 27, 29, Aug. 3, 7, 10, 17, 21, 24, 28, 31, Sept. 4, 14, 18, 21, 25, 28, Oct. 9, 12, 16, 23, Nov. 4, 5, 9, 13, 16, 27, Dec. 4, 11, 21, 1801; Jan. 18, 22, Feb. 5, 12, 19, 22, Mar. 8, 19, Apr. 6, 22, 29, May 21, June 8, 14, Sept. 13, Oct. 6, Dec. 28, 1802; Jan. 14, 21, 27, Feb. 4, Mar. 14, 21, Apr. 4, 10, 18, 25, May 2, 23, 30, June 6, 13, 27, July 25, Aug. 8, 15, 29, Sept. 5, 19, Oct. 10, 31, Nov. 7, 14, 1803; Jan. 2, 9, 16, 30, Feb. 13, 27, Mar. 12, Apr. 9, 30, May 7, 18, 21, 28, June 4, 21, 28, July 2, 9, 12, 16, 19, 23, 26, 30, Aug. 6, 9, 13, 20, 23, Sept. 3, 6, 11, 13, 18, 21, 24, Oct. 2, 9, 16, 18, 23, 30, Nov. 1, 6, 8, 13, 15, 20, 22, 27, 29, Dec. 4, 6, 13, 18, 20, 25, 1804; Jan. 8, 10, 15, 24, 29, Feb. 5, 7, 11, 14, 18, 21, Mar. 5, 7, 12, 14, 19, 21, 28, Apr. 11, 16, 25, 30, May 1, 2, 7, 16, 21, 23, 28, 30, June 4, 6, 25, 27, July 2, 4, 9, 16, 18, 25, 30, Aug. 15, 20, 27, Sept. 3, 12, 18, 19, 23, 26, Oct. 8, 10, 17, Nov. 5, 7, 19, 26, 28, Dec. 5, 10, 12, 17, 1805; Jan. 2, 14, 16, 21, 23, 25, Feb. 6, 11, 18, 20, 25, Mar. 4, 11, 13, 18, 25, 27, Apr. 1, 3, 8, 10, 17, 22, May 6, 13, 22, 23, 26–29, June 3, 10, 12, 18, 19, 20, 24, July 15, 17, 22, 24, 25, 29, 30, Aug. 4, 5, 12, 14, 19, 21, 26, 1806.

York Inst., Saco, has Jan. 2–Oct. 13, 1788; Jan. 31–Sept. 28, 1789.
Boston Pub. Lib. has Aug. 15, Dec. 15, 1786; Apr. 3, 19, 20, June 14, Sept. 13, 14, Dec. 26, 1787; Jan. 1, 14, Feb. 19, Mar. 17, 19, Aug. 6, 11, Nov. 7, 8, 1788; Mar. 20, 24, 25, Apr. 15, 17, 18, May 12, 13, 20, 21, July 9–Nov. 11, 1789; Jan. 7, 8, May 7, 8, 19, 20, July 30, 31, Aug. 2, 3, 7, Sept. 1, 2, 21, 24, 25, Oct. 7, 16, Nov. 8–12, 22, 25, Dec. 24, 27, 31, 1790; June 6, 7, 27, 28, July 4, 5, 21, Aug. 26, 27, Sept. 21, 22, 28, 29, Oct. 3, 4, Nov. 17, 18, 29, Dec. 27, 1791; Feb. 1, 8, 1792; Jan. 19, Nov. 30, Dec. 4, 1793; June 16, 1794; Mar. 26, 1795.
Univ. of Chicago has Jan. 3–5, 8, 11, Feb. 7, Mar. 14, 29, Apr. 8, 10, 23, 25, May 10, 29, July 4, Aug. 12, 1788; Jan. 2–June 30, 1789, fair; Apr. 26, May 4, 1790; Jan. 1–Dec. 31, 1791, fair; Nov. 18, 1794; May 7, 9, 1795; Feb. 1, 1797; Aug. 28, Sept. 18, Nov. 19–Dec. 23, 1799; Jan. 3–Apr. 28, 1800.
Rutgers Univ. has Dec. 14, 19, 1787; Jan. 4, 12–16, 19, Nov. 27, 29, Dec. 1, 4–6, 1788; Jan. 9, 10, 28, 30, 31, Apr. 30, 1789; June 23, July 20, Aug. 7, 24, 31, 1792; June 6, Aug. 5, 1794.
Univ. of Penn. has Jan. 1–June 30, 1790.
Mass. Hist. Soc. has Apr. 19, Nov. 17, 21, 1786; Mar. 6, 19, 1787; June 24, 1788; Aug. 5, Dec. 30, 1791; Mar. 6, 7, 30, 1792; May 31, June 16, 1794; July 3, 1795; May 4, 1797; Mar. 7, 1800.
Duke Univ. has Feb. 25–28, Mar. 3, 4, 15, 18, 22, Apr. 10, May 10, 1788; Feb. 14, Nov. 26, Dec. 5, 10, 1789; Jan. 15, 1790; Oct. 3, 1794; May 29, Oct. 9, 1801.
Hist. Soc. Penn. has Aug. 27, 1787; Mar. 5, 1788; Oct. 4, 1793; Apr. 15, 1795; Jan. 16, 17, 20, 27, 28, 31, Feb. 3, 5, 13, Mar. 24, Apr. 1, 25, 1797.
Cornell Univ. has Apr. 24, 25, Nov. 6, 1805; Jan. 29, 30, 1806.

[New York] Daily Advertiser, 1807.

Daily. Established Aug. 4, 1807, with the title of "The Daily Advertiser," printed and published for the Proprietors, and succeeding "The People's Friend." In the initial issue, an editorial signed by James A. Bayard stated that the paper was to be conducted by himself and Samuel Bayard. It was discontinued with the issue of Dec. 31, 1807, vol. 1, no. 128, being purchased by J[ohn] J. Negrin, who established in its stead "L'Oracle and Daily Advertiser."

Am. Antiq. Soc., N. Y. Hist. Soc., and Lib. Congress have Aug. 4–Dec. 31, 1807.
Boston Athenæum has Aug. 5–Dec. 31, 1807.
Duke Univ. has Sept. 4–Dec. 30, 1807, fair.
N. Y. State Lib. has Aug. 4, 6, 1807.
Univ. of Mich. (Clements) has Dec. 21, 23, 1807.
Yale has Aug. 5, Sept. 14, 1807.
Harvard has Oct. 1, 1807.

[New York] Daily Advertiser, 1808–1809.

Daily. A continuation, without change of volume numbering, of "L'Oracle and Daily Advertiser," the first issue with the new title of "The Daily Advertiser" being that of Sept. 12, 1808, vol. 1, no. 213, published by Joseph Desnoues. With the issue of Jan. 16, 1809, the paper was published by L[ewis] Jones, for the Proprietors, but at some time between Feb. 2 and June 1, 1809, it again was published by Joseph Desnoues. The last issue located is that of June 1, 1809, no. 433.

N. Y. Hist. Soc. has Sept. 12–Dec. 31, 1808.
Lib. Congress has Dec. 9, 1808–Feb. 2, 1809.
Harvard has Sept. 17, 24, Oct. 1, 8, 12, 15, Nov. 14, 23, Dec. 3, 10, 14, 1808; Jan. 25, June 1, 1809.
Am. Antiq. Soc. has Oct. 15, 19, Nov. 3, 10, 1808.
N. Y. State Lib. has Jan. 14, 15, 17, 1809.

New-York Daily Advertiser, 1817–1820+.

Daily. Established Apr. 9, 1817, with the title of "New-York Daily Advertiser," published by John W. Walker, for Theodore Dwight. It succeeded the "New-York Courier," continuing its advertisements, but starting a new volume numbering. With the issue of July 29, 1817, Dwight took Walker into partnership, under the firm name of Dwight & Walker, with Dwight as editor and Walker as printer. With the issue of July 8, 1818, William B. Townsend was added to the firm, which became Dwight, Townsend & Walker. It was so continued until after 1820. A semi-weekly edition was also published from 1817 to 1820, with the title of "New-York Advertiser," which see.

N. Y. Hist. Soc. has Apr. 9, 1817–Dec. 30, 1820.
Lib. Congress has Apr. 17–July 1, 16–Nov. 8, 22–Dec. 31, 1817; Aug. 7, Sept. 17, Oct. 2, 1819; Aug. 24, Nov. 21, 1820.
Am. Antiq. Soc. has Jan. 31, 1818; Mar. 26, Aug. 16, Nov. 25–27, 1819; May 10, 1820.
Wesleyan Univ. has Dec. 30, 31, 1819.
New Haven Col. Hist. Soc. has Feb. 1–29, 1820.
Rutgers Univ. has May 22, 1818.
N. Y. State Lib. has Feb. 19, 1819.

[New York] Daily Express, 1813.

Daily. Established Aug. 28, 1813, judging from the earliest issue located, that of Sept. 3, 1813, vol. 1, no. 6, published by G[arret] C. Tunison, with the title of "Daily Express." It succeeded "The Statesman," starting a new volume num-

NEW YORK 625

bering, but continuing some of its advertisements. The issues of Dec. 11 and Dec. 15 (vol. 1, no. 33), 1813, were published by N[athaniel] T. Eldredge.

Am. Antiq. Soc. has Sept. 3, Dec. 15, 1813.
N. Y. Hist. Soc. has Dec. 11, 1813.

New-York Daily Gazette, 1788–1795.

Daily. Established Dec. 29, 1788, by J. & A. M'Lean [John and Archibald M'Lean], with the title of "The New-York Daily Gazette," succeeding "The Independent Journal." John M'Lean died May 18, 1789, but it was not until the issue of Aug. 5, 1789, that his name was omitted from the imprint and the paper was published by Archibald M'Lean. With the issue of Apr. 2, 1792, the title was altered to "New-York Daily Gazette;" with either Jan. 28 or 29, 1795, to "The New York Gazette," published by A. M'Lean; at some time between Mar. 5, and 28, 1795, to "New-York Daily Gazette;" and at some time between Apr. 27, and May 13, 1795, to "The New-York Gazette and General Advertiser." See under "New-York Gazette," 1795–1820.

N. Y. Hist. Soc. has Dec. 29, 1788–Dec. 31, 1791; Jan. 16, Feb. 3, 4, 7, 8, 14, 17, Mar. 19, 24, 26, 31, Apr. 2, 10, 13, 19–21, May 4, 16, 18, 26–29, June 2, 11, 29, July 2, 5, 16, 18, 26, 30, 31, Aug. 4, 8, 10, 13, 17, 20, 23, 28, 31, Sept. 4, 6, 15, 17, 24, 27, Oct. 10, 11, Nov. 8–13, 15, 17, Dec. 8, 13, 17, 22, 25, 26, 31, 1792; Jan. 3–5, 10, 12, 15, 16, 19, 22, 25, 26, Feb. 2–5, 8–11, 15, 21–25, 28, Mar. 7–11, 19–25, 28, Apr. 3, 4, 8, 10–12, 18, 22, 23, 25, 30, May 1, 13, 15, 28, June 1, 4, 11, 12, 14, July 12, 15, 17, 19, 20, 22, 26, 28, Aug. 6, 7, 12, 13, 30–Sept. 2, 9, 11, 14, 16, 20, 21, 27, Oct. 4, 10, 15, 19–22, 25, 28, Nov. 1, 2, 5, 9–12, 23, 25, 27, Dec. 2, 4, 5, 7, 9, 12, 1793; Jan. 2, 4, 6, 8–15, 18, 21–23, 25–29, 31, Feb. 1, 4, 6–8, 11, 12, 14, 15, 18–20, 22–27, Mar. 1–Apr. 30, May 26, Aug. 14–21, Sept. 1, 22, 23, 25, 26, 29, 30, Oct. 2–6, 9, 25, Nov. 7, 29, Dec. 2–4, 8, 9, 11, 17, 18, 20, 23, 26, 1794; Jan. 1, 6, 7, 15, 16, 26, Apr. 17, 21, 23, 25, 1795.

N. Y. Soc. Lib. has Dec. 29, 1788–July 30, 1791; Jan. 1–Dec. 31, 1794.
Boston Athenæum has Dec. 29, 1788–Dec. 31, 1790.
Lib. Congress has Dec. 29, 1788–Dec. 31, 1789; Apr. 3, 1790; July 26, 1792; July 14, Sept. 29, 1794; Apr. 6, 1795.
N. Y. State Lib. has Dec. 29, 1788–Dec. 31, 1789; Oct. 19, Nov. 1, 8, 1793; May 5, 1794.
Am. Antiq. Soc. has Jan. 24, 28, Feb. 4, 6, 18, 21, 25, Mar. 6, 16, 18, Apr. 15, 17, 18, 25, May 1, 2, 5, 14, 15, 23, June 30, July 4, 21, 28, 30, Aug. 1, 3, 13, 18, 22, 27, Sept. 8, 15, 26, 28, Oct. 3, 6, 10, 13, 20, 27, 29, Nov. 4, 11, 25, Dec. 9, 19, 23, 1789; Jan. 27, 30, Feb. 17, 20, Mar. 3, 10, 19, 30, Apr. 10, 17, May 1, 6, 18–22, 28–Aug. 31, fair; Sept. 9–13, 15, 17–20, 27, 28, Oct. 1–7, 9, 12, 14, 15, 19, 28, Nov. 2, 10, 19, 20, 30, Dec. 3, 11, 22, 29, 1790; Jan. 1, 5, 8, 31, Feb. 1, 2, 5, 9, 12, 16, Mar. 5, 14, 22, 29, Apr. 6–9, 26, May 4, 7, 12,

14, June 4, 11, July 7, 9, 13, Aug. 2, 5, 6, 10, 16, 23, 27–30, Sept. 1, 5, 6, 10, 12, 15, 22, 24, 26, 28, 29, Oct. 3, 15, 24, 25, Nov. 9, 16, 23, 24, 30, Dec. 3, 21, 24–29, 31, 1791; Jan. 16, 21, 28, Feb. 4, Mar. 3, 10, 24, 28, 31, Apr. 28, May 10, 19, 25, June 4, 12, 19, 21, July 2, 10, 17, 25, 30, Aug. 4, 7, 11, 14, 18, Sept. 1, 7, 22, 24, 29, Oct. 6, 13–16, 18, 22, 29, 31, Nov. 7, 10, 12, 24, Dec. 1, 5, 10, 15, 22, 28, 1792; Jan. 5, 16, 21, 28, Feb. 7, 20, 25, 28, Mar. 18, 21, 25, 28, Apr. 4, 11, 22, May 10, 20, 31, June 7, July 19, Aug. 16, 26, 30, Sept. 4, 16, Oct. 7, 12, 21, 26, 28, Nov. 25, Dec. 26, 1793; Jan. 4, 27, Feb. 3, 10, 17, Mar. 6, 10, 17, Apr. 21, May 7, 9, 16, 19, 22, June 5, 7–10, 13, 23, July 15, 29, Aug. 2, 20, 22, 27, Sept. 16, 23, Oct. 4, 7, 29, Nov. 5, 19, Dec. 8, 17, 24, 1794; Jan. 17, Mar. 28, Apr. 8, 24, 1795.

Harvard has June 24, 28, July 5, 8, 12, 15, 22, 26, 29, Sept. 16, 30, Nov. 15, 18, 22, 25, 1791; Mar. 21, Apr. 14, 25, May 31, June 16, 21, July 5, 7, 10, 12, 28, 31, Aug. 2, 8, 14, 25, Sept. 1, 27, 29, Oct. 6, 8, 13, 18, Nov. 9, 10, Dec. 5, 11, 25, 26, 1792; Jan. 2, 5, Feb. 7, 25, 28, Mar. 4, 7, July 8, Aug. 23, 26, Sept. 6, 27, Oct. 11, Nov. 4, 11, 25, Dec. 5, 1793; Jan. 13, 16, Feb. 13, 15, 17, 24, Apr. 17, May 21, June 2, 9, 1794.

N. J. State Lib. has Jan. 10–Dec. 23, 1789.

York Inst., Saco, has Jan. 30–Sept. 28, 1789.

N. Y. Pub. Lib. has Aug. 4, 7, Oct. 10, 28, 29, 1793; July 12, 14, 1794.

Buffalo Hist. Soc. has June 3, 6, 7, 17, 24, July 19, 28, Aug. 1, 13, Nov. 19–21, 1794.

Hist. Soc. Penn. has Jan. 5–19, 1789; May 4, 1793.

Univ. of Mich. (Clements) has Apr. 7, 8, 1789; Mar. 14, 1791; Oct. 7, 1794.

Wis. Hist. Soc. has May 1, 1789.

Cornell Univ. has May 1, Oct. 31, 1789.

Rutgers Univ. has Mar. 22, 1791.

Conn. Hist. Soc. has May 12, 1791.

Phil. Lib. Co. has Oct. 24, 1793.

[New York] Daily Items, 1815–1816.

Daily. Established Nov. 1, 1815, judging from the date of the earliest issue located, that of Nov. 15, 1815, no. 13, published by Alexander Ming, with the title of "Daily Items, for Merchants." It was of quarto size and contained commercial, shipping and business news. The Saturday issues were supplied by Ming's weekly newspaper, "Ming's New-York Price-Current," which, beginning with Nov. 11, 1815, carried in the heading, just before its own serial number, the words "Daily Items," with the serial number of the latter paper. "Daily Items" was suspended for the month of January 1816, but was resumed on Feb. 1, 1816. The last issue located is that of Feb. 16, 1816, no. 66, and the paper was apparently discontinued about two weeks later.

N. Y. Hist. Soc. has Nov. 15–17, 21–24, 27, 1815; Feb. 5–9, 12–14, 16, 1816.

Am. Antiq. Soc. has Nov. 16, 1815.

[New York] Daily Telegraph, 1812–1813.

Daily. The earliest copy located is that of Feb. 19, 1813, no. 42, printed at no. 20 Chatham Street, entitled "The Daily Telegraph." It was of quarto size. The name of the printer was not given in the imprint, but a copy dated Apr. 13, 1813, vol. 2, no. 80, contains an advertisement showing that the printer was Benjamin Brower. A prospectus for the paper was published in "The New-York Phœnix" of Feb. 24, 1813, stating that it was to be printed at 132 Water Street, formerly the office of the "Public Advertiser" and of "The New-York Phœnix."

Am. Antiq. Soc. has Apr. 13, 1813.
H. Armour Smith, Yonkers, has Feb. 19, 1813.

[New York] Deutsche Freund, 1819.

Seidensticker, "First Century of German Printing," 1893, p. 208, says that "Der Deutsche Freund" was established in New York City by Edward Schaffer in 1819 and that only a few numbers appeared. There is said to be a notice in the "Baltimore American" about Nov. 1, 1819 (which reference I cannot find in the file), acknowledging the receipt of the initial issue, consisting of 16 octavo pages and edited by Rev. Frederick C. Schaffer. No copy located.

[New York] Diary, 1792–1798.

Daily. Established Feb. 15, 1792, with the title of "The Diary; or, Loudon's Register," succeeding Loudon's other paper "The New-York Packet." The imprint stated that the paper was published by Samuel Loudon, Jun., although in a later issue, that of Jan. 1, 1793, it was stated that the paper was established by Samuel Loudon and his son Samuel. With the issue of Aug. 15, 1792, the name of Samuel Loudon was given as the printer, and with Jan. 1, 1793, Samuel Loudon & Son. With the issue of Jan. 1, 1794, Abraham Brower was admitted to partnership, under the firm name of Loudon & Brower, and the title was changed to "The Diary; or Evening Register." With the issue of Oct. 22, 1794, the firm name reverted to Samuel Loudon & Son. In February, 1795, the title was changed to "The Diary, & Universal Daily Advertiser" and the publisher to Samuel Loudon, Jun. In May, 1795, the title was changed to "The Diary, & Universal Advertiser." Samuel Loudon, Jun., died Sept. 17, 1795, but there was no change in the imprint. With the issue of Feb. 1, 1796, the paper was published by Cornelius C. VanAlen & Co., and the title was shortened to "The Diary." With the issue of Jan. 25, 1797, this firm was dissolved and the paper published for John I. Johnson, by Crookes & Saunders [John Crookes and Robert Saunders]. With the issue of Mar. 20, 1797, the title was changed to "Diary and Mercantile Advertiser," the last two words being so prominent that the paper might almost be called "Mercantile Advertiser." With the issue of Mar. 31, 1797, it was published by John Crookes, for John I. Johnson; with

628　Newspaper Bibliography

June 16, 1797, by John Crookes, for the Proprietor; with Feb. 21, 1798, by John Crookes, for the Proprietors; and with Sept. 11(?), 1798, by John Crookes for the Proprietor. The last issue located with this title was that of Sept. 13, 1798, no. 1964, and at some time between this date and Nov. 13, 1798, no. 1970 (showing a slight suspension), the title was changed to "Mercantile Advertiser," which see.

A weekly edition was published for the country under the title of "Register of the Times," which see.

 N. Y. Hist. Soc. has Feb. 15, 1792–Aug. 14, 1793; Aug. 20, 30, Sept. 2–5, 13, 18, 30, Oct. 2, 5, 11, 19, Nov. 27, Dec. 10, 1793; Jan. 1–Dec. 31, 1794; Jan. 24, Sept. 9, 21–Dec. 31, 1795, fair; Feb. 20, July 11, Aug. 18, 1796; Jan. 2–June 13, 1797; May 8, 1798.

 Lib. Congress has Mar. 2, 7, 10, 16, 17, 21, 26, 29–31, Apr. 30, May 16, 28, 29, June 1, 2, 9, 20, 21, July 4, 5, Sept. 10, 21, 22, Oct. 3–6, 16, Nov. 22, 23, Dec. 6–8, 12–15, 20, 23, 1792; Apr. 27, June 17, July 25, 30, 31, Aug. 2, 5, 6, 9, 15–19, 21, 24–27, 29–Sept. 2, 4–10, 12, 13, 16, 18, 19, 23, 25, 27, 28, Oct. 1, 4, 28, Nov. 21, 30, Dec. 12, 17, 18, 28, 31, 1793; Jan. 3, 4, 7, 8, 14, 16, 18–21, 24–27, 30–Feb. 1, 3, 12, May 7, June 9, 12, 16, July 4, 1794; Feb. 26, Mar. 2–7, 18, 20, Aug. 10, 1795; Apr. 6, 1796–May 7, 1798, fair.

 Am. Antiq. Soc. has Feb. 16, 18, 23–Mar. 14, 16–27, 29–Apr. 2, 6, 9, 11, 12, 16, 17, 20, 23–27, May 1, 3–9, 11–June 2, 5–16, 19–23, 27, 28, 30, July 2–6, 9, 10, 14, 16, 18, 20–27, 30, 31, Aug. 25, 27, Sept. 1, 5, 6, 12–17, 20–22, 25–27, 29, Oct. 1, 3, 4, 6–10, 12–18, 20, 23–25, 29, 30, Nov. 1–3, 8, 15, 17–20, 22–24, 27, 28, Dec. 3–15, 19–31, 1792; Jan. 3–Dec. 28, 1793; Feb. 1, Mar. 1, Apr. 8–12, 15–May 16, 19–July 28, Aug. 4, Sept. 20, 27, Oct. 3, 4, 16, 22, Nov. 19, 26, Dec. 12, 1794; Feb. 11, May 13, July 24, 25, 28, Aug. 15, 20, 22, Sept. 5, 1795; Jan. 3, June 5, July 8, Nov. 15, Dec. 8, 1797; Apr. 16, 25, May 7, 22, 29, June 23, 25, Sept. 11, 13, 1798.

 Harvard has Mar. 23, 31, Apr. 2, 14, 17, 18, 30, May 1, 8, 23, 25, 26, 29, 31, June 1, 2, 5, 7, 11, 15, 21–23, 27, 30, July 6, 10, 11, 13, 16, 21, 30, 31, Aug. 1, 3, Sept. 8, 11, 14, 15, 18, 19, Oct. 8, 13, 17, 25, Nov. 2, 6, 7, 21, 24, Dec. 1, 10–12, 14, 15, 1792; Jan. 1–4, 7, 9, 11, 14–16, 18, 19, Feb. 1, 8, 12–14, 20, Mar. 2, Apr. 17, July 24, Aug. 16, 27, Oct. 5, 29, Nov. 5, 8, 21, Dec. 3, 7, 17–19, 1793; Jan. 4, 6, 9, 21, Feb. 1, 11, 19, 24, 26, Mar. 18, May 7, 30, June 7, 11, 1794; Feb. 24, 25, Apr. 4, 8, 21, 22, 28, 29, May 2, 4, 6, 13, 26, 30, June 1, 3, 4, 8, 9, 12, 15, 16, 19, 23–25, July 1, Oct. 1, Nov. 3, 1795; Jan. 28–Feb. 1, May 2, June 4, 20, Oct. 14, Nov. 26, 1796; Jan. 18, Feb. 6, 17, Mar. 11, 21, 29, Apr. 1, 20, June 27, July 3, 4, Oct. 2, Nov. 9, 1797; Jan. 2, 5, 17, May 18, July 6, Sept. 1, 1798.

 Wis. Hist. Soc. has Jan. 1–Dec. 31, 1793; Jan. 1–June 17, Oct. 21–Dec. 31, 1794; Mar. 22, 27–31, Apr. 3, 12, 18, 21(?)29, May 12, 13, 16, June 12–July 27, fair, Aug. 9, 11, 14, 19, 21, 25, Oct. 16, 17, Dec. 13, 20, 1797; Feb. 3, 14, 15, 17, 20, 22–26, 28, Mar. 1, 9, 17, 19, 26, 28, 31, Apr. 25, 27, 28, 30–May 3, 5–8, 10, 1798.

N. J. Hist. Soc. has Feb. 20–Dec. 28 1792; Nov. 20, 1795; Aug. 1, 1797–Feb. 3, 1798.
N. Y. Pub. Lib. has Apr. 23, 30, May 1, 4, 18, 28, June 21, 25, 29, July 2, 28, 30, Aug. 4, 1792–June 23, 1794, fair; Apr. 27, 1795; Mar. 28, Apr. 3, 1797; Mar. 22, 1798.
Phil. Lib. Co. has Aug. 15, 1792–Feb. 14, Oct. 16, Nov. 7, 1793; Mar. 4–June 12, 1794; Jan. 22, 1798.
Hist. Soc. Penn. has Feb. 16–Aug. 14, 1792; Apr. 30, Oct. 17, 1793; July 23, 1794; Mar. 21, 24, 25, 1797.
Long Id. Hist. Soc. has Aug. 15–Sept. 14, 29, 1792; Feb. 14, 1793; Nov. 7, 1796.
N. Y. Soc. Lib. has Apr. 12, 1796–Aug. 21, 1797, fair.
N. Y. State Lib. has June 25, 26, Aug. 1, Sept. 5, 1792; Nov. 6, 7, 1793; Jan. 2–Dec. 30, 1797.
Univ. of Mich. (Clements) has Dec. 12, 1792; Sept. 10, 1793; Jan. 3, 4, 1794; Apr. 7, 16, July 5, 29, Nov. 21, 1796; Apr. 11, 15, 19, 26, May 2, 15–19, 22–24, June 20, July 5, 10, 12, Sept. 28, Oct. 23, 30, 1797; Mar. 3, 24, Apr. 2, 5, May 5, 1798.
Buffalo Hist. Soc. has May 14–June 4, Sept. 9, 22, Nov. 4, 1794.
Boston Pub. Lib. has May 28, June 8, 27, July 6, 1792.
Ga. Hist. Soc. has Aug. 27, Sept. 15, 25, 26, 1792.
Rutgers Univ. has Mar. 24, 28, 1796; Apr. 22, May 3, 1797.
Senate House, Kingston, N. Y., has Nov. 22, 23, 1793.
Yale has Mar. 17, 1792.
Mass. Hist. Soc. has June 19, 1794.

[New York] **Dickinson's New-York Price-Current**, 1813, see **New-York Price-Current**.

[New York] **Evening Mercury**, 1793.

Daily. Established Jan. 1, 1793, by John Buel, with the title of "Evening Mercury." It was a quarto of four pages, issued every week-day afternoon, immediately after four o'clock. The last issue located is that of Jan. 3, 1793, vol. 1, no. 3.

Am. Antiq. Soc. has Jan. 1, 3, 1793.

New-York Evening-Post, 1744–1753.

Weekly. Established Nov. 26, 1744, judging from the date of the earliest issue located, that of Dec. 17, 1744, no. 4, printed by Henry DeForeest, with the title of "The New-York Evening-Post." With the issue of May 25, 1747, there was a change in the set-up of the title heading, involving the omission of the dash after the word "Evening." The issue of Mar. 21, 1748, no. 169, is followed in the only known file for this year by Sept. 5, 1748, no. 172, indicating a suspension of several weeks. The last issue located is that of Dec. 18, 1752, no. 300, soon after which the paper was probably discontinued. The "New-York Mercury" of Apr. 30, 1753, refers to "De Foreest's Paper" of Apr. 9, 1753.

Rev. Horace E. Hayden wrote me in 1917 that the Wyoming Historical Society had a file of the New York Evening Post from Feb. 24 to Nov. 27, 1752, but repeated search in the library of that Society has failed to reveal the file.

The N. Y. Historical Society has reproduced by photostat all of the known issues of this paper from 1744 to 1752, which set is to be found in the following libraries: Am. Antiq. Soc., Mass. Hist. Soc., Carter Brown Lib., Yale, N. Y. Hist. Soc., Grosvenor Lib., Western Reserve Hist. Soc., Univ. of Ill., Newberry Lib., Univ. of Mich. (Clements), and Huntington Lib.

N. Y. Hist. Soc. has Dec. 17, 1744–Mar. 21, 1748, lacking 17 issues; Sept. 5–Dec. 26, 1748; Jan. 1–Dec. 31, 1750.
N. Y. Pub. Lib. has Aug. 3, Sept. 7, 1747; Jan. 7–Mar. 4, 18–Dec. 30, 1751.
Lib. Congress has Jan. 9, Mar. 6–June 26, July 10, 24–Oct. 30, Nov. 20, 27, 1749.
Am. Antiq. Soc. has Feb. 10, Dec. 18, 1752.
Duke Univ. has Apr. 22, 1751.
Hist. Soc. Penn. has Sept. 7, Oct. 26, 1747; Feb. 17, Mar. 30, 1752.

New-York Evening Post, 1782–1783.

Tri-weekly. Established as a tri-weekly Sept. 4, 1782, judging from the date of the earliest issue located, that of Oct. 25, 1782, vol. 1, no. 23, a paper of quarto size, published by Sower, Morton, and Horner [Christopher Sower, Jun., William Morton and Samuel Horner], with the title of "The New-York Evening Post." The last issue located is that of Mar. 21, 1783, vol. 2, no. 86. In April, 1783, it became a semi-weekly and the title was changed to "The New-York Morning Post," judging from the volume numbering of the latter paper. Sower also retired from the firm at this time, and later had considerable difficulty in adjusting his accounts with his former partners (see his letter in the "Royal Gazette" of Sept. 27, 1783).

Univ. of Mich. (Clements) has Oct. 25, 1782; Feb. 5, 14, Mar. 7, 1783.
N. Y. Hist. Soc. has Mar. 21, 1783.

New-York Evening Post, 1794–1795.

Tri-weekly. Established Nov. 17, 1794, by L[evi] Wayland, with the title of "The New-York Evening Post," succeeding the "Columbian Gazetteer." With the issue of Dec. 8, 1794, the title was altered to "New-York Evening Post," and it was published by L. Wayland and Matthew L. Davis. It was discontinued with the issue of May 25, 1795, vol. 1, no. 82.

N. Y. Hist. Soc. has Nov. 17, 1794–May 25, 1795.

Am. Antiq. Soc. has Nov. 17–Dec. 31, 1794; Jan. 2, 5, 28, Mar. 16, Apr. 8, 15, 29, May 4, 15, 1795.
N. Y. State Lib. has Nov. 19–24, 1794.
Harvard has Apr. 10–15, May 4, 8, 1795.
Lib. Congress has Mar. 27, 30, 1795.

New-York Evening Post, 1801–1820+.

Daily. Established Nov. 16, 1801, with the title of "New-York Evening Post," published by Michael Burnham and edited by William Coleman. With the issue of Dec. 12, 1811, it was published by Michael Burnham & Co., and with the issue of Oct. 7, 1816, the title was altered to "The New-York Evening Post." It was so continued until after 1820. Throughout this period, Coleman, although his name was not in the imprint, was editor, and it was known as his paper. The Post carried a semi-weekly edition, called the "New-York Herald" (which see) from Jan. 2, 1802 to Nov. 15, 1817, and "New-York Evening Post, for the Country" from Nov. 19, 1817 to after 1820.

N. Y. Hist. Soc. has Nov. 16, 1801–Dec. 30, 1820, lacking only a few issues; also July 8, 15, 18, Aug. 12, 19, Sept. 26, Oct. 7, 10, 28, 31, Nov. 7–18, Dec. 16, 30, 1818; Jan. 6, 1819–Dec. 30, 1820, fair, of the semi-weekly.

N. Y. Soc. Lib. has Nov. 16, 1801–Dec. 30, 1820, fair.

N. Y. Pub. Lib. has Nov. 16, 1801–Dec. 31, 1812; Jan. 3, 1814–Dec. 30, 1820; also Nov. 19, 1817–Dec. 29, 1819; Apr. 8, June 3–Dec. 30, 1820, of the semi-weekly.

Lib. Congress has Nov. 16, 1801–Dec. 31, 1803; Sept. 1–29, 1804; Feb. 1, 1805–Dec. 31, 1819; Jan. 3–5, Feb. 28, Dec. 30, 1820; also Nov. 19, 1817–Dec. 30, 1818; Jan. 6, 9, 16, Feb. 13, 27, Apr. 10, 17, 28, June 30, 1819–May 3, 1820, fair, of the semi-weekly.

Conn. Hist. Soc. has Nov. 16, 1801–Nov. 15, 1817.

Boston Athenæum has Jan. 1, 1802–Dec. 31, 1808; Aug. 12, 1809; Feb. 8–Dec. 31, 1810; Mar. 9–Dec. 31, 1812; Jan. 2, 1818–Dec. 30, 1820.

Columbia Univ. has Nov. 20, 1801–Sept. 28, 1803, fair; Feb. 7, 1807–Nov. 14, 1813, fair; Feb. 7, 1816–Dec. 24, 1819, fair.

Yale has Nov. 16, 1801–May 15, 1805; Jan. 3–Dec. 30, 1807; Mar. 14, Dec. 5, 1808–Mar. 3, 1809, fair; Mar. 16, Dec. 10, 1810; Jan. 5, 8, 12, 23, 24, Mar. 12, 1811–July 7, 31, Aug. 3–7, Nov. 27, 1812; Jan. 2–July 1, 7, 8, 20, 22, Aug. 11, 28, 31, Oct. 4, 7, Nov. 3, 1813; May 26, 1814–Nov. 3, 1817, scattering issues; Jan. 2, 1818–Dec. 30, 1820.

Am. Antiq. Soc. has Nov. 16–Dec. 31, 1801; Jan. 1–June 18, July 12, 13, Aug. 10, 25, Sept. 1–Dec. 30, 1802; Jan. 1, 1803–Dec. 28, 1804; Feb. 6, Mar. 6, 11, 13, May 18, July 10–18, Sept. 10, Nov. 2–Dec. 31, 1805; Jan. 6–Nov. 1, 4, 18, 1806; Jan. 11, 18, Feb. 4, 17, 20, 22, 23, May 2, 6, 21, July 6, 9, Aug. 10, 22, Sept. 23, Dec. 26, 29, 1807; Feb. 18, 24–27, Mar. 30–Apr. 2,

15, May 6, 7, 10, July 9, 1808; Oct. 12, 1809; Mar. 17, Aug. 23, Oct. 1, Dec. 6, 1810; Jan. 28, 31, Feb. 12, 13, Mar. 12, 13, Apr. 27, May 3, 17, 31, July 1, 8, Dec. 2, 1811; Jan. 3, 1812–Dec. 30, 1820; also Nov. 19, 1817–May 3, 1820, fair, of the semi-weekly.

N. Y. State Lib. has Jan. 1, Mar. 2–Apr. 17, fair, Aug. 2, 1802; Jan. 27–29, Feb. 24–Mar. 30, fair, May 9–June 20, July 6–20, Aug. 15, 16, Nov. 9–Dec. 31, 1803; July 18, Oct. 1, 1804–Dec. 31, 1805; May 30, June 25, 1806–Dec. 30, 1808, fair; Jan. 3–Apr. 3, May 22, 23, Oct. 24, 1809; Feb. 3, Mar. 6, 7, 14, 17, 24, Apr. 28, 1810; Mar. 11, Apr. 22, 24, July 26, 1811; Feb. 20, Apr. 29, May 6, July 1, 11, 14, 15, Aug. 1, 6, 18, 19, 26, Oct. 20, 23, 27–30, Dec. 15, 1812; Jan. 12, Mar. 12, 13, 22, Apr. 19, 24, 30, May 1, 8, June 10, 12, July 19, Aug. 27, Oct. 4, 21, 26, Nov. 12, 15, 20, Dec. 4, 9, 11, 24, 1813; Jan. 6, Mar. 8, Apr. 1, 22, 26, 28, June 17, Sept. 1, Nov. 1, 8, 29, 1814; Apr. 4, 17, May 5, 1815; June 17–27, Oct. 22, 1816–Mar. 31, 1817; Feb. 5–7, 1818; Nov. 8, 1819; Jan. 8, May 5, 1820; also Nov. 22, 1817–Dec. 1, 1819, scattering file; Jan. 1–Dec. 27, 1820, of the semi-weekly.

Wis. Hist. Soc. has Jan. 18, 1802–Dec. 31, 1807, fair; Mar. 1–5, Sept. 10, 1808; Jan. 4, 5, 11, May 13–16, July 8, 10–12, 15–18, 22, Aug. 14, 26, 27, Sept. 9–11, 13–23, 25, Oct. 9, 1811; Jan. 3–9, Feb. 11–29, Mar. 30–Dec. 31, 1812; Dec. 19, 1818; also Jan. 2, 1819–Dec. 30, 1820, of the semi-weekly.

Hist. Soc. Penn. has Apr. 14, 1814–Dec. 30, 1820.

N. J. Hist. Soc. has Nov. 21, 1811–Dec. 31, 1814, scattering file; Jan. 7, 1815–Oct. 29, 1816; June 21, 1817–Apr. 30, 1818.

Western Reserve Hist. Soc. has Nov. 18, 1801–Dec. 31, 1803, fair.

No. Tonawanda Pub. Lib. has Nov. 16, 1801–Jan. 24, 1803.

Univ. of Mich. (Clements) has Feb. 1–Mar. 31, Apr. 13, Sept. 1–14, Oct. 12–Dec. 31, 1802; Apr. 25–Dec. 31, 1812, fair; Feb. 17, May 17, 1813; Jan. 24, 25, Mar. 9, July 15, 29–Dec. 29, 1815, fair; May 22, Sept. 7, 1818; Sept. 5–Dec. 30, 1820, fair.

Harvard has Jan. 27–Aug. 16, 1802, fair; Jan. 5, Nov. 18, 1803; July 2, 1804; May 5, 1808.

Newburgh, N. Y., Lib. has July 5, 1803–Jan. 31, 1804.

Duke Univ. has Apr. 21, Aug. 3, Nov. 7, 10, 1803; Jan. 28, July 21, Oct. 28–31, Dec. 3, 24, 29, 1806; July 1–Aug. 9, 1808, fair; July 1–Dec. 31, 1811, fair; July 19–Aug. 11, Nov. 29, 1817; also Jan. 28–Dec. 26, 1818, fair; Jan. 2, 1819; Jan. 1–Dec. 30, 1820, of the semi-weekly.

Minn. Hist. Soc. has Jan. 4–Dec. 31, 1813.

Chicago Hist. Soc. has Feb. 13, 1813–Dec. 30, 1814.

Mass. Hist. Soc. has Feb. 21, 1815–Feb. 24, 1816.

Newberry Lib. has Nov. 19, 1817–Dec. 30, 1820, of the semi-weekly.

H. Armour Smith, Yonkers, has Oct. 6–Nov. 3, Dec. 5, 1818; Mar. 12, June 1–July 12, 1819, fair.

Buffalo Hist. Soc. has Jan. 2, 1819–Dec. 30, 1820.

Lehigh Univ. has June 3–Nov. 29, 1820, of the semi-weekly.

Rutgers Univ. has Mar. 31, 1802; Feb. 15–May 20, 1803, fair; Sept. 18, 1806; Mar. 1, 5, 29, Apr. 2, 7, June 8, 1808.

Many libraries have single or a few scattering issues.

[New York] Exile, 1817–1818.

Weekly. Established Jan. 4, 1817, by Walter Cox, with the title of "The Exile." It was devoted chiefly to Irish intelligence. The last issue located is that of Oct. 18, 1817, vol. 1, no. 42. The Albany "Argus" of Sept. 8, 1818, refers to Walter Cox, "editor of the Exile, a paper lately published in New York."

Lib. Congress has Jan. 4–May 17, July 26–Aug. 9, 30, Sept. 6, 20, 27, Oct. 4, 18, 1817.

Am. Antiq. Soc. has Jan. 4–25, Feb. 8, Apr. 5, 12, May 3, 31, June 21, July 12, Oct. 11, 1817.

[New York] Forlorn Hope, 1800.

Weekly. Established Mar. 24, 1800, with the title of "Forlorn Hope," published from the Prison, New York, and conducted by William Keteltas, who signed the editorial announcement. It was published in the interest of prison reform and especially to bring about the repeal of the law as to imprisonment for debt. The last issue located is that of Sept. 13, 1800, vol. 1, no. 25.

Lib. Congress has Mar. 31–Sept. 6, 1800.

N. Y. Hist. Soc. has Mar. 31, Apr. 19–Sept. 13, 1800.

Univ. of Mich. (Clements) has Apr. 19, May 17, June 7, 14, 28, Aug. 9, Sept. 6, 1800.

Wis. Hist. Soc. has Mar. 24, 1800.

Am. Antiq. Soc. has Sept. 13, 1800.

[New York] French and American Gazette, see Gazette Francaise.

New-York Gazette, 1725–1744.

Weekly. Established, judging from the date of the earliest issue located and from the weight of contemporary evidence, on Nov. 8, 1725. Thomas, in his History of Printing (ed. 1874, vol. 2, p. 98), states that the paper first appeared Oct. 16, 1725, and reconstructs the heading of the second issue published Monday, Oct. 23, 1725, although the only issues mentioned in his text are some of 1736. It is a noticeable fact that Oct. 23, 1725, did not fall on Monday, but on Saturday. The earliest issue known is that of Monday, Mar. 7, 1726, no. 18, entitled "The New-York Gazette," printed by William Bradford (a photographic reproduction is given in Stokes, "Iconography of Manhattan Island," vol. 2, p. 413). This numbering would show that the first issue was published Nov. 8, 1725. In the issue of May 2, 1726, Bradford states "This Numb. 26 of our

Gazette concludes the first half year," and in the issue of June 17, 1728, he says "We began to Publish this Gazette the first of November, 1725." The Philadelphia "American Weekly Mercury" of Nov. 4, 1725, carries news with the New York date line of Nov. 1, 1725, and regularly weekly thereafter. Since the first issue must have been headed "November 1 to November 8," as was the early custom of giving the dating, this statement of Bradford's is entitled to the highest respect. Although Hildeburn, in his "Printers and Printing in New York," as well as many other historians, follow Thomas, later authorities accept Nov. 8, 1725, as the correct date.

In either 1742 or 1743, Bradford took his former apprentice, Henry DeForeest, into partnership and the paper was published by William Bradford & Henry DeForeest. The last issue located is that of Oct. 29, 1744, no. 990, and the paper was probably discontinued with the issue of Nov. 19, 1744, to be succeeded the following week by DeForeest's "New-York Evening-Post."

The New York Historical Society has reproduced by photostat all of the known issues of this paper from 1726 to 1744, which set is to be found in the following libraries: — Am. Antiq. Soc., Lib. Congress, N. Y. Hist. Soc., N. Y. Pub. Lib., N. Y. Geneal. & Biog. Soc., N. Y. Soc. Lib., Columbia Univ., Hunter Coll., N. Y. State Lib., Mass. Hist. Soc., Boston Athenæum, Carter Brown Lib., Yale, Grosvenor Lib., Western Reserve Hist. Soc., Univ. of Ill., Newberry Lib., Univ. of Mich., Wis. Hist. Soc., and Huntington Lib.

- N. Y. Soc. Lib. has Mar. 28–Oct. 31, Nov. 14–28, Dec. 19, 26, 1726; Jan. 2– Mar. 20, Apr. 10–May 15, 29–Dec. 25, 1727; Jan. 1, 22, Feb. 5–Apr. 1, 29– July 22, Aug. 12, 19, Sept. 2, 17–Oct. 28, Nov. 11–Dec. 31, 1728; Jan. 14– Nov. 17, 1729.
- N. Y. Pub. Lib. has Apr. 4, 11, June 13, Oct. 3, Dec. 5, 1726; Apr. 17, 24, July 31, Aug. 7, 28, Sept. 11, 25, Oct. 9–30, Dec. 25, 1727; Jan. 1–15, 29, Mar. 25–Apr. 8, May 6, 20, June 3–17, July 1, Aug. 5–26, Sept. 9–Oct. 21, Nov. 11, 18, Dec. 2, 10, 24, 31, 1728; Jan. 14, 21, Apr. 7–28, May 11, 26, July 14, Aug. 11, Sept. 15, 29–Oct. 13, 1729; Jan. 6, Mar. 23, Apr. 27, May 18, June 1–29, July 13, 20, Aug. 3, 24, 31, Sept. 21, 28, Oct. 19–Nov. 16, 1730; Jan. 4–Mar. 1, 15, 29–Apr. 12, 26, May 24, June 14, July 5–19, Aug. 16, 30– Sept. 20, Oct. 5, Nov. 1, Dec. 13, 1731; Jan. 11, June 19, July 10, Aug. 7, 21, 28, Oct. 30, Dec. 4, 11, 26, 1732; Jan. 9–23, Apr. 9, 30, June 11–Aug. 20, Sept. 3–24, Oct. 15–Dec. 3, 24, 31, 1733; Jan. 7–Sept. 2, 16–Dec. 30, 1734; Jan. 7–21, Feb. 4–May 12, 26–Nov. 10, 24–Dec. 30, 1735; Jan. 6–Feb. 10, 24, Mar. 6–Apr. 12, May 3–Aug. 16, 1736; June 12–July 31, Aug. 21, Sept. 4, Oct. 30, 1738; Jan. 16, 22, Feb. 20, 27, Mar. 20, Apr. 9, 23, June 18–July 9, Sept. 17, 24, 1739; Mar. 4–18, 1740; July 2, Aug. 20, Sept. 24, Oct. 1, 15, 1744.
- N. Y. Hist. Soc. has Oct. 9, 1727; May 11, 18, June 1–22, July 6–Aug. 3, 17, Sept. 7, 21, 28, Oct. 12–Nov. 9, Dec. 7–29, 1730; Jan. 19, Mar. 8, 22, May 3, 10, 31, June 7, 21, 28, July 26, Aug. 9, 23, Oct. 11, Nov. 15–Dec. 6, 21, 1731;

Jan. 18, Feb. 15, Apr. 3, May 8–22, June 12, 26, July 17–31, Sept. 4, 11, 25, Oct. 2, 16, 23, Nov. 20, 27, Dec. 18, 1732; Jan. 23, Feb. 6–20, Mar. 20, Apr. 16, May 21, 28, July 16, 30, Aug. 13, Oct. 8–29, Nov. 12, Dec. 3–31, 1733; Jan. 7–Dec. 30, 1734; Jan. 7–Feb. 11, Mar. 10, 17, 31, Apr. 7, 21– May 19, June 2–16, 30, Aug. 11, 25–Oct. 6, 20, Nov. 3–17, Dec. 1, 23, 30, 1735; Jan. 13–Feb. 24, Mar. 15–Apr. 5, 19, May 31, June 7, 21, 28, July 26, Aug. 2, 30–Oct. 25, Nov. 15, Dec. 13, 21, 1736; Jan. 11, Feb. 10, 24– Mar. 8, 29–Apr. 11, 25–May 30, June 13, 27, July 4, Aug. 1, 29, Sept. 5, 19, Oct. 3, 10, 24–Nov. 7, 28–Dec. 27, 1737; Jan. 23, Feb. 14, Mar. 14, Apr. 7, 10, May 21, June 12, July 3, 24–Aug. 7, 1738; Apr. 16, 1739; May 19, 26, 1740; May 4, 1741.

Hist. Soc. Penn. has Mar. 7, July 4, 11, 25–Aug. 8, 1726; Oct. 2, 1732; Jan. 21, Mar. 11, Dec. 2, 1734; Feb. 4, Aug. 11, 1735; Nov. 1, 1736–Apr. 14, 1740, good; July 23, Oct. 29, 1744.

British Museum has Feb. 18, 1734–Apr. 24, 1738, good.

Lib. Congress has Jan. 23, Feb. 6, Oct. 29, Nov. 12, 1733; Jan. 28, Feb. 11– May 20, June 3–17, July 1–Aug. 12, 26, Sept. 2, 23–Dec. 30, 1734; Aug. 23, Oct. 11, 25, 1736.

Wis. Hist. Soc. has Apr. 3, 1732; Aug. 30, Sept. 6, 1736.

British Public Record Office has Sept. 24, Oct. 1, 1733.

Yale has Apr. 28, 1735.

H. Armour Smith, Yonkers, has Nov. 17, 1735.

Univ. of Mich. (Clements) has Sept. 13, 1736.

Am. Antiq. Soc. has Mar. 22, Sept. 13, 1736.

New-York Gazette, or Weekly Post-Boy, 1747–1773.

Weekly. A continuation, without change of volume numbering, of "The New-York Weekly Post-Boy," the first issue with the title of "The New-York Gazette, revived in the Weekly Post-Boy" being that of Jan. 19, 1747, no. 209, printed by James Parker. With the issue of Jan. 1, 1753, William Weyman was taken into partnership, the paper was printed by J. Parker and W. Weyman and the title was changed to "The New-York Gazette: or, the Weekly Post-Boy." With the issue of Feb. 5, 1759, the partnership was dissolved and the paper printed by James Parker. With the issue of Feb. 12, 1759, upon the retirement of James Parker, the paper was printed by his nephew, Samuel Parker, who changed the title, Mar. 19, 1759, to "Parker's New-York Gazette: or, the Weekly Post-Boy." With the issue of Dec. 10, 1759, the name of the printer was omitted, and with July 31, 1760, the imprint became James Parker, and Company [James Parker and John Holt].

With the issue of May 6, 1762, the firm was dissolved, and John Holt, who stated that he had "had the management of the business for near two years past," became the publisher, changing the title to "The New-York Gazette; or, the Weekly Post-Boy." Hearing that James Parker, from whom he had hired the establishment, was intending to publish a newspaper in New York (see

Mass. Hist. Soc. Proc. ser. 2, vol. 16, pp. 210–216), Holt gave up the title of the Gazette, and on May 29, 1766, called his paper "The New-York Journal, or General Advertiser," no. 1. But learning that Parker declined publishing for the present, he resumed the old title, June 5, 1766, with the former volume numbering, "The New-York Gazette; or, the Weekly Post-Boy," no. 1222. He so continued the paper until Oct. 9, 1766, no. 1240. Again, in view of Mr. Parker's publishing intentions, Holt, on Oct. 16, 1766, adopted a new title "The New-York Journal, or General Advertiser," no. 1241, continuing the volume numbering of the Gazette. For this paper see under "New-York Journal."

James Parker resumed publication Oct. 16, 1766, under the title of "The New-York Gazette: or, the Weekly Post-Boy," no. 1241, also continuing the volume numbering, as well as the title. Parker died July 2, 1770, and with the issue of July 9, 1770, the printer's name was omitted from the imprint. With the issue of Aug. 13, 1770, the paper was printed by Samuel Inslee, and Anthony Car, who leased it from Samuel F. Parker. The last issue with their imprint which has been located is that of July 12, 1773, no. 1577, but they evidently continued the paper until the expiration of their lease on Aug. 13, 1773 (Gaine's "New-York Gazette," Aug. 16, 1773). The paper was then published for a few weeks by Samuel F. Parker and John Anderson (see Thomas, "History of Printing," ed. 1874, vol. 2, p. 107, and advertisement in "The New-York Journal" of Sept. 9, 1773), but no copies with their imprint have been located. In "Rivington's New-York Gazetteer" of Nov. 11, 1773, there is a reference to Parker & Anderson as the printers of a New York newspaper, and in the same paper of Dec. 9, 1773, there is an advertisement stating that the partnership of Parker & Anderson was dissolved on Dec. 9, and that John Anderson would carry on the printing business.

N. Y. Hist. Soc. has negative photostat set of all located issues, 1747–1773.

N. Y. Hist. Soc. has Jan. 19, 1747–Dec. 25, 1752; Feb. 26, 1753–May 5, Aug. 18–Oct. 27, 1755; Feb. 16, Mar. 8, July 5, 26, Sept. 13, Oct. 18, Dec. 13, 1756; Aug. 1, 29, Sept. 5, 19, 26, Oct. 10, 17, Nov. 14, Dec. 5, 12, 1757; Feb. 13, Mar. 6, 27–Apr. 17, May 1–15, June 5, 19, July 3, 10, 24, Aug. 7–21, Sept. 4, 11, Oct. 9, 16, 30–Nov. 20, Dec. 11, 18, 1758; Jan. 1–Feb. 12, 26–Apr. 2, 16, 23, May 21–July 2, 16–Dec. 24, 1759; Jan. 7, 14, Feb. 4–May 12, 26–July 17, Dec. 18, 1760; Jan. 22–Feb. 5, 19–Apr. 2, 16–May 28, June 11, 18, July 2, 9, 23, Aug. 6–Oct. 15, 29, Nov. 5, 19–Dec. 3, 17–31, 1761; Jan. 7–Mar. 4, 18–June 24, Nov. 18, 1762; Jan. 6–Feb. 3, 17, Mar. 3–17, 31–May 12, 26–Sept. 1, 15–Dec. 29, 1763; Mar. 22, 29, Nov. 29–Dec. 20, 1764; Jan. 3, 1765–Dec. 24, 1766; Mar. 14, 1768–Dec. 30, 1771.

N. Y. Pub. Lib. has Jan. 19, 1747–Dec. 18, 1758, good; Jan. 1–Sept. 24, 1759, fair; Feb. 11–Dec. 18, 1760, fair; Apr. 9, Aug. 20, 1761; July 8–Dec. 30, 1762, fair; Apr. 21, 1763; Jan. 5, 1764–Dec. 26, 1765, fair; Jan. 2–Oct. 9, Dec. 25, 1766; Jan. 1, 1767–Dec. 12, 1768, fair; May 22–June 12, Oct. 23, 1769; Mar. 19, May 14, June 11, Aug. 6, 1770; Aug. 12, 1771; May 18, 1772.

NEW YORK 637

Hist. Soc. Penn. has Jan. 19–Dec. 28, 1747; Apr. 24–July 24, Sept. 18–Oct. 9, Nov. 13–Dec. 18, 1749; Jan. 1, 1750–Nov. 6, 1752; Jan. 1, 1753–July 1, 1754, fair; Jan. 27, 1755–Dec. 24, 1760, fair; Jan. 15–29, 1761; Jan. 7, 1762–Dec. 14, 1772, fair; Feb. 1, 1773.

Lib. Congress has Feb. 23–Dec. 28, 1747; Mar. 7, May 30, 1748–Dec. 25, 1749, fair; Feb. 5–Apr. 9, 23–May 14, 28, June 11–25, July 16–30, Aug. 13, 20, Sept. 10–Oct. 29, Nov. 19, 1750; Jan. 7, 1751–Dec. 19, 1757; Oct. 9, 16, Nov. 13, 1758; Feb. 5, 1759; Apr. 30–Dec. 31, 1761; Jan. 26, May 3, 1764; Jan. 17–Feb. 21, June 27, Dec. 5, 1765; Jan. 2, 9, 30–Feb. 20, Apr. 24, July 24, 31, Aug. 21, 1766; Jan. 29, Mar. 26, Apr. 2, July 2, Nov. 26, Dec. 3, 31, 1767; Feb. 1, 1768; Dec. 18, 1769; Mar. 26, Apr. 2, May 6, 1770; Mar. 4, 11, Apr. 8, July 29, Aug. 5, Sept. 30, Oct. 7, Nov. 11, 1771; Mar. 9, May 25, Sept. 28, Oct. 19, Nov. 23, 1772; Jan. 4, Feb. 8, Apr. 12, June 21, July 5, 12, 1773.

Phil. Lib. Co. has Jan. 19–Nov. 30, Dec. 28, 1747; Jan. 4–25, Mar. 7, Apr. 11, 18, Sept. 26–Oct. 24, Nov. 7–21, Dec. 12, 19, 1748; Feb. 6, Mar. 6–Apr. 10, 24, May 1, Sept. 4, 18, 1749; Jan. 8, Mar. 5, Apr. 2, 16, July 13, Sept. 24, Nov. 5, Dec. 10, 1750; Jan. 14–28, Feb. 18, Mar. 4, 25, Apr. 1, 15, May 20, June 10, Aug. 19, Sept. 16, 30, Dec. 30, 1751; Jan. 6, May 4, 11, June 1, July 13, 27, Nov. 13, Dec. 18, 25, 1752; Jan. 1, 1753–Oct. 9, 1766; Feb. 5, 26, Mar. 19, Apr. 30, May 6, July 30, Aug. 27, Sept. 3, Oct. 22, 1770; Jan. 14, Apr. 20, May 1, June 3, 17, 24, Aug. 5, 12, 26, Sept. 9–Oct. 7, 28–Dec. 23, 1771; Mar. 23–Apr. 6, 27–May 25, June 15, July 27, 1772.

N. Y. Soc. Lib. has Mar. 7, 1748; Sept. 23, 1754; Nov. 10, 1755–Mar. 5, 1759; Mar. 31, 1760–Oct. 9, 1766; Nov. 12, 1767–May 30, 1768; June 20, 27, Nov. 7, 1768; Apr. 24, Dec. 11, 1769.

Am. Antiq. Soc. has Mar. 23–Dec. 28, 1747; Jan. 4, 25, Feb. 15, 29, Mar. 28–Apr. 11, 25, June 27, July 11, 25–Aug. 8, 21–Sept. 12, Oct. 3, 10, Nov. 28–Dec. 12, 1748; June 25, 1750; Nov. 1, 22, 1756; May 16, 1757; Aug. 7, Nov. 6–27, Dec. 11–23, 1758; Jan. 1–Feb. 19, Mar. 12, Apr. 9, May 14–July 17, 1759; Jan. 14, Feb. 25, 1762; May 31, 1764; Jan. 3, 1765–Oct. 9, 30, 1766; Jan. 1, 1767–Dec. 25, 1769.

Mass. Hist. Soc. has Nov. 2, 1747; Jan. 18, Nov. 28, 1748; Apr. 30, 1753; Dec. 30, 1754; Apr. 19, Oct. 4, 1756; July 10, 31, Oct. 16, 1758; Oct. 8, 1759; July 19, 1764; Aug. 1, 1765; Jan. 9, Feb. 20, Apr. 17, May 1, July 3, Sept. 4, Nov. 6, 1766; May 28, Dec. 10, 1767; Feb. 1, Mar. 14, 1768–Dec. 31, 1770; Jan. 14, Feb. 11, 25, Mar. 25, Apr. 15, June 10, 24, July 15–Aug. 5, 19–Sept. 9, Oct. 14, Nov. 4–18, Dec. 9, 1771; Jan. 6–Feb. 10, 24, Mar. 2, Apr. 27, May 4, 18, June 22, July 6, 13, 27, 1772.

Yale has June 25, Aug. 20–Sept. 3, 17–Oct. 1, 22, 29, Nov. 19–Dec. 24, 1750; June 3, Sept. 23, 1751; Apr. 20, 1752; Sept. 3, 1753; May 20, June 17, Aug. 12, Sept. 23, 30, Dec. 9–23, 1754; Jan. 13, 20, Feb. 17, Mar. 3, Apr. 14, 21, Nov. 23, Dec. 29, 1755; Mar. 1, 8, Apr. 19, May 24, Aug. 9, Sept. 6, 13, Oct. 11, 25, Nov. 1, 22, 29, Dec. 20, 27, 1756; Jan. 3, 10, 31, Feb. 14, Mar. 7,

Apr. 4, May 23, June 21–July 4, 25–Aug. 8, 22–Oct. 10, Nov. 21–Dec. 5, 1757; Jan. 16, Mar. 6, Apr. 10, 17, May 22–June 12, Dec. 11, 1758; Jan. 15, July 2, 23, 1759; Apr. 14, 28, June 2, 9, 1760; Mar. 5, May 7, June 11, Dec. 10, 1761; Jan. 14, 21, Feb. 25, May 6, July 1, 8, Aug. 5, Oct. 14, 1762; July 7, 1763; July 26, Nov. 1, 1764; Jan. 31, Feb. 14, Aug. 15–Dec. 26, 1765; Jan. 2–Feb. 20, Mar. 6, 13, May 22, Sept. 4, 1766.

Wis. Hist. Soc. has Sept. 25, 1749–Dec. 10, 1750.

Del. Hist. Soc. has Oct. 16, 1766–Oct. 30, 1769.

Boston Pub. Lib. has Dec. 6, 14, 1747; Oct. 22, Nov. 5, Dec. 17, 1750; June 10, 1751; Dec. 31, 1753; June 3, 1754; July 5, Aug. 9, 1756; Jan. 15, 1759; Dec. 12, 1765; Apr. 3, 28, May 15, June 12, Sept. 11, 13, 18, Oct. 2, 1766.

N. Y. State Lib. has Aug. 17, 1747; Jan. 22, Mar. 19, 26, Apr. 9, 23, 1750; Oct. 3, 1757; June 18, 1759; Mar. 21, Apr. 14, 18, May 2, July 28, 1768; June 5, July 10, 31, 1769; Mar. 26, July 23, 1770; June 10, Dec. 9, 1771; May 18, 1772.

Newburgh, N. Y. Lib. has June 4, 1753; Apr. 4, 11, 1757; Nov. 27, 1758; Mar. 19, Apr. 2, 1759.

Univ. of Chicago has May 18, Aug. 17, 31, Oct. 12, Nov. 30, Dec. 14, 1747; Nov. 16, 1772.

Univ. of Mich. (Clements) has May 18, June 29, Aug. 31, Oct. 12, 1747; Aug. 8, 1757; Feb. 15, 1768.

N. J. Hist. Soc. has May 18, Aug. 17, 31, 1747; Mar. 7, 1748; Jan. 8–Feb. 12, Mar. 5–Apr. 9, 23–May 14, 28, June 11–25, 1750; Apr. 22, 1754; June 16, 1755; Jan. 1, 1761; Sept. 29, 1763; Oct. 10, 1765; Jan. 6, 1772.

Duke Univ. has Nov. 16, 1747; Dec. 10, 1750; Dec. 19, 1763; July 3, 1766; Aug. 6, 1770.

Princeton has Feb. 16, 1747; July 7, 1760.

Harvard has Mar. 7, 1748; Oct. 23, 1760.

Rutgers Univ. has Mar. 5, June 25, 1750; Aug. 21, 1760.

Columbia Univ. has May 12, Dec. 15, 1755.

Western Reserve Hist. Soc. has Oct. 16, 1758; Nov. 24, 1768.

Cornell Univ. has Apr. 4, 25, Aug. 8, 1768; Jan. 9–23, 1769.

New-York Gazette [Weyman's], 1759–1767.

Weekly. Established by William Weyman, with the title of "Weyman's New-York Gazette." A prospectus issue, no. 00, was published Feb. 16, 1759, and the initial number, no. 1, appeared Feb. 19, 1759. With the issue of Aug. 13, 1759, the title was changed to "The New-York Gazette." Because of the Stamp Act, the paper was temporarily suspended with the issue of June 10, 1765, no. 340. This was followed by occasional issues: July 15, no. 341; July 22, without numbering; Sept. 16, no. 342; and Nov. 25, no. 343, resuming regular publication. The paper was discontinued with the issue of Dec. 28, 1767, no. 454.

N. Y. Pub. Lib. has Feb. 16, Mar. 26, 1759–Dec. 26, 1763; Jan. 2, 1764–Dec. 30, 1765, fair; Jan. 6, 1766–Dec. 14, 1767.
N. Y. Hist. Soc. has Feb. 19, 1759–Dec. 26, 1763, good; Jan. 30, Mar. 12, 19, Apr. 2–23, May 7–28, 1764; Feb. 3, 17, May 12–June 16, 30–July 14, 28, Sept. 8, 22, Oct. 6, 20, Nov. 24, Dec. 1, 1766; Jan. 19, Feb. 2, 16, Mar. 2, 23, Apr. 13, May 4, 11, 25–June 15, Aug. 31, Sept. 14, 28, Nov. 2, 30, 1767.
Hist. Soc. Penn. has Feb. 25–July 30, 1759, fair; Aug. 13, 1759–Dec. 26, 1763; Feb. 27, Mar. 5, May 14, 1764; Jan. 27, Feb. 10, 24, Apr. 7–May 5, 1766.
N. Y. Soc. Lib. has Nov. 5, 1759; Oct. 30, Nov. 17, 1760; Sept. 28, 1761; Feb. 15, Oct. 18, Dec. 13, 27, 1762; Jan. 3, 1763–Oct. 15, 1764; Jan. 7, 1765–Dec. 14, 1767.
Am. Antiq. Soc. has Sept. 8, 17, 22, 1760; Oct. 18, 1762; Jan. 7, 1765–Dec. 28, 1767.
Univ. of Pittsburgh has Jan. 2, 1764–Nov. 25, 1765.
Boston Pub. Lib. has Nov. 26, 1759; July 14, Aug. 25, Sept. 29, Oct. 20, Nov. 3, Dec. 1, 15, 1760; Feb. 16, 23, Mar. 23–Apr. 20, June 8, 29, Aug. 3, 10, 24–Sept. 7, 28, Oct. 19, 26, Nov. 30, Dec. 14, 1761; Feb. 8, Mar. 1, 1762; Jan. 24, 31, Feb. 28, Mar. 14, Nov. 7, 28, Dec. 26, 1763; Oct. 20, 1766; July 20, 27, 1767.
Yale has Feb. 19, Apr. 2, 30, Sept. 17, 1759; July 21, Sept. 29, Oct. 20–Dec. 29, 1760; Jan. 12, 26, Mar. 16, 30, Apr. 27, May 11–June 8, July 27, Sept. 14, Nov. 30, 1761; Mar. 7, 1763; Apr. 16, July 19, 1764; Dec. 23, 1765; June 9, 1766.
Lib. Congress has Nov. 26, 1759; Aug. 11, Sept. 15, 29, Nov. 10, 17, Dec. 8, 1760; Feb. 9, 16, Mar. 2, 9, 23, 30, Apr. 20, May 25, July 27, Aug. 3, 17, Sept. 7, 14, Oct. 8, 1761; Mar. 3, 1 , Dec. 15, 1766.
Md. Hist. Soc. has Jan. 18, Feb. 1, 15, Mar. 15, 22, Apr. 12, 26, May 3, 17, June 21, July 5, 26, 1762.
Del. Hist. Soc. has Feb. 2, Aug. 3, Nov. 19, Dec. 14, 1767.
Mass. Hist. Soc. has Feb. 25, 1759; July 21, 1766.
N. Y. State Lib. has Feb. 15, 1762; Apr. 14, 1766.
Harvard has Oct. 27, 1760.
Princeton has July 13, Oct. 5, 1761.
Wis. Hist. Soc. has Jan. 18, 1762.
Rutgers Univ. has May 9, 1763.

New-York Gazette, and Weekly Mercury, 1768–1783.

Weekly. A continuation, without change of volume numbering, of "The New-York Mercury," the first issue with the title of "The New-York Gazette; and the Weekly Mercury" being that of Feb. 1, 1768, no. 848, printed by Hugh Gaine. With the issue of Oct. 4, 1773, the semi-colon in the title was changed to a colon. In September, 1776, immediately prior to the British occupation of New York,

Gaine removed to Newark, in New Jersey, where on Sept. 21, 1776, he brought out "The New-York Gazette; and the Weekly Mercury," no. 1301, continuing the volume numbering of his previous New York issue, Sept. 9, no. 1300. Here he published seven issues, to Nov. 2, 1776, no. 1307 (see under Newark in the New Jersey checklist). In the meanwhile, the British, who were without a newspaper in New York, engaged Ambrose Serle to take charge of the printing, and brought out on Sept. 30, 1776, "The New-York Gazette: and the Weekly Mercury," no. 1301, continuing Gaine's former numbering, and even leaving the imprint "Printed by Hugh Gaine." With the issue of Oct. 7, 1776, however, the printer's name was omitted from the imprint. Gaine espoused the Royalist cause, returned to New York and brought out the issue of Nov. 11, 1776, with his name again as printer. He continued to print the paper until the date of the last issue located, that of Nov. 10, 1783, no. 1673, with which it was apparently discontinued.

The N. Y. Historical Society has reproduced by photostat all of the known issues of this paper from 1768 to 1783, which set is to be found in the following libraries: N. Y. Hist. Soc., Am. Antiq. Soc., Lib. Congress, Yale, Grosvenor Lib., Western Reserve Hist. Soc., Newberry Lib., Univ. of Chicago, Univ. of Ill., Univ. of Mich. (Clements), and Huntington Lib.

N. Y. Pub. Lib. has Feb. 1, 1768–Nov. 10, 1783.

N. Y. Hist. Soc. has Feb. 1, 1768–Apr. 22, 1776; June 3–Aug. 12, Oct. 14, 21, Dec. 9–30, 1776; Jan. 6, 1777–Aug. 26, 1782; Jan. 6–Oct. 13, 1783.

Hist. Soc. Penn. has Feb. 1, 1768–Dec. 25, 1769; Jan. 15, June 18, Dec. 3, 1770; Jan. 7, 1771–Dec. 25, 1775; Mar. 18–May 6, July 29, Dec. 2–30, 1776; Jan. 6, 1777–Nov. 10, 1783, good.

Lib. Congress has Feb. 1–Dec. 26, 1768; Jan. 2, 23–Feb. 20, Mar. 13–Apr. 3, May 22, 29, June 12–July 3, 17–Aug. 21, Sept. 4, 11, Oct. 2–Nov. 20, Dec. 11, 18, 1769; Jan. 8–22, 1770; Mar. 11, June 24, July 8, 1771–Dec. 6, 1773; Jan. 10–Nov. 14, 1774, fair; Jan. 2–Dec. 25, 1775; Jan. 1, 8, 22, Feb. 5, Apr. 22, May 6, 20, June 24–July 8, 29, Aug. 5, Sept. 9, 30, Oct. 7, Nov. 25, 1776; Jan. 6–Dec. 29, 1777; Jan. 19, 1778–Dec. 24, 1781, good; June 10, July 1, 1782; Feb. 3–Sept. 29, 1783, fair.

N. Y. Soc. Lib. has Feb. 1, 1768–Dec. 26, 1774; Jan. 1–July 1, 1776; Aug. 26, Sept. 28, Oct. 12, Dec. 2, 1776; May 26, 1777; Aug. 10, 1778.

Am. Antiq. Soc. has Feb. 1, 1768–Dec. 31, 1770; Apr. 1, Aug. 12, 26, Sept. 2, 16, 30, Oct. 7, 21, Nov. 4, 11, 25–Dec. 30, 1771; Jan. 4, 1773–Dec. 25, 1775; Jan. 22, 29, Feb. 12, 26, Mar. 4, May 13, 20, July 8, 29, Nov. 4, 18, 1776; Jan. 6–Feb. 10, Mar. 3, 10, 24, Apr. 14–Aug. 4, 18–Oct. 6, 20–Nov. 10, 24–Dec. 29, 1777; Jan. 5–19, Feb. 2, 16–Apr. 6, May 18, Aug. 10, 31–Sept. 14, 28, Oct. 19, Nov. 2, 9, 30, 1778; Jan. 4, 18–Feb. 8, Mar. 1, Apr. 12, 26, June 7, Sept. 13–27, Oct. 18, Nov. 15, 29, 1779; Jan. 17, Feb. 14, 28, Mar. 20, Apr. 10, 24, May 29, June 26, Sept. 11, Oct. 16, 1780; Feb. 19, Mar. 5, 19, Apr. 23, May 14, 21, Dec. 31, 1781; Jan. 14, May 6, June 10, Nov. 18–Dec. 2, 1782; Jan. 6, 20–Aug. 18, Sept. 1, 8, 29–Oct. 13, 27, 1783.

Mass. Hist. Soc. has Mar. 28, 1768–Dec. 24, 1770, fair; Jan. 7, 14, Feb. 11, Apr. 1, 8, May 13, June 3, 10, July 15, 29, Aug. 12–Sept. 16, 30, Nov. 11, 18, Dec. 2, 16–30, 1771; Jan. 6, 13, Feb. 3–24, Mar. 23, Apr. 13, 27, May 18, June 1–July 13, 27, Sept. 7, Nov. 23, 1772; July 12, Aug. 23, 30, Nov. 1, 1773; Nov. 7, 28, Dec. 12, 26, 1774; Jan. 23–Feb. 6, 27, Mar. 20, Apr. 10, July 31, Oct. 16, 30, Nov. 27, Dec. 11, 18, 1775; Jan. 8, Apr. 1, 8, 29, June 10, 17, Aug. 19, Dec. 16, 1776; Apr. 6, 1778; Mar. 1, 1779; May 29, 1780; Jan. 8, Apr. 9, June 4, July 16, Sept. 17, Nov. 12, Dec. 24, 1781; Mar. 25, Sept. 9, 1782.
Boston Pub. Lib. has Feb. 29, Apr. 4, 1768–Apr. 3, 1769; Aug. 7, Oct. 9, 1775; Feb. 12, 1776; Feb. 2, 1778.
Yale has Jan. 2, 1769–Dec. 30, 1770; May 29, Nov. 13, 1775.
Univ. of Pittsburgh has Apr. 10, 1769–Dec. 14, 1772, fair.
Phil. Lib. Co. has Feb. 19, Mar. 12, June 18, July 2, Aug. 13, Sept. 10, Oct. 1, 15, Nov. 26, Dec. 3, 24, 1770; Jan. 7, 1771–Feb. 10, 1772; Oct. 18, 1773; May 16, 23, Aug. 22, Oct. 17, Dec. 5, 1774; Jan. 16, 23, Mar. 6, Apr. 24, May 15, 22, June 5–26, July 10–24, Oct. 16, 1775; Jan. 1, 22, Feb. 5, 19–Apr. 8, May 6, 27, June 10, July 8, 15, Aug. 12–26, Oct. 26, Nov. 25–Dec. 9, 23, 1776; Jan. 6, 1777.
Univ. of Mich. (Clements) has Sept. 19, Oct. 10, 1768; Jan. 23, 1769; Aug. 19, Sept. 9, Oct. 28, Nov. 18, 1771; Mar. 2, 16, Apr. 20, May 18, Aug. 10, 1772; Jan. 25, Feb. 1, 22, Mar. 1, 15, Apr. 5, 12, 26, May 3, 17, 24, June 7, July 5, 19, Aug. 23, Oct. 4, 18, Nov. 1, 22, 29, 1773; July 25, 1774; Jan. 9–Dec. 11, 1775, fair; May 20, July 8, 1776; June 2, 1777; Apr. 13, 1778; Aug. 2, Dec. 17, 1779; Jan. 3–Dec. 25, 1780, fair; Feb. 26–Dec. 24, 1781, fair; Jan. 27, Apr. 7, May 12, June 2, 16, 23, Aug. 4, 1783.
N. Y. State Lib. has Feb. 1, Mar. 7, 14, 28, Apr. 4, 25–May 16, 30–June 20, July 4–Sept. 12, Oct. 3, 17, 31–Dec. 5, 19, 1768; Feb. 6, Mar. 13, May 22, Dec. 18, 1769; Feb. 26, Apr. 30, May 14, 28, June 11, July 23, Sept. 17, Nov. 5, Dec. 31, 1770; July 29, Sept. 9, 1771; Jan. 6, 1772; Oct. 11, Nov. 15, 1773; Nov. 7, 1774; Sept. 11, 18, Oct. 9–23, 1775; Mar. 19, 1781; May 27, 1782.
British Museum has May 10, Aug. 9, Sept. 6, 27, Oct. 11, 25, Nov. 1, Dec. 27, 1773; Jan. 24, Feb. 7, 14, Mar. 14–Apr. 18, May 2–30, June 13, 27, July 4, 25–Aug. 15, 29, Sept. 19, Oct. 10–31, Dec. 5–26, 1774; Jan. 2, 23, Feb. 6, 27, Mar. 20–Apr. 3, June 5, 1775; Nov. 4, 18, 25, 1776; Feb. 15, 1779; Nov. 6, 1780; June 18–July 2, Sept. 24, Oct. 8–Nov. 5, Dec. 3, 1781; June 9, 16, 1783.
Rutgers Univ. has Feb. 8, June 20, Sept. 5, 19, Oct. 31, Nov. 7, 14, Dec. 5, 1768; Jan. 23, Sept. 25, 1769; Feb. 15, Mar. 8, 1773; Feb. 7–21, Mar. 28, Apr. 18–May 2, 16, 23, June 6, 20, July 25, Aug. 22–Sept. 12, 26–Oct. 10, Nov. 21, 1774; Feb. 20, Aug. 28, Oct. 30–Nov. 13, 27, Dec. 4, 1775; May 27, 1776; Feb. 24, May 12, June 2, 1783.
Univ. of Chicago has Mar. 1, 1773; Mar. 6, May 8, June 12, Aug. 14, 28, Sept. 11, 25, Nov. 6, Dec. 11, 1775; Apr. 5, 1776; Apr. 30, 1781.

Long Id. Hist. Soc. has Jan. 16, 1769; May 24, 1773; Apr. 17, 1775; Nov. 24, 1777.

Wis. Hist. Soc. has Aug. 7, 28, 1775; July 8, 22, 1776; June 5, Dec. 4, 1780; May 6, June 3, 10, 24, Sept. 2, Oct. 28, 1782.

N. J. Hist. Soc. has Nov. 28, 1769; Dec. 16, 1776; Sept. 16, 1782.

Columbia Univ. has May 23, 1768.

Cornell Univ. has Oct. 3, 1768.

New-York Gazette, 1795–1820+.

Daily. A continuation, without change of numbering, of the "New-York Daily Gazette." The first issue with the title of "The New York Gazette" was that of Jan. 27 (or 29), 1795, published by A[rchibald] M'Lean. At some time between Mar. 5 and 28, 1795, the title reverted to "New-York Daily Gazette," but between Apr. 27, and May 13, 1795, was finally changed to "The New-York Gazette and General Advertiser." With the issue of Jan. 3, 1797, M'Lean took John Lang into partnership, the firm name being M'Lean and Lang ("and" changed to "&" with May 17, 1798). Archibald M'Lean died Sept. 22, 1798, but through an arrangement with his widow, the firm name continued. With the issue of Mar. 21, 1799, John Lang became sole proprietor. With the issue of Jan. 26, 1801, John Turner was taken into partnership, the firm name being John Lang & Co. The initial "The" in the title was omitted with the issue of May 2, 1803. The paper was suspended on account of sickness of the editors with the issue of Aug. 25, 1803, but was resumed with Oct. 24, 1803. The initial "The" was restored to the title with the issue of Sept. 6, 1806 (after a suspension of a week because of a fire on Aug. 31), and was again omitted with the issue of Oct. 21, 1806. With the issue of Jan. 3, 1805, the firm name became Lang & Turner. With the issue of July 2, 1814, John West was admitted to the firm, which became Lang, Turner & Co. With the issue of Jan. 6, 1820, John Lang's son, Robert U. Lang, entered the firm, although no alteration was made in the firm name, and the title was changed to "Lang, Turner & Co's New-York Gazette & General Advertiser." It was so continued until after 1820.

N. Y. Hist. Soc. has Jan. 29–31, Feb. 13, 28, Mar. 3–5, Apr. 17, 21, 23, 25, May 13–15, 18, 22, 25–30, June 1–Dec. 31, 1795, fair; May 11, 1796; Jan. 12, 1797–Dec. 31, 1802; Jan. 1, 1803–Dec. 30, 1807, fair; Jan. 4–Mar. 3, Sept. 1–Dec. 31, 1808; Jan. 2, 1809–Dec. 30, 1820.

N. Y. Soc. Lib. has Jan. 2–Dec. 30, 1797; Aug. 27, 29, Sept. 3, 6, 1798; Jan. 8–Feb. 27, Mar. 22–Sept. 4, 1799; Oct. 15, 1799–Dec. 9, 1801; Jan. 17, 1803–Dec. 31, 1804; Jan. 4, 1806–Dec. 5, 1812; Mar. 8, 1813–Dec. 30, 1820.

Lib. Congress has Apr. 4, June 23, July 1–7, Dec. 19, 1796; Jan. 5–Mar. 30, fair; Nov. 11, 1797; May 21, 23, Aug. 3, 16, Sept. 11–15, 21, Nov. 26, 27, 1798; Feb. 11, 22, Mar. 21, Apr. 30, May 6, 9, 24, 27, 28, June 1–Dec. 31, 1799, fair; Jan. 2, 6, 18, Feb. 23, Aug. 11, Dec. 26, 1800; July 14, 1801; Mar. 22, 1802; May 25, June 16, July 23, 1803; Feb. 19, Sept. 23, Oct. 24,

New York

Nov. 22, 1805; Oct. 29, Nov. 8, 19, 20, 1806; Oct. 6, Dec. 8, 31, 1807; Jan. 8, Mar. 4, 7–11, 1808; Apr. 13, 1809–Dec. 30, 1820.
Boston Athenæum has May 20, 1800–Dec. 31, 1808.
N. Y. Pub. Lib. has Feb. 25, Sept. 24, Nov. 16, 20, Dec. 25, 1795; Feb. 1, 1796; Nov. 5, 1801; Feb. 11, 1802; Jan. 1–Dec. 31, 1806; Jan. 1–June 29, 1811; Feb. 11, Mar. 5, 14, 26, Apr. 2, May 1, 4–25, Nov. 2–Dec. 31, 1812; Jan. 1, 1813–Dec. 31, 1815; July 1–Dec. 31, 1816; May 26, July 31, 1817.
Yale has Feb. 11, 1811; June 18, 1812–June 30, 1815.
Am. Antiq. Soc. has Jan. 31, Feb. 4, 11, 18, 25, Mar. 4, 28, Apr. 8, 24, July 22, Aug. 7, 13, 22, Sept. 12, 17, Oct. 1, Nov. 5, 25, 26, 1795; Apr. 8, 9, May 16, 26, June 6, 9, July 26, 27, Aug. 4, 15, Sept. 9, 20, 22, 23, Nov. 1, 1796–Mar. 21, 1799, fair; Apr. 3, 4, 29, May 8, Nov. 5, 7, Dec. 9–23, 27, 31, 1799; Jan. 6, 1800–June 27, 1801, fair; Aug. 18, Nov. 30, 1803; Feb. 7, Aug. 30, 1804; Jan. 30–Dec. 30, 1805; Jan. 9–Feb. 22, Apr. 4–Dec. 16, 1806; Aug. 5, 13, 1807; Jan. 6, 1808; Apr. 20, Nov. 1–Dec. 30, 1809; Jan. 26, Mar. 9, May 16–29, Aug. 27, 1810; Apr. 20, June 10, July 26, Aug. 5, 9, 15, 16, Sept. 27, Oct. 29–31, Dec. 12–31, 1811; Feb. 3, 1812–Dec. 31, 1813; Feb. 4, Sept. 17, 1814; Mar. 23, July 17, 19, 22, 24, 27, 29, Aug. 1–4, 7, 8, 21, 26, Sept. 1–6, 11, 12, 15, 18, 26, 30, Oct. 6, 9, 1815; Aug. 10, 12, 14, 15, Oct. 19, 26, 1816; Jan. 29, July 19, Aug. 20, 21, Dec. 10, 1817; Jan. 1, Mar. 6, May 15, July 24, 1818; Jan. 1, Mar. 17, Apr. 1, 7, July 24, Aug. 4, 1819; Feb. 2–28, Aug. 28, Nov. 22, Dec. 29, 1820.
Harvard has May 29, Aug. 13, Dec. 2, 8–31, 1795, fair; Jan. 13–Apr. 13, fair, July 27, 1796; Mar. 16, 28, Apr. 3, 5, 7, 18, May 15, June 8, 16–20, July 3, 5, 6, 10, Aug. 7, Sept. 30, Oct. 4, Nov. 3–8, 11, 13, 16, 17, 1797; Jan. 3–6, 11, 13, Mar. 27, June 6, Sept. 13, 14, 1798; Jan. 3, Feb. 13, 1799; Jan. 10, 27, Apr. 1, Sept. 27–Dec. 23, 1800, fair; Jan. 3–Nov. 17, 1801, fair; Jan. 18, Feb. 1, 8, 15, 23, Mar. 1, 4, 8, 13, 16, 29, Apr. 2, 5, 12, 14, 16, May 3, 5, 22–25, 29, 31, June 5–8, 14, 17, 19, July 5, 8, 17, 20, 21, 28, 31, Apr. 7, 14, 23, Sept. 3–Dec. 31, 1802, fair; Jan. 1–Aug. 25, Oct. 24–Dec. 31, 1803, fair; Jan. 3, 1804–June 15, 1805, fair; Oct. 18, 1806; Jan. 6–Sept. 24, 1807, fair; Aug. 16, Dec. 3, 8, 1808.
Phil. Lib. Co. has Oct. 27, 29, Nov. 5, 17–23, 27, 28, 30, Dec. 4, 8, 10, 1795; Jan. 9, 21–25, 27–29, Feb. 1–3, 26, Mar. 1–3, 12, 16, 19, 22–24, 26–29, 31, Apr. 4–8, 11, 13, 15, 26–30, May 4, 19–21, 26, 28, 31–June 3, 6, 11–16, 23, 25, July 1, 4, 8, 15, 19, 22–25, 27–30, Aug. 10, 11, 13, 24, 1796; July 22, 25, 1797; Jan. 23, 25–31, Feb. 3–Mar. 7, 9–24, 27–Apr. 2, 4–12, 14–May 8, 10, 12, 15–24, 26–30, June 30–July 5, 7–14, 17, 19, 21–25, 27–31, 1798.
N. Y. State Lib. has Apr. 9, Dec. 22, 1800; Aug. 1, 21, Sept. 19, 1801; Jan. 4, 1802; Aug. 4, 1803; May 1, June 6, 25, 1804; May 6, 20, July 7–Dec. 24, 1806, fair; Jan. 1, 1807–Apr. 5, 1809, fair; Apr. 27, 30, 1810; Jan. 30, June 18, 29, July 17, Aug. 13, 1812; Nov. 25, 1813; Jan. 6, Sept. 7, 1814.
Boston Pub. Lib. has Feb. 27, 1799; Oct. 4, 1808–May 1, 1809, fair; Apr. 8–July 6, 1811; Mar. 18, 1814.

Chicago Hist. Soc. has Mar. 7, 8, June 6, 11–14, 21, Sept. 16, Oct. 11, 1806; May 7, 1807; Aug. 25, 29, 31, Nov. 7, 8, 11, 14, Dec. 19, 20, 22, 1808; Jan. 10, 14, 20, 21, 24, 26, July 27, Aug. 2, 5, 7, 9, 19, 1809; Mar. 23, 24, Oct. 19, 31, Nov. 1, 5, 6, Dec. 5, 1810; Jan. 1, 3, Mar. 5–Oct. 31, 1811, fair; Jan. 1, 3, Feb. 3–Oct. 29, 1812, fair; Jan. 1–Dec. 16, 1813, fair.

Univ. of Pittsburgh has Jan. 1–Dec. 28, 1800.

Western Reserve Hist. Soc. has Jan. 1–Oct. 29, 1811.

Long Id. Hist. Soc. has Jan. 1–June 30, 1812.

Penn. State Lib. has July–Dec., 1812.

N. J. Hist. Soc. has Jan. 27, 1812–Aug. 5, 1816, scattering file.

Univ. of Mich. (Clements) has Nov. 3, 1812; Jan. 1–Apr. 30, June 2, 1813; Aug. 21, 1817; Sept. 7, 8, 1819.

Several libraries have single, or a few scattering issues, represented in other files.

[New York] Gazette Francaise, 1795–1799.

Tri-weekly. Established July 6, 1795, under the title of "Gazette Francaise et Americaine," with a sub-title "French and American Gazette." It carried alternate columns of French and English. No name of a publisher was given, although it was printed at 63 Liberty Street. With the issue of July 17, 1795, J[ohn] Delafond was given as printer and editor. With the issue of Oct. 2, 1795, the paper was bought and published by Labruere, Parisot and Co. [―――― Labruere and Claude Parisot]. The last issue published by them and the last folio issue was that of Mar. 2, 1796, no. 104, and with the succeeding issue the size was reduced to quarto, the title changed to "Gazette Francaise" and the paper printed wholly in French. No publisher was given in the imprint, although according to a manuscript entry on the copy of Jan. 2, 1797, the paper was published by Parisot & Co. With the issue of May 5, 1797, the name of Parisot appeared in the imprint as publisher. The paper was so continued until the date of the last issue located, that of Oct. 4, 1799, no. 555.

N. Y. Hist. Soc. has July 6, 1795–Mar. 2, 1796.

Harvard has Aug. 12, 14, 24, 28, 31, Sept. 4, 7, 14, 18, 27, 30, Oct. 2, 12, 14, 21–26, 30–Nov. 9, 16–20, 25, Dec. 2–28, 1795; Jan. 1–Feb. 15, 17–Mar. 2, 18–23, 28–Apr. 1, 18, 25, May 4–9, July 8, 11, 15–22, 29–Aug. 5, 10–Sept. 9, 16, 17, 21–Oct. 7, 12, 19–Nov. 4, 9, 11, 16–Dec. 5, 9–14, 21, 23, 28, 30, 1796; Jan. 2–Feb. 10, 15–27, Mar. 8, 13–17, 24–Apr. 3, 10–14, 19, 21, 26–May 15, 19, 22, 26–June 2, 7, 12–July 17, 28, Aug. 2, 15, 28, 30, Sept. 4, 6, 11, 20, 25, 29, Oct. 6–11, 16, 20–27, Nov. 6, 10, 13, 20, Dec. 6, 18, 25, 1797; Jan. 15, Feb. 12, 14, 21, 26–Mar. 2, 9–14, 19, 21, 26, 28, Apr. 2, 6, 16, 20, 27, May 7–11, 16, 18, 23, June 1–8, Aug. 3, 13, 15, 1798; Feb. 22, Mar. 1, 4, 8, 13, 15, 20, 27, 29, Apr. 1, May 10, 15, 20, 27, June 3, 17, 19, July 26–Aug. 5, 9, 14–21, 28, Sept. 4–9, 13, 20, 23, 27, Oct. 2, 4, 1799.

Am. Antiq. Soc. has Sept. 23, 1796; Aug. 4, 1797–Dec. 31, 1798.

[New York] Gazette of the United States, 1789–1790.

Semi-weekly. Established Apr. 15, 1789, by John Fenno, with the title of "Gazette of the United States." The last New York issue was that of Oct. 13, 1790, vol. 2, no. 53, when it was removed to Philadelphia, where it was continued with the issue of Nov. 3, 1790.

Am. Antiq. Soc., Harvard, Boston Pub. Lib., Mass. Hist. Soc., Boston Athenæum, York Inst. Saco, Keene Pub. Lib., Yale, N. Y. Hist. Soc., N. Y. Pub. Lib., N. Y. Soc. Lib., N. Y. State Lib., Hist. Soc. Penn., Univ. of Penn., Penn. State Lib., Lib. Congress, Univ. of Chicago, Univ. of Mich. (Clements), Wis. Hist. Soc., Univ. of Texas, and British Museum have Apr. 15, 1789–Oct. 13, 1790.

Duke Univ. has Apr. 15, 1789–Oct. 13, 1790, fair.
Ohio Arch. & Hist. Soc. has Apr. 15–Dec. 2, 1789; Jan. 17–Oct. 13, 1790.
Jersey City Pub. Lib. has Apr. 15, 1789–Apr. 17, 1790.
Princeton has Apr. 15, 1789–Apr. 14, 1790.
Phil. Free Lib. has Apr. 15, 1789–Apr. 10, 1790.
Dartmouth has Apr. 15, 1789–Jan. 27, 1790.
Rutgers Univ. has Apr. 29, 1789–Mar. 17, Apr. 10, 1790.
Conn. Hist. Soc. has Apr. 15–Sept. 26, 1789; May 5–Oct. 13, 1790.
Western Reserve Hist. Soc. has Sept. 26, Oct. 14, 1789; Apr. 14–Oct. 13, 1790.
Md. Hist. Soc. has Apr. 14–Oct. 13, 1790.
Camden Co. (N. J.) Hist. Soc. has Apr. 14–Oct. 13, 1790.
Buffalo Pub. Lib. has Apr. 17–Oct. 13, 1790.
St. Louis Univ. has Apr. 17–Oct. 13, 1790.

New-York Gazetteer, 1783–1787.

Weekly, tri-weekly, semi-weekly, and daily. Established as a weekly, Dec. 3, 1783, by Shepard Kollock, with the title of "The New-York Gazetteer, and Country Journal." With the issue of Jan. 5, 1784, it was changed to tri-weekly, and with July 27, 1784, to semi-weekly. On Dec. 7, 1784, the paper was made an eight-page quarto, with pagination, the title was shortened to "The New-York Gazetteer," and a new volume numbering was adopted. With the issue of Mar. 8, 1785, the title was changed to "The New-York Gazetteer, and the Country Journal." With the issue of Aug. 14, 1786, the paper became a daily, the size reverted to folio, the title was changed to "New-York Gazetteer; or, Daily Evening Post," and the publishing firm became Kollock, Carroll & Patterson [Shepard Kollock, George Carroll and John Patterson]. With the issue of Dec. 18, 1786, the semi-weekly publication was resumed, the title changed to "The New-York Gazetteer; and, Public Advertiser," and the firm became Carroll & Patterson. With the issue of May 7, 1787, the partnership was dissolved and the paper published by J. Patterson. The last issue located is that of Aug. 16, 1787, vol. 3, no. 248.

646 NEWSPAPER BIBLIOGRAPHY

N. J. Hist. Soc. has Dec. 3, 1783–Dec. 14, 1786.
Am. Antiq. Soc. has Dec. 24, 31, 1783; Jan. 7, 12, 14, 30, Feb. 4, 16, 18, Mar. 8–17, Apr. 28, May 7, 12, 19, June 2, 23, 30, July 14, 30, Aug. 24, 31, Sept. 7, 14–21, Oct. 1–19, 26, Nov. 19, Dec. 14, 21–31, 1784; Jan. 4–11, 18, Feb. 11, 22, Mar. 22, Apr. 15, June 21, July 5, 19, 26, Aug. 16, 23, 30, Sept. 6, 20, 27, Oct. 4, 11, 25, Nov. 1, Dec. 9–30, 1785; Jan. 3–Aug. 11, 24, 26, 28, 31, Sept. 2, 4, 6–9, 12, 13, 16, 21, 26, 29, 30, Oct. 3, 4, 6, 7, 10–13, 16, 18, 20, 21, 24, 25, 27, 28, Nov. 3, 4, 7, 8, 10, 11, 14, 17, 18, 21, 22, 24, 25, 29, Dec. 1, 8, 9, 14, 18, 21, 1786; Jan. 1–Aug. 16, 1787.
N. Y. Hist. Soc. has Dec. 10, 1783; Mar. 22, 31, Nov. 16, 23, 1784; Dec. 3, 1784–Aug. 11, 1786; Jan. 15, 1787.
Cortland Co. (N. Y.) Hist. Soc. has Dec. 10, 1783–Dec. 3, 1784.
Lib. Congress has Jan. 5–12, 16–28, Feb. 2–6, 16, 1784; Feb. 25, 1785; Feb. 28, Apr. 11, 1786; Jan. 1, 22, Apr. 5, 12, 19, Aug. 9, 1787.
Mass. Hist. Soc. has May 19, Dec. 24–31, 1784; Feb. 22, 1785; Mar. 7, May 23, Nov. 21, 22, 27, 28, 1786; Jan. 1, 8, 15, Feb. 5, 1787.
N. Y. Pub. Lib. has Aug. 17, Oct. 26, Dec. 17, 1784; May 27–June 28, July 29, Aug. 12, 1785; Jan. 10, 1786.
British Museum has Jan. 19–28, Feb. 4–18, 23, 1784; Aug. 8–14, 1786.
Yale has Apr. 5, May 10, June 14, Sept. 16, 1785.
Harvard has Dec. 3, 1783; Sept. 12, Dec. 8, 1786.
Boston Pub. Lib. has Sept. 20, 1785; Jan. 1, 1787.
N. Y. State Lib. has Jan. 13, Mar. 14, 1786.
Rutgers Univ. has May 17, 1784.
Hist. Soc. Penn. has Dec. 14, 1784.
Long Id. Hist. Soc. has Feb. 22, 1785.
N. J. State Lib. has Feb. 3, 1786.

[New York] **General Shipping & Commercial List**, see **New-York Shipping and Commercial List.**

[New York] **Greenleaf's New Daily Advertiser**, 1796–1800, see **Argus.**

[New York] **Greenleaf's New York Journal**, 1794–1800.

Semi-weekly. A continuation, without change of volume numbering, of "The New-York Journal, & Patriotic Register," the first issue with the new title of "Greenleaf's New York Journal, & Patriotic Register" being that of Jan. 1, 1794, vol. 48, no. 1, published by Thomas Greenleaf. In September, 1798, Greenleaf was seized with the yellow fever, and died Sept. 14, 1798. The issues of Sept. 8, 12, and 16 bore no imprint, and then the paper was suspended until Nov. 7, 1798, when it was resumed, with the publisher given as Ann Greenleaf, his widow. David Frothingham, who had published a newspaper at Sag Harbor, became in 1799 Mrs. Greenleaf's foreman or manager, but on Nov. 21, 1799,

NEW YORK

was tried for libel and was sentenced to four months imprisonment. The paper was discontinued with the issue of Mar. 8, 1800, vol. 52, no. 1370, when it was sold out to David Denniston, who established the "Republican Watch-Tower" in its stead.

From May 11, 1795 to Mar. 8, 1800 "The Argus, or Greenleaf's New Daily Advertiser" (which see) was published as a daily, with arrangement of the text different from "Greenleaf's New York Journal," and with frequent different advertisements.

N. Y. Hist. Soc. has Jan. 1, 1794–Mar. 8, 1800.

Yale has Jan. 3, 1795–Mar. 8, 1800.

N. Y. Pub. Lib. has Jan. 4–25, Feb. 15, 1794–May 9, 1795; Jan. 2, 1796–Dec. 30, 1797; Jan. 2–19, 26–Feb. 2, 9–Apr. 10, 17–June 1, 8–19, 26–Oct. 30, Dec. 25, 28, 1799.

Am. Antiq. Soc. has Jan. 4, 18, 25–Feb. 1, 8, 19, Mar. 8–19, 26, Apr. 16, 23, 30–May 17, June 4, 11, 18, 21, 28, July 5, 9, 23, Aug. 6, 20, 30, Sept. 10, 20, 24, Oct. 1, 4, 11, 18, 25, Nov. 1–19, 26–Dec. 6, 17–31, 1794; Jan. 3, 7, 14, 17, 28–Feb. 7, 18–28, Mar. 14–Apr. 1, 8, 11, 22–29, May 6, 9, 23–30, June 17–27, July 4–29, Aug. 5, 12, 19–Sept. 2, 19, 23, Oct. 3, 24, 31, Nov. 7, Dec. 9, 12, 1795; Jan. 2–19, Feb. 5–16, Mar. 11, 15, 29–Apr. 5, 15–22, 29, May 6, 13, 20, 27–June 7, 17, 24, July 5, 12–19, 26, Aug. 9, 19, 23, 30, Sept. 2, 9, 20, 23, Oct. 4–Dec. 30, 1796; Jan. 4–Dec. 30, 1797; Jan. 3, 10, 17, 24–Feb. 17, 24–Mar. 17, 24, 31, Apr. 7, 14, 18, 25–May 12, 26, 30, June 9, 20–30, July 25, Aug. 8, Nov. 24, Dec. 29, 1798; Jan. 2, 16, 23, Feb. 9, 16–23, Mar. 2–9, 16, 20, 30–Apr. 6, 27–May 4, 22, 29, June 1, 15, July 3–13, 24, 27, Aug. 31–Sept. 11, Oct. 26, Nov. 2, 1799; Jan. 15, 29, 1800.

Winyaw Indigo Soc., Georgetown, S. C., has 1794, 1796–1797.

Lib. Congress has May 3–Dec. 31, 1794; Jan. 3–May 9, July 29, Aug. 1, 29, Sept. 16, Oct. 14, 31, 1795; Jan. 2, Apr. 26, July 5, Aug. 9, Sept. 9, 20, Oct. 4, 11, 18–28, Nov. 8, 23, Dec. 9, 20, 1796; Jan. 11, 18, 21, Feb. 1–8, 15, 25, Mar. 4, 11, 22, 25, Apr. 1–8, 15–26, May 3, 6, 13–June 4, 14–25, July 5–12, 19, 22, Aug. 2–26, Sept. 6–13, 20–Oct. 7, 14, 18, 28, Nov. 4, 8, 18, 29, Dec. 6, 16–30, 1797; Jan. 27, 1798; May 4, Sept. 11, 1799.

East Hampton Free Lib. has Jan. 22, Mar. 8, 26, Apr. 16–May 3, 17, 21, 28, June 4, 21, July 9, 19, 26–Aug. 2, 16, Sept. 6, 20, Oct. 1–15, 25, Nov. 15, 26, Dec. 20, 24, 1794; May 1, Aug. 29, Sept. 5–16, Nov. 21, 25, Dec. 2, 1795; Feb. 19, Mar. 4, July 15, 1796; Mar. 15, 1797; Feb. 6, 13, Nov. 2–Dec. 28, 1799.

Long Id. Hist. Soc. has Jan. 1, 11, 22, Feb. 5, 8, 15, Mar. 12, 19, Apr. 2, 16, May 3, 31, June 4, 11, 18, 28–July 9, 16–26, Aug. 6, 20, 23, Oct. 1, 8, Nov. 1, 19, 29–Dec. 6, 20, 1794; Jan. 28, Feb. 4, Mar. 14, Apr. 25, Oct. 3, 17, 1795; June 3, 1796; Feb. 11, Mar. 1, May 10, June 14, 28, Nov. 7, 1798; Jan. 30, Apr. 27, Aug. 14, Sept. 11, 1799; Jan. 1–8, 15, 22–29, Feb. 26–Mar. 8, 1800.

New Haven Col. Hist. Soc. has Dec. 6, 1794–Dec. 5, 1795.

G. C. Knox, Hermosa Beach, Calif., had Jan. 3, 1795–Dec. 30, 1796, fair; but now not located.

Alfred O. Nicoll, Washingtonville, N. Y., has June 28–Dec. 30, 1796; June 6–Nov. 1, 1797.

Harvard has Jan. 11, 15, Feb. 8, Mar. 15, Apr. 12, 16, May 14, 1794; Apr. 18, Sept. 5, 9, 1795; Apr. 5, 1796; Mar. 15, Apr. 19, Sept. 16, 23, Oct. 11, Nov. 18, 1797; Jan. 3, 13, May 26, June 2, Sept. 16, 1798; Mar. 6, Apr. 6, June 26, July 24, Aug. 17, 21, Sept. 28, Oct. 2, Nov. 9, 13, 1799; Feb. 5, 1800.

N. Y. State Lib. has Feb. 11, 14, Aug. 15, 19–Sept. 2, 9, 19–Oct. 10, 21–Nov. 28, Dec. 26, 1795; Mar. 8, 1796; Jan. 27, Mar. 24, 1798.

Wis. Hist. Soc. has May 23–Sept. 4, 12, 16, Nov. 14, 17, 24, Dec. 1, 8–19, 26, 1798; Jan. 2, 9–16, 23, Feb. 6–23, Mar. 2–13, 20, 23, 30, Apr. 6, 13, 27, May 1, 4, 11–June 5, 12, 19, 22, 29–July 13, 20–31, Aug. 7–Sept. 25, Oct. 2–Nov. 20, Dec. 4, 11, 25, 28, 1799.

Duke Univ. has Jan. 28, 31, Feb. 25, 28, Mar. 25, 28, Apr. 1, May 6, 1795.

Univ. of Rochester has Apr. 29, 1796; Oct. 7, 1797; June 9, 30, July 7, 14, Dec. 12, 1798.

Boston Pub. Lib. has Jan. 24, 31, Mar. 24, June 6, 20, 1798.

Western Reserve Hist. Soc. has June 6, 1795.

Phil. Lib. Co. has Dec. 15, 1798.

Conn. Hist. Soc. has Dec. 21, 1799.

[New York] **Harmer's New York Register,** 1813.

Weekly. Established Feb. 17, 1813, judging from the first and only issue located, that of Mar. 24, 1813, vol. 1, no. 6, published by Joseph Harmer, with the title "Harmer's New York Register."

Am. Antiq. Soc. has Mar. 24, 1813.

[New York] **Herald,** 1794–1797.

Semi-weekly. Established June 4, 1794, under the title of "The Herald; a Gazette for the Country," as the semi-weekly edition of the "American Minerva." It was published by George Bunce & Co. [George Bunce and Noah Webster, Jun.]. With the issue of May 4, 1796, this partnership was dissolved and the paper published by Hopkins, Webb & Co. [George F. Hopkins, Joseph D. Webb and Noah Webster, Jun.]. With the issue of May 17, 1797, Webb retired and Webster and Hopkins continued under the firm name of Hopkins & Co. The last issue was that of Sept. 30, 1797, vol. 4, no. 343, when it was succeeded by "The Spectator," which see.

Am. Antiq. Soc., Boston Pub. Lib., Conn. Hist. Soc., Suffield (Conn.) Lib., N. Y. Hist. Soc., N. Y. Pub. Lib., N. Y. State Lib., and Lib. Congress have June 4, 1794–Sept. 30, 1797.

NEW YORK 649

Harvard and Univ. of Mich. (Clements) have June 4, 1794–Sept. 30, 1797, fair.
Duke Univ. has June 4, 1794–Sept. 30, 1797, fair.
Boston Athenæum has Oct. 16, 1794–Oct. 29, 1796; Nov. 5, 9, Dec. 10, 1796; Jan. 14, May 27, June 7–Sept. 30, 1797.
Yale has June 4, 1794–Jan. 24, 1795; May 6, 16–June 3, 1795; Nov. 23, 29, 1796; Jan. 7–May 13, June 7–Sept. 30, 1797.
Princeton, Ga. Hist. Soc., and Iowa State Dep't of History have June 4, 1794–June 4, 1796.
Conn. State Lib. has June 19, 1794–July 30, 1796, fair.
Mass. Hist. Soc. has Dec. 8, 20, 1794–Aug. 22, Sept. 5, 1795; May 21, 25, June 4, 18, 1796; Mar. 8, 22, 25, May 10, 13, 24, June 7, 10, July 19–Aug. 5, 16, 23–Sept. 30, 1797.
Rutgers Univ. has July 10, 1794–Apr. 11, 1795; July 12, 1797.
Wis. Hist. Soc. has Jan. 3, 1795–Sept. 30, 1797.
York Inst., Saco, has Jan. 9, 1796–Sept. 27, 1797.
Cincinnati Pub. Lib. has June 8, 1796–Sept. 30, 1797.
Cornell Univ. has June 6–Sept. 30, 1795.
New Haven Col. Hist. Soc. has Mar. 22–Sept. 30, 1797.

New-York Herald, 1802–1817.

Semi-weekly. Established Jan. 2, 1802, with the title of "New-York Herald," published by Michael Burnham and edited by William Coleman. With the issue of Dec. 14, 1811, it was published by Michael Burnham, & Co. The title was slightly altered to "New York Herald" with the issue of Aug. 23, 1815, and to "The New-York Herald" with Oct. 2, 1816. The last issue with this title was that of Nov. 15, 1817, no. 1656, and with the succeeding issue it was changed to "New-York Evening Post, for the Country." The Herald from 1802 to 1817 was the semi-weekly edition of the "New-York Evening Post," and like that paper was edited by William Coleman, although his name did not appear in the imprint.

Am. Antiq. Soc. has Jan. 2, 1802–Nov. 15, 1817.
Lib. Congress has Jan. 2, 1802–Nov. 15, 1817.
N. Y. Hist. Soc. has Jan. 2, 1802–Dec. 28, 1811; Feb. 1–Dec. 23, 1812, fair; Jan. 2, 1813–Dec. 31, 1814; Jan. 4, 1815–Nov. 15, 1817, fair.
N. Y. Pub. Lib. has Jan. 2, 1802–Dec. 25, 1805; Feb. 26, Mar. 5, 8, 15, 19, Apr. 5, 12, 26, 1806; Jan. 20, 1808–Nov. 15, 1817.
Yale has Jan. 2, 1802–Dec. 28, 1816.
Boston Athenæum has Jan. 1, 1803–Oct. 5, 1816.
N. Y. State Lib. has Jan. 2, 1802–Jan. 31, 1806; Jan. 3, 15, Feb. 14, Mar. 7, 11, 14, Aug. 29, Sept. 16–Oct. 10, 21, 31, Nov. 7, 21, Dec. 5, 1807; Jan. 2, 1808–Dec. 31, 1814; Jan. 4–Dec. 27, 1815, fair; Jan. 3–Dec. 28, 1816, scattering file; Jan. 22, May 10, 31, 1817.

North Tonawanda Pub. Lib. has Apr. 20, 1803–Oct. 9, 1816.
Conn. Hist. Soc. has Mar. 31, 1802–Oct. 31, 1814.
Wis. Hist. Soc. has Jan. 2, 1802–Dec. 28, 1805; Jan. 27, Apr. 9, 13, June 18, Sept. 14, 24, 1808–Dec. 30, 1809; Nov. 14, 1810–May 19, 1813; Jan. 1–Dec. 31, 1814; July 1, 1815–Sept. 14, 1816.
Dartmouth has Nov. 20, 1802–Nov. 17, 1804, fair; Mar. 9, 1805–Jan. 3, 1816, scattering file.
Univ. of Mich. (Clements) has Jan. 2, 1802–Dec. 31, 1806, fair; Mar. 4, 1807–Feb. 18, 1815, scattering file; Nov. 5, 1817.
Boston Pub. Lib. has Jan. 9, 1802–Oct. 17, 1807; Sept. 26, 1812–Mar. 3, 1813.
Harvard has May 19, Aug. 14, 1802–Dec. 31, 1808, fair; May 31, June 3, 1809.
Bowdoin Coll. has Jan. 30, 1808–Sept. 27, 1815, fair.
Newberry Lib. has May 13, 1802–Apr. 16, 1803, fair; Jan. 4, 1804–June 29, 1805; Jan. 2, 1811–Nov. 15, 1817, fair.
Duke Univ. has Jan. 20, 1802–Dec. 28, 1805, fair; Jan. 4, 1806–June 9, 1810, scattering file; Feb. 10, 1813–Apr. 17, 1816, scattering file.
Western Reserve Hist. Soc. has Jan. 2, 1802–Dec. 6, 1806; Mar. 17, 1813–July 30, 1814.
Peabody Inst., Baltimore, has Sept. 22, 1804–Dec. 29, 1810.
Chicago Hist. Soc. has Aug. 21, 1802–Aug. 31, 1803; Jan. 4–Sept. 4, 1805, fair; Sept. 27, 1806; Jan. 21–June 3, 1807; Jan. 6–Dec. 29, 1810, fair; May 26, June 2, July 14, Sept. 1, 1813.
Cornell Univ. has Jan. 4–Dec. 29, 1804; Jan. 6, 1813–July 29, 1815, fair.
Hudson Lib., Hudson, N. Y., has June 30, 1810–Oct. 3, 1814.
Hist. Soc. Penn. has Jan. 2, 1802–Dec. 31, 1803.
East Hampton Free Lib. has Dec. 19, 1802–Dec. 31, 1803; Mar. 9, Apr. 6, 16, 1814.
Iowa State Dep't of History has Dec. 8, 1802–June 11, 1803.
Pocumtuck Valley Mem. Lib., Deerfield, Mass. has Jan. 1, 1803–Dec. 22, 1804.
Williams Coll. has July 29, 1812–Dec. 29, 1813.
Cincinnati Pub. Lib. has June 18, 1814–Oct. 1, 1817.
Otsego Co. Hist. Soc., Cooperstown, N. Y., has Jan. 2–Dec. 29, 1802.
N. J. Hist. Soc. has Jan. 1–Dec. 31, 1803.
New Haven Col. Hist. Soc. has Jan. 1–Dec. 31, 1803.
Univ. of Texas has May 28–Oct. 29, 1803.
Rutgers Univ. has Jan. 4–Dec. 29, 1804; July 10, 1805; May 24, Aug. 27–Sept. 3, Oct. 8, 15, Dec. 27, 31, 1806.
Detroit Pub. Lib. has Oct. 17, 1804; Jan. 2–Dec. 28, 1805; Apr. 30, 1806.
Many libraries have single, or a few scattering issues.

[New York] Impartial Gazetteer, 1788.

Weekly. Established May 17, 1788, by Harrisson and Purdy [John Harrisson and Stephen Purdy, Jun.], with the title of "The Impartial Gazetteer, and Saturday Evening's Post." It was of quarto size. With the issue of Aug. 9, 1788, the title was shortened to "The Impartial Gazetteer," but with Aug. 16, 1788, was enlarged to "The Impartial Gazetteer, and Saturday Evening Post." The last issue with this title was that of Sept. 13, 1788, no. 18, after which it was changed to "The New-York Weekly Museum," which see.

N. Y. Pub. Lib. has May 17–Sept. 13, 1788.
Lib. Congress has June 28–Sept. 13, 1788.
Am. Antiq. Soc. has June 28–Aug. 2, 16, 30, Sept. 13, 1788.
Boston Pub. Lib. has July 12, 1788.

[New York] Impartial Observer, see Observateur Impartial.

[New York] Independent Gazette, 1783–1784.

Weekly and semi-weekly. A continuation, without change of volume numbering, of "The Independent New-York Gazette." The first issue with the new title of "The Independent Gazette; or the New-York Journal Revived" was that of Dec. 13, 1783, no. 4, published by John Holt. With the issue of Jan. 8, 1784, it changed from a weekly to a semi-weekly. Holt died Jan. 30, 1784, and with the issue of Feb. 5, 1784, the paper was published by E. Holt [Elizabeth Holt, his widow]. With the issue of Feb. 19, 1784, it reverted to a weekly. The last issue with this title was that of Mar. 11, 1784, no. 23, after which it was changed to "The New-York Journal," which see.

N. Y. Pub. Lib. has Dec. 13, 1783–Mar. 11, 1784.
Lib. Congress has Jan. 3–29, Feb. 7–Mar. 11, 1784.
Am. Antiq. Soc. has Dec. 13–27, 1783; Jan. 3–15, Feb. 14, 19, 1784.
N. Y. Hist. Soc. has Dec. 20, 1783; Jan. 17, 22, 29, Feb. 5, 12, 19–Mar. 11, 1784.
British Museum has Jan. 10–Feb. 14, 1784.
Mass. Hist. Soc. has Dec. 13, 1783; Jan. 10, 1784.
N. J. Hist. Soc. has Jan. 22–31, 1784.
Harvard has Feb. 7, 1784.

[New York] Independent Journal, 1783–1788.

Weekly and semi-weekly. Established Nov. 17, 1783, by Webster and M'Lean [Charles Webster and John M'Lean], with the title of "The Independent Journal: or, the General Advertiser." With the issue of Dec. 25, 1783, it was changed from a weekly to a semi-weekly. With the issue of Feb. 18, 1784, the name of the printing firm was changed to J. M'Lean & Co. With the issue of July 2, 1788, Archibald M'Lean was admitted to the firm, and the paper was published by J. and A. M'Lean. The last issue located is that of Dec. 24, 1788, no. 529, and it was discontinued under this title with the following issue, to be succeeded by "The New York Daily Gazette," which see.

N. Y. Hist. Soc. has Nov. 17, 1783–Aug. 28, 1784; Dec. 8, 1784–Dec. 24, 1788.
Am. Antiq. Soc. has Dec. 8–25, 1783; Jan. 7, 14, Feb. 11, Mar. 10, Apr. 7, May 5, 8, 19, 29–June 9, 23, 30, July 7, 17–Aug. 11, 21, 25, Sept. 1–Dec. 29, 1784; Jan. 1, 1785–Dec. 29, 1787; Jan. 2, 5, 12–19, 26, Feb. 16, 20, 27, Mar. 1, 8, 19–Apr. 2, 9, 23, 30, June 4, 14–21, July 5, 19, 23, 30, Aug. 2, 16, 30–Sept. 17, 24, Oct. 4, 15, 18, Nov. 5, 8, 29, Dec. 3, 10, 13, 1788.
N. Y. Soc. Lib. has Jan. 8–Dec. 28, 1785, fair; Jan. 4, 1786–Dec. 24, 1788.
Lib. Congress has Feb. 25, Sept. 8, 29, Oct. 6, 16, 20, 27, Nov. 13, 24, Dec. 18–25, 1784; Jan. 5, 22, 26, Feb. 2, 12–26, Mar. 9, Apr. 6, 27, 30, May 11, 21, 28, June 1, 8, 15, 22, 29–July 9, 20, Aug. 3–31, Sept. 7, 17, 28–Oct. 5, 12, 29, Nov. 9, 19, 26, 30, Dec. 10–24, 1785; Oct. 4, 1786; Jan. 3, Feb. 7, 14, Mar. 3, Apr. 11, 18, 21, July 18, 25, 28, Aug. 4, 8, 22, Sept. 5, 12, Oct. 3–17, 24, 27, Nov. 7, 10, Dec. 15, 1787; Feb. 13, 1788.
N. Y. Pub. Lib. has Dec. 15–22, 1784; Feb. 2, 19–June 8, July 9–Oct. 29, 1785, fair; Jan. 11, Sept. 13, 1786; May 26, June 2, 23, 27, Dec. 26, 29, 1787.
Univ. of Mich. (Clements) has Jan. 7, 11, 21–Feb. 15, 25, Mar. 1–22, Apr. 1, 5, 19, May 27, July 5, 22, Aug. 23–30, Sept. 6–30, Oct. 7–Nov. 8, 15–22, 29, Dec. 9–30, 1786; Jan. 3–Dec. 29, 1787, fair; Apr. 23, Aug. 30, Sept. 6, 1788.
Mass. Hist. Soc. has Sept. 8, Oct. 13, Nov. 3, 1784; Feb. 26, Mar. 2, Apr. 6, 16, 20, 1785; Apr. 5, 1786; Jan. 10, 1787; July 2, 28, 1788.
York Inst., Saco, has Aug. 13–Oct. 11, 1788.
Yale has Mar. 3, Apr. 28, 1784; June 28, Aug. 6, 9, 20, Sept. 6, Oct. 8, Nov. 1, 1788.
British Museum has Jan. 24, 31, Feb. 7, 14, 21, 1784.
Harvard has June 9, 1784; July 16, 1785.
N. Y. State Lib. has Aug. 19, Sept. 2, 1786; Jan. 6, Oct. 27, 1787.
Boston Pub. Lib. has Dec. 22, 1784.
Rutgers Univ. has Sept. 28, 1785.
Univ. of Ill. has July 28, 1787.

[New York] **Independent Mechanic,** 1811–1812.

Weekly. Established Apr. 6, 1811, by Joseph Harmer, with the title of "Independent Mechanic." With the issue of Aug. 3, 1811, John M. Elliott was admitted to partnership and the paper was published by Harmer & Elliott; but with Aug. 17, 1811, Elliott was dropped, George Asbridge took his place and the paper was published by Joseph Harmer & Co. With Jan. 4, 1812, it was published for George Asbridge. The last issue located is that of Sept. 26, 1812, vol. 2, no. 26.

British Museum has Apr. 6, 1811–Sept. 26, 1812.
N. Y. State Lib. has Apr. 6, 1811–Mar. 28, 1812.
Am. Antiq. Soc. has Apr. 20, June 29, 1811; Feb. 1, 1812.

[New York] Independent New-York Gazette, 1783.

Weekly. Established Nov. 22, 1783, by John Holt, with the title of "The Independent New-York Gazette," reviving with a new volume numbering his "New-York Journal," which had been published at Kingston and Poughkeepsie during the War. The last issue with this title was that of Dec. 6, 1783, no. 3, after which it was changed to "The Independent Gazette," which see.

N. Y. Pub. Lib. has Nov. 22–Dec. 6, 1783.
N. Y. Hist. Soc. has Nov. 22, 1783.

[New York] Independent Reflector, 1752–1753.

Weekly. Established Nov. 30, 1752, with the title of "The Independent Reflector," printed by James Parker. It consisted of a series of essays on political and religious subjects, written mostly by William Livingston (see Sedgwick's "Memoir of William Livingston," chap. 3), and might well be classed as a magazine, although it bore the appearance of a newspaper and concerned itself with the topics of the day. It was of folio size and each issue consisted of four pages, excepting those of Feb. 1 and Sept. 27, 1753, which consisted of six pages. The last issue was that of Nov. 22, 1753, no. 52, after which it was suppressed by the authorities. Livingston then brought out a title-page and a preface of 31 pages, dated Jan. 19, 1753 (error for 1754).

Am. Antiq. Soc., New Haven Col. Hist. Soc., John Carter Brown Lib., N. Y. Hist. Soc., N. Y. Pub. Lib., Columbia Univ., N. Y. State Lib., Sage Lib. New Brunswick, Princeton, N. J. Hist. Soc., Rutgers Univ., Western Reserve Hist. Soc., Wis. Hist. Soc., and Lib. Congress have Nov. 30, 1752–Nov. 22, 1753.
Boston Athenæum has Dec. 7, 1752–Nov. 22, 1753.
Yale has Nov. 30, 1752–May 10, 24–Aug. 2, 16–Nov. 22, 1753.
Hist. Soc. Penn. has Dec. 14, 1752–Nov. 22, 1753.
Williams Coll. has Nov. 30–Dec. 28, 1752.
Boston Pub. Lib. has Jan. 11–May 17, June 21–July 5, 1753.
N. Y. Soc. Lib. has Nov. 30, 1752; Aug. 9, 23, 1753.
Mass. Hist. Soc. has May 31, 1753.

[New York] Independent Republican, 1806–1807.

Semi-weekly. A continuation, without change of volume numbering, of the "Bowery Republican," the first issue with the new title of "Independent Republican" being that of Nov. 25, 1806, vol. 1, no. 14, published by Swaine and Jackson [John Swaine and ——— Jackson]. Jackson retired early in 1807, and in April, 1807, J. Swaine became sole publisher, changing the title slightly to "The Independent Republican." The last issue located is that of May 6, 1807, vol. 1, no. 86, and within a month the paper was discontinued. The New York

"Morning Chronicle" of May 25, 1807, says "Died, Last week in this city, of that terrible disease called starvation, the Bowery, alias the Independent Republican."

Am. Antiq. Soc. has Nov. 25–Dec. 9, 26, 1806; Jan. 9, 30, Feb. 13, 17, Mar. 10, 24–31, Apr. 7, 10, 21, May 6, 1807.
Univ. of Mich. (Clements) has Mar. 27, 1807.
N. Y. State Lib. has Mar. 31, Apr. 3, 1807.

[New York] Instructor, 1755.

Weekly. Established Mar. 6, 1755, by J[ames] Parker and W[illiam] Weyman, with the title of "The Instructor." The last issue located is that of May 8, 1755, no. 10. It contained extracts, select pieces and occasional news. It was an octavo, of four numbered pages to the issue, and was ostensibly a periodical, rather than a newspaper. Yet the "New-York Gazette" of Mar. 10, 1755, referred to it as follows: "Last Thursday [Mar. 6] was published in this City, a Small new Paper entitled, The Instructor, to be continued Weekly."

Lib. Congress has Mar. 6–May 8, 1755 (also photostat in N. Y. Pub. Lib.).
N. Y. Hist. Soc. has Apr. 10, 1755.

[New York] John Englishman, 1755.

A series of essays on political and religious subjects, over the pseudonym of "John Englishman," and here classed as a newspaper because of its general appearance and its frequency of issue. The first issue, headed "John Englishman's true Notion of Sister-churches," was without date, but was published on Apr. 9, 1755, according to an announcement in the "New-York Gazette" of Apr. 7, 1755. It was a folio of 2 pages, with pagination, and bore the colophon of J[ames] Parker and W[illiam] Weyman. The second and subsequent issues were entitled "John Englishman, In Defence of the English Constitution," and appeared on Apr. 18, 25, May 2, 16, 30, June 7, 14, 21, and July 5. The issue of July 5, 1755, no. 10, is the last located.

N. Y. Pub. Lib. has Apr. 9–June 14, July 5, 1755.
Lib. Congress has Apr. 18–May 30, June 14, 21, 1755.
Yale has May 2–July 5, 1755.
Harvard has May 16, June 21, 1755.
N. Y. Soc. Lib. has May 16, 1755.
Am. Antiq. Soc. has May 16, 1755.

New-York Journal, 1766–1776.

Weekly. A continuation, without change of volume numbering, of "The New-York Gazette; or, the Weekly Post-Boy," the last issue of which was that of

NEW YORK 655

Oct. 9, 1766, no. 1240. For a premature issue which appeared May 29, 1766, no. 1, see under "New York Gazette, or Weekly Post-Boy." The first regular issue with the title of "The New-York Journal, or General Advertiser" was that of Oct. 16, 1766, no. 1241, published by John Holt. With the issue of Mar. 19, 1767, the title was slightly changed to "The New-York Journal; or, the General Advertiser." The paper was discontinued at New York, because of the British occupation of the city, with the issue of Aug. 29, 1776, no. 1756. For its revival at Kingston, upon July 7, 1777, see under Kingston.

Hist. Soc. Penn. has Oct. 16, 1766–Aug. 29, 1776.

N. Y. Hist. Soc. has Oct. 16, 1766–Dec. 28, 1775; Jan. 4, 11, Feb. 15, May 2–16, June 27, 1776.

N. Y. Pub. Lib. has Oct. 16, 1766–Dec. 28, 1775; Feb. 1, 8, 22–Mar. 14, 28, June 27, July 18, 1776.

N. Y. Soc. Lib. has Jan. 1, 1767–Dec. 28, 1775.

Lib. Congress has Nov. 6–Dec. 18, 1766; Jan. 1, 8, June 4, July 16–Nov. 12, Dec. 3–31, 1767; Jan. 7, 1768–Dec. 21, 1769, good; Jan. 4, 1770–Dec. 30, 1773, fair; Jan. 6, 20, Feb. 17, 24, Mar. 10–Apr. 21, May 19, June 23–July 14, Aug. 4–25, Sept. 8, 22–Nov. 10, 24, Dec. 22, 29, 1774; Jan. 5–Dec. 28, 1775; Jan. 4–Feb. 1, Mar. 7, 14, Apr. 18, 25, May 9, 16, June 13–Aug. 29, 1776.

Phil. Lib. Co. has Oct. 16, 1766–Dec. 26, 1771; Jan. 16–Feb. 6, Mar. 26, 1772; Mar. 31, Apr. 28, Sept. 1, 1774; Jan. 19–Feb. 9, Mar. 9, May 4, 11, 25, June 29, July 6, 20, Aug. 3, Oct. 5–26, Nov. 9, 16, 30–Dec. 28, 1775; Jan. 4–Feb. 29, Mar. 14–Apr. 18, May 2–June 13, 27–July 11, 25–Aug. 22, 1776.

Am. Antiq. Soc. has Oct. 16, 1766–Dec. 27, 1770; Jan. 10–31, Feb. 28, Mar. 14, 28–Apr. 11, 25, May 16, 23, July 25, 1771; Jan. 23–Mar. 12, Apr. 16–May 7, 28, June 11–25, July 23–Aug. 20, Sept. 3–Oct. 15, 29–Nov. 19, Dec. 3–17, 1772; Jan. 7, Feb. 4–Mar. 4, 25, Apr. 1, 29, May 13, 27, Sept. 9, 30, Oct. 14, 1773; Mar. 10, 24, Apr. 14, June 16, July 7, 21, Sept. 1, 15–Oct. 6, 20–Nov. 24, Dec. 29, 1774; Jan. 5–Apr. 27, May 11–July 13, 27, Aug. 17, 31–Sept. 21, Oct. 5–19, Dec. 7–28, 1775; Jan. 4, 11, 25–Feb. 15, 29, Mar. 21, 28, Apr. 18, 25, May 9, 30, June 13, 20, July 18, 25, Aug. 22, 1776.

Yale has Nov. 13, 1766–Dec. 24, 1767; Jan. 7, Feb. 20, 25, Mar. 3, 31, Apr. 28, May 12, June 9, July 7, Aug. 11, 18, Sept. 1, 8, 29, Oct. 13, 20, Nov. 10–Dec. 1, 15, 22, 1768; Jan. 26–Feb. 9, Mar. 9, 16, 30, Apr. 6, 20, May 4, 18, June 29, July 13, 20, Aug. 3–24, Oct. 12–Nov. 9, 30, Dec. 7, 1769; Jan. 4, 1770–Nov. 21, 1771, fair; Jan. 23, Apr. 2, 30, 1772; Feb. 29, Mar. 21, 28, Apr. 11–May 9, June 6–Aug. 1, 22, 29, 1776.

Mass. Hist. Soc. has June 18, 1767; Jan. 9, 16, Oct. 13, Nov. 24, 1768; Jan. 19, Feb. 16, 23, Mar. 9–23, Apr. 6, May 18, June 8, Sept. 14, Dec. 14, 1769; Mar. 8, 15, Apr. 19, 26, June 14, July 19, Aug. 23, Sept. 6–20, 1770; Mar. 28, Apr. 11, 18, May 2, 23, 30, June 6, 13, July 4, 1771; Jan. 2, 9,

656   NEWSPAPER BIBLIOGRAPHY

Feb. 20, Apr. 2, May 21, 28, July 16, Aug. 20, 27, Sept. 24, Oct. 22, Nov. 5, 12, 26, 1772; Jan. 7, 14, Nov. 25, Dec. 9, 16, 1773; Feb. 9, Apr. 6, May 25, June 1, July 6, Aug. 3, Sept. 28, Oct. 26–Nov. 23, Dec. 7–28, 1775; Jan. 4, 11, Feb. 8–29, Mar. 14, Apr. 11, 18, May 16, June 13–July 4, 18, 25, Aug. 15, 1776.

N. J. Hist. Soc. has July 28, 1774–May 18, July 6, 1775.

Wis. Hist. Soc. has May 30, 1771; Jan. 16, July 2, 9, 30, 1772; Dec. 30, 1773–May 5, 1774.

Md. Hist. Soc. has June 23–July 21, 1774.

Univ. of Mich. (Clements) has Nov. 27, Dec. 4, 1766; Jan. 14, 21, Feb. 4–18, Dec. 15, 1768; Jan. 19, Feb. 9, June 8, 15, 1769; June 28, 1770; Mar. 26, July 23, Nov. 12, 1772; Feb. 24, Aug. 25, Oct. 13, 1774; Jan. 12, 26, Feb. 9, 16, Mar. 9, 16, May 11, 18, June 1–July 6, 20, Aug. 10–Sept. 21, Oct. 5, 12, 26, Nov. 16, 23, Dec. 7, 21, 1775; Jan. 4, Feb. 15, May 9, July 4, 11, 1776.

Long Id. Hist. Soc. has Jan. 26, 1769; May 18, June 1, July 27, Aug. 24, Sept. 7, Oct. 5, 19, Nov. 30, Dec. 14, 28, 1775; Jan. 11, 25, Feb. 8, 22, Mar. 7, Apr. 4, May 2, 16, June 13, 27, July 25, 1776.

N. Y. State Lib. has May 11, 1769–Feb. 1, 1770; Apr. 5, July 19, 1770; Mar. 21, 1771; Apr. 16, 23, June 11, Oct. 22, Nov. 26, 1772; Feb. 23, June 1, 1775; May 16, Oct. 6, 1776; and several supplements in 1768–1769.

Rutgers Univ. has June 29, Nov. 30, 1769; Jan. 18, Mar. 8, Apr. 12, 19, May 10, Aug. 16, Dec. 27, 1770; Apr. 4, May 16, 23, 1771.

Boston Pub. Lib. has Oct. 16, Dec. 16, 1766; July 2, Nov. 26, 1767.

Conn. Hist. Soc. has June 18, 1767; Feb. 18, 1773; Jan. 20, 1774.

Duke Univ. has Sept. 20, 1770; July 18, 1776.

Harvard has June 29, 1775.

New-York Journal, 1784–1793.

Weekly, daily, and semi-weekly. A continuation of "The Independent Gazette." The first issue with the new title was called "The New-York Journal, and State Gazette," Mar. 18, 1784, no. 1950, published weekly by Elizabeth Holt. The volume numbering continued the former numbering of "The New-York Journal," suspended at Poughkeepsie, Jan. 6, 1782, no. 1926, adding the 23 numbers of "The Independent Gazette." With the issue of Feb. 17, 1785, the title was changed to "The New-York Journal, and the General Advertiser," and with the issue of Mar. 3, 1785, the paper was published by Eleazer Oswald, for Elizabeth Holt. With the issue of June 23, 1785, the title was changed to "The New-York Journal, or the Weekly Register," and Elizabeth Holt resigned the proprietorship to Eleazer Oswald and Andrew Brown. This firm was dissolved with the issue of Aug. 4, 1785, and the paper published by Eleazer Oswald. With the issue of Jan. 18, 1787, it was transferred to Thomas Greenleaf, who stated that he had had the management of it since September, 1785, and the title was changed to "The New-York Journal, and Weekly Register." With the issue of Nov. 19, 1787, it became a daily, the title being changed to "The New-York Journal, and Daily Patriotic Register." The Thursday paper, however, which was intended for country subscribers, was entitled "The New-York Journal, and Weekly Register," and was included in the volume numbering of the daily paper. The last daily issue was that of July 26, 1788, and with July 31, 1788, the paper was published regularly as a weekly, with the title of "The New-York Journal, and Weekly Register." With the issue of May 4, 1790, it became a semi-weekly and the title was changed to "The New-York Journal, & Patriotic Register." The last issue with this title was that of Dec. 28, 1793, vol. 47, no. 104, after which it was changed to "Greenleaf's New York Journal," which see.

N. Y. Hist. Soc. has Mar. 18–May 6, June 3, 10, July 15, 22, Oct. 14, 1784; Jan. 13, Feb. 10, 24, May 26, June 23, July 14–28, Aug. 11–Sept. 15, Dec. 29, 1785; Jan. 12, 26, Feb. 9–23, Mar. 30, 1786–June 28, 1787; July 19–Aug. 2, 16, 23, Sept. 13, 27, Oct. 11, 1787–Dec. 28, 1793.

N. Y. Soc. Lib. has Sept. 1, 1785–Dec. 25, 1793.

British Museum has Mar. 18, 1784–Dec. 28, 1787, fair; July 31, 1788–Dec. 30, 1790.

N. Y. State Lib. has Mar. 18, 1784–Dec. 28, 1786; Feb. 21, 1788; Jan. 7, 1790–Dec. 29, 1792.

Am. Antiq. Soc. has Apr. 8–22, May 6, June 10–July 15, Sept. 2–16, 30, Oct. 28, Nov. 11, Dec. 2, 9, 23, 30, 1784; Jan. 27, Feb. 24, Mar. 3, 24, Apr. 7, 21, 28, May 19, 26, Aug. 25, Sept. 8, 29, Nov. 3, Dec. 1, 29, 1785; Jan. 19, 1786–Nov. 15, 1787; Nov. 20–24, 28–Dec. 1, 6, 11–13, 15, 19, 20, 24–27, 1787; Jan. 9, 10, 17, 24, 31, Feb. 7, 14, 21, 28, Mar. 1, 6, 8, 20, 27, Apr. 3, 10, 17, 24, 26, May 1, 7, 8, 15, 22, 29, 30, June 5, 12, 19, 21, 23, 26, July 3, 4, 8–11, 14, 17, 24, 31, Aug. 14, 21, Sept. 4, 18, 1788–Dec. 31, 1789; Jan. 7, 21–Feb. 4, 18, Apr. 22, May 4, 11–June 4, 11–Nov. 4, 11, 15, 22–Dec. 9, 16, 20, 27, 1790; Jan. 3–20, Feb. 3, 7, 24, 28, Mar. 7, 14–Dec. 24, 1791; Jan. 4, 1792–Dec. 28, 1793.

Long Id. Hist. Soc. has May 6, 1784–Nov. 16, 1786; Oct. 29, 1791; May 30, Sept. 19, Nov. 7, 1792.

Yale has May 6, 20, 27, June 10, 24–Aug. 5, Sept. 2, 16–Oct. 7, 28–Nov. 25, Dec. 9–30, 1784; Jan. 6, 13, Feb. 3, Mar. 10, 24, Sept. 15, 22, Oct. 27, Nov. 10, 1785; Feb. 9, Mar. 9, 30, Apr. 6, May 4, 25, Aug. 10, 24, 1786; Sept. 6, 27, Oct. 4, 1787; July 5, 26, 31, Aug. 7, 21–Sept. 4, 18, Nov. 13, 1788; June 4, Oct. 1, Dec. 31, 1789; Mar. 11, May 11, June 18, 1790; Jan. 3, 1791–Dec. 28, 1793.

N. Y. Pub. Lib. has Dec. 16, 1784; Jan. 20, 27, Feb. 24, Sept. 8, 15, 29, Oct. 6, 20, 27, 1785; Jan. 4, 1787–Dec. 31, 1791; Jan. 28–Aug. 15, Dec. 29, 1792; Oct. 30, 1793.

Detroit Pub. Lib. has June 23, 1785–Dec. 25, 1788; Jan. 2–Dec. 28, 1793.

Winyaw Indigo Soc., Georgetown, S. C., has Jan. 8, 1789–Dec. 28, 1793.

Lib. Congress has May 20, July 8, Sept. 30, Oct. 14, 1784; Jan. 27, Apr. 21, 1785; Mar. 23, June 15, July 27, Oct. 5, 1786; Jan. 18, Feb. 8, Mar. 8, Apr. 12, 26, June 7, July 12–Aug. 2, 16, Sept. 13, Oct. 4, 18, Nov. 8, Dec. 21–31, 1787; Jan. 1–Dec. 25, 1788; June 11, 18, July 30, Sept. 17, Oct. 15, Nov. 5, 19, Dec. 10, 1789; Feb. 11, May 18, 25, 28, June 8, July 30, Aug. 3, 10, 31, Oct. 15, Nov. 15, 1790; Jan. 6, Sept. 28, 1791; June 16, 1792.

York Inst., Saco, has Nov. 22, 1787–Sept. 24, 1789.

Harvard has Dec. 30, 1784; June 23–Nov. 24, Dec. 15, 1785; Jan. 19, Feb. 23, Mar. 16, July 6, 20, 27, Aug. 10–Dec. 28, 1786; Jan. 4–25, Feb. 8–22, Mar. 22, Apr. 26, Sept. 27, 1787; June 4, 1789; June 15, 18, July 13–20, 30, Sept. 17, Nov. 19, 23, 1791; Apr. 25, May 2, 23, 26, June 16, 20, 30, July 7, 14–25, Aug. 1, 4, 11, 22, Sept. 8–15, 29, Oct. 3–13, 20, 24, 31, Nov. 7, 17, 28, Dec. 1, 12, 15, 26, 29, 1792; Jan. 5, 16, 19, 26, Feb. 2–13, 20, 23, Mar. 2, Apr. 13, Sept. 4, 14, Oct. 2, 16, 30, Nov. 9, 13, Dec. 14, 18, 1793.

Wis. Hist. Soc. has Oct. 4, 1787–Dec. 25, 1788.

Univ. of Penn. has Jan. 3–July 24, 1788.

Mass. Hist. Soc. has July 15, 1784; Nov. 16, Dec. 14, 1786; Feb. 1, Dec. 13, 1787; May 18, 1790; Feb. 22, 1792.

N. J. Hist. Soc. has Mar. 24–June 6, 1792.

Boston Pub. Lib. has Aug. 24, 1786; Feb. 22, 1792; Dec. 11, 1793.

Univ. of Mich. (Clements) has Nov. 3, 1785; Feb. 15, 1787; Aug. 14, Oct. 9, 1788.

Rutgers Univ. has Jan. 14, Apr. 15, June 11, 1790; July 25, 1792.

Duke Univ. has Nov. 1, 1790; Apr. 2, 1791.

New-York Journal, 1802.

Weekly. Established May 22, 1802, by Beach and Mallory [Lazarus Beach and Samuel Mallory], with the title of "New-York Journal." In June, 1802, the title was changed to "New-York Journal and Weekly Monitor," the publishers having bought out a magazine called "The Lady's Monitor." The last issue located is that of Aug. 14, 1802, vol. 1, no. 13, and two months later the paper was sold out to Ming & Young, who established "The Weekly Visitor."

Harvard has May 22, 1802.
Long Id. Hist. Soc. has May 29, July 31, Aug. 14, 1802.

New York Journal, 1809–1811.

Semi-weekly. Established June 10, 1809, by Frank, White & Co. [Jacob Frank and George White], with the title of "The New York Journal." It was issued as the semi-weekly edition of the "Public Advertiser." After Nov. 29, 1809, no imprint was given, although the changes in printers must have been the same as for the "Public Advertiser." With the issue of Feb. 6, 1811, Philip Tabele became publisher. The last issue located is that of Aug. 7, 1811, vol. 3, no. 225. It was succeeded in 1812, as a country paper for the "Public Advertiser," by "The New-York Phœnix."

Am. Antiq. Soc. has June 10–July 22, 29–Aug. 30, Sept. 6–Oct. 4, 11–Dec. 30, 1809; Jan. 10, 17–24, Feb. 7–17, 24–Mar. 3, 10–June 30, July 7–Aug. 4, 11–25, Sept. 1, 12–Nov. 7, 14, 28, Dec. 8–22, 29, 1810; Jan. 2, 5, 12–Feb. 16, 23, 27, Mar. 6–27, Apr. 3, 20, 1811.

Long Id. Hist. Soc. has July 19–Dec. 30, 1809; Mar. 28, 31, Apr. 11, 21–May 9, 30, June 9, 13, 27, July 7–Sept. 22, Nov. 3, 17, 28, Dec. 8, 1810; Jan. 2, Feb. 2, 13, 16, 23, Mar. 13, 27, Apr. 10, 24, Aug. 7, 1811.

N. Y. Pub. Lib. has July 22–Oct. 18, 25, 28, Nov. 4–22, Dec. 3, 9–30, 1809; Jan. 3, Apr. 7, 21–June 30, July 7–Aug. 18, 1810; May 11, 1811.

N. Y. Hist. Soc. has Nov. 1–11, 18–Dec. 2, 13–20, 27, 30, 1809; Jan. 3–10, 20, 27–Feb. 14, 21–Mar. 24, 31, Apr. 4, 11–Dec. 29, 1810.

Lib. Congress has July 29, Aug. 5, Dec. 6, 1809; Apr. 14, 21, 28, May 2, 9, 23–June 5, 16–30, July 11, 14, 21, 25, Aug. 18–25, Sept. 12, 15, 29, 1810.

East Hampton Free Lib. has July 1, Aug. 2, 9, 13, Sept. 16, Nov. 15, 1809; Feb. 2, 1811.

Boston Athenæum has Dec. 12, 29, 1810; Mar. 20, 1811.

Univ. of Mich. (Clements) has Sept. 12, 15, 1810.

[New York] **Journal des Révolutions**, 1793.

Semi-weekly. This paper was evidently established at New York in September 1793, under the title of "Journal des Révolutions de la Partie Française de Saint-Domingue." The Prospectus is a twelve page quarto, French and English in parallel columns, headed "Proposals for printing a Journal of the Revolutions in the French Part of St. Domingo," numbered "Tom II, no. 1." The paper was considered by its editor, Tanguy de la Boissière, as a continuation of his paper of the same name published at St. Domingo, of which ten numbers were printed, with the last on Mar. 28, 1793. The Prospectus contains an announcement headed "New Expositions; or ideas of the reundertaking of this Journal," dated August 29, 1793, and signed by Tanguy. The conditions were that the paper should be issued semi-weekly in French and English, and subscriptions were received by the "Author" at 26 Water Street, New York, by T. Greenleaf, printer, and by several other printers in the various States.

In the "New York Journal" of Sept. 4, 1793, is this advertisement: "The Editor of the Journal of the Revolutions in the French Part of St. Domingo, requests, that those gentlemen who have been supplied with the proposals for this work (which is No. 1 of the work itself) will be so kind as to obtain as many subscriptions as possible, at one dollar each in advance, and to return the names subscribed, and the cash advanced, to T. Greenleaf, Printer, New York, with all possible expedition. New York, Sept. 4, 1793."

The twelve page Prospectus was followed by a Supplement to no. 1, containing four pages. The first regular issue is vol. 2, no. 2, pp. 13–20, dated Sept. 16, 1793. The New York Journal of Sept. 18, 1793, says: "No. 2 of the Journal of the Revolutions of St. Domingo was published yesterday" and adds that subscriptions should be sent to Greenleaf's Printing Office. The issue of Sept. 16, 1793, is the last located of the paper printed at New York, edited by Tanguy and evidently printed in Thomas Greenleaf's office. These New York issues seem to be printed with Adam Mappa's type which had been cast for Greenleaf's use in printing the 1792 Laws of New York. Apparently the paper was discontinued at New York, and established at Philadelphia, as a tri-weekly, with a new numbering. The first Philadelphia issue located is that of Sept. 27, 1793, no. 3, pages 5–8 (see under Philadelphia). Cabon's History of Haiti Journalism (Am. Antiq. Soc. Proc. 1939, vol. 49, p. 151), referring to this Journal, states that Tanguy continued his paper at New York, that his first issue was on Sept. 23, 1793, and that Parent was his printer, as he previously had been in St. Domingo. But Cabon's reference to the date of issue and to the printer clearly referred to the Philadelphia issues.

John Carter Brown Lib. has Prospectus, and Sept. 16, 1793.

Lib. Congress has Suppl. to no. 1, and Sept. 16, 1793 (in Genet Papers).

[New York] **Ladies' Weekly Museum,** 1817.

Weekly. A continuation, without change of volume numbering, of the "New-York Weekly Museum." The first issue with the new title of "The Ladies' Weekly Museum, or Polite Repository of Amusement and Instruction" was that of May 3, 1817, vol. 6, no. 1, published by James Oram. It was of octavo size, contained sixteen numbered pages to the issue, and had a title-page and index. Although it would be considered a magazine from its appearance and the nature of its title, it is here included as a newspaper since it carried current news and death notices and especially because it continued the old established "New-York Weekly Museum." The last issue with this title was that of Oct. 25, 1817, vol. 6, no. 26, when it was succeeded by "The Weekly Visitor," which see.

Am. Antiq. Soc., N. Y. Hist. Soc., N. Y. State Lib., Watkinson Lib., and Lib. Congress have May 3–Oct. 25, 1817.

[New York] **Lady's Weekly Miscellany,** 1806–1807, see **Weekly Visitor,** 1802–1807.

[New York] **Lang, Turner & Co.'s New-York Gazette,** 1820, see **New-York Gazette,** 1795–1820.

[New York] **Loudon's New-York Packet,** 1784–1785, see **New York Packet.**

[New York] Mercantile Advertiser, 1798–1820+.

Daily. A continuation, without change of volume numbering, of the "Diary and Mercantile Advertiser." The earliest issue located with the new title of "Mercantile Advertiser" is that of Nov. 13, 1798, no. 1970, published by John Crookes, for the Proprietor. With the issue of Apr. 22, 1799, it was published by James Chevalier, who died Aug. 23, 1799, it being stated that he had had the direction of the paper for eighteen months. With the issue of Aug. 27, 1799, it was published by John Crookes, for the Proprietor. With the issue of Oct. 16, 1806, the imprint became John Crookes, printer and publisher. With the issue of Mar. 30, 1808, it was published by John Crookes & A[mos] Butler. On May 27, 1816, Crookes retired, and the paper was published by Amos Butler. With the issue of July 5, 1819, George W. Hyer was admitted to partnership and the paper published by Butler & Hyer, and was so continued until after 1820.

> N. Y. Hist. Soc. has Jan. 2, 1799–Dec. 31, 1802, good; Jan. 1–June 14, Sept. 1–Nov. 30, 1803; Jan. 3–14, Feb. 4–May 30, July 2–Nov. 30, 1804; Mar. 1, 1805–Dec. 31, 1812, good; Jan. 1, 1813–May 23, 1815, fair; Nov. 7, 22, 1815; Jan. 8, Feb. 15, 17, 23, Mar. 15, 19, Dec. 6–14, 1816; Jan. 1–Dec. 29, 1820.
>
> Lib. Congress has Nov. 10, 1798; May 7, 18, 21, 23, 27, 30, June 1, Oct. 2, 25, 28, Nov. 25, Dec. 21, 23, 24, 30, 1799; May 21, Aug. 28, Sept. 11, Oct. 1, Nov. 4–Dec. 31, 1800, fair; Feb. 10, 17, 1801; Jan. 21, Apr. 20, May 4–6, Oct. 26, 1802; Apr. 27, 1803; Sept. 28, Dec. 9, 18, 1807; Feb. 17, Mar. 23, June 11, 13, 20, Dec. 5, 1808; Jan. 24, Feb. 20, Apr. 19, Nov. 1–Dec. 23, 1809; Jan. 15, 1810–Nov. 27, 1813; Apr. 21, July 7, 1814; Jan. 9, Apr. 19, 1815; Jan. 1–Nov. 30, 1818; Jan. 1, 1819–Dec. 30, 1820.
>
> Boston Athenæum has Mar. 28, 1799–Mar. 12, 1800.
>
> Am. Antiq. Soc. has Nov. 13, 15, 16, 20, 21, 26–28, 30, Dec. 4, 11, 12, 14, 18, 21, 27, 1798; Jan. 15, 22, 24, 29, 31, Feb. 5, 7, 9, 12, 21, Mar. 5, 19, Apr. 3, 4, 8, 9, 17, May 31, Aug. 2, Nov. 6, Dec. 21, 1799; Mar. 12–14, Apr. 11, 21, May 7, 21, June 5, 11, 1800; Apr. 18, 1801; Sept. 23, 1802; Feb. 8, Apr. 2, July 16, 19, 29, 30, Aug. 3, 17, 23, 30, Sept. 6, 13, 27, Oct. 4, 19, 1803; June 7, Aug. 18, Sept. 7, 10, 1804; Sept. 14–18, 21, Oct. 16–19, 1805; Jan. 3, 1806; July 14, 1807; Mar. 4, May 25, 1808; Feb. 21, Oct. 3, 13, 1809; Feb. 6, Mar. 6, 7, 20, June 4, 5, Aug. 28, Sept. 11, 25, Nov. 30, Dec. 13, 1810; Jan. 1, 5, 12, 15, 17–19, 22, Feb. 4, 8, 11, 15, 18–21, 23–26, 28, Mar. 1, 4, 5, 8–12, 14, 27, 29, Apr. 1, 2, 4, 5, 8, 10, 12, 15–18, 29, 30, May 2–10, 14, 15, 18, June 8, 29, July 4, Aug. 24, 29–Sept. 2, 10–16, 18, 19, 26–Oct. 15, 17, 18, 22–24, 30, Nov. 3, 10, 28, 1811; Feb. 10, Mar. 6, Aug. 22, 1812; Sept. 21, Dec. 13, 1813; Mar. 10, 11, June 22, July 2, 1814; Mar. 3, Apr. 27, 28, 1815; Sept. 11, 1816; Mar. 30, Apr. 1, 7, 28, 1819.
>
> Harvard has Feb. 7, 11, 26, 28, Mar. 6, 8, 9, Sept. 9, 1799; Mar. 22, Aug. 22,

1800; Jan. 4–Nov. 29, 1802, fair; Jan. 6, 1803–Dec. 28, 1808, scattering file; Jan. 16, 1809.

Wis. Hist. Soc. has Apr. 9, 1800; June 27–Nov. 12, 1801, scattering; May 3, June 11, 12, Aug. 27, Dec. 23, 1802; July 23, 1804; Jan. 29, 1805; Jan. 16, Mar. 31, Apr. 2, July 17, Aug. 4, Sept. 12, 1806; Feb. 9, 16, Mar. 2, Dec. 14, 1807; May 12, June 22, 23, 27, 28, Aug. 10, 22, 23, Nov. 3, 18, 21, Dec. 31, 1808; Feb. 9, 22, Mar. 4, Apr. 22, 28, June 9, Aug. 16, Oct. 17, Nov. 7, 1809; Feb. 7, Mar. 28, Aug. 23, 1810; June 4, 1811; Dec. 17, 1818.

N. Y. State Lib. has Nov. 4, 1800; Aug. 4, 1803; Jan. 6, 1808; Feb. 14, Mar. 2, Apr. 28, May 3, Dec. 8, 1809; Aug. 5, Oct. 25, 26, 31, Nov. 7–9, Dec. 30, 31, 1811; Jan. 20, 23, Feb. 1, 26–28, Mar. 2, 4, Dec. 12, 1812; Oct. 15, Nov. 29, 1813; Sept. 6, 13, 1814; Jan. 30, Sept. 12, 14, 18, 19, Oct. 7, 10, 25, 1815; Apr. 27, 30, May 23, 27, 29, July 10, 1816; Apr. 19, 1817.

N. Y. Pub. Lib. has Feb. 13, 1800; July 14, 18, 23, 1804; Sept. 15, 1812; Nov. 23, 1813; Mar. 23, July 29, Aug. 12, 1814; June 3, 1815; Jan. 14, Mar. 2, 9, Apr. 5, 6, 16, Nov. 1, 11, 1817.

N. Y. Soc. Lib. has June 3, 4, 6, 28, Sept. 27, 1805; Sept. 22, 23, 26, 1806.

Rutgers Univ. has May 29, 1805; July 31, 1806; June 30, 1808; Aug. 24, 1811.

Univ. of Chicago has Oct. 21, 28, 1818.

Conn. Hist. Soc. has Dec. 24, 1799.

Hist. Soc. Penn. has Dec. 19, 1800; Mar. 1, 1808.

New-York Mercury, 1752–1768.

Weekly. Established Aug. 3, 1752, judging from the date of the earliest issue located, that of Aug. 31, 1752, no. 5, printed by Hugh Gaine, with the title of "The New-York Mercury." Gaine, however, writing thirteen years later, stated that Aug. 8, 1752, was "the Day this Mercury was first published here." (New-York Mercury, Oct. 28, 1765). With the issue of Jan. 28, 1754, he changed his name in the imprint to H. Gaine, with Feb. 7, 1757, omitted the name entirely, and with Dec. 12, 1757, restored it to Hugh Gaine. The issues of Nov. 4, 11, and 18, 1765, because of the Stamp Act, were published without numbering and entitled "No Stamped Paper to be had," but with Nov. 25, 1765, the former title was resumed. The last issue with the title of "The New-York Mercury" was that of Jan. 25, 1768, no. 847, after which the title was changed to "The New-York Gazette; and the Weekly Mercury," which see.

The N. Y. Historical Society has reproduced by photostat all of the known issues of this paper from 1752 to 1768, which set is to be found in the following libraries: — N. Y. Hist. Soc., Am. Antiq. Soc., Lib. Congress, Yale, Grosvenor Lib., Western Reserve Hist. Soc., Newberry Lib., Univ. of Chicago, Univ. of Ill., Univ. of Mich. (Clements), and Huntington Lib.

N. Y. Hist. Soc. has June 4, 1753–Dec. 27, 1762; Jan. 3, 10, Mar. 21, May 2, Oct. 10, Nov. 28, 1763; Jan. 2–Dec. 31, 1764; Jan. 7–21, Feb. 11–25, Apr. 29,

New York

May 13–July 8, Aug. 5–Oct. 28, Nov. 11–25, Dec. 9–30, 1765; **Jan. 6–** Sept. 1, 15–Oct. 13, 27, Nov. 24, Dec. 15, 29, 1766; Jan. 5, 1767–Jan. 25, 1768.

Lib. Congress has June 4–Dec. 24, 1753, fair; Dec. 16–30, 1754; Jan. 6–Dec. 22, 1755, fair; Jan. 5–Dec. 27, 1756; Jan. 10–Dec. 19, 1757; Jan. 2, 9, Feb. 20–Mar. 20, June 26, Sept. 11, Oct. 23, 1758; Jan. 1–Mar. 26, Apr. 9, 23–May 14, June 11–Aug. 20, Sept. 3, 17, Nov. 12, Dec. 3–31, 1759; Oct. 6, 1760; Oct. 19, 1761; Feb. 15–Aug. 9, Sept. 6, 27, Oct. 18, Nov. 29, 1762; May 2, 30, July 18, Dec. 12, 1763; Jan. 9, June 25, Sept. 24, Oct. 8–Dec. 31, 1764; Jan. 7, 1765–Jan. 25, 1768, fair.

Hist. Soc. Penn. has Dec. 17, 1753–Dec. 23, 1754; July 21, Oct. 13, Nov. 24, Dec. 8, 22, 29, 1755; Jan. 5, 1756–Nov. 5, 1764; Sept. 9, 23, Oct. 21, 28, Dec. 9–23, 1765; Feb. 10–Aug. 18, 1766; Jan. 5–Feb. 23, Mar. 9–May 4, June 22, July 20, Aug. 17, 1767; Jan. 18, 25, 1768.

N. Y. Pub. Lib. has Feb. 17, 24, May 12, 19, June 2, 16, 30, July 14–21, Aug. 4–25, Nov. 10–Dec. 15, 29, 1755; Jan. 5, 1756–Jan. 25, 1768.

Phil. Lib. Co. has Aug. 31, Oct. 2, Nov. 6–Dec. 25, 1752; Apr. 30, May 7, Sept. 10, 17, Oct. 8, 15, Nov. 19, Dec. 3, 10, 1753; Mar. 25–Apr. 15, May 20–July 22, Aug. 12–Dec. 30, 1754; Jan. 6, 1755–Dec. 25, 1758, fair; Jan. 1, Mar. 19, 26, Apr. 9, 16, 30, May 7, 21–June 4, 18, July 2, 16, Sept. 3, Nov. 19–Dec. 24, 1759; Feb. 11, Apr. 21, 28, May 12, July 14, Oct. 6–20, Nov. 4, 10, 24–Dec. 1, 22, 1760; Mar. 23, 30, May 4, 11, 25, July 20, Aug. 3, 10, 24–Sept. 14, 28, Dec. 21, 1761; June 28, 1762; Jan. 31, 1763; Sept. 19, 1764; May 6, July 8, Oct. 21, Nov. 4, 18, Dec. 16, 30, 1765; Jan. 6, 13, Feb. 10, Mar. 3, Apr. 14, June 9, 23, 1766; Mar. 2, 9, May 11, July 6, 1767.

Am. Antiq. Soc. has Jan. 12, 26, Feb. 9, 23–May 10, 24–July 12, 26–Aug. 16, 30, Sept. 13–Nov. 1, 15, 22, Dec. 6–20, 1756; Jan. 10, 24–Feb. 14, 28–Apr. 18, May 2, 9, 23–June 27, July 18–Aug. 1, 22–Nov. 7, 28–Dec. 19, 1757; Feb. 6, 1758; June 11, 18, 1759; Mar. 15, Aug. 2, 1762; Oct. 17–Dec. 26, 1763; Jan. 2–Dec. 24, 1764; Mar. 4–18, Apr. 1, 1765; Oct. 27, 1766; Jan. 5, 1767–Jan. 25, 1768.

Yale has Feb. 3, Mar. 3, May 26, June 16, July 14, 1755; May 28, 1759; Mar. 10, 24, May 26, 1760; Apr. 6, July 27, Aug. 31, Sept. 7, Oct. 5, 12, 26, Nov. 2, 30, Dec. 21, 1761; Jan. 25, Feb. 15, 22, Mar. 1–15, Apr. 19, May 10, 24, 31, June 7, Aug. 30, Oct. 18, 25, Dec. 6, 1762; Jan. 2, 1764–Dec. 29, 1766.

N. Y. Soc. Lib. has Jan. 3–Dec. 26, 1757; Jan. 5, 1767–Jan. 25, 1768.

Univ. of Pittsburgh has Jan. 1, 1753–Dec. 15, 1755, fair.

British Museum has Jan. 20–Dec. 29, 1755.

Mass. Hist. Soc. has Jan. 6–Nov. 17, 1755, fair; Apr. 26, Nov. 8, 1756; Mar. 17, Nov. 17, 1760; Feb. 21, 1763; Jan. 14, Aug. 5, 1765.

Wis. Hist. Soc. has Oct. 7, 14, 1754; Jan. 6–Dec. 8, 1766.

Univ. of Mich. (Clements) has Dec. 22, 1755; Jan. 12, Feb. 23–Mar. 8, 22, Apr. 5, 19–May 10, 24, June 7, 21, 28, July 12, 26, Aug. 16, 30, Oct. 18,

Nov. 8–Dec. 20, 1756; Jan. 24, Feb. 28, Mar. 14–Apr. 18, May 2, 9, 30, June 6, 20, 27, July 18, Aug. 1, Sept. 12, Oct. 10, 17, Nov. 14, 1757; Jan. 15, 22, Mar. 12, 1759.

Long Id. Hist. Soc. has July 12, 26, Aug. 9, Nov. 1, Dec. 27, 1756; July 2, 16, 1759; July 28, 1760; Oct. 12, 1761; June 7, Sept. 27, Nov. 15, 1762; Feb. 28, Sept. 12, Dec. 5, 1763; Jan. 9, Feb. 13, Mar. 26, May 21, July 9, Aug. 13, Sept. 3, Nov. 12, Dec. 10, 1764; Jan. 21, 28, Feb. 25, Mar. 11–25, Apr. 8, 22, July 22, 1765.

Newburgh, N. Y. Lib. has Aug. 11, Sept. 22, Nov. 17, 1755; May 3, 10, June 7, July 12, Oct. 11, 1756; Jan. 31, May 2, June 6, 27, Sept. 19, Oct. 3, Nov. 28, 1757; Apr. 24, May 1, Dec. 4, 1758.

Boston Pub. Lib. has Mar. 29, Apr. 5, 19, May 24, June 7, July 5, 19, Aug. 9, Sept. 27, Nov. 22, Dec. 6, 1756; Mar. 7, 1757.

Md. Hist. Soc. has Mar. 1, May 31, Aug. 2–16, 1762.

Columbia Univ. has June 3, 1754; Aug. 23, 1762; May 28, 1764.

Univ. of Minn. has June 3, 1754; Apr. 15, Dec. 9, 1765; Oct. 26, 1767.

Rutgers Univ. has June 21, 1756; June 21, Aug. 9, Sept. 6, Oct. 18, 25, 1762; Feb. 7, 28, Oct. 3, 1763; Jan. 18, 1768.

Duke Univ. has July 5, 1756.

Harvard has Nov. 4, 1760.

N. Y. State Lib. has Apr. 29, 1765; May 19, June 30, 1766; Mar. 26, June 22, July 6, Sept. 28, 1767.

Amer. Philos. Soc. has Dec. 2, 1765.

New-York Mercury, 1779–1783.

Weekly. Established Sept. 3, 1779, judging from the date of the earliest issue located, that of Sept. 10, 1779, vol. 1, no. 2, published by William Lewis, with the title of "The New-York Mercury; or, General Advertiser." At some time between Mar. 8 and May 24, 1782, Samuel Horner was admitted to partnership, under the firm name of Lewis and Horner. Horner retired in July or August, 1782, and William Lewis again became sole publisher. At some time between Jan. 3 and Aug. 15, 1783, John Ryan was admitted to partnership and the paper was published by William Lewis and John Ryan. The last issue located is that of Aug. 15, 1783, vol. 4, no. 211.

Hist. Soc. Penn. has Sept. 10–24, Oct. 15, Nov. 26, Dec. 10, 1779; Jan. 14–28, Feb. 25, Mar. 3, 31, Sept. 8, 1780; Mar. 2–16, 30, Apr. 19, May 4, Aug. 17, 1781.

Am. Antiq. Soc. has Dec. 3, 10, 1779; Jan. 21, July 14, 1780; Jan. 19, Mar. 9, Apr. 27, May 11, Sept. 28, 1781; Jan. 25, Mar. 1, June 21, July 5, 1782; Aug. 15, 1783.

Mass. Hist. Soc. has Sept. 10, 1779; June 29, Sept. 7–21, Dec. 14, 1781; Sept. 6, 1782.

N. Y. Hist. Soc. has Apr. 28, 1780; Mar. 16, 1781; Feb. 8, May 24, 1782.

N. Y. Pub. Lib. has Apr. 28, June 16, 1780; Mar. 16, 1781.
Lib. Congress has Nov. 5, 1779; June 30, 1780.
N. Y. State Lib. has Sept. 14, 1781.
Wis. Hist. Soc. has Jan. 3, 1783.

New-York Messenger, 1819–1820.

Semi-weekly. Established Dec. 10, 1819, judging from the date of the earliest issue located, that of Dec. 14, 1819, vol. 1, no. 2, published semi-weekly by J[ared] W. Bell & M[oses] Y. Scott, with the title of "The New-York Messenger." The paper was edited by Scott. The last issue located is that of Jan. 21, 1820, vol. 1, no. 11.

N. Y. Hist. Soc. has Dec. 14, 1819.
Am. Antiq. Soc. has Jan. 21, 1820.
Lib. Congress has Jan. 21, 1820.

[New York] Mid-day Courier, 1814.

Daily. Established Nov. 24, 1814, by Lazarus Beach & Co., with the title of "The Mid-day Courier. With the Morning's Mails." The only other copy located is that of Dec. 6, 1814, vol. 1, no. 11, without name of publisher.

East Hampton Free Lib. has Nov. 25, 1814.
N. Y. State Lib. has Dec. 6, 1814.

[New York] Military Monitor, 1812–1814.

Weekly. Established Aug. 17, 1812, with the title of "The Military Monitor, and American Register," printed by Joseph Desnoues, for the Proprietor. It was of quarto size and paged, with eight pages to the issue. Although a magazine in appearance and containing few advertisements, it included current military news and could be regarded as a newspaper. The first four issues, Aug. 17 to Sept. 7, 1812, were not printed until late in 1812, when they were distributed to subscribers in order to complete the volume. The first issue printed was that of Sept. 14, 1812, vol. 1, no. 5, containing the Prospectus, and with the imprint of Printed by [John] Hardcastle & [Peter] Van Pelt, for T[homas] O'Connor and S[tephen] Wall. With the issue of Oct. 12, 1812, the printer became Joseph Desnoues. With the issue of Dec. 14, 1812, T. O'Connor became sole proprietor, the issues of Nov. 30 and of Dec. 7 having been omitted. With the issue of Apr. 12, 1813, O'Connor's name disappeared as editor. The paper was printed by Joseph Desnoues at least as far as Aug. 23, 1813, vol. 1, no. 52, and this first volume had a title-page and index. A broadside notice, dated Nov. 1, 1813, states that the paper had been suspended on Sept. 24, 1813, because of a printers' lock-out by James Bolen, in whose office it was printed. This apparently did not affect the volume numbering, as the issue of Nov. 6, 1813, is numbered vol. 2, no. 11. This issue was printed by Nicholas Van Riper, for the Proprietor. The last issue known, but not seen by me, is that of Apr. 2, 1814, vol. 2, no. 32.

N. Y. Hist. Soc. has Aug. 17, 1812–Aug. 23, 1813; Nov. 6, 1813.
Am. Antiq. Soc. has Aug. 17, 1812–Aug. 23, 1813; Nov. 6, 1813.
Lib. Congress, Huntington Lib., and Boston Athenæum have Aug. 17, 1812–Aug. 23, 1813.
Hist. Soc. Penn. has Aug. 17, 1812–Aug. 9, 1813.
N. Y. State Lib. has Sept. 14, 28–Dec. 21, 1812; Jan. 4, Feb. 22, Mar. 1, Apr. 5, 19–June 21, July 5, Aug. 2, 1813.
Yale has May 3, 1813.
A file sold at Merwin Sales Co., on Mar. 13, 1911, included Aug. 17, 1812–Aug. 23, 1813, scattering; Aug. 28, Sept. 4, 18, 1813; Feb. 19, Mar. 26, Apr. 2, 1814; but its present location is not known.

[New York] Minerva, 1796–1797.

Daily. A continuation, without change of volume numbering, of the "American Minerva," the first issue with the new title of "The Minerva, & Mercantile Evening Advertiser" being that of May 2, 1796, vol. 3, no. 821, published by Hopkins, Webb & Co. [George F. Hopkins, Joseph D. Webb, and Noah Webster, Jun.]. With the issue of May 15, 1797, Webb retired after a disagreement (see issue of May 9, 1796), and Webster and Hopkins continued under the firm name of Hopkins & Co. The last issue was that of Sept. 30, 1797, vol. 4, no. 1162, it being succeeded by the "Commercial Advertiser," which see. A semi-weekly edition was also published under the title of "The Herald; a Gazette for the Country."

N. Y. Hist. Soc., Lib. Congress, Phil. Lib. Co., and Boston Athenæum have May 2, 1796–Sept. 30, 1797.
Univ. of Mich. (Clements) has May 4, 1796–Sept. 30, 1797, fair.
Am. Antiq. Soc. has July 1–6, Sept. 30, Oct. 6, 1796; Jan. 5–Mar. 20, 22–Apr. 28, May 1–June 9, 12–Sept. 30, 1797.
N. Y. Pub. Lib. has May 2–Dec. 31, 1796, fair; Jan. 21–Sept. 30, 1797, scattering file.
Harvard has June 3, 20, Aug. 8, 15, Oct. 4, 5; 1796; Mar. 27, 1797.
Hist. Soc. Penn. has Jan. 30, Aug. 4, 9, 14, 15, 17, 1797.

[New York] Ming & Young's New-York Price-Current, 1804–1805, see New-York Price-Current.

[New York] Ming's New-York Price-Current, 1805–1817, see New-York Price-Current.

[New York] Moniteur Français, 1804.

Tri-weekly. Established in April, 1804, judging from the date of the first and only issue located, that of Nov. 29, 1804, no. 104, published by A [————] P. A. Maulouin, with the title of "Moniteur Français." It was a general newspaper, of quarto size, published tri-weekly from the same building as the Daily Advertiser, and was printed wholly in French, except for a few English advertisements.

In the New York "Morning Chronicle" of Sept. 15, 1804, is an unsigned advertisement dated Sept. 15, headed "French Moniteur" and reading as follows: "For the accommodation of the American and French merchants, and for the public generally, the editor of the French Moniteur has determined to alter the plan of his paper: it will appear on the 17th inst. printed in the French and English language, on a medium paper, it will be printed daily as at present and at the same prices, 8 dollars per annum, 2 dollars per quarter, 1 dollar for a single month. Advertisements inserted at a moderate price. Subscriptions received by the editor no. 8 Division street, and at the office of Deare and Andrews, printers, no. 12 Cedar-street." This advertisement presumably refers to the "Moniteur Français," and if published daily, the date of establishment would be much later than April 1804. If Deare & Andrews [Lewis Deare and Sydney W. Andrews] received subscriptions for the paper, it does not necessarily follow that they printed it.

Am. Antiq. Soc. has Nov. 29, 1804.

[New York] Morning Chronicle, 1802–1807.

Daily. Established Oct. 1, 1802, with the title of "Morning Chronicle," printed for the Proprietor [Peter Irving], by William A. Davis. With the issue of Jan. 19, 1803, Davis's name was omitted from the imprint. With the issue of Nov. 22, 1803, the paper was published, for the Proprietor, by Robert Wilson, but with Nov. 7, 1804, Wilson's name was replaced by that of Lewis Jones, Jun. With the issue of Feb. 9, 1805, Jones became a part proprietor, and the paper was published by Lewis Jones, Jun. & Co. With Aug. 3, 1805, it was published by Lewis Jones, Jun. With the issue of Aug. 20, 1805, it was published by the Proprietor, and with Jan. 6, 1806, for the Proprietor. The Sherburne, N. Y., "Olive Branch" of Sept. 10, 1806, refers to "Stanley's Morning Chronicle" as a New York newspaper; presumably this was Henry Stanley of New York, the proprietor. With the issue of Mar. 16, 1807, it was published by Lazarus Beach, who discontinued it with the issue of June 15, 1807, no. 13599 (error for 1399). From 1802 to at least 1804 a semi-weekly edition was also published under the title of the "Chronicle Express." An attempt was made in June, 1806, to establish a semi-weekly edition, to be called the "Native American," but not enough subscriptions were secured.

N. Y. Hist. Soc. has Oct. 1, 1802–Dec. 31, 1805, fair; May 1, 1806–June 15, 1807, fair.

Lib. Congress has Oct. 2, 1802; Jan. 1, 1803–Dec. 29, 1804, fair; Feb. 2, 1805–Dec. 22, 1806, fair; Jan. 3–June 15, 1807.

N. Y. Pub. Lib. has Oct. 1, 1802–Apr. 19, 1803; Mar. 12, 1805; Oct. 4, 1806.

N. Y. State Lib. has May 2, 1803–June 30, 1804; Jan. 3–May 10, July 9, Aug. 2–Sept. 10, Dec. 25–31, 1805; Jan. 1–16, 20–25, 29, Feb. 13, 18, 20, Mar. 29, 31, June 2, 3, 7, 9, 16, 25, 30, July 7, 12, 14, 17–19, 23, 24, 26, 28, 30, 31, Aug. 2, 4, 6–8, 11–13, 15, 18, 19, 26, 29, Sept. 4, 9, 12, 15, 19, Oct. 3, 4, 10, 16, 17, 20, 22, 30, Nov. 3, 10, 11, 13, 15, 18–24, Dec. 2, 6–10, 12, 27–30, 1806; Jan. 5–12, 15, 17, 20, 27, Feb. 6–9, 11–13, 20, 23, 28, Mar. 5, 6, 12, 13, Apr. 7, 13–June 15, 1807.

Am. Antiq. Soc. has Dec. 24, 1803; Apr. 26–28, June 9, July 3–Dec. 25, 1804, fair; Jan. 1–June 29, 1805, fair; July 8, 1805; Mar. 20–25, Apr. 1, May 8, 14, 16, 17, 21, 22, 24, 30, 31, 1806; Feb. 2, 24, Mar. 13, 16, Apr. 7, 8, 16, 20–22, 25, 27, 29, 30, 1807.

Harvard has Oct. 1, 2, 7, 9–12, 14–16, 19, 23, 27, 30, Nov. 6, 13, 16, 20, 23, Dec. 19, 1802; Jan. 5, Feb. 10, Oct. 20, 1803; Jan. 4, May 26, 29, 31, June 21, 23, 25, July 7, 14, Aug. 4, 25, Sept. 1, 12, 15, 22, 26, Oct. 10, 17, 24, 27, 31, Nov. 3, 14, 17, 21, 28, Dec. 5, 8, 12, 15, 1804; Jan. 5, 9, 16, 23, 26, Feb. 2, 6, 13, 16, 20, 23, 27, Mar. 1, 6, 9, 13, 16, 20, 23, 27, 29, 30, Apr. 3, 6, 24, 27, May 18, 22, 29, June 6, 8, 12, 15, 26, 29, July 3, 17, 20, 24, 27, Aug. 7, 14, 17, 21, 24, Sept. 4, 6, 7, 14, 20, 21, Oct. 4, 11, 16, Nov. 2, 6, 23, Dec. 14, 18, 21, 30, 1805; Jan. 1, 4, 8, 11, 18, 22, Feb. 8, 15, 22, 26, Mar. 1, 5, 8, 12, 15, 22, 29, Apr. 2, 12, 19, 23, 26, 29, 30, May 3, 10, 14, 24, 28, 31, June 14, 21, 25, July 2, 19, 29, Aug. 13, 20, Sept. 8, 9, 22, 24, Oct. 29, Nov. 1, 5, 28, Dec. 20, 24, 1806; Jan. 3, 10, 14, 15, 21, 24, 31, Feb. 4, 7, 11, 13, 21, 25, 28, Mar. 3, 7, 14, 18, 21, Apr. 1, May 6, 16, 27, June 13, 1807.

Duke Univ. has Aug. 16, 17, 27, 28, 30, 31, Sept. 2, 9, 10, 17, 20, 25, Oct. 23, 31, Nov. 1, 2, 6, 9, 11, 12, 14, 15, 21–30, 1805.

N. J. Hist. Soc. has Oct. 6, 1802; Apr. 27–May 5, 1804.

Cornell Univ. has Apr. 25, Nov. 30, 1805.

Univ. of Rochester has Jan. 24, Feb. 2, 1807.

Univ. of Mich. (Clements) has Feb. 9, 1803.

Yale has Nov. 13, 1804.

Rutgers Univ. has June 20, 1805.

Wis. Hist. Soc. has Jan. 15, Apr. 8, 1807.

New-York Morning Post, 1783–1792.

Semi-weekly and daily. A continuation, without change of volume numbering, of "The New-York Evening Post." The first issue with the title of "The

New-York Morning Post" was published in April, 1783, judging from the date of the earliest issue located with a volume number, that of July 25, 1783, vol. 3, no. 125, published by Morton and Horner [William Morton and Samuel Horner]. It was of folio size and published semi-weekly. On Feb. 23, 1785, it became a daily and the title was changed to "The New-York Morning Post, and Daily Advertiser." Horner died Jan. 12, 1786, and William Morton became sole publisher. With the issue of Oct. 6, 1788, the title was changed to "The Morning Post, and Daily Advertiser." With the issue of Jan. 3, 1792, the paper was again published semi-weekly and the title was changed to "The New-York Morning Post." The last issue located is that of June 12, 1792, no. 2300.

Am. Antiq. Soc. has June 25, July 25, Aug. 8, Nov. 7 (also facsim.), Dec. 2, 1783; Feb. 12, May 28, June 1, July 20, Aug. 3, 6, 10, 27–Sept. 7, 28–Oct. 5, 26, 29, Nov. 5–12, 19, Dec. 14, 21, 24, 31, 1784; Jan. 4, 21, Feb. 15, Mar. 7, 10, 17, 24, Apr. 2, 4, 6, 11, 14, 21, 25, May 2, 12, June 6, 13, 27, July 4, 11, 14, 18, 25, 28, Aug. 4, 8, Sept. 1, 5, Oct. 6, 13, 15, 1785; Feb. 1, May 25, June 1, 3, 7, 13, 15, 24, 27, 28, July 4, 11, 25, Aug. 5, 8, 12, 15, 22, 24, 26, 29, Sept. 7, 12, 19, 21, 26, Oct. 10, 14, 17, 19, 21, 26, Nov. 4, 7, 10, 14, 18, 22, 23, 29, Dec. 6, 13, 15, 23, 27–29, 1786; Jan. 3, 10, 17, 26, 29, 31, Feb. 3, 7, 10, 14, 17, 20, 21, Mar. 2, 3, 14, 17, 20, 21, 24, 31, Apr. 4, 7, 10, 13, 14, 17, 18, 25–28, May 4, 5, 9–22, 25, 26, June 5, 7, 15–18, 21, 23, 30, July 3, 7, 14, 19, 21, 30, Aug. 2, 4, 9, 11, 16, 18, 21, 23, Sept. 11, 13, 27, Oct. 6, 9–11, 16, 20, 23, 25, 27, Nov. 1, 3, 14, 20, 21, 28, Dec. 1, 11, 22, 1787; Jan. 9, 23, Feb. 6, 16, 23, 27, Mar. 18, 29, Apr. 1, 5–8, 15, 29, 30, May 6, 17, 20, 27, 31, June 5, 7, 17, 19, 26, 28, July 1, 3, 14, 17, 26, 31, Aug. 4, 7, 13–16, 26, 28, Sept. 3, 5, 12, 15, 18, 20, 27, 30, Oct. 2, 9, 11, 14, 20–22, 25, 30, Nov. 26, Dec. 5, 8, 9, 1788; Jan. 1, 7, 9, 13, 14, 23, Feb. 6, 17, 21, 24, 28, Mar. 10, 18, Apr. 1, 18, 25, May 2, 4, 21, June 23, 29, July 2, 14, 28, Aug. 4, 13, 27, 29, Sept. 17–19, 26, 30, Oct. 22, 29, Nov. 4, 7, 11, 13, 14, 20, 21, 24, 25, 27, 28, Dec. 1, 2, 4, 5, 8, 9, 11, 12, 15, 16, 18, 19, 25, 26, 29, 30, 1789; Jan. 16, 19, 20, 23, 30, Feb. 3, 6, 10, 17, 20, Mar. 3, 10, 13, 17, 24, Apr. 3, 9, 16, 17, 23, 24, 28, May 6, 8, 11, 17, 18, 20, 22, 24, 27, 29, 31, June 8, 10, 12, 15, 22, 25, 28–July 2, 5, 8, 9, 13, 14, 16, 18–27, 29, 31–Aug. 10, 14, 16, 19, 21, 26, Sept. 11, 18, 21, 30, Oct. 5, 9, 12, 16, 19, 23, 27, 28, 30, Nov. 4, 10, 11, 20, 27, Dec. 4, 7, 11, 15, 18, 25, 1790; Jan. 1, 5, 8, Feb. 2, 5, 9, 12, 16, 26, Mar. 2, 9, 12, 16, 19, 23, Apr. 2, 9, 13, 16, 23, 30, May 4, 7, 14, 28, 31, June 16, 21, 30, July 2, 7, 9, 12, 16, 23, 28, 30, Aug. 4, 6, 9, 11, 16–18, 20, 23, 25, 30, Sept. 1, 3, 5, 13, 17, 20, 21, 24, 27, Oct. 1, 4, 6, 8, 11, 15, 18, 20, 22, 25, 29, Nov. 2, 5, 12, 16, 23, 30, Dec. 9, 13, 28, 1791; Jan. 13–Feb. 3, 10, 17, 24–Mar. 20, 30–Apr. 20, 27–May 4, 25–June 5, 12, 1792.

N. Y. Hist. Soc. has July 18, Aug. 22, 1783; Dec. 14, 1784; Mar. 9, Sept. 18, 28, Oct. 5, 16, 1786; Aug. 24, 27, Oct. 15, 17, 1787; Jan. 4, 11, 15, 16, 18–22, 28, 29, Feb. 1, 4, 7, 26, Mar. 3, 6, 11, 18, 22, 29, Apr. 2, 8, 10, 11, 25, May 29,

Aug. 21, 22, 30, Sept. 3, 6, 10, Oct. 8, 16, Nov. 25, 26, 29, 1788; June 29, July 9, 27, Aug. 5, 1790.

York Inst., Saco, has Nov. 20, 1787–Apr. 9, 1789.

British Museum has Aug. 5, Sept. 16, 26, 30, Oct. 3, 10, 14, Nov. 7, Dec. 5, 1783; Feb. 20, 1784; Aug. 8–16, 1786.

Lib. Congress has Feb. 27, 1784; Jan. 3, 22, 25, Feb. 7, 14, 26, 27, Mar. 2, 3, 23, 31, Apr. 6, 12, 18–21, 26, 27, May 3, 4, 8, June 1, 16, July 2, 11, 12, 16, 23, 25–28, Aug. 2, 9, 15, 20, Sept. 7, 10, 13, 26, 28, Oct. 1, 2, 4, 6, 8, 10, 13–17, 22–24, Nov. 3, 8, 10, Dec. 14, 1787; Mar. 28, 1788; Apr. 7, 9, May 26, 1789; July 7, 10, 1790.

Harvard has July 9, 1784; June 17, 22, July 1, 8, 13, 18, 20, 25, 30, Sept. 20, Nov. 14, 23, 24, 1791; Mar. 20, 1792.

N. Y. Pub. Lib. has Aug. 29, Sept. 5, Oct. 13, 21, 29, Nov. 1, Dec. 16, 1785.

Amer. Philos. Soc. has Mar. 17, Apr. 26, 1787; Nov. 23, 30, 1791; Jan. 31, 1792.

N. J. Hist. Soc. has Aug. 17, 1785; Mar. 11, May 31, 1786.

N. Y. Soc. Lib. has Mar. 2, 1785; May 13, 1788.

Wash. & Lee Univ. has Aug. 22, 1783.

N. Y. State Lib. has Mar. 16, 1784.

Univ. of Mich. (Clements) has Jan. 26, 1787.

Rutgers Univ. has Dec. 20, 1787.

Yale has Aug. 22, 1788.

Boston Athenæum has Sept. 12, 1788.

Many libraries have the facsimile of Nov. 7, 1783.

New-York Morning Post, 1810–1812.

Daily. Established Nov. 20, 1810, with the title of "New-York Morning Post," published by G[arret] C. Tunison, for the Proprietor, Joseph Osborn signing as editor. It was really a continuation of the "American Citizen," although having a new title and new volume numbering. On Dec. 1, 1810, it was announced that Mr. Osborn no longer had any connection with the paper. The New York "Columbian" of Jan. 24, 1811, refers to William L. Rose as "editor of the Morning Post." With the issue of May 21, 1811, it was published by Tunison & Mills [Garret C. Tunison and Joseph Mills]; with June 15, 1811, by Tunison & Mills, for W[illiam] L. Rose; and with Aug. 28, 1811, by G. C. Tunison, for W. L. Rose (changed to Wm. L. Rose with the issue of Apr. 24, 1812). It was discontinued with the issue of Aug. 19, 1812, vol. 2, no. 587, to be succeeded by "The Statesman." The "Morning Star" was issued from the same office as a semi-weekly edition.

N. Y. Hist. Soc. has Nov. 20, 1810–Aug. 19, 1812.

N. Y. Soc. Lib. has Nov. 23, 27, Dec. 1, 1810–Aug. 18, 1812.

Lib. Congress has Nov. 20, 1810–Dec. 30, 1811; July 1–Aug. 19, 1812.

Am. Antiq. Soc. has Jan. 1–Feb. 21, 23–Apr. 13, 20–June 30, July 9, 1812.

Duke Univ. has Nov. 20–Dec. 29, 1810; Sept. 26, 1811; Aug. 14, 1812.

N. Y. State Lib. has May 1, 1811; Apr. 3, June 22, 1812.
N. Y. Pub. Lib. has Feb. 7, 1811; Feb. 22, 1812.
Rutgers Univ. has Jan. 15, 1812.

[New York] **Morning Star**, 1810–1813.

Semi-weekly. Established Nov. 27, 1810, with the title of "Morning Star," published by G[arret] C. Tunison, for the Proprietor, Joseph Osborn signing as editor. It was the successor of the "Republican Watch-Tower," although with a new title and a new volume numbering. It was so published, surely to April, 1812, soon after which it was printed by G. C. Tunison, for W. L. Rose. During this period it was issued as the semi-weekly edition of the "New-York Morning Post," which on Aug. 20, 1812, became "The Statesman." The "Morning Star" continued as the semi-weekly edition of the latter paper, changing its imprint with the issue of Aug. 21, 1812, to "Published by G. C. Tunison, for the Proprietor" [Joel Hart], and adopting a new volume numbering. The last issue located is that of Dec. 15, 1812, vol. 1, no. 35, but it was continued under this title until Feb. 26, 1813, when its name was changed to "The Statesman (for the Country").

N. Y. Hist. Soc. has Dec. 4, 1810; Feb. 1, 5, 12–Mar. 5, 12, 15, 22, Apr. 9, 12, 23–30, May 7–24, 31–July 2, 9–19, 26–Aug. 16, 23, 27, Sept. 3–Oct. 8, 15, Nov. 1–Dec. 27, 1811; Apr. 3, 1812.
Am. Antiq. Soc. has Dec. 7, 1810; Mar. 5, 15, Apr. 9, 12, May 24, July 30, Aug. 9, Nov. 8, 1811; Aug. 18, 25, 28, Sept. 18, Nov. 27, Dec. 1, 15, 1812.
Lib. Congress has Sept. 17, 1811; Jan. 29, 1813.
Univ. of Pittsburgh has Jan. 1, 1811.
Univ. of Mich. (Clements) has Mar. 5, 1811.

[New York] **Mott and Hurtin's New-York Weekly Chronicle**, 1795.

Weekly. Established Jan. 1, 1795, by Jacob S. Mott and William Hurtin, Jun., with the title of "Mott and Hurtin's New-York Weekly Chronicle." The last issue with this title was that of Apr. 16, 1795, vol. 1, no. 16, after which the firm was dissolved and the title changed to "The New-York Weekly Chronicle," which see.

N. Y. Hist. Soc. has Jan. 1–Apr. 16, 1795.
Am. Antiq. Soc. has Mar. 19, 1795.
Wis. Hist. Soc. has Apr. 2, 1795.

New-York Museum, 1788.

Semi-weekly. Established May 23, 1788, judging from the date of the earliest issue located, that of June 6, 1788, vol. 1, no. 5, published by John Russell, with the title of "The New-York Museum." It was of quarto size. The last issue located is that of Aug. 15, 1788, vol. 1, no. 25.

Am. Antiq. Soc. has June 6, 17, July 4, 29, 1788.
N. Y. Pub. Lib. has Aug. 15, 1788.

[New York] **National Advocate**, 1812–1820+.

Daily, weekly, and semi-weekly. Established Dec. 15, 1812, as a daily, with the title of "The National Advocate," edited by Henry Wheaton, and published by Geo. White. With the issue of Jan. 4, 1813, the name of the publisher was omitted, but with Mar. 11, 1813, the paper was published for N[aphtali] Phillips, Proprietor. Wheaton last appears as editor in the issue of May 15, 1815, and with the issue of July 21, 1815, Andrew C[aldwell] Mitchell is given as editor. With the issue of Feb. 20, 1817, Mitchell retired and the name of the editor was omitted from the imprint, but Mordecai M. Noah became editor and so continued until after 1820. N. Phillips was the publisher from 1813 to after 1820.

An edition for the country was also published, entitled "The National Advocate, (For the Country)," weekly from January, 1813, and semi-weekly from February, 1814 to after 1820.

N. Y. Hist. Soc. has Dec. 15, 1812–Dec. 31, 1813; Jan. 19–June 30, Dec. 30, 1814; June 27, 1815; July 1–Dec. 31, 1816; May 28–Dec. 31, 1817; Feb. 2, 1818–Dec. 30, 1820; also Aug. 2, Nov. 25, 1814; Mar. 14, 1815; Mar. 24, 27, Apr. 10, 17, 24, July 10, Aug. 7–14, Sept. 1, 22, Dec. 1, 11, 1818; Nov. 21, 24, Dec. 8, 1820, of semi-weekly.

Lib. Congress has Apr. 23, 1813–Dec. 31, 1817, fair; Jan. 1, 1818–Dec. 30, 1820; also Apr. 14, 1813; Jan. 12, 1816; Nov. 13, 1817, of semi-weekly.

Bath, Me., Free Lib. has Jan. 5, 1814–Dec. 22, 1820.

N. Y. Pub. Lib. has Feb. 23–Mar. 24, July 7–Dec. 31, 1813; Sept. 1, 1814–Apr. 29, 1815; Oct. 25, 1815; July 1–Dec. 31, 1817, fair; May 10–Dec. 30, 1820, fair; also Mar. 28, June 9, Aug. 15, 1815; July 1, 1817; Nov. 20, 1818–Dec. 31, 1819, fair; May 2, Oct. 24, 27, Nov. 14, 17, 1820, of semi-weekly.

Am. Antiq. Soc. has Dec. 17, 18, 28, 1812; Jan. 1, 5, 13, Mar. 6, 12, 30, Apr. 27, May 29, July 23, 27, Aug. 3, Sept. 28, Oct. 11, Nov. 18, Dec. 16, 1813; Jan. 11, 31, Mar. 29, Apr. 27, July 1, Aug. 13, Sept. 19, Oct. 2, 4, 7, 11–14, Nov. 10, 23, Dec. 3, 10, 17, 21, 30, 1814; Jan. 7, 11, Feb. 17, Mar. 20, 28, Apr. 8, May 18, June 23, Nov. 28, Dec. 1, 9, 1815; Jan. 6, June 13, 16, July 15, 16, Oct. 25, 1816; July 1, 1818–Dec. 30, 1820; also Mar. 3, June 16, July 7, Aug. 4–18, Sept. 1, 15–Oct. 20, Nov. 17, 24, Dec. 8, 22, 1813; Jan. 5, 26, Feb. 2, 18, Mar. 1, 1814–Dec. 25, 1815, fair; Jan. 1–Feb. 16, 23, Apr. 9, Sept. 27, Oct. 1, 8–22, 29–Dec. 31, 1816; Jan. 3–Dec. 30, 1817, fair; Jan. 1–20, 27, June 19, 1818; Feb. 12, Mar. 2, 5, 30, Apr. 2, 16, 23, 27, May 7, June 20, Aug. 3, 27, Sept. 7, 9, 14, Oct. 1–12, 22, Nov. 2, 26, Dec. 3, 7, 14, 21, 1819; Jan. 28, Feb. 1, 25–Mar. 3, 10, 31, Apr. 7, 11, July 4, 31, 1820, of semi-weekly.

NEW YORK 673

Wis. Hist. Soc. has June 28, 1816–Dec. 31, 1818; also Jan. 5, 1819; June 10–Dec. 29, 1820, of semi-weekly.

N. Y. State Lib. has Feb. 9, Apr. 19, 22, 23, 26–29, May 3, 7, 27, 29, 31, June 1, 5, July 5, 20, 26, Sept. 28, Nov. 2, 26–29, Dec. 3, 20, 24, 31, 1813; Jan. 5, 11, 13–15, 21, 24, 25, Feb. 2, 4, 7, 14, 15, 22, Apr. 4, 6, 12, 14, 19–22, 27, May 2–7, 10, 25, Sept. 20, Oct. 3, 5, 7–10, 27, Nov. 8, 9, 12, 15–17, 19, 23, Dec. 5, 6, 15, 17, 26, 1814; Jan. 2, 6, 18, 1815; Mar. 25, Apr. 18, May 22, July 30, Aug. 12, 1816; also Nov. 17, 20, 1818; Apr. 2, 1819; Aug. 15–Dec. 29, 1820, of semi-weekly.

Dartmouth has Dec. 18, 1813–July 25, 1814, fair.

Boston Athenæum has Jan. 14–Dec. 29, 1820, of semi-weekly.

Long Id. Hist. Soc. has Mar. 10–May 26, Dec. 29, 1813; Apr. 25, Dec. 25, 1815; Jan. 1, 9, 19, 1816, of semi-weekly.

Duke Univ. has Nov. 25, Dec. 30, 1816; July 25–Aug. 6, 24–Oct. 12, Nov. 30, Dec. 2–5, 24, 1818; Jan. 21–26, 28, 30, Apr. 15–21, 27, 28, 30, May 3, June 1, Dec. 8, 1819; also July 1, 15, 18, 1817, of semi-weekly.

Cornell Univ. has Oct. 17, 20, Nov. 10, 14, 21, 24, Dec. 1–25, 1815; Jan. 26, June 18, Dec. 13, 1816; Feb. 18, Mar. 7, Aug. 1, 1817, of semi-weekly.

Univ. of Mich. (Clements) has Jan. 3, Mar. 13, July 8–Aug. 3, 1818; Sept. 8, 1819; also Sept. 2, 1814, of semi-weekly.

Mass. Hist. Soc. has Aug. 28, Sept. 1, 5, 18, Oct. 27–29, Dec. 25, 28, 29, 1818; Jan. 29, Nov. 5, 1819.

Yale has May 26, Nov. 22, 1813; also Mar. 10, 1815, of semi-weekly.

[New York] **No Stamped Paper,** 1765, see **New-York Mercury,** 1752–1768.

[New York] **Observateur Impartial,** 1808.

Semi-weekly. Established Feb. 6, 1808, with the title of "L'Observateur Impartial, et Messager de l'Union," with the alternate title of "The Impartial Observer, and Union Messenger," printed by W[———] Turner & Co. for the editors, at the Minerva Press. It was a large quarto newspaper, of eight pages, the first four in French and the last four in English. The initial issue, which is the only one located, announced that the next issue would appear Feb. 13, but that thereafter it would appear semi-weekly.

N. Y. State Lib. has Feb. 6, 1808.

[New York] **Observer,** 1809–1811.

Weekly. Established Feb. 19, 1809, with the title of "The Observer," published every Sunday. It was of octavo size, paged and with eight pages to the issue. Although a magazine in appearance, it contained the news of the week, as well as local deaths and marriages. The first few issues were without imprint, but with the issue of Mar. 19, 1809, the name of William Elliot was given as printer. The paper was suspended with the issue of Aug. 6, 1809, no. 25. After a suspension of over a year, it was revived, with new volume numbering, Oct. 14, 1810. It carried the same title, but was of quarto size with four pages to the issue, and was printed by Elliot and Crissy [William Elliot and James Crissy]. With the issue of Feb. 3, 1811, the size was increased to eight pages. According to a reference in the "New York Journal" of Feb. 13, 1811, the paper was published on Sunday in two editions, one in the morning and one in the evening. The last issue located is that of Apr. 21, 1811, no. 28. See under "Weekly Observer" for continuation.

    N. Y. Hist. Soc. has Feb. 19–Mar. 5, 19, Apr. 16–30, 1809; Oct. 14, 1810–Apr. 21, 1811.
    N. Y. State Lib. has Feb. 19–Aug. 6, 1809.
    Lib. Congress has Feb. 19–Aug. 6, 1809.

[New York] Occasional Reverberator, 1753.

Weekly. Established Sept. 7, 1753, with the title of "The Occasional Reverberator," printed by J[ames] Parker. It consisted of essays and letters on political and religious subjects, and although it might be considered a magazine, because of its newspaper appearance and its concern with the topics of the day it is here included as a newspaper. It was of folio size and four issues were published on Sept. 7, 14, 21, and Oct. 5, 1753.

    N. Y. Pub. Lib. Congress, Princeton, Sage Lib. New Brunswick, Huntington Lib., Univ. of Mich. (Clements), and Wis. Hist. Soc. have Sept. 7–Oct. 5, 1753.
    Am. Antiq. Soc., N. Y. Hist. Soc., and John Carter Brown Lib. have Sept. 7–21, 1753.
    New Haven Col. Hist. Soc. and Boston Athenæum have Sept. 7, 14, 1753.

[New York] Olio, 1813–1814.

Weekly. Established Jan. 27, 1813, by S[amuel] Marks, with the title of "The Olio." It was of quarto size, paged and with eight pages to the issue. Although a magazine in appearance, it contained current news and marriage and death notices. At the conclusion of the first volume, Jan. 22, 1814, a title-page was printed, and the paper was suspended for one week to give the subscribers time to reflect upon the proposed increase in the price of the subscription. The issue of Feb. 5, 1814, vol. 2, no. 1, is the last located.

    Am. Antiq. Soc. has Jan. 27, 1813–Feb. 5, 1814.
    N. Y. Hist. Soc., N. Y. Pub. Lib., Brown Univ., Allegheny Coll., Yale, and Lib. Congress have Jan. 27, 1813–Jan. 22, 1814.
    N. Y. State Lib. has Feb. 6–Nov. 27, 1813, fair.
    Univ. of Mich. (Clements) has July 31, Aug. 7, 28–Dec. 11, 1813; Jan. 1–22, 1814.

[New York] Oracle, 1808.

Daily. Established Jan. 1, 1808, by J[ohn] J. Negrin, with the title of "L'Oracle and Daily Advertiser." It succeeded "The Daily Advertiser" and was printed partly in French and partly in English. The last issue with this title was that of Sept. 10, 1808, vol. 1, no. 212, when it was bought by Joseph Desnoues and published, without change of volume numbering, under the title of "The Daily Advertiser," which see.

N. Y. Hist. Soc. has Jan. 1–Sept. 10, 1808.
Lib. Congress has Jan. 1–June 30, 1808.
Am. Antiq. Soc. has Jan. 1–June 22, July 20, Aug. 11, 13, Sept. 10, 1808.
Harvard has Jan. 9, 13, Feb. 11, May 25, June 22, 25, July 27, 30, Aug. 10, 13, 17, 20, Sept. 3, 7, 10, 1808.
N. Y. State Lib. has Jan. 5, 1808.
Duke Univ. has Mar. 4, Apr. 11, 1808.
Wis. Hist. Soc. has May 7, 1808.
Dartmouth has July 26, 1808.

[New York] Oram's New-York Price-Current, 1797–1804, see New-York Price-Current.

New York Packet, 1776.

Weekly. Established Jan. 4, 1776, by Samuel Loudon, with the title of "The New York Packet. And the American Advertiser." It was suspended with the issue of Aug. 29, 1776, no. 35, immediately prior to the entry of the British into New York. Loudon re-established the paper at Fishkill in January, 1777, and at the close of the War returned to New York. For the Fishkill issues, see under Fishkill, and for the later New York file, 1783–1792, see the next entry.

Lib. Congress has Jan. 4–May 16, 30–July 18, Aug. 15, 1776.
N. Y. Soc. Lib. has Jan. 4–July 4, 1776.
N. Y. Pub. Lib. has Feb. 8–Mar. 7, 21–Apr. 25, May 9–23, June 6–Aug. 15, 1776.
N. Y. Hist. Soc. has Feb. 1–22, Apr. 25, May 30, July 4, 1776.
Mass. Hist. Soc. has Feb. 8, 22, May 23, June 6, 20, 27, July 11, 25, 1776.
Am. Antiq. Soc. has Apr. 18, Aug. 8, 29, 1776.

New York Packet, 1783–1792.

Semi-weekly, tri-weekly, and weekly. Removed from Fishkill at the close of the War, and re-established at New York, without change of volume numbering, with the issue of Nov. 13, 1783, no. 332, printed semi-weekly by Samuel Loudon, with the title of "The New York Packet. And the American Advertiser." With the issue of Nov. 11, 1784, the title was changed to "Loudon's New-York

Packet," and with that of May 16, 1785, to "The New-York Packet." With the issue of Nov. 14, 1785, his son John Loudon was admitted to partnership, and the paper was published by Samuel and John Loudon. With the issue of May 5, 1789, it became a tri-weekly. John Loudon died Sept. 28, 1789, and with the issue of Oct. 1, 1789, the paper was published by Samuel Loudon. It was changed to a weekly with the issue of Feb. 3, 1791, and was discontinued with the issue of Jan. 26, 1792, no. 1227. Samuel Loudon and his son Samuel established "The Diary; or Loudon's Register," as a daily paper, Feb. 15, 1792.

N. Y. Hist. Soc. has Nov. 13, 24, 1783; Jan. 1–8, 15, 19, Feb. 5–Mar. 18, Apr. 8, 12, 29–Dec. 27, 1784; Jan. 3–13, 20–Mar. 24, 31–May 12, 19–June 20, July 4, Aug. 11–Dec. 29, 1785; Jan. 2, 1786–Jan. 26, 1792.

N. Y. Pub. Lib. has Nov. 20, 1783; Jan. 1, 5, Mar. 4, Apr. 8, May 27, Dec. 9, 13, 1784; Jan. 13, 24, 27, Feb. 3, 21, Mar. 7, 14, 21, 24, 31–Apr. 18, 25–June 9, July 11–23, Aug. 8, Sept. 12, 19, 22, Oct. 3–Nov. 21, 28–Dec. 29, 1785; Jan. 2, 1786–Dec. 30, 1788, fair; Jan. 13, May 1, 1789.

Am. Antiq. Soc. has Dec. 15–29, 1783; Jan. 1–Dec. 30, 1784; Jan. 3, 6, 13, 27–Feb. 3, 14, 24, Mar. 3, 17–Apr. 7, 14, 21, 28, June 23, 30–July 7, 14, 21, Aug. 11, Sept. 1, 8, 15, 26, Oct. 20, Nov. 17, 24, Dec. 22, 29, 1785; Jan. 5, Feb. 6, 16, Mar. 13, 16, 23, 27, Apr. 6, 13–24, May 1, 4, 15, 22, 25, June 5, 9, 15, 19, 29, July 10, 17, 27, Aug. 14, 17, 24, Sept. 4, 28, Oct. 2, 5, 12, 16, 23, 30–Nov. 7, 21–28, Dec. 5, 12–26, 1786; Jan. 2–Dec. 25, 1787, fair; Jan. 8, 11, Feb. 5–Dec. 30, 1788, fair; Jan. 13–27, Feb. 3, 13, 24, 27, Mar. 3, 20–27, Apr. 3, 7, 24, 28, May 1, 5, 14, 23, June 25, July 28, Aug. 11, 20–Dec. 31, 1789, fair; Jan. 2–Feb. 4, 16, Mar. 2, 4, 23, 30–Dec. 30, 1790, fair; Jan. 1–6, 13, 18, 25–29, Feb. 24, Mar. 10, 31–May 5, June 2, 16–30, July 14, 28–Aug. 25, Sept. 29, Oct. 20–Nov. 24, Dec. 8–29, 1791; Jan. 5, 19, 1792.

Lib. Congress has Mar. 14, 1785; Sept. 28, Oct. 5, 1786; Jan. 2–Dec. 28, 1787; Jan. 18, 22, Aug. 22, Sept. 19, Oct. 24, 1788; Mar. 3, 10, 17, 24, Apr. 7, 17, June 18, July 25, Aug. 15, Dec. 5, 10, 24–31, 1789; Jan. 5, 7, 14, 23, 28, July 3, 10, 17, 24, 29, Oct. 21, 30, Nov. 2, 16, 18, Dec. 11, 1790.

Yale has July 1, Oct. 28, 1784; Apr. 14, May 26, Sept. 25, 1785; Apr. 22, 25, June 24, Aug. 5, 19, Sept. 2, Nov. 18, 1788; Feb. 13–May 7, July 2–Dec. 31, 1789; Mar. 11, 30, 1790.

N. Y. State Lib. has Dec. 22, 1785; Jan. 19, Feb. 6, 9, 23, Apr. 20, June 12–19, 26–July 3, Aug. 17, Sept. 4, Oct. 2, 26, Nov. 7, 17, 28, Dec. 12, 22, 26, 1786; Jan. 9, 12, Feb. 2, July 27, Sept. 21, Oct. 9, 1787; May 2, 27, June 3, 6, 20, July 8, 22, 25, Aug. 8, 12, 26, Sept. 5, 16, 23, 30, Oct. 10, 14, 24, Nov. 4–14, 25, 28, Dec. 19, 23, 30, 1788; Jan. 23, 27, 1789; Oct. 30, 1790.

N. Y. Soc. Lib. has July 12, 1784; Jan. 2–Dec. 29, 1786.

York Inst., Saco, has Nov. 20–Dec. 28, 1787; Aug. 8–Oct. 14, 1788; Jan. 30–Sept. 26, 1789.

Boston Pub. Lib. has Oct. 10, 31, 1785; Jan. 1–July 22, 1788, fair; Dec. 10, 1789; June 17, 1790.

Mass. Hist. Soc. has Dec. 22, 1783; Jan. 8, July 22, Oct. 28, Nov. 11, 1784; Mar. 17, 21, Apr. 7, 1785; Nov. 28, 1786; Jan. 16, 30, Feb. 16, 1787.
Univ. of Mich. (Clements) has July 7, 1785; June 5, Sept. 7, 14, 28, Oct. 2, 12, 16, 23, 30, Nov. 6, 16, 1787; Oct. 3, 1789.
Harvard has Nov. 17, 1783; May 3, 17, July 8, Aug. 2, 1784; Oct. 26, Nov. 2, 1787.
British Museum has Feb. 2–23, 1784; Aug. 14, 1786.
Rutgers Univ. has June 15, 1786; Aug. 31, 1787; Aug. 29, Oct. 28, 1788.
Duke Univ. has July 13, 1787; July 25, 1788.
N. J. Hist. Soc. has Jan. 25, 1788.
Newberry Lib. has Feb. 1, 1788.
Wis. Hist. Soc. has Aug. 15, 1789.

New-York Pacquet, 1763.

Weekly. Established by Benjamin Mecom with the title of "The New-York Pacquet." A preliminary issue, no. 0, was published July 11, 1763, and the first numbered issue evidently appeared on July 18. The last issue located is that of Aug. 22, 1763, no. 6.

N. Y. Hist. Soc. has July 11, Aug. 22, 1763.
N. Y. Pub. Lib. has July 11, 1763.

[New York] Parker's New-York Gazette, 1759–1762, see New-York Gazette, or Weekly Post-Boy.

New-York Patriot, 1815–1816.

Weekly. Established Dec. 2, 1815, with the title of "The New-York Patriot," printed by E[phraim] Conrad. The last issue located is that of Mar. 30, 1816, no. 18.

Am. Antiq. Soc. has Dec. 9, 1815; Feb. 10, Mar. 2, 9, 1816.
N. Y. Hist. Soc. has Mar. 2, 1816.
Wis. Hist. Soc. has Mar. 30, 1816.

[New York] Patron of Industry, 1820+.

Semi-weekly. Established June 28, 1820, with the title of "The Patron of Industry," published under the auspices of the National Institution for the Promotion of Industry, and printed for the Editors by J[onathan] Seymour. It was continued after 1820.

Am. Antiq. Soc., N. Y. Hist. Soc., Yale, Phil. Lib. Co., and Lib. Congress have June 28–Dec. 30, 1820.

Huntington Lib. has July 29, Sept. 9, 13, 20–27, Nov. 4, 1820.
Tenn. State Lib. has July 8, 19, Oct. 18–Nov. 18, 1820.

[New York] Pelican, 1808.

Tri-weekly. Established Oct. 6, 1808, with the title of "The Pelican," printed by J[ohn] Hardcastle for the Proprietor. It was a newspaper of quarto size and the editorial announcement was signed by Joseph Forster. This initial issue is the only one located.

Harvard has Oct. 6, 1808.

[New York] People's Friend, 1806–1807.

Daily and semi-weekly. Established Sept. 1, 1806, with the title of "The People's Friend & Daily Advertiser," published, for the Proprietor [Stephen C. Carpenter], by J[acob] Frank. The American Antiquarian Society has Carpenter's printed "Prospectus," undated, but accompanied by a letter regarding his newspaper dated Aug. 25, 1806. It succeeded "The Daily Advertiser" and continued its advertisements. With the issue of Nov. 10, 1806, Frank's name was omitted as printer, and with that of Nov. 11, 1806, the paper was printed and published for the Proprietor by Lazarus Beach. With the issue of Mar. 13, 1807, the name of the printer was changed to John H. Prentiss. In the issue of June 5, 1807, Carpenter stated that he was to withdraw as editor, and that the establishment was for sale. The last daily issue with the title of "The People's Friend & Daily Advertiser" was that of Aug. 3, 1807, vol. 1, no. 285, when it was succeeded by "The Daily Advertiser."

A semi-weekly edition for country subscribers was begun Jan. 1, 1807, with the shortened title of "The People's Friend," printed and published for the Proprietors by Lazarus Beach. The printer's name was changed to John H. Prentiss with the issue of Mar. 14, 1807. When Carpenter sold out the paper to Samuel and James A. Bayard in August, 1807, the new proprietors changed the title of the daily to "The Daily Advertiser," but continued "The People's Friend" as a semi-weekly, which, with the issue of Aug. 5, 1807, was published for the Proprietors, without any printer's name. The semi-weekly was discontinued with the issue of Dec. 31, 1807, vol. 1, no. 104.

N. Y. Hist. Soc. has Sept. 1, 1806–Aug. 3, 1807; also Jan. 1–Dec. 31, 1807, of semi-weekly.
Lib. Congress has Sept. 1, 1806–Aug. 3, 1807.
Harvard has Sept. 2–Dec. 31, 1806, fair; Jan. 1–7, May 6, 1807; also Jan. 17–Dec. 2, 1807, of semi-weekly.
Am. Antiq. Soc. has Prospectus (Aug. 1806); May 7, June 5, July 1–Aug. 3, 1807; also Jan. 7–Dec. 31, 1807, fair, of semi-weekly.
N. Y. State Lib. has Sept. 4, 1806–Feb. 25, 1807, fair; Mar. 9, 12–14, Apr. 30, May 14, 16, June 26, July 27, 1807.

Boston Athenæum has Jan. 1–July 15, 1807.
Duke Univ. has Jan. 1–31, July 2–Aug. 3, 1807.
Long Id. Hist. Soc. has Sept. 1, 3, 15, 19, 22, 27, Nov. 7, 8, 11, 1806; Jan. 23, Feb. 24, June 5, 1807.
N. Y. Soc. Lib. has Mar. 11, 14, Apr. 1, 4, 8, 15, 22, 25, May 1, 6, June 6, 10, 1807.
Univ. of Mich. (Clements) has Dec. 23, 1806; July 10, 1807.

New-York Phœnix, 1812–1813.

Weekly. Established June 3, 1812, judging from the earliest issue located, that of Aug. 12, 1812, vol. 1, no. 11, edited by Geo. White, with the title of "The New-York Phœnix." This paper was the country edition of the "Public Advertiser," published by Samuel Brower. In December, 1812, White's name was omitted from the imprint and the paper was published by Samuel Brower. It was discontinued in February, 1813, and its subscription list relinquished to the "National Advocate (For the Country)," as noted in "The National Advocate" of Feb. 23, 1813.

Am. Antiq. Soc. has Aug. 12, Oct. 15, 1812.
Lib. Congress has Aug. 19, Sept. 2, 1812.
Trinity Coll., Hartford, has Sept. 23, 1812.

[New York] Plebean, 1754.

The "New-York Mercury" of Aug. 12, 1754, announced "On Wednesday next [Aug. 14] will be published, Price, Two Pence; Number I, of a New Paper, entitled 'The Plebean'." The same paper, on Aug. 19, 1754, stated "Next Wed. will be pub. No. II." The paper may have been a magazine in type, or a series of essays. Supposedly Hugh Gaine, publisher of the "New-York Mercury," printed "The Plebean." Frank B. Bigelow, in the "Literary Collector," 1902, vol. 5, p. 38, states that it was edited by "Noah Meanwell," and printed by Hugh Gaine, and that the issue of Sept. 11, 1754, no. 5, was in the N. Y. Society Library. But this issue cannot now be found.

[New York] Political Bulletin, 1810–1811.

Semi-weekly and weekly. Established Dec. 22, 1810, by J[ohn] Hardcastle, with the title of "The Political Bulletin and Miscellaneous Repository." At first issued semi-weekly, it became a weekly on Jan. 12, 1811. It was of quarto size, and although a magazine in appearance, contained current news, advertisements and death notices. The last issue located is that of Mar. 30, 1811, no. 16.

N. Y. Hist. Soc. has Dec. 22, 1810–Mar. 30, 1811, fair.

[New York] Porcupine's Gazette, 1800.

Only one issue of this paper was published at New York, that of Jan. 13, 1800, no. 779, published by Wm. Cobbett, with the title of "Porcupine's Gazette." Cobbett removed from Philadelphia, because of the yellow fever epidemic, in 1799, and after publishing nine issues of his paper at Bustleton, near Philadelphia, he went to New York where he brought out his "farewell number." Instead of being printed in the form of a newspaper, it was printed as a pamphlet, being of 12 mo. size and numbered pp. 49–72.

Am. Antiq. Soc., N. Y. Soc. Lib., N. Y. Pub. Lib., Lib. Congress, Univ. of Mich. (Clements), and Harvard have Jan. 13, 1800.

New-York Post-Boy, 1744–1747, see New-York Weekly Post-Boy.

New-York Price-Current, 1786.

Weekly. First published under the title of "The New-York Price-Current" Aug. 14, 1786, continuing "The American Price-Current," and printed by Francis Childs. Childs's paper, "The Daily Advertiser," from Aug. 10 to Aug. 16, 1786, contained the following notice: — "A Price Current, given (gratis) every Monday, to the Subscribers for this Paper." The issue of Aug. 14, 1786, the only one located, has no volume numbering and contains two pages, small quarto.

Lib. Congress has Aug. 14, 1786.

New-York Price-Current, 1796–1817.

Weekly and semi-weekly. Established early in 1796, judging from the date of the earliest issue located, that of Jan. 2, 1797, no. 54, published weekly by James Oram, with the title of "The New-York Prices Current." It was a paper of quarto size. With the issue of June 3, or 10, 1797, the title was changed to "Oram's New-York Price-Current, and Marine Register;" with May 25, 1799, to "New-York Price-Current;" and with June 26, 1802, to "Oram's New-York Price-Current." With the issue of Sept. 8, 1804, Oram sold out to Alexander Ming and William Young, and the title was changed to "Ming & Young's New-York Price-Current," published by Ming & Young. Young died Sept. 15, 1805, and with the issue of Sept. 21, 1805, the title was changed to "Ming's New-York Price-Current," published by Alexander Ming. With the issue of Jan. 30, 1813, Samuel Dickinson became the publisher and the title was changed to "Dickinson's (Formerly) Ming's New-York Price-Current," but with the issue of Mar. 20, 1813, the title reverted to "Ming's New-York Price-Current," Dickinson continuing as publisher. With the issue of Nov. 19, 1814, Alexander Ming again became publisher. With the issue of May 4, 1816, the size was increased from four to eight pages; with May 24, 1817, it was changed back to four pages and made a semi-weekly; and with Dec. 6, 1817, it was decreased to two pages. The last issue located is that of Dec. 31, 1817, no. 1212.

In 1815–1816 Ming sent out his paper, which was published on Saturday, as the Saturday issue of "Daily Items, for Merchants," giving the serial number of both papers in his headline. See under "Daily Items."

N. Y. Hist. Soc. has Jan. 2, 1797–Dec. 27, 1806; Dec. 17, 1808; Jan. 6, 1810–Dec. 31, 1817.
N. Y. Pub. Lib. has Aug. 10, 1805–Dec. 29, 1810.
Mass. Hist. Soc. has Nov. 25, 1809–Sept. 29, 1810.
Lib. Congress has Jan. 20–Dec. 29, 1810.
Phil. Lib. Co. has Jan. 4, 1813–Dec. 27, 1814.
Harvard has Mar. 20, May 20, July 1, 15, 1797; Apr. 19, May 31, 1800; Apr. 25, May 16, June 13, 20, Aug. 1, 29, Sept. 19, Oct. 3, Dec. 5, 1801; June 26, 1802; Oct. 8, 1803; May 5, 26, 1804; Aug. 31, Sept. 7, 28, Oct. 19, Nov. 2, 16, Dec. 28, 1805; June 21, Oct. 11, 1806; Jan. 31, Feb. 14, May 2, 16, June 6, July 18, Aug. 29, Nov. 7, 21, 1807; Feb. 20, Apr. 9, 16, 30, July 9, 30, Aug. 6, Sept. 10, 1808.
Am. Antiq. Soc. has Nov. 24, 1798; Mar. 16, Dec. 14, 1799; Jan. 18, 1800; May 9, 1801; May 29, 1802; July 20, 1805; July 12, Oct. 4, Nov. 29, 1806; Sept. 12, 19, Oct. 3, 24, 1807; Jan. 9, 1808; Oct. 14, 1809; June 23, Sept. 1, 1810; Dec. 7, 1811; Jan. 25, 1812; Aug. 20, 1814; Feb. 8, Mar. 1, 1817.
British Museum has May 13, 1797; Mar. 9, June 8, 15, July 6, Aug. 3, 7, 31, 1799.
N. Y. State Lib. has Dec. 16, 30, 1809; Jan. 6, 20, Apr. 28, 1810.
Rutgers Univ. has Apr. 23, 1808.
Wis. Hist. Soc. has Jan. 5, 1811.
Univ. of Mich. (Clements) has Apr. 24, 1813.

New-York Prices Current, 1797, see New-York Price-Current.

[New York] Prisoner of Hope, 1800.

Weekly and semi-weekly. Established May 3, 1800, as a weekly, with the title of "Prisoner of Hope." Although published in the interest of "The Society of the Relief of Distressed Prisoners," it was a newspaper of a general type. With the issue of May 10, 1800, the name of the "Conductor" was given as William Sing. With the issue of May 21, 1800, the paper was published semi-weekly, but with Aug. 9, 1800, it reverted to a weekly. It was discontinued with the issue of Aug. 23, 1800, vol. 1, no. 28.

N. Y. Pub. Lib. has May 3–Aug. 23, 1800.
N. Y. Hist. Soc. has May 10, 17, 31, June 4, 11–18, 25, July 5, 12–19, 26–Aug. 2, 16, 1800.
Am. Antiq. Soc. has May 31–July 26, 1800.
New Haven Col. Hist. Soc. has July 12, 1800.

[New York] Public Advertiser, 1807–1813.

Daily and tri-weekly. Established Jan. 5, 1807, as a daily, by J[acob] Frank & Co., with the title of "The Public Advertiser." With the issue of Jan. 5, 1808, George White was added to the firm, which became Frank, White & Co. With the issue of June 23, 1809, the title was altered to "Public Advertiser." This firm was dissolved and there was no imprint from Jan. 4 to Jan. 26, 1810. With the issue of Jan. 27, 1810, the paper was published by J. Frank, for the Proprietors; with Mar. 8, 1810, the imprint was not given; and with Feb. 5, 1811, Philip Tabele became publisher. With the issue of Aug. 15, 1811, vol. 5, no. 1525, the title was changed to "American Patriot, and Public Advertiser" and it was printed by Samuel Brower, for the Proprietors. With the issue of Oct. 7, 1811, the paper became a tri-weekly, printed by Samuel Brower, but with Nov. 18, 1811, it reverted to a daily. On April 20, 1812, the title reverted to "Public Advertiser," the paper still being published by Samuel Brower. With the issue of Aug. 14, 1812, the imprint gave the name of Geo. White as editor, in addition to Samuel Brower as publisher; but with the issue of Dec. 14, 1812, White's name was omitted. It was discontinued with the issue of Feb. 22, 1813, vol. 7, no. 1958, as noted in "The National Advocate" of Feb. 23, 1813, to which paper its list of subscribers was relinquished. The "Public Advertiser" carried a country edition under the following titles: "New-York Aurora," 1807–1809; "The New York Journal," 1809–1812; "The New-York Phœnix," 1812–1813.

- N. Y. Hist. Soc. has Jan. 5–Oct. 14, Nov. 6–Dec. 29, 1807; Jan. 2, 1808–Oct. 3, 16, 1811; Apr. 20–Dec. 31, 1812.
- Lib. Congress has Feb. 23–Dec. 31, 1807, fair; Jan. 1, 1808–Dec. 31, 1810; July 1–Aug. 7, Oct. 4, 5, 1811; Feb. 18, 1812; Jan. 1–Feb. 22, 1813.
- Am. Antiq. Soc. has Feb. 7, Mar. 4, 17, June 29, July 11, Aug. 7, 18, Sept. 8, 28, Oct. 15–19, 21–Nov. 5, 20, Dec. 16, 28, 1807; Jan. 2, 1808–Dec. 31, 1810; Jan. 7–June 29, Aug. 23–29, Sept. 5, Oct. 7, 9, 11, 23, 25, 30, Dec. 9, 1811; Jan. 18, 21, 1812; Feb. 12, 1813.
- N. Y. State Lib. has Jan. 6, Feb. 21, Apr. 9, 10, 18, 25, 1807; Jan. 12, 1808–Apr. 3, 1809, fair; Apr. 18, Nov. 20, 1809–Apr. 6, 28, 1810; Jan. 3–Mar. 30, Apr. 13, 16, 23, 1811; Jan. 12, Mar. 2, 4, 9–13, 16, 20–24, 27, 28, 31, Apr. 1, 12, 20, 21, 27, 29, May 1, June 25, July 1, 11, 14, 16, 17, 20, 23, 25–30, Aug. 6–Oct. 31, Nov. 17–19, 23, 24, 27, 28, Dec. 3–5, 8–9, 12, 15, 16, 19, 21, 1812.
- Univ. of Mich. (Clements) has Jan. 5, 1808–Dec. 30, 1809, fair; Jan. 1, 6, 9, 11–13, Mar. 17, 20, Apr. 19, May 1, 11, 12, July 2–Aug. 31, Sept. 4–6, 8–10, 15, 19, 20, 22–24, 27–Oct. 17, 22, 1810.
- N. Y. Pub. Lib. has Apr. 10, 1808; Jan. 1–July 4, 1810; May 7, 9, July 25, Oct. 7–11, 16, Nov. 6, 20, 27–Dec. 20, 27, 1811; Jan. 7, 8, 13, 14, Mar. 19, 1812.
- Harvard has Jan. 5, 8–10, 15, 19–21, 24, 28–31, Feb. 4, 6, 9, 17, 19, 21, 23, 25, 27, Mar. 9, 12, 14, 17, 18, 21, 25, 28, Apr. 1, 8, 15, 18, 25, 29, May 2, 13, 16, 20, Aug. 17, 1807.

Yale has Feb. 20, 1808–Aug. 31, 1810, scattering issues.
Duke Univ. has Feb. 19, 1808; Jan. 3–Mar. 19, fair; Nov. 9, 11, 25, Dec. 25, 27, 28, 1809; Jan. 1–5, 29, Feb. 1, 1810.
Rutgers Univ. has Dec. 20, 1808; Feb. 11, Mar. 14, 1809; June 27, 1810; Aug. 10, 1811.
Long Id. Hist. Soc. has July 29, 1809; Feb. 3, 1810.
Skaneateles Lib. Assoc. has Dec. 21, 1811.

New-York Public Sale Report, 1814–1816.

Weekly. Established in January, 1814, judging from the earliest issue located, that of Jan. 30, 1815, vol. 1, no. 52, published by N[athaniel] T. Eldredge, with the title of "New-York Public Sale Report." With the issue of Dec. 9, 1816, John Wood was admitted to partnership and the paper published by Eldredge & Wood. The last issue located is that of Dec. 30, 1816, vol. 3, no. 52. It was succeeded by "Wood's New-York Sale Report," which see.

Yale has Nov. 13, 1815–Dec. 30, 1816.
Am. Antiq. Soc. has Jan. 30, 1815.

[New York] Register of the Times, 1796–1797.

Weekly. The weekly edition of "The Diary." It was established June 3, 1796, with the title of "Register of the Times," published by Cornelius C. Van Alen & Co. With the issue of Jan. 27, 1797, it was printed by Crookes & Saunders [John Crookes and Robert Saunders], for John I. Johnson, and with Apr. 7, 1797, by John Crookes for John I. Johnson. The last issue located is that of June 9, 1797, no. 53.

N. Y. Hist. Soc. has June 3, 1796–June 9, 1797.

[New York] Remembrancer, 1804–1805.

Weekly. Established in November, 1804, judging from the first and only issue located, that of June 1, 1805, no. 30, published by G[eorge] & R[obert] Waite, with the title of "The Remembrancer." It was of quarto size, and although containing some local news, was devoted chiefly to advertising stationery, lottery tickets and patent medicines sold by G. & R. Waite.

Am. Antiq. Soc. has June 1, 1805.

[New York] Republican Chronicle, 1817–1819.

Semi-weekly and daily. Established as a semi-weekly Apr. 2, 1817, with the title of "Republican Chronicle," published by Charles N. Baldwin and Abraham Asten. With the issue of Dec. 31, 1817, the publishing firm became Baldwin,

Asten & Co., and S[amuel] Woodworth, who had hitherto served in an editorial capacity, was given as editor. On Mar. 4, 1818, a daily paper was also established, with a new volume numbering, entitled "Republican Chronicle & City Advertiser." The title of the semi-weekly continued as "Republican Chronicle." With the issue of May 27, 1818, the paper was published by Charles N. Baldwin alone, S. Woodworth continuing as editor. With the issue of July 29, 1818, Woodworth's name was omitted from the imprint. The last issue of the semi-weekly located is that of Jan. 27, 1819, vol. 2, no. 191, and of the daily that of Jan. 9, 1819, vol. 2, no. 106. The Utica "Columbian Gazette" of Mar. 23, 1819, states that the "Republican Chronicle," published by Charles N. Baldwin, has been discontinued.

Rutgers Univ. has Apr. 2, 1817–Jan. 27, 1819 of semi-weekly; and Aug. 15, Oct. 10, 1818, of daily.

Am. Antiq. Soc. has Apr. 12, 29, May 3, 1817; Apr. 22, 1815, of semi-weekly; Mar. 18, May 23, June 30, 1818, of daily.

Univ. of Rochester has June 14, July 2, Aug. 20, Oct. 1, 1817; Dec. 19, 1818, of semi-weekly.

Wis. Hist. Soc. has Dec. 2, 1818.

N. Y. Hist. Soc. has Jan. 9, 1819, daily.

[New York] Republican Watch-Tower, 1800–1810.

Semi-weekly. Established Mar. 12, 1800, by D[avid] Denniston, with the title of "Republican Watch-Tower." It was really a continuation of "Greenleaf's New York Journal," although bearing a new title and volume numbering. With the issue of May 6, 1801, Denniston formed a partnership with James Cheetham, the firm name being D. Denniston and J. Cheetham. With the issue of Apr. 9, 1803, the partnership was dissolved and James Cheetham became sole publisher. Cheetham died Sept. 19, 1810, but his name remained in the imprint until Nov. 16, 1810, vol. 10, no. 1014, with which issue the paper was published by G[arret] C. Tunison, for the Proprietor. It was then discontinued under this title, to be succeeded on Nov. 27, 1810, by the "Morning Star." From 1800 to 1810, the "Republican Watch-Tower" was issued as the semi-weekly edition of the "American Citizen."

N. Y. Hist. Soc. has Apr. 25, Sept. 13, 20, 24, 27, Oct. 29, 1800; July 29, 1801; Feb. 27, Mar. 17–Apr. 3, 10, 21, 28, 1802–Oct. 16, 1810.

N. Y. State Lib. has June 3, 6, July 15, 1801; Jan. 16, May 1–Sept. 10, 21–29, Nov. 5, 1802–Apr. 20, 1810.

Yale has Mar. 12, 1800–July 13, 1803.

Conn. Hist. Soc. has May 4, 1803–Apr. 29, 1808.

Am. Antiq. Soc. has Mar. 19, Apr. 12–19, May 28, Oct. 25, Nov. 15, 19, 1800; Jan. 28, Apr. 29, May 20, June 6, 1801; May 1, 22, 26, June 2–9, 16, July 21,

NEW YORK 685

31, Aug. 4, Sept. 22, Oct. 13, 1802; Jan. 19, May 25, June 1-18, 25, July 2, Oct. 29, Nov. 5, 12-26, Dec. 3, 28, 31, 1803; Jan. 4, 21, 25, Feb. 8, 11, 18-Mar. 24, 31, Apr. 14-25, May 9-16, 26, June 1, 6, July 14, Aug. 11, 15, Oct. 6, 10, Nov. 17, 21, 1804; Jan. 5, 16-May 1, June 1, July 13, 1805; Jan. 2, Mar. 18, 25-Apr. 1, May 9, 1806-Dec. 29, 1809; Jan. 9, 16, 23, 30, Feb. 2, 16, 27-Mar. 9, 23-Apr. 6, 13, 24, May 8, 29, June 5, Sept. 4, Nov. 16, 1810.

N. Y. Pub. Lib. has Mar. 12-Dec. 31, 1800, fair; Jan. 3-Feb. 4, 14, Apr. 15, Nov. 28, 1801; Mar. 6, May 8, 1802-Apr. 30, 1803, fair; Jan. 4-Feb. 15, 29-Mar. 28, Apr. 18, May 5, 12-26, June 6, 20, Aug. 8, 11, 25-Sept. 1, 19, 26, Oct. 17, 27, 31, Nov. 21, Dec. 29, 1804; Jan. 2, 5, 12, 19-Feb. 2, 9, Apr. 24, 27, May 11, 29, June 1, 8-12, 19-29, July 17, Aug. 17, 21, Sept. 18-28, Oct. 27, Nov. 6, 13, 16, 23, Dec. 4-28, 1805; May 2, 1806; Mar. 18, 1810.

Lib. Congress has Mar. 14-Dec. 29, 1804; Feb. 13, Aug. 31, Oct. 23, Nov. 9, 1805; Nov. 4, 1806; Apr. 3, May 29, June 2, 30, July 28, Aug. 7, 11, Sept. 1, 29-Oct. 6, 13, 23, 27, Nov. 24, Dec. 6, 22, 1807; Jan. 8, Mar. 4, 11, Apr. 5, 12-19, 29, May 10-17, 24, 27, Aug. 16, 23, 26, Sept. 2-13, 23, Oct. 4, 7, 1808; Jan. 3, 1809-July 10, 1810.

Trinity Coll., Hartford, has Jan. 1-Dec. 27, 1806, fair; Jan. 1-Dec. 30, 1808, fair; Jan. 6-Oct. 29, 1809, fair.

Harvard has Apr. 2, 9, 23, May 10, 17, 21, June 4-July 6, 19-Aug. 20, 30, Sept. 13, 20, Oct. 4, 22, 25, Nov. 29, Dec. 13, 20, 27, 1800; Jan. 3, 7, 28, 31, Feb. 18, 25, Mar. 4, 1801-Dec. 29, 1802, fair; Jan. 1-19, 29, Feb. 2, 26, Apr. 6, June 18, 29, July 2, 13, 16, 30-Aug. 6, 17, 24, 27, Sept. 7, 21-28, Oct. 5-12, 19, Dec. 24, 1803; Jan. 7, 14, 29, Mar. 21, May 9, 26, June 20-30, July 7-18, 25, Aug. 4, 11, 25-Sept. 5, 15, 19, 29, Oct. 10-20, 31, Nov. 10-17, 24, Dec. 8, 26, 1804; Jan. 2, 1805-Dec. 4, 1807, fair; June 21, July 26, Aug. 2-Dec. 23, 1808, fair; Jan. 13, 1809.

Long Id. Hist. Soc. has Mar. 12, 15, May 7-21, 31, June 18, 28, July 6, 16-26, Aug. 2-30, Oct. 1, 4, Nov. 1, 8, 12, Dec. 3, 24, 31, 1800; Jan. 3, 28-Feb. 28, Mar. 14, 18, Apr. 1, May 13-30, June 19, Aug. 6, 19, Sept. 5, 23, Oct. 3, 7, Nov. 7, 21, 25, Dec. 5, 12, 23, 1801; Apr. 3-21, May 5, 10, 15, 22-30, June 23, Sept. 25, 1802; Feb. 23, Apr. 2-June 25, 1803, fair; Jan. 21, Mar. 28, Apr. 4, July 21, Nov. 7, Dec. 12, 1804; July 3, Nov. 30, 1805; Feb. 28, Mar. 11, Apr. 15, 29, Sept. 2-Nov. 4, Dec. 16, 1806; Jan. 16, 20, Mar. 6, 13, May 1-15, June 2-30, July 31, Sept. 6, 23, Oct. 25, 28, Nov. 4, 1808; Jan. 13, Feb. 3, 7, 21, Mar. 17, Apr. 4, 7, 23, 26, May 12-June 2, Sept. 15, 22, Oct. 10, 20-Nov. 7, 1809; Jan. 9, 19, Mar. 2-19, 16, 23, 30, Apr. 3, May 11, 1810.

Duke Univ. has May 9, June 6-July 14, Aug. 4, 1809-Apr. 20, 1810.

Univ. of Mich. (Clements) has Oct. 13, 1802; Aug. 8, 1804; Jan. 19, 1805; Aug. 21, Nov. 10, 1807; Jan. 9, 1810.

Wis. Hist. Soc. has Nov. 5, 1800; Apr. 1, June 10, 1808.

N. Y. Soc. Lib. has Oct. 13, 1802; May 26, 1804; Sept. 7, 1810.

Rutgers Univ. has Mar. 15, Nov. 22, 1800.

[New York] **Rivington's New-York Gazette,** 1777.

Weekly. A continuation, without change of volume numbering, of "Rivington's New-York Gazetteer," the last number of which was that of Nov. 23, 1775, no. 136. The first issue with the title of "Rivington's New-York Gazette: or the Connecticut, Hudson's River, New-Jersey, and Quebec Weekly Advertiser" was that of Oct. 4, 1777, no. 137. With the issue of Oct. 18, 1777, the title was changed to "Rivington's New York Loyal Gazette," which see.

Am. Antiq. Soc., N. Y. Hist. Soc., and Hist. Soc. Penn. have Oct. 4, 11, 1777.

[New York] **Rivington's New-York Gazette,** 1783.

Semi-weekly. A continuation, without change of volume numbering, of "The Royal Gazette," the first issue with the new title of "Rivington's New-York Gazette, and Universal Advertiser," being that of Nov. 22, 1783, no. 747. The paper was finally discontinued with the issue of Dec. 31, 1783, no. 758.

N. Y. Hist. Soc., and Hist. Soc. Penn. have Nov. 22–Dec. 31, 1783.
Am. Antiq. Soc. has Nov. 22–Dec. 27, 1783.
Phil. Lib. Co. has Nov. 22–29, 1783.
Lib. Congress has Dec. 6–20, 1783.
N. Y. Pub. Lib. has Dec. 6, 10, 17, 1783.
Yale has Dec. 3, 17, 1783.
N. Y. State Lib. has Dec. 6, 1783.
Wis. Hist. Soc. has Dec. 6, 1783.
Boston Pub. Lib. has Dec. 20, 1783.

[New York] **Rivington's New-York Gazetteer,** 1773–1775.

Weekly. Established Apr. 22, 1773, by James Rivington, with the title of "Rivington's New-York Gazetteer; or the Connecticut, New-Jersey, Hudson's-River, and Quebec Weekly Advertiser." A preliminary issue, without numbering, had been issued Mar. 18, 1773, headed "To the Subscribers for Rivington's New-York Gazetteer," being delivered gratis to subscribers. With the issue of Dec. 16, 1773, the title was altered to "Rivington's New-York Gazetter: or, the Connecticut, Hudson's River, New-Jersey, and Quebec Weekly Advertiser." With the issue of May 5, 1774, the colon in the title was altered to a semicolon, and the printer's name was omitted from the imprint. The last issue was that of Nov. 23, 1775, no. 136. On Nov. 27, 1775, because of his pronounced Tory sentiments, Rivington's printing-office was attacked by the Sons of Liberty, and his press and type destroyed. He soon sailed for London, not to return until 1777, when he continued his newspaper under the title of "Rivington's New-York Gazette," which see.

Am. Antiq. Soc., N. Y. Hist. Soc., and N. Y. Pub. Lib. have Mar. 18, Apr. 22, 1773–Nov. 23, 1775.

Lib. Congress and Phil. Lib. Co. have Apr. 22, 1773–Nov. 23, 1775.

Univ. of Mich. (Clements) has Apr. 22–Aug. 5, 19, 26, Sept. 9, 16, 30–Oct. 21, Nov. 4–25, 1773; Jan. 20, Feb. 10, 17, Mar. 3, 10, 24–Apr. 28, May 12, 26, June 7, 21, Oct. 6, 13, Nov. 3, 10, 1774; Feb. 2, 9, Mar. 9–Apr. 13, 27–Aug. 3, 17, 31–Sept. 28, Oct. 12, 26, Nov. 9–23, 1775.

East Hampton Free Lib. has May 27–Nov. 25, Dec. 16–30, 1773; Jan. 6–20, Feb. 3–June 30, Sept. 2, 22, 29, Oct. 27, 1774; Jan. 5–Apr. 13, 1775.

Hist. Soc. Penn. has Apr. 22, 1773–Dec. 29, 1774.

Mass. Hist. Soc. has Apr. 22, 1773–July 28, 1774, fair; Sept. 2, 29, Nov. 3–17, Dec. 1, 8, 22, 29, 1774; Jan. 5–Mar. 16, June 8, 29, July 13, Oct. 26, Nov. 9, 1775.

Yale has Apr. 22, 1773–Apr. 14, 1774.

N. Y. Soc. Lib. has Apr. 22–Dec. 30, 1773; Mar. 3, 1774; Mar. 9, 1775.

British Museum has Apr. 29–June 10, July 8, 15, Aug. 5, Sept. 16–Oct. 14, 28, Nov. 11–Dec. 9, 23, 1773; Jan. 6, 20, Feb. 10, 17, Mar. 10, 24, Apr. 7, 28, May 5–June 2, 16, 30–July 14, 28, Aug. 11–25, Sept. 8, 15, 29–Oct. 13, Nov. 24, 1774; Jan. 26, Feb. 23–Apr. 13, 27, May 18, June 1–22, July 6, Sept. 21, Nov. 9, 1775.

Univ. of Pittsburgh has Apr. 29, 1773–Apr. 7, 1774, fair.

Wis. Hist. Soc. has Jan. 6, 1774–Nov. 16, 1775, fair.

N. J. Hist. Soc. has Feb. 17, 1774–May 4, 1775, fair.

N. Y. State Lib. has May 13, June 3, 17, Sept. 16, 23, Dec. 2, 16, 1773; Feb. 10, 24, Mar. 31, Apr. 21, 28, May 19–June 9, 22, 30, July 28, Aug. 4, Sept. 8, 22, Nov. 3, Dec. 22, 1774; Jan. 5, 19, Mar. 2, Apr. 6, June 1, 15, 1775.

Univ. of Chicago has Nov. 11, 1773; Feb. 17, Mar. 10, 24, July 21, 1774; Mar. 30, May 4, Aug. 3, Sept. 7, 14, Oct. 26, 1775.

Boston Pub. Lib. has June 9, Sept. 22, Nov. 3, 10, 1774; Aug. 10, 31, 1775.

Western Reserve Hist. Soc. has July 1, 15, Oct. 7, 21, 1773.

Duke Univ. has July 8, Aug. 5, 26, 1773; Sept. 22, Oct. 27, 1774; Jan. 19, Apr. 20, May 18, July 13, Aug. 17, 1775.

Princeton Univ. has June 10, 24, July 15, 1773.

Rutgers Univ. has Sept. 30, 1773; May 5, 1774.

Long Id. Hist. Soc. has Jan. 20, May 12, 1774.

Univ. of Minn. has Feb. 24, 1774.

Columbia Univ. has Apr. 7, 1774.

Harvard has Mar. 23, 1775.

[New York] **Rivington's New York Loyal Gazette,** 1777.

Weekly. A continuation, without change of volume numbering, of "Rivington's New-York Gazette." The first issue with the new title of "Rivington's New York Loyal Gazette" was that of Oct. 18, 1777, no. 139. The last issue with this title was that of Dec. 6, 1777, no. 146, the title then changing to "The Royal Gazette," which see.

N. Y. Hist. Soc. and Hist. Soc. Penn. has Oct. 18–Dec. 6, 1777.
Am. Antiq. Soc. has Oct. 18–Nov. 1, 15–Dec. 6, 1777.
N. Y. Pub. Lib. has Oct. 18–Nov. 8, 1777.
Buffalo Pub. Lib. has Oct. 18, 1777.
Lib. Congress has Nov. 29, 1777.

[New York] **Royal American Gazette,** 1777–1783.

Weekly and semi-weekly. Established Jan. 16, 1777, as a semi-weekly, by James Robertson, with the title of "The Royal American Gazette." With the issue of Jan. 15, 1778, on account of the departure of James Robertson for Philadelphia, the paper was published by Alexander Robertson, and with May 19, 1778, became a semi-weekly. James Robertson returned to New York and with the issue of Oct. 6, 1778, the paper was published by Alexander and James Robertson, but upon the removal of James to Charleston, it was again published, with the issue of June 27, 1780, by Alexander Robertson. With the issue of Jan. 1, 1782, James Robertson returned to New York, and with his brother Alexander, and Nathaniel Mills and John Hicks, formed the firm of Robertsons, Mills and Hicks. They continued to publish the paper up to the last known issue, that of July 31, 1783, vol. 9, no. 604. It was soon discontinued, as an advertisement in the Royal Gazette of Aug. 6, 1783, announced that the partnership was dissolved Aug. 5, and the property was to be sold at auction.

Hist. Soc. Penn. has Jan. 16, 1777–Dec. 28, 1780; Mar. 6, 27, May 1, 1781; May 14, 1782.

N. Y. Hist. Soc. has Oct. 9, Nov. 6, 13, 1777; Feb. 12, 26, Mar. 12, Apr. 30, May 28, June 11, 16, Aug. 25, Sept. 3, 8, 22, 24, Oct. 29, Nov. 19, Dec. 8, 1778; Jan. 19, 28, Feb. 16–25, Mar. 4, 23, 25, May 20, July 13, 22, 29, Aug. 12, Oct. 7, 12, Dec. 23, 1779; Jan. 13, 18, Apr. 6, May 11, June 6, Aug. 8, 10, Sept. 21, Oct. 26, Dec. 7, 26, 1780; Jan. 2, 4, June 28–July 24, Nov. 1, 1781; July 9, Dec. 19, 1782; Jan. 2, July 31, 1783.

Am. Antiq. Soc. has Apr. 20, June 27, July 11, Oct. 5, 10, 1780; Mar. 13, Apr. 19, June 5, Aug. 14, 16, Sept. 4, 1781; Jan. 24, June 11, July 23, Oct. 22, Nov. 28, Dec. 3, 10, 26, 31, 1782; Feb. 11, Apr. 15–May 27, July 17, 22, 1783.

Mass. Hist. Soc. has Apr. 10, 17, 1777; Mar. 12, Apr. 9, May 7, 28, July 14, Aug. 4, 1778; May 13s, 1779; Mar. 13, 20, Apr. 5, 1781; Jan. 3, July 18, 23, 1782; May 29, 1783.

N. Y. Pub. Lib. has Apr. 10, May 15, Sept. 18, Dec. 18, 1777; Jan. 1, Mar. 19, June 18, Sept. 10, 1778; Feb. 25, 1779; Apr. 26, 1781; Jan. 1, May 14, 1782.

Wis. Hist. Soc. has Aug. 28, 1777; Dec. 14, 1779; June 15, Aug. 3, 29, 1780; Feb. 19, Aug. 20, 1782; June 26, 1783.

Lib. Congress has Aug. 7, 1777; Mar. 12, July 14, 1778; Feb. 2, 9, Oct. 28, 1779; June 13, 1780.

British Museum has Jan. 25, 1781; June 12–19, July 31, 1783.

Boston Pub. Lib. has Mar. 19, 1778.

British Pub. Rec. Office has July 28, 1778; July 4, 1782.
Harvard has Mar. 4, Dec. 23, 1779.
N. Y. Soc. Lib. has Apr. 15, 1783.

[New York] **Royal Gazette,** 1777–1783.

Weekly and semi-weekly. A continuation, without change of volume numbering, of "Rivington's New York Loyal Gazette." The first issue with the new title of "The Royal Gazette" was that of Dec. 13, 1777, no. 147, published by James Rivington. With the issue of May 13, 1778, it changed from weekly to semi-weekly. The last issue to be called "The Royal Gazette" was that of Nov. 19, 1783, no. 746, the title then being changed to "Rivington's New-York Gazette, and Universal Advertiser," for which see under "Rivington's New-York Gazette," 1783.

Am. Antiq. Soc., N. Y. Hist. Soc., and Hist. Soc. Penn. have Dec. 13, 1777–Nov. 19, 1783.

Lib. Congress has Dec. 13, 20, 1777; Jan. 3, 17, 24, Feb. 7, 14, Mar. 7, Apr. 18, May 2–Dec. 30, 1778, fair; Jan. 2–Dec. 18, 1779, fair; Jan. 19, 22, June 17, 26, July 8, Oct. 7, 21, 28, Nov. 8, 1780; Jan. 3–Dec. 29, 1781; Jan. 2–Oct. 9, Nov. 13–27, 1782; Jan. 1–Nov. 8, 1783, fair.

N. Y. Pub. Lib. has Dec. 13, 27, 1777; Jan. 3, May 27, June 3, 13, 17, July 8, 29–Aug. 5, 19–Sept. 2, 19, 23, Oct. 7–17, Nov. 7–14, 1778; Jan. 6–Dec. 25, 1779, fair; Jan. 1–Dec. 30, 1780; Feb. 10, 28–Mar. 10, 17, 28, Apr. 6, 14–28, May 9, Nov. 14, Dec. 5, 1781; Jan. 2–Dec. 28, 1782; Apr. 16, July 23, Sept. 3, Oct. 22, 25, Nov. 8, 15, 1783.

Phil. Lib. Co. has Jan. 3–24, Feb. 7, 14, Mar. 7–May 23, June 3, 1778; Apr. 14, June 26, Sept. 1, 4, 11, 18, 29, Oct. 13, 27, 30, Dec. 11, 1779; Jan. 8, 15, Feb. 5, 23–Mar. 8, 22–Apr. 1, 8, 12, 19, May 6, 10, 1780; Feb. 14, Mar. 14, 17, 31, Apr. 11, 21, 25, May 5, 9, 17, 30, Aug. 8–15, 22, Sept. 1, Oct. 24, 31, Nov. 21, 24, Dec. 12, 22, 1781; Jan. 2, 1782–Nov. 19, 1783.

N. Y. State Lib. has Dec. 4, 1779–Dec. 30, 1780; Mar. 17, Sept. 26, Oct. 27, Nov. 24, 1781; Oct. 23, 30, Nov. 2, 9, 23, Dec. 4–11, 25, 1782; Jan. 29, Aug. 16, 1783.

British Museum has Aug. 29, 1778; Aug. 30, Oct. 11, 18, Nov. 1–11, 1780; Jan. 27, Feb. 17, Mar. 3, 7, June 23, 30, July 21, 28–Sept. 15, 22, Oct. 3, 6, 17, 24–Nov. 7, 17–28, Dec. 5, 1781; Feb. 20, 1782–June 11, 1783; June 18, Sept. 13, Oct. 15, 22, 25, 1783.

Univ. of Mich. (Clements) has Dec. 13, 27, 1777; May 16, 23, Oct. 21–Nov. 11, 18–Dec. 30, 1778; Jan. 2, 9–20, 27, Feb. 6–27, May 22, Sept. 9, 1779; Nov. 9, Dec. 8, 1780; July 4, 11–Sept. 15, 22–Oct. 27, Nov. 3–Dec. 29, 1781; Mar. 26, Apr. 5, 1783.

Boston Pub. Lib. has Jan. 30, Feb. 17, Mar. 27, May 8, June 26, Aug. 4, Nov. 17, 1779; Jan. 22, 29, May 27, Aug. 30, Sept. 2, 16, Nov. 8, 1780; Sept. 5, 12, 1781; Apr. 17, 20, 27, June 5, 19, July 10, Sept. 18, Oct. 2, Nov. 6, 13–

Dec. 4, 14, 21, 28, 1782; Mar. 22, 29, Apr. 2, 9–16, May 10, 28, June 7–28, July 12, Aug. 27, Sept. 24, 1783.

Mass. Hist. Soc. has Jan. 24, Mar. 6, May 23, June 13, Aug. 22, 29, Oct. 14, 1778; Feb. 3, 4, 27, Mar. 6, Sept. 18, Nov. 27, 1779; Apr. 12, 26, 1780; July 7, 18, Sept. 12, 22, Oct. 20, Dec. 26, 1781; May 4, June 26, Sept. 7, 1782.

Wis. Hist. Soc. has July 18, Aug. 29, 1778; Sept. 4, 22, 1779; Aug. 23, 26, Sept. 2, Oct. 18, Nov. 1, 4, 11, 1780; Feb. 24, Apr. 25, Oct. 6, 17–31, Nov. 21, 1781; Nov. 23, 1782; May 31, June 11–18, Sept. 27–Oct. 25, 1783.

Yale has Feb. 20, 1779; Jan. 3–Dec. 29, 1781; July 30, Oct. 1, 15, 29, 1783.

Univ. of Chicago has Nov. 4, 1778; Jan. 2, 13, Feb. 13, 1779; Oct. 27, 1781.

Am. Philos. Soc. has Oct. 28, 1778; Sept. 25, 1782.

Long Id. Hist. Soc. has June 16, Aug. 8, 1781.

N. Y. Soc. Lib. has Aug. 17, Nov. 6, 1782.

Troy Pub. Lib. has July 15, 1778.

Duke Univ. has Mar. 3, 7, 1781; Mar. 20, 1782.

Harvard has July 13, 1782.

[New York] Shamrock, 1810–1817.

Weekly. Established Dec. 15, 1810, with the title of "The Shamrock; or, Hibernian Chronicle," published by Edward Gillespy and printed by Largin & Thompson [George Largin and Thomas Thompson]. It was a folio sized newspaper devoted to Irish interests. With the issue of Sept. 19, 1812, it was printed for Gillespy by Pelsue & Gould [William L. Pelsue and ——— Gould], and with the issue of Nov. 14, 1812, it was printed by the "Shamrock Press." It was suspended by Gillespy with the issue of June 5, 1813, vol. 3, no. 26. A title-page, dated 1811, was printed for volume 1. On June 18, 1814, it was revived, with new volume numbering and with the title of "The Shamrock," published by E. Gillespy & T[homas] O'Connor, and printed by Nicholas Van Riper. It was then of quarto size, paged and eight pages to the issue. With the issue of July 30, 1814, the printer's name was omitted. It was again suspended, with the issue of Jan. 28, 1815, vol. 1, no. 33. On Sept. 2, 1815, it was revived with the title of "The Shamrock," published by T. O'Connor, but without printer's name, and with a new series volume numbering. From July 20 to Aug. 3, 1816, it was printed by Clayton & Fanshaw [Henry Clayton and Daniel Fanshaw], but with the issue of Aug. 17, 1816, the printer's name was again omitted. After another suspension with the issue of Aug. 17, 1816, it was revived Dec. 2, 1816, by T. O'Connor as publisher, still without name of printer. With the issue of Jan. 4, 1817, it was printed by Clayton & Fanshaw, and with Jan. 25, 1817, by Van Pelt & Riley [Peter Van Pelt and Benjamin J. Riley]. O'Connor continued the paper to the last issue located, that of Aug. 16, 1817, vol. 2, new series no. 33. Riley died Nov. 22, 1817.

Lib. Congress has Dec. 15, 1810–June 5, 1813; June 18, 1814–Jan. 28, 1815; Sept. 2, 1815–Aug. 16, 1817.

N. Y. Hist. Soc. has Dec. 15, 1810–June 5, 1813; June 18, 25, July 16–Aug. 20, Sept. 3–17, Oct. 1–22, Nov. 12, 19, 1814; Jan. 14–28, 1815; Dec. 2, 1816; Jan. 4–Aug. 16, 1817.

Am. Irish Hist. Soc., N. Y. City, has Dec. 15, 1810–June 5, 1813; Sept. 2, 1815–Dec. 21, 1816.

Riggs Lib., Georgetown Univ. has Dec. 15, 1810; Jan. 26, 1811–Oct. 17, 1812; Sept. 2, 1815–Mar. 23, 1816.

Am. Antiq. Soc. has Dec. 15, 29, 1810; Jan. 5, 1811–June 5, 1813; Sept. 2, 1815–Aug. 16, 1817.

N. Y. State Lib. has Dec. 22, 1810–Dec. 26, 1812.

Western Penn. Hist. Soc., Pittsburgh, has Dec. 22, 1810; Apr. 13, 1811–Apr. 3, 1813.

Univ. of Penn. has July 30, 1814; Oct. 28, Nov. 4, 1815; Feb. 17–Mar. 2, 16–Apr. 13, 27, May 11, 18, June 8–Aug. 3, Dec. 7, 21, 28, 1816; Jan. 4–Apr. 12, 26, May 10, 24, June 14, July 5, 19, Aug. 16, 1817.

Catholic Univ., Washington, has June 18–Dec. 10, 1814.

N. Y. Pub. Lib. has Feb. 1, Mar. 28, Apr. 11–25, May 9, 23, June 6–July 4, 18, 1812.

Wis. Hist. Soc. has Aug. 29, Sept. 19–Oct. 3, 17, 24, 1812.

Ind. Hist. Soc. has May 18, 25, June 8, 15, July 27, 1816.

Harvard has May 4, 1811.

Huntington Lib. has July 11, Sept. 19, 1812.

New-York Shipping and Commercial List, 1815–1820+.

Semi-weekly. Established Feb. 21, 1815, by Day & Turner [Mahlon Day and Charles Turner], with the title of "General Shipping & Commercial List." It was a paper of quarto size. With the issue of Sept. 13, 1816, the title was altered to "New-York Shipping and Commercial List." With the issue of Sept. 10, 1819, the partnership was dissolved and the paper was published by C. Turner & Co. [Charles Turner and John Johnston]. With the issue of Sept. 12, 1820, the title was altered to "Turner's New-York Shipping and Commercial List," and was so continued until after 1820.

N. Y. Pub. Lib. has Feb. 21, 1815–Dec. 29, 1820.

Lib. Congress has Mar. 14, 1815–Dec. 29, 1820.

Yale has May 2, 1815–Dec. 29, 1820.

Univ. of Mich. (Clements) has June 27, Nov. 7, Dec. 27, 1815; Jan. 3, Feb. 6, 27, Mar. 1, 12, May 7, 21, July 6, 23, Aug. 30, Sept. 13, Oct. 18, Dec. 17, 1816; Feb. 21, Mar. 7–14, 1817.

Mass. Hist. Soc. has Jan. 3, Feb. 17, Mar. 13, 24, 27, Apr. 14–24, May 8, 19, 26, June 9, 16–July 3, 10, Aug. 11, Sept. 15, 22–29, Oct. 6, 9, 23, 27, Nov. 7, 13–20, 27–Dec. 29, 1818; Jan. 1, 8, 12, 19–Mar. 2, 9, 12, 23, Apr. 6, 9, 16, 23, 30, May 11, 14, 21, 28–June 18, 25, July 7, 13–23, 30, Aug. 6–13, 20–Oct. 1,

8, 29–Nov. 5, 12–Dec. 24, 1819; Jan. 11–21, Feb. 1, 11, 15, 25–Mar. 3, 10–31, Apr. 7, 14–May 2, 9–June 6, 16, 1820.
Phil. Lib. Co. has Jan. 7–Dec. 29, 1820.
Am. Antiq. Soc. has Mar. 15, 1816; Mar. 27, May 15, 1818.

[New York] Spectator, 1797–1820+.

Semi-weekly. Established Oct. 4, 1797, with the title of "The Spectator," as the semi-weekly edition of the "Commercial Advertiser," and succeeding "The Herald; a Gazette for the Country." It was published by G[eorge] F. Hopkins, whose name alone appeared in the imprint, although Noah Webster, Jun., was associated with him as editor. With the issue of July 3, 1799, the partnership between Webster and Hopkins was dissolved, the latter withdrew, and Webster took his nephew, Ebenezer Belden, into partnership, the firm name being E. Belden & Co. With the issue of Nov. 5, 1803, the partnership was dissolved, and the paper printed, for the Proprietor [Zachariah Lewis], by J[oseph] Mills. With the issue of Jan. 14, 1804, the title was altered to "New-York Spectator." With the issue of Feb. 6, 1805, the paper was printed, by J. Mills, for Z. Lewis, and with May 22, 1811, it was published by Z. Lewis. With the issue of Jan. 16, 1813, Lewis admitted Francis Hall to partnership, the firm name being Lewis & Hall. With the issue of Apr. 14, 1820, Lewis retired and the paper was published by William L. Stone and Francis Hall under the firm name of Francis Hall & Co. It was so continued until after 1820.

N. Y. Hist. Soc., N. Y. Pub. Lib., and Yale have Oct. 4, 1797–Dec. 29, 1820.
Mass. Hist. Soc. has Oct. 4, 1797–May 15, 1813; June 5, Dec. 8–25, 1813; Jan. 5, 18, 1814; Oct. 25, 1815–Dec. 29, 1820.
N. Y. State Lib. has Oct. 4, 1797–Dec. 31, 1803; Jan. 4–Dec. 29, 1804, scattering; Jan. 9–Mar. 30, Sept. 21, Oct. 15, 1805; Jan. 1–Dec. 31, 1806, fair; Jan. 3–Dec. 26, 1807; May 18, 21, 1808; Jan. 26, 1810–Dec. 29, 1820.
Boston Pub. Lib. has Oct. 4, 1797–July 13, 1803; Jan. 1, 1806–Dec. 29, 1807; Jan. 3, 1810–Dec. 29, 1820.
Am. Antiq. Soc. has Oct. 4, 1797–Dec. 12, 1804; Jan. 2, 1805–Dec. 22, 1810, scattering file; Jan. 2, 1811–Dec. 29, 1820.
Lib. Congress has Oct. 4, 1797–June 18, 1800; June 28, 1800–Dec. 16, 1801, scattering; Jan. 2, 1802–May 5, 1804; May 9, 1804–June 27, 1807, fair; July 1, 1807–Dec. 26, 1820.
Boston Athenæum has Oct. 4, 1797–Oct. 2, 1799; Jan. 2, 1808–Dec. 26, 1810; Jan. 4, 1812–Feb. 15, 1815; Jan. 25, 1817–Dec. 29, 1820.
Cornell Univ. has Oct. 7, 1797–Apr. 11, 1801; July 21, 1801–Sept. 4, 1802; May 26, 1804–Jan. 29, 1819, fair.
Dartmouth has July 6, 1799–Dec. 29, 1820, fair.
Conn. Hist. Soc. has Oct. 4, 1797–Sept. 30, 1801; Jan. 4, 1804–Dec. 31, 1808; Oct. 16, 1811–Oct. 6, 1813.

NEW YORK 693

Western Reserve Hist. Soc. has Jan. 3–Dec. 29, 1798, fair; Aug. 23, 1806–Dec. 29, 1820, fair.
Wis. Hist. Soc. has Oct. 4, 1797–May 29, 1802; Jan. 1–Nov. 5, 1803; Oct. 24, 1804; Nov. 1, 1809; Feb. 1, 1815; Sept. 13, 1815–May 10, 1817; July 4, 1817–Sept. 11, 1818.
Univ. of Mich. (Clements) has Oct. 4, 1797–Dec. 28, 1799; Jan. 1–15, 22, 29, Feb. 5–12, 26–Mar. 12, Apr. 5, 30, May 7, 21, 24, July 12, Aug. 2, 16, Sept. 3, 10, 1800; Feb. 18, 1801; July 6, 1803; Mar. 20, 30, May 4, 8, June 1, 1805, Oct. 11, 1813; June 17, Aug. 9, 1815.
Rutgers Univ. has Oct. 11, 1797–Sept. 7, 1799; July 1, 1815; Dec. 18, 1818-Dec. 31, 1819, scattering.
Univ. of Chicago has Oct. 4, 1797–June 2, Oct. 24, 1798; Apr. 10, 13, 1799; Jan. 11, 1800.
Harvard has Apr. 11, Aug. 25–Dec. 12, 1798; Feb. 9, 1799–June 5, 1805, fair.
York Inst., Saco, Me., has Mar. 17, 1798–June 24, 1801.
Duke Univ. has Feb. 28, 1798–July 4, 1801, scattering issues; Aug. 28, 1802; Feb. 23–Dec. 28, 1811, scattering; Jan. 7–Mar. 1815, fair; Jan. 2, 1818–Jan. 19, 1819, fair.
Middlebury Coll. has Jan. 1, 1800–May 6, 1801.
Hist. Soc. Penn. has June 21, 1806–Feb. 8, 1809.
Conn. State Lib. has Jan. 22, Mar. 22, May 4, 21, 28, 1800; Sept. 17, 1803–Mar. 26, 1808, scattering.
New Haven Col. Hist. Soc. has Jan. 6–Dec. 8, 1810, fair; Dec. 29, 1818–Dec. 29, 1820.
Newburgh, N. Y. Lib. has Jan. 2, 1813–Sept. 27, 1815.
Chicago Hist. Soc. has Jan. 6–Dec. 29, 1813.
Princeton has July 9, 1814–Dec. 28, 1816.
Williams Coll. has Jan. 3, 1816–Dec. 29, 1820.
Danbury, Conn. Lib. has June 24, 1815–May 29, 1816.
Brown Univ. has Aug. 23, 1818–Dec. 29, 1820.
Troy Pub. Lib. has Sept. 1, 1818–Dec. 31, 1819.
N. J. Hist. Soc. has Mar. 23, 1819–Dec. 26, 1820.
Buffalo Hist. Soc. has Jan. 4–Dec. 29, 1820.
Many libraries have single, or a few scattering copies.

[New York] **Spirit of '76,** 1809.

Semi-weekly. Established Mar. 7, 1809, by J[ohn] Hardcastle for the proprietors, with the title of "Spirit of '76." It was of quarto size and was an anti-Jeffersonian paper. The last issue located is that of Apr. 27, 1809, no. 16.

N. Y. Hist. Soc. has Mar. 7–Apr. 27, 1809.
Am. Antiq. Soc. has Mar. 17, 28, 1809.
Lib. Congress has Mar. 28, 1809.

New-York Spy, 1806.

Weekly. Established Nov. 18, 1806, by John C. Totten, with the title of "The New-York Spy." The last located is that of Dec. 2, 1806, vol. 1, no. 3.

Am. Antiq. Soc. has Nov. 18, Dec. 2, 1806.

[New York] Standard of Union, 1813–1814.

Semi-weekly. Established Oct. 5, 1813, with the title of "The Standard of Union," printed for Tunis Wortman at E[phraim] Conrad's printing-office. The name of the printer disappeared with the issue of Feb. 18, 1814. With the issue of Apr. 15, 1814, the paper was printed for the Proprietor, by John H. Sherman. The last issue located is that of May 6, 1814, vol. 1, no. 62.

Hist. Soc. Penn. has Oct. 5, 1813–May 6, 1814.
Am. Antiq. Soc. has Dec. 3–10, 17, 1813–May 3, 1814.
N. Y. Pub. Lib. has Oct. 8, 22, Dec. 17, 21, 28, 31, 1813; Jan. 7, 11, Feb. 11, 22–Mar. 4, Apr. 22–29, 1814.
Univ. of Mich. (Clements) has Dec. 17–28, 1813; Jan. 28, Feb. 1, 8, 11, Mar. 11–22, 29–Apr. 5, 15–22, 1814.
Wis. Hist. Soc. has Oct. 5, 1813.
N. Y. Hist. Soc. has Nov. 19, 1813.
Western Reserve Hist. Soc. has May 6, 1814.

[New York] Star in the West, 1819.

Weekly. Established Mar. 6, 1819, entitled "The Star in the West, or Masonic Chronicle," published by Thomas W. Cummings, and printed by Thompson & Farrand [Edward W. Thompson and Joseph Farrand]. With the issue of Apr. 17, 1819, the printing firm became McDuffee & Farrand [Donald McDuffee, according to N. Y. Directory, and Joseph Farrand], and with May 1, 1819, Charles N. Baldwin. With the issue of June 5, 1819, Luther Pratt became publisher; with July 14, 1819, Luther Pratt and George Frederick Busby; and with Aug. 11, 1819, Luther Pratt alone. Pratt continued as editor and publisher, and Charles N. Baldwin as printer, until the last issue located, that of Dec. 23, 1819, vol. 1, no. 37. In the issue of Dec. 23, the editor stated that only one more number would be published.

Iowa Grand Lodge, Cedar Rapids, Iowa, has Mar. 6–Dec. 23, 1819.
N. J. Hist. Soc. has Mar. 6–May 1, July 14, 21, Aug. 4–25, Sept. 8, 15, Nov. 10–25, 1819.
Am. Antiq. Soc. has May 8, 1819.

[New York] Statesman, 1812–1813.

Daily. Established Aug. 20, 1812, with the title of "The Statesman," published by G[arret] C. Tunison, for the Proprietor [Joel Hart]. It succeeded the "New-York Morning Post," although having a new title and new volume numbering. It was discontinued with the issue of Aug. 23, 1813, vol. 1, no. 314. It carried a semi-weekly edition for the country under the title of "Morning Star," but on Feb. 26, 1813, this title was changed to "The Statesman, (For the Country)." This paper was succeeded by the "Daily Express."

N. Y. Hist. Soc. has Aug. 20, 1812–Aug. 23, 1813.
N. Y. Soc. Lib. has Aug. 20, 1812–Aug. 21, 1813.
Lib. Congress has Aug. 20, 1812–June 30, 1813.
N. Y. State Lib. has Aug. 20, 26, 28, Sept. 8, 10–14, 16, 18, 21, 23, 26, 29, 30, Oct. 2–7, 10, 13, 15–21, 23–26, 29–31, Nov. 11, 12, 28, Dec. 1, 2, 9, 10, 1812; Jan. 1, Mar. 3, Apr. 22–29, 1813.
Am. Antiq. Soc. has Sept. 1, Oct. 9–Nov. 12, 14, 17–Dec. 5, 8, 1812; Jan. 4–18, Feb. 5, 24, Mar. 11, June 21, July 1–Aug. 4, 16–23, 1813; also Feb. 26, Mar. 5–Apr. 13, May 4, 1813, of country ed.

[New York] **Tablet,** 1797–1798.

Weekly. Established Oct. 25, 1797, judging from the earliest issue located, that of Dec. 13, 1797, vol. 1, no. 8, published by Tiebout & Burling [John Tiebout and Thomas Burling], with the title of "The Tablet; and Weekly Advertiser." In April, 1798, the title was shortened to "Tablet," and John Tiebout became sole publisher. The last issue located is that of June 27, 1798, vol. 1, no. 36.

Long Id. Hist. Soc. has Dec. 13, 1797; Apr. 25, June 27, 1798.
Am. Antiq. Soc. has Mar. 28, Apr. 4, June 27, 1798.

[New York] **Temple of Reason,** 1800–1801.

Weekly. Established Nov. 8, 1800, by D[ennis] Driscol, with the title of "The Temple of Reason." It was of quarto size, eight pages to an issue, and with pagination. Although devoted to expounding the principles of deism, it contained current news and advertisements and considered itself a newspaper. The first four numbers were reprinted in two numbers, omitting the political and current news. The paper was suspended at New York with the issue of Feb. 7, 1801, and was resumed at Philadelphia on Apr. 22, 1801.

Am. Antiq. Soc., Harvard, Long Id. Hist. Soc., Hist. Soc. Penn., and Lib. Congress have Nov. 8, 1800–Feb. 7, 1801.
N. Y. Hist. Soc. has Nov. 8, 15 (reprints), 22, Dec. 6, 1800–Feb. 7, 1801.
N. Y. State Lib. has Prospectus, Oct. 4, 1800.

[New York] **Time Piece,** 1797–1798.

Tri-weekly. Established Mar. 13, 1797, with the title of "The Time Piece; and Literary Companion," printed by P. Freneau, & A. Menut [Philip Freneau signs as editor and mentions Alexander Menut as printer]. With the issue of Mar. 20, 1797, the words "Time Piece" in the title were altered to "Time-Piece." With the issue of Sept. 15, 1797, the partnership was dissolved, the paper published by P. Freneau & M. L. Davis, and the title shortened to "The Time Piece." Freneau withdrew and with the issue of Mar. 21, 1798, it was published by M[atthew] L. Davis & Co. This firm was dissolved and with the issue of June 15, 1798, it was published by R. Saunders, for the Proprietors. The imprint was changed to Robert Saunders, for the Proprietors, with June 18, 1798, and the issue of July 9, 1798, shows that the proprietors were John D. Burk and Dr. James Smith, stating that Burk had been arrested for violation of the sedition act. With the issue of July 11, 1798, the paper was published for the Proprietors. The last issue located is that of Aug. 30, 1798, vol. 3, no. 150. John Wood, in his "History of the Administration of John Adams," 1802, p. 223, stated that the two editors were arrested under the sedition act, and that Burk, knowing that he was an alien, left New York without waiting for the trial, and that "The Time Piece" was in consequence dropped.

N. Y. Hist. Soc. has Mar. 13, 1797–Aug. 30, 1798.
Lib. Congress has Mar. 13, 1797–Aug. 28, 1798.
Boston Athenæum has Mar. 13, 1797–Aug. 25, 1798.
N. Y. Pub. Lib. has Mar. 13, 1797–Aug. 18, 1798.
Wis. Hist. Soc. has Mar. 15, 1797–Aug. 30, 1798.
Am. Antiq. Soc. has Mar. 13–May 1, 10, 1797–Aug. 30, 1798.
Univ. of Mich. (Clements) has Mar. 13, 1797–Aug. 21, 1798, fair.
Princeton has Mar. 13, 1797–July 6, 1798, fair.
Ga. Hist. Soc. has Sept. 18, 1797–May 2, 1798.
Harvard has Mar. 17–22, 27–Apr. 7, 12–19, 24, May 1, June 12, 16, 21, 30, July 12, Nov. 3–8, 17, 24, 1797; Jan. 12, 15, 1798.
N. Y. State Lib. has Apr. 3, 1797–May 30, 1798, fair; June 22, July 2, 1798.
Phil. Lib. Co. has Jan. 24, Feb. 5–Apr. 20, 30–May 9, 16, 23–June 13, 20, 1798.
Yale has Apr. 10, May 19, Sept. 25, Oct. 2, 9, 16, 23, Nov. 6, 20, Dec. 4, 1797; Feb. 21, 1798.
Rutgers Univ. has Mar. 24, 31, Apr. 3, 5, 12, 14, May 1, 19, July 17, Aug. 9, Sept. 1, 20–Dec. 27, 1797, fair; Jan. 3, 10, 12, 24, Feb. 21, 23, Mar. 5, 19, May 9, 16, June 15, 1798.
Duke Univ. has Mar. 17, 20, Apr. 10, May 12–31, June 9, 21, July 3, 28, Aug. 11, Nov. 1, Dec. 11, 15, 27, 29, 1797.
Long Id. Hist. Soc. has Aug. 23, Sept. 29, 1797.
Hist. Soc. Penn. has Aug. 14, 1797.

[New York] Times, 1813.

Established Nov. 16, 1813, with the title of "The Times," printed by Nicholas Van Riper, and published by D[avid] Longworth. This initial issue is the only one located. Although a magazine from the nature of its contents and not regarded by its editor as a newspaper, it is here included because of its journalistic title and the inclusion of a "Department of News."

British Museum has Nov. 16, 1813.

[New York] Town and Country Journal, 1783.

Weekly. Established Sept. 11, 1783, judging from the first issue located, that of Oct. 2, 1783, vol. 1, no. 4, printed by W[illiam] Ross, with the title of "The Town and Country Journal; or, the American Advertiser." The last issue located is that of Dec. 11, 1783, vol. 1, no. 14.

Conn. Hist. Soc. has Oct. 2, 1783.
N. Y. Hist. Soc. has Nov. 27, 1783.
Yale has Dec. 11, 1783.

[New York] Turner's New York Shipping and Commercial List, see **New-York Shipping and Commercial List.**

[New York] United States' Shipping List, 1810–1812.

Semi-weekly and weekly. Established late in the year 1810, judging from the earliest issue located, that of Nov. 22, 1811, no. 112, published semi-weekly by Jonathan Elliot, at the Tontine Coffee-House, with the title of "The United States' Shipping List & Prices Current." The next number located, that of Nov. 6, 1812, no. 182, was issued weekly, was entitled "United States' Shipping List and Prices Current," and was published at the Tontine Coffee-House, without name of publisher. The last issue located is that of Nov. 20, 1812, no. 184.

N. Y. Hist. Soc. has Nov. 22, 1811; Nov. 6, 20, 1812.

[New York] War, 1812–1817.

Weekly. Established June 27, 1812, with the title of "The War," published, for the editor, by S[amuel] Woodworth & Co. The paper was of quarto size, paged, provided with title-page and index, and contained chiefly war news. The editor was Thomas O'Connor, judging from his own statement in "The Military Monitor" of Sept. 14, 1812, where he states that he edited the first ten numbers of "The War," and by Woodworth's acknowledgment of his assistance in "The War" of Sept. 19, 1812, with which issue, moreover, the name of S. Woodworth & Co. appeared alone in the imprint. The first eight issues, from June 27 to Aug. 15, 1812, were reprinted late in 1812, omitting, however, certain current news items. The paper was suspended with the issue of Sept. 6, 1814, vol. 3, no. 12. In order to complete the record of the war, it was revived in February, 1817, and three issues were published, vol. 3, nos. 13, 14, and 15, only the first of which had a title and imprint: "The War," published by Samuel

Woodworth and printed by C[harles] N. Baldwin. These issues were undated, except that the first contained an announcement dated Feb. 24, 1817.

>Am. Antiq. Soc., Yale, N. J. Hist. Soc., Rutgers Univ., Columbia Univ., Lehigh Univ., Wis. Hist. Soc., Western Reserve Hist. Soc., Cleveland Pub. Lib., Lib. Congress, and Univ. of Mich. (Clements) have June 27, 1812–Sept. 6, 1814; and the three nos. in 1817.
>N. Y. Hist. Soc. has June 27, 1812–Sept. 6, 1814; and two nos. in 1817.
>N. Y. State Lib., U. S. Naval Academy, Ohio Hist. and Phil. Soc., Cleveland Pub. Lib., and Monitor Publ. Co. at Montreal have June 27, 1812–Sept. 6, 1814.
>Watkinson Lib., Hartford, has June 27, 1812–Sept. 6, 1814, fair.
>Grosvenor Lib., Buffalo, has June 27, 1812–June 14, 1814, and the three nos. in 1817.
>N. Y. Pub. Lib., Buffalo Pub. Lib., Hist. Soc. Penn., Detroit Pub. Lib., Toronto Pub. Lib., and British Museum have June 27, 1812–June 14, 1814.
>Chicago Hist. Soc. has June 27, 1812–May 18, 1813.
>Ohio State Lib. has July 25, 1812–Mar. 22, 1814, fair.
>Many libraries have partial files or scattering numbers.

[New York] Washington Republican, 1809–1810.

>Weekly. Established July 29, 1809, with the title of "Washington Republican; or, True American," printed by T[homas] Hardcastle for the Proprietor. At some time between this date and Nov. 25, 1809, the name of the printer was omitted, although it continued to be printed at 13 Murray street. The last issue located is that of Jan. 13, 1810, vol. 1, no. 24.

>N. Y. Hist. Soc. has July 29, 1809.
>Am. Antiq. Soc. has Nov. 25, 1809; Jan. 13, 1810.

New-York Weekly Chronicle, 1795.

>Weekly. A continuation, without change of volume numbering, of "Mott and Hurtin's New-York Weekly Chronicle," the first issue with the new title of "The New-York Weekly Chronicle" being that of Apr. 23, 1795, vol. 1, no. 17, published by William Hurtin, Jun., and Andrew Commardinger. The last issue located is that of Oct. 1, 1795, vol. 1, no. 40. Commardinger died in the yellow fever epidemic on Oct. 14, 1795.

>N. Y. Hist. Soc. has Apr. 30–Oct. 1, 1795.
>Am. Antiq. Soc. has May 7, 14, 28, July 9, Aug. 20, 27, Sept. 3–17, 1795.
>Boston Pub. Lib. has July 9, 1795.

[New York] Weekly Inspector, 1806–1807.

>Weekly. Established Aug. 30, 1806, with the title of "The Weekly Inspector,"

published for Thomas Green Fessenden, and printed by Hopkins and Seymour [George F. Hopkins and Jonathan Seymour]. It was of octavo size and with eight pages to the issue, but although of magazine appearance it contained current and local news. With the issue of Nov. 29, 1806, the size was increased to sixteen pages. It was discontinued with the issue of Aug. 22, 1807, vol. 2, no. 52.

Am. Antiq. Soc., Harvard, Boston Pub. Lib., Northampton Forbes Lib., Yale, N. Y. Hist. Soc., N. Y. Pub. Lib., N. Y. Soc. Lib., N. Y. State Lib., Buffalo Pub. Lib., Brooklyn Pub. Lib., Princeton, Lib. Congress, Iowa State Lib., Newberry Lib., Wis. Hist. Soc., and British Museum have Aug. 30, 1806–Aug. 22, 1807.

Cornell Univ. has Aug. 30, 1806–Feb. 21, 1807.

Detroit Pub. Lib. has Aug. 30–Nov. 29, Dec. 13–27, 1806; Jan. 3–Feb. 21, Mar. 28, Apr. 18, May 9, 1807.

New-York Weekly Journal, 1733–1751.

Weekly. Established Nov. 5, 1733, by John Peter Zenger, with the title of "The New-York Weekly Journal." This initial issue was misprinted Oct. 5, 1733. Zenger died July 28, 1746, and presumably the first issue after this date was printed by Catherine Zenger, his widow, although the earliest issue with her imprint which has been located is that of Sept. 1, 1746. At some time between Nov. 21 and Dec. 12, 1748, Catherine Zenger (sometimes spelled Catharine in the imprint) retired and the paper was printed by John Zenger, her step-son. He continued the paper until his death, June 18, 1751. The "New York Evening Post" of June 24, 1751, in his death record refers to him as "Printer and Publisher of the New-York Weekly Journal." The last issue located is that of Mar. 18, 1751, no. 1017 (misprinted no. 0117). Zenger's printing-press and type were sold at auction on July 30, 1751, according to an advertisement in the "New York Evening Post" of July 8, 1751, which reads "Mr. John Zenger, Printer in this City, being lately deceased, and leaving no Person qualified to carry on his Business: This is to give Notice, that the Printing Press and Materials lately occupied by him, will be exposed to sale at publick Vendue, on Tuesday the 30th of this July, at the Dwelling-House of the Deceased: — The Press is esteemed a good One; and much of the large letter is in good Order." James Parker, in a broadside "Appeal to the Publick of New-York," 1759 (copy in Lib. Co. of Phil.), states that he bought Zenger's press and types (see Beverly McAnear's article on "James Parker versus William Weyman" in N. J. Hist. Soc. Proceedings, Jan. 1941, vol. 59, p. 3).

The N. Y. Historical Society has reproduced by photostat most of the known issues of this paper from 1733 to 1751, which set is to be found in the following libraries: — N. Y. Hist. Soc., Am. Antiq. Soc., Lib. Congress, Mass. Hist. Soc., Carter Brown Lib., Yale, Grosvenor Lib., Western Reserve Hist. Soc., Newberry Lib., Univ. of Mich. (Clements), and Huntington Lib.

N. Y. Pub. Lib. has Nov. 5, 1733–Dec. 29, 1735; Jan. 5–Oct. 25, Nov. 22–
Dec. 27, 1736; Jan. 10–May 16, June 6, 27–Aug. 1, 15–29, Sept. 13–26, 1737;
Jan. 17, 30–Oct. 15, 30–Nov. 13, 27–Dec. 4, 18, 25, 1738; Jan. 1–June 11,
25–July 9, Oct. 22–Nov. 19, Dec. 3–31, 1739; Jan. 7, 14, 28–Dec. 29, 1740;
Jan. 5–Dec. 28, 1741; Jan. 4–Mar. 31, June 14–Sept. 13, 27–Oct. 18, Nov. 1–
Dec. 27, 1742; Jan. 3–Mar. 7, 21–Aug. 15, 29–Nov. 28, Dec. 11–26, 1743;
Jan. 2–Mar. 5, 1744; Mar. 20, 1749.

Am. Antiq. Soc. has Nov. 5, 1733–Dec. 27, 1736; Jan. 10–31, Feb. 14–Apr. 4,
18, Dec. 26, 1737; Jan. 2, 16–Nov. 13, 27, Dec. 4, 18, 25, 1738; Jan. 1–
Feb. 19, Dec. 24, 1739; Apr. 20, Oct. 18, 1741; Mar. 5, Apr. 30, 1744; June 10,
1745; July 14, Oct. 13, 1746; Feb. 17, Mar. 23, Sept. 14, Oct. 19, Dec. 7,
21, 1747; Jan. 25, Feb. 1, Mar. 7, May 9, 23–June 6, 20–July 4, 18–Sept. 26,
Oct. 17–Nov. 14, Dec. 12, 26, 1748; Jan. 10 supp., 13, May 15, 22, June 5, 12,
26–Aug. 28, Sept. 18, 25, Oct. 16, 1749; Feb. 27–Mar. 19, Apr. 2–15, 31,
May 9, June 4, 11, Aug. 6, 20, Sept. 17, 24, Oct. 8–29, Nov. 26, Dec. 3, 1750;
Jan. 14, 1751.

N. Y. Hist. Soc. has Nov. 5, 1733–Dec. 29, 1735; Jan. 5–Oct. 24, Dec. 6, 13, 27,
1736; Jan. 24, 31, Mar. 14, 28 supp., June 27, July 11, 1737; June 12–Aug. 7,
21–Sept. 4, Oct. 2, Dec. 18, 25, 1738; Jan. 1–15, 29–Feb. 19, Apr. 2–May 14,
Aug. 27, 1739; Feb. 5, Oct. 6, 1740; Jan. 19, 1741; Feb. 22, 1742; Apr. 2, 9,
Sept. 3, Oct. 15, Nov. 19, Dec. 17, 1744; Jan. 28, Feb. 4, 25, Mar. 11, 25–
Apr. 8, June 3, 10, Aug. 5, 27, Sept. 2, 30, Dec. 16, 1745; Jan. 27, Feb. 10, 17,
Mar. 3, Apr. 28, May 19, June 9–23, July 28, Sept. 1, Oct. 27, Nov. 24, Dec.
29, 1746; Jan. 5, Feb. 2, 17, Mar. 23–Apr. 6, 27, May 18, 25, July 6, Aug. 3,
24, 31, Sept. 28, Oct. 12, Nov. 9, Dec. 21, 1747; Feb. 1–15, Mar. 14, Apr. 4,
May 9, June 27, July 18, Aug. 1, 22, Sept. 19, Dec. 12, 1748; Jan. 2, 9, 23,
30, Feb. 13, 27, Mar. 20, Apr. 3s, May 1, 8, June 12, 19, July 3, Aug. 28, Sept.
18, 1749; Jan. 2, Feb. 19, 27, Apr. 2–15, May 9, 28, June 4, July 2, 9, Aug. 20,
Sept. 3, 1750; Jan. 14, Feb. 4, Mar. 18, 1751.

Lib. Congress has Nov. 5, 1733–Dec. 29, 1735; Jan. 5–Oct. 18, Nov. 8–Dec. 27,
1736; Jan. 10–Mar. 21, Apr. 18–Aug. 8, 29, 1737; Jan. 8, 1739; Mar. 3–17,
1740; Jan. 5, Sept. 28, Dec. 14–28, 1741; Jan. 4–Feb. 22, 1742.

Gabriel Wells, New York, has Nov. 12, 1733–Oct. 18, 1736.

Hist. Soc. Penn. has Nov. 12, 1733–Feb. 2, 1736.

Mass. Hist. Soc. has Aug. 15, 1737–Feb. 19, 1739; July 23, 1739–Feb. 22, 1742.

British Pub. Record Office, London, has Dec. 10, 17, 1733; Sept. 23–Oct. 7,
1734; Feb. 2, Mar. 8, 29, Sept. 13, 1736.

N. Y. Soc. Lib. has Feb. 18–Mar. 11, 1734.

Univ. of Mich. (Clements) has Jan. 21, 1733; May 27, 1734.

Rutgers Univ. has May 20, Aug. 12, 1734.

N. J. Hist. Soc. has Sept. 16, 1734; Jan. 21, 1745.

N. Y. State Lib. has Mar. 1, 15, 1735.

N. Y. State Hist. Assoc. has Dec. 24, 1733.

Duke Univ. has Apr. 15, 1734.

Yale has Mar. 29, 1736.

Charles F. Heartman owned 89 issues of 1733–1736, all located in other collections, and in 1934 published a volume entitled "John Peter Zenger and his Fight for the Freedom of the American Press," including in each volume one of the original issues of Zenger's paper.

New York Weekly Messenger, 1811–1813.

Weekly. Established Dec. 7, 1811, according to a statement in the New York "Columbian" of Dec. 7, 1811, and judging from the earliest issue located, that of June 27, 1812, vol. 1, no. 29, published by G[eorge] & R[obert] Waite, with the title of "New York Weekly Messenger." It was of quarto size, and although containing some local news, was devoted chiefly to advertising lotteries conducted by G. & R. Waite. The last issue located is that of Oct. 2, 1813, vol. 3, no. 3.

Am. Antiq. Soc. has June 27, Sept. 5, 1812; Oct. 2, 1813.

New-York Weekly Museum, 1788–1817.

Weekly. A continuation, without change of numbering, of "The Impartial Gazetteer," the first issue with the new title of "The New-York Weekly Museum" being that of Sept. 20, 1788, no. 19, published by Harrisson and Purdy [John Harrisson and Stephen Purdy, Jun.]. It was of quarto size, but in May, 1789, the attempt was made to enlarge it to folio. This was unsuccessful and with the issue of June 20, 1789, the paper resumed quarto size. With the issue of May 7, 1791, the partnership was dissolved and the paper published by John Harrisson. With the issue of May 14, 1791, the title was altered to "The Weekly Museum," and with June 23, 1798, to "Weekly Museum." The paper was suspended from Sept. 8 to Nov. 10, 1798; from Sept. 7 to Nov. 2, 1799, during the yellow fever epidemic; and from Aug. 13 to Nov. 5, 1803. John Harrisson died Aug. 13, 1804, and with the issue of Oct. 6, 1804, the paper was published for the Proprietor. With the issue of Aug. 17, 1805, the title was changed to "New-York Weekly Museum." With the issue of Feb. 15, 1806, it was published by Marg[are]t Harrisson, who stated that she had been the proprietor since her husband's death. Margaret Harrisson died Mar. 22, 1808, and with the issue of Apr. 2, 1808, the paper was published by her son C. Harrisson (changed to Charles Harrisson with the issue of Apr. 20, 1811). With the issue of May 9, 1812, the paper was purchased and published by James Oram, who started a new series volume numbering and slightly altered the title to "The New-York Weekly Museum." With the issue of May 7, 1814, Oram started an octavo series, with a new numbering and with eight pages to the issue, and changed the title to "New-York Weekly Museum, or Polite Repository of Amusement and Instruction." The issues from May 7 to June 4, 1814, had advertising covers entitled "The Advertiser, attached to the New-York Weekly Museum." With the issue of May 6, 1815, the word "The" was inserted at the beginning of the title and the size was increased to sixteen pages. The last issue with this title was that of Apr. 26, 1817, vol. 5, no. 26, after which the title was changed to "The Ladies' Weekly Museum," which see. The octavo volumes, from 1814 to 1817, had title-pages and indexes.

Am. Antiq. Soc. has Sept. 20–Dec. 27, 1788; Jan. 3–May 2, 16, Oct. 31, Nov. 14, 1789; Jan. 16, 30, Mar. 6, 27, Apr. 17, May 8, June 12, 26, July 3, 17, 24, Aug. 21, Sept. 11, Oct. 9–23, Nov. 13, 1790; Apr. 2–30, July 30–Aug. 13, 27, Nov. 5, 1791; Apr. 14, May 5, 12, June 2, July 21, 28, Aug. 18, Sept. 29, Nov. 5, 1792; Jan. 5–Mar. 30, Apr. 13, May 25–Dec. 28, 1793; Jan. 4, 1794–Dec. 30, 1815; Jan. 6–Apr. 27, Sept. 21, Nov. 2–Dec. 28, 1816; Jan. 4–Apr. 26, 1817.

N. Y. Hist. Soc. has Jan. 3–24, Apr. 18–May 9, June 6–Nov. 14, 1789; Jan. 2–30, Feb. 13, 20, Mar. 6–Dec. 25, 1790; Apr. 16, 1791–Dec. 27, 1800; Jan. 3–31, Feb. 28, Mar. 14, 21, Apr. 11–May 16, June 6–Aug. 15, 29, Sept. 12, 19, Oct. 31–Dec. 26, 1801; Jan. 2, 1802–Apr. 26, 1817.

Lib. Congress has Sept. 20, 1788–May 2, July 25, 1789; Feb. 13, May 8, July 17, Dec. 11, 1790; Mar. 5, Apr. 9, 30, 1791–Dec. 31, 1796; Mar. 18, 1797–Apr. 27, 1805; Nov. 30, 1805–Sept. 17, 1808; Jan. 14, 1809–Dec. 29, 1810; Feb. 9–Oct. 26, 1811, fair; May 8, 1813–Apr. 26, 1817.

Wis. Hist. Soc. has July 7–Nov. 10, 1792, fair; Jan. 5, 1793–Nov. 24, 1794; Jan. 3, 1795–May 25, 1799; May 16, 1801–Mar. 11, 1809; Jan. 2, 1811–Apr. 30, 1814; May 6, 1815–Apr. 27, 1816.

N. Y. Pub. Lib. has Sept. 20, 1788–May 9, 1789; Jan. 5, 1793–July 4, 1795; Jan. 7, 1797–Dec. 27, 1800; Mar. 21, July 11, Aug. 28, Sept. 4, 1801; Oct. 16, 30, Nov. 20, 1802; Jan. 1–Dec. 31, 1803, fair; Jan. 7, 1804–Dec. 31, 1808; Jan. 7–Feb. 4, Mar. 3, Apr. 29, July 15, Aug. 12, Oct. 21–Nov. 4, 1809; Feb. 17, Mar. 3, 24, 31, Apr. 14, May 5, 1810; Feb. 9–Dec. 28, 1811; Feb. 8–Dec. 26, 1812; Jan. 2, 1813–Apr. 23, 1814, fair.

Harvard has June 23, 1791; June 18, 1796; Apr. 1, 8, June 3–17, July 1, 15, Aug. 12, 1797–Jan. 19, 1805; June 29, 1805; Jan. 3, 1807–Dec. 30, 1809.

Univ. of Texas has Apr. 14, 1798–May 8, 1802; July 10, 1802–Apr. 6, 1811.

East Hampton Free Lib. has July 4, 1789–Dec. 30, 1797, fair; Mar. 1, 1800–Dec. 29, 1804; May 8, 1813–Apr. 30, 1814.

Watkinson Lib. has June 1, 1793–June 17, 1797; Jan. 7, 1804–Dec. 26, 1807; May 3–Apr. 26, 1817.

N. Y. Soc. Lib. has June 16, 1792–June 10, 1797; May 7, 1814–Sept. 23, Oct. 28, Nov. 25, Dec. 23, 1815; Feb. 10–17, Apr. 20, May 4, 1816; Feb. 1–Mar. 8, 1817.

N. Y. State Lib. has Sept. 8, 1792; June 1, 1793–May 17, 1794; Feb. 6–Dec. 24, 1796; Nov. 10, 1798; Nov. 2, 1799–Dec. 27, 1800; Mar. 28–Dec. 19, 1801, scattering; Jan. 2, 1802–Dec. 29, 1804; Feb. 15, 1806–Feb. 7, 1807; Aug. 15, 1807–Sept. 16, 1809; May 9, 1812–May 29, 1813; Apr. 2, 1814–Apr. 26, 1817.

Newberry Lib. has Aug. 21, Sept. 18, Oct. 2–16, Oct. 30–Nov. 27, 1790; Jan. 1,

NEW YORK 703

22, Apr. 2, 9, 30, May 7, July 16–Aug. 6, 20, 27, Sept. 10, 24–Oct. 22, Nov. 5–Dec. 17, 1791; Jan. 7–Feb. 4, 18, Mar. 10–Apr. 7, 21, 28, May 12, 19, June 2–30, July 14–Oct. 13, 1792; Mar. 29, June 14, Sept. 20–Oct. 4, 18, Dec. 27, 1800; Jan. 3–17, 31, Feb. 7, 21–May 2, June 13, 20, Sept. 19–Oct. 3, 17, 24, 1801; Jan. 2–Apr. 3, 24, May 1, July 24, 31, Aug. 14, 21, Oct. 2, 9, 23–Nov. 20, 1802; Jan. 29–Feb. 19, Mar. 19–Apr. 16, 30, May 7, June 4, July 16, Aug. 13, Dec. 10, 1803; Mar. 10–Apr. 7, July 7–28, Sept. 15–Nov. 3, 17, Dec. 22, 29, 1804; Feb. 13, 1808–Dec. 15, 1810, fair; May 9, 1812–Apr. 29, 1815, fair; Nov. 2, 1816–Apr. 26, 1817.

Duke Univ. has Sept. 25, Dec. 4, 1790; Oct. 6, 1792; Mar. 16, 1793; Nov. 2, 1793–Nov. 14, 1795, fair; Apr. 9, May 21, June 4, 11, 25, Aug. 27, 1796–Aug. 5, 1797, fair; Mar. 24, July 24–Aug. 28, Nov. 17–Dec. 8, 22, 1798; Jan. 12–Feb. 2, 23, Mar. 9, 16, Aug. 17, Nov. 9, 16, 1799; July 5, 1800; July 11, Aug. 15, 1801; Aug. 28, Sept. 4, 1802; June 25, Nov. 26, 1803; Feb. 22, 1806–Oct. 21, 1809; 1810–1813, scattering issues.

Univ. of Mich. (Clements) has Nov. 8, 1788; Mar. 16, Aug. 10, 1793; Feb. 15–Dec. 6, 1794, fair; May 16–Sept. 19, Nov. 14, 1795–June 17, 1797; Nov. 2, 9, 1799; Jan. 9, 1802–Dec. 22, 1804; Jan. 5–June 1, Sept. 7, Nov. 16, Dec. 7, 1805; Jan. 18, Feb. 8, July 12, Sept. 13–Dec. 13, 1806; Feb. 14, 1807–Feb. 4, 1809; Mar. 23, Apr. 6, May 4, Dec. 14, 1811; Aug. 8, 1812; June 17, July 1, 15, 1815.

Univ. of Chicago has Jan. 26, Apr. 27, July 6–Nov. 30, 1793, fair; Jan. 11, Mar. 1–Nov. 22, 1794, fair; Feb. 14, Apr. 4–May 2, 30, June 20, 1795; Mar. 4, 25, May 6–June 3, July 29, Aug. 19, Sept. 2, 9, Oct. 21–Nov. 4, 25, Dec. 2, 16, 1797; May 16, 1812–Apr. 30, 1814; Dec. 7, 1816–Apr. 26, 1817.

Yale has Oct. 11, 1788; Dec. 31, 1808; July 15, 22, 1809; Jan. 13, Aug. 4, 11, Sept. 1, 15, 29, Oct. 13, Dec. 20, 1810; Jan. 4, 1811–Apr. 20, 1816.

N. J. Hist. Soc. has Jan. 5, 1793; July 26, 1794; Apr. 23, July 16–Aug. 20, 1796; Jan. 7–Aug. 5, 1797, fair; Aug. 28, 1802–July 20, 1805.

Hist. Soc. Penn. has Jan. 3, 1795–Dec. 31, 1796.

Western Reserve Hist. Soc. has Jan. 9–Dec. 24, 1796.

Boston Pub. Lib. has Dec. 7, 1799–Oct. 25, 1800.

Conn. Hist. Soc. has Nov. 5, 1803–Sept. 29, 1804; Apr. 9, 1808–July 15, 1809.

Princeton has May 15, 1813–Apr. 23, 1814; May 6–Oct. 28, 1815.

Iowa State Lib. has May 7, 1814–Oct. 28, 1815; May 4–Oct. 26, 1816.

Columbia Univ. has May 6, 1815–Oct. 26, 1816.

Rutgers Univ. has Jan. 1, 1791; May 5, 1792–Dec. 21, 1793, fair; Nov. 29, 1794; Jan. 3, Mar. 21, 1795; Dec. 10, 1803; May 9, 1812–May 1, 1813, fair; Apr. 2–30, 1814.

Many libraries have scattering issues located in other collections.

New York Weekly Observer, 1811.

Weekly. The only issue located is that of Sept. 29, 1811, no. 37, published every Sunday morning by Jonathan Elliot, with the title of "The New York Weekly Observer." It was evidently a continuation of "The Observer."

Lib. Congress has Sept. 29, 1811.

New-York Weekly Post-Boy, 1743–1747.

Weekly. Established Jan. 3, 1743, by James Parker with the title of "The New-York Weekly Post-Boy." It was a paper of quarto size, but with the issue of July 25, 1744, was enlarged to folio. The last issue with this title was that of Jan. 12, 1747, no. 208, and with the succeeding issue it was changed to "The New-York Gazette, revived in the Weekly Post-Boy," which see.

Mass. Hist. Soc. has Jan. 3, 1743–July 16, 1744.
N. Y. Hist. Soc. has July 25, Aug. 8, 15, Oct. 17, 1743; Jan. 2–Dec. 31, 1744; Jan. 7–Feb. 17, Mar. 18, Apr. 15–Oct. 28, Nov. 11, 18, Dec. 23, 30, 1745; Jan. 6–June 9, Sept. 9–Nov. 17, Dec. 1–29, 1746; Jan. 5, 12, 1747.
Hist. Soc. Penn. has Feb. 1, Apr. 25 postscript, 1743; July 9, 25–Dec. 31, 1744; Jan. 7–Dec. 30, 1745; Jan. 6–Sept. 22, Oct. 6–20, Nov. 10–Dec. 29, 1746; Jan. 5, 12, 1747.
N. Y. Pub. Lib. has Aug. 6–Sept. 10, 24–Nov. 12, 26–Dec. 31, 1744; Jan. 7–Feb. 25, Mar. 11–June 24, July 8–Oct. 21, Nov. 18–Dec. 9, 23, 30, 1745; Jan. 6–Mar. 10, 24, 31, Apr. 21–June 2, 16, 30–Oct. 27, Nov. 10–Dec. 29, 1746; Jan. 5, 12, 1747.
Phil. Lib. Co. has Sept. 10–Dec. 31, 1744; Jan. 7–July 15, Aug. 5–19, Sept. 2–Oct. 28, Nov. 11–Dec. 16, 30, 1745; Jan. 6–July 28, Aug. 11–Dec. 29, 1746; Jan. 12, 1747.
N. Y. State Lib. has Jan. 6, 13, 27, Feb. 17, Mar. 17, 31, Apr. 14s, 28s, May 28s, June 9–23, July 7–21, Sept. 8s, 1746.
Wis. Hist. Soc. has Mar. 24, Apr. 7–May 12, 26, June 2, 1746.
N. J. Hist. Soc. has Oct. 28, Nov. 4, 1745; Feb. 17, May 19, 1746.
Lib. Congress has Aug. 20, 1744; Feb. 24, May 26, 1746.
Rutgers Univ. has Oct. 28, Nov. 4, 1745.
Boston Pub. Lib. has July 21, Aug. 17, 31, 1746.

[New York] Weekly Visitor, 1802–1807.

Weekly. Established Oct. 9, 1802, with the title of "The Weekly Visitor, or, Ladies' Miscellany," published by Ming & Young [Alexander Ming and William Young], who announced that the new paper was succeeding the "New-York Journal." It was of quarto size, paged, with eight pages to the issue, and each volume had a title-page and index. Although a magazine in appearance, it contained current news, death notices, and advertisements. The paper was suspended from Aug. 27 to Oct. 29, 1803, to atone for which two numbers were issued each week from Dec. 17, 1803, to Feb. 18, 1804. Young died Sept. 15, 1805, and in the issue of Oct. 1, 1805, vol. 3, no. 52, which had no change of imprint, it was stated that the paper would be "suspended for a few weeks." It was resumed Nov. 2, 1805, published by John Clough, with the title of "The Weekly Visitor; or, Ladies' Miscellany," although the initial "The" was omitted with Dec. 28, 1805. The last issue with this title was that of Oct. 25, 1806, vol. 4, no. 52. On Nov. 1, 1806, vol. 5, no. 1, Clough changed the title to "The Lady's Weekly Miscellany," which continued to Oct. 24, 1807, vol. 5, no. 52. Thereafter there was a change in the form of publication, advertisements were excluded, and the periodical partook more of the nature of a magazine. In this bibliography no issues are described or listed after Oct. 24, 1807.

> Am. Antiq. Soc. has Oct. 9, 1802–Oct. 25, 1806; Feb. 21, May 16, July 4, 1807.
>
> N. Y. Hist. Soc. has Oct. 9, 1802–Oct. 1, 1805; Dec. 28, 1805–Dec. 27, 1806; Jan. 17–May 16, 30, June 13, 20, July 4, 11, Sept. 5–Oct. 10, 24, 1807.
>
> Lib. Congress has Oct. 9, 1802–Sept. 29, 1804; Dec. 7, 1805–Oct. 18, 1806; Nov. 15, 1806–Jan. 10, 1807.
>
> N. Y. Pub. Lib. has Oct. 9, 1802–Apr. 2, 1803; Oct. 6, 1804–Oct. 1, 1805.
>
> Rutgers Univ. has Oct. 16–30, Nov. 13–Dec. 31, 1802; Jan. 8–Feb. 26, Mar. 19–Apr. 16, 30, June 4, 18, July 30, Nov. 12–Dec. 3, 1803; Oct. 13, 1804–Feb. 23, 1805; Mar. 30–Oct. 1, 1805.
>
> N. Y. State Lib. has Oct. 9, 1802–Dec. 10, 1803.
>
> Univ. of Chicago has Oct. 23, 1802–Aug. 20, Nov. 5–19, 1803.
>
> Harvard has Oct. 3, 20, 1804–Sept. 21, 1805; May 31, June 28, 1806–Oct. 24, 1807.
>
> N. Y. Soc. Lib. has Nov. 2, 1805–Oct. 18, 1806.

[New York] **Weekly Visitor,** 1817–1820+.

Weekly. Established Nov. 1, 1817, printed and published by Alexander Ming, with the title of "The Weekly Visitor, and Ladies' Museum." It continued, but with new volume numbering, "The Ladies' Weekly Museum," and like that publication, could only be considered a newspaper since it carried current news, and marriage and death notices. It was of octavo size, contained sixteen numbered pages to the issue, and had title-page and index. With the issue of May 6, 1820, it was printed and published, with a new series volume numbering, by Alexander Ming, and edited by "Jonathan Newstyle." With the issue of July 15, 1820, it was printed by Alexander Ming, Jun., and edited by Alexander Ming. Continued until after 1820.

> Am. Antiq. Soc. and Yale have Nov. 1, 1817–Oct. 30, 1819.
>
> Rutgers Univ. has Nov. 1, 1817–Apr. 25, 1818; May 23, June 6–27, July 25, Aug. 1, 1818; May 1–Oct. 30, 1819; June 17–July 1, 22, Aug. 12–26, Dec. 23, 1820.
>
> N. Y. Pub. Lib. has Nov. 1, 1817–Apr. 4, July 18, 1818; Jan. 9, Apr. 17, May 15, Oct. 16, Dec. 25, 1819.
>
> Univ. of Ill. has Nov. 1, 1817–Nov. 28, 1818.

Boston Pub. Lib. has Nov. 1, 1817–Apr. 25, 1818.
Grosvenor Lib., Buffalo, has Nov. 1, 1817–Apr. 25, 1818.
N. Y. Hist. Soc. has May 2, 1818–Oct. 28, 1820.
N. Y. Soc. Lib. has May 2, 16–30, June 13, July 4–18, Aug. 1–Sept. 12, Oct. 10–24, 1818; Apr. 24, 1819; May 6–Oct. 21, 1820.
N. Y. State Lib. has Oct. 31, 1818–Apr. 24, 1819; Nov. 6, 1819–Apr. 29, 1820.
Pratt Lib., Baltimore, has Oct. 31, 1818–Apr. 24, 1819.
Wis. Hist. Soc. has May 2–Oct. 24, 1818.
Lib. Congress has Oct. 31, 1818–Apr. 24, 1819.

[New York] **Western Star,** 1812–1813.

Weekly. Established May 16, 1812, with the title of "The Western Star, and Harp of Erin," published, for the proprietors, by G[eorge] Douglas. It was of quarto size, with pagination and eight pages to the issue. Although devoted primarily to Irish interests, it contained a considerable amount of current news. With the issue of May 23, 1812, G. Douglas is given as publisher without mention of the proprietors, and with Sept. 12, 1812, he is given in the imprint as editor. The paper was discontinued with the issue of May 1, 1813, vol. 1, no. 51. The volume was provided with a title-page and index.

N. Y. Hist. Soc. and Boston Pub. Lib. have May 16, 1812–May 1, 1813.
Univ. of Mich. (Clements) has May 16, 1812–Apr. 24, 1813.
Riggs Lib., Georgetown Univ., has May 30, 1812–May 1, 1813.
Am. Antiq. Soc. has Jan. 16, Feb. 20, 1813.

[New York] **Weyman's New-York Gazette,** 1759, see under **New-York Gazette [Weyman's]**.

[New York] **Wood's New-York Sale Report and Price Current,** 1820.

Weekly. A continuation of the "New-York Public Sale Report," although when the change of title occurred cannot be told from the only two issues located, Feb. 5 and 19, 1820, vol. 7, nos. 5 and 7, entitled "Wood's New-York Sale Report and Price Current," published by John Wood. It was of quarto size, with eight pages to the issue.

Am. Antiq. Soc. has Feb. 5, 19, 1820.

[New York] **Youth's News Paper,** 1797.

Weekly. Established Sept. 30, 1797, with the title of "The Youth's News Paper," printed by J[acob] S. Mott, for the Editor, and C[harles] Smith. It was of octavo size, eight pages to the issue and with pagination. The last issue located, and undoubtedly the last published, was that of Nov. 4, 1797, no. 6.

Although a magazine in appearance and size, it considered itself a newspaper, and summarized the news of the day for younger readers.

Am. Antiq. Soc., N. Y. Hist. Soc., and N. Y. Pub. Lib. have Sept. 30–Nov. 4, 1797.

[Newburgh] Mirror, 1797–1799.

Weekly. Established in September, 1797, judging from the date of the earliest issue located, that of Oct. 15, 1798, vol. 2, no. 3, published by Philip Van Horne, with the title of "The Mirror." In November, 1798, the paper was transferred to J[oseph] W. Barber. The last issue located is that of Sept. 3, 1799, vol. 2, no. 51.

Am. Antiq. Soc. has Oct. 15, 22, Nov. 26, Dec. 10, 1798.
Newburgh Free Lib. has Oct. 22, 1798; May 28–July 9, 1799.
Sherburne Pub. Lib. has Mar. 5, 1799.
Harvard has May 28, 1799.
Columbia Univ. Lib. has Sept. 3, 1799.

[Newburgh] Orange County Gazette, 1799.

Weekly. Established Dec. 17, 1799, judging from the date of the only issue located, that of Dec. 31, 1799, vol. 1, no. 3, published by J[acob] Schultz, and J[oseph] W. Barber, with the title of "The Orange County Gazette."

N. Y. Pub. Lib. has Dec. 31, 1799.

[Newburgh] Orange County Gazette, 1818–1819.

Weekly. A continuation, without change of volume numbering, of the "Orange County Gazette" of Goshen. The paper was removed from Goshen to Newburgh in October, 1818, by Theophilus L. Houghton, one of its former proprietors. The only issues located are those of Mar. 22 and Apr. 26, 1819 (vol. 13, nos. 1 and 6), published by Theophilus L. Houghton, with the title of "Orange County Gazette, and Newburgh Public Advertiser;" and Nov. 22, 1819, vol. 12, no. 36, entitled "The Orange County Gazette, and Newburgh Public Advertiser," of quarto size, but without publisher's name or imprint. This issue contains a notice of the recent dissolution, on Oct. 12 last, of the firm of Benjamin F. Lewis & Co. [Benjamin F. and Uriah C. Lewis], as booksellers and printers, and that the business would be continued by Uriah C. Lewis. Presumably they were the printers of the paper, succeeding Houghton. The Mount Pleasant "Westchester Herald" of Dec. 7, 1819, says "The Orange County Gazette has been discontinued. It had been published nearly twelve years."

Morristown, N. J., Nat. Park Museum has Mar. 22, Apr. 26, 1819.
Am. Antiq. Soc. has Apr. 26, 1819.
N. Y. Pub. Lib. has Nov. 22, 1819.

[Newburgh] **Orange County Patriot,** 1811–1812, see under **Goshen.**

Newburgh Packet, 1793–1797.

Weekly. Established in December, 1793, judging from the date of the earliest issue located, that of Feb. 3, 1795, vol. 2, no. 62, published by Lucius Carey, with the title of "The Newburgh Packet." With the issue of May 12, 1796, the paper was transferred to David Denniston, who continued as publisher to the last issue located, that of Jan. 10, 1797, no. 163. There is also a supplement of June 5, 1797, but without imprint or volume numbering. E. M. Ruttenber, in his "History of Newburgh," 1859, p. 253, relates a story of how a file of "The Newburgh Packet" was accidentally destroyed or scattered in 1850.

N. Y. State Lib. has Feb. 3–Mar. 10, 24–Apr. 7, 21, 1795; Feb. 11, 1796.
Alfred V. Nicoll, Washingtonville, N. Y., has May 12, 1796–Jan. 10, 1797.
N. Y. Pub. Lib. has June 5, 1797, suppl.

[Newburgh] **Political Index,** 1806–1820+.

Weekly. Established Apr. 17, 1806, judging from the date of the earliest issue located, that of May 1, 1806, vol. 1, no. 3, published by Ward M. Gazlay, with the title of "Political Index," and succeeding the "Recorder of the Times." Continued by Gazlay until after 1820.

Newburgh Free Lib. has May 8, 1806–Dec. 15, 1812; Apr. 27, Aug. 31, Nov. 23, 1813; Jan. 4, Mar. 15, May 24, June 7, Nov. 1, 1814; July 18, 1815; May 7–July 23, Aug. 20, Sept. 3, 17–Oct. 22, Nov. 26–Dec. 31, 1816; Jan. 7, 1817–Dec. 26, 1820.
Am. Antiq. Soc. has May 1, 1806–Oct. 7, 1807; Feb. 17, June 22, 1808; Mar. 8, 1809; Aug. 27–Sept. 17, Oct. 1, 15–29, Nov. 10, Dec. 24, 1811; Jan. 21, Feb. 4, 18, Mar. 3–17, 31–Apr. 21, May 12, June 2, July 7–21, Nov. 17, Dec. 1, 8, 1812; Mar. 30, Apr. 20, Aug. 10, Oct. 12, Nov. 2, 16, Dec. 7, 21, 1813; May 10, 1814; Dec. 12, 19, 1815; June 16, 1818.
N. Y. Hist. Soc. has Feb. 5–May 7, 21–Oct. 8, 22–Dec. 31, 1811; Jan. 7, 21–June 2, 16–Nov. 17, Dec. 1, 1812–Apr. 6, 1813; Apr. 18, 1820.
Lib. Congress has Jan. 4–May 2, 16–July 25, Oct. 31–Dec. 26, 1820.
N. Y. Pub. Lib. has May 1–15, 29, June 5, 26, July 10, 17, Oct. 16, Dec. 11–25, 1806; Jan. 1, May 27, 1807.
N. Y. State Lib. has Mar. 29, 1809; Mar. 13, 1810; Mar. 26, Apr. 23, 1811; Jan. 7, 14, July 14, Nov. 24, Dec. 29, 1812; Apr. 20, 1813; Mar. 15, 1814.
Harvard has Sept. 4–18, Oct. 16, 1806.

[Newburgh] **Recorder of the Times,** 1803–1806.

Weekly. Established June 22, 1803, judging from the date of the earliest issue located, that of Aug. 3, 1803, vol. 1, no. 7, published by Dennis Coles, with the title of "Recorder of the Times." The last issue located is that of Aug. 22, 1805, vol. 3, no. 10. Discontinued under this title in April, 1806, when it was succeeded by the "Political Index."

    Harvard has May 30, June 20–July 4, 18–Aug. 8, 22–Sept. 12, 26, Oct. 17, 31, Nov. 7, 21, 1804; Jan. 17, Feb. 7–28, May 16, June 6, 20, July 18, Aug. 1, 22, 1805.
    Am. Antiq. Soc. has Aug. 3, 1803; Feb. 8, 1804.
    Newburgh Free Lib. has Carrier's Address Jan. 1, 1804; Aug. 29, 1804.

Newburgh Republican, 1811.

Weekly. Established Jan. 15, 1811, judging from the earliest issue located, that of Feb. 5, 1811, vol. 1, no. 4, published by Eldad Lewis, with the title of "The Newburgh Republican." The last issue located is that of Mar. 12, 1811, vol. 1, no. 9. It was discontinued with the succeeding issue, and was then combined with the "Orange County Patriot," which was removed from Goshen to Newburgh. See under Goshen — Orange County Patriot.

    Am. Antiq. Soc. has Feb. 5, Mar. 5, 12, 1811.

[Newburgh] Rights of Man, 1799–1806.

Weekly. Established in November, 1799, judging from the date of the earliest issue located, that of Apr. 14, 1800, vol. 1, no. 24, published by Benoni H. Howell, for Elias Winfield, with the title of "The Rights of Man." At some time between Aug. 25 and Oct. 20, 1800, Howell retired and the paper was printed by Elias Winfield. In January, 1801, Dennis Coles became the publisher and started a new volume numbering. In January, 1803, the paper was transferred to Robert Hinchman, the word "The" was dropped from the title and a new volume numbering was again adopted. David Denniston became editor of the paper soon after April, 1803, although his name was not given in the imprint, but died Dec. 13, 1803. With the issue of Apr. 9, 1804, Hinchman retired, and Thomas Wilson became the publisher and continued the paper to the date of the last issue located, that of Mar. 13, 1806, vol. 4, no. 10. Wilson went to Poughkeepsie, to establish "The Farmer," in April, 1806.

    Newburgh Free Lib. has Apr. 14–28, Oct. 20, 1800; May 13, 1802; Aug. 15, 1803; Mar. 5, July 23, 1804–Jan. 14, 1805.
    Harvard has Aug. 18, 1800; Apr. 12, 1803; Jan. 7, 14, 28, Feb. 4, 25, Mar. 18, Apr. 29, May 6, June 4, 18, 25, July 9, 16, Aug. 13, 27–Oct. 9, 23, Nov. 20, Dec. 4, 11, 25, 1805; Jan. 1, 22–Feb. 12, 27, Mar. 13, 1806.
    Am. Antiq. Soc. has May 26, 1801; Sept. 12, Nov. 14, 1803; Jan. 9, Mar. 5, 12, Apr. 9, May 21, June 11, 1804; Sept. 3, 1805.
    N. Y. Pub. Lib. has Nov. 3, 1800; Oct. 1, 1803.
    Lib. Congress has Jan. 13, 1801; Feb. 22, 1803.

N. Y. State Lib. has Dec. 2, 1801.
Rutgers Univ. has Jan. 28, 1805.
Univ. of Ill. has June 25, 1805; Jan. 8, 1806.
Adriance Lib., Poughkeepsie, has Jan. 22, 1806.

[Newtown] Investigator, 1820+.

Weekly. Established Jan. 1, 1820, judging from the date of the earliest issue located, that of June 17, 1820, vol. 1, no. 25, printed for the Proprietors by J[ob] A. Smith, with the title of "The Investigator," and so continued until after 1820. Newtown was the early name of Elmira.

Chemung Co. Hist. Soc., Elmira, has June 17, 1820.

[Newtown] Telegraph, 1815–1819.

Weekly. Established in November, 1815, judging from the date of the first issue located, that of Mar. 25, 1817, vol. 2, no. 21, published at Newtown Village (now Elmira) by W[illiam] Murphy, with the title of "The Telegraph." In a letter to an Elmira newspaper in 1853, Rev. James Durham gave some reminiscences of early Newtown newspapers (quoted in Wm. H. Arnold's "Newspapers of Elmira" — ms. in AAS). He states that the Telegraph was established in 1815 by Brindle & Murphy [William Brindle and William Murphy] of Williamsport, Pa.; that Murphy became sole proprietor until 1818, when he sold out to Abner and Edson Harkness; that the Harknesses sold out to Erastus Shepard, who improved the paper typographically and called it the Newtown Telegraph; and that the paper was succeeded by the Investigator. The known issues correspond with these facts. The earliest located issue is "The Telegraph," Mar. 25, 1817, vol. 2, no. 21, published by W. Murphy. In a list of New York newspapers of Jan. 1, 1818, it is recorded as published by A. & E. Harkness (Munsell, "Typographical Miscellany," p. 132). The issues of June 4 and Aug. 5, 1819 (vol. 4, no. 35), are entitled "Newtown Telegraph" and are published by Erastus Shepard.

Am. Antiq. Soc. has Mar. 25, 1817; June 4, 1819.
N. Y. Pub. Lib. has Sept. 9, 1817.
Chemung Co. Hist. Soc., Elmira, has Aug. 5, 1819.

[Newtown] Vedette, 1818–1820.

Weekly. Established July 4, 1818, judging from the date of the earliest issue located, that of Aug. 15, 1818, vol. 1, no. 7, published by W[illiam] Murphy, with the title of "The Vedette." The last issue located is that of Oct. 2, 1819, vol. 2, no. 66. The "Geneva Palladium" of Aug. 30, 1820, refers to the "whining little tippling editor of the Newtown Vedette."

Am. Antiq. Soc. has Aug. 15, 1818; July 10, 1819.
Chemung Co. Hist. Soc., Elmira, has Dec. 5, 1818; Oct. 2, 1819.
Mrs. Raymond L. Buell, Richmond, Mass., has Sept. 11, 1819.

[Norwich] **Chenango Weekly Advertiser,** 1811–1812.

Weekly. Established Jan. 25, 1811, by J[ohn] F. Fairchild, with the title of "Chenango Weekly Advertiser." So continued to the last issue located, that of June 25, 1812, vol. 2, no. 75, in which the publisher refers to the lack of advertising patronage and a possible discontinuance of his paper.

Am. Antiq. Soc. has Jan. 25, 1811–June 25, 1812.

[Norwich] **Columbian Telegraph,** 1812–1813.

Weekly. Established Aug. 19, 1812, judging from the date of the earliest issue located, that of Dec. 9, 1812, vol. 1, no. 17, published by J[ames] M. Miller, with the title of "Columbian Telegraph." Within a year, certainly before Jan. 18, 1814, the title was changed to "The Telegraph," which see.

Cornell Univ. has Dec. 9, 1812.

Norwich Journal, 1816–1820+.

Weekly. Established Nov. 14, 1816, by J[ohn] F. Hubbard, with the title of "The Norwich Journal." The paper suspended in December, 1818, but resumed Jan. 9, 1819. It was continued by Hubbard until after 1820.

Guernsey Mem. Lib., Norwich, has Nov. 14, 1816–Nov. 12, 1818; Jan. 9–Dec. 14, 1819; Jan. 26–Dec. 20, 1820.
Univ. of Rochester has Apr. 16, 1817; Apr. 16, Dec. 3, 1818; Feb. 25, Apr. 29, 1819; Jan. 4, July 19, 1820.

[Norwich] **Olive Branch,** 1808–1809.

Weekly. Removed from Sherburne and established at Norwich without change of title or volume numbering. The first issue at Norwich was that of Feb. 13, 1808, vol. 2, no. 91, published by John F. Fairchild & Co., with the title of "Olive Branch." With the issue of Apr. 2, 1808, the paper was enlarged in size and the title altered to "The Olive-Branch." With the issue of July 17, 1809, John F. Fairchild became sole publisher. The paper was discontinued with the issue of Nov. 13, 1809, vol. 4, no. 182.

N. Y. State Lib. has Feb. 13–Mar. 26, Sept. 24, 1808.
Am. Antiq. Soc. has Apr. 2, 1808–Nov. 13, 1809.

[Norwich] Republican Agriculturalist, 1818–1820+.

Weekly. Established Dec. 10, 1818, by Thurlow Weed, with the title of "The Republican Agriculturalist." The initial issue refers to succeeding the Norwich Journal and continuing its advertisements. With the issue of Sept. 14, 1820, Samuel Curtis, Jun. became the publisher and continued the paper until after 1820. Thurlow Weed, in his "Autobiography," p. 85, says that he disposed of the establishment "late in November 1820," evidently an error of memory. The "Norwich Journal" of Feb. 14, 1821, argued to prove that Mr. Curtis was not the real editor of the Agriculturalist, but his name surely appeared in the imprint.

Univ. of Rochester (Thurlow Weed Collection) has Dec. 10, 1818–Dec. 2, 1819.

Emily Weed Hollister in 1919 owned the volume for 1818–1819, and also Dec. 30, 1819–Sept. 14, 1820, which I personally examined. Her daughter, Mrs. Thomas G. Spencer, presumably has this latter volume, which when found will be placed in the Univ. of Rochester Library.

[Norwich] Telegraph, 1813–1814.

Weekly. A continuation, without change of volume numbering, of the "Columbian Telegraph," the change of title occurring at some time in 1813. The earliest issue located is that of Jan. 18, 1814, vol. 2, no. 75, published by James M. Miller, with the title of "The Telegraph." An obituary of James M. Miller in the "Ithaca Journal" of Apr. 11, 1838, states that he died on Apr. 6, and that he was editor of the Norwich Telegraph in 1812.

Rochester Pub. Lib. has Jan. 18, 1814.

[Norwich] Volunteer, 1814–1817.

Weekly. Established Oct. 4, 1814, with the title of "The Volunteer," printed by James M. Miller, for Lot Clark. The issue of Feb. 7, 1816, vol. 2, no. 71, the last located, was printed by John Burgess Johnson. "The Norwich Journal" of Feb. 5, 1817, announced that the "Volunteer" establishment had been transferred to the editor of the "Journal."

Harvard has Oct. 4, 1814.
Lib. Congress has Feb. 7, 1816.

Ogdensburgh Palladium, 1810–1814.

Weekly. Established Nov. 27, 1810, by Kipp & Strong [John C. Kipp and Timothy C. Strong], with the title of "Ogdensburgh Palladium, and St. Lawrence Advertiser." At some time between Feb. 26 and Apr. 23, 1811, Strong retired and the paper was published by J. C. & L. Kipp [John C. and L——Kipp]. Late in 1812, the paper was purchased and published by John P. Sheldon, who shortened the title to "Ogdensburgh Palladium," and continued it until 1814 (see Munsell, "Typographical Miscellany," p. 12). The last issue located is that of Feb. 3, 1813, vol. 3, no. 6.

    Am. Antiq. Soc. has Nov. 27, 1810; Feb. 19, Apr. 23, July 30, 1811; Nov. 3, 1812; Feb. 3, 1813.
    N. Y. Pub. Lib. has Aug. 13, 1811.

[Ogdensburgh] **St. Lawrence Gazette,** 1815–1820+.

Weekly. Established in December, 1815, judging from the date of the earliest issue located, that of Dec. 16, 1817, vol. 3, no. 104, published by Strachan & Fairchild, with the title of "St. Lawrence Gazette." In a sketch of the county press written before 1850 from papers then in existence, it is stated that the "St. Lawrence Gazette" was established by David R. Strachan and Platt B. Fairchild, and was continued by them until after 1820 (Munsell, "Typographical Miscellany," p. 13).

    N. Y. Hist. Soc. has Dec. 16, 1817–Dec. 22, 1818.

[Olean] **Hamilton Recorder,** see under **Hamilton.**

[Onondaga] **Gazette,** 1816–1820+.

Weekly. Established in January, 1816, judging from the date of the earliest issue located, that of Apr. 24, 1816, vol. 1, no. 14, published by Evander Morse, Jun., with the title of "Gazette; and Onondaga Advertiser," issued at Onondaga Court House. William Ray edited the paper, but retired in October, 1816 (see Brooklyn "Long Island Star" of Apr. 27, 1816, and Auburn "Advocate of the People," Oct. 2, 30, 1816). Morse was the publisher certainly as late as Apr. 14, 1819. Continued until after 1820.

    Am. Antiq. Soc. has June 5, Sept. 25, Oct. 2, 1816; July 9, 1817; Apr. 14, 1819.
    Long Id. Hist. Soc. has Apr. 24, 1816.
    N. Y. State Lib. has June 5, 1816; Apr. 30, 1817.
    Skaneateles Lib. Assoc. has Aug. 14, 1816.

[Onondaga] **Lynx,** 1811–1812.

Weekly. Established at Onondaga Hollow in December, 1811, by Thomas C. Fay, with the title of "The Lynx." Fay's prospectus is published in the New York "Columbian" of Nov. 28, 1811. In September, 1812, the name of Thurlow Weed appeared as printer and publisher, and in October, 1812, the paper was discontinued (see J. V. H. Clark, "Onondaga," 1849, vol. 2, p. 132; and Thurlow

Weed, "Selections from Newspaper Articles," 1877, pp. 14, 16, also his "Autobiography," p. 24). No copy located.

Onondaga Register, 1814–1820+.

Weekly. Established Sept. 28, 1814, by L[ewis] H. Redfield & Co., with the title of "Onondaga Register," printed at Onondaga Hollow. On Mar. 12, 1817, the firm of L. H. Redfield & Co. [James D. Bemis] was dissolved and Redfield took Chauncy Morse into partnership under the firm name of Redfield & Morse. The firm was dissolved Mar. 17, 1818, and Redfield continued the paper alone until after 1820.

Onondaga Hist. Assoc., Syracuse, has Sept. 28, 1814–Dec. 27, 1820.
Am. Antiq. Soc. has Sept. 28, 1814; Apr. 30, 1817; Sept. 23, Dec. 30, 1818.
N. Y. Pub. Lib. has Oct. 26, 1814.
N. Y. State Lib. has June 28, 1815; Nov. 21, 1817.
Long Id. Hist. Soc. has May 7, 1817.
Skaneateles Lib. Assoc. has July 9, 1817.

Oswego Gazette, 1817–1819.

Weekly. Established in 1817 by S. A. Abbey and Bro. [Seth A. and Dorephus Abbey], and by them transferred the same year to Augustus Buckingham ("History of Oswego County," 1877, p. 117). In a list of New York newspapers of Jan. 1, 1818, published in the "Albany Argus" of Jan. 6, 1818, it is recorded as published by A. Buckingham. It was succeeded in 1819 by the "Oswego Palladium." No copy located.

Oswego Palladium, 1819–1820+.

Weekly. Established Oct. 7, 1819, by John Haines Lord, Jun., with the title of "Oswego Palladium." Continued by him until after 1820.

Oswego City Lib. has Oct. 14, 1819–Nov. 2, 1820.

Otsego Herald, 1807–1813, see under Cooperstown.

Ovid Gazette, 1817–1820+.

Established apparently in 1817, following the "Seneca Patriot." It appears in a list of newspapers of Jan. 1, 1818 ("Albany Argus," Jan. 6, 1818), where the name of Michael Hayes is given as the publisher. Quoted in "Saratoga Sentinel" of Dec. 27, 1820. No copy located. Edward J. Fowle, writing in 1846 (Follett, "History of Press in Western New York," p. 69), says, "I date my connection with the Press from 1816, when I commenced as an apprentice with Michael Hayes, in the office of the 'Ovid Gazette.'" But since he states that one of the reasons for starting the paper at Ovid was to get back the Courts which had been removed to Waterloo in May 1817, it is probable that the paper was not begun until the latter year.

[Ovid] Seneca Patriot, 1815–1817.

Weekly. Established Aug. 25, 1815, by George Lewis & Co., with the title of "Seneca Patriot." The Auburn "Advocate of the People" of Nov. 26 and Dec. 10, 1817, printed letters to show that Samuel R. Brown of Auburn established the paper, putting in George Lewis as printer and giving James G. Hathaway some proportion of the profits. At the end of a year Lewis became the sole publisher, is given as the editor as late as October 1816 ("Advocate of the People," Oct. 30, 1816), and continued until May 1817 (see Munsell, "Typographical Miscellany," p. 128). J. G. Hathaway published a "Seneca Patriot" at Fayette, N. Y., in 1817–1818. Upon the removal of the county seat to Waterloo, Lewis went to that town, where he established the "Waterloo Gazette" ("Albany Gazette," May 29, 1817).

Am. Antiq. Soc. has Aug. 25–Sept. 15, Oct. 6, 1815.
N. Y. State Lib. has Sept. 1, 8, 1815.
N. Y. Pub. Lib. has Sept. 8, 1815.
H. Armour Smith, Yonkers, has Oct. 13, 1815.

[Owego] American Constellation, 1801–1803.

Weekly. Daniel Cruger, Jr., removed from Union to Owego late in 1801, where he continued "The American Constellation." The only known issue is that of May 8, 1802, vol. 2, no. 77, published at Owego Village by D. Cruger, Jun. Cruger sold out in August, 1803, to Steward & Mack, who changed the title to "American Farmer."

Univ. of Ill. has May 8, 1802.

[Owego] American Farmer, 1803–1814.

Weekly. Established Aug. 24, 1803, judging from the date of the earliest issue located, that of Sept. 14, 1803, vol. 1, no. 4, published by Steward & Mack [Henry Steward and Stephen Mack], with the title of "American Farmer." Apparently from their advertisement the publishers had intended to call the paper the "National Whig." The imprint states that it was published at "Tioga, (Owego Village, N. Y.)." Early in 1804, Steward sold out his interest, and the paper was published by Stephen Mack alone. In August, 1810, the title was changed to "American Farmer, and Owego Advertiser." In the winter of 1813, Stephen B. Leonard purchased a half interest. Mack died Apr. 16, 1814, and in June, 1814, Leonard discontinued the paper under that title, changing the name to "The Owego Gazette" (see history of paper in "Owego Gazette" of Nov. 22, 1900).

    Harvard has Sept. 14, 21, Oct. 5, 1803; Oct. 4, 24, 31, 1804.
    Am. Antiq. Soc. has Sept. 14, Oct. 26, 1803; July 11, 18, 1810.
    Tioga Co. Hist. Soc., Owego, has Mar. 13, July 29, 1807; Feb. 8, 1809; Oct. 9, 1811.
    Broome Co. Courthouse, Binghamton, has Apr. 20, Oct. 19, Nov. 2, 16, 1808; Dec. 18, 1811; Jan. 1, Feb. 19, 1812.
    Cornell Univ. has Aug. 29, 1810–July 2, 1811.
    N. Y. State Lib. has Feb. 11, 1807.

Owego Gazette, 1814–1820+.

Weekly. Established in June, 1814, by Stephen B. Leonard, with the title of "The Owego Gazette," succeeding the "American Farmer." The earliest issue located is that of Dec. 14, 1814, vol. 1, no. 27. On June 15, 1815, Ebenezer Mack entered into partnership with Leonard (see "Owego Gazette" of Nov. 22, 1900), but the partnership did not last long, expiring before February, 1816, when Stephen B. Leonard was again sole publisher. The paper was continued by Leonard until after 1820.

    Tioga Co. Hist. Soc., Owego, has Dec. 14, 1814; Jan. 19, Mar. 30, Aug. 3, 24, 31, Sept. 21, Oct. 5, 19, 1819; Aug. 22, 1820.
    Cornell Univ. has Feb. 13, 20, 1816.
    Lib. Congress has Feb. 27, 1816.
    N. Y. State Lib. has Apr. 11, 18, 1820.

[Oxford] Chenango Patriot, 1809–1811.

Weekly. Established in April, 1809, judging from the date of the earliest issue located, that of Aug. 7, 1810, vol. 2, no. 11, published by John B. Johnson, with the title of "Chenango Patriot." The last issue located is that of Jan. 29, 1811.

    Am. Antiq. Soc. has Aug. 7, 1810.
    Oxford Lib. has Sept. 11, 1810.
    Review-Times Office, Oxford, in 1918 had Jan. 29, 1811, but could not locate it in 1939.

Oxford Gazette, 1813–1820+.

Established Dec. 7, 1813, by Chauncey Morgan, with the title of "Oxford Gazette," and so continued until after 1820.

    Oxford Lib. has Dec. 7, 1813–Nov. 26, 1814; Mar. 6, 1816; Nov. 27, 1816–Nov. 19, 1817; Nov. 24, 1819–Dec. 27, 1820.

Ohio Arch. & Hist. Soc. has Aug. 11–Dec. 22, 1819; Jan. 12, Feb. 16, 1820.
Wesleyan Univ. has Dec. 17, 1814.

[Oxford] President, 1808.

Weekly. Established Feb. 27, 1808, judging from the date of the earliest issue located, that of Apr. 2, 1808, vol. 1, no. 6, published by Theophilus Eaton, with the title of "The President." The last issue located is that of June 19, 1808, vol. 1, no. 18.

Am. Antiq. Soc. has Apr. 2, 1808.
Oxford Lib. has June 19, 1808.

Palmyra Register, 1817–1820+.

Weekly. Established Nov. 26, 1817, by Timothy C. Strong, with the title of "Palmyra Register." With the issue of Oct. 13, 1819, Strong took Charles Bradish into partnership under the firm name of Strong & Bradish. With the issue of Feb. 16, 1820, the partnership was dissolved and T. C. Strong became sole publisher, so continuing until after 1820.

N. Y. State Lib. has Nov. 26, 1817–Dec. 27, 1820.
Am. Antiq. Soc. has Oct. 4, Nov. 29, 1820.

[Peekskill] Westchester Gazette, 1808–1820+.

Weekly. Established in October, 1808, judging from the date of the earliest issue located, that of Aug. 28, 1810, vol. 2, no. 96, published by Robert Crumbie, with the title of "Westchester Gazette; and Peekskill Advertiser." The issue of Aug. 3, 1812, has this same title, but the next issue located, that of Apr. 9, 1814, is entitled "Westchester & Putnam Gazette." The copies located from 1816 to after 1820 are entitled "West-Chester Gazette." Crumbie was still the publisher in 1818, but an issue in 1821 is imperfect and does not reveal the publisher's name.

Am. Antiq. Soc. has Aug. 28, 1810.
H. Armour Smith, Yonkers, has Mar. 23, 1812.
N. Y. Hist. Soc. has Aug. 3, 1812.
N. Y. State Lib. has Apr. 9, 1814.
New Haven Col. Hist. Soc. has July 20, 1816.
Franklin Couch, Peekskill, has Apr. 25, 1818.
N. Y. Pub. Lib. has Apr. 21, 1821.

Penn-Yan Herald, 1818–1820+.

Weekly. Established in May, 1818, judging from the date of the earliest copy located, that of Mar. 2, 1819, vol. 1, no. 43, published by A[braham] H. Bennett and P[————] Youngs, with the title of "The Penn-Yan Herald." There is a reference to its establishment in the "Auburn Gazette" of May 27, 1818, and to the marriage on Oct. 4, of Abraham H. Bennett, "one of the editors," in the issue of Oct. 14, 1818. Between Apr. 6 and June 8, 1819, Youngs retired and the paper was published by A. H. Bennett, who continued to publish it until after 1820.

> Penn Yan Printing Co. has Mar. 2, 16, 30, Apr. 6, June 8, July 6–20, Aug. 3, Sept. 21, Oct. 26, Nov. 9, 23, 30, 1819.
> Am. Antiq. Soc. has Jan. 25, 1820.

[Peterboro] Freeholder, 1807–1813.

Weekly. Established Jan. 23, 1807, judging from the date of the earliest issue located, that of Feb. 18, 1807, vol. 1, no. 4, published by Dockstader & Bunce [Jacob Dockstader and Jonathan Bunce], with the title of "The Freeholder." In the issue of Feb. 10, 1808, it was announced that this partnership had expired on Jan. 16 previous, and that the paper was to be conducted by Jonathan Bunce & Co. At some time between July 17 and Aug. 28, 1811, Jonathan Bunce became sole proprietor. Bunce's printing-office was totally destroyed by fire Jan. 18, 1813 (see Cazenovia "Pilot" of Jan. 20, 1813), and the paper ceased under this title.

> Madison Co. Hist. Soc., Oneida, has Feb. 18, 1807; Feb. 10, May 4, July 13, Nov. 16, 23, 1808; July 26, Nov. 1, Dec. 27, 1809; Jan. 24, Feb. 7, 14, Dec. 26, 1810; July 17, Aug. 28, 1811; May 6, 1812.
> N. Y. State Lib. has Nov. 9, 1808; Nov. 8, 1809; May 15, 1811.
> N. Y. Pub. Lib. has Dec. 26, 1810; May 8, 1811; Jan. 29, 1812.
> Am. Antiq. Soc. has June 27, 1810.

[Peterboro] Gazette, 1817, see under Morrisville.

[Peterboro] Madison County Herald, 1813–1818.

Established in 1813 by Jonathan Bunce, with the title of "Madison County Herald" (Munsell, "Typographical Miscellany," p. 119). It is recorded in a list of New York newspapers given in the "Albany Argus" of Dec. 26, 1815, and also in a list in the "Albany Argus" of Jan. 6, 1818, where the editor is given as Jonathan Bunce. No copy located.

[Plattsburgh] American Monitor, 1809–1810.

Weekly. Established Aug. 4, 1809, by Nichols & Lowell [George W. Nichols and Samuel Lowell], with the title of "American Monitor." On Sept. 1, 1809, Lowell was replaced by Luther Marsh, and the paper was published by Nichols & Marsh. With the issue of Nov. 4, 1809, Samuel Lowell became sole publisher.

The paper was suspended with the issue of Nov. 10, 1810, vol. 2, no. 63, being succeeded by "The Clinton Advertiser."

Am. Antiq. Soc. has Aug. 4–18, Sept. 22, 29, Oct. 14, Nov. 11, 18, Dec. 16, 1809; Jan. 6–20, Feb. 3, 17, Mar. 3, 17, 31, Apr. 7, 28, May 12, June 16–July 14, 28, Aug. 4, 18, 25, Sept. 8, 22–Nov. 10, 1810.

N. Y. Hist. Soc. has Aug. 4–Nov. 4, 18–Dec. 23, 1809; Jan. 6–20, 1810.

N. Y. State Lib. has Oct. 14, 1809; Oct. 20, 1810.

[Plattsburgh] Clinton Advertiser, 1810–1811.

Weekly. Established Nov. 17, 1810, by Samuel Lowell, with the title of "The Clinton Advertiser." It was of quarto size, and succeeded the "American Monitor," continuing the advertisements, but adopting a new volume numbering. It was succeeded in March, 1811, by the "Political Observatory."

Am. Antiq. Soc. has Nov. 17, 1810; Jan. 12, 1811.

Plattsburgh Herald, see **[Plattsburgh] Northern Herald.**

[Plattsburgh] Northern Herald, 1812–1815.

Weekly. Established Jan. 4, 1812, by Samuel Lowell, with the title of "The Northern Herald." It succeeded his other paper, the "Political Observatory," continuing the advertisements, but adopting a new volume numbering. It was suspended in August, 1812, and discontinued in October, 1812 (see Plattsburgh "Republican," Sept. 18, Oct. 30, 1812). In April, 1813, the paper was revised and printed by Frederic C. Powell, for the Proprietor, a new volume numbering being started. Early in 1814, it was printed by F. C. Powell for the Proprietors. The issue of Aug. 26, 1814, vol. 2, no. 21, has the title of "The Northern Herald." Between this date and Jan. 20, 1815, vol. 2, no. 42, the title was changed to "Plattsburgh Herald," still published by F. C. Powell for the Proprietors. The next issue, and the last located, is that of July 21, 1815, vol. 3, no. 16, published by S[amuel] Beaumont for the Proprietors. In a list of currently issued newspapers printed in the "Albany Argus" of Dec. 26, 1815, is recorded the Plattsburgh Herald.

Am. Antiq. Soc. has Jan. 11, 1812; Apr. 10, Oct. 26, Dec. 23, 1813; July 1, Aug. 26, 1814.

H. Armour Smith, Yonkers, has Jan. 20, July 21, 1815.

[Plattsburgh] Political Observatory, 1811.

Weekly. Established Mar. 29, 1811, judging from the date of the earliest issue located, that of Apr. 12, 1811, vol. 1, no. 3, published by Samuel Lowell, with the title of "Political Observatory." It succeeded "The Clinton Advertiser," continuing the advertisements, but adopting a new volume numbering. It was suspended with the issue of Dec. 28, 1811 (see Plattsburgh "Republican" of Jan. 10, 1812), to be succeeded by "The Northern Herald."

Am. Antiq. Soc. has Apr. 12, May 4–18, June 8–July 13, 27–Aug. 24, 1811.

[Plattsburgh] **Republican,** 1811–1820+.

Weekly. Established Apr. 12, 1811, with the title of "Republican," printed for the Proprietors, by L[inus] J. Reynolds. With the issue of Oct. 11, 1811, it was printed by Cady & Flagg [Heman Cady and Azariah C. Flagg], for the Proprietors; but with the issue of Nov. 8, 1811, it was printed by Azariah C. Flagg, for the Proprietors. With the issue of Oct. 9, 1813, the title was changed to "Plattsburgh Republican." The paper was continued by Flagg until after 1820.

N. Y. State Lib. has Apr. 12, 1811–Mar. 25, July 1–Dec. 30, 1820.
Am. Antiq. Soc. has Apr. 20, May 3–June 28, July 12–26, Aug. 16, Sept. 13, Oct. 4, 25–Nov. 29, 1811; Sept. 4, 18, 1812; Jan. 8, Apr. 16, 30, May 7, June 4, Aug. 28, Sept. 4, Oct. 16, 23, Dec. 11, 25, 1813; Apr. 16, June 11, July 16, Oct. 29, Dec. 3, 17, 1814; Jan. 28, May 20, Aug. 12, 26, Sept. 16, Oct. 21, Dec. 2, 1815; Apr. 13, May 18, June 29, July 20, 1816; Apr. 12–July 26, Aug. 9–30, Sept. 27, Oct. 11–25, 1817; Mar. 7, 21–July 4, 18–Dec. 26, 1818; Jan. 2–30, Feb. 13–Mar. 27, Sept. 4, 1819.
Harvard has July 19, Aug. 16, 23, Nov. 22, Dec. 6, 27, 1811; Jan. 3, 17, Feb. 7–Mar. 13, Apr. 17, May 1, 22, June 5, July 3, 24, Aug. 7, 21–Sept. 4, Oct. 30–Nov. 13, Dec. 11–25, 1812; Jan. 8, 15, 29, Feb. 26, Mar. 5, 19–Apr. 16, 30, June 11, 18, July 2, 16, Aug. 7–28, Sept. 18, Oct. 16–30, Nov. 20, Dec. 4–18, 1813; Jan. 8, 15, Feb. 12, Mar. 5, Apr. 9, 30, May 7, June 4, 11, Oct. 8–22, Nov. 12–26, Dec. 10, 24, 1814.
N. Y. Hist. Soc. has Mar. 18, Apr. 8, 1815.
Wesleyan Univ. has July 16, 1814.
H. Armour Smith, Yonkers, has June 4, 1813; Apr. 1, Sept. 26, Oct. 23, 1815; Dec. 25, 1816; Nov. 8, 1817; June 6, 1818; Jan. 30, 1819; Oct. 14, 1820.

Potsdam Gazette, 1816–1820+.

Weekly. Established Jan. 13, 1816, by Powell & Clark [Frederic C. Powell and Zenas Clark], with the title of "Potsdam Gazette." This firm was dissolved on Apr. 19, 1816, according to an advertisement in the issue of June 21, 1816, and F. C. Powell became sole publisher. J. Munsell, in "Typographical Miscellany," p. 13, gives the date of establishment and says that the paper was continued until after 1820.

Am. Antiq. Soc. has June 21, 1816; Aug. 8, 1817; Feb. 27, 1818.
F. R. Woodruff, Potsdam, has Dec. 9, 1819.
H. Armour Smith, Yonkers, has Nov. 29, 1816.

[Poughkeepsie] **American Farmer,** 1798–1800.

Weekly. Established June 8, 1798, by John Woods, with the title of "American Farmer, and Dutchess County Advertiser." Discontinued with the issue of July 22, 1800, vol. 3, no. 8.

N. J. Hist. Soc. has June 8, 1798–July 22, 1800.
Am. Antiq. Soc. has Jan. 3, 17, 31, Feb. 28–Mar. 21, Apr. 25, May 2, 23–June 6, 20, July 25, Oct. 22, 29, Dec. 17, 1799; Apr. 1, 22, 1800.
N. Y. Pub. Lib. has Dec. 24, 31, 1799; Jan. 7–Feb. 11, Mar. 4, 25, Apr. 1, 29, June 10, 17, July 1, 1800.
Adriance Lib., Poughkeepsie, has June 8, July 12, 1798; Jan. 17, May 15, June 13, Sept. 3, Oct. 1, 1799; Apr. 22, 1800.
Lib. Congress has Jan. 28, Feb. 18, 1800.
N. Y. Hist. Soc. has May 23, 1799.
Harvard has Sept. 10, 1799.

[Poughkeepsie] **Country Journal,** 1785–1789.

Weekly. Established Aug. 11, 1785, judging from the date of the earliest issue located, that of Sept. 15, 1785, no. 6, published by Nicholas Power, with the title of "The Country Journal, and the Poughkeepsie Advertiser." With the issue of Sept. 30, 1788, the title was altered to "The Country Journal, and Dutchess and Ulster County Farmer's Register." The last issue with this title was that of July 7, 1789, no. 205. With the issue of July 14, 1789, the title was changed to "The Poughkeepsie Journal," which see.

N. Y. Hist. Soc. has Dec. 15–29, 1785; Jan. 5–July 5, 26–Aug. 23, Sept. 6–20, Oct. 4, 25–Nov. 15, Dec. 6, 13, 27, 1786; Jan. 3, 10, 24–Apr. 18, 1787; Aug. 12, 1788; June 23, July 7, 1789.
Am. Antiq. Soc. has Nov. 1, Dec. 6, 13, 27, 1786; Jan. 10–Mar. 28, Apr. 11, 18, May 9, 23, June 13–July 18, Aug. 1, 8, 22, Sept. 5, 12, 26–Oct. 17, Nov. 14, Dec. 26, 1787; Jan. 9, 22, Feb. 19–Mar. 4, 18, Apr. 8, 15, May 6, 13, June 3, July 1, 15–Sept. 2, 16, Oct. 14–28, Nov. 25, Dec. 2, 23, 1788; Jan. 13, 27, Feb. 10, Mar. 3, 17, Apr. 7, 28, May 19, June 16, July 7, 1789.
N. Y. Pub. Lib. has Sept. 15–29, Oct. 13, 1785; Aug. 8, 1787–July 7, 1789.
Adriance Lib., Poughkeepsie, has Oct. 13, 1785; Jan. 10–31, Feb. 14–June 13, 27, July 4, 18–Aug. 29, Sept. 12–Oct. 24, Nov. 7, Dec. 5–26, 1787; Dec. 9, 1788; Feb. 24–June 23, 1789.
J. Frederick Ham, Millbrook, N. Y., has June 20, Nov. 14, 1787; Feb. 17, Apr. 28, May 12, 1789.
Lib. Congress has Aug. 12, 1788.
Baltus B. VanKleeck, Poughkeepsie, has Aug. 26, 1788.

[Poughkeepsie] **Dutchess Observer,** 1815–1820+.

Weekly. Established May 10, 1815, by Barnum & Nelson [Charles P. Barnum and Richard Nelson], with the title of "Dutchess Observer." With the issue of Jan. 8, 1817, the title was changed to "The Dutchess Observer," but with that of Mar. 17, 1819, reverted to its earlier form. With the issue of Nov. 17, 1819, the partnership was dissolved and the paper published by Charles P. Barnum. With the issue of May 17, 1820, Nicholas Jacacks was admitted to partnership and the paper published by Barnum & Jacacks. With the issue of Nov. 1, 1820, the title was again altered to "The Dutchess Observer." Continued until after 1820.

Adriance Lib., Poughkeepsie, has May 10, 1815–Dec. 27, 1820.
Lib. Congress has Dec. 31, 1817; Mar. 24, Apr. 21–May 12, 26, June 16, 30, July 7, 21, Aug. 4–18, Sept. 1, 8, Oct. 6, 13, 27, Nov. 17, 24, Dec. 8–22, 1819; Jan. 5–19, Feb. 9–Apr. 5, 1820.
Am. Antiq. Soc. has July 24, 1816; Sept. 17, 1817; June 17, 1818.
N. Y. Hist. Soc. has Mar. 25, 1818; Apr. 26, 1820.
Western Reserve Hist. Soc. has Oct. 20, Dec. 1, 1819.

[Poughkeepsie] Farmer, 1806–1807.

Weekly. Established Apr. 15, 1806, by Thomas Wilson, with the title of "The Farmer." The last issue located is that of Feb. 10, 1807, vol. 1, no. 41. The paper was suspended in May, 1807, immediately after the State election (see "Republican Crisis," of Albany, June 19, 1807).

N. Y. Pub. Lib. has Apr. 15, 1806–Feb. 10, 1807.
Am. Antiq. Soc. has Apr. 29, May 13, 20, June 10, Aug. 5, 1806; Jan. 6, Feb. 3, 1807.
Adriance Lib., Poughkeepsie, has Apr. 22, Sept. 30, Nov. 25, Dec. 10, 1806.
Harvard has May 13, 20, June 3, Aug. 12, 1806.
Baltus B. VanKleeck, Poughkeepsie, has Oct. 21, 1806.

[Poughkeepsie] Farmers' & Mechanics' Repository, 1809.

Fortnightly. Established Nov. 25, 1809, with the title of "Farmers' & Mechanics' Repository," printed for Bronson French and others. It was of quarto size. The name of Bronson French was signed to the editorial announcement, and publication was promised fortnightly. In this issue, the only one located, an engraved caricature occupies the upper half of the first page.

N. Y. Pub. Lib. has Nov. 25, 1809.

[Poughkeepsie] Guardian, 1801–1802.

Weekly. Established Nov. 10, 1801, by Buel & Joyner [Jesse Buel and Nathaniel Joyner], with the title of "The Guardian." It was discontinued with the issue of June 1, 1802, vol. 1, no. 30, to be succeeded by the "Political Barometer," which see.

NEW YORK 723

Harvard has Dec. 15, 22, 1801; Jan. 19, 26, Feb. 9–Mar. 2, 16–Apr. 20, May 18, 25, 1802.
Lib. Congress has Mar. 30, May 4, 25, 1802.
Adriance Lib., Poughkeepsie, has June 1, 1802.

Poughkeepsie Journal, 1789–1820+.

Weekly. A continuation, without change of volume numbering, of "The Country Journal," the first issue with the new title of "The Poughkeepsie Journal" being that of July 14, 1789, published by Nicholas Power. At some time between Mar. 30, and May 25, 1796, the imprint became Nicholas Power and Company. A few weeks later, probably with the issue of Sept. 28, 1796, the paper was published by Nicholas Power and Richard Vanderburgh. With the issue of Nov. 9, 1796, the partnership was dissolved and the paper again published by Nicholas Power alone. With the issue of Mar. 27, 1798, Henry C. Southwick was admitted to partnership, and the paper was published by Power and Southwick. On Nov. 25, 1800, Southwick retired and the paper was published by Nicholas Power. With the issue of June 1, 1802, Power took John Aikin as a partner into business, under the firm name of Nicholas Power and Co., and at this time the title was changed to "The Poughkeepsie Journal, and Constitutional Republican." With the issue of Aug. 24, 1802, the initial "The" was omitted from the title. With the issue of May 21, 1805, the paper was published by Power, Bowman & Co. [Nicholas Power, Godfrey Bowman and John Aikin]. With the issue of Jan. 7, 1806, the paper was purchased and published by Bowman and Potter [Godfrey Bowman and Paraclete Potter]. With the issue of Apr. 1, 1806, Chester Parsons was admitted to the firm, which became Bowman, Parsons & Potter. With the issue of Feb. 8, 1809, the firm was dissolved and the paper published by Paraclete Potter. With the issue of May 24, 1815, the title was shortened to "Poughkeepsie Journal." The paper was so continued until after 1820.

Adriance Lib., Poughkeepsie, has Aug. 11, Sept. 1–Oct. 13, 27–Nov. 10, 24, Dec. 8, 15, 1789; Nov. 24, 1791; Jan. 21, 28, Feb. 11, 18, Mar. 4–Apr. 8, 22–May 6, 20, June 3–July 1, 22, 29, Aug. 19–Dec. 30, 1795; Jan. 6, 20, 27, Feb. 17–Mar. 9, June 29–July 20, Aug. 10–24, Sept. 14–Nov. 16, Dec. 28, 1796; Jan. 4, 1797–Dec. 30, 1800; Jan. 6, Mar. 3, 17, 1801; Jan. 5, 1802–Dec. 25, 1804; Mar. 12, 1805–Dec. 28, 1808; Jan. 4–Feb. 8, 22, Mar. 8, May 3, Aug. 16, Oct. 4, 18, 25, Nov. 8–22, Dec. 20, 27, 1809; Jan. 3, 1810–Dec. 27, 1820.

Am. Antiq. Soc. has July 14–Aug. 4, 18–Sept. 15, Oct. 6, 27–Dec. 22, 1789; Jan. 19, 26, Apr. 20–May 15, 29, June 12–Aug. 14, Sept. 4–Oct. 16, Nov. 6–20, Dec. 18, 25, 1790; Jan. 1, 8, Feb. 5, 19, Mar. 5–Apr. 16, 30, May 12, 26, June 2, 16, 30–July 21, Aug. 4, 11, 25–Sept. 8, 22–Nov. 24, Dec. 8, 15, 29, 1791; Jan. 5, 19, Feb. 2, 16–Mar. 15, 29, Apr. 5, May 3, 17, June 14, July 5–19, Aug. 1, 15, Sept. 19, 26, 1792; Jan. 9, Feb. 13, 27–Mar. 13, 27, Apr. 10,

24–May 8, Oct. 23, 1793; Nov. 18, 1795; Mar. 23, May 25, June 2, 15, 29, July 13, Oct. 12–Nov. 2, Dec. 21, 1796; Jan. 25, Feb. 8–Mar. 1, 22, 29, Aug. 15, 1797; Mar. 6, 13, May 8, June 12, 1798; Oct. 28, Nov. 4, 1800; July 6, 1802; Aug. 16, Sept. 6, 27, 1803; Mar. 13, 20, 1804; Feb. 25, June 3, July 1, Oct. 7, Dec. 9, 1806; Feb. 17, 1808; Dec. 5, 1810; June 5, 1811; May 13, June 17–July 1, 15, Aug. 26, Sept. 9, 23, Nov. 18, Dec. 2, 1812; Feb. 3, Mar. 3, 10, 24, 1813; Mar. 22, 1820.

Rutgers Univ. has Jan. 19, 1792–Aug. 13, 1794; May 27, 1812; June 19, 1816.

Wis. Hist. Soc. has May 1–Sept. 18, 1793; Feb. 26–July 9, 1794; Nov. 27, 1798; Oct. 1, 1799.

Lib. Congress has May 20, 1812; Oct. 13, 1813; July 15, 29, Aug. 5, Sept. 9, Oct. 14, Nov. 4–18, Dec. 2, 16, 30, 1818; Jan. 6, 13, 27–Feb. 17, Mar. 3, 17, Apr. 7, Aug. 11, 1819; Feb. 2, Apr. 19, May 3, 24, July 26, Aug. 16, Sept. 13, 1820.

Harvard has Nov. 18, 1795; Apr. 12, Aug. 1, 1797; Mar. 30, 1802; Jan. 4, Oct. 11, 1803; Feb. 14, Apr. 10, Sept. 4, 25, Dec. 25, 1804; Jan. 1, 1805; Apr. 8, Oct. 14, 1806.

N. Y. Hist. Soc. has Dec. 22, 29, 1789; Jan. 12, 19, 1790; Apr. 3, 1793; Aug. 27, Sept. 17, 1799; Aug. 16, 1803; July 19, 1815; May 3, July 19, Aug. 16, 1820.

Yale has Jan. 13–Feb. 3, 17, 24, 1796.

Baltus B. VanKleeck, Poughkeepsie, has May 25, Nov. 23, 30, 1796; Dec. 31, 1799; Jan. 31, 1804; Mar. 10, Nov. 25, 1807.

N. Y. State Lib. has Feb. 9, 1790; June 26, 1804; Oct. 21, 1812.

H. Armour Smith, Yonkers, has Apr. 10, July 10, 24, 1798.

N. Y. Pub. Lib. has July 14, 1789; Aug. 2, 1820.

J. Frederick Ham, Millbrook, N. Y., has Jan. 12, 1790; Sept. 22, 1791.

Boston Pub. Lib. has Apr. 6, May 15, 1790.

J. Lawrence Chapter, Daughters of 1812, Haddonfield, N. J., has Aug. 31, Sept. 7, 1796.

Mrs. D. H. Rikert, So. Royalton, Vt., has Dec. 24, 31, 1799.

Perry Burke, Poughkeepsie, has Dec. 31, 1799.

Vassar Coll. has Jan. 12, 1802; May 13, 1807.

Univ. of Mich. (Clements) has Apr. 3, 1793.

Columbia Co. Hist. Soc., Kinderhook, has Aug. 31, 1796.

Senate House, Kingston, has Sept. 7, 1796.

Univ. of Ill. has June 30, 1801.

Wesleyan Univ. has May 24, 1815.

[**Poughkeepsie**] **New-York Journal**, 1778–1782.

Weekly. A continuation, without change of volume numbering, of "The New-York Journal," suspended at Kingston in October, 1777. The first Poughkeepsie issue was that of May 11, 1778, no. 1772, published by John Holt, with the title of "The New-York Journal, and the General Advertiser." It was suspended from

Nov. 6, 1780, to July 30, 1781, because of scarcity of paper and lack of financial support. After being resumed with the issue of July 30, 1781, it was suspended with the issue of Jan. 6, 1782, no. 1926, to allow Holt to print the State Laws. The paper was revived by Holt at New York, under the title of "The Independent New-York Gazette," Nov. 22, 1783.

N. Y. Pub. Lib. has May 11, 1778–Jan. 6, 1782.

N. Y. Hist. Soc. has May 11–Dec. 28, 1778; Jan. 4–Feb. 15, Mar. 1, 29–Apr. 19, May 3–June 14, 28–Sept. 6, 20, 27, Oct. 11–Dec. 27, 1779; Jan. 31, Mar. 6, May 8, 22, 29, June 19, 26, Sept. 11, Oct. 30, 1780; July 30, Sept. 3, 10, 24, Oct. 1, 15, 22, Nov. 5–26, Dec. 10, 17, 1781.

Am. Antiq. Soc. has July 20, Aug. 10, 24, 31, Oct. 5–19, Nov. 2, 23, 30, Dec. 21, 1778; Jan. 4, Feb. 15–Mar. 1, Apr. 12, May 10, 31, June 7, 21, July 5, Aug. 9, 30, Sept. 6–Oct. 18, Nov. 8, 1779; Feb. 14, Mar. 27, Apr. 17, May 22, June 19, July 17, Aug. 7, Oct. 23, Nov. 6, 1780; July 30, Aug. 6, 20, Sept. 24, Oct. 1, 15, 29, Nov. 5, 19, 1781.

Lib. Congress has May 11–25, June 8–29, July 20, Aug. 3–Sept. 14, 28, Oct. 12–Nov. 30, Dec. 14, 21, 1778; Jan. 11, 18, Feb. 8, Apr. 19, June 7, 14, July 5, 19, Aug. 16, Sept. 20, Oct. 11, 18, Dec. 13, 1779.

Phil. Lib. Co. has June 1, July 13, Oct. 5, Dec. 7, 1778; Feb. 1, 22, Mar. 1, Apr. 19, July 12, Aug. 16, Sept. 6, 1779.

Mass. Hist. Soc. has Aug. 31, Nov. 30, 1778; Sept. 6, Oct. 4, 1779; Oct. 1, 29, 1781.

N. Y. State Lib. has Sept. 3, Dec. 10–31, 1781.

Univ. of Mich. (Clements) has July 20, Aug. 10, 1778; Jan. 4, 1779; Nov. 12, 1781.

Adriance Lib., Poughkeepsie, has Oct. 19, 1778; Jan. 25, Feb. 8, 1779.

Western Reserve Hist. Soc. has Nov. 2, 1778.

Amer. Philos. Soc. has Feb. 15, 1779.

Boston Pub. Lib. has Sept. 20, 1779.

Univ. of Minn. has Apr. 17, 1780.

[Poughkeepsie] **Northern Politician,** 1812.

Weekly. Established Sept. 16, 1812, by Isaac Mitchell with the title of "Northern Politician." It succeeded the "Republican Herald," continuing the advertisements, but adopting a new volume numbering. Mitchell died Nov. 26, 1812, and the issue of Dec. 2, 1812, was printed by P[———] R. Miller, for the Proprietors. The last issue was that of Dec. 9, 1812, vol. 1, no. 13, and with the next issue the paper resumed its former title of "Republican Herald," which see.

Adriance Lib., Poughkeepsie, has Sept. 16–Dec. 9, 1812.

N. Y. State Lib. has Sept. 23, Oct. 21, 1812.

James Lawrence Chap., Daughters of 1812, Haddonfield, N. J., has Oct. 21, Nov. 11, Dec. 9, 1812.

Baltus B. VanKleeck, Poughkeepsie, has Sept. 16, 1812.

[Poughkeepsie] **Political Barometer**, 1802–1811.

Weekly. Established June 8, 1802, by Mitchell & Buel [Isaac Mitchell and Jesse Buel], with the title of "Political Barometer." It succeeded "The Guardian," but adopted a new volume numbering. With the issue of June 4, 1805, the partnership was dissolved, and Isaac Mitchell became sole publisher. With the issue of Sept. 2, 1806, the paper was purchased and published by Thomas Nelson & Son. With the issue of Apr. 13, 1808, the partnership was dissolved and Joseph Nelson, who had been the junior editor, became sole publisher. With the issue of Sept. 12, 1810, the paper was transferred to Charles C. Adams & Co., with Joseph Nelson continuing as printer. The last issue was that of Aug. 21, 1811, vol. 10, no. 13, upon which date Nelson sold the establishment to a new firm, which began the "Republican Herald" in its stead.

- Adriance Lib., Poughkeepsie, has June 8, 1802–May 27, 1806; June 10, 1806–Aug. 21, 1811, fair.
- N. Y. Hist. Soc. has June 5, 1804–Dec. 31, 1805; Jan. 7–May 27, June 24–July 29, Aug. 19–Oct. 21, Dec. 9–30, 1806; Jan. 6–Feb. 17, Mar. 3–May 27, 1807.
- Am. Antiq. Soc. has June 8–July 13, 1802; Apr. 12, Aug. 16, 1803; Jan. 3, 1804; Feb. 18, Apr. 29, May 20, June 3, 1806–May 13, 1807; Aug. 9, Nov. 1, 1809; Aug. 15, 1810; Apr. 3, 17, 30, May 29, June 5, 1811.
- Buffalo Hist. Soc. has May 20, 1807–May 24, 1809.
- N. Y. State Lib. has Mar. 13, 1804; Aug. 6–Dec. 24, 1805; July 29, 1807; May 31, 1809–Aug. 21, 1811.
- Harvard has June 15, Aug. 24, Sept. 7, 21, 1802; Feb. 1, 8, 22, Mar. 8, Apr. 26, May 10, June 7, 28, July 12–Aug. 16, Sept. 6, 13, 27, Oct. 11–25, Nov. 29, Dec. 6, 1803; Jan. 3, Feb. 14, Mar. 20, Apr. 10–May 1, June 19, 26, Aug. 21, Sept. 4–18, Oct. 2, 30–Nov. 20, Dec. 11, 1804; Jan. 1, 15, Feb. 5, 12, 26, Mar. 5, 19, Apr. 16, May 7, 28, June 11, 25, Sept. 3, 24, Oct. 1, 29, Nov. 12, Dec. 3–17, 1805; Jan. 21–Feb. 4, Mar. 11, Apr. 1, May 6, 13, June 3, 24, July 15, 29–Aug. 12, Sept. 9, Oct. 7, 14, Nov. 11–25, Dec. 23, 1806; Jan. 13, Feb. 10–24, Apr. 21–May 5, Sept. 2, 23, Oct. 7, 21, Dec. 2, 1807; June 22, Aug. 10, 24, Sept. 14, 28, 1808.
- Baltus B. VanKleeck, Poughkeepsie, has Nov. 12, 26, 1805; Dec. 23, 30, 1806; May 20, 1807; Mar. 8, 1809; Mar. 21, 1810–July 10, 1811.
- Troy Pub. Lib. has June 15, July 6, 20, Aug. 31, Oct. 12, 26, Nov. 23, Dec. 7, 1802; May 24, 1803.
- Univ. of Ill. has Sept. 17, Oct. 15, 1805; May 13, 1806.
- Newburgh Lib. has Sept. 16, 1807; May 11, June 15, 1808.
- Lib. Congress has Oct. 26, 1802; May 16, 1810.
- East Hampton Free Lib. has Feb. 22, 1803.
- Boston Athenæum has Jan. 21, 1806.
- N. Y. Pub. Lib. has Oct. 28, 1806.

[Poughkeepsie] Republican Herald, 1811–1820+.

Weekly. Established Aug. 28, 1811, by C[harles] C. Adams and D[aniel] MacDuffee, with the title of "Republican Herald," succeeding the "Political Barometer." With the issue of Apr. 15, 1812, MacDuffee retired and the paper was published by Charles C. Adams alone. With the issue of Sept. 12, 1812, vol. 2, no. 3, the paper was discontinued and sold to Isaac Mitchell, who established the "Northern Politician" in its stead. The latter paper ran for thirteen issues, through Dec. 9, 1812. On Dec. 16, 1812, Charles C. Adams bought back the paper from Mitchell, and recommenced it under its former name, assuming its former numbering. Adams died Apr. 6, 1814, and the paper was then published for Mrs. Adams. With the issue of May 11, 1814, the paper was purchased and published by Rudd & Stockholm [Reuben B. Rudd and Derick B. Stockholm]. With the issue of Mar. 22, 1815, Rudd was replaced by Thomas Brownejohn and the paper was published by Stockholm & Brownejohn. With the issue of Nov. 3, 1819, the partnership was dissolved and the paper was published by D. B. Stockholm. It was so continued until after 1820.

> Adriance Lib., Poughkeepsie, has Aug. 28, 1811–Sept. 9, Dec. 16–30, 1812; Jan. 6–Feb. 3, June 9, July 28, Aug. 18, 25, Sept. 22, 29, Oct. 13–Dec. 29, 1813; Jan. 5, 1814–July 9, 1817; Jan. 13, Feb. 3, 10, Mar. 3, 10, 31, Apr. 7, May 5, June 23, July 7, Aug. 25, Sept. 1, 15, 22, Oct. 6, Nov. 3, 10, 24–Dec. 15, 1819; Dec. 20, 1820.
> Am. Antiq. Soc. has Aug. 19, 1812; Mar. 3, Aug. 4, 18, Sept. 22, Oct. 6–Nov. 17, Dec. 1, 29, 1813; Jan. 5, 19, 26, Feb. 16, 23, Mar. 9, Apr. 20, May 18, 25, June 8, 22, July 6, 13, Aug. 17, 24, Sept. 7, Oct. 5, 19–Nov. 9, 1814; Mar. 8, May 3, 1815.
> N. Y. Hist. Soc. has Jan. 4, 11, Feb. 15, Mar. 1, Apr. 12, 26, Sept. 27, Oct. 25, Nov. 15, 29, 1815; May 1, 1816–Apr. 23, 1817.
> James Lawrence Chapter, Daughters of 1812, Haddonfield, N. J., has Jan. 8, Apr. 22–May 6, July 8, Dec. 16, 23, 1812; Jan. 6, May 19, 26, Sept. 15, Nov. 24, 1813.
> N. Y. State Lib. has July 8, 15, Sept. 9, 1812; Jan. 26, Mar. 23, 1814.
> Baltus B. VanKleeck, Poughkeepsie, has Aug. 19, 1812.
> Boston Pub. Lib. has Apr. 27, 1813.
> Western Reserve Hist. Soc. has Oct. 13, 1819.

[Poughkeepsie] Republican Journal, 1795–1796.

Weekly. Established Sept. 30, 1795, judging from the date of the earliest issue located, that of Oct. 21, 1795, vol. 1, no. 4, published by Nathan Douglas, with the title of "Republican Journal." On June 29, 1796, Douglas sold out and the paper was published by Richard Vanderburgh & Co. The last issue located is that of July 6, 1796, vol. 1, no. 41, and the paper was soon discontinued, as Vanderburgh entered the management of "The Poughkeepsie Journal" in September, 1796.

> Phil. Lib. Co. has Oct. 21, Nov. 4, 11, 18, Dec. 2, 1795; June 8, 15, 22, 1796.
> Am. Antiq. Soc. has Nov. 4, 11, 25, Dec. 9, 30, 1795; Feb. 24, 1796.
> Harvard has Nov. 18, Dec. 23, 1795; May 25, June 8, 22, 1796.
> N. Y. Pub. Lib. has June 1, 1796.
> Baltus B. VanKleeck, Poughkeepsie, has July 6, 1796.

Rochester Gazette, 1816–1820+.

Weekly. Established in June, 1816, judging from the date of the earliest issue located, that of June 9, 1818, vol. 2, no. 102, published by A. G. Dauby & Co., with the title of "Rochester Gazette." Frederick Follett, in his "Press of Western New-York," 1847, p. 46, states that the paper was started by Augustine G. Dauby, that John Sheldon was associated with him for ten months immediately prior to removing to Detroit, and that Oran Follett succeeded Sheldon and remained with Dauby for a short time. John P. Sheldon established the "Detroit Gazette," July 25, 1817, and Oran Follett established the "Spirit of the Times" at Batavia, Feb. 3, 1819. In a list of New York newspapers of Jan. 1, 1818 (printed in the "Albany Argus" of Jan. 6, 1818), the "Rochester Gazette" is recorded as published by A. G. Dauby & Co. The issues in 1819 were published by A. G. Dauby. On Dec. 5, 1819, a fire entirely destroyed the printing-office, and it was April 18, 1820, before Dauby was able to resume publication. The issues in 1820 and after were published by Augustine G. Dauby.

> Boston Athenæum has June 9, 1818.
> Am. Antiq. Soc. has May 18, 1819.
> Univ. of Rochester has June 15, 22, 1819; Apr. 18, 1820.
> Rochester Pub. Lib. has May 30, June 13, July 11–Aug. 1, 15, 22, Sept. 19–Nov. 21, Dec. 5, 26, 1820.
> Chicago Hist. Soc. has June 6, 1820.

Rochester Telegraph, 1818–1820+.

Weekly. Established July 7, 1818, by E[verard] Peck, & Co., with the title of "Rochester Telegraph." So continued until after 1820.

> N. Y. Hist. Soc. and Rochester Pub. Lib. have July 7, 1818–Dec. 26, 1820.
> Hist. Soc. Penn. has July 7, 1818–July 6, 1819.
> Univ. of Rochester has July 7, 1818–June 29, 1819.
> Am. Antiq. Soc. has Sept. 22, 1818; July 13–27, 1819.
> Wis. Hist. Soc. has Jan. 4, Nov. 14, 1820.
> Chicago Hist. Soc. has Nov. 21, 1820.

[Rome] Columbian Patriotic Gazette, 1799–1803.

Weekly. Established Aug. 8, 1799, judging from the date of the earliest issue located, that of Sept. 26, 1799, vol. 1, no. 8, published by Ebenezer Eaton & Thomas Walker, with the title of "Columbian Patriotic Gazette." The word "Patriotic" is in different type, so that the paper might possibly be called "Columbian Gazette." With the issue of Aug. 4, 1800, the paper was printed by Thomas Walker, for Eaton & Walker. With the issue of Aug. 3, 1801, the firm of Ebenezer Eaton and Thomas Walker dissolved partnership, and the paper was published by Thomas Walker. The last issue located is that of Sept. 6, 1802, vol. 4, no. 162, and in March, 1803, Walker removed the paper to Utica, where he established it as the "Columbian Gazette."

> Harvard has Sept. 26, 1799; Aug. 25, 1800; Jan. 5–Feb. 2, Mar. 2, Apr. 13, 27, July 13, 1801; Feb. 1, 1802.
> Am. Antiq. Soc. has Feb. 24, Apr. 21, Aug. 11, Oct. 20, Nov. 17, 1800; Apr. 13, Aug. 17, 24, 1801; Sept. 6, 1802.
> N. Y. State Lib. has Dec. 23, 1799; Jan. 6, Apr. 7, Dec. 29, 1800.
> Western Reserve Hist. Soc. has May 19, 1800; Oct. 5, 1801.
> Oneida Hist. Soc., Utica, has Aug. 4, 1800 Extra; Feb. 15, Mar. 8, 1802.
> Hamilton Coll. Lib., Clinton, has Apr. 28, 1800.
> Long Id. Hist. Soc. has July 28, 1800; July 27, 1801.
> Boston Athenæum has Nov. 17, 1800.
> Lib. Congress has Apr. 27, 1801.

[Rome] Oneida Observer, 1818–1819.

Weekly. Removed from Utica, where it was called "The Utica Observer," and established at Rome toward the close of the year 1818 as "The Oneida Observer." The only copy located is that of July 20, 1819, vol. 3, no. 133, entitled "The Oneida Observer," and published by E[liasaph] Dorchester. The paper was returned to Utica later in 1819 (Munsell, "Typographical Miscellany," p. 138, and French, "Gazetteer of New York," 1860, p. 459).

> Am. Antiq. Soc. has July 20, 1819.

Sacket's Harbor Gazette, 1817–1820+.

Weekly. Established Mar. 18, 1817, by George Camp, with the title of "Sacket's Harbor Gazette." On Mar. 17, 1818, the title was changed to "Sacket's-Harbor Gazette & Advertiser." In February, 1820, Mathew M. Cole became the publisher and the title was changed to "The Sacket's Harbor Gazette." The paper was continued until after 1820.

> Jefferson Co. Hist. Soc., Watertown, N. Y., has Mar. 25, 1817–Feb. 15, 1820, fair.

Am. Antiq. Soc. has June 9, 23, 1818; Aug. 3, 1819; also incorrect facsimile of Oct. 8, 1818, which is in several libraries.
Wis. Hist. Soc. has Dec. 1, 1818.
Yale has Oct. 27, 1820.

[Sag Harbor] American Eagle, 1817–1820+.

Weekly. Established Oct. 18, 1817, by Samuel A. Seabury, with the title of "American Eagle." The paper immediately succeeded the "Suffolk County Recorder." Before the end of 1818 the title was enlarged to "American Eagle. And Suffolk County General Advertiser," but was shortened again in 1820 to "The American Eagle." Seabury continued the paper until after 1820.

Am. Antiq. Soc. has Oct. 25–Nov. 22, 1817; Mar. 6, Oct. 23–Nov. 27, Dec. 11–25, 1819; Jan. 1–Feb. 2, 1820.
Long Id. Hist. Soc. has Jan. 10, 1818.
Queens Borough Pub. Lib. has Dec. 12, 1818; Jan. 23, 30, Mar. 13, Apr. 10, May 29, 1819.
East Hampton Free Lib. has Feb. 6, 13, 27, Mar. 27, Apr. 3, Aug. 7, 1819.
Jermain Lib., Sag Harbor, has May 8, 22, June 12, July 17, 24, Sept. 4, 11, 25, 1819; July 8, 1820.
Wis. Hist. Soc. has Dec. 5, 1818.

[Sag Harbor] Frothingham's Long-Island Herald, 1791–1798.

Weekly. Established May 10, 1791, by David Frothingham, with the title of "Frothingham's Long-Island Herald." The last issue located is that of Dec. 17, 1798, vol. 7, no. 317, at about which time Frothingham became foreman in the office of "Greenleaf's New York Journal," aiding Mrs. Greenleaf in the conduct of that paper after her husband's death. Benjamin F. Thompson, in his "History of Long Island," 1839, p. 226, states that Frothingham's paper was transferred to Selleck Osborn who changed the title to "Suffolk County Herald," June 19, 1802. Yet Osborn makes no mention of this fact in his initial issue, and no copies of the Long Island Herald, or even any Sag Harbor imprints, are known from 1799 to 1802. Charles J. Werner in 1918 wrote me that Thompson as late as 1840 had in his possession at Hempstead what he called "A complete file of Mr. Frothingham's Long Island Herald," although most of Thompson's collections of newspapers and documents were subsequently destroyed. Morton Pennypacker, of Kew Gardens, Long Island, who has gathered a large collection of early Long Island documents and newspapers, believes that Frothingham's paper ceased in 1798.

East Hampton Free Lib. (Pennypacker Coll.) has May 10, June 14, 21, Aug. 9, 23, 30, Sept. 13, 27, Oct. 4, Nov. 1, 22, 29, Dec. 20, 1791; Jan. 5, Feb. 9, 16, Mar. 29, Apr. 12, 19, May 3, 1792; Aug. 28, 1794; Oct. 30, 1797.

NEW YORK 731

Long Id. Hist. Soc. has June 7, 1791; July 11, 1793; Aug. 17, 1796; Feb. 1, Mar. 15, 22, Apr. 12, 19, May 3, 10, 24–June 7, 21–July 5, 26, Aug. 9–30, Sept. 13–Oct. 18, 30, Nov. 6, Dec. 18, 1797; Jan. 16, Mar. 19, 26, Apr. 30, May 7, 21, June 4–July 9, 23, 30, Aug. 13–Sept. 3, Nov. 19, Dec. 3, 17, 1798.
N. Y. Hist. Soc. has June 28, Sept. 6, 13, Oct. 4, 11, 25, Nov. 1, 22, Dec. 13–27, 1791; Jan. 5, Feb. 9, Nov. 29–Dec. 20, 1792; Dec. 23, 1794; Apr. 13, May 11, 25, June 8, July 6, Oct. 26, Dec. 14, 1795; Jan. 11, Sept. 21, Oct. 26, 1796; Jan. 25, Feb. 8, 23, May 3, 31, July 19, 26, Aug. 9, Sept. 20, 27, Dec. 18, 1797.
Am. Antiq. Soc. has July 26, Sept. 13, 27, Oct. 4, 1791; Apr. 12, July 12, 1792.
Jermain Lib., Sag Harbor, has Dec. 6, 1792.
Harvard has Mar. 12, 1798.

[Sag Harbor] Suffolk County Herald, 1802–1803.

Weekly. Established June 19, 1802, by Selleck Osborn, with the title of "Suffolk County Herald." The last issue located is that of Jan. 3, 1803, vol. 1, no. 29.

Long Id. Hist. Soc. has June 19–Aug. 7, 21–Sept. 11, Oct. 4, 11, Dec. 13, 1802; Jan. 3, 1803.
East Hampton Free Lib. has Sept. 4, Oct. 18, 1802.
Am. Antiq. Soc. has Nov. 29, 1802.
Harvard has Nov. 29, 1802.

[Sag Harbor] Suffolk County Recorder, 1816–1817.

Weekly. Established Oct. 19, 1816, by Samuel A. Seabury, with the title of "Suffolk County Recorder." Discontinued with the issue of Oct. 11, 1817, vol. 1, no. 52, to be succeeded by the "American Eagle."

N. Y. Hist. Soc. has Oct. 19, 1816–Oct. 11, 1817.
East Hampton Free Lib. (Pennypacker Coll.) has Oct. 19, 1816–Oct. 11, 1817.
Jermain Lib., Sag Harbor, has Oct. 26, Nov. 2, 1816; Jan. 4, 18–Feb. 8, Mar. 1–15, 29–June 7, 21, 28, July 26–Sept. 13, Oct. 4, 11, 1817.
Am. Antiq. Soc. has Oct. 19–Nov. 9, 23, 1816.

[Sag Harbor] Suffolk Gazette, 1804–1811.

Weekly. Established Feb. 20, 1804, by Alden Spooner, with the title of "Suffolk Gazette." Because of the illness of the editor, there were no issues from Aug. 19 to Sept. 16, 1805. With the issue of Sept. 1, 1810, Spooner relinquished his control of the paper to a company, although continuing as printer, and the paper was printed by Alden Spooner, for the Proprietors. In the American Antiquarian Society is a copy of the printed circular sent out by a special committee, Aug. 14, 1810, to secure members of the Company. The paper was discontinued with the issue of Feb. 23, 1811, vol. 6, no. 364.

- Jermain Lib., Sag Harbor, and East Hampton Free Lib. (Pennypacker Coll.) have Feb. 20, 1804–Feb. 23, 1811.
- Am. Antiq. Soc. has Feb. 20, Mar. 5, Aug. 20, Sept. 17–Oct. 1, 15, 29–Nov. 19, Dec. 3, 17–31, 1804; Jan. 7, 28, Feb. 25, Mar. 4, 18, 25, Apr. 8, 22, May 20–June 10, July 1, 15, 29, Sept. 23–Oct. 14, Nov. 25–Dec. 9, 1805; Jan. 6, Feb. 17, Mar. 10, Apr. 7, 21, May 5, 26, June 16–July 14, 28, Aug. 11, Oct. 20–Nov. 10, 24, Dec. 8, 22, 29, 1806; Jan. 5–Feb. 9, 23, Mar. 2, 16, Apr. 6, 20, 27, May 18–June 1, 15–July 6, 20, Aug. 3, 24–Sept. 28, Dec. 7, 14, 28, 1807; Jan. 4–18, July 2, 23, 30, Sept. 10, 17, Oct. 1, 22, Dec. 3, 1808; Jan. 14–Mar. 4, 18, Apr. 15, 22, May 6–20, June 17, July 29, Sept. 9, Nov. 25, Dec. 2, 16–30, 1809; Jan. 13, 20, Feb. 3–Apr. 14, May 5, 19, June 9, July 7, 21, 28, Aug. 25–Sept. 8, 22–Oct. 6, 20, 27, Nov. 17, Dec. 1, 8, 22, 29, 1810; Jan. 5–Feb. 9, 23, 1811.
- Harvard has Feb. 20, Mar. 5–Apr. 2, 23, 30, May 14, 21, June 18, 25, July 2–30, Aug. 13, 20, Sept. 3–17, Oct. 8–Nov. 5, 26–Dec. 31, 1804; Jan. 7–21, Feb. 4–Apr. 8, 22–May 13, 27, June 24, July 15, Aug. 12, Sept. 30, Oct. 14–Dec. 30, 1805; Jan. 6–Feb. 17, Mar. 10, 24–Apr. 14, 1806.
- N. Y. Hist. Soc. has Apr. 2, 9, 30, Sept. 17, Oct. 22, Nov. 5–26, Dec. 10–31, 1804; Jan. 7, 28, Feb. 18–Mar. 11, 25, Apr. 8, June 17, 24, Aug. 12, Sept. 9, Dec. 23, 1805; June 3, July 29, Dec. 2, 1809; Feb. 24, Mar. 3, June 30, July 28, Sept. 22, Nov. 10, 1810.
- Yale has Mar. 5–Aug. 13, 1804.
- Long Id. Hist. Soc. has Sept. 8, 29, 1806; Jan. 21, Feb. 25, Mar. 4, 18, Apr. 1, 29, May 6, 20, 27, June 17, 1809; Feb. 2, 1811.
- N. Y. State Lib. has Jan. 14, Apr. 15, 1809.
- Queens Borough Pub. Lib. has Aug. 31, 1807.
- Lib. Congress has Oct. 1, 1808.
- N. Y. Pub. Lib. has Apr. 15, 1809.

[Salem] Northern Centinel, 1798–1804.

Weekly. Established Jan. 1, 1798, by Henry Dodd, with the title of "Northern Centinel." The last issue was that of May 15, 1804, vol. 7, no. 332, after which the title was changed to "The Northern Post."

- Am. Antiq. Soc. has Jan. 1–Dec. 25, 1798; Mar. 19, Apr. 9, July 16, Aug. 13, 27, Sept. 3, 17, Nov. 5–19, Dec. 10, 1799; Apr. 8, Aug. 26, Sept. 9, Oct. 21, Nov. 11, 18, Dec. 9, 1800.
- N. Y. State Lib. has Apr. 9, 1798; Sept. 10–Oct. 22, 1799; Nov. 18, Dec. 23, 1800; Jan. 6–Dec. 22, 1801; July 27, 1802; Jan. 11, 1803–May 15, 1804.
- Harvard has July 23, 1798; Jan. 7, 1800.
- Lib. Congress has Jan. 7, 21, 1800.

N. Y. Hist. Soc. has Aug. 13, 1798.
N. Y. Pub. Lib. has Nov. 27, 1798.
Hugh McLellan, Champlain, N. Y., has June 25, 1799.

[Salem] **Northern Post**, 1804–1820+.

Weekly. Established May 22, 1804, judging from the date of the earliest issue located, that of May 29, 1804, vol. 1, no. 2, published by Henry Dodd and David Rumsey, Jun., with the title of "The Northern Post." With the issue of May 19, 1814, the firm was dissolved and the paper published by H. Dodd & Co. With the issue of June 9, 1814, a new partnership was formed between Henry Dodd, David Rumsey, and James Stevenson, Jun., under the firm name of Dodd, Rumsey & Stevenson. With the issue of Dec. 29, 1814, Rumsey withdrew and the paper was published by Dodd & Stevenson. With the issue of Nov. 2, 1820, the firm name was changed to H. Dodd & Co., and was so continued until after 1820.

> N. Y. State Lib. has May 29, June 19, 1804–Dec. 25, 1806; Jan. 1–Apr. 9, 23–May 21, July 30, Dec. 31, 1807; May 19, June 2–Aug. 25, 1808; Apr. 13, 20, May 25, 1809; Jan. 4, 1810–May 9, June 6, 1816; Dec. 11, 1817; July 23, 1818; May 4, Sept. 21, Oct. 19, Nov. 9, 23, Dec. 7, 1820.
> Am. Antiq. Soc. has July 4–Dec. 26, 1805; Jan. 2–May 8, July 3, 10, 31–Sept. 4, 18–Dec. 25, 1806; Jan. 1–Mar. 26, May 14, Nov. 12, 1807; May 19, June 9, 1808; May 25, Nov. 30, 1809; Feb. 22, Mar. 8, 15, Apr. 12, 26, May 24, June 7, 28–Aug. 9, Sept. 6–27, Oct. 11, Dec. 27, 1810; Apr. 11–May 16, June 6, 13, 1811; May 20–Dec. 30, 1813; Jan. 6–Feb. 10, 24–May 5, 19–Dec. 29, 1814; Jan. 5, 1815–Apr. 16, 1818.
> N. Y. Hist. Soc. has July 25–Dec. 26, 1805; July 3, 10, 31–Aug. 28, Sept. 18–Dec. 25, 1806; Jan. 1–Mar. 26, 1807; July 5–19, Aug. 9, 1810; Dec. 17, 1812; Apr. 1, 1813; May 12, 1814; Feb. 16, May 16–June 27, July 11–Aug. 1, 15, 1816–May 7, 1818.
> N. Y. Geneal. & Biog. Soc. has May 21, 1807–May 12, 1808.
> Bancroft Lib., Salem, has May 14, 1818–May 11, 1820.
> N. Y. Pub. Lib. has Sept. 5–Nov. 14, Dec. 5–26, 1805; July 31–Aug. 28, Sept. 18–Oct. 23, Nov. 6–Dec. 25, 1806; Jan. 8–Feb. 5, 1807; July 5, 1810.
> Harvard has Aug. 2, 23, 1804.
> Univ. of Ill. has Feb. 7, 1805.
> Troy Pub. Lib. has May 22, 1806.
> Western Reserve Hist. Soc. has Aug. 11, 1807.

[Salem] **Times**, 1794–1795.

Weekly. Established June 18, 1794, by George Gerrish, with the title of "The Times; or, National Courier." Discontinued in January, 1795, according to the statement in the initial number of the "Washington Patrol."

> N. Y. Pub. Lib. has June 18, 26, 1794.

[Salem] Washington Patrol, 1795.

Weekly. Established May 27, 1795, by Wm. W. Wands & S. J. [St. John] Honeywood, with the title of "Washington Patrol." The last issue located is that of Nov. 18, 1795, vol. 1, no. 26.

N. Y. State Lib. has May 27–Nov. 18, 1795.
Harvard has May 27, June 3, 17, July 15, Sept. 16, 1795.
Lib. Congress has Aug. 19–Oct. 28, 1795.
Am. Antiq. Soc. has June 3, July 8, 29, 1795.
N. Y. Pub. Lib. has May 27, 1795.

[Salem] Washington Register, 1803–1820+.

Weekly. Established in October, 1803, judging from the date of the earliest issue located, that of Feb. 7, 1804, vol. 1, no. 19, published by John M. Looker, with the title of "Washington Register." At some time between June 26, 1805, and Nov. 13, 1806, Looker sold out to J[ohn] P. Reynolds. In the Cincinnati "Liberty Hall" of Dec. 22, 1812, is printed a notice of the death, at Cincinnati, Dec. 17, 1812, of John M. Looker, "printer, formerly editor of the Washington Register, a Republican paper, published at Salem, Washington County, New York." With the issue of Jan. 5, 1816, Reynolds sold out to Timothy Hoskins. With the issue of Dec. 31, 1818, Hoskins sold out to James B. Gibson, who continued the paper until after 1820.

Univ. of Ill. has Feb. 7, 1804; June 26, 1805.
Am. Antiq. Soc. has Nov. 13, 1806; June 14, 21, 1810; Jan. 19, Feb. 9, Mar. 1, July 12, 19, Sept. 27, Oct. 11, Nov. 22, Dec. 20, 1816; June 20, 1817; Jan. 9, 16, Mar. 6, 20, 27, Apr. 10, June 5, July 10, 1818; Aug. 21, Sept. 11, 18, Oct. 16, 23, Nov. 9, 16, Dec. 24, 1818; Sept. 23, 1819.
Western Reserve Hist. Soc. has Nov. 16, 1809–Oct. 31, 1811.
Newberry Lib. has Jan. 7, Feb. 4, Mar. 11, 25–Apr. 29, June 3, 17, 24, July 1, Aug. 19, Sept. 9–30, Oct. 14, 21, Nov. 11–Dec. 16, 30, 1814; Jan. 6–20, Feb. 3–17, Mar. 3–31, Apr. 21–June 2, 16, 23, July 7, Aug. 4–25, Oct. 13, 27, Nov. 17, Dec. 1–15, 29, 1815; Jan. 12, Feb. 2, 23, Mar. 15, 29, Apr. 12, 26, May 17, 31, June 14, 21, July 5, 26–Aug. 16, Sept. 6, Nov. 1–15, 29, Dec. 27, 1816; Jan. 3–24, Feb. 14–Apr. 11, 25–May 30, June 13, 27–Sept. 5, 19–Oct. 31, Nov. 21–Dec. 12, 26, 1817; Jan. 2, 30, Feb. 20, Mar. 13, Apr. 3, May 1, June 12, 26, July 3, 31–Aug. 14, Dec. 31, 1818; Jan. 14, 28–Apr. 1, 29–May 27, Sept. 16, 30–Nov. 25, Dec. 9–30, 1819; Jan. 6–May 25, June 15, 22, 1820.
Lib. Congress has Apr. 7, 1808.
N. Y. State Lib. has Jan. 31, Mar. 28, 1811; Apr. 8, 1819.

[Sandy Hill] Times, 1818–1820+.

Weekly. Established Oct. 17, 1818, judging from the date of the first and only issue located, that of Apr. 9, 1819, vol. 1, no. 26, published by E. Gilman Storer, with the title of "The Times." It was established in 1818 by E. Gilman Storer, with Adonijah Emons as editor, in 1819 was printed for the proprietor by William Storer, Jr., and so seems to have been continued until after 1820 (see "History of Washington County," 1894, and "Sandy Hill Herald" of Mar. 9, 1899 in N. Y. State Lib.). The Sandy Hill "Times" is referred to in the Middlebury, Vt., "National Standard" of Aug. 18, 1819; the "Angelica Republican" of Nov. 14, 1820; and the "Cherry-Valley Gazette" of Dec. 5, 1820.

H. Armour Smith, Yonkers, has Apr. 9, 1819.

[Sangerfield] Civil & Religious Intelligencer, 1816–1820+.

Weekly. Established Nov. 18, 1816, by Joseph Tenny, with the title of "Civil & Religious Intelligencer." It was of octavo size, 4 pages to the issue, and although a magazine in appearance, contained current and local news, and death and marriage notices. Included also as part of each issue was "The Christian's Weekly Monitor," separately paged, and with a volume numbering which continued a periodical of that name begun by Tenny two years previous. The title of this section was changed to "The Christian's Monitor" on Mar. 3, 1817. In August, 1817, the title of the magazine was changed to "Civil & Religious Intelligencer, or the Gleaner & Monitor." The issues in 1819 were entitled "Intelligencer, Civil and Religious." It was continued until after 1820.

Am. Antiq. Soc. has Nov. 18, Dec. 16–30, 1816; Jan. 6–Mar. 17, June 7, July 19, Aug. 23, 30, Sept. 13, 1817.
N. Y. State Lib. has Jan. 27, 1817.
Madison Co. Hist. Soc., Oneida, has Jan. 12, 1818.
Hamilton Coll., Clinton, has May 28, Aug. 20–Oct. 15, 1819.

[Sangerfield] Intelligencer, see Civil & Religious Intelligencer.

Saratoga Gazette, 1810.

The "Saratoga Gazette" published at Saratoga, is recorded by Isaiah Thomas, in his list of newspapers published at the beginning of 1810 (History of Printing, ed. 1874, vol. 2, p. 298), but the name of the editor is not given and Thomas evidently was unable to obtain a copy of the paper.

[Saratoga Springs] Saratoga Sentinel, 1819–1820+.

Weekly. Established May 26, 1819, by Gideon M. Davison, with the title of "Saratoga Sentinel." With the issue of Sept. 13, 1820, the paper was transferred to John A. Murray, who continued it until after 1820.

Am. Antiq. Soc. has May 26, 1819–Dec. 27, 1820.
N. Y. State Lib. has June 9, Aug. 4, 11, 25, Sept. 29, 1819; Apr. 19, 1820.

Boston Athenæum has Sept. 1, 1819.
Western Reserve Hist. Soc. has Mar. 1, 1820.

[Schenectady] Cabinet, 1810–1820+.

Weekly. Established May 26, 1810, by I[saac] Riggs, with the title of "The Cabinet." It succeeded the "Western Budget," continuing its advertisements, but adopting a new volume numbering. With the issue of July 6, 1814, Henry Stevens was admitted to partnership and the paper was published by Riggs & Stevens. With the issue of Oct. 2, 1816, the partnership was dissolved, and I. Riggs again became sole publisher. The paper was so continued until after 1820.

- N. Y. State Lib. has Apr. 17, 1811; Mar. 25, 1812; Jan. 20, Mar. 10–24, Apr. 7, 14, 28, May 12, Aug. 4, 18, Sept. 15–Oct. 6, 27, Nov. 3, 24, Dec. 8, 1813; Jan. 5, 26–Feb. 9, 23–Mar. 16, May 25, June 8–29, Sept. 7–Dec. 28, 1814; Oct. 2, 1816–Dec. 27, 1820.
- Am. Antiq. Soc. has July 24, Oct. 16, 1810; Oct. 23, 1811; Sept. 30–Oct. 14, 28–Nov. 11, Dec. 23, 1812; Jan. 6, 13, 27, Mar. 3, 10, 24, 31, June 23, 30, Aug. 18, Oct. 6, Dec. 1, 29, 1813; Feb. 16, Mar. 2, Apr. 27–May 11, June 29, Aug. 10, Sept. 7, 14, 28, Nov. 2–16, 1814; Jan. 18, Apr. 5, 1815; Mar. 25, July 22, Oct. 7, Nov. 25, 1818; Apr. 7, 14, June 2, 1819; Aug. 2, 1820.
- Schenectady Co. Hist. Soc. has Aug. 19–Sept. 9, Oct. 7, Nov. 4, 11, 25, Dec. 23, 30, 1812; Jan. 6, 13, Feb. 17, Mar. 24, 31, Apr. 14, May 5, July 28–Aug. 18, Sept. 1, 15, 29, Oct. 6, 20, Nov. 3, 17, 1813; Jan. 26, Feb. 23, Apr. 20, May 4–18, June 1, Aug. 3, 17, Sept. 21–Oct. 5, 26, Nov. 16, 1814; Jan. 4, Mar. 22, Apr. 19, May 17, Oct. 11–25, Dec. 6, 20, 1815; Jan. 10, 24, Feb. 7, Apr. 10, 24, May 8, June 5, Aug. 7, 1816; Jan. 29, Feb. 5, Apr. 16, June 4, 18, Sept. 3, 10, Oct. 15, 29, Nov. 26, Dec. 3, 1817; Jan. 14, Feb. 25, Apr. 22, June 3, July 29, Aug. 5, Sept. 16, Oct. 14–28, Dec. 2, 23, 1818; Apr. 7, 28, May 19, June 23, July 7, Aug. 11, 25, Oct. 27, Nov. 17, 24, Dec. 22, 29, 1819; Feb. 16, Apr. 12, 26, May 17–June 7, Sept. 28, Dec. 27, 1820.
- Alonzo P. Walton, Schenectady, has Nov. 11, 1812; Mar. 31, Oct. 6, 20, 1813; Feb. 22, 1815; Feb. 25, 1818; Dec. 29, 1819.
- N. Y. Hist. Soc. has Oct. 28, 1812; Aug. 28, Nov. 20, 1816.
- Buffalo Hist. Soc. has May 13, 1812.
- Onondaga Hist. Assoc., Syracuse, has Feb. 10, 1813.
- H. Armour Smith, Yonkers, has Jan. 4, 1815.
- N. Y. Pub. Lib. has Apr. 5, 1820.

Schenectady Gazette, 1799–1802.

Weekly. Established in January, 1799, judging from the date of the earliest issue located, that of Dec. 31, 1799, vol. 1, no. 51, published by John L. Stevenson, with the title of "Schenectady Gazette." The last issue located is that of

Feb. 10, 1801, vol. 3, no. 109, and the paper was probably suspended late in 1802.

Harvard has Dec. 31, 1799.
N. Y. Hist. Soc. has Oct. 7, 1800.
N. Y. State Lib. has Jan. 20, 1801.
Lib. Congress has Feb. 10, 1801.

Schenectady Gazette, 1812.

Weekly. Established July 9, 1812, by Ryer Schermerhorn, with the title of "Schenectady Gazette." The last issue located is that of Aug. 20, 1812, vol. 1, no. 7.

Am. Antiq. Soc. has July 9, 16, 1812.
Harvard has July 9, 1812.
Alonzo P. Walton, Schenectady, has July 23, 1812.
Schenectady Gazette office has Aug. 20, 1812.

[Schenectady] Mohawk Advertiser, 1807–1811.

Weekly. Established July 31, 1807, judging from the date of the earliest issue located, that of Aug. 7, 1807, vol. 1, no. 2, published by Ryer Schermerhorn, with the title of "Mohawk Advertiser." In October, 1810, Schermerhorn disposed of the paper, which was then printed by T[———] Johnson, for William S. Buell, editor and proprietor, and was so published at least until May 7, 1811. The issue of Nov. 12, 1811, vol. 5, no. 5, was published by William S. Buell.

Am. Antiq. Soc. has Aug. 7, 28, Sept. 11, 1807; Oct. 18, 1808; Apr. 10, June 19, July 3, Aug. 14, Oct. 23, Nov. 6–20, 1810; Feb. 19–Mar. 5, 19, Apr. 9, May 7, 1811.
Harvard has Oct. 2, 1807; Oct. 23, Nov. 6, 1810.
N. Y. Soc. Lib. has Dec. 11, 1807.
Willis T. Hanson, Schenectady, had Jan. 22, 1808, now not located.
Utica Pub. Lib. has Sept. 19, 26, 1809.
N. Y. State Lib. has Sept. 4, 1810; Nov. 12, 1811.

[Schenectady] Mohawk Mercury, 1794–1798.

Weekly. Established Dec. 15, 1794, judging from the date of the earliest issue located, that of Feb. 9, 1795, no. 9, published by Wyckoff & Brokaw [Cornelius P. Wyckoff and Abraham Brokaw], with the title of "The Mohawk Mercury." With the issue of Sept. 8, 1795, the partnership was dissolved, and the paper was published by Cornelius P. Wyckoff. The last issue located is that of Mar. 13, 1798, no. 170, in which issue the publisher announced his removal from the town during the following month.

Am. Antiq. Soc. has Feb. 9, 24, Mar. 31, Apr. 14, 21, June 16, 30, July 7, 28, Aug. 11, 18, Sept. 1, 22, Nov. 10, 17, 1795; May 17, 24, June 14, 21, July 12, Sept. 20–Oct. 11, 25, 1796; Jan. 3, 24–Feb. 21, Mar. 28–Apr. 11, 25–May 9, 23–June 6, July 25–Aug. 8, 22–Sept. 12, 26–Oct. 10, 24, Nov. 7, 21–Dec. 5, 19, 26, 1797; Jan. 16–30, Feb. 13–Mar. 13, 1798.

Harvard has Feb. 9, 17, 24, May 19, 26, June 9, 16, 30, Sept. 8, Dec. 22, 1795; Mar. 1, 22, Apr. 12–May 24, June 21, July 12–26, Sept. 13, 20, Oct. 4, 11, Nov. 22, Dec. 13–27, 1796; Jan. 3–24, Feb. 7, 14, Mar. 21–Apr. 4, 18, 25, 1797; Jan. 2, 1798.

Wis. Hist. Soc. has Mar. 24, Aug. 18, 1795.

N. Y. Pub. Lib. has Feb. 24, 1795.

[Schenectady] Western Budget, 1807–1810.

Weekly. Established July 4, 1807, by D[erick] & C[ornelius] VanVeghten, with the title of "Western Budget." With the issue of Aug. 1, 1807, the name of the publishing firm was changed to VanVeghten & Son. In December, 1808, the firm was dissolved, Hermon VanVeghten stating that he was authorized to collect the firm's debts, and I[saac] Riggs became the publisher. The paper was discontinued under this title with the issue of May 19, 1810, vol. 3, no. 156, and was succeeded by "The Cabinet."

Am. Antiq. Soc. has July 25–Aug. 8, 1807; Jan. 10, 24, 31, Feb. 28, Mar. 14–28, Oct. 3, 1809; Jan. 23–Feb. 6, 20, 27, Apr. 24–May 8, 1810.

[Schenectady] Western Spectator, 1802–1807.

Weekly. Established in December, 1802, judging from the date of the earliest issue located, that of Apr. 21, 1803, vol. 1, no. 18, published by John L. Stevenson, with the title of "The Western Spectator; or, Schenectady Weekly Advertiser." The last issue located is that of Apr. 25, 1807, vol. 5, no. 227. The paper was evidently succeeded in July, 1807, by the "Western Budget."

Alonzo P. Walton, Schenectady, has Feb. 17, Dec. 14, 1804; Jan. 11, Nov. 22, 1805; Apr. 25, 1807.
Schenectady Co. Hist. Soc. has Apr. 21, 1803.
Am. Antiq. Soc. has June 30, 1803.
N. Y. State Lib. has Jan. 13, 1804.
Harvard has Nov. 8, 15, 1805.

[Schoharie] American Herald, 1809–1812.

Weekly. Established in June, 1809, judging from the date of the earliest issue located, that of Aug. 18, 1809, vol. 1, no. 12, published by John C. G. Groesbeek, with the title of "American Herald." In January, 1810, the paper was transferred to Derick VanVeghten and the title slightly altered to "The American Herald."

The last issue located is that of Oct. 26, 1811, vol. 3, no. 126. W. E. Roscoe, in his "History of Schoharie County," 1882, p. 79, states that the title was changed to "Schoharie Herald" in 1812, soon after which it was discontinued.

N. Y. Hist. Soc. has Aug. 18–Nov. 18, Dec. 16, 23, 1809; Jan. 6, 13, Feb. 10–Mar. 3, Apr. 14, 1810.
Am. Antiq. Soc. has Dec. 23, 1809; July 7, 1810; Aug. 17, 1811.
Schoharie Co. Hist. Soc. has Sept. 28, 1811.
N. Y. State Lib. has Oct. 26, 1811.

Schoharie Budget, 1817–1819.

Weekly. Established June 11, 1817, judging from the date of the only issue located, that of June 18, 1817, vol. 1, no. 2, published by D[erick] VanVeghten, with the title of "Schoharie Budget." It is recorded in a list of New York newspapers of January, 1818 (see "Albany Argus" of Jan. 6, 1818), where VanVeghten is given as the publisher. The Schoharie Budget is quoted in the "Scioto Gazette" of Jan. 1, 1819. It was succeeded in 1819 by the "Schoharie Republican" (Roscoe, "History of Schoharie County," p. 80).

Univ. of Pittsburgh has June 18, 1817.

Schoharie Gazette, 1815.

A paper with the title of "Schoharie Gazette" is recorded in a list of New York newspapers of December, 1815, printed in the "Albany Argus" of Dec. 26, 1815. No copy located.

Schoharie Herald, see [Schoharie] American Herald.

[Schoharie] Observer, 1818–1820+.

Weekly. Established Oct. 28, 1818, judging from the date of the earliest issue located, that of Nov. 25, 1818, vol. 1, no. 5, published by M[athew] M. Cole, with the title of "The Observer." In July, 1819, Solomon Baker became publisher, changing the title to "Schoharie Observer" late in 1819. Between August and October 24, 1820 [———] Fish was taken into partnership under the firm name of Baker & Fish. Giles H. Hubbard, who was editor, died Dec. 14, 1820. The issues from Oct. 24 to Dec. 19, 1820 were entitled "The Schoharie Observer." Continued after 1820.

N. Y. State Lib. has Apr. 7, extra, May 19, June 30, July 21, Aug. 4, Dec. 15, 1819; Mar. 21, Apr. 11, 18, July 25, Aug. 1, Dec. 12, 19, 1820. This library owned a file, 1818–1823, which was destroyed in the Capitol fire of 1911.
N. Y. Hist. Soc. has May 12, 1819; Apr. 11, Nov. 14, 1820.
Am. Antiq. Soc. has Nov. 25, 1818; Oct. 24, 1820.
Univ. of Pittsburgh has June 30, 1819; Mar. 21, 1820.

Schoharie Republican, 1819–1820+.

Weekly. Established in 1819 by Derick VanVeghten (Roscoe, "History of Schoharie County," p. 80), and continued until after 1820. No copy located. The first issue appeared in December, 1819, judging from a statement in the "Schoharie Observer" of Dec. 15, 1819. VanVeghten disposed of his interest to Peter Keyser, who started a new volume numbering July 26, 1820 (see "National Intelligencer" Oct. 28, 1820).

N. Y. State Library owned a file, 1819–1824, which was destroyed in the Capitol fire of 1911.

[Schoharie] True American, 1809–1815.

Weekly. Established Dec. 9, 1809, judging from the date of the earliest issue located, that of Jan. 20, 1810, vol. 1, no. 7, published by Thomas M. Tillman, with the title of "The True American." The last issue located is that of Feb. 25, 1815, vol. 6, no. 270. The issue of Oct. 2, 1813, is recorded in the "Albany Bi-Centennial Loan Exhibition," 1886, p. 71.

Am. Antiq. Soc. has Jan. 20, May 12, 19, July 14, Nov. 24, 1810.
Lib. Congress has Mar. 17, 31, 1810.
Schoharie Co. Hist. Soc. has Feb. 25, 1815.

[Scipio] Levana Gazette, 1798.

Weekly. Established June 20, 1798, judging from the date of the earliest issue located, that of Nov. 21, 1798, vol. 1, no. 23, published by R[oger] Delano, with the title of "Levana Gazette: or, Onondaga Advertiser." The imprint gives "Scipio, Onondaga County" as the place of publication, although the name of Levana, a small village, then in the township of Scipio, is given at the heading of the local news. In Follett's "Press of Western New York," p. 66, is noted a copy of the third number. Storke, writing in 1877, on the "History of the Press of Cayuga County" (Cayuga Co. Hist. Soc. Coll. no. 7, p. 57), says that a complete file had been recently burned.

N. Y. Pub. Lib. has Dec. 5, 1798.
Cayuga Co. Hist. Soc., Auburn, has Nov. 21, 1798.

[Scipio] Western Luminary, 1801.

Weekly. Established Mar. 31, 1801, judging from the date of the earliest issue located, that of Apr. 7, 1801, vol. 1, no. 2, printed by Ebenezer Eaton, for Eaton, & Co., with the title of "Western Luminary." The imprint states that it was "Printed in Scipio, at Watkins's Settlement, Cayuga County," the present Scipioville. The last issue located is that of July 21, 1801, vol. 1, no. 17.

Lib. Congress has Apr. 7, 1801.

Am. Antiq. Soc. has Apr. 21, 1801.
Cornell Univ. has June 16, 1801.
Cayuga Co. Hist. Soc., Auburn, has July 21, 1801.

[Sherburne] **Morning Star**, 1810.

Weekly. In the prospectus of the "Republican Messenger" of May 22, 1810, it was stated that the junior editor, James Percival, "has recently been employed in printing a Federal newspaper entitled 'The Morning-Star,' in this village; but . . . has thought proper to embark in an undertaking which promises fairer results." The advertisements of "The Morning Star" were evidently continued in the "Republican Messenger," and judging from the dates of these advertisements, the former paper was established Mar. 27, and discontinued May 8, 1810. No copy located.

[Sherburne] **Olive Branch**, 1806–1808.

Weekly. Established May 21, 1806, by Phinney & Fairchild [Elihu Phinney and John F. Fairchild], with the title of "Olive-Branch." With the issue of June 11, 1806, the title was altered to "Olive Branch." With the issue of May 20, 1807, John F. Fairchild became sole publisher, changed with the issue of Jan. 9, 1808, to John F. Fairchild & Co. The last issue at Sherburne was that of Feb. 6, 1808, vol. 2, no. 90, after which the paper was removed to Norwich, without change of title or volume numbering. See under Norwich.

N. Y. State Lib. has May 21, 1806–Feb. 6, 1808.
Harvard has June 18, July 2, 9, 23, 1806.

[Sherburne] **Republican Messenger**, 1810.

Weekly. Established May 22, 1810, by Pettit & Percival [Jonathan Pettit and James Percival], with the title of "Republican Messenger." The paper succeeded "The Morning Star" and continued its advertisements. It was discontinued at Sherburne with the issue of Jan. 1, 1811, vol. 1, no. 33, when the proprietors stated that they proposed to remove the establishment "a short distance to the Westward." Percival established the "Cortland Courier" at Homer, about forty miles west of Sherburne, in March 1811.

Am. Antiq. Soc. has May 22, 1810–Jan. 1, 1811.
N. Y. State Lib. has May 22, June 5–July 3, 17, 24, Aug. 7, Sept. 25, Nov. 27, Dec. 18, 25, 1810.
N. Y. Hist. Soc. has July 26, Aug. 7, 1810.
Harvard has Oct. 2, Nov. 6, 1810.

[Sherburne] **Western Oracle**, 1804–1806.

Weekly. Established Apr. 5, 1804, judging from the date of the earliest issue located, that of May 3, 1804, vol. 1, no. 5, published by Abraham Romeyn, with the title of "The Western Oracle, and Chenango Weekly Magazine." It was of octavo size, 16 pages to the issue, and with pagination. Although a magazine in appearance, it was a newspaper in contents. It was discontinued probably in 1806 (J. H. Smith, "History of Chenango and Madison Counties," p. 107).

> Sherburne Pub. Lib. has May 3–July 12, 1804.
> Am. Antiq. Soc. has May 31, 1804.
> Charles C. Merrill, Sherburne, in 1918 owned Mar. 30, 1805, now not located.

Sing-Sing, see under Mount Pleasant.

[Somers] American Union, 1811.

In the Poughkeepsie "Republican Herald" of Dec. 11, 1811, is the following notice, "Died — At South Salem, on the 15th ult. Milton F. Cushing, Esq. postmaster, and editor and proprietor of the 'American Union,' of Somers, in Westchester County." No copy located. The paper evidently succeeded Cushing's previous paper, the "Somers Museum."

Somers Museum, 1809–1810.

Weekly. Established Nov. 8, 1809, by Milton F. Cushing, with the title of "Somers Museum." The last issue located is that of July 24, 1810, vol. 1, no. 36, which issue is entitled "Somers Museum. And Westchester County Advertiser."

> Am. Antiq. Soc. has Nov. 8, Dec. 20, 1809; July 24, 1810.
> Mrs. John C. Holmes, Katonah, N. Y., has Nov. 15, 1809 (photostat in N. Y. Pub. Lib.).

Stillwater, see under Upton.

Tioga, see [Owego] American Farmer.

[Troy] Farmer's Oracle, 1797–1798.

Weekly. Established Jan. 31, 1797, by Luther Pratt, & Co. [Luther Pratt and Daniel Curtiss, Jun.], with the title of "Farmer's Oracle." It was removed from Lansingburgh to Troy, where it was started with a new volume numbering. With the issue of Apr. 11, 1797, the firm was dissolved and Luther Pratt became sole publisher. The last issue located is that of Apr. 17, 1798, vol. 2, no. 12.

> Am. Antiq. Soc. has Feb. 28, Mar. 14, 21, Apr. 11, 25–May 9, June 27, Aug. 22, Oct. 10, 31, Nov. 21, 1797.
> N. Y. Hist. Soc. has Apr. 18, May 2–23, June 20, July 11–Aug. 1, 15–29, Sept. 12–Dec. 26, 1797; Jan. 16, Feb. 20, Mar. 6, 20–Apr. 3, 17, 1798.

NEW YORK

Harvard has June 27, Sept. 5, 12, Oct. 10, 31, Nov. 28, Dec. 5, 19, 1797; Jan. 16, Feb. 13–Mar. 13, Apr. 3, 1798.
N. Y. Pub. Lib. has Dec. 5, 1797.
Troy Pub. Lib. has Apr. 10, 1798.

[Troy] **Farmers' Register,** 1807–1820+.

Weekly. Removed from Lansingburgh and established at Troy without change of title or volume numbering. The first issue at Troy was that of Nov. 24, 1807, vol. 5, no. 44, published by Francis Adancourt, with the title of "Farmers' Register." It was so continued until after 1820.

Am. Antiq. Soc. has Dec. 22, 29, 1807; Jan. 12, 19, Feb. 2, 16, Mar. 1–15, Apr. 5–19, June 7, July 12, 26, Aug. 23–Sept. 13, 27, Oct. 11–25, Nov. 8–22, Dec. 6, 20, 27, 1808; Jan. 3, 10, 24–Feb. 7, 21–Mar. 14, 28, Apr. 11, 25, May 2, 23, 30, June 20, 27, July 25, Aug. 8, 29–Oct. 10, 31, Nov. 21, Dec. 5, 12, 26, 1809; Jan. 2–30, Feb. 20, 27, Apr. 3–May 8, 22, June 19–July 10, 31, Aug. 21–Sept. 18, Oct. 2–16, 30–Nov. 13, 27, Dec. 11, 18, 1810; Jan. 1–Mar. 12, Apr. 9, 23–May 21, June 4, 11, July 23, 30, Aug. 20, 27, Sept. 24, Oct. 1, 15, 29, Nov. 5, Dec. 3, 1811; Jan. 21, Feb. 18, Mar. 10, Apr. 7, 14, May 5, June 9, 23, Aug. 25, Sept. 1, Oct. 13, 27, Dec. 15, 1812; July 20, Aug. 31, Sept. 14, 21, Dec. 21, 1813; Jan. 18–Feb. 8, Mar. 1, 10, 17, July 26, Aug. 9, Sept. 27, Oct. 4, Nov. 15, 29, Dec. 13, 1814; Jan. 3, Feb. 21, Mar. 21–Apr. 18, June 20, July 4, 11, Sept. 26, Dec. 26, 1815; Jan. 23, Feb. 6–20, Mar. 5, Apr. 2, 9, June 25, July 23–Aug. 6, 1816; Dec. 9, 1817; Nov. 10, Dec. 1, 1818; July 6, 13, 27, Sept. 21, Nov. 16, Dec. 21, 1819; Mar. 28, Oct. 24, Dec. 25, 1820.

Newberry Lib. has Apr. 26–May 31, June 14–Aug. 9, Sept. 6–Oct. 11, 25, Nov. 1, 29–Dec. 13, 27, 1808; Jan. 3, 10, 24–Feb. 28, Mar. 14–Apr. 4, May 2–30, June 20–July 18, Aug. 1, 8, 29, Sept. 12–Oct. 3, Nov. 21–Dec. 12, 1809; Jan. 2, Mar. 13, Sept. 4, Oct. 2, 23, Nov. 13, 1810; Feb. 12, 19, Apr. 23, May 7, 14, 28–June 11, 25, July 9, Sept. 3–24, Oct. 8, 15, Nov. 5, 12, 26, Dec. 24, 1811; Jan. 14–Feb. 4, 25–Mar. 24, Apr. 21, July 28, Aug. 4, Oct. 20, Dec. 8–22, 1812.

Harvard has Dec. 1, 1807; July 19–Oct. 4, 18, Nov. 1, 8, Dec. 6–27, 1808.

Mich. State Lib. has Oct. 25, 1808; Aug. 1–22, Sept. 12–Oct. 17, 31–Nov. 14, 1809; Jan. 23, Feb. 6, Mar. 13, 27, Apr. 10, 24, May 1, 15, 22, 1810.

N. Y. State Lib. has July 12, 1808; Feb. 14, Nov. 21, Dec. 5, 12, 1809; Mar. 13, 1810; Apr. 2, 9, 23, 1811; July 14, Aug. 18, Oct. 6–Nov. 10, 1812; Mar. 23, 1813; Jan. 3, 1815.

N. Y. Hist. Soc. has July 26, Oct. 25, Nov. 15, 1808; Apr. 9, 1811.
Boston Athenæum has June 18, 1811.
Duke Univ. has Aug. 31, 1813.
Lib. Congress has Sept. 26, 1815.

Univ. of Rochester has June 29, 1819.
H. Armour Smith, Yonkers, has Dec. 19, 1815.

Troy Gazette, 1802–1812.

Weekly. Established Sept. 15, 1802, by Thomas Collier, with the title of "The Troy Gazette." With the issue of Sept. 4, 1804, the title was altered to "Troy Gazette," and the paper was transferred to Wright & Willbur [John C. Wright and Solomon Willbur, Jun., changed to Wilbur with the issue of Sept. 18, 1804]. With the issue of Dec. 25, 1804, Henry Stockwell was admitted to the firm, which became Wright, Wilbur & Stockwell. With the issue of Sept. 10, 1805, Sterling Goodenow replaced Wilbur in the firm, which became Wright, Goodenow, & Stockwell. With the issue of Dec. 1, 1807, the paper was printed by John R. Weld, for Wright, Goodenow, & Stockwell, but with that of July 12, 1808, Weld's name was omitted, and the paper was published by Wright, Goodenow, & Stockwell. With the issue of Dec. 20, 1808, the partnership was dissolved and the paper was published for the proprietors by John C. Wright. With the issue of Dec. 5, 1809, the title was changed to "Troy Gazette, and Rensselaer Philanthropist," and the paper was purchased and published by Eldad Lewis. In October, 1810, the title was shortened to "Troy Gazette," Ryer Schermerhorn was admitted to partnership, and the firm name became Lewis and Schermerhorn. With the issue of Dec. 4, 1810, Ryer Schermerhorn became sole publisher. The last issue located is that of Mar. 17, 1812, vol. 8, no. 394, in which issue Schermerhorn announced that the paper was for sale, as he was intending to remove from Troy. He established the "Schenectady Gazette," July 9, 1812.

Troy Pub. Lib. has Sept. 15, 1802–July 17, 1804; Sept. 4, 1804–May 29, 1810.
Harvard has Sept. 15–29, Oct. 13, 20, Nov. 16, 30, Dec. 14, 21, 1802; Jan. 4, 25, Feb. 1, 22–Mar. 15, 29–Apr. 12, 26, May 3, 31, June 14, Aug. 30, Sept. 13, Nov. 1, 8, 22, Dec. 13, 1803; Feb. 21, 28, Mar. 20–Apr. 10, 24–May 8, 22, June 19, 26, July 10, Sept. 4–30, Nov. 13–Dec. 25, 1804; Jan. 1, 8, 22, Feb. 5–Mar. 19, Apr. 9, 23, May 7, 14, 28–June 25, July 9–30, Aug. 13–Oct. 8, 22, Nov. 26, Dec. 10, 24, 1805; Feb. 4, 25, Apr. 15, 29, May 13, 20, June 10, 17, July 29, Aug. 5, Sept. 9, 23, 30, Oct. 14, Nov. 4, Dec. 9, 30, 1806; Jan. 6, 27, Feb. 24, Mar. 10, 31, Apr. 14–May 5, 26–June 16, 30, July 21, 28, Aug. 11–Sept. 8, 22, Oct. 6, 27, Nov. 10, 17, 1807; July 19, Aug. 2, 16–30, Sept. 13, 27, Dec. 20, 27, 1808.
Am. Antiq. Soc. has Oct. 20, 1802; Apr. 12, May 24, Aug. 16, 23, Sept. 6, 1803; Mar. 27, 1804; Mar. 3, July 7, Aug. 4, Sept. 1–Oct. 27, Nov. 10–Dec. 29, 1807; Jan. 5–Oct. 18, Nov. 1–Dec. 27, 1808; Jan. 3–24, Feb. 7, 14, Apr. 11, Nov. 7, Dec. 5, 1809; May 1, 22, 29, June 12, 19, July 3–Aug. 7, Sept. 18, Oct. 23, 30, 1810; Feb. 26, Mar. 5, 26, Nov. 19, 1811; Mar. 17, 1812.
N. Y. Hist. Soc. has Sept. 3–Oct. 29, Nov. 12–Dec. 10, 24, 1805; Jan. 21–Feb. 4, 18–Apr. 15, 29–July 1, 15–Oct. 14, 28–Dec. 30, 1806; Jan. 6–20, Feb. 3–Mar. 31, May 12, July 21, 1807.

NEW YORK 745

Mich. State Lib. has Mar. 21, 1809–Mar. 26, 1810.
Union Coll. has Jan. 23–Mar. 6, 27–Apr. 10, May 22, 29, June 12, 26, July 3, 31, Aug. 14–28, Sept. 11, Oct. 9, Nov. 6, Dec. 18, 1810.
N. Y. State Lib. has Dec. 7, 28, 1802; Jan. 4, 11, Mar. 15, 29, Apr. 19, 26, May 10, July 26, Aug. 23, 1803; Feb. 21, Mar. 7, July 17, Sept. 4, Nov. 6, 1804; May 31, Dec. 27, 1808; Jan. 3, 1809.
Lib. Congress has Mar. 17, May 26, Aug. 4, 11, 1807; May 10, 1808; Nov. 27–Dec. 25, 1810; Jan. 1, 8, 22–Feb. 19, 1811.
Boston Athenæum has Dec. 3–17, 31, 1805; Jan. 14, 28, Feb. 4, 1806.
Univ. of Ill. has June 25, Sept. 17, 1805.
Univ. of Pittsburgh has Nov. 26, 1811.

[**Troy**] **Northern Budget**, 1798–1820+.

Weekly. Removed from Lansingburgh and established at Troy without change of title or volume numbering. The first issue at Troy was that of May 15, 1798, vol. 1, no. 48, published by Robert Moffitt & Co. [Robert Moffitt and Jesse Buel], with the title of "Northern Budget." With the issue of July 7, 1801, this firm was dissolved, Buel retired in favor of Zebulon Lyon, and the paper was issued by Moffitt & Lyon. With the issue of Oct. 16, 1804, Zebulon Lyon withdrew from the firm in favor of his son Oliver Lyon, the firm name remaining unchanged. Moffitt died May 4, 1807, and with the issue of May 12, 1807, Oliver Lyon became the publisher. The printing-office was destroyed by fire on Mar. 18, 1810, and no papers were issued until June 19, 1810. At some time between Nov. 22, 1814, and Feb. 28, 1815, Lyon was replaced as publisher by Ebenezer Hill. With the issue of either Aug. 26, or Sept. 2, 1817, Zephaniah Clark became the publisher and continued the paper until after 1820.

Troy Pub. Lib. has May 15, 1798–June 10, 1801; July 19, 1803; June 11, 1805–June 7, 1808; July 8–Aug. 19, 1817; Sept. 9, 1817–Dec. 26, 1820.
Am. Antiq. Soc. has May 15–Aug. 7, 21, Sept. 11–Oct. 16, 30–Nov. 13, 27–Dec. 25, 1798; Jan. 1–Dec. 11, 25, 1799; Jan. 1–Feb. 12, Apr. 9, June 18–Dec. 31, 1800; Jan. 7, 21, 28, Feb. 11–Mar. 11, 25–Apr. 15, May 6–Dec. 22, 1801; Jan. 5, 19–Feb. 2, 16, Mar. 9, 23, Apr. 6–May 18, July 20, 1802; Jan. 11, May 24, June 7, Aug. 16, 23, Sept. 6, 13, Oct. 25, 1803; Feb. 28, Mar. 13, 27, Apr. 10, July 17, 1804; Apr. 16, 1805; Apr. 22, 29, May 13, June 3–24, July 15, Aug. 12, 19, Sept. 2, Oct. 7, Nov. 11, Dec. 9–30, 1806; Jan. 6–27, Mar. 31–May 26, June 30, July 7, 21, Aug. 25, Sept. 15–Oct. 6, 20, Nov. 10, 17, Dec. 8, 22, 1807; Jan. 12, 26, Feb. 16, Mar. 8, 15, Apr. 5, 19, May 3, June 7, July 12, Aug. 9, Sept. 27, 1808; Apr. 11, June 13–27, Aug. 22, 29, Sept. 12–Oct. 10, Nov. 14, 28–Dec. 26, 1809; Jan. 9–Feb. 6, 20–July 3, 17–Aug. 7, 21–Sept. 25, Oct. 9, 23, 30, Nov. 13, 11–25, 1810; Jan. 8–22, Feb. 12–Apr. 2, 23, 30, May 14, 21, June 4, 11, July 16–30, Aug. 27, Sept. 17–Oct. 1, 15, 29–Nov. 12, 26, Dec. 3, 1811; Jan. 14, 21, Feb. 11, Mar. 10, Apr. 14, May 19, June 23–July 7, Sept. 22, 1812; Jan. 26, Mar. 23, Apr. 6, Nov. 23, 1813;

Feb. 8, June 28, Aug. 23, Nov. 22, 1814; Feb. 28–Mar. 21, July 4, 1815; Jan. 9, Feb. 13, 1816.

Harvard has May 22, July 10, Oct. 2, 1798; Apr. 16, Sept. 3, 1799; Oct. 29, 1800; Oct. 6, 1801; Feb. 9, Oct. 19, Nov. 2, 23, Dec. 14, 1802; Jan. 4, 25, Feb. 8–22, Mar. 15, 29, Apr. 5–May 17, June 7, 28–Oct. 4, 25, Nov. 1, 15–Dec. 6, 27, 1803; Jan. 10–May 1, June 19, July 3–24, Aug. 7–28, Sept. 11–Oct. 2, 23–Nov. 27, Dec. 18, 1804; Jan. 1, 8, 29–Mar. 26, Apr. 9, 30–May 14, June 4, 18, July 2, Aug. 6, 27, Sept. 10–Oct. 1, 29, Nov. 19, Dec. 17, 24, 1805; Feb. 25, Mar. 11, Apr. 1, May 13, 27, June 24, July 22, Aug. 19, Sept. 9, 30–Oct. 21, Nov. 11, 1806; Mar. 3–24, May 19, Sept. 15, 29, Oct. 13, 20, Nov. 17, 1807.

Newberry Lib. has Jan. 22, Feb. 5, 26, Mar. 26–Apr. 16, May 28, June 4, 18, 25, July 30, Aug. 20, Sept. 3–17, Oct. 1, 29–Dec. 31, 1800; Jan. 14, 21, Feb. 4, 11, 25, Mar. 4, 18, Apr. 8–May 20, July 7, 14, 28–Aug. 18, 1801; Apr. 6–27, May 11, June 1–July 27, Aug. 10–Sept. 21, Oct. 5, 19, 26, Nov. 9–23, Dec. 7, 28, 1802; Jan. 4–Feb. 15, Mar. 8–Apr. 12, 26–May 31, June 14, 21, July 5, 12, 26–Sept. 13, 27–Oct. 18, Nov. 1, 29, Dec. 6, 20, 1803; Jan. 3, 10, 24–Feb. 7, 28, Mar. 20, Apr. 24–July 10, 24–Aug. 14, 28–Nov. 27, Dec. 11–25, 1804; Jan. 1–Mar. 12, 26–Apr. 16, May 21–June 11, July 2–23, Aug. 6–Dec. 31, 1805; Jan. 7–Feb. 25, Mar. 11–Apr. 29, May 20–Aug. 12, 26, Sept. 2, Nov. 18–Dec. 30, 1806; Jan. 13–Feb. 10, Mar. 31–Apr. 14, 28, 1807; Apr. 14, May 5, 12, Oct. 13–27, 1812; Mar. 26–Apr. 9, 23, May 7, 1816.

N. Y. State Lib. has June 5, Sept. 25, 1798; May 14, July 2, 23, 30, Aug. 13, Sept. 10, Oct. 2, 16, Nov. 13, 27–Dec. 11, 1799; Jan. 29, Feb. 5, June 11, Aug. 20, 1800; May 6–20, June 3, 10, 1801; Nov. 2, 1802; July 17, Sept. 4, 1804–Dec. 3, 1805; July 10, 1810; Aug. 13, 1816; Sept. 5, 1820.

N. Y. Hist. Soc. has May 15, 29–June 12, July 3, Oct. 9, 1798; Jan. 29, July 23, Sept. 17, 1799; July 16, 1800; July 7, Aug. 11, 25, 1801; May 3, Oct. 25, 1803; June 25, 1805; Mar. 22, 1808; Jan. 24, Aug. 8, 29, Sept. 12, 1809; July 17, 1810; Jan. 22, 1811.

Mich. State Lib. has Apr. 11, 1809–Mar. 13, 1810.

Lib. Congress has Nov. 20, 1799; July 30, 1800; Mar. 4, Sept. 15, Oct. 13, 1801; Jan. 30, Feb. 20, 27, Mar. 13, 1810.

N. Y. Pub. Lib. has June 14, 1803; June 26, 1810; Dec. 31, 1811.

Phil. Lib. Co. has May 22, 1798.

Wis. Hist. Soc. has June 15, 1802; Feb. 9, 1813.

Cornell Univ. has Aug. 11, 1807.

Univ. of Pittsburgh has Dec. 3, 1811.

Boston Athenæum has May 5, 1818.

Troy Post, 1812–1820+.

Weekly. Established Sept. 1, 1812, by Parker and Bliss [William S. Parker and Pelatiah Bliss], with the title of "The Troy Post." With the issue of Nov. 10,

1812, the title was altered to "Troy Post." Bliss died Sept. 30, 1818, but there was no change in the imprint. With the issue of Apr. 6, 1819, the paper was published by William S. Parker, with the announcement of the dissolution of partnership signed by Parker alone and dated Mar. 23. The paper was continued by Parker until after 1820.

> Troy Pub. Lib. has Sept. 1, 1812–Dec. 26, 1820.
> N. Y. State Lib. has Sept. 1, 1812–Aug. 19, 1817; Oct. 6, 1818; Dec. 26, 1820.
> N. Y. Hist. Soc. has Sept. 1, 1812–Aug. 23, 1814.
> Am. Antiq. Soc. has Sept. 29–Oct. 13, 1812; May 28, 1816; Feb. 10, 1818; Feb. 2, 1819.
> Lib. Congress has Oct. 13, 1812.
> Wesleyan Univ. has May 16, 1815.
> Boston Athenæum has Dec. 5, 1820.
> H. Armour Smith, Yonkers, has Aug. 15, 1815.

[Troy] **Recorder,** 1795.

Weekly. Removed from Lansingburgh and established at Troy in May, 1795, without change of title or volume numbering. The last Lansingburgh issue located is that of May 12, 1795, vol. 3, no. 194, and the first Troy issue located is that of May 26, 1795, vol. 3, no. 196. It was entitled "The Recorder" and was published by Gardner & Hill [George Gardner and James Hill]. On June 26, 1795, this firm was dissolved and the paper was published by Gardner and Billings [George Gardner and Nathaniel Billings]. In August, 1795, George Gardner became sole publisher. The last issue located is that of Dec. 8, 1795, vol. 7, no. 224. At some time between Sept. 1 and Nov. 3, 1795, the numbering was changed from vol. 5 to vol. 7, possibly because Gardner assumed that his paper was the successor of "The Federal Herald," established at Lansingburgh in 1788.

> Harvard has May 26, June 16, July 28, Sept. 1, Dec. 8, 1795.
> Am. Antiq. Soc. has July 14, 28, Aug. 4, Nov. 17, 1795.
> Troy Pub. Lib. has Aug. 18, 1795.
> N. Y. Pub. Lib. has Aug. 18, 1795.
> Lib. Congress has Nov. 3, 1795.

[Union] **American Constellation,** 1800–1801.

Weekly. Established Nov. 15, 1800, judging from the date of the earliest issue located, that of Nov. 22, 1800, vol. 1, no. 2, published by D[aniel] Cruger, Jun., with the title of "The American Constellation." Although dated at Union, it was actually printed at Chenango Village (see Lawyer's "Binghamton," 1900, p. 447), and there is evidence to show that the issue of Oct. 3, 1801, was really printed at Chenango Point, the early name of Binghamton. The Ovid "Bee" of June 27, 1855, in a list of early New York newspapers examined, notes a copy of "The American Constellation" of Nov. 15, 1800, published by Daniel Cruger, Jr. The last issue located is that of Oct. 3, 1801, vol. 1, no. 46. Cruger removed to Owego late in 1801, to continue the paper there under the same title.

N. Y. State Lib. has Nov. 22, 1800; Jan. 10, 24, Feb. 21, Mar. 7, 14, May 2, 9, July 25, Aug. 15, 29, Sept. 5, Oct. 3, 1801.
Lib. Congress has Aug. 15, 1801.
Tioga Co. Hist. Soc., Owego, has Sept. 12, 1801.

[Union Springs] Cayuga Tocsin, 1812–1813.

Weekly. Established Jan. 2, 1812, by Royall T. Chamberlain, with the title of "The Cayuga Tocsin." The last issue located which was published at Union Springs is that of Apr. 15, 1813, vol. 2, no. 68. Between this date and June 2, 1813, the paper was removed to Auburn, where it was continued under the same title, without change of volume numbering.

Am. Antiq. Soc. has Jan. 2–30, Feb. 27, 1812; Jan. 20, 1813.
Harvard has Mar. 12, Oct. 22, Nov. 19, Dec. 3, 10, 1812; Apr. 1, 15, 1813.
Wis. Hist. Soc. has Jan. 9, 1812.
Cayuga Co. Hist. Soc., Auburn, has Oct. 15, 1812.

[Upton] Columbian Courier, 1794.

Weekly. Established June 3, 1794, judging from the date of the earliest issue located, that of Sept. 9, 1794, vol. 1, no. 15, published by Gardner and Hill [George Gardner and James Hill], with the title of "Columbian Courier." The paper was published at "Upton, in Stillwater," and an advertisement, dated Sept. 1, 1794, stated that the inhabitants of the village had voted that that portion of the town "near the Church" was to be called Upton. Gardner and Hill removed to Lansingburgh in December, 1794, where they established the "Lansingburgh Recorder."

Am. Antiq. Soc. has Sept. 9, 16, 1794.
Boston Pub. Lib. has Sept. 16, 1794.

Utica Club, 1814–1815.

Weekly. Established Aug. 11, 1814, with the title of "The Club," edited by Henry Goodfellow, Esq. & Company, and published by Seward & Williams [Asahel Seward and William Williams]. It was of quarto size and was suspended before the close of the year (J. C. Williams, "An Oneida County Printer," p. 60, and "Utica Patriot" of Aug. 2, 1814). A new series was announced to begin Jan. 5, 1815, but the day of publication was delayed ("Utica Patriot," Jan. 3, 10, 1815). It was revived Feb. 27, 1815, with new volume numbering, judging from the issue of Mar. 6, 1815, vol. 1, no. 2, entitled "The Club,"

NEW YORK 749

edited by Henry Goodfellow, Esquire and Company, and printed by Willard & Ingersoll [———— Willard and Jonathan Ingersoll, Jun.]. The next issue located, that of May 15, 1815, vol. 1, no. 12, was entitled "The Utica Club," and was published by Jonathan Ingersoll, Jun. The last issue located is that of June 12, 1815, vol. 1, no. 16. Ingersoll is referred to in the "Utica Patriot" of Feb. 20, 1816, as the "late editor" of the "Utica Club."

Am. Antiq. Soc. has Mar. 6, May 15, 1815.
Oneida Hist. Soc., Utica, has June 12, 1815.

[Utica] **Columbian Gazette,** 1803–1820+.

Weekly. Established Mar. 21, 1803, by Thomas Walker, with the title of "Columbian Gazette." It succeeded his "Columbian Patriotic Gazette" published at Rome, continuing the advertisements, but adopting a new volume numbering. With the issue of Jan. 4, 1814, Eliasaph Dorchester was admitted to partnership, under the firm name of Walker & Dorchester. With the issue of Dec. 31, 1816, the firm was dissolved and T. Walker again became sole publisher. The paper was so continued until after 1820.

Oneida Hist. Soc., Utica, has Mar. 28, 1803–Mar. 12, 1804; Mar. 18, 1805–Mar. 10, 1807; Mar. 8, 22, Apr. 6, 1808; Apr. 25, 1809; Mar. 12, 1811–Mar. 3, 1812; July 6, 1813; June 21–Nov. 22, 1814, fair; Feb. 21, Oct. 3, 1815; July 9, 30, Oct. 15–Dec. 17, 1816; Jan. 28, July 22, Sept. 16, 23, Nov. 11, 18, Dec. 9–30, 1817; Jan. 13, 1818–Dec. 26, 1820, fair.

N. Y. Hist. Soc. has Aug. 12, 1805; Mar. 17, 1807–Mar. 5, 1811; Mar. 10, 1812–Feb. 28, 1815; Mar. 4, 1817–Dec. 26, 1820.

Am. Antiq. Soc. has Apr. 25, Sept. 5, 19–Oct. 3, Nov. 28, 1803; Feb. 13, 27, Mar. 12, 19, June 18, Dec. 3, 1804; Apr. 8, 22, 1805; June 3, July 8, Nov. 25, 1806; June 16, Sept. 29, Oct. 13, 1807; Mar. 29, Apr. 19, May 17, July 5, 12, 26, Aug. 16, 23, Sept. 6–Nov. 15, Dec. 20, 1808; Jan. 10, 17, 31, Feb. 7, 21, Mar. 7–May 2, 16–June 6, 27, July 4, 18, Aug. 1, Oct. 31, Nov. 7, Dec. 26, 1809; Jan. 2, 9, 23, Feb. 6, May 1, 8, June 5, July 10–24, Sept. 18, 1810; Feb. 19–Mar. 2, 19, May 28, June 11, 1811; Nov. 3, 1812; Jan. 5, 1813; May 3, 1815; Aug. 5, 1817; July 27, 1819.

Harvard has Apr. 25, May 23, June 20–Aug. 15, 29, Sept. 12, 19, Oct. 3, 24, 31, Nov. 21, Dec. 5, 12, 1803; Jan. 16, 30, Feb. 13–27, Mar. 19, May 14–28, June 18, 25, July 30, Aug. 6, Sept. 10, 17, Oct. 8, 15, 29, Nov. 12, 26, Dec. 3, 17, 24, 1804; Jan. 7, 21, Feb. 4, 25, Mar. 11, 25, Apr. 22, May 20, June 17, July 1, 29, Aug. 26, Sept. 2, 30, Oct. 14–Nov. 11, 25, 1805; Jan. 13, 27, Feb. 10, 24, Mar. 10, 24, 1806; Mar. 31, 1807; Mar. 12, Apr. 30, May 21, July 23–Aug. 27, Sept. 10, 24–Oct. 15, Dec. 3, 31, 1811; Jan. 7–28, Feb. 25, Mar. 3, Nov. 3, 1812; Sept. 14, 21, 1813; Jan. 11, Feb. 22, Apr. 12, May 10, June 21, 28, Oct. 18, Nov. 22, 29, 1814.

Western Reserve Hist. Soc. has July 6, 1813–Aug. 29, 1815.

Hamilton Coll. has Aug. 24, 1813–May 16, 1815; Feb. 16, 1819.
N. Y. State Lib. has July 9, 1804; May 24, 1808; Nov. 21, 1809; Apr. 2, 1811; Apr. 14, June 16, Sept. 8, 29–Oct. 20, Dec. 1, 1812; July 13, Sept. 7, Oct. 19, Nov. 2, Dec. 14, 1813; Jan. 25, Mar. 22, Apr. 12, 19, Aug. 23, Sept. 6, 1814; Feb. 1, 1815; May 28, Nov. 19–Dec. 3, 17–31, 1816; Jan. 7, 28, Mar. 4, 1817; May 23, 1820.
Univ. of Ill. has July 2, Oct. 15, Nov. 5, 1804; July 1, Sept. 23, Dec. 2, 1805; Jan. 13, Mar. 3, Apr. 29, 1806.
Lib. Congress has Aug. 23, Sept. 6, 13, 1808; Sept. 7, 1813; Apr. 27, 1819.
Utica Pub. Lib. has Nov. 4, 1806; Feb. 28, 1815.
Wis. Hist. Soc. has May 9, 1803.
N. Y. Pub. Lib. has Oct. 19, 1813.
Cornell Univ. has July 5, 1814.

Utica Observer, 1817–1818, 1819–1820+.

Weekly. Established Jan. 7, 1817, by E[liasaph] Dorchester, with the title of "The Utica Observer." Toward the close of the year 1818, it was removed to Rome, where it was called the "Oneida Observer," but late in 1819, it was brought back to Utica, where it was continued under its early title until after 1820 (see Munsell, "Typographical Miscellany," p. 138; French, "Gazetteer of New York," 1860, p. 459; and Bagg, "Memorial History of Utica," p. 481).

Am. Antiq. Soc. has July 1, 8, Aug. 5, 1817.

[Utica] Patriot, 1803–1820+.

Weekly and semi-weekly. Established Feb. 28, 1803, with the title of "The Patriot," printed for the Editor [John H. Lothrop], by Merrell & Seward [Ira Merrell and Asahel Seward]. It succeeded the "Whitestown Gazette and Cato's Patrol" and continued its advertisements, although adopting a new volume numbering. With the issue of Feb. 27, 1804, the title was changed to "Utica Patriot." With the issue of Aug. 26, 1806, Seward retired from the firm and the paper was printed for the Editor, by Ira Merrell. In 1811 Lothrop was succeeded as editor by William H. Maynard (M. M. Bagg, "Pioneers of Utica," p. 367). With the issue of May 4, 1813, Merrell took George Camp into partnership, and the paper was printed for the Editor by Merrell & Camp. With the issue of Jan. 2, 1816, the paper was combined with "The Patrol" and issued semi-weekly under the title of "Utica Patriot, & Patrol," printed for the Proprietors by Ira Merrell. The prospectus of the union shows that the Proprietors were Asahel Seward, William H. Maynard and William Williams, and the issue of Apr. 2, 1816, states that Maynard was the editor. With the issue of Apr. 2, 1816, the paper reverted to a weekly. Williams retired as a proprietor in 1817. Merrell continued to print the paper for the other two proprietors until after 1820.

New York

N. Y. Hist. Soc. has Mar. 7–Dec. 26, 1803; Jan. 2–30, Feb. 20–Dec. 10, 31, 1804; Jan. 21, 28, Feb. 11–Mar. 4, 18, 25, Apr. 15–May 13, 27, June 3, 17, 24, July 15, Aug. 5, 12, 26–Sept. 23, Oct. 7–28, Nov. 11–Dec. 2, 16–30, 1805; Jan. 6–27, Feb. 10–Mar. 11, Apr. 1, 15, 22, May 6–Sept. 16, 30–Dec. 9, 30, 1806; Jan. 6–Dec. 29, 1807; Feb. 15, 1814–Dec. 26, 1820.

Oneida Hist. Soc., Utica, has Dec. 19, 1803; Jan. 9, 1804; Feb. 10, Apr. 21, 1807; Jan. 19, 1808–Feb. 13, 1810; May 22, 1810; Sept. 10, 1811; Apr. 21, May 5, June 2, Nov. 24, 1812; July 6, 1813; Mar. 29, May 24, July 5–Aug. 2, 23, Sept. 20, Nov. 22, Dec. 20, 1814; Feb. 7, Mar. 21, Apr. 18, May 2, June 13, July 25, Aug. 8, 22, Oct. 10, 31–Nov. 28, Dec. 19, 26, 1815; Jan. 19, 30, Feb. 2, 9, 13, 23, May 21, June 18, July 23, Aug. 6, 20, Sept. 17, Oct. 8, 29, Nov. 12, 26, Dec. 17, 24, 31, 1816; Dec. 30, 1817; Feb. 3, Mar. 24, 1818; Jan. 26, May 2, 16, July 4, 1819; May 9, 1820.

Am. Antiq. Soc. has Mar. 14–Apr. 25, May 30, June 13–Oct. 31, 1803; Mar. 5, 12, Apr. 2–30, May 14, 21, June 4–25, July 16–Aug. 6, 20, Sept. 3, 17, 24, Oct. 8, 22–Nov. 26, 1804; Apr. 1, 15, 1805; Oct. 14, Dec. 9, 1806; Oct. 27, 1807; Aug. 22, Sept. 26, Nov. 21, 1809; Jan. 30, Apr. 10, 24, May 8, July 10, 1810; Feb. 26, Mar. 19, May 28, June 25, 1811; Sept. 14, 1813; Feb. 24, Mar. 7, 21, Apr. 18, May 9, 1815; Jan. 2–Mar. 26, 1816; Aug. 3, 1819.

Rochester Pub. Lib. has May 21–July 16, 30, Aug. 13–Sept. 3, Oct. 8, 15, Dec. 3, 10, 24, 1811; Jan. 7, 21, Feb. 4–Apr. 21, Nov. 3, 17, Dec. 8, 1812; Feb. 2, 16, May 11, 18, June 1, Aug. 17, Oct. 26, Nov. 16, 1813; July 5, 26, Aug. 9, Oct. 18, Nov. 15, 1814.

Buffalo Hist. Soc. has Feb. 18, 1812–Feb. 8, 1814.

N. Y. State Lib. has Aug. 19, 1806; Apr. 26, July 19, 1808; Apr. 20, July 6, Aug. 3, 10, Sept. 7, Nov. 9, Dec. 14, 1813; Jan. 25, Mar. 2, Apr. 19, 26, May 10, 17, June 28–July 12, Aug. 9, Oct. 18, 1814; Mar. 12, Sept. 17, Nov. 5, 12, 26–Dec. 17, 1816; Jan. 6, Feb. 18–Mar. 4, 1817.

Hamilton Coll. has Sept. 21, 1813; Jan. 11–25, Mar. 15–Sept. 13, Oct. 25–Dec. 27, 1814; Jan. 17–May 2, 16, 23, 1815; Feb. 27, 1816; Apr. 21–May 19, 1818.

Univ. of Ill. has Oct. 8, 22, Nov. 5, 12, 26, Dec. 10, 1804; May 27, June 3, 24, July 29, 1805; Sept. 8, Oct. 6, Dec. 8, 1807; Jan. 19, Feb. 16, Mar. 8, 1808.

Lib. Congress has June 20, Aug. 15, Sept. 12–26, 1803.

Utica Pub. Lib. has Dec. 12, 1803; July 22, 1804; Apr. 22, 1806; Oct. 9, 1810; Mar. 7, 1820.

Western Reserve Hist. Soc. has Oct. 11, 1808; Oct. 30, 1810; July 7, Aug. 25, 1812; Apr. 13, Aug. 31, 1813; Aug. 16, 1816.

Univ. of Mich. (Clements) has Mar. 14, 1803; Mar. 5, 1804.

N. Y. Pub. Lib. has Feb. 22, 1814; Mar. 14, 1815.

Ontario Co. Hist. Soc., Canandaigua, has May 16, 1803.

Yale has May 28, 1811.

Wesleyan Univ. has Jan. 14, 1814.

Cayuga Co. Hist. Soc., Auburn, has Jan. 3, 1815.
Wis. Hist. Soc. has Dec. 8, 1818.

[Utica] Patrol, 1815–1816.

Weekly. Established Jan. 5, 1815, by Seward and Williams [Asahel Seward and William Williams], with the title of "The Patrol." Although a weekly, published on Thursday, another edition, with later news, was frequently issued on Monday. The last issue with this title was that of Jan. 1, 1816, vol. 1, no. 52, after which the paper was combined with the "Utica Patriot," to form the "Utica Patriot, & Patrol," which see.

N. Y. Hist. Soc. has Jan. 5, 1815–Jan. 1, 1816.
Western Reserve Hist. Soc. has Jan. 5, 1815–Jan. 1, 1816.
Am. Antiq. Soc. has Jan. 5–Apr. 24, May 8–June 29, July 10–Aug. 28, Sept. 11, 25, 1815–Jan. 1, 1816.
N. Y. State Lib. has Jan. 12–Dec. 18, 1815.
Lib. Congress has Apr. 6, Aug. 21, Sept. 25, Oct. 2, 16–Nov. 27, Dec. 11–25, 1815; Jan. 1, 1816.
Univ. of Mich. (Clements) has Jan. 12, Mar. 23, June 29, July 31, 1815.
Colgate Univ. has Jan. 5, 1815.
Cayuga Co. Hist. Soc., Auburn, has Mar. 6, 1815.
Wesleyan Univ. has May 11, 1815.
Utica Pub. Lib. has Sept. 18, 1815.

[Utica] Whitestown Gazette, 1798–1803.

Weekly. Removed from Whitestown, without change of volume numbering, in July, 1798. The earliest Utica issue located is that of Sept. 3, 1798, vol. 3, no. 118, published by William M'Lean, with the title of "Whitestown Gazette. And Cato's Patrol." With the issue of June 21, 1802, the title was altered so as to read "Whitestown Gazette and Cato's Patrol." The last issue with this title was that of Feb. 21, 1803, vol. 7, no. 351, when the paper was succeeded by "The Patriot," which see.

Am. Antiq. Soc. has Sept. 3, Oct. 1, 1798; May 5, 26, June 30, Nov. 3, 24, 1800; Mar. 9, 1801; July 19, 1802; Feb. 21, 1803.
Oneida Hist. Soc., Utica, has Sept. 17, Dec. 3, 1798; Mar. 31, Apr. 7, 1800; Jan. 5, 12, 1801.
Univ. of Ill. has Feb. 25, Mar. 4, 25, Apr. 1, 15–May 6, July 8–Aug. 5, Sept. 29, 1799.
N. Y. Hist. Soc. has Oct. 6, 1800; Jan. 12–Dec. 28, 1801; Jan. 4, Feb. 8, 1802–Feb. 21, 1803.
Minn. Hist. Soc. and Williams Coll. have Dec. 30, 1799.
Western Reserve Hist. Soc. has Oct. 12, 1801.
Utica Pub. Lib. has Apr. 5, 12, 1802.

NEW YORK 753

[Wardsbridge] Orange County Republican, 1806–1808.

Weekly. Established May 6, 1806, with the title of "Orange County Republican," published for the Proprietors by Cyrus Beach, and Luther Pratt. The issue of May 6, 1806, has "Montgomery" at the head of the local news, but the issue of May 13 and subsequent issues have "Wardsbridge" at the head of the local news and "Wardsbridge: Montgomery Township" in the imprint. The paper was so continued at least until Dec. 11, 1806, vol. 1, no. 32. The next issue located is that of Mar. 23, 1808, vol. 2, no. 19, published by Cyrus Beach. This issue contains an advertisement of the dissolution of the firm of Cyrus Beach & Co., signed by Cyrus Beach and Joseph Tennery, and dated Jan. 1, 1808. It mentions accounts due from May 6, 1806, to Oct. 1, 1807. No issue has been located after Mar. 23, 1808. The Newburgh "Political Index" of Mar. 19, 1807, has the following reference to the paper: "Wm. H. otherwise called Billy Weller . . . has we understand, condescended to take under his direction and management the editorial part of the Orange County Republican."

> Newburgh Free Lib. has May 6–Sept. 11, 1807; also Carrier's Address, Jan. 1, 1807.
> Am. Antiq. Soc. has May 22–June 5, Nov. 27, Dec. 11, 1806.
> Harvard has May 22, July 3, 1806; Mar. 23, 1808.

[Waterford] Agriculturalist, 1820+.

Weekly. Established September, 1820, judging from the date of the earliest issue located, that of Apr. 3, 1821, vol. 1, no. 31, published by T[ruman] Webster, with the title of "Agriculturalist."

> N. Y. Hist. Soc. has Apr. 3, 1821.

Waterford Gazette, 1801–1818.

Weekly. Established Oct. 27, 1801, judging from the date of the earliest issue located, that of Nov. 17, 1801, vol. 1, no. 4, published by Horace H. Wadsworth, with the title of "Waterford Gazette." Early in October, 1802, John M. Looker was taken into partnership, under the firm name of Wadsworth & Looker, but with the issue of Dec. 7, 1802, Looker retired and Wadsworth became sole publisher. In 1812, or early in 1813, Charles Webster became the publisher, but was succeeded in 1815 by Truman Webster. The last issue located is that of Feb. 20, 1816, vol. 15, no. 719. The paper is recorded, with Truman Webster as publisher, in a list of New York newspapers of Jan. 1, 1818 (see "Albany Argus," Jan. 6, 1818). How long thereafter it was continued is not known.

> Harvard has Nov. 17, Dec. 1, 8, 22, 29, 1801; Jan. 5–19, Feb. 2–Mar. 2, 16–Apr. 6, 20, May 4, 11, June 1–July 6, 20, Aug. 10, 17, Sept. 7–28, Oct. 12–Dec. 28, 1802; Jan. 4–May 3, 17–June 28, July 19–Sept. 6, 20, 27, Oct. 11–Nov. 1, 22, 1803; Jan. 3–17, Feb. 7, 21, Mar. 6–May 29, June 19–Aug. 7, 21,

28, Sept. 18, 25, Oct. 9–Nov. 13, Dec. 4–25, 1804; Jan. 1, 15, 22, Feb. 5, 19, 26, Apr. 30, May 28, June 11, 25, July 2, 16–Aug. 20, Sept. 10–Oct. 1, 15, 29, Nov. 19–Dec. 10, 1805; Sept. 22, Oct. 6, 20, 1807; Sept. 11, 25, 1810.

Am. Antiq. Soc. has Mar. 9, Apr. 6, 1802; July 26, Aug. 23, Sept. 6, 13, 27, 1803; July 3, 1804; Apr. 21, June 16, Dec. 29, 1807; Jan. 5, 12, 1808; May 20 extra, 1809; Feb. 13, May 29, July 24, 31, Oct. 30, 1810; Feb. 26, Mar. 5, 19, Apr. 2, 9, 30, May 7, 21, Nov. 5, 1811; Aug. 3, 1813.

Troy Pub. Lib. has Dec. 29, 1801; Nov. 9, 16, Dec. 14, 1802.

Univ. of Ill. has Sept. 25, 1804; Feb. 5, May 21, Aug. 13, 1805.

N. Y. State Lib. has Jan. 31, 1804; Mar. 5, Apr. 2, 1811; Jan. 21, 1812.

Ohio Hist. & Phil. Soc. has Aug. 18, 1807.

Adriance Lib., Poughkeepsie, has Jan. 19, 1808.

Univ. of Pittsburgh has Dec. 10, 1811.

N. Y. Pub. Lib. has Feb. 20, 1816.

Waterloo Gazette, 1817–1820+.

Weekly. Established May 28, 1817, judging from the date of the earliest issue located, that of July 2, 1817, vol. 1, no. 6, published by George Lewis, with the title of "Waterloo Gazette." In October 1817 (see letter from George Lewis in Auburn "Advocate of the People" of Dec. 10, 1817), Lewis transferred the paper to Hiram Leavenworth. With the issue of Mar. 12, 1818, the paper was published by H. Leavenworth for J[ohn] M'Lean and H. Leavenworth. In October, 1818, H. Leavenworth became sole publisher. In May or June, 1819, the title was altered to "The Waterloo Gazette," but on Nov. 22, 1820, was changed back to "Waterloo Gazette." So continued until after 1820.

Waterloo Lib. has July 2, 16, 30, Aug. 6, 20, Sept. 10, 17, Oct. 1, Dec. 17, 1817; Jan. 7–21, Feb. 4, 11, 25–Mar. 19, Apr. 23, May 7–June 11, July 2–16, Aug. 13, Oct. 1, 22, Nov. 25, Dec. 2, 30, 1818; Jan. 13–Feb. 3, 17, Mar. 17, 31, Apr. 7, 21, May 5–19, June 9, 30–July 28, Aug. 18, Sept. 22–Oct. 6, 20, 1819; May 31, June 21, 28, July 12–Aug. 16, 30–Sept. 13, 27–Oct. 25, Nov. 15–Dec. 13, 1820.

Am. Antiq. Soc. has Dec. 23, 1818; Feb. 10, Apr. 14, Sept. 22, 29, Oct. 20, 27, Dec. 15, 1819; Jan. 5, 26, Apr. 26, May 24, 1820.

Yale has Nov. 11, 1818.

Skaneateles Lib. Assoc. has Jan. 6, 1819.

Western Reserve Hist. Soc. has Nov. 17, 1819.

[Watertown] American Advocate, 1814–1817.

Weekly. A continuation, without change of volume numbering, of the "Northern Luminary." The earliest issue located with the title of "American Advocate" is that of Nov. 23, 1814, vol. 2, no. 96, published by Jairus Rich. It is included in a list of New York newspapers of December, 1815 (printed in the "Albany Argus" of Dec. 26, 1815). It probably was discontinued early in 1817.

Am. Antiq. Soc. has Nov. 23, 1814.

[Watertown] American Eagle, 1810–1812.

Weekly. Established Apr. 10, 1810, with the title of "American Eagle," printed for Henry Coffeen. It succeeded "The Hemisphere," continuing the advertisements, but adopting a new volume numbering. F. B. Hough, in his "History of Jefferson County," 1854, p. 372, states that Coffeen was the proprietor, and Abraham Taylor was the printer, but Taylor's name does not appear in any of the issues located. The last issue located is that of Sept. 25, 1810, vol. 1, no. 25. In 1811 or 1812, the paper was succeeded by the "Republican Watchman."

Am. Antiq. Soc. has Apr. 10, 24, May 29, June 5, 19, Aug. 14, 1810.
N. Y. State Lib. has Sept. 25, 1810.

[Watertown] Hemisphere, 1809–1810.

Weekly. Established Oct. 17, 1809, judging from the earliest issue located, that of Feb. 6, 1810, vol. 1, no. 17, printed by Abraham Taylor, with the title of "The Hemisphere." It was discontinued in April, 1810, to be succeeded by the "American Eagle," which see.

Am. Antiq. Soc. has Feb. 6, 1810.

Watertown Herald, 1808–1809.

Weekly. Established Dec. 5, 1808, judging from the date of the first and only issue located, that of Apr. 3, 1809, vol. 1, no. 18, published by James B. Robbins, with the title of "Watertown Herald."

British Museum has Apr. 3, 1809.

[Watertown] Independent Republican, 1819–1820+.

Weekly. Established Apr. 5, 1819, judging from the date of the earliest issue located, that of June 14, 1819, vol. 1, no. 11, published by S[eth] A. Abbey, with the title of "Independent Republican." So continued until after 1820. (See also F. B. Hough, "History of Jefferson County," 1854, p. 372).

Am. Antiq. Soc. has June 14, 1819.
Watertown Hist. Soc. has Oct. 17, Dec. 19, 26, 1820.

[Watertown] Jefferson and Lewis Gazette, 1817–1819.

Weekly. Established in the spring of 1817 by Dorephus Abbey and John H. Lord, Jr., with the title of "Jefferson and Lewis Gazette," and discontinued in

April, 1819 (F. B. Hough, "History of Jefferson County," 1854, p. 372). It is included in a list of newspapers of Jan. 1, 1818 (printed in the "Albany Argus" of Jan. 6, 1818), where Lord is given as the publisher. No copy located.

[Watertown] Northern Luminary, 1813–1814.

Weekly. Established Jan. 26, 1813, by J[airus] Rich, with the title of "Northern Luminary." It succeeded Coffeen's paper, the "Republican Watchman," continuing the advertisements, but adopting a new volume numbering. The title was not printed across the top of the first page, but was given only in column headings on the second and fourth pages. The last issue located is that of Mar. 2, 1814, vol. 2, no. 58. The paper was succeeded in 1814, without change of volume numbering, by the "American Advocate," which see.

Am. Antiq. Soc. has Feb. 2, 23, Apr. 20, 1813; Mar. 2, 1814.

[Watertown] Republican Watchman, 1812–1813.

Weekly. Established in 1812, or possibly in 1811, by Henry Coffeen, and continuing his other paper, the "American Eagle" (see statement in "Northern Luminary" of Feb. 2, 1813). The only copy located is that of May 12, 1812, vol. 3, no. 109, printed for Henry Coffeen, entitled "Republican Watchman," and continuing the numbering of the "American Eagle." Coffeen sold out the establishment in January, 1813, to Jairus Rich, who changed the title to the "Northern Luminary."

Am. Antiq. Soc. has May 12, 1812.

[West Farms] West-Chester Patriot, 1813.

Semi-weekly. Established in April, 1813, judging from the date of the first and only issue located, that of July 3, 1813, no. 23, published by M[atthias] Lopez, with the title of "West-Chester Patriot."

Am. Antiq. Soc. has July 3, 1813.

Whitesborough, see under **Whitestown, Western Centinel.**

Whitestown Gazette, 1793, 1796–1798.

Weekly. Established July 11, 1793, by Richard Vanderburgh, with the title of "Whitestown Gazette." The Utica Directory of 1828 states that the paper was published in the village of New Hartford, in the town of Whitestown, that the proprietors were Jedediah Sanger, Samuel Wells and Elijah Risley, that the printer was Richard Vanderburgh, and that it was discontinued in the winter of 1793–1794. Under date of Mar. 12, 1794, R. Vanderburgh advertises in "The Western Centinel" of Mar. 26, 1794, that beginning with Apr. 15, 1794, he will publish the "Whitestown Gazette" in a more extensive manner, under the firm of Vanderburgh, Lang and Johnson, and refers to his "former patrons." It was revived on June 7, 1796, judging from the issue of July 5, 1796, vol. 1, no. 5, published by Samuel Wells, with the title of "Whitestown Gazette." With the issue of July 12, 1796, William M'Lean was admitted to partnership and the paper was published by Wells and M'Lean. With the issue of Sept. 27, 1796, Wells withdrew and William M'Lean became sole publisher. The last Whitestown issue was that of July 17, 1798, vol. 3, no. 111, after which the paper was removed to Utica, where it was continued without change of volume numbering.

Oneida Hist. Soc., Utica, has July 11, Aug. 22, 1793; Oct. 4, 1796; July 17, 1798.
Wis. Hist. Soc. has Aug. 9, 1796–May 29, 1798.
Am. Antiq. Soc. has July 5, Oct. 25, 1796; Apr. 4, Aug. 15, 1797; Jan. 30, Feb. 13, 1798.
Harvard has July 19, 26, 1796; Nov. 7, 1797; June 12, 1798.
Otsego Co. Hist. Soc., Cooperstown, has Oct. 4, 1796.
N. Y. State Lib. has Mar. 20, 1798.

[Whitestown] **Western Centinel**, 1794–1800.

Weekly. Established Jan. 8, 1794, judging from the date of the earliest issue located, that of Mar. 26, 1794, vol. 1, no. 12, published by Oliver P. Easton, with the title of "The Western Centinel." The Utica Directory of 1828 states that James Swords of New York was the proprietor and Easton the printer, and that the paper was printed in the village of Whitesborough, in the town of Whitestown. Before June, 1794, the title was changed to "Western Centinel." Easton was the publisher of the issues located to Apr. 19, 1797. The issue of Aug. 3, 1798, and the last issue located, that of Nov. 2, 1798, vol. 5, no. 252, were published by Edward Lewis, Jun. Pomroy Jones, in his "Annals of Oneida County," 1851, p. 521, says that Easton was succeeded by a Mr. Lewis, who was the publisher in the summer of 1799. Whitestown imprints show that Lewis & Webb were printers in that town in 1797, Edward Lewis in 1798 and 1799, and Warren Barnard in 1800.

Harvard has Feb. 25, May 27, July 1, 15, Aug. 19, Sept. 16, Oct. 28, Nov. 11, Dec. 30, 1795; Apr. 6, 13, 27, May 11, 18, June 1, 22–July 13, 27–Aug. 17, 31, Sept. 14, 21, Oct. 5, 26, Nov. 2, 16–Dec. 28, 1796; Jan. 4, 11, 25, Feb. 8–Mar. 1, 15–29, Apr. 12, 19, 1797.
Am. Antiq. Soc. has Mar. 26, 1794; Feb. 4, Aug. 12, 1795; June 15, Oct. 26, 1796.
Wis. Hist. Soc. has Mar. 18, Aug. 12, 1795.
N. Y. Pub. Lib. has June 11, 1794.
Univ. of Ill. has Aug. 3, 1798.
Troy Pub. Lib. has Nov. 2, 1798.

[Williamsville] **Buffalo Gazette**, 1814–1815, see under **Buffalo**.